D1526135

Colonial

Americans

~ of ~

Royal and Noble

Descent

ALLEGED, PROVEN AND DISPROVEN

Patricia Ann Scherzinger

Heritage Books, Inc.

Other Heritage Books by the author:

Accomack County, Virginia, 1850 Census
Northampton County, Virginia, 1850 Census

Published 1996 by

HERITAGE BOOKS, INC.
1540E Pointer Ridge Place
Bowie, Maryland 20716
1-800-398-7709

ISBN 0-7884-0467-9

A Complete Catalog Listing Hundreds of Titles
On History, Genealogy, and Americana
Available Free Upon Request

CONTENTS

Insistent voices call from out of the Past,

"A noble race doth well its own endow
So pure and fine let all thine actions be
None can deny of Royal Race art thou."

(Annah Walker Robinson Watson, *Of Sceptred Race)*

INTRODUCTION

T hrough the years many scholarly men and historians have searched the records and written much about royal pedigrees and lineages. Now as research continues and more records become available, many lineages which were alleged and accepted as authentic royal lineages have been disproved and corrected. Thus, researchers are still using many outdated records which contain errors and omissions that may lead them to the wrong pedigree.

On the other hand, we know that genealogy is a progressive science. We can use new knowledge, methods and technology to interpret the existing records more precisely. Remember the limitations that existed in days gone by: illiteracy prevented many people from recording even the births of their children. One wonders how so many records have survived the mists of time, escaping the destructive elements of fire, water, and careless handling. But, thanks to historians of centuries past, we are able to recreate many pedigrees with accuracy.

People throughout the ages have taken pride in their station in life. They cherish the history of their family, including their trials and triumphs and their ambition to rise above the mundane. This ambition has inspired successive generations to pursue their own adventures and conquests. The cumulative efforts of these people should be a vital part of our nation's history. It should claim and hold a place of dignity and demand the recognition it is due.

In the British colonial period of what is now the United States, many sons of nobility of lesser rank left their homes seeking a new life in the New World. These sons were not, for the most part, first sons. The law of primogeniture, prevalent in England, was not recognized in the New World. These were the sons of nobility seeking opportunities and successes that were not bequeathed them in their native countries.

The "adventurers," (investors) and settlers of Jamestown in 1607, came with dreams of a new and richer life. The English government encouraged the settlement of Virginia by promising the adventurer 50 acres of land for each additional person he brought to the colony. Many a man found his fortune in land with that promise, and to this day many a Virginian lives on the same property that their English ancestor earned by bringing colonists to the New World.

Then the Pilgrims, who took courage and crossed the stormy Atlantic in frail boats, settled in Massachusetts. They left their ancestral homes in pursuit of religious freedom. They found much, much more: a legacy to posterity granting freedom of worship forever. Eventually, vast numbers came and colonized the the eastern shores of North America and yet, for the most part, very few brought their pedigrees and family records. Little did they know, or perhaps did they even think, that their descendants would one day seek this information. The early colonists could not have foreseen that our adventure, unlike theirs, would be to hold in our hands and hearts our pedigrees, to prove to the world who we are and where we came from.

Many did come; they gained land, settled, and lived their lives and dreams in this, the new and promised land. Records were started and kept in many regions of the Eastern Seaboard. Some families brought and continued to keep and cherish their family records. For those Americans who can trace their families now, it is chiefly through land records. Some can trace through wills, deeds and other land transactions back 300 years. The oldest and most continuous land records in the United States are in two little counties on what is known locally as the "Delmarva" Peninsula (*De*laware, *Ma*ryland, *Vir*gin*ia*). They are Accomack and Northampton Counties in the state of Virginia. I am from Northampton County, and so I have been one of the very few who can trace my lineage back to the early 1600's, and in several cases my ancestors were the first English families to settle in America. For the fortunate few who are able to trace their family history to the early 1600's, many have been successful in connecting their ancestors to the royal lines of aristocracy.

Never since the settlement of our beloved country has the want for knowledge of our ancestors been so great. Persons in every station of life are making inquiries respecting the past and for information on their ancestors. The libraries and archives of national and state records offices are open to everyone looking for material, histories, and biographies; and any little bit of information, no matter how minuscule, is received with much appreciation. Many researchers have discovered lineage to famous men and women.

It is very important in America to preserve lines of descent accurately. Not only is this country a "melting pot" of many cultures, but our society also has become very mobile. Families tend to become separated by wide distances; traditional "extended" and "nuclear" families are becoming rarer; and many Americans are losing touch with their roots. We then must carefully preserve the records for future generations.

There have been, over these many years, volumes written on royal pedigrees and the descendants of the immigrant with royal ancestry. It is from these publications I have taken the information for this directory. Since many of the books published are rare and compiled over a span of many years there may be conflicting information and dates. However, in many instances, if reported in periodicals or quarterly magazines and other notable publications these have been corrected and noted in the text.

The cut-off year is 1776, the year of our independence. Some families may go a few years beyond that. Also, some may be included in this work even though they had no issue, but led noble and courageous lives. These have been noted also.

It is hoped that this work will add to the researcher's library and be of noteworthy, positive and practical value. As shown in the text, America has become the home of descendants of the noblest and most royal houses of Europe. Even though I have listed the immigrant with royal ancestry I have not gone into the actual records of the royal ancestor. I have left that to the honorable and most learned professional men who have dedicated their lives to researching royal families. However, I have listed the record in which I found the immigrant and his descendants, and the researcher may review these records for himself.

The legacy our ancestors left us is like no other seen in any part of the world or in any place in time. The dim chapters of time lead us into the dark ages of history through the records of those individuals who rose above the common man into peerages of leadership and nobility. The preservation of our links to these noble men is the reason I have compiled this book.

Patricia Ann Scherzinger

The Consciousness of Noble Ancestry is an
Inspiration to Noble Living

Here I acknowledge my own royally descended ancestors starting with Edward III, King of England. My immigrant ancestor was John Fisher of Northampton County, Virginia, b1603 d1640, his parents were John Fisher and Benetta Dering, she being of royal descent. This line is my maternal side, my mother being Geraldine Virginia Powell Dudley, and her mother Emory Sara Lee Mapp Powell. The line of descent was followed through *The Royal Descents of 500 Immigrants* by Gary Boyd Roberts, pages 159 and 160.

1st	Edward III, King of England, d 1377 = Philippa of Hainault
2nd	John of Gaunt, Duke of Lancaster = Catherine Roet
3rd	Joan Beaufort = Ralph Neville, 1st Earl of Westmoreland
4th	Edward Neville, 1st Baron Abergavenny = Elizabeth Beauchamp
5th	George Neville, 2nd Baron Abergavenny = Margaret Fenne
6th	Elizabeth Neville = Thomas Berkeley
7th	Anne Berkeley = John Brent
8th	Margaret Brent = John Dering
9th	Richard Dering = Margaret Twisden
10th	Benetta Dering = John Fisher
11th	John Fisher of Virginia, The Immigrant = Elizabeth____
12th	Phillip Fisher = Elizabeth Maddox
13th	Bridget Fisher = William Bradford
14th	Fisher Bradford = Mary Mellechoppe
15th	Mary Bradford = Calab Harrison
16th	Leah Harrison = George Thomas Mapp
17th	Edwin Thomas Mapp Sr = Indiana Frances Jones
18th	Edwin Thomas Mapp Jr = Lorraine Lee Coates
19th	Emory Sara Lee Mapp = Victor Mapp Powell
20th	Geraldine Virginia Powell = Lorus Eugene Dudley
21st	Patricia Ann Dudley

ABBREVIATIONS OF PLACE OF BIRTH

CT	Connecticut	NE	New England
DC	District of Columbia	NH	New Hampshire
DE	Delaware	NJ	New Jersey
FL	Florida	NS	Nova Scotia
GA	Georgia	NY	New York
IN	Indiana	OH	Ohio
KY	Kentucky	PA	Pennsylvania
LI	Long Island	RI	Rhode Island
MA	Massachusetts	SC	South Carolina
MD	Maryland	TN	Tennessee
ME	Maine	TX	Texas
MO	Missouri	US	United States
MS	Mississippi	VA	Virginia
NC	North Carolina	VT	Vermont

ABBREVIATIONS

abt	about	desc/o	descendant of
Adjt	Adjutant	doc	doctor
aft	after	Dr	Doctor
adm	administration	Esq	Esquire
anc	ancestor	Gen	General
&	and	Gov	Governor
b	born	Hon	Honorable
bp	baptism	Jr	Junior
bef	before	Lieut	Lieutenant
bet	between	m	married
Brig	Brigadier	Maj	Major
Capt	Captain	Mr	Mister
chr	christened	Mt	Mount
co	county	Pres	President
coh	coheir	reg	regiment
Col	Colonel	ret	retired
d	died	Rev	Reverend
dsp	died without issue	Rev	Revolution
dy	died young	Sergt	Sergeant
dau	daughter	So	South
Dea	Deacon	Sr	Senior
dept	department	Univ	University
desc/o	descendant of		

CHRONOLOGY OF HISTORIC EVENTS
1607-1776

1607: Three ships sent by the London Company land at Cape Henry, Virginia. Captain John Smith and others found Jamestown, the first permanent English town in the present-day U.S.

1608: Frenchman Samuel de Champlain founds the village of Quebec, Canada.

1609: Henry Hudson explores the eastern coast of present-day U.S. for the Netherlands; the Dutch then claim parts of New York, New Jersey, Delaware and Connecticut, and name the area New Netherlands.

1609-10: All but 60 of the 500 settlers in Jamestown die during the "Starving Time."

1610: Town of Santa Fe is founded in New Mexico.

1612: Settlers plant tobacco in Virginia for the first time.

1614: Pocahontas, daughter of Powhatan, marries John Rolfe in Jamestown. John Rolfe exports cultivated tobacco.

1619: The first women and the first African slaves arrive in Virginia, and the first representative government of the European colonies begins with Virginia's House of Burgesses.

1620: The Pilgrims sail from England to Cape Cod on the *Mayflower*. They make a plan of government called the Mayflower Compact. Massachusetts' first permanent town at Plymouth is settled.

1621: Massachusetts Pilgrims and Massasoit, leader of the Wampanoag Indians, establish peace and hold the first Thanksgiving feast in colonial America.

1622: Opechancanough leads a great massacre at Jamestown and kills 347 English settlers.

1623: Colonization of New Hampshire is begun by the English.

1624-1626: The Dutch buy Manhattan Island from the Indians and colonization of present-day New York State is begun at Fort Orange (Albany).

1630: The town of Boston, Massachusetts, is founded by the English Puritans.

1632: Lord Calvert founds Maryland.

1633: Colonization of Connecticut is begun by the English.

The first school in the North American colonies is founded in New Amsterdam.

1636: Roger Williams founds Rhode Island.

Thomas Hooker moves to Connecticut.

Harvard, the colonies' first college, is founded in Massachusetts.

1638: Harvard establishes the colonies' first library.

Delaware colonization begins when Swedish people build Fort Christina at present-day Wilmington.

1640: Stephen Daye of Cambridge, Massachusetts prints *The Bay Psalm Book*, the first English-language book published in what is now the U.S.

1643: Swedish settlers begin colonizing Pennsylvania.

1647: Massachusetts forms the first public school system in the colonies.

1649: King Charles I of England is beheaded; Parliament rules.

Slavery becomes essential to Virginia's tobacco economy.

1650: North Carolina is colonized by Virginia settlers about this year.

Population of colonial U.S. is about 50,000.

1660: New Jersey colonization is begun by the English near Charleston about this year.

Charles II is restored to the English throne.

1664: The British capture New Amsterdam and rename it New York.

1665-1666: London is attacked first by the Great Plague and then by the Great Fire.

1670: South Carolina colonization is begun by the English near Charleston.

1673: Jacques Marquette and Louis Jolliet explore the upper Mississippi River for France.

1675-1676: New England colonists conquer Indians in King Philip's War.

1676: Bacon's Rebellion.

1677: North Carolinians rebel against English taxes.

1680: Pueblo Indians led by Pope attack the Spaniards and drive them out of Santa Fe.

1682: Philadelphia, Pennsylvania is settled by William Penn.

La Salle explores Mississippi River all the way to its mouth in Louisiana and claims the whole Mississippi Valley for France.

1686: King James II sends Sir Edmund Andros to control New England colonists.

1692: Witchcraft trials held in Salem, Massachusetts.

1693: College of William and Mary is founded in Williamsburg, Virginia.

1699: Williamsburg (then called Middle Plantation) becomes the capital of Virginia.

1700: Colonial population is about 250,000.

1704: The *Boston News-Letter*, the first successful newspaper in the colonies is founded.

1706: Benjamin Franklin is born in Boston.

1732: James Oglethorpe founds Georgia.

George Washington, future first president of the United States, is born in Virginia.

1733: English begin colonizing Georgia, their thirteenth colony in what is now the United States.

Daniel Boone is born.

1735: John Adams, future second president, is born in Massachusetts.

John Peter Zenger is acquitted of libel for printing criticism of New York's British governor.

1739: The Great Awakening, a religious revival begins.

1743: Thomas Jefferson, future third president is born in Virginia.

1749: Liberty Hall Academy is founded, forerunner of Washington and Lee University.

1750: Colonial population is about 1,200,000.

1754: Col. George Washington and 150 Virginians defeat a French exploratory party in Pennsylvania and start the French and Indian War.

The colonies reject the Albany Plan, Benjamin Franklin's proposal for a union.

1755: General Braddock's British troops are defeated by French and Indians at Fort Duquesne.

Johnson and Hendrick defeat the French at Lake George.

1755 (cont.) The Acadians leave Nova Scotia because they will not swear loyalty to Britain.

1759: The British are victorious at Quebec.

1760: Johnson and General Amherst capture Montreal. The war in America is won by the British, who gain Canada and most other French lands east of the Mississippi River.

George III becomes king of England.

1763: The Treaty of Paris ends the Seven Years' War.

The Proclamation of 1763 forbids American colonists to settle west of the Appalachians.

1764: British pass Sugar Act to gain tax money from the colonists.

1765: British pass Stamp Act, forcing the colonies to pay taxes on printed matter.

The Sons of Liberty band together against taxation without representation.

1766: British repeal the Stamp Act.

1767: British pass the Townshend Acts, which tax tea and other goods.

1769-1782: Father Junipero Serra and other Franciscan friars establish twenty-one missions in California.

1770: British soldiers kill five Americans in the Boston Massacre.

1773: Fifty colonists dump British tea into Boston Harbor at the Boston Tea Party to protest the tax.

1774: British close up the port of Boston to punish the city for the Tea Party.

Delegates from all the colonies but Georgia meet in Philadelphia at the First Continental Congress.

1775: Apr 19: Revolutionary War begins at Lexington and Concord, Massachusetts.

May 10: Second Continental Congress convenes in Philadelphia and names George Washington Commander-in-Chief of the American forces.

Patriots under Ethan Allen and Benedict Arnold take Fort Ticonderoga.

Britain declares war on America.

Jun 17: Colonists inflict heavy losses on British but lose Battle of Bunker Hill near Boston.

Jul 3: George Washington takes command of Continental Army.

1775 (cont.)   The Wilderness Road opens to pioneers

1776:   Mar 17: Washington's troops force the British out of Boston in the first major American victory of the war.

          May 4: Rhode Island is the first colony to declare itself independent of Britain.

          Jul 4: Declaration of Independence is adopted.

COLONIAL AMERICANS
of ROYAL and NOBLE DESCENT
Alleged, Proven, and Disproven

THE DESCENDANTS

Entries generally consist of the following items when the information is available:

1) surname
2) given names and titles
3) colony of principal residence(s)
4) year of birth
5) year of death
6) marriage year and spouse's name
7) identified as the immigrant of royal or noble ancestry with source(s), or identified as a descendant of one or more such immigrants with sources cited for each such descent separately.

– A –

ABBOTT Anne - of PA, m1723 Jonathan Biles - desc/o Anne Mauleverer AFA238

Jane - of NJ, b1701 d1780, m1726 Joseph Burr d1767, a Quaker & land owner - desc/o Anne Mauleverer CHB357; MCD154; DBR(5)784

Joanna - of MA, b1755, m1776 Simon Winship b1749 d1813 - desc/o Elizabeth St John CHB218; BCD218

John - of NJ, b abt 1674 - desc/o Anne Mauleverer MCD154; RAA1, 59

Oliver - of MA, b1727 d1796, m1752 Joanna French - desc/o Elizabeth St John CHB218; BCD218

Samuel - of NJ, b1749 d1828, m1775 Lucy Laurie - desc/o Anne Mauleverer CHB358; MCD154

Rev Thomas - of MA, b1745, m1776 Hannah Hesilridge dau/o Sir Robert & Sarah Hesilridge - desc/o Thomas Dudley NE(8)316

Timothy - of NJ, b1717, m1746 Ann Satterthwaite - desc/o Anne Mauleverer CHB357, 358; MCD154

William - of NJ - desc/o Anne Mauleverer MCD154

ABELL Abel - of CT, b1757 d1841, m1783 Lucy Hubbard - desc/o Robert Abell BLG2530

Abigail - b1690 - desc/o Robert Abell RAA59

Benjamin - of CT, b abt 1652 d1699, m abt 1678 Hannah Baldwin d aft 1717 dau of John Baldwin - desc/o Robert Abell BLG2530; DBR(4)503; RAA59

Benjamin - of CT, b abt 1687 d1769, m1713/1714 Lydia Hazen -

ABELL (cont.)

    desc/o Robert Abell BLG2530

Sergt Caleb - of MA, b1646 d1731, m1669 Margaret Pose or Post - desc/o Robert Abell BLG2530; LDS40; RAA59; AAP149; FFF202, 254b; GBR226

Caleb - of MA, b1677 d aft 1746, m1704/1705 Abigail Sluman - desc/o Robert Abell BLG2530

Capt Caleb - of MA, b1763 d1842, m1791 Elona Shepherdson - desc/o Robert Abell BLG2530

Daniel - of CT, b1705/1706 d bef 1794, m1727 Sarah Crane - desc/o Robert Abell BLG2530

David - of CT, b1722 d1781, m1742 Alice Roberts - desc/o Robert Abell LDS40; RAA59; FFF255b

Dorothy - of MA, b1677 d1741, m(1)1703 Ebenezer Walker b1676 d1717/1718 son of Deacon Philip Walker - desc/o Robert Abell DBR(2)846; RAA59

Elijah - of CT, b1729 d1798, m1754 Anne Lathrop - desc/o Robert Abell BLG2530

Elizabeth - m1715 John Lathrop b1690 d1752 of Norwich, CT - desc/o Robert Abell III DBR(3)514

Experience - b1674 d1763, m John Hyde - desc/o Robert Abell RAA59; AAP149; FFF202; GBR226

Jemima - of CT, b abt 1692 d1741, m1719 Gershom Mattoon of MA, b1690 d1766 son of Philip Mattoon & Sarah (Hawks) Mattoon - desc/o Robert Abell DBR(4)503

Capt John - of CT, b1678 d1769, m1703 Rebecca Sluman - desc/o Robert Abell LDS40; RAA59; FFF254b

Jonathan - of CT, b1733 d1802, m1754 Lydia Bliss - desc/o Robert Abell BLG2530

Jonathan - of CT, b1767 d aft 1830, m1790 Lucy Treadway - desc/o Robert Abell BLG2530

Joshua - of MA, b1649 d1724, m(2) Bethiah Gadger b1660 d1723 of Norwich, CT - desc/o Robert Abell III DBR(3)514; RAA59

Joshua - of MA, b1695 d1731/1732, m1720 Rebecca Carpenter - desc/o Robert Abell BLG2530

Martha - b1683 - desc/o Robert Abell RAA59

Mary - of MA, b1642, m Elder Samuel Luther, son of Captain John Luther - desc/o Robert Abell DBR(3)711; DBR(5)142; RAA59

Mehitable - b abt 1689 - desc/o Robert Abell RAA59

Lieut Preserved - of MA, b1644 d1724, m(1)1667 Martha Redaway b1648 d1686 dau/o James Redaway, m(2)1686 Sarah Bowen - desc/o Robert Abell BLG2530; DBR(2)845; RAA59; FFF254b

Rebecca - b1746 - desc/o Robert Abell RAA59

Robert III - of MA 1630, b abt 1605 d1663 Rehoboth, MA, who was the 18th generation in line of descent from Alfonso IX, King of Leon, came to Boston with Governor John Winthrop, took the freeman's oath 1631, son of George Abell & Frances Cotton, m Joanna____ d aft 1682, she, m(2) 1667 William Hyde - the immigrant FLW62; BLG2530; LDS40; DBR(2)844, 845; DBR(3)514, 669, 711; DBR(4)503; DBR(5)142; RAA 1, 59; AAP149; FFF202, 253, 254b; GBR226

ABELL (cont.)

Capt Robert - of MA, b1721 d1800, m1747 Mary Thompson - desc/o Robert Abell BLG2530

William - of CT, b1749 d1837 - desc/o Robert Abell FFF255b

William Robert - b1755, m Lois Merry - desc/o Robert Abell LDS40; RAA59

ABERCROMBY James - b1706 d1781 British commander in America during the French & Indian Wars, son of Alexander Abercromby of Glassaugh & Helen Meldrum dau/o George Meldrum of Crombie, m Mary Duff of Dipple & Brace (his third cousin) & had issue a daughter Jane - the immigrant GBR108; DAB(1)28, 29

ABNEY Dannett - of VA, bp 1660 Leicester d1733 Spotsylvania, VA, son of George Abney & Bathusia ____, m(2) Mary Lee dau/o Reverend Joseph Lee - the immigrant FLW79 sufficient proof of alleged royal ancestry is lacking

Nancy - of SC, b1767 d1793, m(1) Thomas Spraggins - desc/o Anne Lovelace DBR(1)121; DBR(2)193; DBR(3)459

ADAMS Abigail - of MA, b1765 d1813, m1786 Col William Stephens Smith - desc/o Elizabeth Coytmore PFA75

Alice - of VA, b1768, m1788 William Marshall of Fauquier Co, VA - desc/o Col Walter Aston CFA(6)10

Ann - of MA, m1694 John Dickenson - desc/o John Fenwick DBR(2)585; DBR(3)372; DBR(4)701

Anne - of VA, b abt 1731 d1775, m abt 1748 Col Francis Smith of South Farnham Parish, Essex Co, member of the House of Burgesses - desc/o Col Walter Aston CFA(6)9

Anne - of VA, b1762 d1820, m1787 Col Mayo Carrington of Boston Hill, Cumberland Co, VA - desc/o Col Walter Aston CFA(6)10

Charles - of MA, b1770 d1800, m1795 Sarah Smith - desc/o Elizabeth Coytmore PFA75

Daniel - b1679, m Thanks Shepard - desc/o Mary Phelps LDS12

Daniel - b1706, m Lucy or Lucia Saxton - desc/o Mary Phelps LDS12

Daniel - of NJ, b1773 d1863, m1818 Elizabeth Good Bartlett - desc/o Elizabeth Denne ECD166 - desc/o George Elkington DBR(1)7

Capt Elihu - of MA, b1741 d1776, m1765 Thankful White - desc/o Elizabeth Coytmore PFA85

John - b1735 d1826, m Abigail Smith - desc/o Elizabeth Coytmore PFA Apx C #5

John - of NH, b1759 d1831, m1787 Abigail Coleman b1743 d1826 - desc/o Thomas Dudley DBR(5)224

Pres John Quincy - of MA, b1767 d1848 President of the United States 1825/1829, m1797 Louisa Catharine Johnson - desc/o Rev William Norton J&K121; CHB164; BCD164; AAP143, 144 - desc/o Elizabeth Coytmore PFA79, 169, Apx C #5

John - of VA, b1773 d1825, physician & prominent citizen of Richmond for many years, m Margaret Winston dau/o Geddes Winston of Richmond - desc/o Col Walter Aston CFA(6)10

Mary Ann - b1773 d1822, m1793 Simeon Francis b1770 d1823 - desc/o Rev Peter Bulkeley DBR(1)680; DBR(2)328, 394, 758; DBR(3)312

Capt Peter Boyleston - of MA, b1738 d1823, m1768 Mary Crosby -

ADAMS (cont.)

desc/o Elizabeth Coytmore PFA85

Col Richard - of VA, b1726 New Kent Co d1800 Richmond, an ardent patriot throughout the Revolution & one of the most enterprising, & public spirited, wealthy & influential citizens of Richmond, m1755 Elizabeth Griffin b1738 d1800 dau/o Leroy Griffin & Mary Anne Bertrand of Richmond - desc/o Col Walter Aston CFA(6)9

Richard - of VA, b1760 d1817, m(1) Mrs Elizabeth Southall of Chatsworth, m(2) Mrs Sarah Travers Daniel Hay - desc/o Col Walter Aston CFA(6)10

Richard Saxton - b1734, m Lucy Matson - desc/o Mary Phelps LDS12

Samuel Griffin - of VA, b1776 Richmond d1821 Richmond, adjutant 19th regiment Virginia militia War of 1812, was projector first water works system of Richmond 1809, served in Virginia Assembly, m1797 Katherine Elizabeth Innes b1779 d1836 dau/o Judge Henry Innes of Caroline Co - desc/o Col Walter Aston CFA(6)10, 11

Sarah - of VA, m Col John Fry b1737, col of the colonial militia, member of the House of Burgesses from Albemarle Co, VA & a vestryman of St Anne's Parish, Albemarle Co - desc/o Col Walter Aston CFA(6)9

Sarah - of VA, b1766 d1806, m1793 William Smith, governor of VA & member of House of Delegates, who was lost in the Richmond Theater fire 1811 - desc/o Col Walter Aston CFA(6)10

Tabitha - of VA, b1728 d1764, m Richard Eppes, member of House of Burgesses - desc/o Col Walter Aston CFA(6)361

Thomas - of VA, b abt 1730 New Kent Co d1788, clerk of Henrico Co, vestryman & warden Henrico Parish, an earnest patriot serving in many civic positions, m Elizabeth Fauntleroy - desc/o Col Walter Aston CFA(6)8, 9

Thomas Bowler - of VA, b1759 d1794 Richmond, m Sarah Mowisin, whose mother was a Miss Bland of Prince George Co - desc/o Col Walter Aston CFA(6)10

AIKENS Nathaniel - b1759, m Mary Tupper - desc/o John Whitcomb LDS93; RAA84

ALBERTSON Mary - of NY, b1709 d1778, m1734 Jeffery Clark b1703 d1782 - desc/o Henry Willis DBR(3)315

ALCOCK Anne - of MA, bp 1650 d1723, m(1)1669/1670 John Williams b1644 d1687 of MA & RI, attorney general of RI 1686, m(2)1689 Robert Guthrie - desc/o Dr Richard Palgrave ECD(3)232; DBR(2)592; DBR(3)572; DBR(5)372

George - of MA 1630 - the immigrant CGA11; sufficient proof of alleged royal ancestry is lacking

Johanna - b1660 - desc/o Richard Palgrave RAA121; GBR266

Mary - b1652 - desc/o Richard Palgrave RAA121

Sarah - of MA, bp 1650 d1715, m1671 Rev Zechariah Whitman b1644 d1726 - desc/o Dr Richard Palgrave DBR(4)693; RAA121

ALDERMAN Daniel II - of NJ, b1748 d1824, m1772 Sarah Newton b1757 d1848 - desc/o Olive Ingolsby DBR(2)655; DBR(3)630

David - of NC, b1775 d1860, m1794 Nancy Ann Morgan b1776 d1841 - desc/o Olive Ingoldsby DBR(2)655; DBR(3)630

ALEXANDER Catherine - of NJ, m Major Walter Rutherford - desc/o
James Alexander CHB23; BCD23

Catherine - of NJ, b1755 d1826, m(1)1779 Col William Duer - desc/o
James Alexander BCD24

Elizabeth - of NJ, m John Stevens - desc/o James Alexander CHB23;
BCD23

Elizabeth Ashton - b1773, m Thomas Harrison - desc/o James
Alexander AMB410

Frances - of VA, b1728, m1749 John Stuart - desc/o James Alexander
AMB410

James - of NJ 1716, b1691 d1756, m Mary Sprott - the immigrant
CHB22; MCB140; BCD22; sufficient proof of alleged royal ancestry
is lacking

Jane - of VA, b1730, m1748 Henry Ashton - desc/o James Alexander
AMB410

Jane - b1771, m Col John Field Slaughter - desc/o James Alexander
AMB410

John - of VA 1659, d1677 - the immigrant MCB186; AMB409; CGA11
sufficient proof of alleged royal ancestry is lacking

John - of VA, b1735, m1756 Lucy Thornton - desc/o James Alexander
AMB410

John Stuart - b1766, m Catherine Foote - desc/o James Alexander
AMB410

Mary - of NJ, b1721 d1767, m1739 Peter Van Brugh Livingston -
desc/o James Alexander CHB22; BCD22

Philip - of VA, m Sarah Ashton - desc/o James Alexander AMB409

Capt Philip - of VA, b1704 d1753, m1726 Sarah Hooe - desc/o James
Alexander AMB410

Philip - b1776, m___Harrison - desc/o James Alexander AMB410

Robert - of VA, d1704, m Anne Fowke - desc/o James Alexander
AMB409

Robert - of VA, b1688 - desc/o James Alexander AMB409

Sarah - of VA, b1700, m Cadwallader Dade - desc/o James Alexander
AMB409

William - of NJ, b1726 d1783, m Sarah Livingston - desc/o James
Alexander CHB24; BCD24

Col William - of VA, b1744 d1814, m1765 Sigismunda Mary Massie -
desc/o James Alexander AMB410

ALLEN Arthur - of VA, b1602 d1670, m Alice Tucker - the immigrant
WAC7; sufficient proof of alleged royal ancestry is lacking

Major Arthur - of VA, d1710, m Katherine Baker - desc/o Arthur Allen
WAC7

Elijah - b1763 - desc/o Joseph Bolles RAA71

Eunice - of MA, b1775 d1843, m1791 Remembrance Hitchcock -
desc/o Richard Lyman CHB148; BCD148

Jane - b1587/1588 d1626 died in England, dau/o Thomas Allen &
Mary Faircloth, m1613 Rev Peter Bulkeley of MA - the immigrant
GBR332; TAG(16)129/136, (39)98, 99

John - of VA, d1741, m Elizabeth Bassett - desc/o Arthur Allen WAC7

Jude - chr 1743, m Sarah Philbrick or Philbrook - desc/o Joseph
Bolles LDS13; RAA71

ALLEN (cont.)

Lewis Buckner - of VA, b1773 d1835, m abt 1805 Mary Catharine Jones - desc/o Col George Reade AWW216

Martha - of IN, m abt 1792 Montgomery Allen - desc/o Nancy Anne Pollock JSK1537

Samuel - b abt 1737/1746 - desc/o Joseph Bolles RAA71

Samuel - b1711, m Anne Clarke - desc/o Joseph Bolles LDS13; RAA71

ALLERTON Isaac - VA, m Elizabeth Willoughby - desc/o Margaret Wentworth NFA49

Sarah Elizabeth - of VA, m Hancock Lee - desc/o Thomas Willoughby NFA46, 49

ALLSTON (or ALSTON) Elizabeth - of SC, m Joseph LaBruce & had issue - desc/o John Allston SCG(1)3

John - of SC 1682, b1666 d1718/1719 son of William of Hammersmith in London, Co Middlesex, England & Thomasine (Brooke) Allston, m Elizabeth Turges Harris wid/o John Harris - the immigrant DBR(2)19; RAA1, 60; BLG2537; GBR149; SCG(1)1/3

John - of SC, d1750, m(1) Deborah____, m(2) Mrs Sarah Belin & had issue - desc/o John Allston SCG(1)3

John Hayes - of SC, m Harriet Middleton Wilkinson - desc/o John Allston DBR(2)19

Mary - of SC, m Joseph Warnock & had issue - desc/o John Allston SCG(1)3

Peter - of SC, d1748, m Sarah Torquet & had issue - desc/o John Allston SCG(1)3

Peter - of SC, d1749, m Sarah Hayes - desc/o John Allston DBR(2)19

Peter Jr - of SC, m Mary Bacot - desc/o John Allston DBR(2)19

Thomasin - of SC, m Abraham Warnock & had issue - desc/o John Allston SCG(1)3

William - of SC, m Esther LaBruce & had issue - desc/o John Allston SCG(1)3

ALLYN Abigail - m John Williams - desc/o Margaret Wyatt GBR396

Anna - of CT, b1678, m(2) Joseph Whiting b Hartford, CT 1640 d1717 - desc/o Margaret Wyatt DBR(2)612, 613; RAA61

Jane - of CT, b1670, m1686 Lieut Henry Wolcott of CT b1670, son of Simon Wolcott - desc/o Margaret Wyatt DBR(1)147

Lieut Colonel John - of CT, b1630 d1696 came to New England with his father Matthew Allyn & was cornet of troop 1657/1658, town clerk of Hartford, deputy & magistrate; secretary of CT 1663/1665, m(1)1651 Ann Smith dau/o Henry Smith & granddau/o Colonel William Pynchon, treasurer of the Massachusetts Colony, m(2) Hannah Lamberton - desc/o Margaret Wyatt CHB27; BCD27; DBR(1)198, 199; DBR(2)612; RAA61; CRL(1)183; NEFGM(1)154

Martha - b1667, m Aaron Cook - desc/o Margaret Wyatt DBR(1)199

Mary - of CT, b1628 d1703, m1646 Capt Benjamin Newberry d1689 deputy to the General Court of CT - desc/o Margaret Wyatt J&K123; ECD106, 241; MCD157; BCD353; DBR(1)336, 418, 557; DBR(2)721; DBR(3)126, 686; DBR(5)726; RAA61; CRL(1)183; GBR397; NEFGM(1)154

Mary - of CT, b1657 d1724, m1686 William Whiting - desc/o Margaret Wyatt CHB27; BCD27

ALLYN (cont.)

Matthew - of CT, bp 1604 of Brompton, Devon, England d1670/1671 son of Samuel Allyn of Chelmsford, England (?), m1626 Margaret Wyatt - the immigrant RAA1, 61; CRL(1)182, 183; sufficient proof of alleged royal ancestry is lacking

Capt Thomas - of CT, d1695/1696, m Abigail Warham - desc/o Margaret Wyatt CHB541; DBR(1)147; CRL(1)183; GBR396; NEFGM(1)153/156

Col Matthew - b1660 d1758 Council & Judge of the Superior Court for the Colony of CT, m1686 Elizabeth Wolcott d1734 in the 69th year of her age, dau/o Henry Wolcott Jr - desc/o Margaret Wyatt NEFGM(1)154

Capt Peletiah - of CT, b1689 d1766, m1711 Mary Stoughton dau/o Thomas Stoughton & Dorothy Talcott - desc/o Margaret Wyatt NEFGM(1)155

Samuel of CT, b1759, m Jerusha Bissell dau/o Capt Ebenezer F Bissell - desc/o Margaret Wyatt NEFGM(1)155

Samuel Wolcott - of CT, b1727 d1801, m1755 Joanna Mills d1794 aged sixty-three - desc/o Margaret Wyatt NEFGM(1)155

Capt Thomas - of CT, d1695/1696 trooper & made a freeman in 1658, m1658 Abigail Warham dau/o Rev John Warham - desc/o Margaret Wyatt NEFGM(1)154

ALMY John - b1720 - desc/o Anne Marbury RAA114

Joseph - b1727, m1750 Abigail Sisson - desc/o Rev Pardon Tillinghast DBR(1)296

Mercy - b1758, m1780 John Wing - desc/o Rev Pardon Tillinghast DBR(1)296

Sanford - b1759 - desc/o Anne Marbury RAA114

ALSOP Elizabeth - of CT, d1688 dau/o John Alsop & Temperance Gilbert, m(1)1642 Richard Baldwin bp 1622 d1685, m(2) William Fowler - the immigrant ECD(2)20, 25; DBR(5)923; RAA1, 65; GBR272 some aspect of royal descent merits further study; NEHGR(46)366/369; DLJ99

ALSTON (see also ALLSTON) Absalom - of NC, d1828, m Elizabeth Briggs - desc/o Col John Alston DBR(2)48; DBR(3)542, 656

Charity - of NC, b1743, m Capt James Jones - desc/o Col John Alston DBR(1)26; DBR(2)135, 177; DBR(5)369

Elizabeth - of NC, m1725 Samuel Williams Sr - desc/o Col John Alston JSW1674; DBR(1)619, 766, 770; DBR(2)817; DBR(4)270

Elizabeth - of NC, b abt 1739, m aft 1756 Thomas Crawford - desc/o Col John Alston DBR(1)630; DBR(2)736; RAA62

Elizabeth Elsie - of NC, m(1) John Gilbert, m(2) Edmund Duggan - desc/o Col John Alston DBR(2)397

Gideon - b1765 d1831, m1789 Frances Atherton - desc/o Col John Alston DBR(1)498; DBR(2)266

James Wright - m Temperance Thomas - desc/o Col John Alston DBR(1)313

Maj James - of NC, d1761, m aft 1741 Christine Lillington - desc/o Col John Alston CHB333; BCD333; DBR(2)16, 48, 665, 174, 190, 192; DBR(3)542, 656; DBR(4)785

Col James - of NC, b abt 1746/1748 d1815, m1774 Grizeal Yancey -

ALSTON (cont.)

desc/o Col John Alston CHB333; DBR(1)378; BCD333; DBR(2)665, 740; DBR(4)785

James - of NC, b1754 d1805, m(1) Sarah Kearney - desc/o Col John Alston DBR(2)214, 491, 564, 588, 839; DBR(3)137, 160, 253, 309

Maj or Col John - of NC 1710, bp 1673 d1758, m abt 1700 Mary Clark - the immigrant CHB333; JSW1673, 1674; BCD333; DBR(1)18, 20, 26, 59, 191, 192, 313, 376, 497, 538, 551, 619, 630, 631, 766, 770, 772; DBR(2)13, 16, 32, 38, 39, 48, 81, 134, 135, 168, 169, 175, 176, 208, 213, 214, 259, 261, 265, 272, 339, 345, 395, 396, 404, 488, 490, 491, 526, 559, 563, 580, 588, 665, 730, 731, 736, 740, 815, 816, 837, 838; DBR(3)136, 137, 157, 190, 224, 251, 307, 308, 309, 542, 656; DBR(4)92, 270, 299, 381, 785; DBR(5)368, 1018; RAA1, 62

John - of SC, son of William Alston & Thomasine Brooke, m Mrs Elizabeth Turgis Harris - the immigrant GBR149

Capt John - of NC, b1750 d1784, m Ann Hunt Macon - desc/o Col John Alston DBR(1)22, 497; DBR(2)32, 38, 266, 581

John - of NC, d1814 - desc/o Col John Alston DBR(2)48; DBR(3)192, 542, 656

Col Joseph John - of NC, b1702 d1780, m(1) Elizabeth Chancy, m(2) Euphan Wilson - desc/o Col John Alston DBR(1)20, 22, 59, 60, 313, 497, 538; DBR(2)32, 38, 82, 263, 265, 266, 526, 580; DBR(3)224; DBR(4)92, 299

Joseph John - of NC, b1767 d1841, m1791 Martha Kearney - desc/o Col John Alston DBR(1)20, 22

Judge Lemuel James - b1760 d1836, m Elisabeth Williams - desc/o Col John Alston DBR(1)192, 551, 772; DBR(2)170

Martha - of NC, d abt 1815, m Henry Meroney - desc/o Col John Alston DBR(1)60, 538; DBR(2)82; DBR(3)92

Mary - of NC, b1730, m Nathaniel Kimbrough - desc/o Col John Alston DBR(4)381

Mary - of NC, m abt 1754 Benjamin Hardee - desc/o Col John Alston DBR(2)345

Nathaniel - of NC, b1775 d1852, m1800 Mary Grey Jeffreys - desc/o Col John Alston CHB333; BCD333; DBR(1)378; DBR(2)665, 740, 741

Phillip - of NC, d1783, m Winifred Whitmel - desc/o Col John Alston DBR(1)18, 631; DBR(2)14

Philip - of NC, b1741, m Mildred McCoy - desc/o Col John Alston DBR(2)396, 397

Rachel - of NC, b1747, m Edmond Jones - desc/o Col John Hinton DBR(5)238

Solomon - of NC, d abt 1784, m Ann (Nancy) Hinton abt 1729 - desc/o Col John Alston DBR(1)26, 192, 551, 772; DBR(2)135, 169, 170, 177, 208, 214, 396, 491, 563, 588, 838; DBR(3)137, 309; DBR(4)381

Solomon - of NC, b1733 d1771, m Sarah____ - desc/o Col John Alston DBR(1)192, 772; DBR(2)170

Thomas Whitmel - of NC, b1755, m Lucy Faulcon - desc/o Col John Alston DBR(1)18, 19, 631; DBR(2)14

ALSTON (cont.)

William - of NC, d abt 1743, m abt 1735 Ann Kimbrough - desc/o Col John Alston DBR(1)630; DBR(2)345, 736; RAA62

Lieut-Col William - of VA, b1736 d1810, m1774 Charity Alston - desc/o Col John Alston DBR(2)208

William - of NC, d1789, m Sarah Yeargan - desc/o Col John Alston DBR(2)263; DBR(3)224; DBR(4)299

Col Willis - of VA, m Elisabeth Wright - desc/o Col John Alston DBR(1)313

Hon Willis "Congress" - of NC, b1770 d1837, m(2)1817 Sallie Madeline Potts - desc/o Col John Alston DBR(1)22; DBR(2)32, 38, 581

AMBLER Richard - of VA - the immigrant EDV91; sufficient proof of alleged royal ancestry is lacking

AMES Daniel - b1712 d1778, m1742 Hannah Keith - desc/o John Washbourne DBR(2)853

Hannah - b1770 d1840, m Imla Parker - desc/o Rev Peter Bulkeley DBR(4)322

Timothy - b1744 d1814, m(2)1786 Ruth Carver - desc/o John Washbourne DBR(2)853

AMORY Jonathan - of the Carolinas, d1699 - the immigrant EDV29; sufficient proof of alleged royal ancestry is lacking

ANDERSON Ann - b1751 d1831, m Dabney Minor b1749 d1797 son of John Minor & Susan (Carr) Minor - desc/o William Clopton DBR(1)517

ANDREWS Alice - of NY, m(1) John Higbee, m(2)1716 John Mathis - desc/o Peter Wright DBR(2)502; DBR(4)577

Edward - b1677/1678 d1716, m1694 Sarah Ong - desc/o Peter Wright DBR(4)241

Elizabeth - of NJ, d1725, m1712 Thomas Ridgway - desc/o Peter Wright DBR(4)241

Esther - of PA, b1673 d1741, m1692 George Parker - desc/o Peter Wright DBR(3)636

John - of CT 1640 - the immigrant EDV41; sufficient proof of alleged royal ancestry is lacking

Mary - of RI, m Simon Smith - desc/o William Arnold CHB18; BCD18

Mordecai - of NJ, b1664 d1736, m1691 Mary ___ - desc/o Peter Wright DBR(2)502; DBR(4)577

Whiting - of CT & NJ, b1764 d1811, m Lucy Curtis - desc/o Elizabeth St John CHB225; MCD310; BCD225

ANGELL Prudence - of RI, m Gideon Austin - desc/o Lawrence Wilkinson CHB277; MCD330

ANTRIM Hannah - b1781 - desc/o Elizabeth Denne RAA101

Joseph - b1748 - desc/o Elizabeth Denne RAA101

Mary - of NJ, b1742 d1823, m Aaron Robbins - desc/o Elizabeth Denne DBR(4)597

APPLETON Anne - of MA, m Thomas Storrow - desc/o Samuel Appleton THJ99

Maj Isaac - of MA, b1664 Ipswich d1747, m1695 Priscilla Baker b1674 d1731 dau/o Thomas Baker of Topsfield - desc/o Samuel Appleton BLG2540; DBR(2)647; DBR(3)454; NEFGM(1)178

Isaac - of MA, b1704 Ipswich d1794, m(1) Elizabeth Sawyer b1710

APPLETON (cont.)

d1785 dau/o Francis Sawyer of Wells, ME, m(2)1785 Mrs Hepzibah Appleton - desc/o Samuel Appleton BLG2540; DBR(3)454; NEFGM(1)178

Capt John - b1622 d1699, m1651 Priscilla Glover dau/o the Reverend Joseph Glover & Elizabeth (Harris) Glover - desc/o Samuel Appleton DBR(1)139; DBR(3)73; DBR(5)601; AAP153; GBR389 - desc/o Judith Everard AAP154; GBR459

Judith - b1634 Reydon, m Samuel Rogers of Ipswich MA - desc/o Samuel Appleton -NEFGM(1)177

Judith - of MA, b1653 d1741, m1678 Samuel Wolcott - desc/o Samuel Appleton DBR(3)73; RAA63

Martha - b1620 d1659, m Richard Jacob - desc/o Samuel Appleton DBR(1)360; DBR(2)463; DBR(3)216; DBR(4)492; RAA63

Priscilla - b1657, m1684 Rev Joseph Capen - desc/o Samuel Appleton DBR(1)139; DBR(5)602; AAP153; GBR390 - desc/o Judith Everard AAP154; GBR459

Priscilla - of MA, b1697 d1774, m1718 Thomas Burnham - desc/o Samuel Appleton DBR(2)647

Rebecca - of MA, m Henry Barlow - desc/o Samuel Appleton THJ99

Samuel - of MA 1635, bp 1586 Little Waldingfield, England d1670 Rowley, MA, son of Thomas Appleton & Mary Isaacke, m(1)1615/1616 Preston, England Judith Everard d abt 1628/1633 dau/o John Everard & Judith (Bourne) Everard, m(2) Martha____ - the immigrant FLW215; MCS98, 99; BLG2540; DBR(1)139, 360; DBR(2)461, 462, 463, 645, 646; DBR(3)73, 216, 454; DBR(4)492; DBR(5)600, 601; THJ97; RAA1, 63; EDV16; AAP153; CGA14; GBR389; EO2(3)688/722; NEFGM(1)176/180

Maj Samuel - of MA, b1624 Little Waldingfield, England d1696, m(1)1651 Hannah Paine dau/o William Paine of Ipswich, m(2)1656 Mary Oliver age 16 at the time of marriage d1698 dau/o John Oliver of Newbury, m(3) Elizabeth Whittingham dau/o William Whittingham & Mary Lawrence - desc/o Samuel Appleton BLG2540; DBR(3)73, 454; RAA63; NEFGM(1)177 THJ99)

Samuel - of MA, d1728, m Anna Gerrish - desc/o Samuel Appleton THJ99

Samuel - of MA, b1738/1739 d1819, m1769 Mary White d1834 dau/o Rev Timothy White of Haverhill - desc/o Samuel Appleton BLG2540; DBR(3)454; NEFGM(1)178

Samuel - of MA, m Mary Wentworth - desc/o Samuel Appleton THJ99

ARCHER Ann - of VA, m James Robertson II - desc/o Capt Henry Isham DBR(1)25; DBR(2)344, 641, 822

Elizabeth - of VA, m Thomas Branch - desc/o George Archer WAC71

George - of VA, d1677 - the immigrant WAC71; sufficient proof of alleged royal ancestry is lacking

George - of VA, b1654 d1731, m Elizabeth Harris - desc/o George Archer WAC71

John - of NY - the immigrant EDV14; sufficient proof of alleged royal ancestry is lacking

John - of VA, m(1) Frances____, m(2) Martha Field - desc/o George Archer WAC71

ARCHER (cont.)

Capt John III - of VA, b1734 d1784, m Elizabeth Trent - desc/o Capt Henry Randolph DBR(3)147

Peter Field - of VA, b abt 1763, m(1) Elizabeth Walthall - desc/o Capt Henry Randolph DBR(3)147

ARGALL Sir Samuel - of VA, b abt 1572 d1626 governor of VA, son of Richard Argall & Mary Scott unmarried - the immigrant DAB(1)345, 346; MCS97; GBR242; VGE199, 200, 346, 347, 394/396, 583, 664/666; GVFHB(4)528/532

ARMISTEAD Capt Anthony - of VA, b1645, m Hannah Ellyson - desc/o William Armistead CFA12; BLG2541

Bowles - of VA, m Mary Fontaine - desc/o William Armistead CFA13

Eleanor Bowles - of MD, m Judge William McMechen - desc/o Maria Horsmanden CHB55; BCD55 - desc/o Sarah Ludlow CHB183; BCD183

Elizabeth - of VA, b1687 d1716, m(1) Ralph Wormley, m(2)1703 William Churchill - desc/o William Armistead CFA13

Frances - of VA, d1685, m(1) Justinian Aylmer, m(2) Lieut Col Anthony Elliott, m(3) Col Christopher Wormley - desc/o William Armistead CFA12; BLG2541

Col Henry - of VA, b1670 d1740, m Martha Burwell - desc/o William Armistead BLG2541

Col John - of VA, b1635 d1698, m Judith Bowles - desc/o William Armistead CFA12; BLG2541

John - of VA, m(1) Elizabeth____, m(2) Susanna Merriwether - desc/o William Armistead CFA13

Col John - of VA, d1799, m 1764 Lucy Baylor - desc/o Martha Bacon CHB34; BCD34 - desc/o William Armistead BLG2541; CFA13

Judith - of VA, d1699, m Robert Carter - desc/o William Armistead CFA12

Lucy - of VA, m Thomas Nelson - desc/o Abigail Smith J&K192 - desc/o William Armistead CFA

Martha - of VA, m Dudley Diggs - desc/o William Armistead CFA13

Robert - of VA, m abt 1750 Elizabeth Burgess - desc/o William Armistead CFA13

William - of VA, bp 1610 d bef 1660, m1608 Anne____ - the immigrant WAC96; BLG2541, 2542; CFA12, 13; CGA14; royal descent not proven

William - of VA, b1671 d1711, m Ann Lee - desc/o William Armistead CFA13

William - of VA, m Maria Byrd - desc/o William Armistead CFA13

William - of VA, d1755, m1739 Mary Bowles - desc/o Martha Bacon CHB34; BCD34 - desc/o William Armistead BLG2541

ARNOLD Abagail - of RI & CT, b1685 d1705/1706, m1704/1705 Gov Jonathan Law - desc/o William Arnold CHB14; BCD14, 15

Alicia - of MD 1723, bp 1700 St Margaret, Westminster d1746 Annapolis, MD dau/o Michael Arnold & Anne Knipe, m1720 St James, Westminster, John Ross b1696 d1766 Annapolis, MD, served as Lord Baltimore's agent & clerk of the Maryland Council 1732/1764, alderman of Annapolis - the immigrant GBR150; FLW80

ARNOLD (cont.)

Benedict - of RI, b1615 d1678, m1640 Damaris Westcott - desc/o
   William Arnold J&K291; CHB14; BCD14; AMB404

Benedict - of RI, b1642 d1727, m(1) Mary Turner - desc/o William
   Arnold J&K291

Benedict - of RI & CN, b1683 - desc/o William Arnold J&K291

Benedict - of RI, b1740 d1801, m(1)1767 Margaret Mansfield,
   m(2)1779 Margaret Pippen - desc/o William Arnold J&K291

Calab - of RI, son of Benedict, m Abigail Wilbur - desc/o Thomas
   Arnold J&K292

Caleb - of RI, b1725 d1784, m1746 Patience Brown - desc/o Thomas
   Arnold J&K297; CHB323; MCB284; BCD323

David - of RI, m1765 Waite Lippitt - desc/o William Arnold AMB405

Eleazer - of RI, b1651 d1722, m Eleanor Smith - desc/o Thomas
   Arnold J&K297; CHB322, 323, MCB284; BCD322, 323

Elizabeth - of RI, b1611 d1683, m William Carpenter - desc/o William
   Arnold CHB13; MCB396; BCD13

Elizabeth - of RI, b1611, m Thomas Hopkins - desc/o William Arnold
   AMB404

Elizabeth - of RI, b1659 d1728, m1680 Peter Greene - desc/o William
   Arnold CHB19; BCD19; AMB404

Elizabeth - of RI, d1747, m1678 Capt Samuel Comstock - desc/o
   Thomas Arnold J&K296; CHB322; BCD322

Elizabeth - of RI, b1775, m Christopher Brown - desc/o Thomas
   Arnold CHB323; BCD323

Elisha - of RI, b1662 d1710, m Susanna Carpenter - desc/o William
   Arnold J&K293; AMB404; PFA Apx C #10

Esther - of RI, b1647 d1688, m(1)1671 James Dexter, m(2)1680
   William Andrews - desc/o William Arnold CHB18; BCD18; AMB404

Israel - of RI, b1649 d1716, m1677 Mary (wid/o Elisha Smith) Barker
   - desc/o William Arnold CHB18; BCD18; AMB405

James - of RI, b1689 d1777, m1719 Elizabeth Rhodes - desc/o
   William Arnold AMB405

Joanna - of RI, b1617 d1692, m(1) Resolved Waterman, m(2) Samuel
   Winson, m(3)1646 Zachariah Rhodes - desc/o William Arnold
   J&K294; CHB15; BCD15; AMB404

Jonathan - of RI, b1708 d1796, m Abigail Smith - desc/o Thomas
   Arnold CHB324; BCD324

Jonathan - of RI, b1741 d1793, m(1)1763 Molly Burr - desc/o Thomas
   Arnold CHB326; BCD326

Joseph - of RI, d1746, m1716 Mercy Stafford - desc/o Thomas Arnold
   J&K297; CHB323; MCB284; BCD323

Capt Josiah - of RI, b1646 d1724/1725, m(1)1683 Sarah Mills -
   desc/o William Arnold CHB14; BCD14

Josiah - of RI, b1717 d1745, m Amy Phillips - desc/o Thomas Arnold
   CHB326; BCD326

Katherine - of RI, m James Ballou II anc/o James Abram Garfield -
   desc/o William Arnold J&K293; PFA Apx C #10

Lydia - of RI, b1749 d1828, m William Buffum - desc/o Thomas Arnold
   CHB326; BCD326

Mary - of RI, m Thomas Steere - desc/o Thomas Arnold CHB323;

ARNOLD (cont.)

    BCD323

    Capt Nathan - of RI, d 1778, m Esther Slack Darling - desc/o William Arnold CHB18; BCD18

    Nehemiah - of RI, b1748 d1835, m1774 Alice Brown - desc/o Thomas Arnold J&K297; CHB323; MCB284; BCD323

    Oliver - of RI, d1770 - desc/o William Arnold EDV30

    Penelope - of RI, m George Hazard - desc/o William Arnold J&K292

    Phebe - of RI, b1670 d173_, m1691 Benjamin Smith Jr - desc/o William Arnold CHB17; BCD17; AMB404

    Phebe - of RI, b1699, m James Cargill Jr - desc/o William Arnold CHB17

    Richard - of RI, b1642 d1710, m(1) Mary Angell - desc/o Thomas Arnold CHB323; BCD323

    Capt Richard - of RI, b1668 d1745, m(1) Mary Woodward, m(2)1715 Dinah Thornton - desc/o Thomas Arnold CHB324. 326; BCD324, 326

    Richard - of RI, m1722 Ruth Aldrich - desc/o Thomas Arnold CHB324; BCD324

    Ruth - of RI, m1738/1739 Gideon Comstock - desc/o Thomas Arnold CHB324; BCD324

    Samuel - of RI, d1736, m Elizabeth ____ - desc/o Thomas Arnold CHB323; BCD323

    Sarah - of RI, d1727, m1708 Silas Carpenter Jr - desc/o William Arnold CHB18; BCD18; AMB404

    Seth - of RI, m Mrs Belinda (Mason) Streeter - desc/o William Arnold CHB18 - desc/o Susan Clinton BCD146

    Stephen - of RI, b1622 d1699, m1646 Sarah Smith - desc/o William Arnold J&K293; CHB17; BCD17; AMB404; PFA Apx C #10

    Stephen - of RI, b1654 - desc/o William Arnold AMB404

    Thomas - of RI, bp 1599 d1674, m(1)1623/1624 ___, m(2)1638/1639 Phebe Parkhurst - the immigrant J&K296; CHB322; MCB284; BCD322; CGA14; no longer accepted as being of royal descent

    Thomas - of RI, b1675 d1727, m1706 Elizabeth Burlingame - desc/o Thomas Arnold CHB324; BCD324

    Thomas - of RI, d1765, m(3) Patience Cook - desc/o Thomas Arnold CHB326; BCD326

    Welcome - of RI, b1745 d1797, m1773 Patience Greene - desc/o Thomas Arnold CHB324; BCD324

    William - of RI 1635, b1587 d abt 1676, m Christian Peake - the immigrant J&K291, CHB13; BCD13; AMB404l; EDV30; PFA Apx C #10; CGA14; sufficient proof of alleged royal ancestry is lacking

    William - of VA, b abt 1772 d aft 1838, m abt 1795 Nancy Berry - desc/o Col John Washington JSW1751

ARUNDEL Anne - of MD, d1649 Anne Arundel Co MD was named after her, dau/o Thomas Arundell & Margaret Howard, m1629 Cecilius (Cecil) Calvert 2nd Lord Baltimore - the immigrant J&K281; ECD147; DBR(1)151; DBR(3)243; GBR136; CFA(2)164

ARUNDEL-HOWARD Matthew - of VA, b1609 d bef 1659, m abt 1625 Ann Hall - the immigrant JSW1770; sufficient proof of alleged royal ancestry is lacking

ASFORDBY Susanna - of NY & MD, d1742, m1691 John Beatty d1721 - desc/o William Asfordby CHB511; DBR(2)739

William - of NY bef 1674, bp 1638 d1698, member of first New York Assembly & high sheriff of Ulster Co, son of John Asfordby & Alice Wolley, m abt 1666 Martha Burton d aft 1711 dau/o William Burton - the immigrant CHB511; MCS60; DBR(2)737, 738, 739; RAA1; 64; GBR213

ASHTON Charles - of VA, d1672 - the immigrant WAC11; sufficient proof of alleged royal ancestry is lacking

Col Henry - of VA, b1671 d1731 - desc/o Charles Ashton WAC11

John - of NJ, m Patience____ - desc/o John Throckmorton ECD(3)262

Rachel - of NJ, d1740, m Richard Stevens - desc/o John Throckmorton ECD(3)262

Rebecca - of NJ, b1672, m David Stout son of Richard & Penelope Stout - desc/o John Throckmorton DBR(1)178; DBR(5)1012

Sarah - of VA, b1769 d1820, m1788 Judge Nicholas FitzHugh - desc/o Col George Reade DBR(5)651

ASTON Anne - of VA, d abt 1749, m1706 Robert Bolling Jr - desc/o Lieut Col Walter Aston ECD(3)8

Elizabeth - of VA, m Francis Mason Jr - desc/o Lieut Col Walter Aston CHB438, 537

Elizabeth - of VA, b abt 169_, m(1)1723 John Carter, m(2) Bowler Cocke - desc/o Lieut Col Walter Aston CHB438

Elizabeth - of VA, d1713, m1656 Thomas Binns - desc/o Lieut Col Walter Aston ECD(3)13; DBR(4)657; DBR(5)580; WAC66; VHG275

Mary - of VA, m(1) abt 1647 Lieut Col Richard Cocke, m(2) Col Edward Hill Jr - desc/o Lieut Col Walter Aston CHB438; ECD(3)8; MCD159; MCS76; DBR(1)669; DBR(2)146, 324, 754, 849; DBR(3)508; DBR(5)257, 1003, 1020; WAC66; GBR361; VGE390, 391; VHG275

Martha - of VA, m Hugh Gifford - desc/o Lieut Col Walter Aston CHB438

Richard - of VA, b1650/1660, m Elizabeth____- desc/o Lieut Col Walter Aston ECD(3)8

Susannah - of VA, d1662, m Lieut Col Edward Major - desc/o Lieut Col Walter Aston CHB438; WAC66; VGE390, 391; VHG275

Lieut Col Walter - of VA 1634, b1607 d1656 son of Walter Aston & Joyce Nason, m(1) ____Norbrow, m(2) Hannah Jordan - the immigrant CHB438; ECD(3)8, 13; MCD159; MCS76; DBR(1)669; DBR(2)125, 145, 322, 323, 430, 432, 754, 849; DBR(3)42, 507; DBR(4)127, 657; DBR(5)257, 580, 858, 888, 1003, 1019; RAA1, 64; WAC66; CGA15; GBR361; VGE390, 391; VHG272/275

Walter Jr - of VA, d1666/1667 - desc/o Lieut Col Walter Aston CHB438; WAC66

ATKINS Catherine - of MA, b1758 d1829, m Samuel Eliot - desc/o Thomas Dudley J&K197; CRL(1)384

Dudley - of MA, b1731, m1752 Sarah Kent - desc/o Thomas Dudley J&K197; CRL(1)384

Dudley - of MA, b1760 d1829 - desc/o Thomas Dudley CRL(1)383, 384

Mary Russell - of MA, b1753 d1836, m1779 George Searle - desc/o Thomas Dudley CRL(1)384

ATTAWAY Elizabeth - of MD, m Capt John Bond - desc/o Thomas Gerard
  DBR(2)233; DBR(3)76; DBR(4)101

ATWOOD (ATTWOOD) Amy - of VA, d1741, m Alexander Legget - desc/o
  Capt Henry Woodhouse APP702

Anne - of MD, m1739 William Diggs - desc/o George Atwood CHB10;
  BCD10

Frances - m Col Lemuel Cornick d1772/1773 - desc/o Capt Henry
  Woodhouse DBR(1)347; DBR(2)445

Frances - of VA, m___Moore - desc/o Capt Henry Woodhouse APP702

George - of MD, d1744, m Anne Petre - the immigrant CHB10; BCD10;
  sufficient proof of alleged royal ancestry is lacking

Heman - b abt 1738, m Jerusha Case - desc/o Abigail Dunham LDS15

John - of VA, d1719/1720, m___ - desc/o Capt Henry Woodhouse
  APP702

Stephen - b1647/1648, m Apphia Bangs - desc/o Abigail Dunham
  LDS15

Thomas - b abt 1695, m(1) Phebe Mayo - desc/o Abigail Dunham
  LDS15

William - of VA, d1720, m Elizabeth___ - desc/o Capt Henry
  Woodhouse APP701, 702

AUBREY (see also AWBREY) Barbara - of PA, dau/o William Aubrey &
  Elizabeth Aubrey, m John Bevan Sr - the immigrant GBR135

Louisa Anna (or Louise Ann) Matilda - of NY, dau/o Anthony &
  Mariana Matilda Lockhart-Wishard Aufrere, m George Barclay - the
  immigrant GBR51, 52

AUSTIN Rose - b1678 - desc/o Rose Stoughton RAA119

Ruth - of RI, m James Cranston - desc/o Lawrence Wilkinson
  CHB277; MCD330

AVERY Abigail - of CT, b1735, m1757 Deacon John Hurlbut - desc/o
  Bridget Tompson DBR(3)684

Anna - of CT, m George Haliburton - desc/o Susan Fienes CHB528

Humphrey - of CT, father of Solomon Avery - desc/o Susan Clinton
  J&K247

John - of CT, b1705 d1789, m1732 Anne Stanton - desc/o Alice
  Freeman DBR(3)682

Jonathan - of CT, m Preserved___ - desc/o Susan Fienes CHB528

Lucy - of CT, m Godfrey Rockefeller anc/o John Davison Rockefeller -
  desc/o Susan Clinton J&K247

Mary - of MA, b1695 d1739, m1720 William Walworth - desc/o Susan
  Clinton CHB417 - desc/o Susannah Palmes ECD(3)185, 188;
  MCD234

Miles - of CT, father of Lucy Avery - desc/o Susan Clinton J&K247

Robert - of CT, m Anna___ - desc/o Susan Fienes CHB528

Solomon - of CT, father of Miles Avery - desc/o Susan Clinton J&K247

AWBREY (see also AUBREY) Martha - of PA, b1662 d1726/1727, m1692
  Rees Thomas - the immigrant CHB299; BCD299; sufficient proof of
  alleged royal ancestry is lacking

AYLETT Anne - of VA, m1743 Augustine Washington, a brother of George
  Washington - desc/o Dr Thomas Gerard MG(1)492

Elizabeth - of VA, b1769, m1787 Alexander Spotswood Moore - desc/o
  Col John West CHB244; BCD244; DBR(3)676; DBR(4)301, 765

AYLETT (cont.)

Mary Macon - of VA, m Philip Fitzhugh - desc/o Col John Henry MCD233

Col Philip - of VA, b1767 d1831, m Elizabeth Henry b1769 d1842 - desc/o Col John West CHB244; BCD244; GVFWM(2)131

Col William - of VA, d1781, m1766 Mary Macon dau/o Col James Macon & Elizabeth Moore - desc/o Col John West DBR(3)676; DBR(4)301, 765; GVFWM(2)131

AYRES Edmond - of VA, d1719, m Ann____ - desc/o Robert Drake DBR(5)1007; SMO25

Francis - of VA, b bef 1688 Accomack Co d1721 Accomack Co, m bef 1700 Accomack Co, Sarah____ d bef 1721 Accomack Co - desc/o Robert Drake SMO25

Francis - of VA, d bef 1737 Accomack Co, m bef 1726 Accomack Co, m Tabitha____ d aft 1744 Accomack Co - desc/o Robert Drake SMO25

Francis - of VA, d abt 1804 Accomack Co, m Margaret____ d aft 1804 - desc/o Col Nathaniel Littleton SMO26

Hulda - of VA, m George Wise - desc/o Robert Drake DBR(5)1007

Jacob - of VA, b abt 1730 Accomack Co d abt 1782 Accomack Co, m bef 1756 Ann____ d aft 1782 Accomack Co - desc/o Robert Drake SMO25

AXEL Hans, Count von Fersen - b1755 d1810, Swedish soldier, aide-de-camp to Rochambeau during the American Revolution, unmarried - the immigrant GBR91

– B –

BACHE Sarah - of NY, b1774 d1852, m James Bleecker - desc/o John Barclay MCB219

BACON Abigail - of VA - desc/o Martha Bacon CHB542

Agnes - of VA, m Matthew Hobson - desc/o Maj Gen Nathaniel Bacon CHB348; BCD348

Anne - of VA, m____Wilkinson - desc/o Col Nathaniel Bacon WAC59

Asa - of MA, b1769 d1855, m(1) Lois Fisk, m(2) Elizabeth Comins - desc/o Michael Bacon BLG2544

Daniel - of MA, b1738 d1813, m Mary Baldwin - desc/o Michael Bacon BLG2544

Edmund - of GA, m Elizabeth Cocke - desc/o Maj Gen Nathaniel Bacon CHB348; BCD348

Elizabeth - of VA, b1674, m Hugh Chamberlain, physician to the King - desc/o Col Nathaniel Bacon GVFWM(1)192

Elizabeth - of VA, m Thomas Burrows - desc/o Col Nathaniel Bacon WAC59

Eunice - of CT, b1755 d1838, m1777 Jehiel Hurlburt - desc/o John Drake DBR(3)661

Sir Francis Baron Verulam, Lord Keeper of the Great Seal, Lord High Treasurer of England, poet - the immigrant J&K187; sufficient proof of alleged royal ancestry is lacking

John - of MA, d1683, m1657 Rebecca Hall - desc/o Michael Bacon BLG2544

John - of MA, b1710 d1806, m Mary____ - desc/o Michael Bacon

BACON (cont.)
> BLG2544
>
> Capt John - of GA, m Agnes Hobson - desc/o Maj Gen Nathaniel Bacon CHB347
>
> John - of GA, b1766 d1812, m Eliza Ruffin - desc/o Maj Gen Nathaniel Bacon CHB348; BCD347, 348
>
> Martha - of VA, d abt 1667, m 1652 Anthony Smith - the immigrant CHB32; BCD32; WAC59; sufficient proof of alleged royal ancestry is lacking
>
> Mehitable - b1706 - desc/o Griffith Bowen RAA72
>
> Michael - of MA 1633, b1579 d1648, m Alice____ - the immigrant BLG2544; sufficient proof of alleged royal ancestry is lacking
>
> Col Nathaniel - of VA 1650, b1620 d1692 member VA Council for forty years, son of Rev James Bacon of Friston Hall, England, m Elizabeth Kingsmill - the immigrant J&K189; EDV61; WAC58, 59; CGA16; GVFWM(1)192, sufficient proof of alleged royal ancestry is lacking
>
> Maj Gen Nathaniel - of VA, b1647 d1676 "the Rebel Patriot of 1676" governor of VA & leader of Bacon's Rebellion, son of Thomas Bacon of Friston Hall, Suffolk & Elizabeth Brooke, m Elizabeth Duke dau/o Sir Edward Duke - the immigrant J&K188; DAB(1)482, 483; CHB347; BCD347; GBR241; GVFWM(1)192
>
> Nathaniel - of VA, b1675/1676 d1743, m Elizabeth Parke - desc/o Maj Gen Nathaniel Bacon CHB347; BCD347
>
> Nathaniel - of VA, b1705 d1779 - desc/o Maj Gen Nathaniel Bacon CHB348; BCD348
>
> Nathaniel Parke - of VA - desc/o Maj Gen Nathaniel Bacon CHB347; BCD347
>
> Sara - of VA, b1740 d1816, m bef 1760 Charles Edwin Crenshaw - desc/o Maj Gen Nathaniel Bacon CHB349; BCD349
>
> Thomas - of MA, b1667 d1749, m1691 Hannah Fales - desc/o Michael Bacon BLG2544

BAGLEY Hannah - of MA, m1750 John Colby - desc/o Anthony Colby DBR(5)685, 769
> John - of MA, b1685 d1727/1728, m1708 Hannah Fowler - desc/o Anthony Colby DBR(5)684, 769
>
> Orlando - of MA, b1658 d1728, m1681 Sarah Sargent - desc/o Anthony Colby DBR(5)684, 769
>
> Sarah - b1663, m John Mack - desc/o Anthony Colby LDS94

BAINTON Anne - of MA, dau/o Ferdinando Bainton & Joan Weare alias Browne, m Christopher Batt - the immigrant GBR249; NE(141)94

BAKER Elizabeth - b1723, m1740 John Low b1714 - desc/o Samuel Appleton DBR(1)139
> Elizabeth - of MA, b1765, m1792 Peter Granger - desc/o Samuel Appleton DBR(5)602
>
> Joseph - of MA, b1741 d1801, m1762 Hephzibah Thorndike - desc/o Samuel Appleton DBR(5)602
>
> Priscilla - m Tarrant Putnam Jr - desc/o Samuel Appleton AAP153; GBR390 - desc/o Judith Everard AAP154; GBR459
>
> Samuel - of MA, d1797, m1778 Patience Chase - desc/o Robert Abell DBR(5)142

BAKER (cont.)
    Capt Thomas - of MA, b1710 d1777, m1729 Sarah Wade - desc/o
      Samuel Appleton DBR(5)602
BALCH or BALCHE John - of MA 1623, b1579 - the immigrant EDV97;
    CGA16; sufficient proof of alleged royal ancestry is lacking
    Rev Thomas - of MD bef 1690 - the immigrant EDV97; CGA16;
      sufficient proof of alleged royal ancestry is lacking
BALDWIN Abiah - of CT, b1733 d1792, m1763 Joel Atwater - desc/o
    Elizabeth Alsop DLJ100
    Abigail - of CT, b1658, m Samuel Baldwin - desc/o Obadiah Bruen
      CHB387; RAA74
    Abigail - b1684? - desc/o Elizabeth Alsop RAA65
    Alexis - bp 1778 d1821, m Comfort Baldwin d1857 aged 73 years
      dau/o Henry Baldwin - desc/o Elizabeth Alsop DLJ103, 104;
      RAA65
    Alsop - of CT, b1741/1742 d1824, m(1)1773 Elizabeth Sherman
      b1751 d1775 dau/o Amos Sherman & Elizabeth Rexford, m(2)1778
      Bathsheba bp 1753 d1815 dau/o Ebenezer Smith & Mabel Smith -
      desc/o Elizabeth Alsop DLJ101
    Amos - bp 1780 d1849, m1799 Molly Downs d1851 aged 70 years
      dau/o Joseph Downs & Rhoda Beecher - desc/o Elizabeth Alsop
      DLJ104
    Andrew - of CT, b1724, m(1)1753 Ann Merwin d1758 aged 35 years,
      m(2) Abigail ___ d1760 aged 37 years, m(3) Mary Hine d1792 -
      desc/o Elizabeth Alsop DLJ100
    Barnabas - of CT, bp 1698/1699 d aft 1779, m1725 Mehitable Tuttle
      b1699 d aft 1779 dau/o Thomas Tuttle & Mary Sanford, wid/o
      John Beecher - desc/o Elizabeth Alsop DLJ99, 100
    Lieut Barnabas - of CT, b1726 d1804, m1748 Mary Terrill b abt 1728
      d1803 dau/o Ephraim Terrill & Elizabeth Lines - desc/o Elizabeth
      Alsop DLJ100
    Capt Barnabas - b abt 1760 d1804, m(1) Huldah Baldwin bp 1764
      d1801 dau/o Enoch Baldwin & Mary Alling, m(2)1803 Jerusha
      Sanford d1811 aged 72 years - desc/o Elizabeth Alsop DLJ100
    Caleb - b1723/1724 - desc/o Obadiah Bruen RAA74
    Charles - b1751 d1818, m1792 Susanna Hine b abt 1775 d1853
      dau/o Stephen Hine & Susanna Smith - desc/o Elizabeth Alsop
      DLJ101
    David - b1755 d1831, m1778 Martha Perkins b1757 d1838 dau/o
      David Perkins & Lydia Bradley - desc/o Elizabeth Alsop DLJ103
    Dorcas - b1738 d1814, m1756 Silas Alling - desc/o Elizabeth Alsop
      DLJ101
    Elijah - of CT, b1740 d1816, m Margaret Lester - desc/o Elizabeth
      Alsop DLJ100
    Elisha - b1741, m1768 Jerusha Coe - desc/o Elizabeth Alsop DLJ101
    Elizabeth - b abt 1670 d aft 1727, m abt 1690 Daniel Tichenor -
      desc/o Obadiah Bruen DBR(1)388; DBR(2)498; DBR(5)170
    Elizabeth - of CT, b abt 1728 d1784, m1746 Jedodiah Andrews -
      desc/o Elizabeth Alsop DLJ100
    Capt Enoch - of CT, b1736 d1815, m(1)1760 Mary Alling bp 1743
      dau/o Ebenezer Alling & Mary Tuttle, m(2) Sarah Pierson b1753

BALDWIN (cont.)

dau/o Oliver Pierson & Hannah___ - desc/o Elizabeth Alsop DLJ100

Enoch - bp 1776 d1815 Batavia, New York, m Lucy Downs dau/o Joseph Downs & Rhoda Beecher - desc/o Elizabeth Alsop DLJ103

Capt Ephraim - b abt 1767 d1835, m Martha Newton b1768 d1826 dau/o Samuel Newton & Mary Camp - desc/o Elizabeth Alsop DLJ101

Esther - of CT, b1731 d1822, m1752 Daniel Beecher - desc/o Elizabeth Alsop DLJ100

Eunice - of CT, b1738, m1758 Jonathan Andrew - desc/o Elizabeth Alsop DLJ101

Eunice - b abt 1770 d1823, m(1) John Woodruff, m(2) Joseph Northrop - desc/o Elizabeth Alsop DLJ101

Hannah - of CT, b1663, m1682 Dr John Fiske - desc/o Obadiah Bruen CHB29; BCD29; DBR(1)17; RAA74

Hannah - of CT, b1674 d1726, m Samuel Sanford - desc/o Obadiah Bruen FFF252

Hannah - b1767 - desc/o Thomas Newberry RAA118

Henry - of CT, b abt 1734 d1801, m1757 Lydia Botsford - desc/o Elizabeth Alsop DLJ101

Hezekiah - b1756 d1831, m1782 Elizabeth Hine bp 1750 d1839 dau/o Stephen Hine & Elizabeth Carrington - desc/o Elizabeth Alsop DLJ102

Huldah - bp 1764 d1801, m Barnabas Baldwin - desc/o Elizabeth Alsop DLJ103

Isaac - of CT, b1740 d1799, m1766 Philena Pardee b1747/1748 d1826 dau/o Samuel Pardee & Rachel Hotchkiss - desc/o Elizabeth Alsop DLJ101

Jared - m Hannah Bronson - desc/o Elizabeth Alsop DLJ101

Joanna - of NJ, m Isaac Nutman - desc/o Obadiah Bruen ECD122

Jonathan - of NJ, b abt 1691 d1726, m Phebe Roberts - desc/o Obadiah Bruen ECD122

Martha - of CT, b1690 d1740, m1710 Enos Camp - desc/o Elizabeth Alsop ECD(2)26

Mary - of CT, b1735, m1771 David Beebe of Trumbull - desc/o Elizabeth Alsop DLJ101

Mary - of CT, b1743 d1826, m1771 Josiah Strong - desc/o Elizabeth Alsop DLJ101

Mary - b1765 d1849, m1783 Ebenezer Beecher - desc/o Elizabeth Alsop DLJ101

Mehitable - of CT, b1728 d1813, m1751 James Thompson - desc/o Elizabeth Alsop DLJ100

Capt Nathaniel - of CT, b1693 d1760, m Elizabeth Parmlee - desc/o Obadiah Bruen CHB387; MCD173

Philemon - b1758 - desc/o Obadiah Bruen RAA74

Richard - of CT, b1622, m Elizabeth Alsop - the immigrant RAA1, 65; CGA16; NE(26)294/303 sufficient proof of alleged royal ancestry is lacking, his wife Elizabeth Alsop of CT was of royal ancestry

Richard - of CT, bp 1745 d1823, m1771 Abiah Botsford d1805 aged 58 years - desc/o Elizabeth Alsop DLJ101

BALDWIN (cont.)

Samuel - b1689 d1764, m Rebecca____ d1793 - desc/o Obadiah
    Bruen RAA74; CGA16

Samuel - b1700 d1785, m1723 Mercy Allen d1790 - desc/o Elizabeth
    Alsop DLJ105

Samuel - of CT, b1725 d1804, m1744 Mercy Stanley - desc/o Obadiah
    Bruen CHB387; MCD173

Samuel Jr - of NY, b1755 d1838, m Lucinda Hill - desc/o Obadiah
    Bruen CHB387; MCD173

Sarah - of CT, bp 1649, m1667 Ensign Samuel Riggs d1738 - desc/o
    Elizabeth Alsop ECD(2)20; MCD173; DBR(5)923; GBR272

Sarah - b1655 - desc/o Obadiah Bruen RRA74

Sarah - b1747/1748, m1784 William Burrit - desc/o Elizabeth Alsop
    DLJ101

Silas - b abt 1770 d1808, m Mary Smith b1774 d1850 dau/o David
    Smith & Huldah Beecher - desc/o Elizabeth Alsop DLJ101

Sylvanus - of CT, b1706 d1785, m1734 Mary French b1711 d1802
    dau/o Francis French & Anna Bowers - desc/o Elizabeth Alsop
    DLJ101

Sylvester - of CT - the immigrant EDV117, 118; sufficient proof of
    alleged royal ancestry is lacking

Temperance - of CT, b1736 d1785, m Samuel Baldwin - desc/o
    Elizabeth Alsop DLJ100

Theophilus - of CT, b1658 d1698, m1682/1683 Elizabeth Canfield -
    desc/o Elizabeth Alsop ECD(2)25; RAA65

Theophilus - of CT, bp 1699 d1784, m Dorothy Munson b abt 1711
    d1790 dau/o John Munson & Sarah Cooper - desc/o Elizabeth
    Alsop DLJ101

Theophilus - of CT, b1735 d1826, m(1)1763 Hephizibah Sherman
    b1742 d1775 dau/o Amos Sherman & Elizabeth Rexford, m(2)1776
    Sarah Strong dau/o Adino Strong - desc/o Elizabeth Alsop DLJ101

Thomas - of CT, bp 1698/1699, m1711/1712 Jerusha Clark - desc/o
    Elizabeth Alsop DLJ99

Thomas - of CT, b1742 d1834, m(1) Eunice____d1780 aged 33 years,
    m(2) Hannah____d1829 aged 66 years - desc/o Elizabeth Alsop
    DLJ100

Thomas - m Eunice____ & had issue - desc/o Elizabeth Alsop DLJ101

Thomas - m Hannah____ & had issue - desc/o Elizabeth Alsop DLJ101

Timothy - of CT, b abt 1695 d1766, m(1)1719 Zerviah Johnson b abt
    1698 d1734 dau/o Jeremiah Johnson & Elizabeth Johnson, m(2)
    Mabel Cooper b1700 d1777 dau/o Samuel Cooper & Elizabeth
    Smith - desc/o Elizabeth Alsop DLJ100

Timothy - of CT, b1722 d1800, m1744/1745 Sarah Beecher b1720
    d1794 dau/o Ebenezer Beecher & Hannah Mix - desc/o Elizabeth
    Alsop DLJ100

BALL Henry - of PA, b1762 d1816, m Elizabeth Fulton - desc/o Thomond
    Ball AFA72

Col Jesse - of VA, b aft 1744, m Agatha Conway - desc/o Col George
    Reade JSW1648; DBR(5)343

Rev John Smith - of VA, b1773 d1849, m1799 Nancy Opie - desc/o
    Col George Reade JSW1648; DBR(2)152; DBR(3)397; DBR(4)167;

BALL (cont.)
DBR(5)343

Lieut Col Joseph - of VA, b1649 d1711, m(2) Mary Johnson or (Bennett?) - desc/o Dr Richard Edwards DBR(1)224 - desc/o Col William Ball TAG(51)167/171

Mary - m William Bates - desc/o Thomas Sargent DBR(1)748

Mary - of VA, b1708/1709 d1789, m(2)1730/1731 Capt Augustine Washington - desc/o Dr Richard Edwards DBR(1)224 - desc/o Col William Ball TAG(51)167/171

Mottrom MD - of VA, b1767 d1842, m1800 Martha Corbin Turberville - desc/o Col Nicholas Spencer CHB530

Spencer - of VA, m____Mottrom - desc/o Col Nicholas Spencer CHB529

Spencer - of VA, b1762 d1832, m Elizabeth Landon Carter - desc/o Col Nicholas Spencer CHB530

Spencer Mottrom - of VA, m Elizabeth Waring - desc/o Col Nicholas Spencer CHB530

Theord - of PA 1769, b abt 1736, m1759 Margaret Denham - the immigrant AFA72; sufficient proof of alleged royal ancestry is lacking

Col William - of VA, - the immigrant TAG(51)167/171; sufficient proof of royal ancestry is lacking

BALLARD Ebenezer - b abt 1740 - desc/o John Deighton RAA86

Sarah - of MA, b1764 d1852, m1783 Micajah Robinson - desc/o Judge Simon Lynde DBR(3)746; DBR(4)835

BALLIE Ann Elizabeth - m John Irvine of Georgia - desc/o Col Kenneth Ballie GBR114

Col Kenneth - of GA, son of John Ballie of Balrobert, m Elizabeth Mackay - the immigrant AAP150; GBR114 some aspect of royal descent merits further study

BALLINGER Bathsheba - b1760, m1772 John Moore b1755 d1834 - desc/o George Elkington DBR(1)107

Joshua - of NJ, b1714 d1761, m1749 Naomi Dunn b1728 - desc/o George Elkington DBR(1)107

Mary - of NJ, d1764, m1733 Thomas Garwood b1707 d1796 - desc/o George Elkington DBR(1)7

BALLORD Lynde - of CT, b1774 d1825, m1794 Polly Bates - desc/o Judge Simon Lynde CHB310; MCB208; BCD310

BANCROFT John - of DE, b1774 d1852, m Elizabeth Wood - the immigrant AFA8; CGA17; sufficient proof of alleged royal ancestry is lacking

BANKS Gershom - of CT, b1752 d1805, m (his cousin) Ruth Banks dau/o Benjamin Banks, Jr - desc/o Grace Chetwoode CHB395

BARBER Daniel - b1719 - desc/o John Drake RAA87

Daniel - b1732/1733 - desc/o Agnes Harris RAA131

David - b1686 - desc/o John Drake RAA87

Joel - of CT, m Mary Drake - desc/o John Drake AFA116

John - of CT, b1676/1677, m Jane Alvord - desc/o John Drake RAA87; AFA116

Joseph - of CT, b1681, m1708 Mary Loomis - desc/o John Drake DBR(3)663; RAA87

Mary - b1758 - desc/o John Drake RAA87

BARBER (cont.)

Mindwell - of CT, b1716, m1740 Ezekiel Scoville - desc/o John Drake DBR(3)663

Naomi - b1721 - desc/o John Drake RAA87

Ruth - of CT, b1683, m(2)1706 William Phelps - desc/o John Drake THC83 - desc/o Thomas Moore THC220

Rosetta - b1758 - desc/o Agnes Harris RAA131

Temperance - b1718 - desc/o John Drake RAA87 William of CT, b1762, m Mary (Polly) Thompson - desc/o John Drake ECD(2)120; AFA116

BARBOUR Brig Gen Philip - of VA, b1770 d1818, m(2)1806 Elizabeth Branch Hopkins - desc/o Col George Reade ECD(2)231

BARCLAY Andrew - of NY, m1737 Helena Roosevelt - desc/o John Barclay MCB219

Anna Dorothea - m Lieut Col Beverley Robinson - desc/o John Barclay AMB343

Anna Dorothy - of NY, b1741 d1795, m1760 Theophylact Bache - desc/o John Barclay MCB219

Anne - b1729 d prior to 1761, m1749 John Craig - desc/o John Barclay CRL(4)390

Anthony - b1755 d1805, m Anna Lent - desc/o John Barclay AMB343

Charles - b1733 d1813, m Rebecca Gordon - desc/o John Barclay CRL(4)390

Charles - of NJ & NY, b1764 d1830, m abt 1784 Anne Van Kirk - desc/o John Barclay CRL(4)390, 391

Cornelia - of NY, m(1) Stephen De Lancey, m(2) General Hudson Lowe - desc/o John Barclay AMB343

David - of NJ, b abt 1610, m Katherine Gordon - the immigrant RAA1, 65; sufficient proof of alleged royal ancestry is lacking

David - of NJ, son of Robert Barclay & Christian Mollison, m Priscilla Freame - desc/o Robert Barclay GBR48

David - b1727 d1772, m1749 Elizabeth Walker - desc/o John Barclay CRL(4)390

Rev Henry - of NY, b1711 d1764, m Mary Rutgers - desc/o John Barclay MCB326; AMB343

Jean (Jane or Joan) - of NJ, b1683 dau/o Robert Barclay & Christian Mollison, m1707 Alexander Forbes - desc/o Robert Barclay ECD247; GBR48

John - of NJ, b1659 d1731, m(1) Katherine Rescarrick, m(2) Cornelia Van Schaick - bro/o Robert Barclay FLW220 - desc/o Catherine Gordon MCB218, 219; GBR48 - the immigrant MCB325; CGA17; CRL(4)388

John - m Susanna Willet - desc/o Robert Barclay GBR48

John - of NJ, b1702 d1786, m(1)1725 Katherine Gordon, m(2)1763 Jane Van Dyke - desc/o John Barclay CRL(4)390

John - of NJ & NY, b1731 - desc/o John Barclay CRL(4)390

Katherine - b1742, m1760 David Stout - desc/o John Barclay CRL(4)390

Lewis - of NJ, b1761 d1820 - desc/o John Barclay CRL(4)390

Lydia - b1739, m Thomas Brown - desc/o John Barclay CRL(4)390

Peter - b1735 d1810 - desc/o John Barclay CRL(4)390

BARCLAY (cont.)

Robert - of NJ, b1648 d1690, Quaker, m Christian Mollison - the
immigrant FLW220; ECD247; MCB325; MCS68; EDV24, 25;
GBR48

Robert - of NJ, b1737 d1818, m(1)1760 Alice (or Elsie) Van Kirk,
m(2)1787 Miriam____ - desc/o John Barclay CRL(4)390

Robert - b1768, m Deborah Barclay - desc/o John Barclay CRL(4)390

Rev Thomas - of NY, b abt 1663 d1734, m1709 Anna Dorothea
Drauyer - desc/o John Barclay MCB219, 325; BLG2547

Col Thomas - of NY, b1753 d1830, m1775 Susan de Lancey - desc/o
John Barclay MCB326; BLG2547; AMB343

William - b1772, m bef 1805 Martha____ - desc/o John Barclay
CRL(4)390

BARHAM Ann - of VA, m Thomas Lane, Jr - desc/o Capt Charles Barham
HSF(8)149; SVF(2)28

Benjamin - of VA, b aft 1711 Surry Co d1797 Southampton Co, m
(perhaps) Mary Judkins dau/o John Judkins of Surry Co - desc/o
Capt Charles Barham HSF(8)147; SVF(2)27

Benjamin - of VA, m Sarah____ & had issue, at least, one son, John
Barham b1771 - desc/o Capt Charles Barham HSF(8)147;
SVF(2)27

Betsy - of VA, m____Gilliam - desc/o Capt Charles Barham HSF(8)148

Capt Charles - of VA, b1626 d1683 high sheriff of Surry Co 1673,
justice 1678/1683 & vestryman 1661, son of Robert Barham &
Katherine Filmer, m bef 1666 Elizabeth Ridley dau/o Peter Ridley -
the immigrant ECD(2)28; MCS97; DBR(1)436; DBR(2)568;
DBR(5)793; RAA1, 66; GBR242; GVE199, 200, 346, 347, 394/396,
583, 664/666; GVFHB(4)528/532; HSF(8)145/153; SVF(2)25/29

Charles - of VA, b abt 1706 d1791 Southampton Co, m(1) Sarah
Judkins dau/o John Judkins of Surry Co, m(2) Ann____Arrington,
a wid/o Southampton Co - desc/o Capt Charles Barham
HSF(8)148; SVF(2)26

Charles - of VA, m____ & had issue 4 childen - desc/o Capt Charles
Barham HSF(8)146; SVF(2)26

Charles - of VA, m Mary (Harwood?) & had issue 5 daughters & 1 son -
desc/o Capt Charles Barham HSF(8)147; SVF(2)26

Elizabeth - of VA, m Thomas Binns - desc/o Capt Charles Barham
HSF(8)146; SVF(2)26

Elizabeth - of VA, m Drewry Parker - desc/o Capt Charles Barham
HSF(8)148; SVF(2)28

Elizabeth - of VA, m James Adams - desc/o Capt Charles Barham
HSF(8)149; SVF(2)28

James - of VA, b abt 1730 d1792 lieutenant of militia 1755
Southampton Co, m (probably) Mary Thorpe - desc/o Capt Charles
Barham HSF(8)148; SVF(2)27

Jesse - of VA, m Faith Judkins - desc/o Capt Charles Barham
HSF(8)149; SVF(2)28

John - of VA, d1771, m Elizabeth Edwards dau/o Thomas Edwards &
Elizabeth Newsom - desc/o Capt Charles Barham HSF(8)146;
SVF(2)26, 28

John - of VA, m____Judkins - desc/o Capt Charles Barham HSF(8)149;

BARHAM (cont.)

> SVF(2)28

> Joseph - of VA, b abt 1745 Surry Co d1823 Surry Co, m1765/1766 Sally Lane b abt 1748 Surry Co d1826 Surry Co, dau/o Thomas Lane & Mary____ - desc/o Capt Charles Barham HSF(8)149; SVF(2)28

> Joseph - of VA, b1768 Surry Co d1834 Surry Co, m1824 Ann Cocke Hunnicutt b1801 Surry Co d1873 Surry Co, dau/o Robert B Hunnicutt Sr & Elizabeth Binns - desc/o Capt Charles Barham HSF(8)149; SVF(2)28

> Lucy - of VA, m____De Loach - desc/o Capt Charles Barham HSF(8)148; SVF(2)28

> Martha of VA, m____Harris - desc/o Capt Charles Barham HSF(8)148

> Mary - of VA, m bef 1770 Benjamin Judkins - desc/o Capt Charles Barham HSF(8)149; SVF(2)28

> Mary - of VA, b abt 1735, m David Newsom - desc/o Capt Charles Barham HSF(8)148; SVF(2)28

> Mary - of VA, m____Cooper - desc/o Capt Charles Barham HSF(8)148

> Mary Ann - of VA, b abt 1776, m Betts Lane - desc/o Charles Barham HSF(8)149; SVF(2)28

> Milly - of VA, m____Hutchinson - desc/o Capt Charles Barham HSF(8)148

> Newsome - of VA, b1768 Sussex Co d1839 Davidson Co, Tennessee, m1794 Wentworth, Rockingham Co, NC, Elizabeth Joyce b1772 Rockingham, NC d1846 Davidson Co, Tennessee - desc/o Capt Charles Barham HSF(8)151

> Patsy - of VA, m____Gilliam - desc/o Capt Charles Barham HSF(8)148

> Priscilla - of VA, m Robert Hart b1666/1667 d1720 - desc/o Capt Charles Barham ECD(2)29; DBR(1)436; DBR(5)793; HSF(8)146; SVF(2)26

> Rebecca - of VA, m William Holliman - desc/o Capt Charles Barham HSF(8)148

> Robert - of VA, b1679 d1760, m abt 1700 Elizabeth Clark dau/o John Clark & Mary Flake of Lawnes Creek Parish - desc/o Capt Charles Barham HSF(8)146; SVF(2)26

> Robert - of VA, b prior to 1711 d1770 Surry Co, m____ & left issue - desc/o Capt Charles Barham HSF(8)146, 147; SVF(2)26

> Robert - of VA, d1797, m Hannah____ - desc/o Capt Charles Barham HSF(8)148; SVF(2)28

> Sarah - of VA, m Edward Fisher - desc/o Capt Charles Barham HSF(8)148

> Susannah - of VA, m____Meacom - desc/o Capt Charles Barham HSF(8)148

> Thomas - of VA, d1764, m Lucy Holt dau/o Benjamin Holt of Surry Co - desc/o Capt Charles Barham HSF(8)146, 167

> Thomas - of VA, b aft 1711 Surry Co d1784 Sussex Co, m Sarah Newsom - desc/o Capt Charles Barham HSF(8)147; SVF(2)26

> Thomas - of VA, m bef 1775 Elizabeth Moss & had issue, at least one dau Mary (Polly) b1775 - desc/o Capt Charles Barham HSF(8)147; SVF(2)26

BARKER Elizabeth - of MA, b1719 d1780, m1752 Samuel Gould - desc/o
Katherine Marbury DBR(2)44

Hezekiah - of RI, b1757 d1834, m(2)1785 Sarah Wood - desc/o Jeremy
Clark FFF129, 132

James - of RI 1634/1635, b1617 d1702, m1644 Barbara Dungan -
the immigrant EDV114; FFF129; CGA17; sufficient proof of alleged
royal ancestry is lacking

Capt James - of RI, b1648 d1722, m1673 Sarah Jeffery - desc/o
Jeremy Clark FFF129

James - of RI, b1675 d1758, m1699 Mary Cook - desc/o Jeremy Clark
FFF129

John - of RI, b1710 d1777, m1735 Rebecca Hour - desc/o Jeremy
Clark FFF129

BARLOW Deborah - b abt 1627, m John Sturges - the immigrant LDS59;
sufficient proof of alleged royal ancestry is lacking

BARNES Ezekiel - b1770, m Fanny Johnson - desc/o Richard Belding
RAA68

Moses - b1714 - desc/o Richard Belding RAA68

Nathan - b1741 - desc/o Richard Belding RAA68

Willard - b1766 - desc/o John Prescott RAA125

BARNET Mary - of VA, m David Taliaferro - desc/o Col George Reade
DBR(5)160

BARNEY Benjamin Jr - of MA, b1732 d1803, m1753 Jemima Jenkins -
desc/o William Gayer DBR(3)749, 754

Luther - b1757 - desc/o Robert Abell RAA59

Lydia - of MA, b1755 d1781, m1776 Matthew Starbuck - desc/o
William Gayer DBR(3)749, 754

BARRETT (BARRET) Isaac - b1752 - desc/o Agnes Harris RAA131

Dr James - of VA, b1772 d1845, m1799 Mary (Polly) Whitfield - desc/o
Lieut Col Walter Aston FFF271

Patty - of MA, b1740/1741 d1819, m1764 Benjamin Spaulding -
desc/o Rev Edward Bulkeley ECD(3)74

William - of VA, b1756 d1815, m Dorothy Winston - desc/o Col George
Reade AWW205

BARRON Hannah - b1709 - desc/o Mary Launce RAA130

John - of MA, m 1721 Hannah Richardson - desc/o Mary Launce
CHB447; MCD291

Lydia - of MA, b1734 d1824, m1753 Lawrence Jackson Harris -
desc/o Mary Launce CHB447; MCD291

Samuel - b1683/1685 - desc/o Mary Launce RAA130

BARROWS Elizabeth - b abt 1715/1718 - desc/o George Morton RAA116

John - b1667 - desc/o George Morton RAA116

BARTLETT Benjamin - of MA, b1658 d bef 1724, m1676/1678 Ruth
Pabodie - desc/o Mary Wentworth ECD(2)304; FFF90

Elizabeth - of MA, b1749 d1779, m1765 Thomas Bartlett - desc/o
Mary Wentworth ECD(2)287

Elizabeth - of MA, b1766 d1811, m1783 Solomon Churchill - desc/o
Mary Wentworth ECD(2)287

Elizabeth - of MA, d1773, m1716/1717 Joseph Bartlett - desc/o Mary
Wentworth ECD(2)287

Major Henry William - of VA - desc/o Rev Hawte Wyatt CHB423

BARTLETT (cont.)

James - of ME, b1759 d1836, m1782 Lois Hill - desc/o Richard Bartlett BLG2552

John - of MA, b1580/1590 d1678, m Joane___ - the immigrant BLG2551; EDV124; CGA22; sufficient proof of alleged royal ancestry is lacking

John - of MA, m1660 Sarah Knight - desc/o John Bartlett BLG2551

John - of MA, b1655 d1736, m1680 Margaret Rust - desc/o Richard Bartlett BLG2552

John - of MA, b1678 d1741, m1701 Mary Ordway - desc/o Richard Bartlett BLG2551

John - of MA & NH, b1711, m1733 Zipporah Flanders - desc/o Richard Bartlett BLG2551

Joshua - of MA, b1707, m Priscilla Jacobs - desc/o Richard Bartlett BLG2551

Capt Nathan - of MA & ME, b1691 d1775, m1714 Shuah Heard - desc/o Richard Bartlett BLG2552

Nathan - of ME, b1737 d1775, m1757 Sarah Shapleigh - desc/o Richard Bartlett BLG2552

Richard - of MA, b1580/1590 d1647 - the immigrant BLG2551; EDV124; CGA23; sufficient proof of alleged royal ancestry is lacking

Richard - of MA, b1621 d1698, m Abigail___ - desc/o Richard Bartlett BLG2551

Richard - of MA, b1648 d1725, m1673 Hannah Emery - desc/o Richard Bartlett BLG2551

Richard - of MA, b1725 d1795, m Mary Bartlett - desc/o Richard Bartlett BLG2551

Richard - of NH, b1750, m1790 Deborah Thurston - desc/o Richard Bartlett BLG2551

Ruth - of MA, d aft 1756, m bef 1711 John Murdock Jr - desc/o Mary Wentworth ECD(2)304; FFF90

Samuel - of MA, b1666 d1713, m1683 Hannah Peabody - desc/o Mary Wentworth ECD(2)287

Samuel - of MA, b1645 d1732, m1671 Elizabeth Titcomb - desc/o Richard Bartlett BLG2551

Samuel - of MA, b1676 d1753, m1704/1705 Abigail Welles - desc/o Richard Bartlett BLG2551

Samuel - of MA, b1748 d1819, m1773 Lois Hix - desc/o Richard Bartlett BLG2551

Sylvanus - of MA, b1719 d1811, m1743 Martha Waite - desc/o Mary Wentworth ECD(2)287

Capt Thomas - of VA - desc/o Rev Hawte Wyatt CHB423; MCD312

Thomas - of MA, b1580/1590 - the immigrant BLG2552; EDV124; CGA23; sufficient proof of alleged royal ancestry is lacking

William - of MA, b abt 1774 d1871, m1801 Ruth Waterman - desc/o Richard Bartlett BLG2551

BARTON Dr John - of MA 1672 - the immigrant EDV118, 119; CGA23; sufficient proof of alleged royal ancestry is lacking

BASS Moses Belcher - m Margaret Sprague - desc/o Anne Marbury DBR(1)760

BASSETT Hon Burwell - of VA, b1734 d1793 member House of
   Burgesses, m1757 Anna Marie Dandridge - desc/o Martha Bacon
   CHB32; J&K190; BCD32

   John Jr - of VA, b1765 d1826, m1786 Betty Carter Brown - desc/o
   Martha Bacon CHB32; BCD32

   Mary - of MA, b1654 Sandwich, MA d1743 Chilmark, MA, m1676
   Chilmark, MA John Redding - desc/o Edward Raynsford
   NE(139)299

   Nathan - of MA, b abt 1657, m1690 Mary Huckins - desc/o Edward
   Raynsford NE(139)299

   Sarah - of MA, m Thomas Lewes of Falmouth - desc/o Edward
   Raynsford NE(139)299

   William - of MA, b abt 1653 d1721, m1675 at Sandwich, MA, Rachel
   Williston of Taunton - desc/o Edward Raynsford NE(139)299

   Col William - of VA, b1709 d174_, burgess 1743, m 1729 Elizabeth
   Churchill - desc/o Martha Bacon CHB32; BCD32; J&K190

   Col William - of VA - the immigrant WAC96; CGA23; sufficient proof of
   alleged royal ancestry is lacking

BATCHELLER Josiah II - b1753 d1827, m Ruth Fletcher - desc/o Ursula
   Scott JSW1762

BATE Rev John - of MD, b1766 d1844, m(1) Agnes Birch - desc/o
   Thomas Gerard DBR(2)233; DBR(3)76

BATES Edward - b1696 - desc/o Olive Welby RAA93

   Fleming - of VA, b1710 d1784, m1737 Sarah Jordan - desc/o John
   Fleming JSW1651

   John - b1668 - desc/o Olive Welby RAA93

   John - b1722 - desc/o Olive Welby RAA93

   Joseph - b1725 - desc/o Olive Welby RAA93

   Mary - of CT, b abt 1667 d abt 1743, m abt 1689 Josiah Cleveland -
   desc/o Olive Welby ECD135; DBR(2)107; DBR(3)620; RAA93

   Mary - b1776, m1790 Stephen Fox - desc/o Thomas Sargent
   DBR(1)748

   Oliver - b1763 - desc/o Olive Welby RAA93

   Sarah - b1767 - desc/o Olive Welby RAA93

   Thomas Fleming - of VA, b1742 d1805, m1771 Caroline Matilda
   Woodson - desc/o John Fleming JSW1651

   Uzal - of NJ, bp 1749, m1803 Elizabeth____ - desc/o Thomas Sargent
   DBR(1)748

BATHURST Lancelot - of VA 1683, d1705 son of Sir Edward of Lechlade,
   Gloucestershire, England & Susan (Rich) Bathurst, m(1)____, m(2)
   Susan Rich - the immigrant WAC12; GBR460; GVFWM(4)569

   Mary - of VA, m bef 1704 Francis Meriwether - desc/o Lancelot
   Bathurst WAC12

   Susan or Susanna - of VA, m abt 1694 Lieut-Col Drury Stith - desc/o
   Lancelot Bathurst WAC12; GVFWM(4)569

BATTE (BATT) Amy - of VA, b1667, m Capt Richard Jones - desc/o
   Thomas Batte DBR(4)394

   Anne - of VA, m Edward Stratton - desc/o Capt Henry Batte SVF(1)26

   Christopher - of MA, b1601 son of Thomas Batt & Joan Byley, m Alice
   Baynton - the immigrant RAA1, 66; GBR374; NE(141)94;
   GDMNH82, 83

BATTE (BATT) (cont.)

Elizabeth - of VA, m William Ligon II - desc/o Capt Henry Batte
  ECD117; MCS81; DBR(5)748; RAA67; SVF(1)26

Elizabeth - of VA, m_____Jones - desc/o Capt Henry Batte SVF(1)27

Capt Henry - of VA 1646, d prior to 1703, burgess 1685/1686, justice
  of Charles City Co, VA 1693, son of Capt John & Martha (Mallory)
  Batte, m Mary Lound, dau/o Henry Lound of Henrico Co, VA - the
  immigrant ECD109, 117; ECD(2)35; MCS81; DBR(1)366;
  DBR(2)437, 468, 470, 620; DBR(3)591; DBR(5)748; RAA67;
  GBR314; VGS(1/5)16; VHG112, 113; SVF(1)26

Henry - of VA, d1770, m Eliza Chamberlain, dau/o Thomas
  Chamberlain & Elizabeth Stratton - desc/o Capt Henry Batte
  SVF(1)27

John - of VA, b abt 1600, m Martha Mallory - the immigrant RAA1, 67;
  GBR314 lists their son Capt Henry Batte as the immigrant

John - of VA, m Mary Poythress dau/o Peter Poythress & Elizabeth
  Bland - desc/o Capt Henry Batte SVF(1)27

Martha - of VA, m(1)_____Jones, m(2)1791 Nathaniel Colley - desc/o
  Capt Henry Batte SVF(1)27

Mary - of VA, m John Poythress, burgess for Charles City Co, 1723
  d1723/1724 - desc/o Capt Henry Batte ECD109; ECD(2)35;
  MCS81; DBR(1)366, 367; DBR(2)437; 470, 620; DBR(3)591;
  RAA67; SVF(1)26

Mary - of VA, m Lieut Peter Jones - desc/o Thomas Batte DBR(1)409;
  DBR(2)58; DBR(4)510

Mary - of VA, m(1)_____Cox, m(2)_____Adderson - desc/o Capt Henry
  Batte SVF(1)27

Mary - of VA, m F Eppes - desc/o Capt Henry Batte SVF(1)27

Paul - b1642 - desc/o Alice Baynton RAA66

Rachael - of VA, m James Parham, removed to Bertie Co, NC - desc/o
  Capt Henry Batte SVF(1)26

Robert - of VA, b1727, m Martha Peterson dau/o John Peterson &
  Martha Thweatt - desc/o Capt Henry Batte SVF(1)27

Sarah - of VA, m Abraham Jones - desc/o Col Henry Batte SVF(1)26

Sarah - b1673 - desc/o Alice Baynton RAA66

Thomas - of VA, son of Capt John Batte & Martha (or Katherine)
  Mallory, m(1) Mary_____, m(2) Mrs Amy_____Butler - the immigrant
  DBR(1)409; DBR(2)58; DBR(4)393, 510; GBR314; VGS(1-5)16;
  SVF(1)25/27

William - of VA, m1704 Mary Stratton dau/o Edward Stratton of
  Henrico Co & Martha Sheepy - desc/o Capt Henry Batte SVF(1)27

BAXTER Mehitabel - of MA, b1740, m1759 Camp Adams b1740 d1823 -
  desc/o Rev Peter Bulkeley DBR(1)680; DBR(2)328, 392, 758;
  DBR(3)312

BAYARD Eliza - of NY, d1846, m1791 John Houston McIntosh - desc/o
  James Alexander BCD22

Katherine Anne - of NY, m Robert Charles Johnson - desc/o James
  Alexander CHB22; BCD22

BAYLOR Ann - of VA, m1774 Temple Gwathney of King & Queen Co, son
  of Owen & Hannah Gwathney & left numerous descendants -
  desc/o Anne Lovelace GVFHB(3)330

BAYLOR (cont.)

Courtney - of VA, educated in England at Croyden, Kent, m Jasper Clayton - desc/o Anne Lovelace GVFHB(3)324

Frances - of VA, m Col Humphrey Hill & had issue - desc/o Anne Lovelace GVFHB(3)329

Frances - of VA, b1748 d1802, m (her first cousin) Col Edward Hill son of Col Humphrey Hill & her aunt Frances (Baylor) Hill - desc/o Anne Lovelace GVFHB(3)330

George - of VA, b1752 at Newmarket, first aid to Washington at the Battle of Trenton & served throughout the Revolution & commanded a VA cavalry regiment bearing his name at the battle of Yorktown, m1778 Lucy Page the dau/o Mann Page of Mannsfield near Fredericksburg, they left issue one child John Walker Baylor who had several daughters. Col George Baylor died in the Barbados 1784 - desc/o Anne Lovelace GVFHB(3)326

Gregory - of VA, lived in King & Queen Co, m bef 1760 Mary (or Maria) Whiting - desc/o Anne Lovelace GVFHB(3)330/331

Col John III - of VA, b1705 of Newmarket, Caroline Co d1772, colonel in the French & Indian War, burgess from Caroline Co, Co Lieut of Orange & leading importer & breeder of thoroughbred horses in VA, m1743/1744 at Yorktown Frances Walker, she died aged 17 on her wedding day dau/o Jacob Walker of Elizabeth City Co - desc/o Col William Bernard DBR(3)450; DBR(4)143; APP120 - desc/o Anne Lovelace GVFHB(3)324

John - of VA, b1750 at Newmarket, educated at Putney Grammar School & at Caius College, Cambridge d1808, m at St. Olave, London Frances Norton dau/o John Norton & Courtney Walker & left issue - desc/o Anne Lovelace GVFHB(3)326

Lucy - of VA, educated in England, m John Armistead & had issue - desc/o Anne Lovelace GVFHB(3)324

Lucy - of VA, b bef 1725, m1742 George Morton d1765 & had issue - desc/o Anne Lovelace GVFHB(3)329

Mary (Mollie) - of VA, b abt 1747 d1820, m Col Benjamin Temple son of Joseph & Ann (Arnold) Temple - desc/o Anne Lovelace GVFHB(3)329

Robert - of VA, justice of King & Queen Co 1727, son of John Baylor & Lucy Todd, m(1) Frances____, m(2) Hannah Gregory dau/o Richard Gregory - desc/o Anne Lovelace GVFHG(3)329

Dr Robert - of VA, b abt 1728 d1760/1762, m Mollie Brooke dau/o Humphrey Brooke Sr & Elizabeth Braxton - desc/o Anne Lovelace GVFHB(3)326

Robert I - of VA, b1754 d1822, m Frances Gwynn of Gwynn's Island - desc/o Col William Bernard DBR(3)450; DBR(4)143; GVFHB(3)326

Walker - of VA, captain in the Revolution & was wounded at Germantown or Brandywine, m Jane Bledsoe dau/o Joseph Bledsoe & left several descendants - desc/o Anne Lovelace GVFHB(3)326

BAYNARD John - of MD, d1705 & left issue. son of Thomas Baynard & Mary Bennett, m Elizabeth Blackwell - the immigrant GBR346; NGS(71)37/40

Robert - of MD, 3rd son of John Baynard & Elizabeth Blackwell -

BAYNARD (cont.)

> desc/o John Baynard NGS(71)37/40

> Thomas - of MD, eldest son of John Baynard & Elizabeth Blackwell - desc/o John Baynard NGS(71)37/40

> William - of MD, 2nd son of John Baynard & Elizabeth Blackwell - desc/o John Baynard NGS(71)37/49

BAYNTON Alice - of MA, bp 1602 d1679, m1629 Christopher Batt - the immigrant FLW214; RAA66; sufficient proof of alleged royal ancestry is lacking

BEALL Amelia Jane - of MD, b1747, m1767 Thaddeus Beall Sr - desc/o Robert Brooke ECD(3)41, 345; DBR(1)529, 705; DBR(2)451

> Brooke - of MD, m Margaret Johns - desc/o Rev Robert Brooke CHB401

> Christina - of MD, b1772 d1849, m Benjamin Mackall Jr - desc/o Rev Robert Brooke CHB401

> Daniel - of MD, b1752, m Martha Peyton - desc/o Rev Robert Brooke DBR(1)84, 218; DBR(2)129

> Elizabeth - of MD, m Rev Stephen Bloomer Balch - desc/o Rev Robert Brooke MCD168

> Col Frederick - of GA, b1768 d1847, m1793 Martha Peyton - desc/o Rev Robert Brooke DBR(1)529

> Col George Jr - of MD, b1729 d1807, m abt 1759 Ann____ - desc/o Col Thomas Brooke ECD(3)44; MCD168; DBR(4)744

> John Brooke Beall - m Eleanor Beatty - desc/o Maj Thomas Brooke DBR(1)393; DBR(2)657

> Ensign Levin Covington - of MD, b1760 d abt 1802, m abt 1781 Esther Best - desc/o Col Thomas Brooke ECD(3)44; DBR(4)744

> Richard - of MD, d1778, m Sarah Brooke - desc/o Rev Robert Brooke DBR(4)547

> Robert Brooke - of MD, b1769, m1791 Elizabeth Berry - desc/o Rev Robert Brooke DBR(4)547

> Thaddeus - of MD, m Mary Jones - desc/o Rev Robert Brooke DBR(2)451

> Thomas - of VA, b1649 d1679, m Ann Gooch - the immigrant WAC13; CGA20 sufficient proof of alleged royal ancestry is lacking

> Thomas - d1823, m Virlinda Beall - desc/o Maj Thomas Brooke DBR(1)393; DBR(2)657

BEATTY John - b abt 1701 d1746, m Henrica Biggs b abt 1716 d1762 - desc/o William Asfordby DBR(2)739

> John - b abt 1738 d1821, m abt 1767 Sarah Parkinson b1739 d1813 - desc/o William Asfordby DBR(2)739

> Mary - of MD, m(1) Isaac Eltinge, m(2)1757 John Cary d1777 - desc/o William Asfordby CHB511

> Susanna - b1768 d1824, m1787 Jacob Gomber b1759 d1819 - desc/o William Asfordby DBR(2)739

> William - of MD, bp 1695 d1757, m Elizabeth Carmack dau/o Cornelius Carmack - desc/o William Asfordby CHB511

BEAUFORD John - of VA, b1707 d1787, m abt 1735 Judith Early - desc/o Richard Perrott JSW1733

> Thomas - of VA, b1663 d1716, m1681 Mary____ - desc/o Richard Perrott JSW1732

BEAUFORD (cont.)

    Thomas Jr - of VA, b1682 d1761, m Elizabeth____ - desc/o Richard
        Perrott JSW1733

    Capt William Early - of VA, b1745 d aft 1814, m1770 Mary Welsh -
        desc/o Richard Perrott JSW1733

BECK Caleb II - of NY, d1733, m1703 Anna (Mol) Fairly bp 1678 dau/o
    Jan Jansen Mol - desc/o Joseph Bolles DBR(1)331; DBR(2)423;
    DBR(4)459

    Engeltie - of NY, bp 1715 d1758, m1745 Isaac Abraham Truax b1715
        d aft 1782 - desc/o Joseph Bolles DBR(1)331, 332, 423, 424;
        DBR(4)459, 460

BECKWITH Barbara - a minor in 1676, m1679 Jacobus Seth - desc/o
    George Beckwith DBR(1)140, 662, 701

    Benjamin - of MD, b1839, m(2) Martha Jones - desc/o George
        Beckwith ECD(3)17

    Charles - of MD, b abt 1669 d1712, m1702 Anne____ - desc/o George
        Beckwith ECD(3)16

    George - of MD, bp 1606 d1676, m1649 Frances Hervey (Harvey) - the
        immigrant ECD(3)16; DBR(1)140, 222, 507, 661, 662, 701;
        DBR(2)314, 648, 651; DBR(3)601, 603, 606; DBR(4)334; RAA1, 67;
        CGA20; royal ancestry not proven

    George - of MD, b abt 1710 - desc/o George Beckwith ECD(3)16

    Hannah - b abt 1697/1700 - desc/o Oliver Mainwaring RAA113

    Jennings - of VA, b1764 d1836 - desc/o Marmeduke Beckwith
        DBR(2)533

    Jonathan - of VA, b1720 d1796, m Rebecca Barnes - desc/o
        Marmeduke Beckwith DBR(2)533; WAC72

    Capt Joseph - of CT, b1640 d1708, m Susannah Way - desc/o Ursula
        Scott JSW1840

    Sir Marmeduke, 3rd Baronet - of VA, b1687, son of Sir Roger, 1st
        Baronet & Elizabeth (Jennings) Beckwith, m Mrs Elizabeth
        (Brockenbrough) Dickenson - the immigrant DBR(1)352;
        DBR(2)533; RAA1, 68; WAC72; CGA20; GBR42

    Marmeduke II - of VA, m Sybil Ellzey - desc/o Marmeduke Beckwith
        DBR(1)352; WAC72

    Mary - m bef 1676 John Miles - desc/o George Beckwith DBR(1)222,
        507; DBR(2)314, 651; DBR(3)603, 607; DBR(4)335

    Matthew - of CT 1636, b1601 d1680, m abt 1636 Elizabeth Lynde -
        desc/o Ursula Scott JSW1840; CGA20

    Newman - of VA, b1767 d1835, m abt 1790 Judith Ann Neal - desc/o
        Marmeduke Beckwith DBR(1)353

    Rebecca - of VA, m Maj John Bellfield - desc/o Marmeduke Beckwith
        WAC72

    Rebecca - b1741 - desc/o Oliver Mainwaring RAA113

    Richard - b abt 1703 - desc/o Oliver Mainwaring RAA113

    Sarah Anne - of CT, b1677, m1691 William Miner - desc/o Ursula
        Scott JSW1840

BEDFORD Ann (Nancy) - of VA, b1765, m1785 Capt Hillary Moseley -
    desc/o of Lieut Col Thomas Lygon DBR(4)660

    Archibald - of VA, b abt 1769 d1827, m1796 Letitia Clay - desc/o Capt
        Thomas Harris ECD(2)158; DBR(1)304; DBR(2)409

BEDFORD (cont.)

 John - b1764 d1841, m1788 Mary Ann Marshall - desc/o Lieut Col Thomas Lygon DBR(1)403; DBR(2)518

 Littleberry - of VA, b1769 d1829, m1790 Mattie Clay - desc/o Lieut Col Thomas Ligon DBR(5)922

 Mary - of VA, m1772 James Hamlett (Hamblett) - desc/o Lieut Col Thomas Ligon DBR(5)999

 Stephen - of VA, b1752 d aft 1807, m abt 1780 Martha____ - desc/o Lieut Col Thomas Ligon ECD(2)172

BEEKMAN William - of NY 1647 - the immigrant EDV25; CGA20; sufficient proof of alleged royal ancestry is lacking

BELCHER Abigail - b1674 - desc/o Richard Billings RAA70

 Abigail - of MA, b1674/1675, dau/o Josiah Belcher d1683, named in her father's will 1683 & partition 1693 - desc/o Edward Raynsford NE(139)300

 Andrew - of MA 1639 - the immigrant EDV32; CGA20; sufficient proof of alleged royal ancestry is lacking

 Andrew - of MA - desc/o Andrew Belcher EDV32

 Anna - of MA, b1671/1672, dau/o Josiah Belcher d1683, named in her father's will 1683 & partition 1693 - desc/o Edward Raynsford NE(139)300

 Benjamin - of MA, b1680/1681, son of Josiah Belcher d1683, named in his father's will 1683 & partition 1693 - desc/o Edward Raynsford NE(130)300

 Benjamin - of MA, b1765 d1833, m1792 Sarah Barney b1771 d1867 dau/o Joseph Barney - desc/o Frances Deighton DBR(1)419; DBR(4)627

 Dorothy - of MA, b1673, dau/o Josiah Belcher d1683, named in her father's will 1683 & partition 1693, m1693/1694 Edmund Gross - desc/o Edward Raynsford NE(139)300

 Edward - of MA, b1669/1670, son of Josiah Belcher d1683, named in his father's will 1683 & partition 1693 - desc/o Edward Raynsford NE(139)300

 Elizabeth - of MA, b1663 bp 1665, dau/o Josiah Belcher d1683, named in her father's will 1683 & partition 1693, m___Payne - desc/o Edward Raynsford NE(139)300

 John - of MA, b1659 bp 1664, son of Josiah Belcher d1683, named in his father's will 1683 & partition 1693 - desc/o Edward Raynsford NE(139)300

 Jonathan - of MA, b1661 bp 1664, son of Josiah Belcher d1683, named in his father's will 1683 & partition 1693 - desc/o Edward Raynsford NE(139)300

 Jonathan - desc/o Andrew Belcher EDV32

 Joseph - of MA, b1665 bp 1665, dau/o Josiah Belcher d1683, named in his father's will 1683 & partition 1693 - desc/o Edward Raynsford NE(130)300

 Josiah - of MA, b1655 bp 1664 d not many weeks before his father Josiah Belcher d1683 - desc/o Edward Raynsford NE(130)300

 Mary - b1709 - desc/o Richard Billings RAA70

 Mary - b1670 - desc/o Richard Billings RAA70

 Moses - b1672 - desc/o Richard Billings RAA70

BELCHER (cont.)

Nathan - of MA, son of Josiah Belcher d1683, named in his father's will 1683 & partition 1693 - desc/o Edward Raynsford NE(130)300

Rebecca - of MA, b1667, dau/o Josiah Belcher d1683, named in her father's will 1683 & partition 1693, m Joseph Fuller - desc/o Edward Raynsford NE(139)300

Ruth - of MA, b1678, dau/o Josiah Belcher d1683, named in her father's will 1683 & partition 1693 - desc/o Edward Raynsford NE(139)300

BELDING (BELDEN) Daniel - b1646 - desc/o Richard Belding RAA68

Elizabeth - b1663 - desc/o Richard Belding RAA68

Elizabeth - b1683/1685 - desc/o Richard Belding RAA68

Elizabeth - b1719 - desc/o Richard Belding RAA68

Esther - b1697 - desc/o Richard Belding RAA68

Esther - b1683 - desc/o Richard Belding RAA68

Eunice - b abt 1735/1736 - desc/o Richard Belding RAA68

Gideon - b1692 - desc/o Richard Belding RAA68

John - b1631 - desc/o Richard Belding RAA68

Lydia - b1675 - desc/o Richard Belding RAA68

Matthew - b1701 - desc/o Richard Belding RAA68

Richard - of CT, bp 1591 - the immigrant RAA1, 68; TAG(XLV)135, 136, 137, 138 - several times an extensive pedigree, shorn of all qualifications such as "probably," "perhaps" or "possibly," has been published presenting an ancestry of considerable distinction. Unfortunately, no documentary evidence has been found to conclusively prove the identity of Richard to royal ancestry

Ruth - b1717 - desc/o Richard Belding RAA68

Samuel - b abt 1629 - desc/o Richard Belding RAA68

Samuel - b1665 - desc/o Richard Belding RAA68

Stephen - b1658 - desc/o Richard Belding RAA68

Susanna - b1651 - desc/o Richard Belding RAA68

William - b abt 1620/1622 - desc/o Richard Belding RAA68

BELL Anne - dau/o Edward Bell & Margaret Barley, m Sir Ferdinando Gorges, m abt 1565 d1647, founder & Lord Proprietor of ME - the immigrant GBR422

Rev Charles - b1770, m Elizabeth Lewis Garland - desc/o Col Richard Lee DBR(3)324

Thomas - of VA, d1809, m Rebecca____ - desc/o Col Richard Lee DBR(3)324, 404

William - of RI, d1737 - the immigrant EDV41; CGA20; sufficient proof of alleged royal ancestry is lacking

William - of VA, d1744, m Mary____ - desc/o Col Richard Lee DBR(3)324, 404

BELLINGER Elizabeth - of SC, m1756 William Simpson, Esq, attorney general & chief justice of South Carolina - desc/o Stephen Bull SCG(1)220

Margaret - of SC, bp 1735 - desc/o Stephen Bull SCG(1)220

BELLINGHAM Gov Richard - of MA 1641, b abt 1590/1592 Boston, Lincolnshire d1672 governor of Massachusetts, son of William Bellingham of Manton & Brombye & Frances Amcotts, m Penelope Pelham - the immigrant EDV41, 42; DAB(2)166, 167; CGA21;

BELLINGHAM (cont.)
GBR225
William - of MA - desc/o Gov Richard Bellingham EDV42

BELLSON Mary - of VA, m 1703 Abraham Ricks - desc/o James Tooke DBR(1)689

BELT Katherine - of MD, b1729/1730 d1773, m1753 Benjamin Brashear - desc/o Giles Brent DBR(4)53, 85, 389, 463; DBR(5)673

BELTY Amy - b1762 - desc/o Alice Freeman RAA132

BEMAN Alvah - b1775 - desc/o Alice Freeman RAA132
Ebenezer - b1719 - desc/o Alice Freeman RAA132
Reuben - b1742 - desc/o Alice Freeman RAA132

BENJAMIN Bethiah - b1754 - desc/o Alice Freeman RAA132
Jabez - b1716 - desc/o Alice Freeman RAA132

BENNET Barbara - of NC, dau/o Andrew of Chesters & Dorothy (Collingwood) Bennet, m James Murray of NC & MA - the immigrant GBR66

BENTON Thomas - of CT, b1766 Windsor d1861 Rutland, MA, m abt 1798 Mary Bunce b1773 Hartford d1864 Rutland, CT - desc/o Col William Leete SMO104

BERKELEY Nelson - of VA, m Elizabeth Wormeley Carter - desc/o Col George Reade CHB250
Norborne, 1st Baron Botetourt - of VA, b abt 1718 d1770 unmarried, governor of VA 1768, son of John Symmes Berkeley & Elizabeth Norborne - the immigrant DAB(2)468; GBR155
Sir William - of VA, b1608 d1677 governor of VA, son of Sir Maurice Berkeley of Bruton, Somerset & Elizabeth Killigrew, m1670 Frances Culpeper dau/o Thomas Culpeper & Katherine St Leger - the immigrant DAB(2)217, 218; MCS50; GBR205; GVFHB(1)61/64

BERNARD Catherine - b abt 1758 - desc/o Richard Bernard RAA68
Elizabeth - of VA, b abt 1653/1665, m Judge Thomas Todd Jr d 1724/1725 son of Capt Thomas & Anna (Gorsuch) Todd - desc/o Col William Bernard DBR(1)215; DBR(3)131, 334, 450, 692; DBR(4)143, 769; WAC72; APP118, 119
Sir Francis, 1st Baronet of NJ, bp 1712 d1779 governor of NJ & MA, only child of Rev Francis Bernard & Margery Winslowe, m1741 Amelia Offley dau/o Stephen Offley of Norton Hall, Derbyshire - the immigrant DAB(2)221, 222; GBR144
George - of VA, living in England 1665 with his his uncle Sir Robert Bernard - desc/o Col William Bernard WAC71, 72; APP118
John - of VA - desc/o Richard Bernard WAC14
Lucy - of VA, m(1) Dr Edmund Gwynne of Gloucester Co, VA d1683/1684, m(2) Edward Creffield Jr, merchant of London d1694 - desc/o Col William Bernard MCD161; BCD38; WAC72; APP118
Philip - of VA, d1709 - desc/o Richard Bernard WAC14
Richard - of VA 1647, b1608 d1652, son of Richard Bernard & Elizabeth Woolhouse, m(1) Dorothy Alwey, m(2)1634 Anne Corderoy - the immigrant RAA1, 68; WAC13, 14; CGA21; GBR144; GVFWM(1)327/331
Richard - of VA, m Elizabeth Hart dau/o Edward Hart, justice of Stafford Co - desc/o Richard Bernard WAC14; GVFWM(1)331
Richard - b1636 - desc/o Richard Bernard RAA68

BERNARD (cont.)

Richard - of VA, b1753 d1785 - desc/o Col William Bernard GVFWM(1)329

Capt Robert - of VA, b abt 1680, m Judith __ - desc/o Col William Bernard ECD(2)44; DBR(4)437

Robert - b abt 1700 - desc/o Richard Bernard RAA68

Thomas - of VA, b1756 d1834, m1792 Mary Hicks - desc/o Col William Bernard ECD(2)45; DBR(4)437

Col William - of VA 1625, b1598 d1665 member of the VA Council 1642/1659 son of Francis Bernard & Mary (Woolhouse) Bernard, m1667 Lucy (Higginson) Burwell d1675 dau/o Robert & Joanna (Tokesey) Higginson and wid/o Lewis Burwell - the immigrant CHB38, 542; ECD(2)44; MCD161; MCS37; BCD38; DBR(1)215, 588; DBR(2)765; DBR(3)131, 334, 445, 449, 450, 688, 691 692; DBR(4)142, 436, 437, 769; RAA1, 68; WAC71, 72; GBR144; APP117/124

William - of VA, b1640 d1704, m____ - desc/o Col William Bernard ECD(2)44; DBR(4)437

William - b abt 1670 - desc/o Richard Bernard RAA68

Capt William - of VA, b abt 1727/1728 d aft 1758, m1748 Mary Fleming - desc/o Col William Bernard ECD(2)44; DBR(4)437; RAA68

William - of VA, b1730, m(1)1750 Winifred Thornton b1729 d1765 dau/o Anthony & Winifred Presley Thornton of Stafford Co, m(2) Sarah Savin of MD - desc/o Col William Bernard GVFWM(1)329, 331

BERRIEN Cornelius - of NY, b1698 d1767, m1719 Sarah Hallett - desc/o Richard Woodhull ECD237

Phebe - of NY, b1735 d1810, m1754 William Warner - desc/o Richard Woodhull ECD238

BERRY Ruth - b1721, m Sylvanus Hopkins - desc/o Richard Sears LDS14

Ruth - of MD, b1762 d1846, m Capt Samuel Griffith - desc/o Anne Lovelace JSW1861

BETHUNE George - the immigrant EDV30; CGA21; EO(1)185/187 royal descent not proven

BETTELL Martha - of NH, b1703, m1724 Israel Young - desc/o Thomas Dudley DBR(1)557; DBR(2)687; DBR(4)839

BETTS Mary - bp 1731, m Ezra Keeler - desc/o Henry Palmer LDS30

Nathan - b1700, m Mary Belding - desc/o Henry Palmer LDS30

Richard - of NY - the immigrant EDV134, 135; CGA21; sufficient proof of alleged royal ancestry is lacking

Thomas - of NY - desc/o Richard Betts EDV134, 135

Uriah - of CT, b1761 d1841, m1783 Sarah Rossiter - desc/o Margaret Wyatt CHB541

BEVAN Anne - of PA, m1696/1697, m Owen Roberts of Merion - desc/o John Bevan Sr CRFP(1)140

Elizabeth - of PA, d1740, m1696 Joseph Richardson son of Samuel Richardson, provincial councillor - desc/o John Bevan Sr MCD165; CRFP(1)141

Evan - of PA, b abt 1666 Wales d1720 Merion, Philadelphia Co, PA,

BEVAN (cont.)

    m1693/1694 Eleanor Wood of Darby d1744/1745 Merion - desc/o John Bevan Sr CRFP(1)140

    Evan - of PA, b1698 d1746 Philadelphia, m____ & left issue - desc/o John Bevan Sr CRFP(1)140

    Jane - of PA, b Glamorganshire, Wales d1703, m1687 Haverford, Chester Co, PA, John Wood of Darby d1705, member of Assembly & commissioned a justice 1728, son of George Wood - desc/o John Bevan Sr CHB80; MCD164; BCD80; DBR(1)376; AFA40, 168; CRFP(1)140, 141

    John Sr "alias," John ap Evan of PA 1683, b1646 Treverigg, parish of Llantrisant, Co Glamorganshire d1726 Treverigg, Wales, minister for the Society of Friends son of Ieuan ap John & Jane Richards, m abt 1665 Barbara Awbrey b1637 d1710/1711 Treverigg, dau/o William Aubrey of Pencoyd, sometime sheriff of Glamorganshire - the immigrant CHB80; MCD164; BCD80; DBR(1)375, 376; AFA40; RAA1, 69; AFA168; TAG(59)1, 2; GBR179; CRFP(1)136/145

    John - of PA, b1694/1695 whom his grandfather devised the paternal estate of Treverigg Glamorganshire & he lived & died there, leaving descendants who still possess a portion of the ancestral estate - desc/o John Bevan Sr CRFP(1)140

BEVERLEY Catharine - of VA, m John Robinson - desc/o Maj Robert Beverley WAC74

    Elizabeth - of VA, b1691 d1723, m1709 William Randolph b1681 d1742 councillor of state eldest son of William Randolph - desc/o Maj Robert Payton CHB168; BCD168; CRL(1)257; VG468

    Elizabeth - of VA, d1730, m Robert Daniel - desc/o Maj Robert Beverley JSW1782

    Elizabeth W - of VA, m Lewis Walker Taylor - desc/o Sarah Ludlow DBR(5)925

    Harry - of VA, b1669 d1730, m Elizabeth Smith - desc/o Maj Robert Beverley JSW1781; BLG2560; WAC74

    Harry - of VA, b1730 d1797, m Jane Wiley - desc/o Maj Robert Beverley BLG2560

    Mary - of VA, m1694 William Jones - desc/o Maj Robert Beverley WAC74

    Col Peter - of VA, d1728, m Elizabeth Peyton - desc/o Maj Robert Beverley WAC74; CRL(1)257

    Maj Robert - of VA, b1635 d1687, m(1) Mary Carter, m(2) Katherine Hone - the immigrant JSW1781; BLG2560; DBR(5)188; WAC74, 75; CRL(1)256; CGA22 - could not find evidence of royal descent

    Robert - of VA, m Ursula Byrd - desc/o Maj Robert Beverley BLG2560; WAC74

    Robert - of VA, b1769, m Jane Tayloe - desc/o Maj Robert Beverley BLG2560 - desc/o Ursula St Leger DBR(5)881

    Robert - of VA, b1740 d1800, m1763 Maria Carter - desc/o Maria Horsmanden CHB58; BCD58 - desc/o Ursula St Leger DBR(5)881

    Robert - of VA, b1701, m Anne Stanard - desc/o Maj Robert Beverley BLG2560

    Robert Gaines - of VA, b1761, m Elizabeth Buckner - desc/o Maj Robert Beverley BLG2560

BEVERLEY (cont.)

Susanna - of VA, b1690 d1737, m John Randolph, attorney general & Speaker of the House of Burgesses - desc/o Maj Robert Beverly CRL(1)285 - desc/o Robert Peyton VG468

William - of VA, bp 1680 d1702, m Judith Wormeley - desc/o Maj Robert Beverley WAC74

Col William - of VA, b1696 d1756, m Elizabeth Bland - desc/o Maria Horsmanden CHB58; BCD58 - desc/o Ursula St Leger DBR(5)881

BEVILLE Essex - of VA, d1682/1683 justice of the peace in 1677 & 1681 for Henrico Co, son of John Beville & Mary Clement, m Mrs Amy____ Butler d1682/1683 - the immigrant GBR182; GVFWM(1)337

BICKERTON Alice - of MD, b abt 1728, m1746 Capt John Winston b1724 of Hanover Co, VA - desc/o Col William Bernard DBR(3)132, 334; DBR(4)769 - desc/o Anne Lovelace GVFHB(3)338

Anne - of MD, m1752 George Webb of New Kent Co, VA & had issue (a) Sara Bickerton Webb b1753 (b) Mary Webb b1756 (c) Bernard Webb - desc/o Anne Lovelace GVFHB(3)338

Elizabeth - of MD, b bet 1712 & 1717, m prior to 27 May 1740 Benjamin Hubbard b1712 in England d1784 burgess from Caroline Co, VA & a member of the Committee of Safety 1774/1775 - desc/o Anne Lovelace GVFHB338, 339

Elizabeth - of MD, m George Webb Jr b1731 of New Kent Co - desc/o Anne Lovelace GVFHB(3)338

John Todd - of VA, b abt 1730 d abt 1775 eldest son & heir of John Bickerton & Mary Todd, m Martha (Patsy)____ - desc/o Anne Lovelace GVFHB(3)337

Martha (Patsy) - of MD, m Benjamin Lewis son of Zachary Lewis & left issue - desc/o Col William Bernard DBR(3)692 - desc/o Anne Lovelace GVFHB(3)337

Philip - of MD, lived & patented land in Lunenberg (now Bedford Co, VA) descendants have not been traced - desc/o Anne Lovelace GVFHB(3)338

BICKLEY Charles - of VA - desc/o Joseph Bickley WAC17

Frances - of VA, m1726 Thomas Tinsley of Hanover Co - desc/o Joseph Bickley WAC17; GVFWM(1)349; GVFHB(1)136

Francis - of VA, settled on land in Hanover Co & was alive in 1766 - desc/o Joseph Bickley WAC17; GVFHB(1)136

James - of VA - desc/o Joseph Bickley WAC17

John - of VA, m (his cousin) Mary Bickley - desc/o Joseph Bickley WAC17; GVFWM(1)348

John - of VA, d1799 3rd son of Joseph Bickley Jr, was of Richmond, Henrico Co. He was captain in the Virginia Troops, War of the Revolution, m (his cousin) Mary Bickley d1800 dau/o Sir William Bickley - desc/o Joseph Bickley GVFWM(1)349

John - of VA, b1713 d1793 m1736 Mary Hurt of Louisa Co, m(2) Susannah Harding wid/o Charles Ellis GVFWM(1)344/350 & GVFHB(1)127/142

Joseph - of VA sometime bef 1703, d bef 1751 he was the first sheriff & justice of the Louisa County Court, son of Sir Francis Bickley, 3rd Baronet & Mary Winch, m Mrs Sarah Shelton Gessedge - the

BICKLEY (cont.)

immigrant WAC16, 17; CGA22; GBR384; GVFWM(1)344/350; GVFHB(1)127/142

Joseph Jr - of VA, d1749, m Elizabeth____ - desc/o Joseph Bickley WAC17; GVFWM(1)348

Joseph - of VA, posthumous son of Joseph Bickley Jr - desc/o Joseph Bickley GVFWM(1)348

Joseph - of VA & TN - desc/o Joseph Bickley WAC16, 17

Mary - of VA, m (her cousin) John Bickley - desc/o Joseph Bickley GVFWM(1)348

Sir William - of VA, succeeded to the baronetcy as 6th Baronet d1771, m____ & left issue - desc/o Joseph Bickley WAC16, 17; GVFWM(1)348; GVFHB(1)136

BIDDLE Col Clement - of PA, b1740 d1814, m(2) Rebekah Cornell - desc/o Rebecca Humphrey CHB158; MCD267; BCD158

Gainor - of PA, b1688, m1706 Jonathan Jones - desc/o Rebecca Humphrey CHB160

Owen - of PA, b1737, m1760 Sarah Parke - desc/o Rebecca Humphrey CHB157; BCD157

Thomas - of PA, b1776, m1806 Christine Williams - desc/o Rebecca Humphrey CHB159; BCD159

BIDWELL Jemima - b1765 - desc/o Richard Harlakenden RAA102

BIGELOW Jabez - of NY, b1760 d1829, m Almy Gardner - desc/o John Drake MCB347; MCD208

Joshua, m Elizabeth Flagg - desc/o John Warren J&K127; PFA Apx C #10

Mercy b1686 d1745, m Lieut Thomas Garfield - desc/o John Warren J&K130; PFA Apx C #10

BILES Joanna - m1753 Edward Morris - desc/o Anne Mauleverer AFA238

BILLINGS Ebenezer - b1669 - desc/o Richard Billings RAA70

Ebenezer - b1750 - desc/o Richard Billings RAA70

Edward - b1707 - desc/o Richard Billings RAA70

Mary - b1645 - desc/o Richard Billings RAA70

Mercy - b1674 - desc/o Richard Billings RAA70

Richard - of MA, b1560, m Elizabeth Strong - the immigrant RAA1, 70; sufficient proof of the alleged royal ancestry is lacking

Richard - b abt 1591 - desc/o Richard Billings RAA70

Roger - b abt 1594 - desc/o Richard Billings RAA70

Roger - b1618 - desc/o Richard Billings RAA70

Samuel - b1638 - desc/o Richard Billings RAA70

William - b abt 1601 - desc/o Richard Billings RAA70

William - b abt 1629 - desc/o Richard Billings RAA70

BINGHAM Doc Ebenezer - of CT, b1719 d1783, m(1) Miriam Phelps - desc/o Thomas Bingham FFF183

Stephen - of CT, b1690 d1770, m(2)1715 Rebecca Bishop - desc/o Thomas Bingham FFF183

Deacon Stephen - of CT, b1740 d1835, m(1)1762 Sarah Long - desc/o Thomas Bingham FFF184

Thomas - of CT 1659, bp 1642 d1729/1730, m1666 Mary Rudd - the immigrant FFF183; sufficient proof of alleged royal ancestry is lacking

BINNS Charles - of VA, b abt 1698 d1749, m Judith Eldridge - desc/o
Lieut Col Walter Aston ECD(3)13; DBR(4)658; DBR(5)580

Lucy - of VA, b abt 1743 d1773, m abt 1768 Col John Cargill III -
desc/o Lieut Col Walter Aston ECD(3)13; DBR(4)658; DBR(5)580

Thomas - of VA, b abt 1658 d1699 - desc/o Lieut Col Walter Aston
ECD(3)13; DBR(4)658; DBR(5)580

BIRD Damaris - b1675, m James Hawes - desc/o Frances Deighton
LDS22

Deighton- of MA b1687, m abt 1711 Isaac Merrick - desc/o Frances
Deighton ECD158; AWW339

Hannah - of MA, b1677 d1748, m1699 John Deane - desc/o Frances
Deighton DBR(3)61; DBR(5)759

BIRGE John - of MA, b abt 1703 d1795, m abt 1726 Experience Stebbins
- desc/o Margaret Wyatt ECD241; DBR(1)418; DBR(2)557

Lucinda - of MA, b1764/1765 d1840, m abt 1784 Thomas Clarke -
desc/o Margaret Wyatt ECD241; DBR(1)418

Simeon - of MA, b1736 d1816, m abt 1764 Lois Kentfield - desc/o
Margaret Wyatt ECD241; DBR(1)418; DBR(2)557

BIRKERTON Martha - of VA, m Benjamin Lewis - desc/o Col William
Bernard DBR(1)215

BISSELL Abigail - b1661, m James Eno - desc/o Thomas Holcomb LDS69

Mary - b1666, m John Pettibone - desc/o Thomas Holcomb LDS68

Sarah - b1734 - desc/o Richard Billings RAA70

Samuel - b1698, m1658 Abigail Holcomb - desc/o Thomas Holcomb
THC169

BLACKBURN Mary - of VA, b1768 d1846, m1789 James Moyers - desc/o
Mary Hinton DBR(2)601

BLADEN Anne - of MD, b1696 d1775, m1711 Benjamin Tasker b1690
d1768 president of the council for thirty-two years and deputy
governor of MD 1752, commissioner to Pennsylvania 1752 & a
delegate to the Colonial Congress of Albany, New York 1754 -
desc/o William Bladen J&K282; CHB45; BCD44; DBR(2)764;
GBR152; MG(1)45, (2)426

Col Thomas - of MD, b1698 d1780 governor of MD 1742/1747 &
member of Parliament, m Barbara Janssen dau/o Sir Theodore
Janssen, Baronet - desc/o William Bladen DAB(2)322; MG(1)45,
(2)426

William - of MD in or bef 1695, b1670/1673 Hemsworth, Yorkshire,
England d1718 clerk of the MD House of Burgesses, publisher &
attorney general of MD, son of Nathaniel Bladen & Isabella Fairfax
dau/o Sir William Fairfax, a general of Cromwell's time, m(1)Letitia
Loftus dau/o Judge Dudley Loftus, m(2)1696 Anne Van Swearingen
dau/o Garret Van Swearingen - the immigrant J&K282;
DAB(2)321/322; CHB44; MCB150; BCD44; DBR(2)764; RAA1, 71;
CGA23; GBR152; MG(1)43/47

BLAIR Sarah - of CT 1795, b1742 d1819 dau/o David & Mrs
Sarah___Lawson Blair, m Samuel Watkinson - the immigrant
DBR(5)226; GBR50; TAG(47)65/69, (48)79, 80

BLAKE William - of New England - the immigrant EDV123; CGA23;
sufficient proof of alleged royal ancestry is lacking

BLAKESLEE Melia - of CT, b1764 d1831, m1786 Lemuel Brooks - desc/o
Thomas Yale ECD(3)306

BLAKISTON Ann - of MD, m Arthur Miller d1739, they had a son Arthur
Miller - desc/o George Blakiston MG(1)58

Ann - of MD, m William Spearman - desc/o George Blakiston MG(1)64

Benjamin - of MD, d1760, m Sarah____d1764 - desc/o George
Blakiston MG(1)63

Capt Ebenezer - of Cecil & Kent Co, MD, b abt 1650 d1709 captain of a
foot company in Cecil Co & justice, m Elizabeth James - desc/o
George Blakiston MG(1)53/55

Maj Ebenezer - of MD, b1684/1685 d1745/1748 represented Kent Co
in the MD Assembly, & was justice of the county, m Sarah Joce
dau/o Thomas Joce of Kent Co - desc/o George Blakiston MG(1)57,
58

Ebenezer - of MD, d1777, m Mary Medford d1780 dau/o George
Medford d1761 - desc/o George Blakiston MG(1)67

Ebenezer - of MD, d1772, m(1)1737 Mary Maxwell, m(2) Hannahretta
Mahon (Mawhawn) b1725 dau/o Thomas Mahon (Mawhawn) &
Mary Moore - desc/o George Blakiston MG(1)61, 66, 67

Elizabeth - of MD, m Roswell Neale b1685 d1751 of St Mary's Co -
desc/o Col Nehemiah Blakiston MG(1)56

Francina - b1736/1737 - desc/o George Blakiston MG(1)62

George - of MD 1668, son of Sir Marmaduke Blakiston & Margaret
James, m Barbara Lawson dau/o Henry Lawson of Newcastle - the
immigrant GBR139; MG(1)48/68

George - of MD, d1778, m Martha____ - desc/o George Blakiston
MG(1)65

John - of MD 1668, d1679, m Sarah____d1683 - desc/o George
Blakiston MG(1)52, 53

John - of MD, b1669 d1733, m Hannah____ - desc/o George Blakiston
MG(1)53, 56, 57

John - of MD, d1724, m Anne Gilbert dau/o Joshua Gilbert - desc/o
Col Nehemiah Blakiston MG(1)55, 56

John - of MD, d1756, m Eleanor Dent dau/o Col George Dent of
Charles Co - desc/o Col Nehemiah Blakiston MG(1)56, 59

John - of MD, d1774, m Frances____ - desc/o George Blakiston
MG(1)65

John - of MD, d1802, m Mary____ - desc/o Col Nehemiah Blakiston
MG(1)59

John - of PA, b1773, grandfather of Kenneth M Blakiston - desc/o
George Blakiston MG(1)64

Joseph - of MD, b1760, m Mary____ - desc/o George Blakiston
MG(1)65

Kenelm - of MD, b1776 d1821, m(1)1800 Chloe Tarlton, m(2)1816
Juliet Locke - desc/o Col Nehemiah Blakiston MG(1)65

Margaret - of VA, dau/o John Blakiston & Phebe Johnston, m Maj
Edward Nott, deputy governor of VA - the immigrant GBR139;
MG(1)48/68

Mary - of MD, m Matthew Mason b1689 d1729 - desc/o Col Nehemiah
Blakiston MG(1)52

Mary - of MD, m____Covington - desc/o George Blakiston MG(1)57

BLAKISTON (cont.)

Michael - of MD, bp 1711 d1758, m 8 Dec 17____ Ann Bradshaw d1771 - desc/o George Blakiston MG(1)63

Michael - of MD, b1738, m Rachel____ - desc/o George Blakiston MG(1)63

Nathaniel - of MD, governor of MD son of John Blakiston & Phebe Johnston, m____ - the immigrant GBR139; MG(1)48/68

Col Nehemiah - of MD, d1693/1694 attorney of the Provincial Court St. Mary's & Charles Co, son of John Blakiston & Susan Chambers, m 1669 Elizabeth Gerard d1716 dau/o Thomas Gerard & Susannah Snow - the immigrant GBR139; MG(1)48/68

Nehemiah Herbert - of MD, d1816 vestryman, m(1)1772 Mary Cheseldine dau/o Kenelm & Chloe Cheseldine, m(2)1801 Eleanor Gardiner Hebb - desc/o Col Nehemiah Blakiston MG(1)64

Presley - of MD & PA, b1741, m1765 Sarah Warnock b1746 - desc/o George Blakiston MG(1)62, 64

Priscilla - of MD, m Simon Worrell - desc/o George Blakiston MG(1)64

Prideaux - of MD, b1696, m1729 Martha Miller dau/o Michael Miller & wid/o William Dunn - desc/o George Blakiston MG(1)59, 60

Prideaux - of MD, of Kent Co - desc/o George Blakiston MG(1)60

Rebecca - of MD, m____ Walters - desc/o Col Nehemiah Blakiston MG(1)52

Rosamond - of MD, b1722, m William Wilmer of Kent Co - desc/o George Blakiston MG(1)58

Sarah - of MD, m Bartus Comegys - desc/o George Blakiston MG(1)64

Susanna - of MD, m(1) Thomas Hatton d1701, m(2) Capt John Attaway - desc/o Thomas Gerard DBR(2)233; DBR(3)76; DBR(4)101; MG(1)52

Susanna - of MD, m Robert Mason of St Mary's Co - desc/o Col Nehemiah Blakiston MG(1)56

Thomas - of MD, bp 1701 d1753, m Margaret Hynson dau/o Col Nathaniel Hynson - desc/o George Blakiston MG(1)60

Vincent - of MD, bp 1703/1704 d1769, m(1) Mary____, m(2) Susanna____ - desc/o George Blakiston MG(1)61

William - of MD, d1737, represented Kent Co in the MD Assembly, m Ann____ - desc/o George Blakiston MG(1)58

William - of MD, d1758, m(1)1735/1736 Ann Glenn b1714 dau/o John Glenn of Kent Co, m(2) Mary Courtney dau/o Thomas Courtney of Kent Co, Delaware & wid/o Thomas Williams - desc/o George Blakiston MG(1)62

William - of MD, d1775, m Ann____ - desc/o George Blakiston MG(1)65

BLAND Anna - of VA, m Robert Munford - desc/o Col William Randolph CRL(3)240

Elizabeth - of VA, b1705, m Col William Beverley, only child of Robert Beverley, the historian, & Ursula Byrd - desc/o Col William Randolph CRL(3)240; APP131

Elizabeth - of VA, b1732/1733, m Col Peter Poythress - desc/o Col William Randolph CRL(3)240

John - b 1739 - desc/o Martha Mallory RAA67 - desc/o Henry Isham RAA104 - desc/o Dorothy Lane RAA126

John - b abt 1765 - desc/o Martha Mallory RAA67 - desc/o Henry

BLAND (cont.)

Isham RAA104 - desc/o Dorothy Lane RAA126

Lucy Atkinson - of VA, m Rev Theodorick Bland Pryor of Dinwiddie Co, VA - desc/o Capt Henry Isham CHB533

Mary - of VA, b1703 d1763/1764, m1728 Col Henry Lee of Lee Hall, Westmoreland Co, lieut-col of militia d1747 - desc/o Col William Randolph CRL(3)240; APP131; PVF132; CFA(5)429

Richard - of Jordans Point VA, b1710 d1776, a member of the Continental Congress, m(1)1729 Anne Poythress b1712 d1758 dau/o Peter Poythress, m(2) Elizabeth Harrison - desc/o Capt Henry Isham CHB533; DBR(2)801; RAA104 - desc/o Col William Randolph CRL(3)240; PVF132; CFA(5)429

Theodorick - of VA 1654, bp 1629 d1669, m Anne Bennett - the immigrant WAC17; CRL(3)139; royal descent not proven

Theodorick - of VA, m Frances Bolling - desc/o Col William Randolph CRL(3)240

BLEECKER Jan Jansen - of NY 1658, m____Jacobson - the immigrant EDV28; CGA24; sufficient proof of alleged royal ancestry is lacking

BLENNERHASSET Harman - of VA, b1765 d1831 adventurer, son of Conway Blennerhasset & Elizabeth Lacy, m Margaret Agnew - the immigrant GBR126

BLISS Alethea - of MA, b1723 d1796, m abt 1748 Joseph Comstock - desc/o John Drake DBR(1)162

Eliphael - b1738 - desc/o John Drake RAA87

Pelethiah - of CT, b1697 d1763, m(1) abt 1730 Sarah (Harris) Brown - desc/o John Drake DBR(1)162; RAA87

BLODGETT Benjamin - b1772 - desc/o George Morton RAA116

BLOODGOOD Aaron - of NJ & NY, m1805 Mary Robinson Chandler - desc/o Edward FitzRandolph AFA46

BLOOMFIELD Ezekiel - of NJ, b1683, m1706 Esther (Hester)____ Dunham wid/o Jonathan Dunham - desc/o Edward FitzRandolph NE(97)279

Jeremiah - of NJ, b1693, m1722 Catherine Weeks - desc/o Edward FitzRandolph NE(97)279

Joseph- of NJ, b1695, m1721 Unis Dunham, dau/o Jonathan & Esther Dunham - desc/o Edward FitzRandolph NE(97)279

Timothy - of NJ, b1681/1682, m1707 Ruth Higgins, dau/o Zedediah Higgins of Somerset Co, NJ - desc/o Edward FitzRandolph NE(97)279

BOARDMAN Anna - b1757 - desc/o Richard Belding RAA68

BOARMAN Ann - of MD, m Ignatius Gardiner - desc/o Rev Robert Brooke CRL(2)69

Catherine - of MD, m Maj William Thomas - desc/o Rev Robert Brooke MCD168

Catherine - of MD, m Richard Gardiner - desc/o Rev Robert Brooke CRL(2)69

Catherine - of MD, m Henry Gardiner - desc/o Rev Robert Brooke CRL(2)69

George - of MD, d1768, m Mary Gardiner - desc/o Rev Robert Brooke CRL(2)69

Ignatius - of MD, m Rebecca Conyers - desc/o Rev Robert Brooke

BOARMAN (cont.)
>> DBR(5)864, 884; - desc/o Thomas Gerard DBR(5)904, 913
> Joseph - of MD, d1826, m bef 1794 Sarah____ - desc/o Rev Robert
>> Brooke CRL(2)69
> Leonard - of MD, d1794, m Elizabeth____ - desc/o Rev Robert Brooke
>> CRL(2)69
> Monica - of MD, m John Edelen - desc/o Rev Robert Brooke CRL(2)69
> Richard Basil - of MD, d1782, m Ann Gardiner - desc/o Rev Robert
>> Brooke CRL(2)68
> William - of MD, m Dorothy Sewall - desc/o Thomas Gerard DBR(5)904
BODDIE Bennett - of NC, b1763, m1793 served as a soldier in the Nash
> County militia during the Revolution & fought at the Battle of
> Guilford Court House 15 Mar 1781 when he was 18 years old, m
> Sarah Smith dau/o Benjamin Smith & Tabitha Exum - desc/o
> William Boddie GVFWM(1)388
> Elijah - of NC, b1765, m Elizabeth Taylor - desc/o William Boddie
>> GVFWM(1)388; HSF(1)340
> Elizabeth - of VA, m Alexander Matthews - desc/o William Boddie
>> HSF(1)340
> Elizabeth - of NC, b1776, m Capt John Perry - desc/o William Boddie
>> GVFWM(1)388; HSF(1)340
> George - of NC, b1769, m(1)1790 Susanna Parham Hill b1760 d1798
>> dau/o Thomas Hill Jr & Rebecca Parham, m(2) Lucy Williams
>> dau/o Major John Williams of Halifax - desc/o William Boddie
>> GVFWM(1)388; HSF(1)340, 345
> John - of VA, b1685, m Elizabeth Thomas dau/o William Thomas &
>> Elizabeth Hill - desc/o William Boddie HSF(1)340
> John - of VA & SC, moved to the Edgefield District, South Carolina
>> where many of his descendants still reside, m Elizabeth Jeffries -
>> desc/o William Boddie GVFWM(1)384; HSF(1)340
> Mary - of VA, m John Browne - desc/o William Boddie GVFWM(1)377;
>> HSF(1)340
> Mary - of NC, b1771, m Joshua Perry d1809 of Franklin Co, NC -
>> desc/o William Boddie GVFWM(1)388; HSF(1)340, 343
> Nathaniel - of NC, b1732 d1797 of Rose Hill, Nash Co, delegate to the
>> State Convention at Halifax, which declared for Independence 4 Jul
>> 1776, member House of Commons 1777 & member Senate
>> 1778/1781, m Chloe Crudup b1745 d1781 dau/o John &
>> Mourning Crudup - desc/o William Boddie GVFWM(1)386;
>> HSF(1)340
> Temperance - of NC, m Capt Solomon Williams d1794 Warren Co, NC,
>> served in Donoho's Company, 6th Regiment, Continental Line, son
>> of Samuel Williams - desc/o William Boddie GVFWM(1)386;
>> HSF(1)340, 341
> Temperance - of NC, b1767, m Col Jeremiah Perry - desc/o William
>> Boddie GVFWM(1)388; HSF(1)340
> William - of VA, bp 1633 d1717 son of John & Mary____Boddie, m(1)
>> Anna____, m(2)1683 Elizabeth____, m(3) Mrs Mary(____) Griffin - the
>> immigrant GBR460 some aspect of royal descent merits further
>> study; GVFWM(1)365; HSF(1)340
> Lieut William - of VA, b1712 in Isle of Wight Co d abt 1772 in

BODDIE (cont.)

Edgecombe Co, North Carolina, was a lieutenant in Northampton Foot in Spanish War 1748, & French & Indian War 1754/1755, m Mary Bennett dau/o Capt William Bennett of the Roanoke Company in the Spanish War - desc/o William Boddie GVFWM(1)384; HSF(1)340

William - of NC, b1749 served as an officer in the Nash County militia in the Revolution, m Martha Jones of Halifax - desc/o William Boddie GVFWM(1)386; HSF(1)340

Willis - of NC, m Catherine Barnes - desc/o William Boddie GVFWM(1)386; HSF(1)340

BODWELL Erastus - of CT, b1776, m1800 Chloe Bird - desc/o John Drake DBR(4)147; DBR(5)372

BOHUN Edmund - of SC, chief justice of South Carolina, son of Baxter Bohun & Margaret Lawrence, m Mary Brampton - the immigrant GBR146

BOLLES (BOWLES) Deliverence - of MA, m1742 Timothy Clifton - desc/o Joseph Bolles ECD(2)51

Elizabeth - of MA, b1652, m John Locke - desc/o Joseph Bolles LDS13; RAA71

Hannah - of MA, b1649 d aft 1690, m Caleb Beck d abt 1690 - desc/o Joseph Bolles DBR(1)331; DBR(2)423; DBR(4)459

Joanna - of MA, b1727, m1744 Ebenezer Record - desc/o Joseph Bolles ECD(2)60; DBR(5)817

John - of CT, b1677 d1767, m(2) Elizabeth Wood - desc/o Joseph Bolles DBR(3)700

Jonathan - of MA, b abt 1700 d1773 Rochester, MA married & had issue - desc/o Joseph Bolles NEFGM(3)1421

Jonathan - of MA, b1732 Rochester d1824 Rockingham, VT, m1754 Elizabeth Randall - desc/o Joseph Bolles NEFGM(3)1421

Joseph - of ME abt 1640, bp 1608 d1678 son of Thomas Bolles & Elizabeth Perkins, m Mary Howell b1624 dau/o Morgan Howell of Cape Porpoise, ME - the immigrant FLW170; ECD(2)51, 57, 60; MCS58; LDS13; DBR(1)331; DBR(2)421, 423; DBR(3)700; DBR(4)459; DBR(5)814; RAA1, 71; GBR214; TAG(37)114, 115, (38)120; NEFGM(3)1420

Lemuel - of NH, b abt 1776 Richmond d1827, m Mary Chamberlain - desc/o Joseph Bolles NEFGM(3)1421

Mary - of ME, b1641 d1704, m1631 Maj Charles Frost - desc/o Joseph Bolles ECD(2)57; RAA71

Samuel - of ME & MA, b1646 d1713, m Mary Dyer dau/o William Dyer - desc/o Joseph Bolles ECD(2)51, 60; DBR(5)814; NEFGM(3)1420, 1421

Samuel - of ME & MA, m bef 1715 Lydia Balch - desc/o Joseph Bolles ECD(2)51, 60; DBR(5)817

Samuel - b1744 d1842, m(1)1766 Margaret Moore - desc/o Joseph Bolles DBR(3)700

Thomas - of ME, b1644 d1727, m(1)1669 Zipporah Wheeler - desc/o Joseph Bolles DBR(3)700; CGA24

BOLLING Agnes - of VA, b1700 - desc/o Robert Bolling WAC19

Anne - of VA, b1690 - desc/o Robert Bolling WAC19

BOLLING (cont.)

Anne - of VA, b1713 d aft 1766, m abt 1730 John Hall - desc/o Lieut Col Walter Aston ECD(3)9

Archibald - m Catherine Payne - desc/o Col William Randolph GBR169 - desc/o Christopher Branch GBR408

Drury - of VA, b1695 - desc/o Robert Bolling WAC19

Edward - of VA, b1687 - desc/o Robert Bolling WAC19 Jane of VA, b1722, m1745 Hugh Miller - desc/o Lieut Col Walter Aston CHB440; MCD159

John - of VA, b1676 - desc/o Robert Bolling WAC19

Robert - of VA 1660, b1646 d1707, m(1)1675 Jane Rolfe, m(2)1681 Anne Stith - the immigrant WAC18, 19; CGA24; GVFWM(1)392; no longer accepted as being of royal descent

Robert - of VA, b1682 - desc/o Robert Bolling WAC19

Robert - of VA, b1730 d1775, m1758 Mary Marshall Tabb - desc/o Lieut Col Walter Aston CHB439

Robert - of VA, m(2)1790 Catherine Stith - desc/o Lieut Col Walter Aston CHB439

Stith - of VA, b1686 - desc/o Robert Bolling WAC19

Stith - of VA, b1753 d1797, m1776 Charlotte Edmunds - desc/o Lieut Col Walter Aston ECD(3)11; DBR(5)258

Susannah - of VA, b1728, m1745 Alexander Bolling - desc/o Lieut Col Walter Aston ECD(3)11; DBR(5)258

Thomas - of VA, b1697 - desc/o Robert Bolling WAC19

BOLTON John - the immigrant EDV36; CGA24; sufficient proof of alleged royal ancestry is lacking

BOND Abigail - of MA, b1680, m1704 Edward Ordway - desc/o Anthony Colby ECD(2)96; DBR(4)758; DBR(5)693

Rebecca - of MD, d1823, m Jonathan Hayden - desc/o Thomas Gerard DBR(4)101

Susannah - of MD & KY, b1740 d1807, m Dr James Bate - desc/o Thomas Gerard DBR(2)233; DBR(3)76

BONNER Capt John - of VA - the immigrant EDV90; sufficient proof of alleged royal ancestry is lacking

John - of MA, d1725 - desc/o Capt John Bonner EDV90; CGA25

Mary - of VA, b1770 d1863, m1789 Edward Lee - desc/o Rev Hawte Wyatt DBR(1)707

BONUM Ruth - b abt 1646 - desc/o George Morton RAA116

BOOTH Bethia - of CT, m1676 Joseph Curtiss - desc/o Edward Booth CHB385; MCD174

Edward - of CT 1640, bp 1608 d1687, m1640 ___Hawley - the immigrant CHB385; CGA24; sufficient proof of alleged royal ancestry is lacking

Elizabeth - of CT, m Capt John Minor - desc/o Richard Booth J&K130, 288; JSW1878; PFA Apx C #9

Isabella - of VA, b1704 d1742, m1726 Rev John Fox - desc/o William Ironmonger DBR(1)643; DBR(5)889

Richard - of CT, bp 1607/1608 d1687, m1640 Elizabeth Hawley - the immigrant J&K130, 288; JSW1878; MCD174; PFA Apx C #9; CGA25; TAG(48)148, 149 no longer accepted as being of royal descent

BOSTWICK Ebenezer - of CT, b1755 d1840, m1777 Rebecca Northrop - desc/o William Leete CHB368

BOSVILE Elizabeth - of MA 1635, d abt 1659 dau/o Godfrey Bosvile & Margaret Grevile, m(1)1635 Lieut Col Roger Harlakenden, m(2) Herbert Pelham of MA, 1st treasurer of Harvard College - the immigrant MCS72; GBR136

John - of MD & VA, b abt 1576, m Jane Elliott - the immigrant RAA1; sufficient proof of alleged royal ancestry is lacking

BOTELER Anne - of MD, dau/o Sir Philip & Elizabeth Langham, m Lionel Copley d1693, governor of MD - the immigrant GBR116

Elizabeth - of VA, b abt 1610/1612 d aft 1668/1669 dau/o John Boteler & Jane Elliott, m1638 Col William Claiborne bp 1600 d aft 1677/1678 son of Thomas Claiborne (Cleyborne) & Sarah (Smith) James, surveyor for the Virginia Company of London, was secretary of the colony 1625/1637; chief commander against the Indians 1664 - the immigrant ECD(3)24; MCS46; DBR(2)100; DBR(3)718; DBR(4)225; DBR(5)328, 337, 339, 340; GBR372; APP184/191; VHG38; CFA(6)152

John - b abt 1576 - the immigrant RAA71; sufficient proof of alleged royal ancestry is lacking

Thomas - of MD, son of John Boteler & Jane Elliott, m Mrs Joan Christopher Mountstephen - the immigrant GBR372

BOURCHIER Mary - of VA, b abt 1598, son of Sir John Bourchier & Elizabeth____, m Jabez Whitaker - the immigrant JSW1796; MCS52; DBR(1)750; DBR(2)273, 456; DBR(3)67, 68; DBR(4)645, 674; GBR146

BOURNE Jane - of VA, d1845, m1781 Lewis Perry - desc/o Rev Hawte Wyatt JSW1636

BOUSH Mary - of VA, d1794, m1744 Josiah Butt - desc/o Capt Henry Woodhouse JSW1656; DBR(1)93

BOUTWELL Phebe - b1741, m Abijah Perry - desc/o Abraham Errington LDS77

BOWDITCH Deborah - of MA, b Salem 1767 d Salem 1823, m1782 Capt Thomas Moriarty b Ireland 1760 d at sea 1787 - desc/o Edward Carleton ECD151; DBR(1)479; DBR(2)591

BOWDOIN Elizabeth - of CT & MA, b1717 d1771, m1732 James Pitts - desc/o Judge Simon Lynde CHB313; BCD313

Margaret - of VA, b1758 d1801 Williamsburg, m1778 Judge Joseph Prentis b1754 d1809 - desc/o Col Nathaniel Littleton SMO301

BOWEN Abigail - of MA, m Caleb Kendrick - desc/o Griffith Bowen AAP146; GBR387 - desc/o Margaret Fleming AAP147

Abigail - of MA, m Benjamin Fiske - desc/o Joseph Peck CRL(2)5

Alice - of MA, m ____Wheaton - desc/o Joseph Peck CRL(2)5

Benjamin - of MA, b1759 d1824, m(1)178_ Hannah Fenner - desc/o Richard Bowen Sr CHB464

Deborah - of RI, b1765 d1809, m Archibald Dorrance - desc/o Joseph Peck CRL(2)6, 23, 27, 31, 47

Elizabeth - of MA, d1712/1713, m 1669 Isaac Addington b1645 d1714/1715 - desc/o Griffith Bowen NE(47)459; EO(1)238

Elizabeth - b1660/1661 - desc/o Griffith Bowen RAA72

Elizabeth - of MA, b1684 - desc/o Richard Bowen Sr CHB463

BOWEN (cont.)

Dr Ephraim - of MA, b1716 d1812, m(1) Mary Fenner, m(2)1746 Lydia Mawney - desc/o Richard Bowen Sr CHB464

Lieut Griffith - of MA 1638/1639, gentleman & Puritan, from parish of Langwith, Gower, Glamorganshire, S. Wales b abt 1600 d abt 1675 son of Francis Bowen, m1627 Margaret Fleming dau/o Henry Fleming & Alice (Dawkin) Fleming - the immigrant DBR(1)466; DBR(4)781; RAA71, 72; AAP146; CGA26; GBR387; NSG(67)163/166; NE(47)453/459; EO(1)232/238; FLW155

Lieut Henry - of MA, b1633 in Wales d1724 in CT, m1658 Elizabeth Johnson b1637 dau/o Capt Isaac Johnson & Elizabeth Porter - desc/o Richard Bowen Sr CHB465 - desc/o Griffith Bowen RAA71,72; AAP146; GBR387; NE(47)459; EO(1)238 - desc/o Margaret Fleming AAP147

Ichabod - of MA, b1693 d1760, m1721 Martha Walker - desc/o Joseph Peck CRL(2)5, 23, 26, 31, 47

Ichabod - of MA, b1735, m1757 Mary Bucklin - desc/o Joseph Peck CRL(2)6, 23, 26, 31, 47

Jabez - of MA, b1739 d1815 - desc/o Richard Bowen Sr CHB464

John - of MA, m Hannah Brewer - desc/o Griffith Bowen AAP146 - desc/o Margaret Fleming AAP147

Col Joseph - of MA, b1774 d abt 1844, m 1796 Mary Tillinghast - desc/o Joseph Peck CRL(2)6

Lucy - of MA, b1758, m1778 Benjamin Waterman - desc/o Joseph Peck CRL(2)6

Lydia - of MA, b1666 d1758, m1686 Joseph Mason - desc/o Richard Bowen Sr CHB465

Margaret - b1667 in Wales d1692, m1647 John Weld, of Roxbury b1623 in England d1691 in Roxbury - desc/o Griffith Bowen RAA72; NE(47)458; EO(1)237

Mary - d1707, m1653 Benjamin Child II, d1678 - desc/o Lieut Griffith Bowen DBR(1)466; DBR(4)781; RAA72; NE(47)459; EO(1)238

Mary - of MA, m____Jones - desc/o Joseph Peck CRL(2)5

Obadiah - of MA, d1699, son of Richard Bowen, freeman, 1658, deputy, 1681, m Mary Clifton - desc/o Richard Bowen Sr CHB465 - desc/o Joseph Peck CRL(2)4, 5

Obadiah Jr - of MA, d1710, m Abigail Bullock dau/o Richard & Elizabeth (Ingraham) Bullock - desc/o Richard Bowen Sr CHB465

Oliver - of MA, b1742 - desc/o Richard Bowen Sr CHB464

Peniel - of MA, bp 1644 d bef his father, m & had issue - desc/o Griffith Bowen NE(47)459; EO(1)238

Richard Sr - of MA, b158_ d1675, m abt 165_ Ann____ - the immigrant CHB463; CGA26; CRL(2)4; RAA no longer accepted as being of royal descent

Richard Jr - of MA, m(1)1646 Esther Sutton, m(2)1689/1690 Martha Saben - desc/o Richard Bowen Sr CRL(2)5

Dr Richard - of MA, b1662 d1736/1737, m1683 Mercy Titus, m1690/1699 Patience Peck - desc/o Richard Bowen Sr CHB463; CRL(2)5

Ruth - of MA, m ____Kinrick - desc/o Joseph Peck CRL(2)5

Sarah - of MA, b1760, m1783 Joseph Rice - desc/o Joseph Peck

BOWEN (cont.)
> CRL(2)6
>> Thomas - of MA, d1663, m Elizabeth____ - desc/o Richard Bowen Sr CHB463
>>
>> Thomas - of MA, b1664 - desc/o Richard Bowen Sr CHB463
>>
>> Col Thomas MD - of MA, b1689, m1710 Sarah Hunt - desc/o Richard Bowen Sr CHB463
>>
>> William - a mariner captured by the Turks & died in captivity abt 1686, m____ & had a son William - desc/o Griffith Bowen NE(47)459; EO(1)237, 238
>>
>> William - of MA, son of William the mariner - desc/o Griffith Bowen NE(47)459; EO(1)238
>>
>> Zerviah - of MA, m____Jones - desc/o Joseph Peck CRL(2)5

BOYD James - of MA, b1732 d1798, m(1)1757 Susanna Coffin, m(2)1791 Ann Bulfinch - the immigrant MCB155; BCD42; sufficient proof of alleged royal ancestry is lacking
> Joseph Coffin - of ME, b1760 d1823, m1796 Isabella Southgate - desc/o Robert Boyd CHB42; BCD42
>
> Robert - of ME 1756, b1732 d1798, m1757 Susannah Coffin - the immigrant CHB42; sufficient proof of alleged royal ancestry is lacking
>
> Robert - of ME, b1758 d1827, m1791 Ruth Smith - desc/o Robert Boyd CHB42; BCD42

BOYLSTON Thomas - of MA, d1653 - the immigrant EDV92; CGA26; sufficient proof of alleged royal ancestry is lacking

BRACE Elizabeth - b1709 - desc/o Nathaniel Browne RAA73

BRADBURY Ann - b1666 d1732/1733, m Jeremiah Allen - desc/o Capt Thomas Bradbury GDMNH104
> Ann - b1701/1702, m Jabez Fox of Falm - desc/o Capt Thomas Bradbury GDMNH104
>
> Ann - of ME, b1743, m1779 Ebenezer Moulton - desc/o Capt Thomas Bradbury DBR(2)210
>
> Anna - of ME, b1702, m1721 Capt William True - desc/o Capt Thomas Bradbury J&K175
>
> Cotton - of ME, b1722 d1806, m Ruth Weare - desc/o Capt Thomas Bradbury J&K170
>
> Crisp - of ME, m1737 Mary Paine - desc/o Capt Thomas Bradbury GDMNH104
>
> Dorothy - m Rev Ammi Ruhamah Cutter - desc/o Capt Thomas Bradbury GDMNH104
>
> Elizabeth - of ME, b1651, m1673 Rev John Buss - desc/o Capt Thomas Bradbury GDMNH104
>
> Elizabeth - of ME, m Lieut Samuel Merrill Jr - desc/o Capt Thomas Bradbury J&K177
>
> Lieut Ephraim - b1756 d1835, m Martha Eaton, m(2)1808 Elizabeth Amlin - desc/o Capt Thomas Bradbury DBR(2)744, 745, 781
>
> Jacob - of ME, b1677 Salisbury d1718, m1698 Elizabeth Stockman - desc/o Capt Thomas Bradbury J&K174; JSW1801; DBR(4)154; DBR(5)325; GDMNH104
>
> Jane - of ME, m Barnabas Soule - desc/o Capt Thomas Bradbury J&K174

BRADBURY (cont.)

Jane - of ME, b1645 Salisbury d1729/1730 Salisbury, m1667/1668 Capt Henry True Jr b1644/1645 Salisbury d1735 Salisbury - desc/o Capt Thomas Bradbury J&K176; ECD(2)64, 84; DBR(1)110, 356, 491; DBR(2)140, 141, 744, 781; DBR(3)318, 431, 521; DBR(5)121; RAA72; FFF90, 107; GDMNH104

John - of ME, b1764 d1851, m Priscilla Burbank - desc/o Capt Thomas Bradbury J&K166

Deacon John - of ME, b1736 d1821, m Elizabeth Ingraham - desc/o Capt Thomas Bradbury J&K166

John - b1699 - desc/o Thomas Bradbury RAA72

Elder John - of ME, b1697 d1778 founder of York, ME, was an elder in the Presbyterian Church, several terms a member of the Provincial Legislature & of the Executive Council 10 years, m Abigail Young - desc/o Capt Thomas Bradbury J&K166; DBR(2)210

John - of ME, m Abigail Young - desc/o Capt Thomas Bradbury GDMNH104

Jonathan - of ME, b1732 d1812, m Abigail Smith - desc/o Capt Thomas Bradbury J&K172

Lieut Josiah - of NH, b1776 d1855, m1804 Almira Tuttle - desc/o Capt Thomas Bradbury DBR(2)745

Judith - of ME, b1638 York d1699/1700, m1665 Caleb Moody brother of Rev Joshua Moody - desc/o Capt Thomas Bradbury J&K164; DBR(2)775; DBR(3)99; RAA72; GDMNH104

Martha - b1727 - desc/o Thomas Bradbury RAA72

Mary - of ME, b1642/1643, m1663 John Stanyan - desc/o Capt Thomas Bradbury J&K165; DBR(3)153; RAA72; GDMNH104

Moses - of ME, b1715, m1737 Abigail Fogg - desc/o Capt Thomas Bradbury JSW1801

Moses - b1731 d1790, m Mary Page - desc/o Capt Thomas Bradbury DBR(4)154

Samuel - of ME, b1757 d1796, m(2)1788 Hannah Noyes - desc/o Capt Thomas Bradbury JSW1801

Samuel - b1762 d1844, m1780 Abigail Cleaves - desc/o Capt Thomas Bradbury DBR(4)154; DBR(5)326

Sarah - of ME, m Ambrose Downes - desc/o Capt Thomas Bradbury GDMNH104

Sarah - b1661 d1708/1709, m abt 1688 Abraham Morrill - desc/o Capt Thomas Bradbury JSW1801; RAA72; GDMNH104

Theophilus - of ME, b1763 d1848, m Lois Pillsbury - desc/o Capt Thomas Bradbury J&K172

Theophilus - of ME, b1739 d1803, m Sarah Jones - desc/o Capt Thomas Bradbury J&K171

Theophilus - of ME, b1706 d1764, m Ann Woodman - desc/o Capt Thomas Bradbury J&K171

Capt Thomas - of ME 1634 , bp 1610/1611 d Salisbury, MA 1695, son of Wymond & Elizabeth (Whitgift) Bradbury, came to New England as agent for his kinsman, Sir Ferdinando Gorges, m 1636 Mary Perkins bp 1615 d1700 - the immigrant J&K164; FLW175; ECD(2)63, 84; JSW1800; MCS91; DBR(1)110, 356, 440, 491; DBR(2)139, 140, 141, 209, 744, 772, 775, 780, 781; DBR(3)97, 98,

BRADBURY (cont.)

    99, 151, 153, 318, 430, 431, 520, 521; DBR(4)151, 154; DBR(5)121, 325; RAA1, 72; FFF89, 102, 107; TAG(18)220, 226; (55)1/4; (53)247; (57)176, 177; GBR461 some aspect of royal descent merits further study; GDMNH104

  Thomas - of ME, b1674, m1700 (his cousin) Jemima True (d six weeks later), m(2)1702 Mary Hilton - desc/o Capt Thomas Bradbury GDMNH104

  Capt Thomas - of ME, b1699 d1775, m Sarah Merrill - desc/o Capt Thomas Bradbury J&K177; DBR(4)154; DBR(5)325

  William - of ME, b1649 d1678, m1671/1672 Rebecca Wheelwright - desc/o Capt Thomas Bradbury J&K174; JSW1801; DBR(4)154; DBR(5)325; RAA72; GDMNH104

  William - of ME, b1672 Salisbury d1756, m Sarah Cotton d1733 & had issue 13 children - desc/o Thomas Bradbury RAA72; GDMNH104

  Wymond - of ME, b1637 d1669, m1661 Sarah Pike - desc/o Capt Thomas Bradbury J&K166; JSW1801; DBR(2)209; RAA72; GDMNH104

  Wymond - of ME, b1669 d1734, m Mariah Cotton - desc/o Capt Thomas Bradbury J&K166; GDMNH104

  Wymond - m Phebe Young - desc/o Capt Thomas Bradbury GDMNH104

BRADFORD Abigail - b1753 - desc/o Olive Welby RAA93

  Dorothy May - of MA - *Mayflower* passenger who drowned off the tip of Cape Cod before the *Mayflower* landed at Plymouth, m Governor William Bradford of the Plymouth Colony - the immigrant TAG(46)117, 118, (47)87; NE(141)94; Dorothy is not listed as of royal descent in the most recent & authoritative book of Gary Boyd Roberts

  Rev Ebenezer - of CT & MA, b1746 d1801, m1776 Elizabeth Green b1758 d1825 - desc/o Olive Welby ECD135; DBR(2)107, 108; DBR(3)620

  Joel - b1773, m Tryphena Smith - desc/o John Dunham LDS21 - desc/o George Morton RAA116

  John - b1717 - desc/o George Morton RAA116

  Molly - b1746 - desc/o George Morton RAA116

  Samuel - b1683 - desc/o George Morton RAA116

  William - of New England 1620 - the immigrant EDV96; CGA27; NE(4)38 no connection with royal ancestry yet available

BRADLEY George - b1732, m Susannah Pierce - desc/o Frances Deighton LDS22

  Pierce - b1764, m Abiah or Abigail Richmond - desc/o Frances Deighton LDS22

BRADSTREET Anne - of MA, m1764 Amos Porter - desc/o Gov Thomas Dudley DBR(4)867

  Dorothy - of NH, d1671/1672, m1645 Rev Seaborn Cotton b1633 d1686 Hampton, NH, eldest son of Rev John Cotton of Boston - desc/o Gov Thomas Dudley DBR(1)557; DBR(2)686; DBR(4)839; RAA89; AFA114; NEFGM(1)77; NE(8)321; GPM(1)pxliv

  Dudley - of MA, b1648 d1702 colonel of militia & for many years magistrate, m1673 Ann (Wood) Price - desc/o Gov Thomas Dudley

BRADSTREET (cont.)
>> DBR(4)399; DBR(5)360; RAA89; AAP155; GBR250; NEFGM(1)78;
>> NE(8)320; GPM(2)pxliv
> Elizabeth - m1729 Joseph Peabody - desc/o Gov Thomas Dudley
>> NE(8)321
> Eunice - m Benjamin Emerson - desc/o Gov Thomas Dudley NE(8)321
> Hannah - of MA, d1707, m1659 Andrew Wiggin b abt 1635 d1710 son
>> of Thomas Wiggin - desc/o Gov Thomas Dudley DBR(5)223;
>> NEFGM(1)77; NE(8)324; GPM(1)pxliv
> Jacob - m Sarah Porter - desc/o Gov Thomas Dudley NE(8)321
> John - of MA, b1653 d1717/1718, m1677 Sarah Perkins dau/o Rev
>> William Perkins of Topsfield - desc/o Gov Thomas Dudley
>> ECD(2)124; DBR(1)487; DBR(2)293; DBR(3)653; RAA89;
>> NEFGM(1)78; NE(8)314; GPM(1)pxliv
> John - m Elizabeth Fisk - desc/o Gov Thomas Dudley NE(8)321
> Lucy - m Robert Andrews - desc/o Gov Thomas Dudley NE(8)321
> Lucy - of MA, m Rev Jonathan Remington d1745, judge of Middlesex
>> 1729, judge of probate & of the Governor's Council - desc/o Gov
>> Thomas Dudley J&K196; NE(8)316
> Lucy - of MA, b1748, m1771 Richard Harris, Collector of the port of
>> Marblehead - desc/o Gov Thomas Dudley NE(8)317
> Margaret - of MA, b1674/1675, m Joy Tyler b1675 d1764 - desc/o
>> Gov Thomas Dudley DBR(4)399; DBR(5)360; RAA89; AAP155;
>> GBR250
> Margaret - m Mr___Andrews - desc/o Gov Thomas Dudley NE(8)321
> Margaret - m Benjamin Bixby Jr - desc/o Gov Thomas Dudley
>> NE(8)321
> Mary - m Elisha Wildes - desc/o Gov Thomas Dudley NE(8)321
> Mary - of MA, m Rev Hull Abbot - desc/o Gov Thomas Dudley
>> NE(8)316
> Mary - of MA, m Thomas Robie, Esq, merchant of Salem, d Salem -
>> desc/o Gov Thomas Dudley NE(8)316
> Mary - m John Dodge of Beverly - desc/o Gov Thomas Dudley
>> NE(8)321
> Mercy - of MA, b abt 1647 d1715, m1672 Major Nathaniel Wade of
>> Medford - desc/o Gov Thomas Dudley NEWGM(1)78; NE(8)324;
>> GPM(1)pxliv
> Mercy - of MA, b1667 d1710 Dr James Oliver b1658 at Boston d1703,
>> physician & graduated from Harvard College, 1680, son of Peter
>> Oliver & Sarah Newdigate, they lived in Cambridge - desc/o Gov
>> Thomas Dudley DBR(3)596; CRL(1)380, 381; NE(8)314, 315;
>> NEFGM(1)78
> Mercy - m Mr___Stone - desc/o Gov Thomas Dudley NE(8)321
> Mercy - of MA, b1689 d1725, m1710 John Hazen of Boxford - desc/o
>> Gov Thomas Dudley ECD(2)124; DBR(1)487; DBR(2)293;
>> DBR(3)653; NE(8)320, 321
> Nancy - of MA, m Richard Harris of Marblehead - desc/o Gov Thomas
>> Dudley NE(8)316
> Priscilla - m Isaac Averill - desc/o Gov Thomas Dudley NE(8)321
> Priscilla - m John Killam of Boxford - desc/o Gov Thomas Dudley
>> NE(8)321

BRADSTREET (cont.)

Rebecca - of MA, m Rev Isaac Story d1816 aged 67 - desc/o Gov Thomas Dudley NE(8)316

Sally - of MA, m Col Gabriel Johonnot of Boston, MA & Hampden, ME - desc/o Gov Thomas Dudley NE(8)316

Dr Samuel - of MA, d1682/1683 Jamaica, physician in Boston, m(1) Mercy Tyng dau/o William Tyng, m(2) Martha____ - desc/o Gov Thomas Dudley J&K195; DBR(3)596; CRL(1)380; NE(18)314; NEFGM(1)78; GPM(1)pxliv

Samuel - m1722 Sarah Clarke - desc/o Gov Thomas Dudley NE(8)321

Samuel - m Ruth Lamson - desc/o Gov Thomas Dudley NE(8)321

Sarah - of MA, m(1) Richard Hubbard d1681 held some principal offices in town & was deputy to the general court in 1660, of Ipswich, m(2) Major Samuel Ward of Marblehead - desc/o Gov Thomas Dudley NEFGM(1)77; NE(8)323; GPM(1)pxliv

Sarah - b1685 - desc/o Gov Thomas Dudley RAA89

Sarah - of MA, bp 1696, m1714 Jacob Wendell d1761 aged 70 merchant of Boston, one of the governor's council & colonel of the Boston regiment - desc/o Gov Thomas Dudley CRL(1)381; NE(18)314, 315

Simon - of MA 1630, b1603 d1697 at Salem, m(1) Anne Dudley dau/o Governor Thomas Dudley, she was the mother of all his children and was of royal descent - the immigrant EDV102, 103; CRL(1)380; CGA27; NE(18)313/333; royal descent has not been proven

Rev Simon - of MA, b1638/1640 d1683, ordained a minister 1670, m1667 (his cousin) Lucy Woodbridge dau/o Rev John Woodbridge - desc/o Gov Thomas Dudley NE(8)316; NEFGM(1)77; GPM(1)pxliv

Simon - m 1711 Elizabeth Capen & had son Simon - desc/o Gov Thomas Dudley NE(8)321

Rev Simon - of MA, ordained 1698 in Charlestown, m(1)____ & had issue, m(2) Mary Strahan dau/o Dr Strahan formerly of Scotland - desc/o Gov Thomas Dudley NE(8)316

BRAINERD Dorothy - of CT, b1710, m Lieut David Smith - desc/o Elizabeth St John CHB222; BCD222

Rev John - of NJ, b1720 d1781, m1752 Experience Lyon - desc/o Elizabeth St John J&K299

Martha - of CT, b1716 d1754, m1738 Maj Gen Joseph Spencer - desc/o Elizabeth St John CHB222; BCD222

Mary - of NJ, b1756 d1792, m Lieut Col John Ross - desc/o Elizabeth St John J&K299

Rev Nehemiah - of CT, b1712 d1744, m Elizabeth Fiske - desc/o Elizabeth St John CHB222

BRANCH Agnes - of VA, m(1) Edward Osborne d1724, m(2)1726 John Worsham Jr d1745 - desc/o Christopher Branch APP135; GVFWM(1)417

Amy - of VA, m (her cousin) Henry Branch - desc/o Christopher Branch APP135; GVFWM(1)418

Arthur - of VA, d1802, m1779 Catherine Moseley - desc/o Christopher Branch GVFWM(1)436

Benjamin - of VA, b1665 d1706, orphan, m1695 Tabitha Osborne - desc/o Christopher Branch BLG2576; APP139

BRANCH (cont.)

Benjamin - of VA, b1700 d1762, m(1) (his cousin) Mary Osborne, m(2) (his cousin) Obedience Turpin - desc/o Christopher Branch BLG2576; APP139

Benjamin - of VA, b1732 d1786, m Anne Bass - desc/o Christopher Branch BLG2576

Bolling - of VA, m Rebecca Graves - desc/o Christopher Branch GVFWM(1)435

Charles - of VA, d1835, m Elizabeth Porter - desc/o Christopher Branch GVFWM(1)436

Christopher - of VA, b1595/1602 d1682/1683, justice 1650 & burgess 1629/1641, son of Lionel Branch & Valentia Sparkes, m1619 Mary Addie dau/o Sir Francis Addie, of Darton, Yorks - the immigrant DBR(1)311, DBR(1)607; DBR(2)228, 229, 754; AAP141; WAC104; BLG2575; GBR407; APP133/139; GVFWM(1)410/443; NEFGM(3)1557

Christopher Jr - of VA, b abt 1627/1628 d1665, m____ - desc/o Christopher Branch DBR(2)229; AAP141; WAC104; BLG2576; GBR407; APP134; GVFWM(1)413

Christopher - of VA, b1659 d1727, m Anne Sherman dau/o Henry & Cicely Sherman & wid/o John Crowley d1687 - desc/o Christopher Branch APP137; DBR(2)229

Cicely - of VA, b1695/1696 d1770, m1718 William Bass d1753 - desc/o Christopher Branch APP138

Daniel - of VA, d1782, m bef Nov 1761 Elizabeth Porter dau/o Thomas Porter of Cumberland Co - desc/o Christopher Branch APP136; GVFWM(1)438

Daniel - of VA, d1793, m Jemima Britton dau/o William Britton - desc/o Christopher Branch GVFWM(1)440

Daniel - of VA, d1811, m(1) Mary Britton dau/o James Britton, m(2)1783 Sally Clarke - desc/o Christopher Branch GVFWM(1)440

Edward - of VA, d1804, m(1) Margaret____ - desc/o Christopher Branch GVFWM(1)434

Edward - of VA, m Judith____ - desc/o Christopher Branch GVFWM(1)440

Elizabeth - of VA, m Melchizedek Richardson b abt 1648 d1700/1701 - desc/o Christopher Branch APP134; GVFWM(1)413

Elizabeth - of VA, d1766, m(1)1710 Robert Goode of Whitby d1718, m(2) by Oct 1725 Page Punch d1727, m(3) Edward Curd d1742 - desc/o Christopher Branch APP135; GVFWM(1)417

Elizabeth - of VA, d1789, m(1)1730 Stephen Woodson d1735/1736, m(2) Charles Bates b abt 1718 d1790 son of John Bates - desc/o Christopher Branch APP136; GVFWM(1)419

Elizabeth - of VA, m John Wooldridge & had a daughter Elizabeth named in her grandmother's will - desc/o Christopher Branch APP136

Elizabeth - of VA, m (Charles?) Burton - desc/o Christopher Branch GVFWM(1)434

Elizabeth - of VA, m____Harris - desc/o Christopher Branch GVFWM(1)436

Frances - of VA, m Lodowick Tanner b1692 d1773 of Henrico & Amelia

BRANCH (cont.)

Co, VA - desc/o Christopher Branch APP135; GVFWM(1)418

Hannah - of VA, m____Hopkins - desc/o Christopher Branch GVFWM(1)436

Henry - of VA, d bef 1748, m Amey Branch - desc/o Christopher Branch APP138

James - of VA, b abt 1666 d1749, m Mary____d1757 - desc/o Christopher Branch APP136; GVFWM(1)419, 420

Johannah - of VA, m____Sandifer - desc/o Christopher Branch GVFWM(1)435

John - of VA, d1688, m Martha____ she, m(2) Thomas Osborne, m(3)1692 Thomas Edwards - desc/o Christopher Branch APP137; GVFWM(1)422, 423

John - of VA, d1769, m____ & had issue - desc/o Christopher Branch GVFWM(1)435

John - of VA, d1750/1751, m Johanna Hancock d1771 dau/o Samuel Hancock - desc/o Christopher Branch APP136

Margery - of VA, m aft Aug 1736 John Goode d1743 - desc/o Christopher Branch APP135

Martha - of VA, m aft Aug 1736 Daniel Willson d1786 - desc/o Christopher Branch APP135

Martha - of VA, m Richard Ward b abt 1659 d1724 - desc/o Christopher Branch APP137; GVFWM(1)413

Mary - of VA, m(1)1677 Thomas Jefferson d1697 son of John Jefferson, m(2)1700/1701 Joseph Maddox - desc/o Christopher Branch DBR(1)311, 607; AAP141; GBR407; APP138

Mary - of VA, m____Cary - desc/o Christopher Branch GVFWM(1)434

Mary - of VA, m (Henry?) Tatum - desc/o Christopher Branch APP135; GVFWM(1)418

Mary - of VA, d1767, m____Walters - desc/o Christopher Branch APP138

Mary - of VA, m____Marshall - desc/o Christopher Branch GVFWM(1)436

Mary Susan - of VA, m John F Wiley - desc/o Christopher Branch GVFWM(1)435

Matthew - VA, b abt 1661 d1726, m____ - desc/o Christopher Branch APP135; GVFWM(1)418; APP136

Matthew - of VA, d1766, m____ & had issue - desc/o Christopher Branch GVFWM(1)432

Matthew - of VA, of Hanna Spring, Chesterfield Co, VA d1767, m____ - desc/o Christopher Branch GVFWM(1)432

Matthew - of VA, d1772, m1750 Ridley Jones - desc/o Christopher Branch GVFWM(1)419, 432

Matthew - of VA, d1786, m Ann Walthall dau/o Henry Walthall - desc/o Christopher Branch GVFWM(1)435

Matthew - of VA, m Martha Cox - desc/o Christopher Branch GVFWM(1)435

Obedience - of VA, d1746, m(1)1696 John Cocke, m(2) Alexander Trent d1703, m(3) Thomas Turpin d1724 - desc/o Christopher Branch APP137; GVFWM(1)423, 424, 425

Obedience - of VA, d1774, m Thomas Cheatham d1752 - desc/o

BRANCH (cont.)

Christopher Branch DBR(2)229; APP138

Olive - of VA, d1782, m (his cousin) Verlinche Branch - desc/o Christopher Branch APP136; GVFWM(1)437

Patience - of VA, m(1)1699 Edward Skerme d1700, m(2) by 1 Apr 1701 Joseph Wilkinson d1752 - desc/o Christopher Branch APP137 (see Priscilla)

Peter - of VA, m(1)1785 Judith Jones dau/o John Jones, m(2) Martha____ - desc/o Christopher Branch GVFWM(1)434

Phoebe - of VA, m____Hill - desc/o Christopher Branch APP136; GVFWM(1)420, 421

Phoebe - of VA, m____Lockett - desc/o Christopher Branch GVFWM(1)440

Polly - of VA, m Thomas May - desc/o Christopher Branch GVFWM(1)435

Priscilla - of VA, d bef 1750, m(1)1699 Edward Skerme of Henrico Co, m(2)1701 Joseph Wilkinson of Henrico Co - desc/o Christopher Branch GVFWM(1)423 (see Patience)

Samuel - of VA, b abt 1663 d1700, m Ursula____ she, m(2) by 1707 Walter Scott d1743 - desc/o Christopher Branch APP138

Samuel - of VA, m Winifred____ - desc/o Christopher Branch GVFWM(1)434

Samuel - of VA, d1789, m____ & had issue - desc/o Christopher Branch GVFWM(1)436

Sarah - of VA, m Edward Gregg - desc/o Christopher Branch GVFWM(1)435

Tabitha - of VA, d1752, m bef 1727 Henry Mitchell d1754 of Sussex Co, VA - desc/o Christopher Branch APP135; GVFWM(1)417, 422

Thomas - of VA, b1623/1624 d1693/1694, m Elizabeth (Gough?) d1697 - desc/o Christopher Branch WAC104; APP132/133; GVFWM(1)412, 413

Thomas - of VA, b abt 1658 d1728, m by 1688 Elizabeth Archer, dau/o George Archer - desc/o Christopher Branch APP134, 135; GVFWM(1)416, 417

Thomas - of VA, b1767 d1818, m1787 Mary Patteson - desc/o Christopher Branch BLG2576

Thomas - of VA, m Mary Eldridge dau/o Thomas Eldridge - desc/o Christopher Branch GVFWM(1)435

Thomas - of VA, of Shampoke d1773, m Mary____ - desc/o Christopher Branch APP136; GVFWM(1)439

Verlinche - of VA, m (her cousin) Olive Branch - desc/o Christopher Branch APP136

William - of VA, b abt 1625/1626 d abt 1670, m Jane____b abt 1640 - desc/o Christopher Branch WAC104; APP134; GVFWM(1)412, 414, 415

William - of VA, d1807, m Sarah Martin - desc/o Christopher Branch GVFWM(1)436

BRASHEAR Sarah - of MD, b1764, m Christian Bingaman - desc/o Giles Brent DBR(4)85, 389, 463; DBR(5)673

Capt Tobias - of MD, b1754 d1807, m1780 Martha Brocus - desc/o Giles Brent DBR(4)53

BRATTLE Elizabeth - of MA, b1660 d1719, m1677 Nathaniel Oliver - desc/o Elizabeth Coytmore ECD(2)101; DBR(5)118

Capt Thomas - of MA, d1683, m1657____Tyng - the immigrant EDV103; CGA27; sufficient proof of alleged royal ancestry is lacking

BRAXTON Carter - of VA, b1736 d1797 of Elsing Green & Chericoke, King William Co, was a signer of the Declaration of Independence, member of Continental Congress & Virginia Legislature, m(1)1755 Judith Robinson d1757 dau/o Col Christopher Robinson & Judith (Wormley-Griffin-Beverley) of Herwick, Middlesex Co, m(2) Elizabeth Corbin dau/o Col Richard Corbin & Elizabeth Tayloe of Laneville, King & Queen Co - desc/o Sarah Ludlow J&K269; CHB183; BCD183; CFSSA84, 85

Carter - of VA, of King William Co, prominent, influential citizen in affairs of church & state, m Miss____Sayre - desc/o Sarah Ludlow CFSSA85

Corbin - of Chericoke, King William Co, physician, m Mary Walker Tomlin dau/o John Walker Tomlin & Margaret Williamson - desc/o Sarah Ludlow CFSSA85, 86

Elizabeth - of VA, m Humphrey Brooke, of King William Co, son of Robert Brooke & Katherine Booth of Essex Co, VA - desc/o Sarah Ludlow CFSSA84

Elizabeth - of VA, m1779 Col Samuel Griffin of Williamsburg, VA, col & deputy adjt gen 1776, member of US Congress 1789 to 1795 - desc/o Sarah Ludlow CFSSA85

Col George - of VA, of King William Co, m Mary Blair, dau/o John Blair & Mary Monroe of Williamsburg, VA - desc/o Sarah Ludlow CFSSA84

Col George - of VA, of Chericoke, King William Co, m Mary Carter b1764 dau/o Charles Carter & Mary Carter - desc/o Sarah Ludlow CFSSA85

Judith - of VA, b1757, m1779 John White of King William Co, son of Rev Alexander White, rector of St David's Parish - desc/o Sarah Ludlow J&K269; CHB184; BCD184; CFSSA85

Mary - of VA, m Robert Carter Burwell, of Isle of Wight Co, b1720 d1779 son of Nathaniel Burwell & Elizabeth Carter of Fairfield, Gloucester Co, VA - desc/o Sarah Ludlow CFSSA84

Mary - of VA, b1756 d abt 1782, m1779 Robert Page Jr b1752 d1794 of Broadneck House, Hanover Co, son of Robert Page & Sarah Walker - desc/o Sarah Ludlow CHB183; BCD183; CFSSA85

BREESE Sidney - of NY 1733/1734 - the immigrant EDV104; CGA27; sufficient proof of alleged royal ancestry is lacking

BRENT Anne - of MD, b abt 1620 bp 1637 Ilmington d bef 1647, m abt 1640 Leonard Calvert, first governor of MD, second son of Sir George Calvert, Lord Baltimore - the immigrant DBR(4)542; RCFA(7)105 lists Anne as the dau/o Sir Richard Brent & Elizabeth Reed

Anne - of VA, d1803, m (her cousin) Daniel Carroll of Duddington - desc/o Col Giles Brent CFA(1)33; CFSSA88; RCFA113

Catherine - d1819, m1754 James Douglas - desc/o Capt George Brent RCFA108

Catherine - m1787 George Diggs - desc/o Capt George Brent RCFA108

BRENT (cont.)

Capt Charles - of VA, of Woodstock, Stafford Co, m Hannah Innes,
daughter or granddaughter Rev Hugh or Josiah Innes - desc/o
Capt George Brent CFSSA89, 90

Charles - of VA, m Ann Gunnell, of Fairfax Co & had issue - desc/o
Capt George Brent CFSSA90

Daniel - of VA, d1814 of Richland, Stafford Co, member of the House of
Delegates, m1782 Ann Fenton Lee, dau/o Thomas Ludwell Lee &
Mary Aylett of Bellevue - desc/o Col Giles Brent CFA(1)33;
CFSSA89

Daniel - b1768 d1841, m1813 Eliza Walsh - desc/o Capt George Brent
RCFA108

Daniel Carroll - of VA, b1759 d1814, member of the House of
Delegates from Stafford Co, m1782 Ann Fenton Lee, dau/o Thomas
Ludwell Lee & Mary Aylett - desc/o Col Giles Brent CFA(1)33;
RCFA113

Eleanor - of VA, m Clement Hill - desc/o Col Giles Brent CFA(1)33;
CFSSA89; RCFA113

Elinor - b1770 d1822, m Francis Digges - desc/o Capt George Brent
RCFA109

Elizabeth - of VA d1719, m1709 Thomas Langman - desc/o Capt
George Brent RCFA107

Elizabeth - of VA, m(1) abt 1735 Samuel Hinton d1771, m(2)1774
Thomas Hunton - desc/o Lieut Col Henry Fleete APP288

Capt George - of VA 1660, d1699, captain of troop of horse 1670,
ranger general of the Northern Neck of VA & receiver general of the
Rappahannock 1690 son of George Brent & Mariana Peyton, m(1)
Elizabeth Greene dau/o William Greene, of Bermuda & ___Layton,
m(2)1687 Mary Sewell dau/o Henry Sewall & Lady Jane Lowe
Sewall Calvert, Baroness Baltimore of MD - the immigrant
BLG2577; WAC20, 21; CFA(1)30; GBR132; CFSSA89; RCFA106,
107

George - of VA, b1703 of Woodstock, Stafford Co d1778, m1730 Mary
Firmingham of Bermuda - desc/o Capt George Brent WAC21;
CFSSA89; RCFA107

George - of VA, m Miss___Wilson, dau/o Dr Wilson of Martinburg, VA
- desc/o Capt George Brent CFSSA90

George - of VA, of Alexandria, served as collector of the port for many
years, m Miss___Persons, of Fredericksburg, VA & had issue -
desc/o Capt George Brent CFSSA90

George - b1762 d1804 lieutenant in the Revolution, m Mary Fitz-Hugh
of Marmion - desc/o Capt George Brent RCFA107

Col Giles - of VA & MD by 1637, b abt 1600/1691 d1671 member of
Assembly & treasurer of the province, 1638; lord of the manor of
Kent Fort, 1642; dep governor of MD, 1643/1644, son of Richard
Brent & Elizabeth Reed, m(1) Princess Mary Kittamaquund (an
Indian) dau/o the emperor of Piscatoway (she was adopted by
Margaret Brent) educated, baptized & given the name of Mary
Brent, m(2) abt 1660 Mrs Frances Whitgreaves Harrison - the
immigrant ECD(3)30; BLG2577; DBR(4)50, 53, 78, 81, 389, 462;
DBR(5)670, 673, 1026, 1027; CFA(1)32, 33; GBR132; CFSSA88;

BRENT (cont.)

RCFA112

Col Giles Jr - of VA, b1652 of Retirement, Westmoreland Co d1679, m1671 (his first cousin) Mary Brent dau/o George Brent & Marianna Peyton of Defford - desc/o Col Giles Brent CFA(1)33; CFSSA88; RCFA112

Henry - d1709, m Jane Thompson - desc/o Capt George Brent RCFA107

Hugh - of VA, of Paris, Kentucky, m Elizabeth Baxter & had issue - desc/o Capt George Brent CFSSA90

Jane - b1738, m1775 Richard Graham - desc/o Capt George Brent RCFA108

John - b1766 d1813, m Anne Brent - desc/o Capt George Brent RCFA108

Katherine - of VA, b abt 1649 d abt 1690, m(1) abt 1665 Richard Marsham - desc/o Giles Brent ECD(3)30; DBR(4)53, 81, 389, 462; DBR(5)673; RCFA112

Katherine - of VA, m Mr____Wrenn - desc/o Capt George Brent CFSSA90

Margaret - of MD, b1600 d1670/1671 unmarried feminist, dau/o Richard Brent & Elizabeth Reed - the immigrant GBR132

Margaret - b1673, m George Plowden - desc/o Col Giles Brent RCFA112

Marianne - of VA - desc/o Capt George Brent WAC21

Mary - of VA, dau/o George Brent & Mariana Peyton, m(1) Col Giles Brent Jr, her 1st cousin, m(2) Francis Hammersley - desc/o Capt George Brent GBR133; RCFA106

Mary - b1675, m John Nutwell - desc/o Col Giles Brent RCFA112

Mary - d1715, m Roswell Neale - desc/o Capt George Brent RCFA107

Mary - of VA, m Mr____Lewis - desc/o Capt George Brent CFSSA90

Nancy - of VA, m Mr____Atwell - desc/o Capt George Brent CFSSA90

Nicholas - of VA - desc/o Capt George Brent WAC21

Richard - of MD & VA, b abt 1570, m Elizabeth Reed - the immigrant RAA1, 73; GBR132 lists their son Giles Brent as the immigrant

Robert - of VA, b bef 1682 of Woodstock, Stafford Co, prominent, influential citizen of affairs, d1721, m1702 Susannah Seymour, dau/o Capt David Seymour, of Bermuda - desc/o Capt George Brent BLG2577; WAC21; CFA(1)30; CFSSA89; RCFA107

Robert Jr - of VA & MD, b1704/1705 d1750 MD, m1729/1732 (recorded in Durham Church, Trinity Parish, Charles Co, MD,) Mary Wharton b1706 d1774 dau/o Henry Wharton & Jane Doyne - desc/o Capt George Brent BLG2577; CFA(1)30; CFSSA89; RCFA108

Robert III - of MD, b1734 of Charles Co d1790, m1750 Anna Maria Parnham b1739/1740, dau/o Dr Francis Parnham & Mary____ - desc/o Capt George Brent BLG2577; CFA(1)30

Robert - d1780, m Anne Carroll, sister of Archbishop Carroll - desc/o Capt George Brent RCFA107

Robert IV - of MD, b1759 d1810, m1783 Dorothy Leigh, dau/o William Leigh & Dorothy Doyne - desc/o Capt George Brent BLG2577; CFA(1)30, 31; RCFA109

BRENT (cont.)

Robert - b1764 d1819 first mayor of Washington, m1787 Mary Young - desc/o Capt George Brent RCFA108

Susannah - m Raphael Neale - desc/o Capt George Brent RCFA107

Susannah - m1756 John Sutherland - desc/o Capt George Brent RCFA107

Thomas - of VA, m Nellie Peyton of VA - desc/o Capt George Brent CFSSA90

William - of VA, b abt 1679/1680 of Richland, Stafford Co d1709 England, m1709 England, Sarah Gibbons dau/o William Gibbons of Wilts Co - desc/o Col Giles Brent CFSSA88; CFA(1)33; RCFA113

William - of VA 1717, of Richland, Stafford Co b1710 England d1742, m Eleanor Carroll, dau/o Daniel Carroll of Rock Spring, MD & Eleanor Darnall, & sister of Archbishop, Bishop of the Roman Catholic Diocese in the United States - desc/o Col Giles Brent CFA(1)33; CFSSA88; RCFA113

Capt William - of VA, of Dumfries, Prince William Co & later Fauquier Co, served with distinction as Capt of Infantry in the Continental Army, Revolutionary War, took a prominent & active part in affairs of both church & state, m Hannah Neal, dau/o Christopher Neal - desc/o Capt George Brent CFSSA90

William - emigrated to Mississippi, m twice & had issue - desc/o Capt George Brent CFSSA90

BRENTON Jahleel - of RI, b1729 d1802 became a rear admiral in the British Navy, m____ - desc/o Gov John Cranston GRFHG(1)282; NE(79)252

Sir Jahleel - of RI, b1770 at Newport - desc/o Gov John Cranston GRFHG(1)282; NE(79)252

William - of MA 1634 - the immigrant EDV120; CGA27; sufficient proof of alleged royal ancestry is lacking

BRERETON or BRIERTON Rev John - of ME, b1572 d1619, explorer & author, third son of Cuthbert Brereton & Joan House or Howes, m Margaret____ - the immigrant DAB(3)39, 40; GBR360

BRERTON Elizabeth - of VA, born after father's death d1749, m Col Robert Jones - desc/o Capt William Claiborne FFF52 - desc/o Elizabeth Boteler APP189

Elizabeth - of VA, d1634, m Capt Thomas Winder, son of Lieut Col John Winder of MD - desc/o Elizabeth Boteler APP180/190

Thomas II - of VA, d1699, m(1)____, m(2) Mary____ - desc/o Capt William Claiborne FFF52 - desc/o Elizabeth Boteler APP189

BRESSIE or BRESSEY Constance - of CT, named for her grandmother Constance (Shepherd) Bressey, m John Morey of Wethersfield, CT - desc/o Thomas Bressey NE(112)43

Hannah (could possibly be a daughter Susannah bp 1647) of CT, b abt 1640, m1659 Thomas Paine d1682 - desc/o Thomas Bressey NE(112)43

John - of CT, b abt 1639 bp 1647 d1708/1709, m abt 1677 Anne Pearce of York, ME d bef 1696 - desc/o Thomas Bressey NE(112)43

Phebe - of CT, m(1) Joseph Dickinson of New Haven, Northfield & Wethersfield, CT, was killed in King Philip's War 4 Sep 1675, m(2) John Rose Sr, of New Haven - desc/o Thomas Bressey NE(112)43

BRESSIE or BRESSEY (cont.)

Thomas - of CT 1634, linen-draper, son of Edmund Bressie & Constance Shepherd, m(1)1626/1627 Hannah Hart, m(2)1631 Phebe Bisby dau/o William Bisby - the immigrant GBR335; NE(112)27/44, (118)251/262, (141)95

Thomas - of CT & MA, m aft 14 Nov 1672 Mary Osborn - desc/o Thomas Bressey NE(112)43

BREWER Abigail - b1705 - desc/o Rev Charles Chauncy RAA79

Charles - of MA - desc/o Rev Charles Chauncy MCD192

Rev Daniel - of MA - desc/o Rev Charles Chauncy MCD192

BREWSTER Abigail - of MA, b1647, m Daniel Burr - desc/o Roger Ludlow CRL(2)321

Abigail - of NY, b1703 d1773 - desc/o Roger Ludlow CRL(2)321

Fear - of MA, m Isaac Allerton - desc/o Mary Wentworth NFA49

Hannah - b1718 - desc/o Robert Abell RAA59

Jonathan - of MA 1621, b1593 d1659, m1624 Lucretia Oldham - desc/o Mary Wentworth ECD(2)301; EDV31

Jonathan - of MA - desc/o Mary Wentworth NFA48

Joseph - of NY, b1709 d1760 - desc/o Roger Ludlow CRL(2)321

Love - of MA, b abt 1595 d1650, m1634 Sarah Collier - desc/o Mary Wentworth ECD(2)287; NFA48; FFF90

Mary - of MA, m Jonathan Owen - desc/o Roger Ludlow CHB413

Mary - of MA, b1627 d aft 1697/1698, m1645 John Turner Sr - desc/o Mary Wentworth ECD(2)301

Mary - of NY, b abt 1695 d1761, m(1) Joshua Wells - desc/o Roger Ludlow LDS29; RAA111; CRL(2)321; CRL(2)365

Nathaniel - of NY, b abt 1689 d1732, m abt 1712 Phebe Smith - desc/o Roger Ludlow ECD192; CRL(2)321

Patience - of MA, b abt 1600 d abt 1634, m1624 Gov Thomas Prence - desc/o Mary Wentworth ECD(2)290, 295

Samuel - of NY, b1718/1720 d1802, m Mary____ - desc/o Roger Ludlow ECD192

Samuel - of NY, b abt 1740 d1824, m(2) abt 1775 Freelove Williams - desc/o Roger Ludlow ECD192

Sarah - of MA, b163_ d bef 1678, m abt 1656 Benjamin Bartlett - desc/o Mary Wentworth ECD(2)287, 304; FFF90

Sarah - of NY, b1701 d1773 - desc/o Roger Ludlow CRL(2)321

Sarah Ludlow - of MA, m Joseph Hawkins - desc/o Roger Ludlow CHB413

Timothy - of NY, b abt 1658 d1741/1745, m abt 1685 Mary Hawkins - desc/o Roger Ludlow ECD192; LDS29; RAA111; CRL(2)321, 365

William - of MA, b abt 1566/1567, m Mary Wentworth - the immigrant RAA1; NFA47, 48; CGA27; sufficient proof of alleged royal ancestry is lacking

BRIDGES Betsey - b1770 d1844, m1792 Silas Holbrook - desc/o John Prescott DBR(1)381

Hackeliah II - of MA, b1737, m1764 Elizabeth Underwood - desc/o John Prescott DBR(1)381

Moody - of MA, m Naamah Frye ancestor of John Ward Dean - desc/o Capt Thomas Bradbury J&K167

BRIDGHAM Mercy - of MA, b1725 d1806, m1750 Dr William Thomas - desc/o Mary Launce DBR(1)545

BRIGGS Rev Isaac - of MA, b1762, m Polly Danforth - desc/o Frances Deighton DBR(2)163

BRIGHT Henry - of MA 1630 - the immigrant EDV44, 45; CGA28; EO(1)314, 315 royal descent not proven

BRINGHURST James - b1730 - desc/o John Claypoole RAA81
James - b1766 - desc/o John Claypoole RAA81

BRINEY Francis - of RI, d1719 - the immigrant EDV42; sufficient proof of royal ancestry is lacking

BRISCO William Dent - of MD, m Sarah Stone - desc/o Humphrey Warren CHB317; BCD317

BRISTOW Robert - of VA 1660, b1643 d1707, m Averilla Curtis - the immigrant WAC22; sufficient proof of alleged royal ancestry is lacking

BROCKENBROUGH John MD - of VA, m Sarah Roane - desc/o Col Moore Fauntleroy CHB143; BCD143

BROCKLEBANK Hannah - b1772 - desc/o Samuel Appleton RAA63

BRODNAX Maj John - of VA, d1657, m Dorothy____ - the immigrant WAC76; sufficient proof of alleged royal ancestry is lacking
William - of VA, b1675 d1727, m Rebecca Travis - the immigrant WAC76; sufficient proof of alleged royal ancestry is lacking

BROME Barbara - of MD, m Philip Dorsay - desc/o Rev Robert Brooke DBR(2)751
Henry - of MD, m bef 1761 Ann Dawkins - desc/o Rev Robert Brooke DBR(2)751
James Mackall - of MD, b1750, m(1) Margaret Mackall, m(2) Ann Brome Marten - desc/o John Brome CFA37
John - of MD, m Margaret____ - the immigrant CFA36; sufficient proof of alleged royal ancestry is lacking
John - of MD, b abt 1656/1658, m Margaret Winifred Jones - desc/o John Brome CFA36
John - of MD, b1680 d1738, m1702 Ann Hooper - desc/o John Brome CFA36
Col John - of MD, b1703 d1749, m Anne Gantt - desc/o John Brome CFA36
Col John - of MD, b1727, m Mary Mackall - desc/o John Brome CFA36
John - of MD b1749 d1778, m1774 Betty Heigh Gantt - desc/o John Brome CFA37
John - of MD, b1775, m1805 Ann Wilson - desc/o John Brome CFA37
Mary - of MD, b1707, m1725 Richard Young - desc/o John Brome CFA36
Mary - of MD, b1729 d1809, m(1) Nathaniel Wilson, m(2) James Duke - desc/o John Brome CFA35
Thomas - of NY - the immigrant CFA35; sufficient proof of alleged royal ancestry is lacking
Thomas - of MD, b1709, m Dorcas Godsgrace - desc/o John Brome CFA36

BROMFIELD Abigail - of MA, b1726 d1775, m1744 William Phillips son of Reverend Samuel Phillips - desc/o Edward Bromfield EO(1)328

BROMFIELD (cont.)

Abigail - of MA, b1753 d1791, m1781 D D Rogers - desc/o Edward Bromfield EO(1)328

Edward - of MA 1675, merchant & trading business b1648/1649 son of Henry Bromfield & Frances Kempe, m(1) abt 1678 Mrs Elizabeth____Brading by whom he had one child, Elizabeth, who died unmarried in 1717, m(2)1683 Mary Danforth d1734 dau/o Reverend Samuel Danforth - the immigrant GBR231; NE(25)182/185, 329/335; EO(1)316/326

Edward - of MA, b1695 d1756, m1723 Abigail Coney b1700 - desc/o Edward Bromfield EO(1)325/328

Edward - of MA, b1723 d1746 unmarried - desc/o Edward Bromfield EO(1)327, 328

Elizabeth - of MA, b1763 d1833, m D D Rogers - desc/o Edward Bromfield EO(1)329

Frances - of MA, b1694 d1721 of smallpox, m1715 Reverend John Webb b1687 son of Mr John Webb, died without issue - desc/o Edward Bromfield EO(1)323

Henry - of MA, b1727 in mercantile business, m(1)1749 Margaret Fayerweather b1732 d abt 1761 of smallpox, dau/o Thomas Fayerweather, m(2)1762 Hannah Clark b1724 d1785 eldest dau/o Richard Clark of Boston - desc/o Edward Bromfield EO(1)328, 329

Henry - of MA, m 1812 in London, Margaret Letitia Fox - desc/o Edward Bromfield EO(1)322

Mary - of MA, b1689, m1724 Thomas Cushing b1693 d1746 son of Thomas Cushing - desc/o Edward Bromfled EO(1)322

Sarah - of MA, b1692 d1775, m Capt Issac Dupee - desc/o Edward Bromfield EO(1)322, 323

Sarah - of MA, b1757 d1831, m1786 Dr E Pearson - desc/o Edward Bromfield EO(1)328, 329

BRONAUGH Jeremiah - of VA - the immigrant CRL(3)114; sufficient proof of alleged royal ancestry is lacking

Col Jeremiah Jr - of VA, b1702 d1749, m Sympha Rosa Enfield (Mason) Dinwiddle - desc/o Jeremiah Bronaugh CRL(3)114

John - of VA, b1743 d1777, m Mary Anne Carter - desc/o Jeremiah Bronaugh CRL(3)115

John Jr - of VA, b abt 1772 d1825 - desc/o Jeremiah Bronaugh CRL(3)115

Mary Mason - of VA, b1770 d1831, m Robert Hereford - desc/o Jeremiah Bronaugh CRL(3)115

BRONSON Mercy - b abt 1742 - desc/o Thomas Dudley RAA89 - desc/o William Leete RAA107

BROOKE Ann - of MD, b1645, m Christopher Beans - desc/o Rev Robert Brooke CFA(1)42; CRL(2)73; MG(1)94; CFA(5)82

Ann - of MD, b1712, m William Carmichael of Queen Anne's Co - desc/o Rev Robert Brooke AMB72; MG(1)102

Ann - of MD, m William Neale - desc/o Rev Robert Brooke MG(1)99; CFA(5)80

Anna - of MD, b1711, m____Harris - desc/o Rev Robert Brook MG(1)105; CFA(1)43, (5)85

Anne - of MD, m bef 1710 Benedict Leonard Boarman b1687 d1757 of

BROOKE (cont.)

    Charles Co - desc/o Rev Robert Brooke CRL(2)68; MG(1)99

Anne - of MD, b1671 d1733, m(1) James Dawkins d1701, m(2) abt
    1702 James Mackall b1671 d1717 - desc/o Rev Robert Brooke
    CHB405; ECD(3)37, 39; MCD169; DBR(1)236; AMB72; MG(1)97;
    CFA(5)82 - desc/o Mary Wolseley DBR(2)333; DBR(3)435;
    DBR(4)355; FLW80

Anne - of VA, b1773 d1802, m William Hammond Dorsey - desc/o Rev
    Robert Brooke CHB406

Baker - of MD 1650, b1628 Battle, Sussex d1679/1680 member of the
    Council of MD & surveyor general of the province, m1664 Anne
    Calvert dau/o Governor Leonard Calvert - desc/o Rev Robert
    Brooke J&K200; CHB399; ECD(3)53; MCD168; BLG2581;
    DBR(2)375; DBR(5)984; AMB71; CFA(1)41; CRL(2)72, 73; MG(1)94;
    CFA(5)80; CRFA178

Baker Jr - of MD, b1666 of St Mary's Co d1698, m1650 Katherine
    Marsham dau/o his step-father Richard Marsham - desc/o Rev
    Robert Brooke ECD(3)53; DBR(5)984; MG(1)95; CFA(5)80 - desc/o
    Anne Arundel APP161, CFA(5)289

Basil - of MD, b abt 1714 of Charles Co d1757, m(1) abt 1735 Dorothy
    Taney dau/o Michael Taney of Calvert Co & Mary Neale, m(2)
    Sarah____ - desc/o Rev Robert Brooke MG(1)107, 235; CFA(5)82

Basil - of MD, b1717 d1761, m Henrietta Neale d1774 dau/o Raphael
    Neale of Charles Co & Mary Brooke - desc/o Rev Robert Brooke
    AMB72; MG(1)107

Basil - of MD, b1738 d1794, m(1)1764 Elizabeth Hopkins d1794 -
    desc/o Rev Robert Brooke BLG2581; AMB72; MG(1)106; CFA(5)81

Basil - of MD, b1748, m Anne Duke dau/o James & Mary (Brown)
    Duke - desc/o Rev Robert Brooke MG(1)106

Basil - of MD, b1772 d1851, m1797 Mary Patrick - desc/o Rev Robert
    Brooke BLG2581

Capt Benjamin - of PA, b1753 d1834, m Anna Davis - desc/o John
    Brooke AFA54

Bennet - of VA, m Mary Hill - desc/o Rev Robert Brooke CHB405;
    MCB333

Bowyer - of MD, (twin to John Brooke d young) b1737 d1815, m(1)
    Mary Browne, m(2) Hannah Reese - desc/o Rev Robert Brooke
    MG(1)106

Catherine - of VA, m Richard Tunstall - desc/o Rev Robert Brooke
    CHB404

Charles - of MD, b1636 d1671 - desc/o Rev Robert Brooke CHB404;
    BLG2581

Clement - of MD, d1732, m Mary____ - desc/o Rev Robert Brooke
    MG(1)105

Clement - of MD, b1676 of Prince George's Co d1737, m Jane Sewall
    d1761 dau/o Maj Nicholas Sewall of St Mary's Co & Susanna
    Burgess - desc/o Rev Robert Brooke J&K202; CHB403; DBR(2)574;
    DBR(3)707; DBR(4)524; CFA(1)42, (5)83; MG(1)100, 101; RCFA179

Clement - of MD, b1732, m Mary____ - desc/o Rev Robert Brooke
    CFA(5)83

Clement - of MD, b1770 d1836 Zanesville, Ohio, m1794 Ann Dillon

BROOKE (cont.)

b1774 d1833 dau/o Moses & Hannah (Griffith) Dillon - desc/o Rev Robert Brooke DBR(2)640; DBR(3)419; MG(1)121, 122

Rev Clement Reverdy - of MD, b1730 d1800, m1774 Anne Murdock of Prince George's Co - desc/o Rev Robert Brooke CFA(1)44, (5)86, MG(1)110

Dorothy - of MD, b1678 d1730, m(1) Michael Taney Jr d1702, m(2) Richard Blundell d1705, m(3) Col John Smith d1717 - desc/o Rev Robert Brooke CHB404; DBR(5)864, 884; AMB72; MG(1)96, 97; CFA(5)82

Dorothy - of MD, b1707 d1780, m abt 1727 Archibald Edmonston of Frederick Co - desc/o Rev Robert Brooke DBR(1)586; AMB72; MG(1)101

Dorothy - of MD, b1776, m Gerard T Hopkins - desc/o Rev Robert Brooke AMB73

Eleanor - of MD, m(1) Philip Darnall d1705 son of her step-father Col Henry Darnall by a former marriage, m(2) William Digges - desc/o Rev Robert Brooke CFA(1)42, (5)84; MG(1)96; RCFA179

Eleanor - of MD, m(1) John Tasker d1711, m(2) Charles Sewall d1742 - desc/o Rev Robert Brooke CFA(1)43, (5)84; MG(1)100

Eleanor - of MD, b1716/1718 d1785, m1734 Col Samuel Beall Jr d1778 of Frederick Co - desc/o Rev Robert Brooke CHB401; ECD(3)41; DBR(1)84, 218, 345, 392, 529, 705; DBR(2)128, 450, 451, 657; DBR(4)547; CFA(1)44, (5)86; MG(1)105

Eleanor - of MD, d1760, m Clement Gardiner d1747 of St Mary's Co - desc/o Rev Robert Brooke MG(1)99; CFA(5)80

Eleanor - of MD, m____Harrison - desc/o Rev Robert Brooke MG(1)101; CFA(5)84

Elizabeth - of MD, b1655 d1687, m1671 Capt Richard Smith of Calvert Co - desc/o Rev Robert Brooke ECD(3)49; AMB71; CFA(1)42, (5)82; CRL(2)73; MG(1)94

Elizabeth - of MD, b1699 d1748, m Col George Beall b1695 d1780 - desc/o Col Thomas Brooke ECD(3)44; MCD168; DBR(4)744; CFA(1)43, (5)85; MG(1)100; RCFA180

Elizabeth - of MD, b1707, m Nathaniel Beall - desc/o Rev Robert Brooke AMB72; MG(1)101

Elizabeth - of MD, m Cuthbert Fenwick d1729 of St Mary's Co - desc/o Rev Robert Brooke DBR(1)788; MG(1)102

Elizabeth - of MD, m Charles Carroll b1702 d1781 of Annapolis - desc/o Rev Robert Brooke J&K202; MG(1)101; CFA(5)84

Elizabeth - of MD, b1740/1741, m1761 Thomas Pleasants of Goochland Co, VA - desc/o Rev Robert Brooke BLG2581; AMB72; MG(1)106

Esther Maxwell - of MD, b1755 d1842, m1780 Henry Hill Jr - desc/o Rev Robert Brooke ECD(3)53; DBR(5)985; MG(1)108

Frederick Thomas - of MD, b1770 - desc/o Rev Robert Brooke MG(1)118

Col George - of VA, d1782 - desc/o Rev Robert Brooke CHB404

Henry - of MD, b1704 of Prince George's Co d1751, m Margaret____ - desc/o Rev Robert Brooke DBR(2)574; DBR(3)707; DBR(4)524; MG(1)105; CFA(5)83

BROOKE (cont.)

Hannah - of MD, b1770, m1794 Isaac Briggs - desc/o Rev Robert Brooke AMB73

Humphrey - of VA, m Elizabeth Braxton - desc/o Rev Robert Brooke CHB404

Isaac - of MD, b1759 of Prince George's Co d1785, m1780 Sarah Ann Magruder dau/o Alex Magruder of Prince George's Co - desc/o Rev Robert Brooke MG(1)110; CFA(5)86

James - of PA, b1678 d1720 - desc/o John Brooke AFA54

James - of MD, b1705 d1784, m1725 Deborah Snowden d1758 dau/o Richard Snowden & Elizabeth Coale - desc/o Rev Robert Brooke J&K203; CHB406; BLG2581; AMB72; MG(1)105; CFA(5)81

James - of PA, b1721 d1787, m Mary Evans - desc/o John Brooke AFA54

James - of MD, b1730/1731 d1767, m Hannah Janney of VA - desc/o Rev Robert Brooke BLG2581; AMB72; MG(1)106; CFA(5)81

Jane - of MD, d1779, m abt 1720 Alexander Contee d1740 of Prince George's Co - desc/o Rev Robert Brooke CHB402; MCD168; CFA(1)43, (5)85; MG(1)100; RCFA179

Jane - of MD, m John Smith d1736 of St Mary's Co - desc/o Rev Robert Brooke CHB399; MG(1)99; CFA(5)80

John - of PA, bp 1638, m Frances____ - the immigrant AFA54; CGA28; royal descent not proven

John - of MD, b1640 d1677, m Rebecca Isaac - desc/o Rev Robert Brooke CRL(2)73; CFA(1)42, (5)82

John - of MD, b1687 d1735, m1709 Sarah (Wargent?) b1691 - desc/o Rev Robert Brooke BLG2581; AMB72; MG(1)102, 235; CFA(5)82

John - of MD, b1710, m Sarah____ - desc/o Rev Robert Brooke CFA(5)82

John - of MD, d1770, m Barbara____ & had a son John Brooke - desc/o Rev Robert Brooke MG(1)102

John - of MD, b1753 d1790, m Mary Wheeler - desc/o Rev Robert Brooke MG(1)106

Jonathan - of PA, b1701 d1731, m Elizabeth Rees - desc/o John Brooke AFA54

Leonard - of MD, d1718 of St Mary's Co, m Anne Boarman dau/o Maj William Boarman of Charles & St Mary's Co, ancestor of James Thomas & - desc/o Rev Robert Brooke J&K200; CRL(2)73; MG(1)95, 98, 99; CFA(5)80 - desc/o Anne Arundel APP161; CFA(5)289

Leonard - of MD, b1697 d1736, m Ann Darnall d1779 - desc/o Rev Robert Brooke ECD(3)53; MCD168; DBR(5)984; MG(1)104

Capt Leonard - of MD, b1728 d1785 sea captain & commander of a vessel called *Horatio*, m(1) Anne Darnall dau/o Henry Darnall of Portland Manor, m(2) abt 1785 Elizabeth (Maxwell?) - desc/o Rev Robert Brooke ECD(3)53; DBR(5)984; MG(1)108

Lucy - of MD, m Thomas Hodgkin - desc/o Rev Robert Brooke CFA(1)43, (5)85; MG(1)100; RCFA180

Lucy - of MD, b1721, m John Estep d1766 of Charles Co - desc/o Rev Robert Brooke CFA(1)44, (5)86; MG(1)105

Mary - of MD, b1630, m(1) Capt James Bowling d1693 of St Mary's Co,

BROOKE (cont.)

m(2) Benjamin Hall d1721 of Prince George's Co, m(3) Henry
Witham - desc/o Rev Robert Brooke CFA(1)42, (5)84; CRL(2)72;
MG(1)96; RCFA179

Mary - of MD, d1763, m1690 Raphael Neale b1683 d1743 - desc/o
Rev Robert Brooke DBR(2)375; CRL(2)73; MG(1)95; CFA(5)80 -
desc/o Anne Arundel CFA(5)289

Mary - of MD, b1709, m Peter Dent b1694 d1757 of Prince George's Co
- desc/o Rev Robert Brooke DBR(2)282; CFA(1)43, (5)85; GBR385;
MG(1)104

Mary - of MD, b abt 1740 d1808, m abt 1757 Stephen Howison d1815
son of John Howison & Anne Wood - desc/o Rev Robert Brooke
MG(1)235

Mary - of MD, d1758, m Patrick Sim MD d1740 of Prince George's Co -
desc/o Rev Robert Brooke CHB401; MG(1)100; CFA(1)43, (5)85;
RCFA179

Mary - of MD, b1760, m1791 Thomas Moore - desc/o Rev Robert
Brooke AMB73

Mary - of MD, m John Boarman - desc/o Rev Robert Brooke MCD168

Mary - of MD, m Philip Fenwick - desc/o Rev Robert Brooke MG(1)108

Monica - of MD, b1752, m Michael Taney, their son Roger Brooke
Taney was Chief Justice of the United States - desc/o Rev Robert
Brooke J&K203; MG(1)106

Lieut Nicholas - of MD, b1752 d1797, m____Hill - desc/o Rev Robert
Brooke DBR(2)574; DBR(3)707; DBR(4)524

Priscilla - of MD b1685 d abt 1760, m1705 Thomas Gantt - desc/o Rev
Robert Brooke ECD(3)46; DBR(2)751; MG(1)100; CFA(1)43, (5)84

Priscilla - of MD, b1717 d1785, m abt 1740 Charles Browne d1766 of
Queen Anne's Co - desc/o Rev Robert Brooke CHB406; MCD169;
AMB72; MG(1)102

Rachel - of MD, m Henry Darnall of Prince George's Co - desc/o Rev
Robert Brooke MG(1)105; CFA(5)83

Rebecca - of MD, d1763, m(1) (her first cousin) John Howard b1688
Somerset Co, MD d1742 of Charles Co, son of Edmund Howard &
Margaret Dent, m(2) Col John Addison, who emigrated to MD in
1667, d during a visit to England 1705 - desc/o Rev Robert Brooke
CFA(1)43, (5)85; MG(1)100; RCFA180

Richard - of MD, d1719 of St Mary's Co, m Clare Boarman d1747
dau/o Maj William Boarman of Charles Co, MD - desc/o Rev Robert
Brooke MG(1)104; CFA(5)80

Dr Richard - of MD, b1716 d1783, m1767 Rachel Gantt b abt 1743
d1793 dau/o Thomas Gantt of Prince George's Co & Rachel Smith -
desc/o Rev Robert Brooke MG(1)110; CFA(5)85

Richard - of MD, d1755, m(1) Monica Gardiner d1772 dau/o Clement
Gardiner of St Mary's Co, m(2) ____Queen dau/o Henry Queen -
desc/o Rev Robert Brooke MG(1)104; CFA(5)80

Richard - of MD, d1771 of Charles Co, m____ & had issue - desc/o Rev
Robert Brooke MG(1)109

Richard - of VA, b1736 d1788, m1758 Jane Lynn d1774 - desc/o Rev
Robert Brooke CHB406; BLG2581; AMB72; MG(1)106; CFA(5)81

Rev Robert - of MD 1650, b1602 d1665 governor of MD 1653, son of

BROOKE (cont.)

    Thomas Brooke & Susan Forrster, m(1)1627 Mary Baker d1634 dau/o Thomas Baker & Mary Engham, m(2)1635 Mary Mainwaring d1663 dau/o Roger Mainwaring - the immigrant J&K200; CHB397; ECD(3)37, 41 & 53; MCB333; MCD167; MCS82; BLG2581; DBR(1)83, 84, 217, 236, 344, 528, 586, 588, 704, 788; DBR(2)281, 282, 375, 450; 454, 455, 572, 574, 607, 639, 656, 751, 833; DBR(3)415, 418, 707; DBR(4)78, 104, 523, 546, 743, 744; DBR(5)105, 863, 864, 984, 1027, 1028; AMB71; RAA1; CFA(1)41; CRL(2)71, 72; GBR258, 385; MG(1)91/123, 235; CFA(5)79; RCFA178

    Robert - of VA, b1639 London, England d1667 Calvert Co, MD, m(1) Katherine Booth, m(2) Elizabeth Thompson dau/o William Thompson of St Mary's Co - desc/o Rev Robert Brooke CHB404; BLG2581; DBR(1)788; AMB71; CFA42; CRL(2)73; MG(1)97, 98; CFA(1)42, (5)82

    Robert - of MD, d1715/1716, m Grace____ Boone b abt 1662 d1725 wid/o John Boone d1689 of Calvert Co - desc/o Rev Robert Brooke DBR(1)788; MG(1)102

    Robert - of MD, b1692 d1753, m Jane Fenwick d1759 dau/o Cuthbert Fenwick of St Mary's Co - desc/o Rev Robert Brooke MG(1)107

    Roger - of MD, b1637 Brecknick College, Wales d1700 of Battle Creek, Calvert Co justice of Calvert Co & high sheriff, m(1) Dorothy Neale dau/o Capt James Neale & Ann Gill, m(2)1676 Mary Wolseley dau/o Walter Wolseley - desc/o Rev Robert Brooke J&K203; CHB404; ECD(3)37; MCB333; MCD168; BLG2581; DBR(1)236, 586; DBR(2)607; DBR(5)864; AMB72; CFA(1)41, 42, (5)81; CRL(2)73; MG(1)96, 235

    Roger Jr - of MD, b1673 of Prince George's Co d1718, m1702 Elizabeth Hutchin(g)s second dau/o Francis Hutchings & Eliza____Hutchings - desc/o Rev Robert Brooke J&K203; CHB405; MCB169; BLG2581; DBR(1)586; AMB72; MG(1)101; CFA(1)42, (5)81

    Roger - of MD, b1714 d1772, m(1) Sarah Bowyer d1645/1646 of Philadelphia, m(2) Elizabeth Boarman - desc/o Rev Robert Brooke AMB72; MG(1)106

    Roger - of MD, d1776, m Mary____ - desc/o Rev Robert Brooke MG(1)106

    Roger - of MD, b1734 d1790, m Mary Matthews d1808 - desc/o Rev Robert Brooke BLG2581; AMB72; MG(1)106; CFA(5)81

    Roger - of MD, b1774, m1804 Mary Younghusband - desc/o Rev Robert Brooke BLG2581; AMB73

    Samuel - of MD, b1758, m Sarah Garrigues - desc/o Rev Robert Brooke AMB72

    Sarah - of MD, b1724, m Philip Lee - desc/o Rev Robert Brooke CFA(1)43, (5)84; MG(1)100

    Sarah - of MD, b1767, m Caleb Bentley - desc/o Rev Robert Brooke AMB73

    Sarah - of MD, m(1) Michael Taney d1743, m(2) Edward Cole, Jr d1761 of St Mary's Co - desc/o Rev Robert Brooke MG(1)102

    Sarah - of MD, b1772 d1849, m1789 Samuel Harper b abt 1765

BROOKE (cont.)

d1834 - desc/o Rev Robert Brooke MG(1)110; CFA(5)85

Sarah Browne - of MD, m(1)___Tomlin, m(2) Capt William Fleete - desc/o Rev Robert Brooke CHB405

Susanna - of MD, d1767, m(1) Walter Smith d1734 of Hall's Craft, Calvert Co, m(2) Hyde Hoxton d1754 - desc/o Rev Robert Brooke CHB403; MG(1)101; CFA(5)84

Maj Thomas - of MD 1650, b1632 d1676 major of militia of Calvert Co, represented Calvert Co in the Provincial Assembly & was high sheriff, m1658 Eleanor Hatton b1642 d1725 dau/o Richard & Margaret Hatton - desc/o Rev Robert Brooke J&K201; CHB400; ECD(3)41, 46; MCD168; BLG2581; DBR(1)84, 217, 344, 392, 705; DBR(2)128,281; 450, 574, 639, 657, 751; DBR(3)418, 707; DBR(4)547, 744; AMB71; CFA(1)41; CRL(2)72; GBR385; MG(1)95, 96; CFA(5)83; RCFA178

Col Thomas - of MD, b1659/1660 d1730/1731 deputy governor of MD 1720, m(1) Anne___, m(2)1699 Barbara Dent b1676 d1754 dau/o Thomas Dent of St Mary's Co & Rebecca Wilkinson - desc/o Rev Robert Brooke J&K201; CHB401; ECD(3)41, 44, 46; MCD168; DBR(1)84, 217, 218, 344, 392, 528, 705; DBR(2)128, 282, 450, 639, 657, 751; DBR(3)418; DBR(4)547, 744; CFA(1)42, (5)84; GBR385; MG(1)100; CRFA179

Thomas - of MD, b1682/1683 d1744 representative for Prince George's Co in the MD Assembly & was high sheriff, m1705 Lucy Smith b1688 d1770 dau/o Col Walter Smith of Calvert Co & Rachel Hall - desc/o Rev Robert Brooke DBR(1)528, 705; DBR(2)128, 282; 450, 657; DBR(3)419; DBR(4)547; CFA(1)43, (5)85; GBR385; MG(1)104

Maj Thomas - of MD, d1798, m Ann Darrell - desc/o Rev Robert Brooke CHB403

Thomas Jr - of MD, b1682/1683 d1744/1745, m1705 Lucy Smith - desc/o Rev Robert Brooke J&K201; CHB401; ECD(3)41; MCD168; DBR(1)84, 218, 345, 392, 639; MG(1)117

Thomas - of MD, b1706 d1749, m(1) bef 1732 Judith Briscoe, m(2) Sarah Mason dau/o Col George Mason of Gunston, Stafford Co, VA - desc/o Rev Robert Brooke DBR(2)640; DBR(3)419; CFA(1)43, (5)85; MG(1)109, 117

Thomas - of MD, b abt 1721 of Prince George's Co d1768, m(1)1753 Frances Jennings dau/o Thomas Jennings of Prince George's Co, m(2) Elizabeth___ - desc/o Rev Robert Brooke MG(1)110; CFA(5)86

Thomas - of MD, b1734 d1788/1789, m1768 Elizabeth Brooke d1784 - desc/o Rev Robert Brooke DBR(2)640; DBR(3)419; MG(1)116, 117, 118

Thomas - of MD, b1744 d1789 - desc/o Rev Robert Brooke BLG2581; AMB72

Thomas - of MD, b1776 - desc/o Rev Robert Brooke MG(1)118

Thomas - died early in the Carolinas, m___ & left issue - desc/o Rev Thomas Brooke MG(1)120

Walter - of MD, b1707 of Prince George's Co d1740/1741, m Mary Ashcom Greenfield dau/o James Greenfield of Prince George's Co - desc/o Rev Robert Brooke MG(1)110

BROOKE (cont.)

Walter - of MD & VA, b abt 1740 d1798 commodore in the VA Navy 1775/1778, m1747 Ann Darrell - desc/o Rev Robert Brooke MG(1)109, 116; CFA(5)85

William Pitt - of VA, d1816, m____ & left issue - desc/o Rev Robert Brooke MG(1)120

BROOKS Cotton Brown - of MA, b1765 d1834, m1794 Jane Williams - desc/o Grace Kaye J&K219 - desc/o Muriel Gurdon ECD(2)235

Eunice - b1771 - desc/o Mary Launce RAA130

Joanna Cotton - of MA, m Nathaniel Hall - desc/o Grace Kaye CHB209; BCD209

Peter Chardon - of MA, b1767 d1849, m1792 Ann Gorham - desc/o Grace Kaye CHB209; BCD209 - desc/o Muriel Gurdon ECD180

William Gray - of MA, m Mary Ann Phillips, father of Rev Phillips Brooks - desc/o Grace Kaye J&K219

BROOME Barbara - of MD, b abt 1762 d abt 1818, m abt 1783 Philip Dorsey Jr - desc/o Robert Brooks ECD(3)46

Henry - of MD, b abt 1730 d1771, m1761 Anne Dawkins - desc/o Robert Brooks ECD(3)46

BROUGHTON Abigail - of MA, m____Callighan & had a daughter Sarah Callighan - desc/o Thomas Broughton NE(37)300

Edward - of MA, b1673 d1744 schoolmaster & merchant, m Martha Wheeler dau/o Josiah Wheeler, & leaving children, Sarah, Copia & Patience - desc/o Thomas Broughton NE(37)299

Elizabeth - of MA, b1646 at Watertown, m Obadiah Reed d abt 1725 - desc/o Thomas Broughton NE(37)299

George - of MA, b1657 Salmon Falls d bef May 1690 killed by Indians, a merchant in Boston & captain of soldiers to fight the Indians, m Perne Rawson b1646 dau/o Edward Rawson, secretary of the colony - desc/o Thomas Broughton NE(37)299

Hannah - of MA, b1658, m1713 John Myrick - desc/o Thomas Broughton NE(37)299

John - of MA, d1680 killed by Indians, m & had issue - desc/o Thomas Broughton NE(37)300

Mary - of MA, m1701 at Woburn, Jacob Fowle - desc/o Thomas Broughton NE(37)300

Rebecca - of MA, m1707 at Boston, Edward Cowell of Truro, MA - desc/o Thomas Broughton NE(37)299

Thomas - of MA, d1700 a rich & active merchant, son of Edward Broughton & Helen Pell, m bef 1643 Mary B(r)iscoe dau/o Nathaniel B(r)iscoe - the immigrant GBR374; NE(37)298/304

BROWN Abigail - of MA, b1732 d1800, m1764 Rev Edward Brooks - desc/o Grace Kaye J&K219; CHB360; MCD285; BCD209 - desc/o Muriel Gurdon ECD180; ECD(2)235

Daniel - of CT, b1743 d1788, m1770 Hannah English - desc/o Rev Peter Bulkeley ECD(3)69; TAG(36)101

Capt Elijah - of MA, b1769 d1806, m1798 Rachael (Joy) Bacon - desc/o Ensign Constant Southworth DBR(2)400; DBR(3)462

Elizabeth - b1671 - desc/o Peter Bulkeley RAA75

Elizabeth - of MA, m John Chipman - desc/o Grace Kaye CHB360; MCD285

BROWN (cont.)

Elizabeth - of RI, m1738 John Gidley, Jr - desc/o Gov John Cranston NE(79)250

Eleazer - of CT, b1696 d1768, m1725 Sarah Rowe - desc/o Rev Peter Bulkeley ECD(3)68

Frances Brown - of MD, b1713 Rich Hill, Charles Co, 2nd child of Dr Gustavus Brown & Frances Fowke, m1741 Rev John Moncure, the first of this name known in VA, was probably b in the parish of Kinoff, Co Mearns, Scotland abt 1709/1710 d1764 - desc/o Col Gerard Fowke VG424

Gershom - of CT, b1665, m1695 Hannah Mansfield - desc/o Rev Peter Bulkeley ECD(3)68

Israel Putnam - m Sally Briggs - desc/o Samuel Appleton AAP153; GBR390 - desc/o Judith Everard AAP154

James - of RI, m1718 Mary Jepson - desc/o Gov John Cranston NE(79)250

John - of RI, b1696 d1764, m1717 Joan Lucas - desc/o Gov John Cranston NE(79)250

Rev Marmaduke - of MA - desc/o Thomas Brown EDV36, 37

Peleg - of RI, m Esther Frebody - desc/o Gov John Cranston NE(79)250

Robert - of RI, m____Kenedy - desc/o Gov John Cranston NE(79)250

Samuel - of MA, b1751 d1831, m1768 Priscilla Harding - desc/o Ensign Constant Southworth DBR(2)400; DBR(3)462

Sarah - of VA, b1715, m abt 1738 Rev James Scott of Dipple & Westwood, VA, b Dipple Parish, Elgin, Scotland d1782 - desc/o Col Gerard Fowke CFA(5)315

Thomas - of MA 1632 - the immigrant EDV36, 37; sufficient proof of alleged royal ancestry is lacking

Zebulon - of NJ - desc/o William Clayton MCD202

BROWNE Abigail - of CT, b1701/1702 - desc/o Nathaniel Browne TAG(22)174

Bennet - of VA - desc/o Robert Brooke MCD169

Edward - of MD, bp 1632 d1678, m Sarah Williams - the immigrant BLG2584; CGA29; sufficient proof of alleged royal ancestry is lacking

Edward - of MD, b1678 d1716, m Mary Erickson - desc/o Edward Browne BLG2584

Elizabeth - of CT, b abt 1653 d1713, m Michael Todd - desc/o Rev Peter Bulkeley DBR(3)86; DBR(5)970

Hannah - of CT, b1651, m1669 Isaac Lane d1711 - desc/o Nathaniel Browne ECD(3)57, 60; TAG(22)163

Rev Isaac - died & buried in Nova Scotia 1787 son of Dr Peter Browne - desc/o Rev Peter Bulkeley TAG(36)101

John - of CT, b1657 d1719, m1685 Anna Porter - desc/o Nathaniel Browne TAG(22)163

John - of CT, b1690 - desc/o Nathaniel Browne TAG(22)164

Maj John - of MD, b1699 d1747, m Jane de Courcy - desc/o Edward Browne BLG2584

Mary - of VA & MA, m1699 Benjamin Lynde - desc/o William Browne CHB138; BCD138

BROWNE (cont.)

Mary - m1760 Isaac Lawrence Jr - desc/o William Hyde THC177

Mary Burnet - of VA, m Herbert Claiborne - desc/o William Browne CHB138; BCD138 - desc/o Sarah Ludlow CHB182; BCD182

Nathaniel - of CT, b abt 1625 of Hartford, Springfield d bef 26 Aug 1658 Middleton, CT, son of Percy Browne & Anne Rich, m 1642/ 1647 Hartford, Eleanor Watts b abt 1627 d1703 Middleton, dau/o Richard & Elizabeth Watts - the immigrant FLW192; ECD(3)57, 60; RAA1, 73; GBR334; TAG(22)158/163, (23)109, (60)91

Nathaniel - of CT, b1654 d1712, m1677 Martha Hughes d1729 dau/o Richard & Mary Hughes - desc/o Nathaniel Browne TAG(22)163

Nathaniel - of CT, b1683 - desc/o Nathaniel Browne TAG(22)163

Robert - of MD, b abt 1746 d1794, m abt 1770 Sarah ____ - desc/o Rev Robert Brooke CHB406; MCD169

Col Samuel - of MA, d1731, m(2)1705 Abigail Keatch - desc/o William Browne CHB138; BCD138

Deacon Samuel - b1703 d1784, m Mercy Patterson - desc/o William Hyde THC 177

Sarah - of VA, m Capt William Fleete - desc/o Robert Brooke MCD169

William - of MA 1634/1635, b1608 d1687, m(1) Mary Young, m(2) Sarah Smith - the immigrant CHB138; MCB165; BCD138; royal descent not proven BCD138

William - of MD, b1738 d1795, m Anne Wickes - desc/o Edward Browne BLG2584

William Burnet - of VA, b1738, m(1) Judith Frances Carter - desc/o William Browne CHB138; BCD138; WAC24, 25

BROWNING Mary Wade - of VA, b1776, m1800 George W Yates, a Strother kinsman - desc/o William Strother GVFTQ(3)418

BROWNELL Bridget - b1713 - desc/o Anne Marbury RAA114

Esther - b1732, m Samuel Howland - desc/o Richard Pearce LDS36

Jeremiah - b1689, m Deborah Burgess - desc/o Richard Pearce LDS36

BRUEN Abigail - of CT, m Samuel Baldwin - desc/o Obadiah Bruen MCD173

Caleb - of CT - desc/o Obadiah Bruen CHB386; MCD173

Caleb - of NJ, b1735 d1818, m Anna Wheeler - desc/o Obadiah Bruen BLG2587

Eleazar - of NJ, b1675, m(1)____, m(2) Ruth Baldwin - desc/o Obadiah Bruen BLG2587

Eleazar - of NJ, b1694 d1778, m Charity Gilbert - desc/o Obadiah Bruen BLG2587

Hannah - of MA, b1643 d abt 1695, m1663 John Baldwin - desc/o Obadiah Bruen ECD122; BLG2587; DBR(1)388; DBR(2)498; DBR(5)170; TAG(26)12

John - of CT, b1560 d1625, m1580 Elizabeth (Hardware) Cowper (or Cooper), m(2) aft 1596 Anne Fox, m(3)1612 (lic) Margaret (Allen) Rutter - the immigrant CHB385; FLW38; DBR(1)16; TAG(26)15; sufficient proof of alleged royal ancestry is lacking

John IV - of NJ, b1646 d1696, m Esther Lawrence - desc/o Obadiah Bruen CHB386 ECD127, 130; MCB318; MCD172; BLG2587; DBR(1)384; DBR(2)117, 494; DBR(3)30; DBR(4)538

BRUEN (cont.)

John - of CT, b1690 d1767, m Mary Tompkins - desc/o Obadiah
Bruen CHB387; ECD131; DBR(2)117

Joseph - of NJ, b abt 1667 d1753 - desc/o Obadiah Bruen ECD127

Mary - of CT, bp 1622 d1670 Milford, CT, m1653 John Baldwin Sr -
the immigrant CHB29, 387; FLW36; MCS73; BLG2587; BCD29;
DBR(1)16; RAA74; FFF262 sufficient proof of alleged royal ancerstry
is lacking

Matthias - of CT - desc/o Obadiah Bruen CHB386; MCD173

Matthias - of NJ, b1766 d1846, m Hannah Coe - desc/o Obadiah
Bruen BLG2587

Obadiah - of CT & NJ, bp 1606 Tarvin d1682/1690 Newark, NJ, m(2)
Sarah___ d abt 25 Mar 1684 - the immigrant CHB386; FLW36,
127, 130; MCB318; MCD172; MCS73; BLG2587; DBR(1)384, 387;
DBR(2)117, 494, 497, 498; DBR(3)28, 29; DBR(4)538; DBR(5)170,
1032; RAA1, 74; EDV119, 120; FFF252; CGA29; GBR356;
TAG(26)12/25

Rebecca - of NJ, m Thomas Montagne - desc/o Obadiah Bruen
CHB386; MCB318; MCD172

Rebecca - of CT, m Samuel Headley - desc/o Obadiah Bruen CHB387

Ruth - of NJ, b abt 1717/1718 d1793, m Caleb Davis - desc/o
Obadiah Bruen ECD127

Sarah - of NJ, b1679 d1745, m Abraham Kitchell - desc/o Obadiah
Bruen DBR(1)384; DBR(2)494; DBR(3)30; DBR(4)539

Sarah - of NJ, b abt 1737 d1803, m Major Samuel Hayes - desc/o
Obadiah Bruen ECD131; DBR(2)117

BRYANT Anne - b1738/1739 - desc/o Henry Norton RAA118

David - b1706/1707 - desc/o Henry Norton RAA118

Deborah - b1718/1720 - desc/o Henry Norton RAA118

Jacob - b1713/1714 - desc/o Henry Norton RAA118

Jacob (BRIANT) - b1748 - desc/o Henry Norton RAA118

BUCHANAN George - of MD, b1763 d1808, m1789 Laetitia McKean
desc/o Rev Robert Brooke CHB403

James - of PA 1783, father of James Buchanan President of the United
States 1857/1861 - the immigrant J&K122; sufficient proof of
alleged royal ancestry is lacking

John - of PA, b abt 1727, m Jane Russell - the immigrant RAA1, 74;
AAP147; sufficient proof of alleged royal ancestry is lacking

John - b abt 1763 - desc/o John Buchanan RAA74

Robert - of PA, b1760 d1820, m1795 Sarah Brown - the immigrant
ECD(2)68; sufficient proof of alleged royal ancestry is lacking

BUCKNER Elizabeth - of VA, b1690 d1770, m abt 1706 Mordecai Cooke
III - desc/o William Ironmonger DBR(1)739; DBR(2)784; DBR(3)697;
DBR(4)220, 442; DBR(5)744

Elizabeth Bankhead - of VA, m Norborne Taliaferro - desc/o Andrew
Monroe PFA157

BUELL Aaron - b1730, m(1) Hannah Post - desc/o Edward Griswold
LDS61

Abigail - b1770 d1847, m1794 Melancthon Woolsey Welles b1770
d1857 - desc/o William Leete DBR(1)483; DBR(2)596; DBR(3)583;
DBR(5)213

BUELL (cont.)

Daniel - b1698, m Elizabeth Post - desc/o Edward Griswold LDS61

Elizabeth - b1755, m Giles Kelsey - desc/o Edward Griswold LDS61

Peter - b1739 d1797, m1766 Abigail Seymour b1745 d1806 - desc/o William Leete DBR(1)482, 483; DBR(2)596; DBR(3)583; DBR(5)213

Samuel - b1663, m Judith Stevens - desc/o Edward Griswold LDS61

BUFFINGTON Lydia - of MA, b1735 d1763, m1754 Joseph Baker - desc/o Robert Abell DBR(5)142

BULKELEY Aaron - b1748 - desc/o Peter Bulkeley RAA75

Abigail - b1734 d1824, m Rev Amos Ames - desc/o Rev Peter Bulkeley DBR(4)322

Abigail - of CT, b1760 d1833, m Josiah Beardsley b1750 d1842 - desc/o Rev Peter Bulkeley DBR(1)50, 51

Benjamin - of CT - desc/o Rev Charles Chauncy CHB85

Billy - of CT, b abt 1772, m(1)1792 Mary Turner b abt 1773, m(2)____ - desc/o Rev Peter Bulkeley TAG(36)153

Catherine - of MA, b abt 1660, m Richard Treat - desc/o Rev Peter Bulkeley GPM(3)417; RCFA126

Dr Charles - of CT, m Hannah Raymond b1668 - desc/o Rev Peter Bulkeley TAG(36)100

Maj Charles - m Ann Latimer & had issue - desc/o Rev Peter Bulkeley AMB431; RCFA126

Capt Charles - of CT, d1752, m Betsy Tainton - desc/o Rev Charles Chauncy CHB86; BCD86 - desc/o Grace Chetwoode CHB394; MCD182

Charles - of CT, b1703 d1758, m1724 Mary Sage - desc/o Rev Charles Chauncy CHB84; BCD84 - desc/o Grace Chetwoode CHB393; ECD(3)90; MCD182

Capt Chauncey - of CT, m(1) Sarah Parmelee wid/o Nathaniel Doane d1771 - desc/o Rev Peter Bulkeley TAG(36)103

Conklin - of CT, b1741 at Saybrook, m1768 Sarah Spencer - desc/o Rev Peter Bulkeley TAG(36)157

Daniel - b1689 d1762, m Hannah____ - desc/o Rev Edward Bulkeley JSW1883

Daniel - of CT, b1744, m1764 Dorothy Olmsted - desc/o Rev Peter Bulkeley GPM(3)418

Daniel - of CT, b abt 1768, m Zilpah____ - desc/o Rev Peter Bulkeley TAG(36)152

David - of CT, b1749, m Hannah Beckwith - desc/o Rev Peter Bulkeley GPM(3)418

Dimmis - of CT, b1766 d1843, m1790 Joel Harris b1766 Salem, CT d1843 - desc/o Rev Peter Bulkeley TAG(36)103

Dorothy - m Sergt David Osborn - desc/o Grace Chetwood ECD248 - desc/o Rev Peter Bulkeley DBR(1)809

Dorothy - of CT, b abt 1662 d1757, m1693 Lieut Thomas Treat - desc/o Rev Peter Bulkeley ECD(3)81, 83; GPM(3)417; RCFA126

Dorothy - of CT, b1716 d1801, m1741 Thomas Curtis - desc/o Rev Charles Chauncy CHB85, 86; BCD85

Rev Edward - of MA, bp 1614 d1695/1696 matriculated at St Catherine's Hall, Cambridge 1629; educated Harvard College, ordained Marshfield, MA 1642/1643 son of Rev Peter Bulkeley &

BULKELEY (cont.)

Jane Allen, m Lucian (Lucy Ann)____ d1695/1696 - the immigrant
MCD(2)261; ECD(3)63, 65, 71, 73; JSW1883; DBR(2)653;
DBR(3)125; DBR(4)266, 322; DBR(5)229, 1034; AMB430; RAA1;
GBR210; RCFA125 - desc/o Jane Allen GBR332; TAG(16)129/136

Edward - of CT, b1673 d1748, m1702 Dorothy Prescott - desc/o Rev
Charles Chauncy CHB84; BCD84 - desc/o Grace Chetwoode
CHB393; ECD(3)90; MCD182 - desc/o Rev Peter Bulkeley AMB430;
THJ77; RCFA126

Brig Maj Edward - of CT, b abt 1736 d1787, m1771 Rachel Lyman
Pomeroy - desc/o Rev Charles Chauncy CHB85; BCD85

Elijah - of CT, b1766, m Pamelia Loomis - desc/o Rev Peter Bulkeley
GPM(3)419

Capt Eliphalet - of CT, b1746 d1816 capt in the Revolutionary War,
was in the Lexington alarm from Colchester, m1767 (his cousin)
Anna Bulkeley dau/o Major Charles Bulkeley - desc/o Rev Charles
Chauncy J&K275; CHB87; MCB258; MCD192; BCD87 - desc/o
Grace Chetwoode CHB394; MCD182 - desc/o Rev Peter Bulkeley
AMB431; TAG(36)102, 103; RCFA126

Elizabeth - of MA, b1590 d1643, m(1) Richard Whittingham, m(2)1618
Atherton Haugh d1650 - the immigrant DBR(4)735, 736; FLW34;
ECD(3)71; MSC74; GBR211

Elizabeth - of MA, b abt 1638 d1693, m1665 Rev Joseph Emerson
b1620 d1679/1680 - desc/o Rev Edward Bulkeley ECD(3)65;
DBR(1)98; DBR(4)266, 687; DBR(5)229; GPM(2)417

Ellen - of CT, bp 1762, m Mark Curtis son of Ebenezer Curtis & Annis
Warner - desc/o Rev Peter Bulkeley TAG(36)101

Esther - of MA, m Jesse Sabin - desc/o Rev Charles Chauncy BCD87

Eunice - of CT, b1747, m1767 Elisha Lord - desc/o Rev Peter Bulkeley
GPM(3)418

Frances - of MA, (sister of Rev Peter Bulkeley) b abt 1568, m abt 1595
Richard Welby - the immigrant FLW34; MCS74; DBR(2)107;
GBR211

Rev Gershom - of MA b1636 Concord d1713 appointed surgeon to the
CT troops in King Philip's War & placed on the Council of War,
honorable in his descent, of rare abilities, excellent in learning,
master of many languages, exquisite in his skill, in divinity, physic
& law, m1659 Sarah Chauncy b1631 Ware, England d1699 dau/o
Rev Charles Chauncey, president of Harvard College - desc/o Grace
Chetwoode CHB393; MCD182; MCS182 - desc/o Rev Peter Bulkeley
ECD(3)81, 90; AMB430; THJ76, 79; GPM(3)417; RCFA126;
NEFGM(3)1209

Capt Gershom - of CT, b abt 1676 d1753, m(2) Rachel Talcott - desc/o
Grace Chetwood ECD139 - desc/o Rev Charles Chauncy BCD88

Capt Gershom - of CT, b1709 Colchester, a prominent citizen of the
town, holding many offices, m1733 Abigail Robbins - desc/o Rev
Charles Chauncy CHB88 - desc/o Rev Peter Bulkeley GPM(3)418;
NEFGM(3)1210

Gershom - of CT, b1763 Colchester, m____ & had issue - desc/o Rev
Peter Bulkeley GPM(3)419

Gershom - of CT & NY, b1748 d1820, m(1)1773 Elizabeth Chapman -

BULKELEY (cont.)

    desc/o Grace Chetwoode ECD139

Grace - of MA, b1670 d1711, m1692 Ebenezer Kilbourn b1665 d1711
- desc/o Rev Peter Bulkeley DBR(1)680; DBR(2)328, 392, 758;
DBR(3)312; RAA75

Hannah - of CT, bp 1758 at Redding d1828, m (may have) 1782 David
Austin of New Preston d1825 - desc/o Rev Peter Bulkeley
TAG(36)102

Hannah - of CT, b1776 at Weathersfield d1804, m Amos Woodruff
b1763 at Farmington d1843 - desc/o Rev Charles Chauncy CHB85
- desc/o Rev Peter Bulkeley TAG(36)154

James - of CT, b1729 d1803, m Elizabeth Whitehead b abt 1738
d1809 dau/o Nathaniel Whitehead - desc/o Rev Peter Bulkeley
DBR(1)50

Rev John - of CT, b1679 Wethersfield d1731, distinguished scholar &
divine; was first minister & settler at Colchester, m1701 Patience
Prentice dau/o John Prentice & Sarah____ - desc/o Rev Charles
Chauncy J&K275; CHB86; MCD192; BCD86 - desc/o Grace
Chetwoode CHB394; MCB258; MCD182 - desc/o Rev Peter
Bulkeley AMB430; GPM(3)417; RCFA126; NEFGM(3)1209, 1210

Col John - b1703 d1772, m Abigail Wright - desc/o Rev Peter Bulkeley
DBR(4)322

Col John - of CT, b1705 of Colchester d1753, judge of the Supreme
Court of CT, m(1)1738 Mary Adams Gardner dau/o Rev Eliphalet
Adams & wid/o Jonathan Gardiner, m(2)1751 Abigail Hastings -
desc/o Rev Charles Chauncy J&K275; CHB86; BCD86 - desc/o
Grace Chetwoode CHB394; MCD182 - desc/o Rev Peter Bulkeley
AMB431; GPM(3)418; RCFA126

John - of CT, b1738 Colchester, m1759 Judith Worthington - desc/o
Rev Peter Bulkeley GPM(3)148; NEFGM(3)1210

John - b1740 d1799, m1773 Sarah Dayton - desc/o Rev Peter
Bulkeley DBR(1)462

John - of CT, b1759, m Theodora Foote - desc/o Rev Peter Bulkeley
GPM(3)418

John Charles - of CT, b1772, m Sally Tainton - desc/o Rev Charles
Chauncy CHB87; MCB258; MCD182; BCD87

Jonathan - desc/o Rev Peter Bulkeley AMB431

Joseph - of CT, b1627, 10th child - desc/o Rev Peter Bulkeley
DBR(1)462

Joseph - of CT, b1741, m1761 Lois Day - desc/o Rev Peter Bulkeley
GPM(3)418

Joseph - of CT, b abt 1644/1648 d1719, m Martha Beers d aft 1720
dau/o James Beers - desc/o Rev Peter Bulkeley ECD(3)79;
JSW1883; DBR(1)50; RAA75

Joseph - b1658/1659 d1701 was a mariner & master of the ketch
Gabriel, m Joanna Shute d1767 dau/o Richard Shute & wid/o
Nathaniel Nicols - desc/o Rev Peter Bulkeley DBR(1)462

Joseph - of MA, b1670 d1748, m Rebecca (Jones) Minott - desc/o Rev
Peter Bulkeley DBR(4)322

Capt Joseph - of CT, m(2) Silence Keene dau/o William & Jane Keane
of Boston & wid/o Arthur Jeffrey - desc/o Rev Peter Bulkeley

BULKELEY (cont.)

   TAG(36)100

   Joshua Robbins - of CT, b1771 d1838 Williamstown, m Sarah Tainter b1770/1771 Colchester d1848 Williamstown - desc/o Rev Peter Bulkeley GPM(3)419; NEFGM(3)1210

   Judith - of CT, b1775, m Solomon Tainter - desc/o Rev Peter Bulkeley GPM(3)419

   Lucy - m Elaphas Lord - desc/o Rev Peter Bulkeley RCFA126

   Lucy - bp 1749, m Capt John Lamb of Groton, CT & had issue - desc/o Rev Peter Bulkeley AMB431; RCFA126

   Lydia - bp 1739, m1761 Capt Robert Latimer - desc/o Rev Peter Bulkeley AMB431; RCFA126

   Lydia - of CT, m Solomon Savage of Middletown, CT - desc/o Rev Peter Bulkeley TAG(36)102

   Martha - of MA, b abt 1572, m Abraham Mellows d1639 Charlestown, MA - the immigrant FLW34; ECD(3)73; RAA75; GBR211

   Martha - b1721 d1812, m Ephraim Wheeler - desc/o Rev Edward Bulkeley JSW1883

   Mary - of CT, b1725 d1762, m1750 David Webb - desc/o Grace Chetwood ECD(3)90

   Mary - bp 1741, m George B Hurlbut - desc/o Rev Peter Bulkeley AMB431; RCFA126

   Mary - of CT, b1774, m Aaron Buckland - desc/o Rev Peter Bulkeley GPM(3)419

   Mary - b1776 d1808, m1799 Richard Brooke Hewes d1844 - desc/o Rev Peter Bulkeley DBR(1)463

   Nabby - of CT, b1769, m Roger Tainter - desc/o Rev Peter Bulkeley GPM(3)419

   Noah Summers - of CT, b1775/1776 at North Stratford, m Anna Newman b1779 - desc/o Peter Bulkeley RAA75; TAG(36)151

   Oliver - desc/o Rev Peter Bulkeley AMB431

   Patience - of CT, b1714, m Ichabod Lord - desc/o Grace Chetwoode CHB394 - desc/o Rev Peter Bulkeley RCFA126

   Rev Peter - of MA, b1582/1583 Odell, Bedfordshire, England d1658/1659 Concord, MA, who was of royal descent from King Edward I, of England, Puritan clergyman & a founder and first minister of Concord, MA, son of Edward Bulkeley & Olive Irby, m(1)1613 Jane Allen d1626 Odell, England after giving birth to twelve children, dau/o Thomas Allen of Coddington, m(2)1635 Grace Chetwoode b1602 d1669 New London, CT, dau/o Sir Richard Chetwoode, Knight, & Dorothy Needham of Odell - the immigrant FLW34; ECD(3)63, 68, 79, 81; JSW1883; MCS74; DBR(1)50, 462, 679, 808; DBR(2)328, 392; DBR(3)86, 312; DBR(4)266, 322, 687; DBR(5)229, 970, 1033, 1034; DAB(3)249, 250 AMB430; THJ77, 78; RAA75; EDV17; CGA30; GBR210, 211; TAG(35)62, 63, 100/106, (37)45/51, (40)95/99; NE(141)100; GPM(3)416/419; RCFA124; NEFGM(3)1208, 1209

   Peter - of MA, b1640/1641 d1688, m1667 Rebecca Wheeler - desc/o Rev Edward Bulkeley ECD(2)262; ECD(3)63; DBR(4)322; AMB430; GBR211; RCFA126 - desc/o Jane Allen GBR332

   Dr Peter - of CT, b1636 1643 d1691, m Margaret Foxcroft - desc/o

BULKELEY (cont.)

Grace Chetwoode CHB395; ECD139, 248; DBR(2)392 - desc/o Rev Peter Bulkeley DBR(1)680; DBR(2)328, 758

Peter - of MA, b1664 d lost at sea, m1700 Rebecca Talcott - desc/o Rev Peter Bulkeley AMB430; GPM(3)417; RCFA126

Peter - of CT, b1683 d1771, m Hannah Bulkeley - desc/o Grace Chetwoode CHB395

Peter - of CT, b1684 d1752, m1707 Hannah Ward b abt 1692 d1772 dau/o Samuel Ward - desc/o Rev Peter Bulkeley ECD(3)79; DBR(1)50; RAA75

Peter - of CT, bp 1715/1716 d1804, m1740 Ann Hill - desc/o Grace Chetwoode ECD139; RAA75

Peter - of CT, bp 1715 d1801, m(1)1741 Sarah Turney b1718, m(2) Hannah Sherwood b1736 - desc/o Rev Peter Bulkeley ECD(3)79; TAG(36)101

Peter - of CT, b1745 d1813, m1768 Mary Green - desc/o Rev Peter Bulkeley ECD(3)79

Rachel - of CT, m Joseph Darling & had issue - desc/o Rev Peter Bulkeley TAG(36)100

Rebecca - of MA, b1681, m1701 (Dr) Jonathan Prescott Jr - desc/o Rev Edward Bulkeley ECD(2)262; ECD(3)63; GBR211 - desc/o Jane Allen GBR332

Richard - of MA, bp 1695 d1767, m1728 Mary Noyes - desc/o Rev Peter Bulkeley DBR(1)462

Roger - of MA, b1751, m Jerusha Root - desc/o Rev Peter Bulkeley GPM(3)418

Roxa Lyman - of CT, b1772, m1793 Col Selah Francis - desc/o Rev Charles Chauncy CHB85; BCD85 - desc/o Richard Lyman CHB152; BCD152

Sarah - of MA, b1640 d1723, m Eleazer Brown - desc/o Rev Peter Bulkeley ECD(3)68, 86; DBR(5)970; RAA75

Sarah - of CT, b1702, m(1) John Trumbull, m(2) John Wells - desc/o Rev Peter Bulkeley AMB431; GPM(3)418; RCFA126

Sarah - of CT, m Joseph Perry - desc/o Grace Chetwoode CHB395

Sarah - of CT, b1733 d1802, m1756 Cephas Smith - desc/o Rev Charles Chauncy CHB85, 86; BCD84

Sarah - of CT, b1735, m1765 Joseph Isham - desc/o Rev Peter Bulkeley GPM(3)418

Sarah - of CT, b1735, m1758 John Tainton - desc/o Rev Charles Chauncy CHB88; BCD88

Sarah - of CT, m Joseph Stow - desc/o Rev Charles Chauncy CHB86; BCD86

Solomon Tainton - of MA, m Mary Welk - desc/o Rev Charles Chauncy CHB87; BCD86

Stephen - of CT & MA, b1759 resided at Buckland, MA, m1785 Rhoda Thaver b1767 - desc/o Rev Peter Bulkeley TAG(36)101

Thomas - of CT, bp 1617 d1685, m Sarah Jones b abt 1620 d1682 dau/o the Reverend John Jones - desc/o Rev Peter Bulkeley ECD(3)68, 79; JSW1883; DBR(1)50; DBR(3)86; DBR(5)970; AMB430; RAA75; GPM(2)417

William - of CT, b1761, m Mary Champion - desc/o Rev Peter Bulkeley

BULKELEY (cont.)
   GPM(3)418

BULL Ann Bryan - of SC, m James Garvey - desc/o Stephen Bull
   SCG(1)220
   Anne - of SC, b1722 d1754, m Joseph Izard, Esq, member of
      Commons - desc/o Stephen Bull SCG(1)218
   Burnaby - of SC, d1754 settled in the Indian land in 1715 &
      afterwards got considerable grants there, member of the Commons
      House of Assembly 1739/1742 for St Paul, m Lucia Bellinger dau/o
      Landgrave Bellinger - desc/o Stephen Bull SCG(1)219
   Catherine - of SC, b1699 d1734, m___Wilson - desc/o Stephen Bull
      SCG(1)209
   Charlotte - of SC, b1719 d1743, m1742 John Drayton, member of the
      Council & left issue - desc/o Stephen Bull SCG(1)212
   Elizabeth - of SC, b1712, m1730 Thomas Drayton, member of the
      Council & left issue - desc/o Stephen Bull SCG(1)212;
      GPFPM(1)413/438
   Capt John - of SC, b1693 d1767 captain of the provincial forces,
      justice of the peace, member of the Commons House of Assembly,
      m(1)___ who was carried off by the Indians in 1715, m(2) Mary___
      b abt 1699 d1771 - desc/o Stephen Bull SCG(1)217, 218
   John - of SC, d1802 of Granville Co, was justice of the peace, member
      of the Commons House & deputy secretary of the province. member
      of the Provincial Congress & subsequently a member of the House
      of Representatives, Senate & United States Congress, m1768
      Eleanor Purry only daughter & heiress of Charles Purry, Esq -
      desc/o Stephen Bull SCG(1)221
   Lucia - of SC, m Jacob Guerard - desc/o Stephen Bull SCG(1)220
   Mary - of SC, m(1) Nathaniel Barnwell b1772 d1800, m(2)___Maxy -
      desc/o Stephen Bull SCG(1)213
   Mary - of SC, b1723 d1760, m Col Thomas Middleton, member
      Commons & colonel Carolina Regiment Indian War 1760/1761 -
      desc/o Stephen Bull SCG(1)218
   Mary Lucia - of SC, bp 1723, m Landgrave Edmund Bellinger, the
      third, (her first cousin) - desc/o Stephen Bull SCG(1)220
   Sarah - of SC, m John Gibbs Barnwell, Esq - desc/o Stephen Bull
      SCG(1)213
   Stephen - of SC 1669, d1706 captain & engineer of the forts
      1671/1675, captain & then colonel of the provincial forces
      1687/1703, justice of the peace, assistant judge, surveyor general
      & was a great explorer among the Indians, son of Josias Bull &
      Katherine Agard - the immigrant GBR171; SCG(1)208/221
   Stephen - of SC, b1707 of Newberry, Esq d1750 served as captain in
      the St Augustine expedition, was a justice of the peace & a member
      of the Commons House of Assembly, m(1)1731 Martha Godin
      dau/o Benjamin Godin of Charlestown, m(2)1747 Judith Mayrant
      dau/o James Nicholas Mayrant - desc/o Stephen Bull SCG(1)212,
      213
   Gen Stephen - of SC, b1707, m(1)1755 Elizabeth Woodward d1771
      only dau/o Richard Woodward, m(2)1772 Anne Barnwell dau/o
      Nathaniel Barnwell & wid/o Col Thomas Middleton - desc/o

BULL (cont.)

    Stephen Bull SCG(1)213

    Stephen - of SC, d1770 of Prince William parish, m1739 Elizabeth Bryan dau/o Joseph Bryan - desc/o Stephen Bull SCG(1)220

    William - of SC, b1683 d1755 member of the Commons House of South Carolina 1706/1719 & served as captain in the Tuscarora & Yemasee wars; was colonel of the Berkeley County regiment; commissioner of Indian affairs 1721 & was appointed to assist Gen Oglethorpe to settle Georgia. He was appointed lieutenant governor 1738 until 1744, m Mary Quintyne d1738/1739 dau/o Richard Quintyne - desc/o Stephen Bull SCG(1)210, 211; DAB(3)252

    William - of SC, b abt 1749 d1805 justice of the peace & elected to the provincial Congress, m1779 Elizabeth Reid b1762 dau/o Dr James Reid - desc/o Stephen Bull SCG(1)214

    William - of SC, b1710 Ashley Hall, South Carolina d1791 The first American to graduate in medicine, was devoted to Carolina, had been five times governor of the province & the most popular governor it ever had. He had a princely fortune at stake in the revolution, but did not waver in his conscientious duty to his King, m1746 Hannah Beale dau/o Othneal Beale but had no issue - desc/o Stephen Bull SCG(1)217; DAB(3)252/253

    William - of SC, planter, second son of Burnaby Bull & Lucia Bellinger, m(1)___, m(2) Anne___ & had issue a son William Robert Bull & a daughter Adriana who married ___Grant - desc/o Stephen Bull SCG(1)221

    William Robert - of SC, b1762, m___ & had issue William Robert Bull & Lucia Bull - desc/o Stephen Bull SCG(1)221

BULLEN John - b1686, m1709 Sarah Underwood - desc/o John Prescott DBR(1)373

    Joseph - b1716, m1739 Mary Marsh - desc/o John Prescott DBR(1)373

    Rev Joseph - of MA, b1750 d1825, m1774 Hannah Morse - desc/o John Prescott DBR(1)373

BULLITT Col Alexander Scott - of KY, b1761 Jefferson Co, Ky d1816, m1785 Priscilla Christian, dau/o Col William Christian & Anne Henry, sister of Patrick Henry - desc/o Col Gerard Fowke CFA(5)315

BULLOCK James - of NC, b1772 d1825, m1795 Nancy Bullock - desc/o Col George Reade DBR(3)354

BURD Col James - of PA, b1725 d1793 son of Edward Burd of Ormiston & Jean Haliburton, m1748 Sarah Shippen - the immigrant ECE(3)87; GBR94

    Jane (Jean) - of PA, b1757 d1814, m1783 George Patterson - desc/o Col James Burd ECD(3)87

BURNAP Martha - of MA, b1697, m1717 Ebenezer Stearns - desc/o Elias Maverick ECD(3)175; DBR(5)737

BURNET Gov William - of NY, b1688 The Hague d1729 governor of New York, NJ, MA, & New Hampshire, son of Gilbert Burnet, Bishop of Salisbury & Mary Scott, m(1) Maria Stanhope, m(2) Anna Maria Van Horne dau/o Abraham Van Horne & Mary Prevoost of New York - the immigrant EDV44; DAB(3)295; CGA31; GBR107

BURNETT Isabel - of NJ, dau/o Robert Burnett of NJ &___Forbes, m William Montgomery - desc/o ___Forbes who, m Robert Burnett of NJ - the immigrant GBR76

BURNHAM Elizabeth - b1744 d1782, m1765 Capt Jabez Treadwell - desc/o Samuel Appleton DBR(2)647

Thomas - of CT 1649, b1617 - the immigrant EDV104, 105; CGA31; sufficient proof of alleged royal ancestry is lacking

Maj Thomas - b1722 d1792, m1744 Judith Lord - desc/o Samuel Appleton DBR(2)647

BURR Ann - of NJ - m1757 George Deacon - desc/o Anne Mauleverer MCD154

Col Aaron - Vice President of the United States - desc/o Rev James Pierrepont J&K242

Hannah - of NJ, b1754, m(1)1774 Henry Ridgway b1749 (her first cousin), m(2) George Harlan - desc/o Anne Mauleverer CHB357; MCD155, 156; DBR(5)784

Henry - of NJ, b1731, played some part in the Revolution, m1751 Elizabeth Foster - desc/o Anne Mauleverer CHB357; MCD155; DBR(5)784

Jane - of NJ, m1762 David Ridgway - desc/o Anne Mauleverer MCD154

Jonathan - b1741 - desc/o Richard Belding RAA68

Mary - of NJ, m1747 Solomon Ridgway - desc/o Anne Mauleverer MCD154

Rachel - of NJ, m Josiah Foster - desc/o Rebecca Humphrey CHB415; MCD267

Timothy - b1767 - desc/o Richard Belding RAA68

BURROUGH (or BURROUGHS) Elizabeth - of MA, m1704 Peter Thomas - desc/o Nathaniel Burrough TAG(56)44

Rev George - of MA, b abt 1650 d1692, executed for witchcraft at Salem, 19 Aug 1692, m(1) Hannah___d1681, m(2) by 1683 Mrs Sarah (Ruck) Hathorne, m(3) Mary___ - the immigrant MCS52; RAA1, 76 - desc/o Nathaniel Burrough GBR223; TAG(48)140/146, (56)43/45, (60)140/142; FLW169

Hannah - of MA, m1705 Jabez Fox - desc/o Nathaniel Burrough TAG(56)44

Nathaniel - of MA & MD, returned to England, d1682, merchant mariner, son of George Burrough & Frances Sparrow, m abt 1649 Rebecca Style(s) - the immigrant GBR223; TAG(60)140/142; NE(33)239; FLW169

Mary - of MA, b abt 1672, m(1)1693 Michael Homer b abt 1650 d abt 1695/1697, m(2)1699/1700 Christopher Hall Jr b abt 1674 d1711 son of Christopher & Sarah___Hall, m(3) bef 9 Jun 1735 Joseph Tiffany of Norton, MA - desc/o Nathaniel Burrough RAA76; TAG(48)140/146

Rebecca - of MA, m(1)1698 Isaac Fowle - desc/o Nathaniel Burrough TAG(56)44

BURT Salome - b abt 1771/1773 - desc/o John Prescott RAA125

BURTON Archer - of VA, b abt 1760 d1832, m Elizabeth Adams - desc/o Henry Randolph DBR(4)171

BURWELL Carter - of VA, m Lucy Grymes - desc/o Martha Bacon CHB33; BCD33 - desc/o Sarah Ludlow CHB133; BCD133; DBR(1)742; DBR(3)694

Elizabeth - of VA, d1734, m Benjamin Harrison - desc/o Abigail Smith J&K133; BCD34

Elizabeth - of VA, m William Nelson - desc/o Abigail Smith J&K191 - desc/o Martha Bacon CHB33 - desc/o Sarah Ludlow CHB132; BCD132; PVF201

Elizabeth - of VA, d1734, m Benjamin Harrison - desc/o Martha Bacon CHB34

Elizabeth - of VA, d1811, m John Page - desc/o Sarah Ludlow DBR(1)400

Frances - of VA, m Gov John Page - desc/o Martha Bacon CHB33; BCD34 - desc/o Sarah Ludlow CHB133; BCD133

Joanna - of VA, b1674 d1727, m1693 Col William Bassett, Jr. - desc/o Abigail Smith J&K190; BCD32

Maj Lewis - of VA 1640, b1621 d1653, m Lucy Higginson - the immigrant EDV121; WAC33; CGA31; sufficient proof of alleged royal ancestry is lacking

Lewis - of VA, d1710, m(1) Abigail Smith, m(2) Martha Lear - desc/o Lewis Burwell WAC33

Lewis - of VA, of Gloucester Co, VA, member of the House of Burgesses & of the Convention 1775/1776, m Judith Page dau/o Mann Page - desc/o Anne Rich PVF272

Lewis - of VA, d bef 1772, m1736 Mary Willis dau/o Col Francis Willis & Anne Rich - desc/o Martha Bacon CHB33, 132; BCD33, 132 - desc/o Sarah Ludlow DBR(1)400

Lewis - of VA, b1716 d1779, m1746 Frances Thacker - desc/o Sarah Ludlow DBR(1)400

Martha - of VA, b1685, m Col Henry Armistead - desc/o Abigail Smith J&K192 - desc/o Martha Bacon CHB34; BCD34

Nathaniel - of VA, m Elizabeth Carter - desc/o Martha Bacon CHB33; J&K191; BCD33

Nathaniel - of VA, m Lucy (Page) Baylor - desc/o Martha Bacon CHB33; BCD33 - desc/o Sarah Ludlow CHB133; BCD133; DBR(1)742; DBR(3)694

Rebecca - of VA, b1746, m1764 Jacqueline Ambler - desc/o Martha Bacon CHB33, 132; BCD33; BCD132 - desc/o Anne Rich PVF272

Col Robert Carter - of VA, m Sarah Nelson - desc/o Martha Bacon CHB34; BCD34 - desc/o Sarah Ludlow CHB133; BCD133

Spotswood - of VA, m Mary Marshall - desc/o Maj Gen Alexander Spotswood CHB291; BCD291 - desc/o Col John West BCD245

Thomas Nelson - of VA, m Elizabeth Nicholson - desc/o Dudley Diggs CHB77; BCD77

BUTLER Ann - b1740, m Daniel Look - desc/o Sarah Palmer LDS55

Elizabeth - b abt 1610/1620 - desc/o John Boteler RAA71

Hannah - m Moses Bass - desc/o Anne Marbury DBR(1)760

Mary - of VA, d bef 1682 dau/o Almleric (Amory) Butler, m bef 1672 Capt William Underwood Jr - the immigrant ECD(2)73; GBR451

Mary - of SC, m Dr Mease, of Philadelphia & had 2 sons, Pierce & John who took the name of Butler - desc/o Stephen Bull SCG(1)219

BUTLER (cont.)

Pierce - of SC, b1744 County Carlow, Ireland d1822, planter, legislator & senator, third son of Sir Richard Butler, 5th Baronet & Henrietta Percy, m1771 Mary Middleton dau/o Thomas Middleton of Prince William parish, SC & Mary Bull - the immigrant DAB(3)364, 365; GBR260; SCG(3)155

BUTT Nathaniel - of VA, d1804, m1790 Frances Butt b aft 1772 d1821 dau/o Malaba & Elizabeth (Bartee) Butt - desc/o Capt Henry Woodhouse JSW1656; DBR(1)93

BUTTERFIELD Abel - b1742, m Mercy or Mary - desc/o John Whitney LDS26

BYE Deborah - of PA, b1709, m Jonathan Ingham of Ingham Spring - desc/o Thomas Bye CFA(6)110

Elizabeth - of PA, b1685 Horselydown, Southwark, England, m Nehemiah Blackshaw of the Falls, Bucks Co, PA, son of Randall Blackshaw of Holingee Manor, Cheshire & The Falls, Bucks Co, PA - desc/o Thomas Bye CFA(6)110

Elizabeth - of PA, b1705, m George Mitchell - desc/o Thomas Bye CFA(6)110

Enoch - of PA, b1757 of Solebury, Bucks Co d1837, m1781 Abigail Kinsey d1824 dau/o Samuel Kinsey & Elizabeth Crew of Buckingham - desc/o Thomas Bye AFA102; CFA(6)111

Hezekiah - of PA, b1717 of Solebury d1790, m1743 Mary Ingham d1790 dau/o Jonas Ingham of Ingham Spring - desc/o Thomas Bye AFA102; CFA(6)110

Hezekiah - of PA, b1754, m1778 Sarah Pettit dau/o William Pettit - desc/o Thomas Bye CFA(6)111

John - of PA, b abt 1675 England d1732 of Solebury, Bucks Co, m1704 Sarah Pearson daughter & co-heiress of Thomas Pearson of Marsden, Lancashire, England & Grace Vipont of Briarcliffe, Westmoreland, England - desc/o Thomas Bye AFA102; CFA(6)110

Jonathan - of PA, b1761, m Sarah Kinsey dau/o Benjamin Kinsey of Buckingham - desc/o Thomas Bye CFA(6)111

Rachel - of PA, b1743, m1764 Zachariah Betts, son of Thomas Betts & Sarah Stevenson - desc/o Thomas Bye CFA(6)110

Sarah - of PA, b1683 came to Pennsylvania 1701 with her mother, m1702 William White of Philadelphia - desc/o Margaret Davis ECD(3)111; DBR(4)230 - desc/o Thomas Bye DBR(5)481

Thomas - of PA, b abt 1645 (probably at) Copyngedbridge House, Basingstoke, Hampshire, England d1726 son of Thomas Bye b1601 d1666 & Elizabeth Alliston, m1670 Margaret Davis d1724 dau/o Nathaniel Davis - the immigrant RAA1, 76; AFA102; DBR(5)480, 481; GBR403; TG(9)226/227; CFA(6)109

BYINGTON David - b1702, m Mercy____ - desc/o Edward Griswold LDS89

Eunice - b1731, m David Rogers - desc/o Edward Griswold LDS89

Mary - b1710, m Moses Foote - desc/o Edward Griswold LDS45

BYRD Abby - of VA, b1767, m Judge William Nelson, of Yorktown, VA, son of William Nelson & Elizabeth Burwell of Yorktown - desc/o Warham Horsmanden GVFTQ(1)315; CFSSA106

Anne - of VA, b1725 d1757, m1742 Charles Carter of Cleves, King

BYRD (cont.)

George Co, son of Col Robert Carter & Elizabeth (Landon-Willis) of
Corotoman - desc/o Warham Horsmanden CHB55; BCD55;
GVFTQ(1)312; CFSSA105

Anne Ursula - of VA, m Robert Beverley - desc/o Warham Horsmanden
CHB58; BCD58

Deighton - of MA, m Isaac Mysick - desc/o Frances Deighton CHB467

Elizabeth Hill - of VA, b1754, m(1) James Parke Farley, who came to
VA in 1762, m(2) Rev John Dunbar, m(3) Col Henry Skipwith -
desc/o Warham Horsmanden GVFTQ(1)314, 315; CFSSA105

Evelyn Taylor - of VA, b1766, m Benjamin Harrison of Brandon,
Surrey Co, son of Nathaniel Harrison & Mary Digges - desc/o
Warham Horsmanden GVFTQ(1)315; CFSSA105

Francis Otway - of VA, d1800 an officer in the British Army but after
the beginning of the American Revolution resigned and offered his
services to America. In 1775 he was appointed an aide to General
Lincoln & two years later was made lieutenant-colonel of the 3rd
Virginia Continental Dragoons, m Anne Munford of Mecklenburg
Co, VA - desc/o Warham Horsmanden GVFTQ(1)316; CFSSA105

Jane - of VA, b1729, m1746 John Page of North End, Gloucester Co,
VA, son of Mann Page & Judith Carter of Rosewell - desc/o
Warham Horsmanden CHB56; BCD56; DBR(3)646; DBR(4)122;
DBR(5)1036; GVFTQ(1)312; CFSSA105

Jane - of VA, b1773, m Carter Harrison - desc/o Warham Horsmanden
GVFTQ(1)315

Maria - of VA, b1727 d1744, m1743 Col Landon Carter of Sabine Hall,
Richmond Co, VA, son of Col Robert Carter & Elizabeth (Landon-
Willis) of Corotoman - desc/o Warham Horsmanden CHB55;
MCD184; BCD55; GVFTQ(1)312; CFSSA105

Maria Horsmanden - of VA, b1761, m1784 John Page of Pagebrook,
Clark Co, son of Robert Page & Sarah Walker of Broad Neck -
desc/o Warham Horsmanden CHB57; BCD57; GVFTQ(1)315;
CFSSA105

Susan - of VA, m John Brayne, of London, England & had issue -
desc/o William Byrd WAC104 - desc/o Warham Horsmanden
CFSSA104

Thomas Taylor - of VA, b1752 d1821 major in the War of the
Revolution, m1786 Mary Anne Armistead dau/o William Armistead
of Hesse, Gloucester Co, VA - desc/o Warham Horsmanden CHB57;
ECD221; BCD57; DBR(3)140; GVFTQ(1)314; CFSSA106 - desc/o
William Byrd BLG2697

Ursula - of VA, b1681 d1698, m Robert Beverley Jr, of James City Co,
son of Robert Beverley & Mary Keeble - desc/o Ursula St Leger
DBR(5)881; WAC104 - desc/o Warham Horsmanden CFSSA104

Wilhelmina - of VA, b1715, m Thomas Chamberlayne, of New Kent Co
& King William Co, son of William Chamberlayne & Elizabeth
Littlepage of New Kent Co - desc/o Warham Horsmanden CHB54;
BCD54; GVFTQ(1)312; CFSSA104, 105

William - of VA abt 1670, b1652 d1704, m1672/1673 Mary (Maria)
Horsmanden - the immigrant BLG2597; DBR(4)172; DBR(5)1036;
RAA1, 76; EDV142, 143; WAC103, 104; Royal descent is from his

BYRD (cont.)

wife Mary (Maria) Horsmanden who is desc/o of Warham
Horsmanden - the immigrant; GVFTQ(1)306/320

Col William II - of VA, b1674 d1744 founder of Richmond in 1733,
successful in commercial, political & cultural activities, m(1)1706
Lucy Parke d1716 dau/o Col Daniel Parke d1710, later governor of
the Leeward Islands, m(2)1724 Maria Taylor dau/o Thomas Taylor
of Kensington, England - desc/o Warham Horsmanden CHB54, 55;
ECD221; MCD184; BCD54; DBR(3)140, 645; DBR(4)122;
DBR(5)1035; CGA32; GVFTQ(1)312 - desc/o William Byrd
BLG2597; DBR(4)175; WAC104; DAB(3)383, 384; CFSSA104

Col William III - of VA, b1728 d1777, of Westover, Charles City Co,
m(1)1748 Elizabeth Hill Carter b1731 d1760, dau/o John Carter &
Elizabeth Hill of Corotoman, m(2)1761 Mary Willing d1814 of
Philadelphia - desc/o Warham Horsmanden CHB57; ECD221;
MCD184; BCD57; DBR(3)140; GVFTQ(1)314; CFSSA105 - desc/o
William Byrd BLG2697

- C -

CADWALADER Anne - of PA, b1771 d1850, m1795 Robert Kemble of New
York - desc/o John Cadwalader CFA(3)116

Elizabeth - of PA, b1773 d1824, m1792 Archibald McCall of
Philadelphia, son of Archibald McCall & Judith Kemble - desc/o
John Cadwalader CHB48; BCD48; CFA(3)116

Hannah - of PA, b1715 d1787, m1737 Samuel Morris - desc/o John
Cadwalader CHB49; BCD49; CFA(3)115

John - of PA 1697, b1677/1678 Penllyn, Merionethshire, Wales d1734
Philadelphia, m1699 Martha Jones d1747, dau/o Edward Jones &
Mary (Wynne) Jones - the immigrant CHB48; MCB375, 376;
MCD188; BLG2598; BCD48; GBR306; CFA(3)114

Maj Gen John - of PA, b1742 d1786, fought with Washington during
the Revolutionary War & had a distinguished military career,
m(1)1776 Elizabeth Lloyd b1742 d1776 Philadelphia, dau/o
Edward Lloyd & Ann Rousby of Wye House, Talbot Co, MD, m(2)
Williamina Bond b1753 d1837, dau/o Dr Phineas Bond &
Williamina Moore of Philadelphia - desc/o John Cadwalader CHB4;
MCB376, 377; MCD188; BLG2598; BCD48; CFA(3)116

Col Lambert - of PA & NJ, b1732 d1813, m1793 Mary McCall - desc/o
John Cadwalader CHB48; BLG2598; BCD48 - desc/o Thomas
Lambert DAB(3)401; MCD239

Martha - of PA, b1739, m1774 John Dagworthy b1721 Trenton, NJ
d1784, a captain in the provincial forces, commissioned captain in
the British Army, colonel & afterwards brigadier-colonel of the
Delaware militia - desc/o John Cadwalader CFA(3)115

Mary - of PA, m1731 Judge Samuel Dickinson & became the mother of
John Dickinson, the signer of the Declaration of Independence & of
Gen Philemon Dickinson - desc/o John Cadwalader CFA(3)115

Rebecca - of PA, m William Morris - desc/o John Cadwalader
CFA(3)115

CADWALADER (cont.)

Thomas MD - of PA, b1707 d1779, physician of Philadelphia, 1776
appointed a medical director of the Army hospitals, m1738 Hannah
Lambert b1712 d1786 dau/o Thomas Lambert, Jr of NJ - desc/o
John Cadwalader CHB48; CFA(3)115; DAB(3)400/401; MCB376;
MCD188; BLG2598; BCD48

CALKINS Lucretia - b1774/1776 - desc/o Robert Abell RAA59 - desc/o
Alice Freeman RAA132

Solomon - b1746 - desc/o Alice Freeman RAA132

CALVERT Anne - of MD 1663, b abt 1645, m(1) abt 1664 Baker Brooke
b1628 Battle, Sussex, England d1678/1679 deputy governor, m(2)
abt 1680 (her cousin) Henry Brent of Calvert Co MD d bef 6 Aug
1694, m(3) abt 1694 Judge Thomas Tasker d1699, m(4) abt 1700
Col Richard Marsham d1713/1714, Justice of Prince George's Co
MD - desc/o Leonard Calvert APP161; MG(1)143/158 notes: The
question of Anne Calvert's husbands is still perplexing, but the
above account seems the most satisfactory & probable; CFA(2)164,
(5)289; RCFA106

Anne - of VA, m William Peasley - desc/o Leonard Calvert CFA(2)164,
(5)288

Anne - of MD, m aft 10 Jul 1694 Edward Somerset - desc/o Cecilius
Calvert CFA(2)165

Anne - of MD & VA, m bef 1714 Thomas Porter d1740 - desc/o
Leonard Calvert MG(1)174

Anne - of MD, b1751 d1822, m1766 Captain William Lindsay d1792 of
Colchester, Prince William & Laurel Hill, Culpeper Co, VA - desc/o
Leonard Calvert MG(1)148; CFA(5)293

Anne (Nancy) Beck - b1773 d1835, m1797 (her first cousin) Cecilius
Calvert - desc/o Leonard Calvert MG(1)152; CFA(5)294

Basil - b1760 d1833, m Nancy Triplett - desc/o Leonard Calvert
MG(1)204

Benedict "Swingate" - of MD, b1724 d1788, m1748 Elizabeth Calvert
dau/o Gov Charles Calvert & Rebecca Gerard - desc/o Anne
Arundel BLG2600; DBR(1)333; CRFP(2)1112 - desc/o Lady
Charlotte Lee GBR9; NE(104)175; MG(1)141, 160, 161

Benedict Leonard, 4th Baron Baltimore - of MD, b1679 d1715 member
of Parliament, m1698/1699 Lady Charlotte Lee d1721 (divorced
1705) dau/o Edward Henry Lee, Earl of Lichfield & Lady Charlotte
FitzRoy, a dau/o King Charles II - desc/o Anne Arundel J&K281;
ECD147; ECD(2)77; MCD190; BLG1600; DBR(1)152; DBR(3)244;
GBR136; MG(1)140; CRFP(2)1110 - desc/o Cecil Calvert MG165;
CFA(2)165

Benedict Leonard - of MD, b1700 d1751/1752 Member of Parliament
for Harwich & in 1727 governor of MD, died & buried at sea -
desc/o Anne Arundel BLG2600; MG(1)140; CRFP(2)111; CFA(2)165
- desc/o Lady Charlotte Lee BCD52

Burr - m Adah Fairfax - desc/o Leonard Calvert MG(1)147

Caroline - of MD, m Sir Robert Eden, Baronet & governor of MD d1786
- desc/o Anne Arundel BLG2600; GBR9; MG(1)141

Cecilius - of MD, b1702 d1765, secretary of the province & managed
the affairs of his Lordship - desc/o Anne Arundel MG(1)140;

CALVERT (cont.)
CFA(2)165

Cecilius (Cecil), 2nd Baron Baltimore - of MD, b1605/1606
d1675/1676 son of George Calvert, 1st Baron Baltimore & Anne
Mynne, m1727/1728 Lady Anne Arundell b abt 1615 d1649 dau/o
Sir Thomas Arundell, 1st Lord Arundell of Wardour Castle & a
Count of the Holy Roman Empire & Anne (Philipson) Thurgood;
from them descended the succeeding Lords (Barons of) Baltimore
extinct in 1771 - the immigrant GBR383, MG(1)138, 139, 165;
APP153/161; CRFP(2)1108/1110; CFA(2)164, (5)288

Cecilius - of MD, b1767 d1852 in Missouri, m1797 (his first cousin)
Nancy Beck Calvert b1773 d1835 dau/o George & Lydia Beck
(Ralls) Calvert, he moved to Kentucky & later to Missouri where he
died - desc/o Leonard Calvert MG(1)149, 166; CFA(5)291

Charles, 3rd Baron Baltimore - of MD, b1637 d1714/1715 governor of
MD & major general in the British Army, m(1) 1656 Mary Darnell
dau/o Ralph Darnell of Loughton, Herefordshire, m(2) abt 1667
Jane (Lady Baltimore) (Lowe) Sewall d1700/1701 dau/o Vincent
Lowe of Denby, Derbyshire & Anne Cavendish of London & wid/o
Henry Sewall, m(3)1701 Mary (Banks) Thorpe d1710/1711,
m(4)1712 Margaret Carleton d1731 dau/o Thomas Carleton of
Hexham, Northumberland - desc/o Anne Arundel J&K281;
ECD147; DAB(3)426, 427; ECD(2)77; MCD190; MCS47; GBR136;
APP159 BLG2600; DBR(1)151; DBR(3)243; RAA1, 77; MG(1)139,
165; CRFP(2)1110; CFA(2)164, (5)288

Charles (alias Lazenby alias Butler) - of MD, governor of MD, son of
Piers Butler & Henrietta Fitz James, m Rebecca Gerard dau/o John
Gerard & Elizabeth___ - the immigrant GBR13 some aspect of
royal descent merits further study, NE(104)175 (reprinted in
EO2:3:413)

Charles - of MD & VA, b1662/1663 d1733, m(1)1690 Mary Howson
dau/o Robert Howson of Stafford Co, VA, m(2) Barbara Kirk dau/o
Martin & Mary Kirk of St Mary's Co - desc/o Leonard Calvert
APP160; MG(1)145, 170; CFA(5)290

Charles, 5th Baron Baltimore - of MD b1699 d1751 governor of MD,
Member of Parliament for Surrey, Fellow of the Royal Society & Lord
of the Admiralty in 1741, m1730 Mary Jansen d1748 in Shaillot
near Paris, dau/o Sir Theodore Jansen - desc/o Anne Arundel
J&K281; CFA(2)165 - desc/o Lady Charlotte Lee CHB52; MCB164;
MCD190; MCS13; BLG2600; GBR9 some aspect of royal descent
merits further study; NE(104)175; MG(1)140, 141 - desc/o Cecil
Calvert MG(1)165; CRFP(2)1111

Charlotte - b1702 d1744, m Thomas Brerewood Esq - desc/o Anne
Arundel MG(1)140; CFA(2)165

Cynthia - of VA, m (her cousin) ___Calvert - desc/o Leonard Calvert
MG(1)203

Dorothy - of MD, m James Talbot - desc/o Anne Arundel CFA(5)288

Edward Henry - of MD b1701 d1730, commissary colonel of MD 1728,
m Margaret Lee - desc/o Anne Arundel BLG2600; MG(1)140

Edward Henry - of MD, b1766 d1846, m1796 Elizabeth Biscoe b1780
d1857, dau/o George Biscoe & Araminto Thompson - desc/o Lady

CALVERT (cont.)

Charlotte Lee MG(1)161 - desc/o Anne Arundel CRFP(2)1113; CFA(2)165

Eleanor - of MD, b1754 d1811, m(1)1774 Col John Parke Custis b1753 d1781, son of Daniel Parke Custis & Martha Dandridge, step-son of George Washington 1st President of the United States, m(2)1787 Dr David Steuart - desc/o Charlotte Lee CHB52; MCB164; MCD190; BCD52; GBR9; NE(104)175; MG(1)160; CRFP(2)1113

Elisha - b abt 1758 d bef 22 Jun 1784 a Revolutionary soldier - desc/o Leonard Calvert MG(1)204

Elizabeth - of MD, b1666 d aft 1684, m1681 Capt James Neale of Wolleston Manor, Charles Co, MD - desc/o Leonard Calvert APP160; MG(1)145; CFA(5)290

Elizabeth - of MD, m Samuel Matthews - desc/o Anne Arundel CFA(5)288

Elizabeth - of MD, b1730 d1798, m1748 Benedict "Swingate" Calvert - desc/o Anne Arundell MG(1)164

Elizabeth - of MD, m1780 Dr Charles Stewart b1750 d1822 - desc/o Lady Charlotte Lee MG(1)161; CRFP(2)1113

Francis - of VA, b1751 d1823, m(1)1791 Elizabeth Witt b1772 d1806 dau/o Lewis Mills & Anne Witt, m(2)1809 Elizabeth Rose - desc/o Anne Brent DBR(4)543 - desc/o Leonard Calvert MG(1)178, 179

Frederick 6th & last Lord Baltimore - of MD, b1732 d1771 in Naples, although he left no legitimate issue he had several natural children by Hester Whelan of Ireland, m1753 Lady Diana Egerton b1732 d sp 1758 dau/o Scrope Egerton, Duke of Bridgewater - desc/o Anne Arundel J&K281; MG(1)141 - desc/o Cecil Calvert MG(1)165

George, 1st Lord Baltimore - of VA & MD, b1578 Kiplin, Yorkshire d1632, promoter of MD, son of Leonard Calvert & Alice Crossland, m(1)1604 Anne Mynne d 8 Aug 1621, aged 42 yrs 9 mo 18 days, dau/o George Mynne & Elizabeth Wroth, m(2) abt 1625, Joane____ d1630 is supposed to have been drowned returning from VA - the immigrant APP153/161; DAB(3)428, 429; CRFP(2)1107/1127; GBR383 lists his son Cecil Calvert, 2nd Baron Baltimore, proprietor of MD - the immigrant; CFA(5)287, 288

George - of MD, b1668 d aft 1739, m1690 Elizabeth Doyne, two other wives have been mentioned, viz: Anne Notley & Hannah Neale - desc/o Anne Brent DBR(4)542 - desc/o Leonard Calvert MG(1)146, 166, 202; CFA(5)290; RCFA105

George - of VA, b abt 1700 d1771, m(1) abt 1725 Sytha Elizabeth Harrison, m(2)1741 Mrs Esther Stone wid/o Francis Stone - desc/o Leonard Calvert MG(1)202, 203

George - of MD & VA, b1712 d1782 commissioned captain of a company of militia in Culpeper Co by Thomas Jefferson then governor of VA, m(1) abt 1740 Anne Crupper, m(2)1779 Mary Deatherage d1810 wid/o Robert Deatherage d1777 & dau/o Francis & Susannah (Dabney) Strother, of St Mark's Parish, Culpeper Co - desc/o Leonard Calvert MG(1)147, 166; CFA(5)290; RCFA105

George - of VA, b1744 d1821 captain in the War of the Revolution from

CALVERT (cont.)

VA & lived & died in Culpeper Co, m1764 Lydia Beck Ralls - desc/o Leonard Calvert MG(1)151; CFA(5)293

George - of MD, b1768 d1838, m1799 Rosalie Eugenia Stier b1778 d1821 dau/o Henri Joseph Stier of Antwerp & Maria Louise Peeters - desc/o Anne Arundel BLG2600; DBR(1)333; CRFP(2)1113 - desc/o Lady Charlotte Lee MG(1)161

George - b1771, m1809 Anne Jennings - desc/o Leonard Calvert CFA(5)294

Gerrard - b1765 d1840, m Rosanna McIlwaine - desc/o Leonard Calvert MG(1)204

Grace - of MD, bp 1611/1612, m abt 1630 Sir Robert Talbot, 2nd Baronet, of Cartown, Co Kildare, Ireland, d1671 - desc/o George Calvert APP157; GBR383; CFA(2)164, (5)288

Helen - of MD, m Thomas Green, second governor of MD - desc/o Anne Arundel CFA(5)288

Humphrey - of VA, d1802, m Catherine____ - desc/o Leonard Calvert MG(1)203

Jacob - of VA, b1720 d1772, m Sarah Crupper - desc/o Anne Brent DBR(4)543 - desc/o Leonard Calvert MG(1)177, 178

Jane - of MD, b1703 d1778, m1720 Col John Hyde, of Kingston Lisle, Berkshire - desc/o Anne Arundel ECD148; ECD(2); DBR(1)152; DBR(2)237; DBR(3)244; CFA(2)165

Jane - of MD, b1746, m(1) abt 1768 Capt John Maddox, of the Royal Navy, m(2) John Settle, m(3)____Grymes - desc/o Leonard Calvert MG(1)147; CFA(5)293

John - of MD & VA, b abt 1692 d1739, m abt 1711 Elizabeth Harrison dau/o Benjamin Harrison III & Elizabeth Burwell of VA - desc/o Anne Brent DBR(4)543 - desc/o Leonard Calvert MG(1)146, 166; CFA(5)290; RCFA105

John - m Mary Calvert dau/o Joseph & granddau/o Cornelius Calvert of Norfolk & Princess Anne Co, VA - desc/o Leonard Calvert MG(1)146

John - of MD & VA, b1742 d1790 captain in the Revolution among the VA forces, m(1)1765 Sarah Bailey, m(2)1772 Hellen Bailey, both of his wives were daughters of John Bailey of Baltimore Co, MD - desc/o Leonard Calvert MG(1)149, 166; CFA(5)291; RCFA106

John - of VA, m Susannah____ - desc/o Leonard Calvert MG(1)203

John - d1812, m Winifred Smith dau/o Peter & Elizabeth Smith of Prince William Co, VA & had issue - desc/o Leonard Calvert MG(1)178

John - of VA, d1788, m Elizabeth____ & had issue - desc/o Leonard Calvert MG(1)203

John - b1762 d1824, m(1) Mary McCurdy, m(2) Grace Appleby - desc/o Leonard Calvert MG(1)204

John - b1775, m1804 Anne Askin - desc/o Leonard Calvert MG(1)152; CFA(5)294

Landon - of VA, b1764 d1809 Lewis Co, Kentucky, m1787 Anne Wood Howison b1766 d1845 dau/o Stephen Howison & Mary Brooke - desc/o Leonard Calvert MG(1)204

Leonard - of MD, b1606 d1647, 1st governor of MD 1634/1647,

CALVERT (cont.)

m1642 Anne Brent dau/o Richard Brent of Stoke Larke, Gloucestershire, England & Elizabeth Reed - the immigrant FFF207; DAB(3)430, 431; CGA33; GBR383; APP156; MG(1)133/228; CFA(2)164, (5)289

Lydia - of MD, b1748, m Archiblad Bigbee - desc/o Leonard Calvert MG(1)148; CFA(5)293

Margaret - of VA, m Hezekiah Fairfax - desc/o Leonard Calvert MG(1)203

Margaret - of VA, b1770, m1794 John Adams - desc/o Leonard Calvert MG(1)151; CFA(5)293

Mary - of VA, m Lawrence Butler - desc/o Leonard Calvert MG(1)178

Ralls - of VA, b1767 d1815 postmaster, m1790 Mary Wade Strother dau/o Capt John & Anne (Strother) Strother - desc/o Leonard Calvert MG(1)152; CFA(5)295

Richard - of MD, b1670 d1718, m Sarah____ in Westmoreland Co, VA - desc/o Leonard Calvert MG(1)146

Robert - emigrated to Texas & founded Calvert City - desc/o Leonard Calvert MG(1)146

Sarah - of MD, b1749, m____Rookard - desc/o Leonard Calvert MG(1)148; CFA(5)293

Sarah Howson - m aft 1717 Nathaniel Jones b1696 d1754 - desc/o Leonard Calvert MG(1)146

Thomas - of MD, b1714, m1734 Sarah Harrison - desc/o Leonard Calvert MG(1)147

William - of MD 1661, b1642/1643 d1682 served as member of MD Assembly, attorney general, secretary of the province & judge of probate, alderman of St Mary's City & was colonel of militia & commander of foot in St Mary's Co, m1661/1662 Elizabeth Stone dau/o Governor William Stone & Verlinda Cotton - desc/o Anne Brent DBR(4)542 - desc/o Leonard Calvert APP159, 160; MG(1)144, 145, 166; CFA(2)164, CFA(5)289; RCFA105

William - of VA, b1732 d1812 in Kentucky, m abt 1757 Hannah (Harrison?) d1807 - desc/o Leonard Calvert MG(1)203

CAMFIELD Abigail - of CT, m1703 Jonathan Rockwell - desc/o Francis Willoughby DBR(3)735; DBR(4)348, 651

CAMP Anna - of CT, b1769 d1810, m1791 Stephen Cogswell - desc/o Elizabeth Alsop ECD(2)26

Isaac - of CT, b1720 d1761, m Sarah Clark - desc/o Elizabeth Alsop ECD(2)26

Isaac Jr - of CT, b1740 d1793, m Jane Baldwin - desc/o Elizabeth Alsop ECD(2)26

CAMPBELL Alexander - of VA, b1761 d1826 - desc/o John Campbell CHB475

Archibald - of VA, b1760 d1830 - desc/o John Campbell CHB475

Ebenezer - of MD, b173_ - desc/o John Campbell CHB475

Francis - of PA, b1724/1745 d1791, m(1)____, m(2) Elizabeth Parker - desc/o John Campbell CHB475

James - of PA, b abt 1755 d1807/8, m Cassandana Miller - desc/o John Campbell CHB479

John - of VA, b1694 d1736/1737 merchant at Glasgow & Jamaica,

CAMPBELL (cont.)

    trading with Falmouth, Dumfries & Blandford in VA, m1718/1719
    Mary Simpson - the immigrant CHB475; CGA33; sufficient proof of
    alleged royal ancestry is lacking

    John - of MA 1696 - the immigrant EDV93; CGA33; sufficient proof of
    alleged royal ancestry is lacking

    John, 4th Earl of Loudoun - b1705 d1782 British commander in
    America during the French & Indian War, unmarried, son of Hugh,
    3rd Earl of Loudoun & Margaret (Dalrymple) Campbell - the
    immigrant GBR51

    John - of PA, b1752 d1819, m Catharine Cutler - desc/o John
    Campbell CHB476

    John - of VA, b1763 d1806 - desc/o John Campbell CHB475

    Margaret - of MD, b1736 d1812, m Alexander Campbell - desc/o John
    Campbell J&K157; CHB475

    Capt Robert - of PA, b1753/1754 d1779, m1779 Mary Hall - desc/o
    John Campbell CHB479

    Robert - of VA, b1768 d1807 - desc/o John Campbell CHB475

    William, Baron Campbell - of SC 1733, d1778 captain in the Royal
    Navy, governor of Nova Scotia 1766 & South Carolina 1773, fourth
    son of John, 4th Duke of Argyll & Mary (Bellenden) Campbell,
    m1763 Sarah Izard dau/o Ralph Izard - the immigrant J&K155;
    DAB(3)464, 465; GBR31

CANDE Sarah - of CT, b1710 d1792, m1731 John Higbee (Higby) - desc/o
    Nathaniel Browne ECD(3)60

CANFIELD Abraham - of CT, b1720 d1813, m1748 Rachel Ketcham -
    desc/o Francis Willoughby DBR(1)493; DBR(2)616; DBR(3)342

    Abraham - b1764 d1836, m Jerusha Roberts - desc/o Francis
    Willoughby DBR(1)493; DBR(2)616

    Esther - b1748 d1816, m John C Carmichael - desc/o Francis
    Willoughby DBR(3)342

    Jedediah - b1681, m Lydia Kellum - desc/o Francis Willoughby
    DBR(1)493; DBR(2)616; DBR(3)342

CAPELL Anne - of MD, m Robert Wiseman - the immigrant DBR(3)650;
    sufficient proof of alleged royal ancestry is lacking

CAPEN Mary - of MA, bp 1688/1689, m1709/1710 Thomas Baker Jr -
    desc/o Samuel Appleton DBR(1)139; DBR(5)602; AAP153; GBR390
    - desc/o Judith Everard AAP154; GBR459

CARGILL Lucy - of RI, m Nathan Arnold - desc/o William Arnold CHB16;
    BCD17

    Sarah Harrison - of VA, b1770 d1837, m1799 John Raines Mason -
    desc/o Lieut Col Walter Aston ECD(3)13; DBR(4)658

CARLETON Benjamin - of MA, b1693 Bradford d1772 Bradford, m(1)
    Abigail Dudley d1726 in her twenty-seventh year, m(2)
    Elizabeth____ - desc/o Edward Carleton NEFGM(1)8

    Bethiah - b1700, m William Hutchins - desc/o Ellen Newton LDS110

    Dudley - of MA, b1721/1722 Bradford, his name appears in the
    Revolutionary rolls of Massachusetts as one of a list of men serving
    as a committee for Essex Co to raise recruits for the campaigns in
    New York & Canada, m1745 Abigail Willson of Bradford d1799,
    aged seventy-four years - desc/o Edward Carleton NEFGM(1)8

CARLETON (cont.)

Edward - of MA 1639, bp 1610 Beeford d1650/1661 son of Walter
  Carleton & Jane Gibbon, m1636 Ellen Newton bp 1614 dau/o
  Mayor Lancelot & Mary (Lee) Newton - the immigrant FLW6, 7;
  ECD151; MCS77; DBR(1)36, 117, 479; DBR(2)590, 702;
  DBR(3)493, 571; RAA1, 78; CGA35; TAG(17)105/109; GBR178;
  NEFGM(1)7/9

Edward - of MA, b1664/1665 Haverhill, m Elizabeth____ - desc/o
  Edward Carleton RAA78; NEFGM(1)8

Edward - of MA, b1690/1691 Haverhill - desc/o Edward Carleton
  RAA78; NEFGM(1)8

Elizabeth - of MA, b1706 d1773, m1724 Jeremiah Stickney b1702
  d1763 - desc/o Edward Carleton DBR(3)493

Ezekiel - of MA, b abt 1701 d1775, m1731 Mercy Kimball b1712/1713
  d1781 - desc/o Edward Carleton DBR(1)36

Hannah - b1747 - desc/o Edward Carleton RAA78

Lieut John - of MA, b1637 d1668/1669, m1658/1659 Hannah Jewett
  b1641 dau/o Joseph Jewett bp 1609 & May Mallingson - desc/o
  Edward Carleton ECD151; DBR(1)36, 117, 479; DBR(2)591;
  DBR(3)493; RAA78; CGA35; NEFGM(1)7, 8 - desc/o Ellen Newton
  LDS110

John - of MA, b abt 1660/1661 d1745, m1688 Hannah Osgood b1668
  d1734 dau/o Capt Christopher Osgood - desc/o Edward Carleton
  ECD151; DBR(1)36, 479; DBR(2)590

John - b1709, m Hannah Platts b1732 d1782 - desc/o Edward
  Carleton DBR(1)117

John - b1718 - desc/o Edward Carleton RAA78

John - b1738 d1807, m Tabitha French b1742 d1807 - desc/o
  Edward Carleton DBR(1)118

John - b1758 d1846, m1794 Sarah Chase b1773 d1846 - desc/o
  Edward Carleton DBR(1)118

Mary - of MA, b1737 d Salem 1805, m1759 John Bowditch b1732 d at
  sea 1793 - desc/o Edward Carleton ECD151; DBR(1)479;
  DBR(2)591

Michael - of MA, b1757 Bradford d1836 Bradford, served in the
  Revolution as a private in several regiments, was stationed near
  Boston in 1778 & served in a regiment raised in Essex & Suffolk
  counties to reinforce Washington's Army, m1795 Haverhill, Ruth
  Ayer b1778 Haverhill d1847 dau/o Nathaniel Ayer & Lydia White -
  desc/o Edward Carleton NEFGM(1)8

Capt Samuel - of MA, b Andover 1696 d Salem 1767, m1726 Deborah
  Stevens - desc/o Edward Carleton ECD151; DBR(1)479; DBR(2)591

Thomas - of MA, b1667 Haverhill, m Elizabeth Hazelton dau/o
  Abraham Hazelton - desc/o Edward Carleton DBR(1)117;
  DBR(3)493; NEFGM(1)8 - desc/o Ellen Newton LDS110

Timothy - of MA, b1752 d1834, m1792 Rebecca Field b1771 d1856 -
  desc/o Edward Carleton DBR(1)37

CARLYLE Anne - of VA, d1778 in childbed of an only son, Carlyle Fairfax
  Whiting, m1777 Henry Whiting, of Gloucester Co - desc/o William
  Fairfax CFA(2)277

Sarah - of VA, m1776 William Herbert, of Alexandria, VA b1743 d1818

CARLYLE (cont.)
- desc/o Hon William Fairfax CHB176; BCD176l; CFA(2)277
CARMAN Abigail - of NJ, m1763 Aaron Bloodgood - desc/o Edward
FitzRandolph AFA46
Mary - m William Terry - desc/o Anne Marbury DBR(4)311; DBR(5)290
Jacob - b abt 1754, m Rachel Weeks - desc/o Henry Willis DBR(2)429
CARNAN Charles North - b1752 d1809, m(1) Mary Boyce b1756 d1776,
m(2) Sarah Johnston, issue by second wife three daughters -
desc/o Anne Lovelace GVFHB(3)355
Robert North - b1756 d1837, m(1) Katherine Risteau, m(2) Mrs Ennals,
nee Goldsborough, issue by his first wife seven children, his eldest
daughter was named Frances Todd Carnan - desc/o Anne Lovelace
GVFHB(3)355
CARNES Thomas Jenner - of MA - desc/o Mabel Harlakenden MCD231
de CARONDELET & de NOYELLE Francois Luis Hector, Vicomte de la
Hestre & du Langue of Louisiana & West Florida, m Maria Castanos
Aragorri Uriarte y Olivide - the immigrant GBR302
CARPENTER Alice - of MA, b abt 1590 d1670, m(1)1613 Edward
Southworth, m(2)1623 Gov William Bradford - the immigrant
FLW15, 16; sufficient proof of alleged royal ancestry is lacking
Amos - of CT, b1693 d1793 - desc/o William Carpenter BLG2603
Benjamin - of RI, m Mary Tillinghast - desc/o William Arnold CHB13;
BCD13
Benjamin - of CT, b1663 d1738, m1691 ____ - desc/o William
Carpenter BLG2603
Benjamin - of RI, b1673 d1766, m Prudence Kingsley - desc/o William
Arnold CHB13; BCD13
Benjamin - of NY, b1767 d1833, m1797 Catherine Solomon - desc/o
William Carpenter BLG2603
Bridget - b1744 - desc/o Alice Freeman RAA132
Charlotte - of RI, m Allen Gladding - desc/o William Arnold CHB14;
BCD14
Edward - of NJ, b1772 d1813, m1799 Sarah Stratton - desc/o Gov
Thomas Lloyd CHB129
Elizabeth - of RI, m Peleg Williams - desc/o William Arnold CHB14;
BCD14
Elizabeth - of NJ, m1767 Ezra Firth - desc/o Gov Thomas Lloyd
CHB128; MCD252; BCD128
Hannah - of NJ, b1743 d1820, m(1)1768 Charles Ellet - desc/o Gov
Thomas Lloyd CHB130; BCD130; DBR(2)515
Hannah - of PA, d1766, m1746 Samuel Shoemaker - desc/o Gov
Thomas Lloyd CHB127; BCD127
John - of MA, b1628 d1695, m Hannah____ - desc/o William
Carpenter BLG2603
John - of MA, b1733 d1821, m(3)1801 Mary Carpenter (his cousin)
b1752 wid/o Edward Ide - desc/o Robert Abell DBR(2)846; RAA59
John - b1756 - desc/o Robert Abell RAA59
Margaret - of NJ, b1756 d1821, m1776 James Mason Woodnut -
desc/o Gov Thomas Lloyd CHB129; BCD129; DBR(1)1; DBR(3)175;
AFA198
Mary - of RI, b1714, m1733 Benjamin Westcott - desc/o William

CARPENTER (cont.)
Arnold CHB19; BCD19
Oliver - of RI, b1739, m Susanna Potter - desc/o William Arnold
CHB13, 14; BCD13, 14
Judge Preston - of NJ, b1721 d1785, m(1)1742 Hannah Smith -
desc/o Gov Thomas Lloyd CHB128; BCD128; DBR(1)1; DBR(2)515;
DBR(3)175; AFA198
Priscilla - of RI, b abt 1648 d aft 1690, m1670 William Vincent -
desc/o William Arnold MCB396
Samuel - of PA 1683, d1714 - the immigrant EDV143; CGA35;
sufficient proof of alleged royal ancestry is lacking
Samuel - of NY, b1666, m Patience____ - desc/o William Carpenter
BLG2603
Samuel - of NY, b1695, m Patience____ - desc/o William Carpenter
BLG2603
Samuel - of NY, b1734 d1800, m Betsy Allison - desc/o William
Carpenter BLG2603
Simon - of VT, b1740 d1830, m1769 Anna Burton - desc/o William
Carpenter BLG2603
Thomas - of NJ, b1742 d1847, m1774 Mary Tonkin - desc/o Thomas
Lloyd CHB128; BCD128
Timothy - of RI, d1726, m Hannah Burton - desc/o William Arnold
CHB14; BCD14
William - of MA, b1605 d1659, m Abigail____ - the immigrant BLG2602
sufficient proof of alleged royal ancestry is lacking
William - of MA, b1631 d1703, m Prissilla Bennett - desc/o William
Carpenter BLG2603
de CARPENTIER Maria - of DE, m Jean (Jan) Paul Jaquet - the immigrant
GBR296
CARR Ann - of NH, b1678/1684, m1702 Robert Bettell - desc/o Thomas
Dudley DBR(1)557; DBR(2)687; DBR(4)839
Dabney - b1773 d1837 - desc/o Capt Henry Isham PFA127
CARRELL Jacob - of PA, b1732 d1817, m1769 Elizabeth Jamieson -
desc/o Rev Thomas Dungan ECD(3)141
James II - of PA, b abt 1699 d1749, m1723 Diana Van Kirk - desc/o
Rev Thomas Dungan ECD(3)141
CARRINGTON Ann - of PA, m____Morris - desc/o Elizabeth Hannah
Carrington NGS(70)248/270
Col Edward - of VA, b1748/1749 d1810 lawyer, lieut col in Virginia's
First Continental Artillery Regiment, deputy quartermaster colonel
of the Southern Army from 1780/1783 & served with distinction at
the battles of Monmouth, Guilford Courthouse, Hobkirk's Hill &
Yorktown. He was a member of the House of Delegates 1784/1788,
member of the Continental Congress 1786/1788, federal marshal,
supervisor of revenue for VA & mayor of Richmond in 1806 & 1809,
m1792 Elizabeth Jaquelin Ambler b1765 d1842 dau/o Jaquelin &
Rebecca (Burwell) Ambler & wid/o Col William Brent. They had no
children - desc/o George Carrington NGS(70)248/270
Elizabeth Gibbs - of PA, m____Alleyne - desc/o Elizabeth Hannah
Carrington NGS(70)248/270
Elizabeth Hannah - of PA, b1739/1740 d1795 in Barbados, m1760

CARRINGTON (cont.)

Charles Willing b1738 d1788 son of Charles & Anne (Shippen) Willing - the immigrant GBR257 some aspect of royal descent merits further study; NGS(70)248/270

George - of VA, bp 1711 d1785 a surveyor, planter & highest civil and military authority in Cumberland Co, VA, son of Paul Carrington & Henningham Codrington, m on or about 26 Jun 1732 Anne Mayo bp 1712 d1785 dau/o William & Frances (Gould) Mayo - the immigrant GBR257 some aspect of royal descent merits further study; NGS(70)248/270

George Jr - of VA, b1737/1738 d1784, vestryman, co clerk, co surveyor & col in the militia, m Margaret Bernard dau/o William Bernard - desc/o George Carrington NGS(70)247/270

Hannah - of VA, b1751 d1817, m1772 Nicholas Cabell b1750 d1803 son of Dr William & Elizabeth (Burks) Cabell - desc/o George Carrington NGS(70)247/270

Henningham - of VA, b1746 d1810, m1767 John Bernard b1736 d1799 son of William Bernard - desc/o George Carrington NGS(70)247/270

Joseph - of VA, b1741/1742 d1802 vestryman, public official & col in the militia, m1763 Theodosia Mosby dau/o Benjamin & Mary (Poindexter) Mosby - desc/o George Carrington NGS(70)247/270

Mary - of VA, b1759 d1829, m1781 Joseph Watkins b1747 d1804 son of Benjamin & Jane Watkins, "The richest man in Goochland County." - desc/o George Carrington NGS(70)247/270

Mayo - of VA, b1753 d1803 served as an ensign in a Cumberland Co minuteman company, a capt during the Revolutionary War & was captured at Charleston in 1780, a surveyor, justice of the peace, sheriff and a member of the House of Delegates 1786/1788. lieut col commandant of the 17th Virginia militia regiment, m1789 Ann Adams b1762 d1820 dau/o Richard & Elizabeth (Griffin) Adams - desc/o George Carrington NGS(70)247/270

Nathaniel - of VA, b1743/1743 d1803 lieut in a Cumberland Co minuteman co, justice of the peace, sheriff & capt in the militia, m Phoebe Harris dau/o Benjamin & Priscilla (Wager) Harris - desc/o George Carrington NGS(70)247/270

Judge Paul Sr - of VA, b1733/1734 d1818 a lawyer, judge and public official serving for 42 years, m(1)1755 Margaret Read b173(4) d1766 dau/o Col Clement & Mary (Hill) Read, m(2)1792 Priscilla Sims b1776 d1803 dau/o David Lewis & Lettice (May) Sims - desc/o George Carrington NSG(70)248/270; DAB(3)522

CARROLL Charles - of MD 1688, b1660 d1720, m(1)1689 Martha Underwood, m(2)1693 Mary Darnall - the immigrant CHB304; BCD304; AMB412; EDV62; CFA(1)66; CGA35; sufficient proof of alleged royal ancestry is lacking

Dr Charles - of MD 1737, b1691 d1755 representative of Annapolis in the Maryland Assembly, son of Charles O'Carroll & Clare Dunne (O'Doyne), m(1) Dorothy Blake, m(2) Anne Plater - the immigrant CHB60; BLG2604; BCD60; AFA86; GBR260

Charles - of MD, b1702 d1782, m Elizabeth Brooke - desc/o Charles Carroll CHB304; BCD304; AMB412; CFA66

CARROLL (cont.)

Charles - of MD, b1723 d1783, m1753 Margaret Tilghman - desc/o Charles Carroll BLG2604

Charles - of MD, b1729 d1763, m Mary Hill - desc/o Charles Carroll CFA67

Charles - of MD, b1737 Annapolis d1832 Revolutionary leader & signer of the Declaration of Independence, m1768 Mary Darnall (his cousin), dau/o Henry Darnall, Jr & Rachel Brooke - desc/o Rev Robert Brooke J&K202; MG(1)101; CFA(2)171 - desc/o Charles Carroll DAB(3)522, 523; CHB304; BCD304; AMB412; CFA(5)84

Charles - of MD, d1861, m1799 Harriett Chew - desc/o Charles Carroll AMB412

Daniel - of MD, b1707 d1734, m Anne Rosier - desc/o Charles Carroll CHB304; BCD304; CFA66, 67

Daniel - of MD, b1752, m Eleanor Digges - desc/o Charles Carroll CHB304; BCD304

Eleanor - of MD, m Daniel Carroll - desc/o Charles Carroll CFA67

Elizabeth - of MD, m Daniel Carroll - desc/o Charles Carroll CHB304; BCD304

James - of MD, m Achsah Ridgely - desc/o Dr Charles Carroll CHB60; BCD60

James Maccubbin - of MD, m Sophia Dorsey Gough assumed surname Carroll - desc/o Dr Charles Carroll CHB60; BCD60

Mary - of MD, m Richard Caton of MD - desc/o Charles Carroll AMB412 - desc/o Rev Robert Brooke CFA(2)171

Mary Clare - of MD, b1727, m1747 Nicholas Maccubbin - desc/o Dr Charles Carroll CHB60; BLG2304; BCD60, AFA86

Nicholas - of MD, m Anne Jennings - desc/o Dr Charles Carroll AFA86

William - b1741 - the immigrant BLG2604 royal ancestry not proven

CARTER Alice - of VA, b abt 1730 Lancaster Co d bef 1776 Lancaster Co, m M Griggs - desc/o Lady Diana Skipwith HSF(5)259

Ann - of VA, m Richard Farris - desc/o Col William Randolph DBR(2)339, 406

Ann Hill - of VA, b1773 d1829, m1793 Gen Henry Lee, son of Henry Lee & Lucy Grymes of Stratford - desc/o Sarah Ludlow ECD(2)184; PVF206; CFSSA112 - desc/o Anne Lovelace GVFHB(3)349

Anne - of VA, b1696, m1722 Benjamin Harrison of Berkeley, Charles City Co d abt 1744 sheriff & burgess, son of Benjamin Harrison & Elizabeth Burwell & had issue - desc/o Sarah Ludlow J&K137; CHB185 ECD194; MCD198; BCD185; DBR(2)276, 522; DBR(3)378; DBR(5)346, 955; AAP144; PFA Apx C #6; GBR229; CFA(1)78; AMB55; DBR(5)167; PVF201; CFSSA110 - desc/o John Carter BLG2605

Anne - of VA, m(1) John Champe of King George Co, m(2) Col Lewis Willis of Fredericksburg, VA, son of Col Henry Willis & Mildred Washington-Gregory - desc/o Sarah Ludlow PVF203; CFSSA118

Anne Walker - of VA, b1764, m1780 John Catlett of Gloucester Co, a distinguished lawyer, son of John Catlett & Mary Eggleston of King William Co - desc/o Sarah Ludlow PVF203; CFSSA118

Carolanna - of VA, m Dr Elisha Hall - desc/o Sarah Ludlow CFSSA118

Col Charles - of VA, b1707 d1764 of Cleves, King George Co, served as

CARTER (cont.)

a burgess & col of King George Co militia, m(1)1728 Mary Walke(r) dau/o Joseph Walke(r), m(2)1742 Ann Byrd dau/o Col William Byrd & Maria Taylor of Westover, m(3)1764 Lucy Taliaferro dau/o Capt William Taliaferro & Ann Walker - desc/o Sarah Ludlow CHB182, 183; MCD1918; BCD182; AMB55; CFA(1)78; PVF202, 203; CFSSA117, 118 - desc/o John Carter BLG2605

Charles - of VA, b1713, m Lucy____ - desc/o Lady Diana Skipwith HSF(5)257

Charles - of VA, b1732 d1806 of Corotoman, Lancaster Co & Shirley, Charles City Co, served as a burgess from Lancaster 1758/1775, m(1)1756 Mary Walker b1736 d1806, dau/o Col Charles Carter & Mary Walker of Cleves, King George Co, m(2)1770/1771 Anne Butler Moore, dau/o Bernard Moore & Anne Catherine Spotswood ancestor of Gen Robert E Lee - desc/o Sarah Ludlow J&K264; CHB136; ECD(2)184; BLG2605; BCD136; DBR(5)925; AMB55; CFA78; PVF202; CFSSA111

Charles - of VA, of Ludlow, King George Co d1796, m Elizabeth Chiswell dau/o Col John Chiswell & had issue - desc/o Sarah Ludlow PVF203; CFSSA118

Charles - of VA, d1806, m(1)1756 Mary W Carter b1736 d1770 dau/o Charles of Cleves & Mary Walker, m(2) Anna Butler Moore dau/o Bernard Moore & Anne Catherine Spotswood of Chelsea, King William Co, VA - desc/o Sarah Ludlow PVF206

Charles - of VA, b1765 Culpepper Co d1829, m1781 Betty Lewis b1765 Spotsylvania Co, VA d1830 dau/o Col Fielding Lewis & Betty Washington - desc/o John Washington HSF(4)163

Charles - of VA, b1765/1766 of Mt Atlas, m Nancy Carter dau/o Robert W Carter of Sabine Hall & Judith Fauntleroy - desc/o Sarah Ludlow AMB56; PVF206; CFSSA112

Charles Ewell - b abt 1771 - desc/o Lady Diana Skipwith RAA130

Doctor Charles Warner Lewis - of VA, m Mary Chastain Cocke - desc/o Col William Randolph DBR(4)201

Dale - of VA, b1710, m(1) Miss Edwards, m(2)____ - desc/o Lady Diana Skipwith HSF(5)257

Dale - of VA, d1847, m Katherine Porter - desc/o Lady Diana Skipwith DBR(2)729

Daniel - of VA, b1700, m Elizabeth Pammil - desc/o Lady Diana Skipwith HSF(5)257

Dorothy - b1710/1711 - desc/o John Prescott RAA125

Edward - of VA, b1671 d1697, m1697 Elizabeth Thornton b abt 1672 Petsworth Parish, Gloucester Co, VA, dau/o William Thornton - desc/o Lady Diana Skipwith DBR(1)285, 342, 452; DBR(2)8; DBR(3)228, 668; RAA130; CRL(3)116; HSF(5)256, 259

Edward - d1784, m1751 Mrs Catherine Brent - desc/o Lady Diana Skipwith DBR(1)342; DBR(2)8

Col Edward - of VA, b1734 of Blenheim, Albermarle Co, served as a member of the House of Delegates, m Sarah Champe dau/o Col John Champe & Ann Carter of King George Co - desc/o Sarah Ludlow CHB135; BLG2605; BCD135; DBR(1)94; DBR(2)158; DBR(3)236, 306; AMB55; CFA(1)78; PVF202; CFSSA111

CARTER (cont.)

Edward - b1766 d1840, m(2) Martha Custis Violet - desc/o Lady Diana Skipwith DBR(1)342; DBR(2)8

Edward - of VA, b1767 of Cloverland, m Jane Carter dau/o John Carter of Sudley, Prince William Co & Janet Hamilton - desc/o Sarah Ludlow AMB56; PVF206; CFSSA112

Elizabeth - of VA, b1680 d1721, m(1) Nathaniel Burwell, son of Lewis Burwell & Abigail Smith of King's Creek, m(2) aft 1721 Dr George Nicholas, of Williamsburg, surgeon in the British Navy - desc/o Sarah Ludlow J&K268; CHB132, 133; ECD197; ECD(2)188; BCD132; DBR(1)113, 400, 742; DBR(2)55; 694; DBR(3)694; AMB55; CFA(1)78; CRL(1)249; PVF199; CFSSA110 - desc/o Lady Diana Skipwith HSF(5)256

Elizabeth - of VA, d aft 1764, m 1742 Col Francis Willis b1742 - desc/o Sarah Ludlow DBR(1)29; CFSSA116

Elizabeth - of VA, m William Stanard, Sheriff 1802/1804 - desc/o Sarah Ludlow CHB135; BCD135; DBR(1)94; DBR(2)158; DBR(3)236

Elizabeth - of VA, m William Churchill son of ____Churchill & Hannah Harrison of Bushby Park - desc/o Sarah Ludlow CHB182; BCD182; PVF203; CFSSA118

Elizabeth - of VA, b1764 d1832, m Col Robert Randolph of Eastern View, Fauquier Co, son of Peter Randolph & Lucy Bolling of Chatsworth - desc/o Sarah Ludlow CFSSA112; CFA(1)79

Elizabeth - of VA, m____Dawson - desc/o Lady Diana Skipwith HSF(5)257

Elizabeth Hill - of VA, b1731 d1760, m1748 Col William Byrd of Westover, Charles City Co, son of Col William Byrd & Maria Taylor of Westover - desc/o Sarah Ludlow AMB55; PVF202; CFSSA111

Elizabeth Hill - of VA, b1764 D1832, m Col Robert Randolph - desc/o Sarah Ludlow CHB136; BLG2605; BCD136; DBR(3)306; AMB56; CFA79

Elizabeth Landon - of VA, m1790 Spencer Ball b1762 d1832 of Portici, Prince William Co, son of Capt Spencer Mottrom Ball & Elizabeth Waring of Coan, Northumberland Co - desc/o Sarah Ludlow CFSSA116

Elizabeth Wormeley - of VA, a Revolutionary heroine, m1756 Nelson Berkeley of Airwell, Hanover Co son of Col Edmund Berkeley & Mary Nelson - desc/o Sarah Ludlow CHB188; BCD188; CFSSA120

Frances - of VA, m Thomas Ludlow Lee d1807 son of Thomas Ludwell Lee & Mary Aylett - desc/o Sarah Ludlow CHB187; BCD187; PVF208

George - of VA, m(2) Eleanor Eltonhead, m(3) Ann Carter - desc/o John Carter BLG2605

George - b abt 1728 - desc/o Lady Diana Skipwith RAA130

George - of VA, b1761 of Corotoman, Lancaster Co, m Lelia Skipwith dau/o Sir Peyton Skipwith & Anne Miller - desc/o Sarah Ludlow AMB56; PVF206; CFSSA112

Capt Henry - desc/o Lady Diana Skipwith DBR(1)123

Henry Skipwith - of VA, b1676, m Anne Harris - desc/o Lady Diana Skipwith HSF(5)256

CARTER (cont.)

James - of VA, b1708, m Joyce____ - desc/o Lady Diana Skipwith HSF(5)257

James - of PA, b1751 d1795 plantation owner of Chester Co, Pennsylvania, m1782 Ann Sharpless b1761 d1844 dau/o Jacob Sharpless - desc/o Oliver Cope DBR(1)516; DBR(2)659

Jane - of VA, m Samuel Kellett - desc/o Sarah Ludlow CHB136; BCD136; DBR(1)501

Job Sr - of VA, b1734 King George Co d Amherst, VA, m Anne____ d aft 1782 - desc/o Lady Diana Skipwith HSF(5)257

Job Jr - of VA, b abt 1757 Lancaster Co d1809 Lexington, KY, m abt 1804 Sarah Newton Lane b abt 1773 Charlestown, VA d abt 1826 Bourbon, KY dau/o Joseph Lane & Mary Newton - desc/o Lady Diana Skipwith HSF(5)257, 258

John - of VA 1649, b1620/1624 d1669, m(1) Jane Glyn, dau/o Morgan Glyn of England, m(2) Eleanor Eltonhead dau/o Richard Eltonhead & Ann Sutton of England & wid/o William Brocas, of royal ancestry, m(3) Anne Carter, dau/o Cleave Carter, of England, m(4) Sarah Ludlow of royal ancestry, dau/o Gabriel Ludlow of Dinton, m(5) Elizabeth Shirley of Gloucester Co - the immigrant BLG2605; DBR(4)252; AMB55; RAA1, 78; WAC97; CFA(1)77; John was not of royal descent

John - of VA, m(2)1714 Margaret Todd - desc/o Lady Diana Skipwith DBR(1)145; DBR(5)376

John - of VA, b1690 d1743, of Corotoman, Lancaster Co & Shirley, Charles City Co secretary of state 1722/1743, m1723 Elizabeth Hill d1777 dau/o Col Edward Hill of Shirley, Charles City Co - desc/o Sarah Ludlow J&K264; CHB135; ECD(2)184; BLG2605; BCD135; DBR(1)94; DBR(2)158; DBR(3)234, 306; DBR(5)925; AMB55; CFA(1)78; PVF202; CFSSA111

John - of VA, d1782, m Miss Spencer - desc/o Lady Diana Skipwith DBR(1)286; DBR(3)228, 668

Capt John - of VA, b abt 1717 d1783 of Caroline Co, m(1) ____Armistead, m(2) abt 1768 Hannah Chew dau/o John Chew & Mary Beverley of Spottsylvania Co - desc/o Lady Diana Skipwith DBR(1)145; DBR(2)803; DBR(3)332; DBR(5)376 - desc/o Sarah Ludlow CFSSA116

John - of VA, m Elizabeth Travers - desc/o Sarah Ludlow BLG2605; AMB54

John - of VA, b1739 d1789 of Sudley, Prince William Co, m1760 Janet Hamilton - desc/o Sarah Ludlow DBR(4)254; DBR(5)946; CFSSA121

John - of VA, of King George Co, m Philadelphia Claiborne - desc/o Sarah Ludlow PVF203; CFSSA118

Joseph - of VA, b1690 d1764, m1713 Ann Pines - desc/o Lady Diana Skipwith DBR(1)280; CRL(3)116

Joseph - of VA, b1697, m Catherine Stevens - desc/o Lady Diana Skipwith HSF(5)257

Joseph Jr - of VA, d1771, m(1)1746 Margaret Mason, m(2)1755 Lettice Lynton - desc/o Lady Diana Skipwith CRL(3)116

Joseph - of VA, b1736, m Elizabeth Presley - desc/o Lady Diana

CARTER (cont.)

Skipwith HSF(5)257

Judith - of VA, b1693, m1718 Mann Page of Roswell, Gloucester Co, son of Col Matthew & Mary Mann - desc/o Sarah Ludlow J&K265; CHB134; BCD134; AWW342; BLG2605; AMB55; CFA(1)78; PVF201; CFSSA110

Judith - of VA, m____Chilton - desc/o Lady Diana Skipwith HSF(5)259

Judith Frances - of VA, m1763 William Burnett Brown son of William Brown & Mary Burnett - desc/o Sarah Ludlow CHB182; BCD182; PVF203; CFSSA118

Kate Spotswood - of VA, m Dr Carter Berkeley - desc/o Sarah Ludlow DBR(5)925

Col Landon - of VA, b1709 d1778, m(1)____Armistead, m(2) Maria Byrd, m(3)1732 Elizabeth Wormeley - desc/o Sarah Ludlow CHB186, 187; BCD186; DBR(4)254; DBR(5)946; AMB55

Landon - of VA, b1713 of Sabine Hall, Richmond Co, m(1) Elizabeth Wormeley b1714 d1740 dau/o John Wormeley of Rosewell, m(2) Maria Byrd dau/o William Byrd of Westover, m(3) Elizabeth Beale dau/o Thomas Beale & Elizabeth Tavener of Chestnut Hill, Raphannock - desc/o Sarah Ludlow PVF203; CFSSA120

Landon - of VA, of Prince William Co, m Judith Fauntleroy dau/o Moore Fauntleroy & Margaret Micou of Richmond Co - desc/o Maria Horsmanden CHB55; BCD55 - desc/o Sarah Ludlow CHB186; BCD187; CFSSA120

Landon - of VA, b1751 of Cleves, King George Co d1811, m(1) Mildred Willis dau/o Col Lewis Willis & Mary Champe of Willis Hill, Spotsylvania Co, m(2) Mrs Eliza (Carter) Thornton of Sabine Hall - desc/o Maria Horsmanden CHB56; BCD56 - desc/o Sarah Ludlow CHB183; BCD183; PVF203, 207; CFSSA112, 119

Landon - of VA, b1756/1757 d1820, m(1)1780 Catherine Griffin Tayloe b1761 d1798 dau/o John Tayloe & Rebecca Plater of Mount Airy, m(2) Mary B Armistead - desc/o Sarah Ludlow CHB187; BCD187; CFSSA120

Lucy - of VA, m(1)1730 Col Henry Fitzhugh of Eagle's Nest, King George Co, son of William Fitzhugh & Ann Lee, m(2) Nathaniel Harrison of Brandon, Surry Co, son of Nathaniel Harrison & Mary Cary of Wakefield, & had issue - desc/o Sarah Ludlow BLG2605; AMB55; CFA(1)78; PVF202; CFSSA111

Lucy - of VA, d bef 1776, m1761 John Smithers - desc/o Lady Diana Skipwith HSF(5)259

Lucy Landon - of VA, m Gen John Minor of Fredericksburg b1761, served with distinction in the Revolution & was present at the surrender of Lord Cornwallis in 1781 son of Major John Minor & Elizabeth Cosby of Topping Castle, Caroline Co - desc/o Maria Horsmanden CHB56; BCD56; BCD183 - desc/o Sarah Ludlow CFSSA119

Margaret Crew - of VA, b1771 d1822, m1802 Zachariah Taliaferro - desc/o Lady Diana Skipwith DBR(1)145; DBR(2)803; DBR(3)333; DBR(5)376

Maria - of VA, William Armistead & had issue - desc/o Maria Horsmanden CHB55; BCD55 - desc/o Sarah Ludlow CHB183;

CARTER (cont.)

> BCD183; CFSSA118

Maria Byrd - of VA, m Robert Beverley of Blandfield, son of William Beverley & Elizabeth Bland - desc/o Sarah Ludlow CHB187; BCD187; CFSSA120

Martha - of VA, m William Armistead of Hesse, Gloucester Co, VA - desc/o Sarah Ludlow PVF203

Mary - of VA, b1712 d1736, m1733 Major George Braxton d bef 1755 of Newington, King & Queen Co - desc/o Sarah Ludlow J&K269; BLG2605; BCD183; AMB55, 56; CFA(1)78; PVF202; CFSSA84/87, 110

Mary - m John Carter - desc/o Lady Diana Skipwith DBR(1)452

Mary - of VA, m Col Robert Randolph of Eastern View, Fauquier Co, VA - desc/o Sarah Ludlow PVF206

Mary - of VA, b1763, m George Braxton of Chericoke, King William Co, son of Carter Braxton & Elizabeth Corbin - desc/o Sarah Ludlow CFSSA112

Mary Ann - of VA, b1747 d1820/1825, m Dr John Bronaugh - desc/o Lady Diana Skipwith CRL(3)117

Mary Walker - of VA, m Charles Carter (her cousin) of Shirley & Corotoman, son of John Carter & Elizabeth Hill - desc/o Sarah Ludlow PVF203; CFSSA118

Millicent - of VA, m1766 Rev Charles Cummings - desc/o Lady Diana Skipwith HSF(5)259

Nancy - of VA, m(1) Cornelius Vaughn, m(2) Edward Carter - desc/o Lady Diana Skipwith HSF(5)257

Norris - of VA, b1748 d1816, m Agnes Allen - desc/o Lady Diana Skipwith DBR(2)729; HSF(5)257

Peter - of VA, b1706 Lancaster Co d1789 Warrenton, m1730 Judith Norris d1785 King George Co - desc/o Lady Diana Skipwith ECD(2)246; DBR(2)728; DBR(4)558; HSF(5)257

Peter Jr - of VA, b1743, m Mary Anne Ellis - desc/o Lady Diana Skipwith HSF(5)257

Priscilla - of VA, b1760 d1823, m Lieut Robert Mitchell - desc/o Sarah Ludlow DBR(3)339

Raleigh - b abt 1740 d1820, m Sarah Sharpe - desc/o Lady Diana Skipwith DBR(1)452

Col Robert, called "King" - of VA, b1663 of Corotoman, Lancaster Co d1732 member & Speaker of the Virginia House of Burgesses, councillor & acting governor, son of John Carter & Sarah Ludlow, m(1) abt 1688 Judith Armistead d1699 dau/o Col John Armistead, m(2)1701 Elizabeth Landon b1684 d1719 dau/o Thomas Landon of England & wid/o Richard Willis - desc/o Sarah Ludlow J&K137, 263; CHB132,182; ECD194, 197; ECD(2)184, 188; MCD198; BCD132; BCD182; DBR(1)29, 94, 113, 400, 501, 742; DBR(2)55, 158, 276, 522, 559, 694; DBR(3)234, 306,339, 378, 557,694; DBR(4)200, 245; DBR(5)167, 868, 925, 946, 955, 1056; AAP144; GBR229, PVF199; BLG2605; AMB55; PFA Apx C #6; CFA(1)77; CRL(1)248, 249; DAB(3)541, 542; AWW342; CFSSA109

Robert - of VA, m Mary Coles - desc/o Sarah Ludlow CHB135; BCD135

CARTER (cont.)

Robert - of VA, m Winifred Beale - desc/o Sarah Ludlow CHB186;
BCD187

Robert - of VA, of Nominy Hall, Westmoreland Co d1732, m1725
Priscilla Bladen - desc/o Sarah Ludlow AMB55; CFA(1)78; PVF202

Robert II - of VA, b1705 of Nominy Hall, Westmoreland Co d aft 1757,
m Priscilla Churchill b1705 d aft 1757 dau/o William Churchill &
Elizabeth Armistead of Middlesex Co - desc/o Sarah Ludlow
BLG2605; DBR(1)29, 501; DBR(3)339; CFSSA116

Robert III - of VA, b1728 of Nominy Hall, Westmoreland Co, a
distinguished member of the King's Council, was known as
"Councillor Carter," m1754 Frances Ann Tasker, dau/o Benjamin
Tasker of Bel Air, Prince George's Co - desc/o Sarah Ludlow
DBR(3)339; PVF202; CFSSA116

Robert - of VA, b1774 of Shirley, Charles City Co, m1792 Mary (Lucy)
Nelson b1774 dau/o Gen Thomas Nelson of Yorktown - desc/o
Sarah Ludlow AMB56; PVF206; CFSSA118

Robert Wormley - of VA, of Sabine Hall, Richmond Co, m Winifred
Tavener Beale, dau/o Capt William Beale of Richmond - desc/o
Sarah Ludlow CFSSA120

Sarah - of VA, m bef 1776 ____ McTrye - desc/o Lady Diana Skipwith
HSF(5)259

Sarah - of VA, m William Thompson & had issue - desc/o Sarah
Ludlow PVF203; CFSSA118

Solomon - of VA, b1739 d1786, m abt 1760 Mary Ann Bickley dau/o
Capt John Bickley - desc/o Lady Diana Skipwith ECD(2)246;
DBR(4)558; HSF(5)257

Tabitha - of VA, b abt 1722/1724 d1759, m1747 Jeremiah Starke -
desc/o Lady Diana Skipwith DBR(1)280

Capt Thomas Jr - of VA, b1672 Lancaster Co d1733 Lancaster Co,
justice 1705/1729, m1695 Lancaster Co, Arabella Williamson d aft
1737 dau/o William Williamson - desc/o Lady Diana Skipwith
ECD(2)246; DBR(1)513; DBR(2)728; DBR(3)225; DBR(4)558;
CRL(3)116; HSF(5)256

Thomas III - of VA, b1696 d1735, m1720/1725 Joanna Miller - desc/o
Lady Diana Skipwith DBR(1)513; HSF(5)257

Thomas - of VA, b1700 d1776, m(1)____, m(2) Mrs Anne (Wale) Hunton
- desc/o Lady Diana Skipwith DBR(1)286, 342, 452; DBR(2)8;
DBR(3)228, 668; RAA130; HSF(5)259

Thomas - of VA, b1731, m Elizabeth____ - desc/o Lady Diana Skipwith
HSF(5)257

Thomas IV - of VA, b1734 d1817, m1764 Winifred Hobson - desc/o
Lady Diana Skipwith DBR(1)513

Thomas - of VA, b1752/1754 d1813, m abt 1776/1777 Susannah
Gaines - desc/o Lady Diana Skipwith DBR(1)286; DBR(3)229, 668

William - of VA & KY, b1757 d1841 in Ohio Co, Kentucky, a
Revolutionary soldier, m1809 Sara (Williams) Evans - desc/o Lady
Diana Skipwith ECD(2)246; DBR(4)558

Wormeley - of VA, m1787 Sarah Edwards - desc/o Maria Horsmanden
CHB55; BCD55 - desc/o Col Moore Fauntleroy CHB143; BCD143 -
desc/o Sarah Ludlow BCD187

de CARTERET Peter - of NC, governor of North Carolina son of Helier de Carteret & Rachel La Cloche, m____ - the immigrant GBR220

Philip - of NJ, b1639 d1682 first governor of NJ son of Helier de Carteret & Rachel La Cloche, m Mrs Elizabeth Smith Lawrence - the immigrant DAB(3)546; GBR220

CARY Ann - of VA - desc/o Miles Cary WAC104

Anne - of VA, m Robert Carter Nicholas - desc/o Miles Cary CFA81

Bridget - of VA - desc/o Miles Cary WAC104

Edward - of MD, b1757, m Martha Stubbs - desc/o Col George Reade DBR(2)644; DBR(3)102

Elizabeth - of VA, m Brian Fairfax - desc/o Miles Cary CFA81

Elizabeth - of VA, m Fernando Fairfax - desc/o Miles Cary CFA82

Elizabeth - of VA - desc/o Miles Cary WAC104

Henry - of VA - desc/o Miles Cary WAC104

Mary of VA, b1704 d1775, m Joseph Selden - desc/o Miles Cary CFA81

Mary - of VA, m E J Ambler - desc/o Miles Cary CFA81

Mary Monroe - of VA, m William S Peachy - desc/o Miles Cary CFA82

Miles - of VA 1650, b1620 d1667, m Anne Taylor - the immigrant EDV65, 66; WAC104; CFA80, 81; CGA36; sufficient proof of alleged royal ancestry is lacking

Col Miles - of VA, b1665 d1708, m1702 Mary Wilson - desc/o Miles Cary WAC104; CFA81

Sarah - of VA, m George William Fairfax - desc/o Miles Cary CFA81

Sarah - of VA, m Capt Thomas Nelson - desc/o Miles Cary CFA82

Maj Thomas - of VA, m Ann Milner - desc/o Miles Cary WAC104; CFA81

William - of VA, b abt 1657 d1713, m Martha Seabrook - desc/o Miles Cary CFA81

William - of MD, b1760 d1806 enlisted and served in Seventh Regiment, Maryland Line, 1778/1780, m1793 Maria Barbara Fritchie dau/o Dr Casper Fritchie & Susan (Whithare) Fritchie - desc/o William Asfordby CHB511

Col Wilson - of VA, b1703 d1772, m Sarah____ - desc/o Miles Cary CFA81

Wilson - of VA, b1760 d1793, m1782 Jean Barbara Carr - desc/o Miles Cary CFA82

Col Wilson Miles - of VA, b1734 d1817, m1759 Sarah Blair - desc/o Miles Cary CFA82

CASE Abigail - b1682 - desc/o Agnes Harris RAA131

Abigail - b1725 - desc/o Agnes Harris RAA131

Eunice - b1703 - desc/o Agnes Harris RAA131

John - b1694 - desc/o Agnes Harris RAA131

Jonathan - b1701 - desc/o Agnes Harris RAA131

Jonathan - b1723 - desc/o Agnes Harris RAA131

Mercy - b1700 - desc/o Agnes Harris RAA131

Oliver - b abt 1765 - desc/o Agnes Harris RAA131

Samuel - b1667 - desc/o Agnes Harris RAA131

CATE Ann - of VA, m1755 Capt Henry Bonner - desc/o Rev Hawte Wyatt DBR(1)706, 707

CATESBY Elizabeth - of VA, m William Cocke, secretary of VA - the
immigrant GBR417 some aspect of royal descent merits further
study

Mark - b abt 1679 d1749, naturalist, traveler & writer on the South,
died unmarried - the immigrant DAB(3)571, 572; GBR417 some
aspect of royal descent merits further study

CATLETT David - of VA, b1669 d bef 1719 - desc/o Capt Henry
Woodhouse JSW1893

Capt John - of VA, b1749, m1775 Allie King - desc/o Capt Henry
Woodhouse JSW1893

Robert - of VA, b1721 d1803, m Mary Floyd - desc/o Capt Henry
Woodhouse JSW1893

William - of VA, d abt 1788 - desc/o Capt Henry Woodhouse JSW1893

CATLIN Honor - of CT, b1745 d1811, m1762 Dr Russell Abernethy -
desc/o Margaret Wyatt DBR(1)199

CAVERLY Charles - of CT - the immigrant EDV62; CGA36; sufficient proof
of alleged royal ancestry is lacking

George - of CT - the immigrant EDV62; CGA36; sufficient proof of
alleged royal ancestry is lacking

CHALLIS Ennos - b1757, m Joanna Chase - desc/o Anthony Colby
LDS47

CHALONER Ninyam - of RI, d1752 - the immigrant EDV43, 44; CGA36;
sufficient proof of alleged royal ancestry is lacking

CHAMBERLAYNE (CHAMBERLAIN) Dorothy - of SC, dau/o Edmund &
Eleanor (Colles) Chamberlayne, m Robert Daniell - the immigrant
GBR44 some aspect of royal descent merits further study

Edward Pye - of VA, m Mary Bickerton Webb - desc/o Warham
Horsmanden CHB54; BCD54; CGA36

Jacob - b1685 - desc/o Griffith Bowen RAA72

Lucy Parke - of VA, m Robert Carter Williamson - desc/o Warham
Horsmanden CHB56; BCD55

Mary - b1687 - desc/o Griffith Bowen RAA72

Mary - b1714 - desc/o Griffith Bowen RAA72

Sarah - b1712 - desc/o Griffith Bowen RAA72

Thomas - of VA, son of Edmund & Eleanor (Colles) Chamberlayne, m(1)
Mary Wood, m(2) Elizabeth Stratton - the immigrant GBR44

CHAMBERS Rebecca - of PA, b1751 d1834, m1768 Robert Wallace -
desc/o James Claypoole CHB94; MCD200; BCD94

CHAMPERNOUN Capt Frances - of ME 1665, d1687 son of Arthur
Champernoun & Bridget Fulford - the immigrant FLW10; MCS24;
RAA1, 79; EDV94; CGA36; sufficient proof of alleged royal ancestry
is lacking

CHAMPLIN Capt William - b1757 d1848, m1781 Content Leeds Brown -
desc/o Alice Freeman DBR(3)424; DBR(4)800

CHANDLER Allen - b1759 d1837, m Sarah Pyle - desc/o William
Chandler AFA158

James - of NY, b1769 d1839, m Huldah Payne - desc/o Samuel
Symonds AFA14

John - of MA - desc/o William Chandler EDV137

William - of MA 1637 - the immigrant EDV137; CGA37; sufficient proof
of alleged royal ancestry is lacking

CHANDLER (cont.)

    William - of PA, b1676 d1746, m Ann Bowater - the immigrant AFA158; sufficient proof of alleged royal ancestry is lacking

    William - of PA, b1718 d1795, m Rebecca Allen - desc/o William Chandler AFA158

CHANNING Francis Dana - b1775 d1810, m1806 Susan Higginson d1810 - desc/o Gov Thomas Dudley NE(8)319

    Rev William Ellery - of RI, religious reformer - desc/o Gov Thomas Dudley J&K196

CHAPIN Abigail - b1732 - desc/o Dorothy Stapilton RAA117

    Abner - b1746 - desc/o Amy Wyllys RAA126

CHAPLIN Joseph - b abt 1765 - desc/o Alice Freeman RAA132

CHAPMAN Throop - b1739, m(2) Deborah Willson - desc/o William Throop LDS28

CHAPPELL George - b1722 - desc/o Oliver Mainwaring RAA113

    Isaac - b1761 - desc/o Oliver Mainwaring RAA113

CHASE Josiah - b1746 - desc/o Gov Thomas Dudley RAA89

    Josiah - b1772 - desc/o Gov Thomas Dudley RAA89

CHAUNCY Abigail - of MA, b1677, m(1) Dr Hudson, m(2) Edward Burroughs - desc/o Rev Charles Chauncy AMB349; NEFGM(1)152

    Abigail - of CT, b1701, m Rev John Graham - desc/o Rev Charles Chauncy CHB69; BCD69

    Abigail - b1717, m Jabez Hamlin - desc/o Rev Charles Chauncy AMB349; NEFGM(1)152

    Catherine - b1676 - desc/o Charles Chauncy RAA79; NEFGM(1)152

    Catherine - of MA - m Rev Daniel Brewer - desc/o Rev Charles Chauncy MCD192

    Catherine - of CT, b1741 d1830, m1759 Rev Elizur Goodrick - desc/o Rev Charles Chauncy AMB349; J&K273; CHB71; MCD192; BCD71; NEFGM(1)153

    Catherine - of CT, b1765 d1841, m1790 Reuben Rose Fowler - desc/o Rev Charles Chauncy CHB70; BLG2612; BCD70; AFA94

    Rev Charles - of MA, bp 1592 Yardley Bury Church, Hertford d1671/1672 Cambridge, MA, second president of Harvard College, fifth son of George Chauncey & Anne Welsh, m1630/1631 Catherine Eyre bp 1604 d1667 dau/o Robert Eyre of Newe Sarum, Wilts & Agnes or Ann Still - the immigrant J&K273; FLW70, 71; CHB68,84; MCB257; MCD191; MCS2; BLG2612; BCD68, 84; DBR(5)1038; AMB348; RAA1, 79; DAB(4)41, 42; EDV43; AFA94; CGA37; GBR423; NE(10)259/262, (11)148/153; NEFGM(1)150, 151

    Charles - of MA, d1781, m Sarah Walley - desc/o Rev Charles Chauncy CHB68; BCD68; DAB(4)42

    Charles - of MA, b1705 d1787 clergyman, m(1)1727 Elizabeth Hirst, m(2)1738 Elizabeth Townsend, m(3)1760 Mary Stoddard - desc/o Rev Charles Chauncy DAB(4)42, 43

    Judge Charles - of CT, b1747 Durham d1823 New Haven, king's attorney for the state & judge of the superior court, m1773 Abigail Darling b1746 d1818 dau/o Thomas Darling & Abigail____ of New Haven - desc/o Rev Charles Chauncy BLG2612; AMB349; NEFGM(1)153

CHAUNCY (cont.)

Col Elihu - of CT, b1710 Durham d1791 commanded a regiment in the French War; chief justice of the county court & member of the CT legislature for 39 years, m1739 Mary Griswold d1801 aged eighty-three years, dau/o Samuel Griswold, Esq, of Killingworth - desc/o Rev Charles Chauncy J&K273; CHB70, 71; MCD192; BLG2612; BCD70; AMB349; NEFGM(1)152

Elizabeth Hirst - b1769, m Jeremiah Clarke of York, ME - desc/o Rev Charles Chauncy NE(11)152

Rev Elnathan - of CT, b1724 d1796, m1760 Elizabeth Worthington - desc/o Rev Charles Chauncy CHB70; BLG2612; BCD70; AMB349; AFA94; NEFGM(1)152

Ichabod - of MA, b1635 d1691, m Mary King - desc/o Rev Charles Chauncy AMB348; NEFGM(1)152

Rev Israel - of CT, b1644 Scituate, MA d1703 Stratford, founder & trustee of Yale College, chaplain King Philip's War 1675/1676, m(1) Mary Nichols d1669 Fairfield, CT, dau/o Isaac Nichols & Margaret Washburn, m(2)1684 Sarah Hudson d1711 dau/o John Hudson - desc/o Rev Charles Chauncy CHB68; FLW71; BCD68; AMB348; NEFGM(1)152

Rev Israel (Issac) - of CT, b1670 d1745, m Sarah Blackleach - desc/o Rev Charles Chauncy CHB68, 69; BCD68, 69

Rev Isaac - of MA, b1632 Ware, Hertford, England d1712 educated at Harvard College & was minister at Woodborough, Wiltshire, m Jane___ & had issue - desc/o Rev Charles Chauncy CHB68; BCD68; AMB348; FLW71; NEFGM(1)152

Mary - of MA, b1707 d1776, m Jacob Cushing - desc/o Rev Charles Chauncy CHB68; BCD68

Rev Nathaniel - of MA, b1639 Plymouth, MA, twin to Elnathan d1685 Hatfield, physician & minister, m1673 Abigail Strong dau/o Elder John Strong & had issue - desc/o Rev Charles Chauncy J&K273; FLW71; MCD192; BLG2612; BCD69; AMB349; NEFGM(1)152 - desc/o Catherine Eyre DBR(1)476; RAA79; AFA94

Rev Nathaniel - of CT, b1681 Hatfield d1756 he was the first graduate of Yale College, m1708 Sarah Judson of Stratford, dau/o Captain James Judson & Rebecca Wells - desc/o Rev Charles Chauncy J&K273; CHB69, 70; MCD192; BLG2612; BCD70; AMB349; AFA94; NEFGM(1)152

Nathaniel - of CT, b1721 d1798, m(1) Mary Stocking, m(2) Susannah Gilbert - desc/o Rev Charles Chauncy AMB349; BLG2612

Nathaniel - of CT, b1758 d1825, m1782 Abigail Olcot - desc/o Rev Charles Chauncey BLG2612

Nathaniel William - of CT, b1761 d1840 - desc/o Rev Charles Chauncy BLG2612

Rev Peter Bulkeley - desc/o Rev Charles Chauncy J&K275; CHB84; FLW71; MCB257; MCD192; BCD84; AMB348; NEFGM(1)152 - desc/o Catherine Eyre DBR(1)476

Sarah - of MA, bp 1631 Ware d1699 Wethersfield, CT, m1659 Concord, MA, Rev Gershom Bulkeley b1635/1636 Cambridge, MA d1713 Glastonbury, CT, son of Rev Peter Bulkeley - desc/o Rev Charles Chauncy J&K275; CHB84; FLW71; MCB257; MCD192;

CHAUNCY (cont.)

> BCD84; AMB348; NEFGM(1)152 - desc/o Catherine Eyre DBR(1)476

> Sarah - of MA, b1683 d1767, m1712 Rev Samuel Whittelsey - desc/o Rev Charles Chauncy CHB69; BCD69; AMB349; NEFGM(1)152

> Sarah - b1711, m Israel Burritt - desc/o Rev Charles Chauncy AMB349; NEFGM(1)152

> Sarah - b1745, m(1) Lemuel Guernsey, m(2) Simeon Parsons - desc/o Rev Charles Chauncy AMB349; NEFGM(1)153

> Sarah - b1765, m John Moore, shipmaster of Portsmouth, NH - desc/o Rev Charles Chauncy NE(11)150

> Worthington Gallup - of CT, b1772 d1814 - desc/o Rev Charles Chauncy BLG2612

CHEATHAM Benjamin - of VA, m1747 Grace Williams - desc/o Christopher Branch DBR(2)229

> Edward - of MD, b abt 1670, m Mary Drake - the immigrant RAA1, 80; sufficient proof of alleged royal ancestry is lacking

> Margaret - of VA, m1789 Poindexter Noell - desc/o Christopher Branch DBR(2)229

> Richard - of VA, m Grace Moore - desc/o Christopher Branch DBR(2)229

CHECKLEY Anthony - of MA - the immigrant EDV111, 112; CGA38; sufficient proof of alleged royal ancestry is lacking

CHESEBOROUGH Bridget - b1669 - desc/o Alice Freeman RAA132

> Margaret - of CT, bp 1677, m1696 Joseph Stanton - desc/o Bridget Tompson DBR(3)684

> Sarah - of CT, b1662 d1729, m Lieut William Gallup - desc/o Alice Freeman DBR(3)424; DBR(4)800; RAA132

CHESTER Leonard - of CT, d1648 - the immigrant EDV112; CGA38; sufficient proof of alleged royal ancestry is lacking

CHETHAM Hannah - of MD, b1703 d1729, m1726 Richard Grafton - desc/o Mary Drake DBR(3)722; DBR(4)48, 471

CHETWOODE or CHETWODE Grace - of CT, b1602 d1669 dau/o Sir Richard Chetwode & Dorothy Needham, m1635 Rev Peter Bulkeley b1582/1583 d1658/1659 founder & 1st minister of Concord, MA - the immigrant CHB392 FLW133; ECD138, 248; ECD(3)90; MCD182; MCS82; DBR(1)98; DBR(2)392, 758; DBR(3)312; GBR269

CHICHELEY (CHICHELE) Sir Henry - of VA 1649, d1682 deputy governor of VA, m Mrs Agatha (Eltonhead) Kellaway - the immigrant WAC78; GBR231; NE(25)182/185

CHICHESTER John - of VA, bp 1681 d1728, m Elizabeth Symes - desc/o Richard Chichester CHB518; MCD196; WAC77, 78

> Mary Symes - of VA, m Bernard Hooe Jr - desc/o Richard Chichester MCD196

> Richard - of VA 1702, bp 1657 d1734, m(1) Anna____ M(2)1719 Ann Chinn - the immigrant CHB518; MCD196; WAC77, 78; sufficient proof of alleged royal ancestry is lacking

> Richard - of VA, d1743, m1734 Ellen Ball - desc/o Richard Chichester CHB518; MCD196; WAC78; CGA38

> Col Richard - of VA, d1796, m(1)1759 Ann Gordon, m(2) Sarah McCarty - desc/o Richard Chichester CHB518; MCD196; WAC78

CHICHESTER (cont.)

Richard McCarty - of VA, b1769 d1817, m Ann Thomson - desc/o Richard Chichester CHB519; WAC78

CHILD Benjamin III - of MA, b1656 d1724, m1683 Grace Morris b1660 d1723 - desc/o Lieut Griffith Bowen DBR(1)466; DBR(4)781; RAA72

Capt Benjamin - of MA, b1685 d1771, m1712 Patience Thayer - desc/o Lieut Griffith Bowen DBR(4)781

Ephraim - b1683 - desc/o Lieut Griffith Bowen RAA72; CGA38

Ephraim - b1711 - desc/o Lieut Griffith Bowen RAA72

Grace - of MA, b1715/1716, m1737 Moses Lyon - desc/o Lieut Griffeth Bowen DBR(4)781

Increase - b1740 - desc/o Lieut Griffith Bowen RAA72

Mark Anthony - b1771 - desc/o Lieut Griffith Bowen RAA72

Mary - b1660 - desc/o Lieut Griffith Bowen RAA72

Mary - b1691 d1730/1732, m1715 Peter Walker b1689 d1760 - desc/o Lieut Griffith Bowen DBR(1)466

Mehitabel- b1669 - desc/o Lieut Griffith Bowen RAA72

CHILTON Capt John - of VA, b1739 d1777, m1768 Letitia Blackwell - desc/o William Ironmonger DBR(4)442

Joseph - of VA, b1774 d1841, m1795 Ann Smith - desc/o William Ironmonger DBR(4)442

Susan - of VA, b1771 d1843, m1792 Chilton Ransdell - desc/o William Ironmonger DBR(1)740; DBR(2)785; DBR(3)697; DBR(5)744

William - of VA, b1730 d1776, m1768 Sarah Orrick - desc/o William Ironmonger DBR(1)740; DBR(2)785; DBR(3)697; DBR(4)220; DBR(5)744, 806

William - of VA, b1773, m Sarah Powell - desc/o William Ironmonger DBR(4)220; DBR(5)806

CHIPMAN Elizabeth - of MA, b1756 d1823, m William Gray - desc/o Grace Kaye CHB360; MCD285

CHISMAN (CHEESMAN) Anne - of VA, b1755, m1777 William Howard - desc/o Col George Reade DBR(3)657

Diana - of VA, b1715 d1735, m James Goodwin d1757 Hanover Co, planter of York Co - desc/o Col George Reade APP174; GVFWM(1)777; HSF(2)195

Edmund - of VA, d1735, m Elizabeth Chapman b1709 d1782 - desc/o Col George Reade DBR(3)657; APP173; GVFWM(1)776

Edmund - of VA, d1784, m Mary Robinson b1759 d1781 dau/o Anthony & Frances Robinson - desc/o George Reade GVFWM(1)777

Elizabeth - of VA, b1681, m___Lucas - desc/o Col George Reade APP172

Ellinor - of VA, b1717 d1765, m John Shield b1719 - desc/o Col George Reade APP174; GVFWM(1)777; HSF(2)195

George - of VA, d1741/1742, m Mary___ - desc/o Col George Reade APP173; GVFWM(1)776

Henry - of VA, b1720 d1770, m Mary___ - desc/o Col George Reade APP174

Col John - of VA, b1682/1683 d1728/1729, colonel in the militia, m1708 Ellinor Hayward (Howard) b1690 d1767 dau/o Henry & Diana Hayward - desc/o Col George Reade APP174; GVFWM(1)777; HSF(2)194, 195

CHISMAN (CHEESMAN) (cont.)

John - of VA, b1713 d1735, m Frances____ - desc/o Col George Reade APP174; GVFWM(1)777; HSF(2)195

John of VA, d abt 1758, m Mary Phillipson dau/o Dr Robert Phillipson - desc/o Col George Reade GVFWM(1)776

John - of VA, m Elizabeth Doswell of Hanover Co - desc/o Col George Reade GVFWM(1)777

John - of VA, d1803, m Mary____, m(2) Elizabeth Cary dau/o Major Miles & Ann Cary - desc/o Col George Reade GVFWM(1)777

Mary - of VA, m____Athey, probably Edward Athey of James City Co - desc/o Col George Reade APP172

Mary - of VA, b1723 d1781, m1744 Harwood Jones d1771, justice of Warwick Co & captain of militia, son of Mathew & Martha Jones - desc/o Col George Reade APP174; GVFWM(1)777; HSF(2)195

Mildred - of VA, b1675/1676, m Col Lawrence Smith of York & Gloucester Co, d1738/1739 captain of the militia, justice, sheriff & a member of the House of Burgesses for York - desc/o Col George Reade APP173

Mount Edward - of VA, m____ & had issue - desc/o Col George Reade GVFWM(1)777

Capt Thomas - of VA, d1770, m(1) Elizabeth ____d1757, m(2) Diana Moss dau/o John Moss & Elizabeth Goodwin - desc/o Col George Reade DBR(3)657; GVFMW(1)776, 777

Thomas - of VA, d1722, captain of militia & held 600 acres in York Co, m Anne____ - desc/o Col George Reade DBR(3)657; APP173; GVFWM(1)776

CHRISTIAN Priscilla - of VA & KY, m1785 Col Alexander Scott Bullitt - desc/o Col John Henry CHB116; BCD116

CHRISTOPHERS Elizabeth - of CT, m Capt Joseph Hurlburt - desc/o Grace Kaye CHB206; BCD206

Lucretia - of CT, m John Mumford Jr - desc/o Grace Kaye CHB207; MCD284; BCD207; DBR(1)700; DBR(2)769; DBR(3)480; DBR(5)594, 938 - desc/o Muriel Gurdon DBR(3)482

Richard - of CT, m Lucretia Bradley - desc/o Grace Kaye CHB206; BCD206

Sarah - b1719 d1801, m1742 James Mumford - desc/o Grace Kaye DBR95)606

CHURCHILL Armistead - of VA - desc/o William Churchill WAC18

Elizabeth - of VA, b1710 d1779, m(1) Col William Bassett, m(2) William Dawson - desc/o William Churchill WAC18

Hannah - of VA, m Benjamin Robinson - desc/o Sarah Ludlow CHB182; BCD182

Harriet - dau/o Charles Churchill & Mary Gould, m(1) Sir Everard Fawkener, m(2) Thomas Pownall b1722 d1805 governor of Massachusetts - the immigrant GBR271

Priscilla - of VA, b1705, m(1) Robert Carter, m(2) John Lewis - desc/o William Churchill WAC18

William - of VA, b1649 d1710, m(1) Mary____, m(2)1703 Elizabeth Armistead - the immigrant WAC17, 18; CGA39; sufficient proof of alleged royal ancestry is lacking

CHUTE James - of MA 1635 - desc/o Lionel Chute Jr EDV46; CGA39
    Lionel Jr - of MA 1635 - the immigrant EDV46; CGA39; sufficient proof
    of alleged royal ancestry is lacking

CILLEY Maj Gen Joseph - of CT, b1734 d1799 officer in the Revolutionary
    War & president of the Society of the Cincinnati, m Sarah
    Longfellow - desc/o Capt Thomas Bradbury J&K165

CLAGETT Elizabeth - of MD, b1708/1709 d bef 1767, m1725 Col Thomas
    Prather II - desc/o Anne Lovelace JSW1634; DBR(2)663
    John - of MD, b1713 d1790, m1739 Sarah Magruder - desc/o Anne
    Lovelace DBR(2)217, 218
    Walter - of MD, b1763 d1803, m Martha Williams - desc/o Anne
    Lovelace DBR(2)218
    Wiseman - of NH, b1721 Bristol, England d1784 lawyer, king's
    attorney for & solicitor general of New Hampshire, son of Wiseman
    Clagett & Martha Clifton, m1659 Lettice Mitchell dau/o Dr Mitchell
    of Portsmouth - the immigrant DAB(4)111, 112; GBR117,
    NGSQ(62)207

CLAIBORNE Anne - of VA, b1748, m1768 Col Richard Cocke - desc/o
    Elizabeth Boteler CHB66; BCD66; AMB232; VHG41; CFA(6)153
    Anne Elizabeth - of VA, m Christopher Freeman - desc/o Elizabeth
    Boteler AFA254
    Col Augustine - of VA, b1721 Sweethall, King William Co d1787
    Windsor, Sussex, attorney & member of the House of Burgesses &
    state senate, m1744 Mary Herbert b1726 d1799 dau/o Buller
    Herbert of Prince George Co & Mary Stith - desc/o Elizabeth Boteler
    CHB65, 243; ECD(2)266; BLG2618; BCD65; AMB232; AFA182;
    APP191; VHG40; CFA(6)153 - desc/o Col/Gov John West
    BCD(2)243, 561; DBR(4)377, 777, 811; DBR(5)558, 872
    Augustine - of VA, b1747 d1796, m Martha Jones dau/o Frederick
    Jones of Dinwiddie - desc/o Elizabeth Boteler AMB232; VHG41;
    CFA(6)153
    Bathurst - of VA, b1774, m(1)___Batte, m(2) Mary Leigh Claiborne -
    desc/o Elizabeth Boteler AMB232; VHG41
    Bernard - of VA, m Martha Ravenscroft Poythress, wid/o Major William
    Poythress - desc/o Elizabeth Boteler AMB232; CFA(6)153
    Bernard - of VA, of Dinwiddie Co, m aft Sep 1738 Hannah
    (Ravenscroft) Poythress, wid/o Francis Poythress & dau/o Thomas
    & Elizabeth Ravenscroft - desc/o Elizabeth Boteler APP190; VHG40
    Buller - of VA, b1745 served in the Revolution as lieutenant, captain &
    subsequently brigadier major & aide-de-camp to General Lincoln,
    after the Revolution was a justice & sheriff of Dinwiddie Co, m Patsy
    Ruffin dau/o Edmund Ruffin of Sussex Co - desc/o Elizabeth
    Boteler AMB232; VHG41, 44; CFA(6)153
    Daniel - of VA, d1795, m Mary Maury - desc/o Col/Gov John West
    CHB242; BCD242 - desc/o Elizabeth Boteler APP190; VHG40
    Elizabeth - of VA, m Benjamin Holmes of King & Queen Co - desc/o
    Elizabeth Boteler APP191
    Elizabeth - of GA, b abt 1750, m(2)1777 David Douglas - desc/o
    Col/Gov John West DBR(4)261; DBR(5)840
    Elizabeth - of VA, b1761, m Thomas Peterson - desc/o Elizabeth
    Boteler AMB232; VHG41; CFA(6)154

CLAIBORNE (cont.)

Gen Ferdinand Leigh - of VA, bp 1772 d1815, m Mary Magdaline Hutchins dau/o Col Anthony Hutchins, a retired British officer who had settled on a large royal grant in what was west Florida - desc/o Col/Gov John West DBR(1)413; DBR(4)378, 777 - desc/o Elizabeth Boteler VHG41

Henry - of VA, m Mary Major - desc/o Elizabeth Boteler APP190

Herbert - of VA, b1746 of Chestnut Grove, New Kent Co, m(1) Mary Ruffin dau/o Robert Ruffin of Sweet Hall, m(2) Mary Burnet Browne dau/o William Burnet Browne & Judith Carter, m(3) Miss Scott - desc/o Elizabeth Boteler CHB66, 243; BCD66; AMB232; AFA182; VHG43; CFA(6)153 - desc/o Col/Gov John West BCD243

Jane - of VA, b abt 1638 d bef May 1671, m bef May 1661 Col Thomas Brereton d abt 1683 of Northumberland Co - desc/o Elizabeth Boteler BLG2618; AMB231; WAC96; FFF52; VHG38; CFA(6)152

John - of VA, b abt 1651 of St John Parish, King William Co, m____ - desc/o Elizabeth Boteler APP188

John - of VA, of St John's Parish King William Co 1704, m____ - desc/o Elizabeth Boteler APP191

John - of VA, of Dale Parish, Chesterfield Co 1765 - desc/o Elizabeth Boteler APP190

John Herbert - of VA, b1763 member of the Sussex volunteers in the Revolution at seventeen, m Mary Gregory dau/o Roger Gregory of Chesterfield, VA - desc/o Col/Gov John West DBR(2)561, 872 - desc/o Elizabeth Boteler AMB232; VHG41; CFA(6)154

Katherine - d1715 aged 34, m Capt John Campbell d1740/1741 - desc/o Elizabeth Boteler APP188; CFA(6)152

Leonard - of VA, d1694 colonel of militia of St Elizabeth's, Jamaica, m Martha ____ - desc/o Elizabeth Boteler CHB475; BLG2618; AMB231; WAC96; APP187, 188; CFA(6)152

Leonard - of VA, b abt 1708 d1785, justice of King William Co 1726 & 1729, sheriff 1732, m(1) Martha Brunell or Burnet b1701 d1720 aged 19 years 3 months & 2 days, dau/o Major Francis Burnell, m(2) Elizabeth Barber of York Co - desc/o Col/Gov John West DBR(1)136; DBR(2)206; DBR(3)363; DBR(4)261; DBR(5)840; AMB232 - desc/o Elizabeth Boteler BLG2618; DBR(4)225; APP190; VHG40; CFA(6)153

Leonard Jr - of VA & GA, d bef 1772 - desc/o Col/Gov John West DBR(4)261; DBR(5)840

Lucy - of VA, m1745 Samuel Duval - desc/o Elizabeth Boteler DBR(2)98; 100

Lucy Herbert - of VA, b1760 d aft 1823, m1776 Col John Cocke - desc/o Col/Gov John West ECD(2)266 - desc/o Elizabeth Boteler AMB232; VHG41; CFA(6)154

Martha - of VA, b aft Feb 1718/1719, m1739/1740 Patrick Napier d1733/1734 - desc/o Elizabeth Boteler APP191; VHG40

Mary - of VA, b abt 1630 d abt 1669, m(1) Edward Rice, m(2) Maj Robert Harris - the immigrant ECD(3)24, 27; DBR(3)718 - desc/o Elizabeth Boteler DBR(5)340; RAA71

Mary - of VA, b1744, m1763 Gen Charles Harrison - desc/o Elizabeth Boteler CHB66; BCD66; AMB232; CFA(6)153

CLAIBORNE (cont.)

Mary Ann - of VA, m John Butts - desc/o Hon Col John West CHB242; BCD242

Mary Cole - of VA, b1738 d1771, m Roger Gregory - desc/o Col/Gov John West DBR(2)372

Mary Gregory - of VA, m John Douglas Wilkins - desc/o Col/Gov John West DBR(5)872

Col Nathaniel - of VA, b1716 d1756 justice 1741 & sheriff 1750, m Jane Cole dau/o William Cole - desc/o Elizabeth Boteler CHB65; BLG2618; AMB232; APP191; VHG40; BCD65; CFA(6)153 - desc/o Col/Gov John West CHB242; BCD242; DBR(1)412; DBR(2)371

Nathaniel - of VA, bp 1775 d1859 member of House of Delegates 1810/1812 & in the Senate 1821/1825, from 1825 to 1837 was a member of Congress from VA, m Elizabeth Archer Benford of Goochland Co by whom he had eleven children - desc/o Elizabeth Boteler VHG42; CFA(6)153

Philadelphia - of VA, m Abner Waugh - desc/o Elizabeth Boteler CHB64, 245; MCD321; BCD64, 245

Philip Whitehead - of VA, m Elizabeth Dandridge - desc/o Elizabeth Boteler CHB64; BCD64

Richard - of VA, b1741 d1776, m Mary Glenn - desc/o Elizabeth Boteler DBR(4)225; BLG2618 - desc/o Col/Gov John West DBR(1)136; DBR(2)206; DBR(3)363

Richard - of VA, b1757 d1818 major Continental Army & member of the House of Delegates from Brunswick, m dau/o Phillip Jones - desc/o Elizabeth Boteler VHG41; AMB232; CFA(6)154 this source states he m Miss Hayward of South Carolina

Richard Henry - of VA, b1764 brigadier major Weedons Brigade, 1777; deputy quartermaster general 1780/1782, m Mary Cook - desc/o Elizabeth Boteler BLG2618; DBR(4)225 - desc/o Col/Gov John West DBR(1)136; DBR(2)206; DBR(3)363

Sarah - of VA, b1713 d1777, m Joseph Thompson b1703 justice 1644/1645, sheriff 1745/1746 & captain of militia of Albemarle Co 1745 d1765 - desc/o Elizabeth Boteler APP191; VHG40

Sarah - of VA, b1765, m Charles Anderson of VA - desc/o Elizabeth Boteler VHG41; AMB232; CFA(6)154

Susanna - of VA, b1751, m Frederick Jones of Dinwiddie - desc/o Gov/Col John West DBR(4)811; DBR(5)558 - desc/o Elizabeth Boteler VHG41; AMB232; VHG42; CFA(6)153

Lieut Col Thomas - of VA, b1647 d1683 killed by an arrow while leading an expedition against the Indians, served as lieutenant colonel of militia, m by 22 Aug 1681 Sarah Fenn d 18 Oct 1716 aged 56 years, 6 months & 27 days dau/o Samuel & Dorothy Fenn - desc/o Elizabeth Boteler CHB64; BLG2618; BCD64; AMB231; WAC96; AFA182, 254; DBR(4)225; APP187; VHG38, 39; CFA(6)152

Capt Thomas - of VA, b1680 of Sweet Hall, King William Co d1732, m(3) Anne Fox b1684 d1733 dau/o Henry Fox & Anne West, dau/o Colonel John West - desc/o Elizabeth Boteler CHB64; BLG2618; BCD64; AMB232; AFA182, 254; DBR(4)225; APP190; VHG39; CFA(6)152, 153

Thomas - of VA, b1704 d1734 clerk of Stafford Co - desc/o Elizabeth

CLAIBORNE (cont.)

Boteler BLG2618; AMB232; CFA(6)153

Thomas - of VA, b1749 sheriff of Brunswick, member of Congress 1793/1805, m____Scott dau/o____Scott a native of Nova Scotia - desc/o Elizabeth Boteler AMB232; CFA(6)153

Capt Thomas - of VA, mentioned in a patent 1723 as son of John Claiborne, dec'd - desc/o Elizabeth Boteler APP191

Ursula - of VA, m William Gough, son of John Gough, burgess from King & Queen Co 1699 - desc/o Elizabeth Boteler APP189; CFA(6)152

Capt William - of VA 1621, bp 1610 d bef 1680 secretary & treasurer of the VA Colony, and surveyor-colonel of the "Old Dominion." Grants of 25,000 acres of land are of record in his name in the VA land office, son of Thomas Clayborn (Clayborne) & Sarah (Smith) James of the parish of Crayford, Co Kent, England, m abt 1635 Elizabeth Boteler (Butler) b bef 1612 dau/o John & Jane (Elliott) Boteler of the parish of Roxwell, Co Essex, England - the immigrant CHB64, 475; MCD194; BLG2618; BCD(1)64; DBR(2)97, 118, 205, 206; DBR(3)164, 715; DBR(4)438, 439, 775; DBR(5)1023; AMB231; EDV63; WAC95, 96; AFA182, 254; CGA40; FFF52; APP184/191; GVFT(1)358/371; not of royal descent, his wife Elizabeth Boteler is of royal descent

William - of MD, b abt 1636 d bef 21 Mar 1677/1678 member of Governor Berkeley's court to try Bacon's followers & captain & lieut col of militia, m Katherine____ - desc/o Elizabeth Boteler APP186; CFA(6)152

Lieut Col William Jr - of VA, d1682, m Elizabeth Wilkes - desc/o Elizabeth Boteler CHB64; MCD194; BLG2618; BCD64; DBR(2)100; AMB231; WAC96

William - of VA, d1705, m Dorothy Dandridge - desc/o Elizabeth Boteler CHB64; MCD194; BCD64; VHG38

William - of VA, b1671 d1705/1706, justice & lieutenant colonel of militia on the formation of King William Co 1701/1702, m____ - desc/o Elizabeth Boteler APP188

William IV - of VA, under 16 in 1705, d1746 justice & sheriff of King William Co, m Elizabeth Whitehead dau/o Col Philip Whitehead of King William Co - desc/o Elizabeth Boteler CHB64; MCD194; BCD64; DBR(2)100; APP189; CFA(6)153

William - of VA, b1753 Sussex d1809 served as a private in the Sussex militia & father of several distinguished sons, m Mary Leigh bp 1739 dau/o John & Mary Leigh of Sussex - desc/o Elizabeth Boteler CHB64; BCD65; DBR(4)777; VHG41 - desc/o Col John West CHB242; BCD242; DBR(1)412

William - of VA, b1753, m____Ruffin dau/o Robert Ruffin - desc/o Elizabeth Boteler AMB232; CFA(6)153

Gov William Charles Cole - of MD, b1775 Sussex d1817 governor of Louisiana - desc/o Capt John West DBR(1)413 - desc/o Elizabeth Boteler VHG41

CLAIK Dr James - of VA 1730, b1730 d1814, m1760 Marianna Ewell - the immigrant CHB98; BCD98; sufficient proof of alleged royal ancestry is lacking

CLAIK (cont.)

Sarah - of VA, b1764, m1785 Daniel Jenifer Jr - desc/o Dr James Claik CHB98; BCD98

CLAPP Aaron - of MA, m1747 Jerima Bartlett - desc/o Margaret Wyatt BCD353

Achach - of MA, m1780 John Dewey - desc/o Margaret Wyatt BCD353

Asabel - of MA, b abt 1717 d1777, m Sarah Wright - desc/o Thomas Newberry ECD(3)224

Benjamin - of MA, b1738 d1815, m abt 1765 Phoebe Boynton - desc/o Thomas Newberry ECD(3)222; DBR(5)727

Lieut David - of MA, b1744 d1823, m1767 Hannah King - desc/o Richard Williams CHB378

Jonathan - of MA, b1713 d1782, m Submit Strong - desc/o Thomas Newberry ECD(3)222; DBR(5)727

Roger - of MA, b1684 d1762, m Elizabeth Bartlett - desc/o Thomas Newberry ECD(3)222, 224; DBR(5)727 - desc/o Margaret Wyatt BCD353

Sarah - of MA, b1743, m Solomon Weller - desc/o Thomas Newberry ECD(3)224

Wait - of CT, b1670 d1716, m1689 Lt John Taylor - desc/o Margaret Wyatt CHB541; DBR(3)126; RAA61 - desc/o Thomas Newberry RAA118

CLARK (CLARKE) Aaron - b1687 - desc/o Thomas Newberry RAA118

Aaron - b1758 - desc/o Elizabeth Alsop RAA65

Abigail - of RI, b1674 d1731, m Samuel Thurston - desc/o Capt Jeremy Clarke DBR(3)672; GRFRP(1)210

Ann - b1698 d1746, m Samuel Dunn - desc/o Anne Marbury ECD258

Ann - of RI, m William Wood - desc/o Capt Jeremy Clarke GRFRP(1)210

Anne - of MA, b1676 d1732, m abt 1703 William Greenman - desc/o Capt Jeremy Clarke ECD154; ECD(2)92; DBR(4)733; DBR(5)232

Anne - of RI, b1682, m1704 Thomas Hicks - desc/o Capt Jeremy Clarke DBR(3)674; DBR(4)817; GRFRP211

Audley - of RI, b abt 1728, m Sarah Weeden - desc/o Capt Jeremy Clarke NEFGM(2)589

Catharine - b1671 d1752, m(1) James Gould, m(2) Nathaniel Sheffield - desc/o Capt Jeremy Clarke GRFRP(1)208

Daniel - b1654 - desc/o Thomas Newberry RAA118

Daniel - of RI, m1743 Margaret Cranston - desc/o Capt Jeremy Clarke DBR(1)811

Deliverance - of RI, b1678 d Portsmouth, Rhode Island 1732, m1699 George Cornell d Newport 11 Apr 1752 son of Thomas Cornell - desc/o Capt Jeremy Clarke ECD253; GRFRP(1)208 - desc/o Katherine Marbury DBR(1)82

Elizabeth - of RI, m John Stanton - desc/o Capt Jeremy Clarke GRFRP(1)210

Esther - b1732/1733 - desc/o Richard Belding RAA68

Frances - of RI, b1638, m Randall Holden - desc/o Capt Jeremy Clarke GRFRP(1)205

Frances - b1673, m James Hart - desc/o Capt Jeremy Clarke GRFRP(1)208

CLARK (CLARKE) (cont.)

George - of NY, b1768 d1835, m(1)1793 Eliza Rochford, m(2)1844
Anne Carey -the immigrant MCB134; royal descent not proven

Hannah - of RI, b1667 d1732, m1691 Dr Thomas Rodman - desc/o
Capt Jeremy Clarke DBR(5)88, 91; GRFRP(1)208

Hannah - b1737 - desc/o Anne Marbury RAA114 Rev James of RI,
b1649 d1736, in 1701 was ordained pastor of the Second Baptist
Church of Newport & held this office until his death, m Hopestill
Power b1650 d1718 dau/o Nicholas & Jane Power of Providence,
Rhode Island - desc/o Capt Jeremy Clarke FLW15; MCS76;
DBR(4)75; NE(74)134; GRFRP(1)205, 211

Capt Jeremy (Jeremiah) - of RI, bp 1605 East Farleigh, Kent
d1651/1652 Newport, RI, governor of Rhode Island, son of William
Clerke & Mary Weston, m 1637 Frances Latham bp 1609/1610
d1677 dau/o Lewis Latham - the immigrant FLW173; ECD154,
253; ECD(2)89; MCS75, 76; DBR(1)811; DBR(2)223, 669, 672;
DBR(4)75, 271, 733, 814, 815; DBR(5)79, 85, 87, 230, 231, 232;
RAA1, 81; FFF132; GBR111, 248; NE(74)68/76, 130/140;
GRFRP(1)201/212; NEFGM(2)588, 589

Jeremiah Jr - of RI, b abt 1643 d1729 deputy governor of Rhode Island
1696/1705, m Anne Audley d1732 probably a dau/o John &
Margaret Audley of Boston, MA - desc/o Jeremy Clarke ECD154;
ECD(2)89, 92; DBR(1)811; DBR(4)75, 733; DBR(5)232; NE(74)134;
GRFRP(1)205; NEFGM(2)581

Jeremiah III - of RI, d1733, m Elizabeth Sisson - desc/o Jeremy Clarke
ECD(2)89

Jerusha - b1721 - desc/o Thomas Newberry RAA118

John - b1656 - desc/o Thomas Newberry RAA118

Joseph - b1694 - desc/o Anne Marbury RAA114

Latham - of RI, b1645 d1719, m(1) Hannah Wilbur dau/o Samuel &
Hannah (Porter) Wilbur, m(2)1698 Anne (Collins) Newberry b abt
1651 d1731/1732 wid/o Walter Newberry - desc/o Jeremy Clarke
DBR(3)672; DBR(4)75; NE(74)134; GRFRP(1)205, 210

Mary - of RI, b1641 d1711, m1658 John Cranston b1625 d1680,
physician & governor of Rhode Island 1678/1680, son of Rev
James Cranston (chaplain to King Charles I), m(2) Robert Stanton
(widower) b1645 d1713 son of Robert & Avis Stanton of Newport,
Mary had 10 children by her 1st husband & 1 by her second
husband - desc/o Capt Jeremy Clarke FLW183; MCS76; GBR248;
NE(74)134; GRFRP(1)205

Mary - b1661, m(1) Daniel Gould, m(2) Ralph Chapman Jr - desc/o
Capt Jeremy Clarke GRFRP(1)208

Mary - of RI, m James Hard b1669 - desc/o Capt Jeremy Clarke
GRFRP(1)211

Mary - of RI, m Joseph Fry - desc/o Capt Jeremy Clarke GRFRP(1)210

Mary - b1690 - desc/o Thomas Newberry RAA118

Mary - of RI, d1756, m Jeremiah Weeden - desc/o Capt Jeremy Clarke
NEFGM(2)589

Mehitabel - of CT, b1701 d1723, m1722 Thomas Downs b1699 d1785
- desc/o Nathaniel Browne TAG(22)164

Miers - of DE, b1761 d1810, m1785 Alletta Clowes b1767 d1832 -

CLARK (CLARKE) (cont.)

    desc/o Margery Maude DBR(1)47; DBR(3)91 - desc/o Thomas
    Fisher AFA56

    Patience - of RI, b1762 d1848, m1794 Gideon Vaughn b1774 d1869 -
    desc/o Capt Jeremy Clarke DBR(1)811

    Peleg - of RI, b1743 d1797, m Mary Gardiner dau/o William Gardiner -
    desc/o Jeremy Clarke NEFGM(2)589

    Rebecca - of MA, bp 1669 Marblehead, m1684 Marblehaed, John
    Sweatland & had issue seven children bapt at Marblehead
    1685/1704 - desc/o Mary Gye NE(96)239

    Samuel - of RI, b1699 of Portsmouth d1710, m1710 Hannah Wilcox
    dau/o Stephen Wilcox & Hannah Hazard - desc/o Capt Jeremy
    Clarke DBR(1)811; NEFGM(2)589

    Samuel - of RI, m Mary Coggeshall - desc/o Capt Jeremy Clarke
    GRFRP(1)210

    Samuel - b1707 - desc/o Richard Belding RAA68

    Samuel - b1724, m1746 Esther Tourtellot - desc/o Anne Marbury
    ECD258

    Sarah - of CT, b1651 bp 1663 d abt 1706, m(1) Sergt Isaac Pinner dsp
    1674, m(2) Caleb Carr b1624 d1695, widower, governor of Rhode
    Island in 1695 - desc/o Thomas Newberry ECD(3)226; RAA118 -
    desc/o Jeremy Clarke NE(74)134; GRFRP(1)206

    Sarah - of RI, b1698, m1721 Edward Greenman Jr - desc/o Jeremy
    Clarke ECD(2)89

    Judge Thomas - of NJ, b1737 d1809 a member of the Proprietors
    Council of West Jersey, m1758 Christian Vanneman b1741 d1809
    - desc/o Henry Willis DBR(3)315

    Gov Walter - of RI, b abt 1638 d1714, held high offices in the colony &
    was governor in 1676/1677, 1686, & 1695/1696-1698, m(1)1660
    Content Greenman b abt 1636 d1666 dau/o John Greenman,
    m(2)1667 Hannah Scott b abt 1642 d1681 dau/o Richard Scott &
    Catharine Marbury, m(3)1682/1683 Freeborn (Williams) Hart
    b1635 d1709 dau/o Roger & Mary Williams & wid/o Thomas Hart,
    m(4)1711 Sarah (Prior) Gould b1664 d1714 dau/o Matthew & Mary
    Prior & wid/o John Gould - desc/o Jeremy Clarke ECD253;
    DBR(4)75; DBR(5)87; NE(74)133, 134; GRFRP(1)205; FLW15

    Weston - of RI, b1648 d1728, held high offices in the colony, serving in
    various years as attorney general, general treasurer & general
    recorder, m(1)1668 Mary Easton b1648 d1690 dau/o Peter Easton
    & Ann Coggeshall, m(2)1691 Rebecca (Thurston) Easton b1662
    d1737 dau/o Edward & Elizabeth (Mott) Thurston & wid/o Peter
    Easton, Jr - desc/o Capt Jeremy Clarke MCS76; DBR(3)673;
    DBR(4)817; NE(74)134; GRFRP(1)205, 210

CLARKSON Ann Margaret - of NY, b1761 d1824, m1784 Gerrit Van
    Horne - desc/o Matthew Clarkson CFA(3)138

    Christiana - m Rev Isaac Stelle - desc/o Edward FitzRandolph
    DBR(2)679; DBR(3)486

    David - of NY, b1694 of New York City d1751, m1724 Ann Margaret
    Freeman b1706 d1759, dau/o Rev Bernardus Freeman - desc/o
    Matthew Clarkson EDV108, 108

    David - of NY, b1726 of New York City d1782, m1749 Elizabeth French

CLARKSON (cont.)

  b1724 d1808 - desc/o Matthew Clarkson CFA(3)138

 Gerardus - of NY, b abt 1737 d1790 studied medicine & was the first treasurer of the College of Physicians at Philadelphia; he was also trustee of the University of Pennsylvania & member of the Philadelphia Medical Society & American Philosophical Society, m1761 Mary Flower - desc/o Matthew Clarkson NYGBR(30)#2p77

 Levinus - of NY, b1765 d1845, m Ann Mary Van Horne - desc/o Matthew Clarkson CFA(3)138

 Matthew - of NY 1687, b abt 1665 England d1702 New York, provincial secretary of New York 1689/1702, son of David Clarkson & Elizabeth Kenrick, m1692 Katherine Van Schaick, dau/o Gerrit Van Schaick of Albany, New York - the immigrant EDV107, 108; CGA40; GBR227; NYGBR(11)#4 p156/158, (12)#1p16, 20, (21)#4p193, (30)#2p77; CFA(3)137

 Matthew Jr - of NY, d1739, m Cornelia Bancker de Peyster - desc/o Matthew Clarkson NYGBR(30)#2p77

 Matthew - of NY & PA, b1735 d1800, mayor of Philadelphia & had a daughter who married Robert Ralston, brother of Gerardus Clarkson - desc/o Matthew Clarkson NYGBR(21)#4p193, (30)#2p77

 Gen Matthew - of NY, b1758 d1825, m(1)1785 Mary Rutherford, dau/o Walter Rutherford, m(2)1792 Sarah Cornell d1803 - desc/o Matthew Clarkson CFA(3)138

 Thomas Streatfeld - of NY, b1763 d1844, m Elizabeth Van Horne b1771 d1852 - desc/o Matthew Clarkson CFA(3)138

 William - of NY & PA, b1763 d1812 graduated 1783 in medical dept of the University of Pennsylvania, founder and fellow of the College of Physicians, but in 1793 gave up that profession & became a Presbyterian minister, m Catharine Floyd dau/o General William Floyd, signer of the Declaration of Independence & Isabella Jones of Long Island - desc/o Matthew Clarkson NYGBR(30)#2p77

CLAY Henrietta - of VA, b1771, m1793 Maj George Michael Bedinger - desc/o Maj Henry Filmer EDC(2)134; DBR(5)355

 Dr Henry III - of VA, b1736 d1820, m1753 Rachel Povall b1739 d1820 - desc/o Maj Henry Filmer ECD(2)134, 136; DBR(1)67; DBR(2)86, 222, 338, 387; DBR(5)355; FFF7

 Mary - of VA, b1742 d1823, m1760 Stephen Lockett - desc/o Maj Henry Filmer DBR(3)322; DBR(4)185

 Mary Ann - of VA, b1770 d1845, m1789 Thomas Dawson - desc/o Maj Henry Filmer DBR(2)388

 Samuel - of VA, b1761 Revolutionary War Soldier, m Lucy Winn dau/o George Winn - desc/o Maj Henry Filmer DBR(1)67; DBR(2)87, 338

CLAYPOOLE Capt Abraham George - of PA, b1756 d1827, m(2)1795 Elizabeth Steele - desc/o James Claypoole CHB95; BCD95

 Edith - of PA, b1723 d1800, m(1)1744 David Chambers - desc/o James Claypoole CHB94; MCD200; BCD94

 Elizabeth - of VA, b abt 1739 d1805, m John Osborne - desc/o James Claypoole ECD(3)94; RAA81

 George - of PA, b1674 in London, England, m Mary___ d1702 - desc/o James Claypoole GPFHB177, 178

 George - of NJ, b1706 d1770, m(1) Hannah___ - desc/o James

CLAYPOOLE (cont.)

Claypoole CHB92; BCD92

George - of NJ, b1733, m1756 Mary Parkhouse - desc/o James Claypoole CHB92; BCD92

Helen - b1662 London, England d1691 Jamaica with two of her children, m ___Bethell - desc/o James Claypoole GPFHB1778

James - of PA 1683, b1634 d1687 son of John Claypoole & Mary Angell, m1657 in Bremen, Germany, Helen Merces (or Mercer) d1688 - the immigrant CHB92; ECD(3)94; MCB162; MCD200; BCD92, 354; RAA81; CGA40; GBR276; TAG(18) 202, 203; TAG(47) 204, 205; TAG(67) 97/107 states, "The descent claimed in different sources (those sources listed in article) from King Edward I has never been properly documented and, in its published versions, contains a number of errors." by Charles M Hansen, FASG Corrected pedigree listed; GBR276; GPFHB177/179

James - of DE, b1664 d abt 1706, m abt 1686 Mary Cann - desc/o James Claypoole ECD(3)94; RAA81; GPFHB177

James - of DE, b1701 d1789, m Jane___ - desc/o James Claypoole ECD(3)94; RAA81

James - of PA, b1720, m(1)1742 Rebecca White, m(2) Mary Chambers - desc/o James Claypoole CHB94, 95; BCD94

James - of PA, m Mary Hood - desc/o James Claypoole BCD354

James - of PA, m Mary Kemp - desc/o James Claypoole BCD354

John - of PA & DE, b1595, m Mary Angell - the immigrant RAA1, 81; sufficient proof of alleged royal ancestry is lacking

John - of PA, b1658 in London, England d1700 - desc/o John Claypoole RAA81; GPFHB177

Joseph - of PA & NJ, b1677 d1744, m(1)1703 in Charlestown, South Carolina, Rebecca Jennings d1715, m(2)1716 Edith Ward - desc/o James Claypoole CHB92; MCD200; BCD92, 94; GPFHB177, 178

Mary - of PA, b1660 in London, England, m1687 Francis Cooke - desc/o James Claypoole GPFHB177, 178

Mary - b abt 1688 - desc/o John Claypoole RAA81

Nathaniel - of PA, b1672 d172-, m Elizabeth___ - desc/o James Claypoole BCD354; GPFHB177

Norton - b abt 1641 - desc/o John Claypoole - desc/o John Claypoole RAA81

Priscilla - of PA, b1666 d1698, m___Crapp - desc/o James Claypoole GPFHB178

Rebecca - of PA, b1711 d1762, m1729 Henry Pratt - desc/o James Claypoole CHB93; BCD93

William M D - of NC, b1758 d1792, m1790 Mary Wright - desc/o James Claypoole CHB92; BCD92

CLAYTON Anne - of VA, m Harry Landon Davis - desc/o John Clayton JEB75

Arthur - of VA, m (his cousin) Jane Hatley Baylor - desc/o Anne Lovelace GVFHB(3)324

Arthur - of VA, d bef 1733 - desc/o John Clayton JEB75

Arthur W - of VA, m Eliza Longwood - desc/o John Clayton JEB75

Catherine - of VA, m Christopher Pryor - desc/o John Clayton JEB75

Courtney Baylor - of VA, m___Harris of Nelson Co, VA - desc/o Anne

CLAYTON (cont.)

Lovelace GVFHG(3)324

Elizabeth - of DE, m1730 Mark Manlove Jr - desc/o Joshua Clayton CRL(1)63

Elizabeth - of VA, m(1)1771 Orlando Jones, m(2)1793 William Walter - desc/o John Clayton JEB75

James - of VA, m Anne Dawson - desc/o John Clayton JEB75

James - of DE, d abt 1761, m Grace____ - desc/o Joshua Clayton CRL(1)64

James Lawson - of DE - desc/o Joshua Clayton CRL(1)63

Jasper - of VA, d1779 - desc/o John Clayton JEB75

John - of VA 1705, b1665 d1737, m Ann Page - the immigrant WAC32, 33; JEB74; CGA40; sufficient proof of alleged royal ancestry is lacking

John - of DE, b abt 1675 d1758/1759, m Grace____ - desc/o Joshua Clayton CRL(1)64

John - of VA, b1685 d1773, m1723 Elizabeth Whiting - desc/o John Clayton WAC32, 33; JEB75

John Jr - of DE - desc/o Joshua Clayton CRL(1)64

John - of NJ - desc/o William Clayton MCD202

John - of DE, b1749 d1802, m Mary Mason Manlove - desc/o Joshua Clayton CRL(1)64

Lieut John Whiting - of VA, d1826, m Elizabeth Willis - desc/o John Clayton JEB75

John Whiting Jr - of VA, m Mary____ - desc/o John Clayton JEB75

Joshua - of PA - the immigrant CRL(1)63, royal descent not proven

Joshua - of DE, b abt 1677 d1761 - desc/o Joshua Clayton CRL(1)63

Dr Joshua - of DE, b1744 d1798, m Mrs Rachel McCleary adopted dau of Richard Bassett - desc/o Joshua Clayton CRL(1)64

Leah - of NJ, m Abraham Brown Jr - desc/o William Clayton MCD202

Lucy Whiting - of VA, m(1) Nathaniel Manson, m(2) Henry Landon Davies - desc/o John Clayton JEB75

Lydia - of DE, m1720 John Cowgill - desc/o Joshua Clayton CRL(1)63

Lieut Philip - of VA, b abt 1745 d1786, m Anne Coleman - desc/o Dr Samuel Clayton JEB76

Samuel - of VA, bp 1688 d bef 1704, m Susannah____ - desc/o Dr Samuel Clayton JEB 75

Samuel - of VA, b abt 1720 d1735, m Elizabeth Pendleton - desc/o Dr Samuel Clayton JEB75

Samuel - of VA, b abt 1775, m Anne Coleman - desc/o Dr Samuel Clayton JEB76

Sarah - of DE, m Thomas Cowgill - desc/o Joshua Clayton CRL(1)63

Sarah - of VA, m(1)____Livingston, m(2) Henry Hughes - desc/o John Clayton JEB75

Dr Thomas - of VA, d1739, m1728 Isabella Lewis - the immigrant WAC32, 33; JEB75 sufficient proof of alleged royal ancestry is lacking

William - of PA 1682 - the immigrant MCD202; JEB58; TG(4)169/173 royal descent refuted

CLEMENT Capt Isaac - d1817, m Anne Denham - desc/o Edmund Jenings DBR(2)603

CLEVELAND Josiah II - of CT, b abt 1690 d abt 1762, m abt 1719 Abigail
Payne b abt 1686 d1762 - desc/o Olive Welby ECD135; DBR(2)107;
DBR(3)620; RAA93

Mary - of CT, b abt 1720 d abt 1765, m1743 William Bradford d1780 -
desc/o Olive Welby ECD135; DBR(2)107; DBR(3)620; RAA93

CLIFTON Dorothy - of MA, b1743 d1838, m1766 Savery Hathaway -
desc/o Joseph Bolles ECD(2)51

CLINTON Alexander - of NJ, b1732 d1758 a physician or surgeon &
apothecary in the College of NJ in 1750, m1757 Mary Kane (or
Keen) & left no children - desc/o Charles Clinton NYGBR(13)#1p10,
#3p139

Catharine - of NY, b1773, m(1)____Taylor, m(2) General Pierre Van
Cortlandt - desc/o Charles Clinton NYGBR(13)#4p179

Charles - of NY, b1690 Ireland d1773 employed as deputy surveyor by
the surveyor-general, commanded a regiment during the French
war in 1758, son of James Clinton & Elizabeth Smith, m in Ireland
Elizabeth Dennison b abt 1705 d1779 dau/o Alexander Dennison -
the immigrant GBR142; NYGBR(12)#4p195/198, (13)#1p5/10,
#3p139

Charles - of NY, b1767 d1829 studied law & was admitted to practice,
also became an excellent surveyor, in 1802 he was a member of the
legislature, m1790 Elizabeth Mulliner b1770 d1865 only dau/o
William Mulliner of Little Britain & Mary Denniston - desc/o
Charles Clinton NYGBR(13)#4p180

Christiana - of NY, dau/o James Clinton & Elizabeth Smith, m John
Beatty - the immigrant GBR143; NYGBR(12)#4p195/198

Cornelia Tappan - of NY, b1774, m Edmond C Genet, the French
Envoy - desc/o Charles Clinton NYGBR(13)#4p179

DeWitt - of NY, b1769 d1827 US senator & governor of New York -
desc/o Charles Clinton GBR143; NYGBR(13)#1p10

Sir George (the Admiral) - of NY, b abt 1686 d1761 governor of New
York, son of Francis, 6th Earl of Lincoln & Susan (Penniston)
Clinton, m Anne Carle - the immigrant EDV26; CGA40; GBR36;
NYGBR(13)#1p9

George - of NY, b1739 d1812 United States vice-president & governor
of New York, m1770 Cornelia Tappen b1744 d1800 only dau/o
Petrus Tappan - desc/o Charles Clinton GBR142;
NYGBR(13)#1p10, #4p179, 180

Gen James Clinton - of NY b1733 or 1736 d1812 Revolutionary
soldier, m(1) 1765 Mary DeWitt b1737 d1795 only dau/o Egbert
DeWitt & Mary Nottingham, m(2) Mary Little b1768 Ireland d1835
dau/o Graham Little - desc/o Charles Clinton GBR142;
NYGBR(13)#1p5/10, #4p173/180

Jesse Eaton - b1762 - desc/o Peter Bulkeley RAA75

Susan (also listed under Fiennes) - of MA 1634, m Gen John
Humphrey - the immigrant J&K246; CHB146, 416; FLW188;
MCB164; BCD146; sufficient proof of alleged royal ancestry is
lacking

CLOPTON Ann - of VA, b bef 1682, m Nicholas Mills - desc/o William
Clopton DBR(1)517; DBR(5)657; GVFWM(1)853, 856

Anne - of VA, b1720/1721, m William Divers - desc/o William Clopton

CLOPTON (cont.)
GVFWM(1)854, 856

Anne Lane - of VA, m Elisha Meredith of Hanover Co, VA - desc/o William Clopton GVFWM(1)857

Benjamin - of VA, m1755 Agnes Morgan dau/o Anthony Morgan - desc/o William Clopton GVFWM(1)857, 858

Cassandra - of VA, b1741 d1782, m1764 Josephus Perrin - desc/o Rev William Clopton DBR(1)797

Elizabeth - of VA, m(1) 1713 William Walker, m(2) Alexander Moss of New Kent & Cumberland Co, VA - desc/o William Clopton GVFWM(1)853, 856

John - of VA, d1816 captain of Virginia militia during the Revolution, m1784 Sarah Bacon dau/o Edmund Bacon of New Kent Co, VA - desc/o William Clopton GVFWM(1)858

Rev Reuben - of VA, b1757 d1795 established as a minister on a glebe in King William Co, m1784 Elizabeth Hales - desc/o William Clopton DBR(1)486; DBR(2)606; GVFWM(1)858

Robert - of VA, m(1)1711 Sarah Scott d1719, m(2) Mary____ - desc/o William Clopton GVFWM(1)853, 856

Robert - of VA, m Frances____ - desc/o William Clopton GVFWM(1)859

Sarah - of VA, m Robert Ellyson - desc/o William Clopton GVFWM(1)857

Thomasine - of MA, dau/o William Clopton & Margery Waldegrave, m (as his 2nd wife) John Winthrop b1587/1588 d1649, statesman, founder & governor of Massachusetts Bay Colony - the immigrant GBR222

Waldegrave - of VA, m Unity Alford b1724 dau/o John & Grace Alford - desc/o William Clopton GVFWM(1)857

Doctor Waldegrave - of VA, b1755 d1832, of Georgia - desc/o William Clopton GVFWM(1)857

Walter - of VA, m1711 Mary Jarratt dau/o Robert & Mary____ Jarrett - desc/o Rev William Clopton DBR(1)797; GVFWM(1)856

William - of VA, bp 1613 d1671, m Elizabeth Sutcliffe - the immigrant MCS4; DBR(1)485, 797; DBR(2)841; RAA1; CGA40; royal descent not proven

William - of VA, b1655 d bef 1733 constable of Hampton Parish in York Co, & clerk of St Peter's Church, New Kent Co, VA, son of William Clopton & Elizabeth Sutcliffe, m Mrs Ann Booth Dennett b1647 d1716 dau/o Robert Booth & wid/o Thomas Dennett - the immigrant DBR(1)517; DBR(2)606; DBR(5)657; RAA81; GBR222; GVFWM(1)856/865; NYGBR(71)#2p207, 208

William - of VA, b1714, m Cassandra____ - desc/o Rev William Clopton DBR(1)797; GVFWM(1)859

William - of VA, d bef 1733, m1718 Joyce Wilkinson dau/o George Wilkinson - desc/o William Clopton DBR(1)485; DBR(2)606; GVFWM(1)853, 854, 856

William - of VA, b1722 d1796, m1752 Elizabeth Darrell Ford - desc/o William Clopton DBR(1)485; DBR(2)606; GVFWM(1)854, 857

COBB Henry Willis - of NC - desc/o Col George Reade DBR(3)187

COCHRANE Alexander - of MA, son of John Cochrane of Glanderston & Isabella Ramsay, m Margaret Rae - the immigrant GBR86;

COCHRANE cont.)
    NE(56)192
COCKE Anne - of VA, b abt 1690 d1749, m1704/1706 Maj Robert Bolling
    Jr - desc/o Lieut Col Walter Aston CHB439, ECD(3)11; MCD159;
    DBR(5)257; GBR361; GVFHB(2)329
    Anne - of VA, m___Waddrup - desc/o Frances Mason CHB441
    Buller - of VA, m Elizabeth Barron - desc/o Capt William Claiborne
    CHB66; BCD66
    Elizabeth - of VA, m Lawrence Woodward - desc/o Lieut Col Walter
    Aston CHB439
    Elizabeth - of VA, m___Stewart - desc/o Frances Mason CHB440
    Elizabeth - of VA, m William Cole - desc/o Frances Mason CHB441
    Elizabeth - of VA, m John Peter - desc/o Frances Mason CHB441
    James - of VA, m___Poythress - desc/o Frances Mason CHB441
    John - of VA d1696, m Mary Davis - desc/o Lieut Col Walter Aston
    CHB438
    John - of VA, m Elizabeth Peter - desc/o Frances Mason CHB441
    Margaret - of VA, m Edward Wyatt - desc/o Frances Mason CHB441
    Martha - of VA, m1699 Joseph Pleasants - desc/o Lieut Col Walter
    Aston FFF271
    Martha - of VA, m(1) Arthur Moseley Jr of Henrico Co, m(2) Edward
    Friend of Henrico Co - desc/o Christopher Branch GVFWM(1)425
    Mary - of VA, b1690 d1754, m Obadiah Smith - desc/o Lieut Col
    Walter Aston CHB439; DBR(1)670; DBR(2)755, 849; DBR(3)508;
    DBR(5)1003 - desc/o Col Richard Cocke DBR(2)432
    Mary Flower - of VA, b1678 d1754, m Obediah Smith - desc/o Lieut
    Col Walter Aston DBR(2)146 - desc/o Col Richard Cocke DBR(2)324
    Obedience - of VA, m Benjamin Branch - desc/o Christopher Branch
    GVFWM(1)425
    Richard - of VA, b1600 d1665/1666 member of the House of
    Burgesses from Henrico 1644, 1654/1655 & commander of the
    county militia, son of John & Elizabeth Cocke of Wallfurlong,
    Stottesdon, Shropshire, England, m(1) Temperance Baley, m(2) abt
    1652 Mary Aston dau/o Lieut Col Walter Aston - the immigrant
    DBR(2)432; FFF270 - desc/o Lieut Col Walter Aston CHB439;
    MCD159; DBR(5)1020; GVFHB(2)405; APP87/95; the royal line
    came through Mary Aston wife of Richard Cocke
    Richard - of VA, b1639 d1706, m Elizabeth Cox - desc/o Lieut Col
    Walter Aston DBR(5)257; FFF227, 271
    Richard - of VA, m Elizabeth (Littleberry?) - desc/o Col Walter Aston
    GBR361; GVFHB(2)411
    Thomas - of VA - desc/o Frances Mason CHB441
    Thomas Everand - of VA - desc/o Frances Mason CHB441
    William (alias Cox) - of VA, d1712, m abt 1695 Sarah Perrin - desc/o
    Lieut Col Walter Aston CHB438
    William - of VA, b1655 d1693, m(1) abt 1678 Jane Clarke, m(2) abt
    1689 Sarah Jane Flower - desc/o Lieut Col Walter Aston CHB439;
    DBR(2)146, 324, 849; DBR(3)508; DBR(5)1003 - desc/o Col
    Richard Cocke DBR(2)432
    William - of VA, d1763, m Sarah Short - desc/o Frances Mason
    CHB440

COCKERCRAFT Elizabeth - m Nathaniel Hering - desc/o Rev John
Oxenbridge BCD166

CODD Mary Anne St Leger - of MD, d1787, m abt 1730 James Stout -
desc/o Col St Leger Codd JSW1720; DBR(4)64, 189, 196, 278;
DBR(5)307, 310, 714, 967

Sarah - m Thomas Pattison d1742/1743 - desc/o Sir Warham St Leger
APP529

Col St Leger - of VA by Apr 1670 & MD, b1635 d1707/1708, son of
William Codd & Mary St Leger, m(1) by 11 May 1670 Ann (Mottrom)
Wright Fox b1639 dau/o Col John Mottrom & wid/o Richard
Wright & David Fox, m(2) Anne (Bennett) Bland d Nov 1688, m(3)
Anne (Hynson) Randall Wickes, dau/o Thomas Hynson & wid/o
Benjamin Randall & Joseph Wickes - the immigrant JSW1720;
MCS38; DBR(4)64, 189, 195, 196, 276, 278; DBR(5)306, 310, 714,
967; RAA1, 82; WAC23, 24; GBR141 - desc/o Sir Warham St Leger
APP528

Capt St Leger - of MD, b1680 d1784 vestryman of St Paul Parish, Kent
Co, MD & captain of militia d bef 3 Apr 1730, m Mary Hanson
b1680 dau/o Col Hans Hanson - desc/o Col St Leger Codd
JSW1720; DBR(4)64, 189, 278; DBR(5)306, 307, 310, 714, 967;
WAC23, 24 - desc/o Sir Warham St Leger APP530

CODDINGTON Ann - b1721 - desc/o Anne Marbury RAA114

Anne - b1677 d1732, m1716 Reverend Samuel Niles b1674 d1762 son
of Nathaniel & Sarah (Sands) Niles - desc/o Katherine Hamby
NE(145)264

Edward - b1687 d probably at sea by 13 Jun 1727, m1724 Elizabeth
King b abt 1706 d1730, they had at least one child, Susanna -
desc/o Katherine Hamby NE(145)264

John - b1690 d1743, m1726 Elizabeth Rogers b abt 1705 d1745 -
desc/o Katherine Hamby NE(145)264

Nathaniel - b1691/1692 d aft 1738, m1719 Hope Brown b abt 1701 d
aft 23 Apr 1739 dau/o James & Ann (Clark) Brown - desc/o Anne
Marbury RAA114 - desc/o Katherine Hamby NE(145)264

William - b1680 d1755, m1700 Content Arnold b1681 d1721 dau/o
Benedick & Mary (Turner) Arnold, m(2)1722 Jane Bernon b1696
d1752 dau/o Gabriel & Esther (Le Roy) Bernon - desc/o Katherine
Hamby NE(145)264

William - of MA 1627/1628 - the immigrant EDV106; CGA40;
sufficient proof of alleged royal ancestry is lacking

CODRINGTON Simon - of VA - the immigrant APP205 until more definite
information becomes available, evidence that there are Virginia
descendants of Simon Codrington is inconclusive. GBR lists that
there was (very probably) a Robert Codrington of Barbados who was
the father of Henningham Codrington who m Paul Carrington their
son was George Carrington of VA that this family merits further
study.

COFFIN Daniel - of MA, b1700, m Lydia Moulton - desc/o Tristram Coffin
BLG2624

Daniel - of ME, b1737, m Mehitable Harmer - desc/o Tristram Coffin
BLG2624

Libni - b1745, m(1) Hepzibah Starbuck - desc/o Richard Sears LDS84

COFFIN (cont.)

Napthali - of ME, b1769 d1837, m Abigail Scribner - desc/o Tristram Coffin BLG2624

Stephen - of MA, b1664, m1685 Sarah Atkinson - desc/o Tristram Coffin BLG2624

Tristram - of MA 1642, b1605 d1681, m1630 Dionis Stephens - the immigrant EDV30; BLG2624; CGA40; sufficient proof of alleged royal ancestry is lacking

Tristram - of MA, b1632 d1705, m1653 Judith Greenleaf - desc/o Tristram Coffin BLG2624

William - b1771, m(2) Mary Duncan - desc/o Richard Sears LDS84 - desc/o Rose Stoughton RAA119

COGGESHALL Caleb - of RI, b1709 d1740, m1732 Mercy Mitchell - desc/o John Coggeshall BLG2625

Job - of RI, b1733 d abt 1780, m1756 Deborah Starbuck - desc/o John Coggeshall BLG2625

John - of RI 1632, b1601 d1647, m Mary___ - the immigrant EDV110; BLG2625; CGA41; sufficient proof of alleged royal ancestry is lacking

John - of RI, b1659 d1727, m Mary Stanton - desc/o John Coggeshall BLG2625

Joshua - of RI, b1626 d1688, m Joan West - desc/o John Coggeshall BLG2625

Josiah - b1752, m(1)1776 Mary Horswell - desc/o Jeremy Clarke DBR(3)672

Peter - of MA, b1766, m Pamela Starbuck - desc/o John Coggeshall BLG2625

COGHILL Frederick - of VA, b abt 1674 d aft 1708, m bef 1707 Sarah___ - desc/o James Coghill DBR(2)440, 682; BLG2625

Frederick - of VA, m Mary Hawes - desc/o James Coghill BLG2625

James - of VA 1644, b abt 1640 d1685, m(1) Alice___, m(2) Mary___ - the immigrant DBR(1)553; DBR(2)439, 440, 681, 682; RAA1, 82; BLG2625; sufficient proof of alleged royal ancestry is lacking

John - of VA 1664 - the immigrant EDV114; CGA41; sufficient proof of alleged royal ancestry is lacking

Lydia - b abt 1722 - desc/o James Coghill RAA82

Susannah - of VA, b bef 1715, m John Rucker - desc/o James Coghill DBR(2)440, 682

William - b abt 1666 - desc/o James Coghill RAA82

William - of VA, b1754 d1826, m Kezia Coleman - desc/o James Coghill BLG2625

COGSWELL Edward - of MA, b1686 d1773, m Hannah Brown - desc/o Samuel Symonds AFA16, 18, 20

Martha - of CT, d1804, m Capt Stephen Payne - desc/o Samuel Symonds AFA16, 18, 20

Nathaniel - of MA, b1714 d1810, m Huldah Kinney - desc/o Samuel Symonds AFA16, 18, 20

COIT Abigail - b abt 1716 - desc/o Alice Freeman RAA132

COKE John - of VA 1724, b1704 d1767 of Williamsburg, goldsmith, son of Richard Coke & Elizabeth Robie, m bef 1738 Sarah Hogg (Hoge) - the immigrant MCS71; WAC41, 42; GBR126; GVFWM(2)72/74

COKE (cont.)

John - of VA, b1762, m1797 Rebecca Lawson, wid/o Col James Shields - desc/o John Coke GVFWM(2)72/74

Judith - of VA, b1763 - desc/o John Coke GVFWM(2)73, 74

Richard - of VA, b1772, m1804 Lucy Henley d1810 - desc/o John Coke GVFWM(2)73, 74

Robie - of VA - desc/o John Coke WAC41

Samuel - of VA, d1773, m1760 Judith Brown b1746 dau/o Dr John Brown of Williamsburg, VA & Judith Armistead - desc/o John Coke WAC41; GVFWM(2)71/74

Sarah - of VA, b1765 - desc/o John Coke GVFWM(2)74

Susan - of VA, b1768 - desc/o John Coke GVFWM(2)74

COLBY Anthony - of MA, b abt 1580 d1660/1661, m1632 Susanna Haddon - the immigrant ECD(2)96; JSW1686; LDS47, 90, 94; DBR(4)757; DBR(5)684, 692, 768, 769; BLG2627; NGSQ(62)263, 264; TAG(15)65/75; NE(141)105/106, (141)105 no conclusive evidence has been found & Anthony Colby's parentage must still be considered unknown

Hannah - of MA, b bef 1674 d aft 1746, m William Osgood - desc/o Anthony Colby JSW1686

John - of MA, bp 1633 d1673, m1655/1656 Frances Hoyt - desc/o Anthony Colby JSW1686

Mary - b1647, m William Sargent - desc/o Anthony Colby LDS47, 90

Molly - b1761 d1831, m1780 Rev Joseph Quimby - desc/o Anthony Colby DBR(5)685, 769

Obadiah - of MA, m Elizabeth Gee - desc/o Anthony Colby BLG2627

Obadiah - of MA, m Mary Merrill - desc/o Anthony Colby BLG2627

Rebecca - of MA, b1643 d1672, m1661 John Williams Jr - desc/o Anthony Colby ECD(2)96; DBR(4)758; DBR(5)693

Samuel - of MA, m Elizabeth Sargent - desc/o Anthony Colby BLG2627

Samuel - of MA, m Dorothy____ - desc/o Anthony Colby BLG2627

Sarah - b1635 d1663, m1653 Orlando Bagley - desc/o Anthony Colby LDS94; DBR(5)684, 769

COLDEN Rev Alexander - of PA 1710 - the immigrant EDV47, 48; CGA41; sufficient proof of alleged royal ancestry is lacking

COLE Curtis - b1742 - desc/o Robert Abell RAA59

Dorothy - m Thomas Freeman - desc/o Constant Southworth DBR(3)245

Ebenezer - b1715 - desc/o Robert Abell RAA59

Hannah - of MA, b1668, m Thomas Place - desc/o Anne Marbury DBR(3)134; DBR(5)948

Hugh - b1706 - desc/o Robert Abell RAA59

Martha - of MA, b1709, m1728 Oliver Mason b1706 d1787 son of Isaac Mason - desc/o Robert Abell DBR(3)711

Martha - b 1734 - desc/o Robert Abell RAA59

Mary - b abt 1705 - desc/o Anne Marbury RAA114

Sisson - b1746 - desc/o Robert Abell RAA59

Susanna - b abt 1653 - desc/o Anne Marbury RAA114

Urania - of MA, b1746 d1828, m1763 James Rounds Jr - desc/o Richard Bowen Sr CHB465

COLE (cont.)
  William - b1671 - desc/o Anne Marbury RAA114
COLEMAN Ann - of VA, b abt 1739/1740 d1804, m Col William Green - desc/o Rev Hawte Wyatt DBR(1)615
  Ann - of VA, m Robert Scott - desc/o Rev Hawte Wyatt DBR(3)409
  Francis - of VA, b abt 1740 d1774 - desc/o Rev Hawte Wyatt DBR(3)409
  Mary Ligon - of VA, b1731 d aft 1769, m1750 Thomas Bedford Sr b1725/1730 d1785 - desc/o Capt Thomas Harris ECD(2)158 - desc/o Lieut Col Thomas Ligon ECD(2)172; DBR(1)304, 400; DBR(2)408, 518; DBR(4)660; DBR(5)922, 999
COLEPEPPER (CULPEPER) Anne - of VA, bp 1630 b1695, m abt 1653 in Virginia, Christopher Danby of Thorpe Perrow, Yorkshire - desc/o Sir Warham St Leger APP528
  Catherine - of VA, m Thomas Fairfax, 5th Baron Fairfax - desc/o Thomas Colepepper (Culpeper) GBR433
  Frances - of VA, bp 1634, m(1)1652 Samuel Stephens b abt 1629, governor of Georgia, son of Capt Richard Stephens, m(2) 1670 Sir William Berkeley b1608 d1677, governor of Virginia, son of Sir Maurice Berkeley & Elizabeth Killebrew, m(3)1680 Philip Ludwell d1717, Virginia councilor & governor of North Carolina & South Carolina - desc/o Katherine St Leger GBR140; APP525
  Thomas - of VA, m Katherine St Leger of Virginia - the immigrant GBR432 some aspect of royal descent merits further study
  Thomas 2nd Baron Colepepper (Culpeper) - of VA, b1635 d1689, governor of Virginia, m Margaret van Hesse - the immigrant GBR433 some aspect of royal descent merits further study
COLESWORTHY Samuel - of MA, m Mary Gibson - desc/o Richard Williams CHB377
COLLAMORE Anthony - of MA, b1640 son of John Collamore & Mary Nicholl, m Sarah Chittenden - the immigrant RAA1, 82; AAP144, 145; GBR444 some aspect of royal descent merits further study
  Elizabeth - m Timothy Symmes - desc/o Anthony Callamore AAP145; GBR444
  Martha - b1744 - desc/o Anthony Callamore RAA82
  Mary - b1667 - desc/o Anthony Callamore RAA82
  Peter - b1671 - desc/o Anthony Callamore RAA82; CGA41
  Thomas - b1709 - desc/o Anthony Callamore RAA82
COLLETON James - of SC, governor of South Carolina son of Sir John Colleton, Baronet & Katherine Amy, m Anne Kendall - the immigrant GBR345; NGS(59)254/262, (60)25/35 royal descent from Henry Fitz Roger
COLLIER Frances - b1735, m Capt James Scott - desc/o Capt Henry Isham DBR(1)40
  James - of VA, b1757 d1832, m(1)1788 Elizabeth Bouldin - desc/o Rev Hawte Wyatt DBR(1)300, 648
  John - b1707 d1749, m Elizabeth Meredith - desc/o Francis Ironmonger DBR(3)44
  Maj John - of VA & KY, b1742, m Hannah Cary - desc/o Francis Ironmonger DBR(3)44; DBR(4)131
  Nancy Elizabeth Wyatt - of VA, m Joshua Hill - desc/o Edward Wyatt

COLLIER (cont.)
>ECD(2)325; DBR(1)212; DBR(2)403

>Capt Nathaniel - of VA, d1814, m Sallie Williamson - desc/o Francis Ironmonger DBR(3)44

COLLINS Avis - of CT, b1714 d1754, m1734 Peter Buell b1710 d1784 - desc/o William Leete CHB371; DBR(1)482; DBR(2)596; DBR(3)583; DBR(5)213

>Cyprian - of CT, b1733, m1756 Azuba Gibbs - desc/o William Leete CHB371

>Capt Daniel - of CT, b1701, m Lois Cornwall - desc/o William Leete DBR(5)575

>Giles - of VA, d1710/1711, m Frances___ - desc/o Capt Henry Woodhouse APP701

>Henry - of VA, m Elizabeth Bennett - desc/o Capt Henry Woodhouse APP701

>Laura - of CT, b1759 d1826, m1759 Reuben Parmalee - desc/o William Leete DBR(5)575

>Mercy - of CT, b1707 d1786, m bef 1734 Samuel Hopson Jr - desc/o William Leete DBR(4)517

>Rev Timothy - of CT, b1699 d1777, m1723 Elizabeth Hyde - desc/o William Leete CHB371

>Triphenia - of CT, b1757, m1778 Abraham Wadhams - desc/o William Leete CHB371

>William - of CT, b1728, m Ruth Cook - desc/o William Leete DBR(5)575

COLT Sylvia Easton - of MA, m Brig Gen Charles Larned - desc/o Gov Thomas Dudley AFA114

COLTON Aaron - b1744 - desc/o Amy Wyllys RAA126

>Benjamin - b1722 - desc/o Amy Wyllys RAA126

>Eli - b1750 - desc/o Amy Wyllys RAA126

>Gideon - b1728 - desc/o Amy Wyllys RAA126

>Sarah - b1757 - desc/o Amy Wyllys RAA126

COMSTOCK Rev Adam - of RI, b1740 d1819, m1763 Margaret McGregor - desc/o Thomas Arnold CHB324, 325; BCD324, 325

>Benjamin - of RI, b1747 d1828, m1776 Mary Winsor - desc/o Thomas Arnold CHB322; BCD322

>Benjamin - of CT, b1755 d1842, m(1) Lucinda Rice, m(2) Mehitable Cressey - desc/o John Drake DBR(1)162

>Betsey - m Daniel Butler - desc/o Elizabeth Marshall GBR264 - desc/o Thomas Lewis GBR465

>Gideon - of RI, father of Amey Comstock - desc/o Thomas Arnold J&K296

>Hazadiah - of RI - desc/o Thomas Arnold J&K296

>John - of RI, b1693 d1750, m Esther Jenks - desc/o Thomas Arnold CHB322; BCD322

>Ruth - of RI, b1763 d1800, m1787 Rev Nicholas Van Vranken - desc/o Thomas Arnold CHB325; BCD325

>Samuel - of RI, d1765, m1738 Anna Brown - desc/o Thomas Arnold CHB322; BCD322

CONEY Samuel - of MA, b1718 d1803, m1742 Rebecca Guild - desc/o Mary Gye ECD(3)177

CONEY (cont.)

Susanna - of MA, b1755 d1844, m1778 John Church - desc/o Mary Gye ECD(3)177/8

CONGDON Frances - b1703, m Stephen Gardiner - desc/o Frances Dungan LDS11

CONSTABLE George - of CT, bp 1635 - the immigrant MCS54; sufficient proof of alleged royal ancestry is lacking

CONTEE Jane - of MD, m John Hanson - desc/o Rev Robert Brooke CHB402; MCD168

CONWAY Agatha - of VA, m1737 Captain Cuthbert Spann, vestryman of St Stephen's Parish, Northumberland Co, 1742 & Burgess 1748 son of Richard Spann of Northumberland Co, VA - desc/o Martha Eltonhead CRL(1)264; GVFWM(2)91; VG243

Agatha - of VA, b1740 d1826 Stafford Co, m1757 Isaac Eustace son of William Eustace & Ann Lee - desc/o Martha Eltonhead CRL(1)264; GVFWM(2)92; VG247, 261

Agatha - of VA, b1746, m1765 Col Jesse Ball - desc/o Col Richard Lee DBR(2)252; DBR(3)397; DBR(4)167; VG246

Anne - of VA, m1729 Robert Edmonds - desc/o Martha Eltonhead CRL(1)264; GVFWM(2)91; VG243

Anne - of VA, b1750, m abt 1770 John Moncure - desc/o Martha Eltonhead CRL(1)264; VG247

Catlett - of VA, b1751 of Hawfield, Orange Co d1827 for many years a Justice in Orange Co & said that he was Captain of Cavalry in the Revolutionary War, but no record of such exists, m abt 1775 Susannah Fitzhugh b1756 d1819 dau/o John Fitzhugh of Belle Air - desc/o Martha Eltonhead VG254, 264; CFA(5)139

Edwin - of VA abt 1640, b abt 1610 Worcestershire, England d1675 Lancaster, VA was the third clerk of Northampton Co, VA, m(1)1640 (?) Martha Eltonhead dau/o Richard Eltonhead, m(2)____ - the immigrant RAA1, 82; CGA42; GVFWM(2)90; sufficient proof of alleged royal ancestry is lacking, royal ancestry is through his wife Martha Eltonhead VG223; CFA(5)136

Edwin Jr - of VA, b abt 1640/1644 d1698 son of Edwin Conway & Martha Eltonhead, m(1) abt 1675/1680 Sarah Walker dau/o Lieut Col John Walker of Gloucester Co, VA & Sarah wid/o Col Henry Fleet, m(2) abt 1695 Elizabeth Thornton or Thompson - desc/o Martha Eltonhead AAP142, 143; WAC68, 69; CRL(1)263, 264; GVFWM(2)89; GBR348; VG229, 231 this source lists Sarah as the dau/o Lieut Col Henry Fleete; CFA(5)136; CFA(5)136

Edwin - of VA, b1681 in Lancaster Co d1763 Lieut Col of Militia & burgess, also vestryman, m(1)1704 Anne Ball dau/o Col Joseph Ball & Elizabeth Romney, m(2) Ann Hack b1697 d1747 probably dau/o Dr George Hack & Anna Herman - desc/o Martha Eltonhead CRL(1)264; CGA42; GVFWM(2)90; VG234, 238; CFA(5)136

Edwin - of VA, b1742, m abt 1765 Sarah Conway McAdam dau/o Dr Joseph McAdam & Sarah Ann Gaskins - desc/o Martha Eltonhead GVFWM(2)92; VG261

Eleanor Rose (Nelly) - of VA, b1731 Caroline Co d1829 at Montpellier, Orange Co, m1749 Col James Madison b1723 d1801 son of Ambrose Madison & Frances Taylor - desc/o Martha Eltonhead

CONWAY (cont.)

AAP142, 143; GBR348; VG245; CFA(5)137 - desc/o Anthony Savage GBR253

Elizabeth - of VA, m1724 Christopher Garlington of Northumberland Co - desc/o Martha Eltonhead CRL(1)264; GVFWM(2)91; VG243

Elizabeth - of VA, b1724, m James Taylor - desc/o Martha Eltonhead VG244; CFA(5)137

Eltonhead - of VA, b1646, m(1) abt 1662 Henry Thacker, vestryman of Middlesex Parish, VA 1664/1700, sheriff of Middlesex 1672, son of Richard Thacker, vestryman of Middlesex Parish 1664/1700, m(2) William Stanard - desc/o Martha Eltonhead RAA82; GVFWM(2)90; VG229, 235; CFA(5)136

Francis - of VA, b1697 at Richmond Co, m1718/1720 Rebecca Catlett d1760 dau/o Col John Catlett & Elizabeth Gaines of Essex Co, VA - desc/o Martha Eltonhead AAP142, 143; GBR348; GVFWM(2)90; VG244; CFA(5)137 - desc/o Anthony Savage GBR253

Francis - of VA, b1722 Richmond Co d1761, m1744/1745 Sarah Taliaferro b1727 d1784 dau/o Colonel John Taliaferro & Sarah Smith of Williamsburg - desc/o Martha Eltonhead VG244, 254; CFA(5)138

Francis - of VA, of Port Conway, King George b1748/1749 d1794, Captain Conway was a member of the King George Committee of Safety 1774/1776, served for three years in the Continental Line 1775/1778, m1770 Elizabeth Fitzhugh b1754 Belle Air, VA, 5th child of John Fitzhugh & Alice Thornton - desc/o Martha Eltonhead VG254, 263; CFA(5)138

Francis - of VA, m Mary Slaughter, dau/o Capt Philip Slaughter - desc/o Martha Eltonhead CFA(5)139

Francis Fitzhugh - of VA, b1772 d1803 in Fredricksburg, killed in a duel with William Thornton, who also fell mortally wounded both being in love with the innocent cause of the duel Lucie H. Macon, the niece of President Madison - desc/o Martha Eltonhead VG264; CFA(5)138

George - of VA, b abt 1710/1715 d1754, m1739 Anne Heath b1721 dau/o Samuel Heath - desc/o Martha Eltonhead CRL(1)264; GVFWM(2)91; VG243, 246, 247

George - of VA, b1744 Lancaster Co d bef 1792, m abt 1770 Ann Downman b1748 dau/o Travers Downman & Grace Ball - desc/o Martha Eltonhead VG247, 262

Hannah - of VA, b1724, m1746 Tunstall Hack - desc/o Martha Eltonhead CRL(1)264; GVFWM(2)91

Mary - of VA, b1686 d1730, m(1)1703 John Daingerfield, m(2)1707 Major James Ball - desc/o Martha Eltonhead GVFWM(2)90; VG234; CFA(5)136

Mary - of VA, m Thomas Gaskins d1737 - desc/o Martha Eltonhead GVFWM(2)91

Milicent - of VA, b1727 d1747/1748, m1742 Colonel James Gordon of Lancaster Co b1714 Newry, Ireland d1768 Lancaster Co - desc/o Martha Eltonhead GVFWM(2)91; VG243

Peter - of VA, of Lancaster Co d1753 Justice of Lancaster Co 1742; licensed to keep an ordinary or public house 1743; Burgess for

CONWAY (cont.)

Lancaster Co 1748 & 1752, m(1) Elizabeth (Betty) Spann dau/o Richard Spann of Northumberland Co, m(2) Elizabeth (Betty) Lee dau/o Richard Lee of Northumberland Co - desc/o Martha Eltonhead GVFWM(2)91; VG243

Peter - of VA, m Fanny____ - desc/o Martha Eltonhead VG246

Sarah - of VA, b1728, m Dr Charles Taylor - desc/o Martha Eltonhead CFA(5)137

Sarah Anne - of VA, b1767 d1783, m1783 Col James Ewell - desc/o Martha Eltonhead GVFWM(2)92; VG262

Walker - of VA, b abt 1748 d abt 1786 drowned in the Potomac River near Dipple Parish, m1775 Anne Moncure b1748 dau/o Reverend John Moncure & Frances Brown - desc/o Martha Eltonhead CRL(1)264; VG247, 262

CONYERS (CONVERSE) Abigail - of MA, b1744, m1764 Joseph Green - desc/o Edward Conyers AMB108

David - of MA, b1746 d1829, m1770 Rachel Elliott - desc/o Edward Conyers AMB108

Dorcas - of MA, b1703, m1723 Daniel Whitmore - desc/o Edward Conyers AMB108

Edward - of MA 1630, b1590 d1663, m(1) Jane Clarke, m Sarah____ - the immigrant ECD(3)97; MCB162; AMB107; sufficient proof of alleged royal ancestry is lacking

Ensign Edward - of MA, b1696 d1784, m1717 Elizabeth Cooper - desc/o Edward Conyers ECD(3)97; AMB108

Capt Edward - of CT, bp 1720 d1800, m Mary Davis - desc/o Edward Conyers ECD(3)97

Elisha - of MA, b abt 1774 d abt 1852, m Lucy Curtis - desc/o Edward Conyers ECD(3)98

James - of MA, b abt 1620 d1715, m(1)1643 Anna Long, m(2) Anna Sparhawke - desc/o Edward Conyers AMB107

Joel - of CT, b1750, m(1)1778 Demaris Wilson - desc/o Edward Conyers AMB108

Josiah - of MA, b abt 1618, m1651 Esther Champney - desc/o Edward Conyers AMB107

Josiah - of CT, bp 1714, m1737 Mary Sabin - desc/o Edward Conyers AMB108

Martha - of MA, bp 1727, m1756 Diah Johnson - desc/o Edward Conyers AMB108

Mary - of MA, b abt 1622 d1663, m(1)1643 Simon Thompson, m(2)1659 John Sheldon - desc/o Edward Conyers AMB107

Pain - of MA, b1706 d1781, m Mary Halford - desc/o Edward Conyers AMB108

Sergt Samuel - of MA, bp 1637/1638 d1669, m1660 Judith Carter - desc/o Edward Conyers ECD(3)97; AMB107

Samuel - of MA, b1662 d abt 1732, m1694 Dorcas Cain (Pain) - desc/o Edward Conyers ECD(3)97; AMB108

Samuel - of MA, b1694, m(1)1716 Hannah Bartlett, m(2) Sarah Atwell - desc/o Edward Conyers AMB108

Samuel - of CT, b1740, m1767 Mereba Burrill - desc/o Edward Conyers AMB108

CONYERS (CONVERSE) (cont.)

Samuel Davis - of MA, bp 1742 d abt 1831, m Mahitabale Harris - desc/o Edward Conyers ECD(3)97

Thomas - of MA, b1699, m(1)1723 Martha Clough - desc/o Edward Conyers AMB108

Thomas - of CT, bp 1738 d1809, m(1)1762 Mary Morse, m(2) Abigail Colton, m(3) Sabarina Smedley, m(4) Mary Colton - desc/o Edward Conyers AMB108

COOK Aaron - of CT, bp 1640/1641 d1716, m1661 Sarah Westwood dau/o William Westwood - desc/o Margaret Wyatt DBR(1)199; TAG(11)179

Aaron II - of CT, m1715 Hannah Wadesworth - desc/o Margaret Wyatt DBR(1)199

Ebeneezer Jr - of CT, bp 1746 d1813, m abt 1770 Mary West - desc/o Mary Wentworth ECD(2)291

Hannah - of CT, bp 1718/1719 d1812, m Major Abijah Catlin - desc/o Margaret Wyatt DBR(1)199

Rebecca - b abt 1721/1724 - desc/o Edward Southworth RAA131

William Walker - of MA, b1773 d1830, m 1795 Rexy Whittlesey - desc/o Mary Wentworth ECD(2)291

COOKE Catherine - of MD, b1774 d1849, m1793 Jonas Clapham b1763 d1837 - desc/o Richard Tilghman MG(2)456

Elizabeth - of VA, d1748, m abt 1689 Richard Buckner - desc/o William Ironmonger DBR(1)739; DBR(2)784; DBR(3)697; DBR(4)219, 220, 442; DBR(5)744

Jemima - of VA, b1707 d1796, m1723 Thomas Chilton - desc/o William Ironmonger DBR(1)740; DBR(2)784, 785; DBR(3)697; DBR(4)220, 442; DBR(5)744

Mary - of VA, b1680 d1723, m abt 1701 Thomas Booth - desc/o William Ironmonger DBR(1)643; DBR(5)889

Mordecai - of VA, b abt 1708 d1751, m Elizabeth Whiting b1713 d1762 - desc/o Col William Bernard APP119, 120 - desc/o Anne Lovelace GVFHB(3)320

Richard - of MD, b1772, took the name of Tilghman in compliance with the will of his uncle Richard Tilghman, m(1) Elizabeth Van Wyck of Baltimore, m(2) (her sister) Frances Van Wyck - desc/o Richard Tilghman MG(2)456

Susannah - of VA, b1693 d1749, m1718 Henry FitzHugh - desc/o William Ironmonger ECD(2)162; DBR(3)46, 698, 702; DBR(5)585, 586

William - of MD, b1776, m Elizabeth Tilghman dau/o Edward Tilghman of Philadelphia - desc/o Richard Tilghman MG(2)456

COOLEY Mary - b1724 - desc/o Thomas Newberry RAA118

Triphosa - of CT, d1841, m1784 Samuel Thrall Jr - desc/o William Leete DBR(4)752

COOLIDGE John - of MA, b1604 d1691, m Mary Maddock - the immigrant EDV54; BLG2631; CGA43; sufficient proof of alleged royal ancestry is lacking

John - b1690, m Hannah Ingram - desc/o John Coolidge BLG2631

Capt John - of MA, b abt 1756 probably at Bolton d1822 Plymouth, served in the Revolutionary War & was the anc/o President (John)

COOLIDGE (cont.)

Calvin Coolidge, 30th United States President, m1779 Lancaster,
Hannah Priest dau/o James Priest & Hannah Lawrence of
Marlborough - desc/o William Goddard NE(77)295

Jonathan - b1647 d1724, m Martha Rice - desc/o John Coolidge
BLG2631

Joseph - b1719 d1771, m Marguerite Olivier - desc/o John Coolidge
BLG2631

Joseph - b1747 d1820, m Elizabeth Boyer - desc/o John Coolidge
BLG2631

Joseph - b1773 d1840, m Elizabeth Bulfinch - desc/o John Coolidge
BLG2631

Josiah - of MA, b1718 Watertown d Lancaster, m Mary Jones - desc/o
William Goddard AAP152; GBR219; NE(77)292, 293

Josiah - of MA, m1772 Bolton, Molly Houghton - desc/o William
Goddard NE(77)293

Lydia - of MA, bp 1725/1726 Watertown, m1745 Westborough, Joseph
Bartlett of Rutland - desc/o William Goddard NE(77)286

Mary - b1680 d1702, m1697 Daniel Livermoore - desc/o Dr Richard
Palgrave DBR(5)762

Mary - of MA, m1762 Bolton, Amos Fuller & had issue 5 children b
Bolton prior to 1775 - desc/o William Goddard NE(77)298

Obadiah - of MA, d1767 (probably), m1750 Roxbury, Sarah Davis &
had issue 8 children under the age of 14 at their father's death in
1767 - desc/o William Goddard NE(77)286

Obadiah - living in Saltash (Plymouth), VT in 1790 with his family,
consisting of one male over 16 years of age (himself), one male
under 16, & two females (United States Census of 1790, VT) -
desc/o William Goddard NE(77)293

Rachel - of MA, b abt 1731 d1766 Northborough, m Seth Rice of
Northborough - desc/o William Goddard NE(77)286

COOPER Matilda - b1762, m1784 Aaron Whipple - desc/o Dr Richard
Palgrave DBR(5)762

COOTE Letitia - m Robert Molesworth, 1st Viscount Molesworth - desc/o
Richard Coote GBR207

Richard, 1st Earl of Bellomont, of NY, MA & NH, b1636 d1701,
governor of New York, MA & NH son of Richard Coote, 1st Baron
Coote of Colony & Mary St George, m Catherine Nanfan - the
immigrant and ancestor of Olivia (Mary) de Havilland (actress) &
Joan de Beauvoir de Havilland, known as Joan Fontaine (actress)
GBR207; NYGBR(48)#3p319/320

COPE Sir Anthony - of VA, son of Sir Anthony Cope, subscribed for stock
in the Virginia Company and he & his brother, Sir Walter Cope were
active in promoting foreign commerce for England and in
establishing colonies in America - the immigrant APP210/211;
proof of royal ancestry is lacking

Caleb - of PA, b1736 d1824, m1760 Mary Mendenhall - desc/o Oliver
Cope AMB52; BLG2632

Caleb - b1770 d1834, m1796 Amy Dixon - desc/o Oliver Cope
DBR(1)159; DBR(2)240

Hannah - of PA, b1724 d1817, m1746 John Carter b1723 d1770 son

COPE (cont.)

of George Carter & Elizabeth (Hull) Carter - desc/o Oliver Cope DBR(1)516; DBR(2)659

Hannah - m Simon Cranston - desc/o Oliver Cope BLG2632

Israel - b1770 d1855, m Margaret Cooper - desc/o Oliver Cope AMB52; BLG2632

Jasper - of PA, b1775, m Rebecca Shoemaker - desc/o Oliver Cope AMB52; BLG2632

John - of PA, b1691 d bef 1773, m1721 Charity Jefferies b1695 d1747 a widow - desc/o Oliver Cope DBR(1)158, 516; DBR(2)240; DBR(3)174, 184; AMB52; RAA83; BLG2632

John - of PA, b1763, m Mary De Graff - desc/o Oliver Cope AMB52; BLG2632

John - of PA, b1730 d1812, m(1) Grace Cloud, m(2)1760 Mary Dickinson - desc/o Oliver Cope DBR(1)158; DBR(2)240; DBR(3)174, 184; AMB52

Joseph - b1739, m Ann Taylor - desc/o Oliver Cope AMB52

Joshua - of PA & VA, b1736 (twin to Caleb), m Jane Brown - desc/o Oliver Cope AMB52

Nathan - b1733, m Amy Bane - desc/o Oliver Cope AMB52; RAA83

Oliver - of PA 1683, b1647 d1697 son of John Cope & Elizabeth____, m Rebecca____ - the immigrant DBR(1)158, 516; DBR(2)240, 658, 659; DBR(3)174, 184; AMB52; RAA1, 83; BLG2632; CGA43; GBR325

Samuel - b1726, m Deborah Parke - desc/o Oliver Cope AMB52

Samuel - b1762 d1854, m1797 Sarah Willits - desc/o Oliver Cope DBR(3)184

Sarah - b1759, m James Miller - desc/o Oliver Cope RAA83; BLG2632

Thomas Pim - of PA, b1768 d1854, m(1) Mary Drinker, m(2) Elizabeth Stokes - desc/o Oliver Cope AMB53; BLG2632

William - of PA, b1687 - desc/o Oliver Cope AMB52

William - of PA, b1766, m Elizabeth Rohrer - desc/o Oliver Cope AMB52; BLG2632

COPLEY Lionel - of MD, d1693 governor of MD, son of Lionel Copley & Frisalina Warde, m Anne Boteler - the immigrant GBR280

Thomas - of MD, b1595 d abt 1652 Jesuit missionary, son of William Copley & Magdalen Prideaux, unmarried - the immigrant GBR240

COPPOCK Sarah - b1712 - desc/o Jane Vaughn RAA120

CORBETT Hannah Margaret - of SC, b1775, m Jacob Emilius Irving of Ironshore, Jamaica - desc/o John Harleston SCG(2)289

Thomas - of SC, b1770, m Eliza Harleston - desc/o John Harleston SCG(2)289

CORBIN Alice - of VA, b1660, m1679 Philip Lightfoot of Teddington, Sandy Point, Charles City Co d1708 son of John Lightfoot, Esq & Elizabeth Philips of Grays Inn, Middlesex Co - desc/o Henry Corbin GVFHB(2)323; CFSSA173

Alice - of VA, b1722, m Benjamin Needler(s)? d bef Apr 1741 son of Culverwell Needler - desc/o Henry Corbin GVFHB(2)327; CFSSA174

Ann - of VA, b1664 d1694, m1685 Col William Tayloe d1710 of Mt. Airy, Richmond Co, member of the House of Burgesses for that

CORBIN (cont.)

    county 1700/1706 - desc/o Henry Corbin GVFHB(2)323; CFSSA173

Ann - of VA, b1724, m(1) Isaac Allerton d1739 of Westmoreland Co, son of Willoughby Allerton, m(2) David Currie d1739 for many years minister of Christ Church Parish, Lancaster Co & had issue including son Gawin - desc/o Henry Corbin GVFHB(2)326; CFSSA174

Ann - of VA, b1767, m(1) William Currie Beale, son of Col Thomas Beale & Jane Currie of Chestnut Hill, Richmond Co, m(2) Capt George Christopher & had issue - desc/o Henry Corbin CFSSA176

Betty - of VA, b1764, m1782 George Turberville d1798 of Westmoreland Co - desc/o Henry Corbin GVFHB(2)344

Courtney - of VA, m Joseph Hutchins - desc/o Henry Corbin CFSSA174

Elizabeth - of VA, m Carter Braxton, of Chericoke, King William Co, son of Col George Braxton & Mary Carter of Newington, King & Queen Co - desc/o Henry Corbin CFSSA175, 176

Elizabeth - of VA, b1764, m1782 (her cousin) Maj George Lee Turberville of Eppings Forest, Richmond Co, son of Col John Turberville & Martha Corbin of Hickory Hill, Westmoreland Co & had issue - desc/o Henry Corbin CFSSA176

Felicia - of VA, b1770, m(1)1791 Orrick Chilton of Curryomen, Westmoreland, son of William Chilton & Sarah Orrick of Maidstone, Westmoreland, m(2) John Chilton, son of Col Charles & Elizabeth Blackwell of Hereford - desc/o Henry Corbin GVFHB(2)344; CFSSA176

Frances - of VA, d1713 in London, m Edmund Jenings b1659 d1727 of Ripon Hall, York Co, VA, member of the Council of Virginia from 1699, attorney general 1680/1691, secretary of state 1702/1712, 1720/1722 & governor of Virginia Aug 1706/Jun 1710, son of Sir Edmund Jenings of Ripon, Yorkshire & Margaret Burkham - desc/o Henry Corbin CRL(1)254; GVFHB(2)324; CFSSA173

Francis - of VA, b1759/1760 of The Reeds d1820/1821, m Anne Beverley dau/o Col Robert Beverley of Blandfield & Maria Carter - desc/o Henry Corbin GVFHB(2)347; CFSSA178

Gawin - of VA, d1744 justice of the peace for Middlesex 1698, member of the House of Burgesses for many years, collector & naval officer of Rappahannock River District, m(1) Katherine Wormeley b1679 dau/o Ralph Wormeley of Rosehill & Catherine Lunsford, m(2) Jane Lane dau/o John Lane & wid/o Willis Wilson, m(3) Martha Bassett b1694 d1738 dau/o Col William Bassett of Eltham, New Kent Co & Joanna Burwell - desc/o Henry Corbin GVFHB(2)326; CFSSA173

Gawin - of VA, b1725 d1760 of Peckatone, Westmoreland Co, m Hannah Lee d1781 dau/o Thomas Lee of Stratford, Westmoreland Co & Hannah Ludwell - desc/o Henry Corbin GVFHB(2)343; CFSSA175

Gawin - of VA, b1738/1740 Corbin Hall, Middlesex Co d1779 Buckingham House, liberal supporter of the Episcopal Church & a vestryman, a burgess 1766/1769 & an influential member of the King's Council, m1762 (his cousin) Joanna Tucker dau/o Col

CORBIN (cont.)

Robert Tucker of Norfolk & Joanna Corbin - desc/o Henry Corbin GVFHB(2)343; CFSSA176

Gawin - of VA, m1776 Elizabeth Jones dau/o Thomas Jones & Sally Skelton of Northumberland Co - desc/o Henry Corbin GVFHB(2)350

Henry - of VA 1654, b1629 Hall End, Warwick, England d1677, of Buckingham House, Middlesex Co, 3rd son of Thomas Corbin & Winifred Grosvenor served as justice, burgess in Colonial Assembly and a member of the council of Virginia, was one of the builders of the first country club in America, m1645 Alice Eltonhead dau/o Richard Eltonhead of Eltonhead, Lancashire & Ann Sutton - the immigrant DBR(5)300, 874, 1052; RAA1, 84; WAC87; CRL(1)254; CGA43; GBR212; GVFHB(2)303/350; CFSSA171/181

Jenny or Jane Lane - of VA, m Col John Bushrod d1760 of Westmoreland Co, son of John Bushrod & Anne Bushrod of Gloucester Co - desc/o Henry Corbin GVFHB(2)326; CFSSA174

Joanna - of VA, b1720 d aft 1779, m1739 Col Robert Tucker b1737 d1780 of Norfolk, merchant, son of Robert Tucker & Frances (Houston) (Courtney) ? - desc/o Henry Corbin GVFHB(2)326; CFSSA174

John - of VA, b1715 of Port Tobago, Caroline Co d1757 justice of the peace, m (his cousin) Lettice Lee b1714 d1768 dau/o Richard Lee & Martha Silk of London - desc/o Henry Corbin GVFHB(2)339; CFSSA180

John Tayloe - of VA, b1739 Lanesville, King & Queen Co, m1772 Mary Waller b1752 dau/o Benjamin Waller & Martha Hall of Williamsburg & had issue - desc/o Henry Corbin GVFHB(2)346; CFSSA177

Laetitia - of VA, b1657 d1706, m1674 Richard Lee II b1646 of Mount Pleasant, Westmoreland Co d1714 son Col Richard Lee & Anne Constable - desc/o Henry Corbin DBR(5)300, 877; GVFHB(2)322; CFSSA173

Martha - of VA, b1738 d1792, m1769 Col John Turberville b1737 d1799 of Westmoreland Co, son of Col George Turberville & Martha Lee of Hickory Hill - desc/o Henry Corbin GVFHB(2)339, 341; CFSSA175

Martha - of VA, m1769 George Turberville d1793 of Westmoreland Co - desc/o Henry Corbin GVFHB(2)343

Martha - of VA, m Thomas Newton - desc/o Henry Corbin CFSSA174

Richard - of VA, b1708 d aft 1783, burgess of Middlesex Co & of the King's Council, receiver-general of the Colony 1754/1776, m1737 (his cousin) Elizabeth Tayloe b1721 dau/o John Tayloe & Elizabeth Gwynn-Lyde of The Old House, Richmond Co - desc/o Henry Corbin GVFHB(2)327; CFSSA175

Richard - of VA, b1766 d1814 raised & equipped an artillery company & served with it with credit in the war of 1812 & was promoted to the rank of major, m 1771 Elizabeth Hill Byrd d1822 dau/o Col William Byrd (3rd) of Westover - desc/o Henry Corbin GVFHB(3)350

Richard Henry - of VA, b1775 Westmoreland Co d1798/1799, prominent, influential citizen in affairs of church & state, member

CORBIN (cont.)

    House of Delegates 1797, m1797 Betty Taylor Corbin - desc/o Henry Corbin GVFHB(2)345; CFSSA176

    Sarah - of VA, m James Taylor - desc/o Henry Corbin CFSSA174

    Winifred - of VA, b1662 d1711, m Col Leroy Griffin of Rappahannock Co - desc/o Henry Corbin GVFHB(2)323; CFSSA173

CORDRAY Anna - of VA, dau/o William Cordray & Bridget Goddard, m Richard Bernard of VA - the immigrant GBR382; GVFWM(1)227/231

CORNELL Caleb - of RI, b1683 d1734, m1705 Elizabeth Hagner - desc/o Thomas Cornell CRL(2)165

    Deliverance - of RI, b1733, m1749 Benjamin Hall d1805 son of Benjamin Hall - desc/o Jeremy Clarke ECD253 - desc/o Katherine Marbury DBR(1)82

    John - of RI, b abt 1637 d1704, m1669 Mary Russell - desc/o Thomas Cornell CRL(2)165

    John - of RI, b1681, m Mary Scarr - desc/o Thomas Cornell CRL(2)165

    Joshua - of RI, b1677, m Sarah Thorne - desc/o Thomas Cornell CRL(2)165

    Hannah - of RI, b1730, m1750 Thomas Coggeshall - desc/o Jeremy Clarke DBR(3)672

    Mary - of RI, b1679, m James Sands - desc/o Thomas Cornell CRL(2)165

    Rebecca - of RI, b1685, m John Starr - desc/o Thomas Cornell CRL(2)165

    Richard - of RI, b1678 d1757, m Hannah Thorne - desc/o Thomas Cornell CRL(2)165

    Richard - of RI, b1709, m1730 Mary Martin dau/o Joseph Martin - desc/o Jeremy Clarke ECD253 - desc/o Katherine Marbury DBR(1)82

    Thomas - of MA bef 1638, d abt 1655, m Rebecca Briggs - the immigrant CRL(2)161, 162, 163; sufficient proof of alleged royal ancestry is lacking

CORNICK Mary - b1753 d1799, m Capt John James - desc/o Capt Henry Woodhouse DBR(1)348; DBR(2)445

CORSON Joseph - of PA, b1764 d1834, m1786/1787 Hannah Dickenson - desc/o Rev Thomas Dungan ECD(3)143

COSBY Amy - of VA, m Francis Anderson - desc/o Thomas Wingfield GVFHB(5)828

    Ann - of VA, m William Yancey - desc/o Thomas Wingfield GVFHB(5)828

    Frances - of VA, b1767, m Samuel Overton - desc/o Thomas Wingfield GVFHB(5)835

    Garland - of VA, b1759 d abt 1842 enlisted 1776 in Capt James Dabney's Co, enlisted again 1781 then commissioned captain, m1782 Molly Poindexter of Louisa Co, VA dau/o Thomas Poindexter, moved to Fayette Co, Kentucky & later to Henderson Co, Kentucky & had issue - desc/o Thomas Wingfield GVFHB(5)834

    Louisa - of VA, b1774, m John Bullock - desc/o Thomas Wingfield GVFHB(5)835

    Overton - of VA, b1772, m Ann Bissett - desc/o Thomas Wingfield

COSBY (cont.)

> GVFHB(5)835

> William - of NY & NJ, b abt 1690 d1735/1736 governor of New York & NJ son of Alexander Cosby & Elizabeth L'Estrange, m Grace Montagu - the immigrant GBR120; NYGBR(2)#4p203

> Wingfield - of VA, b1746, m(1) Mary Morris, m(2) Annie Baker - desc/o Thomas Wingfield GVFHB(5)828

COTTON Anna - of NH, b1661 d1702, m(1) George Carr - desc/o Gov Thomas Dudley DBR(1)557; DBR(2)686; DBR(4)839

> Anne - m Mr____ Johnson - desc/o Gov Thomas Dudley NE(8)321

> Dorothy - of MA, b1693 d1748, m1710 Rev Nathaniel Gookin b1687 d1734 - desc/o Capt Thomas Lake CHB410 - desc/o Gov Thomas Dudley NE(8)321, 322

> Dorothy - m Col Joseph Smith - desc/o Gov Thomas Dudley NE(8)321

> Elizabeth - of MA, b1665, m Rev William Williams b1665 d abt 1746 son of Isaac Williams of Newton - desc/o Gov Thomas Dudley RAA89; AFA114; NE(8)321

> Joanna - of MA, b1694 d1772, m1719 Rev John Brown - desc/o Grace Kaye J&K219; CHB360; MCD284; BCD209 - desc/o Muriel Gurdon ECD180; ECD(2)235

> Rev John - of MA 1633, b1584 d1654, m(1)1613 Elizabeth Harrocks, m(2)1632 Sarah Hawkridge - the immigrant EDV71; BLG2633; FFF202, 258 sufficient proof of alleged royal ancestry is lacking

> Rev John - of MA, b1658 d1710, m Anna Lake dau/o Capt Thomas Lake of Boston - desc/o Gov Thomas Dudley NE(8)321

> Rev John of MA, m 1719 Mary Gibbs - desc/o Grace Kaye CHB208; BCD208

> Leonard - of NH, a teacher at Hampton Falls, NH, m____ & had four children - desc/o Bridget Lisle NE(53)298

> Maria - m(1) Mr____ Atwater, m(2) Samuel Partridge - desc/o Gov Thomas Dudley NE(8)321

> Mary of MA, b1689 d1731, m1712 Rev John Whiting b1682 Lynn d1752 - desc/o Capt Thomas Lake CHB410 - desc/o Gov Thomas Dudley NE(8)321

> Mary of MA, m(1) Rev Mr Cheny, m(2)1748 Rev Dr Joseph Pynchon - desc/o Grace Kaye CHB208; BCD208

> Mercy - m Capt Peter Tufts of Medford - desc/o Gov Thomas Dudley NE(8)321

> Sarah - m Richard Pierce - desc/o Gov Thomas Dudley NE(8)321

> Rev Seaborn - of MA, b1633, m1654 Dorothy Bradstreet - desc/o Rev John Cotton BLG2633

> Thomas - b1695 d1770, m1725 Martha Williams - desc/o Rev John Cotton BLG2633

> Thomas - of CT, b1730 d1808, m1758 Sarah Holbrook - desc/o Rev John Cotton BLG2633

> Willard - of VT, d1829, m1781 Mercy Gallup - desc/o Rev John Cotton BLG2633

COULSON Joseph - of PA & MD, b1663, m Margaret Evans - the immigrant RAA1, 84; sufficient proof of alleged royal ancestry is lacking

> Sarah - b abt 1722 - desc/o Joseph Coulson RAA84

COULSON (cont.)

Thomas - b1703 - desc/o Joseph Coulson RAA84

COUTANT Jean - of NY - the immigrant EDV37, 38; sufficient proof of alleged royal ancestry is lacking

COVERT Elizabeth - of NJ, died in England, m John Fenwick b1618 d1683 - the immigrant GBR251

COVINGTON Anne - of VA, m LeRoy Hill - desc/o William Strother GVFTQ(3)382

Francis Strother - of VA, b1754 d1823, m1774 (his cousin) Lucy Strother b1728 d1836 - desc/o William Strother GVFTQ(3)381

Mary - of VA, m(1) Robert Deatherage, m(2) Capt George Calvert - desc/o William Strother GVFTQ(3)382

Peggy Strother - of VA, b1775 d1835, m1794 Daniel Brown - desc/o William Strother GVFTQ(3)382

Susannah - of VA, m Anthony Hughes - desc/o William Strother GVFTQ(3)382

William - of VA, b abt 1760 d1827, m Mildred Strother - desc/o William Strother GVFTQ(3)382

COWARD Deliverance - m James FitzRandolph - desc/o John Throckmorton GBR236

John - m Alice Britton - desc/o John Throckmorton GBR236

COWDREY Jacob - of MA, bp 1720/1721 d1820, m(1)1755 Mary Ann Beckwith - desc/o Rev Peter Bulkeley DBR(4)267; TAG(36)104

Jacob Jr - of CT, b1762 at Hartland d1846 Chester, Ohio, m1785 Abigail O. Beckwith b1766 at East Haddam, CT d1860 & had issue nine children - desc/o Rev Peter Bulkeley TAG(36)104

Squire - of MA, b abt 1764 d1840, m abt 1790 Sally Ordway - desc/o Rev Peter Bulkeley DBR(4)267

COX Elizabeth - of VA, d1704, m Col John Smith d1719/1720 of Abingdon, Gloucester Co on York River, VA son of Major Lawrence Smith - desc/o William Strachey GVFWM(4)627/631

Fleet - of VA, d1791, justice of Westmoreland Co, m Elizabeth Wright - desc/o Lieut Col Henry Fleete APP289

James S - of PA, b1748 d1821, m 1787 Charlotte Sitgreaves - descendant of George Cox Earl of Somers - the immigrant FFF30, 31; sufficient proof of alleged royal ancestry is lacking

Martha of VA, m1723 Col Henry Wood - desc/o Lieut Col Walter Aston CHB438

Mary Ann - of VA, m Francis Wright d1793 - desc/o Lieut Col Henry Fleete APP289

Philip II - m Susannah Kniseley - desc/o Edward FitzRandolph DBR(2)679

COYTEMORE Elizabeth - of MA, b abt 1617 d1642/1643 dau/o Rowland Coytmore & Mrs Katherine Miles Gray of MA, m abt 1636/1637 Capt William Tyng b abt 1605 d1652/1653 Braintree, MA, treasurer of the MA Bay Colony 1640/1644, they were ancestors of President John Quincy Adams & many other distinguished New Englanders - the immigrant FLW168; ECD(2)101; MCS78; DBR(5)118; AAP144; PFA Apx C #5; GBR165; TAG(32)9/23; EO2(2)107/113

CRABB Lettice (Letias) - of VA, m Gerrard McKenney - desc/o Thomas Gerard DBR(3)56

Osman - of VA, d1719/1720, m Sarah Ocanny - desc/o Thomas Gerard DBR(3)56

CRA(Y)CROFT John - of MD, m Anne___ - the immigrant GBR224 some aspect of royal descent merits further study

CRADDOCK Gov Matthew II - of MA - the immigrant EDV55; sufficient proof of alleged royal ancestry is lacking

CRAIK Dr James - of VA 1750, b1730 d1814, m1760 Mariana Ewell - the immigrant MCB136; sufficient proof of alleged royal ancestry is lacking

CRANDALL Bridget - b abt 1739 - desc/o Anne Marbury RAA114

Hannah - b1745 - desc/o Robert Abell RAA59

CRANSTON Abigail - of RI, m1766 at Newport, Daniel Holloway - desc/o Gov John Cranston GRFHG(1)290; NE(79)260

Ann - of RI, b1715 d1774 at Newport, m James Wilward - desc/o Gov John Cranston GRFHG(1)288; NE(79)258

Ann - of RI, bp 1719 Trinity Church, Newport, m1736 Thomas Brewer - desc/o Gov John Cranston GRFHG(1)285; NE(79)255

Ann - of RI, m(1)___ Beckett, m(2) George Gardner & had issue by both marriages - desc/o Gov John Cranston GRFHG(1)297; NE(79)267

Benjamin - of RI, b1668 at Newport d bef 1718, mariner, elected captain of the Colony forces & also deputy 1707, m Sarah Godfrey dau/o John & Sarah Godfrey - desc/o Gov John Cranston DBR(4)273; GRFHG(1)283; NE(79)253

Benjamin - of RI, b abt 1690/1691, m1735 Philadelphia, PA, Elizabeth___ Baldwin b1694 d1756 at Marcus Hook, PA - desc/o Gov John Cranston GRFHG(1)287/288 No documentary evidence has been found to prove that this Benjamin Cranston was a son of William Cranston; NE(79257

Benjamin II - of RI, b1707 at Newport d bef 1774, m(1)___ Thurber, m(2)1728/1729 Elizabeth Estabrooks & left issue - desc/o Gov John Cranston DBR(4)273; GRFHG(1)287; NE(79)257

Benjamin - of RI, b1719 at Newport d abt 1753 at Newport, admitted a freeman 1 May 1744. 1744 commanded the privateer *King George* of Newport, a sloop of 110 tons, carrying 12 guns & 80 men. In Nov 1745 he was in command of the privateer *Duke of Cumberland* of Newport, a ship of 180 tons, carrying 20 guns, 30 swivels & 130 men. He is said to have been lost at sea when this ship went down., m1742 at Newport, Bathsheba Coggeshall b1725 at Newport d1795 at Newport, dau/o Thomas Coggeshall & Sarah Lancaster - desc/o Gov John Cranston GRFHG(1)289, 290; NE(79)259, 260

Benjamin - of RI, b1727 d aft 1778, was second lieutenant on the sloop *Roby*, a privateer & he was one of those on the colonial ship *General Stark*, which was lost on the coast of ME in the Revolutionary War, m(1)1748/1749 at Warren, Sarah Bowen b1731 at Swansea d1771 at Warren, m(2) Keziah___ - desc/o Gov John Cranston GRFHG(1)296; NE(79)266

Benjamin III - of RI, b1729 d aft 1778, m1748 Sarah Bowen - desc/o Gov John Cranston DBR(4)273

CRANSTON (cont.)

Benjamin - of RI, b1754 at Warren d1823 at Warren, quartermaster & captain's clerk on board the row galley *Spitfire*, under Capt John Crandall in the Revolutionary War, he also served as a private in the Revolutionary Army & served three years in both branches of the service, m1777 at Warren, Mrs Mary Bowen b1756 at Warren d1848 at Warren, wid/o Reuben Bowen - desc/o Gov John Cranston GRFHG(1)310; NE(79)355

Caleb - of RI, b abt 1662 at Newport d bef 1711 at Newport, m at Newport, Judith Parrott b abt 1670 at Newport d1737 at Newport, dau/o Simon Parrott & Elizabeth____ - desc/o Gov John Cranston GRFHG(1)283; NE(79)253

Caleb - of RI, b1703, m Priscilla Jones d1764 at Newport aged 70 years - desc/o Gov John Cranston GRFHG(1)283; NE(79)253

Caleb - of RI, b1730/1731 d1765 at Warren, in 1759 commanded the sloop *Polly* & the sloop *Roby*, privateers, m abt 1753 Mary____ d aft 1774 - desc/o Gov John Cranston GRFHG(1)296; NE(79)262, 266

Caleb - of RI, b abt 1730 d1800, m(1) Mary Gould d bef 1790 dau/o Jeremiah & Elizabeth Gould, m(2)____ - desc/o Gov John Cranston GRFHG(1)292

Caleb - of RI, b1749/1750 at Warren d bef 1825, in 1797 he was master of the brig *Fair America*, m1770 at Warren, Rachel Lewin b1749 d1825 at Warren, dau/o William & Sarah Lewin - desc/o Gov John Cranston GRFHG(1)309; NE(79)354

Caleb - of RI, b1772 at Jamestown d1829, m Sarah Burlingame b1774 d1842 dau/o Peter Burlingame - desc/o Gov John Cranston GRFHG(1)303; NE(79)348

Catherine - of RI, m1766 at Newport, Samuel Brown Jr - desc/o Gov John Cranston GRFHG(1)291; NE(79)261

Deborah - of RI, m Daniel Holloway & had issue, an only child, Benjamin Holloway - desc/o Gov John Cranston GRFHB(1)291; NE(79)261

Deborah - of RI, m1789 at Newport, William Holmes - desc/o Gov John Cranston GRFHB(1)299; NE(79)344

Elizabeth - of RI, b1671 d1736, m(1) abt 1695 John Brown b1671 d1731 Newport, son of James Brown & Elizabeth Carr, m(2) Rev James Honeyman, rector of Trinity Church, Newport - desc/o Gov John Cranston GRFHG(1)280; NE(79)250

Elizabeth - of RI, m1711 at Newport, Charles Tillinghast & had issue - desc/o Gov John Cranston GRFHG(1)283; NE(79)253

Elizabeth - of RI, b1701, m William Almy - desc/o Gov John Cranston GRFHG(1)283; NE(79)253

Elizabeth - of RI, b1714/1715, m1732 Thomas Arnold - desc/o Gov John Cranston GRFHG(1)286; NE(79)256

Elizabeth - of RI, b1752, m Samuel Northrup - desc/o Gov John Cranston GRFHG(1)292; NE(79)262

Elizabeth - of RI, b1757, m1779 at Warren, Lewis D Berssayude - desc/o Gov John Cranston DBR(4)273; GRFHG(1)296; NE(79)266

Elizabeth - of RI, b1759 d1822 in Ohio, m1785 in Foster, Asa Bates of Coventry, RI b1758 d1841 - desc/o Gov John Cranston GRFHG(1)295; NE(79)265

CRANSTON (cont.)

Frances - of RI, b1694 d1740 at Newport, m1715 Trinity Church, Newport, Jahleel Brenton b1691 at Newport d1767 at Newport son of William Brenton & Hannah Davis - desc/o Gov John Cranston GRFHG(1)282

Frances - of RI, b1739 d1809, m1764 at Newport, Samuel Davenport b1741 d1816 son of Joseph Davenport & Elizabeth Wood of Little Compton, RI, & had issue - desc/o Gov John Cranston GRFHG(1)290, 291; NE(79)260

Hannah - of RI, b1754 d1820, m1779 at Scituate, Joab or Jacob Young son of Nathan Young - desc/o Gov John Cranston GRFHG(1)295; NE(79)265

Hannah - of RI, m(1) John Wilkins, m(2) John Hirst & had issue by first husband - desc/o Gov John Cranston GRFHG(1)297; NE(79)267

Hannah - of RI, b abt 1766, m1788 at Middletown, RI, Joseph Manchester b1757 at Middletown RI, son of Isaac & Hannah Manchester - desc/o Gov John Cranston GRFHG(1)300; NE(79)345

Hart - of RI, b1699 d1724/1725 Newport, m1721 at Newport, Nathaniel Hatch - desc/o Gov John Cranston DBR(1)717; GRFHG(1)282

Harte - of RI, b1724 d1762, m1744 Robert Dunbar of Newport & had issue - desc/o Gov John Cranston GRFHG(1)286; NE(79)

James - of RI, b aft 1710 d1740 mariner & lost at sea, m1739 at Newport, Eunice Richmond b1722 dau/o Edward Richmond & Rebecca Thurston - desc/o Gov John Cranston GRFHG(1)291, 292; NE(79)261

James - of RI, b1764 at Newport d1832, m1787 at Foster, Ruth Austin b1767 d1858 dau/o Gideon Austin & Prudence Angell - desc/o Gov John Cranston GRFHG(1)309; NE(79)354

James - of RI, b1768 at Newport d1814 in the military service of the United States, serving in the War of 1812, m1792 Anne Hempstead b1773 d1810 dau/o Robert Hempstead & Anne Avery - desc/o Gov John Cranston GRFHG(1)316, 317

Jeremiah - of RI, b1719 living in Newport as late as 1782, captain's quartermaster on the sloop *King George* of Newport 1747, m1743 Christina Weeden dau/o William Weeden & Phebe Peckham & wid/o ____ Tripp - desc/o Gov John Cranston NE(79)256

Jeremiah - of RI, d1795, m Esther____ & had issue, a son William T b abt 1795 - desc/o Gov John Cranston GRFHG(1)302; NE(79)347

Gov John - of RI abt 1637, b abt 1625 in Scotland or London, England d1679/1680 in Newport, brought to New England by Captain Jeremy Clark in 1638 age 12, governor of Rhode Island, son of James Cranston, a chaplain to King Charles I, m1658 Newport, Mary Clarke b abt 1641 at Newport d1711 dau/o Jeremiah Clarke & Mrs Frances Latham Dungan - the immigrant MCS28; BLG2637; DBR(1)716; DBR(4)273; EDV101; GBR111; TAG(53)152/153; GRFHG(1)277/395; NE(79)247/267, 344/357

Col John - of RI, b abt 1675 at Newport d1751 elected deputy for Newport at least ten times between 1707 & 1744 & was chosen speaker of the House of Deputies in 1711 & 1716. He commanded

CRANSTON (cont.)

    the Rhode Island force of 200 men that took part in the expedition against Port Royal in Aug 1710. He was at one time commander of the armed colony sloop *Tartar*, & was captain of Fort George for the years 1741/1744, m(1) Ann Mercy Newberry d1728 at Newport dau/o Walter Newberry & Ann Collins, m(2)1729 Elizabeth____ d1760 at Newport aged abt 75 years - desc/o Gov John Cranston BLG2637; GRFGH(1)284, 285; NE(79)254

John - of RI, b abt 1684 at Newport d1745 at Newport, a freeman of the colony in 1707 & was a deputy for Jamestown 1734/1735, m abt 1700 Penelope Godfrey b1685 d1761 at Newport, dau/o John & Sarah Godfrey - desc/o Gov John Cranston DBR(1)716; EDV101; GRFHG(1)285; NE(79)255

John - of RI, b abt 1707 d1753 elected captain of the Jamestown company of militia in 1740 & again in 1744, m abt 1733 Deborah Carr b1716 dau/o John & Frances Carr - desc/o Gov John Cranston BLG2637; GRFHG(1)290: NE(79)260

John - of RI, b1752 at Newport d1793 at Newport, m1786 at Newport, Comfort Collins b1752 at Newport d1799 at Newport, dau/o James Collins & Mary Arnold - desc/o Gov John Cranston GRFHG(1)297; NE(79)267

John - of RI, b1755 at Newport d1825, farmer & served in the Revolutionary War as a private, m(1)1790 Phoebe Ann Edwards b1775 d1805 dau/o Ephraim Edwards, m(2)1810 Cynthia Cooke - desc/o Gov John Cranston GRFHG(1)307, 308; NE(79)352

John - of RI, b1759 at Jamestown d1840 at Westerly, RI, served as a private in 1776 in Col Archibald Crary's regiment of RI troops, his name being on the pension roll of 1840, chosen lieutenant of the First Company of South Kingstown militia in 1797 & in 1798 & captain of the Second Company in 1799, m abt 1780 Susannah Helme b1762 at North Kingstown d1842 dau/o Oliver Helme - desc/o Gov John Cranston GRFHG(1)301, 302; NE(79)346/347

John - of RI, b1761 at Warren d1828 enlisted as a private in the Fourth Regiment of Albany County Militia in 1781 just at the close of the Revolutionary War, m abt 1781 Abigail Tisdale b1762 d1847 dau/o Joseph Tisdale & Lucy Hammond of Exeter, RI - desc/o Gov John Cranston GRFHG(1)311; NE(79)356

John - of RI, b1768 d1829, m Miss Green & had issue 8 children - desc/o Gov John Cranston BLG2637; GRFHG(1)299; NE(79)344

Joseph Wanton - of RI, b1774/1775 in Newport d1816 added to his original surname that of Cranston & was known as Joseph Wanton Cranston son of Joseph Wanton & Penelope Cranston, m1796 in Newport, Mary Smith dau/o Capt William Smith & Hannah Carr - desc/o Gov John Cranston GRFHG(1)291, 393, 394

Mary - of RI, m Philip Harwood - desc/o Gov John Cranston GRFHG(1)283; NE(79)253

Mary - of RI, b1713 d1737 in Newport, m Daniel Clarke - desc/o Gov John Cranston GRFHG(1)285; NE(79)255

Mary - of RI, bp 1713 Trinity Church, Newport d1737, m1728 John Gidley Jr d1744 aged 44 years, son of John Gidley, judge of the Vice Admiralty Court - desc/o Gov John Cranston GRFHG(1)285;

CRANSTON (cont.)
NE(79)255

Mary - of RI, b1712/1713, m1731 Thomas Brooks - desc/o Gov John Cranston GRFHG(1)286; NE(79)256

Mary - of RI, b1730 d1751 at Newport, m1750 at Newport, Nathaniel Coggeshall b1729 at Newport d bef 1778 at Newport, son of Nathaniel Coggeshall & Sarah Billings - desc/o Gov John Cranston GRFHG(1)294; NE(79)264

Mary - of RI, m1750 at Jamestown, Daniel Holloway - desc/o Gov John Cranston GRFHG(1)290; NE(79)260

Mary - of RI, b1744/1745 d1801, m(1)1766 at Newport, William Checkley of Boston, m(2)1782 Rev Ezra Stiles of Newport d1795 New Haven, CT, President of Yale College 1778/1795 - desc/o Gov John Cranston GRFHG(1)290; NE(79)260

Mary - of RI, bp 1773 at Newport, m George Brown - desc/o Gov John Cranston GRFHG(1)306; NE(79)351

Patience - of RI, b1753 d1819 at Foster, m1798 at Foster, Benjamin Dexter son of John Dexter of Cranston, RI - desc/o Gov John Cranston GRFHG(1)295; NE(79)265

Peleg - of RI, b1717/1718 at Swansea, MA d1805, m1749 at Jamestown, Sarah Carr b1722 at Jamestown d1791 at Foster dau/o Thomas Carr & Hannah Carr - desc/o Gov John Cranston GRFHG(1)294, 295; NE(79)264/265

Peleg - of RI, b1754 Jamestown, RI d1846 at Newport, m(1) prior to 1780 at Newport, Elizabeth Young b1757 at Newport d1795 at Newport, m(2)1799 at Newport Mrs Freelove G Young b1761 d1836 at Newport, wid/o Henry Young - desc/o Gov John Cranston GRFHG(1)300; NE(79)345

Peleg - of RI, b1757 at Newport d1822 at Foster, m1783 at Foster Elizabeth Babcock b1764 at Foster d1841 at Foster - desc/o Gov John Cranston GRFHG(1)308; NE(79)353

Peleg - of RI, b1770 at Warren, mariner, m1793 Mary Cobb - desc/o Gov John Cranston GRFHG(1)310; NE(79)355

Penelope - of RI, b at Newport d1811 at Newport, m at Newport Joseph Wanton - desc/o Gov John Cranston GRFHG(1)291; NE(79)261

Phebe - of RI, b1762, m1785/1786 at Bristol, RI, Asa West & had issue - desc/o Gov John Cranston GRFHG(1)296; NE(79)266

Rachel - of RI, bapt as an adult 1767, m(1)1763 Henry Miller or Maud from Demerara, British Guiana, m(2)1779 Joseph Atkins of New Bedford, MA, m(3)1785 George Munro - desc/o Gov John Cranston GRFHG(1)297; NE(79)267

Rhoda - of RI, bp 1776 in Newport, m William Carr - desc/o Gov John Cranston GRFHG(1)306; NE(79)351

Richmond - of RI, b1739 at Newport d bet 1774 & 1782, served 1757 during the French & Indian War on the privateer *George* of Newport & in the following year as sailmaker on the same vessel, m1765 at Newport, Sarah Hookey b1742 at Newport, d aft 1782 dau/o William Hookey & Rebecca Coggeshall - desc/o Gov John Cranston GRFHG(1)300; NE(79)344

Gov Samuel - of RI, b1659 at Newport d1727 at Newport, a goldsmith by trade & major of the colony forces in 1698 & was elected

CRANSTON (cont.)

      governor in 1698, holding this office until his death in 1727,
m(1)1680 Mary Williams Hart b1663 at Newport d1710 at Newport
dau/o Thomas Hart & Freeborn Williams, m(2)1711 Judith (Parrott)
Cranston abt 1670 at Newport d1737 at Newport dau/o Simon &
Elizabeth Parrott & wid/o his brother Caleb Cranston - desc/o
Jeremy Clarke FLW183; EO(1)614/623 - desc/o Gov John
Cranston DBR(1)716; BLG2637; GRFHG(1)280; NE(79)250

  Samuel - of RI, b1687 at Newport d1721 at Newport, admitted a
freeman of the colony 6 May 1707 & elected deputy for Newport 1
May 1716, m abt 1706 at Newport, Elizabeth Cornell b abt 1682 at
Newport d1749/1750 at Newport dau/o Thomas Cornell &
Susannah Lawton - desc/o Gov John Cranston GRFHG(1)286;
NE(79)256

  Samuel - of RI, b1707/1708 at Newport d bef 2 Apr 1744, m1726 at
Newport, Amy Almy b1705 at N of the Colony in May 1757 & in
1763 chosen ensign of the Fourth Company of the Newport Militia,
but refused to serve, m1758 at Newport Grace Gibbs b1737 at
Newport d1825 at Newport - desc/o Gov John Cranston
GRFHG(1)305; NE(79)263, 350

  Samuel - of RI, b1746 d1824 at Newport, m1767 Elizabeth Chapman -
desc/o Gov John Cranston BLG2637; GRFHG(1)299; NE(79)344

  Samuel - of RI, b1752 at Newport d1830 in NY, served in the
Revolutionary Army from 1775 to 1783 at which time he was
honorably discharged & was on the pension rolls in 1837/1838,
m1780 Zilpha King b1761 d1844 dau/o Samuel King & Freelove
Phillips - desc/o Gov John Cranston GRFHG(1)306; NE(79)351

  Samuel - of RI, b1757 at Warren d aft 1790, m abt 1783 Elizabeth____
- desc/o Gov John Cranston GRFHG(1)310, 311; NE(79)355

  Samuel - of RI, b1764 at Newport d1813 at Newport, m1786 at
Newport, Rachel Chadwick - desc/o Gov John Cranston
GRFHG(1)321

  Sarah - of RI, b1705, m William Robinson - desc/o Gov John Cranston
GRFHG(1)284; NE(79)254

  Sarah - of RI, bp 1750, m1770 at Newport, Edward Hazard, eldest son
of George Hazard - desc/o Gov John Cranston GRFHG(1)294;
NE(79)264

  Simon - of RI, b1768 d1856 shipbuilder & afterwards a farmer, m(1)
Mary Marshall b1775 d1820 dau/o William Marshall & Mary
Tatnall, m(2) Hannah Cope d1855 - desc/o Gov John Cranston
GRFHG(1)312; NE(79)357

  Stephen - of RI, b1767 at Warren, d1792 drowned in the narrows off
Bristol, m1789 at Bristol, Sarah Salisbury b1754 at Bristol d1840
at Bristol, dau/o Barnard & Elizabeth Salisbury - desc/o Gov John
Cranston GRFHG(1)310; NE(79)355

  Thomas - of RI, b1692 at Newport d prior to 1721, he became
possessed, in right of his wife, a large estate in Swansea, where he
lived after his marriage. From Swansea he went to sea in command
of a vessel, and was lost on this voyage, m at Swansea, MA,
Patience Gardiner b1687 at Swansea, dau/o Samuel Gardiner &
Elizabeth Carr, & left issue 2 daughters - desc/o Gov John

CRANSTON (cont.)

Cranston GRFHG(1)286, 287; NE(79)256

Thomas - of RI, b abt 1710 d1745 at Newport, mariner admitted a freeman of the Colony May 1739, m1738/1739 at Jamestown, Hannah Fry b1715 d1750 dau/o Joseph Fry & Mary Clarke - desc/o Gov John Cranston GRFHG(1)291; NE(79)261

Thomas - of RI, b1710 at Newport d1785 sailmaker & West India merchant, admitted a freeman 4 May 1731. He was elected deputy for that town almost every year from 1746 to 1774 & was speaker of the House in 1754. During the French & Indian War he served on the Committee of War from 1757 to 1760, m1729 at Newport, Mary Coggeshall b1711 at Newport d1792 at Newport, dau/o Joseph Coggeshall & Mary Dyer - desc/o Gov John Cranston GRFHG(1)293; NE(79)263

Thomas - of RI, b1752 at Newport d1792 drowned in Narragansett Bay, m1771 Ann Sweet d1814 dau/o Samuel Sweet - desc/o Gov John Cranston GRFHG(1)305, 306; NE(79)350

Thomas - of RI, b1757 at Jamestown d1825 lieutenant of the second company of North Kingstown Militia in 1799, m Sarah Northrup b176___ at North Kingstown, RI, dau/o Gideon Northrup - desc/o Gov John Cranston GRFHG(1)301; NE(79)346

Thomas - of RI, b1773 at Warren d bef 19 Apr 1816, mariner, m1795 at Warren, Elizabeth Child b1773 at Warren, dau/o Jeremiah Child & Patience Cole - desc/o Gov John Cranston GRFHG(1)332, 333

Thomas - of RI, b1774 at Newport d1827 at sea, m abt 1798 Alice Eldredge or Eldred b1781 d1850 dau/o Joseph Eldredge or Eldred & Abby Carr - desc/o Gov John Cranston GRFHG(1)321

Walter - of RI, b1713 at Newport d1763 at Newport admitted a freeman 30 Apr 1734, in 1740 was appointed second lieutenant of the Colony sloop *Tartar*. He was one of the principal inhabitants of Newport authorized 1742 to form a military company not to exceed 100 men, by the name of the "Artillery Company of the Town of Newport," the object being to train officers to command the militia in time of war. He was one of the signers, 4 Sep 1750 of a petition to the king, praying him to forbid the legislature of Rhode Island to issue any more bills of credit, on account of the depreciation of the currency. He was chosen a warden of Trinity Church Newport, 1749, a vestryman 1756 holding the latter office until his death, m1747 Frances Ayrault b1718 at Newport d1798 at Newport, dau/o Daniel Ayrault & Mary Robineau - desc/o Gov John Cranston GRFHG(1)289; NE(79)259

William - of RI, b abt 1670 at Newport d bef 1697 Newport, m Mary (or Mercy)___ d1732 - desc/o Gov John Cranston GRFHG(1)284; NE(79)254

William - of RI, b1692 at Newport, d abt 1776 at Newport, shipwright, m(1)1713/1714 at Newport, Mariam Norton b1695 at Newport d1727/1728 at Newport, m(2)1728 Mercy Gould b1694 at Newport d1747 at Newport, dau/o Thomas Gould & Elizabeth Mott - desc/o John Cranston GRFHG(1)288; NE(79)258

William - of RI, b abt 1712 d bef 31 Aug 1745, m1735 at Newport, Mary Davis of Bristol, England - desc/o Gov John Cranston

CRANSTON (cont.)
> GRFHG(1)291; NE(79)261
>> William - of RI, b1721/1722 at Newport d1751 at Newport, cooper made a freeman of the colony 30 Apr 1745, m1743 at Newport, Mary Mott - desc/o Gov John Cranston GRFHG(1)297; NE(79)267
>> William - of PA, b abt 1736 at Marcus Hook, PA d1811 at Stanton, DE, m abt 1765 Ann Johnson Ford, dau/o Humphrey & Elizabeth Johnson & wid/o William Ford - desc/o Gov John Cranston GRFHG(1)296; NE(79)266
>> William - of RI, b abt 1764 d abt 1860, served in the Revolutionary War & is said to have been the youngest drummer boy serving in the Revolution, m(1) abt 1792 Abigail Congdon d aft 1854 dau/o John Congdon & Abigail Rose, William Cranston divorced her &, m(2)1813 Olive Hor or Horr b1778 d1863 dau/o George Hor & Wealthy Benjamin - desc/o Gov John Cranston GRFHG(1)302; NE(79)347
>> William - of RI, b1772 at Newport d1823 at Newport, m Lydia or Elizabeth____ b1765 d1836 at Newport - desc/o Gov John Cranston GRFHG(1)321

CRAVEN Christopher - of SC, governor of South Carolina, son of Sir William Craven & Christopher Craven, m Elizabeth Staples - the immigrant GBR130

CRAWFORD Grizelle Yancey - m(1) Thomas Hawkins - desc/o Col John Alston DBR(1)630; DBR(2)736
> Mary - b abt 1766 - desc/o John Alston RAA62

CRENSHAW Mary Temperance of VA, d1807, m William Rice MD - desc/o Maj Gen Nathaniel Bacon CHB349; BCD349

CRISPIN Jacob - of NJ, b1752 d1848, m abt 1782 Anne Chubb - desc/o Joshua Owen ECD(2)209
> Joseph - of NJ, b1737 d1807, m1742 Elizabeth Owen d1811 - desc/o Joshua Owen ECD(2)207; DBR(1)173; DBR(2)248; DBR(3)388; DBR(5)718
> Joseph - of NJ, b1769 d1825, m abt 1796 Elizabeth Hewes b1775 d1857 - desc/o Joshua Owen ECD(2)207; DBR(1)173; DBR(2)248; DBR(3)388; DBR(5)718
> Joshua - of NJ, b1729 - desc/o Joshua Owen ECD(2)209
> Silas - of PA, b abt 1655 d1711, m Hester Holme - desc/o Capt William Crispin DBR(2)246; AFA6; BLG2638
> Silas - of PA, b abt 1725 d1800, m Martha Miles - desc/o Capt William Crispin AFA6; BLG2638
> Silas - of PA, b1767 d1806, m Esther Dougherty - desc/o Capt William Crispin AFA6; BLG2638
> Thomas - of PA, b1694 d1749, m Jane Ashton - desc/o Capt William Crispin AFA6; BLG2638
> Capt William - of PA, b1627 d1681, m Rebecca Bradshaw - the immigrant DBR(2)246; DBR(3)386; AFA6; BLG2638; sufficient proof of alleged royal ancestry is lacking

CRISWELL ____ (Miss) - of VA, m Warren Lewis - desc/o Col William Randolph PVF134
> Elizabeth - of VA, m Charles Carter of Ludlow - desc/o Col William Randolph PVF134

CRISWELL (cont.)

Lucy - of VA, m1770 Col William Nelson of The Dorrile, Hanover Co, VA - desc/o Col William Randolph PVF134

Susan R - of VA, m Speaker John Robinson, of the Virginia House of Burgesses & had issue - desc/o Col William Randolph PVF134

CROCKERCRAFT Elizabeth of MA, m Nathaniel Hering - desc/o Rev John Oxenbridge CHB206; GBR125

CROFT Elizabeth Lanier - of VA, b abt 1760 d1834, m(1)1778 Moses Ingram - desc/o John Washington DBR(1)206; DBR(5)698

CROMMELIN Anna - b1719, m G R Myer - desc/o Robert Sinclair NYGBR(50)#1p48

Charles - b1722, m(1)____ Roosevelt, m(2)____ Fish - desc/o Robert Sinclair NYGBR(50)#1 p48

Daniel - b1707 New York d1768 New York, settled in New Amsterdam, m____ & had issue five children - desc/o Robert Sinclair NYGBR(50)#1p47

Elizabeth - b1715, m Gabriel Ludlow & had issue - desc/o Robert Sinclair NYGBR(50)#1p47/48

Elizabeth - m____ Somers - desc/o Robert Sinclair NYGBR(50)#1p48

Judith - m1761 in New Amsterdam (her cousin) Samuel Ver Planck b1739 d1820 - desc/o Robert Sinclair NYGBR(50)#1p47

Mary - m1737 Gulian Ver Planck b1698 d1751 - desc/o Robert Sinclair NYGBR(50)#1p47

Mary - m Henry Bowers & they had issue two daughters, Mary & Ann Bowers - desc/o Robert Sinclair NYGBR(50)#1p48

CROMWELL Joseph - of MD, b1707 d1769, m Comfort____ - desc/o William Cromwell AFA244

Capt Richard - of MD, b1749 d1802, m1772 Rachel Cockey - desc/o William Cromwell AFA244

William - of MD 1671, m Elizabeth Trahearne - the immigrant AFA244; sufficient proof of alleged royal ancestry is lacking

William - of MD, b1678 d1735, m abt 1700 Mary Woolguist - desc/o William Cromwell AFA244

CROWN or CROWNE Agnes - of NH, b1686 bp 8 Oct 1704 age 18 in Brattle Street Church, Boston, m1710 James Addison & had several children including a son James who administered on her estate, it was granted 1750 - desc/o Agnes Mackworth EO2(1)631

Elizabeth - of NH, b1684 was received into the covenant and Bapt in the North Parish, Portsmouth in 1707, m1717 Elias Constance of Boston - desc/o Agnes Mackworth EO2(1)631

Henry - of MA, b abt 1648 in England d1696 living at Portsmouth, NH in 1672, kept a house of public entertainment, was a notary public & attorney, m1676 Alice Rogers dau/o William Rogers - the immigrant RAA1 - desc/o Agnes Mackworth FLW167; MCS27; RAA84; EO2(1)630, 631

Rebecca - of MA, b1689/1690 bp 1 Feb 1713 in Brattle St Church Boston, m1725 Robert Weston of Boston - desc/o Agnes Mackworth EO2(1)631

CRUGER John - of NY 1688 - the immigrant EDV36; sufficient proof of alleged royal ancestry is lacking

CUDWORTH James - of MA, b abt 1610 son of Reverend Ralph Cudworth
& (probably) Mary Machell, m Mary Masham - the immigrant RAA1,
84; GBR270 some aspect of royal descent merits further study;
NE(30)464; EO2(1)632, 633

James - b1635 - desc/o James Cudworth RAA84

James - b1665/1670 - desc/o James Cudworth RAA84

James - b1696/1697 - desc/o James Cudworth RAA84

James - b1740 - desc/o James Cudworth RAA84

James J - b abt 1762/1765 - desc/o James Cudworth RAA84 - desc/o
Henry Norton RAA118

Mary - b1633 - desc/o James Cudworth RAA84

CUMING Sir Alexander, 2nd Baronet - b abt 1690 d1775 English agent
who persuaded the Creek & Cherokee Indians to accept British
sovereignty, son of Sir Alexander Cuming, 1st Baronet & Elizabeth
Swinton, m Amy Whitehall - the immigrant GBR102

CUMMINGS Capt Josiah of MA, b1763 d1834, m1785 Sarah Taylor -
desc/o John Whitney CHB229; BCD229

CUNYNGHAM Mary - of PA, b1699, m Isaac Roberdeau - the immigrant
DBR(1)228; DBR(3)561; DBR(4)194, 453; GBR93 lists her son
Daniel Robedeau - the immigrant

CURRELL Henry - d1785, m Amy____ d1804 - desc/o Lieut Col Henry
Fleete APP288

Nicholas - d1801, m____ - desc/o Lieut Col Henry Fleete APP288

Spencer - m1757 Judith Bridgeford - desc/o Lieut Col Henry Fleete
APP288

CURSON Richard - of MD, son of Samuel Curson & Rebecca Clark, m
Elizabeth Becker - the immigrant GBR181

CURTIS Hephzibah -of CT, b1757 d1807, m1784 Jason Boardman -
desc/o Rev Charles Chauncy CHB86; BCD86

Joseph - b1769 - desc/o Anne Marbury RAA114

CURTISS Ephriam - of CT, b1684 d1775 - desc/o Edward Booth
CHB385; MCD174

Ephriam - of CT, b1739 d1794 - desc/o Edward Booth CHB385;
MCD174

Rebecca - of CT, m David Birdseye - desc/o Edward Booth CHB386;
MCD174

Stiles - of CT, b1708 d1785 - desc/o Edward Booth CHB385; MCD174

CURWEN Abigail - of MA, b1637, m(1) 1663 Eleazer Hathorne, m(2) Judge
James Russell - desc/o Capt George Curwen J&K250; NE(10)304

Bartholomew - of MA, b1693 d1747, m Esther Burt dau/o Mr John
Burt - desc/o Capt George Curwen NE(10)304

Elizabeth - b1678 d1706, m1702 James Lindall - desc/o Capt George
Curwen NE(10)304

Capt George - of MA 1638, b1610 Sibbertoft, Northamptonshire d1685
Salem, MA, son of John Curwen, m(1)1636 Mrs Elizabeth (Herbert)
White b1611 d1668 Salem, MA, dau/o John Herbert, mayor of
Northampton, England, m(2) Mrs Elizabeth (Winslow) Brooks d aft
1694 dau/o governor Edward Winslow & Mrs Susanna____ White &
wid/o Robert Brooks - the immigrant J&K250; FLW41; RAA85;
EDV42; GBR416; NE(10)304/305

Rev George - of MA, b1682 d1717 graduated Harvard College 1701,

CURWEN (cont.)

m1711 Mehitable Parkman d1718 dau/o Deliverance Parkman - desc/o Capt George Curwen NE(10)304

George - of MA, b1666, m(1) Susanna Gedney, m(2) Lydia Gedney both wives were daughters Bartholomew Gedney - desc/o Capt George Curwen NE(10)304

George - of MA, b1717 d1746, graduated Harvard College 1735, m1739 Sarah Pickman b1718 d1810 - desc/o Capt George Curwen NE(10)304

George - of MA, b1718 d1780 m____ & had issue - desc/o Capt George Curwen NE(10)304

Hannah - of MA, b1642, m1664 Major William Browne Jr - desc/o Capt George Curwen NE(10)304

John - of MA, b1638 d1683, m Margaret Winthrop d1697 dau/o Governor Winthrop - desc/o Capt George Curwen NE(10)304

John - of MA, b1722, m____ & had issue - desc/o Capt George Curwen NE(10)304

John - of MA, b1755 - desc/o Capt George Curwen NE(10)304

Jonathan - of MA, b1640 d1718, m1675 Elizabeth (Sheaf) Gibbs d1718 dau/o Jacob & Margaret Sheaf & wid/o Robert Gibbs - desc/o Capt George Curwen NE(10)304

Joseph - of MA, b1724, m____ & had issue - desc/o Capt George Curwen NE(10)304

Mehitable - of MA, b1741 d1813, m1764 Richard Ward b1741 d1824 - desc/o Capt George Curwen NE(10)304

Penelope - of MA, b1670 d1690, m1684/1685 Josiah Wolcott - desc/o Capt George Curwen NE(10)304

Samuel - of MA, b1715 d1802, graduated Harvard College 1735, m1750 Abigail Russell b1725 d1793 dau/o Daniel Russell of Charlestown - desc/o Capt George Curwen NE(10)304

Samuel - of MA, b1728 d1776, m____ & had issue - desc/o Capt George Curwen NE(10)304

CUSHING Benjamin - of MA, b1739 d1810, m1767 Hannah Hazeltine - desc/o Matthew Cushing CFA115

Caleb - of MA, b1673 d1752, m1698 Elizabeth Cotton - desc/o Matthew Cushing CFA115

Charles of MA, b1744 d1809 a representative & member of the MA Senate, m Hannah Croade - desc/o Rev Charles Chauncy CHB68

Daniel - b1619 d1700, m Lydia Gilman - desc/o Matthew Cushing BLG2645; CFA114

David - b1727 d1800, m Ruth Lincoln - desc/o Matthew Cushing BLG2645

David - b1754 d1827, m Hannah Cushing - desc/o Matthew Cushing BLG2645

Deborah - of MA, bp 1625 - desc/o Matthew Cushing CFA114

Jeremiah - of MA, b1621 - desc/o Matthew Cushing CFA114

John - of MA, b1627 d1708, m1658 Sarah Hawke - desc/o Matthew Cushing CFA114

John Newmarsh - of MA, b1779 d1849, m(1)1799 Lydia Dow, m(2)1815 Elizabeth Johnson - desc/o Matthew Cushing CFA116

Matthew - of MA, bp 1589 d1660, m1613 Nazareth Pitcher - the

CUSHING (cont.)
> immigrant EDV45, 46; BLG2644; CFA114; sufficient proof of
> alleged royal ancestry is lacking
>> Matthew - of MA, bp 1623 - desc/o Matthew Cushing CFA114
>> Theophilus - b1657 d1750, m Mary Thaxter - desc/o Matthew
>> Cushing BLG2645

CUSTIS Betty - of VA, m Thomas Teackle - desc/o Capt Adam
> Thoroughgood CRL(2)115
> Elizabeth - of VA, m Thomas Custis - desc/o Capt Adam Thoroughgood
> CRL(2)115
> Elizabeth Parke - of VA, b1776 d1832, m1796 Thomas Law, son of the
> Bishop of Carlisle - desc/o Lady Charlotte Lee MG(1)160
> John - of VA, d1732, m(2) Ann Kendall - desc/o Capt Adam
> Thoroughgood CRL(2)115

CUTHBERT James - of SC, son of John of Castle Hill & Jean (Hay)
> Cuthbert, m(1) Mrs Patience Stobo Hamilton, m(2) Mrs Mary
> Hazzard Wigg - the immigrant GBR60

CUTLER Betty - of VA, m Michael Hall - desc/o Robert Drake DBR(5)385
> Samuel - b1773, m Cordelia Youngs - desc/o Joan Vincent LDS33

CUYLER Hendricks - of NY 1664 - the immigrant EDV37; sufficient proof
> of alleged royal ancestry is lacking

– D –

DABNEY Elizabeth Price - of VA, b1772 d abt 1806, m(1) Lynn
> Shackelford - desc/o Col William Randolph DBR(1)422

DADE Anne - of VA, m William Lane - desc/o Francis Dade GVFTQ(1)431
> Anne - of VA, m1772 Lieut Col Buckner Stith - desc/o Francis Dade
> GVFTQ(1)442
> Anne Fowke - of VA, b1737, m George West d (sp) 1786 - desc/o
> Francis Dade GVFTQ(1)436
> Baldwin - of VA, b1716 d1783, m(1)1736 Sarah Alexander d1739
> dau/o Robert Alexander & Anne Fowke, m(2) abt 1743 Verlinda____
> d1798 - desc/o Francis Dade GVFTQ(1)441
> Baldwin - of VA, b1760 a cadet in the 3rd Continental Dragoons, 1778,
> in 1807 he stated in a petition that he was planning an "emigration
> to the Western Country," m1781 Catherine West d1804 dau/o Capt
> John West Jr d1777 & Catherine Colville - desc/o Francis Dade
> GVFTQ(1)442
> Behethland - of VA, m1777 Justinian Birch - desc/o Francis Dade
> GVFTQ(1)442
> Cadwallader - of VA, b abt 1693 d1761, m(1) abt 1720 Sarah
> Alexander b1700 d1744 dau/o Philip Alexander & Sarah Ashton,
> m(2)1752 Sarah Berryman - desc/o Francis Dade GVFTQ(1)432,
> 435
> Cadwallader - of VA, d1777, m Mary____ , left an only son Francis who
> dy - desc/o Francis Dade GVFTQ(1)436
> Charles Stuart - of VA, d1812, m Jane Adams dau/o Robert Adams Sr
> - desc/o Francis Dade GVFTQ(1)445
> Elizabeth - of VA, b1658, m Major Edward Griffith of Warwick Co -

DADE (cont.)

desc/o Francis Dade GVFTQ(1)431

Elizabeth - of VA, m1750 Robert Yates - desc/o Francis Dade GVFTQ(1)432

Elizabeth - of VA, b1734, m1751, m (her cousin) Lawrence Washington b1727 d1804 of Digby - desc/o Francis Dade GVFTQ(1)435

Elizabeth - of VA, b1764, m1782 (her cousin) Townshend Dade - desc/o Francis Dade GVFTQ(1)442

Francis - of VA bef 1651, b1621 assumed the name of John Smith owing to his royalist connections or sympathies, after the Restoration in 1660 he resumed his name d1662 at sea, son of William Dade & Mary Wingfield, m abt 1651 Behethland Bernard b abt 1635 d1720 dau/o Major Thomas Bernard of Warwick Co, VA & Mary Behethland dau/o Captain Robert Behethland - the immigrant GBR285; GVFHB(2)654; GVFTQ(1)428/457

Francis - of VA, b1659 d1694, m abt 1683 Frances Townshend d1726 dau/o Col Robert Townshend b1640 d1675 & Mary Langhorne d1685 - desc/o Francis Dade GVFTQ(1)431

Francis - of VA, b abt 1691 d abt 1769, m abt 1716 Jane Alexander b1696 d1744 dau/o Philip Alexander & Sarah Ashton - desc/o Francis Dade GVFTQ(1)432, 434

Francis - of VA, b abt 1756 d1791 an original member of the Society of the Cincinnati in Virginia, entered the army & served until the end of the war as cornet, 3rd Continental Dragoons 1778, lieut 1780 & capt 1781, m1782 Sarah Taliaferro dau/o Capt Lawrence Taliaferro & Mary Jackson - desc/o Francis Dade GVFTQ(1)436, 452

Frances - of VA, b1734 d1814, m1755 Col Francis Peyton d1805 son of Col Valentine Peyton b1688 d1751 & Frances Harrison dau/o Thomas Harrison of Chappawamsic - desc/o Francis Dade GVFTQ(1)434

Frances - of VA, b1732, m1754 Charles Stuart - desc/o Francis Dade GVFTQ(1)435

Frances - of VA, b1753, m1774 James Gwatkins d1817 - desc/o Francis Dade GVFTQ(1)445

Hannah Gibbons - of VA, b1759, m1779 Col Lawrence Ashton b1757 d1812 - desc/o Francis Dade GVFTQ(1)445

Henry - of VA, b abt 1705 d1754, m1726 Elizabeth Massey (probably) dau/o Benjamin Massey - des/o Francis Dade GVFTQ(1)432

Henry - of VA, m1790 Jane Fitzhugh of King George Co, VA - desc/o Francis Dade GVFTQ(1)433

Horatio - of VA, b1724 d1782, m(1)1749 Frances Richards, m(2)1753 Mary (Stuart) Massey b1726 d1799 dau/o Rev David Stuart & Jane Gibbons of St Paul's Parish & wid/o Sigismund Massey - desc/o Francis Dade GVFTQ(1)445

Isaac - of VA, b1756 d1819 at Gloucester, MA, a Revolutionary soldier, m in Westmoreland Co, VA Fanny Blundell b1766 d1843 dau/o Reuben Blundell - desc/o Francis Dade GVFTQ(1)433

Jane - of VA, m1777 Robert Yates - desc/o Francis Dade GVFTQ(1)442

Langhorne - of VA, b1720 d1753, m1742/1743 Mildred Washington dau/o John Washington & Mary Massey - desc/o Francis Dade GVFTQ(1)435, 451

DADE (cont.)

Langhorne - of VA, m1778 Frances Alexander dau/o Col William
Alexander b1744 d1814 of Effingham & Sigismunda and Mary
Massey b1744 d1832 - desc/o Francis Dade GVFTQ(1)442

Langhorne - of VA, b1755 d1811, m1780 Sarah Ashton b1756 d1815
dau/o Henry Ashton & Jane Alexander of Effingham - desc/o
Francis Dade GVFTQ(1)445, 446

Langhorne - of VA, b1768 d1830 justice of the peace for King George
Co 1829, m abt 1794 Mary Anne Harrison b1776 dau/o Burr
Harrison & Mary Anne Barnes - desc/o GVFTQ(1)455

Mary - of VA, b1656 d1699, m(1) abt 1677 Capt Robert Massey d1689,
m(2)1692 Col Rice Hooe d1726 - desc/o Francis Dade
GVFTQ(1)431

Mary - of VA, b1727, m1746 Howson Hooe Jr d1796 - desc/o Francis
Dade GVFTQ(1)432

Robert - of VA, b1684 d bef 1714, m Margaret____ - desc/o Francis
Dade GVFTQ(1)432

Robert - of VA, b abt 1723 d1756 in Charles Co, MD, m1743 Elizabeth
Harrison d1785 in MD - desc/o Francis Dade GVFTQ(1)435

Robert - of VA, b1731 d1776 soldier in the Revolutionary Army, m____
- desc/o Francis Dade GVFTQ(1)432

Robert Townshend - of VA, m in Carteret Co, North Carolina 1773
Elizabeth Parker - desc/o Francis Dade GVFTQ(1)445

Rose Townshend - of VA, b1751 d1791, m(1)1769 Robert Knox d1782,
m(2) George Dent - desc/o Francis Dade GVFTQ(1)435

Sarah - of VA, m Thomas Triplett - desc/o Francis Dade GVFTQ(1)436

Sarah - of VA, b1747, m1774 Lawrence Taliaferro b1734 d1798 -
desc/o Francis Dade GVFTQ(1)442

Sarah - of VA, m1796 James Parke - desc/o Francis Dade
GVFTQ(1)451

Townshend - of VA, b abt 1688 d1761 County Lieutenant of Stafford
Co 1725 High Sheriff in 1731, Captain 1736, Colonel 1737, &
justice of the peace, m(1) abt 1714 Elizabeth Alexander b1698
d1736, m(2)1745 Rose (Newton) Grigsby d1785 wid/o Thomas
Grigsby d1745 & dau/o Garrard Newton of King George Co -
desc/o Francis Dade GVFTQ(1)432, 434

Townshend - of VA, b1707 d1781 in Fairfax Co, VA, a "recognized
Patriot" he signed the Protest Against the Stamp Act, m1736
Parthenia (Alexander) Massey b1709 dau/o Robert Alexander &
Anne Fowke & wid/o Dade Massey Jr - desc/o Francis Dade
GVFTQ(1)434, 436

Townshend - of Frederick Co, VA, (probably) appointed with William
Washington, captain in Stafford Co 1775, m (may have) 1784
Elizabeth Ball dau/o Williamson Ball & had a son, Williamson Ball
Dade, who died in Prince William Co, VA 1833 - desc/o Francis
Dade GVFTQ(1)442

Townshend - of VA, b1760 d1808, m1782 (his cousin) Elizabeth Dade
dau/o Baldwin & Verlinda Dade - desc/o Francis Dade
GVFTQ(1)436, 454

Rev Townshend - of VA, b1742 d1822 in MD, m1784 Mary Simmons
b1765 d1837 dau/o Samuel & Elizabeth Simmons - desc/o Francis

DADE (cont.)

    Dade GVFTQ(1)436, 437

    Townshend - of VA, b1743 d1807, m(1)1769 Jane Stuart b1751 d1774 dau/o Rev William Stuart & Sarah Foote, m(2)1775 Susannah Fitzhugh b1757 d1817 dau/o Henry Fitzhugh & Sarah Battaile - desc/o Francis Dade GVFTQ(1)451

    Townshend - of VA, b1766 (Did he marry Elizabeth Ball in 1784 ?) - desc/o Francis Dade GVFTQ(1)445

    William - of VA, m Mrs Sarah (Taliaferro) Dade - desc/o Francis Dade GVFTQ(1)445

    William Dade - of VA, b1760 d1840, m Orange Co, VA 1792 Mrs Sarah (Taliaferro) Dade dau/o Lawrence Taliaferro & Mary Jackson - desc/o Francis Dade GVFTQ(1)450

DALE Catherine - of VA, b1652 Lancaster Co d1703 dau/o Major Edward Dale & Lady Diana Skipwith, m1670 Lancaster, Capt Thomas Carter Sr b1630 England d1700 Lancaster - desc/o Diana Skipwith ECD(2)246; DBR(1)123, 145, 280, 285, 342, 451, 513; DBR(2)8, 728, 803; DBR(3)228, 668; DBR(4)558; DBR(5)376; RAA130; WAC69

    Elizabeth - of VA, m William Rogers - desc/o Diana Skipwith DBR(4)698; WAC69

DALLAM John Josias Middlemore - son of Richard Dallam & Frances Paca - desc/o Anne Lovelace GVFHB(3)363

    Josias William - of MD, b1747 d1820, m(1)1770 Sarah Smith by whom he had issue nine children, m(2) Henrietta Maria Jones dau/o Judge Thomas Jones of Baltimore Co & had issue five children - desc/o Anne Lovelace GVFHB(3)363

    Richard - of MD, b1743, lived in Harford Co, MD, later settled in Kentucky, m(1)1765 Frances Paca, fourth dau/o John Paca of Baltimore Co by whom he had issue, m(2) Peggy Carlisle, m(3) Mary Hart, m(4) Jane Macall - desc/o Anne Lovelace GVFHB(3)363

    William Winston Smith Dallam - son of Richard Dallam & Frances Paca - desc/o Anne Lovelace GVFHB(3)363

DALSTON Catherine - of VA, dau/o Sir Charles Dalston, 3rd Baronet & Susan Blake, m Francis Fauquier b abt 1704 d1768, lieut governor of Virginia - the immigrant GBR214

DALTON Lucy - b abt 1762, m John Watts - desc/o Capt Thomas Harris LDS107; RAA71, 102

    Mary - of VA, b1748 d1841, m1769 Col Archilaus Hughes - desc/o Col John West DBR(2)843

DAMON Amos - b1729 - desc/o Anthony Collamore RAA82

    Dr Edward - of MA, b abt 1705/1706 d1801 at Ware, m(1) abt 1735 Lois____ d1740 age 30, m(2)1740 at Reading, Elizabeth Smith b1720 dau/o Abraham Smith & Elizabeth Pierce - desc/o Rev Peter Bulkeley TAG(36)100

    Jemima - b1756 - desc/o Anthony Collamore RAA82

    Mehitabale - of MA, b1699 d1763, m1718 Nathaniel Cowdrey b1691 d1751 - desc/o Rev Peter Bulkeley DBR(4)266

    Susannah - of MA, b1697, m Nathaniel Townsend - desc/o Grace Chetwood DBR(1)100

DANDRIDGE Maj Alexander Spotswood of VA, b1753, served in the Revolutionary War, m Ann Stephen, dau/o Gen Adam Stephen - desc/o Col John West CHB244; BCD244; CFA(1)118 - desc/o Maj Gen Alexander Spotswood CHB291; BCD291

    Anne - of VA, m John Spottswood Moore - desc/o Col John West DBR(2)843; CFA(1)118

    Anne - of VA, m William Dandridge Claiborne - desc/o Anne Lovelace GVFHB(3)345

    Dorothea Spottswoode of VA, b1757 d1831, m1777 Patrick Henry - desc/o Col John West CHB243; BCD243; DBR(3)326; CFA(1)118 - desc/o Maj Gen Alexander Spotswood CHB291; BCD292

    Eliza - of VA, b1764, m____ Payne - desc/o Col John West CFA(1)118

    Elizabeth of VA, m Philip Whitehead Clairborne - desc/o Col John West CHB245; MCD321; BCD245

    Francis - of King William Co, VA, m1779 Lucy Webb of New Kent Co, VA - desc/o Col John West GVFWM(2)119

    John - of VA, b1756, m Mrs____ Goode - desc/o Col John West CFA(1)118

    Martha of VA, b1721 d1747, m1739 Philip Aylett - desc/o Col John West CHB244; MCD321; BCD244; DBR(3)676; DBR(4)301, 765; GVFWM(2)119, 120; CFA(1)117

    Martha - of VA, b1748 d1791, m1769 Archer (Archibald) Payne - desc/o Col John West DBR(3)466; GBR112, 115; CFA(1)118

    Mary of VA, m1745 John Spotswood - desc/o Col John West CHB245; BCD245, DBR(1)407; DBR(3)163; GVFWM(2)120; CFA(1)117

    Col Nathaniel West of VA, b1729 King & Queen Co d1789 Hanover Co, captain Virginia Association 1756, burgess Hanover Co 1758/1764, m1747 Dorothea Spotswood b1733 d1773 dau/o Governor Alexander Spotswood & Anne Butler (Brayne) - desc/o Col John West CHB243; BCD243; DBR(1)240; DBR(2)842, 843; DBR(3)326, 466; GBR115; GVFWM(2)119; CFA(1)117

    Nathaniel West - of VA, b1762 d1810, m Sallie Watson dau/o John Watson & Mary Bigger & had issue - desc/o Col John West GVGWM(2)131; CFA(1)118 information in this reference is different including date of d1847, m1797 Martha Fontaine b1781 d1845

    Robert - of VA, b1760, m Mildred Aylett Allen - desc/o Col John West CFA(1)118

    William - of VA, m (his cousin) Agnes West dau/o Col Francis West of King William Co & had issue - desc/o Col John West GVFWM(2)119; CFA(1)117

    William - of VA, b1750, m Anne Bolling or Bolton - desc/o Col John West CFA(1)118

DANIEL Robert - of VA, b1666 d1723, m1687 Margaret Price - desc/o Col William Daniel JSW1784

    Robert - of VA, m Elizabeth Beverley - desc/o Col William Daniel JSW1784

    Samuel - b1729 d1823, m Elizabeth Thomas - desc/o Col William Daniel JSW1784

    Col William - of VA, b1626 d1695, m(1) bef 1665 Dorothy Forth - the immigrant JSW1783, 784; sufficient proof of alleged royal ancestry is lacking

DARE Virginia - of NC, b1587 the first English child born in America - desc/o Eleanor White JSW1540

DARLING Esther Slack of RI, m Capt Nathan Arnold - desc/o Susan Clinton CHB146; BCD146

Samuel - of RI, b1695 d1750 - the immigrant EDV115, 116; sufficient proof of alleged royal ancestry is lacking

Samuel MD - of CT, b1751 d1842, m1779 Clarinda Ely - desc/o Mabel Harlakenden MCB404; MCD229

DARLINGTON Abraham - of PA - the immigrant EDV115, 116; sufficient proof of alleged royal ancestry is lacking

John - of PA - the immigrant EDV115, 116; sufficient proof of alleged royal ancestry is lacking

DARNALL Mary - of MD, m1768 Charles Carroll of Carrollton - desc/o Rev Robert Brooke MG(1)105; CFA(5)83

DASHIELL Elizabeth - of MD, d1820, m John Upshur Dennis - desc/o Nathaniel Littleton CFA(4)127

DAUBENEY Lloyd Jr - of NY, b1746, m1770 Mary Coventry - the immigrant MCB366; MCD206; sufficient proof of alleged royal ancestry is lacking

DAVENPORT Abigail - b1672 d1691/1692, m1691 Rev James Pierpont - desc/o Rev John Davenport AMB104; DLJ522

Abigail - b1696, m1718 Rev Stephen Williams of Springfield, MA - desc/o Rev John Davenport AMB104; DLJ522

Abraham - of CT, b1715 d1789, m(1)1750 Elizabeth Huntington b1725 d1773 dau/o Jabez Huntington & Elizabeth Edwards, m(2)1776 Martha Fitch a widow - desc/o Rev John Davenport AMB104; DLJ523

Deodate - of CT, b1706 d1761, m(1)1730 Lydia Woodward b abt 1706 d1758 dau/o John Woodward & Sarah Rosewell, m(2)1760 Mercy Ball dau/o Alling Ball & Sarah Thompson, wid/o Eleazer Morris b abt 1693 - desc/o Rev John Davenport AMB104; DLJ522

Deodate - of CT, b1730 d1808, m(1)Lydia Raymond, m(2) Elizabeth Jones - desc/o Rev John Davenport AMB104

Elizabeth - b1666 d1744, m1700 Rev Warham Mather - desc/o Rev John Davenport AMB104; DLJ522

Elizabeth - b1708, m Rev William Gaylord of Wilton - desc/o Rev John Davenport AMB104; DLJ523

Hezekiah - b1769 d1854, m1804 Philena Piepont d1827 aged 40 - desc/o Rev John Davenport DLJ523

Rev James - of NY, b1716 d1755, m & had issue - desc/o Rev John Davenport AMB104; DLJ523

Rev John - of MA & CT, bp 1597 Coventry d1669/1670 clergyman, author & founder of the New Haven Colony & minister there, son of Henry Davenport & Winifred Barnaby, m bef 1619 Elizabeth (Wooley ?) b abt 1603 d1676 - the immigrant FLW190, 191; MCS90; DBR(2)778, 779; DBR(3)710; AMB103; THJ36, 39; RAA1, 86; EDV46; GBR334, 335; TAG(52)216, 217; DLJ521, 522

John II - of MA, b abt 1635 d1677, m1663 Abigail Pierson dau/o the Reverend Abraham Pierson - desc/o Rev John Davenport DBR(2)779; DBR(3)710: AMB104; DLJ522

Reverend John III - of MA, b1668 d1731, m(1)1695 Martha (Gould)

DAVENPORT (cont.)

Selleck d1712, m(2) Elizabeth (Morris) Maltbie d1758 dau/o John Morris & Hannah Bishop & wid/o William Maltbie b1675 - desc/o Rev John Davenport DBR(2)779; DBR(3)710; AMB104; DLJ522

John - of CT, b1698 d1742, m1722 Sarah Bishop - desc/o Rev John Davenport AMB104; DLJ522

John - of CT, b1724 d1756, m1748 Deborah Amblar - desc/o Rev John Davenport AMB104

John - of CT, b1749 d1820, m(1) Prudence Bell, m(2)1795 Sarah Gaylord - desc/o Rev John Davenport AMB105

Joseph - of CT, b1725, m1753 - desc/o Rev John Davenport AMB104

Hezekiah - of CT, b1738 d1777, m1763 Ruth Ketchams - desc/o Rev John Davenport AMB104

Lydia - b abt 1746 d1801, m1779 Samuel Holt - desc/o Rev John Davenport DLJ523

Martha - of MA, b1700, m(1)1731 Rev Thomas Goodsell, m(2) Samuel Baker - desc/o Rev John Davenport DBR(2)779; AMB104; DLJ522

Martha - of CT, b1731, m1757 John Crissey - desc/o Rev John Davenport AMB105

Martha - b1733, m Gould S Silliman - desc/o Rev John Davenport DLJ522

Martha - b1771 d1843, m1793 Eli Potter - desc/o Rev John Davenport DLJ523

Mary - b1676, m(1)1694 Nathaniel Weed or Wade - desc/o Rev John Davenport AMB104; DLJ522

Mary - b1771 d1858, m1794 John Woodward - desc/o Rev John Davenport DLJ523

Phoebe - of MA, b1713, m Thomas Underhill son of Nathaniel Underhill - desc/o Rev John Davenport DBR(3)710, 711

Capt Richard - of MA - the immigrant EDV46; sufficient information of alleged royal ancestry is lacking

Rhoda - of CT, b1754, m1775 Thaddeus Huested - desc/o Rev John Davenport AMB105

Roswell - b1768, m1793 Esther Hemingway dau/o Samuel Hemingway & Hannah Morris - desc/o Rev John Davenport DLJ523

Samuel - b abt 1736 d1810, m(1) May Morris b abt 1740 d1765 dau/o Eleazer Morris & Mercy Ball, m(2) Mary Street b1738 d1803 dau/o Elnathan Street & Damaris Hull - desc/o Rev John Davenport DLJ522

Sarah - b1701/1702, m(1) Capt William Maltby, m(2) Rev Eleazar Wheelock of Lebanon - desc/o Rev John Davenport AMB104; DLJ522

Sarah - b1731 d1806, m John Mix - desc/o Rev John Davenport DLJ522

Sarah - of CT, b1751, m1770 Manmouth Lounsbury - desc/o Rev John Davenport AMB104

Sarah - b1767, m1784 Ira Smith - desc/o Rev John Davenport DLJ523

Silas - of CT, b1736, m1765 Mary Webb - desc/o Rev John Davenport AMB104

Street - b1775, m1827 Nancy M Shultz - desc/o Rev John Davenport

DAVENPORT (cont.)
>DLJ523

DAVIDSON Eunice - of CT, b1757 d1849, m1781 Sylvanus Willes - desc/o Olive Welby ECD(3)272

>Sarah - b1755 - desc/o Olive Welby RAA93

DAVIE Elizabeth - of MA, m Daniel Taylor - desc/o Humphrey Davie TAG(23)211, 212

>Elizabeth - of MA, b1715/1716, m1739 James Butler b1713 d1739 son of James Butler & Abigail Eustis - desc/o Humphrey Davie TAG(23)214

>Humphrey - of MA 1662, bp 1625 d1688/1689, merchant & acted on committees for Boston, represented Billerica as a deputy to the General Court, was elected an assistant overseer of Harvard College, son of Sir John Davie, 1st Baronet & Juliana Strode, m(1) bef 25 May 1655 Mary White d1681 dau/o Edmund White & Elizabeth Wilson, m(2)1683 Mrs Sarah Gibbon Richards b1645 dau/o William & Ursula Gibbon & wid/o James Richards - the immigrant GBR121; TAG(23)207/217

>Humphrey - of MA, b1684/1685, m1714 Margaret Gedney b1694 dau/o William & Hannah (Gardner) Gedney - desc/o Humphrey Davie TAG(23)214, 215

>Sir John, 5th Baronet - of CT, a Harvard graduate & patentee of New London, CT, first clerk of the town of Groton, CT, returned to Sandford, Devonshire where his descendants now live - desc/o Humphrey Davie TAG(23)206, 207

>Margaret - of MA, b1666, m1702 Henry Franklin d1713 - desc/o Humphrey Davie TAG(23)212, 213

>William - of MA, b1686 - desc/o Humphrey Davie TAG(23)215

DAVIS Amy - of NJ, m1741 John Gill - desc/o Dorothea Scott CHB90; BCD90

>Maj Benjamin - of GA, b abt 1742 d1817, m abt 1770 Tabitha Rose - desc/o Capt Thomas Warren ECD(3)312; DBR(1)189; DBR(2)270

>Daniel - b1719 - desc/o Griffith Bowen RAA72

>Judge David - of NJ, m Dorothy Cousins - desc/o Dorothea Scott CHB90; MCB226; MCD288; BCD90

>Eleanor - of VA, m John Bourne III - desc/o Rev Hawte Wyatt JSW1636

>Elizabeth - of NJ, m1731 Samuel Morgan - desc/o Dorothea Scott ECD(2)240

>Hannah - of NJ, b1728, m Richard Wood - desc/o Dorothea Scott CHB90; BCD90

>Isaac - of NJ, d1739, m Elizabeth___ - desc/o Dorothea Scott ECD(2)240

>Jacob - of NJ, b1734 d1820, m(1)1761 Esther Wilkins - desc/o Dorothea Scott MCB226, 227

>Joseph - of NJ, b abt 1753 d1827, m(1) Abby Farrand - desc/o Obadiah Bruen ECD127

>Lucy - of MA, b1738 Concord d bef Dec 1776, m Benjamin Hutchins - desc/o Rev Peter Bulkeley TAG(36)105

>Margaret - of PA, d1724 dau/o Nathaniel & Mary___ Davis, m1670 Thomas Bye VIII - the immigrant ECD(3)111; DBR(4)230; GBR163

DAVIS (cont.)
some aspect of royal descent merits further study
Mary - b1744 - desc/o Griffith Bowen RAA72
Sally - of NJ, b1774 d1853, m abt 1795 Sayres Coe - desc/o Obadiah
Bruen ECD127
Susanna of VA, m William Bartlett - desc/o Rev Hawte Wyatt CHB423;
MCD312
DAVISON Christopher - of VA - the immigrant WAC85; sufficient proof of
alleged royal ancestry is lacking
DAWSON Benoni II - of MD, b1769 d1844, m1792 Katherine P D
McKennon - desc/o Anne Brooke ECD(3)39; DBR(1)236;
DBR(2)333; DBR(3)436; DBR(4)355
Mary - of VA, b1734 d1788, m1752 Ludwell Grymes of Brandon,
Middlesex Co, VA b1733- - desc/o Henry Isham CHB534 - desc/o
Col William Randolph DBR(2)672; PVF132
DAY Elizabeth - m Capt Nathaniel Ridley - desc/o Peter Montague FFF80c
DAYTON Elizabeth - b1711 - desc/o Peter Bulkeley RAA75
Hannah - of CT, b1718, m1738/1739 Stephen Jacobs - desc/o Rev
Peter Bulkeley DBR(5)971
DEANE Damaris - of MA, b1689, m Matthew White - desc/o Frances
Deighton DBR(2)163
Lieut Joseph - of MA, b1717 d1803, m1741 Katherine Willis - desc/o
Frances Deighton DBR(3)61; DBR(5)759
Lydia - b1767 - desc/o Margaret Wyatt RAA61 - desc/o Thomas
Newberry RAA118
Mehitable of MA, b1697, m Josiah Richmond - desc/o Richard
Williams CHB377; MCD308
Sarah - of MA, b1743, m1765 Jacob Williams - desc/o Frances
Deighton DBR(3)61; DBR(5)759
DEBEVOISE Carel - of NY, b abt 1620, m Sophia Van Lodensteyn - the
immigrant RAA1, 86; sufficient proof of alleged royal ancestry is
lacking
Carel - b1680 - desc/o Carel DeBevoise RAA86
Carel - b abt 1711 - desc/o Carel DeBevoise RAA86
Jacobus - b1651 - desc/o Carel DeBevoise RAA86
Maria - b1744 - desc/o Carel DeBevoise RAA86
DEIGHTON Frances of MA, bp 1611 St Nicholas, Gloucester d1705/1706
Taunton, MA, dau/o Dr John Deighton & Jane Bassett, m1632
Witcombe Magna, Gloucester, Richard Williams bp 1607 Wootton-
under-Edge d1693 Taunton, MA - the immigrant CHB374, 67;
FLW84; ECD(2)106; MCD308; MCS20; LDS22; DBR(1)419, 563,
762; DBR(2)162, 163, 365, 688, 690; DBR(3)60, 61, 161, 364, 367;
DBR(4)428, 627, 860; DBR(5)96, 759; RAA86; AWW339; GBR205
Jane - of MA, bp 1609 dau/o Dr John Deighton & Jane Bassett,
m(1)1627 St Nicholas, John Lugg, came to NE 1638 d aft 1644,
m(2) bef 1647 Jonathan Negus b1602 d aft 1678 & had issue by
both husbands - desc/o Katharine Deighton CHB376; FLW84;
ECD(3)114; MCS20; GBR205
Dr John - of MA, b abt 1581, m Jane Bassett - the immigrant RAA1,
86; sufficient proof of alleged royal ancestry is lacking
Katharine - of MA, bp 1614/1615 Gloucester, England d1671 dau/o

DEIGHTON (cont.)

Dr John Deighton & Jane Bassett, m(1) Samuel Haighburne or Hackburne, m(2)1644 Roxbury, MA, Governor Thomas Dudley b1576 d1653 governor of MA, m(3) Rev John Allyn & had issue by all 3 husbands - the immigrant CHB375; FLW83, 84; ECD(2)110; JSW1826; MCS20; DBR(2)569; DBR(4)729; DBR(5)79, 82, 84; RAA86; GBR205

DELAFIELD John - of NY, b1748 d1824, m1784 Anne Hallett - the immigrant CHB104; BCD104; AMB270; sufficient proof of alleged royal ancestry is lacking

DE LANCEY Etrenne - of New England 1681 - the immigrant EDV24; sufficient proof of alleged royal ancestry is lacking

DELANO (DE LANNOY) Hester - of MA, b1638 d1678, m John Soule - desc/o Philippe Delano CHB505

Hannah - of MA, b1711 d1768, m1733 Ezekiel Soule - desc/o Philippe Delano CHB487

Jonathan - of MA, m Mary Warren - desc/o Philippe Delano CHB505

Jonathan Sr - of MA, b1676 d1765, m1699 Hannah Doty - desc/o Philippe Delano CHB487

Jonathan Jr - of CT 1722, m Hannah Doten - desc/o Philippe Delano CHB505

Philippe - of MA 1635, b1603 d1681, m1634 Hester Dewsbury the immigrant CHB487, 504; EDV47; sufficient proof of alleged royal ancestry is lacking

Priscilla - b abt 1686 - desc/o Miles Standish RAA131

Susanna - of CT b1724, m1746 Capt Noah Grant Jr - desc/o Phillipe Delano CHB505

Dr Thomas of MA, b1642 d1723, m1667 Mary Alden - desc/o Philippe Delano CHB487

DE PEYSTER Johannes - of NY 1652 - the immigrant EDV24; sufficient proof of alleged royal ancestry is lacking

DENISON or DENNISON Maj Gen Daniel - of MA, d1673 - desc/o William Denison EDV57

Elizabeth - of MA, bp 1642 d1723, m1660 Rev Dr John Rogers - desc/o Gov Thomas Dudley DBR(1)71; DBR(2)90

Hannah - of CT, b1643, m1659 Capt Nathaniel Cheseborough - desc/o Alice Freeman DBR(3)424, 684; DBR(4)800; RAA132

John - of MA, d1747 - desc/o William Denison EDV57

Prudence - b1743 - desc/o Alice Freeman RAA132

Sarah - of CT, b1641 d1701, m Thomas Stanton - desc/o Alice Freeman DBR(4)483

William - of MA 1631 - the immigrant EDV57; sufficient proof of alleged royal ancestry is lacking

DENNE Elizabeth - of NJ, bp 1662/1663, m(1)1680 Richard Hancock d1689 - the immigrant ECD166; DBR(1)6; DBR(4)596; RAA101; sufficient proof of alleged royal ancestry is lacking

DENNIS Donnack - of MD, b1669 d1740, m Sarah___ - desc/o Nathaniel Littleton CFA(4)126

Eleanor - of MD, m Jeremiah Morris - desc/o Nathaniel Littleton CFA(4)126

Eliza - of MD, b1743, m Thomas Maddux - desc/o Nathaniel Littleton

DENNIS (cont.)
CFA(4)127

Elizabeth - of MD, b1665, m George Lyle of Somerset Co, MD - desc/o Nathaniel Littleton CFA(4)126

Elizabeth - of MD, b1760 d1811, m1776 John Teackle b1753 of Kegotank, Accomack Co d1817 & had issue - desc/o Nathaniel Littleton HSF(10)198; CFA(4)128

Henry - of MD, b1757 d1785, member of MD Assembly 1778/1779, was second lieutenant in Revolutionary Army 1776/1777, lost at sea 1785, m1780 Anne Purnell, dau/o Judge Lemuel Purnell - desc/o Nathaniel Littleton HSF(10)197; CFA(4)128

John - of MD, b1676 of Beverly, Worcester Co d1741, appointed one of the justices of the Provincial Court, m(1) Sarah Littleton d1732, dau/o Col Southey Littleton & Sarah Bowman, m(2) Elizabeth Day, dau/o Capt George Day - desc/o Nathaniel Littleton CFA(4)126

John - of MD, b1704 d1766, m Mary Purnell d1768 - desc/o Nathaniel Littleton HSF(10)196; CFA(4)127

John - of MD, b1771 of Beckford, Princess Anne's Co d1807, m1793 Elinor Jackson d1827 dau/o Henry Jackson of Somerset Co MD & had issue among whom was Elizabeth W Dennis who married Abel Parker Upshur I - desc/o Nathaniel Littleton HSF(10)198

Littleton - of MD, b1728/1729 of Beverly, Worcester Co d1774, m1754 Susanna Upshur b1733 d1784 eldest dau/o Abel Upshur I & Rachel Revell - desc/o Nathaniel Littleton HSF(10)196, 197; CFA(4)128

Littleton - of MD, b1765 d1833, m1788 Elizabeth Upshur b1769 d1819, dau/o John Upshur II & Ann Emmerson & had issue - desc/o Nathaniel Littleton HSF(10)198

Sarah - of VA, b1768 d1804, m1785 Francis Hutchins Waters b1764 d1826 & had issue - desc/o Nathaniel Littleton HSF(10)198

DENNY William - of PA & DE, lieut governor of Pennsylvania & governor of Delaware son of Hill Denny & Abigail Berners, m Mary Hill - the immigrant GBR240

DENT Ann of MD, m Samuel Brisco - desc/o Humphrey Warren CHB317; BCD317

Ann Herbert - of MD, b1756 d1813, m1774 Capt William Mackall Wilkinson son of William & Barbara (Mackall) Wilkinson - desc/o Col Gerard Fowke DBR(1)655; DBR(2)200, 309, 753

Elizabeth - of MD d1760, m Richard Tarvin of Charles Co, MD d1742 - desc/o Col Gerard Fowke APP616

Col George - of MD, b1690 d1754, chief justice of MD, m1712 Ann Herbert d1764 dau/o Captain William Herbert - desc/o Col Gerard Fowke DBR(1)654; DBR(2)199, 308, 752, 753; APP616

George Washington - of MD, b1776, m Anne Hutchinson - desc/o Gov Robert Brooke DBR(2)282

Brig-Gen John - of MD, b1733 d1809 delegate from Charles Co to MD Convention, Commissioner of payment to troops in Canada, m1753 Sarah Marshall dau/o Thomas Marshall - desc/o Col Gerard Fowke DBR(1)654; DBR(2)199, 308, 753

Peter - of MD, bp 1694/1695 d1757, m1726 Mary Brooke b1709 - desc/o Col Gerard Fowke GBR363; APP615

DENT (cont.)

    Peter Jr - m Mary Eleanor____ - desc/o Col Gerard Fowke GBR364 - desc/o Robert Brooke GBR385

    Thomas - of MD 1658, b1630 - the immigrant DBR(2)281 royal ancestry not proven

    Thomas - of MD, b1685 d1725, justice of Charles Co, sheriff, & captain of militia, committed to debtor's prison 1722, as a result of gambling debts, m1705 Anne Bayne d1725 - desc/o Col Gerard Fowke APP615

    Capt Thomas - of MD, b1735 d1789, m Elizabeth Edelen - desc/o Rev Robert Brooke DBR(2)282

DENWOOD Esther - m____ King - desc/o Col Nathaniel Littleton APP466

    John - d bef 12 May 1725, m Mary Elizabeth Hack - desc/o Col Nathaniel Littleton APP466

    Priscilla - m1720 Thomas Gillis b1697 d1780, of Somerset Co, MD - desc/o Col Nathaniel Littleton APP466

    Thomas - d1765, m(1) Mary Waters d bef Sep 1752, m(2) Mary____ - desc/o Col Nathaniel Littleton APP466

DEVOTION Jemima - b1727 - desc/o Richard Harlakenden RAA102

DEWEY David I - of CT, b1676 d1712, m1699 Sarah____ - desc/o John Drake DBR(5)799

    David II - of MA, b1700 d1746, m Abigail Ashley - desc/o John Drake DBR(5)799

    David III - of MA, b1725 d1813, m1751 Rebecca Phelps - desc/o John Drake DBR(5)799

    Electa - of MA, b1772 d1849, m1798 Oliver Bush - desc/o Benjamin Moseley ECD(3)217; DBR(2)721

    Hannah - of CT, m1704 Phillip Loomis - desc/o John Drake DBR(5)618; RAA87

    Josiah of MA, anc/o George Dewey - desc/o Richard Lyman J&K204

    Timothy - of MA, b1755 d1839, m1776 Aseneth Sexton - desc/o John Drake DBR(5)799

    Zerviah - b1726 - desc/o Alice Freeman RAA132

DICKENSON Brainerd - of NJ, b1752 d1819, m Sarah Baldwin - desc/o Philemon Dickenson BLG2658

    Nathaniel - of MA 1629 - the immigrant EDV94; sufficient proof of alleged royal ancestry is lacking

    Peter - of NY, b1647 d1723, m Abigail Reeve - desc/o Philemon Dickenson BLG2658

    Peter - of NJ, b1710 d1798, m Sarah Brainerd - desc/o Philemon Dickenson BLG2658

    Philemon - of MA 1637, b1613 d1672, m Mary Paine - the immigrant EDV94; BLG2658; sufficient proof of alleged royal ancestry is lacking

    Philemon - of NY, b1682 d1718, m Hannah Case - desc/o Philemon Dickenson BLG2658

DICKESON John - b1718 d1777, m1739 Mary____ - desc/o John Fenwick DBR(2)585; DBR(3)372; DBR(4)701

    Thomas - b1742 d1789, m1773 Hannah Hudson - desc/o John Fenwick DBR(2)585; DBR(3)372; DBR(4)701

    William - b1696 d1764, m abt 1716____ - desc/o John Fenwick

DICKESON (cont.)
> DBR(2)585; DBR(3)372

DICKINSON Christopher - b1729 - desc/o Anne Marbury RAA114
> Charity - b1776 - desc/o Anne Marbury RAA114
>
> Dorcas - b1750 - desc/o Dorothy Stapilton RAA117
>
> George - b1707 - desc/o Dorothy Stapilton RAA117
>
> Jemima - m1770 Sylvanus Lawrence - desc/o Francis Mapes DBR(3)500
>
> Peter - of NJ, d1773, m1736/1737 Sarah Brainard - desc/o Francis Mapes DBR(3)500
>
> Philemon - of NY, d1718, m1709 Hannah Case - desc/o Francis Mapes DBR(3)500
>
> Samuel - b abt 1750 - desc/o Anne Marbury RAA114

DIGGS/DIGGES Ann - of VA, b abt 1657 d1688, m Col William Cole of Bolthrope, Warwick Co - desc/o Dudley Diggs BLG2659; AMB297; APP252; GVFWM(2)170; HSF(12)262, 263
> Ann - of MD, d aft Jun 1751, m1704 Henry Darnall b abt 1682 - desc/o Dudley Diggs BLG2659; APP151, 152
>
> Anne of MD, m Dr George Steuart - desc/o Dudley Diggs J&K225; CHB76; BCD76
>
> Anne - of VA, m____ Baylor - desc/o Dudley Diggs HSF(12)268
>
> Catherine - of VA, b1654 d1727, m1677 William Herndon - desc/o Dudley Diggs JSW1605; DBR(4)791; DBR(5)772, 870; FFF284
>
> Charles - of MD, m Miss Dulany(?) - desc/o Dudley Diggs J&K225; BCD76
>
> Charles - of MD, b1676 d1744, m Susannah Maria Lowe - desc/o Dudley Diggs BLG2659; DBR(3)320; APP251
>
> Col Cole of VA, b1691/1692 d1744 commander in chief of the militia for Warwick, York & Elizabeth City Co, VA, m Elizabeth Power dau/o Dr Henry Power of York Co - desc/o Dudley Diggs CHB77; MCD210; BCD77; DBR(1)103, 350, 597; DBR(2)64, 698, 726, 727; DBR(3)106, 108, 343, 557; DBR(4)679; DBR(5)704, 710, 780, 822; AMB297; APP253; GVFWM(2)173; HSF(12)264, 265
>
> Cole - of VA, b1748, m Martha Walker - desc/o Dudley Diggs GVFWM(2)179; HSF(12)270
>
> Cole - of VA, b1754 d1817 major of cavalry during the Revolution, member of the House of Delegates & Virginia Convention of 1788, m Mary Purdie b1767 d1826 dau/o George Purdie & Mary Robinson - desc/o Dudley Diggs GVFWM(2)178; HSF(12)268, 269
>
> Sir Dudley of VA, b1583 d1638 member of the London Company for Colonizing Virginia, eldest son of Thomas Digges & Anne St Leger, m Mary Kempe dau/o Sir Thomas Kempe of Olantigh, Kent & Dorothy Thompson - the immigrant J&K255; CHB75, 76; ECD(3)119; JSW1605; MCD210; BLG2659; BCD75; DBR(1)103, 182, 183, 350, 596; DBR(2)64, 698; DBR(3)106, 557; DBR(4)679; DBR(5)703, 709, 772, 821 , 870, 986; AMB296, 297; WAC32; FFF284; GBR140; APP247/253 states there is no record that Sir Dudley Digges or his sons Thomas and John, both members of the Virginia Company, 1612, came to Virginia; HSF(12)257/271
>
> Dudley of VA, b1664/1665 d1710 Virginia agent for the London merchant Micajah Perry, member of the House of Burgesses &

DIGGS/DIGGES (cont.)

Colonel of Warwick County militia, m Susannah Cole b abt 1674 d1708 dau/o Col William Cole of Warwick Co - desc/o Dudley Diggs CHB77; BLG2659; BCD77; DBR(1)103, 350, 597; DBR(2)64, 698, 726; DBR(3)106, 343, 557; DBR(4)679; DBR(5)704, 709, 780; AMB297; APP253; GVFWM(2)171; HSF(12)264

Dudley of VA, b1729 d1790 appointed colonel of horse & foot 1748, lawyer by profession, m(1) Martha Armistead, m(2) Elizabeth Wormeley dau/o Ralph Wormeley of Rosegill, Middlesex Co - desc/o Dudley Diggs CHB77; BCD77; DBR(1)103, 350, 597; DBR(2)64, 698, 727; DBR(3)108; 343; DBR(4)679; DBR(5)704, 710, 780, 822; AMB297; GVFWM(2)179; HSF(12)270

Dudley - of MD, d1752, m Mary Lilly - desc/o Dudley Diggs BLG2659

Dudley - of VA, Burgess & justice from Goochland, m Mary Hubard dau/o James & Elizabeth Hubard - desc/o Dudley Diggs AMB297; APP253; GVFWM(2)172; HSF(12)264

Dudley - of VA, b1760, m Mary Diggs dau/o Dudley Diggs - desc/o Dudlley Diggs AMB198; GVFWM(2)177; HSF(12)268

Dudley - of VA, b1765, m Alice Page dau/o Gov John Page & wid/o Dr Augustine Smith - desc/o Dudley Diggs GVFWM(2)180; HSF(12)270

Gov Edward of VA shortly after 11 Dec 1650, bp 1621 d1675 member of the Governor's Council 1654/1675, governor Virginia Colony 1655/58, son of Sir Dudley Diggs & Mary Kempe, m Elizabeth Brayne (or Page) d abt 1691 - desc/o Dudley Diggs J&K255; ECD(3)119; JSW1605; MCB153; MCD210; MCS39; BLG2659; BCD76; DBR(1)103, 350, 597; DBR(2)64, 696, 698, 726; DBR(3)106, 320, 343; DBR(4)679, 791; DBR(5)703, 772, 779, 780, 822, 870; AMB297; RAA1, 87; EDV125; WAC32; FFF284 - the immigrant GBR140; GVFTQ(1)546/555; GVFWM(2)169/180; HSF(12)260

Col Edward - of VA, d1769 justice of the peace for York Co & commissioned county lieutenant 1748, m1739 Anne Harrison b abt 1719 d1775 dau/o Nathaniel Harrison - desc/o Dudley Diggs AMB298; GVFWM(2)174; HSF(12)266, 267

Edward - of VA & MD, d1714 surveyor general & examiner general of MD's Eastern Shore, m Elizabeth Darnell d1705 - desc/o Dudley Diggs BLG2659; APP251

Edward - of VA, b1746 d1818, m1775 Elizabeth Gaskins b1756 dau/o Col Thomas Gaskins - desc/o Dudley Diggs AMB298; GVFWM(2)175; HSF(12)267, 268

Eleanor - of MD, m Raphael Taney - desc/o Dudley Diggs BLG2659

Eliza - of MD, d1722, m1698 Anthony Neale - desc/o Dudley Diggs ECD(3)119, 120

Elizabeth - of MD, m Anthony Neal of Charles Co, MD b in Spain abt 1659 d1723, lieutenant in the Charles Co militia & participated in the Nanticoke Indian War - desc/o Dudley Diggs BLG2659; DBR(5)986; APP251

Elizabeth - of MD, m Raphael Neale - desc/o Dudley Diggs BLG2659

Elizabeth - of VA, b1761, m Dr Robert Nicholson of Yorktown - desc/o Dudley Diggs BCD77; GVFWM(2)180; HSF(12)270

Elizabeth - of VA, b1752, m Dr Thomas Powell - desc/o Dudley Diggs

DIGGS/DIGGES (cont.)

AMB298

Elizabeth - of VA, m William Diggs of Newport News, son of Edward Digges - desc/o Dudley Diggs HSF(12)269

Frances - of VA, m William Sumner & had issue, three children - desc/o Dudley Diggs HSF(12)267

George Atwood of MA, b1746 d1792, m1789 Catherine Brent - desc/o George Atwood CHB10,76; BCD10; BCD76; DBR(3)320

Henry - of MD, d1795, m Jane Brent - desc/o Dudley Diggs BLG2659

Jane - of MD, m Notley Rozer b1673 d1727 - desc/o Dudley Diggs BLG2659; APP251

John - of MD, m Eleanor Hall - desc/o Dudley Diggs BLG2659

John - of Frederick Co, MD, received large grants from Lord Baltimore in what is now Baltimore, Carroll & Frederick Counties, MD, & in York Co, PA, m____ - desc/o Dudley Diggs APP251

Dr Joseph Sr - of VA, b1725 - desc/o Edward Diggs GVFT(1)547

Lucy - of VA, b1771, m John Stratton of the Eastern Shore of VA & had issue, two daughters who married two Parkers - desc/o Dudley Diggs GVFWM(2)180; HSF(12)270

Lucy B - of VA, m Dudley Fitzhugh - desc/o Dudley Diggs GVFWM(2)177

Martha (Patsy) of VA, b1757 d1848, m1780 Capt Nathaniel Burwell - desc/o Dudley Diggs CHB77; BCD77; DBR(1)103, 350, 597; DBR(2)64, 698, 727; DBR(3)108, 343; DBR(4)679; DBR(5)704, 710, 780, 822

Mary - of VA, b1660 d1690, m Capt Francis Page son of Col John Page - desc/o Dudley Diggs BLG2659; AMB297; GVFWM(2)170; HSF(12)262

Mary of VA, b1717 d1743, m1739 Nathaniel Harrison Jr b1703 d1791 of Brandon, Prince George Co, VA - desc/o Dudley Diggs CHB77, 78; BCD77, 78; AMB297

Mary - of MD, m____ Okey - desc/o Dudley Diggs APP252

Mary - of VA, b1748 d1814, m George Fitzhugh of Fauquier Co & left 4 children - desc/o Dudley Diggs AMB298; GVFWM(2)177; HSF(12)268

Mary - of VA, m____ Henshaw - desc/o Dudley Diggs HSF(12)268

Mary - of VA, m Dudley Diggs, of Louisa Co, son of Col Edward Diggs of Bellfield - desc/o Dudley Diggs GVFWM(2)180; HSF(12)270

Mary - of VA, m William Hill - desc/o Dudley Diggs HSF(12)269

Patsy - of VA, b1757 d1848 Rustic Lodge, m1780 Capt Nathaniel Burwell - desc/o Dudley Diggs GVFWM(2)179, 180; HSF(12)270

Sarah - of VA, b1757, m William Fitzhugh of Fauquier Co - desc/o Dudley Diggs AMB298; GVFWM(2)177; HSF(12)268

Sarah Dudley - of VA, m (her cousin) Whiting Diggs - desc/o Dudley Diggs HSF(12)263

Susannah - of VA, m1739 Benjamin Harrison of Wakefield, Surry Co, son of Nathaniel Harrison - desc/o Dudley Diggs AMB297; HSF(12)266

Thomas - of VA, b1750 d1818, m____ & had issue - desc/o Dudley Diggs AMB298; GVFWM(2)177; HSF(12)268

Whiting - of VA, m Sarah Dudley dau/o Edward Dudley (his uncle) -

DIGGSDIGGES (cont.)

desc/o Dudley Diggs GVFWM(2)177; HSF(12)268

Col William - of VA & MD 1678/1679, b1650 d1697, justice of York Co 1671, captain of horse 1674 & sheriff 1679, m Elizabeth Sewall d1710 dau/o Henry Sewall & wid/o Dr Jesse Wharton - desc/o Dudley Diggs J&K255; CHB76; ECD(3)119; MCS39; BLG2659; BCD76; DBR(3)320; DBR(5)986; AMB297; APP250; GVFWM(2)170; HSF(12)262

William - of MD, b1713 d1783, m1739 Anne Atwood - desc/o Dudley Diggs CHB76; BCD76; DBR(3)320

Maj William - of VA, of Denbigh, Burgess, justice of the peace from Warwick Co, m Frances Robinson dau/o Major Anthony & Diana Robinson of York Co - desc/o Dudley Diggs CHB78; MCD210; BCD78; AMB297; GVFWM(2)177; HSF(12)268

William - of VA, b1742 sheriff of York Co & was involved in the Revolution also a member of the House of Delegates from Warwick Co for several years, m Elizabeth Diggs dau/o Col William Diggs of Denbigh (his uncle) - desc/o Dudley Diggs AMB298; GVFWM(2)175; HSF(12)267

William - of VA & MD, d1740, m Eleanor (Brooke) Darnell d1740 wid/o Philip Darnell - desc/o Dudley Diggs BLG2659; APP251

William Dudley of MD, m Eleanor Carroll - desc/o George Atwood CHB10,76; BCD10 - desc/o Dudley Diggs BCD76

DIMMOCK Ensign Shubael - of MA, b1640 d1732, m Joanna Bursley - desc/o Rev Thomas Dimmock J&K220; BLG2660

Shubeal - of MA, m Tabatha Lathrop - desc/o Rev Thomas Dimmock BLG2660

Shubeal - of MA, m Esther Pierce - desc/o Rev Thomas Dimmock BLG2660

Thankful - of MA, m Edward Waldo - desc/o Rev Thomas Dimmock J&K221

Rev Thomas - of MA 1639, d1658, m Ann Hammond - the immigrant J&K220; BLG2660; sufficient proof of alleged royal ancestry is lacking

DINSMORE John - of ME 1723, m Hannah ____ - the immigrant FFF92; sufficient proof of alleged royal ancestry is lacking

Robert - of ME, b1692, m Margaret Orr - desc/o John Dinsmore FFF92

William - b1731, m Elizabeth Cochran - desc/o John Dinsmore FFF92

William - m Elizabeth Barnett - desc/o John Dinsmore FFF92

DISBROW Peter - of NY 1666 - the immigrant EDV37; sufficient proof of alleged royal ancestry is lacking

DIVOLL Elizabeth - b1701, m Eleazer Houghton - desc/o John Whitcomb LDS46

DIXON Mildred - of VA, d1799, m1772 Philip Clayton - desc/o Col George Read DBR(4)804; DBR(5)365

Roger - of VA, b1763 d1833, m bef 1795 Mildred____ - desc/o Col George Read DBR(1)132; DBR(2)204; DBR(4)804; DBR(5)365

DIXWELL John - of CT, b abt 1607 d1688/1689, English regicide & Cromwelliam politician, son of William Dixwell & Elizabeth Brent, m(1) Mrs Joanna____ Ling, m(2) Bathsheba Howe - the immigrant GBR373

DODGE William - of MA 1629 - the immigrant EDV32; sufficient proof of alleged royal ancestry is lacking

DONGAN Thomas, 2nd Earl of Limerick - of NY, b1634 d1715, governor of New York & soldier, son of Sir John Dongan, Baronet & Mary Talbot, m Mary___ - the immigrant GBR216

DOOLITTLE Daniel - b1741 - desc/o Peter Bulkeley RAA75

    Johnson - b1765 - desc/o Peter Bulkeley RAA75

DORMER Fleetwood - of VA - the immigrant WAC42; sufficient proof of alleged royal ancestry is lacking

    Fleetwood - of VA - desc/o Fleetwood Dormer WAC42

DORSEY Elizabeth - d1749, m1741 Henry Griffith b1720 d1794 - desc/o Anne Lovelace DBR(1)652

    Jemima - of MD, d1770, m1750 Joseph Hobbs - desc/o Rev Hawte Wyatt DBR(2)286

    John - of MD, b1691 d1764, m1708 Honor Elder - desc/o Rev Hawte Wyatt DBR(2)286

    Sarah - of MD, b1739, m Richard Berry - desc/o Anne Lovelace JSW1861

DOUGLAS or DOUGLASS Elizabeth - of VA, b Accomack Co d1792 Accomack Co, m abt 1755 Skinner Wallop b Accomack Co d 1815 Accomack Co - desc/o Robert Drake SMO205

    James - of SC & AL, b bet 1760/1765 d1839, m abt 1792 Susanna Rogers - the immigrant ECD(2)116; sufficient proof of alleged royal ancestry is lacking

DOWD Rebecca - b1767 - desc/o Agnes Harris RAA131

DOWDALL Matilda Cecilia - of NJ, dau/o Walter Dowdall & Anne Johnson, m Thomas Shadden - the immigrant GBR217

DOWNING Margaret - b1714 - desc/o Amy Wyllys RAA126

DOYLE Elizabeth - of PA, m Joseph Fell - desc/o Rev Thomas Dungan AFA52

DRAKE Abigail - of CT, b1648 d1696, m1668 Israel Dewey - desc/o John Drake DBR(5)618, 799; RAA87

    Catherine - b1699, m Jonathan Fowler - desc/o John Drake LDS42

    Elizabeth of CT, b1621 d1716, m(1)1644 William Gaylord, m(2) aft 1657 John Elderkin - desc/o John Drake J&K312; CHB108; MCB346; MCD208; BCD108; DBR(1)162; RAA87; CRL(1)172

    Elizabeth - of CT, b1664 d1697/1698, m Nicholas Buckland - desc/o John Drake CRL(1)173

    Elizabeth - of CT, b1675, m Joseph Rockwell - desc/o John Drake MCD208; DBR(1)195; RAA87

    Enoch - of CT, b1655 d1698, m1680 Sarah Porter - desc/o John Drake ECD(2)120; LDS23; RAA87; CRL(1)173

    Enoch - of CT, b1683 d1776, m(1)1704 Elizabeth Barber, m(3) Dorcas Eggleston - desc/o John Drake ECD(2)120; LDS23; RAA87

    Enoch - of CT, b1705/1706 d1782, m1735 Mary Barber - desc/o John Drake ECD(2)120

    Esther (Hester) - of CT, b1662 d1691/1692, m1681 Thomas Griswold - desc/o John Drake DBR(4)146

    Hannah - of CT, b1653 d1694, m Capt John Higley - desc/o John Drake J&K311; MCD209; DBR(3)660; RAA87; CRL(1)173

    Hannah - of CT, b1678, m John Hoyt - desc/o John Drake DBR(5)59

DRAKE (cont.)

Isaac - of MA, b1753 d1800, m Jane Crossman - desc/o Thomas
Drake AMB59; CFA137

Jacob - of CT, b1683 d1762, m Hannah Loomis - desc/o John Drake
CRL(1)194

Jacob - of MA, d1689, m Mary Bissell - desc/o John Drake CRL(1)172;
THC81

James - b1746 d1816, m Amy____ - desc/o John Throckmorton
DBR(1)178

Jerusha - b1720, m Samuel Filley - desc/o John Drake LDS23; RAA87

Sergt Job - of CT, d1689, m1646 Mary Wolcott - desc/o John Drake
J&K308; CHB106; MCB430; BCD106; DBR(1)727; DBR(4)146;
DBR(5)618, 799; AFA82; RAA87; CRL(1)193, 194; THC81

Lieut Job - of CT, b1652 d1711, m1677 Elizabeth (Clarke) Cook -
desc/o John Drake J&K308; CHB106; MCD208; BCD106;
DBR(1)727, 728; RAA87; CRL(1)173, 194

Deacon Job - m Elizabeth Alvord - desc/o John Drake DBR(1)195

John - of CT 1635, b1585 d1659, m Elizabeth Rodgers - the immigrant
J&K308; CHB106, 107; FLW197; ECD(2)120; JSW1881; MCB346,
430; MCD208; MCS16; LDS23, 42; BCD105; DBR(1)162, 195, 727;
DBR(2)165, 166, 777; DBR(3)78, 79, 81, 82, 660, 662, 663;
DBR(4)146; DBR(5)50, 59, 372, 618, 798, 1040; AFA82; RAA1, 87;
EDV31, 32; CRL(1)172; AFA116; THC81, 82; TAG(41) 239/243;
TAG(63) 193/206 "The proposed parentage for John Drake of
Windsor should no longer be considered sound," Robert Charles
Anderson, FASG; NE(141)104 further research on identification of
possible Drake royal lines is currently being undertaken

John II - of CT, b1612 d1688/1689, m1648 Hannah Moore - desc/o
John Drake J&K311; CHB107; ECD(2)120; JSW1881; MCD208;
LDS23, 42; BCD107; DBR(1)195; DBR(2)167; DBR(3)79, 82, 660,
663; DBR(5)50, 59; RAA87; CRL(1)172; AFA116; THC81, 82

John - of CT, b1649 d1689, m1671 Mary Watson - desc/o John Drake
DBR(5)59; CRL(1)173

Lydia - of CT, b1661 d1702, m1681 Joseph Loomis - desc/o John
Drake CHB107; JSW1881; BCD107; DBR(2)167; DBR(3)79, 82;
DBR(5)50; CRL(1)173

Mary - of CT, d1683, m John Gaylord - desc/o John Drake CRL(1)172

Mary - of VA, b1625 d aft 1688, m abt 1670 Capt Richard Hill - desc/o
Robert Drake ECD(3)123; DBR(5)381, 1007; SMO25, 133

Mary - of CT, b1649 d1728, m1686 Thomas Marshall - desc/o John
Drake MCB430; LDS42; AFA82; RAA87; CRL(1)173

Mary - of MD, b1672, m Dr Edward Chetham - the immigrant
DBR(3)722; DBR(4)48, 471 sufficient proof of alleged royal ancestry
is lacking

Mary - of CT, b1680 d1717, m John Porter - desc/o John Drake
CRL(1)194

Mary - of CT, b1736 d1824, m1758 Joel Barber - desc/o John Drake
ECD(2)120

Mindwell - of CT, b1671 d1736, m James Loomis - desc/o John Drake
CRL(1)173

Robert - of VA 1636, bp 1591 Messtham, Surrey, England d1641

DRAKE (cont.)

Accomack-Northampton Co fourth son of Henry Drake & Mary Lee, m1622 Surrey, England, Joan Gawton bp 1607 Norfolk, England d Northampton Co - the immigrant ECD(3)123; DBR(5)380, 381, 1007; RAA1, 88; GBR390; SMO133

Ruth - of CT, b1657 d1731, m Samuel Barber - desc/o John Drake DBR(3)663; RAA87; CRL(1)173; AFA116; THC88 - desc/o Thomas Moore THC220

Sarah of CT, b1686 d1747, m1702 Maj Gen Roger Wolcott - desc/o John Drake J&K308; BCD106; DBR(1)729; CRL(1)195

Simon - of CT, b1659 d1711, m Hannah Mills - desc/o John Drake CRL(1)173

Thomas - of MA 1653, b1635, m(1) Jane Holbrook, m(2)1681 Mellicent Ford - the immigrant AMB58; CFA137; RAA no longer accepted as being of royal descent

William - of MA, b1661 d1727, m Sarah Nash - desc/o Thomas Drake AMB58; CFA137

William - of MA, b1695, m Mary Townsend - desc/o Thomas Drake AMB58; CFA137

William - of MA, b1729, m1752 Phoebe Leonard - desc/o Thomas Drake AMB58; CFA137

DRAPER Thomas - b1739, m Lydia Rogers - desc/o Samuel Hyde LDS37

DRAYTONS Charles - of SC, b1743 d1820 medical doctor, m Hester Middleton - desc/o Stephen Bull GPFPM(1)422

John - b1766 d1822, m Hester Rose Tidyman - desc/o Stephen Bull GPFPM(1)427

Mary - of SC, b1734 d1806, m(1)1753 Edward Fenwick of Charleston, m(2)1776 John Williams de Brahm, surveyor-general of South Carolina - desc/o Stephen Bull GPFPM(1)420

Mary Charlotte - b1766, m Daniel Wilson & had issue - desc/o Stephen Bull GPFPM(1)424

Mary - m1791 Thomas Parker, Esq, attorney-at-law - desc/o Stephen Bull GPFPM(1)427

Stephen - of SC, b1736 d1810, m(1)___ Betts, m(2)1769 Elizabeth Waring dau/o John Waring - desc/o Stephen Bull GPFPM(1)420

Thomas - of SC, b1759 d1801 - desc/o Lady Mary Mackenzie GPFPM(1)420

William - of SC, b1732 d1790 lawyer & was appointed aide-de-camp to Gov Lyttleton & took part in the expedition against the Cherokee Indians in 1759, m(1) Mary Motte, m(2) Mary Gates - desc/o Stephen Bull GPFPM(1)420, 423, 424

William - b1776 d1846, m(1) Ann Gadsden, m(2) Maria Miles Heyward - desc/o Stephen Bull GPFPM(1)424

William Henry - of SC & PA, b1742 d1779 judge, m1764 Dorothy Golightly - desc/o Stephen Bull GPFPM(1)422

DRUMMOND Ann - of MD, d bef 1799, m Capt John Selby - desc/o Richard Wright ECD(3)286

Barbara - of VA, b1703 d1756, m Daniel Welbourne - desc/o Robert Drake DBR(5)381

Elisha - of VA, b abt 1760 Accomack Co d1809 Accomack Co, m1779 Thomas Fletcher b1749 d 1820 - desc/o Robert Drake SMO134

DRUMMOND (cont.)

Hill - of VA, d1728 - desc/o Robert Drake DBR(5)381

Capt Richard - of VA, m abt 1690 Ann Tilney (?), m Elizabeth Scarburgh - desc/o Robert Drake ECD(3)123; SMO133 (the wife of Capt Richard Drummond is different with this source)

Capt Richard II - of VA, b Accomack Co d1730/1732 Accomack Co, m Anne Hacke b Accomack Co d aft 1732 - desc/o Robert Drake ECD(3)124; SMO134

Spencer - of VA, b Accomack Co d1759 Accomack Co, m Anne____ d1774 - desc/o Robert Drake SMO134

Tabitha - of VA, b Accomack Co d1761, m abt 1726 Accomack Co, George Douglas b abt 1698 Scotland d1758 Accomack Co - desc/o Robert Drake SMO205

DRURY Caleb - b1688, m Elizabeth Eames - desc/o Henry Rice LDS38

Caleb - b1713, m Mehitable Maynard - desc/o Henry Rice LDS38

Zachariah - b1748, m Ruth Sawyer - desc/o Henry Rice LDS38

DU BOIS Jacques - of NY 1675 - the immigrant EDV98, 99; sufficient proof of alleged royal ancestry is lacking

Jeremiah - b1760 d1844, m Sarah Shute - desc/o Jeremy Clarke ECD154

Joel - b1759 d1803, m1783 Elizabeth Sparks - desc/o Jeremy Clarke ECD156; ECD(2)92; DBR(4)734

Louis - of NY 1660/1661, d1696 - the immigrant EDV98, 99; sufficient proof of alleged royal ancestry is lacking

DUDLEY Abigail - of MA, m Mr Watson - desc/o Gov Thomas Dudley CRL(4)543

Alexander - b1727 - desc/o Edward Dudley RAA88

Ambrose - of VA, b1649 became a member of the vestry of Kingston Parish, Gloucester Co in 1667 & in 1699 he became a justice of the peace, m____ & left issue - desc/o Edward Dudley DBR(3)532; DBR(4)433, 550; GVFTQ(1)633

Ambrose - of VA, m Judith Scott - desc/o Edward Dudley DBR(4)550

Ambrose William - of KY, b abt 1750 d1825 in Lexington, Kentucky, captain in the Revolutionary Army in Virginia & a minister, m1773 Ann Parker dau/o William Parker - desc/o Edward Dudley DBR(2)820; DBR(3)181, 739; GVFTQ(1)627

Ann - of MA, b1641 Salisbury, m Col Edward Hilton d1699 - desc/o Gov Thomas Dudley DBR(1)74; DBR(2)97; CRL(4)543; NE(10)135; GDMNH209

Ann - of MA, b1684 d1776, m(1)1707 John Winthrop, m(2) Jeremiah Miller - desc/o Katherine Deighton ECD(2)111; DBR(5)84, 85, 1042 - desc/o Gov Thomas Dudley DBR(5)81; CRL(1)405; GPM(1)34

Ann - of NC, b abt 1727 d1763/1799, m abt 1746 William Simpson - desc/o Edward Dudley ECD(3)134; DBR(4)669

Ann - of MA, d1775, m John Lovell - desc/o Gov Thomas Dudley GPM(1)34

Anna - of CT, b1752 d1819, m1768 Capt Timothy Field - desc/o Anna Lloyd J&K321; ECD(3)193

Anne - of MA 1630, b abt 1612 d1672, an author & published the first book of poems by an Englishwoman in America, m1628 Simon Bradstreet bp 1603/1604 Horbling, Lincolnshire, England d1697

DUDLEY (cont.)

Salem, of MA 1630, secretary of the colony, assistant & was governor 1679/1686, 1689/1692, son of Rev Simon & Margaret Bradstreet - desc/o Gov Thomas Dudley J&K195; ECD(2)124; DBR(1)487, 557; DBR(2)293, 686; DBR(3)596, 653; DBR(4)399, 838, 839, 867; DBR(5)223, 360; RAA89; AAP155; CRL(1)401; AFA114; CRL(4)543; GBR250; RAA89; FLW54; NEFGM(1)77; NE(8)312/325; GPM(1)pxliii, 33

Armistead - of VA, served with Gen George Rogers in the Northwest - desc/o Edward Dudley GVFTQ(1)634

Benjamin Winslow - of KY, celebrated surgeon & greatest lithologist of his time - desc/o Edward Dudley GVFTQ(1)627

Betsy - of VA, m Capt Peter Bernard - desc/o Edward Dudley GVFTQ(1)634

Biley - of MA, b1647 d1728, Juror & selectman, m1682 Elizabeth Gilman - desc/o Gov Thomas Dudley GDMNH209

Bishop - of NC, d1788 in Topsail Co militia of New Hanover at the beginning of the French & Indian War, m Rebecca Ward - desc/o Edward Dudley DBR(1)251, 262; DBR(2)363, 858; DBR(3)15; GVFTQ(1)637

Catharine - of MA, b1690 d1760, m(1)1714 William Dummer, m(2) Lieut governor William Wainwright - desc/o Gov Thomas Dudley CRL(1)405; GPM(1)34

Catharine - of MA, b1729 d1769, m Peter Johonnot - desc/o Gov Thomas Dudley GPM(1)34

Catharine - of MA, b1761, m1779 Nehemiah Davis - desc/o Gov Thomas Dudley GPM(1)34

Christopher - of VA, b1670 d1746, m1705 Mary Lewis - desc/o Edward Dudley ECD(3)134; DBR(1)251, 262; DBR(2)363, 858; DBR(3)15; DBR(4)669; GVFTQ(1)631

Christopher II - of NC, b abt 1712 d1764, in 1748 served as sergeant in the military company under the command of Capt John Ashe to repel the Spanish invasion of North Carolina, m(1) Elizabeth Bishop dau/o George Bishop, m(2) Margaret____ - desc/o Edward Dudley DBR(1)251, 262; DBR(2)363, 858; DBR(3)15; GVFTQ(1)631, 636, 637

Christopher - of VA & NC, b1715 d1781, m____ & left issue - desc/o Edward Dudley GVFTQ(1)633

Christopher III - of NC, b1763 d1828, ship builder & actively interested in establishing public schools in Onslow Co, for many years treasurer of Onslow Co & presiding justice of the co court, served as a member of the Senate of North Carolina from Onslow Co, m Margaret Snead b1764 d1827 dau/o Robert Snead - desc/o Edward Dudley DBR(1)251, 264; DBR(2)363, 858; DBR(3)15; GVFTQ(1)637

Deborah - of MA, b1645 d1683, m Major Jonathan Wade d1689 of Medford - desc/o Katharine Deighton CHB375; MCS20; DBR(2)571; CRL(1)401; CRL(4)543; FLW83; NEFGM(1)77; GPM(1)33

Dorcas - of VA, m William Rowntree - desc/o Edward Dudley DBR(3)532; DBR(4)433, 550

Dorothy - of MA, b1662, m1681 Moses Leavitt - desc/o Gov Thomas

DUDLEY (cont.)

Dudley LDS64; DBR(5)68; RAA89; CRL(4)543; GDMNH209

Dorothy - of VA, b abt 1695 d1751, m bef 1714 Henry Gatewood - desc/o Edward Dudley DBR(1)326; DBR(2)244, 419; DBR(5)777

Edward - of VA, b1602 d1655 son of Robert Dudley of Bristol, England, m Elizabeth Pritchard d1691 she, m(2) abt 1657 John Robinson d1688 - the immigrant ECD(3)127; JSW1679; DBR(1)251, 262, 326; DBR(2)242, 243, 363, 418, 732, 818, 819, 858; DBR(3)14, 179, 180, 531, 532, 738, 739; DBR(4)432, 433, 550, 668; DBR(5)776; RAA1, 88; GVFTQ(1)623/641 sufficient proof of alleged royal ancestry is lacking

Edward - of VA & NC, b abt 1706 d1745, m1726 Hasten Starkie - desc/o Edward Dudley ECD(3)134; DBR(4)669

Eleanor - of VA, m____ Jackson - desc/o Edward Dudley GVFT(1)630

Elizabeth - of NH, b1652, m1674 Capt Kingsley Hall - desc/o Gov Thomas Dudley DBR(1)63; NE(10)137; GDMNH209

Elizabeth - of MA, m Simon Gilman - desc/o Gov Thomas Dudley GDMNH210

Elizabeth - of MA, b1724 d1765, m(1)1749 Dr Joseph Richards, m(2)1765 Samuel Scarborough - desc/o Gov Thomas Dudley GPM(1)34

Elizabeth - m Joseph Greely - desc/o Gov Thomas Dudley DBR(5)916

Elizabeth - b1751, m1779 Jonathan Lovering - desc/o Gov Thomas Dudley DBR(1)747

Frances - of VA, b1697, m ____ Munden - desc/o Edward Dudley GVFTQ(1)628

George - of VA, in 1722 was church warden of Kingston Parish, m prior to 1718 Judith Armistead dau of William Armistead of Matthews Co, VA - desc/o Edward Dudley GVFTQ(1)623/641

George - of VA, elected to the vestry of Kingston Parish 1769, m1758 Dorothy Tabb b1736 dau/o William Tabb - desc/o Edward Dudley GVFTQ(1)634

George - of VA, d1835 & left son George Dudley residing in Georgia - desc/o Edward Dudley GVFTQ(1)634

Guilford - of NC, d1781 is said to have organized the first volunteer military company in America in 1774 at Halifax, North Carolina, served under General Greene by whom he was made a major in Guilford Court House & was later appointed lieutenant colonel of militia, m Anna Bland Eaton dau/o Col Thomas Eaton of Granville Co, North Carolina - desc/o Edward Dudley GVFTQ(1)633

James - of VA, b abt 1670 vestryman of Petsworth Parish, Gloucester, VA in 1682, m(1)1679 Mary Welch, m(2) Elizabeth____ d1688, m(3) Ann Fleet - desc/o Edward Dudley ECD(3)128; DBR(2)820; DBR(3)180, 181, 739; DBR(4)669; GVFTQ(1)627

James - of VA, d1702, styled himself as "son & heir apparent of William Dudley, gentleman," m____ & left issue - desc/o Edward Dudley GVFTQ(1)627, 628

Lieut James - of MA, b1690 Exeter d1746, cooper, m Mercy Folsom b abt 1691 Exeter - desc/o Gov Thomas Dudley GDMNH210; NEFGM(3)1601

James - of VA, d1711, m____ & had issue - desc/o Edward Dudley

DUDLEY (cont.)
GVFTQ(1)628

James - of VA, m1727 Jean Staunton d1744 dau/o Theophilus
Staunton & had issue - desc/o Edward Dudley GVFTQ(1)628

Jean - of VA, m1760 Mary Berry - desc/o Edward Dudley
GVFTQ(1)628

John - of MA, b1697 d1762, m Nicholas Perriman - desc/o Gov
Thomas Dudley GDMNH210

John - of VA, m(1) Elizabeth____, m(2) Edith____ d1708, m(3) prior to
1715 Mary Milwood & inherited land located on James River from
her father, Robert Milwood - desc/o Edward Dudley GVFTQ(1)630

John - of VA, m1720 Ann Hill dau/o William & Ann Hill of Middlesex
Co - desc/o Edward Dudley GVFTQ(1)630

John - of NH, b1769 d1833, m1801 Hannah Dudley Young - desc/o
Gov Thomas Dudley DBR(1)496

John - of ME, b1775 Winthrop, ME d1847 China, ME, m Eunice
Winslow & had issue - desc/o Gov Thomas Dudley NEFGM(3)1601

Jonathan - of MA, d1761/1762, m1720 Dinah Bean - desc/o Thomas
Dudley DBR(5)916; GDMNH209

Joseph - of MA & NH, b1647 Roxbury d1720 member of parliament,
president of New England, governor of MA & NH, m1669 Rebecca
Tyng dau/o Major General Edward Tyng - desc/o Thomas Dudley
J&K197; DBR(5)80, 81; CRL(1)401, 402; CRL(4)543; NEFGM(1)77;
GPM(1)pxliii, 33/34 - desc/o Katharine Deighton CHB375, 376;
FLW84, 84; ECD(2)110; MCS20; DBR(5)84

Joseph - of MA, d1727 age 25, m1724 Maria Gilman - desc/o Gov
Thomas Dudley GDMNH210

Joseph - b1728, m1750 Hannah Leavitt - desc/o Gov Thomas Dudley
DBR(1)747; DBR(5)752

Joseph - of MA, b1732, m Lucy____ - desc/o Gov Thomas Dudley
GPM(1)34

Joseph - of NC, in 1714 was appointed overseer of roads in Chowan Co
North Carolina - desc/o Edward Dudley GVFTQ(1)633

Joyce - of VA, m____ Goodaker - desc/o Edward Dudley GVFTQ(1)628

Judith - of VA, b1765 d1817, m1788 Capt Louis Booker of Essex Co
b1754 d1814 - desc/o Edward Dudley GVFTQ(1)634, 639

Louis - of NC, b1734, m Frances Alden dau/o James Alden - desc/o
Edward Dudley GVFTQ(1)633

Lucy - of MA, b1728 d1768, m1749 Dr Simon Tufts - desc/o Gov
Thomas Dudley GPM(1)34

Lucy - of MA, b1759, m1783 Seth T Whiting - desc/o Gov Thomas
Dudley GPM(1)34 Margaret of MA, bp Cambridge, had a child by
Francis Pofat - desc/o Gov Thomas Dudley GDMNH209

Marlow - of NC, b1730, m1763 Maria Ashton - desc/o Edward Dudley
GVFTQ(1)633

Mary - of MA, b1650, m1675/1676 Dr Samuel Hardy of Beverly, living
at Exeter 1713/1714 - desc/o Gov Thomas Dudley CRL(4)543;
GDMNH209

Mary - of MA, b1692 d1774, m(1)1713 Francis Wainwright, m(2) Capt
Joseph Atkins - desc/o Thomas Dudley J&K197; CRL(1)406;
GPM(1)34

DUDLEY (cont.)

Mary - of MA, m David Watson - desc/o Gov Thomas Dudley GDMNH209

Mary - of MA, b1736 d1796, m John Cotton - desc/o Gov Thomas Dudley GPM(1)34

Mary - of NC, m 1779 Samuel Williams Jr - desc/o Edward Dudley JSW1679; DBR(2)732

Mercy - of MA, b1621 d1691, m1639 Rev John Woodbridge son of the Rev John Woodbridge, & had issue, twelve children - desc/o Gov Thomas Dudley J&K196; ECD256; LDS101; DBR(1)13, 319; DBR(2)110, 415; DBR(3)520; DBR(4)70, 71, 338; DBR(5)1042; RAA89; CRL(1)401; CRL(4)543; FLW54; NEFGM(1)77; GPM(1)pxliii, 33

Mercy - of MA, m by 1746 Nathaniel Thing - desc/o Gov Thomas Dudley GDMNH209

Micajah - of NH, b1751 Brentwood d1798 Durham, ME, m Susanna Forster b1751 Attleboro, MA, d1838 China, ME dau/o Timothy Forster & Sibylla Freeman - desc/o Gov Thomas Dudley NEFGM(3)1601

Molly - of VA, m Abraham Iveson - desc/o Edward Dudley GVFTQ(1)634

Nicholas - of MA, b1694 Brentwood d1766, m Elizabeth Gordon - desc/o Gov Thomas Dudley DBR(1)747; DBR(5)752; GDMNH210

Nicholas Gilman - of NH, b1746 d1818, m Sarah Kimball - desc/o Gov Thomas Dudley DBR(1)496

Patience - of MA, b1615 d1689/90, m1632 Maj-Gen Daniel Denison - desc/o Gov Thomas Dudley DBR(1)70; DBR(2)90; CRL(1)401; CRL(4)543; NEFGM(1)77; GPM(1)pxliii, 33

Paul - of MA, bp 1650 d1681, m abt 1676 Mary Leverett dau/o Governor John Leverett - desc/o Katharine Deighton CHB376; MCS20; CRL(1)401; FLW84 - desc/o Gov Thomas Dudley CRL(4)543; NEFGM(1)77; GPM(1)pxliii, 33

Paul - of MA, b1675 d1751, m1703 Lucy Wainwright - desc/o Gov Thomas Dudley CRL(1)405; GPM(1)34

Paul - of MA, b1757 d1847, m1779 Martha Foster - desc/o Gov Thomas Dudley GPM(1)34

Peyton - of VA, d1757, m Mary____ - desc/o Edward Dudley GVFTQ(1)630

Phyllis - of VA, m Samuel Hyde Saunders - desc/o Edward Dudley GVFTQ(1)633

Polly - of VA, m Major Richard Ayers - desc/o Edward Dudley GVFTQ(1)634

Rebecca - of MA, b1681, m1702 Samuel Sewall Jr - desc/o Gov Thomas Dudley CRL(1)405; GPM(1)34

Rebecca - of MA, m1681 Francis Lyford - desc/o Gov Thomas Dudley DBR(1)791; CRL(4)543; GDMNH209

Rebecca - of MA, b1726 d1775, m(1) Benjamin Gerrish, m(2)1775 John Burbige - desc/o Gov Thomas Dudley GPM(1)34

Rebecca - of MA, b1763 d1834, m1788 Major Nathaniel Parker - desc/o Gov Thomas Dudley GPM(1)34

Col Richard - of VA, b abt 1623 in Bristol, England d abt 1687, 1657

DUDLEY (cont.)

was Sheriff of Gloucester Co, 1667 elected a member of the vestry
of Kingston Parish in Gloucester Co & was later appointed colonel of
militia, m1645 Mary Sewell (Seawell) - desc/o Edward Dudley
ECD(3)127/8; JSW1679; DBR(1)326; DBR(2)243, 419, 732, 819,
820; DBR(3)180, 532, 739; DBR(4)433, 550, 668, 669; DBR(5)777;
RAA88; GVFTQ(1)631

Richard - of VA, m Elizabeth Stephens - desc/o Edward Dudley
DBR(1)326; DBR(2)243, 244, 419; DBR(5)777; RAA88

Richard - of VA, d1716, m Elizabeth____ - desc/o Edward Dudley
DBR(1)326; DBR(2)244, 419; DBR(5)777

Robert - of VA, b abt 1650 d abt 1700, m____ Green sister of Edward
Green - desc/o Edward Dudley GVFTQ(1)634

Robert - of VA, b abt 1647 d1701 elected a member of the vestry of
Christ Church, Middlesex Co, & four years later made church
warden, 1685 elected member of the House of Burgesses, m abt
1690 Elizabeth Ransom dau/o George Ransom - desc/o Edward
Dudley GVFTQ(1)632

Robert - of VA, b1675 d1709, m1701 Elizabeth Dudley wid/o Major
Robert Dudley - desc/o Edward Dudley GVFTQ(1)634

Robert - of VA, of Princess Anne Co prior to 1713, d abt 1746, m
Elizabeth White dau/o Solomon White of Isle of Wight Co - desc/o
Edward Dudley GVFTQ(1)629

Robert - of VA, b1708 moved to King & Queen Co, VA & became a
member of the vestry of Stratton Major Parish 1729 to 1745 -
desc/o Edward Dudley GVFTQ(1)628

Robert - of VA, d abt1745, m Elizabeth Curtis dau/o James Curtis -
desc/o Edward Dudley GVFTQ(1)632

Robert - of VA, b1726 d1766, m1746 Joyce Gale (Gayle) - desc/o
Edward Dudley ECD(3)128; DBR(2)820; DBR(3)181, 739;
GVFTQ(1)627

Robert - of VA & KY, m Ann Punis dau/o James Punis - desc/o
Edward Dudley GVFTQ(1)627

Robert - of KY, m Nancy Parrish - desc/o Edward Dudley
GVFTQ(1)627

Robert - of NC, m Jane Marlow & had issue - desc/o Edward Dudley
GVFTQ(1)633

Robert - of VA, lieutenant in the Fifth Virginia Continental Line &
served from Feb 12, 1776 to the end of the war, m____ & had issue
- desc/o Edward Dudley GVFTQ(1)628

Robert Ballard - of VA, m Ann____ & left issue - desc/o Edward Dudley
GVFTQ(1)634

Rev Samuel - of NH, bp 1608 All Saints, Northamptonshire
d1682/1683, merchant, magistrate & preacher, m(1)1632/1633
Mary Winthrop d1643 dau/o Governor John Winthrop, m(2) Mary
Byley b abt 1616, m(3) by 1651 Elizabeth____ aged 43 in 1671 -
desc/o Gov Thomas Dudley FLW54; LDS64; DBR(1)63, 74, 495,
747, 791; DBR(2)96; DBR(5)68, 752, 916, 1042; RAA89;
CRL(1)401; NEFGM(1)77, (3)1601; NE(10)134/135; GDMNH209;
GPM(1)pxliii, 33

Samuel Jr - of NH, d1732, m Elizabeth or Hannah Tyne - desc/o Gov

DUDLEY (cont.)

Thomas Dudley DBR(5)752, 916; NE(10)137; GDMNH209; NEFGM(3)1601

Samuel - of MA, b1686 d1717/1718, m Hannah Colcord - desc/o Gov Thomas Dudley GDMNH210

Samuel - of NH, b1720, m(1)___ Ladd, m(2) Mrs Sleeper, m(1) Mrs Clark - desc/o Gov Thomas Dudley NEFGM(3)1601

Sarah - of MA, bp 1620 Sempring, England d1659 Roxbury, m(1) Maj Benjamin Keane, m(2) Thomas Pacey of Boston - desc/o Gov Thomas Dudley CRL(1)401; CRL(4)543; NEFGM(1)77; GPM(1)33

Sarah - of MA, b1716, m___ Leavitt - desc/o Gov Thomas Dudley GDMNH209

Sarah - of MA, b1706, m Ezekiel Gilman - desc/o Gov Thomas Dudley GDMNH210

Stephen - of NH, d1734, m(1)1684 Sarah Gilman b1664 d1712/1713 dau/o John Gilman of Exeter, m(2) Mary Thing, m(3) Mercy Gilman - desc/o Gov Thomas Dudley DBR(1)495, 747; DBR(5)752; RAA89; GDMNH209; NEFGM(3)1601

Col Stephen - of NH, b1687/1688 d1734, m1708 Sarah Davison - desc/o Gov Thomas Dudley DBR(1)496; RAA89; GDMNH210

Deacon Stephen - of NH, b1724 d1811, m1745 Hannah Sanborn - desc/o Gov Thomas Dudley DBR(1)496; RAA89

Stephen - b1762 - desc/o Thomas Dudley RAA89

Susan - of VA, m Robert Ransom - desc/o Edward Dudley GVFTQ(1)634

Governor Thomas - of MA 1630, bp 1576 Yardley-Hastings, Northamptonshire d1653 Roxbury, MA, who was the 20th generation in line of descent from King Henry I, of England & of royal descent from King Robert II, of France. Also a descendant of King Henry II, of England. Son of Captain Roger Dudley & Susanna (Thorne) Dudley. One of the supporters of the MA Bay Co 1629, was governor, deputy governor, or assistant every year of his life. A man of large ability and noble character. No other man in MA ever held such power over government before or since. m(1)1603 Dorothy Yorke b1582 Northamptonshire, England d1643 Roxbury, dau/o Edmund Yorke, m(2)1644 Katharine Deighton d1671 - the immigrant J&K195; FLW53; ECD256; ECD(2)123; MCS40; LDS64, 101; DBR(1)13, 62/3, 70, 74, 319, 487, 495, 557, 746, 791; DBR(2)88, 90, 96,106, 110, 293, 414, 415, 569, 685, 686; DBR(3)519, 520, 595, 596, 651, 653; DBR(4)49, 70, 112, 338, 395, 396, 838, 866, 867; DBR(5)68, 79, 80, 120, 222, 223; DBR(5)359, 372, 610, 752, 916, 1041, 1042; RAA1, 89; EDV57; AAP155; CRL(1)391, 392; AFA114; CRL(4)541; 542; GBR250/252 Some aspect of royal descent merits further study, alternate descent outlined, the best royal descent is through his maternal line Susanna Thorne; TAG(44)129/137, (62)43/47; TG(5)131/39, 150/51, 154/56; NE(1)71/72, (10)133, (47)120, (49)507, (56)189, 206, (66)340/343, (97)342, (99)130/131; EO2(1)689/692; NEFGM(1)77; GPM(1)pxliii, 33; NEFGM(3)1600, 1601, 1602

Thomas - of VA, b abt 1651 in York Co, VA d1719, engaged in business as a merchant from 1673 until Bacon's Rebellion, m

DUDLEY (cont.)

Frances____ - desc/o Edward Dudley GVFTQ(1)628

Thomas - of VA, d1736, m1706 Elizabeth Meecham - desc/o Edward Dudley GVFTQ(1)630

Thomas - of VA, m____ - desc/o Edward Dudley JSW1679; DBR(2)732

Thomas - of VA & NC, d abt 1755, moved to Currituck Co, North Carolina, m Mary Booth dau/o George Booth - desc/o Edward Dudley GVFTQ(1)629

Thomas - of MA, living 8 Apr 1713, schoolmaster, m(1) abt 1697 Mary____, m(2) Rebecca____ the returned Indian Captive & wid/o Edward Taylor, living 1732 Newmarket, m(3) Elizabeth____ b1652 - desc/o Gov Thomas Dudley CRL(4)543; GDMNH209

Thomas - of MA, b1731 d1769 Roxbury, m1753 Hannah Whiting - desc/o Gov Thomas Dudley GPM(1)34

Thomas - of MA, b1755 Roxbury d Roxbury, m1778 Abigail Weld - desc/o Gov Thomas Dudley GPM(1)34

Thomas - of KY, succeeded his father as pastor of Bryant's Church in 1825 - desc/o Edward Dudley GVFTQ(1)627

Thomas - b1768 - desc/o Edward Dudley RAA88

Capt Treworthy - of MA, d1751, m Hannah Gilman - desc/o Gov Thomas Dudley GDMNH210

Trustworthy - b1757 d1814, m abt 1783 Sarah Stevens - desc/o Gov Thomas Dudley DBR(5)752

William - of VA, b abt 1621 probably in Bristol, England d1677, vestryman of Christ Church Parish, Middlesex Co & in 1668 became church warden, m Elizabeth Cary - desc/o Edward Dudley ECD(3)134; DBR(1)251, 262; DBR(2)363, 858; DBR(3)15; GVFTQ(1)626/627

William - of VA, d prior to Nov 1692, member of the vestry of Christ Church Parish, Middlesex Co, m1682 Mary Bawd dau/o William Bawd of Lancaster Co, VA - desc/o Edward Dudley GVFTQ(1)629

William - of VA & NC, b1683 d abt 1740 moved to Bath Co, North Carolina in 1716, m Jemima____ & had a son Arthur Dudley - desc/o Edward Dudley GVFTQ(1)629

William - of MA, b1686 d1743, m Elizabeth Davenport dau/o Judge Addington Davenport - desc/o Gov Thomas Dudley CRL(1)405; GPM(1)34

William - of VA, b1696 d1760, m1721 Judith Johnson - desc/o Edward Dudley ECD(3)128; DBR(2)820; DBR(3)181, 739; RAA88; GVFTQ(1)627

William - of VA, m abt 1741 Jane Ballard in York Co & had issue - desc/o Edward Dudley GVFTQ(1)634

William - of VA, b1731 d1794, settled at Dudley's Ferry, West Point, King & Queen Co, m Ann____ - desc/o Edward Dudley GVFTQ(1)630

William - of MA, b1753 Roxbury d1780, m1774 Sarah Williams - desc/o Gov Thomas Dudley GPM(1)34

Col William - of VA, b abt 1766 d1813, m1792 Lucy Smith - desc/o Edward Dudley ECD(3)128

William - of VA, d1760, m Rebecca____ & had issue - desc/o Edward Dudley GVFTQ(1)628

DUDLEY (cont.)

Capt William Aylett - of VA, b1775 d1851, m1798 Mary "Polly" Smith - desc/o Edward Dudley DBR(3)740 DULANY

Col Benjamin Tasker - of VA, m1773 Elizabeth French dau/o Daniel French of Virginia - desc/o William Bladen CHB45; BCD45

Major Walter - of MD, d1807, m Elizabeth Brice - desc/o Mary Drake DBR(3)722; DBR(4)48, 471

DUMARESQ Anne - b1746, m1761 William Turner - desc/o Philip Dumaresq NE(19)318; EO2 (1)696

Anne - bp 1765, m(1) John Ferguson Esq. son of Sir John Ferguson of Ayrshire, m(2) Charles Gow Esq. - desc/o Philip Dumaresq NE(19)318; EO2 (1)696

Edward - d1721, m1743 Mary Boutineau dau/o Stephen Boutineau - desc/o Philip Dumaresq NE(19)318; EO2 (1)696

James - bp 1772, entered the Royal Navy as a midshipman afterwards studying law, he was a man of charming address and polished manners, a good musician, a true lover of poetry & a keen sportsman, m1797 Sarah Farwell dau/o Eben Farwell of Vassalboro, ME - desc/o Philip Dumaresq NE(19)318; EO2 (1)697

Philip - of MA, d abt 1744 2nd son of Elias Dumaresq & Frances De Carteret, eldest daughter & coh of Sir Francis De Carteret, m1716 Susannah or Susan Ferris (Ferry) dau/o Capt Henri Ferry of Boston - the immigrant EDV32; GBR220; NE(17)317/321; EO2 (1)693/696

Philip - of MA, b1737 a loyalist & aide-de-camp to Lord Dunmore, m1763 Rebecca Gardiner dau/o Sylvester Gardiner of Boston - desc/o Philip Dumaresq NE(19)318; EO2 (1)696

Susan - of MA, d1743, m1741 Mathew Saumarez - desc/o Philip Dumaresq NE(19)318

DUMMER John - of MA, - desc/o Prichard Dummer EDV55

Prichard - of MA 1638 - the immigrant EDV55; sufficient proof of alleged royal ancestry is lacking

Gov William - of MA - desc/o Prichard Dummer EDV55

DUNBAR Robert - of RI, m Eunice Barker & had issue at least three children - desc/o Gov John Cranston GRFHG(1)286; NE(79)256

William - of Mississippi - b1749 d1810 planter & scientist, son of Sir Archibald of Newton & Thurnderton (de jure 4th Baronet of Northfield) & Anne (Bayne) Dunbar, m Dinah Clark - the immigrant GBR90

DUNCAN Sarah - of NY, m1768 William Wickham & had issue 2 sons & 1 daughter - desc/o Gabriel Ludlow NYGBR(50)#1p38

Thomas - of NY, m Margaret Bourhout & had issue two daughters, Margaret & Amelia - desc/o Gabriel Ludlow NYGBR(50)#1p38

DUNCH Deborah - of NY, d abt 1659 known as Lady Deborah Moody, founder of a colony at Gravesend, L.I. dau/o Walter Dunch & Deborah Pilkington, m Sir Henry Moody, 1st Baronet - the immigrant GBR383

DUNDAS Elizabeth of PA, b1764 d1793, m1785 Henry Pratt - desc/o James Dundas CHB100; BCD100

James of PA 1757, b1734 d1788 son of John Dundas of Manour & Anne Murray, m Elizabeth Moore - the immigrant CHB100; MCB145; MCD212; BCD100; GBR107

DUNDAS (cont.)

Thomas - of PA, son of John Dundas of Manour & Anne Murray, m___ sister of Mrs Hannah Russell - the immigrant GBR107

DUNGAN Barbara - of RI, m James Barker - desc/o Jeremy Clark FFF132

Elizabeth - of RI, m William Dungan - desc/o Jeremy Clark FFF132

Frances - of RI, bp 1632 d1697, m1648 Randall Holden - the immigrant ECD(3)138; LDS11, 76, 112; sufficient proof of alleged royal ancestry is lacking

Joseph - of PA, b1710 d1785, m Mary Ohl - desc/o Rev Thomas Dungan ECD(3)143

Rebecca - of RI, m Edmund Doyle - desc/o Rev Thomas Dungan AFA52

Sarah - of RI, b abt 1675/8 d1760, m(1) abt 1697 James Carrell - desc/o Rev Thomas Dungan ECD(3)141

Sarah - of PA, b1742 d1811, m1761 Benjamin Corson - desc/o Rev Thomas Dungan ECD(3)143

Rev Thomas - of RI, b abt 1632/4 d1687/8, m1663 Elizabeth Weaver - the immigrant ECD(3)141, 143; AFA52; sufficient proof of alleged royal ancestry is lacking

Thomas Jr - of RI, b1671 d1759, m abt 1697 Mary Drake - desc/o Rev Thomas Dungan ECD(3)143

DUNHAM Abel - of VA, b1772 d1857, m1795 Ann Marlatt - desc/o John Dunham BLG2666

Abigail - b abt 1626, m Stephen Atwood - the immigrant LDS15; sufficient proof of alleged royal ancestry is lacking

Azariah - of NJ, b1718 d1790, m1753(2) Mary Stone Ford - desc/o John Dunham BLG2666

Benajah - of NJ, b1640 d1680, m1660 Elizabeth Tilson - desc/o John Dunham BLG2666

Benajah - of NJ, b1684 d1742, m1704 Dorothy Martin - desc/o John Dunham BLG2666

Daniel - b1727 d1778, m1749 Elizabeth Martin - desc/o Edward FitzRandolph JSW1528

Rev Edward - of NJ, b1661 d1734, m1681 Mary Bonham - desc/o John Dunham BLG2666

Hannah - b1630, m Giles Rickard - desc/o John Dunham LDS21

Hezekiah - of NJ, b1707 d1739, m1733 Elizabeth Drake - desc/o John Dunham BLG2666

Hezekiah - of NJ, b1740 d1799, m1769 Elizabeth Campbell - desc/o John Dunham BLG2666

Isabella - d1824, m Abraham Wyckoff - desc/o Edward FitzRandolph JSW1528

John - b1588 d1668, m(1) Susanna Kenney, m(2)1622 Abigail Barlow - the immigrant LDS21; BLG2666; RAA no longer accepted as being of royal descent - parentage of John unknown, see TAG(30)143/144

John - of NJ, b1756 d1799, m Ann Sherred - desc/o John Dunham BLG2666

Rev Jonathan - of NY, b1693 d1777, m1714 Jane Pyatt - desc/o John Dunham BLG2666

Mary - b1642, m James Hamblen or Hamblin - the immigrant LDS48;

DUNHAM (cont.)
> sufficient proof of alleged royal ancestry is lacking

DUNN Esther - m1777 Thomas Jones - desc/o Anne Marbury ECD258

DUTCH Susannah - of MA, bp 1683 d aft 1762, m1705 Benjamin
> Knowlton - desc/o Richard More ECD(3)212

DUTTON Edward - of PA, b1676/1677 d1731/1732, m1701 ____
> Williams - desc/o John Dutton TAG(66) 65/73

> John - of PA, bp 1648 d1693 Quaker, m1674 Mary Darlington - the
> immigrant DBR(1)456; DBR(2)542, 545, 546; RAA1, 90; CRL(2)230;
> TAG(66) 65/73 states, "A detailed analysis of the pedigree and its
> sources, coupled with additional research, revealed that the line
> was based on wishful interpretations and at times a careless
> reading of the sources. No connection with the gentry Duttons can
> be established." by Col Charles M Hansen, USA (ret), FASG

> John - of PA, b1675 d1735/1736, m1704 Elisabeth Kingsman -
> desc/o John Dutton TAG(66) 65/73

> Lydia - of PA, was a dau/o David & possibly Jane McClasley &
> granddau/o Thomas Dutton & Lucy Barnard, m John Mansell -
> desc/o John Dutton DBR(1)456; DBR(2)545; TAG(66) 65/73

> Mary - of PA, b1721 d1760, m1745 Richard Grubb - desc/o John
> Dutton CRL(2)230

> Robert - of PA, b1681/1682 d at sea abt 1725 engaged in West Indies
> trade - desc/o John Dutton TAG(66) 65/73

> Sarah Catherine - of VA, m William Henry Howard - desc/o Elizabeth
> Boteler DBR(2)100

> Thomas - of PA, b1679 d1732, m1701 Jane McClasley - desc/o John
> Dutton DBR(1)456; DBR(2)545; CRL(2)230 (this source states he
> married in 1701 Lucy Barnard); TAG(66) 65/73 states DBR is in
> error omitting one generation stating Lydia was his granddaughter
> not daughter

> Maj William - of VA, m(2) Susan Brown Christian - desc/o Elizabeth
> Boteler DBR(2)100

DWIGHT Benjamin Woolsley - of NJ, father of Theodore William Dwight -
> desc/o Rev James Pierrepont J&K239

> Elizabeth - of NJ, m Wm Woolsey - desc/o Rev Jas Pierrepont J&K241

> Elizabeth B - of NJ, m Charles Sedgwick - desc/o Rev James
> Pierrepont J&K236

> James - of NJ, father of Rev Timothy Dwight, Pres Yale Univ - desc/o
> Rev James Pierrepont J&K237

> Mary - of MA, b1721 d1809, m1738 Daniel Hall Jr - desc/o Richard
> Lyman CHB149; MCD249; BCD149

> Maurice - of NJ, anc/o Winston Churchill - desc/o Rev James
> Pierrepont J&K240

> Rev Sereno Edwards - of NJ, President of Hamilton College - desc/o
> Rev James Pierrepont J&K238

> Timothy - of NJ, President of Yale University - desc/o Rev James
> Pierrepont J&K237

DYER Anne - of MA, b abt 1674 d aft 1693, m1693/1694 Carew Clarke
> son of Joseph Clarke of Newport - desc/o Anne Marbury ECD258;
> RAA114 - desc/o Katherine Hamby NE(145)263

> Barrett - of MA, b abt 1678 bp as an adult 1697 d1753, m(1)1699

DYER (cont.)

  Hannah Stewart b abt 1672 d1729, m(2)1730 Elizabeth Bull d by
    1744, m(3)1744 Abigail Blake d aft 1754 (one son Barrett b1703
    d1718) - desc/o Katherine Hamby NE(145)263

  Edward - of MA, b abt 1670 d aft 1744, m Mary Green b1677 d aft
    1705 dau/o William & Mary (Sayles) Green - desc/o Katherine
    Hamby NE(145)262

  Elisha - of MA b abt 1672 d by 1755, m Parnell___ d1771 - desc/o
    Katherine Hamby NE(145)262

  Henry - of MA, b abt 1676 bp as an adult 1693 d1740/1742,
    m(1)1697 Mary___ d bet 1723/1726, m(2)1726 Hannah (Adams)
    Holbrook b1685 d1760 dau/o Captain John & Hannah (Webb)
    Adams & wid/o Samuel Holbrook Jr - desc/o Anne Marbury
    DBR(3)170 - desc/o Katherine Hamby NE(145)263

  Mary - of CT, b1698 m1725 Deacon Nathaniel Loomis - desc/o Anne
    Marbury DBR(3)170

  Nathaniel - of MA, b abt 1667 d1729, m1688 Elizabeth Parrot dau/o
    Simon & Elizabeth (___) Parrot - desc/o Katherine Hamby
    NE(145)262

  Samuel - of MA, b abt 1665 d17(?24), housewright, m(1) Lydia
    Williams b1671 d bef 1692 dau/o Joseph & Lydia___ Williams,
    m(2) Mary (Cotta) Sampson b1667/8 d1729 dau/o John & Mary
    (Moore) Cotta & wid/o Hugh Sampson by whom she had sons
    Jeremiah & Hugh Sampson - desc/o Katherine Hamby NE(145)262

DYMOKE Edward - of MA - the immigrant AWW; sufficient proof of royal
    ancestry is lacking

  Joseph Judson - of NJ - desc/o Edward Dymoke AWW

  Thomas - of MA, d1658, m Ann Hammond - desc/o Edw Dymoke AWW

– E –

EARLE William - of MA, b1775, m Martha Pinto - desc/o Obadiah Bruen
    CHB386; MCB318; MCD172

EASTMAN Abigail - of ME, b1761, m1779 James Melee - desc/o Ursula
    Scott JSW1833

  Nathaniel - of ME, b1719, m(2) Susannah Flanders - desc/o Ursula
    Scott JSW1833

EASTON Amey - of RI, d1810, m1749 Samuel Gardiner - desc/o Jeremy
    Clarke DBR(5)88, 91

EATON David - of PA, b abt 1737/1738 d1793/1800, m(1)1760 Mary
    Eaton, m(2) Elizabeth Razon - desc/o John Eaton FFF51, 58

  Elizabeth - b1729, m1754 Simon Noyes - desc/o Capt Thomas
    Bradbury JSW1801

  Hannah - of CT, bp 1632 d1707, m1659 William Jones - desc/o Anna
    Lloyd J&K321; CHB73; ECD(3)192; BCD73

  James II - of PA - the immigrant FFF50; sufficient proof of alleged royal
    ancestry is lacking

  John - of PA 1683, d1716, m Joan___ - the immigrant FFF50, 58;
    sufficient proof of royal ancestry is lacking

  John - of PA, b1700 d1753, m1732 Martha (Todd) Lunn - desc/o John

EATON (cont.)

> Eaton FFF50, 51, 58
>
> Joseph - of DE, b1679 d1749, m(1)1700 Gwenllian Morgan, m(2)1724 Uriah (Gill) Humphrey - desc/o John Eaton FFF50, 58
>
> Joseph - of OH, b1765 d1825, m1790 Bathsheba Sacket - desc/o John Eaton FFF51, 58
>
> Sarah - b1723 - desc/o Thomas Bradbury RAA72

EDDOWES Ralph - of PA, son of John Eddowes & Catherine Moulson, m Sarah Kenrick - the immigrant GBR238

EDEN Frederick Morton - of MD, b abt 1767 d1809, m1792 Anne Smith - desc/o Sir Robert Eden ECD169

> Sir Robert, 1st Baronet - of MD, b1741 d1784 governor of MD, son of Sir Robert, 3rd Baronet & Mary (Davison) Eden, m1763 Caroline Calvert - the immigrant ECD169; GBR32

EDGECOMB Rachel - of ME, b1703, m1746 William Haley - desc/o Judith Lewis DBR(2)173

> Robert - of ME, b1695 d1764, m Sarah Elwell - desc/o Judith Lewis DBR(2)173

EDMONSTON Dorothy - of MD, b1741 d1816, m Ninian Edmonston - desc/o Gov Robert Brooke DBR(1)587

> James Brooke - of MD, b1763 d1816, m Sarah____ - desc/o Gov Robert Brooke DBR(1)587

EDSALL Ruth - of NY, m1697 Lieut John Berrien - desc/o Richard Woodhull ECD237

EDWARD Jane - of PA, m John Jones, son of Rees Jones & Mrs Hannah Price Jones David Evans - the immigrant GBR306

EDWARDS Dorothy - of MA, b1745/1746 at Littleton, m1770 Clement Coburn - desc/o Rev Peter Bulkeley TAG(36)105

> Eleanor - of MA, b1765, m1782 Rufus Bacon - desc/o Rev Peter Bulkeley TAG(36)105
>
> Esther of NJ, m Rev Aaron Burr - desc/o Rev James Pierrepont J&K242
>
> John - of PA, son of Edward ap John, m____ - the immigrant GBR309
>
> John - of PA, son of Evan ab Edward, m Mary Hughes - the immigrant GBR309
>
> John - of MA, b1751 d1837, m1778 Sabra Curtis - desc/o Rev Peter Bulkeley TAG(36)105
>
> Jonathan - of NJ, President of Union College - desc/o James Pierrepont J&K235
>
> Mary - of NJ, m Timothy Dwight - desc/o Rev James Pierrepont J&K237
>
> Dr Richard - of VA, - the immigrant DBR(1)224, royal descent not proven
>
> Sarah - of MA, b abt 1748 d1820 Oxford, m1768 Richard Coburn & had issue - desc/o Rev Peter Bulkeley TAG(36)105
>
> Sarah - of NJ, m Elihu Parsons - desc/o Rev James Pierrepont J&K243
>
> Timothy - of NJ, father of Rhoda Edwards who, m Josiah Dwight - desc/o James Pierrepont J&K236
>
> William - of CT 1639, b1620 - the immigrant EDV150, 151; sufficient proof of alleged royal ancestry is lacking

EDWARDS (cont.)

William - of PA, son of Edward ap John, m(1) Katherine Roberts, m(2) Jane Jones - the immigrant GBR309

EGERTON Charles Calvert - of MD, b abt 1748 d1778, m Mary (Bennett?) - desc/o Leonard Calvert MG(1)424, 425

James - of MD, b abt 1703 d1768, m____ & had issue - desc/o Leonard Calvert MG(1)424

James - of MD, b abt 1770, m(1)1792 Matilda Bond dau/o Col Richard Bond & Susanna Key, m(2)1805 Eliza Chesley - desc/o Leonard Calvert MG(1)425

Mary Ann - of MD, d1765, m Michael Jenifer - desc/o Leonard Calvert MG(1)424

ELDERKIN Abigail of CT, m Edward Waldo Jr - desc/o John Drake J&K312

Anne - of CT, b1661 d1748, m1681 Samuel Bliss - desc/o John Drake DBR(1)162; RAA87

Betty - b1747/1748 - desc/o John Drake RAA87

James - b1698 - desc/o John Drake RAA87

James - b1725 - desc/o John Drake RAA87

John Jr - of CT, b1664, m Abigail Fowler - desc/o John Drake J&K312; MCB346; MCD208; RAA87

Col John - of CT, b1694 d1736, m Susannah Baker - desc/o John Drake J&K312; MCB347; MCD208

Susanna - of CT, b1722 d1797, m Jabez Bigelow - desc/o John Drake MCB347; MCD208

ELDRED Grace - b abt 1690 - desc/o Anne Marbury RAA114

ELDREDGE Mary A - b abt 1688 - desc/o Anne Marbury RAA114

ELIOT Aaron - of CT, b1718 d1785, m Mary Worthington - desc/o Mabel Harlakenden CHB272; BCD272

Abial - of CT, b1686/1687 d1776, m1726 Mary Leete - desc/o John Haynes MCB236, 237; MCD230; BCD273

Benjamin - of CT, b1762 d1848, m Frances Panca - desc/o Mabel Harlakenden CHB272; BCD272

Rev Jared - of CT, b1685 d1763, m1710 Elizabeth Smithson - desc/o Mabel Harlakenden CHB272; BCD272

Jared - of CT, b1761 d1841, m1785 Clarissa Lewis - desc/o Judge Simon Lynde CHB312; BCD312

John - the immigrant 1631 EDV21; sufficient proof of alleged royal ancestry is lacking

Nathaniel - of CT, m Beulah Parmalee - desc/o Mabel Harlakenden BCD273

Sarah - of CT, b1772 d1852, m John Scoville - desc/o William Leete CHB370; MCD246 - desc/o John Haynes MCB237 - desc/o Mabel Harlakenden MCD230

William - of CT, m Ruth Rossiter - desc/o Mabel Harlakenden BCD273

Wyllys - of CT, b1731 d1777, m Abigail Ward - desc/o William Leete CHB370; MCD246 - desc/o John Haynes MCB236/237 - desc/o Mabel Harlakenden MCD230

ELKINGTON Amy - of NJ, b1724 d1817, m1746 Enoch Stratton b1720 d1781 - desc/o George Elkington DBR(2)391

Elizabeth - of NJ, b abt 1696, m1713 Thomas Ballinger - desc/o

ELKINGTON (cont.)

George Elkington DBR(1)7, 107

George - of NJ 1677, bp 1650 d1713, was 23rd generation in line of descent from King Henry I, of England (son of Joseph Elkington b1608 d1688), m1688 Mary (Humphries) Core b1660 dau/o Walter Humphries - the immigrant MCS7; DBR(1)7, 107, 530; DBR(2)347, 389, 390; DBR(3)88, 89; RAA1, 91; GBR402; TAG(22)179/180

George II - of NJ, b abt 1698 d1728/1729, m Ann Kemble (Kimball) dau/o Samuel Kimball - desc/o George Elkington DBR(1)530; DBR(2)347; DBR(3)89

George III - of NJ, b1727 d1748, m1748 Sarah Pimm dau/o John Pimm - desc/o George Elkington DBR(1)530; DBR(2)347; DBR(3)89

Jemima - b abt 1748 d1781, m Samuel Wills son of Daniel Wills of Burlington Co, NJ - desc/o George Elkington DBR(1)530

Joseph - of NJ, b1691 d1724, m1713 Elizabeth Antrim dau/o George Antrim - desc/o George Elkington DBR(2)391

Sarah - of NJ, b1759, m(1)1778 Darling Conrow II, b abt 1742 d1788 son of Darling & Deliverance (Stokes) Conrow - desc/o George Elkington DBR(2)348; DBR(3)89

ELLERY Almy - b1759 d1839, m William Stedman d1831 aged 66 Newburyport, member of Congress - desc/o Gov Thomas Dudley NE(8)318

Benjamin - of RI, b1669 d1746 - desc/o William Ellery EDV108, 109

Elizabeth - of RI, b1751 d1807, m Francis Dana, studied law & chosen delegate to Congress, appointed Minister to Russia & chief justice of MA d1811 aged 68 son of Richard Dana - desc/o Gov Thomas Dudley NE(8)318

Lucy - of RI, b1752 d1834, m1773 Judge William Channing b1751 Newport, RI, attorney general & district attorney holding both offices at the same time until his death 1793 son of John Channing - desc/o Gov Thomas Dudley J&K196; NE(8)318

William - of MA 1663 - the immigrant EDV108, 109; sufficient proof of alleged royal ancestry is lacking

ELLET John - of NJ, b1769 d1824, m(1)1792 Mary Smith - desc/o Thomas Lloyd CHB130; BCD130

ELLIS Daniel - of NJ, b1727 d1794, m1753 Bathsheba Howe - desc/o Rowland Ellis III ECD(3)149

Ellen - of PA, b1689 d1765, m John Evans - desc/o Rowland Ellis MCD266

Rowland - of PA 1686, b1650 d1731 son of Ellis ap Rees (alias Ellis Price) & Anne Humphrey, m(1) Margaret ferch Ellis Morris, m(2) Margaret Owen - the immigrant MCB152; MCD266; GBR80; GPFHB283, 284

Rowland III - of NJ, b abt 1692 d1762/1763, m1715 Sarah Allison - the immigrant ECD(3)149; sufficient proof of alleged royal ancestry is lacking

ELLSWORTH Jemima - of NY, b1742 d1828, m1761 David Hayden - desc/o Elizabeth Coytemore ECD(2)101; DBR(5)118

ELLYSON Anne Clopton - of VA, m(1) William Lightfoot of Charles City, m(2) John Golgin - desc/o William Clopton GVFWM857

ELMER John - b1776 - desc/o Griffith Bowen RAA72

ELTONHEAD Agatha - of VA, dau/o Richard Eltonhead & Anne Sutton, m(1) William Kellaway, m(2) Ralph Wormeley, m(3) Sir Henry Chichele deputy governor of VA - the immigrant GBR349 some aspect of royal descent merits further study - alternate descent outlined

Alice - of VA, dau/o Richard Eltonhead & Anne Sutton, m(1) Rowland Burnham, m(2) Henry Corbin of VA, m(3) Henry Creek - the immigrant GBR349 some aspect of royal descent merits further study - alternate descent outlined

Jane - of MD, dau/o Richard Eltonhead & Anne Sutton, m(1) Robert Moryson, m(2) Cuthbert Fenwick of MD - the immigrant GBR349 some aspect of royal descent merits further study - alternate descent outlined

Martha - of VA, dau/o Richard Eltonhead & Anne Sutton, m abt 1640 England, Edwin Conway b (probably) abt 1610 Worcestershire, England d1675 Lancaster Co, VA, third clerk of Northampton Co, VA - the immigrant AAP142, 143; CRL(1)255; GBR348 some aspect of royal descent merits further study - alternate descent outlined; VG225; CFA(5)136

ELY Joshua - of NJ 1685 - the immigrant EDV109, 110; sufficient proof of alleged royal ancestry is lacking

Nathaniel - of MA 1635 - the immigrant EDV109, 110; sufficient proof of alleged royal ancestry is lacking

Richard - of CT 1660 - the immigrant EDV109, 110; sufficient proof of alleged royal ancestry is lacking

EMERSON Ebenezer - of MA, d1751, m1716 Mary Boutwell - desc/o Rev Edward Bulkeley ECD(3)65; DBR(4)687; DBR(5)229; RAA75

Elizabeth - b1638 - desc/o Peter Bulkeley RAA75

Hannah - of MA, b1745 d1825, m Rev Manasseh Smith - desc/o Capt Thomas Bradbury J&K168

Hannah - of MA, m Rev Daniel Emerson - desc/o Capt Thomas Bradbury J&K168

James - of MA, b1720, m1744 Mary Farrar - desc/o Rev Edward Bulkeley ECD(3)65; DBR(4)687; DBR(5)229; RAA75

Kendall - of MA, b1745 d1805, m(2) Elizabeth Pratt - desc/o Rev Edward Bulkeley ECD(3)65; DBR(4)687; DBR(5)229

Lucian - of MA, b1667 d1739/1740, m1683 Thomas Damon b1658/1659 d1723 - desc/o Grace Chetwood DBR(1)100, 101; DBR(4)266

Lucy - of MA, b1770 Reading d1806 Windsor, VT, m1788, Reading Lieut Aaron Damon d1833 Windsor, VT & had issue - desc/o Rev Peter Bulkeley TAG(36)104

Martha - of MA, m William Cogswell - desc/o Samuel Symonds AFA14, 18, 20

Mary - b1747 - desc/o Peter Bulkeley RAA75

Nathaniel - of MA, d1712 - the immigrant EDV21, 22; sufficient proof of alleged royal ancestry is lacking

Sarah - of NH, b1771 d1850, m abt 1787/1789 Edward Williams Robie - desc/o Henry Sherburne ECD(3)250

Rev William - of MA, m Phebe Bliss - desc/o Capt Thomas Bradbury J&K164

EMERSON (cont.)

    William - of MA, m Ruth Haskins father of Ralph Waldo Emerson & - desc/o Capt Thomas Bradbury J&K164

EMMES Hannah - of MA, m Samuel Colesworthy - desc/o Richard Williams CHB377

EMMET Thomas Addis - of NY, b1764 d1827, lawyer & Irish patriot, son of Robert Emmet & Elizabeth Mason - the immigrant GBR126; NYGBR(46)#3p313

ENDICOTT John - of MA 1628 - the immigrant EDV110, 111; sufficient proof of alleged royal ancestry is lacking

ENO James Jr - of MA, b1651 d1714, m1678 Abigail Bissell - desc/o Thomas Holcomb THC169

    Susannah - of MA, b1699, m Joseph Phelps - desc/o Thomas Holcomb LDS69; THC169

EPPES (EPES) Ann - b1696 d1765, m1713 Capt John Collier - desc/o Capt Henry Isham DBR(1)40

    Ann - of VA, d1787, m Benjamin Harris - desc/o Capt Henry Isham DBR(1)592

    Anne - of VA, m1711 William Kennon b1688 d1751 son of Richard & Elizabeth (Worsham) Kennon, vestryman of Dale & Bristol Parishes, justice of Henrico Co & colonel of militia - desc/o Capt Henry Isham APP264

    Daniel - of MA, m Martha Boardman - desc/o Dorothy Harlakenden DBR(1)273

    Elizabeth - m Edward Eveleth - desc/o Dorothy Harlakenden DBR(1)273

    Elizabeth - of VA, d1777, m1714 Henry Randolph III b1689/1690 d1726, justice, captain of militia & vestryman of Henrico Co - desc/o Capt Henry Isham DBR(1)25; DBR(2)344; RAA104; DBR(3)201; APP265

    Col Francis - of VA, b abt 1683 d1734, Burgess & Sheriff from Henrico Co, m Sarah (Hamlin, Hamblin ?) d1748 - desc/o Capt Henry Isham DBR(1)592; DBR(5)1065; APP264

    Francis IV - m Sarah____ - desc/o Capt Henry Isham GBR339

    Isham - of VA, b abt 1681 d1717, was called Captain, m____ who died abt ten days before 28 Nov 1709 - desc/o Capt Henry Isham APP264

    Martha - of MA, b1654 d1686, m1679 Robert Greenough - desc/o Dorothy Harlakenden CHB281; BCD281

    Martha - of VA, m John Wayles - desc/o Capt Henry Isham GBR339

    Mary - of VA, b abt 1700 d1753, m(1) William Randolph, m(2)Dr James Thompson d1747 - desc/o Capt Henry Isham APP265

    Sarah - of VA, b abt 1702 d1750, m abt 1725 William Poythress b abt 1695 d1763 of Dinwiddie Co, vestryman & churchwarden of Briston Parish, captain, major & colonel of militia, justice & sheriff of Prince George Co - desc/o Capt Henry Isham APP265

    William - of VA, b1686 d bef 8 Sep 1725, m Lucy Hamlin - desc/o Capt Henry Isham APP264

ERRINGTON (or HARRINGTON) Abraham - b abt 1622, m Rebecca Cutler - the immigrant LDS31, 77; sufficient proof of alleged royal ancestry is lacking

ERRINGTON (or HARRINGTON) (cont.)

Rebecca - b1650, m John Gibson - desc/o Abraham Errington LDS31, 77

ERSKINE Henry - of MD abt 1750, m Jean Thompson - the immigrant AFA268; sufficient proof of alleged royal ancestry is lacking

Michael - of MD & VA, m abt 1782 Margaret Hanly Paulee or Paudee - desc/o Henry Erskine AFA268

Robert - of NJ, b1735 d1780 geographer & hydraulic engineer, son of Ralph Erskine of Dunfermline & Margaret Simpson, m Elizabeth____ - the immigrant GBR94; VGS(1-5)69

EUSTACE Agatha Ann - of VA, b1765, m1779 General John Blackwell b1765 Captain 3rd Reg Virginia Line Revolutionary Army; married his first wife when she was 14 years old - desc/o Martha Eltonhead VG261, 265

Anne - of VA, m(1) Capt Edward Hull, 1778 an officer of the 15th VA Reg, killed during the Revolutionary war while enforcing the conscription, m(2)1783 Major Joseph Blackwell b1750, vestryman of Dittengen Parish, Prince William Co 1773 & was a major in the Subsistence Department Virginia Line, Revolutionary War, son of Joseph Blackwell & Lucy Steptoe - desc/o Col Richard Lee DBR(4)214 - desc/o Martha Eltonhead VG261, 271, 272

Captain Hancock - of VA, b1768 of Woodford, Stafford Co d1829, Justice of Stafford Co 1793 & was president justice for many years, m1789 Tabitha Henry dau/o Judge James Henry of Fleet's Bay & Sarah Scarborough, dau/o Edmund Scarborough of Northumberland Co, VA - desc/o Martha Eltonhead VG261, 277

Capt Isaac - of VA, m1757 Agatha Conway - desc/o Col Richard Lee DBR(4)214

John - of VA, Ensign 3d Reg VA Line 1781, m Maria____ & had issue - desc/o Martha Eltonhead VG261

William - of VA, d1800, m Ann____ & had issue - desc/o Martha Eltonhead VG261

EVANS Cadwalader - of PA 1698, b1664 d1745 son of Evan Lloyd Evan, m Ellen Morris of PA - the immigrant MCD187; PFA Apx C #8; GBR306

Cadwallader - of PA 1770, a Quaker - the immigrant J&K137; sufficient proof of alleged royal ancestry is lacking

Elizabeth - b1756 - desc/o Joshua Owen RAA120

Gwen - of PA, m Thomas Foulke, son of Edward Foulke of PA - the immigrant GBR306

Hugh - of PA, b1782 d1772, m(3)1716 Lowry William - desc/o Thomas Evans CHB191; BCD191

Jane - of PA, m John Hubbs - desc/o Cadwalader Evans MCD187 - desc/o Rowland Ellis MCD266

John - of PA 1683 - d1707, m1686 Mary Hughes - the immigrant DBR(1)678; DBR(3)489; RAA1, 92; sufficient proof of alleged royal ancestry is lacking

John - of PA - desc/o Cadwalader Evans MCD187; PFA Apx C #8

John - of MA, b1775 d1826, m1804 Mary Hill b1785 d1845 dau/o Charles Hill - desc/o Edward Carleton DBR(3)493

Joseph - of PA, m Nancy Shipley - desc/o Cadwalader Evans PFA Apx

EVANS (cont.)

    C #8

    Joshua - b1731 - desc/o Joshua Owens RAA120

    Mary - of PA, b1687 d1772, m1720 John Sturgis - desc/o John Evans
        DBR(1)678; DBR(3)489

    Sarah - of PA, m John Hank (s) - desc/o Cadwalader Evans J&K137;
        MCD187; PFA Apx C #8

    Susannah - of PA, b1719 d1801, m1740 Owen Jones Sr - desc/o
        Thomas Evans CHB19; BCD191 - desc/o Hannah Price CHB295;
        BCD295

    Thomas - of PA 1698, b1651 d1738 son of Evan Lloyd Evan, m(1)
        Anne____, m(2) Mrs Hannah Price Jones David - the immigrant
        CHB191; BCD191; GBR306

EVELETH Sarah - m John Powars - desc/o Dorothy Harlakenden
    DBR(1)273

EVERAND (EVERARD) Judith - of MA, dau/o John Everard & Judith
    (Bourne) Everard, m1615/1616 Samuel Appleton - the immigrant
    AAP154; GBR459; TAG(27)208/210

    Sir Richard, 4th Baronet of NC 1725, d1732 governor of North
        Carolina 1725/1731, son of Sir Hugh, 3rd Baronet & Mary (Brown)
        Everard, m Susannah Kidder - the immigrant J&K249; CHB180;
        BCD180; RAA1, 92; GBR37

    Susannah of NC, m David Meade - desc/o Sir Richard Everand
        J&K249; CHB180; BCD180

EYRE Catherine - of MA, b1601 d1667, m1630 Rev Charles Chauncy -
    the immigrant DBR(1)476; sufficient proof of alleged royal ancestry
    is lacking

    George - of NJ 1727 - the immigrant EDV121, 122; sufficient proof of
    alleged royal ancestry is lacking

– F –

FAIRBANKS (FAIRBANK) Deacon Cyrus - b1752 d1852, m1779 Mercy
    Hale - desc/o John Prescott DBR(1)128

    Grace - d1689, m Ephraim Bullen - desc/o John Prescott DBR(1)373

    Capt Jabez - of MA, b1670 d1758 was in the Lancaster Garrison 1704
        commander 1711, m1692 Mary Wilder - desc/o John Prescott
        J&K150; BLG2678; DBR(1)128; RAA125

    Deacon Joseph - of MA, b1693 d1772, m1718 Mary Brown - desc/o
        John Prescott - BLG2678; DBR(1)128

    Capt Joseph - of MA, b1722 d1802, m Mary Willard, m(2) 1749 Abigail
        Tarbell- - desc/o John Prescott BLG2678; DBR(1)128

    Joseph - b1741 - desc/o John Prescott RAA125

    Joseph - of MA, b1743 d1784, m Asenath Osgood - desc/o John
        Prescott BLG2678

    Deacon Joshua - of MA, m Eunice Wilder - desc/o John Prescott
        J&K150

    Luther - of MA, served in Revolutionary War, m Thankful Wheelock -
        desc/o John Prescott & anc/o Charles Warren Fairbanks, Vice
        President of the United States with President Theodore Roosevelt

FAIRBANKS (FAIRBANK) (cont.)

J&K150

Mary - b1767 - desc/o John Prescott RAA125

Thomas - b1707 - desc/o John Prescott RAA125

FAIRFAX Anne - of VA, b1728 Salem, MA d1761, m(1)1743 Maj Lawrence
Washington d1752 elder brother of General George Washington,
m(2) Col George Lee b1714 London, England d1761 Westmoreland
Co - desc/o William Fairfax BLG2918; PVF173; CFA(2)277

Bryan - of VA, d1688 - desc/o William Fairfax BLG2918; EDV16, 17;
WAC93

Rev Bryan, 8th Lord Fairfax - of VA, b1736/1737 Belvoir d1802,
served in the French & Indian Wars 1755/1758 under Washington,
was the chief mourner at the funeral of Gen George Washington &
rector of Christ Church, Alexandria, VA, m(1)1759 Elizabeth Cary
b1738 d1778, youngest dau/o Col Wilson Cary of Ceelys, VA, m(2)
bef Oct 1780 Jane Donaldson d1805, dau/o James Donaldson, a
neighboring farmer - desc/o William Fairfax J&K232; BCD176;
PVF176

Elizabeth - of VA, b1770, m1792 Frederick Griffith, son of Rev David
Griffith - desc/o William Fairfax CFA(2)281

Fernando - of VA, b1763 of Shannon Hill, Jefferson Co bp 1769 at
Towlston (Gen Washington was his godfather) d1820 Mount Eagle,
Fairfax Co, VA, m1796 Elizabeth Blair Cary (his first cousin) d1822
Shannon Hill, dau/o Col Wilson Miles Cary of Ceelys - desc/o
William Fairfax CHB177; BCD177; PVF177; CFA(2)279

George William - of VA, b1724 Bahama Islands, of Belvoir in VA &
Towlston, Yorkshire, England d1787, m1748 Sarah Cary d1811 at
Bath aged 81 years dau/o Col Wilson Cary of Ceelys, near Hampton
- desc/o William Fairfax BLG2918; PVF173; CFA(2)276

Hannah - of VA, m Warner Washington, first cousin of General
Washington - desc/o William Fairfax PVF174

Robert - of VA, b1709/1710 - desc/o William Fairfax BLG2918

Sarah of VA, m Maj John Carlyle of Alexandria, VA - desc/o William
Fairfax CHB176; BLG2918; BCD176; PVF174

Thomas - of VA, b1657 d1719, m Catherine Colepepper (Culpeper) -
the immigrant BLG2918; sufficient proof of alleged royal ancestry is
lacking

Thomas, 6th Baron Fairfax - of VA, b1692 d1781/1782 died
unmarried, son of Thomas, 5th Baron Fairfax & Catherine
(Colepepper or Culpeper) Fairfax - the immigrant GBR43; EDV16,
17; PVF174 - desc/o Thomas Colepepper (Culpeper), 2nd Baron
Colepepper GBR433

Thomas, 9th Lord Fairfax of Cameron of VA, b1762 d1846 Vaucluse,
m(1)1795 Mary Aylett d 30 Apr 1796, aged 20, in the 6th month
after marriage, dau/o Col William Aylett of Fairfield, King William
Co, m(2)1798 Laura Washington (his first cousin) d 28 in 3rd
month after marriage, dau/o Warner Washington, m(3)1800
Margaret Herbert b1784 d1858, dau/o William Herbert & Sarah
Carlyle - desc/o William Fairfax J&K232; BCD176; WAC93;
PVF177, 178; CFA(2)281

William of VA, b1691 bp Newton Kyne d1757, served in the English

FAIRFAX (cont.)

army & navy, president of the Council of Virginia, governor of the Bahamas, son of Henry & Anne (Harrison) Fairfax, m(1)1717 Sarah Walker dau/o Major Thomas Walker, chief justice of the Bahama Islands (2)1731 Deborah Gedney b1708 d1744 - the immigrant J&K232; CHB176; MCB154; MCD213; MCS54; BLG2918; BCD176; EDV16, 17; WAC93; GBR43; PVF167/179; CFA(2)264

FAIRWEATHER Joseph - of NY - the immigrant EDV69; sufficient proof of alleged royal ancestry is lacking

FARNHAM Jemima - b1773, m Ephriam Knowlton - desc/o Henry Spring LDS62

FARNSWORTH Aaron - b1709 - desc/o John Prescott RAA125

Hannah - b1716, m Josiah Butterfield - desc/o John Whitney LDS26

Hannah - b1734 - desc/o John Prescott RAA125 - desc/o Mary Launce RAA130

Reuben - b1705, m Mary Holden - desc/o John Whitney LDS43

Reuben - b1751, m(2) Anna Kellogg - desc/o John Whitney LDS43

FARNUM Sarah - b1767 d1853, m1787 Seth Winslow - desc/o Ursula Scott JSW1871

FARR Daniel - m Leah____ - desc/o John Whitney JSW1808

Leah - of MA, d1832, m1774 Amos Hubbard - desc/o John Whitney JSW1808

FARRAR Abner - of VA, b1768 in Mecklenbury Co d in Marietta, Georgia, m Catherine____ - desc/o William Farrar GVFHB(2)762

Absolam - of VA, removed to Georgia, m Mrs Phoebe (Avery) Clark - desc/o William Farrar GVFHB(2)761

Elizabeth - of VA, b1769, m John Lee & went west - desc/o William Farrar GVFHB(2)761

Elizabeth - of VA, m Dr John Selman of MD, surgeon, USA, during Revolutionary War - desc/o William Farrar GVFHB(2)761

Esther - of VA, b1756 d1826, m1775 Isaac Bogan b1750 d1805, a Revolutionary soldier - desc/o Christopher Branch DBR(1)311

Fanny - of VA, m John Hancock & went west - desc/o William Farrar GVFHB(2)761

Field - of VA, m____ & had at least one son, Field Jr, who was alive in 1772 - desc/o William Farrar GVFHB(2)759

Garland - of VA, m Mary L Shepherd of Fluvanna Co & had 9 children, one of whom is B J Farrar of Nashville, Tennessee - desc/o William Farrar GVFHB(2)763

George - of VA, b abt 1725 d1772, m Mrs Mary (Hillsman) Howard - desc/o Christopher Branch DBR(1)607 - desc/o William Farrar GVFHB(2)758, 759

George - of VA, d1772, m Judith Jefferson dau/o Thomas Jefferson - desc/o William Farrar APP277, 278; GVFHB(2)759

Jane - of VA, m Dr Coleman Rogers of Louisville, Kentucky - desc/o William Farrar GVFHB(2)761

John - of VA, b abt 1670 d bef 1729, m1691 Temperance (Brown) Batte wid/o Thomas Batte & dau/o John Brown & Sarah (later Mrs John Woodson) - desc/o William Farrar APP279; GVFHB(2)755, 756

John - of VA, d1749, m____ - desc/o William Farrar APP278

FARRAR (cont.)

John - of VA, d1769 Albemarle Co, m____ & had issue - desc/o William Farrar GVFHB(2)760

John - of VA, b1754, m1775 Rebecca Warthen - desc/o William Farrar GVFHB(2)762

John Sutton - of VA, d bef 16 Mar 1730, m(1) Elizabeth Hancock, m(2) Martha____ - desc/o William Farrar APP279; GVFGH(2)757

Joseph - of VA, d1749, m Mary (Royal) Woodson wid/o Josiah Woodson - desc/o William Farrar APP278; GVFHB(2)756

Joseph - of VA, lived in Goochland Co, m1755 Susannah Jordan & had issue a son Charles b 6 Dec 1758 - desc/o William Farrar GVFHB(2)760

Joseph Royal - of VA, b abt 1740 & lived in Goochland Co for many years, commissioned captain of militia in 1766, removed to Kentucky in 1785 d Fayette Co, m(1)1762 Phoebe Harris dau/o James Harris of Cumberland Co, m(2) Martha Gaines, m(3) abt 1783 Jane Ford dau/o Thomas Ford of Goochland Co - desc/o William Farrar GVFHB(2)761

Joseph Royal - of VA, m____ dau/o Benjamin Smith of Fayette Co, Kentucky & left issue - desc/o William Farrar GVFHB(2)761

Judith - of VA, m John Flournoy - desc/o William Farrar GVFHB(2)761

Katherine - of VA, m John Barnet d1756 - desc/o William Farrar APP278

Lucy - of VA, m Landsie Jones of Hanover Co - desc/o William Farrar GVFHB(2)761

Lucy - of VA, b1769, m John Crouch - desc/o William Farrar GVFHB(2)761

Martha - of VA, b1665, m Walter Shipley of Charles City Co, sub-sheriff, Apr 1678 - desc/o William Farrar APP277; GVFHB(2)749

Mary - of VA, b abt 1750 d aft 1796, m Thomas Moore d1795 - desc/o Christopher Branch DBR(1)607

Mary - of VA, b1767, m William Harris - desc/o William Farrar GVFHB(2)761

Mary Chastain - of VA, m (her first cousin) Richard Beverley Eggleston son of Edmund Eggleston & Jane Langhorne - desc/o William Farrar GVFHB(2)762

Mary Magdalen Chastain - of VA, b1776, m John Swann of Powhatan Co, VA - desc/o William Farrar GVFHB(2)762

Matthew - of VA, b1726 of Goochland Co d1844 a soldier in the Revolution, m Martha Murrell of Goochland Co - desc/o William Farrar GVFHB(2)763

Matthew - of VA, removed to Mississippi, m(1) ____ Holland & had a daughter who married Henry Baskette, m(2)____, m(3)____ & had issue - desc/o William Farrar GVFHB(2)763

Perrin - of VA, lived in Goochland Co & afterwards Louisa Co where he died at the age of 60, m Sarah Lacy of St Martin's Parish, Hanover Co & had issue - desc/o William Farrar GVFHB(2)761

Peter - of VA, b1730, m1754 Mary Magdalene Chastaine dau/o Stephen Chastaine of Goochland Co & wid/o James Cocke - desc/o William Farrar GVFHB(2)759

Rebecca - of VA, b1764, m Robert Porterfield of Augusta Co, who

FARRAR (cont.)

    served as captain, 2nd Virginia Regiment Continental Line, in the Revolution & was a brigadier-general of Virginia militia in the war of 1812 - desc/o William Farrar GVFHB(2)759

Richard - of VA, lived in Goochland Co, m Elizabeth Saunders & had issue - desc/o William Farrar GVFHB(2)760

Sally - of VA, b1765, m Matthew Anderson of Goochland Co - desc/o William Farrar GVFHB(2)761

Samuel - of VA, b1762 d1818, m Betty Eggleston dau/o Richard Eggleston & Mary Chubb & had issue - desc/o William Farrar GVFHB(2)762

Sarah - of VA, (perhaps), m her cousin William Farrar - desc/o William Farrar APP278

Sarah - of VA, m Major Thomas Shelton - desc/o William Farrar GVFHB(2)763

Sarah - of VA, b1765, m John Royster - desc/o William Farrar GVFHB(2)761

Stephen - of VA, m____ Duncan - desc/o William Farrar GVFHB(2)763

Thomas - b abt 1662 d1742, m(1) Mary Ligon, m(2)1685/1686 Katherine Perrin dau/o Richard Perrin - desc/o William Farrar APP278; GVFHB(2)754

Thomas - of VA, signed his father's title bond to Thomas Randolph 1727/1728 - desc/o William Farrar APP278

Col Thomas - of VA, b1726 d1810 near Carnesville, Franklin Co, Georgia at the home of his son Abner, served in the Revolution as colonel (probably of militia) & was sheriff 1790, m Elizabeth Howard - desc/o Christopher Branch DBR(1)311 - desc/o William Farrar GVFHB(2)758

Thomas - of VA, lived in Goochland Co, m Elizabeth____ & had issue a daughter Mary Ann b 23 Nov 1756 & a son John b 1 Aug 1758 - desc/o William Farrar GVFHB(2)760

Thomas - removed from South Carolina to Claiborne Co, Mississippi d1811, m his cousin Martha Farrar dau/o Thomas Farrar - desc/o William Farrar GVFHB(2)762

Thomas - of VA, removed from Virginia to South Carolina then to Georgia & finally to Claiborne Co, Mississippi d1833, m Margaret Prince - desc/o William Farrar GVFHB(2)762

William - of VA 1618, bp 1583 at Croxton, Lincolnshire, d 1637 bef 11 Jun, third son of John Farrar the Elder & Cicily Kelke, appointed to the Council & served there for the rest of his life, m Mrs Cecily____ Jordan of VA 1611 - the immigrant GBR224, TAG(40)25, 26; APP273/277; GVFHB(2)744

William - of VA, b1627 d1677/1678, son & heir to his father William, Capt of militia, justice & member of House of Burgesses from Henrico Co, m Mary____ - desc/o William Farrar APP276; GVFHB(2)745

William - of VA, b abt 1657 d1721, capt of militia, justice & member of the House of Burgesses, m(1)1680 Priscilla Baugh dau/o William Baugh Jr & Jane____ Baugh, m(2)1707 Mary (Tanner) Ligon - desc/o William Farrar APP277; GVFHB(2)753, 754

William - of VA, of Goochland Co, eldest son & heir to Farrar's Island,

FARRAR (cont.)

d1744, m Sarah____ - desc/o William Farrar APP277; GVFHB(2)756

William - of VA, d bef 5 Dec 1715, m Martha____ - desc/o William Farrar APP278

William - of VA, lived in Goochland Co, m(1) Mary Williamson, m(2)1762 Elizabeth Bibb & had issue - desc/o William Farrar GVFHB(2)760

William - of VA, m____ & died young living issue in Indiana - desc/o William Farrar GVFHB(2)761

FARRIS William - of VA, m Mary Sherwood - desc/o Col William Randolph DBR(2)339, 406

William - of VA, m1758 Martha Truman - desc/o Col William Randolph DBR(2)339, 406

William - of VA, b abt 1776, m1796/1797 Elizabeth Johns - desc/o Col William Randolph DBR(2)339, 407

FARWELL Abel - of MA, b abt 1744 d1817, m Hannah Russell - desc/o Olive Welby JSW1710

Anna - of MA, b1721 Groton, m1741 Josiah Brown - desc/o Olive Welby GPM(1)156

Daniel - of MA, b1717 d1808, m1739 Mary Moon - desc/o Olive Welby ECD250; ECD(3)278; GPM(1)156

Edward - of MA, b1706 d1772, m abt 1730 Hannah Russell - desc/o Olive Welby JSW1710

Elizabeth - of MA, m____ Wilkins - desc/o Olive Welby GPM(1)155

Elizabeth - of MA, b1672, m1693 John Richardson - desc/o Olive Welby GPM(1)156

Elizabeth - of MA, b1713, m1730 Jonathan Gates - desc/o Olive Welby ECD(3)275

Ephraim - of MA, b1760 Groton d1825, m Annie____ - desc/o Olive Welby GPM(1)156

Hannah - b1667 - desc/o Olive Welby RAA93

Henry - of MA & CT 1639, d1670, m Olive Welby - the immigrant CHB352; MCB182; BCD352; RAA1, 93; sufficient proof of alleged royal ancestry is lacking; GBR211 the royal ancestry is through his wife Olive Welby

Henry - of MA, b1674, m Susannah Richardson - desc/o Olive Welby GPM(1)156

Isaac - b abt 1678 - desc/o Olive Welby RAA93

Isaac - of MA, b1744 d abt 1786, m1770 Lucy Page - desc/o Olive Welby ECD250; ECD(3)278

John - of MA, b abt 1639 Concord, m(1) Sarah Wheeler, m(2) Sarah Fisk - desc/o Olive Welby GPM(1)155

John - b1711 - desc/o Olive Welby RAA93

Jonathan - of MA, b1726 Groton d1761 Charlestown, NH, m Eunice____ - desc/o Olive Welby GPM(1)156

Ensign Joseph - of MA, b1641/1642 Concord d1722 highway surveyor 1706, m1666 Hannah Learned b1649 Woburn dau/o Isaac Learned & Mary Stearns - desc/o Henry Farwell CHB352; BCD352 - desc/o Olive Welby ECD250; ECD(3)275, 278; JSW1710; MCB182; DBR(4)664; RAA93; GPM(1)155

Joseph - of MA, b1670 Chelmsford d1740 Groton, m1695/1696

FARWELL (cont.)

Chelmsford, Hannah Colburn - desc/o Olive Welby ECD250; ECD(3)278; DBR(4)665; RAA93; GPM(1)156

Joseph - of MA, b1696 Chelmsford, m1719 Mary Gilson b1703 dau/o Joseph & Elizabeth Gilson - desc/o Olive Welby GPM(1)156

Levi - of MA, b1770 Groton d1858 Washington, m Sarah Smith - desc/o Olive Welby GPM(1)156

Lucy - of NH, b1771 d1849, m1790 Porter Flint - desc/o Olive Welby ECD(3)278

Lydia - of MA, b1749, m1767 John Ireland - desc/o Olive Welby DBR(4)665

Mary - of MA, b abt 1642 d abt 1713/1714, m abt 1665 John Bates d abt 1722 - desc/o Olive Welby ECD134; DBR(2)107; DBR(3)620; RAA93; GPM(1)155

Mary - b1709 - desc/o Olive Welby RAA93

Olive - of MA, b abt 1645, m1668 Chelmsford, Benjamin Spalding - desc/o Olive Welby ECD(3)271; RAA93; GPM(1)155

Olive - b1740 - desc/o Olive Welby RAA93

General Samuel - of MA, b1714 d1757, m Elizabeth Moors - desc/o Olive Welby DBR(4)665

Sarah of MA, m1707 Jonathan Howard - desc/o Henry Farwell CHB352; MCB183; BCD352

Sarah - of MA, b1768 Groton d1850 Nashua, NH, m William Lawrence - desc/o Olive Welby GPM(1)156

Susanna - of MA, b1742 Groton, m John Cheney of Groton - desc/o Olive Welby GPM(1)156

Thomas - of MA, b1698 Chelmsford d1731, m1723 Elizabeth Pierce b Groton - desc/o Olive Welby GPM(1)156

Thomas - of MA, b1733 Groton d1825 Washington, NH, served as lieutenant in various companies during the Revolutionary War, m Sarah Davis d1813 aged seventy years - desc/o Olive Welby GPM(1)156

Thomas - of MA, b1763 Groton d1829, m___ Waite & resided in Hopkinton, NH - desc/o Olive Welby GPM(1)156

William - of MA, b1688 d1756, m1710 Elizabeth Soldine - desc/o Olive Welby ECD(3)275

FAUNCE Joanna - b1689 - desc/o George Morton RAA116

Mary - b abt 1636 - desc/o George Morton RAA116

Mercy - b1651 - desc/o George Morton RAA116

Patience - b abt 1640 - desc/o George Morton RAA116

Priscilla - b abt 1634 - desc/o George Morton RAA116

Thomas - b1647 - desc/o George Morton RAA116

FAUNTLEROY Ann - of VA, m Mr.___ Pettit - desc/o Col Moore Fauntleroy CRL(4)550

Apphia Lewis - m Mr.___ Daingerfield - desc/o Col Moore Fauntleroy CRL(4)550

Bushrod - of VA, b1720 d1778, m Elizabeth Fouchee - desc/o Col Moore Fauntleroy DBR(2)10; DBR(3)195

Elizabeth - of VA, m1685 Richard Metcalfe - desc/o Col Moore Fauntleroy DBR(5)332

Elizabeth - of VA, m Col William Brockenbrough - desc/o Col Moore

FAUNTLEROY (cont.)
    Fauntleroy CHB143; BCD143
    Elizabeth - of VA, m Francis Settle - desc/o Col Moore Fauntleroy
      DBR(4)408
    Griffin - of VA, b1681 d1730, m(1) Elizabeth Taylor, m(2) Ann Bushrod
      - desc/o Col Moore Fauntleroy MCD218; DBR(2)10, 69, 296;
      DBR(3)195; CRL(4)550
    Capt Griffin - of VA, b1716 d1755, m Judith Swann - desc/o Col
      Moore Fauntleroy DBR(2)69, 296
    Griffin Murdock - of VA, b1747 d1794, m1770 Anne Bellfield - desc/o
      Col Moore Fauntleroy DBR(3)156
    Hannah - of VA, m Mr Robinson - desc/o Col Moore Fauntleroy
      CRL(4)550
    Jane - of VA, b1749, m Col Thomas Turner - desc/o Col Moore
      Fauntleroy CRL(4)550
    John - of VA, b1745 d1798, m Judith Ball - desc/o Col Moore
      Fauntleroy CHB144; BCD143
    Joseph - of VA, b1754 d1815, m Elizabeth Foushee - desc/o Col Moore
      Fauntleroy CHB143; BCD143; CRL(4)550
    Judith - of VA, m Landon Carter - desc/o Col Moore Fauntleroy
      CHB143; BCD143
    Judith Swann - of VA, b1751 d1813, m1771 George Boswell - desc/o
      Col Moore Fauntleroy DBR(2)69, 296
    Katherine - of VA, m John Lewis - desc/o Col Moore Fauntleroy
      CRL(4)550
    Col Moore - of VA, b1616 d bef 1665, m(1)1639 Dorothy Colle,
      m(2)1648 Mary Hill - the immigrant CHB142; MCB136; MCD218;
      BCD142; DBR(2)9, 69, 295, 296, 375; DBR(3)46, 156, 193, 195;
      DBR(4)407, 408; DBR(5)328, 331, 332, 1045; RAA1, 93; WAC12;
      AWW172; CRL(4)549, royal ancestry in question
    Col Moore - of VA, b1679 d1739, m Margaret Micou - desc/o Col
      Moore Fauntleroy CHB143; BCD143
    Moore - of VA, married and had a son George - desc/o Col Moore
      Fauntleroy CRL(2)550
    Sarah - of VA, m Mr____ Gray - desc/o Col Moore Fauntleroy
      CRL(4)550
    Thomas - of VA - desc/o Col Moore Fauntleroy MCD218
    Col William - of VA, b1656 d1686, m1680 Katharine Griffin - desc/o
      Col Moore Fauntleroy CHB143; MCD218; BCD143; DBR(2)10, 69,
      296; DBR(3)156, 195; CRL(4)549, 550
    Col William - of VA, b1684 d1757, m1712 Apphia Bushrod - desc/o
      Col Moore Fauntleroy CHB143; BCD143; DBR(3)156; WAC12;
      CRL(4)550
    Col William - of VA, b1713 d1793, m1737 Margaret (Peggy) Murdock -
      desc/o Col Moore Fauntleroy CHB143; BCD143; DBR(3)156;
      WAC12; CRL(4)550
FAY Dinah - b1705 d1782, m1722 David Goodnow - desc/o Dr Richard
    Palgrave DBR(1)784
    James - of MA, b1707 d1777, m1727 Lydia Child - desc/o Dr Richard
      Palgrave DBR(4)430
    John (III) - son of John Fay, Jr & Elizabeth Wellington, m Hannah

FAY (cont.)

Child - desc/o Dr Richard Palgrave GBR266

Jonathan - m Joanna Phillips - desc/o Dr Richard Palgrave GBR266

Jonathan Jr - m Lucy Prescott - desc/o Dr Richard Palgrave GBR266

Lydia - of MA, b1730 d1817, m1750 Amaziah Spooner - desc/o Dr Richard Palgrave DBR(4)430

Samuel Prescott Phillips - m Harriet Howard - desc/o Dr Richard Palgrave GBR267 - desc/o Jane Allen GBR332

FELCH Hannah - b1672 - desc/o William Sargent RAA129

FELL Joyce - of PA, m1779 Isaac Buckman - desc/o Rev Thomas Dungan AFA52

Titus - of PA, m1747 Elizabeth Heston - desc/o Rev Thomas Dungan AFA52

FELSHAW Lemuel - b1769 - desc/o Griffith Bowen RAA72

FELTON Susan - of VA, dau/o Sir Henry Felton, 2nd Baronet & Susan Tollemache, m(1) Philip Harbord, m(2) Francis Howard, 5th Baron Howard of Effingham, governor of Virginia - the immigrant GBR119

FELYPSEN (PHILIPSE) Vrederijck - of NY - the immigrant EDV14, 15; sufficient proof of alleged royal ancestry is lacking

FENWICK Ann - of NJ, m Samuel Hedge d1694/1697 - desc/o John Fenwick DBR(1)316; DBR(2)413; DBR(3)439

Bennett - d1800 - desc/o Rev Robert Brooke DBR(1)788

Charlotte - of SC, b1766, m(1) William Leigh Pierce was from Virginia & was commissioned a captain in 1st Regiment Continental Artillery on 30 Nov 1776, he served on the staff of General Greene until the end of the war. He must have settled in Georgia soon after the Revolution, for in 1787 he sat as a delegate from that state to the Convention that framed the Constitution of the United States, m(2) Ebenezer Jackson was from MA, commissioned 2nd Lieutenant of 3rd Continental Artillery 27 Jun 1781, their daughter Harriet Jackson, m1821 Commodore Tattnall, her 1st cousin - desc/o John Fenwick SCG(2)186

Cuthbert - of MD, son of George Fenwick & Barbara Mitford, m(1)____, m(2) Mrs Jane Eltonhead Moryson of MD - the immigrant GBR354 some aspect of royal descent merits further study

Edward - of SC, b1726 d1775, m(1) Martha Izard dau/o Ralph Izard, m(2)1753 Mary Drayton b1734 d1806 dau/o Thomas Drayton & Elizabeth Bull - desc/o John Fenwick SCG(2)181, 188

Elizabeth - of NJ, m abt 1663 John Adams - desc/o John Fenwick DBR(2)584; DBR(3)372; DBR(4)701

Elizabeth - of SC, d1776, m1776 John Barnwell - desc/o John Fenwick SCG(2)181

George - of CT, b1603 d1756/1757, a founder of Seybrook, CT, son of George Fenwick & Dorothy Forster, m(1) Alice Apsley, m(2) Catherine Haselrige - the immigrant GBR153

Harriett - of SC, b1769, m1786 Governor Josiah Tattnall Jr d1804 - desc/o John Fenwick SCG(2)186

Col James - of MD, b1763 d1823, m Henrietta Maria Lancaster - desc/o Rev Robert Brooke CHB404

John - of NJ, b1618 d1683/1684 son of William Fenwick & Elizabeth Gargrave, m(1) abt 1641 Elizabeth Covert bp 1610 dau/o Sir Walter

FENWICK (cont.)

Covert, m(2) Mary Marten - the immigrant DBR(1)316; DBR(2)411, 412, 582, 584; DBR(3)372, 437, 439; DBR(4)699, 701; RAA1, 94; GBR238; GPFHB285/307

John - of SC, b1691 d1747 a planter & merchant with a business on a large scale, but like other men of that day he found time to serve the public in many capacities, youngest son of Robert Fenwick & Anne Culcheth, m Elizabeth Gibbes dau/o Governor Robert Gibbes of South Carolina - the immigrant GBR238; SCG(2)181, 187

Margaret - of DE, m Edward Stretcher - desc/o Thomas Fenwick MCD216

Martha - of SC, b1760, m abt 15 Oct 1778 Thomas Gadsden d1791, captain in 1st Regiment South Carolina Continentals, son of General Christopher Gadsden - desc/o John Fenwick SCG(2)186

Mary - of SC, b1757, m1779 Walter Izard son of Ralph Izard - desc/o John Fenwick SCG(2)185

Matilda - of SC, b1767, m Robert Giles d1803 - desc/o John Fenwick SCG(2)186

Robert - of MD, d1778, m bef 1751 Susanna Hopewell - desc/o Rev Robert Brooke DBR(1)788

Sarah - of SC, b1756, m(1)1777 Macartan Campbell, m(2) Dr George Jones of Savannah & left issue by both marriages - desc/o John Fenwick SCG(2)185

Selina - of SC, b1764 unmarried at the date of her mother's will 1805 - desc/o John Fenwick SCG(2)186

Thomas - of MD & DE, b abt 1632/1635 d1708 son of Walter Fenwick & Magdalen Hunt, m(1) Mrs Mary Savill Porter Lawson, m(2) Mary____ - the immigrant MCD216; GBR340

FERMOR Lady Juliana - of PA, b1729 dau/o Thomas, 1st Earl of Pomfret & Henrietta Louisa (Jeffreys) Fermor, m1751 Thomas Penn b1702 d1775 of PA, son of William & Hannah (Callowhill) Penn - the immigrant GBR79; GPFPM(2)566/70; CRFP(1)6, 7

FIELD Deacon Aaron - of MA, b1721 d1800, m1743 Eunice Frary - desc/o Zachariah Field THC103, 104

Abraham II - of VA - desc/o William Ironmonger DBR(3)347, 349

Ann - m John Brown - desc/o Thomas Lawrence MCD241

Anna - of MA, b1747, m(1)1786 Ziba Allen, m(2) Samuel Clapp - desc/o Zachariah Field THC104

Chloe - of MA, b1743 d1781, m1764 Samuel Shattuck - desc/o Zachariah Field THC104

Dioma - of MA, m1790 Shubal Fuller - desc/o Zachariah Field THC105

Ebenezer - of MA, b1688 d1723, m1714 Elizabeth Arms - desc/o Zachariah Field THC103

Ebenezer - of MA, b1715, m(1) Sarah Mattoon, m(2) Mrs Christian Field - desc/o Zachariah Field THC103

Elizabeth - of MA, b1723 d1784, m1745 Capt Ebenezer Wells - desc/o Zachariah Field THC103

Eunice - of MA, b1743 d1785, m abt 1760 Joseph Wells - desc/o Zachariah Field THC104

Henry - of VA, b1769 d1850, m Fanny Hill - desc/o William Ironmonger DBR(3)347, 349

FIELD (cont.)

Irene - of MA, b1745, m1769 Lieut Daniel Newcomb - desc/o Zachariah Field THC104

Jesse - of MA, b1749, m Sarah Burke - desc/o Zachariah Field THC104

Joanna - of MA, b1717, m1737 Col Phineas Wright - desc/o Zachariah Field THC103

John - of MA, b abt 1648, m Mary Edwards - desc/o Zachariah Field THC102

John - of VA, d1774, m Ann Rogers Clark - desc/o William Ironmonger DBR(3)347, 349

Joshua - of MA, b1695, m Elizabeth Cooley - desc/o Zachariah Field THC102

Josiah - of MA, b1692, m Elizabeth____ - desc/o Zachariah Field THC102

Joseph - of MA, b abt 1658, m Joanna Watt - desc/o Zachariah Field THC102

Mary - of MA, m 1663 Joshua Porter - desc/o Zachariah Field THC102

Mary - of MA, b1690, m1712 Jonathan Hoyt - desc/o Zachariah Field THC102

Mehitable - of MA, b abt 1748 d1797, m Deacon Jonathan Sheldon - desc/o Zachariah Field THC105

Moses - of MA, b1719, m(1) Anne Dickinson, m(2) Martha Root - desc/o Zachariah Field THC103

Olive - of MA, m Reuben Sheldon - desc/o Zachariah Field THC104

Rachel - of MA, b1751, m1774 Dr Polycarpus Cushman - desc/o Zachariah Field THC104

Sergt Samuel - of MA, b abt 1651 d1697, m(1)1676 Sarah Gilbert, m(2) Mary Belding - desc/o Zachariah Field THC102

Samuel - of MA, b1678, m Mrs Hannah E Hoyt - desc/o Zachariah Field THC103

Sarah - of MA, b1683, m1702 Samuel Warner - desc/o Zachariah Field THC103

Thomas - of MA, b1680, m Abigail Dickinson - desc/o Zachariah Field THC103

Rev Timothy - of CT, b1775 d1844, m(1)1801 Wealthy Ann Bishop - desc/o Anne Lloyd ECD(3)194, 195

Zachariah - of MA, b1606 d1666, m Mary Stanley - the immigrant THC102; sufficient proof of alleged royal ancestry is lacking

Zachariah - of MA, d1674, m1668 Sarah Webb - desc/o Zachariah Field THC102

Zachariah - of MA, b1685, m Sarah Mattoon - desc/o Zachariah Field THC102

FIELDING Frances - of VA - desc/o Henry Fielding WAC78, 79

Henrietta - dau/o Henry Fielding & Charlotte Craddock, m James Gabriel Montresor b1702 d1776, British military engineer who served in the American colonies - the immigrant GBR128

Henry - of VA, d1712 - the immigrant WAC78, 79; GBR list his daughter Henrietta - the immigrant

FIENNES Arbella - of MA, m Isaac Johnson - the immigrant FLW188; MCS43; sufficient proof of alleged royal ancestry is lacking

FIENNES (cont.)

Susan - of MA 1634, b1595 d1661, m John Humfrey - the immigrant CHB528; FLW188; MCD234; MCS43; sufficient proof of alleged royal ancestry is lacking

FIFIELD Abraham - of MA, b1696 d bef 22 Jun 1743, m1722 Boston, Mary Southwick & had issue, at least one son Jonathan Armitage aged abt 19 in 1743 when he chose Jonathan Armitage as his guardian - desc/o Edward Raynsford NE(139)303

FILLEY Sarah - b1742, m Henry Mumford - desc/o John Drake LDS23; RAA87

FILMER Maj Henry - of VA, an officer in the British Army, member of the House of Burgesses for James City & Warwick Co, VA son of Sir Edward Filmer & Elizabeth Argall d1638, m Elizabeth____ - the immigrant ECD(2)133; DBR(1)67; DBR(2)84, 86, 219, 221, 335, 337, 385, 387; DBR(3)321, 322; DBR(4)184; DBR(5)265, 354, 355, 1046; RAA1, 95; WAC31, 32; FFF7; GBR242; VGE199, 200, 346, 347, 394/396, 583, 664/666; GVFHB(4)528/532

Martha - of VA, m Thomas Green Jr, born at sea en route to America, son of Thomas & Martha Green, emigrants from Holland - desc/o Maj Henry Filmer ECD(2)133, 136; DBR(1)67; DBR(2)86, 337, 387; DBR(3)322; DBR(4)185; DBR(5)265, 355; FFF7

FIRTH Hannah - of PA, m Isaac Cooper Jones - desc/o Thomas Lloyd MCD252

FISHER Abigail - of VA, m____ Bradford - desc/o John Fisher APP282

Anne - of VA, m Robert Gascoigne b abt 1673 d1709, justice 1704 & sheriff 1706, son of Robert & Elizabeth Gascoigne - desc/o John Fisher APP282

Anthony - d1671, m Mary____ - the immigrant AFA104; royal ancestry not proven

Bridget - of VA, possibly, m John Milton - desc/o John Fisher APP282

Bridget - of VA, m William Bradford - desc/o John Fisher APP282

Elizabeth - of VA, m(1)____ James, m(2)____ Floyd - desc/o John Fisher APP282

Isaac - b1694, m Esther Mann - desc/o Jonathan Whitney LDS60

John - of VA 1623/1624, b abt 1600 d1639/1640. 2nd son of John Fisher of Maidstone, Kent, England & Benetta (Dering) Fisher, m Elizabeth____ b abt 1610 - the immigrant GBR159; APP279/283; VAG(30)83/89

John - of VA, d1720, m by 28 Mar 1698 Elizabeth (Benthall) Marshman, wid/o Luke Marshman & dau/o Joseph Benthall Sr & his wife Mary____ - desc/o John Fisher APP282; VAG(30)83/89

John - of VA, d1743/1744, m Elizabeth____ d1757 - desc/o John Fisher APP282

Joshua of PA, b1775, m1807 Elizabeth Powell - desc/o James Logan CHB344; BCD344

Lydia - of MA, d1690, m Daniel Morse - desc/o Anthony Fisher AFA104

Maddox - of VA, m Sarah____ - desc/o John Fisher APP282, 283

Margaret - b1728, m Jabez Hills - desc/o Jonathan Whitney LDS60

Margery - of DE, m1722 James Miers b bef 1700 d abt 1737 - desc/o Margery Maude DBR(1)47; DBR(3)91 - desc/o Thos Fisher AFA56

FISHER (cont.)

Mary - of VA, m____ Smith - desc/o John Fisher APP283

Philip - of VA, b abt 1637 d1702/1703, justice of Northampton Co, VA & captain of militia, m Elizabeth Maddox, eldest dau/o Alexander Maddox - desc/o John Fisher AAP279/283; VAG(30)83/89

Philip - of VA, d1709, m Elizabeth____ - desc/o John Fisher APP283

Rebecca - of VA, m(1) by 30 Dec 1679 William Wanton d1686, commissioner of Somerset Co, MD, m(2) Roger Odene (Odewe) - desc/o John Fisher AAP279/283

Sarah - of VA, m____ Gore - desc/o John Fisher APP282

Stephen - of VA, b abt 1636 d by 1658, m shortly aft 20 Apr 1657 Rebecca Bagwell d1658 issue of this marriage a daughter Rebecca Fisher b1658/1659, dau/o John Bagwell of Accomack Co, VA & wid/o Robert Andrews - desc/o John Fisher AAP279/283; VAG(30)83/89

Thomas - of PA 1682, m1692 Margery Maude - the immigrant AFA56; RAA1, 95; sufficient proof of alleged royal ancestry is lacking

Thomas - of VA, d1727, m Sarah____ - desc/o John Fisher APP282

Thomas - of VA, m Patience____, she m(2) Francis Wainhouse Jr d1717/1718 - desc/o John Fisher APP282

Thomas - of VA, d1772, m Mary Bell dau/o Thomas Bell of Accomack Co, VA - desc/o John Fisher VAG86

FISKE Anne - of MA, b1605 d1649, m Francis Chickering - the immigrant AFA16; sufficient proof of alleged royal ancestry is lacking

Anna - of MA, m1776 Rev John Hammond - desc/o Mary Bruen DBR(1)17

Benjamin - of CT, b1683 d1765, m1701 Abigail Bowen - desc/o Mary Bruen CHB29; BCD29; DBR(1)17; RAA74

Benjamin - of MA, b1706 d1771, m Susannah Briggs - desc/o Mary Bruen DRB(1)17

Daniel - of CT, b1710 d1804, m1732 Freelove Williams - desc/o Mary Bruen CHB29; BCD29

Daniel - of RI, b1753 d1810, m1785 Freelove Knight - desc/o William Arnold CHB14, BCD14 - desc/o Mary Bruen CHB29; BCD29

Hezekiah - b1704 - desc/o Obadiah Bruen RAA74

Hezekiah - b1775 - desc/o Obadiah Bruen RAA74

Moses - b1733 - desc/o Obadiah Bruen RAA74

Robert - m Sybil Gold - the immigrant EDV70; sufficient proof of alleged royal ancestry is lacking

FITCH Abel - of CT, b1771 d1822, m Fannie Hinchley - desc/o Rev James Fitch BLG2685

Capt Abraham - of CT, b1737 d1821, m Elizabeth Bissell - desc/o Rev James Fitch BLG2685

Ebenezer - of CT, b1729 - desc/o Thomas Fitch BLG2684

Edward - of CT, b1772 - desc/o Thomas Fitch BLG2684

Elizabeth - m(1) Joshua Raymond, m(2) Rev Elisha Kent - desc/o Thomas Fitch BLG2684

Rev James - of CT, b1622 d1702, m(1) Abigail Whitfield, m(2) Priscilla Mason - the immigrant BLG2685; sufficient proof of alleged royal ancestry is lacking

James - desc/o Thomas Fitch BLG2684

FITCH (cont.)

John - b1633, m1674 Rebecca Lindall - desc/o Thomas Fitch BLG2684

Jonathan - of CT, b1727 - desc/o Thomas Fitch BLG2684

Mary - b1668, m Daniel Terrell - desc/o Thomas Fitch BLG2684

Mary - of CT, b1744 d1774, m1759 Ebenezer Reed - desc/o John Drake CHB107; BCD107

Nathan - of CT, b1705, m Hannah Huntington - desc/o Rev James Fitch BLG2685

Nathaniel - of CT, b1679, m(1) Ann Abell, m(2) Mindwell Higley - desc/o Rev James Fitch BLG2685

Samuel - desc/o Thomas Fitch BLG2684

Sarah - b1663, m John Ford - desc/o Thomas Fitch BLG2684

Thomas - of CT 1638, b1590 d1632/1633, m Anna Reve - the immigrant EDV57; BLG2684; sufficient proof of alleged royal ancestry is lacking

Gov Thomas - of CT, b1612 d1704, m1622 Anne Stacie - desc/o Thomas Fitch EDV57; BLG2684

Thomas - of CT, b abt 1630 d1684, m abt 1662 Ruth Clark - desc/o Thomas Fitch BLG2684

Thomas - of CT, b1665 d1731, m(1) Sarah ___, m(2) Rhoda___, m(3) Rachel___ - desc/o Thomas Fitch BLG2684

Thomas - of CT, b1700 d1774, m1724 Hannah Hall - desc/o Thomas Fitch BLG2684

Thomas - of CT, b1725 - desc/o Thomas Fitch BLG2684

Timothy - of CT, b1735 d1802, m1764 Esther Platt - desc/o Thomas Fitch BLG2684

Timothy - of CT, b1769 - desc/o Thomas Fitch BLG2684

William - b1768 - desc/o Thomas Fitch BLG2684

FITZHUGH Anna - of VA, m George May - desc/o Dudley Diggs CHB78; BCD78

Anne - of VA, b1720 d1789, m1740 Rev Robert Rose - desc/o William Ironmonger DBR(3)702; CRL(4)332

Henry - of VA, b1686/1687 d1768, m1718 Susanna Cooke - desc/o Col William Fitzhugh WAC65; CRL(4)332

Henry - of VA, b1723 d1783, m1746 Sarah Battaile - desc/o William Ironmonger ECD(2)163; DBR(3)698; DBR(5)586

Henry - of VA, b1750 d1773, m1770 Elizabeth Stith - desc/o William Ironmonger DBR(3)698

Henry - of VA, b1773 d1830, m1792 Elizabeth Catlett Conway - desc/o William Ironmonger DBR(3)698

John - of VA, b1727, m1746 Alice Thornton - desc/o William Ironmonger DBR(3)47

John Thornton - of VA, b1749 d1809, m abt 1779 Margaret Helm - desc/o William Ironmonger DBR(3)47

Lettice - of VA, b1707 d1732, m1727 George Turberville - desc/o William Fitzhugh WAC65

Sarah - of VA, b1710 d1743, m1735 Edward Barradall - desc/o Col William Fitzhugh WAC65

Susannah - of VA, b1757, m Col Townshend Dade - desc/o William Ironmonger ECD(2)163; DBR(5)586

FITZHUGH (cont.)

Col William - of VA, bp 1651 d1704, m1674 Sarah Tucker - the immigrant EDV143, 144; WAC65; CRL(4)331; sufficient proof of alleged royal ancestry is lacking

William Henry - of VA, d1713/1714, m Anne Lee - desc/o William Fitzhugh WAC65

FITZRANDOLPH Aratas - of NJ, b1761/1762 Woodbridge d1831, m Abraham Johnson b1762 d1849 - desc/o Edward FitzRandolph NE(97)339

Capt Asher - of NJ, b1755 Woodbridge d1817 Blazing Star, m Katherine Brown b1756 Blazing Star d1817 Blazing Star, dau/o John Brown & Esther Frazee - desc/o Edward FitzRandolph NE(98)52

Benjamin - of NJ, b abt 1665 d1746 Stoney Brook, near Princeton, NJ, m(1)1689 Sarah Dennis b1673 Piscataway d1732 Stoney Brook, dau/o John Dennis & Sara Bloomfield, m(2)1733 Margaret Robinson - desc/o Edward FitzRandolph RAA96; GBR446; NE(97)279

Benjamin - of NJ, b1699 Stoney Brook d1758 Princeton, m1727/1728 Princeton, Elizabeth Pridmore - desc/o Edward FitzRandolph NE(97)279

Bethia - of MA, m John Clarkson - desc/o Edward FitzRandolph DBR(2)679; DBR(3)486

Catherine - of NJ, b1739 Old Vail Farm d1810 Plainfield, m1760 Plainfield, John Vail b1734 near Plainfield d1814 Plainfield, son of John Vail & Margaret Laing (originally Veal) of Plainfield - desc/o Edward FitzRandolph NE(97)338

Catherine - of NJ, b1751, m1778 Plainfield, Robert Miller of Morris Co, NJ - desc/o Edward FitzRandolph NE(97)338

Christopher - Christian - of NJ, b1682 Woodbridge d1715 Cohansey (now Shilo) NJ, m Sarah____ & had issue a daughter Grace b1703 Woodbridge - desc/o Edward FitzRandolph NE(97)331

David - of NJ, b1690/1691, m Sarah Molleson - desc/o Edward FitzRandolph - desc/o Edward FitzRandolph NE(97)278

David - of NJ, b1750 Woodbridge d1793, m Martha Journay b1753 d1810 - desc/o Edward FitzRandolph NE(98)50

Dinah - of NJ, b1700, m1717 Edmund Dunham b1691 son of Rev Edmond Dunham & Mary Bonham - desc/o Edward FitzRandolph JSW1528; NE(97)278

Edward - of MA & NJ, bp 1607 d1684/1685 son of Edward FitzRandolph & Frances Howis, m1637 Elizabeth Blossom b abt 1620 at Leiden d abt 1713 dau/o Thomas Blossom & Anne Helsdon - the immigrant ECD(2)141; JSW1527; MCS111; DBR(2)679; DBR(3)486; DBR(4)477; DBR(5)1047; AFA46; RAA1, 96; FFF227; GBR446; EO2(1)859/861; NE(97)275

Edward - of NJ, b1706 Woodbridge d1750, m1734 Phebe Jackson b1712 Flushing, NY d1777 Plainfield, dau/o James Jackson & Rebecca Hallett of Flushing & sister of James Jackson who married Mary FitzRandolph - desc/o Edward FitzRandolph NE(97)337/338

Edward - of NJ, b Barnstable, MA d1760 Woodbridge, m1704 Middletown, NJ, Katharine Hartshorne b1682 Middletown d1759

FITZRANDOLPH (cont.)

Woodbridge, dau/o Richard Hartshorne & Margaret Carr - desc/o Edward FitzRandolph NE(97)334

Edward - of NJ, b1749 Plainfield d1831 Somerset Co, NJ, m1782 Plainfield Mary Webster b1750 Plainfield d1833 Plainfield, dau/o Hugh Webster & Sarah Marsh - desc/o Edward FitzRandolph NE(98)45

Edward - of NJ, b1754 Perth Amboy d1837 Philadelphia, PA, was a first lieutenant in a Pennsylvania regiment during the Revolutionary War also dropped the "Fitz" from his name after two or three of his children were born, m1779 Philadelphia, PA, Anna Julianna Steele b1761 Germantown, PA d1810 Philadelphia, dau/o Henry Steele of Germany & Anna Margaret Ebright of Zurich, Switzerland - desc/o Edward FitzRandolph NE(98)43

Elizabeth - of NJ, b1657, m1676 Piscataway, Andrew Wooden - desc/o Edward FitzRandolph NE(97)278

Elizabeth - of NJ, b1708 Stoney Brook d1759 Princeton, m1730/1731 Princeton, Ephraim Manning - desc/o Edward FitzRandolph NE(97)280

Elizabeth - of NJ, m Woodbridge, Samuel Moore - desc/o Edward FitzRandolph NE(97)336

Elizabeth - of NJ, m Captain ____ Henderson - desc/o Edward FitzRandolph NE(97)337

Elizabeth - of NJ, b1756, m1779 Mendham, David Shotwell son of Samuel & Ann Shotwell of Elizabeth, NJ - desc/o Edward FitzRandolph NE(97)340

Eseck - of NJ, b1718 Woodbridge d1813 kept a tavern in Milton, NJ, m abt 1756 Mary Robinson b1734 dau/o John Robinson - desc/o Edward FitzRandolph NE(97)339

Eunice - b1730 - desc/o Edward FitzRandolph RAA96

Eunice - of NJ, b1765, m1784 Mendham, ____ Moore & had issue, a son, Hartshorne - desc/o Edward FitzRandolph NE(97)340

Experience - of NJ, b1696 Woodbridge d1758 Woodbridge, m abt 1716/1717 Samuel Moores b1694 Woodbridge d1756 Woodbridge, son of James Moores & Margaret Crage - desc/o Edward FitzRandolph AFA46; NE(97)332

Francis - of NJ, b1738 Woodbridge, twin with her sister Elizabeth, Francis spelled the masculine way both in Quaker records & tombstone in Woodbridge d1796, m1759 Woodbridge, James Crowell d1805 aged 67 years, son of Edward Crowell & Christian Brown Stewart - desc/o Edward FitzRandolph NE(97)333

George - of NJ, b1738, living in Macon, GA in 1759, m1764 Sarah Robinson - desc/o Edward FitzRandolph NE(97)337

Hannah - b1648, m1668 Barnstable Jasper Taylor - desc/o Edward FitzRandolph NE(97)276

Hannah - of NJ, b1688/1689, m1705 Piscataway, Andrew Drake b1684/1685 Piscataway d1743, son of George Drake & Mary Oliver - desc/o Edward FitzRandolph NE(97)277

Hannah - of NJ, b1765 Plainfield d1845, m David Laing b1763 near Princeton d1823 - desc/o Edward FitzRandolph NE(98)44

Hartshorne - of NJ, b1723 Woodbridge, d1806 Mendham, NJ, m1746

FITZRANDOLPH (cont.)

    Piscataway, Ruth Dennis b1727 Piscataway d1770 Randolphville, NJ, dau/o Robert Dennis & Sarah Howland - desc/o Edward FitzRandolph NE(97)340

    Hope - of NJ, b1661, m1680 Piscataway, Ezekiel Bloomfield b1653 Newburyport, MA d1702 Woodbridge, NJ, son of Thomas & Mary Bloomfield - desc/o Edward FitzRandolph NE(97)278

    Hope - of NJ, b1696/1697 Stoney Brook d1741 Princeton, m1718 Princeton Henry Davis - desc/o Edward FitzRandolph NE(97)279

    Grace - of NJ, b1706 Stoney Brook d1786 Princeton, m1728 Princeton, Stephen Johns d1785 - desc/o Edward FitzRandolph NE(97)280

    Grace - of NJ, m Job Runyon of Newark, NJ - desc/o Edward FitzRandolph NE(97)42

    Isaac - of NJ, b1664 Barnstable d1694 Woodbridge, m(1)1690 Woodbridge, Martha Bingla d1691 Woodbridge, dau/o William Bingla, m(2)1692 Woodbridge, Ruth Higgins b1668 Eastam, MA, d1709/1710 Camden, NJ, dau/o Richard Higgins & Mary Yates - desc/o Edward FitzRandolph NE(97)331

    Isaac - of NJ, b1693 Woodbridge d1750 Monmouth Co, NJ, m Hannah Dove b Freehold, Monmouth Co, NJ, dau/o Alexander & Jane Dove of Freehold - desc/o Edward FitzRandolph NE(97)331

    Isaac - of NJ, b1701 Stoney Brook d1750 Princeton, m(1)1728 Princeton, Rebekah Seabrook d1744, m(2)1745/1746 Princeton, Hannah Lee (widow) - desc/o Edward FitzRandolph GBR446; NE(97)279

    Isaac - m Eleanor Hunter - desc/o John Throckmorton GBR236 - desc/o Edward FitzRandolph GBR446

    Isaac - of NJ, b1730/1731 Blazing Star, NJ d abt 1768, m1753 Catherine Hoff dau/o Charles Hoff - desc/o Edward FitzRandolph NE(98)42

    Jacob - of NJ, b1708 Woodbridge d1782 Blazing Star, NJ, m Woodbridge, Mary____ - desc/o Edward FitzRandolph NE(97)335

    Jacob - of NJ, b1737 Blazing Star, NJ d during the Revolution, m Abigail____ - desc/o Edward FitzRandolph NE(97)42

    Jacob - of NJ, b1743 Woodbridge d aft 1798 Isle of Wight Co, VA, m1777 Elizabeth Pretlow, born & died in Isle of Wight Co - desc/o Edward FitzRandolph NE(97)334

    Jacob - of NJ, b1755 Kingwood Township d1839 Blazing Star, m1780 Plainfield, Anna Webster b1760 Plainfield d1822 Plainfield, dau/o John Webster & Anna Taylor of Plainfield - desc/o Edward FitzRandolph NE(98)49

    James - m Deliverance Coward - desc/o Edward FitzRandolph GBR446

    James - of NJ, b1735 d1828 Westland, PA, m(1)1760 Plainfield, Hannah Skinner b1742 Plainfield d1772 Plainfield, dau/o John & Elizabeth Skinner, m(2)1775 Plainfield, Elizabeth Laing b1755 Plainfield d1828 Westland, PA - desc/o Edward FitzRandolph NE(98)44

    James - of NJ, b1767 Plainfield d1840, m1790 Rahway, Catherine Baker b1776 Rahway d1866, dau/o Cornelius Baker & Susanna

FITZRANDOLPH (cont.)

Lee - desc/o Edward FitzRandolph NE(98)127

Janet - of NJ, b1758 Woodbridge d Woodbridge, m1781 Col John
Taylor b1751 Amboy, NJ d1801 Schenectady, NY, son of Jacob
Taylor & Rachel Potter of Amboy - desc/o Edward FitzRandolph
NE(97)337

Jeremiah - of NJ, b1728/1729 Woodbridge d1759 Woodbridge,
m(1)1755 Woodbridge Janet Edgar b1733 Scotland d1756 dau/o
Thomas Edgar & Janet Knox of Scotland, m(2)1757 Rachel Ford
b1733 Piscataway d1799 Woodbridge dau/o William & Mary Ford -
desc/o Edward FitzRandolph NE(97)336

John - of MA, b1653, m1681 Piscataway, Sarah Bonham b1664
Barnstable d1737 Belvedere, dau/o Nicholas Bonham & Hannah
Fuller - desc/o Edward FitzRandolph RAA96; FFF227; NE(97)277

John - of NJ, b1663 Barnstable d1727, m(1)1681 Woodbridge,
Martha____, m(2) 1702 Woodbridge, Sarah Potter d1738 Middlesex
Co, NJ - desc/o Edward FitzRandolph NE(97)331

John - of NJ, b1693, m abt 1713 Ann Elizabeth____ - desc/o Edward
FitzRandolph FFF227; NE(97)277

John - b1716 - desc/o Edward FitzRandolph FFF227

John or Jonathan - b1750, m Charlotte____ - desc/o Edward
FitzRandolph FFF227

John - of NJ, b1763 Plainfield d1837 New York City, m1793 Rahway,
Mary King b1772 Elizabethtown d1826 New York City, dau/o
Nathan King & Sarah Moore - desc/o Edward FitzRandolph
NE(98)126

John - of PA, b1775 d1810, m abt 1805 Catharine Simpson - desc/o
Edward FitzRandolph BLG2686

Jonathan - of NJ, b1692/1693, m1716 Piscataway, Mary Bonham
b1691 Piscataway, dau/o Hezekiah Bonham & Mary Dunn - desc/o
Edward FitzRandolph NE(97)278

Jonathan - of NJ, m1769 Woodbridge ____Thorn dau/o Jacob Thorn -
desc/o Edward FitzRandolph NE(97)336

Joseph - of MA, b1656 d abt 1726 Piscataway, m1687/1688
Woodbridge, Johanna Conger b1670 Woodbridge, dau/o John
Conger & Mary Kelley - desc/o Edward FitzRandolph DBR(2)679;
DBR(3)486; BLG2686; NE(97)277

Joseph - of MA, b1667 Barnstable d1718 Woodbridge, m Isabella
Laing d1754/1755 Woodbridge, dau/o John & Margaret Laing of
Piscataway - desc/o Edward FitzRandolph ECD(2)142; DBR(4)477;
NE(97)333

Joseph - b1691, m1714 Rebekah Drake - desc/o Edward
FitzRandolph BLG2686

Joseph - of NJ, b1704 Woodbridge d1741, boat captain, m Abigail Bird
d Woodbridge, dau/o Jeremiah Bird & Abigail Jones - desc/o
Edward FitzRandolph NE(97)336

Joseph - of NJ, b1703/1704 Woodbridge d1740/1741 Woodbridge,
Joseph & his brother Samuel were captains of sloops, the *Seaflower*
& the *Elizabeth*, plying between Amboy & Boston & Carolina, later
to Jamaica & Curaçao, m1731 Woodbridge, Elizabeth Kinsey b1707
Woodbridge d1738 Woodbridge, dau/o John Kinsey & Grace Hull

FITZRANDOLPH (cont.)

FitzRandolph - desc/o Edward FitzRandolph NE(97)333

Joseph - of NJ, d1782 Blazing Star, m Abigail Ludlam - desc/o Edward FitzRandolph NE(97)335

Joseph - of NJ, b1752 Woodbridge d1814 Woodbridge, m(1) Sarah Edgar b1755 d1790 dau/o Alexander Edgar & Mary E Smith, m(2) Ann Dissosway b1757 d1806 dau/o Cornelius Dissosway & Catherina Corsell - desc/o Edward FitzRandolph NE(97)98

Katherine - of NJ, b1742 d1776 Perth Amboy, m1763 Gilbert Sherer of New York City - desc/o Edward FitzRandolph NE(97)337

Katherine - of NJ, b1753 d Philadelphia, PA, m Dr John Ross b1762 New Garden, Bucks Co, PA - desc/o Edward FitzRandolph NE(97)340

Margaret - of NJ, b1710 Woodbridge d1750 Woodbridge, m1726/1727 Woodbridge, Thomas Hadden b Woodbridge d1778 Woodbridge - desc/o Edward FitzRandolph ECD(2)142; DBR(4)477; NE(97)333

Margaret - of NJ, b1744 Woodbridge d1826 Fayette Co, PA, m1768 Woodbridge, Abraham Vail b1744 d1839, son of Stephen Vail & Esther Smith. This Abram Vail was known as "Black Abram" to distinguish him from Abraham Vail who married Margaret FitzRandolph who was known as "Red Abraham" - desc/o Edward FitzRandolph NE(97)338

Margaret - of NJ, b1746 Plainfield d1812 Greenbrook, m1766 Woodbridge, Abraham Vail b1744 Greenbrook d1824 - desc/o Edward FitzRandolph NE(97)338

Martha - of NJ, b1693 Woodbridge, twin with her brother John, d1766 Woodbridge, m1712 Woodbridge, Reverend John Vail b1685 West Chester, NY d1777 Woodbridge son of Samuel Vail & Elizabeth (Hunt?) - desc/o Edward FitzRandolph RAA96; NE(97)331

Martha - of NJ, b1758 d1837 Monroe, Butler Co, Ohio, m Elias Marsh d1820 New Garden, son of Joseph Marsh - desc/o Edward FitzRandolph NE(97)335

Mary - b1650 d1738 West Barnstable, m1669 Samuel Hinckley b1642 Barnstable d1727 West Barnstable, son of Samuel Hinckley & Sarah____ - desc/o Edward FitzRandolph NE(97)276, 277

Mary - of NJ, b1693 Woodbridge, m1711 Woodbridge, Joseph Ashton of Monmouth Co, NJ - desc/o Edward FitzRandolph NE(97)332

Mary - of NJ, b1710 Woodbridge, m1729 William Thorne b1684 Flushing, Long Island, NY d1735 Woodbridge, son of Joseph Thorne & Mary Browne, m(2)1736/1737 James Jackson b1704 Rocky Hill, Flushing, Long Island, NY d1750 Woodbridge, son of James Jackson & Rebecca Hallett, m(3) Jacob FitzRandolph - desc/o Edward FitzRandolph NE(97)334

Mary - of NJ, b1731, m Israel Dissosway & had issue - desc/o Edward FitzRandolph NE(97)334

Mary - of NJ, m(1)1756 Woodbridge, Samuel Coddington d1757 Woodbridge, m(2)1760 Woodbridge Gabriel Compton d aft 1776 Woodbridge, son of David & Sarah Compton of Bonhamton, NJ - desc/o Edward Woodbridge NE(97)336

Mary - of NJ, b1744 Old Vail Farm d1828 Plainfield, m1765 Rahway, John Hedger (Edgar ?) b Chesterfield, NJ - desc/o Edward

FITZRANDOLPH (cont.)

FitzRandolph NE(97)338

Mary - of NJ, b1746 Woodbridge d1808, m(1)1763 Woodbridge, Dr
Jonas Baldwin d1764 Woodbridge, m(2)1765 Woodbridge,
Cornelius Dissosway b1731 d1785 Staten Island - desc/o Edward
FitzRandolph NE(97)339

Mary - of NJ, b1751 d Wilmington, Del, m1783 Capt Elisha Brown b
Philadelphia, PA, drowned at sea - desc/o Edward FitzRandolph
NE(97)337

Mary - of NJ, b1759 d1787 Woodbridge, m Woodbridge, Gen Clarkson
Edgar, graduate from Princeton College in 1770 age 19 b1751
Woodbridge d1816 Woodbridge, son of William Edgar & Experience
Clarkson - desc/o Edward FitzRandolph NE(97)337

Mary - of NJ, b1773 Blazing Star d1825 Woodbridge, m Robert
Williams - desc/o Edward FitzRandolph NE(97)335

Mary - of NJ, b1775 Woodbridge d1850 Digaby, NS, m Henry Edward
Oakes b1772 Digby d1860 Digby - desc/o Edward FitzRandolph
NE(98)48

Mercy - of NJ, b1744 Old Vail Farm d1766 Plainfield, m Robert
FitzRandolph - desc/o Edward FitzRandolph NE(97)338

Mercy - of NJ, b1771 Elisabeth Town, m1793 James Journay b1765
Staten Island, NY d1857 Weymouth, son of John & Martha Journay
- desc/o Edward FitzRandolph NE(98)48

Nancy - of NJ, b1775 Woodbridge d1865 Darien, CT, m(1)1793 Dr
Thomas Hearn of Dublin, Ireland, m(2), M____ Anthony - desc/o
Edward FitzRandolph NE(98)48

Nathaniel - of NJ, bp 1642 Barnstable, MA d1713 Woodbridge, NJ,
associate justice of Middlesex Co, NJ & represented Woodbridge in
the Provisional Assembly, m1662 Mary Holley b Sandwich d1703
Woodbridge, dau/o Joseph Holley & Rose____, m(2) 1706
Haddonfield, NJ, Jane Curtis d1731 Buckingham, PA dau/o
Thomas & Jane Curtis & the wid/o Samuel Osborne & John
Hampton - desc/o Edward FitzRandolph ECD(2)141; DBR(4)477;
AFA46; RAA1642; NE(97)276/331

Nathaniel - of NJ, d1703 Woodbridge, m1692 Woodbridge, Grace Hull
b1672 Piscataway d1752 Woodbridge, dau/o Benjamin Hull &
Rachel York - desc/o Edward FitzRandolph AFA46; NE(97)332

Nathaniel - of NJ, b1700 Woodbridge, m Mary____ & left issue - desc/o
Edward FitzRandolph NE(97)332

Nathaniel - of NJ, b1703 Stoney Brook d1743 Princeton, donated some
of the land on which Princeton University now stands, m1729
Princeton, Rebekah Mershon b1711/1712 Sassafras, Kent Co, MD,
dau/o Henry Mershon & Ann____ - desc/o Edward FitzRandolph
RAA96; NE(97)279

Nathaniel - of NJ, b1714 Woodbridge d1773 Woodbridge, m(1)1735
Woodbridge, Mary Brooks d1743 Woodbridge, m(2)1745
Woodbridge, Mary Shotwell b1722 Woodbridge dau/o Joseph
Shotwell & Mary Manning - desc/o Edward FitzRandolph -
NE(97)339

Nathaniel - of NJ, b1730 Woodbridge d1744 Woodbridge, owned the
ferry from Woodbridge to Staten Island, NY, m1748 Woodbridge,

FITZRANDOLPH (cont.)

Ursula Stewart b1730 d1798 Woodbridge dau/o Dr David Stewart & Christian Brown - desc/o Edward FitzRandolph NE(97)42

Nathaniel - of NJ, b1747 Woodbridge d1780 Woodbridge, captain of the Middlesex Militia, then elected naval officer of the Eastern District of NJ on 12 Dec 1778; died of wounds received in the Battle of Springfield, NJ, m1772 Woodbridge, Experience Inslee b1748 Woodbridge d1813 Woodbridge, dau/o Jonathan Inslee & Grace Moores - desc/o Edward FitzRandolph NE(98)48

Paul - of PA, b abt 1720, m abt 1745 Anna Smith - desc/o Edward FitzRandolph BLG2686

Phineas - of NJ, b1749 Woodbridge d aft 1823, m Rebecca Dunn b1746 d1809 - desc/o Edward FitzRandolph NE(98)49

Prudence - of NJ, b1696 Woodbridge d1766 Woodbridge, m1716 Shobal Smith b1692 Woodbridge d1767/1768 Woodbridge, son of Samuel Smith & Elizabeth Pierce - desc/o Edward FitzRandolph NE(97)333

Rachel - of NJ, b1698 Woodbridge, m(1)1717 Thomas Vail b Woodbridge d1717/1718 Woodbridge, son of Samuel Vail & Elizabeth (Hunt ?), m(2) William Farson of Delaware - desc/o Edward FitzRandolph NE(97)332

Rebecca - of NJ, b1737 Old Vale Farm d1813 Plainfield, m1758 Woodbridge, Robert Clarkson b & d Woodbridge, son of John Clarkson & Bethia FitzRandolph - desc/o - Edward FitzRandolph NE(97)338

Rebecca - of NJ, b1761 Plainfield d1841 Princeton, NJ, m1780 John Stockton b1742 Princeton d1841 Princeton, son/o Joseph Stockton & Elizabeth Doughty of Princeton - desc/o Edward FitzRandolph NE(98)44

Reuben - of NJ, b1733 d1784 Blazing Star, founder of the Blazing Star ferry from Rahway Neck, NJ to Staten Island, m1734 Woodbridge, Elizabeth Moores d1817 New Garden, Columbiana Co, Ohio, dau/o John Moores - desc/o Edward FitzRandolph NE(97)335

Richard - of NJ, b1705 Woodbridge d1754 Perth Amboy, NJ, m1735 Shrewsbury, NJ, Elizabeth Corlies b1716 Shrewsbury d Perth Amboy, dau/o John Corlies & Naomi Edwards - desc/o Edward FitzRandolph NE(97)337

Richard - of NJ, b1760 Woodbridge, m Rebecca_____ & had issue - desc/o Edward FitzRandolph NE(98)49

Richard - of NJ, b1769 Perth Amboy d1854 Redstone, m(1) Lydia Mackay (Mackey) b1776 d1831 Redstone, m(2)1833 Redstone, Jane (Morrison) Dixon b1774 d1834 Redstone - desc/o Edward FitzRandolph NE(98)53

Robert - of NJ, b1712 Woodbridge d1804 Greenbrook, m1737 Woodbridge, Catherine Taylor, dau/o John Taylor & Sarah Hartshorne - desc/o Edward FitzRandolph NE(97)338

Robert - of NJ, b1737 Woodbridge d1830, m(1)1761 Mercy FitzRandolph b1742 d1764 Plainfield, m(2)1768 Woodbridge, Phebe Pearsall b1749/1750 d1832, m(2)1768 _____ - desc/o Edward FitzRandolph NE(98)47

Robert - of NJ, b1741 Woodbridge d1830 Meadville, PA, joined Col Wm

FITZRANDOLPH (cont.)

Crook's regiment in the Rev War & fought in the Battle of Germantown 1777, m abt 1767 Sarah Taylor d1849 near Meadville - desc/o Edward FitzRandolph NE(98)46

Rosier - of NY, b1689 called Desire when appointed administratrix to the estate of her husband, m William Wright d1744 - desc/o Edward FitzRandolph NE(97)331

Ruth - of NJ, b1695 Piscataway d1780, m(1)1711 Princeton, Edward Harrison d1715 Griggstown, NJ - desc/o Edward FitzRandolph NE(97)279, m(2)1720 Princeton, John Snowden of Philadelphia, PA - desc/o Edward FitzRandolph NE(97)279

Samuel - of NJ, b Barnstable, MA d1754 Woodbridge, m1693 Woodbridge Mary Jones b Elizabeth Town, NJ d1760 Woodbridge dau/o Jeffrey Jones of Elizabeth, NJ - desc/o Edward FitzRandolph NE(97)333

Samuel - of NJ, b1694 Woodbridge d Woodbridge, m1729 Woodbridge, Johannah Kinsey b1705 Woodbridge d1752 Woodbridge, dau/o John Kinsey & Grace Hull FitzRandolph - desc/o Edward FitzRandolph NE(97)334

Samuel - of NJ, m1750 Mary Gach - desc/o Edward FitzRandolph NE(97)336

Samuel - of NJ, b1762 Blazing Star d1794, m abt 1790 Phebe Brundage b1762 Elizabeth, NJ d1796 Elizabeth, NJ - desc/o Edward FitzRandolph NE(98)50

Sarah - b1682, m1707 Piscataway, Jonathan Smalley b1683 son of John Smalley & Lydia Martin - desc/o Edward FitzRandloph NE(97)277

Sarah - of NJ, b1739 d Perth Amboy, m Stephen Taylor - desc/o Edward FitzRandolph NE(97)337

Sarah - of NJ, b1739, m1764 Woodbridge, Mootrey Kinsey, son of Jonathan Kinsey & Annabel Mootrey - desc/o Edward FitzRandolph NE(97)338

Sarah - of NJ, b1763 d bef 1806 Mendham, m1782 Mendham, John Marsh b1756 d1801 son of Samuel Marsh & Mary Shotwell - desc/o Edward FitzRandloph NE(97)340

Stephen - of NJ, b1772 Perth Amboy d1849 Redstone, m1797 Redstone, Pamela Nutt b1780 d1857 - desc/o Edward FitzRandolph NE(98)53

Susannah - of NJ, b1699 Woodbridge, twin with her brother Isaac who died unmarried 1720, m1724 Ephraim Heady - desc/o Edward FitzRandolph NE(97)333

Taylor - of NJ, b1756 Woodbridge d Wellsville, Ohio, m1782/1783 Plainfield, Mary Baum d Wellsville - desc/o Edward FitzRandolph NE(98)47

Temperance - b1687, m abt 1713 John Martin b1683 Piscataway, son of Thomas Martin & Rebecca Higgins - desc/o Edward FitzRandolph NE(97)277

Thomas - of NJ, b1659 d1745 Piscataway, m1686 Piscataway, Elizabeth Manning b1667 Barnstable d1732 Piscataway, dau/o Jeffrey Manning & Hepzibah Andrews of Piscataway - desc/o Edward FitzRandolph JSW1528; NE(97)278

FITZRANDOLPH (cont.)

Thomas - of NJ, b1687 d1732 Piscataway, m1710 Piscataway, Margaret Manning - desc/o Edward FitzRandolph NE(97)278

Thomas - of NJ, b1740 Perth Amboy d1801 Redstone, PA, m1763 Plainfield, Abigail Vail b1742 Greenbrook, NJ d bef 1809 Redstone, dau/o Stephen Vail & Esther Smith of Greenbrook - desc/o Edward FitzRandolph NE(98)43

Thomas - of NJ, b abt 1765 Woodbridge d1848, m & had issue - desc/o Edward FitzRandolph NE(98)49

Ursula - of NJ, b1771 d1841 Woodbridge, m1792 Furman Brown b1765 Woodbridge d1826 son of John & Letitia Brown - desc/o Edward FitzRandolph NE(98)43

Zipporah - of NJ, m1780 Rahway, Samuel Marsh of Elizabeth, NJ d1784 Westfield, NJ - desc/o Edward FitzRandolph NE(97)42

FLAGG Sarah - b1726, m Benjamin Jewett - desc/o Abraham Errington LDS31

FLANDERS Jacob - of VT, b1759 d1840, m(1) Nancy Kenerson - desc/o Anthony Colby JSW1687

Zebulon - of NH & VT, b1737 d abt 1799, m Mariam____ - desc/o Anthony Colby JSW1687

FLEETE Ann - of VA, m____ Brent - desc/o Dorothea or Deborah Scott WAC108

Ann - of VA, m1722 Leonard Howson of Wicomico, Northumberland Co d1737, issue one daughter, Elizabeth - desc/o Lieut Col Henry Fleete APP288; GVFHB(3)5; VG235

Edward Fleete - of MD - desc/o Dorothea or Deborah Scott MCB332; WAC108

Elizabeth - of VA, m Abraham Currell of Lancaster Co d1757 (she died before her husband) - desc/o Lieut Col Henry Fleete APP288; GVFHB(3)5

Lieut Col Henry - of MD & VA abt 1621, b abt 1595/1600 d1660/1661, in 1623 while on an expedition to the Indians along the Potomac River, was captured by them & kept a prisoner for five years, associated with the Calverts in establishing the Province of MD & a member of the first Assembly 1637. Later moved to Lancaster Co Virginia & became a justice and burgess, son of William Fleete of Chatham, Co Kent, England & Deborah Scott, m Sarah____ d1679 - desc/o Dorothea or Deborah Scott CHB469; MCB332; MCD220 - the immigrant WAC107, 108; GBR123; APP284/289; GVFHB(3)1/7; VG234/235

Henry - of VA, d1728/1729 was a justice 1695, sheriff 1718 & captain of militia, m bef 18 Jul 1683 Elizabeth Wildey dau/o William & Jane Wildey - desc/o Dorothea or Deborah Scott CHB469; MCB333; MCD220 - desc/o Lieut Col Henry Fleete WAC108; APP286; GVFHB(3)3, 4, 5

John - of VA, d abt 1667, m Anne____ - desc/o Lieut Col Henry Fleete VG235

John - of VA, b1724 d1793, justice of Lancaster Co, major of militia, m1746 Mary Edwards - desc/o Lieut Col Henry Fleete APP287; VG235

John - of MD - desc/o Dorothea or Deborah Scott MCB332; WAC108

FLEETE (cont.)

Judith - of VA, d1766, m1723 William Hobson of Northumberland Co
b1700 d1739 son of Thomas Hobson & Clark____ - desc/o Lieut Col
Henry Fleete WAC108; APP288; GVFHB(3)5; VG235

Margaret - of VA, m1723 Presley Cox of Cople Parish, Westmoreland
Co d1766 son of Charnock Cox - desc/o Lieut Col Henry Fleete
WAC108; APP289; GVFHB(3)5

Mary Ann - of VA, b1722, m(1) Robert Dudley, m(2)____ Tebbs - desc/o
Lieut Col Henry Fleete APP287; GVFHB(3)7

Reginald - of MD - desc/o Dorothea or Deborah Scott MCB332;
WAC108

Sarah - of VA, m Edwin Conway - desc/o Dorothea or Deborah Scott
CRL(1)266

Sarah - of VA, d bef 10 Mar 1717/1718, m William Brent b abt 1685
d1740 - desc/o Lieut Col Henry Fleete APP287, 288

Capt William - of VA, d1734/1735 sheriff of Lancaster Co 1720,
m1718 Ann Jones dau/o William Jones of Middlesex Co - desc/o
Dorothea or Deborah Scott CHB470; MCB333; MCD220 - desc/o
Lieut Col Henry Fleete APP287; GVFHB(3)7

William - of VA, b1726 d1773, justice of King & Queen Co, m(1)1744
Ann Temple d1754, m(2)1755 Susannah Walker b1736 dau/o
John & Elizabeth (Baylor) Walker - desc/o Dorothea or Deborah
Scott CHB470; MCB333 - desc/o Lieut Col Henry Fleete APP287;
GVFHB(3)7

Capt William - of VA, b1757 d1833, m Sarah Tomlin - desc/o Dorothea
or Deborah Scott CHB470; MCB333, 334

FLEMING Col Charles - of VA, d1720, m Susanna Tarleton - desc/o John
Fleming JSW1651 - desc/o Col William Randolph DBR(2)231 -
desc/o John Fleming DBR(2)484

Elizabeth - of VA, b1680 d1758, m Col Samuel Jordan - desc/o John
Fleming DBR(2)484

John - of VA abt 1616 d1686, m____ - the immigrant JSW1651;
DBR(2)484; sufficient proof of alleged royal ancestry is lacking

Judith - of VA - desc/o John Fleming DBR(2)484

Margaret - of MA, dau/o Henry & Alice (Dawkin) Fleming, m1627
Griffith Bowen - the immigrant AAP147; GBR388; NGS(67)163/166

Susanna Tarleton - of VA, m abt 1709 John Bates III - desc/o John
Fleming JSW1651

Tarleton - of VA - desc/o John Fleming DBR(2)484

Thomas Mann Randolph - of VA, b1767, m Anne Spotswood Payne -
desc/o Capt Henry Isham ECD(2)167; DBR(3)359 - desc/o Col
William Randolph DBR(2)352; DBR(4)365

Ursula - of VA, m1710 Tarleton Woodson - desc/o Col William
Randolph DBR(2)231

FLINT Rufus Frederick - b1768 - desc/o George Morton RAA116

FLOYD Nicoll - of NY, - desc/o Margaret Nicolls J&K260

Gen William of NY, a signer of the Declaration of Independence -
desc/o Margaret Nicolls J&K260

FOLIOT (FOLLIOT) Rev Edward - of VA, b1610 d1690 son of Sir John
Foliot & Elizabeth Aylmer - the immigrant MCS50; RAA1, 97;
WAC110, 111; GBR205

FOLIOT (FOLLIOT) (cont.)

Elizabeth - of VA, m(1) Josias Moody, m(2) Capt Charles Hansford - desc/o Rev Edward Foliot WAC110, 111

Mary - of VA, m(1) Dr Henry Power, m(2) John Seal - desc/o Rev Edward Foliot WAC110, 111

FOOTE Ebenezer - bp 1740, m Rebecca Barker - desc/o Edward Griswold LDS45

FORBES Christian of NJ, d1733, m1732 William Penn III - desc/o Robert Barclay ECD247; GBR49

James Grant - of MA & NY, b1769 d1825, m1804 Frances E Blackwell - desc/o Rev John Forbes BLG2688

John - of PA, b abt 1710 d1759 British army officer, son of John Forbes of Pittencrieff & Elizabeth (Graham) Forbes, m____ - the immigrant GBR88

Rev John - of FL - b abt 1740 d1783, Anglican clergyman & magistrate in East Florida son of Archibald Forbes & Agnes Lumsden, m1769 Dorothy Murray dau/o James Murray of North Carolina & MA and Mrs Barbara Bennet Murray of North Carolina - the immigrant BLG2688; GBR370

Ralph Bennet - of MA, b1773 d1824, m Margaret Perkins - desc/o Rev John Forbes BLG2689

FORDE Standish of MD 1730, d1766, m(1) Hannah____, m(2) Parthenia____ - the immigrant CHB234; MCB186; BCD234; AFA128, 130; sufficient proof of alleged royal ancestry is lacking

Standish Jr of PA, b1759 d1806, m1795 Sarah Britton - desc/o Standish Forde CHB234, 235; BCD234; AFA128, 130

FOSTER Elizabeth - of CT, b1776 d1807, m1796 Titus Chapman - desc/o Grace Chetwood ECD(3)91

Reginald - of MA 1638 - the immigrant EDV137; sufficient proof of alleged royal ancestry is lacking

Thomas - of NY, b1750/1756 d1832, m(2)1780 Hannah Bliss - desc/o Mary Wentworth ECD(2)297

FOULKE Amos of PA, b1740 d1792, m1779 Hannah Jones - desc/o Edward Foulke CHB118; ECD(3)156; MCD223; BCD118

Caleb - m Jane Jones dau/o Owen Jones of Wynnewood, Lower Merion - desc/o Edward Foulke GPFHB347

Caleb Jr - m(1)1795 Margaret Cullen dau/o Thomas Cullen & Sibina____, m(2)1814 Sarah Hodgkiss (widow) - desc/o Edward Foulke GPFHB347

Edward - b1651 d1741, m1680 Eleanor Cadwalader - the immigrant CHB118; MCD223; ECD(3)153; BCD118; AMB386; RAA1; GPFHB347; royal ancestry not proven

Edward - of PA, son of Foulke ap Thomas & Lowri ferch Edward ap Dafydd, m Ellen Hughes (Hugh or Pugh) of PA - the immigrant GBR312

Everard - of PA, b1755 d1827, m1778 Ann Dehaven - desc/o Edward Foulke AMB386

Hugh - of PA, b1685 d1760, m1731 Ann Williams - desc/o Edward Foulke ECD(3)154; AMB386

Israel - of PA, b1760 d1824, m1782 Elizabeth Roberts - desc/o Edward Foulke ECD(3)154

FOULKE (cont.)

Jane - of PA, m Ellis Hughes - desc/o Edward Foulke MCD223

Samuel - of PA, b1718/1719 d1797, m1743 Ann Greasley - desc/o Edward Foulke ECD(3)154

Thomas - of PA, b1724 d1786, m Jane Roberts - desc/o Edward Foulke AMB386

Thomas - of PA, b1679 d1762, m1706 Gwen Evans - desc/o Edward Foulke CHB118; ECD(3)156; MCD223; BCD118; GPFHB347

William - of PA, b1708 d1798, m1734 Hannah Jones - desc/o Edward Foulke CHB118; ECD(3)156; MCD223; BCD118; GPFHB347

FOWKE Anne - of VA, m Major William Dent, lawyer, Charles Co, MD - desc/o Col Gerard Fowke VA156; CFA(5)314

Anne - of VA, b1689/1690 d1739, m Robert Alexander Jr d1735, justice of Stafford Co & major of militia - desc/o Col Gerard Fowke CRL(3)122; APP613; VG156; CFA(5)314 - desc/o Adam Thorowgood CRL(3)122

Catherine - of VA, b1694, m Elsworth Bayne of Charles Co, MD - desc/o Col Gerard Fowke CRL(1)274, (3)122; APP613; VG156; CFA(5)314 - desc/o Adam Thorowgood CRL(3)122

Chandler - of VA, b1732 d1810, m1759 Mary Harrison d1831 dau/o Thomas & Ann Harrison - desc/o Col Gerard Fowke VG157

Capt Chandler - of VA, d1744/1745, m abt 1716 Mary Fossaker b abt 1700 d1783 eldest dau/o Col Richard Fossaker of Stafford Co, VA - desc/o Col Gerard Fowke ECD(3)161; APP613; VG156, 157; CFA(5)314

Elizabeth - of VA, b abt 1666, m1684/1685 Col William Dent of MD, b1660 d1704, lawyer, held many civil & government offices, son of Judge Thomas & Rebecca (Wilkinson) Dent - desc/o Col Gerard Fowke DBR(1)654; DBR(2)199, 308, 752; CRL(3)121; GBR363; APP615

Elizabeth - of VA, b1727, m Zachariah Brazier, son of Robert Brazier, of Isle of Thanel, Kent, England - desc/o Col Gerard Fowke VG157

Elizabeth - of VA, m Col William Phillips,b1744 d1797, Colonel in the Revolutionary War & High Sheriff of Stafford Co, son of James Phillips of Wales, who came to Stafford Co, VA 1714 & Elizabeth Griffin - desc/o Col Gerard Fowke VG158

Frances - of VA, b1691/1692 d1744, m1710 Dr Gustavus Brown b1689 d1762 of Rich Hill, Charles Co, MD - desc/o Col Gerard Fowke CRL(1)274, (3)122; APP613; VG156; CFA(5)315 - desc/o Adam Thorowgood CRL(3)122

Frances - of VA, m Bradford Grayson, went West & left issue - desc/o Col Gerard Fowke VG158

George - of VA, b1764, m Sarah Bartlett, of Western Virginia; moved 1780 to Kentucky & murdered by robbers - desc/o Col George Fowke VG158

Col Gerard - of VA or MD 1650, d1669 son of Roger & Mary (Bayley) Fowke, sometime gentleman in the household of King Charles I & a colonel in the royalist army, burgess for Westmoreland Co to Virginia House of Burgesses & burgess for Charles Co to MD House of Burgesses, m aft 1659 Ann Thoroughgood dau/o Captain Adam Thoroughgood & wid/o Col Job Chandler of Port Tobacco, MD - the

FOWKE (cont.)

immigrant ECD(3)160; DBR(1)654; DBR(2)199, 308, 752; RAA97; EDV117; CRL(1)273, (3)121, 122; GBR363 some aspect of royal descent merits further study; APP612/616; VG154, 155, 156; CFA(5)314

Col Gerard Jr - of MD, b1662 d1734, planter & represented Charles Co in the Lower House of the MD Assembly, vestryman & sheriff, m(1)____ Lomax, m(2)1686 Sarah Burdett of Charles Co, MD d bef 25 Feb 1745/1746 - desc/o Col Gerard Fowke ECD(3)160; CRL(1)274, (3)122; APP612; VG157; CFA(5)314 - desc/o Adam Thorowgood CRL(3)122

Gerard - of VA, b1718 (?) d1781, m1745 Elizabeth Dinwiddie dau/o John Dinwiddie & Sempha Rosa Enfield - desc/o Col Gerard Fowke VG157

Capt Gerard - of VA, b1719 d1769, m1745____ Harrison - desc/o Col Gerard Fowke VG157

Judith - of VA, m1792 Enoch Berry - desc/o Col Gerard Fowke VG157

Lucy - of VA, m1794 Alexander Hawes, son of William Hawes - desc/o Col Gerard Fowke VG158

Mary - of VA, d possibly summer of 1701, m (her cousin) Col George Mason Jr, major commanding a company of militia, captain of rangers, Co Lieutenant of Stafford & member of the house of Burgesses - desc/o Col Gerard Fowke CRL(3)122; APP613; VG156; CFA(5)314 - desc/o Adam Thorowgood CRL(3)122

Richard - of VA, b1741 d1777 in Revolutionary Army, m1760 Ann B Bunbury b1741 dau/o Thomas & Sarah Bunbury - desc/o Col Gerard Fowke ECD(3)161; VG157

Roger - of VA, d bef 31 Jan 1727/1728, m Anne Stone d1761, dau/o Thomas Stone - desc/o Col Gerard Fowke CRL(3)122; APP613; VG156, 157; CFA(5)314 - desc/o Adam Thorowgood CRL(3)122

Roger - of VA, b1773 d1818, m1799 Susan Hawes - desc/o Col Gerard Fowke ECD(3)161; VG158

Sarah - of VA, m ____ Hewlett of Charles Co, MD - desc/o Col Gerard Fowke VG158

Susanna - of VA, b1739, m1764 Henry Peyton - desc/o Col Gerard Fowke VG157

Susanna - of VA, b1761, m Benjamin Berry - desc/o Col Gerard Fowke VG158

William - of VA, d1742, m Mary Fowke dau/o Roger Fowke of Charles Co, MD - desc/o Col Gerard Fowke VG157

FOWLER Catherine - b1723, m Samuel Noble - desc/o John Drake LDS42; RAA87

John - b1714/1715 - desc/o Samuel Appleton RAA63

Sarah - b1745 - desc/o Samuel Appleton RAA63

FOX Amy - b1740, m John Kendrick - desc/o Col/Gov John West LDS100

Anne West - of VA, b1684 d1733, m1703 Capt Thomas Claiborne b1680 d1732 captain of horse, only child of Lieut Colonel Thomas Claiborne, who was slain by Indians in battle 1683 - desc/o Col/Gov John West CHB242; DBR(1)135, 412; DBR(2)206, 371,

FOX (cont.)

561; DBR(3)363; DBR(4)1, 377, 777, 811; DBR(5)558, 840; APP661

Henry - b abt 1680 - desc/o Col/Gov John West LDS100

John - of VA, lieutenant in militia, merchant & land owner, m abt 1697 Frances Lightfoot - desc/o Col/Gov John West DBR(1)641; DBR(2)807; DBR(3)116; DBR(4)157, 287, 568; DBR(5)858, 896; APP661

Rev John - of VA, b1700 d aft 1763, m Isabella Booth - desc/o Col/Gov John West DBR(1)641; DBR(2)807; DBR(3)116; DBR(4)157; DBR(5)859, 896

Capt John - of VA, d1785, m Ann Macon - desc/o Col/Gov John West DBR(1)641; DBR(2)807; DBR(3)116; DBR(4)158; DBR(5)859, 889, 897 - desc/o William Ironmonger DBR(1)643

Joseph - of VA, m Susanna Smith - desc/o Col/Gov John West DBR(4)288, 568

Lucy - of VA, b1747 d1831, m1766 Luke Matthews - desc/o Col/Gov John West DBR(3)178

Mary - of PA, dau/o Francis Fox & Tabitha Croker, m Andrew Ellicott - the immigrant GBR279 some aspect of royal descent merits further study

Nathaniel - of VA, b1763 d1821, m(1) Mary Carver King, m(2) Susan (Brokins) Prosser - desc/o Col/Gov John West DBR(2)31

Col Richard - of VA, b1700/1701 d1771, m1742 Hannah or Joanna Williamson - desc/o Col/Gov John West LDS100; DBR(3)178

Susanna - of VA, b1736, m1765 George Johnson - desc/o Col/Gov John West DBR(4)288, 568

Thomas - of VA, m1707/1709 Mary Tunstall dau/o Edmund & Katherine Tunstall of King & Queen Co, VA - desc/o Col/Gov John West DBR(2)31, 369; APP661

William - of VA & NC, m Sarah Lewis - desc/o William Ironmonger DBR(5)889, 897

William - of VA, d1832, m Sarah____ - desc/o Col/Gov John West DBR(1)641 - desc/o William Ironmonger DBR(1)643

FOXCROFT Francis - of MA, m1682 - the immigrant EDV98; sufficient proof of alleged royal ancestry is lacking

Judge Francis - of MA - desc/o Francis Foxcroft EDV98

Rev Thomas - of MA - desc/o Francis Foxcroft EDV98

FRANKLAND Sir Charles Henry, 4th Baronet, British officer, son of Henry & Mary (Cross) Frankland, m Lady Agnes Surriage b1726 d1783 social leader - the immigrant GBR43

FRANKLIN Benjamin - the immigrant EDV18; sufficient proof of alleged royal ancestry is lacking

John - the immigrant EDV18; sufficient proof of alleged royal ancestry is lacking

FREEMAN Alice - of CT, b abt 1595 d1664/1665 dau/o Henry Freeman & Margaret Edwards, m(1) abt 1615 John Thompson b abt 1580/1590 of Little Preston, Northamptonshire d1626/1627 London, m(2) aft 1644 Robert Parke - the immigrant MCS109; DBR(1)339, 594; DBR(2)442; 537; DBR(3)238, 239, 424, 428, 429, 679, 682, 763; DBR(4)480, 799; DBR(5)186, 187, 540, 796; RAA131; GBR436; TAG(13)1/8, (14)145/146, (29)215/218;

FREEMAN (cont.)

NE(141)105; TG(4)176/179, 184, 185; FLW32; TG(4)176/179, 184, 185

Alice - b abt 1673, m Nathaniel Merrick - desc/o Ensign Constant Southworth LDS56; RAA131

Alice - of MA, b1719/1720 d1790, m1740 George Brown - desc/o Ensign Constant Southworth DBR(2)399, 400; DBR(3)462

Apphia - m Isaac Pepper - desc/o Constant Southworth DBR(3)245

Bennett - of MA, b1671 d1716, m1689 John Paine - desc/o Mary Wentworth ECD(2)290

Constant - of MA, b1669 d1745, m1694 Jane Treat - desc/o Ensign Constant Southworth MCB293

George - of VA & KY, b1763 d1831, m Keziah Yancy - desc/o Capt William Claiborne AFA254

John - of NY, b1754 d1815, m abt 1780 Sybil Lewis - desc/o Ensign Constant Southworth MCB293

Mercy - of MA, b1674 d1747, m abt 1693 Paul Sears - desc/o Mary Wentworth ECD(2)295

Rebecca - of MA, b1694, m(2)1723 John Wing - desc/o Mary Wentworth ECD(2)297

Robert - of MA, b1696 d1755 m1722 Mary Paine - desc/o Ensign Constant Southworth MCB293

Robert - of MA, b1727 d1798, m Anna____ - desc/o Ensign Constant Southworth MCB293

Samuel - of MA, b1662 d1742, m1684 Elizabeth Sparrow - desc/o Ensign Constant Southworth DBR(2)399; DBR(3)461, 462; TAG(11)171/179

Samuel - of MA, b1688 d1751, m1712 Mary Paine - desc/o Ensign Constant Southworth DBR(2)399; DBR(3)462

Thomas - of MA, b1653 d1715/1716, m1673 Rebecca Sparrow - desc/o Mary Wentworth ECD(2)295, 297

FRINK Henry - b1749, m Desire Palmer - desc/o John Gallup JSW1884

Nathan Palmer - b1772, m Betsy____ - desc/o John Gallup JSW1884

Samuel - m Hannah Miner - desc/o John Gallup JSW1884

Samuel - b1693, m Margaret Wheeler - desc/o John Gallup JSW1884

Samuel - b1715, m Mary Stanton - desc/o John Gallup JSW1884

FROST Mary - of ME, b1676, m1694 Capt John Hill - desc/o Joseph Bolles ECD(2)57; RAA71

FULFORD Mary - of ME, dau/o Thomas Fulford & Ursula Bamfield, m(1) Thomas Achims, m(2) Sir Ferdinando Gorges b abt 1565 d1647, founder of ME - the immigrant GBR163

Mary - of NY, dau/o Francis Fulford & Ellen Edgecombe, m Joseph Lovecraft - the immigrant GBR137

FULLER Aaron - b1738 - desc/o John Prescott RAA125

Robert - b abt 1760 - desc/o John Prescott RAA125

– G –

GABRIEL Jean Antonin, Vicomte de Sibour, - of Washington D C, French consular office, son of Jean Baptiste Joseph, Count de Sibour &

GABRIEL (cont.)
  Pauline de Sallmard, m Mary Louisa Johnson - the immigrant
    GBR300
GAGE Daniel - of MA, b1676 d1748, m(1)1698 Martha Burbank - desc/o
    Ursula Scott JSW1871
  Naomi - of MA, m David Hall - desc/o Ursula Scott JSW1871
GALLUP Elizabeth - m Henry Stevens - desc/o John Gallup JSW1884
  John - b1615 d1675, m Hannah Lake - the immigrant JSW1884;
    sufficient proof of alleged royal ancestry is lacking
  Mary - of CT, b1695, m1714/1715, m Deacon John Noyes - desc/o
    Alice Freeman DBR(3)424; DBR(4)800; RAA132
GANTT Anne - of MD, b1708 d1761, m1725 Col John Broome IV - desc/o
    Robert Brooke ECD(3)46; DBR(2)751; CFA187
  Edward - of MD, m Anne Baker - desc/o Thomas Gantt CFA186, 187
  Edward - of MD, b1738 - desc/o Thomas Gantt CFA187
  Elizabeth Heighe - of MD, b1757 d1789, m John Broome - desc/o
    Thomas Gantt CFA187
  Rachel - of MD, b1733/1734, m Dr Richard Brooke - desc/o Thomas
    Gantt CFA187
  Thomas - of MD 1650, bp 1615, m Mary Graham - the immigrant
    CFA186; sufficient proof of alleged royal ancestry is lacking
  Thomas - of MD, m1707 Priscilla Brooke - desc/o Thomas Gantt
    CFA187
  Dr Thomas - of MD, b1710, m1725/1726 Rachel Smith - desc/o
    Thomas Gantt CFA187
  Thomas - of MD, b1736, m(1) Susanna Mackall - desc/o Thomas Gantt
    CFA187
GARDINER Amy - b1725, m Stephen Harding - desc/o Frances Dungan
    LDS11
  Benjamin - of RI, b1705, m1726/1727 Mary Howland - desc/o George
    Gardiner BLG2699
  Benjamin - of NY, b1731 d1809, m Elizabeth Olin - desc/o George
    Gardiner BLG2699
  Benoni - of RI, b1636, m 1667 Mary Eldred - desc/o George Gardiner
    BLG2699; TAG(21)193, 196
  Caleb - of NY, b1768 d1842, m Eunice Northrop - desc/o George
    Gardiner BLG2699
  Elizabeth - of RI, m Capt Peter Wanton - desc/o Jeremiah Clarke
    GRFRP(1)210
  Frances - of RI, m William Benson & was the mother of George Benson
    - desc/o Jeremiah Clarke GRFRP(1)209
  George - of RI, bp 1599 d1677, m(1)1630 Sarah Slaughter, m(2)
    Herodias Hicks, m(3) Lydia Ballou - the immigrant BLG2698;
    TAG(14)243 (Sufficient proof of the alleged royal ancestry is
    lacking); TAG(21)191, 192
  James - b1750 - desc/o Anne Marbury RAA114
  Jerusha - of CT, m1742 John Christophers - desc/o Grace Kaye
    CHB207; MCD284; BCD207; DBR(1)700; DBR(2)769; DBR(3)480;
    DBR(5)594, 938 - desc/o Muriel Gurdon DBR(3)482
  John - of MA, b1737 d1793, m1763 Margaret Harris - desc/o George
    Gardiner BLG2699

GARDINER (cont.)

Rev John - of MA, b1765 d1830, m1794 Mary Howard - desc/o George Gardiner BLG2699

John - of RI - desc/o Joseph Gardiner EDV27

Joseph - of RI, b1669 d1726 - the immigrant EDV27; sufficient proof of alleged royal ancestry is lacking

Lydia - of RI, m William Rodman - desc/o Jeremiah Clark GRFRP(1)209

Nathaniel - of RI, b1674 d1734, m Mary____ - desc/o George Gardiner BLG2699

Nicholas - b1710 - desc/o Anne Marbury RAA114

Dr Sylvester - of MA, b1708 d1786, m(1)1732 Anne Gibbins - desc/o George Gardiner BLG2699

Walter Clarke - of RI & VA, d1817, m Elizabeth Wickham - desc/o Jeremy Clarke DBR(5)88, 91

William - of RI, b1671 d1732, m1695 Abigail Remington - desc/o George Gardiner BLG2699

William - b abt 1775/1779 - desc/o Anne Marbury RAA114

GARFIELD Thomas - b1713 d1774, m Rebecca Johnson - desc/o John Warren J&K127; PFA Apx C #10

Thomas - b1773 d1801, m Asenath Hill - desc/o John Warren PFA Apx C #10

Solomon - b1743 d1807, m Sarah Stimson - desc/o John Warren J&K127; PFA Apx C #10

GARLAND Hudson Martin - of VA, b abt 1775/1776 son of James Garland & Ann Wingfield, m Elizabeth Penn Phillips - desc/o Thomas Wingfield TVG(36)259

GARLINGTON Edwin Conway - of VA, b1746 Lancaster Co d Laurens Co, South Carolina, m1774 Susannah Dickie b1755 d1795 - desc/o Martha Eltonhead VG245, 259

GARRIGUE Rudolph Pierre - of NY, son of Jacques Louis Garrigue & Cecile Olivia Duntzfelt, m Charlotte Lydia Whiting - the immigrant GBR297

GARWOOD Margaret - of NJ, b1704 d1825(?), m1763 John Adams b abt 1738 d1798 - desc/o Elizabeth Denne ECD166; DBR(1)6 - desc/o George Elkington DBR(1)7

Mary - of NJ, m1726 John Antrim - desc/o Elizabeth Denne DBR(4)597; RAA101

Thomas - of NJ, b1707 d1796, m1733 Mary Ballinger d1764 - desc/o Elizabeth Denne ECD166; DBR(1)6

GASCOIGNE Harmanson - of VA, d1772, m Rachel____ - desc/o John Fisher APP283

GASKELL Peter (PENN-GASKELL) - of PA, b abt 1763 d1831 son of Peter Gaskell & Christiana Gulielma of PA, m abt 1793 Elizabeth Edwards b abt 1773 d1831 dau/o Nathan Edwards - desc/o Robert Barclay BCD238; ECD247; MCB137 - the immigrant GBR49; GPFPM(2)574, 575, 579/583; CRFP(1)13, 14

GASKINS Ann - of VA, m Capt William Eustace son of Capt William Eustace & Ann Lee dau/o Hancock Lee - desc/o Martha Eltonhad GVFWM(2)92

Elizabeth - of VA, m Col Richard Hull b1717 d1776 - desc/o Martha

GASKINS (cont.)

Eltonhead GVFWM(2)91

Sarah Ann - of VA, m(1) bef 1741 John Pinkard, m(2)1744 Dr Joseph McAdam - desc/o Martha Eltonhead GVFWM(2)92

Thomas - of VA, m Sarah Eustace dau/o Capt William Eustace & Ann Lee dau/o Hancock Lee - desc/o Martha Eltonhead GVFWM(2)92

GATES Abigail - b abt 1740/1741 - desc/o Alice Freeman RAA132

Dorcas - b1770 - desc/o Richard Palgrave RAA121

Isaac - b1746, m Mary Wheeler - desc/o Samuel Rice LDS20

John - of MA, b1749, m1773 Catherine Coolidge - desc/o Olive Welby ECD(3)275

Thomas - b1776, m Patty Plumley - desc/o Samuel Rice LDS20

GATEWOOD Dolly - of VA, m Francis Higginbotham - desc/o Edward Dudley DBR(2)244

Keziah - of VA, m John Sandidge - desc/o Edward Dudley DBR(1)327; DBR(2)419; DBR(5)777

Larkin - of VA, m Catherine Penn - desc/o Edward Dudley DBR(2)244

GAYER Damaris - of MA, b1673 d1764, m1692 Nathaniel Coffin - desc/o William Gayer CRL(4)46

Dorcas - of MA, b1675 d1747, m1694 Jethro Starbuck - desc/o William Gayer DBR(1)56, 242, 248, 270, 443, 532; DBR(2)77, 198, 357, 675; DBR(3)51, 525, 526, 748, 754, 757; DBR(5)857; CRL(4)45

William - of MA, d1710, m(1) abt 1672 Dorcas Starbuck, m(2) Mary Cundy - the immigrant DBR(1)56, 242, 248, 270, 443, 532; DBR(2)77, 196, 198, 354, 356, 357, 358, 673, 675; DBR(3)51, 525, 743, 747, 748, 754, 755, 757; DBR(4)75; DBR(5)856, 857; RAA98 states no longer accepted as being of royal descent William was not the son of Humphrey Gayer sources used NE(141)106 & PA Genealogical Magazine Vol(28)14/29; CRL(4)45

GAYLES Ann - of MA, m Adam Knox - desc/o Mary Gye NE(97)57

Elizabeth - of MA, m Levi Lane - desc/o Mary Gye NE(97)57

Mary - of MA, m1771 Ebenezer Howard - desc/o Mary Gye NE(97)57

Mercy - of MA, m1784 Richard Roberts - desc/o Mary Gye NE(97)57

Sarah - of MA, m Joseph Mountfort - desc/o Mary Gye NE(97)57

GAYLORD Josiah - of CT, b1686, m1713 Naomi Burnham - desc/o John Drake CHB108; BCD108

Lucy - of CT, b1749 d1837, m1769 Zachariah Mather - desc/o John Drake CHB108; BCD108

Nathaniel - of CT, b1656, m1678 Abigail Bissell desc/ of John Drake CHB108; BCD108

Nehemiah - of CT, b1722 d1801, m1748 Lucy Loomis - desc/o John Drake CHB109; BCD108

GEER Moses - b1774 - desc/o Griffith Bowen RAA72 - desc/o Agnes Harris RAA131

James - b1715 - desc/o Agnes Harris RAA131

James - b1747 - desc/o Agnes Harris RAA131

Joseph - b1692 - desc/o Agnes Harris RAA131

Moses - b1774 - desc/o Alice Freeman RAA132

GERARD Anne - of MD, m(1) Walter Broadhurst, m(2)1665 or 1667 Henry Brett d bef 1668, m(3)1668 Col John Washington - desc/o Dr Thomas Gerard MG(1)491, 493

Elizabeth - of MD, m1748 Benedict Calvert - desc/o Dr Thomas Gerard MG(1)491

Elizabeth - of MD, d1715/1716, m(1)1669 Col Nehemiah Blackiston d1693, m(2) Ralph Rymer - m(3) Joshua Guibert - desc/o Dr Thomas Gerard DBR(2)233; DBR(3)76; DBR(4)101

Frances - of MD, m(1) Col Thomas Speake, m(2) Col Valentine Peyton, m(3) Capt John Appleton - d1676, m(4)1676 Col John Washington, m(5) William Hardwick - desc/o Dr Thomas Gerard MG(1)491, 493; VG487

Jane or Janette - of MD, m____ - desc/o Dr Thomas Gerard MG(1)491

John - of MD, d prior to 1678, m Elizabeth____ - desc/o Dr Thomas Gerard MG(1)491

John - of MD, son of John & Elizabeth Gerard, m____ & had issue - desc/o Dr Thomas Gerard MG(1)491

Judith - of MD, m(1) John Goldsmith, m(2) Richard Clouds - desc/o Dr Thomas Gerard MG(1)497

Justinian - of MD, m Sarah____ , wid/o Wilkes Maunders - desc/o Dr Thomas Gerard MG(1)490

Mary - of MD, m Kenelm Cheseldine - desc/o Dr Thomas Gerard MG(1)491

Rebecca - of MD, m1722 Charles Calvert, governor of MD - desc/o Dr Thomas Gerard MG(1)491

Susanna - of MD, d aft 1670, m(1)1654 Capt Robert Slye, m(2) John Coode - desc/o Dr Thomas Gerard DBR(5)841, 904; MG(1)491

Temperance - of MD 1650, d1711/1712, m(1)1669 Mr Daniel Hutt, m(2) abt 1675 John Crabb, m(3) Benjamin Blanchflower - desc/o Dr Thomas Gerard DBR(2)360; DBR(3)56, 95; MG(1)491, 499

Dr Thomas - of MD 1650, b abt 1605 New Hall, Lancashire, England bp 1608 d1673 Westmoreland Co, VA, practiced medicine & active in provincial affairs, son of Sir Thomas Gerard, m(1)1629 Susanna Snow dau/o John & Judith Snow of Staffordshire, m(2)Mrs Rose Tucker - the immigrant DBR(1)242, 532; DBR(2)233, 360; DBR(3)56, 76, 95; DBR(4)99, 101; DBR(5)841, 904, 1047; RAA1, 99; GBR255; MG(1)478/503; VG487; FLW195

Thomas - of MD, m Susannah Curtis - desc/o Dr Thomas Gerard MG(1)490

GIBBINS Rachel - of ME, b1660, m abt 1690 Roger Edgecomb - desc/o Judith Lewis DBR(2)172

Hannah - m ____ Hibbert - desc/o Elizabeth Marshall GBR265 - desc/o Thomas Lewis GBR465

GIBBS (GIBBES) Ann - of SC, b1752 d1781 St Thomas Parish, m1767 Edward Thomas - desc/o Robert Gibbs SCG(2)218; CFA(5)230

Anne - of SC, b1730 d1755, m1752 William Ladson & had issue - desc/o Robert Gibbs SCG(2)217

Culcheth - of SC, b1724 d1777, m(1) Jane Jackson, wid/o ____ Butler & had issue, m(2) Martha____ - desc/o Robert Gibbs CFA(5)230

Elizabeth - of SC, b1691, m Col John Fenwicke - desc/o Robert Gibbs SCG(2)215; CFA(5)229

GIBBS (GIBBES) (cont.)

Elizabeth - of SC, b1728, m1744 John Ladson, branches of Ladson, Bee & Alston came from this marriage, m(2)1752 Dr James Carson - desc/o Robert Gibbs SCG(2)217

Elisabeth - of SC, b1756, m(1)1775 Capt Charles Shepherd who was killed at the seige of Savannah in 1779, m(2) Samuel Hunt of Boston - desc/o Robert Gibbs SCG(2)218

Henry - of MA, b1668 d1723, minister of Watertown, m1692 Mercy Greenough - desc/o Robert Gibbs NE(19)208, 209

Henry - of MA, b1709, m(1) Margaret Fitch dau/o Jabez Fitch, m(2) bef 27 May 1747 Katherine Willard - desc/o Robert Gibbs NE(19)208/209

Henry - of MA, b1749, m1781 Mercy Prescott dau/o Benjamin Prescott - desc/o Robert Gibbs NE(19)208, 209

Henry - of SC, b1764, m1787 Sarah Moore d1790 age 23 years 8 months & 17 days dau/o John & Elisabeth Moore of St Thomas Parish & had issue 2 children William Henry b1789 d1790 a few hours after his mother & Sarah Elisabeth b1790, m(2)1791 Mary Dunbar - desc/o Robert Gibbs SCG(2)218; CFA(5)230

John - of SC, very probably - the immigrant to Goose Creek, South Carolina, son of Basil Gibbes & Ann Murey, m Elizabeth____ - the immigrant GBR377 some aspect of royal descent merits further study

John - of SC, b1696 d1764, m(1)1719 Mary Woodward b1703 dau/o John Woodward, son of Dr Henry Woodward the first white settler in South Carolina, m(2)1748 Elizabeth Bedon wid/o Paul Jenys & William Raven, m(3)1760 Ann Barnwell Wigg dau/o John Barnwell & wid/o Thomas Stanyarne, Ambrose Reeve & Thomas Wigg - desc/o Robert Gibbs SCG(2)216, 217; CFA(5)229

John - of SC, b1733, m1754 Margaret Ann Stevens - desc/o Robert Gibbs SCG(2)217

John - of SC, b1765, m1787 Mary Smith dau/o Benjamin Smith - desc/o Robert Gibbs SCG(2)222

Josiah Willard - of MA, b1752 d1822, the father of 10 children - desc/o Robert Gibbs NE(19)208, 209

Lewis Ladson - of SC, b1771 d1828, m1809 Marie H Drayton b1784 d1826 & had issue - desc/o Robert Gibbs SCG(2)223

Mary - of SC, m Thomas Elliott - desc/o Robert Gibbs SCG(2)215; CFA(5)229

Mary - of SC, b1719 d1743 on Edisto Island, m1740 William Tilly & had issue - desc/o Robert Gibbs SCG(2)216; CFA(5)230

Mary - of SC, b1722 d1801 Beaufort, Port Republic, m1738 Col Nathaniel Barnwell & had issue - desc/o Robert Gibbs SCG(2)217

Mary - of SC, b1758 d1775, m1774 Thomas Middleton, Esq b175____ d1779 of Crowfield, South Carolina - desc/o Robert Gibbs SCG(2)217, 222

Mary - of SC, b1758 d1833, m1784 William Charles Warham - desc/o Robert Gibbs SCG(2)218

Mary Anna - of SC, b1767, m1784 Major Alexander Garden son of Dr Alexander Garden - desc/o Robert Gibbs SCG(2)222

Robert - of SC, b1644 d1715 proprietors deputy, governor & chief

GIBBS (GIBBES) (cont.)

Justice of South Carolina, son of Robert Gibbs of Barbados & Mary Coventry dau/o Thomas Coventry, m(1)____, m(2) Mary____ - the immigrant GBR377; CFA(5)229

Robert - of MA 1660, son of Sir Henry Gibbs, merchant of Boston, & Elizabeth Temple, m Elizabeth Sheafe - the immigrant EDV110; GBR431 some aspect of royal descent merits further study; NE(19)208, 209

Robert - of RI, d1769 - desc/o Robert Gibbs EDV110

Robert - of SC, b1718 at Wappoo, St Andrew Parish d1751, m1741 Elizabeth Haddrell dau/o George & Elizabeth Haddrell of Christ Church Parish, SC - desc/o Robert Gibbs SCG(2)216; CFA(5)230

Robert - of SC, b1732 d1794, m(1)1753 Ann Stanyarne dau/o Thomas Stanyarne, Esq , m(2)1764 Sarah Reeve d 19 Jan 1825 age 78 years 10 months dau/o Ambrose Reeve & Ann Barnwell - desc/o Robert Gibbs SCG(2)217, 221, 222

Robert Reeve - of SC, b1769, m____ Ann Smith & had issue - desc/o Robert Gibbs SCG(2)222

Sarah - of SC, b1725, m1741 John Mathews, Esq , from this marriage came Gov John Mathews & branches of families of Heyward, Ingraham, Hazelhurst & Plant, of Georgia - desc/o Robert Gibbs SCG(2)217

Sarah - of SC, b1775 d1804 - desc/o Robert Gibbs SCG(2)223

Thomas - of SC, son of Robert Gibbs of Barbados & Mary Coventry dau/o Thomas Coventry, m Elizabeth____ - the immigrant GBR377

Thomas Stanyarne - of SC, b1770, m____ Ann Morgan of NJ - desc/o Robert Gibbs SCG(2)223

William - of SC, b1689 d1733, m Alice Culcheth b abt 1700 d1739 age 39 years dau/o Ralph Culcheth of Canahatty, Tipperary - desc/o Robert Gibbs SCG(2)215, 216; CFA(5)229

William - of SC, b1722 d1789 Charleston, m(1)1744 Mary Benison d1747 dau/o Col George & Elisabeth Benison, m(2)1748 Elisabeth Hasell d1762 dau/o Rev Thomas & Elisabeth Hasell, m(3) Mary Michael dau/o Henry Michael & Mary Cook - desc/o Robert Gibbs SCG(2)216; CFA(5)230

William Hasell - of SC, b1754 Charleston d1834, m1782 Elizabeth Allston dau/o William & Ann Allston of Waccamaw, m(2)1808 Mary Philp Wilson dau/o Dr Robert & Ann Wilson - desc/o Robert Gibbs SCG(2)218, 219; CFA(5)230

GIBSON Abraham - of MA, b1701 d1740, m Mary Wheeler - desc/o John Gibson BLG2704

Abraham - of MA, b1735 d1813, m1760 Esther Fox - desc/o John Gibson BLG2704

Abraham - of MA, b1760 d1816, m(1)1792 Frances Davis, m(2)1805 Susan Norcross - desc/o John Gibson BLG2704

Elizabeth - of MA, b1760 d1798, m1778 Jonathan Piper - desc/o John Prescott DBR(1)560

John - of MA 1634 - b1601 d1694, m(1) Rebecca Thompson - the immigrant BLG2703; sufficient proof of alleged royal ancestry is lacking

John - of MA, b1641 d1679, m1668 Rebecca Errington - desc/o John

GIBSON (cont.)

Gibson BLG2703

Martha - b1672, m(2) Joseph Knight - desc/o Abraham Errington LDS31 & 77

Robert - of MD, b abt 1678/1681 d1704 son of Miles Gibson & Anne Todd, m1702 Mary Goldsmith - desc/o Anne Lovelace GVFHB(3)295, 363

Sarah - of MD, b1678/1683, m Thomas Bale b abt 1664 of Baltimore Co d1707 - desc/o Anne Lovelace GVFHB(3)295, 365

Timothy - of MA, b abt 1679 d1757, m(1)1700 Rebecca Gates, m(2)1755___ - desc/o John Gibson BLG2703, 704

GIDDINGS Joseph - of MA, m Susanna Rindge - desc/o Jane Lawrence J&K216; AAP151, GBR456

Joseph Jr - of MA, m Grace Wardwell - desc/o Jane Lawrence J&K216; AAP151; GBR456

Mary - m Thomas Manning - desc/o Jane Lawrence J&K217

Susannah - of MA, m William Torrey - desc/o Jane Lawrence J&K216; AAP151; GBR456

Thomas - father of Mary Gittings - desc/o Jane Lawrence J&K217

GIFFORD Lois - b1731 - desc/o Robert Abell RAA59

GIGNILLIAT Jean Francois - of SC, b1652 d1699 son of Abraham Gignilliat & Marie de Ville, m Susanne Le Serrurier - the immigrant GBR453; TAG(53)129/131

GILBERT Elizabeth - b1732 - desc/o Richard Belding RAA68

John - b1744 - desc/o Richard Belding RAA68

John - b1685 - desc/o Richard Belding RAA68

Mercy - b1691 - desc/o Richard Belding RAA68

Rufus - b1767 - desc/o Richard Belding RAA68

Thomas - b1695 - desc/o Richard Belding RAA68

GILES Edward - of MA 1634 - the immigrant EDV59; sufficient proof of alleged royal ancestry is lacking

GILKYSON Andrew - of PA, d1842 - desc/o James Gilkyson DBR(2)223

James - of PA, b1748 d1840, m Rachel Gilbert - the immigrant DBR(2)223; sufficient proof of alleged royal ancestry is lacking

GILL Anna Maria - of MD, m James Neale - desc/o Mary Mainwaring GBR255

John of NJ, m1788 Anna Lovet Smith - desc/o Dorothea Scott CHB90; BCD90

GILLAM Hannah - m Peter Butler III - desc/o Anne Marbury DBR(1)760

GILMAN Abigail - b1737, m___ Sanborn of Sanbornton, NH - desc/o Gov Thomas Dudley NE(8)324

Benjamin Clarke - b1763 d1835, m Mary Thing Gilman - desc/o Edward Gilman CFA195

Betsy Mary - of NH, m1763 Simeon Smith - desc/o Capt Thomas Bradbury DBR(3)153

Deborah - m Joseph Sanborn - desc/o Gov Thomas Dudley NE(8)324

Edward - of MA 1638 & NH, b1587 d1681, m Mary Clark - the immigrant EDV33, 34; CFA193; TAG(10)137, 138; sufficient proof of alleged royal ancestry is lacking

Major Ezekiel - of NH, commander of the NH forces at capture of Louisberg 1745, m Sarah Dudley b1706 - desc/o Gov Thomas

GILMAN (cont.)

Dudley DBR(5)223

Israel - m(1) Deborah Thing dau/o Samuel Thing, m(2)____ Sanborn - desc/o Gov Thomas Dudley NE(8)324

Joanna - of NH, m Dr Joseph Adams b1723 d1801, surgeon, NH forces American Revolution - desc/o Gov Thomas Dudley DBR(5)224

Jodah - m____ Cochran - desc/o Gov Thomas Dudley NE(8)324

John - of NH, b1624 d1708, m1657 Elizabeth Treworgye - desc/o Edward Gilman CFA193; NE(18)258, 259

Col John - of NH, b1676/1677 d1740, m(1)1698 Elizabeth Coffin d1720 dau/o Peter & Abigail Coffin, m(2)1720 Elizabeth (Clark) Hale dau/o Nathaniel Clark & wid/o Robert Hale - desc/o Edward Gilman CFA194; NE(18)258, 259

John - of NY, b1712, m1738 Jane Deane - desc/o Edward Gilman CFA194

John - m____ Colcord - desc/o Gov Thomas Dudley NE(8)324

Nathaniel - b1704, m1725 Sarah Emery dau/o Rev Mr Emery - desc/o Edward Gilman NE(18)258, 259

Rev Nicholas - b1707/1708, m1730 Mary Thing b1703 d1789 dau/o Bartholomew Thing & Sarah Kent - desc/o Edward Gilman NE(18)258, 259

Sally - m John Sanborn - desc/o Gov Thomas Dudley NE(8)324

Samuel - b1698 d1785, m(1)1719 Abigail Lord dau/o Robert Lord, m(2) Mary Woodbridge d1759 - desc/o Edward Gilman NE(18)258, 259

GILPIN Alice - of PA, b1714, m1739 Richard Eavenson - desc/o Joseph Gilpin CRL(1)140, (4)202

Ann - of PA, b1702 d1759, m(1)1724 Joseph Miller, m(2)1739 Richard Hallett - desc/o Joseph Gilpin CRL(1)140, (4)202

Bernard - b1763 d1747, m1807 Letitia Gilbert - desc/o Joseph Gilpin AFA60; BLG2707

Betty - of PA, b1742, m abt 1764 William Cleaney or Clenny - desc/o Joseph Gilpin CRL(1)141

Esther - of PA, b1718/1719 d1795, m1741 Samuel Painter - desc/o Joseph Gilpin CRL(1)140, (4)202

George - of PA, b1708 d1773, m(1) Ruth Caldwell, m(2)1760 Mrs Sarah (Woodward) Sharples - desc/o Joseph Gilpin CRL(1)140, (4)202

Gideon - of PA, b1738 d1825, m1762 Sarah Gregg - desc/o Joseph Gilpin AFA60; BLG2707; CRL(1)141

Hannah - of PA, b1692 d1746/1747, m William Seal - desc/o Joseph Gilpin CRL(1)140, (4)202

Hannah - of PA, b1746, m1769 John Grubb - desc/o Joseph Gilpin CRL(1)141

Isaac - of PA, b1709/1710 d1754, m Mary Painter - desc/o Joseph Gilpin CRL(1)140, (4)202

Israel - of PA, b1740 d1834, m Elizabeth Hannum - desc/o Joseph Gilpin CRL(1)141

John - b1765 d1808, m1797 Mary Hollingsworth - desc/o Joseph Gilpin BLG2707

Joseph - of PA, b1664 d1741, m1691/1692 Hannah Glover - the

GILPIN (cont.)
    immigrant AFA60; EDV89; BLG2707; CRL(1)140; CRL(4)202;
    GPFHB366/369 descent is in error as to royal ancestry
    Joseph - of PA & DE, b1703/1704 d1792, m1729 Mary Caldwell -
      desc/o Joseph Gilpin AFA60; EDV89; BLG2707; CRL(1)140, (4)202
    Joseph - b1725 d1790, m1764 Elizabeth Read - desc/o Joseph Gilpin
      BLG2707
    Joseph - of PA, b1748 d1836, m ____ Giles - desc/o Joseph Gilpin
      CRL(1)141
    Lydia - of PA, b1698/1699 d1750, m William Dean - desc/o Joseph
      Gilpin CRL(1)140, (4)202
    Mary - of PA, b1716/1717 d1806, m(1)1736 Philip Taylor, m(2) abt
      1768 George Strode - desc/o Joseph Gilpin CRL(1)140, (4)202
    Mary - of PA, b1752 or 1756, m1774 Adam Williamson - desc/o
      Joseph Gilpin CRL(1)141
    Moses - of PA, b1711/1712, m1742 Ann Buffington - desc/o Joseph
      Gilpin CRL(1)140, (4)202
    Orpha - of PA, b1734, m1754 Joseph Shallcross - desc/o Joseph
      Gilpin CRL(1)140
    Rachel - of PA, b1695 d1776, m Joshua Pierce - desc/o Joseph Gilpin
      CRL(1)140, (4)203
    Ruth - of PA, b1697 d1718, m Joseph Mendenhall - desc/o Joseph
      Gilpin CRL(1)140, (4)202
    Ruth - of PA, b1730 d1781, m Daniel Stubb - desc/o Joseph Gilpin
      CRL(1)141
    Samuel - of MD, b1693 d1761, m Jane Parker - desc/o Joseph Gilpin
      BLG2707; CRL(1)140, (4)202
    Sarah - of PA, b1706 d1783, m Peter Cooke - desc/o Joseph Gilpin
      CRL(1)140
    Thomas - of PA, b1700 d1756, m(1)1726 Ruth Mendenhall, m(2)1728
      Hannah Knowles, m(3)1757 Ann Caldwell - desc/o Joseph Gilpin
      CRL(1)140, (4)202
    Thomas - of PA, b1750 d1802, m(1) Lydia Rice, m(2) Sarah Grey, m(3)
      Sarah Council - desc/o Joseph Gilpin CRL(1)141
    Vincent - of PA, b1732 d1810, m Abigail Woodward - desc/o Joseph
      Gilpin CRL(1)140
GLASSELL Helen Buchan - of VA, m1785 David Grinnan - desc/o James
    Taylor NFA29
GODDARD Benjamin - of MA, b1704 - desc/o William Goddard BLG2710
    Calvin - of CT, b1768 d1842, m1794 Alice Hart - desc/o William
      Goddard BLG2710
    Daniel - of MA, b1734 d1807, m1756 Mary Willard - desc/o William
      Goddard BLG2710
    Rev David - of MA, b1706 - desc/o William Goddard BLG2710
    Ebenezer - b1713/1714 d1762, m Sybil Brigham - desc/o William
      Goddard LDS58; RAA99; BLG2710
    Edward - of MA, b1674/1675 d1754, m1697 Susannah Stone - desc/o
      William Goddard LDS58; RAA99; BLG2710
    Edward - of MA, b1698 d1777, m Hepzibah Hapgood - desc/o William
      Goddard BLG2710
    Elizabeth - b1687 - desc/o William Goddard RAA99

GODDARD (cont.)

Dr Giles - of CT, b1705 d1757, m Sarah Updike - desc/o William Goddard AFA274

Hannah - b1736 - desc/o William Goddard RAA99

Hezekiah - b1771 - desc/o William Goddard BLG2710

John - b1699 - desc/o William Goddard RAA99

Joseph - of MA, b1655 d1728, m Deborah Treadway - desc/o William Goddard RAA99; AFA274

Joseph - of MA, b1682 married and had 3 sons - desc/o William Goddard AFA274

Josiah - b abt 1672 - desc/o William Goddard RAA99; AAP152; GBR219

Rachel - of MA, b1699 Watertown, dau/o Josiah Goddard & Rachel Davis, m1717 Watertown, Obadiah Coolidge Jr b1695 Watertown d aft 1739, cordwainer, son of Obadiah Coolidge - desc/o William Goddard RAA99; AAP152; GBR219; NE(77)286

Susannah - b1742, m Phineas Howe - desc/o William Goddard LDS58; RAA99

William - of MA, chr 1627 d1691 son of Edward Goddard & Elizabeth D'Oyley, m Elizabeth Miles - the immigrant LDS58; RAA1, 99; AAP152; BLG2710; AFA274; GBR219

William - b abt 1653 - desc/o William Goddard RAA99

William - b abt 1701/1702 - desc/o William Goddard RAA99

William - of RI, b1740 d1817, m1786 Abigail Angell - desc/o William Goddard AFA274

GOLD Major Nathan - of CT - the immigrant EDV111; sufficient proof of alleged royal ancestry is lacking

GOLDSBOROUGH Charles - of MD, b1707 d1767, m(1)1730 Elizabeth Ennalls, m(2)1739 Elizabeth Dickinson - desc/o Nicholas Goldsborough BLG2712; CFA197; CRL(1)107; NFA23; CRL(2)198

Charles - of MD, b1740 d1782, m Anna Maria Tilghman - desc/o Nicholas Goldsborough BLG2712; CRL(1)107

Charles - of MD, b1761 d1801, m1783 Williamina Smith - desc/o Nicholas Goldsborough BLG2712

Charles - of MD, b1765 d1734, m1804 Sarah Yerbury Goldsborough - desc/o Nicholas Goldsborough BLG2712; CRL(1)107

Elizabeth - of MD, b1760 d1827, m1784 Dr James Sykes - desc/o Nicholas Goldsborough BLG2712

Elizabeth Greenberry - of MD, b1731 d1820, m1754 William Ennalls - desc/o Nicholas Goldsborough BLG2712; CRL(1)107; CRL(2)198

Howes - of MD, m Rebecca Goldsborough - desc/o Nicholas Goldsborough BLG2712

Howes - of MD, b1715 d1746, m1743 Rosannah Piper - desc/o Nicholas Goldsborough BLG2712; CFA197; CRL(2)198

Howes - of MD, b1775, m Mary Washington - desc/o Nicholas Goldsborough BLG2712

John - of MD, b1711 d1778, m Ann Turbutt - desc/o Nicholas Goldsborough BLG2712; CFA196; CRL(1)106; CRL(2)198

Mary - of MD, b1702 d1742, m Francis Mooney - desc/o Nicholas Goldsborough BLG2712; CRL(1)106; CRL(2)198

Nicholas - of MD 1670, bp 1639 d1670, m1659 Margaret Howes - the

GOLDSBOROUGH (cont.)

immigrant BLG2712; CFA196; CRL(1)106; NFA23; CRL(2)197 sufficient proof of alleged royal ancestry is lacking

Nicholas - of MD, b1662 d1705, m Ann Powell - desc/o Nicholas Goldsborough BLG2712

Nicholas - of MD, b1690 d1766, m1721 Sarah Turbutt - desc/o Nicholas Goldsborough BLG2712

Nicholas - of MD, b1704 (twin to Robert) d1756, m1746 Jane____ - desc/o Nicholas Goldsborough BLG2712; CFA197; CRL(1)106; CRL(2)198

Rachel - of MD, b1692, m1712 Samuel Turbutt - desc/o Nicholas Goldsborough BLG2712

Rachel - of MD, b1769 d1811, m Horatio Ridout - desc/o Nicholas Goldsborough BLG2712

Rebecca - b1757 d1802, m & had issue - desc/o Nicholas Goldsborough BLG2712

Richard - of MD, b1768 d1815, m Achsah Worthington - desc/o Nicholas Goldsborough BLG2712

Robert - of MD, b1660 d1746, m1697 Elizabeth Greenberry - desc/o Nicholas Goldsborough BLG2712; CFA196; CRL(1)106; CRL(2)197

Robert - of MD, b1704 d1777, m(1)1739 Sarah Nicholas, m(2)1742 Mary Ann Turbutt - desc/o Nicholas Goldsborough BLG2712; CFA196; CRL(1)106; CRL(2)198

Robert - of MD, b1733 d1788, m1755 Sarah Yerbury - desc/o Nicholas Goldsborough BLG2712; CRL(1)107; CRL(2)198

Sarah - of MD, b1758 d1821, m(1) Henry Ennalls, m(2)Robert North Carnan - desc/o Nicholas Goldsborough BLG2712

Sarah Fauntleroy - of MD, b1776 d1821, m1808 Dr John Bennett - desc/o Nicholas Goldsborough BLG2712

Thomas - of MD, b1728 d1793, m1775 Katharine Fauntleroy - desc/o Nicholas Goldsborough BLG2712

William - of MD, b1709 d1760, m(1)1734 Elizabeth Robbins, m(2)1747 Henrietta Maria Tilghman - desc/o Nicholas Goldsborough BLG2712; CFA197; CRL(1)106; CRL(2)198

William - of MD, b1762 d1826, m1792 Sarah Worthington - desc/o Nicholas Goldsborough BLG2712; CFA210; CRL(2)198

GOLITZIN (or GALLITZIN) Demetrius Augustine, Prince Golitzin or Gallitzin - of MD & PA, b1770 d1840, Roman Catholic clergyman, colony founder & writer, son of Dimitri, Prince Golitsyn & Adelaide Amalia, Countess von Schmettau, died unmarried - the immigrant GBR414

GOODE Bennett - of VA, b1710 d1771, m1740 Martha Jefferson b1719 d1796 dau/o Captain Thomas Jefferson - desc/o John Goode DBR(1)601

Edmund - of VA, m Elizabeth Woodson - desc/o John Goode DBR(1)89

Edward - of VA, b abt 1720 d aft 1760 - desc/o John Goode BLG2714

Edward - of NC, b abt 1740 d1798, m Mary Turpin - desc/o John Goode BLG2714

Francis - of VA, m Alice Harris - desc/o Christopher Branch GVFWM(1)426

John - of VA prior to 1660, b1620/1630 d bef 1708 son of Richard

GOODE (cont.)

Goode, m(1) Frances Mackarness, m(2) Anne Bennett d bef 1708 - the immigrant DBR(1)89, 601; DBR(2)145; DBR(3)517, 732; RAA1, 100; BLG2714; GBR337 some aspect of royal descent merits further study

John - of VA, b1675 d1720, m Elizabeth___ - desc/o John Goode DBR(1)601

Martha - of VA, m William Minter - desc/o John Goode DBR(1)89

Mary - of VA, m Seth Ward - desc/o Christopher Branch GVFWM(1)426

Philip - of VA, d1776, m Ann Watkins - desc/o John Goode DBR(1)89

Philip - of VA, b1771 d1824, m Rebecca Hayes b1770 d1855 - desc/o John Goode DBR(3)732

Robert - of VA, m Elizabeth Branch - desc/o John Goode DBR(3)517

Robert - of VA, b1711 d1765, m Mary Turpin b1720 d1765 dau/o Thomas & Obedience (Branch) Turpin - desc/o Christopher Branch GVFWM(1)418

Robert - of VA, m Elizabeth Turpin - desc/o John Goode DBR(3)517

Col Robert - of VA, b1743 d1809, m Sallie Bland dau/o Richard Bland & Anne (Poythress) Bland - desc/o John Goode DBR(3)517 - desc/o Christopher Branch GVFWM(1)426

Sallie Bland - of VA, m James Lyle - desc/o John Goode DBR(3)517

Samuel - of VA, m Martha Jones - desc/o John Goode DBR(1)89; DBR(3)732

Samuel II - of VA, d1797, m___ Burwell - desc/o John Goode DBR(3)732

Samuel III - of VA, b1749, m1770 Mary Collier b1756 dau/o John & Elizabeth (Meredith) Collier - desc/o John Goode DBR(3)732

Samuel - of VA, m Mary Burwell - desc/o Christopher Branch GVFWM(1)426

Thomas - of VA, m Eliza Prosser - desc/o Christopher Branch GVFWM(1)426

Thomas - of VA, b abt 1690 - desc/o John Goode BLG2714

William - of VA, b1765 d1837, m1789 Sarah James b1770 d1817 dau/o John James of VA & SC - desc/o John Goode DBR(1)601

GOODNOW Bannister - b1773 d1804, m Submit Temple - desc/o Dr Richard Palgrave DBR(1)784

Daniel - b1724, m1746 Martha Bannister - desc/o Dr Richard Palgrave DBR(1)784

GOODRICH Abigail - of CT, b1754 d1811, m1773 Isaac Lee - desc/o William Leete CHB369; MCD245

Judge Elizur - of CT, b1761 d1849 member of Congress; mayor of New Haven; professor at Yale College; chief justice of the probate court for 13 years & judge of the probate court for 17 years, m1785 Anne Willard Allen - desc/o Rev Charles Chauncy J&K273; BCD71

Rev Samuel - of CT, b1763 d1835, m1784 Elizabeth Ely - desc/o Rev Charles Chauncy CHB71; MCD192; BCD71

GOODSELL Sarah - b1740 d1802, m1758 Jeremiah Wolcott - desc/o Rev John Davenport DBR(2)779

GOODWIN Diana Chisman - of VA, b1760 Hanover Co d1850 Cedar Hill, Hanover Co, m1780 Hanover Co, William Overton Harris b1756

GOODWIN (cont.)

>Cedar Hill, Hanover Co d1802 Cedar Hill, Hanover Co, farmer desc/o Col George Reade HSF(2) 195

>John - of VA, b1735 d1763 Hanover, m Elizabeth Doswell b1743 d1814 dau/o Thomas Doswell & Rebecca Drummond - desc/o Col George Reade HSF(2)195

GOOKIN Charles - of PA - desc/o Daniel Gookin EDV64

>Daniel - of VA & MA, b1621 d1686 - the immigrant EDV64; WAC88; sufficient proof of alleged royal ancestry is lacking

>Daniel Jr - of MA, d1686/1687 - desc/o Daniel Gookin WAC88

>Daniel - b1756 of North Hampton d1831 Saco, ME, m1787 Abigail Dearborn dau/o Dr Levi Dearborne - desc/o Gov Thomas Dudley NE(8)322

>Dorothy - m Rev Peter Coffin of Kingston, NH - desc/o Gov Thomas Dudley NE(8)322

>Elizabeth - m Dr Edmund Chadwick of Deerfield, NH - desc/o Gov Thomas Dudley NE(8)322

>Hannah - m Rev Timothy Upham of Deerfield, NH, b1748 Malden d1811, first minister of Deerfield, NH - desc/o Gov Thomas Dudley NE(8)322

>Hannah - of MA, b1724 d1756, m1749 Patrick Tracy of Newberry - desc/o Capt Thomas Lake CHB410 - desc/o Gov Thomas Dudley NE(8)322

>Capt John - of VA, d1643, m Sarah Offley - the immigrant WAC88, 89; sufficient proof of alleged royal ancestry is lacking

>Mary - of VA, m(1) William Moseley, m(2) Col Anthony Lawson - desc/o Capt John Gookin WAC88, 89

>Rev Nathaniel - b1713 d1763, m(1) Judith Coffin, m(2) Anne Finch, m(3) Love Wingate - desc/o Gov Thomas Dudley NE(8)322

>Samuel - m Sarah Haskell - desc/o Gov Thomas Dudley NE(8)322

GORDON Ann - of VA, b1743 d1765, m1759 Richard Chichester - desc/o Martha Eltonhead VG249

>Katherine - b1620/1621, m David Barclay - the immigrant RAA65; sufficient proof of alleged royal ancestry is lacking

>Thomas - of NJ, b abt 1652 d1722 chief justice of NJ, son of Robert of Pitlurg & Catherine (Burnet) Gordon, m(1) Helen____, m(2)1695 Janet Mudie - the immigrant FLW224; RAA1, 100; GBR76

GORE Elizabeth - b1703/1704 - desc/o Griffith Bowen RAA72

>Samuel - b1681 - desc/o Griffith Bowen RAA72

GORGES Elizabeth - dau/o Tristram Gorges & Elizabeth Cole, m Sir Ferdinando Gorges - the immigrant GBR244; EO2(2)63/78

>Lady Elizabeth - bp 1578 d abt 1658 third dau/o Sir Thomas Gorges, Knight & Helena Shackenburgh or Snakenborg, m(1) Sir Hugh Smith, m(2) Sir Ferdinando Gorges - the immigrant GBR244; EO2(2)63/78

>Sir Ferdinando of ME 1639, b abt 1565 d1647 Lord Proprietor of the Province of ME 1639 son of Edward Gorges & Cecily Lygon, m(1)1589/1590 Westminster, Anne Bell d1620 London, dau/o Edward Bell & Margaret Barley of Writtle, Essex, England, m(2)1621 Mary Fulford dau/o Sir Thomas Fulford d1623, m(3)1627 Ladock, Cornwall, (his 2nd cousin) Elizabeth Gorges daughter

GORGES (cont.)

d1629 of Tristram Gorges & Elizabeth Cole, m(4)1629 (his cousin) Lady Elizabeth Gorges Smith bp 1578 d abt 1658, third dau/o Sir Thomas Gorges, Knight & Helena Shackenburgh - the immigrant J&K284; GBR204, 244; EO2(2)63/78; GDMNH273, 274; FLW174

Ferdinando - b1630 at Wendon Loftus, Essex d1718, m1660 London, Mary Archdale dau/o Thomas Archdale of Loaks nr Chipping Wycomb, Bucks - desc/o Sir Ferdinando J&K284; EO2(2)63/78; GDMNH274

John - of ME, b1593 d1657 eldest son of Sir Ferdinando Gorges & Ann Bell, m(1)1620 Lady Frances Fynes dau/o the Earl of Lincoln, m(2) Mary Meade d1657 dau/o Sir John Meade of Wendon Loftus, Essex - desc/o Sir Ferdinando Gorges J&K284; EO2(2)63/78; GDMNH275

Robert - of ME, governor of New England in 1623 - desc/o Sir Ferdinando Gorges J&K284

GORSUCH Anne or Anna - of VA, bp 1639/1640 Walkern, Hertfordshire d1694/1697, m1655 Capt Thomas Todd bp 1619 d1676, m(2) abt 1667 Capt David Jones d1687, m(3) bef Aug 1693 John Oldston, commander of the Baltimore Rangers - desc/o Anne Lovelace CHB501; ECD(2)178; JSW1860, 1861; DBR(1)121, 652; DBR(2)192, 621, 725; DBR(3)458; APP406

Anne - of MD, d prior to 1796, m William Jones d1830 age 83 years & left issue - desc/o Anne Lovelace GVFHB(3)396

Averilla - of MD, m(1)1782 John Worrell, m(2)1790 Nathaniel Wheeler - desc/o Anne Lovelace GVFHB(3)397

Barbara - of MD, b1726, m(1)1750/1751 George Pickett of Baltimore Co, MD, m(2) (may have) ____ Wilkinson - desc/o Anne Lovelace GVFHB(3)395

Benjamin - of MD, b1730, m(1)____, m(2)1760 Karenhappuck Johnson dau/o Jacob Johnson & left issue - desc/o Anne Lovelace GVFHB(3)395, 407

Benjamin - of MD, b1755 d1794, m1783 Mary Holland & left issue - desc/o Anne Lovelace GVFHB(3)405, 427

Charity - of MD, m1781 Thomas Kelly d1822 & mentions numerous children - desc/o Anne Lovelace GVFHB(3)400

Charles - of MD, bp 1642 Walkern, Hertfordshire d1716 Quaker & large land holder, m(1)1677 Sarah Cole d abt 1690 dau/o Thomas Cole of Baltimore Co, MD, m(2)1690/1691 Anna Hawkins dau/o John & Mary Hawkins of Anne Arundel Co, MD - the immigrant ECD(3)165 - desc/o Anne Lovelace JSW1860; MCD225; DBR(2)37; DBR(3)4; DBR(4)823; APP407; GVFHB(3)383/389

Charles - of MD, b1676/1677, m1700 Sarah____ - desc/o Anne Lovelace APP405

Charles - of MD, b1686 d1746/1748, m(1) abt 1712____, m(2) abt 1720 Sarah Cole dau/o John Cole - desc/o Anne Lovelace MCD225; APP407; GVFHB(3)389, 393, 394

Charles - of MD, b abt 1720 d1806, m(1) Susanna____, m(2) bef 1765 Margaret Harvey dau/o William Harvey of Baltimore Co, MD - desc/o Anne Lovelace GVFHB(3)395, 396

Charles - of MD, b1728/1729 d1792, m Sarah____ - desc/o Anne

GORSUCH (cont.)

Lovelace MCD225; GVFHB(3)404

Charles - of MD, b1725 d1792, m abt 1750 Sarah____ & had issue - desc/o Anne Lovelace GVFHB(3)395

Charles - of MD, b abt 1720 d1806, m(1) Susanne____, m(2) Margaret Harvey - desc/o Anne Lovelace GVFHB(3)391

Charles - of MD, b abt 1736/1740, m1763 Eleanor Bond b1726 d1805 dau/o John & Keturah Bond & left issue - desc/o Anne Lovelace GVFHB(3)402, 421

Charles - of MD, b1753/1754 d1816, m abt 1777 Hannah Bosley d1810 age 61 years & left issue - desc/o Anne Lovelace GVFHB(3)405, 425

Charles - of MD, b prior to 1757 Moved to Kentucky, m1784 Delia Dimmitt dau/o James Dimmit of Baltimore Co & Rachel Sinclair - desc/o Anne Lovelace GVFHB(3)407, 433

Charles - of MD, m1786 Rebecca Gorsuch - desc/o Anne Lovelace GVFHB(3)404

Charles - of MD, b abt 1760/1770, m1809 Susanna Paul - desc/o Anne Lovelace GVFHB(3)423

Chiscilla - of MD, m(1) prior to 1788____ Gorsuch by whom she had issue at least one son Nicholas Gorsuch, m(2)1802 Charles Shipley & had issue Elias, Lovelace, Margaret & Sarah Shipley as shown by his will 1815 - desc/o Anne Lovelace GVFHB(3)399

David - of MD, b1734 d1784, m abt 1760 Elizabeth Hanson b1741 dau/o Jonathan Hanson & Sarah Spicer & had issue - desc/o Anne Lovelace GVFHB(3)395, 407

David - of MD, b1760/1765 d1841, m1786 Rebecca Gorsuch d1841 & left issue - desc/o Anne Lovelace MCD225; GVFHB(3)405, 428

Deborah - of MD, m1793 Nicholas Bryan & left issue - desc/o Anne Lovelace GVFHB(3)402

Dickinson - of MD, d1815, m1794 Mary Talbott & left issue - desc/o Anne Lovelace - desc/o Anne Lovelace GVFHB(3)402

Dorcus - of MD, b1752, m1772 John Ensor - desc/o Anne Lovelace GVFHB(3)405

Eleanor - of MD, b1774 d1858, m1793 Joseph Merryman - desc/o Charles Gorsuch ECD(3)166 - desc/o Anne Lovelace GVFHB(3)402

Eleanor - of MD, b abt 1776, m1801 Thomas Price - desc/o Anne Lovelace GVFHB(3)422

Elisha - of MD, b1757 d1820, m1803 Susanna Miller & left issue - desc/o Anne Lovelace GVFHB(3)405, 427

Elizabeth - of VA & MD, bp 1641 at Walkern, Hertfordshire, m abt 1658 Howell Powell b1623 d1704, of Corotoman River, Lancaster Co, VA & later Baltimore & Talbot Co, MD, affiliated with the Tred Avon Meeting of the Quakers, son of Hugh Powell of Castle Madac, Brecknockshire, Wales - desc/o Anne Lovelace JSW1860; APP407; GVFHB(3)374/379

Elizabeth - of MD, m abt 1774 ____ Kelly - desc/o Anne Lovelace GVFHB(3)393

Elizabeth - of MD, living 1796, m John Lane - desc/o Anne Lovelace GVFHB(3)396

Elizabeth - of MD, m1778 Henry Bond - desc/o Anne Lovelace

GORSUCH (cont.)
> GVFHB(3)399

> Elizabeth - of MD, b abt 1764, m(1) prior to 1783____ Gorsuch & had issue William Gorsuch, m(2)1783 Elijah Stanbury, who had previously married her sister Sarah Gorsuch - desc/o Anne Lovelace GVFHB(3)408

> Hannah - of MD, b1712/1719, m1735 Thomas Stansbury b1714 d1798 son of Thomas & Jane (Hays) Stansbury - desc/o Anne Lovelace GVFHB(3)395

> Jane - of MD, b by 1760 d prior to 1800, m prior to 1788 Joseph Hawkins & left issue three daughters Sarah, Rebecca, & Mary Hawkins - desc/o Anne Lovelace GVFHB(3)399

> Jemima - of MD, m(1)1789 James Stansbury, m(2)1795 Lavallin Berry & left issue by her first husband - desc/o Anne Lovelace GVFHB(3)408

> John - of MD, b1678 d abt 1733, m Elizabeth____ - desc/o Anne Lovelace APP407; GVFHB(3)389

> John - of MD, b abt 1712/1714 d1796, m1735 Mary Price & had issue - desc/o Anne Lovelace GVFHB(3)395, 402

> John - of MD, b abt 1730 d1808, m1755 Elizabeth Merryman b1734 d1795 dau/o John Merryman & Sarah Rogers - desc/o Charles Gorsuch ECD(3)165 - desc/o Anne Lovelace GVFHB(3)393

> John - of PA, b1735, m Sarah Reese - desc/o Anne Lovelace GVFHB(3)440, 441

> John - of MD, b abt 1740 farmer, m prior to 1770 Belinda Bosley dau/o Charles & Elizabeth (Cox) Gorsuch & left issue - desc/o Anne Lovelace GVFHB(3)402, 423

> John - of MD, b abt 1740/1750, m (may have)1767 Mary Wright - desc/o Anne Lovelace GVFHB(3)396

> John - of MD, b abt 1755, m1791 Mary McClung dau/o Robert McClung of Baltimore Co, MD - desc/o Anne Lovelace GVFHB(3)403

> John - of MD, b abt 1760, m1797 Mary Riley - desc/o Anne Lovelace GVFHB(3)405

> John - of MD, b1769/1770 d1833, m1795 Sarah Galloway d1851 age 85 years & left issue - desc/o Anne Lovelace DBR(3)6; DBR(4)823 - desc/o Anne Lovelace GVFHB(3)400, 412, 413

> John (Merryman) - of MD, b1767 d1840, m(1)1804 Sarah (Stansbury) Bowen dau/o Tobias Stansbury & wid/o Josias Bowen, m(2)1811 Ariana Sollers dau/o Thomas Sollers & Arianna Dorsey & wid/o Tobias Stansbury - desc/o Anne Lovelace GVFHB(3)401, 417

> John - of MD, b1770 d1843, m1791 Elizabeth Price dau/o Stephen Price - desc/o Anne Lovelace GVFHB(3)424

> John - of MD, b1772 d1838, m1803 Nancy Goodwin - desc/o Anne Lovelace GVFHB(3)399, 411

> Joshua - of MD, b abt 1770 d1844 a sea captain, Baltimore merchant & a farmer, m(1)1795 Ann Smith, m(2)1806 Eleanor Lynch d1863 dau/o Patrick Lynch & left issue - desc/o Anne Lovelace GVFHB(3)402, 418

> Katherine - of VA by 1652, bp 1633 Walkern, Hertfordshire d by 6 Dec 1669, m William Whitby d by 9 Oct 1655, justice of Warwick Co, represented that county in the House of Burgesses - desc/o Anne

GORSUCH (cont.)

Lovelace JSW1860; APP404

Kesiah - of MD, b1772 d1840, m1790 Christopher Buck b1765 d1807 son of Benjamin Buck & Dorcus Sutton - desc/o Anne Lovelace GVFHB(3)408

Keturah - of MD, b abt 1766, m1790 Norman Gorsuch - desc/o Anne Lovelace GVFHB(3)422

Lovelace - of VA & MD, b abt 1644 d1702/1703, m(1)1679 Rebecca Preston dau/o Richard Preston, m(2)1696 Hannah Walley of PA d1705 - desc/o Anne Lovelace JSW1860; APP407, 408; GVFHB(3)437, 438

Lovelace - of MD, b abt 1715 d1783, foreman of Baltimore Co Grand Jury 1744 & overseer of highways eldest son of Thomas Gorsuch & Jane Ensor, m bef 1752 Sarah____ - desc/o Charles Gorsuch DBR(2)37 - desc/o Anne Lovelace GVFHB(3)392, 398, 399

Lovelace - of MD, b abt 1750, m prior to 1793 Elizabeth____ & had issue - desc/o Anne Lovelace GVFHB(3)400, 412

Margaret - of MD, m1790 Thomas Pindell - desc/o Anne Lovelace GVFHB(3)397

Mary - of MD, b1662, m bef Apr 1680 Richard Keene II - desc/o Anne Lovelace JSW1634; DBR(2)217, 663; APP405

Mary - of MD, m abt 1700 Capt Thomas Clagett Jr - desc/o Anne Lovelace DBR(2)217

Mary - of MD, m abt 1774____ Simpkin - desc/o Anne Lovelace GVFHB(3)393

Mary - of MD, m1779 John Gittings - desc/o Anne Lovelace GVFHB(3)403

Mary - of MD, b abt 1740/1749, m1785 Joseph Peregoy - desc/o Anne Lovelace GVFHB(3)422

Mary - of MD, b1767 d1832, m1786 Charles Jessop b1759 d1828 of Vaux Hall, Baltimore Co, MD son of William Jessop & Mary Walker & left issue several children - desc/o Anne Lovelace GVFHB(3)408

Nancy (Anne) - of MD, m Benjamin Bond - desc/o Anne Lovelace GVFHB(3)399

Nicholas - of MD, d1796, m1785/1795 possibly as his 2nd wife Mary Lavely dau/o William Lavely of Baltimore Co, MD & wid/o Andrew Granchet & left issue - desc/o Anne Lovelace GVFHB(3)402, 417

Nicholas - of MD, b1774 d1839, m(1) Nancy Glenn, m(2)1803 Agnes Glenn b1767 d1848, left no issue - desc/o Anne Lovelace GVFHB(3)406, 433

Nathan - of MD, b prior to 1758 d1813, m1779 Polatia (Pelatiah) Pearce - desc/o Anne Lovelace GVFHB(3)407

Norman - of MD, d prior to 1831 in Muskingum Co, Ohio, m1790 Kitty (Keturah) Gorsuch - desc/o Anne Lovelace GVFHB(3)397, 408, 409

Prudence - of MD, m1789 Benjamin Williams by whom she appears to have had issue - desc/o Anne Lovelace GVFHB(3)400

Rachael - of MD, b abt 1735/1743, m1760 James Bosley - desc/o Anne Lovelace GVFHB(3)402

Rachael - of MD, m1783 James Hooper - desc/o Anne Lovelace GVFHB(3)401

Rachael - of MD, m1796 Abednego Griffith - desc/o Anne Lovelace

GORSUCH (cont.)
>GVFHB(3)400

>Rachel - of MD, b abt 1770, m1792 Stephen Cole - desc/o Anne Lovelace GVFHB(3)422

>Rebecca - of MD, b1767, m1786 David Gorsuch - desc/o Anne Lovelace GVFHB(3)422

>Richard - of VA & MD, bp 1637 Walkern, Hertfordshire, d1677 deputy commissioner & justice for Talbot Co MD, m Elizabeth___ she, m(2) Samuel Hatton d1687/1688, m(3) Herman Foakes - desc/o Anne Lovelace JSW1860; APP405

>Richard - of MD, b1672/1673 d1705, m1696 Elizabeth Martin - desc/o Anne Lovelace APP405

>Richard - of MD, b by 1765 d1834, m___ & left issue - desc/o Anne Lovelace GVFHB(3)401, 416, 417

>Robert - of VA & MD, bp 1635 Walkern, Hertfordshire, m___ killed 1661 by Indians - desc/o Anne Lovelace JSW1860; APP405

>Robert - of MD, d1720, appeared in Baltimore Co, MD in 1700, m Johanna___ d bef 12 Jul 1728 - desc/o Anne Lovelace APP405; GVFHB(3)389

>Robert - of MD, b1757 d1828, m1782 Sarah Donovan b1765 d1826 dau/o Lieut Richard Donovan of Waterford, Ireland & Ann Delafield of Dublin - desc/o Anne Lovelace GVFHB(3)401, 415, 416

>Ruth - of MD, d bef 1796, m1770 John Barton - desc/o Anne Lovelace GVFHB(3)397

>Ruth - of MD, d prior to 1800, m1791 John Williams & leaving issue at least three daughters Sarah, Rachael & Chiscilla - desc/o Anne Lovelace GVFHB(3)400

>Ruth - of MD, m prior to 1777 William Welsh d1802 - desc/o Anne Lovelace GVFHB(3)401

>Ruth - of MD, b abt 1766, m1785 Charles Peregoy, she had two daughters living 1849, Ann, m Elias Read & Elizabeth, m George Shipley - desc/o Anne Lovelace GVFHB(3)406

>Sarah - of MD, d1724, m1709 Thomas Bowdle - desc/o Anne Lovelace APP405

>Sarah - of MD, b1721, m abt 1751 William Parlett d1780 - desc/o Anne Lovelace GVFHB(3)395

>Sarah - of MD, b abt 1740, m1758 John Gill b1737 son of John Gill & Mary Rogers - desc/o Anne Lovelace GVFHB(3)403

>Sarah - of MD, m prior to 1788 Thomas Beaseman by whom she had issue - desc/o Anne Lovelace GVFHB(3)399

>Sarah - of MD, b abt 1760 d1793, m1779 Elijah Stansbury b1751 son of Dixon Stansbury & Penelope Body, m as his 2nd wife, her sister Elizabeth Gorsuch, Sarah & Elijah had issue one son Charles Stansbury - desc/o Anne Lovelace GVFHB(3)408

>Sarah - of MD, b abt 1764, m1781 Abraham Hicks - desc/o Anne Lovelace GVFHB(3)406

>Sarah - of MD, m1791 Benedict Hurst - desc/o Anne Lovelace GVFHB(3)404

>Sarah - of MD, b abt 1774 d aft 1813, m (probably) 1804 Thomas Rutledge - desc/o Anne Lovelace GVFHB(3)422

>Stephen - of MD, b abt 1772, m1798 Tabitha Johnson dau/o Jacob

GORSUCH (cont.)

Johnson - desc/o Anne Lovelace GVFHB(3)422

Thomas - of MD, b1678/1680 d1774, m1714 Anne (Jane) Ensor - desc/o Anne Lovelace ECD(3)165; DBR(2)37; DBR(3)6; DBR(4)823; APP407; GVFHB(3)389, 391

Thomas - of MD, b abt 1720 d1777, m____ & left issue - desc/o Anne Lovelace GVFHB(3)393, 400

Thomas II - of MD, b1730 d1783, m Martha Matthews - desc/o Anne Lovelace DBR(3)6; DBR(4)823

Thomas - of MD, b1750/1751 d1800, m1779 Kesiah Wheeler dau/o Benjamin Wheeler of Baltimore Co & left issue - desc/o Anne Lovelace GVFHB(3)405, 424

Thomas - of MD, b1752 d1815, m1778 Helen Chapman b1763 dau/o Robert & Margaret Chapman - desc/o Anne Lovelace DBR(2)37; GVFHB(3)399, 410, 411

Thomas - of MD, m1787 Rachael McClung dau/o Robert McClung of Baltimore Co, MD - desc/o Anne Lovelace GVFHB(3)407

Urith - of MD, m1779 John Ensor - desc/o Anne Lovelace GVFHB(3)401

William - of MD, b1697/1702 removed to Chester Co, Pennsylvania, m Rebecca____ - desc/o Anne Lovelace GVFHB(3)440

William - of MD, b abt 1700 d1744, m1730 Rebecca____ - desc/o Anne Lovelace APP408

William - of MD, b abt 1715/1718 d1797, m____ & had issue - desc/o Anne Lovelace GVFHB(3)395, 403

William - of MD, m(1)1785 Caroline Tipton, m(2)1786 Penelope Tipton - desc/o Anne Lovelace GVFHB(3)404

William - of MD, b1769 d1846, m(1)1793 Averilla Vaughan b1777 d1800, m(2)1803 Ann McIntire d1832 left issue by both wives - desc/o Anne Lovelace MCD225; GVFHB(3)406, 431

GOSS John - of MA, b1693 d bef 1765, m1711 Mary Woods - desc/o John Prescott DBR(1)559

Sarah - of MA, b1719 d1802, m1744 Deacon Stephen Gibston - desc/o John Prescott DBR(1)559, 560

GOTHERSON Dorothea - of NJ 1705, bp 1657 d1709, m1680 John Davis - desc/o Dorothea Scott CHB90; ECD(2)240; MCB226; MCD288; BCD90

GOUGH Claiborne - of VA, had land in New Kent Co 1748 from which a ferry operated across the York (Pamunkey) River to "Sweet Hall" in King William Co, m____ - desc/o Elizabeth Boteler APP189

GOULD Lydia - of RI, b1758 d1813, m1785 Smith Brown - desc/o Katherine Marbury DBR(2)44, 45;

GOVE Daniel - b1749 - desc/o Thomas Bradbury RAA72

Moses - b1774 - desc/o Thomas Bradbury RAA72

GRAEME Thomas MD - of PA 1717, d1772, m1719 Anne Digges - the immigrant MCB138; sufficient proof of alleged royal ancestry is lacking

GRAFTON Elizabeth - of MA, b1667, m William Hughes d aft 5 Dec 1698 - desc/o Mary Gye NE(96)360

Mary - of MD, b1727, m Walter Dulany - desc/o Mary Drake DBR(3)722; DBR(4)48, 471

GRAFTON (cont.)

Priscilla - of MA, b1671, m Thomas Jackson d aft 5 Dec 1698 - desc/o
Mary Gye NE(96)360

GRAHAM Henrietta - of PA, m1785 Richard Flower - desc/o William
Graham AFA246

Judge Henry Hale - of PA, b1731 d1790, m1760 Abigail Pennell -
desc/o William Graham AFA246

Sarah - of CT, m Gideon Hurd - desc/o Rev Charles Chauncy CHB69;
BCD69

William - of PA, b1692 d1758, m1729 Eleanor Wyatt - the immigrant
AFA246; sufficient proof of alleged royal ancestry is lacking

GRANT Anne - m John Marsh - desc/o Grace Minor PFA Apx D #5

Beriah - b1698 - desc/o Richard Billings RAA70

Deliverance - of CT, m Dr Samuel Cary - desc/o Richard Booth
J&K130

Capt Ebenezer - desc/o Grace Minor PFA Apx D #5

Joshua - b1725 - desc/o Richard Billings RAA70 - desc/o Alice
Freeman RAA132

Joshua - b abt 1758 - desc/o Richard Billings RAA70 - desc/o Alice
Freeman RAA132

Noah I - of CT, b1693 d1727, son of Samuel Grant, m1717 Martha
Huntington - desc/o Richard Booth J&K130, 288; JSW1878 -
desc/o Grace Minor PFA Apx C #9, Apx D #5

Noah II - of CT, b1718 d1756, m1746 Susanna Delano - desc/o
Richard Booth J&K130; JSW1878 - desc/o Grace Minor PFA Apx C
#9, Apx D #5

Capt Noah III - of CT & KY, b1748 d1819, m(2)1792 Rachel Miller -
desc/o Philippe Delano CHB505 - desc/o Richard Booth JSW1878 -
desc/o Grace Minor PFA Apx C #9, Apx D #5

de GRASSE Francois Joseph Paul, Count De Grasse, Marquis de Tilly -
b1722 d1788, French Admiral, commander of the French fleet in
Chesapeake Bay that helped force Cornwallis's surrender at
Yorktown, son of Francois de Grasse-Rouville, Seigneur de Valett &
Veronique de Villeneuve-Trans, m(1) Antoinette Rosalie Accaron,
m(2) Catherine de Pien, m(3) Christine de Cibon - the immigrant
GBR292

Sylvie - m Francois de Pau - desc/o Francois Joseph Paul de Grasse
GBR292

GRAVES Thomas - of MA, d1746 - the immigrant EDV68; BLG2719;
sufficient proof of alleged royal ancestry is lacking

Thomas - of MA - desc/o Thomas Graves EDV68

GRAY Daniel - of VA, m (his cousin) Mary Strother - desc/o William
Strother GVFTQ(3)405

French Strother - of VA, m (his cousin) Sarah Bailey Taylor - desc/o
William Strother GVFTQ(3)405

George Weedon - of VA, b1740 d1823 captain in the 3rd Virginia
Regiment Revolutionary War, m Mildred Thompson - desc/o
William Strother GVFTQ(3)404

John - of VA, m Mary Ormsby - desc/o William Strother GVFTQ(3)405

GREELY Samuel - of NH, b1747 d1824, m Mary Leavitt - desc/o Thomas
Dudley DBR(5)916

GREEN Elizabeth - of NJ, b1758 d1825, m 1776 Rev Ebenezer Bradford - desc/o Thomas Dudley ECD256; DBR(2)110 - desc/o George Wyllys DBR(4)115 - desc/o Mabel Harlakenden DBR(4)118

Elizabeth - of KY, m 1777 Anthony Garrard - desc/o Robert Green CHB286; BCD286

Esther - b1764, m John Pate - desc/o Frances Dungan LDS76

Lieut Col Grief - of VA, b1770, m Rebecca Mayo - desc/o Maj Henry Filmer DBR(5)265

Lucy - of VA, b1717 d1764, m1735 Henry Clay Jr d1764 son of Henry & Mary (Mitchell) Clay - desc/o Maj Henry Filmer ECD(2)134, 136; DBR(1)67; DBR(2)86, 222, 337, 387; DBR(5)355; FFF7

Marston - of VA, b abt 1726, m Eliza Aperson - desc/o Maj Henry Filmer DBR(5)265

Martha - of VA, b1719 d1793, m1741 Charles Clay - desc/o Maj Henry Filmer DBR(3)322; DBR(4)185

Mary - of VA, m1780/1785 George Thomas - desc/o Rev Hawte Wyatt DBR(1)615

Nicholas - of KY, m Elizabeth Price - desc/o Robert Green CHB286; BCD286

Nicholas - of KY, m Lucy____ - desc/o Robert Green CHB286; BCD286

Rebecca - b1712, m Joel Parish - desc/o John Prescott LDS75; RAA125

Robert - of VA, m Eleanor Dunn - the immigrant CHB286; BCD286; sufficient proof of alleged royal ancestry is lacking

Thomas III - of VA, b1665/1669 d1730, m Elizabeth Marston b1672 d1759 dau/o Thomas Marston & Elizabeth (Marvell) Marston - desc/o Maj Henry Filmer ECD(2)133, 136; DBR(1)67; DBR(2)86, 221, 337, 387; DBR(3)322; DBR(4)185; DBR(5)265, 355; FFF7

Willis - of VA, lieutenant in Grayson's regiment, Continental Line, removed to Kentucky where he held many public offices, m1783 Sarah Reed - desc/o George Reade JSW1638 - desc/o Anne Rich GVFTQ(4)508

GREENE Almy - b1728, m1762 Oliver Arnold - desc/o John Greene AMB43; CFA211

Anne - of RI, b1662, m1686 Thomas Greene - desc/o John Greene AMB42; CFA211

Audrey - b1667, m1692 John Spencer - desc/o John Greene AMB42; CFA211

Barlow - of RI, b1695, m1717 Lydia Harding - desc/o John Greene AMB141

Benjamin - of RI, b1702, m1730 Almy Angell - desc/o John Greene AMB42; CFA211

Benjamin - b1764, m1790 Penelope Westcott - desc/o John Greene AMB43; CFA212

Caleb - of RI, b1737 d1813, m1760 Mary Tibbitts - desc/o John Greene AMB43; CFA211, 212

Caleb - b1772 d1853, m(1)1795 Sarah Robinson Greene, m(2) Elizabeth Taylor AMB43; CFA212

Catharine - of RI, b1665, m1688 Charles Holden - desc/o John Greene AMB42; CFA211

Charles - of RI, b1749, m1768 Wait Baily - desc/o Jeremy Clarke

GREENE (cont.)

ECD(2)90

Christopher - of RI, b1740, m1770 Abigail Davis - desc/o John Greene AMB43; CFA212

David - of RI, b1677 d1736, m(1) Mary Slocum, m(2)1706 Sarah Barber - desc/o John Greene AMB324

Deborah - of RI, b1649, m1669 William Torrey - desc/o John Greene AMB43; CFA210

Dinah - b1715, m1735 Randall Rice - desc/o John Greene AMB325

Dorcas - b1769, m Isaac Hall - desc/o John Greene CFA212

Elisha - of RI, b1692 d1767, m Mary Greene - desc/o John Greene AMB141

Elisha - of RI, b1698, m(1)1723 Martha Brown, m(2)1727 Abigail Dexter - desc/o John Greene AMB324

Elizabeth - b1668 d1722, m Francis Reynolds - desc/o John Greene AMB324

Fones - of RI, b1690 d1758, m(1)1711 Dinah Batty, m(2)1712 Rebecca Tibbitts - desc/o John Greene AMB325

Fones - of RI, b1754 d1842, m1810 Patience Cornell - desc/o John Greene AMB325

Gardiner - of MA, b1753 - desc/o John Greene EDV58, 59

Giles - of RI, b1745 d1765, m1764 Phebe Rhodes - desc/o John Greene AMB141

Giles - of RI, b1765, m abt 1784 Rhoda Arnold - desc/o John Greene AMB141

Jabez - of RI, b1673 d1741, m(1)1698 Mary Barton, m(2)1716 Grace Whitman - desc/o John Greene J&K182; AMB324

James - of RI, bp 1626, m(1) abt 1658 Deliverance Potter, m(2)1665 Elizabeth Anthony - desc/o John Greene AMB42, 324; CFA210; THC125

James - of RI, b1659 d1712, m1689 Mary Fones - desc/o John Greene J&K182; AMB324

James - of RI, b1692 d1758, m Roley Carr - desc/o John Greene AMB324

James of RI, b1713 d1792, m1738 Desire Slocum - desc/o William Arnold CHB19; BCD19

James - of RI, b1713, m1740 Patience Waterman - desc/o John Greene AMB325

James - of RI, b1754 d1825, m(1)1782 Rebecca Pitman, m(2) Mercy Waterman - desc/o William Arnold CHB19; BCD19; AMB141

Jeremiah - of RI, b1708, m1749 Anne Wylis - desc/o John Greene AMB324

Job - of RI, b1656 d1745, m1684 Phebe (Williams) Sayles - desc/o John Greene AMB42; CFA211

Job - of RI, b1717 d1798, m1745 Mercy Greene - desc/o John Greene AMB325

Job - of RI, b1746 d1820, m1767 Mary Dexter - desc/o John Greene AMB325

John - of RI & MA, b1597 d1658 surgeon, was one of the twelve original members of the Baptist Church, m1619 Joane Tattersall - the immigrant J&K178; AMB42, 141; CFA210; EDV58, 59;

GREENE (cont.)

CFA210; THC124, 125; sufficient proof of alleged royal ancestry is
   lacking

Maj John - of RI, b1620 d1708 deputy governor of RI, m Ann Almy -
   desc/o John Green J&K178, 179; AMB42; CFA210; THC124

John - of RI, b1685 d1757, m1710 Mary Allen - desc/o John Greene
   AMB324

John - of RI, b1686 d1758, m1719 Mary Greene - desc/o John Greene
   AMB141

John - of RI, b1713 d1792, m1738 Desire Slocum - desc/o John
   Greene AMB141

John - of RI, b1767 d1840, m1789 Lavina Cranston - desc/o John
   Greene AMB325

John - m Azubah Ward - desc/o Anne Marbury GBR234 - desc/o
   Catherine Hamby GBR394

John Coddington - b abt 1751 - desc/o Anne Marbury RAA114

Jone - of RI, bp 1630, m John Hade - desc/o John Greene AMB42;
   CFA210

Joshua - of RI, b1729 d1795, m1753 Mehitable Manton - desc/o John
   Greene AMB43; CFA211

Mary - bp 1633, m(1)1654 James Sweet, m(2) bef 1671 Thomas
   Hungerford - desc/o John Greene AMB42; CFA210; THC125

Mary - b1660, m1685 James Reynolds - desc/o John Greene AMB324

Mary - b1698, m1719 Thomas Fry - desc/o John Greene AMB43;
   CFA211

Mary - of RI, b1703, m1724 Resolved Rhodes - desc/o John Greene
   AMB324

Mary - of RI, b1752 d1851, m1772 George Tillinghast - desc/o John
   Greene AMB325

Mary - b1762, m1791 Richard Burke - desc/o John Greene CFA212

Mercy - b1731, m1750 John Walton - desc/o John Greene AMB43;
   CFA211

Mercy - b1762 d1830, m1801 William Rice - desc/o John Greene
   AMB325

Gen Nathaniel - of RI, officer of the Revolution, father of George Green -
   desc/o John Green J&K182

Peter - of RI, b1621/1622 d1659, m Mary Gorton - desc/o John
   Greene CFA210; THC125

Peter - of RI, b1654 d1723, m1680 Elizabeth Arnold - desc/o John
   Greene AMB42, 141; CFA210

Peter - b1666 d1708, m1695 Elizabeth Slocum - desc/o John Greene
   AMB324

Maj Peter - of RI, b1682 d1767, m1710 Keziah Davis - desc/o John
   Greene AMB141

Philipi(?) - of RI, b1658, m Caleb Carr - desc/o John Greene CFA211

Ray - of RI, b1765 d1849 Attorney General of RI, United States
   senator, m Mary Flagg - desc/o John Green J&K180

Richard - of RI, b1660 d1711, m1692 Eleanor (Williams) Sayles -
   desc/o John Green AMB42; CFA211

Capt Richard - of CT, b1765 d1848, m1803 Sally Webb - desc/o John
   Drake MCB431

GREENE (cont.)

Samuel - of RI, b1671 d1720, m1694 Mary Gorton - desc/o John Green J&K180; AMB42; CFA211

Capt Samuel - of RI, son of William whose dau Patience, m Welcome Arnold - desc/o John Green J&K181

Samuel - of RI, b1700 d1780, m1724 Sarah Coggeshall - desc/o John Greene AMB42; CFA211

Samuel - of RI, b1769 d1861, m(1)1793 Barbara Sheldon, m(2)1820 Mary Lippitt - desc/o John Greene AMB325

Samuel - b1776 d1804, m1696 Elizabeth Stafford - desc/o John Greene AMB43

Sarah - of RI, b1685 d1724, m1706 Stephen Arnold - desc/o John Greene AMB141; CFA212

Sarah - b1664 d1716, m Henry Reynolds - desc/o John Greene AMB324

Sarah - b1774, m(1)1798 William Henry Rice, m(2)1804 Rufus Greene - desc/o John Greene AMB43; CFA212

Stephen - of RI, b1723 d1756, m1753 Mary Hammett - desc/o John Greene AMB141

Stephen - of RI, b1757 d1829, m1782 Sarah Chase - desc/o John Greene AMB325

Susanna - b1688 d1748, m1712 Joseph Hull - desc/o John Greene AMB324

Susanna - b1763, m1780 Caleb Westcott - desc/o John Greene CFA212

Thomas - of RI, bp 1628, m1659 Elizabeth Barton - desc/o John Greene AMB42; CFA210; THC125

Thomas - of RI, b1719 d1806, m(1)1749 Phebe Greene, m(2)1758 Mary Waterman, m(3)1766 Hannah Hill - desc/o John Greene AMB325

William - of RI, b1653 d1723, m1674 Mary Sayles - desc/o John Greene AMB42; CFA210

William - of RI, b1690 d1766, m1712/1713 Sarah Medbury - desc/o William Arnold CHB19; BCD19; AMB141

William - of RI, b1696 d1758 governor of RI for eleven years, m Catherine Greene - desc/o John Greene J&K180; AMB42; CFA211

William - of RI, b1731 d1809 governor of RI 1778/1785, m Catherine Ray - desc/o John Green J&K180

William - of RI, b1748, m Mercy Knight - desc/o John Greene AMB325

GREENMAN Amey - b1727 d1807, m1758 Capt Peter Du Bois - desc/o Jeremy Clarke ECD154; ECD(2)92; DBR(4)733; DBR(5)232

Jeremiah - of MA, m1720 Sarah Blackman - desc/o Jeremy Clarke ECD154; ECD(2)92; DBR(4)733

Margaret - of RI, b1723, m1747 Joseph Greene - desc/o Jeremy Clarke ECD(2)89

GREENOUGH Anna - of MA, b1688, dau/o Capt William Greenough & Elizabeth (Raynsford) Greenough - desc/o Edward Raynsford NE(139)301

Ebenezer - of NH, b1753 d1827, m Mary Flagg - desc/o Dorothy Harlakenden CHB281; BCD281

Edward (recorded as William) - of MA, b1684, son of Capt William

GREENOUGH (cont.)

Greenough & Elizabeth (Raynsford) Greenough, m1703 Rebecca Haggett - desc/o Edward Raynsford NE(139)301

Elizabeth - of MA, b1686, dau/o Capt William Greenough & Elizabeth (Raynsford) Greenough - desc/o Edward Raynsford NE(139)301

Daniel - of MA, abt 1686 d1746, m(1)1722 Elizabeth Hatch - desc/o Dorothy Harlakenden CHB281; BCD281

Newman - of MA, b1681, son of Capt William Greenough & Elizabeth (Raynsford) Greenough - desc/o Edward Raynsford NE(139)301

Symonds - of NH, b1724, m Abigail Chadwick - desc/o Dorothy Harlakenden CHB281; BCD281

GREENWOOD Nathaniel - of MA 1654, b1631 - the immigrant EDV100; sufficient proof of alleged royal ancestry is lacking

Samuel - of MA - desc/o Nathaniel Greenwood EDV100

GREGORY Christine - of VA, m Samuel Meredith - desc/o Col/Gov John West SVF(2)400

Ebenezer - of CT, b1683 d1761, m Mary Fitch - desc/o Henry Gregory AFA222

Elizabeth - m Reuben Thornton - desc/o Henry Gregory NFA71

Elizabeth - b1759 d1841, m1775 Daniel Gregory - desc/o Henry Gregory FFF127

Elnathan - b1734/1735 d1816, m1756/1757 Hannah Whitney - desc/o Henry Gregory FFF127

Ephraim Sanford - of CT, b1708 d1761/1762, m Elizabeth Mix - desc/o Henry Gregory THC126

Ezekeel Sanford - of CT, b1668, m1696 Rebecca Gregory - desc/o Henry Gregory THC126

Frances - of VA, m Mr William Phillips - desc/o Col/Gov John West SVF(2)400

Frances - of VA, d1794, m1736 Col Francis Thornton III - desc/o Col George Reade DBR(2)633; DBR(4)847; DBR(5)159, 210, 547, 555, 567, 571; NFA71

Henry - of MA, d1655 - the immigrant AFA222; FFF126; THC126; EO2(2)124/127 sufficient proof of alleged royal ancestry is lacking

Isaac - b1729, m Hannah Nash - desc/o Margaret Wyatt DBR(3)126

Isaac II - bp 1756, m1775 Sarah St John - desc/o Margaret Wyatt DBR(3)126

Isaiah Hungerford - of CT, b1756 d1833, m Esther Mead - desc/o Esther Mead THC126

John - of CT, b1612/1615 d1689, m Sarah____ - desc/o Henry Gregory AFA222; FFF126; THC126

John - of CT, b1668/1669 d1746 - desc/o Henry Gregory FFF127

John - of CT, b1695/1697 d1764/1765, m Hannah Cornell - desc/o Henry Gregory FFF127

Judah - of CT, b abt 1643/1644 d1730/1733, m1664 Hannah Hoyt - desc/o Henry Gregory FFF127; THC126

Judah or Jochin - of CT, m Sarah Burt - desc/o Henry Gregory THC126

Mildred - of VA, m1740 Col John Thornton - desc/o Col George Reade DBR(3)570; NFA71

Molly - of VA, b1769 Herbert Claiborne of Dinwiddie - desc/o Col/Gov

GREGORY (cont.)

    John West SVF(2)401

Nathan - of CT, d1754, m Sarah St John - desc/o Henry Gregory
AFA222

Nathaniel - of VA, b1763, m Mary Ann Bickerley - desc/o Col/Gov
John West DBR(2)371, DBR(3)165; SVF(2)401

Noah - of NY, b1760, m Phebe Higgins - desc/o Henry Gregory AFA222

Richard - of VA, b1758 d1844, m1777 Mary Ward b1749 d1787 dau/o
Col Seth Ward & wid/o William Brodnax, m(2)1787 Elizabeth
Wilkerson dau/o Nathaniel Wilkerson of Henrico Co - desc/o
Col/Gov John West SVF(2)401

Roger Sr - of VA, b1729 d1803 justice, member of the vestry &
member of the House of Delegates, sheriff, m(1)1756 (his cousin)
Mary Cole Claiborne b abt 1730 d1771 dau/o Nathaniel Claiborne
of King William Co & Jane Cole, m(2)1776 Lunenburg Co, Frances
Garland d1816 wid/o Thomas Loury - desc/o Col/Gov John West
DBR(3)165, 166, 167, 329, 600; SVF(2)400

Roger - of VA, b1761, m Sarah____ - desc/o Col/Gov John West
SVF(2)401

Samuel - of CT, b1676, m____ Wheeler - desc/o Henry Gregory
THC126

Stephen Mead - of CT, b1728 d1806, m1751 Rachel Sanford - desc/o
Henry Gregory THC126

Thomas - of CT - desc/o Henry Gregory AFA222

West - of VA, m Susanna West (first cousin) - desc/o Col/Gov John
West SVF(2)400

William - of VA, b1767, m Marion Ellett - desc/o Col/Gov John West
SVF(2)401

William - of MA, d1740 - the immigrant EDV131; sufficient proof of
alleged royal ancestry is lacking

GRIFFITH Henry - of MD, b1720 d1794, m(2)1751 Ruth Hammond -
desc/o Matthew Arundel-Howard JSW1770/1771 & 1866

Col Henry - b1745 d1809, m Sarah Davis - desc/o Anne Lovelace
DBR(1)652

Joshua - of KY, b1764 d1845, m1783 Elizabeth Ridgely - desc/o
Matthew Arundel-Howard JSW1771

Thomas - d1838, m1811 Harriet Worthington Simpson - desc/o Anne
Lovelace DBR(1)652

GRIGG Ursula - of VA, b abt 1753 d1814 Anderson Co, SC, m1779 John
Hall b Virginia d1814 Anderson Co, SC - desc/o Lady Diana
Skipwith HSF(5)259

GRISWOLD (GRISWALD) Bathsheba - of CT, b1682, m Daniel Clark -
desc/o Edward Griswold CRL(1)160

Benjamin - of CT, b1690, m1718 Ann Norton - desc/o Edward
Griswold CRL(1)160

Daniel - of CT, b1696 d1737, m Jerusha Stevens - desc/o Edward
Griswold BLG2722; CRL(1)160

Daniel B - of CT, b1722, m Mary Bushnell - desc/o Edward Griswold
BLG2722

Deborah - of CT, bp 1646 d1719, m Samuel Buell - desc/o Edward
Griswold LDS61; CRL(1)159; THC130

GRISWOLD (GRISWALD) (cont.)

Edward - of CT, b1607 d1691, m(1)1630 Margaret Hicks - the
immigrant LDS45, 61; 89, 109; BLG2721; CRL(1)158; THC129,
130; TAG(39)176/181 royal descent does not appear to be fully
proved & further confirmatory evidence is sought.

Edward - of CT, b1758 d1843, m Asenath Hurd - desc/o Edward
Griswold BLG2722

Elizabeth - of CT, b1694 d bef 1736, m1747 John Raymond - desc/o
Judge Simon Lynde CHB312; BCD312

Elizabeth - of CT, b1717/1718 d1788, m1742 Haynes Woodbridge -
desc/o DBR(4)147

Francis - chr 1635, m Mary Tracy - the immigrant LDS66; royal
ancestry unproven

Francis - of CT - desc/o Edward Griswold BLG2721

George - of CT, b1633 d1704, m Mary Holcomb - desc/o Edward
Griswold CRL(1)159; THC130

Giles - of CT, b1723 d1804, m1746 Mary Chatfield - desc/o Alice
Freeman DBR(4)483

Hannah - or Ann - bp 1642, m Jonah or Jonas Westover - desc/o
Edward Griswold LDS45, 89, 199

Hannah - of CT, b1729 d1779, m1747 John Raymond - desc/o Judge
Simon Lynde CHB312

John - of CT, b1652 d1717, m Bathsheba____ - desc/o Edward
Griswold BLG2722; CRL(1)159

John - b1703, m Susannah Sanders - desc/o Francis Griswold LDS66

John - of CT, b1719 d1777, m Elizabeth____ - CRL(1)160

John - b1730, m(1)Ruth Hewitt - desc/o Francis Griswold LDS66

John of CT, b1752 d1812, m Sarah Johnson - desc/o John Drake
CHB106; BCD106

Joseph - of CT, m Mary Gaylord - desc/o Edward Griswold BLG2721

Joseph - of CT, bp 1647 d1738, m1670 Abigail Gaylord - desc/o
Edward Griswold CRL(1)159; THC130

Lucretia - b1731, m1747/1748 Col Jonathan Latimer - desc/o Francis
Willoughby DBR(2)856; DBR(3)568

Lucy - of CT, b1721 d abt 1811, m Ebenezer Stevens - desc/o Edward
Griswold CRL(1)160

Mary - of CT, bp 1644, m1661 Timothy Phelps - desc/o Edward
Griswold CRL(1)159; THC130

Mary - of CT, b1747 d1811, m1767 Josiah Pelton - desc/o Alice
Freeman DBR(4)483

Matthew - the immigrant 1639 EDV27; royal ancestry not proven

Millicent - of CT, b1770 d1853, m1787 John Smith - desc/o Mary
Launce DBR(2)552; DBR(3)121

Roger - of CT, m Fanny Rogers, governor of CT - desc/o John Drake
J&K309; BCD355

Ruth - b1757, m(1) Elias Lyman - desc/o Francis Griswold LDS66

Samuel - b1665, m(1) Susannah Huntington - desc/o Francis Griswold
LDS66

Samuel - of CT, b1685 d1736, m(2)1713 Elizabeth Gaylord - desc/o
John Drake DBR(4)147 - desc/o Edward Griswold CRL(1)160

Sarah - of CT, b1638, m(1)1650 Samuel Phelps, m(2)1670 Nathaniel

GRISWOLD (GRISWALD) (cont.)

Pinney - desc/o Edward Griswold CRL(1)159; THC130

Ursula - of CT, b1775 d1811, m Richard McCurdy - desc/o John Drake CHB106; BCD106

Walter - of CT, b1700, m____ Wright - desc/o Edward Griswold CRL(1)160

GROSS Rebecca Hines - b1712 - desc/o Mary Gye RAA115

GROSVENOR Aaron - of MA, b1767 doctor of Pelham, MA, m1791 Sally French - desc/o Rev Peter Bulkeley TAG(36)149

Hannah - of MA, b1769 d1843 at Petersham, m (intention, 18 Jun 1825) Deacon Joel Goddard d1843 age 80 - desc/o Rev Peter Bulkeley TAG(36)149

Lucy - of MA, b1773, m1796 Ithiel Cargill - desc/o Rev Peter Bulkeley TAG(36)149

GROUT Phoebe - m Jacob Will III - desc/o Gov Thomas Dudley GBR250

GRUBB Adam - of DE, b1724, m Mary Russell - desc/o John Grubb CRL(2)226; CRL(4)406

Charity - of DE, m Richard Beeson - desc/o John Grubb CRL(2)225; CRL(4)405

Emanuel - of DE, b1682 d1767, m1708 Ann Hedge Cock (Koch) - desc/o John Grubb CRL(2)225; CRL(4)405

George - of DE, d1791, m Susanna Collett - desc/o John Grubb CRL(2)227 - desc/o John Dutton CRL(2)235

Hannah - of DE, b1728, m(1)1746 Richard Flower, m(2) John Wall - desc/o John Grubb CRL(2)226; CRL(4)406

John - of PA & DE, b1652 d1708, m abt 1681 Frances Vane - the immigrant CRL(2)224, 225; CRL(4)405; sufficient proof of alleged royal ancestry is lacking

John - of DE, b1684 d1758, m Rachel Buckley - desc/o John Grubb CRL(2)226; CRL(4)405

Joseph - of DE, d1747, m____ - desc/o John Grubb CRL(2)225

Margaret - of DE, b abt 1771 d1864, m Peter Rambo - desc/o John Grubb CRL(2)227 - desc/o John Dutton CRL(2)235

Mary - of DE, b1715, m Robert Molder - desc/o John Grubb CRL(2)226; CRL(4)406

Nathaniel - of DE, d1760, m1725 Ann Moore - desc/o John Grubb CRL(2)226; CRL(4)405

Peter - of DE, b1702 d1754, m(1)1732 Martha (Bates) Wall, m(2)1741/ 1742 Hannah Mendenhall - desc/o John Grubb CRL(2)226; CRL(4)405

Phebe - of DE, d1769, m(1) Richard Buffington Jr, m(2)1752 Simon Hadley - desc/o John Grubb CRL(2)225; CRL(4)405

Rachel - of DE, b1726, m John Pedrick - desc/o John Grubb CRL(2)226; CRL(4)406

Richard - of DE, b1720 d1770, m1745 Mary Dutton - desc/o John Grubb CRL(2)227

Samuel - of DE, b1722 d1769, m(1)1746 Rebecca Hewes, m(2)1752 Lydia Baker - desc/o John Grubb CRL(2)226; CRL(4)406

Samuel - of DE, d1760, m1745 Mary Bellerby - desc/o John Grubb CRL(2)226; CRL(4)405

William - of DE, b1713 d1775, m1738/1739 Lydia Huse or Hewes -

GRUBB (cont.)
    desc/o John Grubb CRL(2)226; CRL(4)406

GRYMES Benjamin - of VA, b1750, m1773 Sarah Robinson - desc/o Col William Randolph DBR(3)345

    Bettie Jane - of VA, b1765 d1852, m abt 1781 Rev William Moore - desc/o Col William Randolph DBR(2)672

    Rev Charles - of VA, m Frances Jenings dau/o governor Edmund Jenings & Frances (Corbin) Jenings - desc/o Col George Reade DBR(2)830; PFA Apx D #1

    Lucy - of VA, m Henry Lee - desc/o Col George Reade PFA Apx D #1

    Mary - of VA, b1753 d1739, m1777 Rev Walker Maury of Norfolk, VA b1752 d1788 son of Rev James Murrey of Albemarle Co, VA - desc/o Henry Isham CHB534 - desc/o Col William Randolph PVF132

    Sarah - of VA, m Robert Taliaferro - desc/o Col George Reade DBR(2)830

GUERARD Mary Lucia - of SC, m Edward Lowndes, Esq - desc/o Stephen Bull SCG(1)220

GUNN Asahel - b1757 - desc/o Richard Belding RAA68
    Asahel - b1730 - desc/o Richard Belding RAA68

GURDON Muriel - of MA, b1613 d1694, dau/o Brampton Gurdon & Muriel Sedley, m1633 Maj Richard Saltonstall b abt 1610 d1694 of MA, colonial official - the immigrant FLW8; ECD175, 177, 180; ECD(2)234; MCD228; MCS14; DBR(1)574, 699; DBR(2)766; DBR(3)480, 482; DBR(5)605; NE(95)72; GBR146

GWINNETT Button - of GA, b abt 1735 d1777, governor of Georgia, merchant, planter, signer of the Declaration of Independence, son of Samuel Gwinnett & Anne Emes, m Anne Bourne - the immigrant GBR303

GWYNN (or GWYNNE) Humphrey - of VA, b1727 d1794 - desc/o Col George Reade HSF(2)194

    Lucy - of VA, m Thomas Reade - desc/o Col William Bernard CHB38; MCD161; BCD38; APP118

    Martha - of VA, b1766, m(?) Robert Graham - desc/o Major Robert Peyton VG469

    Thomas Peyton - of VA, b1762 d bef 1810, m Ann____ & had issue - desc/o Major Robert Peyton VG469

GYE Mary - of MA 1630, b abt 1580 dau/o Robert Guy & Grace Dowrish, m1600 Ilsington, Devon, Rev John Maverick bp 1578 Awliscombe, Devon d1635/1636 Dorchester, MA, was chosed one of the teachers of the Puritan church that was organized at Plymouth in the Mary & John, one of the ships of Winthrop's fleet, with the colonists who arrived in New England 30 May 1630 & founded the town of Dorchester, MA, took the oath as freeman 1631 & was minister at Dorchester until his death, son of Peter Maverick & Dorothy Tucke - the immigrant FLW232; ECD(3)174, 177; DBR(5)736; RAA115; GBR295 some aspect of royal descent merits further study, alternate descent noted & referenced but not outlined; NE(96)232/241, 358/366, (97)56/63, (115)248/253, (122)282/283

– H –

HACK Anne - of VA, b abt 1695 d 1770, m(1) aft 1711 Capt Richard
Drummond, m(2) Alexander Buncle - desc/o Richard Wright
ECD(3)286

HACKBURNE (HAIGHBURNE) Elizabeth - of MA, b1635 d1677, m Dr
John Chickering - desc/o Katharine Deighton JSW1826;
DBR(4)729

Hannah - b1642 - desc/o John Deighton RAA86

HADDEN Joseph - of NJ, b1742 d1833, m1774/1775 Martha Oliver -
desc/o Edward FitzRandolph ECD(2)142; DBR(4)477

HAINES Sara - b1737 d1820, m1755 Caleb Newbold - desc/o Peter
Wright DBR(4)98

HALEY Polly - b1774 d1862, m1792 Thomas Anderson - desc/o Rev
Hawte Wyatt DBR(1)511

Sarah - of ME, bp 1764, m David Bryant - desc/o Judith Lewis
DBR(2)173

HALIBURTON Anna - of CT, m Henry McClintock - desc/o Susan Fienes
CHB528

HALL Caleb - of MA, b1700 Attleboro d1791 Peekskill, New York, m1721
Attleboro, Jean (or Jane) Daggett b1700 d1778 Peekskill, New York
dau/o John & Sarah (Pease ?) & had issue at least 12 children -
desc/o Nathaniel Burrough RAA76; TAG(48)144

Christopher - b1723 - desc/o George Burroughs RAA76

Deborah - of MA, b1756 at Sutton d1841 at Petersham, m1776 Rev
Daniel Grosvenor b1750 at Pomfret, CT d1834 at Petersham son of
Ebenezer Grosvenor & Luce Cheney - desc/o Rev Peter Bulkeley
TAG(36)150

Elizabeth Hugh - of VA, b1748 d1782, m1767 Charles Hines - desc/o
Lieut Col Walter Aston ECD(3)9

Hannah - of MA, b1740 at Sutton d1834 at Reading, m1766 Capt Asa
Grosvenor b1745 at Pomfret, CT d1834 at Reading, MA son of
Ebenezer Grosvenor & Luce Cheney - desc/o Rev Peter Bulkeley
TAG(36)149

Hannah - of MA, m Nath'l Bassett - desc/o Herbert Pelham MCD321

Hugh - of VA, b abt 1730 d abt 1771, m abt 1748 Mary Dixon - desc/o
Lieut Col Walter Aston ECD(3)8

Dr Jonathan - of MA, b1754 d1815, m1781 Bathsheba Mumford -
desc/o Rev Peter Bulkeley ECD(3)63

Joseph Jr - of MA - desc/o Herbert Pelham MCD321

Joshua - of MA, b1702 Attleboro d1791 Plainfield, CT, m Abigail
(McIntyre ?). He resided for a few years in Cumberland, Rhode
Island before moving to Plainfield, where he left many descendants
- desc/o Nathaniel Burrough TAG(48)144

Josiah - of MA, b abt 1675, m1712 Mary Woodbury - desc/o Gov
Thomas Dudley DBR(1)63

Judith - m Ephraim Farnum - desc/o Ursula Scott JSW1871

Laban - b1755 - desc/o George Burroughs RAA76

Mary - of CT, b1742 d1833, m1765 Judge Eliphalet Terry - desc/o
Richard Lyman CHB149; MCD249; BCD149

HALL (cont.)

Mary Teresa - of MD, b1760 d1814, m1776 Dr Thomas Bennett Wilson - desc/o Dudley Diggs ECD(3)120; DBR(5)986

Mary Woodbury - of NH, b1717 d1789, m John Langdon - desc/o Gov Thomas Dudley DBR(1)63

Patience - of RI & MA, b Portsmouth 1753 d1825, m1772/1773 Job Lawton b Portsmouth 1753 d1777 son of George Lawton - desc/o Jeremy Clarke ECD253 - desc/o Katherine Marbury DBR(1)82

Dr Robert - of VA & NC, d abt 1780/1786, a surgeon in 3rd North Carolina Infantry Regiment, son of William & Susanna (Poythress) Hall, m abt 1742 Anne Leary, dau/o Cornelius Leary - desc/o Capt Henry Batte ECD110; ECD(2)35; DBR(1)367; DBR(2)438, 470, 620; DBR(3)591

Sicily (or Cecily) Ann Hall - of VA, m abt 1772 John Agee b Buckingham Co abt 1749 d abt 1810, son of James Agee, a Revolutionary soldier - desc/o Capt Henry Batte ECD110; ECD(2)35; DBR(1)367; DBR(2)438, 470, 620; DBR(3)591

Tabitha - b1734, m John Hanks - desc/o William Sargent LDS41; RAA129

HALLETT Sarah - of MA, b1763 d1793, m1791 Barnabas Hallett - desc/o Edward Southworth DBR(5)834

HALLOCK Henry - m 1780 Mary Jayne - desc/o Peter Wright DBR(3)302

HALSNODE Margaret - of NJ by 1679, dau/o John & Margaret (Ladd) Halsnode, m John Denn(e) - the immigrant GBR464

HAMBY C(K)atherine - of MA, bp 1615 d bet 1649/1651 dau/o Robert Hamby & Elizabeth Arnold, m1636 Edward Hutchinson bp 1613 d1675 son of William Hutchinson & Anne Marbury - the immigrant GBR394; NE(141)96, 97, (145)99/121, 258/268; FLW187

HAMILTON Alexander - of MD, b1712 d1756 physician & historian, son of William Hamilton, professor of divinity and principal University of Edinburgh & Mary Robertson, m Margaret Dulany - the immigrant GBR96

Alexander - of NY, b1755/1757 d1804 aid & private secretary to General Washington & has been called the leading spirit of the Continental Congress, of which, he was a member from New York 1787, 1st United States secretary of the treasury, son of James Hamilton of Nevis, British West Indies & Mrs Rachel Faucette Levine, m Elizabeth Schuyler - the immigrant GBR68; NYGBR(20)#2p62/64, (22)#1p57, (79)#1p41/42 - desc/o James Hamilton J&K152

James - of NY, father of Alexander Hamilton - the immigrant J&K152; GBR lists his son as the immigrant

HAMLIN Barnabas - b1747, m Mary Bassett - desc/o Mary Dunham LDS48

Elkanah - b1685, m Abigail Hamblin or Hamblen - desc/o Mary Dunham LDS48

Joseph - of MA, b1702 d1777, m1726/1727 Elizabeth Mathews - desc/o Edward Southworth DBR(5)834

Rebecca - b1694, m Judah Berry - desc/o Richard Sears LDS14

Sarah - of MA, b1733, m1754 Thomas Hallett - desc/o Edward Southworth DBR(5)834

HAMLIN (cont.)

Sylvanus - b1712, m Dorcas Fish - desc/o Mary Dunham LDS48

HAMMERSLEY William - of NY 1716 - the immigrant EDV127; sufficient proof of alleged royal ancestry is lacking

HANCOCK Asa - b1753 - desc/o William Goddard RAA99

Benjamin - b1728 - desc/o William Goddard RAA99

Elizabeth - of VA, m John Sutton - desc/o Lieut Col Thomas Lygon APP359

Johan - of VA, b1680, m1700 Samuel Hancock d1761 of Henrico Co, carpenter - desc/o Lieut Col Thomas Lygon DBR(5)767; GVFWM(3)504; APP359

John - b1688, m(1) Anna Webb - desc/o John Leonard LDS49

Margaret - of NJ, b abt 1684, m1705 Thomas Garwood d1752 - desc/o Elizabeth Denne ECD166; DBR(1)6; DBR(4)597; RAA101

Mary - of VA, m1708 John Hatcher of Henrico Co & Edgecombe Co, North Carolina, son of Edward Hatcher - desc/o Lieut Col Thomas Lygon APP358, 359

Phoebe - of VA, m(1) Thomas Bailey of Varina Parish in Henrico Co d1723, m(2) Nicholas Giles - desc/o Lieut Col Thomas Lygon APP359

Richard - b 1650, m(2) Elizabeth Denne - the immigrant RAA1; royalty not proven

Robert - of VA, living 1729, m1712/1713 Margaret____ - desc/o Lieut Col Thomas Lygon APP358

Samuel - of VA, b1701 d1760 - desc/o Lieut Col Thomas Lygon DBR(5)767

Sarah - of VA, m1688/1689 Arthur Moseley Jr b1655 of Henrico Co - desc/o Lieut Col Thomas Lygon APP358

Simon - of VA, b1720 d1790/1791, m Jane Flournoy - desc/o Lieut Col Thomas Lygon DBR(5)767

Susan - of VA, m Samuel Watkins - desc/o Lieut Col Walter Aston CHB537

Thomas - b1727, m Jemima Wright - desc/o John Leonard LDS49

Thomas - b1763, m Amy Ward - desc/o John Leonard LDS49

William - of VA, d1837, m(2) Mrs Mary Eliza (Fisher) Emmerson - desc/o Lieut Col Thomas Lygon DBR(5)767

HANK Jane - of PA, m John Roberts - desc/o Cadwalader Evans MCD187

HANKS Anna - b1756, m Micah Eldredge - desc/o William Sargent LDS41, RAA129

Elijah - b1761 - desc/o William Sargent RAA129

John Jr - of PA & VA, father of Joseph Hanks - desc/o Cadwallader Evans J&K137

Joseph - of KY, m Nancy Shipley & anc/o Pres Abraham Lincoln - desc/o Cadwallader Evans J&K137

HANSON Ezekiel - of MI, b1767 d1848, m1794 Mary Plumer - desc/o Elder William Wentworth DBR(1)807; DBR(3)231

HARDEE Martha - of NC, m Lieut Col William Alston - desc/o Col John Alston DBR(2)345

HARDIN Rosannah - b1760 - desc/o James Neale RAA117

HARDING Lucretia - d1814, m Asa Williams Stoddard - desc/o Alice Freeman DBR(5)797

HARDING (cont.)

Stephen - b1748/1749, m(1) Prudence Gustin - desc/o Frances Dungan LDS11

HARLAKENDEN Dorothy - of MA 1637, bp 1596 d1636, m1617 Samuel Symonds - the immigrant CHB279; MCS64; BCD279, 280; DBR(1)273; royal descent not proven

Elizabeth - of MA, b1636 - desc/o Col Roger Harlakenden MCS72

Mabel - of MA, bp 1614 Earl's Colne Priory, Essex d1655 dau/o Richard Harlakenden & Margaret Huberd, m(1) abt 1626 Col John Haynes b abt 1594 England d1653/1654 Hartford, CT, governor of MA 1635/1636, 1st governor of CT 1639 & governor or deputy-governor thereafter until his death, m(2)1654 Samuel Eaton - the immigrant J&K252; CHB267, 268; MCB236, 301, 354, 403, 404, 411; MCD229; MCS64; BCD267; FLW72; DBR(4)118; RAA102; TAG(14)208/213; GBR424; NE(15)327/329, (120)243/247; EO2(2)210/212, 215/219

Margaret - of MA, b1638 - desc/o Col Roger Harlakenden MCS72

Richard - of CT & MA, b abt 1565 d1631, m Margaret Hubbart dau/o Edward Hubbart (Hobart) - the immigrant RAA1, 102; TAG(14)208/213; EO2(2)210/212, 215/219; GBR lists their son Col Roger the immigrant

Col Roger - of MA, bp 1611 d1638 son of Richard Harlakenden & Margaret Huberd, m(1) Emlin___ d1634, m(2)1635 Elizabeth Bossevile (Boseveile) b abt 1617 dau/o Godfrey Bosseville of Gunthwayte, York - the immigrant MCS64, 73; EDV122; GBR424; TAG(14)208/213; NE(15)327/329, (120)243/247; EO2(2)210/212, 215/219

HARLESTON Ann - of SC, b1719 d1740, m1757 Jonathan Scott - desc/o John Harleston SCG(2)300

Edward - of SC, b1722 d1775 elected a delegate to the Second Provincial Congress 1775, m Miss___Moore of Cape Fear, North Carolina - desc/o John Harleston SCG(2)285

Edward - of SC, b1761 d1825, m1787 Annabella Moultrie dau/o James Moultrie, British lieutenant-governor & chief justice of East Florida - desc/o John Harleston SCG(2)291

Elizabeth - of SC, dau/o John Harleston & Elizabeth___, m Elias Ball - desc/o John Harleston GBR119

Elizabeth - of SC, m Thomas Corbett Jr & had issue - desc/o John Harleston SCG(2)297

Elizabeth Ann - of SC, d1768, m1759 Benjamin Smith - desc/o John Harleston SCG(2)297

Isaac Child - of SC, b1745 member of the First Provincial Congress & was elected a captain by ballot of the Provincial Congress of South Carolina, served in the Revolutionary War - desc/o John Harleston SCG(2)268

Jane - of SC, m Edward Rutledge - desc/o John Harleston SCG(2)297

John - of SC, d1738 justice of the peace & was one of the trustees of the Free School at Childsberry son of John Harleston & Elizabeth___, m1707 Elizabeth Willis - the immigrant GBR119; SCG(2)279/303

John - of SC, b1708 d1767 generally designated as Captain Harleston,

HARLESTON (cont.)

a planter and an owner of the greatest portion of Harleston a suburb of Charles Town, m1740 Hannah Child - desc/o John Harleston SCG(2)285

John Sr - of SC, b abt 1733 colonel of militia of South Carolina during the Revolutionary War under Moultrie he served at the siege of Charles Town, m1766 Elizabeth Faucheraud - desc/o John Harleston SCG(2)296

John - of SC, b abt 1756 d abt 1781 served in the Revolutionary War, m abt 1777 Elizabeth Lynch dau/o Thomas Lynch Sr - desc/o John Harleston SCG(2)301

Margaret - of SC, b1749 d1819, m1769 Thomas Corbett, merchant of Charleston - desc/o John Harleston SCG(2)289

Nicholas - of SC, b1710 d1768 captain in the Berkeley Regiment of foot, m(1)1732 Sarah Child, m(2)1756 Ann Ashby - desc/o John Harleston SCG(2)285, 296

Nicholas - of SC, b1768 d1832, m1794 Ann Olney Somers & had issue - desc/o John Harleston SCG(2)297

Sarah - of SC, m Dr William Reid - desc/o John Harleston SCG(2)297

William - of SC, b1757 d1816 served in the Revolution & was in charge of the plantation at an early age, m(1) ____Pinckney, m(2) Sarah Quash - desc/o John Harleston SCG(2)290

HARMANSON Catherine - of VA, m(1) John Shepherd d1740, m(2) Richard Drummond Jr d1751, m(3)1756 Ralph Justice d1759 - desc/o Col Nathaniel Littleton APP467

Elishe - of VA, m(1)1740 George Mason Kendall d1755, son of William Kendall & Sorrowful Margaret Custis, m(2) Patrick Harmanson d1775 - desc/o Col Nathaniel Littleton APP467

Elizabeth - of VA, m(1)1741 John Kendall, justice of Northampton Co, m(2)1766 Major John Repass, justice of Northampton Co - desc/o Col Nathanial Littleton APP467

Esther - of VA, m(1) ____Burton, m(2)1746 John Respass - desc/o Col Nathaniel Littleton APP467

Gertrude - of VA, m Severn Eyre - desc/o Col Nathaniel Littleton NE(41)364/368

Sophia - of VA, m1721 William Tazewell - desc/o Col Nathaniel Littleton NE(41)364/368

HARMAR Gen Josiah - of PA - desc/o John Bevan Sr MCD165

Rachel - of PA, d1754, m William Harmar - desc/o John Bevan Sr MCD165

HARRINGTON Benjamin (Harrington or Hearnden) - b abt 1624, m Elizabeth White - the immigrant LDS18, 71; sufficient proof of alleged royal ancestry is lacking

Daniel - b abt 1748, m Sarah Carpenter - desc/o Benjamin Harrington LDS18

Elizabeth - b abt 1650, m Stephen Northrop - desc/o Benjamin Harrington LDS71

John - b1651, m Hannah Winter - desc/o Robert Harrington LDS82

John - b1662, m Lydia Cranston - desc/o Benjamin Harrington LDS18

Jonathan - b1704, m Sarah Foster - desc/o Benjamin Harrington LDS18

HARRINGTON (cont.)
>Patience - chr 1697, m David Stowell - desc/o Robert Harrington
>LDS82
>Robert - b1616, m Susannah George - the immigrant LDS17; royalty
>not proven
>Sarah - b1671, m Joseph Winship - desc/o Robert Harrington LDS17
>Susanna - b1688, m Joshua Kendall - desc/o Robert Harrington
>LDS85
>Thomas - b1665, m Rebecca Bemis - desc/o Robert Harrington LDS85

HARRIS Abigail - of NJ, b1720, m Daniel Alderman b1711 d1785 -
>desc/o Olive Ingoldsby DBR(2)655; DBR(3)630
>Agnes - of CT, b1604/1605 d soon aft 1680 dau/o Bartholomew
>Harris & Elizabeth Collamore, m(1) abt 1634 William Spencer bp
>1601 d1640 son of Gerard & Alice (Whitbread) Spencer, m(2)1645
>William Edwards b1618 - the immigrant FLW211; RAA131;
>GBR445; TAG (63)33/45
>Benjamin - of NC, d1832, m1792 - desc/o Mary Claiborne ECD(3)25
>Christopher Sr - of VA, b1725 d1794, m(1)1745 Mary Dabney - desc/o
>Mary Claiborne ECD(3)27 - desc/o Thomas Harris LDS87;
>DBR(5)336, 340 - desc/o John Boteler RAA71 - desc/o William
>Harris RAA102
>Claiborne - of VA, d1810, m Judith____ - desc/o Mary Claiborne
>ECD(3)24
>Edward - of VA, b1663 d1734, m1685 Mary Turner - desc/o John
>Harris DBR(4)421
>Edward Lanier - of VA, b1769 d1831, m(2)1816 Julia Carden - desc/o
>John Harris DBR(4)421
>Ephraim - of NJ, b1732 d1794, m(1)1755 Jane Pierson - desc/o Olive
>Ingoldsby DBR(2)704; DBR(3)124
>Henry - of VA, b1730 d1773, m Elizabeth Avery - desc/o Col Robert
>Carter DBR(5)346
>Jane - of NJ, b1768 d1803, m(1) Henry Westcott, m(2) Isaac Sheppard
>- desc/o Olive Ingoldsby DBR(2)704; DBR(3)124
>John - of VA, b1588/1589 d bef 1638, m Dorothy____ - the immigrant
>DBR(3)382; DBR(4)418, 636, 637; royal descent not sufficiently
>proven
>Jonathan - of NJ, b1727 d1802, m(2) Martha____ b1736 d1815 -
>desc/o Olive Ingoldsby DBR(2)292
>Jonathan Jr - of NJ, b1763 d1837, m Catherine Casto b1758 d1834 -
>desc/o Olive Ingoldsby DBR(2)292
>Lucy - of VA, b1734, m William Shelton - desc/o Capt Thomas Harris
>ECD(2)159
>Mary - of VA, b1625 d1704, m(2)1648/1650 Col Thomas Ligon -
>desc/o Capt Thomas Harris ECD(2)158; RAA102
>Mary - of VA, m(2) Matthew Swan - desc/o John Harris DBR(4)637
>Mourning - of VA, b1754, m Foster Jones - desc/o Mary Claiborne
>ECD(3)27; DBR(5)336, 340
>Nathan - of VA, b1716 d1793, m1737 Catherine Walton - desc/o John
>Harris DBR(4)421
>Nathan - b1758 - desc/o Edward Rainsford RAA126
>Nathaniel - of NJ, b1693 d1775, m(1) Miriam Brooks b1698 d1772,

HARRIS (cont.)

m(2) Elizabeth ____ d1773 - desc/o Olive Ingoldsby DBR(2)291, 655; DBR(3)630

Paletea - of VA, b abt 1758 d1821, m George Cabiness - desc/o Col Robert Carter DBR(5)346

Rachel - b1744, m William Dalton - desc/o Capt Thomas Harris LDS107; RAA102 - desc/o John Boteler RAA71

Robert - of VA - desc/o John Harris DBR(4)637 - desc/o John Boteler RAA71

Maj Robert - of VA b1615, m abt 1650 Mary Claiborne - desc/o Capt Thomas Harris ECD(2)159; LDS87, 107; DBR(5)336; RAA102

Maj Robert - of VA, b1696 d abt 1765, m abt 1720 Mourning Glenn - desc/o Capt Thomas Harris ECD(2)159; ECD(3)27; LDS87, 107; DBR(3)718; DBR(5)336, 340 - desc/o John Boteler RAA71 - desc/o William Harris RAA102

Robert - of VA, b1741, m Lucretia Brown - desc/o Elizabeth Boteler DBR(3)718

Robert II - of VA, b1761/1763, m Martha____ - desc/o Elizabeth Boteler DBR(3)718

Samuel - b1696 - desc/o Olive Ingoldsby RAA75

Sarah - b1747, m James Martin - desc/o Thomas Harris LDS87 - desc/o John Boteler RAA71 - desc/o William Harris RAA102

Silas - b1760 - desc/o Olive Ingoldsby RAA75

Silas - of ME, b1766 d1844, m1790 Mercy Haskell - desc/o Mary Launce CHB447; MCD291

Silas - b abt 1737 - desc/o Olive Ingoldsby RAA75

Tabitha - of VA, b1757 d1806, m1783 Lieut John Peyton Powell - desc/o Capt Henry Isham DBR(1)592

Capt Thomas - b1587 d1611, m(1) Adria Gurganey - the immigrant RAA102; LDS87; ECD(2)157, 159; DBR(3)248; DBR(4)439; DBR(5)1059; royal descent not proven

Thomas - of VA, b abt 1614 d1672, m Alice West - desc/o John Harris DBR(4)418, 419

Thomas - of VA, b1636 d1688, m Ann____ - desc/o John Harris DBR(4)421

Thomas - of VA, b abt 1665 d1725, m abt 1700 Mary Giles - desc/o Mary Claiborne ECD(3)24

Thomas II - of NJ, b1689 d1749, m Anna____ - desc/o Olive Ingoldsby DBR(2)704; DBR(3)124

Thomas III - of NJ, b1710 d1783, m(1) Sarah Dayton - desc/o Olive Ingoldsby DBR(2)704; DBR(3)124

Walton - of VA, b1739 d1809, m1760 Rebecca Lanier - desc/o John Harris DBR(4)421

William - b1556, m Alice Smith - the immigrant RAA1, royal descent not proven

Capt William - of VA, b1669 d abt 1730, m Temperance Overton - desc/o Capt Thomas Harris ECD(2)159; ECD(3)27; LDS87, 107; DBR(3)718; DBR(5)336, 340 - desc/o John Boteler RAA71 - desc/o William Harris RAA102

HARRISON Ann - of VA, m Thomas Drew - desc/o Col William Randolph PVF142

HARRISON (cont.)

Anne - of VA, b abt 1723, m(1) William Randolph of Wilton, son of William Randolph & Elizabeth Shirley of Turkey Island, m(2) John Carter, son of William Carter & Elizabeth Hill - desc/o Sarah Ludlow PVF201; CFSSA283

Anne - of VA, b1753 d1821, m1775 David Coupland - desc/o Sarah Ludlow PFA215; CFSSA284

Benjamin - of VA - the immigrant WAC102; sufficient proof of alleged royal ancestry is lacking

Benjamin - of VA, b1673 d1710, lawyer, treasurer, attorney general & Speaker of the House of Burgesses, m Elizabeth Burwell, dau/o Lewis Burwell & Abigail Smith - desc/o Benjamin Harrison WAC102

Benjamin (IV) of VA, d1744 high sheriff & burgess, m1722 Anne Carter - desc/o Abigail Smith J&K133; BCD34 - desc/o Martha Bacon CHB34 - desc/o Sarah Ludlow DBR(1)432; DBR(3)557; DBR(5)1056; CFSSA283

Gov Benjamin of VA, b1726 d1791 governor of Virginia, member of the Continental Congress and signer of the Declaration of Independance, m Elizabeth Bassett dau/o Col William Bassett & Elizabeth Churchill - desc/o Sarah Ludlow J&K133; CHB185; ECD194; BCD185; AAP144; PFA Apx C #6; GBR229; CFSSA284 - desc/o Abigail Smith BCD34

Benjamin - of VA, b1755 d1799, m(1)1785 Anna Mercer, dau/o John Mercer & Anne Roy of Marlborough, Stafford Co, m(2)1787 Susan Randolph - desc/o Sarah Ludlow PFA215; CFSSA284

Burr - of VA, b1637 d1706, m Mary____ - the immigrant WAC102; sufficient proof of alleged royal ancestry is lacking

Capt Burr - of VA, b1699, m1722 Ann Barnes - desc/o Burr Harrison WAC102

Carter Bassett - of VA, m(1) Mary Howell, m(2) Jane Byrd - desc/o Sarah Ludlow PFA215; CFSSA284

Carter Henry of VA, b1732, m Susan Randolph dau/o Isham Randolph of Dungenness - desc/o Martha Bacon CHB36 - desc/o Sarah Ludlow CHB186; BCD186; DBR(3)378; PVF201; CFSSA284

Charles - of VA, brigadier general in the Revolutionary army d1796, m Mary Claiborne dau/o Augustine Claiborne - desc/o Sarah Ludlow PVF202; CFSSA283, 284

Edmund of VA, b1761 d1826, m Martha Wales Skipwith - desc/o Sarah Ludlow J&K 271; BCD186 - desc/o Martha Bacon CHB35

Elizabeth Randolph of VA, m Gen Daniel Claiborne Butts - desc/o Capt William Claiborne CHB66; BCD66

Elizabeth - of VA, b abt 1725, m Peyton Randolph, son of Sir John Randolph & Susannah Beverley - desc/o Sarah Ludlow CFSSA283

Elizabeth - of VA, b1737, m1760 Maj John Fitzhugh - desc/o Dudley Diggs CHB78; BCD78

Elizabeth - of VA, b1751, m(1) William Rickman M.D., m(2) ____Edmonson - desc/o Sarah Ludlow PFA215

Elizabeth - of VA, b1764 d1845, m William R Bradley - desc/o Col William Randolph DBR(3)377; PVF142 - desc/o Sarah Ludlow DBR(3)378

HARRISON (cont.)

Elizabeth - of NC, b1772 d1838, m1792 Maj Samuel Smith - desc/o Col George Reade DBR(5)525

Henry - of VA, b1730 d1773, m Elizabeth Avery b1736 - desc/o Sarah Ludlow DBR(2)276, 523; DBR(5)167, 955

Lucy - of VA, m(1) Maj Peyton Randolph of Wilton, Henrico Co, son of William Randolph & Ann Harrison, m(2)1788 Anthony Singleton - desc/o Sarah Ludlow PFA215; CFSSA284

Margaret - of MD, b1753 d1794, m1777 David Weems - desc/o Rev Robert Brooke CHB403

Mary Hopkins - of VA, m Samuel Q Richardson - desc/o Sarah Ludlow CHB186; BCD186

Nathaniel - of VA, b1742 Speaker of the state senate, sheriff of Prince William Co 1779, m(1) Mary Ruffin dau/o Edmund Ruffin, m(2) Anne Gilliam dau/o William Gilliam - desc/o Sarah Ludlow J&K271; CHB161; MCD198; BCD185; PVF202 - desc/o Martha Bacon CHB35

Nathaniel - of VA, member of the Virginia state senate in 1780 - desc/o Abigail Smith J&K133

Nathaniel - of VA, b1717 d1744, m Mary Diggs - desc/o Benjamin Harrison WAC103

Palatea (Peletiah) - of VA, b abt 1758 d1821, m George Cabiness b1744 d1815 - desc/o Sarah Ludlow DBR(2)276, 523; DBR(5)167, 955

Peyton - of VA, m Elizabeth Barclay - desc/o Col William Randolph PVF142

Randolph - of VA, d1769 of Clifton, Cumberland Co, m1790 Dungenness (his first cousin) Mary Randolph - desc/o Col William Randolph PVF142

Robert - of VA, d bef 1771, & had two daughters, who were killed by lightning with their father - desc/o Sarah Ludlow PVF202

Robert Carter of VA, removed to Kentucky, m Anne Cabell - desc/o Martha Bacon CHB36 - desc/o Sarah Ludlow CHB186; BCD186 - desc/o Col William Randolph PVF142

Sarah - of VA, b1770 d1812, m John Minge of Weyanoke, Charles City Co, son of David Minge & Christian Shields - desc/o Sarah Ludlow PFA215; CFSSA284

Thomas - of VA, b1665 d1746 - desc/o Burr Harrison WAC102

Virginia - of VA, m David Castleman - desc/o Sarah Ludlow CHB186

Pres William Henry - of VA, b1773 d1841, 9th President of the United States, m1795 Ann Tuthill Symmes, dau/o Col John Symmes & Anna Tuthill; he was grandfather of Gen Benjamin Harrison President of the United States 1888/1892 - desc/o Sarah Ludlow CHB 185; J&K133; BCD185; EDC194; AAP144; PFA Apx C #6; GBR229; CFSSA285 - desc/o Abigail Smith J&K133; BCD35 - desc/o Martha Bacon CHB35

HARRY Ann - b abt 1745/1746 - desc/o Hugh Harry RAA102

Daniel - of PA, son of Harry Thomas Owen, m Sybil ____ - the immigrant GBR168

Hugh - of PA, b abt 1660 son of Harry Thomas Owen, m Elizabeth Brinton - the immigrant RAA1, 102; PFA Apx C #13; GBR168

HARRY (cont.)

    John - d1763, m Frances____ - desc/o Hugh Harry PFA Apx C #13; GBR168

    Miriam - d1809, m Record Hussey - desc/o Hugh Harry PFA Apx C #13; GBR168

HART Anne - of VA, d abt 1733, m abt 1715 Allen Warren Jr, grandson of the immigrant Thomas Warren who build the Warren House on Smith's Fort Plantation, now the oldest house in Virginia - desc/o Capt Charles Barham ECD(2)29; DBR(1)436; DBR(5)793

    Nathaniel - of NJ, d1830, m Abigail Scudder - desc/o Edward Howell AFA50

HARTWELL Jonathan - b1691 - desc/o Oliver Mellows RAA75

    Mary - b1738 - desc/o Oliver Mellows RAA75

HARWOOD Humphrey - of VA - desc/o Capt Thomas Harwood WAC94

    Capt Thomas - of VA - the immigrant WAC94; sufficient proof of alleged royal ancestry is lacking

    Thomas - of VA - desc/o Capt Thomas Harwood WAC94

HARVEY Nicholas - of MD 1642 - the immigrant DBR(1)207; sufficient proof of alleged royal ancestry is lacking

HARWOOD Agnes - of VA, m Fielding Lewis - desc/o Frances Mason CHB441

    Dorothy - of VA, m Johnson Tabb - desc/o Col George Reade GVFWM(4)270

    Elizabeth - of VA, m Henry Lee of York Co, VA - desc/o Col George Reade GVFWM(4)270

    Judith - of RI, b1724 d1762, m William Vernon & had issue - desc/o Gov John Cranston GRFHG(1)283

    Mary - of RI, m William Paul - desc/o Gov John Cranston GRFHG(1)283

    Sarah - of VA, m Littleton Kendall of Northampton Co, VA - desc/o Col George Reade GVFWM(4)270

HASELRIGE Catherine - of PA, dau/o Sir Arthur Haselrige, 2nd Baronet, Puritan leader & Dorothy Grevile, m George Fenwick b1603 d1656/1657 a founder of Saybrook, CT - the immigrant GBR132

HASTINGS Elizabeth - b1753, m Joseph Oliver Goodrich - desc/o John Whitcomb LDS46

    Jonathan - b1769 - desc/o Oliver Mellows RAA75

HATCH Anna - chr 1706, m David Butler - desc/o Sarah Palmer LDS55

    Benjamin - b1655, m(2) Alice or Elizabeth Eddy - desc/o Sarah Palmer LDS51

    Jeremiah - b1766, m Elizabeth Haight - desc/o Sarah Palmer LDS51

    John - b1689/1690, m Mariah Fish - desc/o Sarah Palmer LDS51

    Nathaniel - b1726, m Achsah Parmelee - desc/o Sarah Palmer LDS51

    Samuel - b1659, m Lydia Young - desc/o Sarah Palmer LDS55

HATHAWAY Love - of MA, b1766 d1841, m Salathiel Hathaway - desc/o Joseph Bolles ECD(2)51

    Stephen - b1746 d1819, m1767, m Hope Pierce - desc/o Frances Deighton AWW339, 340

HATTON Elizabeth - of MD 1649, m(1) Luke Gardiner, m(2) Clement Hill - the immigrant CRL(2)76, 77; sufficient proof of alleged royal ancestry is lacking

HATTON (cont.)

Thomas - of MD - the immigrant CRL(2)76; sufficient proof of alleged royal ancestry is lacking

HAUGH Atherton - of MA, b1677/1678, m1699 Boston, Mercy Winthrop - desc/o Edward Raynsford NE(139)301

Rev Samuel - of MA, b1621 Boston, Lincoln d1662 Boston, MA, minister at Reading, now Wakefield, MA, m Sarah Symmes - desc/o Rev Peter Bulkeley FLW34; MCS74

Samuel - of MA, b1675/1676, m1697 Boston, Margaret Johnson - desc/o Edward Raynsford NE(139)301

HAVILAND Jane - of MA, bp 1612 d bef 1642, dau/o Robert Haviland & Elizabeth Guise, m1629 Capt William Torrey bp 1608 d1690 son of Philip & Alice (Richards) Torrey - the immigrant FLW167; DBR(4)45, 204; DBR(5)603; RAA135; GBR142; NE(108)177, 178

HAWES Amity or Ametee - b1709, m Nathaniel Bradley - desc/o Frances Deighton LDS22

Edmond - of MA, b1608 son of Edmond Hawes & Jane Porter, m____ - the immigrant GBR335; EO2(2)271/298

Experience - b1686 - desc/o John Hawes RAA102

John - of MA, b abt 1640, m Desire Gorham dau/o John Gorham & Desire Howland - the immigrant RAA1, 102 - desc/o John Hawes GBR335; EO2(2)271/298

HAWKINS Eleanor - m(1)1796 Lieut Edward Hamilton - desc/o Sampson Waring DBR(1)202; DBR(2)299

Freegift - of MA, m Hannah Tomlinson - desc/o Roger Ludlow CHB413

Joseph - of MA, m Mercy Riggs - desc/o Roger Ludlow CHB413

Moses - of VA, d1817, m1800 Sarah Castleman b1783 - desc/o William Strother GCFTQ(3)386

Roger - of CT, b1768 d1861, m1793 Miriam Gray - desc/o Edward Southworth DBR(3)594

Sarah Bailey - of VA, m James Thornton - desc/o William Strother GVFTQ(3)38

William Strother - of VA, b1772 d1858, m1802 Katherine Keith dau/o Capt Isham Keith & Charlotte Ashmore - desc/o William Strother GVFTQ(3)386

HAWKS Moses - of MA, b1659 d aft 5 Dec 1698 - desc/o Mary Gye NE(96)359

HAWLEY James - b1760 d1836, m1793 Martha Stevens - desc/o Alice Tomes THC310

Matthew - b1680 - desc/o Alice Tomes THC310

Matthew - b1720 d1790, m Bethia____ - desc/o Alice Tomes THC310

HAY Daniel - of PA - d1797, m Catherine____ - the immigrant BLG2735; sufficient proof of alleged royal ancestry is lacking

James - of NY 1745 - the immigrant EDV40, 41; sufficient proof of alleged royal ancestry is lacking

HAYDEN Jemima - of CT, b1764 d1842, m1797 Nehemiah Hubbell - desc/o Elizabeth Coytemore ECD(2)101; DBR(5)118

John - of CT 1664 - the immigrant EDV58; sufficient proof of alleged royal ancestry is lacking

John - of MD, b abt 1770 d1831, m Elizabeth Jordan - desc/o Thomas Gerard DBR(4)101

HAYDEN (cont.)

William - of MA 1630 & CT - the immigrant EDV58; sufficient proof of alleged royal ancestry is lacking

HAYES Abigail - of NH, b1742 d1819, m Lieut Ichabod Hanson - desc/o Elder William Wentworth DBR(1)807; DBR(3)231

Elizabeth - of NH, b1722 d1795, m Ichabod Hayes - desc/o Elder William Wentworth DBR(1)806; DBR(3)231

Doc Samuel - b abt 1776 d1839, m Elizabeth Ogden Keen - desc/o Obadiah Bruen DBR(2)117

HAYNES John - of MA 1633, b1594 d1654, m Mabel Harlakenden - the immigrant MCB236; EDV123; EO2(2)301/310 sufficient proof of alleged royal ancestry is lacking

Rev Joseph - of CT, b1641, m1668 Sarah Lord - desc/o Mabel Harlakenden MCB404; MCD229

Mabel - of MA, b1645 d1676, m James Russell - desc/o Mabel Harlakenden MCD231

Mercy - b aft 1757 d1819, m1777 Jonathan Montgomery - desc/o Elder William Wentworth DBR(1)44

Capt Paul - of NH, b1713 d1776, m(1) Mary Evans, m(2) aft 1757 Tamsen Drew - desc/o Elder William Wentworth DBR(1)44

Ruth - of MA & CT, b1639 Hartford, CT d abt 1688 Hartford, CT, m1654/1655 Samuel Wyllys bp 1631/1632 Fenny Compton, Warwick, England d1709 Hartford, CT son of Governor George Wyllys & Mary Smith - desc/o Mabel Harlakenden J&K252, 253; CHB268; MCB301, 354, 355, 4111; MCD230; MCS64; FLW73; BCD268; DBR(4)118; DBR(5)610; RAA102 - desc/o John Haynes MCB236

Samuel MD - b abt 1776, m Elizabeth Ogden Keen - desc/o Obadiah Bruen ECD131

Sarah - of CT, b1673 d1696, m1694 Rev James Pierpont - desc/o Mabel Harlakenden MCB404; MCD229

HAYWARD Sarah - b1727 d1797, m1742 Capt Nathaniel Wales - desc/o Rev John Oxenbridge DBR(1)370

HAZARD Mercy - m Judge Freeman Perry - desc/o William Arnold J&K292

Oliver - m Elizabeth Raymond - desc/o William Arnold J&K292

HAZEN Caleb - of CT, b1720 d1777, m1740 Sarah Hamlin - desc/o Thomas Dudley ECD(2)124; DBR(1)487; DBR(2)294

Charity - b1744 d1811, m Elisha Cole - desc/o Thomas Dudley DBR(3)653

Eleazor - of NY, b1755 d1793, m Hannah Fuller - desc/o Thomas Dudley ECD(2)124

Sarah - of NY, b1742 d1801, m Isaac Merrick - desc/o Thomas Dudley DBR(1)488; DBR(2)294

HEADLEY Rhoda - of CT, b1756 d1837, m Jonas Wade - desc/o Obadiah Bruen CHB387

HEALD Mary - of MA, b1698 d1758, m abt 1716 Deacon John Heald - desc/o Rev Edward Bulkeley ECD(3)73

Martha - of MA, b1718 d1795, m1738 John Barrett - desc/o Rev Edward Bulkeley ECD(3)74

HEALE Philip - of VA, m Catherine Douglas - desc/o Col George Reade DBR(1)550

    Smith - of VA, b1765 d1817, m Nancy Douglas - desc/o Col George Reade DBR(2)212, 307

HEARD Susannah - of MD, m1795 William Beale - desc/o John Wiseman DBR(2)834

HEATHCOTE Col Caleb - of NY - the immigrant EDV14; sufficient proof of alleged royal ancestry is lacking

HEATON Mary - of CT, d1816, m Elisha Sill - desc/o Margaret Wyatt DBR(2)613

HEDGE Dorcas - m Daniel Smith b1660 d1716 - desc/o John Fenwick DBR(1)316; DBR(2)413; DBR(3)439

HENRY Abraham - of PA, b1768 d1811, m Elizabeth Martin - desc/o John Bevan Sr CRFP(1)142

    Anne - of VA & KY, m Col George William Christian, who was killed by the Indians near Louisville, Kentucky in 1784 - desc/o Col John Henry CHB116; BCD116; AMB449; CFA(5)243

    Anne - of VA, m Judge Spencer Roane, Judge of Court of Appeals of VA d1822 & left issue - desc/o Col John Henry MCD232; AMB449; CFA(5)244

    Edmund - of TN - desc/o Col John Henry AMB449

    Elizabeth - of VA, b1769 d1842, m1786 Philip Aylett of King William Co, VA - desc/o Col John Henry CHB116; MCD233; BCD116; CFA(5)244

    Elizabeth - of VA, m(1) Gen William Campbell, m(2) Gen Edward Carrington or Gen William Russell - desc/o Col John Henry AMB449; CFA(5)243

    Elizabeth - of PA, b1765 d1798, m Rev John Molther - desc/o John Bevan Sr CRFP(1)142

    Elizabeth - of VA, b1769 d1841, m1786 Philip Aylett - desc/o Col John Henry AMB449

    Jane - of VA, m Col Samuel Meredith & had issue - desc/o Col John Henry MCD233; BCD328; AMB449; CFA(5)243

    Col John - of VA 1730, b abt 1705 of The Retreat, near Richmond d1773 son of Alexander & Jean (Robertson) Henry, of Aberdeen, Scotland, m1772/1773 Sarah Winston, dau/o Isaac Winston & Mary Dabney & wid/o Col John Syme - the immigrant J&K153; CHB115; MCB156; MCD232; BCD115; BCD328; AMB449; FFF280; GBR70; CFA(5)243

    John - of VA - desc/o Col John Henry AMB449

    John Joseph Henry - of PA, b1758 d1811 member of General Arnold's army of invasion of Canada, captured on assault of Quebec, Judge of Second Judicial District of PA, m Jane Chambers - desc/o John Bevan Sr CRFP(1)142

    Lucy - of VA, m Col Valentine Wood of Goochland Co, VA - desc/o Col John Henry AMB449; CFA(5)243

    Martha - of VA, m John Fontaine, son of Rev Peter Fontaine - desc/o Col John Henry AMB449; CFA(5)244

    Mary - of VA, m Luke Bowyer - desc/o Col John Henry CFA(5)243

    Patrick - of VA, b1736 d1799 Red Hill, Charlotte Co, VA member of the Continental Congress, first governor of Virginia, m(1)1754 Sarah

HENRY (cont.)
>Shelton d1775 dau/o John Shelton, m(2)1777 Dorothea Spotswood
>Dandridge b1757 dau/o Col Nathaniel West Dandridge & Dorothea
>Spotswood - desc/o Col John Henry J&K153; CHB116; MCD232;
>BCD116; DBR(2)205; AMB449; FFF280; GBR70; CFA(5)244
>
>Sarah - of VA, m Thomas Thomas of Bristol, England - desc/o Col
>John Henry CFA(5)243
>
>Susanna - of VA, m Gen Thomas Madison & had issue - desc/o Col
>John Henry AMB449; CFA(5)243
>
>William of PA, b1757 d1821 Philadelphia, m1781 Sabina Schropp
>b1759 Nazareth, Northampton Co d1848 Bethlehem, dau/o
>Matthew Schropp & Anna Maria____ - desc/o John Bevan Sr
>CHB81; BCD81; MCD164; DBR(1)376; AFA40; CFRP(1)142, 143

HENSHAW Joshua - of MA, b1703 d1777 in the mercantile business &
>was a public official son of William Henshaw & Katherine Houghton,
>m1733 Elizabeth Sumner d1782 aged 70 years dau/o William
>Sumner & left issue 4 children of whom 3 left no issue - the
>immigrant GBR177 some aspect of royal descent merits further
>study; NE(22)105/115; EO2(2)329/336

HERING Capt Julines - of MA, m1761 Mary Inglis - desc/o Rev John
>Oxenbridge CHB166; BCD166; GBR125
>
>Mary Helen - of SC, dau/o Julines Hering & Mary Inglis, m Henry
>Middleton b1770 d1846 governor of South Carolina, congressman
>& diplomat - the immigrant MCB160; GBR125
>
>Oliver of MA, m Elizabeth Hughes - desc/o Rev John Oxenbridge
>CHB166; BCD166; GBR125
>
>Oliver Jr - of MA, m Anna Maria Morris - desc/o Rev John Oxenbridge
>BCD166; GBR125

HERNDON Benjamin - of VA, b1765 d1805, m1787 Susan Ahart - desc/o
>Dudley Diggs JSW1606
>
>Benjamin - of VA, m Rosannah Wade - desc/o Gov Edward Diggs
>DBR(4)791; DBR(5)772
>
>Dabney - m Elizabeth Hull - desc/o Mary Waller GBR332
>
>Edward - of VA, b1678 d1745, m1698 Mary Waller - desc/o Dudley
>Diggs JSW1605, 1606; DBR(4)791; DBR(5)772, 870; GVFHB(4)8
>
>Edward - of VA, d1759, m Mary Brock dau/o Joseph Brock - desc/o
>Mary Waller GVFHB(4)8, 9
>
>Edward - of VA, b1730 d1799, m Mary Colston dau/o Charles &
>Rebecca (Travers) Colston - desc/o Mary Waller GVFHB(4)9
>
>Edward - of VA, m Elizabeth Stubblefield - desc/o Dudley Diggs
>DBR(5)870 - desc/o Mary Waller GBR332
>
>Edward - of VA, m Mary Duerson - desc/o Dudley Diggs DBR(5)870
>
>Edward - of VA, m Mary Elizabeth Sharpe - desc/o Dudley Diggs
>DBR(5)870
>
>Edward - of VA, b1738 d1831, m1762 Mary Gaines - desc/o Dudley
>Diggs JSW1606
>
>James - of VA, b1722, m Sara____ - desc/o Dudley Diggs FFF285
>
>James - of VA & KY, b1740 d1815, m abt 1761 Isabella Thompson -
>desc/o Dudley Diggs FFF285
>
>James - of VA, m Valentine Haley - desc/o Gov Edward Diggs
>DBR(4)791; DBR(5)772

HERNDON (cont.)

John - of VA, b1756 d1812, m1783 Judith Hampton b1767 d1853 dau/o Phillip & Hannah (Hammond) Hampton - desc/o Dudley Diggs JSW1606

John - of VA, d1786, m Mary George - desc/o Dudley Diggs FFF284/285

Joseph - of VA, m Mary Minor - desc/o Mary Waller GBR332

Susannah - m Thomas Tuggle - desc/o Dudley Diggs DBR(5)772

William - of VA, b1706 d1783, m1730 Ann Drysdale dau/o Lieut-Governor Hugh Drysdale - desc/o Dudley Diggs JSW1605, 1605; DBR(4)791; GVFHB(4)8

HERON Capt Benjamin - of NC, b1722 d1770, clerk of the Pleas of province of North Carolina & naval officer for the province; lieut general of the Hillsborough Camp 1768, chairman of the King's Council of North Carolina 1769, son of Patrick Heron & Anne Vining, m1754 Mary Howe b1736 d1763 dau/o Job Howe - the immigrant DBR(1)758; GBR367 some aspect of royal descent merits further study

Elizabeth - of NC, b1762, m1785 Capt John McKenzie - desc/o Capt Benjamin Heron DBR(1)758

HERRICK Rev Claudius - of NY, b1775 d1859, m1802 Hannah Pierpont - desc/o Henry Herrick BLG2737

Ebenezer - of NY - desc/o Henry Herrick BLG2737

Edward - of MA, b1695 d1775, m1725 Mary Dennison - desc/o Henry Herrick BLG2737

Ephraim - of MA, bp 1636 d1693, m1661 Mary Cross - desc/o Henry Herrick BLG2737

Henry - of MA, b abt 1600 d1661, m Edith Laskin - the immigrant BLG2737; EDV109; TAG(XIV)96, 97, 98; sufficient proof of alleged royal ancestry is lacking

Henry - of NY, b1739 d1821, m1772 Jerusha Foster - desc/o Henry Herrick BLG2737

James - of NY, b1633 d1687, m Martha____ - desc/o Henry Herrick BLG2737

John - of NY - desc/o Henry Herrick BLG2737

John - b1766 d1838, m1789 Nancy Platt - desc/o Henry Herrick BLG2737

Joseph - of NY, b1735, m Elizabeth Burton - desc/o Henry Herrick BLG2738

Josiah - of NY, m Margaret Hicks - desc/o Henry Herrick BLG2738

Nathan - of NY, b1700 d1783, m1729 Eunice Rogers - desc/o Henry Herrick BLG2737

Col Rufus - of MA, b1734 d1811, m1761 Lydia Leonard - desc/o Henry Herrick BLG2737

Samuel - of MA, b1675, m1698 Mehetable Woodward - desc/o Henry Herrick BLG2738

Stephen - of MA, b1670, m1692 Elizabeth Trask - desc/o Henry Herrick BLG2737

Stephen - of CT & NY, b1705, m1726 Phebe Guile - desc/o Henry Herrick BLG2738

William - of NY, b1654 d1736, m Mehetable____ - desc/o Henry

HERRICK (cont.)

Herrick BLG2737

HESILRIGGE Hannah - of MA, m Rev Thomas Abbot - desc/o Robert Hesilrigge MCB144

Robert - of MA, m Sarah Waller - the immigrant MCB144; sufficient proof of alleged royal ancestry is lacking

Sarah - of MA, m Col David Henley - desc/o Robert Hesilrigge MCB144

HEWES Sarah Hunt - of MA, b1752 d1863, m1797 John Alexander Etheridge - desc/o Thomas Dudley DBR(3)597

HEYWOOD Elizabeth - m bef 1680 Thomas Hayes of Barbados - desc/o Thomas Lewis NE(101)21

Hannah - b1757 - desc/o William Goddard RAA99

Hester - m(1) bef 1680 John Orpen d1696, m(2) 1701 Mr Richard Turner - desc/o Thomas Lewis NE(101)21/22

John - Chief Marshal of His Majesty's court of common pleas 1699 & Chief Justice of the court of common pleas in 1704, m1677 Mary Whitehead & had issue, children bp 1681/1688 in Barbados - desc/o Thomas Lewis NE(101)21

Judith - bp 1626, m abt 1646 Saco, James Gibbins - desc/o Thomas Lewis NE(101)23

Martha - m bef 1680 William Charles of Barbados - desc/o Thomas Lewis NE(101)21

Nathaniel - d1704 merchant, m1683 Mrs Alice Homeyard & had children bp 1686/1691/2 - desc/o Thomas Lewis NE(101)23

Richard - mariner, m & the father of a son, Richard, in 1680 - desc/o Thomas Lewis NE(101)21

Richard - of St Michael's parish, wheelwright d1735/1736, m 1714 Prudence Hart - desc/o Thomas Lewis NE(101)22

Robert - m Mary____ & had issue a daughter Susanna bp 1681 d1694 in Barbados - desc/o Thomas Lewis NE(101)21

Thomas - m 1680 Mary Harding d1730 - desc/o Thomas Lewis NE(101)22

HIBBARD Roger - b1757, m Sarah Davidson - desc/o William Throop LDS25

HIBBERT Mary - m Joseph Jewett - desc/o Elizabeth Marshall GBR264 - desc/o Thomas Lewis GBR465

HICKMAN Edwin - b abt 1692 - desc/o Edwin Conway RAA82

Edwin - b1744 - desc/o Edwin Conway RAA82

William - b1770 - desc/o Edwin Conway RAA82

HICKS Freeborn - of RI, b1744 d1782, m1761 Benjamin Rider - desc/o Jeremy Clarke DBR(4)817

John - of RI, b1715, m1740 Elizabeth Russell - desc/o Jeremy Clarke DBR(3)674

John - of RI, b1755 d1815, m1777 Sarah Church - desc/o Jeremy Clarke DBR(3)674

Robert - of MA bef 1630 - the immigrant EDV133; BLG2739; sufficient proof of alleged royal ancestry is lacking

Weston - of RI, b1707, m Susannah Freeborn - desc/o Jeremy Clarke DBR(4)817

HIDE Ann - of VA, dau/o Jonathan Hide &____(Todd) Hide, she left her father's estate when aged 18 - desc/o Col William Bernard APP123

HIGBEE Sarah - of CT, b1739 d1835, m1758 Daniel Rathbone - desc/o Nathaniel Browne ECD(3)60

HIGBY Hannah - of CT, m Joseph Trumbull - desc/o John Drake J&K311

HIGLEY or HIGHLEY Ann - of CT, b1726 d1761, m1744 Mascall Bacon - desc/o John Drake DBR(3)661

Brewster - b1680 - desc/o John Drake RAA87

Brewster - b1709 - desc/o John Drake RAA87

Elizabeth - b1724, m Gideon Mills - desc/o Thomas Holcomb LDS96 - desc/o John Drake RAA87

Eunice - b1776 - desc/o John Drake RAA87

Job - b1768, m(2) Dorcas Eggleston - desc/o Thomas Holcomb LDS54

Joel - b1739 - desc/o John Drake RAA87

John - b1722, m(2)____ - desc/o Thomas Holcomb LDS54

Katherine - of CT, b1679 d1741, m James Nobel - desc/o John Drake MCD209

Dr Samuel - of CT, b1687 d1737, m1719 Abigail Beaumont - desc/o John Drake DBR(3)660

HILL Charles - of ME, b1734 d1819, m1756 Sarah Prentice - desc/o Joseph Bolles ECD(2)58; RAA71

Col Clement - of VA, b1736 of Charlotte Co, served as clerk of Charlotte Co, m1757 Mary Nash, dau/o Judge John Nash of Prince Edward Co - desc/o Edmund Jennings CFSSA302

Rev Clement - of VA, b1770, m1789 Clarissa Edmunds b1772 d1854, dau/o Col Thomas Edmunds of Brunswick Co - desc/o Edmund Jennings CFSSA302

Daniel - of MA, b1675 - desc/o Ralph Hill BLG2742; CFA(1)239

Deborah - of MA, b1663, m John Sheldon - desc/o Ralph Hill BLG2742; CFA(1)238

Deborah - of MA, b1705 d1745, m1729 Samuel Whiting - desc/o Ralph Hill BLG2742; CFA(1)239

Deborah - of PA, b1728 d1763 Madeira, m Robert Bissett d1801 Madeira - desc/o Thomas Lloyd CRFP(1)44

Ebenezer - of MA, b1766 d1854, m(1)1791 Polly Boynton, m(2)1795 Rebecca Bancroft, m(3)1799 Abigail Jones - desc/o Ralph Hill CFA(1)239

Major Edmund - of VA, d1802, served with distinction in the Revolutionary War, m(1) Miss Lewis, m(2)1782 Paulina Cabell b1763, dau/o Col William Cabell & Martha Jordan of Union Hill - desc/o Edmund Jennings CFSSA302

Col Edward - of VA, d1663 - the immigrant WAC46; sufficient proof of alleged royal ancestry is lacking

Col Edward - of VA, b1637 d1700 - desc/o Col Edward Hill WAC46

Col Edward - of VA - desc/o Col Edward Hill WAC46

Elizabeth - of MA, b1661 d1704, m1687 Timothy Baldwin - desc/o Ralph Hill BLG2742; CFA(1)238

Elizabeth - of VA, m1723 John Carter - desc/o Col Edward Hill WAC46

Elizabeth - b1723, m1755 Abraham Jaquith - desc/o Ralph Hill CFA(1)239

Elizabeth - of VA, m Burwell Lanier of Brunswick Co, VA, son of Sampson Lanier & Elizabeth Chamberlayne - desc/o Edmund Jennings SVF(1)283

HILL (cont.)

Elizabeth - b abt 1764 - desc/o Joseph Bolles RAA71

Harriet - of PA, b1729 d1795 Bath, England, m1755 John Scott, merchant of London, England - desc/o Thomas Lloyd CRFP(1)44

Henry - of PA, b1732 d1798 Philadelphia, m Anne Meredith dau/o Reese Meredith of Philadelphia - desc/o Thomas Lloyd CRFP(1)44

Col Isaac - of VA, b1738 of Lunenburg Co d1777 served with distinction in the Revolutionary War, m ____Embry, dau/o Henry Embry of Lunenburg Co - desc/o Edmund Jennings CFSSA302

Isaac - of VA, b abt 1774 of Greenfield, Charlotte, m Mayo Venable b1784 d1869 dau/o Col Samuel Venable & Mary Carrington - desc/o Edmund Jennings CFSSA302

Jane - of MA, m Francis Littlefield - desc/o Ralph Hill BLG2742; CFA(1)238

John - of ME, b1703 d1772, m Elizabeth Gerrish - desc/o Joseph Bolles ECD(2)58; RAA71

Capt John - of VA, served in the Revolutionary War, m Elizabeth Julia Spencer, m(2) Elizabeth____, m(3) Mary Barksdale, 1806 moved to Rutherford Co, Tennessee - desc/o Edmund Jennings CFSSA302

Jonathan - of MA, b1646, m1666 Mary Hartwell - desc/o Ralph Hill BLG2742; CFA(1)238

Capt Jonathan - of VA, of Charlotte Co, served with distinction in the Revolutionary War, m Jane Lewis - desc/o Edmund Jennings CFSSA303

Margaret - of MD, b1737 d1816, m1758 Philadelphia, William Morris b1735 Philadelphia d1766 eldest son of John Morris & Mary Sutton of Spring Mill, Philadelphia - desc/o Thomas Lloyd CHB122; MCD251; BCD122; AFA74; CRFP(1)44, 45

Hon Mark Langdon - of MA, b1772 d1842, m(1)1797 Mary McCobb - desc/o Gov Thomas Dudley DBR(1)63

Martha - of MA, b1709 d1747 - desc/o Ralph Hill BLG2742; CFA(1)239

Mary - of VA, b1646 Accomack Co d1704, m abt 1666 Accomack Co, John Ayres d bef 1697 Accomack Co - desc/o Robert Drake DBR(5)1007; SMO25

Mary - of VA, d1780, m1730 Col Clement Reade b1707 d1763, clerk of Lunenburg Co - desc/o Edmund Jennings HSF(4)130; SVF(1)283; CFSSA302

Mary - of VA, m Thomas Nash of Charlotte Co & had issue - desc/o Edmund Jennings CFSSA303

Nathaniel - of MA, d1706, m1667 Elizabeth Holmes - desc/o Ralph Hill BLG2742; CFA(1)238

Patience - of VA, b abt 1650 Accomack Co d bef 1713 Accomack Co, m abt 1670 Capt John Drummond b1635 d1713 Accomack Co - desc/o Robert Drake ECD(3)123; DBR(5)381; SMO133

Rachel of PA, b1735 d1796, m1759 Richard Wells b1734 near Hull, England, prominent merchant, secretary of American Philosophical Society, director of Library Company, member Pennsylvania Assembly & for a long time cashier of Bank of North America, son of Dr Gideon Wells of Cottness & Mary Partridge dau/o Richard Partridge of London - desc/o Thomas Lloyd

HILL (cont.)

CHB123; BCD123; CRFP(1)44

Ralph - of MA bef 1637, m(1) Elizabeth Parker, m(2)1638 Margaret____
- the immigrant BLG2742; CFA(1)238; sufficient proof of alleged
royal ancestry is lacking

Capt Ralph - of MA, d1695, m1660 Martha Toothaker - desc/o Ralph
Hill BLG2742; CFA(1)238

Ralph - of MA, b1707 d1789, m1733 Mehitable Patten - desc/o Ralph
Hill BLG2742; CFA(1)239

Rebecca - of MA, d1669, m1666 Caleb Farley - desc/o Ralph Hill
BLG2742; CFA238

Rebecca - of MA, b1666 - desc/o Ralph Hill BLG2742; CFA(1)238

Rebecca - of MA, b1711 d1789, m1746 Isaac Marshall - desc/o Ralph
Hill BLG2742; CFA(1)239

Capt Samuel - of MA, b1672 d1755, m Deborah____ - desc/o Ralph
Hill BLG2742; CFA(1)239

Samuel Jr - of NH, b1715/1716 d1798, m1760/1761 Sarah Cutler -
desc/o Ralph Hill BLG2742; CFA(1)239

Samuel - of MA & NH, bp 1764 d1813, m(1) Dorcas Wyeth, m(2) Mary
Adams - desc/o Ralph Hill BLG2742; CFA(1)239

Sarah - of MA, b1713 d1750, m1737 David Baldwin - desc/o Ralph
Hill BLG2742; CFA(1)239

Susanna - of VA, m Capt Benjamin Clement - desc/o Edmund
Jennings DBR(2)603

Col Thomas - of VA, b1740 of Ingleside, Lunenburg Co d1817
surveyor, deputy clerk of Charlotte Co 1765, m Elizabeth Nash,
dau/o Judge John Nash of Prince Edward Co - desc/o Edmund
Jennings CFSSA302

William - of VA, d bef Aug 1799, moved to Carteret Co, NC, m(1)
Catherine Major (?), m(2)1758 Priscilla ____ wid/o Henry Embry Jr,
m(3)1790 Sarah Lanier - desc/o Edmund Jennings SVF(1)283

Zachariah - b1759 d1814 a Revolutionary soldier, m1781 Abigail
Blodgett b1762/1763 dau/o Thomas Blodgett, a Revolutionary
soldier, & Charity (Raymond) Blodgett - desc/o Dr Richard Palgrave
DBR(1)176

HILLS Joseph - b1758, m Esther Ellis - desc/o Jonathan Whitney LDS60

HILTON (HYLTON) Daniel Lawrence - of NY & VA, b abt 1746 d1811,
prominent in many state & local civic activities, m Sarah____ -
desc/o Ralph Hilton TAG(50)81/86

Dudley - of MA, b abt 1676, m Mercy Hall - desc/o Gov Thomas
Dudley DBR(1)74; DBR(2)97

Jane - m 1699 Richard Mattoon of Ipswich & Newmarket - desc/o Gov
Thomas Dudley NE(10)135

John - of NY, b abt 1742 d1782, m(1)1764 Mary Braine, dau/o
Thomas Braine, m(2)1779 Ann Coomes (Combs) - desc/o Ralph
Hilton TAG(50)81/86

Joseph - b abt 1681 d1765, m(1) Hannah Jose dau/o Richard Jose,
m(2) Rebecca____ wid/o____Adams - desc/o Gov Thomas Dudley
NE(10)135

Mercy - of MA, b1709 d1782, m1735 Kinsley James - desc/o Gov
Thomas Dudley DBR(1)74; DBR(2)97; NE(10)135

HILTON (HYLTON) (cont.)

Ralph - of NY, b1710 d1753, shipping & mercantile interests in the Caribbean, Jamaica, & possibly Virginia, son of John Hilton & Mrs Hannah____Moore Hilton, m1741 Mehitabel Lawrence b1719 dau/o Daniel & Mary (Redwood) Lawrence - the immigrant GBR34; TAG(50)81/86

William - of NY, b1749/50 d1837 continued his father's interests in Jamaica, was the father of eight sons & four daughters, m1771 Mary Johnson dau/o Jacob & Christian (Barrett) Johnson of Springfield, Jamaica - desc/o Ralph Hilton TAG(50)81/86

HINCKLEY Ebenezer - of NJ, b1685 West Barnstable d1751, m(1)1717 Barnstable, Sarah Lewis (or Lewes) b1690 Barnstable d1737 dau/o Ebenezer Lewis & Anna Lothrop, m(2)1739 Yarmouth, Thankful Miller b1685 Yarmouth d1763 North Yarmouth - desc/o Edward FitzRandolph NE(97)277

Isaac - of NJ, b1674 West Barnstable d1762 West Barnstable, m1712 Elizabeth Gookin b1690 Sherborn, MA d1767 West Barnstable, dau/o Rev Mr____Gookin - desc/o Edward FitzRandolph NE(97)277

Joseph - of NJ, b1671 West Barnstable d1753 West Barnstable, m1699 Mary Gorham b1679 d1748 West Barnstable, dau/o Lieut Col John Gorham & Mercy Otis - desc/o Edward FitzRandolph NE(97)277

Nathaniel - chr 1738, m Mercy Nickerson - desc/o Ensign Constant Southworth LDS56; RAA131

Nathaniel - b1769, m Rhoda Barber - desc/o Ensign Constant Southworth LDS56; RAA131

HINES Martha "Patsey" Hall - of VA, b1773 d1817, m1793 Henry Dixon - desc/o Lieut Col Walter Aston ECD(3)9

Rebecca - b1686 - desc/o Mary Gye RAA115

HINMAN Enoch - b1758 - desc/o Jane Haviland RAA135

HINTON Alice - of NC, m Capt John James - desc/o Col John Hinton CRL(4)457

Ann (Nancy) - of NC, m Solomon Alston - desc/o Col John Hinton DBR(3)158, 159; DBR(5)238

David - of NC, b1774 d1850, m1791 Jane Lewis - desc/o Col John Hinton DBR(3)264; CRL(4)457

Dempsey - of NC, m Sarah____ - desc/o James Hinton Jr JSW1597

Dempsey Jr - of NC, b1751 d1780, m Mary Ann Bennefield - desc/o James Hinton Jr JSW1597

Elizabeth - of NC, m Thomas James - desc/o Col John Hinton CRL(4)457

Giselle - m Judge Henry Seawell - desc/o Col John Hinton DBR(1)155

James Jr - of PA & NC, d aft 1743, m ____Dempsey - the immigrant JSW1596; sufficient proof of alleged royal ancestry is lacking

Col James - of NC, m Delilah Hunter - desc/o Col John Hinton CRL(4)457

Col John - of NC, d1732 son of James Hinton, m Mary Hardy - the immigrant DBR(1)155, 753; DBR(2)39, 564, 823; DBR(3)158, 252, 262, 263; DBR(5)238, 369; BLG2745; CRL(4)456, 464; GBR134 some aspect of royal descent merits further study

Col John II - of NC, d1784 of the Revolutionary Army, m Griselle

HINTON (cont.)

>>Kimbrough - desc/o Col John Hinton DBR(1)155, 753, DBR(3)263; CRL(4)456, 464

>Col John III - of NC, m Spoebe Smith - desc/o Col John Hinton DBR(1)155; CRL(4)457

>Jonas - of NC, d1770 - desc/o James Hinton Jr JSW1597

>Kimbrough - of NC, married & moved West - desc/o Col John Hinton CRL(4)457

>Martha - of NC, m Col Joel Lane - desc/o Col John Hinton CRL(4)457

>Mary - of VA 1622, d bef 1628 dau/o Sir Thomas Hinton, m1622 Gov Samuel Mathews b1592 d1659/1660 governor of Virginia for life, son of Tobias Mathews, Archbishop of York - the immigrant JSW1643; DBR(2)599, 601; DBR(3)38; DBR(4)411; DBR(5)178, 328, 1050; royal descent not proven

>Mary - of NC, d1795, m Col Joel Lane - desc/o Col John Hinton DBR(1)753; CRL(4)457, 464

>Nancy Ann - of NC, b1710 d1765, m1729 Solomon Alston - desc/o Col John Hinton DBR(2)564; DBR(3)252, 253; DBR(5)369

>Sarah - of NC, m Needham Bryan - desc/o Col John Hinton CRL(4)457

>Thomas - of NC & VA, b1574, m Catherine Palmer - the immigrant RAA1, 103; sufficient proof of alleged royal ancestry is lacking

HITCHCOCK Anna - b1717 - desc/o Amy Wyllys RAA126

HOAR Bridget - of MA, b1673 Cambridge, dau/o Dr Leonard Hoar & Bridget Lisle, m1689 London, Rev Thomas Cotton b1653 near Wortley, England d1730 & left issue, Leonard, Thomas & Alicia - desc/o Bridget Lisle NE(53)298

>Daniel - of MA, b1651, m Hannah Shepard - desc/o Johanna Hoar EDV27; NE(53)299

>Johanna - of MA, bp 1624 d1661 youngest dau of Charles & Joanna Hoar, m1648 Col Edmund Quincy b1627 d1698 - the immigrant EDV27; NE(53)299; EO2(2)344/381 unable to give the authority of records to vouch for proof of alleged royal ancestry

HOBART Dorothy - of CT, b1679 d1733, m(1)1704 Daniel Mason b1674 d1705, m(2)1707 Hezekiah Brainerd - desc/o Elizabeth St John J&K299; CHB221; BCD221, 222; DBR(1)683

>Rt Rev John Henry DD - of NY, b1775 d1830, m1800 Mary Goodin - desc/o James Claypoole CHB94; BCD94

HOBBS Joseph II - of MD, d1791, m Elizabeth Higgins - desc/o Rev Hawte Wyatt DBR(2)286

HOBSON Agnes - of VA, m John Langston Bacon - desc/o Maj Gen Nathaniel Bacon CHB348; BCD348

>Betty - of VA, b1736/1737, m abt 1753 John Corbell - desc/o Lieut Col Henry Fleete APP289

>John - of VA, b1730 d1762, m Winifred Wildey - desc/o Lieut Col Henry Fleete - desc/o Lieut Col Henry Fleete APP288

>Judith - of VA, b1725, m Stephen Chilton - desc/o Lieut Col Henry Fleete APP288

>Mary Ann - of VA, b1732, m(1) William Chilton d1749, m(2) aft Jul 1766 Moses Williams d1772 - desc/o Lieut Col Henry Fleete APP289

>Sarah - of VA, b1725, m Charles Fallin d1773 justice of

HOBSON (cont.)
Northumberland Co, son of Charles & Hannah (Harcum) Fallin - desc/o Lieut Col Henry Fleete APP288

HODGES Dr Samuel - m Elizabeth Johnson - desc/o Gov Thomas Lloyd DBR(1)720

HOFFMAN Philip Livingston - of NY, b1767 d1807, m1787 Helena Kissam - desc/o Col Robert Livingston DBR(3)536

HOLCOMB Abigail - b1639, m Samuel Bissell - desc/o Thomas Holcomb LDS68, 69; THC169
Deborah - of MA, b1650, m1668 Daniel Birge - desc/o Thomas Holcomb THC169
Elizabeth - of MA, m1654 Josias Ellsworth - desc/o Thomas Holcomb THC169
Esther or Hester - b1684, m Brewster Higley - desc/o Thomas Holcomb LDS54, 96
Capt Hezekiah - of CT, b1726 d1794, m1748 Susanna Alderman - desc/o Thomas Holcomb BLG2746
Hezekiah - of CT, b1750 d1820, m1768 Chloe Pinney - desc/o Thomas Holcomb BLG2746
Joshua - of CT, b1640 d1690, m1663 Ruth Sherwood - desc/o Thomas Holcomb BLG2746
Joshua - of CT, b1672 d1727, m1694 Mary or Hannah Carrington - desc/o Thomas Holcomb BLG2746
Joshua - of CT, b1697 d1772, m Mary Griffin - desc/o Thomas Holcomb BLG2746
Mary - of MA, m abt 1655 George Griswold - desc/o Thomas Holcomb THC169
Nathaniel - b1648, m(1) Mary Bliss - desc/o Thomas Holcomb LDS54, 96
Thomas - of CT, b abt 1601 d1657, m Elizabeth Ferguson - the immigrant LDS54, 68, 69, 96; BLG2746; EDV141, 142; THC167, 168, 169; RAA no longer accepted as being of royal descent

HOLDEN Barbara - of RI, b1688 d1707, m1690/1691 Samuel Wickham - desc/o Frances Dungan ECD(3)138
Barbara - b1717, m(2) John Wells - desc/o Frances Dungan LDS76
Catharine - of RI, b1717 d1807, m1736 Christopher Lippitt - desc/o William Arnold CHB16; BCD16
Charles - of RI, b1666, m Catherine Green - desc/o Frances Dungan LDS76
Charles - b1695, m(1) Penelope Bennett - desc/o Frances Dungan LDS76
Sarah - of RI, b1658, m Joseph Stafford - desc/o Frances Dungan LDS11, 112

HOLDER Mary - of RI, b1661 d1737, m1680 Reverend Peleg Slocum - desc/o Katherine Marbury DBR(2)44; DBR(5)833; RAA114

HOLIDAY Ruth - b abt 1747/1751 - desc/o Nathaniel Browne RAA73

HOLLISTER Samuel - b1764 - desc/o Robert Abell RAA59

HOLLOWAY Abigail - of RI, m1782 at Exeter, RI, Simon Sprague - desc/o Gov John Cranston GRFHG(1)290; NE(79)260
Molly - of RI, m Samuel Babcock - desc/o Gov John Cranston GRFHG(1)290; NE(79)260

HOLLOWAY (cont.)

Penelope - of RI, b1751, m Christopher Brown - desc/o Gov John Cranston GRFHG(1)290; NE(79)260

HOLMES Eleazer - b1688 - desc/o George Morton RAA116

Elizabeth - b1721 - desc/o George Morton RAA116

Experience - b1731/1732 - desc/o John Hawes RAA102

John - b1663 - desc/o George Morton RAA116

John - b1682 - desc/o George Morton RAA116

Josiah - b1716 - desc/o George Morton RAA116

Oliver Wendall - of VA, Chief Justice Supreme Court of MA & Associate Justice Supreme Court of the United States - desc/o Gov Thomas Dudley J&K195; CRL(1)381

Simeon - b1741 - desc/o George Morton RAA116

Thomas - b1709 - desc/o George Morton RAA116

William - b1770 - desc/o George Morton RAA116

HOLT Elizabeth - of VA, m Nicholas Cocke - desc/o Frances Mason CHB440

Jane - of VA, m John Hancock - desc/o Lieut Col Walter Aston CHB537

HOLYOKE Edward - of MA 1639 - the immigrant EDV89; sufficient proof of alleged royal ancestry is lacking

Edward - of MA, president of Harvard College - desc/o Edward Holyoke EDV89

Edward Augustus - of MA - desc/o Edward Holyoke EDV89

Elizar - of MA, d1711 - desc/o Edward Holyoke EDV89

HOME George - of VA, son of Sir George, 3rd Baronet & Margaret (Home) Home, m Elizabeth Proctor - the immigrant GBR30

Maj Theophilus - of VA, m abt 1672 ____ - the immigrant WAC91; sufficient proof of alleged royal ancestry is lacking

HOOKER Mercy - of CT, b1719 d1800, m1750 Jedediah Goodrich - desc/o William Leete CHB369; MCD245

HOOPES Elisha - b1765 - desc/o Hugh Harry RAA102

HOPKINS Elijah - b1741, m(3) Joanna Parish - desc/o Richard Sears LDS14; RAA6

Frances - b1614, m William Mann - the immigrant LDS50; royal ancestry unproven

Lydia - of RI, b1733 d1793, m1763 Col Daniel Tillinghast - desc/o Lawrence Wilkinson CHB277; BCD277

Stephen - of RI, b1707 d1785 governor of RI, member of the Continental Congress & signer of the Declaration of Independence, m1726 Sarah Scott - desc/o Lawrence Wilkinson J&K183; CHB277; BCD277

William - of RI, m Ruth Wilkinson - desc/o Joanna Arnold J&K295

HOPSON Simeon - of CT & NY, b1747 d aft 1836, m1776 Naomi Moss - desc/o William Leete DBR(4)517, 518

HORNER Deliverance - b1685 d1714, m1704 Thomas Stokes II - desc/o Peter Wright DBR(4)98

HORSMANDEN Rev Daniel - b abt 1656 d1726, m1690 Mrs Susanna (Woolston) Bowyer b abt 1666 d1714/1715 - desc/o Ursula St Leger GBR141; APP528; GVFTQ(2)240

Daniel Jr - b1694 d1778 last chief justice of New York, m(1) abt 1747

HORSMANDEN (cont.)

Mary Reade, m(2) Anne Jevon - desc/o Ursula St Leger GBR141; GVFTQ(2)240

Maria or Mary - of VA, b abt 1652 d1699, m(1)1667 Samuel Filmer d1670 of East Sutton, Kent, m(2) abt 1673 Col William Byrd b abt 1652 d1704, son of John Byrd & Grace Stegg - desc/o Col Warsham Horsmanden CHB54; ECD221; MCB151; MCD184; BCD54; DBR(3)139, 237, 645; DBR(4)122, 172; DBR(5)880, 881, 1035, 1036; GBR141; APP527; GVFTQ(2)239; CFSSA104

Col Warham - of VA abt 1649, bp 1628 Ulcombe, Kent d1691 member of Governor's council 1658, son of Daniel Horsmanden & Ursula St Leger, m1650/1651 Susanna Beeching b abt 1627 d1691 - desc/o Ursula St Leger ECD221; MCD184; DBR(3)139, 237, 645; DBR(4)122, 172; DBR(5)880 - the immigrant GBR141; APP524; GVFTQ(2)239/252; CFSSA104

HOUGH Atherton - of MA, b1677/1678, son of Samuel Hough & Ann (Raynsford) Hough, m1699 Mercy Winthrop - desc/o Edward Raynsford NE(139)301

Ferdinando - of ME, b1633/1640 d aft 1702, m1665 Mary Moses - desc/o Rev Edward Bulkeley ECD(3)71

George Banfield - of ME, b1730 d bef 1790, m1759 Susanna Colby - desc/o Rev Edward Bulkeley ECD(3)71

Moses - of ME, b1764 d1849, m1786 Elizabeth Chase - desc/o Rev Edward Bulkeley ECD(3)72

Samuel - of MA, b1675/1676, son of Samuel Hough & Ann (Raynsford) Hough, m1697 Margaret Johnson - desc/o Edward Raynsford NE(139)301

Thomas I - of NH, b1660/1675 d aft 1745, m1700 Grace Ferris - desc/o Rev Edward Bulkeley ECD(3)71

Thomas II - of NH, b1703 d aft 1765, m(1)1729 Hepsibah Banfield - desc/o Rev Edward Bulkeley ECD(3)71

HOUGHTON Lois - b1722, m Nathaniel Hastings - desc/o John Whitcomb LDS46

HOUSTOUN Patrick - d bef 1717, m Isabel Johnstone - GBR lists their son as the immigrant Sir Patrick, 5th Baronet of GA, b abt 1698 d1762 president of the Colonial Council of Georgia, son of Patrick & Isabel (Johnstone) Houston, m1740 Priscilla Dunbar - desc/o Patrick Houston MCS69 - the immigrant GBR54

HOVEY Aaron - b1735 - desc/o Olive Welby RAA93

Olive - b1761 - desc/o Olive Welby RAA93

HOWARD Catherine Greenberry - of MD, b1702 d1783, m1717 Orlando Griffith - desc/o Matthew Arundel-Howard JSW1770, 1866

Eleanor - m John Douglass - desc/o Robert Brooke RCFA180

Elizabeth - m____Stone, before Dec 1768 - desc/o Robert Brooke RCFA180

Francis, 5th Baron Howard of Effingham - of VA, bp 1643 d1695 governor of Virginia son of Sir Charles Howard & Frances Courthope, m(1)1673 Philadelphia Pelham, m(2) Susan Felton, m(3) Margaret Vane - the immigrant J&K277; ECD186; GBR283

Harriet - m Samuel Prescott Phillips Fay - desc/o Catherine Hamby GBR394

HOWARD (cont.)

Jacob - of MA, b1719 d1798, m1745 Rachel Fletcher - desc/o Henry Farwell CHB352; MCB183; BCD352

John - of VA, b1635 d1696, m(1)1665 Susanna Norwood - desc/o Matthew Arundel-Howard JSW1770, 1866

Capt John - of MD, b abt 1667 d abt 1704, m(2)1702 Katherine Greenberry - desc/o Matthew Arundel-Howard JSW1770, 1866

Lydia - of MA, b1665, m1694 Joseph Jenkins - desc/o Edward Southworth DBR(3)161

Sarah - b1669 - desc/o Agnes Harris RAA131

Sarah - of MA, m1776 John Cummings - desc/o Henry Farwell CHB352; MCB183; BCD352

William - of NY 1660 - the immigrant EDV67; sufficient proof of alleged royal ancestry is lacking

HOWE Abigail - b1766 - desc/o William Goddard RAA99

George Augustus, 3rd Viscount Howe - b abt 1724 d1758, British commander in America during the French & Indian wars died unmarried, son of Emanuel Scrope Howe, 2nd Viscount Howe & Sophie Charlotte Marie von Kielmansegge - the immigrant GBR187

Miriam - b1765 - desc/o William Goddard RAA99

Rhoda - b1762 - desc/o William Goddard RAA99

Sarah - b1686, m Isaac Learned - desc/o Samuel Hyde LDS92

HOWELL Daniel - of NY, b1680 d1732, m Mary____ - desc/o Edward Howell AFA184

Edward - of MA & NY, bp 1584 d abt 1636, m Frances____ - the immigrant AFA50, 184; sufficient proof of alleged royal ancestry is lacking

Margaret - of NY, bp 1622, m Rev John Moore - desc/o Edward Howell AFA50

Phebe - m 1732 John Scudder - desc/o Edward Howell - desc/o Edward Howell AFA184

Richard - of NY, bp 1629 d aft 1657, m(1) Elizabeth Halsey, m(2) Eleanor Raynor - desc/o Edward Howell AFA184

HOWISON Anne Wood - b1766 d1845, m Landon Calvert - desc/o Rev Robert Brooke MG(1)235

Sarah Anne - b1768, m Peter Trone - desc/o Rev Robert Brooke MG(1)235

HOWLAND Elizabeth - of MA, m1798 Isaac Hamlin - desc/o Edward Southworth DBR(5)834

Esther - b abt 1760, m Peter Barton - desc/o Richard Pearce LDS36

Joseph - m Lydia Bill - desc/o Thomas Southworth GBR245

Lydia - of MA, b1665, m1694 Joseph Jenkins son of John & Mary (Ewer) Jenkins - desc/o Thomas Southworth DBR(3)161

Nathaniel - m Martha Cole - desc/o Thomas Southworth GBR245

Nathaniel Jr - m Abigail Burt - desc/o Thomas Southworth GBR245

HOYT Ensign Jonathan - of CT, b1707 d1779, m1736 Rebecca Benedict - desc/o John Drake DBR(5)59

Jonathan Jr - of CT, b1737 d1821, m1761 Sarah Wood - desc/o John Drake DBR(5)59

Stephen - of CT, b1767 d1835, m1796 Huldah Hawley - desc/o John Drake DBR(5)59

HUBBARD Anne - of VA, b1738 d1789, m1758 Col James Taylor Jr
b1732 at Midway, near Bowling Green, Caroline Co, VA d1814
ensign in the French & Indian War & was colonel of the Caroline Co
militia during the Revolution, a justice, burgess & sheriff also a
member of the Virginia Senate 1788, son of James Taylor of
Bloomsbury, Orange Co, VA & Alice Thornton - desc/o Anne
Lovelace CHB501; GVFHB(3)339 Daniel of CT, b1706 d1741, m
Martha Coit - desc/o Mabel Harlakenden CHB269; BCD269

Daniel Jr - of CT, m Mary Greene - desc/o Mabel Harlakenden
CHB270; BCD270

Col John - of CT, m1724 Elizabeth Stevens - desc/o Mabel
Harlakenden CHB269; MCD230; BCD269

Leah - of MA, b1774, m abt 1792 Adams Cummings - desc/o John
Whitney JSW1808

Col Leverett MD - of CT, b1725 d1794, m1746 Sarah Whitehead -
desc/o Mabel Harlakenden CHB269; MCB302, 303; MCD230;
BCD269

Mary - b1712, m Amos Gates - desc/o Samuel Rice LDS20

Mary - of CT, b1752 d1786, m1777 Rev John Lewis - desc/o Mabel
Harlakenden MCB303; MCD230; BCD270

Mary - of CT, m1777 Lieut David Nevins - desc/o Mabel Harlakenden
CHB270

Mary Todd - of VA, m1767 Dr Thomas Hinde b1734 Oxfordshire,
England, studied medicine in London, settled in Essex Co, VA &
served as a surgeon in the Revolution - desc/o Anne Lovelace
GVFHB(3)340

Russell of CT, b1732, m1755 Mary Gray - desc/o Mabel Harlakenden
CHB269; BCD- 269

Samuel - b1687, m(1) Sarah Clark - desc/o Samuel Rice LDS20

Sarah - m Rev John Cotton of Yarmouth b1661 Guilford, CT
d1705/1706 son of Rev John Cotton of Plymouth - desc/o Gov
Thomas Dudley NE(8)323

Sarah - of CT, m1776 Judge John Trumbull - desc/o Mabel
Harlakenden CHB269; BCD269

HUBBS Rachel - of PA, m Amos Lewis - desc/o Cadwalader Evans
MCD187 - desc/o Rowland Evans MCD266

HUDSON Mary (Polly) - of VA, b abt 1704, m1720 John Wingfield - desc/o
Capt Henry Isham DBR(2)508

HUGER Daniel - of SC - the immigrant EDV67; sufficient proof of alleged
royal ancestry is lacking

Col Francis Kinloch - of SC, b1773 d1855 was trained in medicine in
England. In 1794 he made a daring attempt to rescue Lafayette at
Olmutz & was imprisoned in Austria for eight months. He was
commissioned in 1796 captain in the United States Army, rose to
the rank of colonel & served during the War of 1812, m1802 Harriet
Lucas Pinckney d1824 dau/o General Thomas Pinckney of
Philadelphia - desc/o James Kinloch SCG(3)66

HUGHES (HUGH or PUGH) Ellen - of PA, dau/o Hugh ap Cadwaladr ap
Rhys & Gwen Williams, m Edward Foulke - the immigrant GBR309

Ellis - of PA - desc/o Edward Foulke MCD223

William - of PA - desc/o Edward Foulke MCD223

HULETT Mason Jr - of NY, b1775 d1847, m Abigail Andrews - desc/o Thomas Arnold CHB324; BCD324

HULL Edward - of RI, b1714/1715 d1804, m1762 Mary Weeden - desc/o Dr Richard Palgrave ECD(3)233

Robert - of RI, b1718 d1768, m1738 Thankful Ball - desc/o Dr Richard Palgrave ECD(3)233

HUME (HOME) Armistead - of VA, m Priscilla Colvin dau/o John & Sarah Colvin - desc/o George Hume GVFWM(3)89

Charles - of VA - desc/o George Hume WAC45

Francis - of VA, d1813, m Elizabeth Duncan - desc/o George Hume CHB434; GVFWM(3)89

George - of VA 1721, b1697 Wedderburn Castle, Berwickshire, Scotland d1760 engaged in land surveying as an occupation, son of Sir George Home, 3rd Baronet & Margaret Home, m1727/1728 Elizabeth Proctor - the immigrant CHB434; WAC45; MCS30; GBR30; GVFWM(3)88/91

George - of VA, b1729 d1802, m1754 Jane Stanton - desc/o George Hume CHB434; WAC45

Rev George - of VA, b1755/1756 d1821, m1780/1781 Elizabeth Procter - desc/o George Hume CHB434

George - of VA, b1759 d1816, m Susannah Crigler - desc/o George Hume CHB434

James - of VA - desc/o George Hume WAC45

John - of VA - desc/o George Hume WAC45

William - of VA - desc/o George Hume WAC45

William - of VA, b1734 d1782, m(2) Miss Granville - desc/o George Hume CHB434

HUMPHREY Anne - of MA, b1621 dau/o John Humphrey & Elizabeth Pelham, m(1) William Palmer (or Palmes), m(2) Rev John Myles of Swansea, MA - desc/o Susan Fiennes or Clinton J&K247; CHB146, 416 & 528; FLW189; MCD234; BCD146 - the immigrant GBR116

Mercy - of CT, m Michael Humphrey - desc/o William Leete CHB366; MCD246

Rebecca - of PA 1690, m1678 Robert Owen - the immigrant CHB157, 415; MCD266; BCD157; RAA120; royal descent not proven

HUMPHREY(S) Anne - of PA, m Ellis ap Rees (alias Ellis Price) - the immigrant GBR158

Anne - of PA, m Edward Roberts - the immigrant GBR157

Benjamin - of PA, m Mary Llewelyn - the immigrant GBR157

Daniel - of PA 1682, son of Samuel Humphrey & Elizabeth Rees, m1695 Hannah Wynne, dau/o Dr Thomas Wynne of PA - the immigrant CHB156; BCD156; GBR157; GPFPM(2)72/89

Joseph - of PA, m Elizabeth Medford - the immigrant GBR157

Joshua - of PA, b1710 d1793, m1742 Sarah Williams dau/o Edward Williams - desc/o Daniel Humphreys CHB156; BCD156; GPFPM(2)78

Joshua - of PA, b1751 d1838 the first naval constructor & master shipbuilder to the government, 1774, m Mary Davids b1757 d1805 - desc/o Daniel Humphreys CHB156; BCD156; GPFPM(2)78

Lydia - of PA, m Ellis Ellis - the immigrant GBR157

Rebecca - of PA, m Edward Rees - the immigrant GBR157

HUNGERFORD Benjamin - of CT - desc/o Sir Thomas Hungerford
THC171

Benjamin - of CT, b1705 d1790 - desc/o Sir Thomas Hungerford
THC171

David - of CT, b1710 d1758 - desc/o Sir Thomas Hungerford THC171

Deborah - of CT, b1764, m1786 Nathan Waldo - desc/o Sir Thomas
Hungerford THC171

Eleanor (or Uranah) - of CT, b1747 - desc/o Sir Thomas Hungerford
THC172

Elizabeth - of CT, b abt 1670 d1758, m abt 1695 Joseph Gates -
desc/o Sir Thomas Hungerford THC171

Elizabeth - of CT, b1707, m Joseph Gates - desc/o Sir Thomas
Hungerford THC171

Elizabeth - of CT, b1769 d1853, m(1) early in 1800 Samuel Tuttle,
m(2) abt 1807 Solomon Jones - desc/o Sir Thomas Hungerford
THC172

Esther - of CT, b1687 d1749, m1711 Samuel Gates - desc/o Sir
Thomas Hungerford THC171

Eunice - of CT, b1751, m Joseph Soule - desc/o Sir Thomas
Hungerford THC172

Ezra - of CT, b1761, m Caroline Wilcox - desc/o Sir Thomas
Hungerford THC172

Green - of CT, b1684 d1735, m1709 Jemimi Richardson - desc/o Sir
Thomas Hungerford THC171

Hannah - of CT, b abt 1659, m____ - desc/o Sir Thomas Hungerford
THC171

Hannah - of CT, b1700, m(1)1727 Samuel Ackley Jr, m(2) David Gates
- desc/o Sir Thomas Hungerford THC171

Isaiah - of CT, b1756 d1833, m Esther Mead - desc/o Sir Thomas
Hungerford THC172

John - of CT, b abt 1674, m1702 Deborah Spencer - desc/o Sir
Thomas Hungerford THC171

Capt John - of CT, b1718, m twice - desc/o Sir Thomas Hungerford
THC171

Jonathan - of CT, bp 1715 d1771 - desc/o Sir Thomas Hungerford
THC171

Margaret - of CT, b1767 d1851, m1787 Job Hurlbut - desc/o Sir
Thomas Hungerford THC172

Mary - of CT, b1681 d1763, m Stephen Cone - desc/o Sir Thomas
Hungerford THC171

Mary - of CT, b1749, m Alexander Steward Jr - desc/o Sir Thomas
Hungerford THC172

Samuel - of CT, b1725 d1789, m Mary Graves - desc/o Sir Thomas
Hungerford THC171, 172

Sarah - of CT, b abt 1654, m Lewis Hugh - desc/o Sir Thomas
Hungerford THC171

Sarah - of CT, b1679 d1753, m abt 1697 Nathaniel Cone - desc/o Sir
Thomas Hungerford THC171

Susannah - of CT, b abt 1676, m abt 1700 Samuel Church - desc/o
Sir Thomas Hungerford THC171

Sir Thomas - of CT 1638, b1602 d1671, m(1)____, m(2) abt 1658

HUNGERFORD (cont.)

Hannah Wiley - the immigrant THC170; RAA no longer accepted as being of royal descent

Thomas - of CT, b1648 d1714, m bef June 6, 1671 Mary Green - desc/o Sir Thomas Hungerford THC171

Thomas - of CT, b abt 1672/1673 d1750, m abt 1699 Elizabeth Smith - desc/o Sir Thomas Hungerford THC171

Thomas - of CT, b1702 d1786 - desc/o Sir Thomas Hungerford THC171

Capt Uriel - of CT, b1755, m Hannah Wilcox - desc/o Sir Thomas Hungerford THC172

Zeruah - of CT, b1763, m Amos Northrop - desc/o Sir Thomas Hungerford THC172

HUNT Charity - b1755 - desc/o Edward FitzRandolph RAA96

Dorothy - of MA, b1723/1724 at Littleton, m at Littleton 1744 John Edwards Jr - desc/o Rev Peter Bulkeley TAG(36)104, 105

Elizabeth - m Lemuel Pope - desc/o Richard Palgrave GBR266

Elizabeth - of MA, b1752 d1785, m1773 Solomon Hewes - desc/o Thomas Dudley DBR(3)597

Rebecca - b1724 - desc/o Thomas Bradbury RAA72

Samuel - b1681/1682 ? - desc/o Richard Palgrave RAA121

Sarah - b1722 ? - desc/o Richard Palgrave RAA121

Thomas - of NY 1667 - the immigrant EDV124; sufficient proof of alleged royal ancestry is lacking

HUNTER Edward - b1747 - desc/o Rebecca Humphrey RAA120

Robert - of NY & NJ, d1734 governor of New York & NJ, lieut governor of Virginia, governor of Jamaica, son of James & Margaret (Spalding) Hunter, m Elizabeth Orby - the immigrant GBR68

HUNTING Mary - b1718 - desc/o John Deighton RAA86

Samuel - b1666 - desc/o John Deighton RAA86

Samuel - b1697 - desc/o John Deighton RAA86

HUNTINGDON Olive - b1757 d aft 1800, m1777 Asa Robinson b1757 d aft 1799 - desc/o Elizabeth St John DBR(1)683

HUNTINGTON Lois - b1765 - desc/o Robert Abell RAA59

Theophilus - b1726 - desc/o Robert Abell RAA59

HURD Love - of CT, m Phineas Chapin - desc/o Rev Charles Chauncy CHB69; BCD69

HURLBUT David - b1746 - desc/o Richard Belding RAA68

HURLBURT Anna - of CT, b1762 d1828, m1788 Elisha Blackman - desc/o Bridget Tompson DBR(3)684

Hannah - of CT, b1769 d1855, m Rev William Patten - desc/o Grace Kaye CHB206; BCD206

HUSSEY Jonathan - b1753 - desc/o Rose Stoughton RAA119

Lydia - b1757 d1843, m Jacob Griffith - desc/o Hugh Garry PFA Apx C #13; GBR168

HUSTON James - of MA & ME, m Mary Sloss - the immigrant BLG2758; sufficient proof of alleged royal ancestry is lacking

Robert - of ME, b1752 d1824, m1782 Jane Houston - desc/o James Huston BLG2758

William - of ME, b1719 d1761, m abt 1747 Agnes Lermond - desc/o James Huston BLG2758

HUTCHINS Abigail - b1771, m1792 Henry Chandler of Chester, VT - desc/o Rev Peter Bulkeley TAG(36)105

Basmoth Eleanor - b1769, m John Whipple - desc/o Ellen Newton LDS110

Bulkeley - of VT, b1765 at Putney d1850 at Pawlet, Revolutionary War soldier, m Elizabeth Johnson - desc/o Rev Peter Bulkeley TAG(36)105

Silence, m___Howe of Westmoreland, VT - desc/o Rev Peter Bulkeley TAG(36)105

Simon - of MA, b1761 at Harvard d1832 at Burlington, VT , Revolutionary War soldier - desc/o Rev Peter Bulkeley TAG(36)105

William Gordon - b1739, m(2) Hepzibah Cressey - desc/o Ellen Newton LDS110

HUTCHINSON Abigail - m(1)___Moore, m(2)___Kellond, m(3) Col John Foster - desc/o Anne Marbury NE(19)16

Abigail - b1709, m(1)1732 John Davenport, m(2) William Merchant - desc/o Anne Marbury NE(19)16

Anne - of MA, bp 1643 d1716/1717, m(1)1660/1662 Samuel Dyer bp 1635 d bef 1679 son of William DyeR & Mary (Barrett) Dyer, (who was martyred in Boston in 1660 for her Quaker beliefs), m(2)1679 Daniel Vernon b1643 d1715 son of Samuel Vernon - desc/o Anne Marbury ECD258; RAA114; NE(19)13/20 - desc/o Katherine Hamby NE(145)262

Bridget - b1618 - desc/o Anne Marbury RAA114

Catherine - b1653, m Henry Bartholomew - desc/o Anne Marbury NE(19)15

Capt Edward - of MA, bp 1613 d1675, killed by Indians during King Philip's War, son of William & Anne (Marbury) Hutchinson, m(1)1636 Katherine Hamby d abt 1649/1650 dau/o Counsellor Hamby of Ipswich, m(2)1650 Abigail (Firmage/Vermais) Button b abt 1622 d1689, wid/o Robert Button, & dau/o___& Alice (Blessing) Firmage - desc/o Anne Marbury J&K160; ECD258; DBR(3)170; DBR(4)311; DBR(5)290; RAA114; GBR233; NE(19)13/20, (145)99/121, 258/268; EO2(2)447/484

Edward - of MA, b1678 d1752, m1706 Lydia Foster b1687 dau/o Col John Foster (ancestors of Franklin Delano Roosevelt, President of the United States) - desc/o Anne Marbury GBR233; NE(19)16 - desc/o Katherine Hamby GBR394; NE(145)261

Hon Elisha - of MA, b1641 d1717, m(1)1665 Hannah Hawkins bp 1644 d1676 dau/o Captain Thomas & Mary (Welles) Hawkins, m(2)1677 Elizabeth Clark b1642 d aft 14 Aug 1702 dau/o Major Thomas & Mary___Clark & wid/o John Freak d1675 by whom she had at least two children, Clark & John - desc/o Anne Marbury J&K160; GBR233; NE(1)15 - desc/o Katherine Hamby GBR394; NE(145)261

Elisha - b1745 d1824, preceptor & Canon of Lichfield, m Mary Watson dau/o Col Watson - desc/o Anne Marbury NE(19)17

Elizabeth - of MA, b1639 d1728, m1668 Edward Winslow b abt 1635 d1682 son of John & Mary (Chilton) Winslow & grandson of *Mayflower* passenger James Chilton - desc/o Anne Marbury GBR234; NE(19)13/20 - desc/o Katherine Hamby GBR394;

HUTCHINSON (cont.)

NE(145)261

Elizabeth - of MA, m1757 Rev Nathaniel Robbins - desc/o Anne Marbury GBR233; NE(19)16 - desc/o Katherine Hamby GBR394

Elizabeth - of MA, b1669 d abt 1730, m Dr John Clarke - desc/o Katherine Hamby NE(145)261 - desc/o Anne Marbury NE(19)15

Faith - m Thomas Savage - desc/o Anne Marbury DBR(1)760

Foster - b1724 d in Nova Scotia 1799, m1750 Margaret Mascarene - desc/o Anne Marbury NE(19)16

Hannah - of MA, b1658 d1704, m abt 1689 Peter Walker b abt 1650 d1711, iron dealer, son of James & Bathsheba (Brooks) Walker - desc/o Anne Marbury NE(19)15, (145)265

Hannah - of MA, b1671/1672 d abt 1740, m John Ruck, a merchant, living in Boston in 1739 (ancestors of George Herbert Walker Bush, President of the United States) - desc/o Anne Marbury DBR(4)311; DBR(5)290; GBR234; NE(19)15 - desc/o Katherine Hamby GBR394; NE(145)261

Hannah - b1714, m1733 Rev Samuel Mather - desc/o Anne Marbury NE(19)16

Job - b1757 d1834, m1783 Experience Mack - desc/o John Prescott DBR(1)568

Katherine - of MA, b1652/1653 d aft 1730, m bet 1675/1692 Henry Bartholomew bp 1656 d1694/1698 son of Henry & Elizabeth (Scudder) Bartholomew, m(2)1699 Capt Richard Janverin/Jeanverin, his name afterwards spelled Chamberlain - desc/o Anne Marbury NE(145)265

Lydia - b1717, m1736 George Rogers - desc/o Anne Marbury NE(19)16

Mary - b1773, m1811 William Sanford Oliver d1833 - desc/o Anne Marbury NE(19)17

Samuel - of MA, b1667 - the immigrant EDV19; royal ancestry not proven

Sarah - b1709, m1728 Rev William Welsteed - desc/o Anne Marbury NE(19)16

Sarah - m Dr Peter Oliver - desc/o Anne Marbury NE(19)17

Susanna - of MA, bp 1633, m1651 John Cole - desc/o Anne Marbury DBR(3)134; DBR(5)948; RAA114

Susanna - b1649 d aft 26 May 1716, m1677 Nathaniel Coddington b1653 d1724 son of Governor William & Anne (Brinlley) Coddington - desc/o Anne Marbury RAA114; NE(19)13/29 - desc/o Katherine Hamby NE(145)263

Hon Thomas of MA, m1703 Sarah Foster dau/o Col John Foster - desc/o Anne Marbury J&K160; NE(19)16

Thomas - of MA, b1711, governor of MA at the outbreak of the Revolutionary War & chief justice, m1734 Margaret Sanford - desc/o Anne Marbury J&K160; NE(19)17

Thomas - of MA, b1740, m1771 Sarah Oliver dau/o Lieut Governor Oliver - desc/o Anne Marbury NE(19)17

Thomas - b1774/1775, barrister at law, m(1)1799 Elizabeth Hagen d1808, m(2) Mrs Tolfrey - desc/o Anne Marbury NE(19)17

William - of MA - the immigrant EDV19; EO2(2)447/484 sufficient

HUTCHINSON (cont.)
proof of alleged royal ancestry is lacking
HUTT Gerard - of VA, b1671/1675 d1739/1740, m Anne Jackson - desc/o Dr Thomas Gerard DBR(2)360; DBR(3)95

Gerard II - of VA, d1770, m Mary____ - desc/o Dr Thomas Gerard DBR(3)96

Gerard III - of VA, b1734, m1760 Mate Spence - desc/o Dr Thomas Gerard DBR(3)96

Jane - of VA, d1732, m William McKenney - desc/o Dr Thomas Gerard DBR(2)360

Mary - of VA, d1808, m James Smith Dozier - desc/o Dr Thomas Gerard DBR(3)96

HYDE Abiah - m Aaron Cleveland IV - desc/o Robert Abell AAP149; GBR226

Benjamin - b1756 - desc/o Richard Billings RAA70

Bethia - of CT, b1677/1678, m1708 Jacob Hyde - desc/o William Hyde THC177

Charles - of CT, b1748 d1839, m(1)1768 Mary Abel, m(2) Roxanna Rogers - desc/o William Hyde BLG2760

Capt Daniel - of CT, b1694 d1770, m Abigail Wattles - desc/o William Hyde BLG2760

David Abel - of NY, b1772 d1856, m1797 Margaret Burt - desc/o William Hyde BLG2760

Edward, 3rd Earl of Clarendon - of NY & NJ, b1661 d1723 governor of New York & NJ, son of Henry, 2nd Earl of Clarendon & Theodosis (Capell) Hyde, m Catherine O'Brien, Baroness Clifton - the immigrant GBR41

Elijah - of CT, b1754 d1820, m Elizabeth Edgerton - desc/o William Hyde BLG2761

Elizabeth - of CT, b1660 d1736, m1682 Lieut Richard Lord - desc/o William Hyde BLG2760

Erastus - of NY, b1775 d1810, m1797 Fannie Bell - desc/o William Hyde BLG2760

Experience - b1700 - desc/o Robert Abell RAA59

Hannah - of CT, b1680 d1720, m Eleazer Hyde - desc/o William Hyde THC177

Capt Jacob - of CT, b1703 d1782, m1727 Hannah Kingsbury - desc/o William Hyde BLG2761

Jacob - of CT, b1730 d1815, m Hannah Hazen - desc/o William Hyde BLG2761

Capt James - of CT, b1707 d1793, m1743 Sarah Marshall - desc/o William Hyde BLG2760; AAP149; FFF195, 202; GBR226

Capt James - of CT, b1752 d1809, m1774 Martha Nevins - desc/o William Hyde BLG2760; FFF195, 202

James - b1761 - desc/o Richard Belding RAA68

Job - of MA, b1643 d1685, m Elizabeth Fuller - desc/o William Hyde LDS37; THC177

John - of CT, b1667 d1727, m1698 Experience Abell - desc/o William Hyde BLG2760; FFF195

John - of CT, b1681/1682, m(1)1707 Sarah Prentice, m(2) Hannah Williams - desc/o William Hyde LDS37; THC177

HYDE (cont.)

Jonathan - of CT, b1767 d1829, m Hannah Bronson - desc/o William Hyde BLG2761

Mary - of CT, b1673 d1723, m abt 1691 Capt Abraham Brown - desc/o William Hyde THC177

Mary Calvert - m abt 1766 George Mitchell - desc/o Anne Arundel ECD148; ECD(2)77; DBR(1)152; DBR(2)237; DBR(3)244

Mathew - b1711 - desc/o Robert Abell RAA59

Relief - b1708, m Thomas Draper - desc/o William Hyde LDS37

Deacon Samuel - of MA, b1610, m Temperance____ - desc/o William Hyde LDS37, 92; THC176, 177; RAA no longer accepted as royal descent

Samuel - of CT, b1637 d1677, m1659 Jane Lee - desc/o William Hyde BLG2760; FFF194; THC176

Samuel - of CT, b1665 d1742, m1690 Elizabeth Calkins - desc/o William Hyde BLG2760

Samuel - of CT, b1666/1667 d1741, m Deliverance Dana - desc/o William Hyde THC177

Sarah - b1644, m Thomas Woolson - desc/o William Hyde LDS92

Sarah - of CT, b1675 d1754, m1796/1797 Daniel Hyde - desc/o William Hyde THC177

Thomas - of CT, b1672, m Mary Backus - desc/o William Hyde BLG2761

Thomas - of CT, b1699 d1782, m1732 Elizabeth Huntington - desc/o William Hyde BLG2761

Walter - b1735 - desc/o Richard Billings RAA70

William - of CT 1659, d1681 - the immigrant BLG2760; FFF194; THC176, 177

HYRNE Benjamin - of SC, b1735 d1790, m(1)1759 Elizabeth Ann Harleston b1742 d1769 & had issue, m(2)1773 Catherine Ball b1751 d1774, m(3)1775 Sarah Smith d1785 dau/o George Smith & Elizabeth Waring & had issue, m(4)1787 Rebecca Singleton d1814 aged 62 years wid/o Benjamin Coachman, Esq - desc/o Elizabeth Massingberd SCG(2)402

Col Edward - of SC & Hyrneham, New Hanover Co, North Carolina, b1694 or earlier d1750/1758, m Barbara Smith b1697 d bef 1738 dau/o Thomas Smith, Second Landgrave & Anna Cornelia (van Myddah ?) - desc/o Elizabeth Massingberd SCG(2)401, 403, 404

Elizabeth - of SC, b1722 d1756, m1745 Thomas Dixon b1720 d1769 of James Island & had issue - desc/o Elizabeth Massingberd SCG(2)402

Elizabeth - of SC, m1747/1748 Daniel Britton d1749 of Craven Co, North Carolina & had issue Moses, Mary, Henry & Francis including a son Daniel Britton who died in infancy before 24 Jul 1751 - desc/o Elizabeth Massingberd SCG(2)404, 405

Elizabeth - of SC, b1752 d1790, m1779 Daniel Tucker, Esq b1752 d1797 of Georgetown & had issue - desc/o Elizabeth Massingberd SCG(2)407

Harriet - of SC, b1760, m Richard Bohun Baker & had issue - desc/o Elizabeth Massingberd SCG(2)408

Col Henry - of SC, b1704 d1764, m(1)1733 Susannah Bellinger b1715

HYRNE (cont.)

    d1749 dau/o Landgrave Edmund Bellinger & Elizabeth Baker of the Province of Carolina, m(2)1751 Elizabeth Clark d1752 aged 41 years dau/o Alexander Clark & wid/o Joshua Sanders, m(3)1759 Mary Butler the dau/o Richard Butler wid/o Culcheth Golightly - desc/o Elizabeth Massingberd SCG(2)401, 406, 407

Henry - of SC, b1727 d1780, m(1)1753 Ann Filbein b1736 d1762, m(2)1764 Elizabeth Ball b1746 d1787 & had issue by both wives - desc/o Elizabeth Massingberd SCG(2)402

Henry - of SC, b1734 of St Bartholomew's Parish d abt 1785 captain from the district of Chehaw 1775, captain of militia Dec 1775, lieutenant in 5th South Carolina Regiment (Continental) & received a bounty grant of land for his services, m1756 Mary Ann Girardeau - desc/o Elizabeth Massingberd SCG(2)410

Henry - of SC, b1760, m1790 at Ashepoo, Ann Pinckney Webb, dau/o Dr William Webb, issue a son Henry Hyrne - desc/o Elizabeth Massingberd SCG(2)410

Margaret - of SC, b1720, m Benjamin Coachman & had issue - desc/o Elizabeth Massingberd SCG(2)402

Mary - of SC, b1690 or 1697 d1776 of St James Goose Creek, m1713 Thomas Smith b1669? d1738 - desc/o Elizabeth Massingberd SCG(2)401

Mary - of SC, b1717, m James Screven & had issue - desc/o Elizabeth Massingberd SCG(2)402

Mary Ann - of SC, b1757, m1785 William Basquen - desc/o Elizabeth Massingberd SCG(2)410

Sarah - of SC, b1763, m abt Sep 1788 Col James Simons & had issue - desc/o Elizabeth Massingberd SCG(2)408

Thomas - of SC, b1729 d1782, m1751 Susannah Walker - desc/o Elizabeth Massingberd SCG(2)402

Dr William Alexander - of SC, b1754 d1784 Island of St Thomas, m1779 Sarah Mitchell & left issue - desc/o Elizabeth Massingberd SCG(2)407

- I -

IJAMS Plummer Sr - of MD, b abt 1697 d1792, m1718 Ruth Childs - desc/o Frances White ECD(2)309

    Plummer Jr - of MD, b1748 d1795, m Jemima Welsh - desc/o Frances White ECD(2)309

INGLIS Mungo - of VA - the immigrant WAC29; sufficient proof of alleged royal ancestry is lacking

INGOLDSBY Olive - of MA, bp 1602, m Rev Thomas James bp 1595 d1682/1683 B.A. Emmanuel College, Cambridge 1614/1615 M.A. 1618, ordained Charlestown, MA - the immigrant FLW35; MCS74; DBR(2)291, 654, 703; DBR(3)123, 124, 630; RAA75; TAG(11)143, 144, 145; GBR211 lists her son Rev Thomas James as the immigrant

IRELAND John Jr - of MA, b1768 d1844, m1789 Sarah Hunt - desc/o Olive Welby DBR(4)665

IRONMONGER Elizabeth - of VA, b1685 d1709, m(2)1706 John Collier - desc/o Frances Ironmonger DBR(3)44; DBR(4)131

Frances - of VA, d 1695, m abt 1670 Mordecai Cooke II - desc/o William Ironmonger ECD(2)162; DBR(1)643, 739; DBR(2)125, 784; DBR(3)46, 697, 698, 702; DBR(4)219, 442; DBR(5)105, 585, 744, 889

Francis - of VA, son of Samuel Ironmonger & Bridget Cordray, m Elizabeth____ - the immigrant DBR(3)44; DBR(4)131, 215; GBR382

Mary - of VA, m Abraham Field - desc/o William Ironmonger DBR(3)347, 349

Samuel - b1607, m Bridget Cordray - GBR382 lists their son as the immigrant;

William - of VA 1652, b abt 1628/1629 d1695 son of Samuel Ironmonger & Bridget Cordray, m Elizabeth Jones - the immigrant ECD(2)162; DBR(1)643, 739; DBR(2)784; DBR(3)46, 346, 347, 348, 349, 695, 697, 698, 702; DBR(4)155, 422; DBR(5)585, 741, 744, 858, 889; GBR382

IRVINE Anne - of GA, b1770, m(1)1786 Capt James Bulloch - desc/o John Irvine MD ECD142; MCD236; BCD330; AAP150; PFA Apx C #11; GBR78 - desc/o Col Kenneth Baillie GBR114

John MD - of GA abt 1765, b1742 d1808, son of Charles of Over Boddam & Euphemia (Douglas) Irvine, m(1)1765 Ann Elizabeth Baillie - the immigrant J&K142; CHB329, 330; ECD142; MCD236; MCS70; BCD329, 330; AAP149, 150; PFA Apx C #11; GBR78

William - b1731 - the immigrant EDV68; sufficient proof of alleged royal ancestry is lacking

ISHAM Anne - of VA, m bef 1676 Col Francis Eppes b abt 1718/1719, member of the House of Burgesses for Henrico Co Virginia - desc/o Capt Henry Isham CHB533; DBR(1)25, 40, 592; DBR(2)344, 507; DBR(3)201; DBR(5)1065; RAA104; GBR339

Capt Henry - of Bermuda Hundred VA, b1628 d1676 son of William Isham & Mary (Brett) Isham, m abt 1650 Katharine (Banks) Royall d1686 wid/o Joseph Royall - the immigrant J&K135, 161; CHB532; ECD(2)166; DBR(1)24, 25, 40, 589, 592, 744; DBR(2)34, 343, 344, 504, 506, 507, 641, 801, 821; DBR(3)146, 199, 201, 359; DBR(4)307; DBR(5)105, 724, 1065; RAA1, 104; AAP141; PFA Apx C #3; WAC47, 48; CRL(3)242; GBR338

Henry - of VA, d1680 (dsp) - desc/o Capt Henry Isham CHB533; WAC47, 48

Mary - of VA, b1659, m bef 1676 Col William Randolph of Turkey Island, James River, VA, a member of the Virginia House of Burgesses & the Governor's Council d1711 aged 80, m(2) Capt Joseph Royall - desc/o Capt Henry Isham J&K133; CHB533; ECD(2)166, 744; DBR(2)34, 508, 801; DBR(3)359; DBR(4)307; DBR(5)724; RAA104; AAP141; PFA Apx C #3; CRL(3)242; GBR338

IVES Ebenezer - of CT, b1692 d1759, m1714/1715 Mary Atwater - desc/o Thomas Yale ECD(3)306

Eunice - of CT, b1732 d1801, m1757 Zophar Blakeslee - desc/o Thomas Yale ECD(3)306

Joel - b1760 - desc/o Obadiah Bruen RAA74

IZARD Elizabeth - m176_ Daniel Blake, left no issue - desc/o Stephen Bull SCG(1)218

    Mary - of SC, m1759, m Miles Brewton, Esq - desc/o Stephen Bull SCG(1)218

– J –

JACKSON Judge Charles - of MA, b1775 d1855, m1809 Fanny Cabot - desc/o Capt Thomas Lake CHB410

    Eleazer - b1669 - desc/o George Morton RAA116

    John - of VA, d1826, m Catherine White - desc/o William Clopton DBR(5)657

    Mercy - b1697 - desc/o George Morton RAA116

JACOB (JACOBS) Israel - of NY, b1767, m(2) Elizabeth Winchell, living 1815 - desc/o Samuel Appleton DBR(1)360; DBR(2)464; DBR(3)216; DBR(4)492

    John - of CT, b1725 d1837 known as "the Landlord," being proprietor of the "Half-Way House" on the post road between Boston & Hartford, m1751 Sarah Plank b1726 d1789 - desc/o Dr Richard Palgrave DBR(4)693

    John - of CT, b1754 d1837 known as "Squire," justice of the peace & representative, a soldier in the American Revolution, m Dinah Tourtelotte b1760 d1819 - desc/o Dr Richard Palgrave DBR(4)693

    Joseph - of MA, b abt 1655 d1697, m Susanna Symonds b1668 - desc/o Samuel Appleton DBR(1)360; DBR(2)464; DBR(3)216; DBR(4)492; RAA63

    Joseph - of MA, b1692/1693 d1786, m1723 Mary Bartlett d bef 1736 - desc/o Samuel Appleton DBR(1)360; DBR(2)464; DBR(3)216; DBR(4)492; RAA63

    Mary - b1686 - desc/o Samuel Appleton RAA63

    Richard - of MA, b1724 d1809, m(1) bef 1747 Thankful Kellogg b1726 d1787 - desc/o Samuel Appleton DBR(1)360; DBR(2)464; DBR(3)216; DBR(4)492; RAA63

    Richard - b1760 - desc/o Samuel Appleton RAA63, 68

    Stephen - of CT, b1743 d1825, m(2)1770 Mary Ives - desc/o Rev Peter Bulkeley DBR(5)971

    Thomas - b1641 - desc/o Samuel Appleton RAA63

JADWIN John - of VA - the immigrant WAC107; sufficient proof of alleged royal ancestry is lacking

    Robert - of VA, d1727 - desc/o Thomas Jadwin WAC107

    Thomas - of VA - the immigrant WAC107; sufficient proof of alleged royal ancestry is lacking

JAFFREY George - of NH, d1707 - the immigrant EDV89; sufficient proof of alleged royal ancestry is lacking

    George - of NH, m ___Jeffries - desc/o George Jaffrey EDV89

    Sarah - of NH, m David Jeffries - desc/o George Jaffrey EDV89

JAMES Alice - of VA, m James R Dermott - desc/o William Strother GVFTQ(3)377

    Benjamin - of VA, b1768 d1825, m Jean Stobo - desc/o William Strother GVFTQ(3)377

JAMES (cont.)

Elizabeth - m Joshua Leavitt - desc/o Gov Thomas Dudley DBR(1)74; DBR(2)97

Frances - d1823, m1799 Jonathan Hunter - desc/o Capt Henry Woodhouse DBR(1)348

Jesse - of PA, b1750 d1816, m1779 Phoebe Townsend - desc/o Hannah Price MCB418

Lucy - of VA, m Col Henry Towles - desc/o William Strother GVFTQ(3)377

Nancy - m Dade Hooe - desc/o William Strother GVFTQ(3)377

Ruth - of NY, b abt 1664, m Thomas Harris d1697 - desc/o Olive Ingoldsby DBR(2)291, 655, 704; DBR(3)124, 630; RAA75

Rev Thomas - of NY, b1620/1622 England d1696 East Hampton, Long Island, first minster at Southampton 1650/1696, son of Rev Thomas James & Olive Ingoldsby, m Ruth Jones b abt 1628 d1668 - desc/o Olive Ingoldsby FLW171; MCS74; DBR(2)291, 655, 703; DBR(3)124, 630; RAA75; TAG(11)143, 144, 145 - the immigrant GBR211

JAMESON David - of VA, b1757 d1793, m Milderd Smith - desc/o James Jameson WAC33

James - of VA, d1736, m Mary____ - the immigrant WAC33; sufficient proof of alleged royal ancestry is lacking

James - of VA, b1720 d1766, m Mary Gaines - desc/o James Jameson WAC33

Thomas - of VA - desc/o James Jameson WAC33

JANNEY Elisha - of VA, b1761, m Mary Gibson - desc/o Thomas Janney AFA70

Jacob - of PA, d1786, m1742 Hannah Ingledue - desc/o Thomas Janney AFA70

Joseph - of PA, b1672, m Rebecca Biles - desc/o Thomas Janney AFA70

Thomas - of PA, bp 1634, m1660 Margery Heath - the immigrant AFA70; sufficient proof of alleged royal ancestry is lacking

JEFFERSON Anna Scott - of VA, b1755 d1828, m1788 Hastings Marks - desc/o Capt Henry Isham PFA127 - desc/o Christopher Branch GVFTQ(2)436

Elizabeth - of VA, m1803 (her first cousin) Samuel Allen Jefferson b1776 d1855 - desc/o Christopher Branch GVFTQ(2)452

Field - of VA, b1702 d1765, m Mary Frances Robertson d1750 - desc/o Christopher Branch GVFTQ(2)451

John Robertson - of VA, m1763 Elizabeth Broome dau/o Dr Thomas Broome - desc/o Christopher Branch GVFTQ(2)452

Judith - of VA, b1698 d1730, m George Farrar b1690 d1772 son of Major William Farrar & Priscilla (Baugh) Farrar - desc/o Christopher Branch DBR(1)311, 607

Lucy - of VA, b1752, m1769 Col Charles Lilburn Lewis - desc/o Capt Henry Isham PFA127 - desc/o Christopher Branch GVFTQ(2)436

Maria - of VA, m1796 John Wayles Eppes of Bermuda Hundred, Chesterfield Co, VA & had issue - desc/o Col Thomas Randolph PVF142; CFA(5)428

Martha - of VA, m Robert Wynne (Winn) of Surry Co - desc/o

JEFFERSON (cont.)

Christopher Branch APP139

Martha - of VA, b1746 d1811, m1765 Dabney Carr - desc/o Capt Henry Isham PFA127 - desc/o Christopher Branch GVFTQ(2)436

Martha (Patsy) - of VA, b1772 d1836, m1790 Gov Thomas Mann Randolph Jr of Edge Hill, Albemarle Co, VA & father of Col Thomas Jefferson Randolph of the same place - desc/o Henry Isham PFA98 - desc/o Christopher Branch GVFTQ(2)438 - desc/o Col Thomas Randolph PVF142; CFA(5)428

Mary - of VA, d1745, m Thomas Harris d1730 - desc/o Christopher Branch APP139

Mary - of VA, b1741 d1817 (sister of Thomas Jefferson, 3rd President of the United States), m1760 Col John Bolling III, 3rd-great-grandson of Pocahontas & John Rolfe - desc/o Capt Henry Isham PFA127, GBR169, 338 - desc/o Christopher Branch GBR408; GVFTQ(2)436

Peter - of VA, b1708 d1757 surveyor, colonel in the militia & was a member of the first court, also a delegate in the House of Burgesses, m1739 Jane Randolph d1776 dau/o Isham Randolph - desc/o Christopher Branch AAP141; GBR407; GVFTQ(2)435

Peterfield - of VA, b1735, m1762 Elizabeth Allen b1739 dau/o Samuel Allen of Cumberland Co, VA - desc/o Christopher Branch GVFTQ(2)451

Randolph - of VA, b1755 d1815, m(1)1781 Anna Lewis, m(2) Mitchie B Pryor - desc/o Capt Henry Isham PFA127 - desc/o Christopher Branch GVFTQ(2)438

Samuel Allen - of VA, b1776 d1855, m(1)1803 (his first cousin) Elizabeth Jefferson dau/o John Jefferson - desc/o Christopher Branch GVFTQ(2)452

Capt Thomas Jr - of VA, b1677/1679 d1725/1731, m(1)1697 Mary Field b1679/1680 d1715 dau/o Major Peter Field & Judith (Soane) Randolph, m(2) Alice (Ailsey) Ward - desc/o Christopher Branch DBR(1)311, 607; AAP141; APP139; GVFTQ(2)432/434

Pres Thomas - of VA, b1743 d1826, President of the United States 1801/1809, m1772 Mrs Martha Wayles Skelton b1748 dau/o John Wayles of The Forest, Charles City Co, VA & wid/o Bathurst Skelton - desc/o Capt Henry Isham J&K135; CHB533; DBR(1)744; AAP141; PFA Apx C #3, Apx #3; GBR338 - desc/o Col William Randolph AAP140; GBR169; PVF142; CFA(5)428 - desc/o Christopher Branch GBR407; GVFTQ(2)436, 450

Thomas - of VA, d1814, m1806 Elizabeth Ball d1857 dau/o John & Mary Ball - desc/o Christopher Branch GVFTQ(2)451

JEFFREYS Edward - of VA abt 1715, m1730 Miss Burt - the immigrant MCS23; sufficient proof of alleged royal ancestry is lacking

Sir Herbert - of VA, governor of Virginia, son of William Jeffreys & Jane Berkeley, m Susanna____ - the immigrant GBR282

Jeffrey - of VA, d1707, m Sarah Dawes - the immigrant MCS22; sufficient proof of alleged royal ancestry is lacking

JEFFRIES David - of MA 1677 - the immigrant EDV34; sufficient proof of alleged royal ancestry is lacking

JENKINS Benjamin - of MA, b1707 d1789, m1730 Mehitable Blish b1711 d1737/1738 dau/o Joseph & Hannah (Child) Blish - desc/o Thomas Southworth DBR(3)161

Lydia - of MA, b1735/1736 d1813, m1758 Joshua Nye b1733 d1813 son of Jonathan & Remember Nye - desc/o Thomas Southworth DBR(3)161

JENINGS (JENNINGS) Ariana - b1729 d1801, m John Randolph, attorney general of Virginia - desc/o Edmund Jennings CRL(1)254; SVF(1)282

Edmund - of VA 1680, b1659 d1727 attorney general of Virginia, sheriff of York & James City Co; president of the council, secretary of state & acting governor of Virginia, third son of Sir Edmund Jennings & Margaret Barkham, m Frances Corbin d1713 London, dau/o Henry Corbin & Mrs Alice Eltonhead Burnham Corbin (Creek) - the immigrant DBR(2)603; WAC26; CRL(1)253; GBR287; HSF(4)130; SVF(1)281/283; CFSSA301

Edmund - of MD, b1697 d1756, m1728 Ariana Vanderheiden dau/o Mathias Vanderheiden - desc/o Edmund Jennings WAC26; CRL(1)253; SVF(1)282; CFSSA301

Elizabeth - of VA, m Richard Porteus - desc/o Edmund Jennings WAC26; CRL(1)253

Elizabeth - of VA, b1684 - desc/o Col Peter Jenings WAC26

Frances - of VA, m Charles Grymes of Morattico, VA - desc/o Edmund Jennings WAC26; CRL(1)253; SVF(1)282; CFSSA301

Hannah - b1768 - desc/o Richard Belding RAA68

Margaret - of VA, m(1)1708 Christ Church, Middlesex Co, Isaac Hill d1734, m(2) Nicholas or Josias Randle d1748 - desc/o Edmund Jennings DBR(2)603; HSF(4)130; SVF(1)282; CFSSA301

Col Peter - of VA, d1671, m Catharine Lunsford - the immigrant WAC26; sufficient proof of alleged royal ancestry is lacking

Peter - of VA, m Sarah_____ - desc/o Col Peter Jenings WAC26

Philip - of VA, bp 1678 - desc/o Col Peter Jenings WAC26

Priscilla - m William Hill, an officer in the British Navy - desc/o Edmund Jennings SVF(1)282

Rebecca - of VA, bp 1690 - desc/o Col Peter Jenings WAC26

Thomas - of VA, bp 1686 - desc/o Col Peter Jenings WAS26

JENNER Joanna - of MA, b1734 d1785, m Edward Carnes - desc/o Mabel Harlakenden MCD231

Thomas - of MA, b1693 d1765 - desc/o Mabel Harlakenden MCD231

JENNEY Isabel - dau/o Sir Arthur Jenney & Helen Stonard, m John Talbot b abt 1645 d1727 Anglican missionary clergyman - the immigrant GBR275

JERDONE Francis - of VA, b1720/1721, m1753 Sarah Macon - the immigrant WAC29, 30; sufficient proof of alleged royal ancestry is lacking

JEWETT David - m Sarah Selden - desc/o Elizabeth Marshall GBR264

Elizabeth - m Anselm Comstock - desc/o Elizabeth Marshall GBR264 - desc/o Thomas Lewis GBR465

Hepzibah - b1759, m Caleb Blood - desc/o Abraham Errington LDS31

Nathan - m Deborah Lord - desc/o Elizabeth Marshall GBR264 - desc/o Thomas Lewis GBR465

JEWETT (cont.)

Susannah - of MA, b1758, m1782 Benjamin Tenney - desc/o Grace Chetwode DBR(1)100

JOHN Jane - of PA, dau/o John ap Evan, m Robert Cadwalader, their children & descendants took the surname Roberts - the immigrant GBR306

JOHNES Edward - of MA 1630, d1660 - the immigrant EDV90, 91; sufficient proof of alleged royal ancestry is lacking

JOHNSON Daniel - b1711 - desc/o Mary Gye RAA115

Elizabeth - of MA, b1659 d bef 16 Feb 1710/1711, m Thomas Flint of Salem, MA - desc/o Mary Gye NE(96)240

Elizabeth - of MA, b1696 d1773, m1715 Joshua Bailey, physician - desc/o Mary Gye NE(97)60

Elizabeth - of MD, b1719, m1737 William Dallam son of Richard Dallam of Calvert Co - desc/o Anne Lovelace GVFHB(3)362, 363

Frances Pope - of VA, b abt 1770, m1787 David Poindexter - desc/o Col/Gov John West DBR(4)288, 568

Guy - of NY, b1740 d1788, northern superintendent of Indian Affairs, 1774/1782 son of John Johnson & Catherine Nagle, m Mary Johnson (his first cousin) - the immigrant GBR217

Israel - b1737 - desc/o Richard Palgrave RAA121

John - b1657 - desc/o Mary Gye RAA115

Mary - of NY, dau/o Sir William Johnson, 1st Baronet & Catherine Weissenburg, m Guy Johnson of NY, b abt 1740 d1788 (her first cousin) - desc/o Sir William Johnson 1st Baronet GBR217

Ruth - of MA, b1669/1670, m Robert Wyer of Charlestown, tailor - desc/o Mary Gye NE(96)240

Sarah - of MA, b1665, m Henry Franklin of Boston, vintner - desc/o Mary Gye NE(96)240

Thomas - b1685 - desc/o Mary Gye RAA115

Timothy - of MA, b1672 d1696, m1695 Haverhill, Anne Maverick - desc/o Mary Gye NE(96)240

Timothy - b1737 - desc/o Mary Gye RAA115

Timothy - b1768 - desc/o Mary Gye RAA115

Sir William, 1st Baronet - of NY, b1715 d1774, Mohawk Valley pioneer & superintendant of Indian affairs in the American colonies, son of Christopher Johnson & Anne Warren, m Catherine Weissenburg - the immigrant GBR217; NYGBR(18)#4p150/152

Zebediah - b1704 - desc/o Richard Palgrave RAA121

JOHNSTON David - of NJ & NY, b1724 of New York City & Lithgow, Duchess Co, NY, where he owned a large tract of land & built a large mansion which was standing in 1910, m Magdalin Walton, dau/o Jacob Walton, who was a lieutenant in the Colonial Army - desc/o Euphan Scott CFA(2)394

James - of VA, m1779 Mildred Moorman - desc/o John Johnston BLG2768

John - of NJ, b1691 of Perth Amboy d1731 commissioned a member of the King's Council of NJ 1718/1727, appointed to His Majesty's Council for the Eastern Division of NJ 1720 until his death, m1717 Elizabeth Jamison, dau/o David Jamison, chief justice of NJ 1711, recorder of New York 1712/1723 & attorney general for New York

JOHNSTON (cont.)

in 1720 - desc/o Euphan Scott CFA(2)393

John - of MD & VA, m Lucretia Massie - the immigrant BLG2768; sufficient proof of alleged royal ancestry is lacking

John - of VA - desc/o John Johnston BLG2768

John - of VA, m1725 Elizabeth Ellyson - desc/o John Johnston BLG2768

John - of VA, m1754 Lydia Watkins - desc/o John Johnston BLG2768

John - of NY, b1762 resided at Hyde Park, Dutchess Co, was presiding judge of the court of common pleas, m1792 Susannah Bard, dau/o Samuel Bard of New York - desc/o Euphan Scott CFA(2)394

JONES Alexander - of MA, b1764 d1840, m1790 Mary Farquhar - desc/o John Whitney CHB230; BCD230

Anne - of VA, m John Hawkins - desc/o William Strother GVFTQ(3)379

Behethland - of VA, b1748, m1770 John Peed - desc/o Leonard Calvert MG(1)173

Brereton - of VA, m Lettice____ - desc/o Capt William Claiborne FFF52

Maj Cadwallader - of VA, m aft 18 Jul 1643 & bef 1646 Anne Bluet, the second but eldest surviving daughter & co-heiress of John Bluet, Esq, of Holcombe Rogus, Devon - the immigrant WAC51; EO2(2)570/575 there remains a rather serious gap in the chain of evidence to prove alleged royal ancestry

Calvert - of VA, overseer of the highways in Westmoreland Co 1757 - desc/o Leonard Calvert MG(1)173

Charles Calvert - of VA, b1746 - desc/o Leonard Calvert MG(1)173

David - of VA, m1763 Mary Boswell - desc/o Leonard Calvert MG(1)173

Dorothy - of VA, m1762 Lieut Col Thomas Short - desc/o Thomas Batte DBR(1)409; DBR(2)58

Eleanor - of VA, m1774 Daniel Hamet - desc/o Leonard Calvert MG(1)173

Elizabeth - of CT, m1689 Capt John Morgan - desc/o Anna Lloyd CHB73; BCD73

Elizabeth - of PA, b1693 d1759, m1724 Rees Thomas - desc/o Dr Thomas Wynne ECD(2)331; DBR(3)762

Elizabeth - of VA, b1707 d1749, m Rev John Bell - desc/o Col Richard Lee DBR(3)324, 404

Elizabeth - m Col James Absolom Alston - desc/o Peter Montague FFF80

Elizabeth - of VA, m John Lewis - desc/o John Jones WAC46, 47 - desc/o William Strother GVFTQ(3)379

Gabriel - of VA, b1724 d1806, m1749 Margaret Strother - desc/o John Jones WAC46, 47

Hannah - of PA, b1749 d1829, m1779 Amos Foulke - desc/o Rebecca Humphrey CHB160; BCD160 - desc/o Thomas Evans CHB191; BCD191 - desc/o Hannah Price CHB295; BCD295

Hugh - of PA, son of John Thomas Ellis & Gainor John, m(1)____, m(2) Margaret David, m(3) Anne Williams, m(4) Margaret Edwards - the immigrant GBR309

Jane - of VA, b1762, m1782 Samuel Marshall - desc/o Leonard Calvert MG(1)173

JONES (cont.)

Jenkins - of RI, b1770 d1842, m(1) Dorcas____ - desc/o Anne Marbury DBR(3)134

John - of VA, b1706, m Anne____ - desc/o Martha Mallory DBR(4)510

John - of VA 1720, m Elizabeth____ - the immigrant WAC46, 47; sufficient proof of alleged royal ancestry is lacking

John - of VA, d1762, m1744 Eleanor Moss dau/o John & Margaret Moss - desc/o Leonard Calvert MG(1)173

John - of MA, bp 1708 d1772 son of William Jones & Martha Smith, m1734 Hannah Francis b1715 d1782 dau/o Abraham Francis & Hannah Fayerwether - the immigrant GBR137; NE(113)216/21

Joseph Jr - of MA, b1737 d1799, m Ruth Nelson - desc/o John Whitney CHB230; BCD230

Lowry - of PA, b1680 d1762, m(1) Robert Lloyd, m(2)1716 Hugh Evans - desc/o Hannah Price CHB295; MCB418; BCD295 - desc/o Rees Jones AFA260

Lowry - of PA, b1743 d1804, m1760 Daniel Wister - desc/o Rebecca Humphrey CHB160; MCD267; BCD160 - desc/o Thomas Evans CHB191; BCD192

Margaret - of VA, m Col John Harvie Jr d1807 colonel in the Revolution, a member of the House of Burgesses, a member of Congress & mayor of Richmond in 1785 son of John Harvie & Martha Gaines - desc/o John Jones WAC46, 47; GVFTQ(3)378

Mary - of PA, dau/o Gilbert Jones & Mary____, m Thomas Lloyd b1640 d1694 deputy governor of Pennsylvania, physician & statesman - the immigrant GBR277

Mary - of VA, m____Peck - desc/o Leonard Jones MG(1)173

Mordecai - of VA, b1742 d1805, m Elizabeth Jones - desc/o Martha Mallory DBR(4)510

Owen - of PA, b1711 d1793, m1740 Susannah Evans - desc/o Rebecca Humphrey CHB160; MCD267; BCD160

Maj Peter - of VA, m1727 Dorothy Chamberlain - desc/o Thomas Batte DBR(1)409; DBR(2)58

Prudence - of VA, b1725, m1746 Henry Ward - desc/o Thomas Batte DBR(4)394

Rachel - of NC & GA, m1788 Ralph Banks - desc/o Col John Alston DBR(1)26; DBR(2)135

Rebecca - of PA, b1709 d1779, m1733 John Roberts - desc/o Rebecca Humphrey CHB161; BCD161

Rees (alias) - of PA 1684, (otherwise known as John William Rees), m Hannah____ - the immigrant AFA260; sufficient proof of alleged royal ancestry is lacking

Col Richard - of VA, d1759, m(1) Sarah Stratton - desc/o Thomas Batte DBR(4)394

Robert - of PA, son of John Thomas & Katherine Roberts, m Ellen Jones - the immigrant GBR392 some aspect of royal descent merits further study

Sabra - of VA, b1753, m1778 William Crank - desc/o Leonard Calvert MG(1)173

Sarah - of CT, b1662, m(1)1687 Andrew Morrison, m(2) John Dudley - desc/o Anna Lloyd J&K321; ECD(3)192, 193

JONES (cont.)

Sarah - of VA, m____Franklin - desc/o Leonard Calvert MG(1)173

Thomas - of NC, b1771 d1852, m Catherine McKelroy - desc/o Col John Alston DBR(2)177; DBR(5)369

Col Tignal (Tingnall) - b1735 d1807, m Penelope Cain - desc/o Peter Montague FFF80

William - of MA, d1805 returned to England, m1762 Jane Madgwick dau/o Edward Madgwick & Jane Kittier, they had 7 children all of whom married and lived in England - desc/o John Jones NE(113)220

William Strother - of VA, b1756 d1788, m1780 Frances (Thornton) Buckner of "Fall Hill" - desc/o John Jones WAC46, 47 - desc/o William Strother GVFTQ(3)379

JORDAN Thomas - of VA, b1758 d1850, m1790 Priscilla Applewhite - desc/o James Tooke DBR(1)690

JOSSELYN Henry - of ME 1634, b abt 1606 d1683 son of Sir Thomas Josselyn & Theodora Cooke, m Margaret Cammock - the immigrant FLW176; MCS96; GBR432 left no known descendants; NE(70)248/250, (71)249; EO2(2)578/583

John - of ME, b abt 1608 d aft 1675, author & naturalist, died unmarried, son of Sir Thomas Josselyn & Theodora Cooke - the immigrant FLW176; GBR432 some aspect of royal descent merits further study; NE(71)248, 249

JOY Mary - b1680 - desc/o Agnes Harris RAA131

- K -

KAYE Grace - of MA & CT, m Sir Richard Saltonstall - the immigrant J&K218; CHB205, 206, 359; MCB313; FLW7; MCD283; MCS36; BCD205, 206; DBR(2)268; DBR(3)479; DBR(5)593, 606, 938; AWW179; NE(95)72; GBR164, 421 lists her son Richard Saltonstall as the immigrant

KEEBLE George - of VA - the immigrant WAC8; sufficient proof of alleged royal ancestry is lacking

KEELER David - b1753, m Sarah Barse or Bearss - desc/o Henry Palmer LDS30

Jonah - b1690 d1767, m Ruth Smith - desc/o Matthias St John FFF49

Capt Nehemiah - b1753 d1834, m Eleanor Rockwell - desc/o Mattias St John FFF49

Samuel - b1716 d1781, m Mary Kendrick - desc/o Matthias St John FFF49

KEEN Elizabeth - b1760, m1778 Charles Fladger - desc/o Col George Reade DBR(2)384

KEENE Mary - of MD, b1680/1681 d1759, m1699 Capt Thomas Clagett II - desc/o Anne Lovelace JSW1634; DBR(2)663

KEEP Hannah - b1673, m Ebenezer Miller - desc/o John Leonard LDS35

KEITH Alexander - of VA, of Fauquier Co, served with distinction in the Revolutionary War, after which he moved to Tennessee, m____Thornton, a widow, & had issue a son Charles Edward, a distinguished jurist of Tennessee - desc/o Col William Randolph

KEITH (cont.)
CFSSA312
Alexander - of VA, m Miss___Dawson - desc/o Col William Randolph
CFSSA313
Catherine - of VA, m Dr Anderson Keith of Augusta, KY, son of John
Keith & Mary Doniphan - desc/o Col William Randolph CFSSA312
Catherine - of VA, m John Railey - desc/o Col William Randolph
CFSSA312
Eliza - of VA, m Mr___Berry - desc/o Col William Randolph CFSSA312
Elizabeth - of VA, m Edward Ford of Bourbon Co, Kentucky & had
issue - desc/o Col William Randolph CFSSA313
Elizabeth - of VA, m Clifton Thompson - desc/o Col William Randolph
CFSSA313
Isham - of VA, of Fauquier Co, served with distinction in the
Revolutionary War, m___ & had issue - desc/o Col William
Randolph CFSSA312
Isabella - of VA, m William Strother Hawkins - desc/o Col William
Randolph CFSSA312
James - of VA, clerk of the county court for many years, m___ & had
issue - desc/o Col William Randolph CFSSA312
James - of VA, m Nancy Ireland - desc/o Col William Randolph
CFSSA313
Jane - b abt 1708 d1760, m1724 William Yelles of St Elizabeth,
Goshen, Jamaica - desc/o Sir William Keith GPFHB478
Jane - of VA, m Thomas Clarke - desc/o Col William Randolph
CFSSA313
John - of VA, m Miss Doniphan & had issue - desc/o Col William
Randolph CFSSA312
John - of VA, m Lucie Cox & had issue - desc/o Col William Randolph
CFSSA312
Judith - of VA, m James Key, son of Francis Key & Anne Arnold, of
Maryland & had issue - desc/o Col William Randolph CFSSA313
Judith - of VA, m Thomas Keith - desc/o Col William Randolph
CFSSA313
Louisa - of VA, m Alexander Keith, son of Alexander Keith - desc/o Col
William Randolph CFSSA312
Marshall - of VA, m Harriet Selman - desc/o Col William Randolph
CFSSA313
Mary - of VA, m(1) Mr___Applegate - desc/o Col William Randolph
CFSSA312
Mary - of VA, m Thomas Winn - desc/o Col William Randolph
CFSSA313
Mary Isham - of VA, m Marshall Martin, son of Abraham Martin &
Elizabeth Marshall - desc/o Col William Randolph CFSSA313
Mary Randolph - of VA, b1737 d1809, m1754 Col Thomas Marshall,
son of John Marshall & Elizabeth Markham - desc/o Capt Henry
Isham J&K133; ECD(2)219; DBR(2)35; DBR(3)336, 703; DBR(5)111
- desc/o Col William Randolph DBR(5)316; PFA Apx D #3;
CFSSA312
Mary Randolph II - of VA, m Capt James Payne - desc/o Capt Henry
Isham DBR(5)724

KEITH (cont.)

Priscilla - of VA, m Mr___ Sangster - desc/o Col William Randolph CFSSA313

Rhoda - b1768 - desc/o John Deighton RAA86

Sir Robert, Baronet - b1714 d1771, m Margaritha Albertina Conradina von Suhm - desc/o Sir William Keith GPFHB478

Susan - of VA, m James C Claybrook - desc/o Col William Randolph CFSSA312

Capt Thomas - of VA, served with distinction in the Revolutionary War, m Judith Blackwell, dau/o Joseph Blackwell & Lucy Steptoe of Fauquier Co - desc/o Col William Randolph DBR(3)336; DBR(5)724; CFSSA313

Thomas - of VA, m (his first cousin) Judith Key & had issue - desc/o Col William Randolph CFSSA312

Thomas - of VA, m Miss___Foley - desc/o Col William Randolph CFSSA313

Sir William, 4th Baronet - of PA & DE, governor of Pennsylvania & Delaware, son of Sir William, 3rd Baronet & Jean (Smith) Keith, m Anne Newbury b1675 - the immigrant GBR73; GPFHB473/480

KELLOGG Amos - b1716 - desc/o Richard Belding RAA68

Anna - b1755 - desc/o Richard Belding RAA68

Moses - b1720 - desc/o Richard Belding RAA68

Prudence - b1754 - desc/o Richard Belding RAA68

Stephen - b1695 - desc/o Richard Belding RAA68

Thankful - b1726 - desc/o Richard Belding RAA68

KEMEYS William - of NY, son of Edward Kemeys & Hannah Fowler, m Elizabeth Thornton - the immigrant GBR401; TG(4)148, (6)149

KEMPE Edmund - of VA, son of Arthur Kempe & Dorothy Harris, brother of Richard Kempe - the immigrant GBR222

Edmund - of VA, nephew named in the will of Richard Kempe - the immigrant or descended from one of the three brothers of Richard Kempe who immigrated to Virginia GBR223

Edward - of VA 1644, son of Arthur Kempe & Dorothy Harris, brother of Richard Kempe - the immigrant MCS52; WAC34; GBR222

Elizabeth - of VA, m William Plummer - desc/o Matthew Kempe DBR(3)579

John - of VA, son of Arthur Kempe & Dorothy Harris, brother of Richard Kempe - possible immigrant GBR222

Matthew - of VA, d1704 patented land 1674 in Kingston Parish, Gloucester Co, VA, m Dorothy___ - the immigrant DBR(3)579; GBR223

Matthew - of VA, a burgess of Gloucester Co, VA 1693 - desc/o Matthew Kempe DBR(3)579

Richard - of VA, secretary & active governor of Virginia, son of Robert Kempe & Dorothy Harris, m Elizabeth Wormeley - the immigrant GBR222

Robert - of VA, b1565/1567, m Dorothy Harris - the immigrant RAA1, 104; sufficient proof of alleged royal ancestry is lacking

KENDALL Susanna - b1711/1712, m(1) Joseph Remington - desc/o Robert Harrington LDS85

KENDRICK Anna - m Benjamin Pierce Jr - desc/o Griffith Bowen GBR387
    Benjamin - m Sarah Harris - desc/o Griffith Bowen AAP146; GBR387 -
      desc/o Margaret Fleming AAP147
    Sarah - b1761, m John Patrick - desc/o Col/Gov John West LDS100
KENNEDY Alexander - of MD, b1738, m(2) Mary (Tanday) Thomas -
      desc/o John Kennedy DBR(2)303; DBR(3)625; DBR(4)316
    Andrew - of PA, b1747 d1800 - desc/o John Kennedy CFA297
    Archibald - of NY, b abt 1685 d1763 British colonial official, son of
      Alexander Kennedy of Craigoch and Kilhenzie & Anna Crawford,
      m(1)___Massan, m(2) Mrs Mary Walter Schylmer - the immigrant
      GBR87
    Archibald, 11th Earl of Cassilis - of NY - desc/o Archibald Kennedy
      GBR87
    David - of MD, b1768 d1837, m1788 Joanna Moore - desc/o John
      Kennedy DBR(2)303; DBR(3)625; DBR(4)319
    Elizabeth - of PA, m Anthony McCoy - desc/o John Kennedy CFA297
    Jannette - of PA, m David Risk - desc/o John Kennedy CFA297
    John - of PA, b abt 1710, d aft 1786, m Lilly___ - the immigrant
      DBR(3)625; DBR(4)316; CFA296; sufficient proof of alleged royal
      ancestry is lacking
    John - of PA, b1769 d1836, m1794 Nancy Clayton Pendleton - desc/o
      John Kennedy CFA297
    Robert - of PA, b1693 d1776, m Mary___ - the immigrant CRL(2)222;
      sufficient proof of alleged royal ancestry is lacking
    Col Robert - of PA, b1770 d1849, m1792 Jean McCalla - desc/o Robert
      Kennedy CRL(2)223
    Maj William - of PA, b abt 1746 d1785, m Grace Crier - desc/o Robert
      Kennedy CRL(2)222
KENNON Lieut John - of NC & GA, m1779 Elizabeth Woodson - desc/o
      Col George Reade CHB420
    Mary - of NC, d1782, m1768 Maj Thomas Harrison - desc/o Col
      George Reade DBR(5)525
    Richard - of VA, b1775 - desc/o Col George Reade AWW173
KENRICK Sarah - of PA, b1755 d1815 dau/o John Kenrick & Mary
      Quarrell, m1777 Ralph Eddowes - the immigrant MCS78; GBR166;
      TAG(32)9/23, (24)219/22
KENT Susan - of MA, b1768 d1839, m1788 Judge Hezekiah Huntington -
      desc/o Richard Lyman CHB153; BCD153
KEY John Ross - of MD, b1754 d1821 Redlands, Frederick Co, MD, a
      soldier in the Revolution, m1778 Anne Phoebe Penn Dagworthy
      Charlton b1756 d1830 & had issue among other children, son
      Francis Scott Key b1779 d1843, author of the *Star Spangled
      Banner*, & Ann, wife of Roger Brooke Taney b1777 d1843, 2nd
      Chief Justice of the United States - desc/o Alicia Arnold FLW80
KILBOURN (KILBURN) Josiah - b1702 - desc/o Rev Peter Bulkeley
      RAA75
    Ozias - b1769 - desc/o Agnes Harris RAA131
    Richard - b1735 - desc/o Rev Peter Bulkeley RAA75 - desc/o George
      Morton RAA116
    Sarah - of MA, b1710 d1785, m1726 Timothy Baxter b1706 d1777 -
      desc/o Rev Peter Bulkeley DBR(1)680; DBR(2)328, 392, 758;

KILBOURN (KILBURN) (cont.)
> DBR(3)312

KIMBALL Daniel - of NY, b1752 d1836, m1773 Mary Sterry - desc/o
> Ursula Scott BLG2777

> Hannah - of MA, m1711 Roger Eastman - desc/o Ursula Scott
> JSW1833

> Hannah - of MA, b1713, m1740 Josiah Batcheller - desc/o Ursula
> Scott JSW1762

> Henry - of MA, b1615 d1676, m(1) abt 1640 Mary Wyatt - desc/o
> Ursula Scott JSW1833, 1871

> Jacob - of CT, b1706 d1788, m1730 Mary Parke - desc/o Ursula Scott
> BLG2777

> John - of MA 1634, b1631 d1697, m Mary Bradstreet - desc/o Ursula
> Scott BLG2777

> John - of MA, b1645 d1726, m(1) Mary Jordan - desc/o Ursula Scott
> JSW1833

> John - of CT, b1688/1689 d1761, m1692 Sarah Goodline - desc/o
> Ursula Scott BLG2777

> Jonathan - of MA, b1686 d1758, m1709 Hannah Hopkins - desc/o
> Ursula Scott JSW1762

> Richard Jr - of MA, b abt 1623, m(1) Mary____, m(2) Mary____ - desc/o
> Ursula Scott JSW1762

> Samuel - of MA, b abt 1651 d1716, m1676 Mary Witt - desc/o Ursula
> Scott JSW1762

> Sarah - of MA, b abt 1654 d1692, m1674 Daniel Gage - desc/o Ursula
> Scott JSW1871

KIMBROUGH Mary - of NC, b1773 d1825, m1797 John Martin - desc/o
> Col John Alston DBR(4)381

KING Benjamin - b1722, m Sarah Taylor - desc/o Deacon Edmund Rice
> LDS104

> Daniel Jr - of PA, b1770 d1836 - desc/o John Bevan Sr MCD165

> Michael - of VA - the immigrant WAC50; sufficient proof of alleged royal
> ancestry is lacking

> Michael Jr - of VA - desc/o Michael King WAC50

> Miles - of VA, b1747 d1814 - desc/o Michael King WAC50

> Peter - b1695, m(1) Elizabeth Flagg - desc/o Deacon Edmund Rice
> LDS104

> Sarah - b1754, m William Orreon Hewett - desc/o Deacon Edmund
> Rice LDS104

> William - of VA - desc/o Michael King WAC50

KINGSBURY Absalon - b1730 - desc/o Robert Abell RAA59

> James - b1767 - desc/o Robert Abell RAA59

KINGSLEY Susanna - of MA, m abt 1725/1728 Samuel Packard - desc/o
> John Washbourne DBR(2)529

KINGSMILL Elizabeth - of VA, b1625, m(1) Col William Tayloe - desc/o
> Richard Kingsmill WAC36

> Nathaniel - of VA, b1619 - desc/o Richard Kingsmill WAC36

> Richard - of VA, m Jane____ - the immigrant WAC36; sufficient proof of
> alleged royal ancestry is lacking

> Susan - of VA, b1623 - desc/o Richard Kingsmill WAC36

KINLOCH Cleland - of SC, b1759 Charleston d abt 1823, member from Prince George, Winyah, of the South Carolina Convention which ratified the Federal Constitution 23 May 1788 & the South Carolina General Assemble 1791 to 1793, large plantation owner & was a successful rice planter, m1786 Harriett Simmons dau/o Ebenezer Simmons of Charleston - desc/o James Kinloch SCG(3)62, 63

Francis - of SC, b1720 of Boone Hall & Kensington d1767, member of the Commons House for St James Parish, Santee, 1751/1754, m1751 Ann Isabella Cleland b abt 1735 d1802, only daughter & heiress of John Cleland, Esq - desc/o James Kinloch SCG(3)59, 60

Francis - of SC, b1755 in Charleston d1826 served as captain in the American Army from 1778 to 1781 taking part in the Battle of Beaufort, the siege of Savannah & the defense of Charleston, a member of the Continental Congress 1780/1781 & South Carolina House of Representative served as a delegate from St Philip & St Michael's to the convention which ratified the Federal Constitution May 23, 1788, m(1)1781 Mildred Walker d1781 dau/o Col John Walker of Albemarle Co, VA, m(2)1785 Martha Rutledge b1764 d1816 eldest dau/o Governor John Rutledge - desc/o James Kinloch SCG(3)61, 62

James - of SC 1703, b abt 1685 member of the Commons House of Assembly for Berkeley 1711/1713 & the Council 1717/1757, he lived at Grove Hall, St James Parish, Santee, son of Sir Francis, 2nd Baronet & Mary (Leslie) Kinloch, m(1) abt 1712 Mrs Susannah ____ Strode wid/o John Strode, m(2) Marie Esther Page, wid/o John Gaillard, Esq - the immigrant GBR28; SCG(3)58/67

Mary Esther - of SC, m1772 Major Benjamin Huger of Kensington d1779 killed before the lines at Charlestown - desc/o James Kinloch SCG(3)63, 64

KIRKBRIDE Jonathan - of PA, b1739 d1824, m Elizabeth Curtis - desc/o Joseph Kirkbride BLG2779

Joseph - of PA 1681, b1662 d1737/1738 son of Matthew Kirkbride & Magdalen Dalston, m(1) Phebe Blackshaw, m(2)1702 Sarah Stacy, m(3) Mrs Mary Fletcher Yardley - the immigrant DBR(3)213; RAA1, 104; BLG2779; GBR130

Joseph - of PA, b1775 d1838, m Eleanor Baldwin - desc/o Joseph Kirkbride BLG2779

Letitia - b1734 d1771, m1762 Timothy Taylor - desc/o Joseph Kirkbride DBR(3)213

Mahlon Stacye - of PA, b1703 d1776/1777, m1724 Mary Sotcher - desc/o Joseph Kirkbride DBR(3)213; BLG2779

KIRKPATRICK Alexander of NJ, b abt 1725 d1758, m Elizabeth____ - the immigrant CHB112; BCD112; sufficient proof of alleged royal ancestry is lacking

Anne of NJ, m Capt Moses Este - desc/o Alexander Kirkpatrick CHB112; BCD112

David of NJ, b1724 d1814, m1748 Mary McEowen - desc/o Alexander Kirkpatrick CHB112; BCD112

KITCHELL John - of NJ, b1714 d1777, m1753 Mercy Parkhurst - desc/o Obadiah Bruen DBR(4)539

Judge Joseph - b1710 d1789, m Rachel Bates - desc/o Obadiah

KITCHELL (cont.)

    Bruen DBR(1)384, 385; DBR(2)494; DBR(3)30

    Moses - b1754 d1820, m Phoebe Hedges - desc/o Obadiah Bruen
        DBR(1)385; DBR(2)494; DBR(3)30

    Phineas - of NJ, b1763 d1853, m1782 Esther Mulford - desc/o
        Obadiah Bruen DBR(4)539

KNAPP Joseph II - of MA, d1839, m1784 Eunice Carver - desc/o John
    Washbourne DBR(2)529, 530

    Mary - b abt 1615, m Thomas Smith - the immigrant LDS27; sufficient
        proof of alleged royal ancestry is lacking

KNIGHT Ann - d1828, m Benjamin Albertson - desc/o Giles Knight
    CRL(2)403

    Daniel - of PA, b1757 d1821, m Rachel Walton - desc/o Giles Knight
        CRL(2)403

    Giles - of PA, d1726, m Mary English - the immigrant CRL(2)402;
        sufficient proof of alleged royal ancestry is lacking

    Hannah - b1706, m Eleazer Flagg - desc/o Abraham Errington LDS31

    James - of PA, b1753 d1784, m Gaynor Lukens - desc/o Giles Knight
        CRL(2)403

    Jane - m Joseph Bolton - desc/o Giles Knight CRL(2)403

    Jonathan - of PA, d1745, m Jane Allen - desc/o Giles Knight
        CRL(2)403

    Jonathan - of PA, b1730, m(1)1748 Ann Paul, m(2) Margaret Baldwin,
        m(3) Martha Lloyd - desc/o Giles Knight CRL(2)403

    Jonathan - of PA, b1755 d1830, m Eliza Thomas - desc/o Giles Knight
        CRL(2)403

    Joseph - of ME, b1746 d1829, m(1) abt 1768/1769 Phoebe Colley -
        desc/o Capt Thomas Bradbury DBR(2)775; DBR(3)100

    Mary - m Josiah Costill - desc/o Giles Knight CRL(2)403

    Paul - m Eliza Boucher - desc/o Giles Knight CRL(2)403

    Rebecca - b1703, m John Boutwell - desc/o Abraham Errington
        LDS77

    Rodolphus - b1768 - desc/o John Drake RAA87

    Sarah - of PA, d1838, m John Stackhouse - desc/o Giles Knight
        CRL(2)403

    Tacy - m Robert Croasdale - desc/o Giles Knight CRL(2)403

    Thomas - of NJ 1683, m Elizabeth Browne - the immigrant CRL(2)401;
        sufficient proof of alleged royal ancestry is lacking

    Thomas - of PA, b1736 d1806, m1759 Mary Walmsley - desc/o Giles
        Knight CRL(2)403

    Thomas - b1769 d1824, m Mary Worrell - desc/o Giles Knight
        CRL(2)403

KNOWLTON Abigail - of MA, b1771 d1870, m1795 Benjamin Preston -
    desc/o Richard More ECD(3)213

    Benjamin Jr - of MA, bp 1718 d1789, m1738 Susanna Potter - desc/o
        Richard More ECD(3)213

    Ezra - of MA, bp 1739 d1814, m1762 Abigail Dodge - desc/o Richard
        More ECD(3)213

    Isaac - of NY 1657 - the immigrant EDV16; sufficient proof of alleged
        royal ancestry is lacking

LABAW David - of NJ, b1746 d1814, m Mary Stout - desc/o John
Throckmorton DBR(5)1012

Francis Stout - of NJ, b1769 d1837, m1791 Elizabeth Hutchinson
b1775 d1861 dau/o Jonathan Hutchinson Jr - desc/o John
Throckmorton DBR(5)1012

LAKE Ann - of MA, b1663 d1737, m1686 Rev John Cotton - desc/o Capt
Thomas Lake CHB410

Capt Thomas - of MA 1655, b1615 d1676, m Mary Goodyear - the
immigrant CHB410; sufficient proof of alleged royal ancestry is
lacking

LAMB Dorothy - of MA, b1679, m(2)1712 Rev Timothy Woodbridge -
desc/o John Drake DBR(5)372 - desc/o Richard Palgrave RAA121

LAMBERT Hannah - of NJ, m Dr Thomas Cadwalader - desc/o Thomas
Lambert MCD238

Thomas - of NJ, b1621 d1694, m(1) Ellen Stacy, m(2)1672 Elizabeth
Hooton - the immigrant MCD238; sufficient proof of alleged royal
ancestry is lacking

Thomas - of NJ - desc/o Thomas Lambert MCD238

LANE Dorothy - b abt 1585, m(2) William Randolph - the immigrant
RAA126; GBR169 lists their son Henry Randolph, of VA as the
immigrant

Eleanor - of CT, b1674, m(1)1695/1696 Ebenezer Brown b1670
d1707, m(2)1709/1710 Samuel Blakeslee b1685 d1753 - desc/o
Nathaniel Browne TAG(22)164

Elizabeth - of CT, b1672/1673 d1708, m1693 Joseph Clark b1668
d1703 - desc/o Nathaniel Browne TAG(22)164

Hannah - of CT, b1670/1671 d1734, m1704 Benjamin Smith b abt
1652 d1730/1731 - desc/o Nathaniel Browne ECD(3)57;
TAG(22)164

Sir Ralph - of VA, b abt 1530 d1603, Virginia colonist (commander of
the Roanoke Island settlement 1585/1586) died unmarried, son of
Sir Ralph Lane & Maud Parr - the immigrant GBR171;
TAG(52)15/17; SVF(2)290, 291

Sarah - of CT, b1678 d1737, m1702 Zaccheus Cande - desc/o
Nathaniel Browne ECD(3)60; RAA73

Susanna - m Nathaniel Davis - desc/o Elizabeth St John AAP152;
GBR210

LANGBORNE William - of VA, b1723, m Susannah Smith - the immigrant
WAC9; sufficient proof of alleged royal ancestry is lacking

Col William - of VA - desc/o William Langborne WAC9

LANGDON Mary - b1734 d1806, m(1)1768 Capt Jeremiah Hill - desc/o
Gov Thomas Dudley DBR(1)63

LANGFORD Northrup Holderbee - b1724, m Mary Sanford - desc/o
Benjamin Harrington LDS71

Phebe - b1761, m Abraham Morton - desc/o Benjamin Harrington
LDS71

LANIER Elizabeth - of VA, b aft 1724 d1796, m(1) John Burch, m(2)
Thomas Croft - desc/o John Washington DBR(1)206; DBR(5)698

LAPHAM Nicholas - b1689, m Mercy Arnold - desc/o Frances Hopkins LDS50

Rhoda - b1759, m Nathan Harris - desc/o Frances Hopkins LDS50 - desc/o Edward Rainsford RAA126

Solomon - b1730, m Sylvia Whipple or Lapham - desc/o Frances Hopkins LDS50

LARRABEE Dorothy - b1686 - desc/o Alice Freeman RAA132

LARRIBEE Phoebe - b1680 - desc/o Alice Freeman RAA132

LATHAM Hannah - of MA, m Joseph Washburn - desc/o John Winslow THC341

LATHE Asa - b1761 - desc/o William Sargent RAA129

LATHROP Azel - m Elizabeth Hyde dau/o Phineas and Ann (Rogers) Hyde - desc/o Robert Abell III DBR(3)514

Lieut Ebenezer - of CT, b1743 d1804, m1768 Deborah Lathrop - desc/o Lieut Thomas Tracy FFF143, 156

Erastus - of CT, b1772 d1830, m(1)1801 Judith Crafts, m(2) Mrs Lucy Morse Johnson - desc/o Lieut Thomas Tracy FFF143, 156

Eunice - of CT, b1753 d1823, m1772 Rev Thomas Brockway - desc/o Judge Simon Lynde ECD(3)200

Rev John - of MA 1639, d1675 - the immigrant EDV22; sufficient proof of alleged royal ancestry is lacking

LATIMER Charles - b1759 d1827, m Mary____ - desc/o Francis Willoughby DBR(2)856

Joseph - b1766, m Ann Carson Dobbins - desc/o Simon Lynde DBR(3)568

Robert - of CT, bp 1762 New London d1796 at sea, m1784 Hannah Burnham b1762 dau/o Capt Asahel Burnham & Hannah Sage - desc/o Rev Peter Bulkeley TAG(36)102

LAUNCE Mary - of MA, b aft 1620 d1710 Watertown, MA, dau/o John Launce & Isabella Darcy, m abt 1648 Rev John Sherman of Watertown, MA b1613/1614 d1685, was one of the most learned men of his day & an able & eloquent preacher, son of Edmond Sherman & Grace Stevens - the immigrant J&K184; CHB446; FLW17; MCD291; MCS23; DBR(1)545; DBR(2)551; DBR(3)120, 121; RAA130; GBR176; TAG(21)169/77; NE(24)66

LAW Benedict Arnold - of CT, b1740 d1819, m1770 Sarah Bryan - desc/o William Arnold CHB15; BCD15

Jonathan Jr - of CT, b1705/1706 d1790, m1737 Eunice Andrew - desc/o William Arnold CHB15; BCD15

LAWRENCE Abigail - of NY, m Major Alexander Forbes of the British Army - desc/o Capt William Lawrence RCFA13

Anna - of NY, b1749, m1769 Samuel Riker - desc/o Thomas Lawrence MCB427; MCD242

Asubah - m1750 Samuel Hyde - desc/o Henry Lawrence THC192

Augustine - of NY, b1727 d1794, m Johanna Van Zant - desc/o Capt William Lawrence MCB246; MCD242

Augustine Hicks - of NY, b1769 d1828, m Catharine Luqueer - desc/o Capt William Lawrence MCB246; MCD242

Caleb - of NY, b1723/1724, m1754 Sarah Burling dau/o James Burling & Elizabeth____ - desc/o Capt William Lawrence RCFA14

Capt Daniel - of MA, b1681 d1777, m Sarah____ - desc/o Henry

LAWRENCE (cont.)

Lawrence THC189

Daniel - b1773 d1837, m1796 Sibelar Doty - desc/o Francis Mapes DBR(3)500

Effingham -' of NY, b1734/1735 d1806, m Catherine Farmer - desc/o Capt William Lawrence RCFA14

Effingham - of NY, b1760, m1786 Elizabeth Watson - desc/o Maj Thomas Lawrence BLG2783; NYGBR(5)#1p40, 41

Elisha - of NY, b1666 d1724 - desc/o Capt William Lawrence J&K213

Elisha - of NY, bro of John, father of John Browne Lawrence - desc/o Capt William Lawrence J&K213

Elizabeth - of NY, m John Browne - desc/o Capt William Lawrence RCFA13

Elizabeth - of NY, m1672 Thomas Stevenson Jr - desc/o Thomas Lawrence MCD241

Elizabeth - of NY, m1683 John Saunders & died leaving issue a daughter Elizabeth living in 1703 - desc/o Thomas Lawrence RCFA11

Elizabeth - of NY, b1719, m John Embree - desc/o Capt William Lawrence RCFA14

Elizabeth - of NY, b1765, m Silus Titus & had issue - desc/o Capt William Lawrence RCFA14

Enoch - of MA, b1648/1649, m1676/1677 Ruth Whitney - desc/o Henry Lawrence THC190

Hannah - of NY, m Moses Molyneux of Westchester - desc/o Capt William Lawrence RCFA13

Hannah - of NY, b1726, m Abraham Willett - desc/o Capt William Lawrence RCFA14

Hannah - b1750, m Willard Kingsbury - desc/o Henry Lawrence THC192

Hannah - of NY, b1758 d1838, m1780 Jacob Schieffelin - desc/o Thomas Lawrence MCB341

Henry - of MA 1635 - the immigrant THC189; NYGBR(3)#1p26/29 sufficient proof of alleged royal ancestry is lacking

Henry - of NY, b1767 d1824, m(1) Harriet Van Wyck b1771 d1812, m(2) Amy Pearsall - desc/o Capt William Lawrence CRFA14

Isaac - of MA, b1704/1705 d1793, m Lydia Hewitt - desc/o Henry Lawrence THC191

Isaac Jr - of MA, m1760 Mary Brown - desc/o Henry Lawrence THC192

Isaac III - b1767, m Debby Root - desc/o Henry Lawrence THC192

Isaac - of NY, b1768 d1841 a prominent New York merchant & for twenty years president of the Branch Bank of the United States, m Cornelia Beach dau/o Rev Abraham Beach - desc/o Capt John Lawrence NYGBR(13)#2p62

James - of NY - desc/o Capt Thomas Lawrence MCD243

Jane - of MA 1635, b1614 dau/o Thomas Lawrence & Joan Antrobus of MA, m1633 at St Albans, George Giddings bp 1609 at Clapham, Bedford d1676 at Ipswich, MA son of John Giddings & Joan Purrier - the immigrant J&K216; AAP151; GBR456; EO2(2)1/13

John - of MA, bp 1609 d1667, m Elizabeth___ - desc/o Henry

LAWRENCE (cont.)

Lawrence THC189

John - of NY, d bef 1714/1715, m Elizabeth Cornell b1662 dau/o Richard Cornell - desc/o Capt William Lawrence RCFA12

John - of Flushing, Long Island, New York - son of Thomas Lawrence & Joan Antrobus, m Susanna____ - the immigrant GBR456; NYGBR(3)#1p26/29, #2p102, (3)#3p121/131, (13)#2p62

Capt John - of NY, b1659 d1729 Captain of a troop of horse & also sheriff of the county, m Deborah Woodhull dau/o Richard Woodhull - desc/o Thomas Lawrence J&K212; MCD242; BLG2783; NYGBR(13)#2p62

Judge John - of NY, b1695 Newtown d1765 a wealthy farmer, m1720 Patience Sackett dau/o Joseph Sackett - desc/o Thomas Lawrence J&K212; MCB427; MCD242; NYGBR(13)#2p62

John - of NY, b1731 d1794, m1755 Ann Burling d1821 - desc/o Thomas Lawrence MCB341; MCD242; BLG2783; NYGBR(5)#1p40, 41; RCFA14

Jonathan - of NY - desc/o Maj Thomas Lawrence BLG2783

Jonathan - of NY, m Mary Betts - desc/o Maj Thomas Lawrence BLG2783

Jonas - of MA, b1728, m Tryphena Lawrence - desc/o Henry Lawrence THC192

Joseph - of NY, m Patience Moore - desc/o Thomas Lawrence MCB427; MCD242

Joseph - of NY, b1665/1668 d1759, m1690 Mary Townley - desc/o Thomas Lawrence MCB341; MCD242; BLG2783; RCFA12

Joseph - of NY, b1741 d1781, m Phoebe Townsend dau/o Henry Townsend of Oyster Bay, Long Island - desc/o Capt William Lawrence RCFA14

Lyddya - of NY, b1728, m1745 Stevanus Hunt - desc/o Capt William Lawrence RCFA14

Lydia - b1761/1762 d1813, m Phineas Phelps - desc/o Thomas Hyde THC178

Lydia - of NY, m Anthony Franklin - desc/o Capt William Lawrence RCFA14

Mary - of NY, b1665 d1713, m(1)1682/1683 James Emott, secretary of the province of NJ; clerk of the Council 1683; deputy secretary 1684, he left his widow with four sons & a fortune, m(2)1714 Rev Edward Vaughan d1747 - desc/o Capt William Lawrence RCFA12

Mary - m Thomas Walton - desc/o Thomas Lawrence GBR457 cites source very probable - TAG(17)74/78

Mary - of NY, b1718, m Edward Burling - desc/o Capt William Lawrence RCFA14

Mary - of MA, dau/o Thomas Lawrence & Joan Antrobus, m Thomas Burnham - the immigrant GBR457; NYGBR(3)#1p26/29

Norris - of NY, b1737/1738, m1765 Ann Pell dau/o Caleb Pell & Mary Ferris - desc/o Capt William Lawrence RCFA14

Phebe - of NY, m Obadiah Townsend - desc/o Capt William Lawrence RCFA14

Richard - of NY, m1699 Charity Clarke, dau/o Thomas Clarke - desc/o Capt William Lawrence RCFA12

LAWRENCE (cont.)

Richard - of NY, b1691 d1781, m(1)1717 Hannah Browne b1697 dau/o Samuel Browne, m(2)1691 Mary Becket - desc/o Capt William Lawrence MCB341; MCD242; BLG2783; RCFA13

Richard - of NY, m Betsey Talman - desc/o Capt William Lawrence RCFA14

Samuel - of NY, d1760, m Mary Hicks - desc/o Capt William Lawrence MCB246; MCD242

Sarah - of NY, m James Tillett - desc/o Capt William Lawrence RCFA12

Sarah - of NY, m Joseph Ridgway - desc/o Capt William Lawrence MCD243

Maj Thomas - of NY, bp 1619/1620 d1703 Newtown, active in the affairs of the colony accepting command of the troops raised in Queen's Co to defend Albany against the French, his commission with the rank of major is dated Dec 30, 1689, son of Thomas Lawrence & Joan Antrobus, m Mary or Mercy____ - the immigrant J&K212; MCB424; MCD242; BLG2783; RAA1; EDV33; GBR456; NYGBR(3)#1p26/29, #2p102, (3)#3p121/131, (13)#2p62; RCFA9

Thomas - of NY, m Eleanor Legett - desc/o Maj Thomas Lawrence BLG2783

Thomas - of NY, b1753 d1836/1837, m1779 Eleanor Earle - desc/o Maj Thomas Lawrence BLG2783

Capt William - of Flushing, Long Island, New York, b1622 d1680; 1658 magistrate at Flushing under the Dutch government & after 1664 under the English government, he held a military commission, son of Thomas Lawrence & Joan Antrobus, m(1) Elizabeth ____, m(2)1664 Elizabeth Smith dau/o Richard Smith - the immigrant J&K213; MCB245, 246, 341; MCD241; EDV33; BLG2783; GBR457; NYGBR(3)#1p26/29, #2p102, (3)#3p121/131, (13)#2p62; RCFA11

William - of NY, d1719, m1680 Deborah Smith dau/o Richard Smith - desc/o Capt William Lawrence MCB246; MCD242; RCFA12

William - of NY, b1729 d1794, m(1)1752 Anna Brinkerhoff dau/o Isaac & Diana Brinkerhoff, m(2)1771 Mary Palmer dau/o Charles Palmer - desc/o Capt John Lawrence NYGBR(13)#2p62

William - of NY - desc/o Capt William Lawrence MCD243

William Jr - of NY - desc/o Capt William Lawrence MCD243

LAWSON Christopher - of NH, b abt 1616 son of John Lawson & Anne Wentworth (sister of William Wentworth), m Elizabeth Fitton - the immigrant MCS55; GBR351 some aspect of royal descent merits further study

Susan - of MD, b1743 d1798, m1760 Andrew Buchanan - desc/o Rev Robert Brooke CHB403

LAWTON Capt Benjamin Hall - of MA, b Portsmouth 1774 d1838, m1792 Betsey Paget b1773 d1801 dau/o George Paget - desc/o Jeremy Clarke ECD253 - desc/o Katherine Marbury DBR(1)82

LAY Temperance - of CT, b1691 d1773, m1714 Joseph Griswald DBR(4)483

LEACH Ephraim - of MA, b1761 d1840, m1785 Chloe Shattuck - desc/o John Winslow THC341

LEACH (cont.)

Hannah - b1725, m1743 Sergt Solomon Leach - desc/o John Winslow THC341

Jonathan - of MA, b1741 d1829, m1763 Abigail Leach - desc/o John Washbourne DBR(3)470

Sarah - of MA, b1711, m1732 Timothy Leach - desc/o John Washbourne DBR(3)470

Thomas - of MA, b1766 d1828, m1790 Anna Bradley - desc/o John Washbourne DBR(3)470

LEARNED Experience - b1711, m Jeremiah Shumway - desc/o Samuel Hyde LDS92

LEAVITT Dorothy - of NH, b1773, m John Hunt Sr - desc/o Gov Thomas Dudley DBR(5)68

Jeremiah - b1760, m Sarah Shannon - desc/o Gov Thomas Dudley LDS64; RAA89

Joseph - of NH, b1699, m(1) Mary Wadleigh - desc/o Gov Thomas Dudley LDS64; DBR(5)68; RAA89

Nathaniel - b1727, m Lydia Sanborn - desc/o Gov Thomas Dudley LDS64; RAA89

LECHMERE Thomas - of MA, d1765, m1709 Anne Winthrop - the immigrant MCB161; sufficient proof of alleged royal ancestry is lacking

LEE Alice - of VA, b1736 d1817, m Dr William Shippen Jr of Philadelphia, PA - desc/o Col Richard Lee CFA(1)314; CRL(1)105 - desc/o Henry Corbin CFSSA323; CFA(1)314 - desc/o Alice Eltonhead CFSSA323; CFA(1)314

Ann - of VA, b1693 d1732, m(1) William Fitzhugh of Eagle Nest, King George Co, son of Col William Fitzhugh, m(2)1714 Capt Daniel McCarty of Westmoreland Co, son of Dennis McCarty of Norfolk Co - desc/o Col Richard Lee BLG2785; CFA(1)314; CRL(1)104 - desc/o Henry Corbin CFSSA321; CFA(1)314 - desc/o Alice Eltonhead CFSSA321; CFA(1)314

Anna - of VA, m(1) William Armistead of Mathews Co, son of Col John Armistead & Judith___ of Gloucester Co, m(2) William Eustace - desc/o Col Richard Lee DBR(4)214 - desc/o Henry Corbin CFSSA334 - desc/o Alice Eltonhead CFSSA334

Anne - of VA, b1770 d1804, m Charles Lee - desc/o Col Richard Lee CRL(1)106

Anne - of VA, b1776 d1857, m abt 1793 William Byrd Page of Fairfield, Clark Co, son of Mann Page & Mary Mason (Seldon) - desc/o Col Richard Lee CFA(1)317; CRL(1)105 - desc/o Henry Corbin CFSSA325 - desc/o Alice Eltonhead CFSSA325

Doctor Arthur - of VA, b1740 of Middlesex Co d1792, practiced medicine in Williamsburg, studied law in England & was admitted to the bar in 1770, State Assembly of Virginia 1781/1782, U.S. Congress 1784/1785 d unmarried - desc/o Henry Corbin CFSSA324 - desc/o Alice Eltonhead CFSSA324

Capt Charles - of MD, b1655, m Elizabeth Metstand - desc/o Col Richard Lee DBR(3)324, 404; CFA(1)312; NFA58

Charles - b1731 d1782 unmarried, general in the Revolutionary War, son of John & Isabella (Bunbury) Lee - the immigrant GBR85

LEE (cont.)

Charles - of VA, b1758 of Fauquier Co d1815, member of the American Whig Society, member of the Continental Congress & the Virginia Assembly, naval officer of the Southern Potomac, 1784, Attorney General for President Washington, m(1)1789 Anne Lee, dau/o Richard Henry Lee & Anne (Gaskins-Pinckard), m(2)1809 Margaret Christian (Scott) Peyton of Fauquier Co & dau/o Rev John Scott & Elizabeth Gordon - desc/o Col Richard Lee CFA(1)316; WAC94; CRL(1)105 - desc/o Henry Corbin CFSSA329 - desc/o Alice Eltonhead CFSSA329

Lady Charlotte - of MD, dau/o Edward Henry Lee, 1st Earl of Lichfield & Charlotte Fitzroy, m(1)1698 Benedict Leonard Calvert, m(2) Christopher Crewe - the immigrant CHB52; MCS13; BCD52; DBR(2)236; GBR9

Edmund Jennings - of VA, b1772 of Alexandria d1843, m abt 1796 Sarah Lee, dau/o Richard Henry Lee & Anne (Gaskins-Pinckard) - desc/o Col Richard Lee CRL(1)105; AWW345 - desc/o Henry Corbin CFSSA331 - desc/o Alice Eltonhead CFSSA331

Elizabeth - of VA, b1709 - desc/o Col Richard Lee NFA58

Elizabeth - of VA, m Zachary Taylor, of Orange Co & son of James Taylor & Martha Thompson - desc/o Margaret Wentworth NFA49, 59 - desc/o Henry Corbin CFSSA334 - desc/o Alice Eltonhead CFSSA334

Elizabeth - of VA, b abt 1726, m Maj Peter Conway of Lancaster Co & son of Col Edwin Conway & Ann Ball - desc/o Col Richard Lee DBR(2)151; DBR(3)397; DBR(4)167 - desc/o Henry Corbin CFSSA334 - desc/o Alice Eltonhead CFSSA334

Elizabeth - of VA, m Thomas Bell - desc/o Col Richard Lee AWW120

Flora - of VA, b1765, m (her cousin) Ludwell Lee, of Loudoun Co, son of Richard Henry Lee & Anne Aylett - desc/o Henry Corbin CFSSA324 - desc/o Alice Eltonhead CFSSA324

Francis - of VA - desc/o Col Richard Lee WAC94

Francis Lightfoot - of VA, b1734 of Menokin, Richmond Co d1797, Continental Congress, 1775/1779, signer of the Declaration of Independence 4 Jul 1776, framer of the Articles of Confederation, Virginia Senate, m1769 Rebecca Tayloe, dau/o John Tayloe & Rebecca Plater of Mount Airy - desc/o Col Richard Lee CFA(1)314; CRL(1)105 - desc/o Henry Corbin CFSSA323; CFA(1)314 - desc/o Alice Eltonhead CFSSA323; CFA(1)314

George - of VA, b1714 England d1761, served as a burgess & justice, m(1)1738 Judith Wormley, dau/o John & Elizabeth Wormley of Rosehill, m(2) Anne Fairfax, dau/o Gov William Fairfax & Sarah Walker of the Bahamas & later of Virginia, & wid/o Major Lawrence Washington - desc/o Col Richard Lee CFA(1)313 - desc/o Henry Corbin CFSSA320, 321; CFA(1)313 - desc/o Alice Eltonhead CFSSA320, 321; CFA(1)313

George - of VA, m Frances Ball, dau/o Col James Ball of Bewdley, Lancaster Co - desc/o Henry Corbin CFSSA334 - desc/o Alice Eltonhead CFSSA334

George Fairfax - of VA, b1754 Mt Vernon d1804, m the wid/o Dr Travers of Berkeley Co - desc/o Col Richard Lee CFA(1)313 - desc/o

LEE (cont.)

Henry Corbin CFA(1)313 - desc/o Alice Eltonhead CFA(1)313 - desc/o William Fairfax CFA(2)277

Hancock - of VA, b1653 of Ditchley, Northumberland d1709, served as Justice of Northampton Co, m(1)1675 Mary Kendall, dau/o Col William Kendall of Northampton Co, m(2) Sarah Elizabeth Allerton, dau/o Col Isaac Allerton & Elizabeth Willoughby - desc/o Col Richard Lee DBR(1)695; DBR(2)151, 714; DBR(3)397, 742; DBR(4)167, 213; DBR(5)805; CFA(1)312; WAC94; AWW344, 345; NFA58 - desc/o Henry Corbin CFSSA333, 334 - desc/o Alice Eltonhead CFSSA333, 334

Hancock - of VA, b1709 of Fauquier Co d1780, m1733 Mary Willis d1798, dau/o Col Henry Willis & Anne (Alexander-Smith) - desc/o Col Richard Lee DBR(5)805 - desc/o Henry Corbin CFSSA334 - desc/o Alice Eltonhead CFSSA334

Hannah - of VA, m(2) Joseph Sprigg - desc/o Henry Corbin DBR(5)300

Hannah - of VA, b1728, m Gawin Corbin of Peckatone, Westmoreland Co, son of Col Gawin Corbin & Martha Bassett of Peckatone & Lanesville - desc/o Col Richard Lee CFA(1)314; CRL(1)105 - desc/o Henry Corbin CFSSA322; CFA(1)314 - desc/o Alice Eltonhead CFSSA322; CFA(1)314

Hannah - of VA, m Corbin Washington of Westmoreland Co, son of Col John Augustine Washington & Hannah Bushrod - desc/o Henry Corbin CFSSA322 - desc/o Alice Eltonhead CFSSA322

Lieut Col Henry - of VA, b1691 of Lee Hall, Westmoreland Co d1747/1749, m abt 1723/1724 Mary Bland, dau/o Richard Bland & Elizabeth Randolph of Berkley - desc/o Col Richard Lee BLG2785; CFA(1)314; CRL(1)104; AWW345; NFA57 - desc/o Henry Corbin CFSSA324; CFA(1)314 - desc/o Alice Eltonhead CFSSA324; CFA(1)314

Lieut Col Henry Jr - of VA, b1729 of Leesylvania, Prince George Co d1787, served as justice of the peace, burgess, & state senator, m1750 Lucy Grymes, (Washington's Lowland Beauty) - desc/o Col Richard Lee CFA(1)315; CRL(1)104; AWW345; NFA57 - desc/o Col William Randolph PVF132 - desc/o Henry Corbin CFSSA325; CFA(1)315 - desc/o Alice Eltonhead CFSSA325; CFA(1)315

Gen Henry (Light Horse Harry) - of VA, b1756 of Stratford, Westmoreland Co d1818 Cumberland Island, GA, graduated at Princeton 1773, recruited a company of light horse of which he was chosen capt 1775, promoted major for gallantry in battle 1778, captured the British at Paulus Hook, NJ 1779, for which Congress voted him a gold metal, served as a member of Virginia Assembly, governor of Virginia, appointed major general of the US Troops 1794, by President Washington, m(1)1782 Matilda Lee b1763 Stratford d abt 1790 dau/o Philip Ludwell Lee & Elizabeth Steptoe, m(2)1793 Anne Hill Carter b1773 d1829 dau/o Charles Carter & Anne Butler (Moore) of Corotomon & Shirley - desc/o Col George Reade PFA Apx D #1 - desc/o Col Richard Lee CFA(1)315; CRL(1)104 - desc/o Henry Corbin CFSSA325; CFA(1)315 - desc/o Alice Eltonhead CFSSA325; CFA(1)315

John - of VA, b1678 - desc/o Col Richard Lee BLG2785; WAC94;

LEE (cont.)

> CRL(1)104; NFA57
>
> John - of VA, b1709 - desc/o Col Richard Lee NFA58
>
> John - of VA, b1724 of Cabin Point, Westmoreland Co d1767, burgess, m1749 Mary Smith - desc/o Col Richard Lee CFA(1)314; CRL(1)104 - desc/o Henry Corbin CFSSA324; CFA(1)314 - desc/o Alice Eltonhead CFSSA324; CFA(1)314
>
> John Hancock - of VA, b1733/1734 d1803 lieutenant in Continental Line, major VA State Line, m(3)1781 Elizabeth Bell - desc/o Col Richard Lee DBR(5)805 - desc/o Anne Rich GVFTQ(4)508
>
> Joseph - of SC, b1742 d1814 - desc/o Col Richard Lee DBR(4)827
>
> Kendall - of VA, of Wicomico Parish, Northumberland Co d1780, m1749___Heale, dau/o William Heale & Priscilla Downman of Lancaster Co - desc/o Henry Corbin CFSSA334 - desc/o Alice Eltonhead CFSSA334
>
> Laetitia - of VA, b1730/1731, m1746/1747 Col William Ball - desc/o Col Richard Lee CFA(1)314 - desc/o Henry Corbin CFA(1)314 - desc/o Alice Eltonhead CFA(1)314
>
> Launcelot - of VA, b1756 Mt Vernon, m(1) Mary Bathhurst Jones, dau/o Col Thomas Jones & Sallie Skelton, m(2)___Cockrell - desc/o Col Richard Lee CFA(1)313 - desc/o Henry Corbin CFA(1)313 - desc/o Alice Eltonhead CFA(1)313 - desc/o William Fairfax CFA(2)277
>
> Leanna - of VA, m abt 1707 Capt William Jones II - desc/o Col Richard Lee DBR(3)324, 404
>
> Letitia - of VA, d1776, m(2) Dr Adam Thompson - desc/o Col Richard Lee DBR(4)107; DBR(5)877
>
> Lettice or Letitia - of VA, b1715 London, England d1768, m Col John Corbin of Port Tobago, Caroline Co b1710 son of Gawin Corbin & Jane (Lane-Wilson) - desc/o Col Richard Lee CFA(1)313 - desc/o Henry Corbin CFSSA321; CFA(1)313 - desc/o Alice Eltonhead CFSSA321; CFA(1)313
>
> Ludwell - of VA, of Loudoun Co, m (his cousin) Flora Lee, dau/o Philip Ludwell Lee & Elizabeth Steptoe of Stratford - desc/o Henry Corbin CFSSA322 - desc/o Alice Eltonhead CFSSA322
>
> Martha - of VA, b1716 London, England, m(1) Maj George Turberville of Hickory Hill, son of John Turberville of Northumberland Co, m(2) Col William Fitzhugh of Virginia & Maryland, son of George Fitzhugh & Mary Mason of Stafford Co - desc/o Col Richard Lee CFA(1)313 - desc/o Henry Corbin CFSSA321; CFA(1)313 - desc/o Alice Eltonhead CFSSA321; CFA(1)313
>
> Mary - of VA, m William Augustine Washington of Bridges Creek, Westmoreland Co, son of Augustine Washington & Ann Aylett - desc/o Henry Corbin CFSSA323 - desc/o Alice Eltonhead CFSSA323
>
> Mary - of VA, b1775, m1792 Philip Richard Fendall of Alexandria - desc/o Col Richard Lee CFA317 - desc/o Henry Corbin CFSSA325 - desc/o Alice Eltonhead CFSSA325
>
> Needham Sr - of VA, b1770 d1820, m1795 Susan Bailey - desc/o Col Richard Lee DBR(1)696; DBR(2)714; DBR(3)742
>
> Philip - of VA & MD, b1681 d1744 councillor, commissary general,

LEE (cont.)

    justice & naval officer of the North Potomac district, m(1) Sarah
    Brooke d1724, dau/o Col Thomas Brooke & Anne____ of
    Brookefield, Prince George's Co, Maryland, m(2) 1725/1726
    Elizabeth (Lawson) Sewall wid/o Henry Sewall, m(3) Grace Ashton,
    dau/o Col Henry Ashton & Mary____ - desc/o Col Richard Lee
    DBR(4)107; DBR(5)300; BLG2785; CFA(1)313; CRL(1)104; NFA57 -
    desc/o Henry Corbin DBR(5)300, 877; CFSSA321; CFA(1)313 -
    desc/o Alice Eltonhead CFSSA321; CFA(1)313

Philip Ludwell - of VA, b1726/1727 of Stratford, Westmoreland Co
    d1775, burgess & on the King's Council, m1761/1762 Elizabeth
    Steptoe, dau/o Col James Steptoe & Hannah Ashton of Homany
    Hall, Westmoreland Co - desc/o Col Richard Lee CFA(1)314;
    CRL(1)104 - desc/o Henry Corbin CFSSA324; CFA(1)314 - desc/o
    Alice Eltonhead CFSSA324; CFA(1)314

Col Richard - of VA, b abt 1613 d1664, m1641 Anne Constable - the
    immigrant FLW228; MCS92; DBR(1)547, 695; DBR(2)39, 151, 680,
    691, 713, 714; DBR(3)8, 31, 324, 335, 397, 404, 741; DBR(4)106,
    107, 167, 213, 827; DBR(5)328, 805; 850, 863, 873, 1051, 1052;
    RAA1, 106; EDV66; BLG2785; CFA(1)312; WAC94; CRL(1)103;
    AWW344, 345; NFA56; royal ancestry of Col Richard Lee has not
    been sufficiently proven

Richard II - of VA, b1646 d1714, m Letitia Corbin b1657 d1706 dau/o
    Henry Corbin & Alice Eltonhead of Buckingham House, Middlesex -
    desc/o Col Richard Lee DBR(4)107; BLG2785; CRL(1)104;
    AWW345; NFA57

Richard - of VA, b1679 d1718, m Martha Silk - desc/o Col Richard Lee
    BLG2785; CFA(1)313; CRL(1)104; NFA57 - desc/o Henry Corbin
    CFSSA320; CFA(1)313 - desc/o Alice Eltonhead CFSSA320;
    CFA(1)313

Richard - of VA, b1691 of Northumberland Co d1740, m1720 Judith
    Steptoe, dau/o Anthony Steptoe of Lancaster Co - desc/o Col
    Richard Lee DBR(1)695; DBR(2)151, 714, DBR(3)397, 742;
    DBR(4)167 - desc/o Henry Corbin CFSSA334 - desc/o Alice
    Eltonhead CFSSA334

Richard - of VA, b1726 d1795, burgess, m Sally Poythress, dau/o
    Peter Poythress - desc/o Col Richard Lee CFA(1)314; CRL(1)104 -
    desc/o Henry Corbin CFSSA324; CFA(1)314 - desc/o Alice
    Eltonhead CFSSA324; CFA(1)314

Richard - of VA, b1741, m1779 Sarah Dabney Strother - desc/o Col
    Richard Lee - AWW121

Richard Bland - of VA, b1761 d1827, served as a member of the House
    of Delegates, & a distinguished member of the US Congress, m1794
    Elizabeth Collins, dau/o Stephen Collins & Mary Parish - desc/o
    Col Richard Lee CFA(1)316; CRL(1)105 - desc/o Henry Corbin
    CFSSA325 - desc/o Alice Eltonhead CFSSA325

Richard Henry - of VA, b1732 of Chantilly, Westmoreland Co d1794,
    signer of the Declaration of Independence, 4 Jul 1776, Articles of
    Confederation, 1778, legislature of Virginia, 1780/1784, elected
    president of U. S. Congress, & U.S. Senate & selected for the Hall of
    Fame Oct 1900, m(1)1757 Anne Aylett, dau/o Col William Aylett &

LEE (cont.)

    Elizabeth Eskridge, m(2)1769 Anne Gaskins, dau/o Col Thomas
       Gaskins & wid/o Thomas Pinckard - desc/o Col Richard Lee
       CFA(1)314; CRL(1)105 - desc/o Henry Corbin CFSSA322;
       CFA(1)314 - desc/o Alice Eltonhead CFSSA322; CFA(1)314

  Robert - of VA, b abt 1648 - desc/o Col Richard Lee WAC94

  Sarah - of VA, b1729 d1761 in childbirth, m1748 Col John Carlyle of
       Alexandria, VA b1720 Scotland d1780 - desc/o William Fairfax
       CFA(2)277

  Theodorick - of VA, b1766 of Eckington d1849, m Catherine Hite,
       dau/o John Hite of Winchester - desc/o Col Richard Lee CFA(1)316;
       CRL(1)105 - desc/o Henry Corbin CFSSA325 - desc/o Alice
       Eltonhead CFSSA325

  Thomas - d1749, m Christiana Sim - desc/o Col Richard Lee BLG2785

  Thomas - of VA, b1690 of Stratford, Westmoreland Co d1750, m1722
       Hannah Ludwell dau/o Col Philip Ludwell & Hannah Harrison -
       desc/o Col Richard Lee BLG2785; CFA(1)313; CRL(1)105; NFA57 -
       desc/o Henry Corbin CFSSA321; CFA(1)313 - desc/o Alice
       Eltonhead CFSSA321; CFA(1)313

  Thomas - of VA, b1710 d1757 - desc/o Col Richard Lee DBR(4)827

  Capt Thomas - of VA, b1729 d1816, (2)1761 Mary Bryan - desc/o Col
       Richard Lee DBR(1)696; DBR(2)714; DBR(3)742

  Thomas - of VA, of Prince William Co, m Mildred Washington, dau/o
       Col John Augustine Washington & Hannah Bushrod - desc/o
       Henry Corbin CFSSA322 - desc/o Alice Eltonhead CFSSA322

  Thomas Ludwell - of VA, b1730 of Bell View, Stafford Co d1778, judge
       of the Supreme Court of Virginia, m Mary Aylett, dau/o Col William
       Aylett & Elizabeth Eskridge - desc/o Col Richard Lee CFA(1)314 -
       desc/o Henry Corbin CFSSA322; CFA(1)314 - desc/o Alice
       Eltonhead CFSSA322; CFA(1)314

  Thomas Sim - of MD, b1745 d1819 governor of Maryland 1779/1782
       & 1792/1794, m1771 Mary Diggs - desc/o Col Richard Lee
       BLG2785 - desc/o Rev Robert Brooke MG(1)100

  William - of VA, b1737 of Green Spring, James City Co d1795, agent
       for Virginia in England, appointed by Continental Congress
       commercial agent to Nantes, U. S. Commissioner to The Hague,
       Berlin & Vienna, 1778 negotiated a loan for the U. S. & arranged a
       commercial treaty with Holland, m Hannah Philippa Ludwell, dau/o
       Philip Ludwell & ___Grymes - desc/o Col Richard Lee WAC94 -
       desc/o Henry Corbin CFSSA323 - desc/o Alice Eltonhead
       CFSSA323

  William - of VA, m Jane Payne - desc/o Henry Corbin CFSSA334 -
       desc/o Alice Eltonhead CFSSA334

  William - of MD, b1775 d1845, m Mary Holliday - desc/o Col Richard
       Lee BLG2785

LEEDS Dorothy - of NY, b1756 d1823, m1772 Robert Smith - desc/o
       Peter Wright DBR(2)502

LEETE Abigail - of CT, d1711, m1671 Rev John Woodbridge - desc/o Gov
       William Leete CHB366; MCD246; RAA107

  Abigail - of CT, b1762, m1798 Calvin Crittenden - desc/o Gov William
       Leete CHB369

LEETE (cont.)

Allen - of CT, b1728 d1783, m1758 Rachel Morgan - desc/o Gov William Leete DBR(2)514; DBR(3)65; DBR(4)583

Amos - of CT, b1769 d1852, m1795 Casemilia Mills - desc/o Gov William Leete ECD(2)147; DBR(2)381

Andrew - of CT, b1643 d1702, m1669 Elizabeth Jordan - desc/o Gov William Leete CHB369; MCD245; DBR(2)380, 549, 595; DBR(3)198, 529; DBR(4)208; DBR(5)604; RAA107

Andrew - d1808, m(1)1763 Esther Blatchley - desc/o Gov William Leete DBR(4)208; DBR(5)604

Anne - of CT, b1671 d1724, m1691 John Collins b1665 d1751 - desc/o Gov William Leete CHB371; DBR(1)482; DBR(3)583; DBR(4)517; DBR(5)213, 575

Ann - of VA, b1731, m John Lewis - desc/o Col George Reade DBR(4)485

Caleb - b1673 - desc/o Gov William Leete RAA107

Edward Allen - of CT, b1762 d1841, m1792 Amy Morgan - desc/o Gov William Leete DBR(2)514; DBR(3)66; DBR(4)583

Gideon - of CT, b1703 d1781, m1727 Abigail Penfield Rossiter - desc/o Gov William Leete DBR(2)513, 514; DBR(3)65; DBR(4)583

James - of CT, b1751 d1793, m Jemima Caldwell - desc/o Gov William Leete DBR(3)529

Jane - of VA, b abt 1755, m Dr Zachary Lewis Meriwether - desc/o Col George Reade DBR(4)485

Jared - d1844, m1784 Elizabeth Scranton - desc/o Gov William Leete DBR(4)208; DBR(5)604

John - of CT, b1639 Guilford d1692 Guilford, m1670 Guilford, Mary Chittenden b1647 Guilford d1712 Guilford - desc/o Gov William Leete CHB370; MCD246; DBR(1)482; DBR(2)513, 595; DBR(3)65, 583; DBR(4)583, 751; DBR(5)213; DBR(5)574; SMO103

John II - of CT, b1674 d1730, m Mehitabel (Sarah) Allen - desc/o Gov William Leete CHB370; MCD246; DBR(2)513; DBR(3)65; DBR(4)517, 583

John - of CT, d1822, m1770 Lydia Leete - desc/o Gov William Leete DBR(3)198

Mary - of CT, b1701 d1778, m1726 Abial Eliot - desc/o Gov William Leete CHB370; MCD246

Mary - of CT, m Judge James Hooker - desc/o Gov William Leete NEFGM(1)175

Mercy - of CT, b1685 d1751, m1711 Samuel Hooker - desc/o Gov William Leete CHB369; MCD245

Mina - of CT, d1833, m1813 Joseph Carman - desc/o Gov William Leete DBR(3)198

Pelatia - of CT - desc/o Gov William Leete CHB370

Rachel - b1718 - desc/o Gov William Leete RAA107

Roland - of CT, d1767, m1738 Mercy Dudley - desc/o Gov William Leete DBR(3)198

Samuel - of CT, b1677 d1751, m1723 Hannah Graves - desc/o Gov William Leete ECD(2)146; DBR(2)380, 549; DBR(4)208; DBR(5)604

Samuel - of CT, b1726 d1799, m1765 Mary Kelly - desc/o Gov William Leete ECD(2)147; DBR(2)380, 549

LEETE (cont.)

Samuel - of CT, b1766, m Sarah Case - desc/o Gov William Leete DBR(2)549

Sarah - of CT, b1677 Guilford, m1704 Windsor, Eliakim Marshall b1699 Windsor, CT - desc/o Gov William Leete DBR(4)751; SMO103

Solomon - of CT, b1722, m Zipporah Stone - desc/o Gov William Leete CHB369; DBR(3)529

Gov William - of CT 1639, b1613 Doddington, Huntingtonshire, England d1683 governor of CT 1676/1683 son of John Leete & Anne Shute, m(1)1636 Hartford, CT, Anne Payne bp 1621 d1668 dau/o Reverend John & Anne Underhill Payne, m(2) Sarah Rutherford, m(3) Mrs Mary Newman Street - the immigrant CHB366; ECD(2)146; MCD245; MCS93; DBR(1)482; DBR(2)380, 512, 513, 549, 595; DBR(3)64, 65, 196, 197, 527, 529, 582; DBR(4)207, 208, 517, 579, 583, 751; DBR(5)211, 213, 574, 604, 1053; RAA1, 107; TAG(31)114/117; GBR336 some aspect of royal descent merits further study; NEFGM(1)176; SMO103

William - of CT, b1645 d1687 Guilford, CT, member of the general court of CT, eight terms, m Mary Fenn b1647 Milford d1701 Guilford - desc/o Gov William Leete NEFGM(1)176

William - of CT, b1671 d1736, m1699 Hannah Stone - desc/o Gov William Leete CHB369; DBR(3)198, 529

William - of CT, - desc/o Gov William Leete CHB370

LEFFINGWELL Lydia - of CT, m Capt Ebenezer Lathrop - desc/o Lieut Thomas Tracy FFF143, 156

LEGGETT Gabriel - of NY 1676, d1697 - the immigrant EDV49, 50; sufficient proof of alleged royal ancestry is lacking

LEIGH Margaret - of VA, d1804, m Matthew Heard - desc/o John Wiseman DBR(2)834; DBR(3)650

LEMON or LEMMON Joseph - of MA bef 1680 - the immigrant EDV124, 125; sufficient proof of alleged royal ancestry is lacking

LEONARD John - b abt 1615, m Sarah Heath - the immigrant LDS35, 49, 70; RAA no longer accepted as being of royal descent

Martha - b1649, m Benjamin Waite - desc/o John Leonard LDS70

Rachel - b1665, m Thomas Hancock - desc/o John Leonard LDS49

Sarah - b1645, m John Keep - desc/o John Leonard LDS35

LEVERETT Gov John - of MA, d1724, m Anna Sedgwick - desc/o Thomas Leverett EDV35

Thomas - of MA 1663 - the immigrant EDV35; sufficient proof of alleged royal ancestry is lacking

LEWIS Agatha - of VA, b1753 d1836, m(1) (her cousin) Capt John Frogg Jr, m(2) Col John Stuart - desc/o William Strother GVFTQ(3)380

Apphia Fauntleroy - of VA, m1771 Lieut David Allen - desc/o Col George Reade AWW216; CRL(4)550

Ann - of VA, b1726 d1748, m1747 George Wythe b1726 d1806 of Williamsburg; later became one of Virginia's most distinguished citizens. He was one of the Virginia signers of the Declaration of Independence and an eminent lawyer & jurist - desc/o Col John Waller GVFHB(5)716

Ann - of VA, b1731, m John Lewis - desc/o Col George Reade

LEWIS (cont.)

DBR(3)701; DBR(5)191; AWW91, 211; NFA84

Anne - of VA, b1732 d1809/1810;, m Edmund Taylor - desc/o Col
George Reade CHB255; ECD214; BCD255; DBR(1)209, 687 -

Anne - of VA, m(1) H, m Douthat, m(2)____French - desc/o William
Strother GVFTQ(3)380

Anne Overton - of VA, b1772 Spotsylvania Co d1795, m1795 James
McClure Scott, M.D. b abt 1770 Pennsylvania, no issue - desc/o
Col John Waller VG385, 386

Apphia Fauntleroy - m Lieut David Allen - desc/o Col George Reade
DBR(1)658

Benjamin - of VA, b1744 King & Queen Co, m Martha (Patsy) Bickerton
- desc/o Col John Waller GVFHB(5)716; VG386

Catherine - m 1771 John Bullock - desc/o Col Geo Reade DBR(3)354

Col Charles - of VA, b1696 d1779, m1717 Mary Howell - desc/o Col
George Reade CHB255, 420; ECD212, 214; BCD255; DBR(1)209,
474, 687; DBR(2)384, 825; DBR(3)187, 331, 352, 587; DBR(5)525,
646; AWW173; FFF269; CRL(3)103

Charles - of VA, b1721 d1782, m1746 Mary Randolph - desc/o Col
George Reade DBR(3)587; DBR(5)646

Col Charles - of VA, b1729/30 d abt 1770, m1750 Lucy Taliaferro -
desc/o Col George Reade CHB259; BCD259; DBR(3)623;
DBR(5)562; CRL(3)104

Col Charles - of VA, m Mary Randolph Lewis - desc/o Col George
Reade DBR(5)646; AWW91; NFA84

Charles - of VA, d1822 Lynchburg, m Susan R Waller - desc/o Col
John Waller VG384

Charles II - of VA, m Elizabeth Mary Horry - desc/o Col George Reade
DBR(2)384

Dorothea - of VA, b1737, m Christopher Smith - desc/o Col John
Waller GVFHB(5)716

Eleanor - of PA, m Jesse Lukens - desc/o Cadwalader Evans MCD187
- desc/o Rowland Ellis MCD266

Elizabeth - of ME, bp 1623 d1680/1682, m Robert Heywood, planter of
the parish of St Thomas, Barbados d bef 1680 - desc/o Thomas
Lewis NE(101)21

Elizabeth - of VA, m Col John Bollings of Cobbs, Chesterfield b1700
d1757 - desc/o Col George Reade HSF(2)187

Elizabeth - of VA, bp 1706, m1728 William Rush - desc/o Col George
Reade DBR(1)10; DBR(2)6

Elizabeth - of VA, m Rev Robert Barret - desc/o Col George Reade
AWW92, 205

Elizabeth - of VA, m1744 William Kennon - desc/o Col George Reade
CHB420; DBR(5)525; AWW173

Elizabeth - of VA, b1732 d1809, m(1) Col James Littlepage b1714
d1766, m(2) Maj Lewis Holladay b1751 d1820 - desc/o Col John
Waller GVFHB(5)716

Elizabeth - of VA, b1765 d1855, m Thomas Meriwether Gilmer b 1765
d1817 - desc/o William Strother GVFTQ(3)380

Elizabeth - of VA, b1769, m1788 William Douglas - desc/o Col George
Reade AWW102; NFA80

LEWIS (cont.)

Elizabeth - of VA, m____Barrett - desc/o Col George Reade NFA84

Elizabeth - of VA, m George Greenhow - desc/o Col John Waller VG386

Ellis - of PA, b1680 d1750 son of Lewis ap Robert & Mary____,
    m(1)1713 Elizabeth Newlin, m(2) Mrs Mary____Baldwin - the
    immigrant CHB110; BCD110; GBR80; GPFHB483

Ellis - of PA, b1734 d1776, m(2)1763 Mary Deshler - desc/o Ellis
    Lewis CHB110; BCD110

Col Fielding - of VA, b1725 d1781, m(1)1746 Catherine Washington,
    m1750 Betty Washington - desc/o Col George Reade DBR(1)626;
    DBR(3)448; CRL(3)104, 105

Fielding - of VA, b1751, m Ann Alexander - desc/o Col George Reade
    CRL(3)105

Frances - m 1750 Robert Lewis Jr - desc/o Col George Reade
    DBR(1)474

Frances - of VA, b1769 d1849, m Col Layton Yancey of the Revolution -
    desc/o William Strother GVFTQ(3)380

Francis - of VA, m Lucy Dudley - desc/o Col George Reade AWW173

Gabriel Jones - of VA & KY, b1775 d1864, m Mary Bibb - desc/o Col
    George Reade DBR(3)448, 449

Col George - of VA, b1757 d1821, m Catherine (Kate) Daingerfield -
    desc/o Col John Washington PFA51 - desc/o Col George Reade
    CRL(3)105

George Harvey - of VA, d1798, m1793 Hannah Thomas - desc/o Col
    George Reade DBR(4)721

Maj Howell - of VA, b1731 d abt 1814, m Mary Isabel Willis - desc/o
    Col George Reade CHB257; ECD212; BCD257; DBR(2)825;
    DBR(3)187

Howell - of VA & W VA, b1771 d1822, m Ellen Hackney Pollard -
    desc/o Col George Reade BCD254; CRL(3)105

Isabella - of VA, bp 1707 d1742, m Dr Thomas Clayton - desc/o Col
    George Reade CRL(3)103

Isabella - of VA, m1770 Bennett Goode - desc/o Col George Reade
    AWW91

James - m 1774 Susanna Anderson - desc/o Col George Reade
    DBR(1)474

Col James B - b1726 d1764, m1752 Elizabeth Taylor - desc/o Col
    George Reade DBR(3)353, 354; FFF269

James - of NC, b1772 d1855, m1797 Edith Walters - desc/o Col
    George Reade DBR(4)592

Jane - of VA, b1755 d1790, m Capt Thomas Hughes of the Revolution
    - desc/o William Strother GVFTQ(3)380

Jane - of VA, b abt 1755, m(1) Maj Thomas Meriwether - desc/o Col
    George Reade CHB258; BCD258; DBR(5)191

Jane - of VA, d1760, m Jonathan Read - desc/o Col George Reade
    DBR(3)331

Jane - of VA, m John Hudson - desc/o Col George Reade DBR(3)587

Jane - of VA, m1791 David Hinton - desc/o Col George Reade
    DBR(2)825

Jane - of VA, m(1) Meriwether Lewis, m(2) John Lewis - desc/o Col
    George Reade AWW91; NFA84

LEWIS (cont.)

Col John - of VA, b1672 d1719/1720, m Elizabeth Warner - desc/o
Col George Reade NFA71, 72, 77, 79; CRL(3)102, 103

John - of VA, b1694 d1754, m(1) abt 1718 Frances Fielding (d1731),
m(2) abt 1735 Priscilla (Churchill) Carter - desc/o Col George Reade
CHB259; BCD259; DBR(1)535, 626; DBR(3)448, 623; DBR(4)592,
720; DBR(5)562; FFF206; NFA79; CRL(3)103

John - of VA, b1720 d1794, m1741 Jane Lewis - desc/o Col George
Reade CHB257; BCD257; DBR(3)331

Col John - of VA, b1726 d1789, m Catherine Fauntleroy - desc/o Col
George Reade DBR(1)606, 657, 658; AWW91, 172, 213; CRL(4)550

John - of VA, b1728 (no further record) - desc/o Col George Reade
CRL(3)104

John - of VA, b1729 d1780, m(1) Sarah Iverson, m(2) Mildred Lewis
dau/o Col Robert Lewis & Jane Meriwether - desc/o Col George
Reade AWW211 - desc/o Col John Waller GVFHB(5)716, 719,
VG383

Capt John - of VA & KY, b1747 d1825, m Elizabeth Bates Jones -
desc/o Col George Reade DBR(3)448

Col John - b1753 d1817, m1776 Elizabeth Howell Kennon - desc/o Col
George Reade DBR(1)606

John - of VA, b1754 d1842, m1770 Delilah (Zila) Powell - desc/o Col
George Reade DBR(4)592

John - of VA & TX, b1754 d1825, m Elizabeth Harvey - desc/o Col
George Reade DBR(4)720, 721

John - of VA, m Matilda Nelson & had issue - desc/o Col John Waller
VG386

Dr John Taliaferro - of VA, m(2)1782 Susannah Waring - desc/o Col
George Reade DBR(5)562

John Taylor - of VA, b1757 d1835, m Lucy Maclin - desc/o Col George
Reade FFF269

John Zachary - m Miss Woolfolk - desc/o Col George Reade DBR(3)701

Judith - of ME & NH, bp 1626, m abt 1646 James Gibbins of Saco -
desc/o Elizabeth Marshall FLW21; MCS89; DBR(2)171, 172;
GBR264; TAG(19)10/15; NE(101)16/23, 88/91 - desc/o Thomas
Lewis GBR465

Maj Lawrence - of VA, b1767 d1839, m1799 Eleanor Parke Custis -
desc/o Col George Reade ECD217; CRL(3)105 - desc/o Col John
Washington PFA51

Lucy - of VA, b1735 d1788, m Christopher Ford - desc/o Col John
Waller GVFHB(5)716

Margaret Anne - of VA, b1751 d1834, m(1) John McClanahan, m(2) Col
William Bowyer - desc/o William Strother GVFTQ(3)379

Mary - of NH, bp 1619, m aft 1638 Saco, Rev Richard Gibson of
Portsmouth, New Hampshire, Church of England clergyman -
desc/o Elizabeth Marshall FLW21; MCS89 - desc/o Thomas Lewis
NE(101)20, 21

Mary - of VA, b1727 d1803, m1750 Francis Meriwether - desc/o Col
John Waller GVFHB(5)715

Mary - of VA, b1762 d1829, m Capt John McElhany - desc/o William
Strother GVFTQ(3)380

LEWIS (cont.)

Mary - of VA, d1801, m1784 David Wood Meriwether b1756 d1795 son of William Meriwether & Martha Wood - desc/o Col George Reade AWW211 - desc/o Col John Waller VG384

Mary - of VA, m Waddy Thompson - desc/o Col George Reade DBR(2)836

Mary - of VA, d1813, m Capt William Williams - desc/o Col George Reade CHB257

Mary - of VA, d1748, m1730 Maj Robert Throckmorton - desc/o Col George Reade ECD(2)231; CRL(3) (believed to be the dau/o Col John and Elizabeth Warner Lewis, although documentary proof of her parentage is lacking)

Mary - of VA, m Samuel Cobb of Georgia - desc/o Col George Reade AWW91; NFA84

Mary - of VA, m Buckingham Keen - desc/o Col George Reade DBR(2)384

Mary Randolph - of VA, m Edward Hill Carter - desc/o Col William Randolph DBR(4)201; DBR(5)646

Mary Warner - of VA, m(1) Phillip Lightfoot, m(2)1787 Dr John Bankhead - desc/o Col George Reade CHB259; BCD259; DBR(3)623

Mildred - of VA, m Maj John Lewis - desc/o Col George Reade AWW91; NFA84

Mildred - of NC, m1769 Maj John Cobb(s) - desc/o Col George Reade ECD212; BCD257; DBR(3)187

Nicholas - of VA, b1742, m Mary Walker - desc/o Col George Reade CHB258; MCD272; BCD258; DBR(4)588; AWW91, 92; NFA72, 77, 79, 84, 85

Nicholas Hunter - of VA, b1765, m1812 Ann Meriwether dau/o Nicholas Meriwether & Rebecca Terrell - desc/o Col John Waller VG384

Nicholas Meriwether - of VA, b1767 d1818, m Mildred Hornsby - desc/o Col George Reade CHB258; MCD272; BCD258; AWW102; NFA72, 77, 80, 85

Patsy Bickerton - of VA, m Smelson Smith - desc/o Col John Waller VG386

Phebe - of PA, b1767 d1845, m1787 Robert Waln Jr - desc/o Ellis Lewis CHB110; BCD110

Richmond - of VA, b1774 Spotsylvania Co d1831, surgeon USA in the War of 1812, m(1)1802 Elizabeth Travers b1778 d1827 dau/o Travers Daniel & Frances Moncure, m(2)1830 Margaret B Richardson b1813 - desc/o Col John Waller VG385, 388

Col Robert - of VA, bp 1704 d1757, m abt 1694 Jane Meriwether - desc/o Col George Reade CHB258; MCD272; BCD258; DBR(1)606, 657; DBR(2)835; DBR(3)615, 701; DBR(4)485, 588; DBR(5)191; AWW90, 91; NFA72, 77, 79; CRL(3)103 (death & marriage dates are different)

Robert - of PA, b1714 d1790, m1733 Mary Pyle - desc/o Ellis Lewis CHB110; BCD110

Robert - of VA, b1739, m1760 Jane Woodston - desc/o Col George Reade CHB420

LEWIS (cont.)

Robert - of VA, m Francis Lewis - desc/o Col George Reade AWW91

Maj Robert - of VA, b1769 d1829, m1791 Judith Walker Browne - desc/o Col George Reade DBR(1)626; CRL(3)105 - desc/o Col John Washington PFA51

Robert - of VA, d1802, m1786 Mary Gilchrist Bryce - desc/o Col George Reade CHB420

Robert - of VA, m Judith Walker Browne - desc/o Col George Reade BCD254

Robert - of VA, m ____Fauntleroy - desc/o Col George Reade NFA84

Sallie - of VA, m Philip Taylor - desc/o Col George Reade AWW215, 216

Sarah - b1748, m Dr Waller Lewis - desc/o Col George Reade DBR(3)615; NFA84

Sophia - of VA, m John Carthrae - desc/o William Strother GVFTQ(3)380

Thomas - of ME 1631, b abt 1590 Shrewsbury d by 1640, vintner or wine merchant son of Andrew & Mary (Herring) Lewis, m1618 St Chad's, Elizabeth Marshall of ME, dau/o Roger Marshall & Katherine Mitton - the immigrant RAA1; GBR465; NE(101)3/23; EO(2)2p627/648

Thomas Walker - of VA, b1763 d1807, m1788 Elizabeth Meriwether - desc/o Col George Reade DBR(4)588; AWW92; NFA80

Waller - of VA, b1739, m Sarah Lewis - desc/o Col George Reade GVFHB(5)716

Waller II - b1773 d1818, m Sally Wynne - desc/o Col George Reade DBR(3)615

Col Warner - of VA, b1720, m abt 1746 Mrs Eleanor Bowles Gooch - desc/o Col George Reade DBR(1)535; DBR(4)592, 720; FFF206; CRLL(3)104

Warner Jr - m Mary Chiswell - desc/o Col George Reade DBR(1)535

William - of VA, m Lucy Meriwether - desc/o Col George Reade AWW91; NFA84

Col Zachary - of VA, b1731 King & Queen Co d1803 appointed captain Spotsylvania Co Foot Company 1758 & was captain & colonel, Continental Line in the Revolutionary War, m1771 Ann Overton Terrell b1748 d1820 dau/o Richmond Terrell of Louisa Co & Ann Overton dau/o William Overton - desc/o Col John Waller GVFHB(5)716; VG385

LIDE Mary - m Robert Hodges - desc/o Gov Thomas Lloyd DBR(1)720

LIGHTFOOT Alice - of VA, b1698 - desc/o John Lightfoot WAC36

Ann - of VA, b1708 - desc/o John Lightfoot WAC36, 37

Elizabeth - of VA - desc/o John Lightfoot WAC36, 37

Goodrich - of VA, m Susannah____ - desc/o John Lightfoot WAC36, 37

Goodrich - of VA, bp 1713 - desc/o John Lightfoot WAC36, 37

John - of VA, d1707, m(1) Ann Goodrich, m(2) Mary____ - the immigrant WAC36, 37; sufficient proof of alleged royal ancestry is lacking

John - of VA, b1711 - desc/o John Lightfoot WAC36, 37

Mary - of VA, b1717 - desc/o John Lightfoot WAC36, 37

Philip - of VA, m Alice Corbin - the immigrant WAC36, 37; sufficient proof of alleged royal ancestry is lacking

LIGHTFOOT (cont.)

Philip - of VA, m Sallie Savigne Bernard - desc/o Col George Reade
    CHB259

Philip Bernard - of VA, m Sarah Bee Ross - desc/o Col George Reade
    CHB259

William - of VA - desc/o John Lightfoot WAC36, 37

LIGON (LYGON) Anne (Nancy) - of VA, b abt 1765 d abt 1842, m abt 1781
    Harrison Jones - desc/o Capt Henry Batte ECD117

Blackman - of VA & SC, b1757 d1831, m1782 Elizabeth Townes -
    desc/o Lieut Col Thomas Ligon DBR(3)635; DBR(5)193, 956

Elizabeth - of VA, m1770 Sherwood Purson (Peerson) - desc/o Lieut
    Col Thomas Ligon DBR(5)643

Henry - of VA, d1762, m Sarah Ligon (his cousin) d1785 - desc/o Lieut
    Col Thomas Ligon DBR(5)44, 202, 991; APP359, 360

Henry - of VA, d1778, m bef 1756 Elizabeth____ - desc/o Lieut Col
    Thomas Ligon DBR(5)202

Hugh - of VA, b1661, m(1)1688/1689 Elizabeth Walthall, orphan
    dau/o William Walthall, m(2) bet Jun 1711 & Dec 1713 Jane (Pew)
    Price wid/o John Price - desc/o Lieut Col Thomas Ligon BLG2788;
    APP356, 357

Johan - of VA, b1653 d1728, m abt 1672 Robert Hancock
    d1708/1709 - desc/o Lieut Col Thomas Ligon BLG2788;
    DBR(5)767; GVFWM(3)504; APP358

John - of VA - desc/o Lieut Col Thomas Ligon DBR(5)738, 961

John - of VA, m Mary Moseley - desc/o Lieut Col Thomas Ligon
    DBR(5)778

John - b abt 1732 - desc/o Martha Mallory RAA67 - desc/o William
    Harris RAA102 - desc/o Roger Ludlow RAA111

John Turner - of VA, b1760 d1822, m1786 Jane Haskins - desc/o
    Lieut Col Thomas Ligon DBR(5)47, 991

Joseph - of VA, b1704 d1752, m(2) Judith Stewart - desc/o Lieut Col
    Thomas Ligon DBR(3)35, 634, 635; DBR(4)236, 328; DBR(5)193,
    778, 956; RAA67, 111 - desc/o Thomas Harris RAA102

Capt Joseph - of VA, b1725/1730 d1780, m Judith____ - desc/o Lieut
    Col Thomas Ligon DBR(3)635; DBR(5)193, 956

Joseph - of VA, b1759 d1797, m1780 Frances Netherland - desc/o
    Lieut Col Thomas Ligon BLG2788

Joseph - of VA, d1830, m Nancy Ketura - desc/o Lieut Col Thomas
    Ligon DBR(5)62

Leonard Seth - of VA, m Jannett Mayo - desc/o Lieut Col Thomas
    Ligon DBR(5)740

Leonard Ward - of VA, m Catherine Mayo - desc/o Lieut Col Thomas
    Ligon DBR(5)740

Leonard Ward II - of VA, m Elizabeth Atkinson - desc/o Lieut Col
    Thomas Ligon DBR(5)740

Mary - of VA, b abt 1694 d1749, m1714/1719 Capt John Coleman
    d1714/1719 - desc/o Capt Thomas Harris ECD(2)158 - desc/o
    Lieut Col Thomas Ligon ECD(2)172; DBR(1)304, 403; DBR(2)408,
    518; DBR(4)660; DBR(5)922, 999; APP360

Mary - of VA, m(1)1698 William Anderson, m(2) by 1 Jan 1716/1717
    Peter Rowlett of Bristol Parish d1750 - desc/o Col Thomas Ligon

LIGON (LYGON) (cont.)
APP358

Mary - of VA, b abt 1663 d bef 1686, m Thomas Farrar - desc/o Lieut Col Thomas Ligon BLG2788; APP360

Mary - of VA, m William Moseley - desc/o Lieut Col Thomas Ligon DBR(3)35; DBR(4)236, 328

Mary - b abt 1749/1757 - desc/o Martha Mallory RAA67 - desc/o William Harris RAA102, 111

Matthew - of VA, m(2) Ann Ward - desc/o Lieut Col Thomas Ligon DBR(5)740

Matthew - of VA, d1764, m bef 1710 Elizabeth Anderson - desc/o Lieut Col Thomas Ligon BLG2788; DBR(4)372; DBR(5)643; APP359

Matthew - of VA, m Susanna____ - desc/o Lieut Col Thomas Ligon DBR(4)372

Phoebe - of VA, b abt 1698 d1756/1757, m Henry Walthall - desc/o Lieut Col Thomas Ligon DBR(5)639; GVFWM(3)503

Richard - of VA, b1657 d1724 surveyor of Henrico Co, m1680 Mary Worsham dau/o William Worsham & Elizabeth (? Littlebury) - desc/o Capt Thomas Harris ECD(2)158 - desc/o Lieut Col Thomas Ligon ECD(2)172; BLG2788; DBR(1)304, 403; DBR(2)408, 518; DBR(4)236, 372, 660; DBR(5)202, 643, 740, 922, 999; GVFWM(3)504; APP359

Richard - of VA, m Ann Ward - desc/o Lieut Col Thomas Ligon BLG2788

Richard - of VA, m Olive Jeter - desc/o Lieut Col Thomas Ligon DBR(4)372

Samuel - of VA, b1720 d1783, m Agnes____ - desc/o Lieut Col Thomas Ligon DBR(5)739, 961

Sarah - of VA, m Henry Ligon - desc/o Lieut Col Thomas Ligon APP358

Sarah - of VA, m by 1708 Richard Grills d1720 moved to North Carolina - desc/o Lieut Col Thomas Ligon APP360

Susanna - of VA, b1745, m Samuel Williams - desc/o Lieut Col Thomas Ligon DBR(5)748

Lieut Col Thomas - of VA 1641/1642, bp 1623/1623 d1675 surveyor & burgess of Henrico Co, lieutenant colonel of militia & surveyor of Henrico Co, son of Thomas Lygon b abt 1577 d1626 & Elizabeth Pratt b1602 d1631, m(1)____Pratt, m(2)1648/1650 Mary Harris dau/o Capt Thomas Harris - the immigrant ECD(2)169, 171; MCS49; BLG2788; DBR(1)304, 403; DBR(2)408, 517, 518; DBR(3)35, 634; DBR(4)328, 371, 659, 660; DBR(5)44, 62, 192, 193, 201, 636, 643, 738, 740, 748, 766, 767, 778, 922, 956, 961, 991, 999, 1058, 1059; RAA1, 102, 111; GBR204; GVFWM(3)481/505; APP356; VHG342, 343

Thomas - of VA, m Tabitha____ - desc/o Capt Henry Batte ECD117

Thomas - of VA, d bef Apr 1705, m1697 Elizabeth Worsham - desc/o Lieut Col Thomas Ligon DBR(5)636; GVFWM(3)503; APP358

Thomas - of VA, d bef 1689, m Mary____ & had issue - desc/o Lieut Col Thomas Ligon GVFWM(3)504

Thomas - of VA, b1724, m Ann____ - desc/o Lieut Col Thomas Ligon DBR(5)643

Thomas P - of VA, m Elizabeth Perkinson - desc/o Lieut Col Thomas

LIGON (LYGON) (cont.)

Ligon DBR(5)778

William - of VA, b1616 or abt 1653, d1689 major in Henrico Co militia, m bef 1680 Mary Tanner dau/o Joseph & Mary Tanner - desc/o Lieut Col Thomas Ligon BLG2788; DBR(3)35, 634; DBR(4)236, 328; DBR(5)44, 62, 193, 636, 738, 778, 956, 961, 991; GVFWM(3)502, 503; RAA111; APP357, 358

William II - of VA, b1682 of Prince Edward & Amelia Counties d1764, m Elizabeth Batte - desc/o Lieut Col Thomas Ligon DBR(3)35, 634; DBR(4)236, 328; DBR(5)62, 193, 778, 956; RAA111; APP358

William III - of VA, d1696, m abt 1744 Ann Webber - desc/o Capt Henry Batte ECD117; DBR(5)748 - desc/o Lieut Col Thomas Ligon DBR(5)62

William - of VA, b abt 1732 d1828, m1767 Elizabeth East - desc/o Lieut Col Thomas Ligon BLG2788

William - of VA, b1736 d1788, m1759 Edith Turner - desc/o Lieut Col Thomas Ligon DBR(5)47, 991

William - of VA, b1756 d1838, m Sarah Herring - desc/o Lieut Col Thomas Ligon DBR(5)202

Willis - of VA, b1763 d1826, m Nancy Gaddy - desc/o Lieut Col Thomas Ligon DBR(5)961

LILLIE Anna - m Samuel Howard - desc/o Anne Marbury GBR234 - desc/o Catherine Hamby GBR394

Eunice - b1737 - desc/o Griffith Bowen RAA72

John - m Abigail Breck - desc/o Anne Marbury GBR234

LINCOLN John - of CT, b1726 d1810, m1758 Anna Martin - desc/o Thomas Lincoln BLG2789

Jonah - of CT, b1760 d1845, m1783 Lucy Webb - desc/o Thomas Lincoln BLG2789

Samuel - of CT, b1658 d1704, m1692 Elizabeth Jacobs - desc/o Thomas Lincoln BLG2789

Samuel - of CT, b1693 d1794, m1723 Ruth Huntington - desc/o Thomas Lincoln BLG2789

Thomas - of MA, b1600 d1683, m1665 Elizabeth Harvey - the immigrant BLG2789 sufficient proof of alleged royal ancestry is lacking

Thomas - of MA, b abt 1628 d1720, m(1) Mary Austin, m(2) Susanna Smith - desc/o Thomas Lincoln BLG2789; sufficient proof of alleged royal ancestry is lacking

LINDSAY Christopher - of MA 1629 d1669, m Margaret____ - the immigrant CFA324; sufficient proof of alleged royal ancestry is lacking

Daniel - of VA 1645 - desc/o Rev David Lindsay EDV105

Daniel - of MA, b1753 d1827, m Deborah Ingalls - desc/o Christopher Lindsay CFA325

Rev David - of VA, bp 1603 d1667 son of Sir Jerome Lindsay of Annatland & the Mount & Margaret Colville, m(1)____, m(2) Susannah____ - the immigrant JSW1650; MCB146; MCS33; DBR(2)149; DBR(5)277, 278; RAA1; EDV105; WAC43; GBR100

Eleazer - of MA, b1644 d1716, m Sarah Alley - desc/o Christopher Lindsay CFA324

LINDSAY (cont.)

Eleazer - of MA, b1716/1717 d1793, m Lydia Farrington - desc/o Christopher Lindsay CFA325

Ellen (Helen) - of VA, b1643 d1698, m(2)1671 Capt Thomas Opie Sr - desc/o Rev David Lindsay JSW1650; MCB146; DBR(2)149; DBR(5)278; WAC43

George Waller - of MD, b1771 d1810, m1801 Judith Grayson - desc/o Leonard Calvert CFA(5)293

Ralph - of MA, b1684 d1747, m Mary Breed - desc/o Christopher Lindsay CFA325

William Henry - of MD, b1773 d1823, m1804 Catherine Washington Sanford - desc/o Leonard Calvert CFA(5)293

LINTON John - of PA, b1727 d1786, m(2)1772 Mary Moon b1736 - desc/o Margaret Davis ECD(3)111; DBR(4)230 - desc/o Thomas Bye DBR(5)481

LINZEE Capt John - of MA, m1772 Susanna Inman - the immigrant EDV94, 95; no further connection confirming royal ancestry

LIPPITT Charles of RI, b1754 d1845, m1783 Penelope Low - desc/o William Arnold CHB16; BCD16

Col Christopher of RI, b1744 d1824, m1777 Waite Harris - desc/o William Arnold CHB16; BCD17

LISLE Bridget - of MA, dau/o John Lisle & Alice (Beckenshaw) Lisle, m(1) Leonard Hoar b abt 1630 d1675, 3rd president of Harvard College, m(2) Hezekiah Usher - the immigrant GBR206; NE(53)292; EO2(2)367/371

John - of MA 1640 - the immigrant EDV125; sufficient proof of alleged royal ancestry is lacking

LITTLE Elizabeth - b1719, m1738 Joseph Otis - desc/o Ensign Constant Southworth DBR(5)828

Elizabeth - of NC, b1765 d1829, m1784 Morgan Brown 4th - desc/o Patrick Stuart CHB338; BCD338

Faith - of CT, b1754, m1781 Rev Lemuel Parsons - desc/o Mabel Harlakenden CHB271; BCD271

LITTLEFIELD Martha - b1750 - desc/o John Deighton RAA86

LITTLETON Bowman - of MD, d1696 - desc/o Col Nathaniel Littleton APP580

Col Edward - of VA, d1663, m(1)1658 Sarah Douglass age (12), died in childbirth dau/o Col Edward Douglas of Northampton Co, VA, m(2)1661 Frances Robins dau/o Col Obedience Robins - desc/o Col Nathaniel Littleton WAC38; NE(41)364/368; APP578; HSF(10)190; GVFTQ(18)21

Elizabeth - of VA, d1753, m1662/1663 Richard Waters d1720 of Somerset Co, Maryland - desc/o Col Nathaniel Littleton NE(4)364/68; APP580

Esther - of VA, b1646, m1662/1663 Col John Robins of Cherrystone, b1636 d1709, son of Obedience Robins & Grace O'Neil - desc/o Col Nathaniel Littleton NE(4)364/368; APP462; GVFTQ(18)21; SMO300

Esther - of VA, inherited land at Chincoteague called King Neck, m by 16 Jul 1683 Col William Whittington - desc/o Col Nathaniel Littleton APP580; GVFTQ(18)22

Esther - of VA, b abt 1699 d1764, m1722 Thomas Savage, son of

LITTLETON (cont.)

Thomas Savage & Alicia Harmanson - desc/o Col Nathaniel Littleton WAC38; NE(4)364/368; APP79; GVFTQ(18)22; RCFA(7)70

Gertrude - of VA, d1738/1739, m Henry Harmanson d1709 of Northampton Co, VA - desc/o Col Nathaniel Littleton NE(4)364/368; APP580; GVFTQ(18)22

Leah - of VA, m Col George Gale of Somerset Co, Maryland - desc/o Col Nathaniel Littleton NE(4)364/368

Mary - of VA - desc/o Col Nathaniel Littleton WAC38

Col Nathaniel - of VA 1635, bp 1605 Hopton Castle, Salop d1654 Northampton Co, VA in 1640 he was chief magistrate of Accomack Co in 1652 a member of the House of Burgesses & one of the governor's Executive Council under Governor Richard Burnet & William Claiborne secretary of the colony. 6th son of Sir Edward Littleton (Lyttelton) Baronet, Lord Chief Justice of England, of Shropshire, England & Mary Walter, m abt 1638 Ann Southey b abt 1620 Somerset, England d1656 Northampton Co, VA dau/o Henry & Elizabeth_____ Southey - the immigrant FLW5; DBR(5)1054; RAA1; WAC38; GBR84; NE(41)364/368; APP577/580; GVFWM(3)442; GVFTQ(18)20/23; CFA(4)126; RCFA(7)70; SMO300

Col Nathaniel - of VA, d1703, sheriff, justice, colonel in the Colonial Army, m Susanna Waters, dau/o Col William Waters & Isabel Harmanson - desc/o Col Nathaniel Littleton NE(4)364/368; RCFA(7)70

Nathaniel - of VA, d1702/1703, captain of Northampton Co militia, m Susanna Andrews - desc/o Col Nathaniel Littleton APP79, 579, 580; GVFTQ(18)22

Sarah - of VA, m John Dennis of Somerset Co, Maryland - desc/o Col Nathaniel Littleton NE(4)364/368; HSF(10)196; GVFTQ(18)22

Sarah - of VA, b abt 1669 d1720, m(1) Adam Michael, m(2) Col John Custis desc/o Col Nathaniel Littleton APP577/580

Col Southey - of VA, b1645 d1679 Albany, New York, member of Governor Berkeley's court, officer in the Colonial Army, justice & sheriff, m(1) Sarah_____, m(2) Elizabeth Bowman dau/o Major Edmund Bowman of Accomack Co, VA - desc/o Col Nathaniel Littleton WAC38, 39; NE(4)364, 368; APP579; GVFWM(3)442; GVFTQ(18)22; RCFA(7)70

Southey - of VA, d abt 1702, m Mary Brown dau/o Thomas Brown & Susanna (Denwood) Brown of Northampton Co - desc/o Col Nathaniel Littleton NE(4)364/368; APP580; GVFTQ(18)22

Southey - of VA, d1712/1713, m Mary_____ - desc/o Col Nathaniel Littleton APP79

Susan Custis - of VA, d1716, m_____King - desc/o Col Nathaniel Littleton GVFTQ(18)22

LIVERMORE Mary - b1702, m1726 Nathaniel Sherman - desc/o Dr Richard Palgrave DBR(5)762

LIVINGSTON Alida - of NY, b1728 d1790, m(1)1750 Henry Hansen, m(2)1766 Col Martinus Hoffman - desc/o Col Robert Livingston DBR(3)536; CFA(5)337

Alida - of NY, b1761 d1822, m1785 General John Armstrong, United States Minister to France 1804/1810 d1843 - desc/o Col Robert

LIVINGSTON (cont.)

Livingston CFA(5)336

Catherine - bp 1733, m1759 John L Lawrence - desc/o Col Robert Livingston CFA(5)337

Catherine of NY, b1743 d1798, m1762 Nicholas Bayard - desc/o James Alexander CHB22; BCD22

Catherine - of NY, bp 1745 d1810, m(1)1764 Stephen Van Rensselaer, m(2)1775 Dominie Eilardus Westerlo - desc/o Col Robert Livingston CFA(5)337

Catherine - of NY, b1752 d1849, m1793 Rev Freeborn Garretson - desc/o Col Robert Livingston CFA(5)336

Edward - of NY, b1764 d1836 Montgomery Place, Dutchess Co; member of Congress 1795/1801, United States Attorney, New York & Mayor, New York City, 1801, member of Congress 1822/1829, U.S. secretary of state 1831, Minister to France 1833, m(1)1788 Mary McEvers d1801 dau/o Charles McEvers, m(2)1805 Louise Moreau de Lassy nee D'Avezac de Castera, dau/o Jean D'Avezac De Castera of New Orleans & wid/o Capt Moreau De Lassy - desc/o Col Robert Livingston BLG2793; CFA(5)336

Gertrude - of NY, b1757, m1779 General Morgan Lewis, governor of the state of New York 1804 - desc/o Col Robert Livingston CFA(5)336

Gilbert - of NY, b1689/1690 d1746, m1711 Cornelia Beekman b1693 d1742 dau/o Henry Beekman - desc/o Col Robert Livingston BLG2793; DBR(5)183, 920; GBR92; CFA(5)336

Gilbert - of NY, b1742 d1806, m Catherine Grannell - desc/o Col Robert Livingston DBR(5)920

Gilbert James - of NY, m Susanna Lewis - desc/o Col Robert Livingston GBR92

Henry - of NY, b1714 d1799, m1741 Susanna Conklin - desc/o Col Robert Livingston DBR(5)183, 920

Lieut Col Henry - of NY, b1753 d1823 - desc/o Col Robert Livingston BLG2793

Henry Beekman - of NY, b1750 d1831, colonel 4th New York Regiment, Continental Army, m1781 Ann Hume Shippen dau/o Dr William Shippen - desc/o Col Robert Livingston BLG2793; CFA(5)335

Henry Walter - b1764 d1810, m S Fox - desc/o Col Robert Livingston BLG2792

James - of NY, m Judith Newcomb - desc/o Col Robert Livingston GBR92

Janet - of NY, b1743 d1828, m1773 Gen Richard Montgomery, who was killed at the storming of Quebec 1775 - desc/o Col Robert Livingston CFA(5)335

Johanna - of NY, b1694, m Cornelius Gerrit Van Horne - desc/o Col Robert Livingston CFA(5)336

Col John - of CT, b1680 d1720, m(1)1701 Mary Winthrop dau/o Fitz John Winthrop, governor of CT 1698/1707, m(2)1713 Elizabeth Knight dau/o a Mrs Sarah Knight - desc/o Col Robert Livingston BLG2792; CFA(5)334

John - of NY, bp 1714 Albany d1788, m1742 Catherine De Peyster dau/o Abraham De Peyster - desc/o Col Robert Livingston

LIVINGSTON (cont.)

BLG2793; DBR(1)79; DBR(2)121; DBR(5)528, 529; CFA(5)337

John - of NY, b1755 of Massena, Dutchess Co d1851, m(1)1779
Margaret Sheape or Sheaffe d1784, m(2)1789 Eliza McEvers dau/o
Charles McEvers of New York - desc/o Col Robert Livingston
BLG2793; CFA(5)336

John - m 1785 Ann Cummings - desc/o Col Robert Livingston
DBR(1)79; DBR(2)121; DBR(5)531

John ADC - of NY, b1750 d1822, m1775 Mary Ann LeRoy - desc/o Col
Robert Livingston BLG2793

John Swift - of NY - desc/o Col Robert Livingston BLG2792

Judith - m Samuel Herrick Butler - desc/o Col Robert Livingston
GBR92

Margaret - of NY, b1681, m1700 Colonel Samuel Veitch d1758 first
English Governor of Annapolis Royal - desc/o Col Robert Livingston
CFA(5)334

Margaret - of NY, bp 1747 d1830, m1776 Dr Thomas Jones - desc/o
Col Robert Livingston CFA(5)337

Margaret Beekman - of NY, b1749 d1823 Rhinebeck, New York,
m1776 Dr Thomas Tillotson of Maryland, Surgeon-General,
Northern Department, Continental Army - desc/o Col Robert
Livingston DBR(1)287; CFA(5)335

Moncrieff - b1770 d1853, m(1)1790 Frances Covert, m(2) Catharine
Thorn - desc/o Col Robert Livingston BLG2792

Peter - of MA, b1737 d1794, m1758 Margaret Livingston - desc/o Col
Robert Livingston BLG2792; NYGBR(10)#2p98

Peter Van Brugh - of NY, bp 1710 d1793, member of the Committee of
One Hundred 1775, member and first president of Provincial
Congress 1775, m1739 Mary Alexander b1721 d1769, sister of
William Alexander, Lord Stirling. They had 12 children - desc/o Col
Robert Livingston BLG2793; CFA(5)337

Peter William - b1767 d1826, m1793 Elizabeth Williams - desc/o
Col Robert Livingston BLG2792

Philip - of NY, b1686 Albany d1756 New York, second Lord of the
Manor of Livingston, secretary for Indian Affairs 1722, clerk of the
County of Albany 1721/1749, member of the Provincial Council
1724/1749, m1707 Catherine Van Brugh dau/o Peter Van Brugh -
desc/o Col Robert Livingston JSW1612; BLG2792; DBR(3)536, 726;
CFA(5)336

Philip - of NY, b1716/1717 d1778 Alderman of New York 1754/1763,
member of the Provincial Assembly 1759/1769, Speaker 1768,
signer of the Declaration of Independence 1776, state senator 1777,
m1740 Christian Ten Broeck b1718 d1801 dau/o Col Dirck Ten
Broeck - desc/o Col Robert Livingston BLG2793; AMB36;
CFA(5)337

Philip - of NY, b1741 d1787, m1768 Sarah Johnson - desc/o Col
Robert Livingston BLG2793; AMB36; CFA(5)337

Philip Henry - of NY, b1769 d1831, m Maria Livingston - desc/o Col
Robert Livingston BLG2793; AMB36

Col Robert (the elder) - of NY 1674, b1654 Ancram, Edinburgh,
Scotland d1728 Lord of the Manor of Livingston, New York state &

LIVINGSTON (cont.)

speaker of the New York Legislature 1718/1725, colonel in the provincial militia, son of John Livingston, rector of Ancrum, & Janet Fleming; m1679 Alida Schuyler (Van Rensselaer) dau/o Philip Pieterse Schuyler & wid/o the Rev Nicholas Van Rensselaer - the immigrant JSW1612; BLG2792; DBR(1)77, 79, 287; DBR(2)121; DBR(3)320, 534, 535, 726; DBR(5)183, 528, 919; RAA1; EDV14; GBR92; NYGBR(9)#3p148, 149, (10)#2p98, (32)#3p129/135, #4p193/200; CFA(5)334

Robert, the younger - of NY, m Margareta Schuyler - desc/o Col Robert Livingston GBR92

Robert - of NY, b1688 d1775, first Proprietor of Clermont, m1717 Margaret Howarden of New York d1775 - desc/o Col Robert Livingston BLG2793; DBR(1)287; CFA(5)335

Robert - of NY, b1708 d1790, third Lord of the Manor of Livingston, member of the House of Assembly 1737/1759, m(1)1731 Maria Thong b1711 d1765 dau/o Walter Thong, m(2) Gertrude Van Rensselaer Schuyler b1714 d1790 dau/o Kiliaen Van Rensselaer & wid/o Adoniah Schuyler - desc/o Col Robert Livingston JSW1612; BLG2792; NYGBR(10)#2p98; CFA(5)336

Robert - of NY, b1718 New York d1775 judge of the Admiralty Court 1760, justice of New York Supreme Court 1763, member of the Provincial Assembly 1759/1768, m1742 Margaret Beekman dau/o Col Henry Beekman - desc/o Col Robert Livingston BLG2793; DBR(1)287; CFA(5)335

Robert Cambridge - of NY, b1742 d1790, m1778 Alice Swift - desc/o Col Robert Livingston JSW1612; BLG2792

Robert Gilbert - of NY, b1713 d1789, m1740 Catherine McPhaedres - desc/o Col Robert Livingston BLG2793

Robert Gilbert - of NY, bp 1749 d1791, m1769/1770 Margaret Hude - desc/o Col Robert Livingston BLG2793

Robert Henry - of NY, b1760 d1804, m1792 Catharine Tappen - desc/o Col Robert Livingston DBR(5)183

Robert L - b1775 d1843, m1799 Margaret Livingston - desc/o Col Robert Livingston BLG2792

Robert R - of NY, b1746 New York d1813, one of the most distinguished men of his day in America; member of the Continental Congress; one of the Committee of Five appointed to draw up the Declaration of Independence; member of the Provincial Congress 1775/1777; chancellor of the state of New York 1777/1801, secretary of Foreign Affairs; Minister to France; negotiator of the Louisiana Purchase, m1770 Mary Stevens dau/o John Stevens of Hunterdon, NJ - desc/o Col Robert Livingston BLG2793; CFA(5)335

Robert Thong - b1759 d1813, m1787 Margaret Livingston - desc/o Col Robert Livingston BLG2792

Sarah - of NY, m Major John Ricketts - desc/o James Alexander CHB23; BCD23

Sarah - bp 1725 d1805, m1748 Maj General William Alexander, Lord Stirling - desc/o Col Robert Livingston DBR(3)726; CFA(5)337

Sarah - of NY, b1752 d1814, m1775 (her cousin) Rev John Henry

LIVINGSTON (cont.)

    Livingston b1746 d1825, president of Queen's College New, Jersey - desc/o Col Robert Livingston AMB36; CFA(5)337

    Walter - of NY, b1740 d1797, m1769 Cornelia Schuyler - desc/o Col Robert Livingston BLG2792

    William - of NY, b1723 d1790, member of the Provincial Assembly 1759/1761, governor of NJ 1776/1790, m abt 1745 Susannah French bp 1723 d1789 - desc/o Col Robert Livingston CFA(5)337

LLOYD Anna or Anne - of CT, dau/o George Lloyd, Bishop of Chester & Anne Wilkinson, m(1)1612 Thomas Yale of Plas Grono, Wales d1619, m(2) abt 1627 Gov Theophilus Eaton b abt 1590 d1657/1658 statesman, merchant & governor of the New Haven Colony - the immigrant J&K321; ECD(3)192; BCD73; GBR321; TAG(52)142/144; DLJ2030

    Charles - son of Charles Lloyd & Elizabeth Stanley, brother of Deputy Governor Thomas, m Elizabeth Lort - the immigrant GBR82

    Charles - of PA, b1776 d1860 Chester, now Delaware Co, m1798 Darby, Frances Paschall b1771, dau/o Dr Henry Paschall of Paschallville & Ann Garret - desc/o Robert Lloyd CRFP(1)505

    Lieut Col Cornelius - of VA, m Elizabeth____ - the immigrant WAC41; sufficient proof of alleged royal ancestry is lacking

    David - of PA, b1707 d1773, m abt 1720 Anna Crawford - desc/o Gov Thomas Lloyd DBR(1)720; DBR(2)94, 298, 319, 472, 477, 479, 481, 668, 771, 791; DBR(3)150, 270, 274, 278, 282, 286, 289, 293, 296, 300

    Deborah - of PA & MD, b abt 1682 d172_, m1704 Dr Mordecai Moore d1721 Maryland, of Anne Arundel Co, Maryland practitioner in physick & chirurgery who had come to America with Lord Baltimore as his family physician - desc/o Thomas Lloyd CHB122; MCD251; BCD122; AFA74; CRFP(1)42, 43

    Edward - of VA & MD, m(1) Alice Crouch, m(2) Frances Watkins, m(3) Grace Parker - the immigrant BLG2793; sufficient proof of alleged royal ancestry is lacking

    Edward - of MD, b1670 d1719, m1703 Sarah Covington - desc/o Edward Lloyd BLG2793

    Edward - of MD, b1711 d1770, m1739 Anne Rousby - desc/o Edward Lloyd BLG2793

    Edward - of MD, b1744 d1796, m1767 Elizabeth Taylor - desc/o Edward Lloyd BLG2793

    Elizabeth - of PA, b1677 d1704, m1700 Daniel Zachary - desc/o Thomas Lloyd CRFP(1)42

    Gainor - of PA, b1705 d1728, m1727 Mordecai James d1776 - desc/o Robert Lloyd CRFP(1)497

    Hannah - of PA, b1666, m(1) John Delaval, Provincial Councillor 1692, m(2) Richard Hill, Provincial Councillor 1704/1728 - desc/o Thomas Lloyd CRFP(1)42

    Hannah - of PA, b1699 Merion d1762/1763 Philadelphia, m(1) John Roberts, m(2)1722 William Paschall d1732, third son of Thomas Paschall & Margaret Jenkins of Philadelphia, m(3)1734 Peter Osborne d1765 Philadelphia - desc/o Hannah Price MCB418 - desc/o Robert Lloyd CRFP(1)497, 500, 501

LLOYD (cont.)

Henry - of MA, m1708 ____Nelson - desc/o James Lloyd EDV135, 136

Col Hugh - of PA, b1741/1742 Merion d1832 Kensington, Philadelphia, served in the Revolutionary War, Col of the 3rd Battalion, Chester Co militia, 1776, m1767 Darby, Susanna Pearson b1746 Darby, dau/o Thomas Pearson & Hannah Blunston - desc/o Rees Jones AFA260 - desc/o Robert Lloyd CRFP(1)498; CFA(2)463

Isaac - of PA, m Ann Gibbons - desc/o Robert Lloyd CFA(2)463

Isaac - of PA, m(1) Hannah S Boulton, m(2) Catharine W Boutcher - desc/o Robert Lloyd CRFP(1)499

James - of MA - the immigrant EDV135, 136; sufficient proof of alleged royal ancestry is lacking

Margaret - m William Henry Smith - desc/o John Nelson AAP156; GBR148

Mary of PA, b1674, m1694 Judge Isaac Norris, Provincial Councillor 1709/1734, Speaker of Assembly - desc/o Thomas Lloyd CHB124; BCD124; CRFP72

Mary - of PA, b1763 d1816, m1779 Robert Hodges - desc/o Gov Thomas Lloyd DBR(2)94, 298, 319, 472, 478, 479, 481, 668, 771, 791; DBR(3)150, 151

Mary - of SC, d1816, m1779 Robert Hodges - desc/o Thomas Lloyd DBR(3)270, 271, 275, 278, 283, 286, 289, 293, 296, 300

Miss Lloyd - b abt 1662/69 - desc/o James Neale RAA117

Mordecai - of PA, b1708, m Hannah Fishbourne - desc/o Thomas Lloyd CRFP(1)43

Peter - of PA, b London, England d1744/1745 Philadelphia, common councilman 1729/1744, merchant, m1729 Mercy Masters - desc/o Thomas Lloyd CRFP(1)42

Col Philomen - of MD, b1647 d1685, m abt 1668 Henrietta Maria Neal - desc/o Edward Lloyd BLG2793

Rachel of PA, b1667/1668, m(1)1688 Samuel Preston, Provincial Councillor 1714/1743 - desc/o Thomas Lloyd CHB127; MCD252; BCD127; DBR(1)1; DBR(2)515; DBR(3)175; AFA198; CRFP42

Rees - of PA, b1707 d1743, m1735 Catharine Humphrey d1782 - desc/o Robert Lloyd CRFP(1)497

Richard - of PA, b1713/1714 Merion d1755 Darby, PA, m1736 Hannah Sellers b1717 dau/o Samuel Sellers Jr of Derby & Sarah Smith - desc/o Rees Jones AFA260 - desc/o Robert Lloyd CRFP(1)497, 498; CFA(2)463

Richard Pearson - of PA, b1773 d1814, m Edith Lane - desc/o Robert Lloyd CRFP(1)504

Robert - of PA 1683, b1669 Merionethshire, Wales d1714, m1698 Lowry Jones b1680 Wales, dau/o Rees John William Jones & Mrs Hannah Price Jones David Evans of PA - desc/o Gov Thomas Lloyd DBR(1)720; DBR(2)94, 298, 319, 472, 477, 479, 481, 668, 771, 791; DBR(3)150, 270, 274, 278, 282, 286, 289, 292, 296, 300; GBR326, 327 some aspect of royal descent merits further study; CRFP(1)494/508; CFA(2)463

Robert - of PA, m Catherine Humphrey - desc/o Robert Lloyd CFA(2)463

LLOYD (cont.)

Maj Robert (Lloyd-Lide) - of PA, b1734 d1802, m1760 Sarah Kolb - desc/o Gov Thomas Lloyd DBR(1)720; DBR(2)94, 298, 319, 472, 477; 479, 481, 668, 771, 791; DBR(3)150, 270, 275, 278, 283, 286, 289, 293, 296, 300

Sampson - m Mary Carowley - desc/o Charles Lloyd GBR82

Sampson - m Rachel Champion - desc/o Charles Lloyd GBR82

Sarah - of PA, b1703 d1739, m1729 Gerard Jones d1765 - desc/o Robert Lloyd CRFP(1)497

Sarah - of PA, d1788, m1757 Judge William Moore d1793, native of Isle of Man, member Council of Safety 1776, Board of War 1777, delegate to Continental Congress 1777, member Supreme Executive Council 1779, vice-president 1779, president 1781, Judge High Court of Appeals 1783 - desc/o Thomas Lloyd CHB126; BCD126; CRFP(1)43

Susannah - of PA, d1772, m1762 Thomas Wharton Jr, president Supreme Executive Council 1777/1778 - desc/o Thomas Lloyd CHB125; BCD125; CRFP(1)43

Dep Gov Thomas - of PA 1683, b1640 Dolobran, Montgomeryshire, Wales, d1694, physician in Wales, deputy governor of Pennsylvania, son of Charles Lloyd & Elizabeth Stanley, m(1)1665 Mary Jones, m(2) Mrs Patience (Gardiner) Story - the immigrant CHB122; MCB149; MCD251; BCD122; DBR(1)1, 720; DBR(2)93, 297, 298, 319, 382, 472, 476, 477, 479, 481, 515, 667, 668, 770, 771, 791; DBR(3)150, 175, 270, 271, 274, 278, 279, 282, 286, 289, 292, 296, 297, 299, 300, 678; AFA74; RAA1; AFA198; GBR82; CRFP40/47

Thomas Jr - of PA, b1675 Great Britain d1717/1718 London, England, merchant of Goodmansfield, London, m1734 Sarah Young b1676 d Philadelphia - desc/o Thomas Lloyd CHB125; BCD125; CRFP(1)42

Thomas III of PA 1718, b London, England d1754, m1734 Philadelphia, Susanna Kearny, dau/o Philip Kearney, of Philadelphia & Rebecca Britain, wid/o Dr Edward Owen - desc/o Thomas Lloyd CHB125; BCD125; CRFP(1)43

Thomas - of PA, b1768 Darby, Chester Co, Pennsylvania d1814 Darby, m1788 Darby, Mary Wood dau/o George Wood & Margaret Fisher & had issue - desc/o Robert Lloyd CRFP(1)504, (2)1125; CFA(2)464

LOCKE Deborah - b abt 1685, m Jude Allen - desc/o Joseph Bolles LDS13; RAA71

Hannah - b1754 - desc/o John Prescott RAA125 - desc/o Mary Launce RAA130

LOCKEY Henry - of NC, d aft 1819, m Susanna Burnes dau/o Otway Burns - desc/o Robert Peyton DBR(4)531, 601, 607, 621, 731, 732; FFF40

LOGAN Dr Charles - of VA, d1794, m1779 Mary Pleasants - desc/o James Logan CHB344; BCD344

Dr George of PA, b1753 d1821, m1781 Deborah Norris - desc/o James Logan CHB345

Hannah - of PA & NJ, b1719 d1761, m1748 John Smith - desc/o James Logan CHB345; BCD345

James - of PA, b1674 d1751 son of Patrick Logan & Isabel Hume,

LOGAN (cont.)

m(1)1714 Sarah Reade, m(2) Amy Child - the immigrant CHB343; MCB148; BCD343; GBR112

Sarah - of PA, b1751 d1796, m1772 Thomas Fisher - desc/o James Logan CHB344; BCD344

William - of PA, b1718 d1776, m1740 Hannah Emlen - desc/o James Logan CHB343; BCD343

LOMBARD Daniel - of CT, b1732 d1795, m Jemima Shaylor - desc/o John Drake JSW1881

Roswell - of CT, b1766 d1843, m Cornelia Hall - desc/o John Drake JSW1881

LONG Catherine Marie - of NY, dau/o Samuel Long & Mary Tate, m Sir Henry Moore, 1st Baronet b1713 d1769, governor of New York - the immigrant GBR155

LONGLEY Sarah - b1740 - desc/o John Prescott RAA125

William - b1708 - desc/o John Prescott RAA125

LOOK Damaris - b1764, m Samson Hillman - desc/o Sarah Palmer LDS55

LOOMIS Abigail - of CT, b1711, m1731 David Noble - desc/o John Drake DBR(5)618

Capt Joseph - of CT, b1684 d1748, m1708 Sarah Bissell, m1710 Mary Cooley - desc/o John Drake CHB107; BCD107; DBR(2)167; DBR(3)79, 82; DBR(5)50

Lieut Joseph - of CT, b1710 d1760, m1735/1736 Sarah Woodward - desc/o Col John Drake DBR(2)167; DBR(3)80, 82; DBR(5)50

Mary - of CT, b1720/1721 d1744, m1742 Elijah Fitch - desc/o John Drake CHB107; BCD107

Rachael - of CT, b1693, m Ebenezer Lombard - desc/o John Drake JSW1881

Ruth - b1759 - desc/o John Drake RAA87

Sarah - of CT, b1736 d abt 1794, m Josiah Webster - desc/o John Drake DBR(2)167; DBR(3)80, 82; DBR(5)50

Sarah Irene - of CT, b1729, m1751 David Townsend - desc/o Anne Marbury DBR(3)170

Timothy - b1717 - desc/o John Drake RAA87

LORD Elizabeth - of CT, b1735, m1760 Jared Eliot Jr - desc/o Judge Simon Lynde CHB312; BCD312

Capt Enoch - of CT, b1726 d1814, m Hepzibah Mervin - desc/o Thomas MacGehee CHB288 - desc/o Judge Simon Lynde CHB313; BCD313

Jerusha - of CT, b1755, m Rev David Perry CHB394

Mary Sheldon - m John Pierpont - desc/o Richard Lyman J&K208

Richard - of CT, b1752 d1818, m Ann Mitchell - desc/o Thomas MacGehee CHB288 - desc/o Judge Simon Lynde CHB313; BCD313

Susanna - of CT, b1724 d1808, m1745/1746 Elijah Lathrop - desc/o Judge Simon Lynde ECD(3)200

Thomas - of New England 1635 - the immigrant EDV22; sufficient proof of alleged royal ancestry is lacking

LORING Caleb - of MA, b1689 d1756, m(2) Susanna Cocks - desc/o Deacon Thomas Loring BLG2795

Caleb - of MA, b1736 d1787, m(1) Sarah Bradford - desc/o Deacon

LORING (cont.)

    Thomas Loring BLG2795

    Caleb - of MA, b1764 d1850, m Ann Greely - desc/o Deacon Thomas Loring BLG2795

    John - of MA, b1630 d1714, m(2)1630 Mrs Rachel Buckland - desc/o Deacon Thomas Loring BLG2795

    Deacon Thomas - of MA 1635, m Jane Newton - the immigrant EDV59, 60; BLG2795; sufficient proof of alleged royal ancestry is lacking

    Thomas - of MA, bp 1625/1626 d1678 - desc/o Deacon Thomas Loring BLG2795

LORT Elizabeth - dau/o Charles Lloyd & Elizabeth Lort, m Charles Lloyd - the immigrant GBR82, 83

LOVELACE Anne - of VA by 1652, b1611 d bef 1 Jun 1652 dau/o Sir William Lovelace, Knight & Anne Barne dau/o Sir William Barne, m 1628 Rev Dr John Gorsuch killed in 1647, son of Daniel Gorsuch & Alice (Hall) Gorsuch - the immigrant CHB500; ECD(2)178; JSW1634; MCD225; MCS84, 85; DBR(1)121, 652; DBR(2)36, 190, 191, 217, 621, 663, 725; DBR(3)4, 130, 458; DBR(4)823; DBR(5)1055; GBR237; APP401/408

    John, 4th Baron Lovelace, - of NY, governor of New York, m Charlotte Clayton - the immigrant GBR353 some aspect of royal descent merits further study

    John Baptist - of MD, d1765 - desc/o Anne Lovelace DBR(1)577

    William - of VA & NY, b1583/1584, m Anne Barne - the immigrant RAA1; sufficient proof of alleged royal ancestry is lacking

LOW Thomas - of MA, b1751, m____ - desc/o Samuel Appleton DBR(1)139

LOWE Lieut Col Henry - of MD, commander of St Mary's Co militia, judge of the Provincial Court & deputy commissioner, son of John Lowe & Catherine Pilkington, m Mrs Susannah Maria Bennett Darnall, dau/o Richard Bennett Jr, governor of Virginia & Maryland - the immigrant GBR161; NGS(51)32/43

    Jane - of MD, d1700/1701 dau/o Vincent Lowe & Anne Cavendish, m(1) Henry Sewall d1664/1665, secretary of Maryland, son of Richard Sewall & Mary Dugdale, m(2)1666 Charles Calvert, 3rd Baron Baltimore b1637 d1715 governor of Maryland - the immigrant GBR161; NGS(51)32/43

    Nicholas - of MD, d1717, Roman Catholic, served as clerk of St Mary's Co, & in 1687 as coroner, son of John Lowe & Catherine Pilkington, m Mrs Elizabeth Roe Combes b abt 1666 d1714, dau/o Edward Roe & wid/o Maj William Combes of Talbot Co, Maryland - the immigrant GBR161; NGS(51)32/43

LOWELL Percival - of New England 1639 - the immigrant THJ31; EDV20; sufficient proof of alleged royal ancestry is lacking

    Timothy - b1754 - desc/o Thomas Bradbury RAA72

LOWNDES Amarinthia - of SC, b1754, m1776 Roger Parker Sanders, m(2)___Champney Esq - desc/o Charles Lowndes NE(30)152

    Benjamin - of MD, b1749 d1802, m Dorothy Buchanan b1762 dau/o Gen Andrew Buchanan of Baltimore Co, Maryland - desc/o Capt Christopher Lowndes MG(2)188; CFA(3)301

    Charles - of SC 1730, d1736 Charlestown, son of Charles &

LOWNDES (cont.)

Sarah____Lowndes, m Ruth Rawlins d1763 dau/o Henry Rawlins - the immigrant EDV63; GBR358; NE(30)141/147

Charles - of SC, d1763, appointed Provost Marshal 1752, m Sarah Parker - desc/o Charles Lowndes NE(30)141/147

Charles - of SC, m Jeannie Perry - desc/o Charles Lowndes NE(30)141/147

Charles - of MD & VA, b1765 d1846, merchant in Georgetown, D.C., but settled in Jefferson Co, VA, m(1)1794 Eleanor Lloyd b1776 d1805 dau/o Col Edward Lloyd of Wye, m(2) Francis Whiting of Virginia d1841 - desc/o William Bladen CHB45; BCD45 - desc/o Capt Christopher Lowndes MG(2)189; CFA(3)302

Capt Christopher - of MD 1740, bp 1713 Sandbach, Chester, England d1785 merchant, justice of Prince George's Co 1753 to 1775 & judge of the Orphans' Court, 5th son of Richard Lowndes of Hassall, Cheshire, England & Margaret Poole, m1747 Elizabeth Tasker b1726 d1789 dau/o Benjamin Tasker, president of the Council of Maryland & Anne Bladen - the immigrant EDV63; GBR358; MG(2)187/189; CFA(3)301

Francis - of MD, b1751 d1815, m Jane Maddox d1829 of Yorkshire, England - desc/o Capt Christopher Lowndes MG(2)189; CFA(3)301

Harriet - of SC, m____Brown & had issue Lowndes Brown who, m Margaretta Livingston - desc/o Charles Lowndes NE(30)152

Harriot - of MD, m abt 1781 Levi Gantt, of Prince George's Co, Maryland - desc/o Capt Christopher Lowndes MG(2)188; CFA(3)301

Rawlins - of SC, b1721 d1800 Charleston, m(1) 1748 Amarithia Elliott d1750 dau/o Thomas Elliott of Rantoules, Stone River, m(2) 1751 Mary Cartwright of Charleston, m(3) Sarah Jones of Georgia - desc/o Charles Lowndes NE(30)152

Rebecca - of MD, b1757 d1802, m1781 Benjamin Stoddert b1751 d1813, first secretary of the Navy of the United States - desc/o Capt Christopher Lowndes MG(2)188; CFA(3)301

Richard Tasker - of Blenheim, Bladensburg & Prince George's Co, Maryland, b1763, m Anne Lloyd b1769 d1840 dau/o Col Edward Lloyd of Wye & Elizabeth Tayloe - desc/o Capt Christopher Lowndes MG(2)189; CFA(3)302

Sarah Ruth - of SC, b1764 d1852, m____Simmons - desc/o Charles Lowndes NE(30)152

William - of SC, m1739 Mary Taylor dau/o Nicholas & Mary Taylor - desc/o Charles Lowndes NE(30)141/147

LUCAS Barnabas - b1729 - desc/o George Morton RAA116

Elijah - b abt 1757 - desc/o George Morton RAA116

Joseph - b1689 - desc/o George Morton RAA116

LUCE (LUSE) Benjamin - of NY, b1702 d1744, m(2) Abigail Clark - desc/o John Mapes ECD(2)195; DBR(2)280

Lieut Eleazer - of NJ, b1740 d1820, m(1) abt 1760 Elizabeth____ - desc/o John Mapes ECD(2)195; DBR(2)280

LUCKIN Alice - of VA, b1625 d1698, m1656 Col John Page - the immigrant WAC42; sufficient proof of alleged royal ancestry is lacking

LUDLOW Ann - of NY, m1779 Francis Dashwood - desc/o Gabriel Ludlow
NYGBR(50)#1p54

Cary - of NY, b1736 Haverstraw, appointed master of the court of
chancery in New York 1776 & was surrogate of New York in 1782,
m1766 Hester Lynsen b1750 d1814 dau/o Abraham Lynsen &
Catharine Rutgers - desc/o Gabriel Ludlow NYGBR(50)#2p143

Charles - of NY, m Elizabeth Van Horne youngest dau/o David Van
Horne - desc/o Gabriel Ludlow NYGBR(50)#2p141, 142

Daniel - of NY, b1750 d1814 was in the banking business &
acquainted himself with foreign language, m1773 Arabella Duncan
b1756 d1803 dau/o Thomas Duncan - desc/o Gabriel Ludlow
NYGBR(50)#1p50

Elizabeth - of NY, m Charles Shaw - desc/o Gabriel Ludlow
NYGBR(50)#1p39

Gabriel - of NY 1694, b1663 Castle Cary, Somerset d1736 New York,
clerk of New York House of Assembly 1699/1733, merchant, son of
Gabriel Ludlow & Martha___, m1697 Sarah Hanmer dau/o Rev
Joseph Hanmer, formerly of Iscoyd, Flint, chaplain to His Majesty's
Forces, New York & Martha Eddowes formerly of Whitchurch, Salop
- the immigrant FLW16, 17; MCS62; DBR(3)306, 694; DBR(4)253;
DBR(5)166; EDV26, 27; CRL(1)166; GBR230; NYGBR(47)#1p213,
(50)#1p34/55, #2p134/157

Gabriel - of NY, b1704 d1773 member of the New York Assembly
1739/1745 & vestryman of Trinity Church 1742/1769, m(1)
Frances Duncan, sister of Thomas Duncan, m(2) Elizabeth
Crommelin b1715 dau/o Charles Crommelin banker of Amsterdam,
Holland, & Anna Sinclair, & had issue - desc/o Gabriel Ludlow
NYGBR(50)#1p40

Gabriel - of NY, m A Williams - desc/o Gabriel Ludlow
NYGBR(50)#1p39

Gabriel George - of NY, b1736 d1808 colonel of militia & justice of the
peace, a staunch Loyalist & in 1776 became colonel of the Third
Battalion of Long Island Brigade of Royal Americans, became first
mayor of St John, New Brunswick 1785/1795; judge of the Vice
Admiralty Court 1787/1803; president of the King's Council in New
Brunswick 1803/1808, m1760 Ann Ver Planck b1742 d1822 -
desc/o Gabriel Ludlow NYGBR(50)#1p43

Gabriel Ver Planck - of NY, b1768 d1825 master of the court of
chancery for New York, m1798 Elizabeth A Hunter dau/o Robert
Hunter - desc/o Gabriel Ludlow NYGBR(50)#1p44

Gabriel William - of NJ b1734 Bergen Co, NJ d1805, m1764 Cornelia
Crooke dau/o Charles Crooke & Anneke Rutgers - desc/o Gabriel
Ludlow NYGBR(50)#2p141

George Duncan - of NY, b1734 d1808 councillor & judge of the
Supreme Court of the Colony of New York 1769/1778, senior
councillor & governor of New Brunswick, Canada & chief justice of
the province 1784, m (his cousin) Frances Duncan dau/o Thomas
Duncan - desc/o Gabriel Ludlow NYGBR(50)#1p40, 41

George Duncan - of NY, b1773 d1847, m(1)1825 Mrs Carson b Island
of Nevis, West Indies, m(2) Paris, France, Camille Bernier - desc/o
Gabriel Ludlow NYGBR(50)#1p41

LUDLOW (cont.)

Gulian - of NY, b1764 d1826, m1792 Maria Ludlow b1772 (his second
cousin) dau/o Thomas Ludlow & Mary____ - desc/o Gabriel Ludlow
NYGBR(50)#1p44

Henry - of NY, b1701 Vestryman in Trinity Church for 12 years,
m1725 Rockland, Orange Co, NY, Mary Corbett dau/o Capt John
Corbett - desc/o Gabriel Ludlow NYGBR(50)#1p39

Henry - of NY, m Frances Duncan, dau/o George Duncan & Martha
Ludlow - desc/o Gabriel Ludlow NYGBR(50)#1p39

Henry - of NY, m Mary Price - desc/o Gabriel Ludlow
NYGBR(50)#2p149

Harriet - of NY, b1774, m Grove Wright an eminent & wealthy New
York merchant - desc/o Gabriel Ludlow NYGBR(50)#1p50

James - of NY, b1750, m Elizabeth Harrison - desc/o Gabriel Ludlow
NYGBR(50)#2p149

John - of VA - the immigrant WAC49; sufficient proof of alleged royal
ancestry is lacking

John - of NY, b1706 d1775 moved from NY 1734 to reside near
Newark, NJ on the Passaic River, m1731 Susan Broadbury -
desc/o Gabriel Ludlow NYGBR(50)#2p137

John - of NY, m Mary Ross dau/o Colonel Ross of the British Army -
desc/o Gabriel Ludlow NYGBR(50)#2p137

John - of NY, b1759 d1814 Schenectady, NY, m Phoebe Dunham of
Westfield, NY - desc/o Gabriel Ludlow NYGBR(50)#1p13

John C - of NY, m Lacune Poine - desc/o Gabriel Ludlow
NYGBR(50)#1p39

John Richard - of NY, b1769 d1849, m(1)1787 Elizabeth Vreeland
b1766 d1807, m(2)1810 Carolina Ditmars - desc/o Gabriel Ludlow
NYGBR(50)#2p138

Maria - of NY, b1772, m (her second cousin) Gulian Ludlow - desc/o
Gabriel Ludlow NYGBR(50)#2p149

Martha - of NY, b1698, m George Duncan - desc/o Gabriel Ludlow
NYGBR(50)#1p38

Mary - of NY, m Peter Goelet - desc/o Gabriel Ludlow NYGBR(50)#1p39

Mary - m Francis Dashwood resided in Jamaica - desc/o Gabriel
Ludlow NYGBR(50)#1p44

Mary W - of NY, b1748 d1831, m (her first cousin) Thomas Ludlow son
of Henry Ludlow & Mary Corbett - desc/o Gabriel Ludlow
NYGBR(50)#2p149

Richard - of NY, b1745, m(1)1768 Dinah Van Nostrand dau/o General
Van Nostrand of NJ, a major in the Revolutionary army under
Washington - desc/o Gabriel Ludlow NYGBR(50)#2p134

Robert Crommelin - of NY, b1758, m1781 Elizabeth Conklin & had
issue - desc/o Gabriel Ludlow NYGBR(50)#1p52, #2p155

Roger - of MA & CT, bp 1590 Dinton d1666 Dublin, Ireland, deputy
governor of MA & author of the *Fundamental Orders of CT*, 3rd son
of Thomas Ludlow & Jane Pyle, m(1) Mary Endicott, m(2) Mary
Cogan - the immigrant CHB412; FLW16; ECD192; LDS29; RAA1,
111; CRL(1)166, 167; CRL(2)323; GBR229; TAG(15)129/143,
(25)138/143; NYGBR(50)#1p34

Sarah - of CT, b1639 Fairfield, m1656 Rev Nathaniel Brewster of

LUDLOW (cont.)

Brookhaven, Long Island - desc/o Roger Ludlow CHB412; FLW16;
ECD192, 197; LDS29; RAA111; CRL(2)325

Sarah - of VA abt 1643, b abt 1635 d abt 1668, dau/o Gabriel Ludlow
& Phyllis____, m Col John Carter - the immigrant J&K133;
CHB181, 182; FLW16; ECD(2)184, 188; MCB113, 446,447;
MCD198; BCD131; BCD181, 182; DBR(1)29, 94, 113, 400, 742;
DBR(2)55, 156, 158, 276, 522, 694; DBR(3)202, 234, 306, 338,
339, 378, 693, 694; DBR(4)253; DBR(5)167, 346, 858, 925, 953,
954, 1055, 1056; AAP144; CRL(1)167; GBR229; PVF199/239

Sarah - of NY, m Richard Morris - desc/o Gabriel Ludlow
NYGBR(50)#1p39

Sarah Frances - of NY, b1744 d1823, m1767 Abraham Ogden b1743
d1798 appointed by Washington, United States District Attorney for
the state of NJ son of Judge David Ogden of Newark, NJ - desc/o
Gabriel Ludlow NYGBR(50)#2p153/154, 156

Lieut Col Thomas - of VA, bp 1624 - the immigrant WAC49; sufficient
proof of alleged royal ancestry is lacking

Thomas - of NY, m Mary Ludlow dau/o William Ludlow & Mary
Duncan - desc/o Gabriel Ludlow NYGBR(50)#1p39

Thomas - of NY, b1717, m Catharine Le Roux bp 1725 dau/o Charles
Le Roux - desc/o Gabriel Ludlow NYGBR(50)#2p161

Thomas William - of NY, m F W Morris - desc/o Gabriel Ludlow
NYGBR(50)#2p149

William - of NY, m Mary Gouverneur - desc/o Gabriel Ludlow
NYGBR(50)#1p39

William - of NY, b1707, m1731 Mary Duncan b1713/1714 d1779
dau/o Captain George Duncan & sister of Thomas Duncan - desc/o
Gabrial Ludlow NYGBR(50)#2p141

William Henry - of NY, b1740 d1803, m(1)1771 Catharine Van
Rensselaer of Albany, NY, sister of Kilian Van Rensselaer, m(2)1778
Mary Broughton b1744 d1795 youngest dau/o John Broughton &
Alida Gouverneur - desc/o Gabriel Ludlow NYGBR(50)#2p154

LUDLUM Sarah (Susannah) - m 1754 Richard Hallock - desc/o Peter
Wright DBR(3)302

LUDWELL Sir Philip - of VA, d1717, m(1) Lucy Higginson, m(2)1690
Frances Colepepper (Culpeper), dau/o Thomas Colepepper &
Katherine St Leger, wid/o Sir William Berkeley b1608 d1677
governor of Virginia 1639/1677 - the immigrant WAC10; sufficient
proof of alleged royal ancestry is lacking

LUGG Esther of MA, b abt 163_, m(1) James Bell, m(2)1677 Richard
Marshall - desc/o Katharine Deighton CHB376

LUNSFORD Catherine - of VA, m(1) Peter Jennings, m(2) abt 1672 Ralph
Wormeley - desc/o Thomas Lunsford WAC40

Sir Thomas - of VA 1649, b abt 1610 d1653 secretary & acting
governor of Virginia son of Thomas Lunsford & Katherine Fludd,
m(1) Anne Hudson, m(2)1640 Katherine Neville, m(3) Elizabeth
Wormeley, wid/o Richard Kemp - the immigrant MCS63; GBR284;
GVFWM(3)477

William - of VA - desc/o Thomas Lunsford WAC40

LUQUER Jan - of NY 1658 - the immigrant EDV28; sufficient proof of alleged royal ancestry is lacking

LUTHER Consider - b1698 - desc/o Robert Abell RAA59

James - of MA, b1693 d1771, m Martha Slake - desc/o Robert Abell DBR(5)142

Martha - b1681 - desc/o Robert Abell RAA59

Mehitable - of MA, b1675 d1764, m Ebenezer Cole b1671 d1719 son of James Cole - desc/o Robert Abell DBR(3)711; RAA59

Samuel Jr - of MA, b1663 d1714, m Sarah____ - desc/o Robert Abell DBR(5)142; RAA59

Sarah - of MA, b1718 d1777, m1735 Jonathan Buffington - desc/o Robert Abell DBR(5)142

Sarah - b abt 1718/1723 - desc/o Robert Abell RAA59

LYDDALL Col George - of VA - the immigrant WAC27; sufficient proof of alleged royal ancestry is lacking

LYFORD Moses - of MA, b abt 1725 d1799, m Mehitable Smith - desc/o Gov Thomas Dudley DBR(1)791

Oliver Smith - of MA, b1754 d1788, m Elizabeth Johnson - desc/o Gov Thomas Dudley DBR(1)791

Stephen - of MA, b1683 d1774, m Sarah Leavitt - desc/o Gov Thomas Dudley DBR(1)791

LYMAN Aaron - of MA, b1705 d1788, m1733 Eunice Dwight - desc/o Richard Lyman CHB153; BCD153

Abner - of MA, b1701 d1774, m1738 Sarah Allis - desc/o Richard Lyman CHB148; BCD148

Lieut Benjamin - of MA, b1674 d1723, m1698 Thankful Pomeroy - desc/o Richard Lyman CHB152; BCD152

Col Daniel - of RI, chief justice of the Supreme Court of RI - desc/o Richard Lyman J&K205

Elias - b1715 d1803, m Anne Phelps - desc/o Richard Lyman FFF140b

Deacon Elias - ancestor of Curtis Dwight & Ray Lyman Wilbur - desc/o Richard Lyman J&K207

Gad - father of Oliver Lyman who was father of Mary Lyman - desc/o Richard Lyman J&K208

Hepzibah - of MA, m Josiah Dewey and had Josiah Dewey - desc/o Richard Lyman J&K204

Rev Isaac - of ME, b1724/1745 d1810, m1750 Ruth Plummer - desc/o Richard Lyman J&K206; CHB150; BLG2798; BCD150

Joel - b1764 d1840, m Achsah Parsons - desc/o Richard Lyman FFF140b

Lieut John - of MA, b1623 d1690, m1655 Dorcas Plum - desc/o Richard Lyman J&K206; CHB149; MCD249; BLG2798; BCD149; FFF140b

John - of MA, b1655 d1727, m1694 Abigail Holton - desc/o Richard Lyman CHB148; MCB263; MCD248; BCD148

Lieut John - of CT, b1662, m1686 Mindwell (Sheldon) Pomeroy - desc/o Richard Lyman J&K208

Joshua - of MA, b1704 d1777, m Sarah Norman - desc/o Richard Lyman MCB263; MCD248

Mary - of MA, b1696 d1776, m1719 Samuel Dwight - desc/o Richard

LYMAN (cont.)

    Lyman MCD249; BCD149; CHB149

    Mary - of CT, m Lynde Lord - desc/o Richard Lyman J&K208

    Mary - of MA, m1750 Lieut Oliver Pomeroy - desc/o Richard Lyman
        CHB152; BCD152

    Mindwell - m Ebenezer Pomeroy III - desc/o Margaret Wyatt GBR397

    Moses - of MA, b1662/1663 d1701, m Ann Chaunsey - desc/o
        Richard Lyman J&K206; BLG2798; BCD149; FFF140b

    Capt Moses - of MA, b1689 d1762, m1712 Mindwell Sheldon - desc/o
        Richard Lyman J&K207; CHB150; BLG2798; BCD150; FFF140b

    Moses - of CT, b1713 d1768, m1742 Sarah Heighton (or Hayden) -
        desc/o Richard Lyman CHB151; BCD151

    Col Moses - of CT, b1743 d1829, m(2) Mary Buel - desc/o Richard
        Lyman CHB151; BCD151

    Phoebe - of MA, b1719 d1802, m Caleb Strong - desc/o Richard
        Lyman CHB151; BCD151

    Richard - of MA 1631, b1580 d1640, m bef 1617 Sarah Osborne - the
        immigrant J&K204; CHB148; JSW1871; MCB263; MCD248;
        BLG2798; BCD148; FFF140b royal ancestry not fully proven

    Richard - of MA, b1617 d1662, m Hepzibah Ford - desc/o Richard
        Lyman J&K204; CHB148; MCB263; MCD248; BCD148

    Sarah - of CT, b abt 1646 d aft 1688, m1666 Sergeant John Marsh -
        desc/o Richard Lyman J&K209; JSW1871

    Sarah - of MA, b1740, m1758 Joseph Allen - desc/o Richard Lyman
        CHB148; BCD148

    Seth - of MA, b1736 d1817, m Eunice Graves - desc/o Richard Lyman
        MCB263; MCD248

    Susannah - of MA, b1734 d1770, m1763 Maj Elihu Kent - desc/o
        Richard Lyman CHB153; BCD153

    Tertius - of NH, b1761 d18__, m Hannah Alexander - desc/o Richard
        Lyman MCB264; MCD248

    Theodore - of MA, b1755 d1839, m(2)1786 Lydia Williams - desc/o
        Richard Lyman J&K206; CHB150; BLG2798; BCD150

    Thomas - of MA, m Ruth Holton - desc/o Richard Lyman J&K205

    Thomas - of MA, m Elizabeth____ - desc/o Richard Lyman J&K205

    Thomas - of MA, m Ann____ - desc/o Richard Lyman J&K205

    Capt William - of MA, b1715 d1774, m Jemima Sheldon - desc/o
        Richard Lyman CHB152; BCD152

    Gen William - of MA, b1755 d1811, m1803 Jerusha Welles - desc/o
        Richard Lyman CHB152; BCD152

LYNDE Chief Justice Benjamin - of MA, m1669 Mary Browne - desc/o
    Judge Simon Lynde CHB314; BCD314

    Chief Justice Benjamin Jr - of MA, b1700 d1781, m Mary Goodrich
        Bowles - desc/o William Browne CHB139; BCD139 - desc/o Judge
        Simon Lynde BCD314

    Elizabeth - of CT, b1662 d1746, m George Pordage - desc/o Judge
        Simon Lynde CHB313; BCD313

    Elizabeth - of CT, b1694 d1778, m1720 Judge Richard Lord - desc/o
        Francis Willoughby CHB288 - desc/o Judge Simon Lynde CHB312;
        ECD(3)200; BCD312

    Hannah - of MA & CT, b1694 d1736, m1725 Rev George Griswold -

LYNDE (cont.)

  desc/o Judge Simon Lynde CHB312; BCD312; DBR(2)856; DBR(3)568

 Lydia - of MA, m Rev William Walter - desc/o William Browne CHB139; BCD139 - desc/o Judge Simon Lynde CHB314; BCD314

 Mary - of MA, b1680 d1732, m1702 John Valentine - desc/o Judge Simon Lynde CHB310; MCB208; MCD253; BCD310; DBR(3)746; DBR(4)835; AWW192

 Judge Nathaniel - of MA, b1659 d1729, m1683 Susannah Willoughby b1664 d1709/1710 dau/o Deputy-Governor Francis Willoughby - desc/o Judge Simon Lynde CHB311, 12; ECD(3)200; MCS42; BCD311, 312; DBR(3)568

 Judge Samuel - of MA, b1653 d1721, m1674 Mary Ballord - desc/o Judge Simon Lynde CHB310; MCB208; MCD253; BCD310; AWW192

 Judge Simon - of MA 1650, bp 1624 London d1687 Boston, son of Enoch Lynde & Elizabeth Digby, m1652/1653 Hannah Newdigate - the immigrant CHB30, 31; FLW96; ECD(3)200; MCB207, 208; MCD253; MCS42; BCD309; DBR(2)855; DBR(3)568, 746; DBR(4)834; RAA1, 112; AWW1911, 192; GBR371

 Judge Simon - of MA, b1653 d1721, m1674 Mary Ballard - desc/o Judge Simon Lynde DBR(3)746; DBR(4)835

LYON Edward - b1710 - desc/o Griffith Bowen RAA72

 Elfelda - of MA, b1749 d1792, m1768 Eliphalet Janes - desc/o Lieut Griffith Bowen DBR(4)781

 Rebecca - b1737 - desc/o Griffith Bowen RAA72

LYTTELTON William Henry 1st Baron Lyttelton - of SC, b1724 d1808 governor of South Carolina & Jamaica, diplomat, son of Sir Thomas Lyttelton, 4th Baronet & Christian Temple, m(1) Mary Macartney, m(2) Caroline Bristow - the immigrant GBR124

– M –

MACALESTER Charles Jr - of PA, b1766 d1832, m Anna Sampson - the immigrant CHB174; MCB156; BCD174; sufficient proof of alleged royal ancestry is lacking

MACCUBBIN Charles - of MD, b1757 d1799, m1793 Sarah Allen - desc/o Dr Charles Carroll CHB61; BCD61

MACDONNELL Bryan - of DE - d1707, m Mary Doyle - the immigrant MCB141; sufficient proof of alleged royal ancestry is lacking

MACGEHEE (MCGEHEE) Daniel - of VA, m Jane Brooke Hodnet - desc/o Thomas MacGehee CHB284; MCD256; BCD284

 Edward - of VA, m Katherine de Jarnette - desc/o Thomas MacGehee CHB284; MCD256; BCD284

 Katherine Brooke Garterey - of VA, m David Urquhart - desc/o Thomas MacGehee CHB284; MCD256; BCD284

 Micajah - b1745 d1811, m1769 Anne Scott - desc/o Capt Henry Isham DBR(1)40

 Thomas (James MacGregor) - of VA, d1727 - the immigrant CHB284; MCD256; BCD284 lacks sufficient proof of alleged royal ancestry

MACINTOSH George - of GA, m Anne Houstoun - desc/o Capt John Mohr
MacIntosh CHB171; BCD171

Capt John Mohr - of GA 1733, b1700 d1761 son of Lachlan
Mackintosh of Knocknagel & Mary Lockhart, m1725 Marjory Frazer
- the immigrant CHB170; MCB275; MCD257; BCD170; GBR110

Maj Gen John - of GA, d1826, m1781 Sarah Swinton - desc/o Capt
John Mohr MacIntosh CHB170; BCD170

John Hampden - of GA, m Charlotte Nephew - desc/o Capt John Mohr
MacIntosh MCB276; BCD171

John Houston - of GA, m1791 Eliza Bayard - desc/o Capt John Mohr
MacIntosh CHB171; MCD257

Maj Gen Lachlan - of GA, b1727 d1806, m Sarah Treadcroft - desc/o
Capt John Mohr MacIntosh MCB276; MCD257

Col William - of GA, b1726 d1796, m Jane MacCoy - desc/o Capt John
Mohr MacIntosh CHB170; BCD170

MACK Ebenezer - b1697, m Hannah Huntley - desc/o Anthony Colby
LDS94

Lucy - b1775, m Joseph Smith - desc/o Anthony Colby LDS94

Solomon - b1732, m Lydia Gates - desc/o Anthony Colby LDS94

MACKALL Benjamin - of MD, d1767, m Mary Taylor - desc/o Rev Robert
Brooke CHB405; ECD(3)39; MCD169; DBR(1)236 - desc/o Mary
Wolseley DBR(2)333; DBR(3)436; DBR(4)355

James - of MD, b1708 d1751, m Mary Howe - desc/o Robert Brooke
ECD(3)37

Capt John - of MD, b1738 d1813, m1758 Margaret Gough - desc/o
Robert Brooke ECD(3)37; MCD169

John - of MD, m Martha Duke - desc/o Rev Robert Brooke CHB405

Rebecca - of MD, m1764 Benoni Dawson - desc/o Anne Brooke
ECD(3)39 - desc/o Mary Wolseley DBR(2)333; DBR(3)436;
DBR(4)355

Rebecca - of MD, b1763 d1825, m1781 Thomas Loker - desc/o Robert
Brooke ECD(3)37; DBR(1)236

Sarah Taylor - of MD, b1771 d1816, m Cosmo MacKenzie - desc/o Rev
Robert Brooke CHB544; MCD169

MACKENZIE Lady Anne - of SC, b abt 1733 d1768 Charleston, South
Carolina, a sister of Lady Mary, m(1)1760 Edmund Atkins
b1707/1708 d1761, president of His Majesty's Council for South
Carolina & first superintendent of Indian Affairs for the Southern
District of the American Colonies, m(2)1764 John Murray, a native
of Scotland d1761 in South Carolina, assistant secretary of the
province of South Carolina - the immigrant GBR28; NGS(52)25

Colin - of MD, b1775 d1827, m1799 Sarah Pinkerton - desc/o Thomas
MacKenzie CFA336, 340

Cosmo - of MD, b1770 d1809, m1793 Sarah Mackall - desc/o Thomas
MacKenzie CFA336, 339

Elizabeth - of MD, b1772, m1792 Anthony Reeves - desc/o Thomas
MacKenzie CFA336, 340

George - of MD, b1773, m1798 Mary Jackson - desc/o Thomas
MacKenzie CFA336, 340

Lady Mary - of SC, b abt 1731 d1788 at sea, dau/o George MacKenzie,

MACKENZIE (cont.)

3rd Earl of Cromarty & Isabel (Gordon) MacKenzie, m(1)1750 Capt Robert Clarke, m(2) 1757 Thomas Drayton b1700 d1760 planter & member of His Majesty's Council for South Carolina, m(3)1762 John Ainslie d1774 planter & captain First Regiment South Carolina militia, m(4)1776 Henry Middleton b1717 d1784 president of the Continental Congress - the immigrant GBR28; NGS(52)25; SCG(3)133, 136; GPFPM(1)413/435

Thomas - of MD, m(1) Rebecca Johnson, m(2)1768 Ann Johns - the immigrant CFA336, 339; sufficient proof of alleged royal ancestry is lacking

MACKINTOSH (MCINTOSH) Elizabeth - m Lachlan Mackintosh (McIntosh), her cousin - desc/o Col Henry Mackintosh GBR109

Col Henry - of MA & RI, son of Lachlan Mackintosh of Borlum & Helen Gordon, m Elizabeth Byfield - the immigrant GBR109

Lachlan (McIntosh) - of RI, son of William Mackintosh of Borlum & Mary Reade, m Elizabeth Mackintosh (McIntosh), his cousin - the immigrant GRB109

MACKWORTH Agnes - of MA, dau/o Richard Mackworth & Dorothy Cranage, m(1) Richard Watts of London d1635 son of Sir John Watts of Hertfordshire, Knight, m(2) bef 1640 Col William Crowne of MA, b abt 1617 d1683 Boston, MA, a soldier in Cromwell's service - the immigrant FLW167; MCS26; GBR128; NE(108)176/177; EO(2)627/631

MACLEAN (MCLEAN) Allan - of CT, son of Allan MacLean of Grisiboll & Catherine MacLean of Balliphetrish, m(1) Susanna Beaucham, m(2) Mary Loomis - the immigrant GBR71

John - of NJ, b1771 d1814, chemist & educator, son of John MacLean & Anne Long or Lang, m Phebe Bainbridge - the immigrant GBR72

Neil - of CT, son of Allan MacLean of Grisiboll & Catherine MacLean of Balliphetrish, m Mrs Hannah (Stillman) Caldwell - the immigrant GBR71

MACOMBER Elijah of MA, d1732, m Sarah Pitts - desc/o Richard Williams CHB376 - desc/o Frances Deighton DBR(2)365

Elijah - of MA, b1750/1751, m1770 Zilpha Briggs - desc/o Frances Deighton DBR(1)763

Elizabeth - of MA, b1756 d1849, m1785 Philip Padelford - desc/o Richard Williams CHB376 - desc/o Frances Deighton DBR(2)365

James - of MA, b1717 d1803, m1747 Rachel Drake - desc/o Frances Deighton DBR(1)762

MACON Elizabeth - of VA, b bef 1742/1743 d bef 1779, m Bartholomew Dandridge and had issue - desc/o Anne Lovelace GVFHB(3)345

Mary - of VA, m Col William Aylett d1780 of Fairfield, King William Co, VA, son of Philip Aylett & left issue - desc/o Anne Lovelace GVFHB(3)345

MACY George - of MA, b1761 d1813, m1785 Matilda Folger - desc/o William Gayer DBR(1)271, 444; DBR(2)198

Matthew - of MA, b1732 d1804, m1761 Abigail Gardner - desc/o William Gayer DBR(1)271, 444; DBR(2)198

MADDOX (or MADDUX) Anne - of MD, b1747, m Robert Caldwell, justice of provincial court - desc/o Nathaniel Littleton CFA(4)127

MADDOX (or MADDUX) (cont.)

Elizabeth - of MD, b1727, m Samuel Handy - desc/o Nathaniel Littleton CFA(4)127

John - of MD, b1729 member Maryland Assembly 1755, m____ & had issue - desc/o Nathaniel Littleton CFA(4)127

Leah - of MD, b1745, m Rev James Robertson - desc/o Nathaniel Littleton CFA(4)127

Mary - of MD, b1772 d1816, m1789 William Deatherage - desc/o Anne Arundel CFA(5)293

Sarah - of MD, b1725, m Dr Thomas Holbrook - desc/o Nathaniel Littleton CFA(4)127

MADISON Ambrose - of VA, b abt 1700 d1732, m1721 Frances Taylor - desc/o Anne Lovelace ECD(2)178

Ambrose - of VA, b1755, m____Lee dau/o Hancock Lee - desc/o Martha Eltonhead VG256; CFA(5)137

Gabriel - of VA, m Miriam Lewis - desc/o William Strother GVFTQ(3)379

George - of VA, m Jane Smith - desc/o William Strother GVFTQ(3)379

Eleanor (known as Nelly) - of VA, b1760, m Major Isaac Hite, of Belle Grove, near Middleton, VA & had issue - desc/o Martha Eltonhead VG256, 257; CFA(5)138

Eliza - of VA, m Col Andrew Lewis Jr - desc/o William Strother GVFTQ(3)379

Frances - of VA, b1774, m Dr Robert H Rose, moved to Tennessee & had issue - desc/o Marth Eltonhead VG257; CFA(5)138

Isabella - of VA, b1740 d aft 1817, m Capt Nathaniel Abney - desc/o Anne Lovelace DBR(1)121; DBR(2)193; DBR(3)459

Col James Sr - of VA, b1723 d1801, m1749 Eleanor Rose Conway - desc/o Anne Lovelace ECD(2)178

James - of VA, b1748 d1812 first native Bishop of the Episcopal Church in Virginia, m1779 Sarah Tate - desc/o William Strother GVFTQ(3)379

Pres James Madison Jr - of VA, b1750/1751 d1836, 4th & 5th President of the United States 1809/1816, m1794 Mrs Dorothea (Payne) Todd (known as Dolly Madison) b1772 North Carolina d1849 wid/o John Todd, lawyer of Pennsylvania & dau/o John Payne & Mary Coles - desc/o Martha Eltonhead AAP142, 143; GBR348; VG256; CFA(5)137 - desc/o Anthony Savage GBR253

Jane - of VA, b1731 d1830, m1749 Thomas Lewis b1718 d1790 son of Col Andrew Lewis & Margaret Lynn - desc/o William Strother GVFTQ(3)379

John - of VA, m Agatha Strothers - desc/o Anne Lovelace DBR(1)121; NFA63

John III - of VA, b abt 1700 d1783, m(1) Isabella Todd - desc/o Anne Lovelace DBR(2)192, 193; DBR(3)458

Margaret - of VA, m1786 Judge William McDowell b1765 d1821 son of Judge Samuel McDowell & Agatha McDowell - desc/o William Strother GVFTQ(3)379

Richard - of VA, m____Preston - desc/o William Strother GVFTQ(3)379

Roland - of VA, m Anne Lewis dau/o General Andrew Lewis - desc/o William Strother GVFTQ(3)379

MADISON (cont.)

Sarah - of VA, b1764, m Thomas Macon - desc/o Martha Eltonhead VG257; CFA(5)138

Sarah Cattlett - of VA, b1764 d1849, m1790 Thomas Macon - desc/o Anne Lovelace ECD(2)178

Thomas - of VA, m Susannah Henry, sister of Patrick Henry - desc/o William Strother GVFTQ(3)379

William - of VA, b1762 studied law under Thomas Jefferson, m___Throckmorton - desc/o Martha Eltonhead VG257; CFA(5)138

William Strother - of VA, d1782, m Elizabeth Preston - desc/o William Strother GVFTQ(3)379

MAGRUDER Alexander (McGruder) - of MD, b1610 d1677 son of Alexander McGruder & Margaret Campbell, m(1) Sarah___, m(2) Elizabeth___- the immigrant ECD(3)204; BLG2814; CFA(1)348; GBR99

Alexander - of MD, d1746, m Susanna___ - desc/o Alexander Magruder CFA(1)348

Alexander - of MD, d1751, m Anne___ - desc/o Alexander Magruder CFA(1)349

Eleanor - of MD & KY, b1746 d aft 1813, m William Kidd Marquiss - desc/o Alexander Magruder ECD(3)204

Elinor - of MD, m Nehemiah Wade - desc/o Alexander Magruder CFA(1)349

Elizabeth - of MD, b abt 1664, m John Pottenger - desc/o Alexander Magruder CFA(1)348

Elizabeth - of MD, m William Beall - desc/o Alexander Magruder CFA(1)349

Elizabeth - of MD, b1764 d1835, m___Belmear - desc/o Alexander Magruder CFA(1)349

Haswell - of MD, b1736 d1811, m Charity Beall - desc/o Alexander Magruder BLG2814

Hugh - of MD - desc/o Alexander Magruder CFA(1)348

Isaac - of MD, d1809, m Sophia Baldwin - desc/o Alexander Magruder CFA(1)351

James - of MD, d1676, m___ & had issue - desc/o Alexander Magruder CFA(1)348

James - of MD, d1775, m Barbara Combs or Coombs - desc/o Alexander Magruder CFA(1)349

Jeoffred - of MD, b1762 d1805, m Susanna Bowie - desc/o Alexander Magruder CFA(1)351

John - of MD, b1694 of Dumblane, Prince George's Co d1750, House of Burgesses 1728/1745, m1715 Susanna Smith, dau/o Nathan Smith & Elizabeth Coale - desc/o Alexander Magruder CFA(1)349

John - of MD, b1709 d1782, m Jane Offutt - desc/o Alexander Magruder ECD(3)204

Mary - of MD, m George C Claggett - desc/o Alexander Magruder CFA(1)349

Nathan - of MD, d1786, m Rebecca Beall - desc/o Alexander Magruder CFA(1)351

Nathaniel - of MD, d1734, m Mary___ - desc/o Alexander Magruder CFA(1)348

MAGRUDER (cont.)

Ninian - of MD, b abt 1686 d1751, m Elizabeth Brewer - desc/o
  Alexander Magruder ECD(3)204; CFA(1)349

Samuel - of MD, b1654 of Good Luck, Prince George's Co, d1711, civil
  & military officer, member of House of Burgesses, m Sarah Beall -
  desc/o Alexander Magruder CFA(1)349

Samuel - of MD, d1779, m Elinor or Eleanor Wade - desc/o Alexander
  Magruder CFA(1)349 BLG2814

Col Samuel - of MD, b1661 d1734, m1711 Sarah Beall - desc/o
  Alexander Magruder - ECD(3)204; BLG2814

Capt Samuel - of MD, b1708 d1790, m Jane Haswell - desc/o
  Alexander Magruder BLG2814

Sarah - of MD, b1755, m Rev Thomas Read - desc/o Alexander
  Magruder CFA(1)349

Verlinda - of MD, m John Beall, son of Alexander Beall - desc/o
  Alexander Magruder CFA(1)349

Zadoch - of MD, b1729 d1811, m(1) Widow Bowie, m(2) Rachel
  Pottenger - desc/o Alexander Magruder CFA(1)349

Zadoch - of MD, b1765 d1809, m Martha Wilson - desc/o Alexander
  Magruder CFA(1)349

MAINWARING (MANWARING) Mary - of MD ?, sister of Oliver Mainwaring
  - the immigrant, m Benjamin Gill - GBR255 whether Mary died in
  England or immigrated to Maryland is uncertain

Mary (Mercy) - of CT, bp as an adult 1702 d1739, m1706 Jonathan
  Palmer b1668 d1726 - desc/o Oliver Manwaring ECD(2)191;
  ECD(3)208; DBR(4)249; FFF42

Oliver - of CT, bp 1633/1634 d1723 a mariner, m Hannah Raymond
  bp 1643 d1717 - the immigrant FLW182; ECD(2)191; ECD(3)208;
  DBR(4)249; RAA1, 113; FFF42; GBR255; NE(79)110/111,
  (141)104/105; TAG(41)225/227

Prudence - b abt 1668 - desc/o Oliver Mainwaring RAA113

MALLORY ____ (Miss) - of VA, m John Quarles d aft 1718 - desc/o Roger
  Mallory VHG116

Charles - of VA, m____ & left issue - desc/o Roger Mallory VHG116

Elizabeth - of VA, m Martin Palmer - desc/o Roger Mallory VHG116

Francis - of VA, d1744, m1719/1720 Anne Johnson dau/o Phillip
  Johnson d1699 & Winifred Proby - desc/o Roger Mallory VHG119

Joanna - b1771, m Nathaniel Wilcox - desc/o Peter Mallory LDS111

Mary - b1656, m Eli Roberts - desc/o Peter Mallory LDS67, 81

Mary - of VA, m John Reade - desc/o Roger Mallory VHG119

Martha - of VA, m Capt John Batte - the immigrant DBR(4)510;
  RAA67; sufficient proof of alleged royal ancestry is lacking

Oliver - b1746, m Margaret____ - desc/o Peter Mallory LDS111

Peter - b abt 1610, m Mary Preston - the immigrant LDS67, 81, 111;
  RAA no longer accepted as being of royal descent

Peter - b1718, m Joanna Hall - desc/o Peter Mallory LDS111

Philip - of VA, b1617 d1661, m Catherine Batte - the immigrant
  WAC70; sufficient proof of alleged royal ancestry is lacking

Phillip - of VA, m(1) Sallie Morton, m(2) Rebecca Gray - desc/o Roger
  Mallory HSF(5)279

Roger - of VA, d aft 22 Dec 1695 captain in the militia & justice in King

MALLORY (cont.)

    & Queen Co 1693, son of Thomas Mallory & (probably) Jane____ - the immigrant WAC70; GBR313; VHG103/121; HSF(5)278

    Roger II - of VA - desc/o Roger Mallory HSF(5)278, 279

    Roger III - of VA, d1743, m Sarah____ - desc/o Roger Mallory HSF(5)278, 279

    Uriel - of VA, b1738 d1824 captain in the Revolutionary militia, eldest son of Roger Mallory III, m Hannah Cave b1748 d1817 dau/o Benjamin Cave of Orange Co & Hannah Bledsoe - desc/o Roger Mallory HSF(5)278, 279

    Uriel Jr - of VA, b1775 Orange Co, VA d1840 Alpine, Alabama, m1803 Madison Co, VA, Melinda Welch b1787 Madison Co, VA d1842 Alpine, Alabama dau/o Nathaniel Welch & Betsy Terrill - desc/o Roger Mallory HSF(5)279

    William - of VA, b abt 1660 d1720, m Anne Wythe dau/o Thomas Wythe, Sr, burgess of Elizabeth City, 1680 - desc/o Roger Mallory VHG115, 117, 120

    William - b1675, m Anna____ - desc/o Peter Mallory LDS111

    William - of VA, m Mary Gibson of Orange Co, VA - desc/o Roger Mallory HSF(5)279

    William - of VA, m Mary Allen - desc/o Roger Mallory VHG119

    William - of VA, d bef 20 Jul 1753, m Mary____ - desc/o Roger Mallory VHG120

    William - of VA, d1801, m____ & had issue - desc/o Roger Mallory VHG120

MANCHESTER Gilbert - b1745 - desc/o Edward Southworth RAA131

MANN Mary - b1640, m John Lapham - desc/o Frances Hopkins LDS50

MANNING John - father of Richard Manning, ancestor of Nathaniel Hawthorne - desc/o Jane Lawrence J&K217

MANSELL (MANCILL) Joseph - d180_, m1805 Mary Squibb - desc/o John Dutton DBR(2)545

MANSFIELD Ebenezer - of CT, b1757 d1819, m Mary Lewis - desc/o Rev Peter Bulkeley DBR(3)86

MAPES Francis - of VA, b abt 1588 d1639, m Anne Loveday - the immigrant DBR(2)277, 280; DBR(3)500; sufficient proof of alleged royal ancestry is lacking

    John - of NY, b abt 1613 d1682, m____ - the immigrant ECD(2)194; sufficient proof of alleged royal ancestry is lacking

    Mary - of NY, b abt 1638 d1727, m Barnabas Wines (Winds) Jr - desc/o John Mapes ECD(2)194

    Mary - of NY, b1662, m Barnabas Wines II - desc/o Thomas Mapes DBR(2)280

    Naomi - of NY, b1667 d1724/1725, m Peter Dickinson - desc/o Francis Mapes DBR(3)500

    Thomas - of NY, b1628 d1686, m1650 Sarah Purrier - the immigrant DBR(2)280; DBR(3)500; RAA114 no longer accepted as being of royal descent

MARBURY Anne - of MA 1634 & RI, bp 1591 d1643 killed by the Indians, was the leader of the Antinomians tried for heresy & sedition & banished from MA, founded the town of Portsmouth RI, dau/o Rev Francis Marbury & Bridget Dryden, m1612 London, England,

MARBURY (cont.)

William Hutchinson bp 1586 Alford, Lincoln, England d1642
Boston, son of Edward Hutchinson of Alford - the immigrant
J&K160; FLW18; ECD258; MCS24; DBR(1)760; DBR(2)691;
DBR(3)134, 170, 368; DBR(4)311; DBR(5)290, 947, 948; RAA114;
GBR233, 234, 351; TAG(67)201/210; NE(19)13/20, (123)180/81;
NE(145)14/21; EO2(2)447/484

K(C)atherine - of RI, b abt 1610 d Newport, Rhode Island 1687, dau/o
Francis Marbury & Bridget Dryden, m Berkhampstead, Hertford
1632 Richard Scott bp 1605 Glemsfod, Suffolk d Providence, Rhode
Island bef Mar 1681 - the immigrant FLW20; ECD260; MCS24;
DBR(1)81, 82; DBR(2)44; DBR(4)368; DBR(5)79, 89, 91, 832, 833;
RAA114; GBR233, 351; TAG(67) 201/210; NE(96)8/17,
(123)180/81, (145)14/21; EO2(3)82/117; NYGBR(2)174/178

Francis - of MA & RI, b1555 son of William Marbury & Agnes Lenton,
m Bridget Dryden & was the father of Anne & Katherine Marbury -
the immigrants - the immigrant RAA1, 114; GBR233, 351 listed as
the father but not - the immigrant; TAG(67) 201/210

MARIS Hannah - b1755 - desc/o Rebecca Humphrey RAA120

MARQUIS Mary - of MD, b1773 d1861, m1792 James Allen - desc/o
Alexander Magruder ECD(3)204

MARRIOTT Mary - of VA, b abt 1712 d abt 1764, m abt 1732 Henry
Davis d1767 of Surry Co VA - desc/o Thomas Warren ECD(3)311;
DBR(1)189; DBR(2)270

William - of VA, b abt 1688 d1766, m abt 1710 Sarah Collier d1728
dau/o Thomas Collier of Surry Co, VA - desc/o Thomas Warren
ECD(3)311; DBR(1)189; DBR(2)270

MARSH Mary - of CT, b1716 d1788, m Rev Stephen Heaton - desc/o
Margaret Wyatt DBR(2)613

Mary - m William Watson - desc/o Grace Minor PFA Apx D #5

Sarah - of CT, b1674, m1694 Lieut John Merrill - desc/o Richard
Lyman J&K209; JSW1872

MARSHALL Abiel - whose dau Sarah, m James Hyde - desc/o Margaret
Wyatt J&K123

Abigail - of CT, b1682, m1702 John Birge - desc/o Margaret Wyatt
ECD241; DBR(1)418; DBR(2)557

Catherine - b1699 - desc/o John Drake RAA87

Charles - m Lucy Pickett - desc/o Col William Randolph DBR(3)703

Elizabeth - of ME, d bef 1640 dau/o Roger & Katherine (Mitton)
Marshall, m1618 St Chad, Shrewsbury, Thomas Lewis b abt 1590
Shrewsbury d bef 1640 son of Andrew Lewis of Shrewsbury, Salop
& Mary Herring - the immigrant FLW21; MCS89; GBR264

Elizabeth - VA, b1756 d1842, m Raleigh Colston - desc/o Col William
Randolph DBR(5)111

John - of CT, b1701 d1772, m Elizabeth Winslow - desc/o John Drake
MCB430

Hon John - of VA, b1755 d1835 1st Chief Justice of the Supreme
Court, m1783 Mary Willis Ambler - desc/o Capt Henry Isham
J&K133; DBR(1)744; DBR(2)35 - desc/o Col William Randolph PFA
Apx D #3

Mary - of CT, b1715 Windsor d1797 Windsor, m Nathaniel Stanley

MARSHALL (cont.)

    b1707 Hartford d abt 1761 Windsor - desc/o Col William Leete SMO104

    Ruth - of CT, b1737 d1816, m1754 Capt James Greene - desc/o John Drake MCB430

    Capt Samuel - of CT, m Mary Wilton - desc/o Thomas Marshall AFA84

    Sarah - of CT, b1710/1711 d1800, m1734 Timothy Mather - desc/o William Leete DBR(4)751

    Seth - of CT, d1841, m Susan Frisbie - desc/o John Drake AFA82, 84

    Thomas - of CT, b1693, m Elizabeth Tudor - desc/o John Drake AFA82, 84

    Thomas - of CT, m Desire Tuttle - desc/o John Drake AFA82, 84

    Thomas - of MA, m Alice____- the immigrant AFA84; sufficient proof of alleged royal ancestry is lacking

    Deacon Thomas - of CT, m Mary Drake - desc/o Thomas Marshall AFA84

    William - of VA, b1767 d1815, m(2) Mary Macon - desc/o Capt Henry Isham ECD(2)219 - desc/o Col William Randolph DBR(5)316

MARSHAM Katherine - of MD, b1672 d1712, m1683 Basil Waring, m(2) Samuel Queen - desc/o Giles Brent ECD(3)30; DBR(4)53, 85, 389, 462, 463; DBR(5)673; CRL(2)74

MARSTON Elizabeth - of MA, b1732, m William Watson - desc/o Herbert Pelham NE(4)302/303

    Lucia - of MA, m1756 John Watson - desc/o Herbert Pelham NE(4)303

    Patience - of MA, b1733, m Elkana Watson - desc/o Herbert Pelham NE(4)303

MARTIN Christopher - b abt 1766, m Ann Turner - desc/o Thomas Harris LDS87; RAA102 - desc/o John Boteler RAA71

    Michael - of MA - desc/o Richard Martin (MARTYN) EDV95, 96

    Richard (MARTYN) - of MA - the immigrant EDV95; sufficient proof of alleged royal ancestry is lacking

MASCARENE Jean Paul - of MA 1711, d1760 - the immigrant EDV34; sufficient proof of alleged royal ancestry is lacking

MASON Anne Fowke - of VA, m(1) William Darrell, m(2) Thomas Fitzhugh, clerk of Stafford Co, m(3) Thomas Smith of Fairfax Co d1764 - desc/o Gerard Fowke APP614

    Elizabeth - of VA, d1708/1709, m Capt Thomas Holt - desc/o Lieut Col Walter Aston CHB537

    Elizabeth - of VA, m William Roy of Essex Co - desc/o Gerard Fowke APP614

    Elizabeth - of CT, m1786 Judge John Griswold Hillhouse - desc/o Elizabeth St John CHB222; BCD222

    Frances - of VA 1621, m Thomas Holt - the immigrant CHB440; sufficient proof of alleged royal ancestry is lacking

    Freelove - of MA, b1720, m1738 Joseph Cole - desc/o Richard Bowen Sr CHB465

    French - of VA, d1748, justice of Stafford Co, m Mary Nicholson - desc/o Gerard Fowke APP614

    Col George - of VA, b1627 d1686, m(1) Mary French, m(2) Frances Norgrave - the immigrant WAC42; CRL(3)118, 119; sufficient proof of alleged royal ancestry is lacking

MASON (cont.)

Col George Jr - of VA, b abt 1670 d1716, m(1) Mary Fowke, m(2)____, m(3)____ (the father of 12 children) - desc/o Col George Mason CRL(3)119

George - of VA, b1690 d1735/1736 (drowned in the Potomac River), county lieutenant of Stafford 1719, member of the House of Burgesses, m(1)____ Thomson of Chappawamsic, m(2)1721 Ann Thomson b abt 1699 d1762 - desc/o Gerard Fowke APP614

James - of VA, d1702, m Elizabeth____ - desc/o Lieut Col Walter Aston CHB537

Jeremiah - of CT, b1705 d1779, m1727 Mary Haddam (Clark) b1705 d1799 - desc/o Elizabeth St John CHB221; BCD221; DBR(1)683

Col Jeremiah - of CT, b1730 d1813, m1754 Elizabeth Fitch - desc/o Elizabeth St John CHB221; BCD221

Jeremiah - b1757 d1848, m1782/1783 Phoebe Luther b1762 d1831 - desc/o Robert Abell DBR(3)711

Capt Joseph - of MA, b1687, representative & captain 1732, m1714 Elizabeth Barney - desc/o Richard Bowen Sr CHB465

Mary - of VA, m(1) George Fitzhugh of Stafford Co, member of the House of Burgesses 1718 d1722, m(2) Major Benjamin Strother, tobacco inspector & vestryman b abt 1700 d1765 - desc/o Gerard Fowke APP614

Mary - b1736 d aft 1777, m1756 Nathan Huntingdon b1736 d1818 - desc/o Elizabeth St John DBR(1)683

Simeon - b1735 d1809, m(1)1754 Hannah Thomas b1734 dau/o John Thomas - desc/o Robert Abell DBR(3)711

Sympha Rosa Enfield - of VA, b1703 d1761, m(1) Major John Dinwiddie born Glasgow, Scotland d1726, brother of Gov Robert Dinwiddie, merchant & sheriff of King George Co, m(2) by 4 Aug 1727 Col Jeremiah Bronaugh Jr b1702/1703 d1749, justice of Fairfax Co & vestryman of Truro Parish - desc/o Col George Mason CRL(3)119 - desc/o Gerard Fowke APP614

MASSINGBERD Elizabeth - of SC, dau/o Sir Dra(y)ner Massingberd, Knight of the Co Lincoln, England, & Anne Mildmay, m Edward Hyrne - the immigrant GBR214; SCG(2)397/416

MATHER Atherton - of MA, b1663 d1734, m(1)1694 Rebecca Stoughton, m(2)1705 Mary Lamb - desc/o Rev Richard Mather BLG2820

Rev Cotton - of New England - desc/o Rev Richard Mather EDV96

Rev Eleazar - of MA, b1637 d1669, m Esther Warham - desc/o Rev Richard Mather BLG2820

Rev Increase - of MA, b1639 d1723, m(1) Maria Colton, m(2) Anne Lake - desc/o Rev Richard Mather BLG2820

John - of CT, b1721 d1804, m1745 Nancy Higgins - desc/o Rev Richard Mather BLG2820

John - of CT, b1746, m Elizabeth Peck - desc/o Rev Richard Mather BLG2820

John - of MA, b1775/1776 d1847, m1798 Sophia Taylor b1774 d1847 dau/o Major Edward Taylor - desc/o Margaret Wyatt ECD106; DBR(1)337

Joseph - of CT, b1686 d1749, m Phebe____ - desc/o Rev Richard Mather BLG2820

MATHER (cont.)

Lucy of CT, b1770 d1862, m1788 John Field Fitch - desc/o John Drake CHB108; BCD108

Moses - of NY, b1774 d1832, m1799 Sarah Dresser - desc/o Rev Richard Mather BLG2820

Rev Nathaniel - of MA, b1631 d1697, m Maria Benn - desc/o Rev Richard Mather BLG2820

Rev Richard - of MA 1635, b1659 d1669, m(1)1624 Catherine Holt, m(2)1656 Sarah Storey - the immigrant EDV96; BLG2820; sufficient proof of alleged royal ancestry is lacking

Richard - of MA, b1653, m1680 Catherine Wise - desc/o Rev Richard Mather BLG2820

Rev Samuel - of MA, b1626 d1671, m____Stevens - desc/o Rev Richard Mather BLG2820

Sarah - of CT, b1737 d1822, m1759 William Cooley - desc/o William Leete DBR(4)751

Timothy - of MA, b1628 d1684, m(1) Catherine Atherton, m(2)1678/1679 Elizabeth Weeks - desc/o Rev Richard Mather BLG2820

William - of MA, b1698 d1747, m1721 Silence Buttolph - desc/o Rev Richard Mather BLG2820

William - of NY, b1735 d1810, m(1)1760 Helen Allyn Talcott, m(2) Martha Dickinson - desc/o Rev Richard Mather BLG2820

MATHEWS Baldwin - of VA, b1670 d1736, m Mary Diggs - desc/o Mary Hinton JSW1646

Edmond - of VA 1622, b1606 - desc/o John Mathews JSW1601, 602

Capt Francis - of VA, b1625 d1674/1675 captain of militia & justice of York Co, m____ d1675 in England dau/o William Baldwin - desc/o Gov Samuel Mathews JSW1646; APP445/446

Janet - b1747 d1818, m1765 John Blackburn - desc/o Mary Hinton DBR(2)601

Rev James - of VA & SC, b1755 d1828, m(2)1786 Rebecca Carleton - desc/o John Mathews JSW1602, 603; DBR(3)39; DBR(4)411; DBR(5)178

John - of VA, m Mary Plumley - the immigrant JSW1601/602 royalty not proven

Capt John - of VA, b1661 d1702, m1683 Elizabeth Tavenor - desc/o Gov Samuel Mathews JSW1601; DBR(2)601; DBR(3)38; DBR(4)411; DBR(5)178

John - of VA 1622, b abt 1608 - desc/o John Mathews JSW1601, 602

Mary - of VA, m1711 J Philip Smith - desc/o Mary Hinton JSW1646

Mary - of VA, b1702 d1775, m abt 1723 Isaac Mathews - desc/o Gov Samuel Mathews JSW1601; DBR(2)601; DBR(3)38; DBR(4)411; DBR(5)178

Moses - of VA & SC, b1725 d1806, m1748 Sarah Finley or Findley - desc/o John Mathews JSW1601; DBR(3)39; DBR(4)411; DBR(5)178

Gov Samuel - of VA 1622, b1592 d1657 Governor of Virginia for life, son of Tobias Mathews, Archbishop of York, m(1) Frances Greville wid/o Nathaniel West, m(2)1622 Mary Hinton, dau/o Sir Thomas Hinton - the immigrant JSW1601; DBR(2)60, 147, 599, 601; DBR(4)409; DBR(5)328 - APP442/447 does not give the name of his

MATHEWS (cont.)

wife but does name her father, any claim to royalty comes through the dau/o Sir Thomas Hinton

Lieut Col Samuel - of VA, b abt 1629 d1671 became governor of Virginia early in 1657 and continued until his death, m____ - desc/o Gov Samuel Mathews JSW1601; DBR(2)601; DBR(3)38; DBR(4)411; DBR(5)178 - desc/o Mary or____ Hinton APP445

Capt Samuel - of VA, b abt 1684/1685 d1718, m(1) Elizabeth Braxton - desc/o Gov Samuel Mathews JSW1601; DBR(2)601; DBR(3)38; DBR(4)411; DBR(5)178

Thomas - of VA 1622, b abt 1610 - desc/o John Mathews JSW1601, 602

MATHIS Micajah Sr - of NJ, b1717 d1804, m Mercy Shreve - desc/o Peter Wright DBR(4)577

Sarah - of NJ, b1721 d1799, m(2) John Leeds - desc/o Peter Wright DBR(2)502

Sarah - of NJ, m Samuel Leek - desc/o Peter Wright DBR(4)578

MATTHEWSON Elizabeth - of RI & MA, b1742 d1822, m(1)1763 Mason Helett - desc/o Thomas Arnold CHB324; BCD324

MATTOON Abel - of CT, b1752 d1838, a soldier in the American Revolution, m1778 Mary Allin b abt 1756 d1840 - desc/o Robert Abell DBR(4)503

Philip - of CT, b1721 d aft 1806, m1751 Elinor Roberts d bef 1783 - desc/o Robert Abell DBR(4)503

MATTOX Mary - of MD, b1772 d1816, m1789 William Deatherage - desc/o Leonard Calvert MG(1)148

MAUDE Margery - of DE, b1671 dau/o Joshua Maude & Elizabeth____, m1692 Thomas Fisher b1669 d1713 - the immigrant DBR(1)47; DBR(3)91; GBR180

MAULEVERER Anne - of NJ, b1678 d1754 dau/o Edmund Mauleverer & Anne Pearson, m1696 John Abbott - the immigrant CHB357; MCD154; DBR(5)784; RAA59; AFA238; GBR164

MAVERICK Abigail - bp 1613/1614 Huish d1644 Boston, MA, m John Manning of Boston, merchant who joined the Ancient & Honorable Artillery Company in 1640 & had issue a son & daughter John & Mary - desc/o Mary Gye NE(96)234

Abigail - of MA, b1637 d1690 Beverly, MA, m(1)1655 Matthew Clark of Winnissimet & Marblehead, MA 1668/1674, mariner, m(2) 1688/1689 Marblehead, Benjamin Balch - desc/o Mary Gye NE(96)239

Abigail - of MA, b1644/1645 d bef Jan 1685/1686, m Major Samuel Ward of Marblehead, bp 1638 Hingham, MA d1690 in the expedition to Canada, son of Samuel Ward of Hingham & Charlestown, MA - desc/o Mary Gye RAA115; NE(96)359

Abigail - m 1674 Edward Gilman of Exeter b abt 1649 d abt 1690/1692 selectman & tavern keeper, son of Edward Gilman & Elizabeth Smith - desc/o Mary Gye NE(96)234

Abigail - of MA, b1675 Boston d1750 Saybrook, CT, m1697/1702 William Tully of Saybrook, farmer & shoemaker b1676 d1744 son of John Tully & Mary Beamont - desc/o Mary Gye NE(96)364

Abigail - of MA, b1725 Sudbury d1817 Gardner, MA, m1749 Sudbury

MAVERICK (cont.)

Moses Hill, a soldier in the militia in 1757 b1728 Sherborn d1780 Gardner, son of Nathaniel Hill & Elizabeth Phipps - desc/o Mary Gye NE(96)365

Andrew - of New York City, b1728/1729 Boston d bef 1765 New York City, m1754 New York City, Sarah Rushton b1735 dau/o Peter Rushton & Bethia Reeder - desc/o Mary Gye NE(97)57/58

Ann - of MA, m1695 Haverhill, MA, Timothy Johnson b1672 Haverhill d1696 Haverhill, son of John Johnson & Elizabeth Maverick - desc/o Mary Gye NE(97)60

Ann Nancy - of MA, b1721, m1747 Boston, Nathaniel Phillips of Boston, owner of an apothecary shop d1811 Boston - desc/o Mary Gye NE(97)57

Antipas - of MA, b abt 1619 d1678 by falling out of a boat while intoxicated, took the oath of allegiance 1652 & was an innkeeper 1659, grand juror & juror, m____ & had issue - desc/o Mary Gye NE(96)234

Elias - of MA, b abt 1604 England d1684, m abt 1633 Ann Harris d1697 Reading, MA, dau/o Thomas Harris & Elizabeth____ - the immigrant ECD(3)174; LDS106; DBR(5)736; RAA115; could not have been - the immigrant - desc/o Mary Gye NE(96)239

Elias - of MA, b1643/1644 d1696 Barbados, mariner, m1669 Charlestown, MA, Margaret Sherwood (perhaps) dau/o Thomas Sherwood of Fairfield, CT - desc/o Mary Gye NE(96)363

Elias - of MA, b1670 d1696 Barbados, m1695/1696 Sarah Smith - desc/o Mary Gye NE(96)363

Elizabeth - of MA, b1639 d1673/1674 Haverhill, MA, m1656 John Johnson of Charlestown, a settler in the fall of 1658 at Haverhill, where he became an early proprietor, blacksmith, farmer, deacon, tithingman, selectman, juror, lieutenant, moderator, an officer in King Philip's War & representative to the Provincial Legislature b1633 d1708 killed by the Indians at Haverhill, son of William Johnson & Elizabeth____ - desc/o Mary Gye NE(96)240

Elizabeth - of MA, bp 1649 d bet 1685/1686 & 1698, m(1)1665 Nathaniel Grafton of Salem b1642 d1670/1671 Barbados, son of Joseph Grafton, m(2)1679 Thomas Skinner - desc/o Mary Gye ECD(3)177; RAA115; NE(96)360

Elizabeth - d aft 1710, m____Barrow - desc/o Mary Gye NE(96)362

Elizabeth - of MA, b1715/1716 d1743 Chelmsford, MA, m1738 Boston, Major Sampson Stoddard b1709 Chelmsford d1777, son of Sampson Stoddard & Elizabeth ____ - desc/o Mary Gye NE(97)56

Elizabeth - of MA, bp 1743, m1766 Boston, Ebenezer McIntosh - desc/o Mary Gye NE(97)56

James - of MA, d abt 1695, ferryman & mariner, m Hester____ & left issue - desc/o Mary Gye NE(96)364

James - of MA, b1699 of Sudbury, Framingham & Sherborn, MA d1750 Sudbury, m(1) Mary____, m(2) Mary Walker b1706 Sudbury d1740 Sudbury, dau/o William Walker & Sarah Goodnow, m(3)1742 Lydia Sanderson - desc/o Mary Gye NE(96)365

Jemima - of MA, b1719 d1788 Boston, m1738 Boston, Capt Benjamin White, an officer in the British Army - desc/o Mary Gye NE(97)57

MAVERICK (cont.)

John - of MA, b1578, m Mary Gye - the immigrant RAA1, 115; sufficient proof of alleged royal ancestry is lacking; royal ancestry is through his wife Mary Gye

John - of MA, b abt 1621 England, was one of the original settlers of Charleston, SC 1670/1680 & was a member of the first Colonial Parliament in that state, m (probably) 1649 All Hallows, London, Jane Andrewes & had issue - desc/o Mary Gye NE(96)234/235

John - of MA, b1635/1636 d bef 27 Apr 1680 of Boston, shipwright, m1656 Catherine Skipper, killed by the Indians at Haverhill, MA 1708 in her 70th year - desc/o Mary Gye NE(96)239

John - of MA, bp 1687 aged one year, Charlestown, MA, importer of hard woods at the sign of the "Cabinet & Chest of Drawers," m1710 Boston, Elizabeth Mattox b1691 Boston, dau/o Samuel Mattox & Ann____ - desc/o Mary Gye NE(97)56

Jotham - of MA, b1717/1718, m(1)1742 Boston Mehitable Banks, m(2)1748 Boston Mary Williams, wid/o John Williams - desc/o Mary Gye NE(97)56

Jotham - of MA, b1660 Boston, m1690 Marblehead, MA, Elizabeth Hanniford b1669 Marblehead, dau/o Richard Hanniford & Mariam - desc/o Mary Gye NE(97)59

Katherine - of MA, d aft 1706, m aft 18 Jul 1668 Stephen Paul of Kittery, d1696 shipwright, son of Daniel Paul & Elizabeth - desc/o Mary Gye NE(96)234

Margaret - of MA, bp 1675 Charlestown d1759 Salem, m1691 Boston, John Pratt of Salem, MA b abt 1664 d1729/1730 Salem - desc/o Mary Gye NE(96)363

Martha - of MA, b1693, m1716 Framingham, MA, Thomas Bellows of Marlborough, Hopkinton, Southborough & Framingham, MA b1693 son of Eleazer Bellows & Esther Barrett - desc/o Mary Gye NE(96)365

Mary - of MA, bp 1609/1610 South Huish d aft 1652, m abt 1635 Rev James Parker d1652 Barbados - desc/o Mary Gye NE(96)233

Mary - of MA, b abt 1635 d1707, m(1)1655/1656 John Palsgrave b1633/1634 of Boston, son of Richard Palsgrave & Ann____, m(2)1660 Boston, Capt Francis Hooke d1694/1695, of Kittery, Maine, Clerk of the Writs, justice of the peace, treasurer for the eastern district of the province, selectman, county treasurer, chief justice, councillor, captain, major, son of Humphrey Hooke, alderman of Bristol, England - desc/o Mary Gye NE(96)238

Mary - of MA, b1661, m Samuel Smith d bef 1685, mariner - desc/o Mary Gye NE(96)238

Mary - of MA, d aft 1696, m Aaron Way of Winnissimet bp 1650 Dorchester, MA d aft 1696, moved to South Carolina 1696, son of Aaron Way & Joanna Sumner - desc/o Mary Gye NE(96)240

Mary - under 18 years of age 16 Aug 1670, m (probably) 1688/1689 St Michael's Parish, Barbados, James Drinkwater - desc/o Mary Gye NE(96)362

Mary - of MA, bp 1657 d1695 Marblehead, m Archibald Ferguson of Marblehead, a soldier in the expedition to Canada in 1690, was deposed 16 Jul 1686 aged abt 37 years d aft 5 Dec 1698 & left

MAVERICK (cont.)

issue - desc/o Mary Gye NE(96)360

Mary - of MA, b1720/1721 Sudbury, m1744 Framingham, David Mellen b1721/1722 Framingham d1801 Oxford, MA, son of Simon Mellen & Esther Towne - desc/o Mary Gye NE(96)365

Mary - of MA, b1725 d177_ Boston, m1752 Boston, John Gyles of Boston, importer of fancy goods b1725 Boston, son of Charles Gyles & Mary Cruft - desc/o Mary Gye NE(97)57

Moses - of MA, bp 1611 Huish, Devon, England d1685/1686 Marblehead, proprietor at Dorchester, MA 1633, proprietor at Marblehead in 1637, constable in 1643, selectman, justice of the peace & town clerk, solemnized marriages at Marblehead previous to his death, m(1) bef 6 May 1635 Remember Allerton, who came to New England in the *Mayflower* in 1620 d aft 1652, dau/o Isaac Allerton & Mary Norris, m(2)1656 Boston, Eunice____ b abt 1628 d aft 5 Dec 1698 wid/o Thomas Roberts - desc/o Mary Gye ECD(3)177; RAA115; NE(96)358

Nathaniel - of MA, d1673/1674, m____ & had issue - desc/o Mary Gye NE(96)361/362

Nathaniel - of St Peter's Parish, Barbados d abt 1714 Barbados, m Mary____ d abt 1761 & had issue - desc/o Mary Gye NE(96)362

Nathaniel - of St Michael's Parish, Barbados, under 21 years of age on 16 Aug 1670 d1700/1701, m1682 St Michael's Parish, Mrs Jone Battin - desc/o Mary Gye NE(96)362/363

Paul - of MA, b1657 Boston d aft 1709, m Jemimah Smith b1665 Winnisimett, MA, dau/o Lieut John Smith & Mary Bill - desc/o Mary Gye NE(96)365/366

Paul - of MA, b1714 d abt 1746, m1740 Stratford, CT, Gloria Margaretta Nichols daughter (perhaps) of Benjamin Nichols - desc/o Mary Gye NE(97)56

Peter - of MA, d bef 1681, m Martha Bradford, dau/o Robert Bradford & Martha____ - desc/o Mary Gye NE(96)364

Peter Rushton - of NY, b1755 New York City d1811, engraver, etcher, silversmith & copper plate printer of ability & owned a shop in the city & in 1775 he was an ensign Second Regiment, New York militia, m(1)1772 New York City, Ann Reynolds d1787, m(2)1788 New York City, Rebecca Reynolds d1852 in her 96th year - desc/o Mary Gye NE(97)58

Rebecca - of MA, bp 1639 d1659 Lynn, MA, John Hawkes of Lynn d1694 - desc/o Mary Gye NE(96)359

Rebecca - of MA, b1659/1660 d aft 3 Nov 1696, m George Thomas of Boston d aft 3 Nov 1696 - desc/o Mary Gye NE(96)241

Remember - of MA, bp 1652 d bet 1685/1686-1691, m Edward Woodman, mariner d1693/1698 - desc/o Mary Gye NE(96)360

Ruth - of MA, b abt 1654 d1717 Reading, m1679/1680 Reading, Deacon Francis Smith b1658 d1744 Reading, son of Lieut John Smith & Catherine Morrell of Winnisimet - desc/o Mary Gye RAA115; NE(96)240

Samuel - of MA, b abt 1602 d1670/1676, m abt 1628 Amias Cole dau/o William Cole of Plymouth, Devon, England, shipwright & wid/o David Thompson of Plymouth - desc/o Mary Gye NE(96)235

MAVERICK (cont.)

Capt Samuel - of Barbados, under 21 years of age on 16 Aug 1670 d aft 1710, m____ & had issue - desc/o Mary Gye NE(96)362

Samuel - of MA, d1663/1664 Boston, m1660 Boston, Rebecca Wheelwright d1679 dau/o Rev John Wheelwright & Mary Hutchinson of Wells, Maine - desc/o Mary Gye NE(96)238

Sarah - of MA, b1640/1641 d1714 Reading, MA, m Samuel Walton b1639 Marblehead, MA d1717/1718 Reading, son of Rev William Walton & Elizabeth____ & had issue five children - desc/o Elias Maverick ECD(3)175; LDS106; DBR(5)736; RAA115 - desc/o Mary Gye NE(96)240

Sarah - of MA, d aft 31 Aug 1706, m1683 Marblehead, John Norman deposed 16 Jul 1686 aged abt 26 years & d aft 1706 - desc/o Mary Gye NE(96)360

Sarah - of MA, b1718 Sherborn, m1737 Sudbury, John Putnam b1715 Salem Village d1762 Oswego, New York, son of Samuel Putnam & had issue ten children - desc/o Mary Gye NE(96)365

Silence - of MA, b1735, m1755 Jedidiah Parmenter of Sudbury - desc/o Mary Gye NE(96)365

MAY John - of MA 1640, d1671 - the immigrant EDV126; BLG2821; sufficient proof of alleged royal ancestry is lacking

John - of MA, b1631, m Sarah Bruce - desc/o John May BLG2821

John - of MA, b1663 d1730, m1684 Prudence Brydges - desc/o John May BLG2821

John - of MA, b1686, m Elizabeth Child - desc/o John May BLG2821

Col John - of MA, b1738 d1812, m ____May - desc/o John May BLG2821

Joseph - b1743 - desc/o John May BLG2821

Joshua - b1716 - desc/o John May BLG2821

Joshua - desc/o John May BLG2821

MCCONIHE John - of MA 1718, d1760, m Mary Kennedy - the immigrant FFF190; sufficient proof of alleged royal ancestry is lacking

John - of MA, b1740, m Sarah Campbell - desc/o John McConihe FFF190

MCKEAND Elizabeth Carter - of VA, b1773 d1807, m1802 Robert West - desc/o Sarah Ludlow DBR(1)30

MCKEE Milley - b1762 - desc/o Richard Billings RAA70

Nathaniel - b abt 1731/1733 - desc/o Richard Billings RAA70

MCKENNEY George Sr - of VA, d1801, m(2) 1791 Elizabeth McGuire - desc/o Dr Thomas Gerard DBR(2)360; DBR(3)56, 57

Gerrard - of VA, d1760/1761, m Letias (Lettice) Crabb - desc/o Dr Thomas Gerard DBR(2)360

MCKIM Isaac - of MD, b1775 d1838, m Ann Hollins - desc/o Thomas McKim CFA345

John - of MD, b1742 d1819, m Margaret Duncan - desc/o Thomas McKim CFA345

Thomas - of PA, b1710 d1784 - the immigrant CFA345; sufficient proof of alleged royal ancestry is lacking

MCKNIGHT Dr Charles - of NJ, b1750 d1791, m1778 Mary Morin Scott - desc/o John Throckmorton ECD(3)263

MCLEOD Alexander - of NY, b1774 d1833, Reformed Presbyterian
    clergyman; son of Neil & Margaret (MacLean) McLeod, m Maria
    Anne Agnew - the immigrant GBR72

MCNEILL Henry - of KY, b1755 d1820, m Dorothy Pryor - the immigrant
    DBR(4)39, 60, 345; sufficient proof of alleged royal ancestry is
    lacking

MEADE (MEAD) Anne of NC & VA, m Richard Randolph Jr - desc/o
    Richard Everand CHB180

    Esther - b1760 d1836, m abt 1777 Isiah Hungerford - desc/o Matthias
      St John THC271

    Mary of NC, m George Walker - desc/o Sir Richard Everand J&K249

    Stephen - b1728 d1806, m1751 Rachel Sanford - desc/o Matthias St
      John THC271

MEARS James - b abt 1775 - desc/o John Drake RAA87

MEECH Zilpha - b1734 - desc/o Alice Freeman RAA132

MELLOWES Elizabeth - of MA, bp 1625 d1690/1691, m(1) Thomas
    Barrett, m(2) abt 1653 Edward Wright - the immigrant ECD(3)73,
    76; RAA75; sufficient proof of royal ancestry is lacking

    Elizabeth - b1656 - desc/o Rev Edward Bulkeley RAA75

    John - b1622 - desc/o Rev Edward Bulkeley RAA75

    Oliver - of MA, b abt 1598 d1638, m(1)1620 Mary James - desc/o Rev
      Edward Bulkeley ECD(3)73; RAA75

MERCER Gen Hugh - of VA, b1726 d1777 physician & Revolutionary
    officer, son of William Mercer & Anne Munro, m bef 1764 Isabel
    Gordon - the immigrant MCS67; GBR97 some aspect of royal
    descent merits further study

MERIWETHER David - of VA - desc/o Nicholas Meriwether WAC106

    Col David - of VA, b1690 d1744, m abt 1713 Ann Holmes - desc/o
      Capt Henry Woodhouse JSW1893

    David - of GA, m Mary Harvie - desc/o Col George Reade DBR(5)210

    Francis - of VA, m Martha Jamison - desc/o Col George Reade
      DBR(5)160

    Francis - of VA, d1713, m Mary Bathurst - desc/o Capt Henry
      Woodhouse DBR(5)284 - desc/o Nicholas Meriwether WAC106

    Jane - of VA, m Col Robert Lewis - desc/o Capt Henry Woodhouse
      DBR(2)709

    Col John - of VA, b1728 d1789, m Catherine Fauntleroy - desc/o Capt
      Henry Woodhouse DBR(2)711

    Col John - of VA, b1753 d1817, m1776 Elizabeth Howell Kennon -
      desc/o Capt Henry Woodhouse DBR(2)711

    Lucy - of VA, m Col Francis Smith - desc/o Capt Henry Woodhouse
      DBR(5)284

    Martha - m Benjamin Taliaferro - desc/o Col George Reade DBR(5)210

    Mary - of VA, m Col William Barnett - desc/o Col George Reade
      DBR(5)160

    Mary - of VA, m Capt Richard P White - desc/o Col George Reade
      CHB258

    Nicholas - of VA, d1678 - the immigrant WAC106; sufficient proof of
      alleged royal ancestry is lacking

    Nicholas - of VA, b1647 d1744, m Elizabeth Crawford - desc/o Capt
      Henry Woodhouse DBR(2)709 - desc/o Nicholas Meriwether

MERIWETHER (cont.)

> WAC106
>
> Susannah - of VA, m bef 1668 Nicholas Catlett - desc/o Capt Henry
> Woodhouse JSW1893
>
> Thomas - of VA, d1708 - desc/o Nicholas Meriwether WAC106, 107
>
> William - of VA, m Elizabeth Bushrod - desc/o Nicholas Meriwether
> WAC106

MERONEY Elizabeth - of NC, b1770 d1856, m1791 Robert Riddick -
> desc/o Col John Alston DBR(1)60, 538; DBR(2)82; DBR(4)92

MERRICK Deighton - bp 1750, m1770 David Millard (or Miller) - desc/o
> Frances Deighton ECD158
>
> Hannah - b1731 - desc/o Charles Chauncy RAA79
>
> Isaac - of MA b abt 1712 d1765, m abt 1736 Hannah Hathaway -
> desc/o Frances Deighton ECD158
>
> Ruth - b abt 1712, m Thomas Hinckley - desc/o Ensign Constant
> Southworth LDS56

MERRILL Abel - b1748 d1828 son of Samuel Merrill Jr - desc/o Capt
> Thomas Bradbury J&K177
>
> Caleb - of CT, b1735 d1812, m1753 Susanna Tompkins - desc/o
> Richard Lyman JSW1872
>
> Daniel - of MA, b1642 d1717, m1667 Sarah Clough - desc/o Nathaniel
> Merrill FFF88
>
> Ebenezer - of CT, father of Hannah Merrill - desc/o Richard Lyman
> J&K209
>
> Esther - m Amasa Scoville - desc/o Richard Lyman JSW1872
>
> Hannah - of CT, b1728 d1779, m1748 Ebenezer Griswold - desc/o
> Richard Lyman J&K209
>
> Hannah - of CT, b1754 d1833, m1773 Jesse Tenney - desc/o Richard
> Lyman J&K209
>
> John - of MA 1633 - the immigrant EDV129; sufficient proof of alleged
> royal ancestry is lacking
>
> Nathaniel - of MA 1633, bp 1601 d1654, m Susanna___ - the
> immigrant EDV129; FFF88 sufficient proof of alleged royal ancestry
> is lacking
>
> Nathaniel - of CT, b1702 d1772, m1729 Esther Warner - desc/o
> Richard Lyman JSW1872
>
> Nehemiah - of MA, b1708, m1728, m Mary True - desc/o Nathaniel
> Merrill FFF88
>
> Ruth - of MA, b1681 d1710, m Onesiphorus Page - desc/o Nathaniel
> Merrill FFF88

MESSERVY Clement - of NH 1673, b1655, m Elizabeth___ - the
> immigrant AFA64; sufficient proof of royal ancestry is lacking
>
> Clement - of NH, b1678 d1746, m Elizabeth Jones - desc/o Clement
> Messervy AFA64
>
> John - of MA, b1708 d1762, m Jemima Hubbard - desc/o Clement
> Messervy AFA64
>
> John - m Hannah Libby - desc/o Clement Messervy AFA64
>
> William - m Margery Deering - desc/o Clement Messervy AFA64

MESSINGER Ebenezer - b1697 - desc/o Rev Edward Bulkeley RAA75

> Samuel - b1761 - desc/o Rev Edward Bulkeley RAA75
>
> Sweetser - b abt 1736 - desc/o Rev Edward Bulkeley RAA75

METCALFE Anne - of VA, d1724, m1713/1714 Capt John Opie - desc/o Col Moore Fauntleroy DBR(5)332

    Anne Lea - of VA, b1760 d1844, m Claudius Levert b1750 d1810 had issue a daughter Caroline Ann Elizabeth Levert who married Francis Turner Mastin & had issue - desc/o John Strachey GVFWM(4)629

MICHAEL Margaret - of VA, m Col John Custis - desc/o Capt Adam Thoroughgood CRL(2)116

MIDDLETON Benedict - b abt 1758 - desc/o James Coghill RAA82

    Mary - of SC, m1771 Pierce Butler, United States senator of South Carolina & died leaving issue - desc/o Stephen Bull SCG(1)219, (3)155

    Sarah - of SC, m1766 Benjamin Guerard, governor of the state of South Carolina & died leaving issue - desc/o Stephen Bull SCG(1)218, (3)155

MIERS Mary - of DE, d1785, m abt 1760 John Clarke b1736 - desc/o Margery Maude DBR(1)47; DBR(3)91 - desc/o Thomas Fisher AFA56

MILES Ignatius - b1758 d1827, m1781 Mary Manning - desc/o George Beckwith DBR(1)222; DBR(2)315; DBR(3)603; DBR(4)335

    John II - of MD, d1727, m Mary Manning - desc/o George Beckwich DBR(1)507; DBR(2)651; DBR(3)607

    John III - of MD, b1700 d1761, m Elizabeth Barton - desc/o George Beckwith DBR(1)507; DBR(2)651; DBR(3)607

    John Barton - of MD, b1730 d1761, m1752 Elizabeth Fenwick - desc/o George Beckwith DBR(1)507; DBR(2)651; DBR(3)607

    Katherine - of MA, d1659, m(1) Thomas Gray, m(2)1610 Rowland Coytemore - the immigrant FLW164; sufficient proof of alleged royal ancestry is lacking

    Nicholas - of MD, d1728/1729, m Elizabeth Heard - desc/o George Beckwith DBR(1)222; DBR(2)314; DBR(3)603; DBR(4)335

    Nicholas - of MD, d1768 - desc/o George Beckwith DBR(1)222; DBR(2)314; DBR(3)603; DBR(4)335

    Nicholas - of MD, d1785, m Anastasia____ - desc/o George Beckwith DBR(1)222; DBR(2)314; DBR(3)603; DBR(4)335

    Richard Henry - m Jane Gardiner - desc/o George Beckwith DBR(1)507; DBR(2)651; DBR(3)607

MILLER Ebenezer - b1692, m Elizabeth Smith - desc/o John Leonard LDS35

    Elizabeth - bp 1756, m Hugh Johns - desc/o John Leonard LDS35

    Hannah - of MA, m Joseph Hall - desc/o Herbert Pelham MCD321

    Hannah - of MA, b abt 1776 d1851, m1805 Ephraim Macomber - desc/o Frances Deighton ECD159

    Lillias - of VA, m Patrick Stewart - desc/o Lieut Col Walter Aston MCD160

    Reuben - b1727, m Elizabeth Thrall - desc/o John Leonard LDS35

    Samuel - m____Belcher - the immigrant EDV97; Royal descent not proven

MILLS Abigail Elizabeth Ann - of CT, b1756 d1831, m1776 Ephraim Wooster b1755 d1838 a sergeant in the CT militia during the Revolutionary War - desc/o Elizabeth Alsop ECD(2)20; DBR(5)924

MILLS (cont.)

Ann - of VA, m Thomas Jackson - desc/o William Clopton DBR(5)657

Elizabeth - m David Anderson son of Robert Anderson and Mary (Overton) Anderson - desc/o William Clopton DBR(1)517

Faith Ann - b1765, m Roswell Spencer - desc/o Thomas Holcomb LDS96 - desc/o John Drake RAA87

Thomas Delaun - b1770/1771 - desc/o Thomas Newberry RAA118

MINER Amy - of CT, b1768 d1831, m1789 Ezra Gillett Sr - desc/o Mary Wentworth ECD(2)301

Clement - of MA, bp 1638 d1700, m(1)1662 Grace (or Frances) Burcham - desc/o Capt Thomas Miner JSW1845

David - of CT, b1737 d1799, m1761 Amy Smith - desc/o Mary Wentworth ECD(2)301

Elisha - chr 1745, m Anna Smith - desc/o John Miner LDS78

Ephraim - of MA, b1642 d1724, m Hannah Avery - desc/o Capt Thomas Miner JSW1884

Ephraim - b1675, m Rebecca Curtis - desc/o John Miner LDS78

Hannah - of MA, b1671 d1692, m Samuel Frink - desc/o Capt Thomas Miner JSW1884

Hannah - of CT, b1731 d1813, m1751 Constant Searle(s) - desc/o Dorothy Thompson ECD(2)153; DBR(1)340, 594; DBR(2)442; DBR(3)239; DBR(5)187, 797

Jehu - b1705, m Mary Judson - desc/o John Miner LDS78

Capt John - of VA, b1635, m Elizabeth Booth - desc/o Capt Thomas Miner JSW1876

John - of VA, b1747 d1835, m(2)1767 Cassander Williams - desc/o Capt Thomas Miner JSW1845, 1846

Lovisa - b1776, m Thaddeus Pond - desc/o John Miner LDS78

Stephen - of MA & VA, b1706, m1732 Athalia Updike - desc/o Capt Thomas Miner JSW1845

Capt Thomas - of MA, b1608 d1690, m1634 Grace Palmer - the immigrant JSW1845, 1876, 1884; EDV35; sufficient proof of alleged royal ancestry is lacking

William - of MA, b1670 d1725, m1691 Sarah (Anne) Beckwith - desc/o Capt Thomas Miner JSW1840, 1845

MINOR Grace - of CT, b1670 d1753, m Samuel Grant - desc/o Richard Booth J&K130, 288; JSW1879; PFA Apx C #9, Apx D #5

MINTER Mackarness - d1837, m Rebecca Minter - desc/o John Goode DBR(1)89

MITCHELL Dr Alexander - of VA, m Elizabeth Kearsley - the immigrant AFA66; sufficient proof of alleged royal ancestry is lacking

George Calvert - of NY, b1772 d1825/1826 - desc/o Anne Arundel ECD148; ECD(2)77; DBR(1)152; DBR(2)237; DBR(3)244

Henry - of VA, d1771, m Priscilla___ - desc/o Christopher Branch GVFWM(1)422

Gen Henry - of VA & GA, m Frances Hobbs - desc/o Christopher Branch GVFWM(1)422

Nathaniel - of VA, d1771, m Elizabeth___ - desc/o Christopher Branch GVFWM(1)422

Thomas - of VA, d1761/1762, m Amy Goodwynne dau/o John Goodwynne & Winifred Tucker - desc/o Christopher Branch

MITCHELL (cont.)
GVFWM(1)422
Thomas - of VA & GA, m Ann Raines dau/o Captain Nathaniel Raines
of Prince George Co, VA - desc/o Christopher Branch
GVFWM(1)422
MOALE Elizabeth - of MD, b1759 d1822, m1794 Richard Curson Jr, of
Baltimore, son of Richard Curson & had issue - desc/o Anne
Lovelace GVFHB(3)358
John - of MD, b1761 d1809, m1790 Lucy Morton & had issue one
daughter Ellin Moale who, m John B Bernabue eldest son of
Chevalier Bernabue - desc/o Anne Lovelace GVFHB(3)358
Rebecca - of MD, b1763 d1840, m1780 Thomas Russell - desc/o Anne
Lovelace GVFHB(3)358
Richard - of MD, b1765 d1802, m1797 Judith Carter Armistead b1774
d1863 dau/o William Armistead of Hess, Gloucester (now Mathews)
Co, VA & Maria Carter & left issue - desc/o Anne Lovelace
GVFHB(3)358, 359
Robert - of MD, b1771 d1852, m1801 Frances Owings & left one
daughter Ellin North Moale who, m George Howard Elder of
Baltimore Co - desc/o Anne Lovelace GVFHB(3)359
Samuel - of MD, b1773 d1857, m(1) Ann M Howard dau/o Samuel H
Howard of Annapolis, m(2) Anne G White dau/o Abraham White of
Baltimore & left issue by both wives - desc/o Anne Lovelace
GVFHB(3)359
Thomas - of MD, b1766 d1822, m1793 Eleanor Owings & left issue -
desc/o AnneLovelace GVFHB(3)359
MOLESWORTH Richard - m Catherine Cobb - desc/o Richard Coote
GBR207
William - m Anne Adair - desc/o Richard Coote GBR207
MONCKTON Robert - of NY, b1726 d1782 unmarried, governor of New
York, British commander in America during the French & Indian
Wars, son of John, 1st Viscount Galway & Elizabeth (Manners)
Monckton - the immigrant GBR40
MONCURE Anne - of VA, b1748, m1775 Walker Conway - desc/o Col
Gerard Fowke VG428
Frances - of VA, b1745 Dipple, Strafford Co, m1762 Travers Daniel -
desc/o Col Gerard Fowke VG428
Jean - of VA, b1753 Clermont d1823 Richmond, m abt 1775 General
James Wood b1750 d1813 at Olney, near Richmond, governor of
Virginia 1796/1799, son of Col James & Comfort Wood of Frederick
Co - desc/o Col Gerard Fowke VG428
John - of VA, b1746/1747 Dipple, Stafford Co, m abt 1770 Anne
Conway b abt 1750 dau/o George Conway & Anne Heath - desc/o
Col Gerard Fowke VG428
John - of VA, b1772 Dipple, Strafford Co d1822 justice of Stafford Co
1796 & sheriff 1798, m1792 Alice Peachy Gaskins b abt 1774
d1860 dau/o Col Thomas Gaskins & Hannah Hull of Wicomico,
Northumberland VA - desc/o Col Gerard Fowke VG428
William - of VA, b1774 Clermont d1832 Windsor Forest, Stafford Co,
m179_ Sarah Elizabeth Henry dau/o James Henry of Fleet's Bay,
Northumberland & Sarah Scarborough dau/o Col Edmund

MONCURE (cont.)
   Scarborough of Seaside, Accomack Co - desc/o Col Gerard Fowke
      VG428, 438
MONROE Andrew - of VA 1668, d1668, m1652 Elizabeth Alexander - the
      immigrant J&K140; PFA154, Apx C #4; not of royal descent
   Andrew 2nd - of VA, d1714 - desc/o Andrew Monroe J&K140
   Andrew - of VA, d1735, m Christian Tyler - desc/o Andrew Monroe
      PFA154, Apx C #4
   Sheriff Andrew - of VA, d1770 - desc/o Andrew Monroe J&K140
   Andrew - of VA, d1836, m1789 Ann Bell - desc/o Andrew Monroe
      PFA157
   Elizabeth - of VA, b1754, m William Buckner - desc/o Andrew Monroe
      PFA157
   Pres James of VA, b1759 d1831 President of the United States
      1817/1825, m1786 Elizabeth Kortright - desc/o Andrew Monroe
      J&K140; PFA154, Apx C #4
   Joseph Jones - of VA, b1764 d1824, m(1)1790 Elizabeth Kerr,
      m(2)1801 Sarah Gordon, m(3)1808 Elizabeth Glasscock - desc/o
      Andrew Monroe PFA157
   Spence - of VA, d1774, m1752 Elizabeth Jones - desc/o Andrew
      Monroe J&K140; PFA154, Apx C #4
   William - of VA, b1666 d1737, m1689 Margaret Bowcock - desc/o
      Andrew Monroe PFA154, Apx C #4
MONTAGNE Ann - of VA, m John Jadwin - desc/o Peter Montagne
      WAC87
   Elizabeth - of VA - desc/o Peter Montagne WAC87
   Ellen - of VA, b abt 1633, m1659 William Thompson - desc/o Peter
      Montagne WAC87; FFF80
   Hannah - of NY, b1737, m1755 Morris Earle - desc/o Obadiah Bruen
      CHB386; MCB318; MCD172
   Margaret - of VA - desc/o Peter Montagne WAC87
   Peter - of VA, b1603 d1659, m1633 Cicely____ - the immigrant
      WAC87; FFF80c; NE(141)106, 107 further investigations into the
      correct descent or into other forebears of this family may disclose
      an alternative royal line
   Peter - of VA - desc/o Peter Montagne WAC87
   Peter - b abt 1651 - the immigrant RAA115; sufficient proof of alleged
      royal ancestry is lacking
   William - of VA - desc/o Peter Montagne WAC87
MONTAGU Charles Greville Baron - of SC, governor of South Carolina,
      son of Robert, 3rd Duke of Manchester & Harriet (Dunch) Montagu,
      m Elizabeth Bulmer - the immigrant GBR46
   Grace - dau/o Edward & Elizabeth (Pelham) Montagu, m William
      Cosby b abt 1690 d1735/1736 governor of New York & NJ - the
      immigrant GBR38
   Lady Mary - of NY, dau/o George, 1st Earl of Halifax & Mary (Lumley)
      Halifax, m Sir Danvers Osborne, 3rd Baronet & governor of New
      York - the immigrant GBR33
MONTFORT Clarissa - m John Shellman Jr - desc/o Col Walter Aston
      GBR361

MONTGOMERY Alexander - of PA, b1735 d1798, m Eunia West - desc/o William Montgomery CHB240; BCD240

Hugh - of NJ - the immigrant EDV17; sufficient proof of alleged royal ancestry is lacking

James - of NJ, m Mary____ - desc/o William Montgomery CHB240; BCD240

James - of NJ, b1720 d1760, m1746 Esther Wood - desc/o William Montgomery CHB240; MCD259; BCD240

Robert - of NJ, b1687 d1766, m1710 Sarah Stacy - desc/o William Montgomery CHB240; MCD259; BCD239, 240

Thomas West MD - of NY, b1764 d1820, m1788 Mary Berrien - desc/o William Montgomery CHB240; BCD240

William - of NJ 1706, son of Hugh Montgomery of Brigend & Katharine Scott, m1684 Isabel Burnett dau/o Robert Burnett & Mrs ____Forbes Burnett of NJ - the immigrant CHB239; MCB144; MCD259; BCD239; GBR96

William - of PA, b1752 d1831, m1781 Rachel Henry - desc/o William Montgomery CHB240; MCD259; BCD240

MOODY Caleb - of MA, m Ruth Morse - desc/o Capt Thomas Bradbury J&K167

Joshua - of MA, b1671, m1696 Mary Greenlief - desc/o Capt Thomas Bradbury DBR(2)775; DBR(3)99

Judith - of MA, b1705, m1725/1726 Lieut George Knight - desc/o Capt Thomas Bradbury DBR(2)775; DBR(3)100

Mary - of MA, m Rev Joseph Emerson - desc/o Capt Thomas Bradbury J&K164

Rebecca - b1766 - desc/o Griffith Bowen RAA72

Rev Samuel - of MA, b1676 d1745 chaplain of the MA forces at the reduction of Louisburg 1745, m Hannah Sewall - desc/o Capt Thomas Bradbury J&K164

Sarah - b1695 - desc/o Thomas Bradbury RAA72

Thomas - b1668 - desc/o Thomas Bradbury RAA72

MOORE (MORE) Abigail - m Mr____Gilman - desc/o Gov Thomas Dudley NE(8)324

Alexander Spotswood - of VA, b1763, m1787 Elizabeth Aylett dau/o Col William Aylett of Fairfield, King & Queen Co, VA & left descendants - desc/o Maj Gen Alexander Spotswood CHB292; BCD292 - desc/o Anne Lovelace GVFHB(3)350

Andrew - b1719 d17174, m1751 Dorothy Sweat - desc/o Gov Thomas Dudley NE(8)324

Andrew Leiper - m Ann Fitzhugh - desc/o Maj Gen Alexander Spotswood CHB293

Ann Dandridge - of VA, m George Redd - desc/o Col John West DBR(2)843

Anna - m Joseph Jewett - desc/o Gov Thomas Dudley NE(8)324

Anne Butler - of VA, m prior to 1771 Charles Carter of Shirley - desc/o Anne Lovelace GVFHB(3)349

Augustine - of VA, d1777 burgess from King & Queen Co, VA, m Sarah Rind & left descendants - desc/o Anne Lovelace GVFHB(3)349

Bernard - of VA, m(1) Lucy Ann Hebbred Leiper dau/o Dr James Hamilton Leiper of Chester Co, Pennsylvania & Elizabeth

MOORE (MORE) (cont.)

Smallwood & left issue - desc/o Maj Gen Alexander Spotswood CHB293; BCD293 - desc/o Anne Lovelace GVFHB(3)349

Bernard - of VA, b abt 1720 justice of King William Co, colonel of militia, member of the House of Burgesses & House of Delegates, m abt 1741 Anne Catherine Spotswood b1725 d1802 dau/o Governor Alexander Spotswood - desc/o Col William Bernard APP121, 122 - desc/o Anne Lovelace GVFHB(3)348, 349

Coffin - a physician, m____ & had issue - desc/o Gov Thomas Dudley NE(8)324

Deborah - of MD, b1705 d1751 island of Madeira, m1720/1721 South River, Maryland, Dr Richard Hill b1698 South River, Maryland d1762 Philadelphia, studied medicine, practiced at his native place for some years, & also engaged in the shipping trade, son of Henry Hill of Maryland & Mary Denwood dau/o Levin Denwood - desc/o Thomas Lloyd CHB122; MCD251; BCD122; AFA74; CRFP(1)43

Elizabeth - of VA, b abt 1716 d1779, m(1) Lyonell Lyde d1737/1738 son of Cornelius Lyde of King William Co, VA, m(2) Col James Mason b1721 d1768 justice & sheriff of King William Co, VA - desc/o Col William Bernard APP121 - desc/o Anne Lovelace GVFHB(3)343

Elizabeth - of NY, m Content Titus - desc/o Edward Howell AFA50

Elizabeth - of VA, d1809, m abt 1764 Dr John Walker d1809 of Belvoir, Albemarle Co, VA & left descendants - desc/o Anne Lovelace GVFHB(3)349

Hannah - of CT, d1686, m1648 John Drake - desc/o Thomas Moore THC220

Hannah - of MD, d1805, m Hugh Roberts - desc/o Thomas Lloyd CHB127; BCD127

John - of VA, m (his cousin) Anna Dandridge & left descendants - desc/o Anne Lovelace GVFHB(3)349

Lucy - of VA, b abt 1720 d abt 1759, m abt 1737 Hon John Robinson b1704/1705 d1766 of King & Queen Co, Speaker of the House of Burgesses & treasurer of Virginia 1738/1765 - desc/o Col William Bernard APP121 - desc/o Anne Lovelace GVFHB(3)347

Lucy - of VA, m 1774 Rev Henry Skyren & left descendants - desc/o Maj Gen Alexander Spotswood CHB292; BCD292 - desc/o Anne Lovelace GVFHB(3)350

Martha - b1682 - desc/o Agnes Harris RAA131

Mary - m Gideon Colcord - desc/o Gov Thomas Dudley NE(8)324

Mary - m Mr____Perkins - desc/o Gov Thomas Dudley NE(8)324

Peter - m Mary Norris - desc/o Gov Thomas Dudley NE(8)324

Richard - of MA, bp 1614 d abt 1697 a passenger on the *Mayflower*, son of Samuel More & Katherine More, m(1)1636 Christian Hunt(er?), m(2) Mrs Jane____Crumpton - the immigrant ECD(3)212; GBR350 some aspect of royal descent merits further study; NE(114)163/168, (124)85/87; EO2(2)763/770

Richard - of MD, d1760, m Mary West - desc/o Thomas Lloyd CHB127; BCD127

Sarah - m Mr____Hill - desc/o Gov Thomas Dudley NE(8)324

Susanna - of MA, bp 1652 d aft 1728, m abt 1676 Samuel Dutch -

MOORE (MORE) (cont.)

desc/o Richard More ECD(3)212

Sybil - b1717, m Isaac Ward - desc/o Deacon Edmund Rice LDS114

Taffenia - of VA, b1769 d1830, m William Hudson d1831 - desc/o Christopher Branch DBR(1)607

Thomas - of CT, d1645 - the immigrant THC220; sufficient proof of alleged royal ancestry is lacking

Thomas - of VA, d1796/1797, colonel of militia & justice of King William Co, m Joanna____d1801 - desc/o Col William Bernard APP122 - desc/o Anne Lovelace GVFHB(3)350

William - m Abigail Gilman dau/o Maj John Gilman - desc/o Gov Thomas Dudley NE(8)324

MOORES Margaret - of NJ, m Samuel Carman - desc/o Edward FitzRandolph AFA46

MORGAN Anna - of CT, b abt 1751 d aft 1824, m1770 Rev Aaron Kinne - desc/o Susannah Palmes ECD(3)185

Charles - of VA & KY, b abt 1745 - desc/o Col Moore Fauntleroy DBR(4)408

Christopher of CT, m1768 Deborah Ledyard - desc/o Anna Lloyd CHB74; BCD74

David - b1700 - desc/o Olive Welby RAA93

Dorothy - b1676 - desc/o Alice Freeman RAA132

Elisha - m Abigail Morgan - desc/o Susan Clinton CHB417

Isaac - b1730 - desc/o Olive Welby RAA93

John - of PA, son of James Morgan & Jane____, m Sarah Evans dau/o John & Mary (Hughes) Evans - the immigrant GBR405

Mary - b1755 - desc/o Olive Welby RAA93 - desc/o Alice Freeman RAA132

Samuel II - of NJ b bef 1739 d1773, m Elizabeth (Garrison ?) - desc/o Dorothea Scott ECD(2)240

Samuel III - of NJ, b1762 d1831, m1788 Rebecca Richmond - desc/o Dorothea Scott ECD(2)241

William - of CT, m1716 Mary Avery - desc/o Anna Lloyd CHB74; BCD74

William Jr - of CT, m1744 Temperance Avery - desc/o Anna Lloyd CHB74; BCD74

MORRILL Sarah - b1696, m1718 Benjamin Eaton - desc/o Capt Thomas Bradbury JSW1801; RAA72

MORRIS Anna - m Edward Antill - desc/o Col Lewis Morris CFA376

Anthony - of NJ & PA, b1654 d1721, m(1)1675 Mary Jones, m(2)1689 Agnes____, m(3)1694 Mary____, m(4)1700 Elizabeth Watson - the immigrant AFA48; BLG2832

Anthony - of PA, b1681/1682 d1763, m 1704 Phebe Guest - desc/o Anthony Morris AFA48; BLG2832

Anthony - of PA, b1705 d1780, m(1)1730 Sarah Powell, m(2)1752 Elizabeth Hudson - desc/o Anthony Morris AFA48; BLG2832

Maj Anthony - b1738 d1777 - desc/o Anthony Morris BLG2832

Anthony - b1766 d1860, m1790 Mary Smith Pemberton - desc/o Anthony Morris BLG2833

Anthony Cadwalader - of PA, d1798, m1770 Mary Jones - desc/o John Cadwalader CHB49

MORRIS (cont.)

Benjamin Wistar - of PA, b1762 d1825, m1785 Mary Wells - desc/o Anthony Morris BLG2833

Caspar Wistar - b1764 d1828, m1795 Elizabeth Giles - desc/o Anthony Morris BLG2833

Catharine - m 1778 Thomas Lawrence - desc/o Col Lewis Morris CFA376

Deborah - b1736 d1787, m1756 John Franklin - desc/o Anthony Morris BLG2832

Deborah - of PA, b1760 d1822, m(1)1789 Benjamin Smith, m(2)1809 Isaac Collins, of Trenton, NJ, printer - desc/o Thomas Lloyd CRFP(1)45

Edward - b1688 - desc/o Griffith Bowen RAA72

Elizabeth - b1697, m(1)1716 Samuel Lewis, m(2) William Dury - desc/o Anthony Morris BLG2832

Elizabeth - b1716, m1739 Benjamin Shoemaker - desc/o Anthony Morris BLG2832

Elizabeth - m Col Anthony White - desc/o Col Lewis Morris CFA376

Ellen - of PA, dau/o John Morris & Eleanor Williams, m Cadwalader Evans of PA - the immigrant GBR309

Eunice - b1728/1729 - desc/o Griffith Bowen RAA72

Euphemia - m Capt Matthew Norris - desc/o Col Lewis Morris CFA376

Gouverneur - b1752 d1794 - desc/o Col Lewis Morris CFA376

Gulielma Maria - of PA, b1766 d1826, m1784 John Smith Jr - desc/o Thomas Lloyd CHB123; BCD123; CRFP(1)45

Hannah - m 1771 Jacob Evans - desc/o Anne Mauleverer AFA238

Hannah - of PA, d1832, m1791 Nathaniel Mitchell - desc/o John Cadwalader CHB49

Isaac - of PA, b1701 d aft 1755 - desc/o Anthony Morris BLG2832

Isaac Wistar - b1770 d1831, m1795 Sarah Paschall - desc/o Anthony Morris BLG2833

Israel - b1705 d1729 - desc/o Anthony Morris BLG2832

Israel - b1741 d1806, m Mary Harrison - desc/o Anthony Morris BLG2832

Jacob - of NY, m Mary Cox - desc/o Col Lewis Morris CFA376

James - b1688, m1709 Margaret Cook - desc/o Anthony Morris BLG2832

James - b1707 d1750, m1734 Elizabeth Kearney - desc/o Anthony Morris BLG2832

James - of NY, m Helen Van Cortlandt - desc/o Col Lewis Morris CFA377

John - b1709 d1782, m1734 Mary Sutton - desc/o Anthony Morris BLG2832

Dr John - of PA, b1759 Philadelphia d1793, m1783 Abigail Dorsey dau/o Benedict & Sarah Dorsey of Philadelphia - desc/o Thomas Lloyd CHB122; MCD251; BCD122; AFA74; CRFP(1)45, 46

Joseph - b1715 d1785, m(1)1741 Martha Fitzwater, m(2)1765 Hannah Mickle - desc/o Anthony Morris BLG2832

Col Lewis - of NY 1697, b1671 d1746, m Isabella Graham - the immigrant EDV14; CFA375; sufficient proof of alleged royal ancestry is lacking

MORRIS (cont.)

Lewis - of NJ, b1698, m(1)1723 Katrintje Staats, m(2)1746 Sarah Gouverneur - desc/o Col William Lewis CFA375, 376

Lewis - b1726, m1749 Mary Walton - desc/o Col Lewis Morris CFA376

Lewis - m Ann Elliott - desc/o Col Lewis Morris CFA376

Luke - b1707 d1793, m1749 Mary Richards - desc/o Anthony Morris BLG2832

Luke - b1760 d1802, m1786 Ann Willing - desc/o Anthony Morris BLG2833

Luke Wistar - b1768 d1830, m(1)1791 Elizabeth Morris Buckley, m(2)1800 Ann Pancoast BLG2833

Magdalena (or Helena) - m John Rutherford - desc/o Col Lewis Morris CFA376

Mary - m Capt Vincent Pearse - desc/o Col Lewis Morris CFA375

Mary - b1713 d1759, m1732 Samuel Powell - desc/o Anthony Morris BLG2832

Mary - b1724, m1743 Thomas Lawrence - desc/o Col Lewis Morris CFA376

Mary - d1776, m1775 Thomas Lawrence - desc/o Col Lewis Morris CFA376

Capt Richard - of NY, d1672, m1669 Sarah Pole - the immigrant DBR(1)321; BLG2831 sufficient proof of alleged royal ancestry is lacking

Richard - m Sarah Ludlow - desc/o Col Lewis Morris CFA376

Gen (Judge) Richard - desc/o Sarah Ludlow DBR(1)321

Richard Hill - of PA, b1762 d1841, m(1)1786 Mary Mifflin, m(2)1798 Mary Smith - desc/o Thomas Lloyd CHB123; BCD123; CRFP(1)45

Richard Valentine - b1768 d1815, m1797 Anne Walton - desc/o Col Lewis Morris CFA377

Samuel - b1711 d1782, m1737 Hannah Cadwallader - desc/o Anthony Morris BLG2832

Samuel - of PA, b1734 d1812, m1755 Rebecca Wistar - desc/o Anthony Morris AFA48; BLG2833

Sarah - b1743 d1830, m1771 William Buckley - desc/o Anthony Morris BLG2832

Sarah - b1758 d1831, m1782 Richard Wistar - desc/o Anthony Morris BLG2833

Staats - m Catalina Van Braem - desc/o Col Lewis Morris CFA377

Thomas - b1745 d1808, m1768 Mary Saunders - desc/o Anthony Morris BLG2832

William - b1695 d1776, m(1)1718 Sarah Dury, m(2) Rebecca Cadwallader - desc/o Anthony Morris BLG2832

William - m Sarah Carpenter - desc/o Col Lewis Morris CFA376

William Hudson - b1753 d1807, m1776 Sarah Warder - desc/o Anthony Morris BLG2833

MORRISON Abigail - of NH, b abt 1720 d1790, m1743 Israel Gilman - desc/o Capt Thomas Bradbury DBR(3)153

Ann or Anna - of CT, b1693 d1773, m1714 Dr Ebenezer Talman - desc/o Anna Lloyd J&K321; ECD(3)193

MORSE Bethia - of MA, m John Perry - desc/o Anthony Fisher AFA104

MORTON Abraham - b1676 - desc/o George Morton RAA116

Abraham - b1762, m Phebe Langford - desc/o John Leonard LDS70; RAA116

Benjamin - b1739, m Mary Dexter - desc/o John Leonard LDS70; RAA116

Charles - of MA, b abt 1627 d1698, Puritan clergyman & schoolmaster, son of Nicholas Morton & Frances Kestell, m Joan___ - the immigrant GBR419

Daniel - b1720 - desc/o George Morton RAA116

Deborah - m 1687 Francis Coombs - desc/o George Morton AMB119

Deborah - b1698, m Caleb Stetson - desc/o George Morton AMB119

Deborah - of MA, b1730, m1749 Ichabod Morton - desc/o George Morton AMB119

Ebenezer - of MA, b1696 d1750, m1720 Mercy Foster - desc/o George Morton AMB119

Ebenezer - of MA, b1726 d1775, m1753 Sarah Cobb - desc/o George Morton AMB119

Eleazer - of MA, b1659, m1691 Rebecca Dawes Marshall - desc/o George Morton BLG2835

Elizabeth - b1680 - desc/o George Morton RAA116

Elizabeth - of VA, b1754 d1828, m abt 1772 John Minor Daniel - desc/o Col Walter Aston DBR(2)324, 849; DBR(3)508

Lieut Ephriham - of MA, b1623 d1693, m(1)1644 Ann Cooper, m(2)1692 Mary Shelley - desc/o George Morton BLG2835; AMB118

George - of MA, b1585 d1624, m1612 Julianna Carpenter - the immigrant BLG2835; AMB118; RAA1, 116; sufficient proof of alleged royal ancestry is lacking

Hannah - m 1666 John Fuller - desc/o George Morton AMB119

Hannah - b1694, m John Cook - desc/o George Morton AMB119

Hannah - of MA, b1728, m1748 Abishai Washburn - desc/o George Morton AMB119

Icabod - of MA, b1726 d1809, m1749 Deborah Morton - desc/o George Morton BLG2835

Joanna - of MA, b1682, m1705 Elisha Vaughan - desc/o George Morton 119

John - of MA, b1616 d1673, m1648 Lettice Hanford - desc/o George Morton AMB118

John - of MA, b1650 d1718, m(1)1680 Phebe Shaw, m(2)1687 Mary Ring - desc/o George Morton AMB119

Livy - of MA, b1760 d1838, m(1)1788 Hannah Dailey, m(2)1808 Catherine Richmond - desc/o George Morton AMB120

Lucia - of MA, b1738, m1755 Dr Samuel Clark - desc/o George Morton AMB119

Mary - b1698, m1711 Joseph Hall - desc/o George Morton AMB119

Mary - of MA, b1723, m(1)1743 Ebenezer Spooner, m(2)1778 Capt Jonathan Ingell - desc/o George Morton AMB119

Mercy - of MA, b1722, m1737 Zachary Eddy - desc/o George Morton AMB119

Mercy - b1751 - desc/o George Morton RAA116

Mordicai - of MA, b1773, m Priscilla Bennett - desc/o George Morton BLG2835

MORTON (cont.)

Nathaniel - of MA, b1613, m(1)1635 Lydia Cooper, m(2)1674 Ann Pritchard - desc/o George Morton AMB118; RAA116

Nathaniel - of MA, b1695 d1727, m Rebecca Clark - desc/o George Morton BLG2835.

Patience - of MA, b1615, m1633 John Faunce - desc/o George Morton AMB118; RAA116

Phebe - b1685, m1719 John Murdock - desc/o George Morton AMB118

Phebe - of MA, b1758 d1839, m1782 Samuel Wood - desc/o George Morton AMB119

Priscilla - of MA, b1763 d1847, m1789 Seth Morton - desc/o George Morton AMB119

Remember - b1637 - desc/o George Morton RAA116

Richard - b1640/1649 - desc/o George Morton RAA116

Richard - b1704 - desc/o George Morton RAA116

Sarah - of MA, b1618, m1644 George Bonum - desc/o George Morton AMB118; RAA116

Sarah - of MA, b1734, m1769 John Barrows - desc/o George Morton AMB119

Col William - of VA, d1820, m1764 Susanna Watkins - desc/o Col Richard Cocke DBR(2)432

MORYSON Charles - of VA, m Rebecca Yeo - desc/o Maj Richard Moryson WAC49

Francis - of VA, deputy & acting governor of Virginia, son of Sir Richard Moryson & Elizabeth Harington, m____ - the immigrant GBR262

Maj Richard - of VA, d1648 - the immigrant WAC49; sufficient proof of alleged royal ancestry is lacking

MOSELEY Abigail - m John Lyman III - desc/o Margaret Wyatt GBR397

Abigail - of CT, m Rev Thomas Potwin - desc/o Margaret Wyatt MCD157

Abner - of CT - desc/o Margaret Wyatt MCD157

Benjamin - of MA - the immigrant ECD(3)217; sufficient proof of alleged royal ancestry is lacking

David - of MA, b1705 d1768, m1729 Margaret Dewey b1706 d1762 - desc/o Margaret Wyatt EDC106; DBR(1)336

Edward - of VA, b1661 d1736, m____Stringer - desc/o William Moseley WAC57

Edward Hack - of VA - desc/o William Moseley WAC57

Grace - of MA, b1739, m1761 Dr Samuel Mather b1737 d1808 - desc/o Margaret Wyatt EDC106; DBR(1)336, 337

Hillary - of VA, d1730, m Hannah____ - desc/o William Moseley WAC57

Joseph - of MA, b1670 d1719, m1696 Abigail Root b1680 dau/o Thomas Root - desc/o Margaret Wyatt ECD106; MCD157; DBR(1)336; DBR(2)721; GBR397 - desc/o Benjamin Moseley ECD(3)217

Mary - (sister of Joseph), m Eleazer Weller Jr - desc/o Margaret Wyatt GBR397

Mary Gookin - m(2)1672 Lieut Col Anthony Lawson - desc/o William

MOSELEY (cont.)

Moseley WAC57

Rachel - of MA, b1715 d1797, m1736 Daniel Pomeroy - desc/o Benjamin Moseley ECD(3)217 - desc/o Margaret Wyatt DBR(2)721

Sophia - of MA, b1773 d1821, m John Abbot - desc/o Richard Lyman BCD151

William - of VA, d1655, m Susanna____ - the immigrant WAC57; sufficient proof of alleged royal ancestry is lacking

William - of VA, d abt 1671, m Mary Gookin - desc/o William Moseley WAC57

MOTIER Marie Joseph Paul Yves Roch Gilbert, Marquis de La Fayette (Lafayette) - b1757 d1834 American revolutionary general & French statesman, son of Michel Louis Christophe Roch Gilbert Motier, Marquis de La Fayette & Marie Louise Julie de La Riviere, m Marie Adrienne Francoise de Noailles - the immigrant GBR64

MOUNTFORT Edmund - of MA 1656 - the immigrant EDV106, 107; sufficient proof of alleged royal ancestry is lacking

MUMFORD Elizabeth - b1769 d1843, m Col Richmond Pearson - desc/o Grace Kaye DBR(5)609

Henry - b1769, m Sarah Thompson - desc/o John Drake LDS23; RAA87

Robinson - m 1761 Sarah Coit - desc/o Grace Kaye DBR(5)609

Thomas III - of CT 1720, b1687 d1760, m1704/1705 Hannah Remington - the immigrant FFF67; sufficient proof of alleged royal ancestry is lacking

Thomas IV - of CT, b1706 d1750, m1727 Abigail Chesebrough - desc/o Thomas Mumford III FFF67

Thomas - of CT, b1770, m1795 Mary Sheldon Smith - desc/o Grace Kaye CHB207; BCD207

MUNFORD or MONTFORT Robert - m Anne Brodnax - desc/o Col Walter Aston GBR361

MUNRO Rev Andrew - of VA, son of David Munro of Katewell & Agnes Munro of Durness, m Mrs Sarah Smith Pitt - the immigrant & brother of Rev John Munro GBR89

Rev John - of VA, son of David Munro of Katewell & Agnes Munro of Durness, m Christian Blair - the immigrant GBR89

Mary - of VA, m John Blair (her 1st cousin) - desc/o Rev John Munro GBR89

MUNROE Rev Henry - the immigrant 1757 EDV38; sufficient proof of alleged royal ancestry is lacking

MUNSELL Jacob - of CT, b abt 1690 d1741, m(1)1713 Sarah Calkins, m(2)1718 Phebe Loomis - the immigrant EDV38; CRL(1)167; sufficient proof of alleged royal ancestry is lacking

Robert - of VA 1621 - the immigrant EDV38; sufficient proof of alleged royal ancestry is lacking

MURDOCK Hannah - b1726, m Moses Hibbard - desc/o William Troop LDS25

Janet - of MA, b1711 d bef 1759, m1740 Stephen Tilson - desc/o Mary Wentworth ECD(2)302; FFF90

MURRAY Barbara - of NC, dau/o John of Unthank & Anne (Bennet) Murray, m Thomas Clarke - the immigrant GBR67

MURRAY (cont.)

James - of NC & MA, son of John of Unthank & Anne (Bennet) Murray, m Barbara Bennet - the immigrant GBR66

John, 4th Earl of Dunmore - of NY & VA, b1730 Taymouth, Perthshire, Scotland d1809 Ramsgate, England, governor of New York 1770 & Virginia, eldest son of William Murray, 3rd Earl of Dunmore & Catherine Murray, m1759 Lady Charlotte Stewart dau/o Alexander Stewart, 6th Earl of Galloway & Catherine Cochrane, by whom he had eight children - the immigrant GBR18; NYGBR(40)#4p225/228

John Boyles - of New York, son of John & Mary (Boyles) Murray, m Martha McClenachan - the immigrant GBR67; NYGBR(5)#4p187

MYLES Rev Samuel - of MA - desc/o Anne Humphrey FLW189

MYRICK Rebecca - b1725 d1800, m Nicholas Hathaway - desc/o Frances Deighton AWW339

Ruth - b abt 1712 - desc/o Edward Southworth RAA131

– N –

NANFAN Catherine - dau/o Bridges & Catherine (Hastings) Nanfan, m Richard Coote, 1st Earl of Bellomont b1636 d1701, governor of New York, MA, & New Hampshire - the immigrant GBR35

NEALE Anne - of MD, b1707 d1773, m1730 James Thompson - desc/o Rev Robert Brooke DBR(2)375

Lieut Anthony - of MD, b1659 d1723, m(1) Elizabeth Roswell - desc/o Capt James Neale DBR(5)977

Dorothy - of MD, naturalized 1666, m Roger Brooke son of Governor Robert Brooke - desc/o Capt James Neale DBR(5)884

Edward - of MD, b1700 d1760, m(1) Mary Lowe - desc/o Dudley Diggs ECD(3)120; DBR(5)986

Henrietta Marie Gill - b1647 - desc/o James Neale RAA117

Henry - of MD, d1767, m Mary Gardiner - desc/o Capt James Neale DBR(5)977

Col Henry - of MD, d1816, m(1) Margaret Brent Plowden, m(2) Eleanor Hammersley - desc/o Capt James Neale DBR(5)977

Capt James - of MD 1636/1637, b1615 d1684, Provincial Council & commissioner of the treasury 1643, special agent to Duke of York in Portugal and Spain, agent of Lord Baltimore in Amsterdam, councillor and burgess for Charles Co Maryland, m Anne Gill - the immigrant DBR(5)884, 918, 977, 1062, 1063; RAA1, 117; GBR375

Martha - of MD, b1737 d1789, m Francis Hall - desc/o Dudley Diggs ECD(3)120; DBR(5)986

Mary - of MD, b1683 d173_, m(1)1702 Charles Egerton Jr d1703, m(2)1707 Jeremiah Adderton d1713, m(3)1718 Joseph van Swearingen d1721, m(4)1726 William Deacon - desc/o Leonard Calvert MG(1)145

Roswell - of MD, m(1) Mary Brent - desc/o Capt James Neale DBR(5)977

William - of MD, b1666 d aft 1696 in St Mary's Co, Maryland - desc/o Leonard Calvert MG(1)145

NEGUS Capt Isaac - of MA, b1650 d1700, m1679 Hannah Andrews - desc/o Jane Deighton ECD(3)114

Isaac Jr - of MA, b abt 1685 d1718, m Hannah____ - desc/o Jane Deighton ECD(3)114

John - of NJ, b1753 d1823, m1779 Mary Shreve - desc/o Jane Deighton ECD(3)115

Thomas - of MA, b1718 d1754, m1748 Lavina West - desc/o Jane Deighton ECD(3)114

NEILSON John - of AL & FL, b1771, m1810 Maria Dent - the immigrant CHB492; sufficient proof of alleged royal ancestry is lacking

Mary Hall - of IL, b1773 d1834, m 180_ John More Campbell - the immigrant CHB492; sufficient proof of alleged royal ancestry is lacking

NELSON Elizabeth - of MA, m Nathaniel Hubbard - desc/o John Nelson THJ94

Gershom - b1672 - desc/o Dorothy Stapilton RAA117

John - of MA, b1654 d1734, merchant & public official, son of Robert Nelson & Mary Temple, m Elizabeth Tailer - the immigrant DBR(1)611; DBR(2)796; THJ94; RAA1, 117; AAP156; GBR148

John - of NH, b1731 - desc/o John Nelson THJ95

Margaret - of VA, dau/o Robert Nelson of Gray's Inn, London & Mary Temple, m Rev Thomas Teackle b1624 d1695/1696 - the immigrant CRL(2)144, 118; GBR149; HSF(10)188

Martha - b1677 - desc/o Dorothy Stapilton RAA117

Mary - b1711 - desc/o Dorothy Stapilton RAA117

Mary - of VA, m Edmund Berkeley - desc/o Col George Reade CHB250

Mehitable - of MA, b1691 d1775, m1721 Capt Robert Temple DBR(1)611 - desc/o John Nelson DBR(2)796

Philip - b1634/1635 - desc/o Dorothy Stapilton RAA117

Rebecca - of MA, m Henry Lloyd - desc/o John Nelson THJ95, 96; AAP156; GBR148

Robert - of VA, m(2) Susan Robinson - desc/o Martha Bacon CHB33; BCD33 - desc/o Sarah Ludlow CHB133; BCD133

Temple - of MA, m Mary Wentworth - desc/o John Nelson THJ95

Thomas - of MA, b abt 1604, m(1) Dorothy Stapilton - the immigrant RAA1; sufficient proof of alleged royal ancestry is lacking

Thomas - b1635 - desc/o Dorothy Stapilton RAA117

Thomas - of VA, b1738 d1789 signer of the Declaration of Independence, commander state militia at Yorktown, governor of Virginia, m1762 Lucy Grymes - desc/o Abigail Smith J&K191; AMB122 - desc/o Sarah Ludlow PVF201

NEVILLE (NEVILL, NEVILLS) Lieut Col George Nevill - of VA & NC, b1734 d1811, m Rachel Earle - desc/o John Neville JSW1855

George - of VA, b abt 1760 d1816, m1785 Sarah Foster - desc/o John Neville JSW1856

James - of MD, b1640 d abt 1698, m Elizabeth____ - desc/o John Neville JSW1855

John - of MD 1634, b1612 d1664, m(1) Bridget Thomsley (Thornbay) - the immigrant JSW1855; sufficient proof of alleged royal ancestry is lacking

John - of VA, b abt 1644 d1697 - the immigrant WAC64; sufficient

NEVILLE (NEVILL, NEVILLS) (cont.)
> proof of alleged royal ancestry is lacking
>
> John - of VA, b abt 1665, m1685 Elizabeth Bohannon - desc/o John Neville JSW1855
>
> Joseph - of VA, b1693 d1766, m1730 Ann Bohannon - desc/o John Neville JSW1855

NEWBERRY (NEWBURY) Abigail - of CT, b1659 d1715/1716, m Rev Ephraim Howard - desc/o Thomas Newberry CRL(1)179
> Capt Benjamin - of CT, b1624 d1689, m1646 Mary Allyn - desc/o Thomas Newberry ECD(3)217, 222; DBR(3)686; DBR(5)727; RAA118; CRL(1)179
>
> Capt Benjamin - of CT, b1669 d1709/1710, m1690/1691 Hannah Sackett - desc/o Thomas Newberry CRL(1)180
>
> Benjamin - of CT, b1692/1693 d1718, m Ruth Porter - desc/o Thomas Newberry CRL(1)180
>
> Hannah - of CT, b abt 1633 d bef 1661, m Rev Thomas Hanford - desc/o Thomas Newberry CRL(1)179
>
> Hannah - of CT, b1673 d1718, m John Wolcott - desc/o Thomas Newberry CRL(1)179
>
> Joseph - of CT, married & had issue - desc/o Thomas Newberry CRL(1)179
>
> Margaret - of CT, b1662, m Return Strong - desc/o Thomas Newberry CRL(1)179
>
> Martha - of CT, b1709/1710 d1758, m Maj Roger Wolcott - desc/o Thomas Newberry CRL(1)180
>
> Mary - of CT, bp 1626, m1644 Capt Daniel Clark - desc/o Thomas Newberry ECD(3)226; RAA118; CRL(1)179; FFF73
>
> Mary - of CT, b1647/1648 d1690, m1664 Lieut John Moseley d1690 - desc/o Margaret Wyatt ECD106; MCD157; DBR(1)336; DBR(2)721; GBR397 - desc/o Thomas Newberry ECD(3)217; CRL(1)179
>
> Rebecca - of CT, b1655 d1718, m1675 Samuel Marshall Jr - desc/o Margaret Wyatt J&K123; ECD241; DBR(1)418; DBR(2)557; CRL(1)179
>
> Rebecca - of MA, b abt 1631 d1688, m abt 1652 Rev John Russell - desc/o Thomas Newberry AAP148; CRL(1)179
>
> Capt Roger - of CT, b1706 d1740, m Elizabeth Wolcott - desc/o Thomas Newberry CRL(1)180
>
> Sarah - of CT, b abt 1622 d1684, m Henry Wolcott Jr - desc/o Thomas Newberry CRL(1)179
>
> Sarah - of MA, b1650 d1716, m1668 Capt Preserved Clapp - desc/o Margaret Wyatt CHB541; BCD353; DBR(3)126; RAA61 - desc/o Thomas Newberry ECD(3)222; DBR(5)727; RAA118; CRL(1)179
>
> Thomas - of MA, b1594 d1635, m(1) abt 1619 Jane Dabinott, m(2)1630 Jane____ - the immigrant FLW221; ECD(3)222, 226; DBR(5)727; RAA1, 118; AAP148; CRL(1)178; FFF73; royal ancestry has not been proven
>
> Thomas - of CT, b1657 d1688, m Ann Ford - desc/o Thomas Newberry CRL(1)179

NEWBOLD Daniel - b1757 d1815, m1780 Rachel Newbold - desc/o Peter Wright DBR(4)98

NEWCE Thomas - of VA 1623, d1623 - the immigrant WAC27; sufficient proof of alleged royal ancestry is lacking

William - of VA 1621, d1621 - the immigrant WAC27; sufficient proof of alleged royal ancestry is lacking

NEWDIGATE Mary - of GA, dau/o Sir Richard Newdigate, 2nd Baronet & Mary Bagot, m William Stephens, governor of Georgia - the immigrant GBR262; NE(103)102/107, 287/295

NEWTON Benjamin - of VA - desc/o John Newton WAC89

Elizabeth - of VA - desc/o John Newton WAC89

Ellen - of MA, chr 1614 dau/o Lancelot Newton & Mary Lee, m Edward Carleton of MA - the immigrant LDS110; GBR313; EO2(2)777/792

Gerrard - of VA - desc/o John Newton WAC89

John - of VA, d1697, m Rose____ - the immigrant WAC89; sufficient proof of alleged royal ancestry is lacking

John Jr - of VA - desc/o John Newton WAC89

Joseph - of VA - desc/o John Newton WAC89

Thomas - of VA - desc/o John Newton WAC89

NICHOLAS Elizabeth - of VA, m Edmund Randolph - desc/o Sarah Ludlow PVF201

Judge George - of KY, m Margaret Smith - desc/o Sarah Ludlow CHB134; BCD134

John - of VA, of Seven Islands, Albemarle Co, served as clerk of Albemarle 1749 to 1815, burgess 1756 to 1768 & a member of the Convention of Buckingham Co 1774/1775, m Martha Frye dau/o Col Joshua Fry, of Williamsburg, VA - desc/o Sarah Ludlow DBR(1)113; CFSSA110

Capt Lewis Valentine Nicholas - of VA, b abt 1766 d1840, m Frances Harris - desc/o Sarah Ludlow ECD198

Margaret - m Col Patrick Rose - desc/o Sarah Ludlow DBR(1)113

Judge Philip Narborne - of VA, m Maria Carter Byrd - desc/o Sarah Ludlow CHB133; BCD133

Judge Robert Carter - of VA, b1725 of Williamsburg d1788, statesman, jurist & patriot, served as a member of the King's Council, treasurer of the colony & a vestryman, m1752 Anne Cary, dau/o Col Wilson Cary & Sarah____of Celey's & had issue - desc/o Sarah Ludlow J&K268; CHB133; ECD197; ECD(2)188; BCD133; DBR(2)55, 694, 695; PVF201; CAFSSA110

Wilson Cary - of VA, b1761 d1820, m1785 Margaret Smith - desc/o Sarah Ludlow J&K268; CHB134; ECD(2)188; BCD134; DBR(2)55, 695; PVF201

NICHOLS David - b1757 - desc/o Anne Marbury RAA114

Francis - of NY, b1595 d1650, m(1)____, m(2)1645 Anna Wines - desc/o Col Richard Nichols BLG2842

Isaac - of NY, b1625 d1694, m1646 Margary Washborne - desc/o Col Richard Nichols BLG2842

Col Richard - of NY, b abt 1624 d1672 first gov of NY, died unmarried, son of Francis Nichols (Nicolls) & Margaret Bruce - the immigrant BLG2842; GBR203; TAG(68)113/14

NICHOLSON Francis - of SC - desc/o Robert Nicholson EDV63

Robert - of VA 1655, m Elizabeth Diggs - the immigrant EDV63; WAC86; sufficient proof of alleged royal ancestry is lacking

NICOLA (NICOLAS) Ann - of PA, b1770/1771 d1793, m1790 John Fisher - desc/o Louis Nicola (Nicolas) TAG(57)143

    Charlotte - of PA, b1761 d1830's, m(1)1781 Dr Matthew Maus b1731 in Germany d1787, surgeon, m(2)1794 Dr William R Cozens d shortly bef 20 Feb 1824 - desc/o Louis Nicola (Nicolas) TAG(57)142

    Jane - of PA, b1765 d1795, m1782 Lieut Talmadge Hall d1793 - desc/o Louis Nicola (Nicolas) TAG(57)143

    Louis - of PA 1766, b abt 1717 d1807, revolutionary soldier & public official son of Charles Nicola (or Nicholas) & Charlotte des Vignolles, m(1)1740 Christiana D'Oyly, m(2)1760 Jane Bishop b abt 1740 d1797 - the immigrant GBR344; TAG(57)139/144

    Margaret - of PA, b1764 d1797, m1781 Lieut John Bigham (or Bingham) - desc/o Louis Nicola (Nicolas) TAG(57)143

    Mary - of PA, b1766 d1831, m1785 Thomas Nast b1743 d1815 - desc/o Louis Nicola (Nicolas) TAG(57)143

NICOLL Benjamin - of NY, b1694 d1724, m1714 Charity Floyd - desc/o Judge Matthias Nicoll CHB212, 213; MCD325; BCD212, 213; AMB396

    Benjamin Jr - of NY, b1718 d1760, m Mary Magdalen Holland - desc/o Judge Matthias Nicole CHB213: MCD325; BCD213; AMB397

    Catharine - of NY, m Jonathan Havens - desc/o Judge Matthias Nicoll AMB396

    Frances - of NY, m Edward Holland - desc/o Judge Matthias Nicoll AMB396

    Henry - of NY, b1756 d1790, m Elizabeth Woodhull - desc/o Judge Matthias Nicoll AMB397

    John - of NY 1734 - the immigrant EDV53; sufficient proof of alleged royal ancestry is lacking

    Margaret - of NY, b1662 d1718, m1686 Col Richard Floyd - desc/o Judge Matthias Nicoll AMB396

    Mary - of NY, m John Watts - desc/o Judge Matthias Nicoll AMB396

    Judge Matthias - of NY 1664, b1621 d1687, m Abigail Johns - the immigrant J&K259; CHB212; MCD325; BCD212; AMB396

    Matthias - of NY, d1827 - desc/o Judge Matthias Nicoll AMB397

    Dr Samuel of NY, b1754 d1796, m(1)1782 Anne Fargie - desc/o Judge Matthias Nicoll CHB213; MCD325; BCD213

    Dr Samuel - of NY, m___Nicoll - desc/o Judge Matthias Nicoll AMB397

    Van Rensselaer - of NY, m___Salisbury - desc/o Judge Matthias Nicoll AMB396

    William - of NY 1664, b1657 d1723, m1693 Anne Van Rensselaer - desc/o Judge Matthias Nicoll J&K259; CHB212; MCD325; BCD212; AMB396

    William - of NY, b1715 d1780, m Joanna De Honneur - desc/o Judge Matthias Nicoll AMB396

NICOLLS Margaret - of NY, (sister of Judge Matthias), m Col Richard Floyd - the immigrant J&K260; sufficient proof of alleged royal ancestry is lacking

NILES Elizabeth - b1706 d1770, m1723 Lieut Joshua Hayward - desc/o Rev John Oxenbridge DBR(1)369, 370

    Mary - b1713 d1792, m1730 Rev Atherton Wales - desc/o Rev John

NILES (cont.)

Oxenbridge DBR(2)511, 609

de NOAILLES Anne Jeanne Baptiste Pauline Adrienne Louise Catherine Dominique - dau/o Jean Louis Francois Paul de Noailles, Duc de Noailles & Henriette Anne Louise d'Aguesseau, m Louis Marie de Noailles, Vicomte de Noailles b1756 d1804 leader in the American & French Revolutions - the immigrant GBR104

Louis Marie, Vicomte de Noailles - b1756 d1804 leader in the American & French Revolutions, fought at the battles of Savannah and Yorktown, son of Philippe de Noailles, Duc de Mouchy & Anne Claudine Louise d'Arpajon, m Anne Jeanne Baptiste Pauline Adrienne Louise Catherine Dominique de Noailles - the immigrant GBR104

Marie Adrienne Francoise - dau/o Jean Louis Francois Paul de Noailles, Duc de Noailles & Henriette Anne Louise d'Aguesseau, m Marie Joseph Paul Yves Roch Gilbert Motier, Marquis de La Fayette (Lafayette) b1757 d1834, American Revolutionary general & French statesman - the immigrant GBR104

NOBLE Aurelia - of PA - desc/o John Drake MCD209

David - of CT, b1709 d1761 - desc/o John Drake MCD209

David - of CT, b1732 d1776, m1753 Ruth Noble - desc/o John Drake DBR(5)618

Enoch - of CT, b1763 d1851, m1809 (Mrs) Dorothy (Holcomb) Adams - desc/o John Drake DBR(5)618

James - of CT - desc/o John Drake MCD209

John - of VT - desc/o John Drake MCD209

Lydia - b1768, m Isaac Ensign - desc/o John Drake LDS42; RAA87

NORMAN Eunice - of MA, b1686 Marblehead, m1704 Samuel Raymond of Beverly, MA - desc/o Mary Gye NE(96)360

John - of MA, b1690 Marblehead, fisherman, m1720 Marblehead, Mary Coes dau/o Nicholas Coes - desc/o Mary Gye NE(96)360/361

Sarah - of MA, b1693, m1718 John Broughton - desc/o Mary Gye NE(96)361

NORRIS Charles - of PA, b1712 d1766, m(2)1759 Mary Parker - desc/o Thomas Lloyd CHB124; BCD124

Isaac - of PA, b1701 d1764, m1739 Sarah Logan - desc/o Thomas Lloyd CHB124; BCD124

Joseph Parker - of PA, b1763 d1841, m1790 Elizabeth Hill - desc/o Thomas Lloyd CHB125; BCD125

Mary - of PA, b1740 d1803, m1770 Brig Gen John Dickinson - desc/o Thomas Lloyd CHB124; BCD124

NORTH Elizabeth - of MD, b1731 d1805, m(1)1751 Christopher Carnan b abt 1730 d1769, merchant & importer of Baltimore, Maryland, son of Charles & Prudence Carnan of Reading, Berks & London, England, m(2) Samuel Johnston b abt 1726 in Ireland d1810 - desc/o Col William Bernard APP123 - desc/o Anne Lovelace GVFHB(3)354

Ellin - of MD, b1741 d1825 was a woman of forcible personality & occupied a very promoinent position in the social life of the community, m1758 John Moale b1730/1731 d1798 justice, member of Assembly & Lieut Col of the Baltimore town battalion of

NORTH (cont.)

militia, took an active part in the Revolution, son of John Moale Sr & Rachael Hammond - desc/o Col William Bernard APP123/124 - desc/o Anne Lovelace GVFHB(3)356

NORTHROP Hannah - b abt 1699, m Thomas Langford - desc/o Benjamin Harrington LDS71

Joseph - b abt 1670, m Hopestill Smith - desc/o Benjamin Harrington LDS71

NORTON Col Ebenezer - of CT, b1715 d1785, m1740 Elizabeth Baldwin - desc/o Thomas Norton BLG2843

Ebenezer - of CT, b1748 d1795, m1782 Charity Mills - desc/o Thomas Norton BLG2843

Elizabeth - b abt 1638 - desc/o Henry Norton RAA118

Elizabeth - of MA, m Col John Quincy - desc/o Rev William Norton J&K121; CHB164; MCD261; BCD164

Elizabeth - of MA, m Rev William Smith - desc/o Rev William Norton CHB164

Henry - of ME, b1617 son of Henry Norton & Sarah Lawson, m Margaret____ - the immigrant RAA1, 118; GBR420 some aspect of royal descent merits further study

Rev John - of MA, b1651 d1716, m Mary Mason - desc/o Rev William Norton J&K120; CHB164; MCD261; BCD164

Mary - of CT, m1660 Samuel Rockwell - desc/o Thomas Norton MCD262

Samuel - of CT, b1681 d1767, m1713 Dinah Birdsey - desc/o Thomas Norton BLG2843

Thomas - of CT 1639, b1582 d1648, m1625 Grace Wells - the immigrant MCD262; BLG2843; RAA no longer accepted as being of royal descent

Thomas - of CT, b1626 d1712, m1671 Elizabeth Mason - desc/o Thomas Norton BLG2843

Walter - of MA, son of Thomas Norton & Alice Cranmer, m(1) Mrs Jane Reeve Reynolds, m(2) Eleanor____ - the immigrant GBR420 some aspect of royal descent merits further study

Rev William - of MA, b1610 d1694, m Lucy Downing - the immigrant J&K120; CHB164; MCB161; MCD261; BCD164; EDV119; sufficient proof of alleged royal ancestry is lacking

NORWOOD Benjamin - of VA, d1847, m1782 Mary Aiken - desc/o William Norwood DBR(2)812

Charles - of VA - the immigrant MCS50; sufficient proof of alleged royal ancestry is lacking

George - of VA, d1749 - desc/o William Norwood DBR(2)811; DBR(4)358

Henry - of VA 1647, d1689 - the immigrant MCS49; sufficient proof of alleged royal ancestry is lacking

John - of VA & MD - the immigrant MCS49; sufficient proof of alleged royal ancestry is lacking

Nathaniel - of VA - desc/o William Norwood DBR(2)812

Nathaniel - of VA, d1784, m Mary____ - desc/o William Norwood DBR(2)812

William - of VA 1656, d1703 - the immigrant DBR(2)317, 811;

NORWOOD (cont.)

DBR(3)398; DBR(4)358; RAA1; royal ancestry not proven

William - of VA, b1700/1702 d1763/1790, m Mary____ - desc/o William Norwood DBR(4)358

William - of VA, b1731 d1803, m1764 Ruth Wyche - desc/o William Norwood DBR(4)358

William - of VA, b1769 d1825, m1801 Sarah Howard - desc/o William Norwood DBR(4)358

NOTT Edward - of VA, d1705/1706 lieutenant & governor general of the Colony of Virginia, son of Sir Thomas Nott & Anne Thynne, m Margaret Blakiston - the immigrant GBR151; VGE171, 172

NOURSE Catherine Burton - of KY, b1759 d1833, m1778 John Cooke - the immigrant ECD209; sufficient proof of alleged royal ancestry is lacking

James - of PA, son of John & Elizabeth (Gregory) Nourse, m Sarah Faunce - the immigrant GBR42

NOYES Abigail - of CT, b1724 d1797, m1745 Judge Thomas Darling - desc/o Mabel Harlakenden MCB404; MCD229

Enoch - of MA, b1730, m(2)1759 Judith Knight - desc/o Nicholas Noyes FFF191

Hannah - m Samuel Bradbury - desc/o Capt Thomas Bradbury JSW1801

James - of MA 1633 - the immigrant FFF190

James - of MA, b1657, m1683 Hannah Knight - desc/o Nicholas Noyes FFF191

James - of MA, b1705, m Sarah Little - desc/o Nicholas Noyes FFF191

James - of NH, b1760 d1817, m1781 Hannah Hutchins - desc/o Nicholas Noyes FFF191

John - b1718 - desc/o Alice Freeman RAA132

Joseph - b1731 - desc/o Alice Freeman RAA132

Mary - b1725, m1753 Col Joseph Champlin - desc/o Alice Freeman DBR(3)424; DBR(4)800; RAA132

Mary or Mercy - b1748 - desc/o Alice Freeman RAA132

Nicholas - of MA 1633, b1615/1616 d1701, m abt 1640 Mary Cutting - the immigrant FFF190; sufficient proof of alleged royal ancestry is lacking

Prudence - b1764 - desc/o Alice Freeman RAA132

NUTMAN Phebe - of NJ, b abt 1742 d1826, m Matthias Pierson MD - desc/o Obadiah Bruen ECD122

NYE Lydia - of MA, b1766 d1839, m Levi Chamberlain b1769 d1838 son of Samuel Chamberlain & Lydia Willson - desc/o Thomas Southworth DBR(3)161

– O –

O'BRIEN Catherine, Baroness Clifton - of NY & NJ, dau/o Henry, Lord Ibrackan & Catherine (Stuart) Baroness Clifton O'Brien, m Edward Hyde, 3rd Earl of Clarendon, b1661 d1723, governor of New York & NJ - the immigrant GBR42

O'CARROLL Dr Charles - of MD 1737 b1691 d1755, m Dorothy Blake - the immigrant MCD263; sufficient proof of alleged royal ancestry is lacking

O'SULLIVAN John (Owen) ("Master John") - of ME, b1690 d1795, m Margaret Browne - the immigrant MCB157; MCD298; CHB203; sufficient proof of alleged royal ancestry is lacking

OFFLEY Amelia - of MA, dau/o Stephen Offley & Anne Shute, m Sir Francis Bernard, 1st Baronet, b1712 d1779 governor of NJ & MA - the immigrant GBR315

Sara - of VA, bp 1609 d1627, m1627 Adam Thorowgood - the immigrant WAC12; sufficient proof of alleged royal ancestry is lacking

OGLETHORPE James Edward - of GA, b1696 d1785, soldier & founder of Georgia, son of Sir Theophilus Oglethorpe & Eleanor Wall, m Elizabeth Wright - the immigrant GBR289

OLIVER James - of MA, b1687 d1754, m1711 Rebecca Lloyd - desc/o Elizabeth Coytemore ECD(2)101; DBR(5)118

Mary - of MA, b1712, m1737 William Ellsworth - desc/o Elizabeth Coytemore ECD(2)101; DBR(5)118

Sarah - of MA, bp 1696, m1714 Boston, Col Jacob Wendell bp 1691 Albany, New York d1761 age 70 years, merchant of Boston, one of the governor's council & a colonel of the Boston regiment, he was in 1733 director of the first banking institution in the province, son of Johannes Wendell & Elizabeth Staats - desc/o Gov Thomas Dudley J&K195; DBR(3)597; CRL(1)381; NE(8)313, 314; NEFGM(1)78

OLNEY Emor - of RI, b1741 d1830, m1760 Amy Hopkins - desc/o William Arnold CHB16; BCD15

James - of RI, d1770, m1733 Hannah Winsor - desc/o William Arnold CHB15; BCD15

Paris - of RI, b1770 d1850, m Mercy Winsor - desc/o William Arnold CHB16; BCD16

OPIE Anne Nancy - of VA, b abt 1773 d1849, m1799 Rev John Smith Ball - desc/o Rev David Lindsay DBR(2)149

Jerome (Hierome) L Sr - of VA, b1776/1773 d1839, m Margaret Muse - desc/o Rev David Lindsay DBR(5)278

Capt John Lindsay - of VA, bp 1675 d1722, m1713 Anne Metcalfe - desc/o Rev David Lindsay JSW1650; DBR(5)278

Lindsay II - of VA, b1714 d1746, m1734 Sarah Heale - desc/o Rev David Lindsay JSW1650; DBR(5)278 - desc/o Col Moore Fauntleroy DBR(5)332

Lindsay III - of VA, b1740 d1785, m(2) aft 1773 Elizabeth McAdam - desc/o David Lindsay JSW1650; DBR(5)278 - desc/o Col Moore Fauntleroy DBR(5)332

Capt Thomas Jr - of VA, d1702 - desc/o Rev David Lindsay WAC43

ORDWAY Joseph - of MA, b1707, m1729 Mehitable Burbank - desc/o Anthony Colby ECD(2)96; DBR(4)758; DBR(5)693

Joseph Sr - of MA, b1732, m Mehitable____ - desc/o Anthony Colby ECD(2)96; DBR(4)758; DBR(5)693

Joseph Jr - of NH, b1756 - desc/o Anthony Colby ECD(2)96; DBR(4)758; DBR(5)693

ORR Alexander Dalrymple - of VA & KY, b1761 elected a member of
Congress from that state, m Caroline Taylor, an Englishwoman -
desc/o John Orr GVFTQ(2)786

John - of VA, b1726 son of Alexander of Hazelside & Agnes (Dalrymple)
Orr, m Susannah Monroe Grayson dau/o Benjamin Grayson &
Susannah Monroe - the immigrant GBR58; GVFTQ(2)783/789

John Dalrymple - of VA, b1771 physician, educated in Scotland m____
Lee dau/o Thomas Lee - desc/o John Orr GVFTQ(2)787

William Grayson - of VA, m a Philadelphia lady & is believed to have
left a son - desc/o John Orr GVFTQ(2)787

OSBORN (OSBORNE) Alice - m John Peyton - the immigrant CRL(1)260;
sufficient proof of alleged royal ancestry is lacking

Sir Danvers, 3rd Baronet - of NY, governor of New York, son of Sir
John Osborne, 2nd Baronet & Elizabeth Strode, m Lady Mary
Montagu - the immigrant GBR156

David - b abt 1774 - desc/o John Claypoole RAA81

Elizabeth - of PA, m1789 Philadelphia, Peter Henri son of Pierre Henri,
native of France & Henrietta____ - desc/o Robert Lloyd CRFP(1)501

Grace - of CT, b1724/1725 d abt 1807, m 1749/1750 John Stratton -
desc/o Rev Peter Bulkeley DBR(1)809

Hezekiah - d1814 age 78 - desc/o Rev Peter Bulkeley TAG(36)104

Peter - of PA, m1763 Wilmington, Delaware, Elizabeth Stevens & had
issue - desc/o Robert Lloyd CRFP(1)501

Sarah - of CT, bp abt 1711 d aft 1793, m abt 1731 Joseph Sherwood -
desc/o Grace Chetwood ECD248

Sarah - of VA, b1760, m1781 George Alderson - desc/o James
Claypoole ECD(3)94

OSGOOD Mehitable - of MA, b1706 d1782, m1725 Josiah Flanders -
desc/o Anthony Colby JSW1687

OTIS Ann - b abt 1657/1658 - desc/o Rose Stoughton RAA119

David - b1743 d1825, m1766 Mary Day - desc/o Edward Southworth
DBR(5)828

John - of MA 1635 - the immigrant EDV149; sufficient proof of alleged
royal ancestry is lacking

Joseph - b1771 d1840/1850, m abt 1795 Huldah Hill - desc/o
Edward Southworth DBR(5)828

Mary - b abt 1674 - desc/o Rose Stoughton RAA119

Richard - of NH, b abt 1629, m(1) Rose Stoughton - the immigrant
RAA1, 119; sufficient proof of alleged royal ancestry is lacking

Stephen - b abt 1652 - desc/o Rose Stoughton - RAA119

OWEN Gainor - of PA, b1688, m1705 Jonathan Jones - desc/o Rebecca
Humphrey MCD267; BCD160

Griffith - b1647 - desc/o Jane Vaughn RAA120

Hannah - of PA, b1720 d1791, m(1) John Ogden, m(2)1752 Joseph
Wharton CHB157; BCD157

Jane - of PA, m Hugh Roberts, of PA, son of Robert Pugh & Mrs
Elizabeth Williams Pugh - the immigrant GBR306

Jane - of PA, b abt 1690 - desc/o Jane Vaughn RAA120

John - b1692 - desc/o Rebecca Humphrey RAA120

Joseph - of NY, m1729 Hannah Helmes - desc/o Roger Ludlow
CHB413

OWEN (cont.)

Joseph Jr - of NY, m1761 Millicent Horton - desc/o Roger Ludlow CHB413

Joshua - of NJ, d1727, son of Owen Humphrey, m1697 Martha Shinn - the immigrant ECD(2)205, 207, 209, 212; MCS78; DBR(1)173; DBR(2)247, 248; DBR(3)387; DBR(5)717; RAA1, 120; GBR157

Margaret - of NJ, b abt 1701 d1753, m1722 Benjamin Crispin b1699 d1753 - desc/o Joshua Owen ECD(2)207, 209; MCS78, 79; DBR(1)173; DBR(2)248; DBR(3)387, 388; DBR(5)718

Mary - of PA, m Henry Burr - desc/o Rebecca Owen Humphrey CHB415; MCD267

Owen - of PA, b1690 d1741 - desc/o Rebecca Owen Humphrey CHB157; BCD157

Rebecca - of PA 1690, (sometimes called Rebecca Humphrey[s], dau/o Owen Humphrey, m1678 Robert Owen - the immigrant CHB157, 415; MCD266; BCD157; RAA120 (also listed under Rebecca Humphrey); GBR157

Rebecca - b abt 1702 - desc/o Joshua Owen RAA120

Rebecca - b abt 1726/1731 - desc/o Rebecca Owen Humphrey RAA120

Robert - of DE & PA, son of Humphrey Owen b abt 1620, m Jane Vaughn - the immigrant RAA1, 120; GBR167

Robert - of PA, son of Owen ap Evan & Gainor John, m Rebecca Owen Humphrey[s] - the immigrant GBR306

Robert - of PA, m Susannah Hudson - desc/o Rebecca Owen Humphrey CHB157, 415; MCD267; BCD157

Rowland - of NJ, d bef 1777, m1738 Prudence Powell - desc/o Joshua Owen ECD(2)205

Sarah - of NJ, b abt 1702/1703 d aft 1750, m Samuel Pyle MD - desc/o Joshua Owen ECD(2)212

Sarah - of PA, m1736 John Biddle - desc/o Rebecca Owen Humphrey CHB157; MCD267; BCD157

Sarah - of NJ, d aft 1804, m Jonathon Stratton - desc/o Joshua Owen ECD(2)205

OWENS Jane - of PA 1683, d1686, m(1) Hugh Roberts - the immigrant MCD187; sufficient proof of alleged royal ancestry is lacking

OWSLEY Mary - b1768 d1848, m1786 John Bryant - desc/o Col/Gov John West DBR(3)129

Thomas - of VA, son of John Owsley & Dorothea Poyntz, m Anne_____ - the immigrant GBR286

Thomas III - b1731 d1796, m1746 Mary Middleton - desc/o Col/Gov John West DBR(2)630; DBR(3)129

William - b1749, m1770/1777 Catherine Bolin - desc/o Col/Gov John West DBR(2)630

OXENBRIDGE Bathshua - of MA, m Richard Scott - desc/o Rev John Oxenbridge TAG(31)60/63

Elizabeth - of MA, m Caleb Cockercraft - desc/o Rev John Oxenbridge CHB166; BCD166; GBR125; TAG(31)60/63; NE(108)178

Rev John - of MA, b1608/1609 Daventry d1674 Boston, Puritan & pastor of the First Church Boston MA in 1670, son of Daniel Oxenbridge & Katherine Harby, m(1) Jane Butler d1655, m(2)1656

OXENBRIDGE (cont.)

Frances Woodward d1659 dau/o Rev Hezekiah Woodward of Uxbridge, England, m(3)1660/1661 Mary Hackshaw, m(4) Susannah____ - the immigrant CHB166; FLW170; MCB153; MCS71; BCD165, 166; DBR(1)276, 369, 622, 673; DBR(2)316, 509, 511, 609; DBR(3)23, 26, 27; THJ80; RAA1, 121; GBR125; TAG(31)60/63; NE(108)178

Theodora - of MA, b1658 d1697 Milton, MA, m1677 Rev Peter Thacher - desc/o Rev John Oxenbridge CHB166; FLW170; MCS71; BCD166; DBR(1)276, 369, 623, 673, 674; DBR(2)316, 511; DBR(3)23, 27; GBR125; TAG(31)60/63

- P -

PACKARD Susanna - of MA, b1736, m1760 Joseph Knapp - desc/o John Washbourne DBR(2)529

PADDOCK Nathaniel - b1677, m Ann Bunker - desc/o Richard Sears LDS84

Patience - b1727 - desc/o George Morton RAA116

Priscilla - b1722, m William Coffin - desc/o Richard Sears LDS84

PAGE Major Carter - of VA, b1758, m(1) Mary Cary - desc/o Col Warham Horsmanden DBR(4)122

Catharine - of VA, m Benjamin C Waller - desc/o Sarah Ludlow CHB135; BCD135

Jane Burwell - of VA, b1774 d1796, m1794 Edmund Pendleton - desc/o Sarah Ludlow DBR(1)400

Jane Byrd - of VA, b1770 d1812, m Thomas Swann - desc/o Sarah Ludlow J&K266

John - of VA 1650, b1628 d1692, m Alice Larkin - the immigrant EDV65; sufficient proof of alleged royal ancestry is lacking

John - of VA, b abt 1720 Rosewell, Gloucester Co, m1746 Jane Byrd of Westover, James River, Charles City Co, VA - desc/o Sarah Ludlow J&K266; PVF201

John - of VA, b1744 d1808, m(1)1765 Frances Burwell - desc/o Sarah Ludlow J&K265; CHB134; BCD134

John - of VA, m Maria Horsmanden Byrd - desc/o Sarah Ludlow CHB134; BCD134; DBR(5)1036; AWW342

Judith - of VA, m1775/1776 Col Hugh Nelson - desc/o Maria Horsmanden CHB56; BCD56; DBR(3)646

Lucy - of VA, m1792 Francis Nelson - desc/o Maria Horsmanden CHB56; BCD56

Mann - of VA, b1719, m(1)1743 Alice Grynes, m(2)1748 Anne Corbin Tayloe - desc/o Sarah Ludlow J&K265, 266; CHB134; BCD134; PVF201

Robert - of VA, b abt 1722 Rosewell, Gloucester Co d1768, m1750 Sarah Walker - desc/o Sarah Ludlow J&K267; CHB135; BCD134; AWW342; PVF201

Robert - of VA, m1779 Mary Braxton - desc/o Sarah Ludlow J&K267

Sarah - of MA, b1737 d1809, m1762 John Woodman - desc/o Thomas Bradbury ECD(2)84, 102; FFF108

PAINE Antoinette - of MA, m Samuel Greele - desc/o Mary Launce CHB448

Charles - of MA, b1775 d1810, m1799 Sarah Sumner Cushing - desc/o Mary Launce CHB448

Eles - of MA, m Samuel Varnon - desc/o Edward Raynsford NE(139)306

John - of MA - the immigrant EDV126, 127; sufficient proof of alleged royal ancestry is lacking

John - of RI, b abt 1718/1720 d1775, deputy from New Shoreham, m1744/1745 Bathsheba Rathbone b1725 d1803 - desc/o Dr Richard Palgrave DBR(2)592; DBR(3)572

Margaret - of RI, b1750 d1838, m Lieut Simon Ray Littlefield b1751 d1780 - desc/o Dr Richard Palgrave DBR(2)592; DBR(3)573

Mary - of MA, d bef 1727 m____ Drown - desc/o Edward Raynsford NE(139)306

Mary - of MA, m Rev Elisha Clap - desc/o Mary Launce CHB448

Mercy - of MA, b1712 d1774, m1735 Ebeneezer Cook - desc/o Mary Wentworth ECD(2)291

Robert Treat - of MA, b1731 d1814 attorney general & judge of the Supreme Court of MA, member of the Continental Congress & signer of the Declaration of Independence - desc/o Mary Launce J&K185; CHB448

Robert Treat Jr - of MA, poet - desc/o Mary Launce J&K185; CHB448

Urania - b1706 - desc/o Edward Rainsford RAA126

William Littlefield - of RI & CT, b1776 d1842, m abt 1798 Mary Clarke b1776 d1835 - desc/o Dr Richard Palgrave DBR(2)592; DBR(3)573

PALGRAVE Elizabeth - of MA, b abt 1625 d1707, m abt 1659 Joshua Edwards - the immigrant FLW19; MCS15; TAG(18)209; sufficient proof of alleged royal ancestry is lacking

Mary - of MA, b abt 1619 (sister of Sarah), m abt 1637 Roger Wellington of Watertown, MA b1609 d1697 - desc/o Dr Richard Palgrave MCS15; DBR(1)176, 784; DBR(4)430; DBR(5)762; RAA121; TAG(18)209; FLW19; NE(102)95/97

Dr Richard - of MA, b1580/1585 d1651, who was of royal descent from King Edward I, of England. Came over with the Winthrop fleet & was one of the earliest of New England's physicians; son of Edward Palgrave, m Anna____ d1668/1669 age 75 years - the immigrant ECD(2)232; MCS15; DBR(1)176, 649, 784; DBR(2)591, 592; DBR(3)60, 572; DBR(4)429, 693; DBR(5)372, 762; RAA1, 121; TAG(18)206/209, (25)24/27; GBR266; NE(102)87/98, 312/31, (103)102/107, 287/295, (116)79; FLW19

Sarah - of MA, b1621 d1665 skilled in medicine & surgery, m1648 Dr John Alcock M A Harvard College, 1646, physician - desc/o Dr Richard Palgrave ECD(3)232; MCS15; DBR(2)592; DBR(3)572; DBR(4)693; DBR(5)372; RAA121; TAG(18)209; GBR266; FLW19

PALMER Henry - b1615, m(2) Judith Feake - the immigrant LDS30; sufficient proof of alleged royal ancestry is lacking

Jerusha - b1705 - desc/o Alice Freeman RAA132

Judith - b1654, m John Reynolds - desc/o Henry Palmer LDS30

Love - of CT, b1719, m1736 Jonathan Shepard - desc/o Oliver Manwaring ECD(2)192; ECD(3)208; DBR(4)249; FFF42

PALMER (cont.)

Sarah - b1609, m Henry Rowley - the immigrant LDS51, 55; sufficient proof of alleged royal ancestry is lacking

Susan - of MA, b 1665, m Samuel Avery - desc/o Susan Clinton J&K247; BCD146

PALMES Edward - of CT, son of Andrew Palmes & Elizabeth____, m(1) Lucy Winthrop dau/o John Winthrop Jr & Elizabeth Reade Winthrop, m(2) Mrs Sarah Farmer Davis - the immigrant GBR227

Susan or Susannah - of MA, b1665 d1747, m1686 Samuel Avery - desc/o Susan Clinton CHB416 - desc/o Susan Fienes CHB528 - the immigrant ECD(3)185; MCD234; sufficient proof of alleged royal ancestry is lacking

PARHAM Stith - of VA, will dates 1793, m Elizabeth____ - desc/o Col William Randolph DBR(2)126

Thomas - of VA, b1749, m1799 Elizabeth Moody dau/o Henry Moody - desc/o Col William Randolph DBR(2)126

PARISH Ezekiel - b1742, m Mary Pennock - desc/o John Prescott LDS75

Joel - b1769, m Sarah de Wolf - desc/o John Prescott LDS75

PARKE Abigail - of CT, b1686 d1713, m1704 Christopher Avery - desc/o Alice Freeman DBR(3)682

Alice - b1658 - desc/o Alice Freeman RAA132

Deborah - m Benejah Williams - desc/o Alice Freeman DBR(3)430

Dorothy - b1651/1652 - desc/o Alice Freeman RAA132

Dorothy - bp 1704, m1725 Thomas Woodward - desc/o Alice Freeman DBR(2)537; RAA132

Capt John - of CT, b1660 d1716, m Mary Witter - desc/o Alice Freeman DBR(3)682

Margaret - of CT, b abt 1697 d1772, m(1) Jabez Spicer - desc/o Alice Freeman DBR(5)540; RAA132

Martha - of CT, b abt 1650 d1717, m1667/1668 Isaac Wheeler - desc/o Dorothy Thompson ECD(2)150; DBR(1)340, 594; DBR(2)442; DBR(3)239; DBR(5)187, 797; RAA132

Martha - b1699 - desc/o Alice Freeman RAA132

Nathaniel - of CT, b abt 1621 d1718, m1676/1677 Sarah Geer - desc/o Alice Freeman DBR(5)540; RAA132

Phebe - b abt 1692 - desc/o Alice Freeman RAA132

Robert - b1651 d1707, m Mary Rose - desc/o Alice Freeman DBR(2)537; RAA132

Rose - b1707 - desc/o Alice Freeman RAA132

William - b1670, m Hannah Frank - desc/o Alice Freeman DBR(3)430; RAA132

PARKER Fearnot - m1660/1661 St John, Barbados, Capt John Parnell - desc/o Mary Gye NE(96)234

Rebecca - of PA, m1736 Budd Robinson - desc/o Peter Wright DBR(3)636

Submit - b1715 - desc/o John Prescott RAA125

Eunice - b1712 - desc/o William Sargent RAA129

PARMENTER Hannah - of MA, m John Emmes - desc/o Richard Williams CHB377

PARRAN Alexander - of MD & ME 1796, b1740 d1779, m Elizabeth Eveleth - desc/o Mary Joanna Somerset CHB383

PARRAN (cont.)

Sarah Eveleth - of MA, b1774 d1859, m1803 William Presson - desc/o Mary Joanna Somerset CHB383

PARRISH (PARISH) Ezekiel - b1742 - desc/o John Prescott RAA125

Isaac - of PA, m Sarah Mitchell - desc/o Jane Owen ap Evan CHB191

Joel - b1769 - desc/o John Prescott RAA125

Patience - of PA, m Charles Marshall - desc/o Jane Owens MCD188

PARSHALL James - b abt 1649, m(2) Elizabeth Gardiner - the immigrant RAA no longer accepted as being of royal descent

PARTRIDGE Oliver - b1712 - desc/o Thomas Dudley RAA89

William - b1753 - desc/o Thomas Dudley RAA89

PASCHALL Joanna - of PA, b1725, m1746 Samuel James - desc/o Hannah Price MCB418

Sarah - of PA, m Chester Co, PA, Henry Troth b1728 MD d1768 MD, son of Henry Troth & Elizabeth Johns - desc/o Lady Juliana Fermor CRFP(1)501

PATE Elizabeth - of VA, m James Shelburn - desc/o Col George Reade ECD(2)224; DBR(4)34, 574; DBR(5)219

Jacob - b1710 - desc/o Col George Reade RAA127

Jeremiah - of VA, b1716/1717 m___ Bender - desc/o Col George Reade ECD(2)224; DBR(4)34, 574; DBR(5)219

de PAU Caroline de Grasse - m Henry Walter Livingston Jr - desc/o Francois Joseph Paul de Grasse GBR292

PATTEN Mary - of MA, b1773 at Andover, m1794 James Tidder of Andover, VT - desc/o Rev Peter Bulkeley TAG(36)150

Rhoda - of MA, b1775 at Andover, m1795 Joshua Warner of Andover, VT - desc/o Rev Peter Bulkeley TAG(36)150

PAYNE Edward - of MA, b1710, m Lois Kinney - desc/o Ann Fiske AFA16

George - of VA, d abt 1789, m Frances Stone - desc/o William Payne AFA134

Huldah - of CT, m James Chandler - desc/o Samuel Symonds AFA20

John - of VA, b abt 1614 d abt 1685, m Margaret___ - desc/o William Payne AFA134

John - of VA, b1670 d1750, m Jane Monroe - desc/o William Payne AFA134

Richard - of VA, b1633 - desc/o William Payne AFA134

Smith - b1764, m Margaret Morton Payne - desc/o Col George Reade DBR(1)469

Stephen - of MA, b1654 d1710, m Mary Brintnall - desc/o Ann Fiske AFA16

Stephen - of MA, b1745/1746 d1815, m Martha Cogswell - desc/o Ann Fiske AFA16

William - of VA - the immigrant AFA134; sufficient proof of alleged royal ancestry is lacking

Capt William - of VA, b1755 d1837, m1801 Marion Andre Morson - desc/o William Payne AFA134

PAYTON or PEYTON Benjamin - of NC, b abt 1705 d1748 Beaufort Co, North Carolina, m abt 1725/1726 Eleanor___ Bell (widow) d1753 - desc/o Major Robert Peyton VG470

Celia - of VA, d1774, m Henry Lockey d1773/1774 son of Joseph Lockey - desc/o Robert Peyton DBR(4)530, 601, 607, 621;

PAYTON or PEYTON (cont.)
   DBR(5)75, 730, 732; FFF40
   Elizabeth - of VA, b abt 1670, m abt 1688 Col Peter Beverley, clerk of
      the House of Burgesses 1691/1696; Surveyor General 1719/1728;
      Treasurer 1719/1723 - desc/o Maj Robert Payton CHB168;
      MCB150; BCD168; CRL(1)259; VG468
   Elizabeth - of VA, b1756, m1773 Mr John Dixon, Jr d1788 merchant
      of Gloucestershire - desc/o Major Robert Peyton VG477, 478
   Frances - of VA, b abt 1753/1754 d1828, m1770 John Tabb d bef
      1828 - desc/o Major Robert Payton VG477
   Frances - of VA, d1809, m1755 Humphrey Gwynn b1727 d1794 -
      desc/o Major Robert Payton VG469
   Harriet - of VA, b1761, m1776 Thacker Washington b1740 son of
      Henry Washington & had issue - desc/o Major Robert Peyton
      VG478
   Henry - of VA, b1631 d1659, m Ellen Partington or Packington -
      desc/o John Payton DBR(3)144, 145, 207; DBR(4)445; DBR(5)297,
      622, 624, 628, 711, 950, 951
   Henry - of VA, b1656, m Anne____ - desc/o John Payton DBR(3)145,
      207; DBR(4)445; DBR(5)622, 711, 952
   Henry - of VA, b abt 1744 d1815, m1764 Susanna Fowke - desc/o
      Henry Peyton DBR(5)952
   Henry - of VA - b1765 d aft 1824, m Elizabeth Bronaugh - desc/o
      Henry Peyton DBR(5)952
   James - of VA, b1730 d1789, m1755 Susannah Threlkeld - desc/o
      John Payton DBR(3)145, 207; DBR(4)445
   John - of VA 1644, bp 1596 - the immigrant DBR(3)145, 592;
      DBR(4)444, 445; RAA1, 122; EDV63; sufficient proof of alleged
      royal ancestry is lacking
   John - of VA, b1691 d1760, m(2)1752 Elizabeth Rowzie - desc/o Henry
      Payton DBR(5)711, 952
   Sir John - of VA, b abt 1710/1720 d1790, m(1) abt 1735 Frances____,
      m(2) abt 1786 Mary Dick dau/o Charles Dick of VA - desc/o Major
      Robert Peyton VG469, 475
   Martha - of VA, m1751 Matthew Whiting - desc/o Major Robert Peyton
      VG469
   Mary - of VA, m1756 Humphrey Toye Tabb - desc/o Major Robert
      Peyton VG469
   Mary - of VA, b1758, m1773 Mordecai Throckmorton d abt 1788 -
      desc/o Major Robert Peyton VG478
   Philip - of VA, b abt 1705 d1790, m1748 Winifred Buford - desc/o
      John Payton DBR(5)297, 624, 628
   Maj Robert - of VA bef 1679, b abt 1640 of Roughamn, Co Norfolk,
      England & Iselham, Gloucester, VA d aft 1693, attorney & major
      1680 son of Thomas Peyton III & Elizabeth Yelkverton, m abt
      1665____ & had issue - the immigrant CHB168; MCB150; BCD168;
      DBR(4)530, 601, 607, 621; DBR(5)75, 730, 732; RAA1; CRL(1)259;
      FFF40; GBR185; VG468
   Robert - of VA, b1677/1680 Gloucester Co d bef 1746 North Carolina,
      m Mary____ - desc/o Major Robert Peyton DBR(4)530, 601, 607,
      621; DBR(5)75, 730, 732; VG468

PAYTON or PEYTON (cont.)

Robert - of VA, b1718 d1792, m Sarah West - desc/o Major Robert Peyton FFF40

Ruth - of VA, b1767 d1803, m1784 James Thompson - desc/o John Payton DBR(3)145 207; DBR(4)446

Sarah - of NC, b abt 1726, m abt 1742 Captain Henry Snoad & had issue - desc/o Major Robert Peyton VG470

Seigniora - of VA, b1767 d1810, m Thomas Tabb Bolling b1763 son of Robert Bolling & Mary Cocke - desc/o Major Robert Peyton VG478

Thomas - of VA, b abt 1675 Gloucester Co, vestryman in Prince William Co, 1749, m abt 1700 Frances Tab dau/o John Tabb - desc/o Major Robert Peyton VG468/469

Thomas - of VA, b abt 1751 vestryman of Kingston Parish 1778, m Anne____ d1777 - desc/o Major Robert Peyton VG477

Valentine - of VA, b1657 d1705 - desc/o Henry Payton DBR(5)624, 628

Col Valentine - of VA, b1686 d1751, m Frances Harrison - desc/o John Payton DBR(3)145, 207; DBR(4)445; DBR(5)297

Lieut Valentine - of VA, b1749/1750 d1831, m Mary Elizabeth Edwards - desc/o John Peyton DBR(5)297, 622, 627, 631

Dr Valentine - of VA, b1756, m Mary Butler Washington - desc/o Henry Peyton DBR(5)711

William - of VA, bp 1718 d1792, m Sarah West - desc/o Robert Peyton DBR(4)530, 607, 621; DBR(5)75, 730, 732

PEAKE Lemuel - b1733 - desc/o Griffith Bowen RAA72

PEARCE Mary - b1654, m Thomas Brownell - desc/o Richard Pearce LDS36

Richard - b1615, m Susannah Wright - the immigrant LDS36; RAA no longer accepted as being of royal descent

PECK Elizabeth - of MA, b1657, m Maj Samuel Mason - desc/o Joseph Peck CRL(2)10

Hannah - of MA, b1653, m1677 Daniel Reed - desc/o Joseph Peck CRL(2)10

Ichabod - of MA, b1666 d abt 1690 - desc/o Joseph Peck CRL(2)10

Israel - of MA, bp 1644 d1723, m Bethiah Bosworth - desc/o Joseph Peck CRL(2)10

Jathniel - of MA, b1660, m1688/1689 Sarah Smith - desc/o Joseph Peck CRL(2)10

Jerusha - b1727 - desc/o Agnes Harris RAA131

John - of MA, b abt 1626, m(1)____, m(2) Elizabeth, m(3) Rebecca____ - desc/o Joseph Peck CRL(2)10

Joseph - of MA 1638, b1587 d1663, m(1)1617 Rebecca Clark (d1637), m(2)1638 ____ - the immigrant EDV108; CRL(2)9, 10, 22, 26, 30, 47; sufficient proof of alleged royal ancestry is lacking

Joseph - of MA, bp 1623 d1701, m Hannah____ - desc/o Joseph Peck CRL(2)10, 23, 26, 30, 47

Mary - of MA, b1662, m1690/1691 Benjamin Hunt - desc/o Joseph Peck CRL(2)10

Mary - b1726/1727 - desc/o Elizabeth Alsop RAA65

Nathaniel - of MA, bp 1641 d1676, m Deliverance____ (d1675) - desc/o Joseph Peck CRL(2)10

PECK (cont.)

Nicholas - of MA, bp 1630 d1710, m(1) Mary Winchester, m(2) Rebecca____ - desc/o Joseph Peck CRL(2)10

Patience - of MA, b1669 d1746, m Richard Bowen III - desc/o Joseph Peck CRL(2)10, 23, 26, 31, 47

Rebecca - of MA, bp 1620, m ____ Hubbert - desc/o Joseph Peck CRL(2)10

Samuel - of MA, bp 1638/1639 d1736, m(1)1666 Sarah Hunt (d1673), m(2)1677 Rebecca (Paine) Hunt - desc/o Joseph Peck CRL(2)10

Capt Samuel - of MA, b1672 d1736, m Rachel____ - desc/o Joseph Peck CRL(2)10

PELHAM Capt Edward - of RI, b abt 1650/1652 d1730, m1682 Freelove Arnold b1661 d1711 dau/o Governor Benedict Arnold of Rhode Island - desc/o Herbert Pelham FLW189, 185; MCS57, 72; EDV17, 18; TAG(18)144; NE(33)292

Edward - of RI, d1740/1741, m1717/1718 Arabella Williams - desc/o Herbert Pelham TAG(18)145

Elizabeth - of RI, m(1)1711 John Goodson, m(2)1719 Peter Coggeshall - desc/o Herbert Pelham TAG(18)145

Frances - of MA, b1643, m Jeremiah Stonnard - desc/o Herbert Pelham MCS72; TAG(18)144; NE(33)292

Henry - d1699, m Elizabeth____ d1713 - desc/o Herbert Pelham NE(33)292

Hermione - of RI, b1718 d1765, m1737 John Banister - desc/o Herbert Pelham TAG(18)145

Herbert - of MA 1639/1640, b abt 1600 d1673, 1st treasurer of Harvard College 1643; Commissioner of the United Colonies 1645, son of Herbert Pelham & Penelope West, m(1)1626 Jemima Waldegrave dau/o Thomas Waldegrave & Margaret Holmstead, m(2) Elizabeth Bosville dau/o Godfrey Bosville of Gunthwaite, Yorkshire - the immigrant CHB195; FLW189; MCB159; MCD321; MCS57; ECD195; EDV18; NE(33)287/291; GBR116; TAG(14)197/201, (18)137/149, 210/218, (19)197/202

Mary - of MA, b1640 - desc/o Herbert Pelham MCS72

Penelope - of MA, b abt 1619 d1702, dau/o Herbert Pelham & Penelope West, m1641 Richard Bellingham b abt 1592 Boston, Lincolnshire, England d1672 governor of MA, son of William Bellingham & Frances Amcotts of Manton & Bromby, Lincoln, no issue - the immigrant MCS57; GBR116; FLW189

Penelope - of MA, bp 1633 Bures d1703, m1657 Governor Josiah Winslow of Plymouth Colony - desc/o Herbert Pelham CHB195; ECD(3)238; MCD321; MCS57; BCD195; TAG(18)144; NE(33)291

Penelope - of RI, b1724, m1741 Joseph Cowley - desc/o Herbert Pelham TAG(18)146

Philadelphia - of VA, dau/o Sir Thomas Pelham, 2nd Baronet & Margaret Vane, m Francis Howard, 5th Baron Howard of Effingham - the immigrant GBR123

Thomas - of RI, b abt 1724 d1786, m Abigail____ - desc/o Herbert Pelham TAG(18)145, 146

William - bp 1677 Bures d1714/1715, m Elizabeth____ & had two young children, Henry & Elizabeth the latter being baptized at

PELHAM (cont.)

Bures in 1713 - desc/o Herbert Pelham NE(33)292

PELL Benjamin - of NY, b1753 d1823, m(1)1798 Mary Ferris, m(2) Mary Titus, m(3) Phoebe Folger - desc/o Rev John Pell BLG2859; CFA410

Caleb - b1712 d1768, m Mary Ferris - desc/o Rev John Pell CFA410

Edward - m Mary Deveraux - desc/o Rev John Pell CFA410

Gilbery - m Mary Honeywell - desc/o Rev John Pell CFA410

Rev John - of NY, b1610/1611 d1685, m1632 Tamer Reginolles - the immigrant BLG2859; sufficient proof of alleged royal ancestry is lacking

Lieut Col John - of NY, b1643 d1702, m1675 Rachel Pinckney - desc/o Rev John Pell BLG2859; CFA410

John - b1702 d1773 m____ Totten - desc/o Rev John Pell CFA410

Joseph - of NY, b1700 d1752, m Phoebe Deane - desc/o Rev John Pell BLG2859; CFA410

Joseph - of NY, b1710 d1781, m Phoebe Palmer - desc/o Rev John Pell BLG2859; CFA410

Joseph - of NY, b1740 d1776 - desc/o Rev John Pell BLG2859

Joshua - b1737 d1821, m Abigail Archer - desc/o Rev John Pell CFA410

Philip - m1731 Phoebe Fitch - desc/o Rev John Pell CFA410

Thomas - of NY 1666, bp 1612/1613 d1669, m1647 Lucy____ - the immigrant EDV17, 18; BLG2859; CFA410; sufficient proof of alleged royal ancestry is lacking

Thomas - of NY, b1675 d1739, m Anna dau of Wampage, an Indian chief - desc/o Rev John Pell BLG2859

Thomas - b1704 d1753, m Dorothy Ward - desc/o Rev John Pell CFA410

PELTON Lydia - of CT, b1772 d1864, m1795 John Lane - desc/o Alice Freeman DBR(4)483

PEMBERTON Thomas Jr - of VA, son of Thomas Pemberton & Rebecca Wingfield - desc/o Thomas Wingfield TVG(37)246

PENHALLOW Benjamin - of NH, m(1) Lucy Hart - desc/o Samuel Penhallow BLG2861

Deborah - of NH, b1702, m William Knight - desc/o Samuel Penhallow BLG2861

Elizabeth - of NH, b1698, m(1) John Drummer, m(2) Rev Christopher Toppan BLG2861

Hannah - of NH, b1688, m James Pemberton - desc/o Samuel Penhallow BLG2861

Hulking - of NH, b1766 d1826, m Harriet Pearce - desc/o Samuel Penhallow BLG2861

John - of NH, b1693 d1735, m Elizabeth Butler - desc/o Samuel Penhallow BLG2861

John - of NH, m(1) Sarah Wentworth - desc/o Samuel Penhallow BLG2861

John - of NH, m Sarah Phillips - desc/o Samuel Penhallow BLG2861

Lydia - of NH, b1700 d1718, m Henry Sloper - desc/o Samuel Penhallow BLG2861

Mary - of NH, b1689, m Benjamin Gambling - desc/o Samuel Penhallow BLG2861

PENHALLOW (cont.)

Phoebe - of NH, b1695, m(1) Capt Gross, m(2) Maj Leonard Vassall, m(3) Thomas Graves, m(4) Francis Borland - desc/o Samuel Penhallow BLG2861

Richard Wibird - of NH - desc/o Samuel Penhallow BLG2861

Samuel - of NH, b1665 d1726, merchant, jurist, historian & public official son of Chamond Penhallow & Anne Tamlyn, m(1)1687 Mary Cutts, m(2)1714 Abigail Atkinson - the immigrant MCS17; BLG2860; RAA1, 121; GBR419

Samuel - of NH, b1691, m1732____ - desc/o Samuel Penhallow BLG2860

Samuel - of NH, b1757, m Hannah Sherburne - desc/o Samuel Penhallow BLG2861

Susannah - b1708, m William Winkley - desc/o Samuel Penhallow BLG2861

Thomas - of NH, m Hannah Bunbury - desc/o Samuel Penhallow BLG2861

PENN Christiana Gulielma - b1733 d1803, m abt 1761 Peter Gaskell b abt 1730 d1785 - desc/o Robert Barclay ECD247; GBR49; GPFPM(2)574, 575; CRFP(1)12, 13

Granville - b1761 d1844, m1791 Isabella Forbes b1771 d1847 eldest dau/o General Gordon Forbes & Mary Sullivan - desc/o Lady Juliana Fermor GPFPM(2)569; CRFP(1)7

John "the Younger" - of PA, b1760 d1830 unmarried - desc/o William Penn EDV40 - desc/o Lady Juliana Fermor GPFPM(2)568

Juliana - of PA, b1753 d1772, m1771 William Baker - desc/o Lady Juliana Fermor GPFPM(2)568; CRFP(1)6, 7

Sophia Margaretta - b1764 d1847, m1796 William Stuart Archbishop of Armagh, Established Church & was Primate of that church in Ireland, son of John, Earl of Bute & Lady Mary Wortley Montagu - desc/o Lady Juliana Fermor CRFP(1)7

William - of PA - the immigrant EDV40; Sufficient proof of the alleged royal ancestry is lacking

William - of PA - desc/o William Penn EDV40

PENNOCK Betsy or Betty - b1771, m James Hyde - desc/o Deborah Barlow LDS59

PENNOYER Col Jesse - of NY, b1760 d1825, m Martha Ferguson - desc/o Thomas Pennoyer BLG2862

John - of CT & NY, b1698 - desc/o Thomas Pennoyer BLG2862

Rev Joseph - of NY, b1734, m Lucy____ - desc/o Thomas Pennoyer BLG2862

Thomas - b1658, m1683 Lydia Knapp - the immigrant BLG2862, royalty not proven

PENROSE Bartholomew - of PA, b1674 d1711, m Esther Leech - the immigrant AFA36; sufficient proof of alleged royal ancestry is lacking

Clement Biddle - of PA, b1771 d abt 1820, m1796 Anne Howard - desc/o Bartholomew Penrose AFA36

James - of PA, b1737/1738 d1771, m1766 Sarah Biddle - desc/o Bartholomew Penrose AFA36

Thomas - of PA, b1709/1710 d1757, m1731 Sarah Coats - desc/o

PENROSE (cont.)

Bartholomew Penrose AFA36

PEPPER Apphia - m Timothy Cole - desc/o Constant Southworth DBR(3)245

PERCIVAL Elizabeth - of MA, b1675, m Joseph Ashley - desc/o Edward Raynsford NE(139)299

James - of MA, b1671/1672 Sandwich, MA d1738 East Haddam, CT, m1695/1696 Sandwich, MA, Abigail Robinson - desc/o Edward Raynsford NE(139)299

John - of MA, d aft 3 Apr 1738 Barnstable, MA, m1703 Sandwich, MA, Mary Bourne - desc/o Edward Raynsford NE(139)299

Mary - of MA, m Nathan Bassett - desc/o Edward Raynsford NE(139)200

PERCY George - of VA, b1580 d1632, governor of VA, died unmarried, son of Henry Percy, 8th Earl of Northumberland & Katherine Neville - the immigrant GBR172

PERKINS Betty - b1756 - desc/o John Hawes RAA102 - desc/o George Morton RAA116

Charles - of CT, m Clarissa Deming - desc/o Mabel Harlakenden CHB268; BCD268

Constantine - of VA, b1682 d1676, m(2) Ann Pollard - desc/o Nicholas Perkins DBR(2)746

Hannah - b1756, m Jesse Bowles - desc/o Nicholas Perkins DBR(2)746

Isaac - of NH, bp 1611, m Susanna___ - the immigrant AFA76; sufficient proof of alleged royal ancestry is lacking

John - b abt 1722 - desc/o George Morton RAA116

John - b1748 - desc/o George Morton RAA116

Joseph - of NH & DE, m Martha___ - desc/o Isaac Perkins AFA76

Joseph - of MD, m Mary Hilton - desc/o Isaac Perkins AFA76

Nicholas - of VA 1640, d1656, m Mary Parker - the immigrant DBR(2)746; sufficient proof of alleged royal ancestry is lacking

Nicholas - of VA, b1640 d1711, m Sarah Childress - desc/o Nicholas Perkins DBR(2)746

Stephen - of VA, b1710 d1772, m Mary Hughes - desc/o Nicholas Perkins DBR(2)746

William - of MD & KY, m Nancy Gilpin - desc/o Isaac Perkins AFA76

PERLEY Rev Humphrey Clark of MA, b1761 d1838, m1797 Elizabeth Mighill - desc/o John Putnam CHB429

Capt William - of MA, b1735/1736 d1812, m1761 Sarah Clarke - desc/o John Putnam CHB429

PERNE Rachel - of MA 1650, m Edward Rawson - the immigrant J&K143; PFA Apx C #12 sufficient proof of alleged royal ancestry is lacking

PERRIN Mehitable - b1710 - desc/o Griffith Bowen RAA72

PERROTT Elizabeth - of VA, b1645, m1662 John Beauford - desc/o Richard Perrott JSW1732

Richard - d1686, m(1), m(2), m(3) - the immigrant JSW1732 royal ancestry unproven

PERRY Abijah - b1766, m Elizabeth Tippets or Tibbetts - desc/o Abraham Errington LDS77

Lieut Asa - of MA, m1769 Lydia Leland - desc/o Anthony Fisher

PERRY (cont.)
    AFA104
    Capt Christopher Raymond, United States Navy - m Sarah Wallace
        Alexander - desc/o William Arnold J&K292
    Ezra - b1741 d1821, Revolutionary soldier, m1762 Jemima Titus
        b1744 d1808 - desc/o Lieut Griffith Bowen DBR(1)466
    Frances - of VA, m Francis Whiting - desc/o Robert Throckmorton
        CFA(1)524
    Mary - of CT, b1725 d1807, m Gershom Banks b1712 - desc/o Grace
        Chetwoode CHB395
    Samuel - of MA, m1698 Johanna Lovett - desc/o Anthony Fisher
        AFA104
    Samuel - of MA, m1735 Ruth Leland - desc/o Anthony Fisher AFA104
PETER Robert - of VA, b1760 d1791, m Claramond Holt - desc/o Frances
    Mason CHB441
PETERS Hugh - of MA, b1598 d1660 Puritan clergyman & Cromwellian
    politician, son of Thomas Dyckwood, alias Peters & Martha Treffry,
    m(1) Mrs Elizabeth Cooke Reade, m(2) Deliverance Sheffield - the
    immigrant GBR319 some aspect of royal descent merits further
    study; EO2(2)925/931
    John - b1740, m Ann Barnett - desc/o Thomas Holcomb LDS69
PETTIBONE Abigail - b1706, m(1) David Phelps - desc/o Thomas
    Holcomb LDS68
PHELPS Abigail - b1754, m Jared Merrill - desc/o Thomas Holcomb
    LDS68
    David - b1734, m(1) Abigail Griswold - desc/o Thomas Holcomb LDS68
    Ebenezer - b1745 - desc/o Mary Guy RAA115
    Joel - of CT, b1732, m1757 Jerusha Nash - desc/o John Drake THC83
        - desc/o Henry Griswold THC131 - desc/o Thomas Holcomb
        THC169 - desc/o Thomas Moore THC220
    Lydia - b1723 m John Peters - desc/o Thomas Holcomb LDS69
    Lydia Gould - b1775 - desc/o Mary Guy RAA115
    Mary - b1658, m Daniel Adams - the immigrant LDS12; sufficient
        proof of alleged royal ancestry is lacking
    Phineas - of CT, b1767 d1813, m Lydia Lawrence - desc/o John Drake
        THC83 - desc/o Henry Griswold THC131 - desc/o Thomas Holcomb
        THC169 - desc/o Thomas Moore THC220
    Ruth Barber - of CT, b1713, m Lieut Samuel Phelps - desc/o Thomas
        Moore THC220
    Lieut Samuel - of CT, b1675, m Abigail Eno - desc/o Henry Griswold
        THC130, 169
    Lieut Samuel - of CT, b1708 d1754, m1731 Ruth Phelps - desc/o
        John Drake THC83 - desc/o Henry Griswold THC130, 169
    Temperance - b1739 - desc/o John Drake RAA87
    Ursula - of CT, b1740 d1819, m1762 Deacon Ezekiel Mills - desc/o
        Thomas Newberry ECD(3)229; RAA118
PHILBRICK Esther - b1699, m Amos Rand - desc/o Gov Thomas Roberts
    LDS65
    Joseph - b1663, m Tryphena Marston - desc/o Gov Thomas Roberts
    LDS65

PHILLIPS Abigail - of MA, m Josiah Quincy Jr - desc/o Edward Bromfield
EO(1)328

Elizabeth - m1779 Boston, John Parker, Esq - desc/o Mary Gye
NE(97)57

John - of MA, b1770 d1823 judge of the court of common pleas, was
chosen the first mayor of Boston, m1794 Sally Walley dau/o
Thomas Walley, a merchant of Boston - desc/o Gov Thomas Dudley
NE(8)315

Letitia Bland - m William Magruder Beall - desc/o Col George Reade
DBR(2)436

Margaret - of MA, m Judge Samuel Cooper - desc/o Gov Thomas
Dudley NE(8)315

Nancy - of MA, m1789 Boston, Joseph Lovering - desc/o Mary Gye
NE(97)57

Polly - of MA, m(1)1781 Boston, Jabez Fox, m(2)1787 Boston, William
Lovering - desc/o Mary Gye NE(97)57

Sarah - of MA, m Deacon Mark Newman of Andover - desc/o Gov
Thomas Dudley NE(8)315

William - of VA, m Margaret Bland - desc/o Col George Reade
DBR(2)436

PIERCE Caleb - of PA, b1727/1728 d1815, m1755 Hannah Greaves -
desc/o Joseph Gilpin CRL(4)198

Caleb - b1757 d1796, m Priscilla Wickersham - desc/o Joseph Gilpin
CRL(4)198

Edward - of PA 1737 - the immigrant EDV128, 129; sufficient proof of
alleged royal ancestry is lacking

Jacob - of PA, b1761 d1801, m1784 Hannah Buffington - desc/o
Joseph Gilpin CRL(4)198

Joshua P (twin) b1766, m abt 1811 Susanna Bennett - desc/o Joseph
Gilpin CRL(4)198

PIERPONT Abigail - of CT, b1696 d1768, m1716 Rev Joseph Noyes -
desc/o Mabel Harlakenden MCB404; MCD229

Juliet - m Junius Spencer Morgan and had John Pierpont Morgan -
desc/o Richard Lyman J&K208

PIERREPONT Hezekiah - of CT, b1712 d1741, m1736/1737 Lydia
Hemingway - desc/o James Pierrepont AFA30

Hezekiah Beers - of CT & NY, b1768 d1838, m 1802 Anna Maria
Constable - desc/o James Pierrepont AFA30

James - m Margaret ____ - the immigrant J&K235; AFA30 royal
ancestry unproven

Rev James - of CT, b1659/1660 d1714, a founder of Yale College, m(3)
Mary Hooker - desc/o James Pierrepont J&K235; AFA30

John - of MA, b1617 d1682, m Thankful Stow - desc/o James
Pierrepont J&K235; AFA30

John - of CT, b1740 d1805, m1767 Sarah Beers - desc/o James
Pierrepont AFA30

Sarah - of CT, b1710 d1758, m1727 Rev Jonathan Edwards - desc/o
James Pierrepont J&K235

PIERSON Elizabeth - b1726, m1757 Rev Jacob Green - desc/o Thomas
Dudley ECD256; DBR(2)110 - desc/o George Wyllys DBR(4)115 -
desc/o Mabel Harlakenden DBR(3)118

PIERSON (cont.)

Fanny - of NJ, b1733 d1828, m Israel Crane - desc/o Obadiah Bruen
ECD123

PINKHAM Abijah - b1734 - desc/o Rose Stoughton RAA119

Otis - b abt 1694/1695 - desc/o Rose Stoughton RAA119

Rose - b abt 1655 - desc/o Rose Stoughton RAA119

Sarah - b abt 1761 - desc/o Rose Stoughton RAA119

PINNEY Anne (Anna) - of CT, b1712/1713 d1789, m Asahel Phelps -
desc/o Thomas Newberry ECD(3)229; RAA118

Isaac Jr - of CT, b1686/1687 d1717, m1709/1710 Abigail Fillery -
desc/o Thomas Newberry ECD(3)226, 229; RAA118

Judge Isaac III - of CT, b1716 d1791, m Susannah Phelps - desc/o
Thomas Newberry ECD(3)226

Sarah - of CT, b1756 d1805, m1779 Col Josiah Edson - desc/o
Thomas Newberry ECD(3)226

PITCAIRN John - b1722 d1775 British commander at the Battle of
Lexington in April 1775 son of David & Katherine (Hamilton)
Pitcairn, m Elizabeth Dalrymple - the immigrant GBR69

PITKIN Catherine - of CT, b1757 d1837, m1774 Rev Nathan Perkins -
desc/o Mabel Harlakenden CHB272; BCD272

Rev Timothy - of CT, b1727 d1812 minister of Farmington, CT, m1753
Temperance Clap dau/o Rev Thomas Clap president of Yale College
- desc/o Mabel Harlakenden CHB272; BCD272 - desc/o Gov
Thomas Dudley NE(32)294

Timothy - of CT, m1801 Elizabeth Hubbard - desc/o Mabel
Harlakenden BCD272

PITTS Samuel - of MA, b1745 d1805, m1776 Johanna Davis - desc/o
Judge Simon Lynde CHB313; BCD313

PLACE Benajah - b1742 d1815, m Mary Perkins - desc/o Anne Marbury
DBR(5)948

Enoch - b1704 d1789, m Hannah Wilcox - desc/o Anne Marbury
DBR(5)948

John - b1763 d1846, m Lydia Wilcox - desc/o Anne Marbury
DBR(5)948

Sarah - of RI, b1728 d1805, m1749 Josiah Jones - desc/o Anne
Marbury DBR(3)134

Thomas - of MA, b1697 d1779, m Margaret Stafford - desc/o Anne
Marbury DBR(3)134

PLATT Capt Epenetus - of NY, b1640 d1693, m1667 Phebe Wood -
desc/o Richard Platt BLG2867; CFA(1)415

Maj Epenetus - of NY, b1674 d1744 - desc/o Richard Platt BLG2867

Epenetus - of NY, b abt 1630 d1777, m1753 Catherine Lawrence -
desc/o Richard Platt BLG2867

Epenetus - of NY, b1763 d1796, m Mary Simonson - desc/o Richard
Platt BLG2867

Ephenetus - of CT, b1706 - desc/o Richard Platt CFA(1)415

Lieut Gideon - of CT, bp 1700, m1726 Mary Buckingham - desc/o
Richard Platt CFA(1)415, 416

Gideon - of CT, bp 1734 d1796, m Mehitable Platt - desc/o Richard
Platt CFA(1)416

Gideon - of CT, b1757 d1836, m1783 Hannah Clark - desc/o Richard

PLATT (cont.)

Platt CFA(1)416

Hannah - of CT, b1643 - desc/o Richard Platt CFA(1)415

Hannah - of PA, b1732 d1776, m1755 Enoch Hobart - desc/o James Claypoole BCD94

Henry - of PA, m Elizabeth Dundas - desc/o James Claypoole BCD93

Jonah - of CT, b1645 - desc/o Richard Platt CFA(1)415

Joseph - of CT, b1649, m1680 Mary Kellogg - desc/o Richard Platt CFA(1)415

Joseph - of CT, b1683 - desc/o Richard Platt CFA(1)415

Mary - m(1) Luke Atkinson, m(2) Thomas Wetmore - desc/o Richard Platt CFA(1)415

Mary - of CT, b1704 - desc/o Richard Platt CFA(1)415

Matthew - of PA, m____ - desc/o James Claypoole BCD93

Richard - of CT, b1603 d1684, m Mary____ - the immigrant BLG2867; CFA(1)415; sufficient proof of alleged royal ancestry is lacking

Samuel - of CT, bp 1690 - desc/o Richard Platt CFA(1)415

Sarah - m(1) Thomas Beach, m(2) Miles Erwin - desc/o Richard Platt CFA(1)415

Uriah - of NY, b1707 d1762, m(1) abt 1728 Mary Smith - desc/o Richard Platt BLG2867

PLEASANTS Martha - of VA, m Nathaniel Vandewall - desc/o Lieut Col Walter Aston FFF271

PLOWDEN Dorothy - m Col James Fenwick - desc/o Col Giles Brent RCFA112

Edmund - m Henrietta Slye - desc/o Col Giles Brent RCFA112

PLUMMER Elizabeth - of MD, bp (aft her marriage) 1698 d1762, m1696 William Ijams Jr - desc/o Frances White ECD(2)309

Kemp - b1769 d1826, m1794 Susannah Martin - desc/o Matthew Kempe DBR(3)579

William - of VA, d1774, m Mary Hayes - desc/o Matthew Kempe DBR(3)579

POLK Capt Ezekiel - of SC, served in the Revolutionary War - desc/o Robert Polk J&K140

Robert - of MD abt 1750, m ____ Gullet - the immigrant J&K141; sufficient proof of alleged royal ancestry is lacking

Samuel - of TN, m1794 Jane Knox, father of James Knox Polk President of the United States 1845/1849 - desc/o Robert Polk J&K140

POLLARD Oliver - of MA, b1727 d1812, m1759 Mary Townsend - desc/o John Prescott DBR(1)521

Sarah - of MA, b1751 d1820, m1774 Aaron Whitney - desc/o John Prescott DBR(1)31

POLLOCK Nancy Anne - of KY, b1743 d1805, m1760 Major John Allen - the immigrant JSW1537; sufficient proof of alleged royal ancestry is lacking

POMEROY Eleanor - of MA, b1752 d1823, m1771 Nobel Dewey - desc/o Benjamin Moseley ECD(3)217; DBR(2)721

Eunice - m Ebenezer Clark III - desc/o Margaret Wyatt GBR397

George (Holmes) - of PA, son of Thomas Holmes Pomeroy & Andriah Towgood, m Margaret____ - the immigrant GBR406

POMEROY (cont.)

Luther - b1757 - desc/o Charles Chauncy RAA79

Rachel Lyman - of CT, b1754 d1774, m1771 Brig Maj Edward Bulkeley - desc/o Richard Lyman CHB153; BCD152

Samuel Wyllys - of OH, b1764 d1841, m1793 Clarissa Alsop - desc/o Mabel Harlakenden CHB269; MCB412; BCD269

POOLE Bethesda - of MA, m John Filer - desc/o Capt William Poole MCS19; TAG(31)170/172

John - of MA, m1672 Elizabeth Brenton - desc/o Capt William Poole MCS19; TAG(31)170/172

Mary - of MA, m Daniel Henchman - desc/o Capt William Poole MCS19; TAG(31)170/172

Capt William - of MA abt 1630, bp 1593 d1674 schoolmaster & a founder of Taunton, MA, son of Sir William Poole & Mary Perlham, m Mary____ - the immigrant MCS19; TAG(14)222, 223, (31)170, 172; RAA123; GBR134

POPHAM George - of ME, d1608 son of Edward Popham & Jane Norton - the immigrant GBR134; TAG(31)171, 172, (32)9/12

PORDAGE Hannah of CT, m(2)1714 James Bowdoin - desc/o Judge Simon Lynde CHB313; BCD313

PORTER Calvert - of VA, Revolutionary soldier from VA, m1749 Elizabeth Cash & had issue - desc/o Leonard Calvert MG(1)174

Howson - of VA, m1746 John Starke d1755 & had issue - desc/o Leonard Calvert MG(1)174

Joseph - of VA, b1726/1727, m1756 Jemima Smith of Overwharton Parish, Stafford Co - desc/o Leonard Calvert MG(1)174

POWARS John - b1738 d1820, m Affa Bixbee d1829 age 82 years - desc/o Dorothy Harlakenden DBR(1)273

POWELL Anne - of MD, m1725 Daniel Cox of Dorchester Co, MD - desc/o Anne Lovelace GVFHB(3)381

Daniel - of MD, b abt 1670 d1731, planter of Talbot Co, MD, m1694 Susanna Pitt d1745 dau/o John Pitt of Talbot Co - desc/o Anne Lovelace APP407; GVFHB(3)380, 381

Daniel - of MD, b1708, m1734 Mary Sherwood - desc/o Anne Lovelace GVFHB(3)383

Elizabeth - of MD, m1680 William Dickinson b1689/1690 d1717/1718 of Talbot Co, MD, Quaker, son of Walter Dickinson - desc/o Anne Lovelace APP407; GVFHB(3)379, 380

Frances - of MD, m prior to 1719/1720 William Harrison d1719/1720, planter of Talbot Co, MD, William Harrison left issue by a previous marriage, but there was no issue by William & Frances - desc/o Anne Lovelace GVFHB(3)381

Howell - of MD, b abt 1673 d1740, planter of Talbot Co, MD, m(1)1698 Joanna Pryor, m(2)1704 Esther Bartlett d1717 age 35 years dau/o Thomas Bartlett of Tredhaven Creek, Talbot Co, MD, m(3)1718 Sarah Edmondson - desc/o Anne Lovelace APP407; GVFHB(3)382

James - of MD, b1705/1706 d1734, m1728 Hannah Parrot, they had issue at least one son Howell Powell - desc/o Anne Lovelace GVFHB(3)382

Joanna - of MD, b1715/1716, m1734 William Thomas - desc/o Anne Lovelace GVFHB(3)383

POWELL (cont.)

Mary - of MD, b1713, m1733/1734 Solomon Kenton - desc/o Anne Lovelace GVFHB(3)383

Rebecca - of MD, b abt 1697/1698 d1728, m1724 John Dickinson of Talbot Co, MD - desc/o Anne Lovelace GVFHB(3)381

Sarah - of MD, b1721, m by 1739 ____ Thomas - desc/o Anne Lovelace GVFHB(3)383

Susanna - of MD, d1735/1736, m1734 George Maynard of Queen Anne Co, MD - desc/o Anne Lovelace GVFHB(3)381

Thomas - of MD, b1710/1711, m(1)1737____, m(2)1741____ - desc/o Anne Lovelace GVFHB(3)383

POWER Olive - b1760 - desc/o James Cudworth RAA84

POYTHRESS Ann - b 1712 - desc/o Martha Mallory RAA67

Elizabeth Bland - of VA, b1759 d1806, m William Mayo - desc/o Col William Randolph CRL(3)240

Peter - b abt 1686 - desc/o Martha Mallory RAA67

Susannah - of VA, m William Hall of Buckingham Co VA b abt 1700 - desc/o Capt Henry Batte ECD109; ECD(2)35; DBR(1)367; DBR(2)438, 470, 620; DBR(3)591

Thomas - of VA, m Elizabeth Pleasants Cocke, dau/o James Cocke, clerk of court & burgess abt 1699 - desc/o Capt Henry Batte ECD109; ECD(2)35; DBR(1)367; DBR(2)437, 470, 620; 801; DBR(3)110, 591

PRATHER Lieut Thomas Clagett - of MD, b1726 d1758, m Margaret Prather - desc/o Anne Lovelace JSW1635; DBR(2)663

Thomas - of KY, b1751 d1786, m1775/1776 Mary____ - desc/o Anne Lovelace JSW1635; DBR(2)663

PRATT Hannah - of PA, b1732, m1755 Enoch Hobart - desc/o James Claypoole CHB94

Henry - of PA, m Elizabeth Dundas - desc/o James Claypoole CHB93

Matthew - of PA, m____ - desc/o James Claypoole CHB93

PRENCE Mercy - of MA, b abt 1631 d1711, m1649/1650 John Freeman - desc/o Mary Wentworth ECD(2)290, 295

PRESCOTT (Dr) Abel - of MA, b1718 d1805, m Abigail Brigham - desc/o Rev Edward Bulkeley ECD(2)262; GBR210/211 - desc/o Jane Allen GBR332

Abigail - b1688 - desc/o John Prescott RAA125

Benjamin - b1708 - desc/o James Prescott RAA124

David - b1727/1728 d1813, m1752 Abigail Wright - desc/o John Prescott DBR(1)460

Dorothy - of MA, b1681, m John Varnum - desc/o John Prescott DBR(1)524; RAA125

Ebenezer - b1700 d1771, m1721 Hannah Farnsworth - desc/o John Prescott DBR(1)460

Elizabeth - b1676, m Eleazer Green - desc/o John Prescott LDS75; RAA125

Elizabeth - of MA, abt 1713 d1803, m1731 Rev David Hall - desc/o Rev Peter Bulkeley ECD(3)63

Hannah - of MA, bp 1639 d1697, m1660 John Rugg - desc/o John Prescott DBR(1)381; CRL(1)226; AWW351

Huldah - b1738 - desc/o James Prescott RAA124

PRESCOTT (cont.)

James - of NH, b abt 1643 or 1648 d1728, m Mary Boulter b1648
d1735 dau/o Nathaniel Boulter & Grace Swain - the immigrant
DBR(1)396; FLW26; RAA1, 124 TAG(34)180, 181 sufficient proof of
alleged royal ancestry is lacking

James Jr - of NH, b1671, m1695 Maria Marston - desc/o James
Prescott DBR(1)396;

Jeremiah - b1767 - desc/o James Prescott RAA124

Jeremiah - of NH, b1718 d aft 1780, m(1)1741 Mary Hayes - desc/o
James Prescott DBR(1)397; RAA124

Col Jeremiah - of NH, b1741 d1817, m1764 Sarah Sherburne - desc/o
James Prescott DBR(1)398; RAA124

John - b1681 - desc/o James Prescott RAA124

John - of MA 1645, b abt 1604 d1681 served in the garrison at
Lancaster against the Indians 1675/1676, m1629 Mary Platts or
Gawkroger bp 1607 Sowerby Parish, Halifax, Yorkshire d aft 1678
Lancaster, MA, dau/o Abraham Gawkroger-Platts & Martha Riley -
the immigrant FLW39. The identification of John Prescott of
Lancaster, MA is still challenged. See TAG34:180. While evidence is
not conclusive, the alternatives are not conclusive either. This line
requires further work; MCS87; LDS34, 75; DBR(1)31, 127, 128,
291, 307, 372, 381, 459, 520, 524, 559, 568; EDV113,114; RAA1,
125; CRL(1)225, 226; AWW329, 351; J&K150; NE(95)8

John - of MA, b1743 d1821, m1765 Grace Potter - desc/o Rev Edward
Bulkeley ECD(2)262

John - of NH, b1764 d1857, m1792 Deborah Hill - desc/o James
Prescott DBR(1)397

Capt John Jr - of MA, bp 1635, m1668 Sarah Hayward - desc/o John
Prescott DBR(1)31, 307, 521, 559; CRL(1)226; FLW39

Jonas - b1676 d1750, m1699 Thankful Wheeler - desc/o John
Prescott DBR(1)460

Jonas - of MA, b1648 d1723, m1672 Mary Loker - desc/o John
Prescott LDS75; DBR(1)459, 524; RAA125; CRL(1)226

Jonathan - of MA, d1721, m(1)Dorothy____, m(2) Elizabeth____, m(3)
Rebecca Wheeler, m(4) Ruth Brown - desc/o John Prescott
CRL(1)226

Lucy - sister of Dr Samuel Prescott who completed Paul Revere's
Midnight Ride & ancestor of George Herbert Walker Bush 41st
President of the United States, m Jonathan Fay, Jr b1754 at
Westborough, MA - desc/o Rev Peter Bulkeley GBR211;
TAG(36)150 - desc/o Jane Allen GBR332

Lydia - of MA, b1641, m(1)1658 Jonas Fairbank, m(2) Elias Barron -
desc/o John Prescott DBR(1)128, 373; J&K150; RAA125;
CRL(1)226

Martha - of MA, b1632 d1656, m John Rugg - desc/o John Prescott
CRL(1)226

Martha - of MA, b1679/1680 d1748, m Josiah Wheeler - desc/o John
Prescott DBR(1)31, 521

Mary - b1674 - desc/o John Prescott RAA125

Mary - of MA, b1669, m(2) Philip Goss - desc/o John Prescott
DBR(1)559

PRESCOTT (cont.)

Mary - of MA, bp 1630, m1624 Thomas Sawyer - desc/o John Prescott LDS34; DBR(1)291, 568; RAA125; CRL(1)226

Rachel - b1766, m1790 Amos Reed - desc/o John Prescott DBR(1)460

Samuel - of NH, b1697, m1717 Mary Sanborn - desc/o James Prescott DBR(1)396, 397; RAA124

Samuel Potter - of MA, b1769 d1820, m1798 Elizabeth Brown - desc/o Rev Edward Bulkeley ECD(2)262

Sarah - b1686 - desc/o John Prescott RAA125

Sarah - bp 1637, m(1) Richard Wheeler, m(2)____ Rice - desc/o John Prescott CRL(1)226

PRESTON Anne - b1738 - desc/o Mary Gye RAA115

Hannah - of PA, b1693 d1772, m1711 Samuel Carpenter Jr - desc/o Gov Thomas Lloyd AFA198; CHB127; MCD252; BCD127; DBR(1)1; DBR(2)515; DBR(3)175

Margaret - of MD, b1689 d1734, m1709 Dr Richard Moore - desc/o Gov Thomas Lloyd BCD127; CHB127

PRICE Elizabeth - of VA, b abt 1745 d1819, m1761 Capt George Dabney - desc/o Col William Randolph DBR(1)422

Hannah - of PA 1684, b1656 d1741 dau/o Richard Price & ____, m(1) Rees Jones, m(2) Ellis David, m(3) Thomas Evans - the immigrant CHB294; MCB418; BCD294; GBR312

John - of VA, m(1) Jane____, m(2) Ann Mathews - the immigrant BLG2872, 2873; sufficient proof of alleged royal ancestry is lacking

John - of VA, m____ Rowan - desc/o John Price BLG2873

John - of VA, m Jane Pew - desc/o John Price BLG2873

John - of VA, m Hannah Williamson - desc/o John Price BLG2873

Maraday (or Meredith) - of VA, b1770, m1795 Mary McDaniel - desc/o John Price BLG2873

William - of VA, b1730, m Susanna Burton - desc/o John Price BLG2873

PRINCE John - of MA - the immigrant EDV129, 130; sufficient proof of alleged royal ancestry is lacking

PRIOLEAU Elias - of SC 1687, d1699, m Jeanne Burgeaud - the immigrant BLG2873; sufficient proof of alleged royal ancestry is lacking

Philip - of SC, b1755 d1846, m1783 Alice Edith Homeyard - desc/o Elias Prioleau BLG2873

Col Samuel - of SC, b abt 1690 d1752, m abt 1713 Mary Magdalen Gendron - desc/o Elias Prioleau BLG2873

Col Samuel - of SC, b1717 d1792, m1739 Providence Hext - desc/o Elias Prioleau BLG2873

PROUT Deborah - of MA, b1742 d1825, m1763 Jabez Griswold - desc/o Mary Launce DBR(2)552; DBR(3)121

John - of MA, b1697 d1751, m1736 Abigail Clark Royce - desc/o Mary Launce DBR(2)552; DBR(3)121

PRYOR Judge Roger A - of NY, m Sara Agnes Rice - desc/o Henry Isham CHB533

PULSIPHER John - b1749, m Elizabeth Dutton - desc/o Robert Harrington LDS82

PUTNAM Capt Benjamin - son of Nathaniel Putnam & Elizabeth
    Hutchinson - desc/o John Putnam J&K126
  Deliverance - of MA, b1656, m1685 Capt Jonathan Wolcott - desc/o
    John Putnam CHB428
  Ebenezer - of MA, bp 1717 d1788, m1764 Margaret Scollay - desc/o
    John Putnam CFA(1)422
  Ebenezer - of MA, b1768 d1826, m(1) Sarah Fiske, m(2)1796 Elizabeth
    Fiske - desc/o John Putnam CFA(1)422
  Huldah - of MA, b1716, m1734 Capt Francis Perley desc/o John
    Putnam CHB429
  Gen Israel Revolutionary War General - desc/o John Putnam J&K126
  Lieut James - of MA, b1661 d1727, m(1) Sarah Brocklebank,
    m(2)1719/1720 Mary Rea - desc/o John Putnam CFA(1)422
  James - of MA, b1689 d1763/1764, m1714/1715 Ruth Hathorne -
    desc/o John Putnam CFA(1)422
  Capt Jeremiah - of MA, b1737 d1799, m1763 Rachael Fuller - desc/o
    John Putnam BLG2874
  John - of MA, bp 1579/1580 d1662, m Priscilla____ - the immigrant
    J&K126, 158; CHB428; BLG2874; CFA(1)421; sufficient proof of
    alleged royal ancestry is lacking
  Capt John - of MA, b1627 d1710, m1652 Rebecca Prince - desc/o
    John Putnam BLG2874; CFA(1)421
  Capt Jonathan - of MA, b1659 d1739, m1683 Lydia Potter - desc/o
    John Putnam BLG2874
  Jonathan - of MA, b1691 d1732, m1714 Elizabeth Putnam - desc/o
    John Putnam BLG2874
  Jonathan - of MA, b1715 d1762, m1736 Sarah Perley - desc/o John
    Putnam BLG2874
  Joseph - of MA, b1669, m1690 Elizabeth Porter - desc/o John Putnam
    J&K126; CHB429
  Nathaniel - d1700, m Elizabeth Hutchinson - desc/o John Putnam
    J&K126
  Priscilla - m Adam Brown Jr - desc/o John Putnam J&K126; AAP153 -
    desc/o Judith Everard AAP154; GBR459 - desc/o Samuel Appleton
    GBR390
  Deacon Tarrant - m Priscilla Baker - desc/o John Putnam J&K126
  Lieut Thomas - of MA, bp 1614/1615 d1686, m(1)1643 Ann Holyoke,
    m(2)1666 Mrs Mary Veren - desc/o John Putnam J&K126, 158
  Thomas - of MA, b1763 d1822, m Mary Fitz - desc/o John Putnam
    BLG2874
  William, m Elizabeth Putnam - desc/o John Putnam J&K158
PYLE Col John MD, of PA, b1723 d1804, m1744 Sarah Baldwin - desc/o
    Joshua Owen ECD(2)212
  Capt John MD - of PA, b abt 1746 d abt 1818, m abt 1770 Sarah
    Brayshear - desc/o Joshua Owen ECD(2)212
  Rev William - of NC, b1773 d aft 1827, m1798 Elizabeth Kirby - desc/o
    Joshua Owen ECD(2)212
PYNCHON Elizabeth - b1702 - desc/o Amy Wyllys RAA126
  George - b1717 - desc/o Amy Wyllys RAA126
  George - b1739 - desc/o Amy Wyllys RAA126
  John - of MA, b abt 1625 d1702/1703, m Amy Wyllys - the immigrant

PYNCHON (cont.)

    RRA1, 126; TAG(39)86/89 royal descent is from his wife Amy Wyllys

    Col John - of MA, b1647 of Springfield d1721 in Springfield, m Margaret Hubbard - desc/o Amy Wyllys RAA126; TAG(39)89

    John - of MA, b1674 - desc/o Amy Wyllys RAA126

    John - b1702 - desc/o Amy Wyllys RAA126

    Margaret - of MA, b abt 1680, m Capt Nathaniel Downing - desc/o Amy Wyllys RAA126; TAG(36)72, (39)89

    Margaret - of CT, m1779 Stephen Keeler - desc/o Grace Kaye CHB208; MCD261; BCD208

    Margaret - b1774/1775 - desc/o Amy Wyllys RAA126

    Mary - of MA, b1650 d abt 1674/1676, m1669 Joseph Whiting - desc/o Amy Wyllys RAA126; TAG(39)89

    William - of MA - desc/o Amy Wyllys TAG(39)89

PYNE John - of SC, b1766 d1813 son of John Pyne & Isabella Pyne, m Honora Smith - the immigrant BLG2875; GBR346

    Thomas - of NY, son of John Pyne & Mary Craze, m(1) Sarah Gainesford, m(2) Anna Rivington - the immigrant GBR346

– Q –

QUEEN Margaret - of MD, b1709, m1727/1728 John Belt - desc/o Giles Brent DBR(4)53, 85, 389, 463; DBR(5)673

QUIMBY or QUINBY Moses - b1755, m Hannah Kennedy - desc/o Anthony Colby LDS90

QUINCY Edmund - of MA 1633 - the immigrant EDV23; sufficient proof of alleged royal ancestry is lacking

    Elizabeth - of MA, m Rev William Smith - desc/o Rev William Norton J&K121; BCD164 - desc/o Elizabeth Coytmore AAP144; PFA Apx C #5

    Hannah - of MA, d1833, m Samuel Shaw - desc/o Edward Bromfield EO(1)328

    John - of MA, m Elizabeth Norton - desc/o Elizabeth Coytmore AAP144; PFA Apx C#5

    Josiah - of MA, mayor of Boston & president of Harvard University - desc/o Edward Bromfield EO(1)328

    Sarah - of MA, d1839, m Capt Edward Dowse - desc/o Edward Bromfield EO(1)328

    William - of MA, d1827 lieut-governor of MA, m1774 Miriam Mason dau/o Jonathan Mason - desc/o Edward Bromfield EO(1)328

QUINTON Rachael - d bef 1771, m James Smith b abt 1712 d1779 - desc/o John Fenwick DBR(1)317; DBR(2)413; DBR(3)439

– R –

RAILEY Jane - of VA, b1763 d1824, m1797 Aaron Darnell - desc/o Capt Henry Isham DBR(4)307

RAND Anne - b1727, m Thomas Shannon - desc/o Gov Thomas Roberts LDS65

RAND (cont.)

Moses Wentworth - of NH, b1774 d1812, m1794 Mary Sanborn - desc/o Elder William Wentworth DBR(1)663

RANDOLPH (formerly FITZRANDOLPH) Benjamin - of MA - desc/o Edward FitzRandolph BLG2878

Edward - of MA, b abt 1607 d1676, m1637 Elizabeth Blossom - the immigrant BLG2878; sufficient proof of alleged royal ancestry is lacking

Edward - of NJ, b1678 d1760, m1704 Katherine Hartshorne - desc/o Edward FitzRandolph BLG2878

Edward - of PA, b1754 d1837, m1779 Anna Juliana Steel - desc/o Edward FitzRandolph BLG2878

John - of PA, b1775 d1810, m1805 Catharine Simpson - desc/o Edward FitzRandolph BLG2686

Jonathan - m Mary Bonham - desc/o Edward FitzRandolph BLG2879

Joseph - of MA, b1650 - desc/o Edward FitzRandolph BLG2878

Joseph - of MA, b1656 d abt 1726, m1688 Hannah Conger - desc/o Edward FitzRandolph BLG2686

Joseph - of MA, b1691, m1714 Rebekah Drake - desc/o Edward FitzRandolph BLG2686

Nathaniel - of NJ, b1642 d1713, m1662 Mary Holly - desc/o Edward FitzRandolph BLG2878

Paul - of PA, b abt 1720, m abt 1745 Anna Smith - desc/o Edward FitzRandolph BLG2686

Richard - of NJ, b1705 d1754, m1735 Elizabeth Corlies - desc/o Edward FitzRandolph BLG2878

Samuel - m Margaret FitzRandolph - desc/o Edward FitzRandolph BLG2879

Thomas - m Elizabeth Manning - desc/o Edward FitzRandolph BLG2879

RANDOLPH Anne - of VA, m William Fitzhugh of Chatham - desc/o Col William Randolph CRL(4)555; GVFWM(4)234

Anne - of VA, b1755, m(1)1775 Daniel Scott, m(2) Jonathan Pleasants, m(3) James Pleasants of Goochland Co, VA - desc/o Col William Randolph PVF143

Anne Cary - of VA, b1775 Tuckahoe, m1795 Gouverneur Morris of Morrisana, NY, minister to France - desc/o Col William Randolph PVF136

Archibald (called Archie) Cary - of VA, b1769 Dungeness, m1794 Lucy Burwell dau/o Col Nathaniel Burwell of Carter Hall, Clark Co, VA - desc/o Col William Randolph PVF143

Ariana - of VA, b1750 Williamsburg, m James Wormeley, Captain of the King's Guard, Windsor - desc/o Col William Randolph PVF154

Beverley - of VA, b1706 of Turkey Island, justice of Henrico & burgess for the college, m Elizabeth Lightfoot dau/o Francis Lightfoot & died without issue - desc/o Col William Randolph CRL(4)554; GVFWM(4)233; PVF132

Beverley - of VA, m___ Wormeley - desc/o Col William Randolph PVF147; CFA(5)428

Beverley - of VA, b1744 of Green Creek, Cumberland d1797 commanded a regiment in General Lawson's brigade in campaign of

RANDOLPH (cont.)

> 1780, member of the council, lieut-governor 1784 & governor from 1788 to 1791, m Martha (Patty) Cocke dau/o James Cocke of Williamsburg - desc/o Col William Randolph CRL(4)555; GVFWM(4)234; PVF133

Brett - of VA, b1732 d1759 settled in Gloucestershire, England, m Mary Scott of London - desc/o Col William Randolph GVFWM(4)243

Charlotte - of VA, m Dr Skelton - desc/o Col William Randolph GVFWM(4)243

Dorothy - of VA, m1773 John Woodson of Goochland Co, VA - desc/o Col William Randolph PVF143

Edmund Jennings - of VA, b1753 d1813 Frederick Co, VA, attorney general & governor of VA, member of the Constitutional Convention 1787, Attorney General of the United States & secretary of state, m1796 Elizabeth Nicholas dau/o Robert Carter Nicholas - desc/o Capt Henry Isham J&K162 - desc/o Col William Randolph CRL(1)243; DBR(3)413; GVFWM(4)242; PVF149

Capt Edward - of VA, b1690 a sea captain, m Elizabeth (Grosvenor) Graves (Groves) of Bristol, England - desc/o Col William Randolph DBR(3)413, (5)861; CRL(3)242, (4)554; GVFWM(4)233; PVF131; CFA(5)428 - desc/o Capt Henry Isham CRL(3)242

Edward - of VA, b1690 d1750 - desc/o Col William Randolph DBR(3)473

Edward - of VA, m Lucy Harrison - desc/o Col William Randolph DBR(3)413; PVF131; CFA(5)429

Edward - of VA, m Thomassa Meaux & had issue Margaret, Mary & Lucy - desc/o Col William Randolph GVFWM(4)243

Elizabeth - b1680 - desc/o Dorothy Lane RAA126

Elizabeth - of VA, b1695 Turkey Island, m Theoderick Carter - desc/o Col William Randolph DBR(2)339, 406; DBR(3)516; PVF132

Elizabeth - of VA, b1695 Turkey Island d1719/1720, m1701 Richard Bland, of Jordans Point, James River, VA d1720 - desc/o Capt Henry Isham CHB533; RAA104; CRL(3)242 - desc/o Col William Randolph CRL(3)242; CRL(4)554; GVFWM(4)233; PVF132; CFA(5)429

Elizabeth - of VA, m Rev William Yates of Gloucester Co, VA - desc/o Col William Randolph DBR(5)861; PVF131

Elizabeth - of VA, b1725, m1745 Col John Chiswell - desc/o Col William Randolph CRL(4)555; GVFWM(4)234; PVF134; CFA(5)427

Elizabeth - of VA, b1727 d1782, m1750 John Railey - desc/o Capt Henry Isham DBR(4)307

Elizabeth - of VA, b1742, m1762 Philip Grymes of Middlesex, VA - desc/o Col William Randolph PVF133

Elizabeth - of VA, m1771 John Bailey - desc/o Col William Randolph PVF143

Elizabeth - of VA, m Roland Richard Kidder Meade, of Coggins Point, a distinguished Revolutionary officer - desc/o Col William Randolph GVFWM(4)243

Elizabeth - of VA, d abt 1776, m1763 Col Samuel Sherwin d1789 Colonel Amelia Co militia during American Revolution - desc/o Henry Randolph ECD(2)216; DBR(2)179; DBR(3)201; DBR(4)178

RANDOLPH (cont.)

Elizabeth - of VA, b abt 1765, m1785 Robert Pleasants of Filmer - desc/o Col William Randolph GVFWM(4)238; PVF135

Harrison - of VA, b1743 d1803, m(1) Elizabeth Starke, m(2) Mary Jones - desc/o Col William Randolph DBR(3)413, 414

Henry - of VA abt 1642, bp 1623 d1673, clerk Henrico Co 1643/1656 VA Assembly 1656/1673 son of William Randolph & Dorothy Lane, m(1)1652 Elizabeth____, m(2)1660/1661 Judith Soane dau/o Henry Soane - the immigrant ECD(2)215; DBR(2)179, 641, 821; DBR(3)147; DBR(4)170, 178; DBR(5)152; WAC15; GBR169; GVFWM(4)229

Capt Henry II - of VA, b1665 d1693, m1687 Sarah Swann dau/o Thomas Swann and Mary Mansfield - desc/o Henry Randolph ECD(2)215; DBR(2)179, 641, 821; DBR(3)147; DBR(4)178; RAA126; GVFWM(4)230

Henry III - of VA, b1689 d1726 captain Henrico Co milita, magistrate 1713/1720, sheriff 1723, m1714 Elizabeth Eppes d1777 dau/o Francis Epps III & Anne Isham - desc/o Henry Randolph ECD(2)216; DBR(2)179, 641, 821; DBR(3)147; DBR(4)178; RAA126; GVFWM(4)230

Henry IV - of VA, b1721 d1771 Captain Henrico militia 1748, justice, Chesterfield Co 1749, m Tabitha Poythress b1725 d1805 dau/o Robert & Elizabeth Poythress - desc/o Henry Randolph ECD(2)216; DBR(2)179; DBR(3)201; DBR(4)178; RAA126 - desc/o Henry Isham RAA104

Isham - of VA, b1681 Turkey Island, of Dungeness, Goochland Co d1742, adjutant general of VA 1738, burgess for Goochland Co, agent for the colony to England, m1717 Jane Rogers b1705 d1766 of London, England - desc/o Capt Henry Isham J&K135; CHB533; DBR(3)377; DBR(4)201, 307; AAP141; PFA Apx C #3, Apx D #3; CRL(3)242; GBR338 - desc/o Col William Randolph AAP140; PFA Apx D #3; CRL(3)242; CRL(4)554; GBR169; GVFWM(4)233; PVF131, 141

Isham - of VA, b1770 Dungeness, Goochland Co, m1795 Nancy Coupland of Richmond - desc/o Col William Randolph PVF145

Jane - of VA, b1720, m1739 Peter Jefferson of Shadwell, near Rivanna River, Albemarle Co, VA b1708 d1757 - desc/o Capt Henry Isham J&K133 CHB533; AAP141; PFA Apx C #3, Apx D #3; GBR338 - desc/o William Randolph AAP140; GBR169; GVFWM(4)240; PVF141; CFA(5)428

Jane - of VA, b1729, m1750 Anthony Walke of Fairfield, Princess Anne Co - desc/o Col William Randolph GVFWM(4)243; PVF161

Sir John - of VA, b1689 or 1693 Turkey Island, of Williamsburg, VA d1737, studied law at Gray's Inn was one of the leading lawyers of the colony, treasurer, attorney-general & Speaker of the House of Burgesses, m1718 Susanna Beverly dau/o Col Peter Beverly of Gloucester Co - desc/o Col William Randolph DBR(3)345; CRL(1)242, 243; CRL(3)242; CRL(4)554; GVFWM(4)233; PVF131, 146; CFA(5)428 - desc/o Capt Henry Isham CRL(3)242

John - of VA, b1727/1728 Williamsburg d1784 attorney general of VA & lawyer, m1752 Arianna Jennings dau/o Edmund Jennings -

RANDOLPH (cont.)

desc/o Col William Randolph CRL(1)243; GVFWM(4)241; PVF146, 147; CFA(5)428

John - of VA, b1742 of Mattox, Chesterfield Co d1775, m Frances Bland dau/o Col Theodorick Bland of Causons - desc/o Col William Randolph GVFWM(4)243; PVF161

John - of VA, m Ariana Jennings - desc/o Col William Randolph CRL(1)243

John - of VA, Attorney General of the United States - desc/o Capt Henry Isham J&K162

Judith - of VA, b1724, m1744 Rev William Stith, president of William & Mary College b1707 d1755 - desc/o Col William Randolph GVFWM(4)236, 566; PVF134; CFA(5)427

Judith - of VA, b abt 1736, m Edmund Berkeley of Barn Elms - desc/o Col William Randolph GVFWM(4)237

Judith - of VA, b1773, m1793 (her cousin) Richard Randolph of Bizarre - desc/o Col William Randolph PVF136

Lucy - of VA, b1744, m1761 Lewis Burwell of King's Mill, York, VA - desc/o Col William Randolph PVF133

Marianna - of VA, m James Wormeley - desc/o Col William Randolph GVFWM(4)242

Martha - of VA, b abt 1643/1645 d1725, m1673/1674 Edward Traylor - desc/o Henry Randolph DBR(4)170

Mary - of VA, m William Bolling - desc/o Richard Everand CHB180

Mary - of VA, b1692 Turkey Island d bef May 1738, m1712 William or John Stith of Williamsburg, VA - desc/o Capt Henry Isham CHB533; DBR(2)126, 672; CRL(3)242 - desc/o Col William Randolph CRL(3)242; PVF132

Mary - of VA, d1768 Williamsburg, m1742/1743 Philip Grymes of Brandon, Middlesex, VA - desc/o Col William Randolph DBR(3)345; PVF147; CFA(5)428

Mary - of VA, b1718, m abt 1742 John Price, a native of Wales - desc/o Col William Randolph DBR(1)422; CRL(4)555; GVFWM(4)234

Mary - of VA, b1726, m William Keith, these were ancestors of Chief Justice John Marshall - desc/o Col William Randolph PVF134; CFA(5)427

Mary - of VA, b1727 d1781 of Curl's Neck, m1744 Archibald Cary of Ampthill a distinguished Revolutionary patriot - desc/o Col William Randolph GVFWM(4)243; PVF129, 160, 161; CFA(5)429

Mary - of VA, b1738, m1758 Capt Tarlton Fleming of Rock Castle, Goochland - desc/o Capt Henry Isham ECD(2)167; DBR(3)359 - desc/o Col William Randolph DBR(2)231, 352; DBR(4)365; GVFWM(4)237; PVF135

Mary - of VA, m Capt John Smith d abt 1724, son of Major John Smith - desc/o Col William Randolph DBR(2)126; CRL(4)554; GVFWM(4)233, 590; CFA(5)429

Mary - of VA, m Robert Yates of Gloucester Co, VA - desc/o Col William Randolph DBR(3)473; DBR(5)861; PVF131; CFA(5)429

Mary - of VA, m1770 Charles Lewis - desc/o Col William Randolph DBR(4)201; PVF143

RANDOLPH (cont.)

Mary - of VA, b1762, m1782 David Meade Randolph of Presque Isle, Chesterfield - desc/o Col William Randolph GVFWM(4)237; PVF135

Mary - of VA, b1773 Ampthill, Chesterfield Co, m1790 (her first cousin) Randolph Harrison of Clifton, Cumberland Co - desc/o Col William Randolph PVF146

Mary Isham - of VA, b1726, m Rev Thomas (James) Keith - desc/o Capt Henry Isham J&K133; ECD(2)219; DBR(2)34; DBR(3)336; DBR(5)724 - desc/o Col William Randolph DBR(3)703; DBR(5)111, 316; PFA Apx D #3; GVFWM(4)236; CFSSA311, 312

Mary Judith - of VA, b1736, m1756 Edmond Berkeley Jr of Barn Elms, Middlesex, VA, eldest son of Col Edmond Berkeley & Mary Nelson, dau/o Thomas Nelson of Yorktown, VA - desc/o Col William Randolph PVF146

Col Peter - of VA, b1708 Turkey Island, of Chatsworth, Henrico, justice for Henrico, clerk of burgesses, treasurer, surveyor-general of the customs for the middle district of North America d1767, m1733 Lucy Bolling dau/o Robert Bolling of Bollingbrook - desc/o Maj Robert Payton CHB168 - desc/o Col William Randolph CRL(4)555; GVFWM(4)233; PVF133; CFA(5)427

Peter - of VA, m Elizabeth Southall - desc/o Col William Randolph CRL(4)555

Peyton - of VA, b1722 lawyer & attorney general of VA 1748, m1763 (his cousin) Elizabeth Harrison dau/o Benjamin Harrison - desc/o Col William Randolph GVFWM(4)242; PVF133; CFA(5)428

Dr Philip Grymes - of VA, b1769, m1784 Mary O'Neal, of Washington DC & had issue two daughters - desc/o Col William Randolph PVF143

Richard - b1621 - desc/o Dorothy Lane RAA126

Col Richard - of VA, b1686 Turkey Island, of Curl's Neck, Henrico Co, justice of Henrico, burgess & treasurer d1742, m1714 Jane Bolling dau/o Major John Bolling of Cobb's Chesterfield Co & Mary Kennon, she was great-great-granddau/o Pocahontas - desc/o Capt Henry Isham CRL(3)242 - desc/o Col William Randolph CRL(3)242; CRL(4)554; GVFWM(4)233; PVF131, 159; CFA(5)428/429

Richard - of VA, b1715 Curles, justice of Henrico, member of House of Burgesses, m1750 Anne Meade dau/o David Meade of Nansemond Co - desc/o Col William Randolph GVFWM(4)242; PVF159

Richard - of VA, b1770 of Bizarre, m1790 Judith Randolph (his cousin) dau/o Thomas Mann Randolph of Tuckahoe - desc/o Col William Randolph PVF161

Col Robert - of VA, b1760 of Eastern View, Fauquier Co, d1825 entered the Revolutionary army at the age of 16 as an ensign, promoted to captain & served in Baylor's dragoons, & was captured at Tappan; afterwards aide to General Wayne, m Elizabeth Carter dau/o Charles Carter of Shirley - desc/o Maj Robert Payton CHB168; BCD168 - desc/o Col William Randolph CRL(4)555; GVFWM(4)234

Sarah - of VA, b1715, m1733 John Archer II - desc/o Capt Henry Isham DBR(1)25; DBR(2)344, 641, 821; DBR(3)147

Susan - of VA, m John Randolph Grymes - desc/o Col William

RANDOLPH (cont.)

Randolph GVFWM(4)242

Susannah - of VA, b1738, m Carter Henry Harrison son of Benjamin Harrison IV & Anne Carter - desc/o Col William Randolph DBR(3)377

Thomas - of VA, b abt 1683 Turkey Island, of Tuckahoe d1730/1733, justice of Henrico Co, m1710 Mary Judith Churchill (Fleming) of New Kent Co - desc/o Capt Henry Isham J&K133; ECD(2)166, 167, 219; DBR(2)34; DBR(3)359; DBR(5)724; CRL(3)242 - desc/o Col William Randolph DBR(2)352, 484; DBR(3)336, 703; DBR(4)364; DBR(5)110, 111, 316; PFA Apx D #3; CRL(3)242; CRL(4)554; GVFWM(4)233; PVF131, 134; CFA(5)427

Thomas - of VA, (twin to Isham) b1770 Dungenness, Goochland Co, m(1)____ Skipwith, m(2)____ Laurence, granddau/o Gov Findlay of Kentucky - desc/o Col William Randolph PVF146

Thomas Isham - of VA, b1745 of Dungenness, Goochland Co, m1768 Jane Cary b1751 third child of Col Archibald Cary of Ampthill, Chesterfield Co, VA & Mary Randolph of Curls - desc/o Col William Randolph GVFWM(4)240; PVF129, 143; CFA(5)428

Thomas Mann - of VA, b1741 of Tuckahoe; vestryman of Northam Parish, burgess of Goochland, m(1)1761 Anne Cary b1745 dau/o Col Archiband Cary of Ampthill, Chesterfield Co - desc/o Col William Randolph GVFWM(4)237; PVF129, 135

Thomas Mann - of VA, b abt 1767 of Edge Hill, Albemarle Co d1828, served in the U S Army & became col of the 25th infantry 1813, governor 1819/1822, m1790 Martha Jefferson dau/o President Thomas Jefferson - desc/o Col William Randolph GVFWM(4)238; PVF136

Col William - of VA 1674, b1651 Yorkshire, England d1711 member House of Burgesses 1700/1705, captain Henrico Co Forces 1680, lieut col 1699, attorney general & member Royal Council of VA, son of Richard Randolph & Elizabeth Ryland, m 1680 Mary Isham dau/o Henry Isham of VA and Mrs Katherine Banks Royall - the immigrant ECD(2)219; MCS50, 51; DBR(1)422, 588, 744; DBR(2)125, 126, 231, 339, 343, 349, 352, 406, 484, 670, 801; DBR(3)8, 110, 199, 336, 345, 375, 412, 414, 472, 473, 516, 703, 763; DBR(4)201, 364, 466; DBR(5)105, 110, 315, 860, 861, 1064, 1065; RAA1; EDV65; AAP140; PFA Apx C #3, Apx D #3, CRL(1)242; CRL(3)242; CRL(4)554; GBR169; GVFWM(4)232; PVF129; CFA(5)426, 427

William - of VA, b1681 Turkey Island d1741, m1705 Elizabeth Peyton Beverly dau/o Col Peter Beverly of Gloucester Co & Eliza Peyton - desc/o Col William Randolph DBR(1)422; CRL(3)242; CRL(4)554; GVFWM(4)233; PVF131, 132; CFA(5)427 - desc/o Capt Henry Isham CRL(3)242; PVF131, 132

William - of VA, b1710 of Wilton, Henrico, burgess for Henrico d1761, m1735 Anne Harrison dau/o Benjamin Harrison of Berkeley, on James River, VA & Anne Carter - desc/o Col William Randolph CRL(4)555; GVFWM(4)234; PVF133; CFA(5)427

William - of VA, b1713 of Tuckahoe d1745 burgess for Goochland, m1735 Maria Judith Page dau/o Mann Page of Rosewell & Judith

RANDOLPH (cont.)

Wormeley - desc/o Capt Henry Isham ECD(2)167; DBR(3)359 - desc/o Col William Randolph DBR(2)352; DBR(4)364; GVFWM(4)236; PVF134, 135; CFA(5)427

William - of VA, of Chatsworth d1774 justice of Henrico 1770, m Mary Skipwith dau/o Sir William Skipwith, baronet, of Prestwould, Mecklenburg Co - desc/o Col William Randolph CRL(4)555; GVFWM(4)234

William - b1745/6 - desc/o Henry Isham RAA104 - desc/o Dorothy Lane RAA126

William - b1747, removed to Bristol m____ Little - desc/o Col William Randolph PVF143

William - of VA, b abt 1769 of Chitower, m1794 Lucy Bolling dau/o Col Peter Randolph of Chatsworth - desc/o Col William Randolph GVFWM(4)238; PVF136 states Lucy Bolling was the dau/o Beverly Randolph of Cumberland Co, VA & left issue, two sons

RAPALYE George - of NY 1623 - the immigrant EDV46; sufficient proof of alleged royal ancestry is lacking

William - of NY 1623 - the immigrant EDV46; sufficient proof of alleged royal ancestry is lacking

RATHBONE Valentine - of MA, b1768 d1844, m Love Reddington - desc/o Nathaniel Browne ECD(3)60

RAWSON Abner - of MA, m Mary Allen - desc/o Rachel Perne J&K143

Daniel - b1771 - desc/o Dorothy Stapilton RAA117

Edmund - of MA, m Elizabeth Howard - desc/o Rachel Perne J&K143; PFA Apx C #12

Edward - of MA, d1747, m1724 Deborah Green - desc/o Rachel Perne BLG2880

Rev Grindal - of MA, b1659 d1715 chaplain of the fleet in the Port Royal expedition 1690, m1682 Susanna Wilson - desc/o Rachel Perne J&K143; BLG2880; PFA Apx C #12

Joshua - of MA, b1755 d1804, m1776 Rebecca Griffith - desc/o Rachel Perne BLG2880

Levi - of MA, d1819, m1775 Thankful Warren - desc/o Rachel Perne BLG2880

Nathaniel - of MA, b1671 d1731, m1712 Hannah Thompson - desc/o Rachel Perne BLG2880

Rhoda - of MA, m Aaron Taft, ancestors of Pres William Howard Taft - desc/o Rachel Perne J&K143; PFA Apx C #12

William - of MA, b1651 d1726, m Anne Glover - desc/o Rachel Perne BLG2880

William - of MA, b1692 d1726, m1712 Margaret____ - desc/o Rachel Perne BLG2880

William - of MA, b1713, m1738 Abigail Temple - desc/o Rachel Perne BLG2880

RAYMOND Anna of CT, b1758 d1842, m1787 Stephen Billings - desc/o Judge Simon Lynde CHB312; BCD312

RAYNSFORD (RAINSFORD) Ann - of MA, b1651 d1690 Boston, m Samuel Hough b1651 d1679 Boston, son of Samuel & Sarah (Symmes) Hough - desc/o Edward Raynsford NE(139)299

David - of MA, bp 1644 Boston d1691 Boston, m(1) Abigail____, m(2)

RAYNSFORD (RAINSFORD) (cont.)

Hannah Griggs bp 1659 Roxbury dau/o John Griggs & Mary Patten - desc/o Edward Raynsford NE(139)306/307

David - of MA, b1691, m(1) 1721 Newton, MA, Hannah Hammond, m(2) 1725 Watertown, MA, Abigail Chenery, m(3) 1728 Weston, MA Rebecca (Sanger) Flagg - desc/o Edward Raynsford NE(139)308

Dorothy - of MA, b1663 d1755 Bristol, RI, m abt 1680/1681 Nathaniel Paine b1661 d1723 of Swansea, MA & RI - desc/o Edward Raynsford NE(139)306

Edward - of MA, bp 1609 Staverton, Northampton, England d1680 Boston, MA, 3rd son of Robert Rainsford Esq & Mary Kirton, m(1)___ d1632, m(2) bef Oct 15,1633 Elizabeth___ d1688 & had issue - the immigrant RAA1, 126; GBR439 some aspect of royal descent merits further study; NE(139)229/238, 296/301

Edward - of MA, bp 1654 Boston d1688 Barbados, merchant, m Huldah Davis b1659 Boston b1721 Boston - desc/o Edward Raynsford NE(139)310

Edward - of MA, b abt 1685 d1770 Canterbury, CT, m1705 Abigail Balch b1682 Beverly, MA d1763 Canterbury, CT, dau/o Benjamin Balch & Elizabeth Woodbury of Beverly, MA - desc/o Edward Raynsford NE(139)308; TAG(56)174/178

Elizabeth - of MA, bp 1648 d1688, m abt 1680 Capt William Greenough d1693 Boston - desc/o Edward Raynsford NE(139)300

Elizabeth - of MA, b abt 1659 d1743 Boston, m Giles Fifield d1718 Boston aged 60 years, son of Giles Fifield & Mary Perkins - desc/o Edward Raynsford NE(139)303

Elizabeth - of MA, m by 1702 Samuel Avery of Seabrook, New London, CT, cordwainer - desc/o Edward Raynsford NE(139)313

Hannah - of MA, b1671 d aft 1721, m abt 1693 Peter Leech - desc/o Edward Raynsford NE(139)304

Huldah - of MA, under 16 in May 1688, m1714 Boston, Francis Archibald d1746 merchant - desc/o Edward Raynsford NE(139)311

John - of MA, b1634 Boston d1688 ship carpenter of Boston, m(1) abt 1660 Susannah Vergoose d1681 dau/o Peter & Susannah (Firmage) Vergoose of Boston, m(2) Sarah___ d1705 - desc/o Edward Raynsford NE(139)301/302

Captain John - of MA, b1661/1662 Boston d1710 Barbados, mariner, m Rebecca ___ - desc/o Edward Raynsford NE(139)312/313

Jonathan - of MA, b1636 Boston, m1656 Mary Sunderland - desc/o Edward Raynsford NE(139)305/306

Jonathan - of MA, b1661 Boston d1680, m Martha Raymond bp 1675 dau/o Joshua Raymond & Elizabeth Smith - desc/o Edward Raynsford NE(139)313

Mary - of MA, twin to her brother Joshua or Josiah who died an infant 1632, b1632 d1894 Saconesset, MA, m(1) abt 1652 William Bassett d1670 Sandwich, m(2) abt 1671 James Percival d1691/2 Sacpmesset - desc/o Edward Raynsford NE(139)299

Mary - of MA, b1662/1663 d bef 23 Dec 1681, m Michael Shute d bef 23 Oct 1706 Boston, son of Richard Shute - desc/o Edward Raynsford NE(139)304

Mary - of MA, b1659, m(1) abt 1700 John Rogers of New London, CT,

RAYNSFORD (RAINSFORD) (cont.)

 m(2) abt 1710 Robert Jones of Block Island - desc/o Edward
  Raynsford NE(139)306

 Nathan - of MA, b1641 Boston d bef 3 Apr 1676, m1665 Charlestown,
  Mary Allen b 1643/1644 Charlestown d1672 dau/o John Allen &
  Sarah____ - desc/o Edward Raynsford NE(139)306

 Priscilla - of MA, b abt 1685, m1703 Boston, Thomas Beard (or Board)
  d1711/1712 - desc/o Edward Raynsford NE(139)310

 Ranis - of MA, b1638 d1691 Boston, m1655 Josiah Belcher d1683
  wheelwright, son of Gregory & Catherine____ Belcher of Braintree,
  MA - desc/o Edward Raynsford NE(139)300

 Sarah - of MA, b1677 d1723, m1702 Boston, Henry Sanders, mariner
  d1717 - desc/o Edward Raynsford NE(139)310

 Solomon - of MA, bp 1646 Boston d1692/1693 buried as Sergt
  Solomon Raynsford, m abt 1668 Priscilla Gretchell dau/o Samuel
  Gretchell & Dorcas____ - desc/o Edward Raynsford
  NE(139)308/309

 Solomon - of MA, b1673 d1702 of St Michael's Parish Barbados, m St
  Michael's Parish 1700, Hope or Hopestill (Davice) bp 1668 St
  Michael's Parish, dau/o Damasin Sherwood & wid/o John Dixon -
  desc/o Edward Raynsford NE(139)309/310

READE Anne - of VA, m Matthew Pate bp 1686/1687 - desc/o Col George
  Read ECD(2)224; DBR(4)34, 574; DBR(5)219; RAA127; APP425;
  GVFWM(4)270; HSF(2)190

 Benjamin - of VA, d1731 of Kingston Parish, Gloucester Co, m Lucy
  (Gwyn ?) - desc/o Col George Reade NFA76; CRL(3)112; APP425;
  GVFWM(4)265; HSF(2)193

 Elizabeth - of VA, b1672 d1719/1720, m Col John Lewis II - desc/o
  Col George Reade DBR(4)641; HSF(2)187

 Elizabeth - of VA, m Capt Thomas Chesman (Chisman) b abt 1651 d
  abt 1715 justice of York, capt of militia, vestryman & General
  Assembly of York, son of Edmund Chisman d1678 - desc/o Col
  George Reade DBR(3)657; AWW86; NFA76; CRL(3)112; HSF(2)186,
  194, 195

 Elizabeth - of VA, b1751 d1777, m Col Edward Harwood of Warwick -
  desc/o Col George Reade GVFWM(4)263; HSF(2)188

 Elizabeth - of VA, m Col George Reade - desc/o Col George Reade
  AWW81

 Elizabeth - of VA, m Paul Watlington bp 1678 of Gloucester Co -
  desc/o Col George Reade DBR(2)525; AWW84; APP425;
  GVFWM(4)263, 264; HSF(2)192

 Elizabeth - of VA, m1741 Aaron Phillips - desc/o Col George Read
  DBR(2)436; GVFWM(4)262; HSF(2)188

 Frances - of VA, d1762, m1757 Major Anthony Robinson d1762 -
  desc/o Col George Reade AWW84; GVFWM(4)263; HSF(2)189

 Francis - of VA, b abt 1667 d1694, m(1) Jane Cheesman or Chisman
  dau/o Edmund Chisman, m(2) Alice Reade - desc/o Col George
  Read ECD(2)224, 525; DBR(4)34, 573; DBR(5)219; AWW84; NFA76;
  APP424/425; GVFWM(4)263; HSF(2)190, 191

 Col George of VA 1637, b1608 d1671 burgess for James City Co
  1644/49 & for Gloucester Co 1656, secretary of the colony 1640,

READE (cont.)

acting governor of VA, member of the Council 1657 till his death, son of Robert Reade & Mildred Windebank, m bef 1657 Elizabeth Martiau d1686/7 dau/o Capt Nicholas Martiau of York Co & his wife Jane Berkeley - the immigrant J&K146, 227; CHB248, 419; ECD212, 216; ECD(2)224, 230; MCD271; MCS60; BCD248; DBR(1)10,131, 254, 354, 469, 474, 510, 535, 549, 606, 626, 657, 686, 722/23, 724, 732, 735, 764; DBR(2)6, 61, 102, 130, 204, 211, 212, 225, 305, 306, 307, 317, 382, 383, 417, 435, 525, 525, 632, 642, 643, 823, 824, 826, 830, 835; DBR(3)102, 186, 262, 330, 331, 352, 383, 405, 443, 446, 487, 570, 587, 614, 622, 623, 657, 677, 689, 701; DBR(4)34, 135, 379, 485, 496, 534, 573, 586, 587, 588, 590, 591, 592, 641, 720, 773, 804, 844, 845; DBR(5)102, 155, 159, 190, 209, 219, 239, 328, 340, 342, 364, 365, 525, 555, 562, 564, 570, 571, 646, 651, 678, 804, 1067, 1068; RAA1, 127; EDV52; AAP139; BLG2881; PFA Apx C #1; WAC95; AWW80, 81; FFF123, 268; NFA75; CRL(3)112; GBR183, 468; TAG(51)167/171; APP419; GVFWM(4)260/273; HSF(2)185/200

George - of VA - desc/o Col George Reade BLG2881

Gwyn - of VA, d1762, m Dorothy Clark b1714 d1797 - desc/o Col George Reade APP425/426; GVFWM(4)264; HSF(2)193

John - of VA, vestryman of Petsworth Parish, Gloucester, VA d aft 1731/1732, m(1)____ - desc/o Col George Reade APP422; GVFWM(4)262

John - of VA, m Sarah____ b1732 d1800 - desc/o Col George Reade GVFWM(4)263; HSF(2)188

Rev John - of VA, d bef 1760 rector of Stratton Major Parish in King & Queen Co, m1738 Frances Yates b1718 dau/o Rev Bartholomew Yates & Sarah Mickleburrough - desc/o Col George Reade GVFWM(4)265; HSF(2)190

Rev John - of VA, d1769 - desc/o Col George Reade AWW85; NFA76

Hon John - of PA, b1769 d1854, m Martha Meredith - desc/o Col George Reade BLG2881

John - of VA, m Elizabeth____ - desc/o Col George Reade DBR(2)436

John - of VA, d1739, m Mary Mallory - desc/o Col George Reade DBR(2)103

John - of VA, b1746, m Judith Plummer - desc/o Col George Reade HSF(2)194

Joseph - of VA, m1692 Phoebe Walker - desc/o William Reade CHB336; BCD336

Joseph - of NY - desc/o Lawrence Reade AWW79

Joyce - of VA, b1702/1703 d1771, m Christopher Tompkins b1705 d1779 lieutenant of Caroline Co militia & vestryman of St Margaret Parish - desc/o Col George Reade DBR(3)383, 677; DBR(4)534; APP424; HSF(2)190

Lawrence - of NY - the immigrant EDV52; AWW79 sufficient proof of alleged royal ancestry is lacking

Lucy - of VA, b1701, m1731 John Dixon - desc/o Col George Reade DBR(4)804; DBR(5)365; AWW85; GVFWM(4)270; HSF(2)190

Lucy - of VA, b1735, m John Armistead - desc/o Col George Reade

READE (cont.)
HSF(2)194

Margaret - of VA, m Thomas Nelson of Yorktown, b1677/1678 d1745, he, m(2) Frances (Courtenay) Tucker - desc/o Col George Reade CHB250; BCD250; AWW84; APP423;GVFWM(4)262; HSF(2)188

Martiau - of VA, m Mary Lilly - desc/o Col George Reade AWW84

Mary - of VA, m Capt Mordecai Throckmorton, sheriff of King & Queen Co - desc/o Col William Bernard CHB38; MCD161; BCD38 - desc/o Col George Reade CHB250; MCD272; BCD250; AWW85; APP424; GVFWM(4)270; HSF(2)190

Mary - of NY, m Rev William Vesey - desc/o Lawrence Reade AWW79

Mary - of VA, d1700, m1680 Capt John Smith II - desc/o Col George Reade DBR(2)307

Mary - of VA, m Col John Scarbrook - desc/o Col George Reade AWW81

Mary - of VA, d bef 1763, m John Cary d1763 - desc/o Col George Reade DBR(2)643, 644; DBR(3)102; HSF(2)188

Mary - of VA, m Edward Davis of King & Queen Co - desc/o Col George Reade AWW84; APP425; GVFWM(4)263; HSF(2)192

Mildred - of VA, b1643 d1694, m abt 1671 Augustine Warner Jr b1642/1643 d1681 son of Capt Augustine Warner - desc/o Col George Reade J&K146, 227; CHB251, 420; ECD212, 216, 230; MCD272; MCS60; BCD251; DBR(1)10, 209, 255, 354, 469, 474, 535, 549, 606, 626, 657, 686, 723, 724, 732, 736, 764; DBR(2)6, 61, 73; 212, 307; 383, 617, 632, 825, 829, 835; DBR(3)8, 186, 331, 352, 405, 443, 446, 570, 587, 614, 623, 701; DBR(4)485, 496, 588, 592, 641, 720, 773, 847; DBR(5)102, 159, 190, 210, 239, 240, 342, 525, 555, 562, 564, 571, 646, 651; AAP1, 139; PFA Apx C #1; WAC95; AWW81; FFF124; NFA76; CRL(3)112; GBR183, 468; TAG(51)167/171; APP426; HSF(2)186

Mildred - of VA, b abt 1703, m Major Philip Rootes b abt 1693 of Rosewall, King & Queen Co d1756, justice of King & Queen Co & vestryman of Stratton Major Parish - desc/o Col George Reade J&K229; CHB248, 419; MCD272; BCD248; DBR(1)131; DBR(2)204; DBR(3)689; AWW85; APP424 - desc/o Col William Bernard CHB38; MCD162; BCD38; HSF(2)190

Mildred - of VA, m(1) James Goodwyn d1719 (no issue), m(2) by 1720 Col Lawrence Smith - desc/o Col George Reade DBR(4)135; DBR(5)678; APP423; GVFWM(4)262; HSF(2)188

Mildred - of VA, m John Gwyn - desc/o Col George Reade GVFWM(4)264; HSF(2)194

Ralph - of MA, b1630 d1711, m Mary Peirce - desc/o William Reade CHB336; BCD336

Robert - of VA, m Elizabeth____ - desc/o Col George Reade AWW84

Robert (John) - of VA, d1712 justice of York Co & lived near Yorktown, m Mary Lilly d1722 dau/o John Lilly - desc/o Col George Reade DBR(2)436, 643; DBR(3)102; DBR(4)135; DBR(5)678; AWW81; BCD250; CHB250; NFA76; CRL(3)112; APP422; GVFWM(4)262; HSF(2)187

Rev Robert - of VA, b1734, m Martha Short dau/o William Short of Surry - desc/o Col George Reade GVFWM(4)270; HSF(2)193

READE (cont.)

Robert - of VA, of Gloucester Co, yeoman, m Margaret____ - desc/o Col Geoge Reade HSF(2)194

Samuel - of VA - desc/o Col George Reade AWW84

Samuel - of VA, d abt 1758, m Mary Schlater b1712/1713 d1773 dau/o Richard & Mary (Nutting) Schlater or Sclater - desc/o Col George Reade DBR(2)643; DBR(3)102; APP423; GVFWM(4)263; HSF(2)188

Sarah - of VA, m1760 John Rootes - desc/o Col George Reade AWW85; NFA76; GVFWM(4)266; HSF(2)190

Sarah - of NY, m Dr Thomas Braine - desc/o Lawrence Reade AWW79

Sarah - of VA, m Capt William Fuller - desc/o Col George Reade AWW81

Thomas - of VA, d1693/1694, m Lucy Gwynne dau/o Edmund Gwynne & they had 11 children - desc/o Col George Reade J&K229; CHB2481, 419; MCD271; BCD248; DBR(1)131; DBR(2)204, 383; DBR(3)677, 689; DBR(4)534, 804; DBR(5)365; AWW84; NFA76; CRL(3)112; APP423; GVFWM(4)270; HSF(2)189

Thomas - of VA, d1721, m Ann Allen - desc/o Col George Reade DBR(2)103; HSF(2)193

Thomas - of VA, b1748 at Gwyn's Island, Matthews Co, VA d1838, m1779 Sarah Magruder b1755 Montgomery Co, MD d1822 dau/o Zadok & Rachel Magruder - desc/o Col George Reade GVFWM(4)265

William - of MA, d1656, m Mabel Kendall - the immigrant CHB336; BCD336 sufficient proof of alleged royal ancestry is lacking

William - of VA, d1798, m Joanna Jones - desc/o Col George Reade DBR(2)103

RECORD Simon - of MA, b abt 1750 d1843, m1777 Bethia Packard - desc/o Joseph Bolles ECD(2)60; DBR(5)817

REDD Nancy (Ann) - of VA, m1740 Samuel Dalton - desc/o Col John West DBR(2)843

REED Dr Elijah Fitch - of CT, b1767 d1847, m1792 Hannah McLean - desc/o John Drake CHB107; BCD107

Capt Joshua - of MA, b1739 d1805, m 1759 Rachel Wyman - desc/o William Reade CHB336; BCD336

Nathaniel - of MA, b1704, m Hannah Flagg - desc/o William Reade CHB336; BCD336

Mary - of MA, b1760 d1796, m1779 Eleazer Flagg Poole - desc/o William Reade CHB336; BCD336

REES Sidney - of PA, m Robert Roberts son of John Roberts - the immigrant GBR392 some aspect of royal descent merits further study

REMINGTON (REMMINGTON) Anne - of MA & RI, d1764, m1750 William Ellery b1727 Newport, RI, in 1776 was elected delegate to the Continental Congress, of which he became a useful & active member. Took his seat on the 14th of May 1776 & affixed his name to the Declaration of Independence, 1786 elected by Congress commissioner of the continental loan office for RI, & in 1790 was appointed collector of the customs for the District of Newport, which office he held til his death 1820, son of William Ellery, a wealthy

REMINGTON (REMMINGTON) (cont.)

merchant of Newport & judge; assistant & deputy governor of the colony of Rhode Island - desc/o Gov Thomas Dudley NE(8)317; J&K196

David - chr 1744, m Sybil____ - desc/o Robert Harrington LDS85

Esther - b1772 - desc/o John Prescott RAA125

Martha - of MA, m Edmund Trowbridge b1709 Newton, d1793 Cambridge, judge of the Superior Court - desc/o Gov Thomas Dudley NE(8)317

Mary - of MA, m Rev Benjamin Stevens, only surv child of Rev Joseph Stevens of Charlestown & Sarah Lynde - desc/o Gov Thomas Dudley NE(8)217

REYNOLDS Judith - b1672, m Samuel Betts - desc/o Henry Palmer LDS30

RHODES (RODES) Ann - of VA, b1734 d1802, m1752 William Thomson - desc/o Charles Rodes ECD(3)243

Charles - of VA, b1661 d aft 1719, m abt 1695 Frances____ - the immigrant ECD(3)243; sufficient proof of alleged royal ancestry is lacking

John - of RI, b1658 d1716, m(1)1685 Waite Waterman - desc/o William Arnold CHB16; BCD16

John - of VA, b1697 d1775, m1723 Mary Crawford - desc/o Charles Rodes ECD(3)243

Phebe - of RI, b1698 d1761, m(1) Anthony Holden - desc/o William Arnold CHB16; BCD16

Rebecca - of RI, d1727, m(1) Nicholas Power, m(2)1676 Daniel Williams - desc/o William Arnold J&K294; CHB15; BCD15

RICE Aaron - b1700, m(1) Hannah Wright - desc/o Deacon Edmund Rice LDS52

Amos - of MA, b1743 d1827, m1766 Sarah Graves - desc/o Deacon Edmund Rice BLG2885

Asaph - of MA, b1768 d1856, m1795 Keziah Wood - desc/o Deacon Edmund Rice BLG2885

Caleb - of MA, b1666 d1738/1739, m1696 Mary Ward - desc/o Deacon Edmund Rice BLG2885

Charles - of MA, b1757 - desc/o Deacon Edmund Rice BLG2885

Daingerfield - of VA, b1775 d1827, m Margaret Looney - desc/o Deacon Edmund Rice BLG2585

Deacon Edmund - of MA, b1594 d1663, m(1) Tamazine Hosmer - the immigrant J&K285; BLG2884; LDS52, 104, 114; RAA no longer accepted as being of royal descent; TAG(11)14/21

Edward - of MA, b1653 d1719, m1680 Joyce Russell - desc/o Deacon Edmund Rice BLG2884; LDS52

Elijah - of MA, b1728 d by 1786, m1751 Elizabeth Rice - desc/o Deacon Edmund Rice BLG2884

Ezekiel - b1700 d1760, m1722 Hannah Whitney - desc/o Deacon Edmund Rice BLG2884

Grace - b1675, m Nathaniel Moore - desc/o Deacon Edmund Rice LDS114

Hannah - b1658, m(1) Jonathan Hubbard, m(2) Richard Taylor - desc/o Deacon Edmund Rice LDS20, 39

RICE (cont.)

Henry - b1617 d1711, m1644 Elizabeth Moore - desc/o Deacon
Edmund Rice LDS38, 39; BLG2884

Isaac - b1738, m Mehitabel Stearns - desc/o Deacon Edmund Rice
LDS52

Jacob - of MA, b1660 d1746, m Mary Bannister - desc/o Deacon
Edmund Rice BLG2885

Jacob - b1697 - desc/o Obadiah Bruen RAA74

Jacob - of MA, b1707 d1788, m Hannah Howe - desc/o Deacon
Edmund Rice BLG2885

James - b1726 d1782, m1766 Mary Rhodes Stearns - desc/o Deacon
Edmund Rice BLG2884

James Rhodes - d1848, m1788 Mary Taylor - desc/o Deacon Edmund
Rice BLG2884

John - b abt 1647, m Tabitha Stone - desc/o Deacon Edmund Rice
LDS52

John - of MS, b1751 d1808, m1775 Mary Comee - desc/o Deacon
Edmund Rice BLG2884

Jonathan - b1654, m(1)1674 Martha Eames, m(2)1677 Rebecca
Watson, m(3)1691 Elizabeth Wheeler - desc/o Deacon Edmund Rice
BLG2884

Joseph - of MA, d1663, m(2)1655 Mercy Brigham - desc/o Deacon
Edmund Rice BLG2884

Joseph - b1637 d abt 1668, m(1) Mercy King, m(2) Martha____ -
desc/o Deacon Edmund Rice BLG2885

Josiah - of MA, b1700 d1792, m Thankful Rice - desc/o Deacon
Edmund Rice BLG2885

Josiah - of MA, b1727 d1792, m1749 Eunice Harrington - desc/o
Deacon Edmund Rice BLG2885

Josiah - of MA & VA, b1751, m1774 Hannah Marble - desc/o Deacon
Edmund Rice BLG2585 ·

Lucinda - b1776, m Ira Hatch - desc/o Deacon Edmund Rice LDS52

Rachel - b1664, m Thomas Drury - desc/o Deacon Henry Rice LDS38

Samuel - of MA, bp 1634, m(1) Elizabeth King - desc/o Deacon
Edmund Rice LDS20, 104; BLG2884

Samuel (Rice or King) - of MA, b1667, m Abigail Clapp - desc/o Deacon
Edmund Rice LDS104

Thomas - chr 1626, m Mary King - desc/o Deacon Edmund Rice
LDS114

William - of MS, b abt 1697 d1769, m1719 Martha Rice - desc/o
Deacon Edmund Rice BLG2884

RICH Lady Anne - of VA, b abt 1696 d1727 dau/o Edward Rich & ____, m
Col Francis Willis b1690 Ware River Parish, Gloucester Co, VA,
founded Fredericksburg, VA & was a member of the House of
Burgesses 1748 - the immigrant MCS45; GBR422; PVF270/275;
GVFTQ(4)494/512

Thomas - b1763 - desc/o Joseph Coulson RAA84

RICHARDS Benjamin - of PA - desc/o Lewis Richards DBR(2)762

Henry - of PA - desc/o Lewis Richards DBR(2)762

John - of MA - the immigrant EDV130, 131; sufficient proof of alleged
royal ancestry is lacking

RICHARDS (cont.)
    Joseph - b1762 - desc/o William Goddard RAA99
    Lewis - of PA 1680/1681, m Bridget Lewis - the immigrant DBR(2)762;
        RAA1, 127; sufficient proof of alleged royal ancestry is lacking
    Lewis - of KY, b1763 d1864, m1788 Lucy Hunton - desc/o Lewis
        Richards DBR(2)762
    Philemon - of KY, d1794, m Elizabeth Lewis - desc/o Lewis Richards
        DBR(2)762
    William - b1742 - desc/o Miles Standish RAA131
RICHARDSON Eleanor - of PA, m1717 William Harmar Jr - desc/o John
        Bevan Sr MCD165
    John - of PA - desc/o John Bevan Sr MCD165
    Josiah - of MA, m Sarah Powers - desc/o Rev Peter Bulkeley
        TAG(36)151
    Lucy - of MA, b1759 at Dracut, m1786 David Drury b1763
        Shrewsbury, MA d1818 at Weston, VT, served as a soldier in the
        Revolutionary War - desc/o Rev Peter Bulkeley TAG(36)150
    Molly or Mary - of MA, b1753 d1834, m John Patten b1745 at
        Tewksbury, MA d1807 son of John Patten & Elizabeth Frost -
        desc/o Rev Peter Bulkeley TAG(36)150
    Rebecca - of PA, m Daniel King - desc/o John Bevan Sr MCD165
    William - b1758 - desc/o Mary Gye RAA115
RICHMOND Lemuel - of MA, b1733 d1802, m Molly Richmond - desc/o
        Richard Williams CHB377; MCD308
    Polly - of MA, b1766 d1857, m George Townsend - desc/o Richard
        Williams CHB377; MCD308
RICKARD Abigail - b1655, m James Whiton - desc/o John Dunham
        LDS21
RICKS Mourning - of VA, m Josiah Jordan - desc/o James Tooke
        DBR(1)689/90
RIDER Job - of MA, abt 1746, m1772 Rebecca W Diman - desc/o Henry
        Southworth ECD(2)257; DBR(5)149
    Joseph - of MA, b abt 1714 d1779, m1739 Elizabeth Crossman -
        desc/o Henry Southworth ECD(2)257; DBR(5)149
RIDGWAY Andrew - of NJ, b1762 d1837, m1788 Lydia Clark - desc/o
        Peter Wright DBR(4)241
    Jacob - of NJ, b1723 d1799, m1750 Isabella Schooley - desc/o Peter
        Wright DBR(4)241
    Rachel - of PA, m1792 John Evans - desc/o Edmund Mauleverer
        MCD154
RIGBY Edward - of ME - the immigrant FLW194; MCS79; sufficient proof
        of alleged royal ancestry is lacking
RIGGS Ebenezer - m Lois Hawkins - desc/o Elizabeth Alsop GBR272
    Elizabeth - of CT, b1733 d1824, m(1)1755 Philo Mills d1765 son of
        Reverend Jedediah Mills & Abigail (Treat) Mills - desc/o Elizabeth
        Alsop ECD(2)20; DBR(5)924
    George - m Phebe Caniff - desc/o Elizabeth Alsop GBR272
    James - m Sarah Clark - desc/o Elizabeth Alsop GBR272
    Capt John - of CT, b1676 d1755, m1699 Elizabeth Tomlinson - desc/o
        Elizabeth Alsop ECD(2)20; DBR(5)924
    John - m Hannah Johnson - desc/o Elizabeth Alsop GBR272

RIGGS (cont.)

Samuel - of CT, b1700, m1726 Abigail Gunn b1699 - desc/o Elizabeth Alsop ECD(2)20; DBR(5)924

RIDLEY Mary - m Francis Jones - desc/o Peter Montague FFF80c

ROBBINS Edward Hutchinson - m Elizabeth Murray - desc/o Catherine Hamby GBR394

Melia - of MA, b1764 d1852, m Phinehas Butler Jr - desc/o Katharine Deighton JSW1827; DBR(4)729

Solomon - of CT, b1743 d1794, m1770 Mary (Molly) Harmon - desc/o Samuel Appleton DBR(3)73

ROBERDEAU Daniel - of PA, b abt 1727 d1795 Philadelphia merchant & Revolutionary patriot; a captain in the French & Indian Wars & a colonel in the Revolutionary War, son of Isaac Roberdeau & Mary Cunyngham, m(1)1761 Mary Bostwick, m(2)1778 Jane Milligan - the immigrant ECD(3)107; CHB262; MCB143; BCD262; DBR(1)228; DBR(2)182; DBR(3)562; DBR(4)194, 453; DBR(5)276, 753, 754; GBR93

Mary Horn - of PA, b1774 d1805, m1793 Thomas M Patten - desc/o Daniel Roberdeau ECD(3)107; CHB262; BCD262

ROBERTS Abial - b1693, m(2) Hepzibah Prindle - desc/o Peter Mallory LDS67

Lieut-Col Algernon - of PA, b1750/1751 Pencoed d1815 served in the Revolutionary War, Fifth Company, Third Battalion of Philadelphia Co militia & held many political offices, m1781 Tacy Warner dau/o Col Isaac Warner, of Blockley & Lydia Coulton - desc/o Rebecca Humphrey CHB161; BCD161 - desc/o John Roberts CRFP(1)455

Anne - b abt 1631, m(1) James Philbrick - desc/o Gov Thomas Roberts LDS65

Benjamin - of PA, b1746 removed to VA m____ & left issue - desc/o John Roberts CRFP(1)455

Eli - b1691, m Mary McKay - desc/o Peter Mallory LDS81

Elizabeth - of PA, m Isaac Parrish - desc/o Jane Owens CHB191

Elizabeth - of PA, b1705, m John Parish - desc/o Jane Owens MCD188; CFA435

Elizabeth - b abt 1734, m Ebenezer Saxton - desc/o Peter Mallory LDS67

Elizabeth - of PA, b1740 d1782, m Thomas Palmer - desc/o John Roberts CRFP(1)455

Esther - of PA, m1770 Jonathan Palmer - desc/o John Roberts CRFP(1)459

Gainor - of PA, sister of Katherine & Hugh John Roberts, of PA - the immigrant GBR310

Hannah - of PA, m____ Streaper & d bef her father, leaving five children - desc/o John Roberts CRFP(1)459

Hugh - of PA, son of John Thomas Ellis & Gainor John, brother of Mrs Katherine Roberts Edwards, m Jane Owen of PA, a cousin - the immigrant GBR310

Isaac - of PA, b1711, m Hannah Pascal - desc/o Jane Owens CFA435

Isaac - of PA, d bef his father leaving four children - desc/o John Roberts CRFP(1)459

Job - of PA - desc/o Cadwalader Evans MCD187

ROBERTS (cont.)

John - of PA 1683, b1648/1649 son of Richard Roberts & Margaret Evans, m Gainor Roberts of PA - the immigrant GBR323 some aspect of royal descent merits further study; CRFP(1)451/461

John - of PA, b1710 Pencoed d1776, m1733 Rebecca Jones d1779 dau/o Jonathan Jones & Gainor Owen of Merion - desc/o John Roberts CRFP(1)454, 455

Dr Jonathan - of PA, b1734 d aft 1778, removed to Prince George's Co, MD, m1757 Prince George's Co, MD, Elizabeth Carter, a widow - desc/o John Roberts CRFP(1)455

Margaret - of PA, dau/o Robert ab owain & Margaret ferch John ap Lewys, m Rowland Ellis of PA - the immigrant GBR80

Patience - of PA, b1725, m(1) Samuel Gray, m(2) Isaac Howell - desc/o Jane Owens CFA436

Peter - b1721, m Mary Howe - desc/o Peter Mallory LDS81

Phineas - of PA, b1722 Pencoed d1801, m1743 Philadelphia, Ann Wynne b1724/1725 d1807 eldest dau/o Thomas Wynne of Blockley & Mary Warner - desc/o John Roberts CRFP(1)454, 459

Richard - of PA, b1706/1707, m1732/1734 Elizabeth Allen - desc/o Jane Owens CFA435, 436

Richard - of PA, b1735, m Mary Harris - desc/o Jane Owens CFA436

Robert - of PA & VA, b1673 d1729, m(1) Catherine Jones, m(2)1703 Priscilla Jones - desc/o Jane Owens CHB191; MCD188; CFA435

Robert - of PA, b1685 Merion d1768, m1709 Sidney Rees b1680 Pemaen, parish of Llanwawr, Merionethshire d1764, dau/o Evan Rees & Elizabeth Thomas - desc/o John Roberts CRFP(1)454

Robert - of PA, b1741/1742 d1791, m1775 Catherine Deshler - desc/o Jane Owens CFA436

Samuel - b1754, m Patience Straight - desc/o Peter Mallory LDS81

Sidney - of PA, b1729 d1793, m John Paul - desc/o John Roberts CRFP(1)454

Sidney - of PA, b1756 d1812, m1780 John Jones b1748 d1821, quartermaster of militia during the Revolutionary War, son of Evan Jones & Ann Evans - desc/o John Roberts CRFP(1)459, 460

Tacy - of PA, b1744 d1791, m John Palmer - desc/o John Roberts CRFP(1)455

Gov Thomas - b1600, m Rebecca Hilton - the immigrant LDS65; RAA no longer accepted as being of royal descent

ROBERTSON Dr Andrew - of VA, d1795 - desc/o Dr Richard Edwards DBR(1)224

Elizabeth - m B.F.A.C. Dashiell - desc/o Nathaniel Littleton CFA(4)127

George - m Mary Waters - desc/o Nathaniel Littleton CFA(4)127

Col James III - of VA, m(2) Frances Lightfoot Poindexter - desc/o Capt Henry Isham DBR(1)25; DBR(2)344, 641

Leah - m B.F.A.C. Dashiell, after her death he, m her sister Elizabeth - desc/o Nathaniel Littleton CFA(4)127

Marie Elizabeth - m John Upshur Dennis - desc/o Nathaniel Littleton CFA(4)127

Sarah Anne - m Littleton Upshur Dennis - desc/o Nathaniel Litttleton CFA(4)127

ROBIE Mary - m Joseph Sewall, merchant in Boston & was treasurer of MA - desc/o Gov Thomas Dudley NE(8)316

Mehetable - of MA, m Jonathan Stearns son of Henry Sterns of Springfield - desc/o Gov Thomas Dudley NE(8)316

Simon Bradstreet - of Nova Scotia - desc/o Gov Thomas Dudley NE(8)316

ROBINS Barbara - of VA, m Argall Harmanson d1734, son of George Harmanson & Elizabeth Yeardley - desc/o Col Nathaniel Littleton APP464, 465

Bowdoin - of VA, b1700, m Joyce Gore - desc/o Col Nathaniel Littleton APP465

Edward - of VA, d1728, m Elizabeth____ - desc/o Col Nathaniel Littleton APP464

Col Edward - of VA, b1706 d1779, author of the family manuscript, justice of Northampton Co, m Margaret Teackle b1720/1821 d1794 - desc/o Col Nathaniel Littleton APP464; HSF(10)189

Edward - of MD, b1769 d1857, m1792 Elizabeth Parnell - desc/o Col Obedience Robins BLG2893

Elizabeth - of VA, m Thomas Harmanson d1725 - desc/o Col Nathaniel Littleton APP466

Esther - of VA, d1724, m Arthur Denwood b1671/1672 d abt 1720 of Somerset Co, MD, son of Levin & Priscilla Denwood, prominent Quakers - desc/o Col Nathaniel Littleton APP466

Esther - of MD, m Rouse Fassitt d1768 of Worcester Co, MD - desc/o Col Nathaniel Littleton APP465

Esther - of VA, b1722 d1775, m(1)1738/1739 Col Theophilus Pugh d1745/1746 of Nansemond Co, m(2)1761 Col Lemuel Reddick b1711 d1775, vestryman & churchwarden - desc/o Col Nathaniel Littleton APP464

Esther Littleton - of VA, m John Kendall - desc/o Col Nathaniel Littleton APP465

Grace - of VA, d1722, m Hillary Stringer II - desc/o Col Nathaniel Littleton APP466; SMO301

John - of VA, b1635 at Cherrystone d1709, m1662/1663 Esther Littleton - desc/o Col Obedience Robins BLG2893

John - of VA, b1669 d1740, justice & coroner of Northampton Co, VA, colonel of militia, m1703/1704 Katherine Teackle d1754 dau/o Reverend Thomas Teackle & Margaret (Nelson) Teackle - desc/o Col Nathaniel Littleton APP464, HSF(10)189

Col John - of VA, b1704/1705 d1734/1735, m(1)1729 Sarah Harmanson, m(2)1734 Susanna Godwin - desc/o Col Nathaniel Littleton APP464

Littleton - of VA, d1718/1719, m bef 31 Jan 1698/1699 Margaret (Teackle) Stringer, dau/o Reverend Thomas & Margaret (Nelson) Teackle & wid/o John Stringer - desc/o Col Nathaniel Littleton APP465

Margaret - of VA, m(1)1728/1729 Major William Waters b abt 1623 d1731, m(2) William Burton d1770, sheriff of Accomack Co 1741 - desc/o Col Nathaniel Littleton APP464

Mary - of MD, m John Fassitt d1773 of Worcester Co, MD - desc/o Col Nathaniel Littleton APP465

ROBINS (cont.)

    Col Obedience - of VA 1621, b1601 d1662, m1634 Grace O'Neill - the immigrant BLG2893 sufficient proof of alleged royal ancestry is lacking

    Susanna - of MD, m Jabez Pitt of Dorcester Co, MD - desc/o Col Nathaniel Littleton APP465

    Thomas - of VA, b1677 d1731/1732, of Chincoteague, mariner, m1669 at Boston, MA, Elizabeth Bowdoin dau/o Pierre & Elizabeth Bowdoin - desc/o Col Obedience Robins BLG2893 - desc/o Col Nathaniel Littleton APP465

    Thomas - of MD, b1702 d1765, member of the Lower House of the MD legislature & captain of militia, m1738 Leah Walley d1740, dau/o Elias Walley & Sarah (Peale) Walley of Worcester Co, MD, m(2)1745 Aralanta Purnell, dau/o John Purnell - desc/o Col Obedience Robins BLG2893 - desc/o Col Nathaniel Littleton APP465

    Thomas - of MD, b1740 d1815, m1768 Isabella McClanahan - desc/o Col Obedience Robins BLG2893

ROBINSON Abigail - b1737 - desc/o George Morton RAA116

    Benjamin - b1703/1704 - desc/o George Morton RAA116

    Douglas - of NY, son of William Rose of Clermiston & Mary (Douglas) Robinson, m Fanny Monroe - the immigrant GBR77

    Henry - of VA - desc/o Col Moore Fauntleroy CRL(4)550

    Israel - b1696 - desc/o George Morton RAA116

    John - b abt 1693 - desc/o Thomas Bradbury RAA72

    Lucy - of VA, b bef 1742/1743 (may have), m Col Boyd & whose descendants moved to the South - desc/o Anne Lovelace GVFHB(3)347

    Lydia - of NH, b abt 1700, m1718 John Morrison - desc/o Capt Thomas Bradbury DBR(3)153

    Lydia - b1741/1742 - desc/o George Morton RAA116

    Peter - b1655 - desc/o George Morton RAA116

    Rebecca - of PA, b1744, m Luke Shield - desc/o Peter Wright DBR(3)636

    Sarah - b1720 d1807, m1745 Ebenezer Spooner - desc/o Gov Thomas Dudley DBR(3)520

    Simeon - b1752 - desc/o Thomas Bradbury RAA72

ROCKWELL Benjamin - m Margaret Park - desc/o John Drake DBR(1)195

    James - b1704 - desc/o John Drake RAA87

    Jonathan - of CT, b1711 d1784, m Esther____ - desc/o Francis Willoughby DBR(3)735; DBR(4)351, 651

    Jonathan - of CT, b1728, m Hannah Bennet - desc/o Francis Willoughby DBR(3)735; DBR(4)351, 651

    Jonathan - of CT & IN, b1745 - desc/o Francis Willoughby DBR(3)735; DBR(4)351, 651

    Joseph - of CT, b1670 d1733 - desc/o Thomas Norton MCD262

    Joseph - of CT, b1695 d1746 - desc/o John Drake MCD208 - desc/o Thomas Norton MCD262

    Lucy - b1735 - desc/o John Drake RAA87

    Martin - of CT, b1772 d1851 - desc/o John Drake MCD208 - desc/o Thomas Norton MCD262

    Samuel - of CT, b1726 d1794 - desc/o John Drake MCD208 - desc/o

ROCKWELL (cont.)

Thomas Norton MCD262

Sarah - m Deacon Nathaniel Loomis - desc/o John Drake DBR(1)195

RODES Charles - of VA, son of John Rodes & Elizabeth Jason - desc/o John Rodes WAC80 - the immigrant GBR225

Clifton - of VA - desc/o John Rodes WAC80

David - of VA - desc/o John Rodes WAC80

John - of VA, b1697 d1775, m Mary____ - the immigrant WAC79, 80; sufficient proof of alleged royal ancestry is lacking

John - of VA - desc/o John Rodes WAC80

RODMAN Patience - of RI, b1706 d1739, m Jonathan Easton - desc/o Jeremy Clarke DBR(5)88, 91

RODNEY Caesar - of PA, b1706/1707 d1745 - desc/o William Rodney J&K245; TAG(64)97/111

Judge Caesar - b1730 d1783 delegate to the Continental Congress & signer of the Declaration of Independence - desc/o William Rodney J&K245; TAG(64)97/111

Caesar Augustus - of DE, b1772 d1824, Attorney General of the United States, member of Congress & senator from Delaware - desc/o William Rodney J&K245

Judge Daniel of DE, b1764 d1846, m1788 Sarah Fisher - desc/o William Rodney CHB340; BCD340

John of DE, b1725 d1792, m1752 Ruth Hunn - desc/o William Rodney CHB340; BCD340

Col Thomas - of PA, b1744 d1811 member Council of Safety, delegate to the Continental Congress & United States Judge for the Territory of Mississippi - desc/o William Rodney J&K245

William - of DE by Dec 1681 & of PA. b1652 d1708 Quaker for a short period of time. Came to Pennsylvania with William Penn. Became a member & first speaker of the Assembly of Delaware, sheriff of Sussex county & a member of Penn's Council in 1698. Court clerk & attorney, son of William Rodney & Rachel____, m(1)1688 Mary Hollyman, m(2) Sarah Jones - the immigrant J&K245; CHB340; MCB158; MCS26; BCD340; RAA1, 127; GBR121; TAG(64)97/111

William - of PA, b1689 d1732 sheriff of Kent Co, Delaware, m Ruth Curtis - desc/o William Rodney CHB340; BCD340

ROGERS Andrew - of VA. d1820/1821 - desc/o Gov Thomas Dudley DBR(1)71

Charles - of VA, b abt 1735 d1793, m1762 Catherine Brent - desc/o Diana Skipwith DBR(4)698

Jeremiah Dummer - of MA, b1743 d1784, m1769 Bathsheba Thatcher - desc/o Elizabeth St John CHB220; BCD220

Rev John - of MA, b1666 d1745, m(2)1691 Martha Whittingham - desc/o Gov Thomas Dudley DBR(1)71; DBR(2)90

John - of VA, d1752, m1723 Mrs Jane (Fallin) Walters - desc/o Diana Skipwith DBR(4)698

John - of VA, b abt 1768 d1851, m Sarah Tunstall - desc/o Diana Skipwith DBR(4)698

John - of VA, d1827, m Sara (Salley) Saxon - desc/o Gov Thomas Dudley DBR(2)91

Joseph - of New England - desc/o Thomas Rogers FFF137

ROGERS (cont.)

Rev Nathaniel - of MA 1636 - the immigrant EDV114, 115; sufficient proof of alleged royal ancestry is lacking

Philemon - b1755, m Sarah Prichard - desc/o Edward Griswold LDS89

Phoebe - of RI, b1757 d1847, m Thomas Wall - desc/o Lawrence Wilkinson MCD330

Sarah of MA, b1755 d1835, m1784 Samuel Parkman - desc/o Elizabeth St John CHB221; BCD221

Thomas - of New England, b1586/1587 d1621, m abt 1606 Grace____ - signer of the Mayflower Compact - the immigrant FFF137; RAA no longer accepted as being of royal descent

Thomas - of MA, b1725 d1786, m Elizabeth Ann Carr - desc/o Gov Thomas Dudley DBR(1)71; DBR(2)91

Capt William - of MA, b1689 d1749, m1720 Mary Caldwell - desc/o Gov Thomas Dudley DBR(1)71; DBR(2)90

ROOTES Elizabeth - of VA, m Rev John Thompson - desc/o Col George Reade J&K230; CHB249, 419; BCD249 - desc/o Col William Bernard CHB38; BCD38

Lucy - m bef 1754 Roger Dixon - desc/o Col George Reade DBR(1)132

Col Philip - of VA, m1756 Frances Ann Wilcox - desc/o Col George Reade DBR(3)689

Dr Philip Jennings - of VA, m Sarah Buford Davis - desc/o Col George Reade DBR(3)690

Thomas Reade - of VA, m Maria Smith - desc/o Col George Reade J&K229; CHB248; MCD272; BCD248 - desc/o Col William Bernard MCD162

Thomas Reade Jr - of VA, m(1) Serenah Ryng Battaile - desc/o Col George Reade J&K229; CHB248; MCD272; BCD248 - desc/o Col William Bernard MCD162

ROSE Charles - of VA, b1747 d1802, m(1) Sarah Jordan, m(2) Sarah Winston - desc/o Rev Robert Rose CRL(4)329

Col Hugh - of VA, b1743 d1797, m Caroline Matilda Jordan - desc/o Rev Robert Rose CHB198; MCD275; BCD198; AWW313; CRL(4)329 - desc/o William Ironmonger DBR(3)702

Jane - m James E Taliaferro - desc/o Sarah Ludlow DBR(1)113

Col John - of VA, b1735 d1803, m Catherine Rose - desc/o Rev Robert Rose CRL(4)329

Judith Scott - of VA, m Landon Cabell - desc/o Rev Robert Rose AWW313

Patrick - of VA, b1745 d1822, m(1) Mary Selden, m(2) Mary Nichols - desc/o Rev Robert Rose CRL(4)329

Rev Robert of VA 1725, b1704 d1751, son of John Rose of Lochiehills & Margaret Grant, m(1)1733/1734-Mary Tarrent, m(2)1740 Anne Fitzhugh - the immigrant CHB198; MCB146; MCD275; BCD198; AWW161; 313; CRL(4)328; GBR101 corrected information of ancestors & descendants of Rev Robert Rose, sources listed

Susanna - of VA & NY, b1749 d1825, m Gavin Lawson - desc/o Rev Robert Rose CRL(4)329

ROSS Anne Arnold - of MD, b1727 d1811 Belvoir, MD, m1752 Francis Key b1731/1732 St Paul's Covent Garden, London d1770 Charlestown, Cecil Co, MD - desc/o Alicia Arnold FLW80

ROSS (cont.)

Rev George - of DE, son of David Ross of Balbair & Margaret Stronack, m(1) Joanna Williams, m(2) Catherine Van Gezel - the immigrant GBR415

George Jr - b1730 d1779, signer of the Declaration of Independence, Pennsylvania patriot & jurist - desc/o Rev George Ross GBR415

Gertrude - m(1) Isaac Till, m(2) George Reade b1733 d1798, a signer of the Declaration of Independence, statesman & United States senator - desc/o Rev George Ross GBR415

ROUNDS Mary - of MA, b1773, m Ezekiel Salisbury - desc/o Richard Bowen Sr CHB465

ROWELL Philip - of NH, bp 1745 d1826, m Dorcas Redington - desc/o Thomas Dudley DBR(1)558; DBR(2)687; DBR(4)839

ROWLEY Sarah - b abt 1625, m Jonathan Hatch - desc/o Sarah Palmer LDS51 & 55

ROWNTREE Mary - of VA & MS, b1772 d1851, m1790/1791 Major Elijah Wilbourne - desc/o Edward Dudley DBR(3)532; DBR(4)433, 551

Capt Richardson - of VA, m Mildred (Mary) Hart - desc/o Edward Dudley DBR(3)532; DBR(4)433, 551

William II - of VA, d1766, m Elizabeth Turner - desc/o Edward Dudley DBR(3)532; DBR(4)433,551

ROYAL Sarah Ann - of VA, b abt 1690, m Capt Charles Hudson - desc/o Capt Henry Isham DBR(2)508

ROYCE Experience - b1727 - desc/o Obadiah Bruen RAA74

Rehumah - b1762 - desc/o Oliver Mainwaring RAA113

RUCK Hannah - m Theophilus Lillie - desc/o Anne Marbury GBR234 - desc/o Catherine Hamby GBR394

RUCKER Margaret - of VA, d bef 1802, m bef 1741 Isaac Smith - desc/o James Coghill DBR(2)440, 682

RUDYARD Thomas - deputy governor of East Jersey - son of Anthony Rudyard & Anne Newton, m Alice____ - the immigrant GBR274

RUGG Daniel - of MA, b1678, m1704 Elizabeth Priest - desc/o John Prescott AWW351

Jonathan - of MA, b1661 d1708, m(1)1710 Sarah Newton - desc/o John Prescott DBR(1)381

Lydia - of MA, b1733 d1803, m1754 Lieut Asa Wilder - desc/o John Prescott AWW351

Reuben - of MA, b1705, m1730 Lydia Ross - desc/o John Prescott AWW351

Sarah - of MA, b1705, m1728 Hackeliah Bridges - desc/o John Prescott DBR(1)381

RUGGLES Abigail - b abt 1698 - desc/o Thomas Dudley RAA89 - desc/o William Leete RAA107

Rev Benjamin - of CT, b1676 d1708, m Mercy Woodsbridge - desc/o Thomas Ruggles BLG2895

Benjamin - b1700, m Dorcas Whiting - desc/o Thomas Dudley LDS101; RAA89

Benjamin - b1726, m(1) Sarah Hunt - desc/o Thomas Dudley LDS101; RAA75, 89

Elizabeth - of MA, b1707, m(1) Samuel Dummer, m(2)1739 Rev Daniel Rogers - desc/o Elizabeth St John CHB220; BCD220

RUGGLES (cont.)

Ephraim - b1757, m Olive Powers - desc/o Thomas Dudley LDS101; RAA75, 89 - desc/o Richard Palgrave RAA121

John - of MA, b1591 d1664 - desc/o Thomas Ruggles BLG2895

John - of MA, b1635 d1713, m Mary Gibson - desc/o Thomas Ruggles BLG2895

Capt John - of CT - desc/o William Leete MCD246

Capt Joseph - of MA, b1696 d1742, m1720 Joanna White - desc/o Gov Thomas Dudley DBR(4)71

Capt Joseph - of CT, b1701 d1791, m1722 Rachel Tolle - desc/o William Leete CHB366; BLG2895

Joseph - of CT, b1757, m Mercy Warner - desc/o William Leete CHB366; BLG2895

Capt Lazarus - of CT, b1730 d1797, m1764 Hannah Bostwick - desc/o William Leete CHB366; BLG2895

Mercy - of CT, m Jonathan Humphrey - desc/o William Leete CHB366; MCD246

Mercy - of OH, b1732 d1822, m1754 Edmund Bostwick - desc/o William Leete ChB368

Nathaniel - b1761 d1819, m1786 Sarah (Sally) Fellows - desc/o Gov Thomas Dudley DBR(4)71

Oliver - of CT, NY & PA, b1767 d1850, m Phoebe Moore - desc/o William Leete CHB367

Patience - b1689 d1768, m1711 James Robinson - desc/o Gov Thomas Dudley DBR(3)520

Sarah - b1760 - desc/o Edward Bulkeley RAA75 - desc/o Thomas Dudley RAA89

Thomas - of MA 1637 - the immigrant BLG2895; sufficient proof of alleged royal ancestry is lacking

RUSH David - of MD, b abt 1735 d1783, m1764 Mary Alexander - desc/o Col George Reade DBR(1)10; DBR(2)6

RUSSELL Daniel - of MA, b1737, m Rebecca Chambers - desc/o Capt George Curwen J&K250

James - of MA, m Katherine Graves, anc/o James Russell Lowell - desc/o Capt George Curwen J&K251

James - desc/o Richard Russell EDV18, 19

John - m Sarah Trowbridge - desc/o Thomas Newberry AAP148

Mabel - of MA, b1678/1679 d1722, m(1)1701 Rev John Hubbard, m(2)1707 Rev Samuel Woodbridge - desc/o Mabel Harlakenden CHB269, 271; MCB302; MCD230; BCD269, 271

Mabel - of MA, m David Jenner - desc/o Mabel Harlakenden MCD231

Rebecca - m Ezekial Hayes - desc/o Thomas Newberry AAP148 - desc/o Thomas Trowbridge AAP149; GBR448

Richard - b1611 - the immigrant EDV18; sufficient proof of alleged royal ancestry is lacking

Ruth - b1741 - desc/o Mary Launce RAA130

Samuel - m Abigail Whiting - desc/o Thomas Newberry AAP148

RUTHERFORD John - of NJ, b1760 d1840 admitted to the bar 1781 & clerk of the vestry of Trinity Church, 1788 elected to the legislature, NJ, & to the Senate of the United States 1790, m1781 Magdalene Morris dau/o Lewis Morris - desc/o James Alexander CHB23,

RUTHERFORD (cont.)

    BCD23 - desc/o Walter Rutherford CHB301; BLG2898; BCD301; NYGBR(12)#1p16

    Major Walter - of NY, b1723 d1804 son of Sir John of Edgerston & Elizabeth (Cairncross) Rutherford, m(1)1758 Catherine Alexander - the immigrant CHB301; MCB143; BLG2897; BCD301; EDV29; GBR67; NYGBR(12)#1p14/16

– S –

ST CLAIR Arthur - of MA, d1818, m1760 Phoebe Bayard - the immigrant MCB154; CFA458; sufficient proof of alleged royal ancestry is lacking

    Daniel - of MA, b1762, m Rachel Shannon - desc/o Arthur St Clair CFA458

    Elizabeth - of PA, b1768 d1825, m(1) Lieut Col John Lawrence, m(2) Gen James Dill - desc/o Arthur St Clair CFA458

    John Murray - of MA, b1764, m1783 Jane Parker - desc/o Arthur St Clair CFA458

ST JOHN Daniel - b1700 d1761, m Mary Benedick - desc/o Matthias St John THC270

    Ebenezer - b abt 1660 d1723/1724, m Elizabeth Comstock - desc/o Matthias St John THC270

    Lady Elizabeth - of CT 1636, bp 1604/1605 Bletsoe d1677 Lynn, MA, dau/o Sir Oliver St John, member of Parliament, m1629 Rev Samuel Whiting b1597 d1679 minister at Lynn, MA 1636/1679 son of John Whiting, Mayor of Boston, England - the immigrant J&K299; CHB218; MCB134; MCD310; FLW34, 85; MCS74; BCD218; DBR(1)683; RAA75; AAP152; TAG(34)15/17, (45)256; GBR210; EO2(3)59, 60

    Hannah - b1703 d1746, m1723/1734 Jeremiah____ - desc/o Matthias St John THC270, 271

    James - b1674 d1754, m1693 Mary Comstock - desc/o Matthias St John THC270, 271

    James - b1708 d1756, m(1)1738 Abigail____, m(2) Experience____ - desc/o Matthias St John THC270

    Mark - b1633/1634, m(1) bef 1655/1656 Elizabeth Stanley, m(2)1690 Dorothy Smith - desc/o Matthias St John THC270; FFF49

    Mary - alive in 1696, m1677 Thomas Hyatt - desc/o Matthias St John THC270

    Mary - alive 1750, m1721 David Keeler - desc/o Matthias St John THC270

    Matthias - of MA 1631/1732 & CT 1640, b1603 d1699 - the immigrant THC270, 271; RAA no longer accepted as being of royal descent

    Matthias - b1630 d1728/1729, m Elizabeth____ - desc/o Matthias St John THC270, 271

    Matthias - of CT, b1667/1668 d1748, m abt 1690 Rachel Bouton - desc/o Matthias St John THC270

    Mercy - m1665 Ephraim Lockwood - desc/o Matthias St John THC270

ST JOHN (cont.)

Moses - b1705 d1785, m(1) Mercy Olmstead, m(2) Mary____ - desc/o Matthias St John THC270

Samuel - b1637/1638 d1685, m1663 Elizabeth____ - desc/o Matthias St John THC270

Samuel - b1698 d1779, m(1) Eunice Sherman, m(2)1776 Esther ____ - desc/o Matthias St John THC270

Sarah - b1659 d1714, m1682 Samuel Keeler - desc/o Mattias St John FFF49

Sarah - b abt 1705 d1751, m Elnathan Hanford - desc/o Matthias St John THC270

ST LEGER Katherine - of VA, d bef 28 Aug 1658, dau/o Sir Warham St Leger & Mary Heyward, m Thomas Colepepper (Culpeper) d probably in VA bef 1652, member of the VA Company 1623 & one of the original patentees of the Northern Neck of VA - the immigrant GBR140; APP525

Mary - of VA, bp 1612 dau/o Sir Warham St Leger & Mary Heyward, m1632 William Codd b1604 d1653 - the immigrant GBR141 lists her as the mother of St Leger Codd - the immigrant; APP526

Ursula - of VA, b abt 1672, m abt 1627 Rev Daniel Horsmanden - the immigrant ECD221; DBR(3)139, 237, 645; DBR(4)172; DBR(5)880; GBR141 lists her son Warham Horsmanden of VA the immigrant; APP524

SAFFORD Elizabeth - b1724/1725 - desc/o Alice Freeman RAA132

SALE Cornelius - m Jane Dawson - desc/o Col John Washington DBR(2)132

Judith - m Col LeRoy Pope - desc/o Col John Washington DBR(2)132

SALISBURY Avisa - b abt 1770 - desc/o Robert Abell RAA59

Edward - the immigrant EDV22; sufficient proof of alleged royal ancestry is lacking

SALTONSTALL Abigail - of MA, b1728, m Col George Watson of Plymouth - desc/o Richard Saltonstall AMB124 - desc/o Muriel Gurdon CFA(5)413 - desc/o Grace Kaye CFA(5)413

Dudley - of MA, b1738 d1796, m1765 Frances Babcock - desc/o Muriel Gurdon ECD177 - desc/o Richard Saltonstall AMB276

Elizabeth - of MA, b1668 d1726, m(1)1692 Rev John Denison d1689, m(2)1692 Rev Roland Cotton of Sandwich - desc/o Grace Kaye J&K219; CHB208, 360; MCD284; BCD208; AWW191; AMB124; FFF174; CFA(5)412 - desc/o Muriel Gurdon ECD180; ECD(2)235; CFA(5)412

Elizabeth - of CT, b1690 d1726, m(1)1710 Richard Christophers, m(2) Isaac Ledyard - desc/o Grace Kaye CHB206; BCD206; DBR(5)606; AMB275

Gilbert - b1752, m Harriet Babcock - desc/o Richard Saltonstall AMB276

Gov Gurdon - of CT, b1666 Haverhill, MA d1724 the distinguished minister of New London & was the governor of the Connecticut colony 1707/1724, m(1) Jerusha Richards d1697 dau/o James Richards, m(2) Elizabeth Rosewell d1710 daughter & sole heir of William Rosewell of Branford, m(3) Mary Whittingham Clarke d1730 dau/o William Whittingham & wid/o William Clarke of Boston -

SALTONSTALL (cont.)

desc/o Grace Kaye CHB206, 207, 360; MCB315; MCD284; BCD206, 207; DBR(2)769; DBR(3)480; DBR(5)593, 606; CFA(5)412 - desc/o Muriel Gurdon ECD177; DBR(1)700; DBR(3)482; DBR(5)938; AMB124, 275; EDV42, 43; CFA(5)412

Brig Gen Gurdon Jr - of CT, b1708 d1785 served as delegate to several colonial conventions, a member of several committees of New London conducting Revolutionary affairs & was appointed a brigadier general in 1776, m1732 Rebecca Winthrop - desc/o Grace Kaye CHB207, 360; MCD284; BCD207 - desc/o Muriel Gurdon ECD177 - desc/o Richard Saltonstall AMB275

Henrietta - b1750 d1824, m1772 John Still Miller - desc/o Richard Saltonstall AMB276

Katherine - b1704, m Thomas Brattle - desc/o Richard Saltonstall AMB275

Mary - of CT, b1692, m Jeremiah Miller MD - desc/o Richard Saltonstall AMB275

Mary - of MA, b1749 d1791, m Rev Moses Badger d1792 Providence, Rhode Island - desc/o Richard Saltonstall AMB125 - desc/o Grace Kaye CFA(5)413 - desc/o Muriel Gurdon CFA(5)413

Muriel - b1634, m Edward Moseley - desc/o Richard Saltonstall AMB124

Col Nathaniel - of MA, b1639 Ipswich, MA d1707 Colonel of the Essex Regiment, court official, refused to serve in witchcraft trials, m1663 Elizabeth Ward d1714 dau/o Rev John Ward, of Haverhill - desc/o Grace Kaye J&K218, 219; CHB206, 360; MCB315; MCD284; BLG2899; BCD206; DBR(2)768, 769; DBR(3)480; DBR(5)938; AMB124; AWW189; CFA(5)412 - desc/o Muriel Gurdon ECD176, 177, 180; ECD(2)235; MCD228; DBR(1)575, 699; DBR(3)482; DBR(5)593, 606; FFF174; CFA(5)412

Nathaniel - of MA, b1707, m1733 Lucretia Arnold - desc/o Richard Saltonstall AMB275

Nathaniel MD - of MA, b1746 of Haverhill d1815, m1780 Anna White d1841 dau/o Samuel White of Haverhill - desc/o Grace Kaye CHB361; DBR(5)593; AMB125; CFA(5)413 - desc/o Muriel Gurdon ECD176; BLG2899; CFA(5)413

Rebecca- of CT, b1734, m1758 David Mumford - desc/o Grace Kaye CHB207; BCD207

Sir Richard - of MA 1630, b1586 of Huntwicke Co, Yorkshire bp 1586 Halifax d abt 1661 was one of the first named associates of the original patentees of the MA Bay Colony & was one of the original patentees of Connecticut, m(1) Grace Kaye, dau/o Robert Kaye, of Woodsome, Yorkshire, m(2) Elizabeth West, m(3) Martha Cammock - the immigrant BLG2898, 2899; AMB124; AWW179; FFF173, 174, 181; CHB205/06; FLW7; NE(95)72; sufficient proof of alleged royal ancestry is lacking; his wife (1) Grace Kaye was of royal ancestry; CFA(5)411

Maj Richard - of MA 1630, b1610 Woodsome, Yorkshire d1694 Hulme, Lancastershire, came to New England in 1630 with his father, court official, sergeant-major in Colonel Endicott's Regiment Oct 1641, son of Richard Saltonstall & Grace Kaye, m1633 Muriel Gurdon

SALTONSTALL (cont.)

dau/o Brampton Gurdon of Assington Hall, sheriff of Norfolk 1625/1629 - desc/o Grace Kaye J&K218; CHB206, 359, FLW7; MCB135, 313; MCD284; MCS36; BLG2899; BCD206; DBR(2)768; DBR(3)479, 480; DBR(5)606, 610, 938; AMB124; RAA1; AWW179; FFF174 - the immigrant GBR164; EO2(3)61/63; CFA(5)411

Col Richard - of MA, b1672 d1714, representative from Haverhill 1600, major 1704, afterwards colonel, m1702 Mehitabel Wainwright dau/o Capt Simon Wainwright of Haverhill - desc/o Grace Kaye CHB361; BLG2899; AMB125; CFA(5)412 - desc/o Muriel Gurdon ECD176; DBR(1)575; CFA(5)412

Judge Richard - of MA, b1703 Haverhill, MA d1756, judge of Superior Court 1736/1756, m(1)1726 Abigail Waldron d1735, m(2) Mary Jekyll dau/o John Jekyll, collector of customs at Boston, m(3) Mary Cooke - desc/o Grace Kaye CHB361; BLG2899; AMB125; CFA(5)413 - desc/o Muriel Gurdon ECD176; DBR(1)575; CFA(5)413

Rosewell - of CT, m Mary Haynes - desc/o Richard Saltonstall AMB275

Rosewell - of CT, b1741 d1804, m1763 Elizabeth Stewart - desc/o Grace Kaye CHB360; MCB314 - desc/o Muriel Gurdon ECD178 - desc/o Richard Saltonstall AMB276

Sarah - of CT, b1694, m(1)1716 John Gardiner Jr d1725, m(2) Samuel Davis - desc/o Grace Kaye CHB207; MCD284; BCD207; DBR(1)700; DBR(2)769; DBR(3)480; DBR(5)594, 938 - desc/o Muriel Gurdon DBR(3)482 - desc/o Richard Saltonstall AMB275

Sarah - b1754 d1828, m1775 Daniel Buck - desc/o Richard Saltonstall AMB276

William - of NY, d1842, m Maria Hudson - desc/o Grace Kaye CHB360; MCB314

Winthrop - b1737 d1784, m Ann Wanton - desc/o Gov Gurdon Saltonstall AMB276

SANDERS Sarah - of MA, m1726 John Bossell - desc/o Edward Raynsford NE(139)310

SANDERSON Benjamin - b1707, m Elizabeth Green - desc/o Mary Knapp LDS27

Mary - b1742, m Joseph Call - desc/o Mary Knapp LDS27

SANDIDGE Capt Benjamin - of VA, d1829, m1783 Elizabeth Childress - desc/o Edward Dudley DBR(1)327; DBR(2)419

Dorothy (Dolly) - of VA, m William H Higginbotham - desc/o Edward Dudley DBR(5)777

SANDS (or SANDYS) Abijah - of RI, m____ Warring - desc/o James Sands CFA461

Bathsheba - of RI, m Thomas Everitt - desc/o James Sands CFA461

Edward - of RI, b1673, m Mary Williams - desc/o James Sands CFA461

George - of VA, b1577/1578 d1643/1644, poet & treasurer of VA, son of Edwin Sandys, Archbishop of York & Cecily Wilsford - the immigrant GBR430

Capt James - of RI 1640, b1622 d1695, m Sarah Walker - the immigrant CFA461; AFA156; CRL(2)151, 152; EDV48; sufficient proof of alleged royal ancestry is lacking

Capt James - of NY, b1673 d1731, m abt 1697 Sarah Cornwell -

SANDS (or SANDYS) (cont.)

desc/o Anne Marbury DBR(4)311; DBR(5)290 - desc/o Capt James Sands AFA156; CRL(2)152

James - of RI, b1672 d1731, m1697 Mary Cornell - desc/o James Sands CFA461

James - of RI, b1702, m Rebecca Bailey - desc/o James Sands CFA461

Jerusha - of RI, m John Cannon - desc/o James Sands CFA461

Jerusha - of NY, m John Carman - desc/o Anne Marbury DBR(4)311; DBR(5)290

John - of RI, b1652, m1676 Sybil Ray - desc/o James Sands CFA461

John - of RI, b1710 d1775, m1735 Catherine Greiner - desc/o James Sands CFA461; AFA156; CRL(2)153

John - of PA, b1738, m Hannah Trump - desc/o James Sands CFA461

Margaret - of VA, dau/o Sir Samuel Sandys & Mercy Colepepper (Culpeper), m Sir Francis Wyatt b1588 d1644, governor of VA - the immigrant GBR430

Mary - of RI, m____ Sutton - desc/o James Sands

Mercy - of RI, b1654, m Joshua Raymond - desc/o James Sands CFA461

Othniel - of RI, b1699, m Susannah Lang - desc/o James Sands CFA461

Othniel - of RI, b1756 d1831, m1784 Catherine Rittenhouse - desc/o James Sands CFA461; AFA156

Samuel - of RI, b1652, m Dorothy Ray - desc/o James Sands CFA461

Samuel - of PA, b1736 d1792, m Catherine Bechtel - desc/o James Sands CFA461

Sarah - of RI, b1651, m1671 Nathaniel Niles - desc/o James Sands CFA461

Sarah - of RI, b1692/1694, m1711 Tiddeman Hull - desc/o Dr Richard Palgrave ECD(3)232, 233

Sarah - of RI, b1728, m John Aspinwall - desc/o James Sands CFA461

Sarah - of RI, b1759, m Jacob Colladay Jr - desc/o James Sands CRL(2)153

SANFORD Abel - b1763 d1843, m Deborah Sperry - desc/o Obadiah Bruen FFF252

Bridget - b1682 - desc/o Anne Marbury RAA114

Isaac - b1731 d1801, m Jerusha Baker - desc/o Obadiah Bruen FFF252

Peleg - b1639 - desc/o Anne Marbury RAA114

Samuel - b1698 d1787, m Abigail Holbrook - desc/o Obadiah Bruen FFF252

SARGENT Anna - of MA, b1767 d1850, m1795 John Hayward - desc/o Rev William Sargent CFA(3)481

Charles - b1694, m Hepzibah Heath - desc/o Anthony Colby LDS47

Deborah - of MA, m1801 Thomas Waite, of Malden - desc/o Rev William Sargent CFA(3)480

Ebenezer - of MA, b1690 d1771, m(1)1716 Esther Willis d aft 1735, m(2) Mary____ d1781 - desc/o Rev William Sargent CFA(3)480

Elizabeth - of MA, bp 1630 d1657/1658, m(1) abt 1651 David Nichols

SARGENT (cont.)

of Boston d1652/1653, m(2)1653 Thomas Bill of Boston - desc/o
Rev William Sargent GBR435; NE(75)141; CFA(3)478

Hannah - of MA, bp 1629 d1717 Reading, MA, m1649 Henry Felch of
Reading d1699 they were the parents of 11 children - desc/o Rev
William Sargent RAA129; GBR435; NE(75)141; CFA(3)479

John - of MA, bp 1639 Charelstown d1716 Malden, m(1)1662/1663
Deborah Hillier b1643 Yarmouth, Plymouth Colony d1669 dau/o
Hugh Hillier, m(2)1669 Mary Bense d sp 1670/1671, m(3) Lydia
Chipman b1654 Barnstable d1729/1730 dau/o Elder John
Chipman & Hope Howland - desc/o Rev William Sargent LDS32,
41; RAA129; NE(75)141; CFA(3)479

John - of MA, b1664/1665 1755, m Mary Linnell d1755 dau/o David
Linnell - desc/o Rev William Sargent LDS41; RAA129; CFA(3)479

John - of CT, b1720 of Mansfield, m1740 Hannah Wadkins - desc/o
Rev William Sargent CFA(3)480

John - of MA, b1759 of Leicester d1829 served as a soldier during the
Revolution, m(1)1783 Sarah Gates b1761 d1817 dau/o Simon
Gates, m(2)1818 Grace Tidd b1773 dau/o Joseph Tidd & wid/o
Joseph Denny - desc/o Rev William Sargent CFA(3)481

Jonathan - of MA, b1677 d1754, selectman of Malden for three years
& representative, seven years, m(1)1699/1700 Mary Lynde b1678
d1716, dau/o John Lynde, m(2)1717 Mary Sprague b1696 d1787
dau/o Jonathan Sprague - desc/o Rev William Sargent CFA(3)480

Jonathan - of MA, b1700/1701 of Leicester d1777, m1726 Deborah
Richardson b1708 d1770 dau/o Nathaniel Richardson - desc/o Rev
William Sargent CFA(3)480

Joseph - of MA, b1663 of Malden & Charlestown d1717, m1685 Mary
Green b1668 d1759 - desc/o Rev William Sargent RAA129;
CFA(3)479

Lydia - of MA, m1701 Joseph Waite, Jr, of Malden - desc/o Rev
William Sargent CFA(3)480

Lydia - of MA, b1743 d1816, m(1)1764 Johnson Watson, m(2)1795
Nathaniel Kellogg - desc/o Rev William Sargent CFA(3)481

Lydia Chipman - b abt 1682, m Joseph Waite - desc/o Rev William
Sargent LDS32; RAA129

Mariam - b1720, m John Challis - desc/o Anthony Colby LDS47

Martha - b1725, m John Quinby or Quimby - desc/o Anthony Colby
LDS90

Mary - of MA, b1667, m Nathan Toby of Sandwich - desc/o Rev
William Sargent CFA(3)479

Mary - of MA, b1722 d1794, m1743 Josiah Storrs - desc/o Rev
William Sargent CFA(3)480

Mary - of MA, b1755 d1831, m1773 David Henshaw - desc/o Rev
William Sargent CFA(3)481

Mercy - of MA, b1751 d1823, m1796 Micah Reed - desc/o Rev William
Sargent CFA(3)481

Nathan - of MA, b1718 Malden d1799, m(1)1742 Mary Sargent b1721
d1750 dau/o Joseph Sargent, m(2)1751 Mary Denny b1727 d1822
dau/o Daniel Denny - desc/o Rev William Sargent CFA(3)480

Nathan - of MA, b1746 of New Braintree d1826, m Mary Waite b1754

SARGENT (cont.)

d1816 dau/o Nathaniel Waite - desc/o Rev William Sargent CFA(3)481

Philip - b1672, m Mary Tewksbury - desc/o Anthony Colby LDS47, 90

Philip - b1703, m Martha Hadley - desc/o Anthony Colby LDS90

Phineas - of MA, b1702 of Malden d1761, m1724 Abigail Pratt b1699 d1776 dau/o John Pratt - desc/o Rev William Sargent CFA(3)480

Ruth - of MA, b1642 Charlestown d1711, m(1) abt 1663 Jonathan Winslow b1638 d1676 son of Josiah & Margaret Winslow, m(2)1677 Richard Bourne of Sandwich b England, m(3)1684 Elder John Chipman of Sandwich - desc/o Rev William Sargent NE(75)141, 142; CFA(3)478

Ruth - b1696, m Theophilus Hall - desc/o Rev William Sargent LDS41; RAA129

Samuel - of MA, b1688 d1721, m1714 Elizabeth Pratt b1692/1693 dau/o Thomas Pratt - desc/o Rev William Sargent CFA(3)480

Samuel - b1703/1704 - desc/o Rev William Sargent RAA129

Samuel - of MA & VT, b1754 d1825 served in the Continental Army & was in the Battle of Bunker Hill & at the surrender of Burgoyne's Army, m1781 Mary Washburn b1759 d1848 - desc/o Rev William Sargent CFA(3)481

Sarah - m Caleb Ball - desc/o Thomas Sargent DBR(1)748

Sarah - of MA, b1763 d1837, m1783 William Sprague - desc/o Rev William Sargent CFA(3)481

Susanna - b1750 - desc/o Rev William Sargent RAA129

Thomas - of CT 1644 - the immigrant DBR(1)748; sufficient proof of alleged royal ancestry is lacking

Rev William - of MA, bp 1602 Northampton d1682 Barnstable, MA, deacon & lay preacher at Malden, MA, son of Roger Sargent, m(1) abt 1627 Hannah____ d1632, m(2) abt 1634 Mary____ d1637, m(3) abt 1638 Sarah____ Minshall d 1688/1689 wid/o William Minshall - the immigrant FLW46; LDS32, 41; RAA1, 129; GBR435; NE(74)231/283, (75)57/63, 129/42, (79)358/378; EO2(2)18/38; CFA(3)479

William - of MA, b1680 d1731/1732, m1702 Mary Lewis b1681 d1743/1744 dau/o Isaac Lewis - desc/o Rev William Sargent CFA(3)480

SAVAGE Alice - of VA, m Francis Thornton - desc/o Anthony Savage AAP143, 145; GBR253

Anthony - of VA, son of Ralph Savage & ____, m (possibly) Sarah Constable - the immigrant AAP143, 145; GBR253 some aspect of royal descent merits further study

Hannah - m Capt Benjamin Gillam - desc/o Anne Marbury DBR(1)760

Rebecca - of CT, m Richard Dowd - desc/o Rev Charles Chauncy CHB86; BCD86

SAWYER Abijah - b1765, m Meletiah Graves - desc/o John Prescott LDS34; RAA125

Aholiab - b abt 1702 - desc/o John Prescott RAA125

Benjamin - b1697/1698 - desc/o John Prescott RAA125

Caleb - b1659, m Sarah Houghton - desc/o John Prescott LDS34; RAA125

SAWYER (cont.)

Caleb - b1720, m Lydia Reed - desc/o John Prescott LDS34; RAA125

Caleb - b1740, m(1) Sarah Rogers - desc/o John Prescott LDS34; RAA125

Daniel - b1775 d1819, m1794 Theodosia Pennoyer Bouton (Boughton) - desc/o John Prescott DBR(1)308

Edward - of MA, b1681 d1776, m1707 Elizabeth Mack - desc/o John Prescott DBR(1)568

Elias - b1692 - desc/o John Prescott RAA125

Elias - b1747, m Hannah Farrar - desc/o John Whitcomb LDS16 - desc/o John Prescott RAA125

Elisha - b1718 - desc/o John Prescott RAA125

Ephraim - b1678 - desc/o John Prescott RAA125

Esther - b1739 - desc/o John Prescott RAA125

Eunice - b1714 d1804, m1736 Joshua Woodman - desc/o Thomas Welles FFF119

Hannah - b1728 d1802, m1747 Jonathan Hutchinson - desc/o John Prescott DBR(1)568

Humphrey - b1716/1717 - desc/o Thomas Bradbury RAA72

James - of MA, b1657 d1755, m(2) Mary Prescott - desc/o John Prescott DBR(1)307; RAA125

Jeduthan - b1713 - desc/o John Prescott RAA125

John - of MA, b1661, m1686 Mary Ball - desc/o John Prescott DBR(1)568; RAA125

Jonathan - b1690, m Elizabeth Wheelock - desc/o John Prescott LDS34; RAA125

Joshua - b1732 - desc/o John Prescott RAA125

Mary - of MA, b1653, m1673 Lieut Nathaniel Wilder - desc/o John Prescott DBR(1)291; RAA125

Mary - b1723 - desc/o John Prescott RAA125

Moses - b abt 1690 - desc/o John Prescott RAA125

Ruth - b1717 - desc/o John Prescott RAA125

Ruth - b1757 - desc/o Thomas Bradbury RAA72

Sarah - b1752 - desc/o John Prescott RAA125

Thomas - b1726, m1751 Sara Ross - desc/o John Prescott DBR(1)308

Thomas - b1649 - desc/o John Prescott RAA125

William - b1679 - desc/o John Prescott RAA125

Zilpha - b1765 - desc/o John Prescott RAA125

SAXTON Jerusha - b1682 - desc/o Alice Freeman RAA132

John - b1761, m Mary Fenn - desc/o Peter Mallory LDS67

Mercy - b1686 - desc/o Alice Freeman RAA132

SCHENCK Johannes - of NY 1683, b1656 - the immigrant EDV50; sufficient proof of alleged royal ancestry is lacking

SCHUYLER Philip - of NY 1650 - the immigrant EDV15; sufficient proof of alleged royal ancestry is lacking

SCOTT Amos - b1751 - desc/o Richard Belding RAA68

Ann - of SC, dau/o Jonathan Scott & Ann Harleston - desc/o John Harleston SCG(2)300

Anne Baytop - b1750 d1816, m1769 Micajah McGehee - desc/o Capt Henry Isham DBR(1)40

Betsey - of RI, b1754 d1823, m Capt John Short - desc/o Catherine

SCOTT (cont.)

Marbury ECD260

Catharine - b1696, m Nathaniel Jenkes son of Governor Joseph Jenkes - desc/o Katharine Marbury NYGBR(2)176

Catherine - of VA, b1741, m Dr William Brown - desc/o Col Gerard Fowke CFA(5)315

Christian - of VA, b1745, m Col Thomas Blackburn - desc/o Col Gerard Fowke CFA(5)315

Deliverance - of RI, d1676, m1670 William Richardson, shipmaster of Newport RI & Flushing, Long Island - desc/o Katherine Marbury EO2(3)96; NYGBR(2)175; NE(96)10

Dorothea or Deborah - of VA, m William Fleete - the immigrant CHB469; MCB332; sufficient proof of alleged royal ancestry is lacking

Dorothea - of NY 1680, bp 1611, m(1) abt 1636 Maj Daniel Gotherson, m(2) abt 1670 Joseph Hogben - the immigrant CHB90; ECD(2)240; MCB226; MCD287; BCD89, 90 sufficient proof of alleged royal ancestry is lacking

Edward - of RI, b1703 d unmarried 1768, called "of Newport, Schoolmaster", was one of the incorporators of the Redwood Library at Newport, in 1734; director & librarian in 1747/1748; moderator in 1755 and held various offices. For upwards of twenty years he was head of a grammar school at Newport, the first classical school in Rhode Island, for twenty-five years was one of the judges of the inferior court of common pleas for the county of Newport, the last fifteen he was chief justice. In religious belief he was an Episcopalian, & not a Quaker - desc/o Katharine Marbury EO2(3)103, 104

Elizabeth - of RI, m1717 at Newport, Thomas Rodman son of John Rodman of Long Island - desc/o Katharine Marbury EO2(3)102

Emma - m Caleb Greene - desc/o Katharine Marbury NYGBR(2)177

Esther - of RI, m1721 Thomas Sayles, of Smithfield, Rhode Island - desc/o Katharine Marbury NYGBR(2)177

Euphan - of NJ, dau/o George Scott, the Laird of Pitlochie & Margaret Rigg, m1686 Dr John Johnstone b1661 Edinburgh, Scotland, represented Middlesex Co in the General Assembly, Province of New Jersey, for thirteen years, during ten of which he was Speaker of the House, member of the King's Council 1716/1723 & was mayor of the city of New York 1714/1718 - the immigrant GBR97 some aspect of royal descent merits further study; CFA(2)393

George - of RI, b1706 d1740, m1732 Mary Neargrass b1726 d1760 dau/o Edward Neargrass - desc/o Katharine Marbury EO2 (3)105

George - of RI, b1742 d1798 while in Newport, during the Revolution, Count Christian de Deux Ponts, of the royal Regiment, was quartered at the house of George Scott, m1764 Mary Ayrault d1812 dau/o Stephen Ayrault, shopkeeper - desc/o Katharine Marbury EO2(3)104, 105

Gustavus - of VA, b abt 1753, m1777 Margaret Hall Caile - desc/o Col Gerard Fowke CFA(5)315

Hannah - of RI, b abt 1642 d1681, m1667 Governor Walter Clarke b abt 1638 d Newport, Rhode Island 1714 son of Jeremy Clarke &

SCOTT (cont.)

Frances Latham - desc/o Katherine Marbury DBR(1)82; DBR(5)91; EO2(3)95; NYGBR(2)176; NE(96)9

Hannah - of RI, b1746 d1767, m1766 George Gibbs, merchant - desc/o Katharine Marbury EO2(3)105

Helen - of VA, b1739 Overwharton Parish, Stafford Co d1795, m1791 Cuthbert Bullit b1740 d Prince William Co, a delegate to the VA Assembly 1777 to 1787 & Speaker of the House, member VA Convention, son of Benjamin Bullitt & Elizabeth Harrison of Fauquier Co, VA - desc/o Col Gerard Fowke CFA(5)315

James - of VA, b1742, m Elizabeth Harrison - desc/o Col Gerard Fowke CFA(5)315

Jeremiah - of RI, b1709 d1795, m Rebecca Jenkes - desc/o Katherine Marbury ECD260

Jeremiah - m Sarah Brown - desc/o Katharine Marbury NYGBR(2)177

Jesse - b1767 d1813 at Fairfield, New York, m Susannah Chaffe & left issue 3 sons & 2 daughters - desc/o Katharine Marbury NYGBR(2)178

Joanna - of RI, m Judge Daniel Jenks, a member of the General Assembly for forty years - desc/o Katharine Marbury NYGBR(2)177

Joanna - b1771 d1856, m Charles Jenkes & had issue a son Linden - desc/o Katharine Marbury NYGBR(2)178

Job - of RI, b1731 d1793 at Ballitore, Dublin, Ireland of smallpox, celebrated Quaker preacher by convincement & not by birthright; in 1792 he had a call to preach in Europe & preached through England & Ireland - desc/o Katharine Marbury NYGBR(2)177

John - of RI, b1640 d1677 is said to have been wounded by an Indian while standing in the doorway of his own house at Pawtucket Ferry, took the oath of allegiance to Charles II in 1668, m Rebecca____ d aft 1701 - desc/o Katharine Marbury NE(96)10; EO2(3)96; NYGBR(2)175

John - of RI, b1664 d1724 house carpenter & merchant of Providence & Newport, Rhode Island, m Elizabeth Wanton b1668 dau/o Edward & Elizabeth Wanton - desc/o Katharine Marbury EO2(3)96, 101

John of NY 1702, son of Sir John Scott, 1st Baronet & Elizabeth Scott, m1702 Magdalen Cooper (Vincent) - the immigrant CHB265; MCB165; BCD265; AMB336; AFA68; EDV115; GBR67

John of NY, b1702 d1733, m Marian Morin - desc/o John Scott CHB265; BCD265; AMB336; AFA68

John - of RI, d1798 he was not a Quaker, owned large possessions on the plain in the great meadow hollow, Providence, m Lydia Comstock & left issue - desc/o Katharine Marbury NYGBR(2)177

John - of SC, son of Jonathan Scott & Ann Harleston - desc/o John Harleston SCG(2)300

John - of RI, b1739 d1773, m Sarah Cookson d1770 dau/o Capt Cookson, late commander of His Majesty's Sloop *Senegal* - desc/o Katharine Marbury EO2(3)106

John - of VA, b abt 1747 d1785, m1768 Elizabeth Gordon - desc/o Col Gerard Fowke CFA(5)315

John Bennett - of RI, b1740 d1767, m1764 Phebe Thurston - desc/o

SCOTT (cont.)

Katharine Marbury EO2(3)104

John Cookson - of RI, b1768 d1808 merchant of Newport, m1791
Martha English b1767 d1805 dau/o Capt William English - desc/o
Katharine Marbury EO2(3)106

Brig Gen John Morin of NY, b1730 d1784, m Helena Rutgers - desc/o
John Scott CHB265; BCD265; AMB336; AFA68; RAA72

Joseph - b1697, m Elizabeth Jenkes - desc/o Katharine Marbury
NYGBR(2)176

Joseph - of RI, b1709 d1764, m1739 Elizabeth Bennett - desc/o
Katharine Marbury EO2(3)104

Katherine - of RI, m1719 Col Godfrey Malbone of Newport, Rhode
Island, b1695 at Princess Anne Co, VA d1768 at Newport,
merchant, he was authorized to command & lead 500 soldiers in
the expedition against the French settlements at Cape Breton
1744/1745 - desc/o Katharine Marbury EO2(3)102

Lewis Allaire of NY, b1759 d1798, m1785 Juliana Sitgreaves - desc/o
John Scott CHB165; BCD265; AMB336; AFA68

Mary - of RI, d1665, m1660 Christopher Holder b1631 d1688 had his
right ear cut off by the hangman at Boston 16 Sep 1658, for the
crime of being a Quaker - desc/o Katherine Marbury DBR(2)44;
DBR(5)833; RAA114; EO2(3)95; NE(96)9; NYGBR(2)176

Mary - of RI, b1666 d aft 1734, m Joshua Davis d1736, miller son of
Aaron & Mary Davis of Newport, Rhode Island - desc/o Katherine
Marbury EO2 (3)96

Mary - of RI, m1707 George Goulding b1685 d1742 son of Major Roger
Goulding & Penelope Arnold - desc/o Katharine Marbury NE(96)10;
EO2(3)102

Mary - b1757 - desc/o Griffith Bowen RAA72

Mary - or RI, m Augustus Lapham, a Quaker d1860 leaving numerous
descendants - desc/o Katharine Marbury NYGBR(2)177

Mercy - m Philip Mason & had issue - desc/o Katharine Marbury
NYGBR(2)177

Nathaniel - of RI, m Mercy Smith b1714 d1799 & had issue - desc/o
Katharine Marbury NYGBR(2)177

Nathaniel - of RI, b1769 in Smithfield, m1791 Charlotte Bowen -
desc/o Katharine Marbury NYGBR(2)178

Patience - of RI, b1648 d aft 1707, m1668 Henry Beere of Newport
d1691 son of Edward Beere - desc/o Katherine Marbury EO2(3)95,
96; NYGBR(2)176; NE(96)9

Rachel - b1710 - desc/o Richard Belding RAA68

Rebecca - of RI, b1738 d1764, m1762 James Brenton b1736 at
Newport, 13th child of Jehleel Brenton & Frances Cranston & had
issue 1 son James Brenton - desc/o Katharine Marbury EO2(3)105

Rebeckah - b1669, m John Whipple - desc/o Katharine Marbury
NYGBR(2)175

Rebeckah - b1699, m John Wilkinson - desc/o Katharine Marbury
NYGBR(2)176

Robert - of VA, b abt 1749 d abt 1782, m Catherine Stone of Charles
Co, MD - desc/o Col Gerard Fowke CFA(5)315

Sarah - b1707 d1733, m1726 Stephen Hopkins, signer of the

SCOTT (cont.)

>Declaration of Independence - desc/o Katharine Marbury NYGBR(2)177

>Sarah - m Eleazor Brown - desc/o Katharine Marbury NYGBR(2)177

>Maj Silvanus - of RI, b1672 d1742, m abt 1792 Joanna Jencks b1672 d1756 dau/o Governor Joseph Jencks of Rhode Island & Ester Ballard of Providence & sister of Gov Jenckes - desc/o Katherine Marbury ECD260; NE(96)10; EO2(3)96; NYGBR(2)176

>Sylvanus - of RI, d1829 aged 84 years, m Jerusha Brown d1819 age 72 & had issue - desc/o Katharine Marbury NYGBR(2)177

>Ursula - of MA, m abt 1615 Richard Kimball - the immigrant JSW1762, 1832, 1870; sufficient proof of alleged royal ancestry is lacking

>William - b1773 d1859 at Tioga Co, New York, m Sarah Hunt & left issue - desc/o Katharine Marbury NYGBR(2)178

SCOVILLE Abner - of CT, b1769 d1836, m Comfort Bristol - desc/o John Drake DBR(3)664

>Ezekiel II - of CT, b1744 d1821, m1766 Rebecca Thompson - desc/o John Drake DBR(3)664

>Irene - b1770 - desc/o John Drake RAA87

SCRANTON Elizabeth - of CT, b1757 d1824, m1784 Jared Leete - desc/o Jane Haviland DBR(4)45

SCUDDER Amos - b1738 d1824, m1763 Phebe Rose - desc/o Edward Howell AFA184

>John - of NY, b1765 d1830, m1791 Mary Keen - desc/o Edward Howell AFA184

SEARLE Hannah - of CT, b1753 d1841, m1776 Henry Harding - desc/o Dorothy Thompson ECD(2)153; DBR(1)340, 594; DBR(2)442; DBR(3)239; DBR(4)187; DBR(5)797

SEARLES Abigail - b1721 - desc/o Agnes Harris RAA131

SEARS Deborah - b1639, m Zachariah Paddock - desc/o Richard Sears LDS84

>Edmund - of MA, b1712 d1796, m1743 Hannah Crowell - desc/o Mary Wentworth ECD(2)295; LDS57

>Edmund - of MA, b1743/1744 d1832, m1771 Hannah Taylor - desc/o Mary Wentworth ECD(2)295

>Elizabeth - b1745, m Thomas Homer - desc/o Richard Sears LDS57

>Lydia - b1666, m(1) Eleazer Hamlin - desc/o Richard Sears LDS14

>Paul - b1637/1638, m Deborah Willard - desc/o Richard Sears LDS14, 57

>Paul - b1669, m Mercy Freeman - desc/o Richard Sears LDS57

>Richard - b1590, m Dorothy Thacher or Thaker - the immigrant LDS14, 57, 84; EDV99; BLG2905; RAA; EO2(3)132, 133 there are discrepancies in the pedigree, seemingly irreconcilable & research proves beyond question that not one step of the pedigree can be substantiated by records & on the contrary some portions are impossible & others in conflict with known authorities

SEATON Augustine - of VA, m1776 Mary Winston youngest dau/o Samuel Winston of Louisa Co, VA & had issue including a son William Winston Seaton b1785 - desc/o Anne Lovelace GVFHB(3)342

SEATON (cont.)

Elizabeth - of VA, m Col John West d1743 of West Point, York, VA, son of Capt Thomas West of King & Queen Co, VA - desc/o Anne Lovelace GVFHB(3)342

George - of VA, b1711 d1750, m1734 Elizabeth Hill dau/o Leonard Hill of King & Queen Co, VA & had issue - desc/o Col William Bernard APP121 - desc/o Anne Lovelace GVFHB(3)342

SEELEY John - b abt 1683, m Martha____ - desc/o Deborah Barlow LDS59

Joseph - b1714, m(1) Thankful Bartlett - desc/o Deborah Barlow LDS59

Margaret - b1741, m(1) James Pennock - desc/o Debroah Barlow LDS59

SELBY James - of MD, d bef 1802, m Mary (Polly, Molly) Sturgis - desc/o Richard Wright ECD(3)286

SETH Charles - of MD, b1691, m Elizabeth Jennings - desc/o George Beckwith DBR(1)140, 662, 701

Charles II - of MD, d1769, m Rachel Clayland - desc/o George Beckwith DBR(1)662, 701

James - of MD, b1750, m Hannah Bennett - desc/o George Beckwith DBR(1)140

John - b abt 1720, m Lucy Montgomery - desc/o George Beckwith DBR(1)140

William Clayland - of MD, b1757, m Martha Chamberlain - desc/o George Beckwith DBR(1)662, 701

SETON Margaret - of NY, dau/o John & Elizabeth (Seton) of Balsies, Seton, m Andrew Seton of Barnes - the immigrant GBR75; NYGBR(13)#1p49

William - of NY, son of John & Elizabeth (Seton) of Balsies, Seton, m(1) Rebecca Curson dau/o Richard & Elizabeth (Becker) Curson, m(2) Anna Maria Curson - the immigrant GBR75; NYGBR(13)#1p49, (22)#2p111, (28)#4p247

William Magee - m Elizabeth Ann Bayley, foundress of the American Sisters of Charity - desc/o William Seton GBR75

SETTLE Isaac - of VA, b1700 d1752, m1726 Charity Browne - desc/o Col Moore Fauntleroy DBR(4)408

John - of VA, b abt 1679 d1738, m Mary Strother - desc/o Col Moore Fauntleroy DBR(4)408

Phoebe - of VA, b abt 1728, m Benjamin Morgan - desc/o Col Moore Fauntleroy DBR(4)408

SEVER John - of MA, b1766 d1803, m1790 Nancy Russell - desc/o Penelope Pelham ECD(3)238

William of MA, b1759 d1798, m1785 Mary Chandler - desc/o Herbert Pelham CHB196; BCD196

SEWALL Anne - m(1) Col Benjamin Rozer d1681, m(2) Col Edward Pye - desc/o Jane Lowe NSG(51)40

Anne - of MD, d1789, m Joseph Douglas - desc/o Jane Lowe NGS(51)40

Charles - of MD, d1742 - desc/o Jane Lowe NGS(51)40

Clare - of MD, m(1) Thomas Tasker d1733, m(2) William Young d1772 - desc/o Jane Lowe NGS40

SEWALL (cont.)

Clement - of MD, d1740, m Mary Smith dau/o Col John Smith - desc/o Maj Nicholas Sewall DBR(5)913 - desc/o Jane Lowe NGS(51)40

Dorothy - of MD, d1814, m William Boarman - desc/o Gov Robert Brooke DBR(5)864 - desc/o Maj Nicholas Sewall DBR(5)913

Elizabeth - d1710, m Dr Jesse Wharton d1676, m(2) Col William Diggs d1697 - desc/o Jane Lowe NGS(51)40

Elizabeth - of MD, d1752, m Capt Peregrine Frisby b1688 d1738 of Cecil Co, MD - desc/o Jane Lowe NGS(51)40

Henry - of MA 1634, m Jane Dummer - the immigrant THJ68, 69; EDV100; sufficient proof of alleged royal ancestry is lacking

Henry - of MA - desc/o Henry Sewall EDV100

Henry - of MD, d1722, m Elizabeth____ - desc/o Jane Lowe NGS(51)40

Jane - b1664, m Philip Calvert - desc/o Jane Lowe NGS(51)40

Jane - of MD, b bef 1685 d1761, m1700 Clement Brooke - desc/o Jane Lowe NGS(51)40

Mary - b1658 d1693/1694, m Col William Chandler d1685, m(2)1687 Capt George Brent of Woodstock, Stafford Co, VA - desc/o Jane Lowe NGS(51)40

Mary - of MD, m(1) William Frisby b1699 d1724, m(2)1725 Dominick Carroll of Cecil Co, MD - desc/o Jane Lowe NGS(51)40

Major Nicholas - of MD 1661, b1655 d1737, m Susanna Burgess, dau/o Col William Burgess & Sophia____ - the immigrant DBR(5)912, 913; THJ69; NGS(51)40 - desc/o Jane Lowe NGS(51)40

Samuel - of MA, bp 1652 - desc/o Henry Sewall THJ69; EDV100

Sophia - of MD, m John Cooke of Prince George's Co, MD - desc/o Jane Lowe NGS(51)40

Susanna - of MD, m George Douglas of Kent Co, MD - desc/o Jane Lowe NGS(51)40

SEYMOUR Richard - b1604/1605, m Mercy Ruscoe - the immigrant RAA no longer accepted as being of royal descent

SHANNON Dr Richard Cutts - of NH, b1773 d1828, m Mary Tebbets - desc/o Maj William Vaughan DBR(2)27, 627

Sarah - b1765/1766, m Jeremiah Leavitt - desc/o Gov Thomas Roberts LDS65

Thomas - of NH, b1749 d1800, m1771 Lillias Watson - desc/o Maj William Vaughan DBR(2)27, 627

SHATTUCK Chloe - b1766, m Ephraim Leach - desc/o Zachariah Field THC104

Consider - b1768, m Anne Atherton - desc/o Zachariah Field THC104

Levi - of MA, b1742 d1823, m1770 Margaret Robbins - desc/o John Prescott DBR(1)525

Lydia - b1774, m Arad Root - desc/o Zachariah Field THC104

Ruth - b1668, m Jonathan Farnsworth - desc/o John Whitney LDS26, 43

Samuel - b1765, m Prudence Healey - desc/o Zachariah Field THC104

Seth - b1770, m(1) Sylvia Chapin, m(2) Anna Smith - desc/o Zachariah Field THC104

SHEAFFE William - of MA 1685 - the immigrant EDV131; sufficient proof of alleged royal ancestry is lacking

SHED Daniel - b1746 - desc/o John Prescott RAA125

SHELBURN Robert - of VA, d abt 1713, m Catherine (Vaughn) Saunders - desc/o Col George Reade DBR(5)219

SHELDON Elizabeth - b1713, m Francis Tanner - desc/o Joan Vincent LDS98

Hannah - b1751, m Joseph Cutler - desc/o Joan Vincent LDS33

Isaac - b abt 1687, m(1) Susannah Potter - desc/o Joan Vincent LDS33, 98

John - b1663, m ____ Palmer - desc/o Joan Vincent LDS33, 98

Mary - b1699 - desc/o Amy Wyllys RAA126

Thomas - b1709, m Harriet Winters - desc/o Joan Vincent LDS33

SHELTON James - of VA 1610, d1668, m Ann____ - the immigrant JSW1516; sufficient proof of alleged royal ancestry is lacking

James - of VA, m Mary Bathurst - desc/o James Shelton JSW1516

John - of VA, d1726, m Jane____ - desc/o James Shelton JSW1516

Capt John - of VA, b1705 d1777, m Eleanor Parks - desc/o James Shelton JSW1517

Sarah - of VA, m Patrick Henry - desc/o James Shelton JSW1517

Sarah - of VA, m Augustine Shepherd - desc/o James Shelton JSW1517

Thomas - of VA & MD, d1684, m Miss Wood - desc/o James Shelton JSW1516

Thomas - of VA, d1794, m Elizabeth Woods - desc/o Capt Thomas Harris ECD(2)159

Col William - of VA, m1698 Hannah Armistead - desc/o James Shelton JSW1516/7

William - of VA, d1789, m(1) Patience Thomas - desc/o James Shelton JSW1517

SHEPARD (SHEPHERD) Anna - b1663, m(1)1682 Daniel Quincy - desc/o Elizabeth Coytmore AAP144; PFA Apx C #5; TAG(32)17

Eleony - of MA, b1727, m1746 Oliver Robbins - desc/o Katharine Deighton JSW1827

Elisha - of CT, b1758 d aft 1820 a revolutionary soldier, m(1) Mary__ - desc/o Oliver Mainwaring ECD(2)192; ECD(3)208

John - of MA, b1704 d1809, m1726 Eleony Pond - desc/o Katharine Deighton JSW1827

Jonathan II - of VA, b1739/1740 d aft 1790, m Hanna Benjamin - desc/o Oliver Mainwaring ECD(2)192; ECD(3)208

SHEPHERD (SHEPARD) Eleony - b1727 d1772, m1746 Oliver Robbins - desc/o Katherine Deighton DBR(4)729

Elisha - b1758 d aft 1820, m(1) Mary____ - desc/o Oliver Mainwaring DBR(4)249; FFF42

John - b1704 d1809, m1726 Eleony Pond - desc/o Katherine Deighton DBR(4)729

Jonathan II - of VT, b1739/1740, m Hanna Benjamin - desc/o Oliver Mainwaring DBR(4)249; FFF42

Mary - of VA & KY, b1760 d1844, m John Haggard - desc/o James Shelton JSW1517

SHERBURNE Andrew Sr - of NH, b1738 d1780, m1760 Susanna Knight - desc/o Henry Sherburne ECD(3)253

Henry - of NH, b1611 d bef 1681, m(1)1637 Rebecca Gibbons - the

SHERBURNE (cont.)
> immigrant ECD(3)249; DBR(3)595; sufficient proof of alleged royal ancestry is lacking
>> John - of NH, bp 1615 d1693, m Elizabeth Tuck - the immigrant ECD(3)253; DBR(3)595; sufficient proof of alleged royal ancestry is lacking
>> Capt John - of NH, b abt 1650 d1730/1731, m(1)1700 Mary Jackson - desc/o John Sherburne ECD(3)253
>> Margaret - of NH, b1678/1679 d1717, m1698 Capt Joseph Tilton - desc/o Henry Sherburne ECD(3)249
>> Capt Samuel - of NH, b1638 d1691, m1668 Love Hutchins - desc/o Henry Sherburne ECD(3)249
>> Deacon Samuel - of NH, b1698 d1760, m1726 Mercy Wiggin - desc/o Henry Sherburne ECD(3)253

SHERMAN Abigail - of MA, b1647/1648 d167_, m1664 Rev Samuel Willard - desc/o Mary Launce J&K184; CHB447; DBR(1)545
> Grace - of MA, b1658/1659, m Ebenezer Prout - desc/o Mary Launce DBR(2)552; DBR(3)121
> James - b abt 1647/1655 - desc/o Mary Launce RAA130
> John - b1683 - desc/o Mary Launce RAA130
> Lucy - b1766, m Job Shaw - desc/o John Whitney LDS91
> Mary - of MA, b1657, m1679 Ellis Barron Jr - desc/o Mary Launce CHB447; MCD291; RAA130
> Mary - b1713 - desc/o Mary Launce RAA130
> Mary - b1726, m1748 Deacon John Cooper - desc/o Dr Richard Palgrave DBR(5)762

SHERWIN Sophia - of VA, d1803, m(1) Samuel Pincham, m(2) abt 1799 William Cabaniss - desc/o Henry Randolph ECD(2)216; DBR(3)201; DBR(4)178

SHERWOOD Eleazer - of CT, b abt 1733 d1808, m1770 Mary Squires - desc/o Grace Chetwood ECD248

SHIELD Mary (Polly) - m abt 1804 Selby Hickman - desc/o Peter Wright DBR(3)636

SHIRLEY Cecily - of VA, dau/o Sir Thomas Shirley & Anne Kempe, m Thomas West, 3rd Baron Delaware (de la Warr) b1577 d1618 governor of VA - the immigrant GBR231
> James - b abt 1735 d abt 1785, m Mary____ - desc/o Walter Shirley JSW1668
> James - of VA, b1768 d1840, m(1) Ruth Hiatt - desc/o Walter Shirley JSW1668
> Maj Gen Thomas - of MA - desc/o William Shirley EDV71
> Walter - of NJ 1725, b1690 d1755, m Dorcas Avis - the immigrant JSW1668; sufficient proof of alleged royal ancestry is lacking
> William - of MA, b abt 1694 d1771, governor of MA & the Bahamas, son of William Shirley & Elizabeth Godman, m Frances Barker - the immigrant EDV71; GBR246

SHOEMAKER Benjamin of PA, b1746 d1808, m1773 Elizabeth Warner - desc/o Thomas Lloyd CHB127; BCD127

SHORT Thomas - of VA, b1763 d1815, m1787 Martha Jones - desc/o Thomas Batte DBR(1)410; DBR(2)58

SHUMWAY Parley - b1774, m Polly Johnson - desc/o Samuel Hyde
LDS92

Peter - b1735, m Rebecca Leavens - desc/o Samuel Hyde LDS92

SHUTE Elizabeth - of MA, b1683, m1701 John Blue - desc/o Edward
Raynsford NE(139)304

Joanna - of MA, b abt 1694, m (prob) 1715 Joseph Landon - desc/o
Edward Raynsford NE(139)304

Mary - of MA, b1689, m1707 Ebenezer Paine - desc/o Edward
Raynsford NE(139)304

Col Samuel - of MA, b1662 d1742, governor of MA, son of Benjamin
Shute & Patience (or Anne) died unmarried - the immigrant
EDV144, 145; GBR315

Susanna - of MA, b abt 1685/1686, m(1)1704 Charles Hause, m(2)
Susana Hawes - desc/o Edward Raynsford NE(139)304

SIM Barbara - of MD, m Clement Smith MD - desc/o Rev Robert Brooke
CHB401

SIMMONS Hannah - b1718 - desc/o Miles Standish RAA131

SIMPSON Mary Ann - of NC, b1755 d1840, m Benjamin Williams - desc/o
Edward Dudley ECD(3)134; DBR(4)669

SINCLAIR Anna - of NY, b1693 d1743, m1706 Charles Crommelin d1739
aged 60 years, founded in 1720 the Holland Trading Company
which conducted a lucrative business between Amsterdam & New
York, also founded the great Amsterdam banking house of
Crommelin & Zoon, son of Daniel Crommelin a French Huguenot -
desc/o Robert Sinclair NYGBR(10)#4p170/177, (50)#1p46, 47

Robert - of NY 1679, d1704 a Scotchman by birth, descendant of the
Earls of Orkney & a Presbyterian by profession also mariner, son of
James of Kirkwall & Anna (Sinclair) Sinclair, m1683 Maria
Duyckinck b1659 d abt 1736 dau/o Gerardus Duyckinck & Mary
Duyckinck - the immigrant EDV29; GBR29 some aspect of royal
descent merits further study; NYGBR(10)#4p170/177,
(23)#1p33/37, (50)#1p46, 47

SISSON Mercy - b1771 - desc/o Alice Freeman RAA132

SKINNER Abigail - of MA, b abt 1685 d1728, m1711 Nathaniel Coney -
desc/o Mary Gye ECD(3)177

SKIPWITH Cassandra - of VA, b1678, m1697 Philip Coale - desc/o Sir
Henry Skipwith AMB470; CFA(3)496

Diana - of VA, b1625 d1695 dau/o Sir Henry Skipwith & Amy Kempe,
m abt 1750 Major Edward Dale d1695 high sheriff of Lancaster, a
burgess, justice & commissioner (a distinguished royalist who
sought refuge in VA after the death of King Charles I) - desc/o Sir
Henry Skipwith ECD(2)246; DBR(1)123, 145, 280, 285, 342, 451,
513; DBR(2)8, 728, 803; DBR(3)228, 487, 668; DBR(4)558, 696,
697; DBR(5)376, 1072, 1073; RAA130 - the immigrant GBR213;
HSF(4)256

Elizabeth - of VA, m William Short, U. S. Minister to France & the
Netherlands - desc/o Sir Grey Skipwith CFA(3)497

Fulwar - of VA, b1720, US Consul in France, m Martha Waldron dau/o
Francis Waldron - desc/o Sir Grey Skipwith DBR(4)705; AMB471;
CFA(3)497

Sir Grey, 3rd Baronet of VA, d1680 son of Sir Henry Skipwith, 1st

SKIPWITH (cont.)

Baronet & Amy Kempe, m Elizabeth or Bridget_____ - the immigrant CHB233; MCD292; MCS60; BCD233; DBR(4)705; AMB470; WAC86; GBR213; CFA(3)496

Sir Henry - of VA, m(1) on or bef 1616 Amy Kempe dau/o Sir Thomas Kempe - the immigrant ECD(2)246; DBR(1)123, 145, 280, 285, 342, 451, 513; DBR(2)8, 728, 803; DBR(3)668; DBR(4)558; AMB470; RAA1, 130; EDV128

Col Henry - of VA, b1751 d1815, m1772 _____ Wayles - desc/o Sir Grey Skipwith - CHB233; BCD233; AMB471; CFA(3)497

Jane - of VA, m Edmund Ruffin - desc/o Sir Grey Skipwith CFA(3)497

Lelia - of VA, b1767, m(1) George Carter, m(2)1791 Judge St George Tucker - desc/o Sir Henry Skipwith AMB471; CFA(3)497

Mary - of VA, m William Randolph of Chatsworth & had issue - desc/o Sir Grey Skipwith CFA(3)497

Sir Peyton, Baronet of VA, d1805, m(1) Ann Miller dau/o Hugh Miller, m(2) Jean Miller another dau/o Hugh Miller - desc/o Sir Grey Skipwith CHB233; BCD233; AMB471; WAC86; CFA(3)497

Peyton - of VA & TN, b1771 Prestwould d1852 moved to Maury Co, TN, m1802 Cornelia Greene - desc/o Sir Grey Skipwith CHB233; BCD233; CFA(3)497; CFA(3)497

Robert - of VA, b1748 m_____ Nicholas & had issue - desc/o Sir Henry Skipwith AMB471; CFA(3)497

Sarah - of VA, b abt 1747 d abt 1790, m Thomas Black d1814 capt of Pittsylvania Co militia 1777 to 1781 son of Thos Black Sr progenitor of this family in America - desc/o Sir Grey Skipwith DBR(4)706

Sarah - of VA, m Robert Kennon - desc/o Sir Henry Skipwith AMB471; CFA(3)497

Sir William, 4th Baronet of VA, b abt 1670 d aft 1730, m Sarah Peyton d1727 dau/o John Peyton - desc/o Sir Grey Skipwith CHB233; MCD2912; MCS60; BCD233; DBR(4)705; AMB470; WAC86; CFA(3)497

Sir William, Baronet of VA, b1707 of Prestwould d1764, m1733 Elizabeth Smith dau/o John Smith, high sheriff of Middlesex Co, VA - desc/o Sir Grey Skipwith CHB233; MCB158; MCD292; BCD233; AMB471; WAC86; CFA(3)497

SLAUSON (SLASON) Isaac - b1733 - desc/o Richard Belding RAA68

James - b1680/1681 - desc/o Richard Belding RAA68

James - b1706 - desc/o Richard Belding RAA68

Jedediah - b1769 - desc/o Richard Belding RAA68

SLOCUM Elizabeth - of MA, b1689 d1774, m1707 Isaac Barker - desc/o Katherine Marbury DBR(2)44

Capt Holder - of MA, b1697, m1733 Rebecca Almy - desc/o Katherine Marbury DBR(5)833; RAA114

Mary - b1736 - desc/o Katherine Marbury RAA114

Peleg - of MA, b1740, m1760 Any Russell - desc/o Katherine Marbury DBR(5)833

Peleg - of MA, b1764 d1856, m1788 Elizabeth Ricketson - desc/o Katherine Marbury DBR(5)833

SLYE Anne - of MD, m Francis Ignatius Boarman - desc/o Dr Thomas Gerard DBR(5)904

SLYE (cont.)

Capt Gerard - of MD, b1654 d1703/1704, m1676 Jane (Notley) Saunders - desc/o Dr Thomas Gerard DBR(5)904

Gerard - of MD, b1679 d1733, m(1) Teresia Van Sweringen - desc/o Dr Thomas Gerard DBR(5)904

Robert Jr - of MD, m Priscilla Goldsmith dau/o John & Judith Goldsmith - desc/o Dr Thomas Gerard MG(1)497

SMITH Abigail - of VA, b1656 d1692, m Major Lewis Burwell Jr - the immigrant J&K133; - desc/o Martha Bacon CHB32; BCD32

Abigail - of MA, b1744 d1818, m1764 Pres John Adams - desc/o Rev William Norton J&K121; CHB164; BCD164 - desc/o Elizabeth Coytmore AAP144; PFA75 Apx C #5

Ann - of MD, b1724 d1775, m Samuel Parran - desc/o Mary Joanna Somerset CHB383

Anne - of VA, m Richard Woodson - desc/o Col Walter Aston DBR(1)670; DBR(2)146, 755, 849; DBR(3)508; DBR(5)1003 - desc/o Col Richard Cocke DBR(2)432

Arabella Maria - of PA, dau/o George Smith & ____ Barlow, m Alexander James Dallas b1759 d1817, lawyer & secretary of the treasury - the immigrant GBR320 some aspect of royal descent merits further study

Ariana Ambler - of VA, m William D Holliday - desc/o Col George Reade CHB251; BCD251

Augustine - of VA, b1689, m1711 Gloucester Co, Sarah Carver b1694 d1726, dau/o John Carver - desc/o Col George Reade HSF(2)197, 198

Augustine - of VA, b1738 d1774, m(2) Margaret Boyde - desc/o Col George Reade CHB252; MCD273; BCD252; DBR(1)732; DBR(5)103, 240

Augustine Jaquelin - of VA, m Susanna Taylor - desc/o Col George Reade DBR(1)732

Augustine Warner - of VA, b1687 d1756, m1711 Sarah Carver - desc/o Col George Reade CHB251; MCD273; BCD251; DBR(1)724, 732; DBR(4)496, 773; DBR(5)102, 103, 240; AWW83

Aurora - of CT, b1773 d1834, m(1)1794 Samuel Eells - desc/o Nathaniel Browne ECD(3)58

Benjamin - of MD, m Mary Neale - desc/o Rev Robert Brooke CHB399

Cephas Jr - of CT, b1760/1761 d1815, m1794 Mary Gove - desc/o Rev Charles Chauncy CHB85; BCD85

Charles Somerset - of MD, d1738, m Margaret ____ - desc/o Mary Joanna Somerset CHB382

Charles - of VA, m Catherine Teackle - desc/o Margaret Nelson HSF(10)199

Charles Somerset - of MD, m____ Sothern - desc/o Mary Joanna Somerset CHB382

Daniel - b1642, m Mary Grant - the immigrant LDS63, 113; sufficient proof of alleged royal ancestry is lacking

Daniel - of NH, b1768 d1832, m1792 Betsy Belle Moulton - desc/o Capt Thomas Bradbury DBR(3)153

David - b1757 - desc/o Griffith Bowen RAA72

Dicandia - of MD, m & had issue - desc/o Mary Joanna Somerset

SMITH (cont.)

CHB382

Dorothy - of MD, m Alexander Lawson - desc/o Rev Robert Brooke CHB403

Downing Rucker - of VA, d1825, m Catherine Beaman - desc/o James Coghill DBR(2)440, 682

Edith - of NJ, b1751 d1820, m1772 Benjamin Weatherby b1747/1749 d1812 - desc/o John Fenwick DBR(1)317; DBR(2)413

Edmund - of VA, d1750/1751, surveyor & sheriff of York Co, m Agnes Sclater b1707 - desc/o Col George Reade APP173

Edward - of VA, m Elizabeth Bush - desc/o Col George Reade CHB251; MCD273; BCD251; DBR(4)774

Elizabeth - of VA, m1708 Henry Harrison - desc/o Col George Reade HSF(2)197

Elizabeth - b1706 - desc/o Mary Gye RAA115

Elizabeth - of VA, b1730, m1749 Philip Aylett - desc/o Col George Reade HSF(2)198

Elizabeth - of VA, b1737 d1792, m1755 William Young - desc/o Capt Henry Woodhouse DBR(5)284

Elizabeth - of MD, d aft 1772, m(1)1737 Francis Wilkinson, m(2)1739/1741 Young Parran - desc/o Mary Joanna Somerset CHB382

Ephraim - b1704, m(1) Hannah Witter - desc/o Daniel Smith LDS63

Hale - of KY, b1763/1765 d1817, m1782 Nancy Douglas - desc/o Col George Reade DBR(2)61, 62

Hannah - of NJ, b1773 d1830, m1794 Henry S Drinker - desc/o James Logan CHB345; BCD345

Henry - b1705, m(2) Mary Smith - desc/o Daniel Smith LDS113

Isaac - of VA, b1734 d1813 - desc/o Anthony West CRL(1)113

Isaac - of VA, m1759 Elizabeth Custis Teackle - desc/o Anthony West CRL(1)114

J Philip - of VA, b1695, m1711 Mary Mathews - desc/o Col George Reade JSW1648

Jaduthan - of CT, b1709 d1781, m(1)1733 Mary Kimberly - desc/o Nathaniel Browne ECD(3)57

James - of NJ, b1750 d1833, m1772 Esther Heulings - desc/o James Logan CHB345; BCD345

Jane - of MD, m Col Reeder - desc/o Mary Joanna Somerset CHB382

Jane - of VA, m1757 John Payne - desc/o Col George Reade DBR(1)255, 354, 469

Jerusha - b1728 - desc/o Alice Freeman RAA132

Jerusha - of CT, m Ezra Brainerd - desc/o Elizabeth St John CHB222; BCD222

John - b1672, m Susanna____ - desc/o Daniel Smith LDS63

John - b1680/1681 - desc/o Mary Gye RAA115

John - of VA, b1685, m1700 Anne Alexander - desc/o Col George Reade HSF(2)197

Col John - of MD, d1738, m Sarah Young - desc/o Robert Brooke ECD(3)49

Maj John - of MD, d1759, m Mary Hamilton - desc/o Robert Brooke ECD(3)49

SMITH (cont.)

John - of VA, b1715 d1771, m1737 Mary Jacquelin - desc/o Col
George Reade CHB251; BCD251; DBR(1)732; DBR(4)496, 773;
DBR(5)103, 240; HSF(2)198

Gen John - of VA, b1750 d1836, m1781 Animus Bull - desc/o Col
George Reade DBR(1)724

John - of NJ, b1761 d1803, m1784 Gulielma Maria Morris - desc/o
James Logan CHB345; BCD345

Capt John - of VA, m Elizabeth Cox - desc/o Col George Reade
DBR(4)135; DBR(5)678

Joseph - b1680, m Hannah____ - desc/o Daniel Smith LDS113

Joseph Sim - of MD, m Elizabeth Price - desc/o Rev Robert Brooke
CHB402

Lawrence - of VA, son of Christopher Smith & Elizabeth Towneley, m
Mary (Hitchen?) - the immigrant GBR331 some aspect of royal
descent merits further study

Margaret Hamilton - of MD, b1769 d1833, m1785 Capt Richard
Waters - desc/o Robert Brooke ECD(3)49

Martha - b1710 - desc/o Robert Abell AAR59

Mary - b abt 1647, m John Stratton - desc/o Mary Knapp LDS27

Mary - of VA, m Jesse Ball - desc/o Col George Reade HSF(2)200

Mary - of MD, d1761, m Clement Sewall - desc/o Gov Robert Brooke
DBR(5)864, 884

Mary - of VA, b1744 d1791, m1765 Rev Thomas Smith - desc/o Col
George Reade CHB251; BCD251; DBR(4)497

Mary - of MD - desc/o Mary Joanna Somerset CHB382

Mary - of VA, m Capt John Stubbs - desc/o Col George Reade
DBR(4)135

Mary Jacquelin - of VA, b1773 d1846, m John Crapps - desc/o Col
George Reade CHB252; MCD273; BCD252; DBR(5)103, 240

Mildred - of VA, b1681/1682, m1700 Robert Portens - desc/o Col
George Reade HSF(2)197

Mildred - of VA, b1719 Shooter's Hill, Middlesex Co d1769
Beddingfield Hall, Brunswick Co, m1743 John Willis b1719 White
Hall, Gloucester Co d1766 Beddingfield Hall, farmer & an
Episcopalian & a vestryman of St Andrews Parish, Brunswick Co -
desc/o Col George Reade HSF(2)198

Mildred - of VA, b1725, m abt 1744 Col James Ball Jr - desc/o Col
George Reade JSW1648; DBR(5)343

Mildred - m Capt John Stubbs Jr - desc/o Col George Reade
DBR(5)678

Rev Nehemiah - of CT 1636 - the immigrant EDV49; sufficient proof of
alleged royal ancestry is lacking

Parker - b1758, m Sarah Loomis - desc/o Daniel Smith LDS63 -
desc/o Richard Billings RAA70 - desc/o Alice Freeman RAA132

Phebe - of RI, b1699, m James Cargill Jr - desc/o William Arnold
BCD17

Philemon Hamilton - of MD, b1744 d1772, m Betsey Rawlings - desc/o
Robert Brooke ECD(3)49

Philip - of VA, b1695 Purton, Gloucester Co d1743 Fleets Bay,
Northumberland Co, m1711/1712 York Co, Mary Mathews d bef

SMITH (cont.)

1742 dau/o Baldwin Matthews & Mary Digges - desc/o Col George Reade DBR(1)255, 354, 469, 550; DBR(2)61, 212, 307; DBR(5)343; HSF(2)197, 200

Rachel - of MD, b1720 d1786, m Richard Harrison - desc/o Rev Robert Brooke CHB403

Rebecca - m John Aspinwall - desc/o John Nelson GBR148

Rebecca Price - of MD, m Reuben Worthington - desc/o Rev Robert Brooke CHB402

Richard - of MD - desc/o Mary Joanna Somerset CHB382

Sarah - of VA, m Benjamin Dabney - desc/o Col George Reade CHB251; BCD251

Sarah - of VA, m Robert Throckmorton - desc/o Col George Reade AWW83

Sarah - of VA, b1717, m1735 Mordecai Cook - desc/o Col George Reade HSF(2)198

Sarah - b1743, m Deliverance Wilson - desc/o Daniel Smith LDS113

Sarah - of VA, b1730/1732 d1782, m1746 George Heale - desc/o Col George Reade DBR(1)550; DBR(2)61, 212, 307; HSF(2)200

Seth - b1733, m Sarah Tyler - desc/o Daniel Smith LDS63 - desc/o Alice Freeman RAA132

Simon - of RI, m1766 Freelove Fenner - desc/o William Arnold CHB18; BCD18

Simon - of RI, b1710 d1753, m Elizabeth Turpin - desc/o William Arnold CHB18; BCD18

Temperance - b1700/1701 d1775, m Edward Quinton b1696 d1756 - desc/o John Fenwick DBR(1)316, 317; DBR(2)413; DBR(3)439

Thomas - of CT, b1741 d1773, m1768 Margaret Olcott - desc/o Nathaniel Browne ECD(3)58

Col William - of NY, b1654 d1704 - the immigrant EDV49; sufficient proof of alleged royal ancestry is lacking

Judge William - of NY, b1697 - the immigrant TAG(21)77; sufficient proof of alleged royal ancestry is lacking

William True - b1772 d1859, m Martha Ambrose - desc/o Capt Thomas Bradbury J&K176

SNELL Charles - of MA, b1717 d1771, m1745 Susanna Packard - desc/o Frances Deighton ECD(2)107; DBR(1)564; DBR(2)690; DBR(3)367; DBR(4)861; DBR(5)96

Silence - of MA, b1751 d1821, m1773 Ebenezer Howard - desc/o Frances Deighton ECD(2)107; DBR(1)564; DBR(2)690; DBR(3)367; DBR(4)861; DBR(5)96

SNELLING Capt Abraham - of MA, b1693 d1746, sea captain, m1719 Hannah Sears b1696/1697 d1768 dau/o Alexander & Rebecca (Staines) Sears - desc/o John Snelling NE(108)179/187

Anne - of MA, b1654 d1697, m Francis Davenport - desc/o Dr William Snelling NE(52)342/346

Benjamin - of MA, b1672, blockmaker, m(1)1693/1694 Jemima Andrews b1675 d1707 dau/o James Andrews Jr, m(2)1707/1708 Margaret (Rule) (Page) Johnson dau/o John & Emma (Seeley) Rule - desc/o John Snelling NE(108)179/187

Benjamin - of MA, b1704 d1739, blockmaker, m(1)1722 Hannah

SNELLING (cont.)

      (Porter) Penny, sister of Mathew Porter, m(2)1731 Eliza Lewis
        d1737 aged 32yrs 11 mo 14 days - desc/o John Snelling
        NE(108)179/187

Dorcas - of MA, bp 1702, m1725 Elijah Doubleday b1701 son of Elijah
    & Sarah (Paine) Doubleday - desc/o John Snelling NE(108)179/187

Elizabeth - of MA, bp 1725/1726, m1745 Bethel Blair bp 1724 -
    desc/o John Snelling NE(108)179/187

Elizabeth - of MA, b1726/1727, m1748 Capt Giles Harris, a trader at
    Halifax, Nova Scotia in 1754 - desc/o John Snelling
    NE(108)179/187

Elizabeth - of MA, bp 1771 d1813, m1796 Charles Jacobs son of Col
    John & Hannah (Tolman) Jacobs - desc/o John Snelling
    NE(108)179/187

Hannah - of MA, 1723, m1745/1746 Willing Richardson b1720/1721
    son of Job & Hannah (Cleveland) Richardson - desc/o John
    Snelling NE(108)179/187

Hannah - of MA, b1730, m (intentions) 1757 Abraham Pritchard -
    desc/o John Snelling NE(108)179/187

Hepzibah - of MA, bp 1763 may have, m1798 John Mumford of RI -
    desc/o John Snelling NE(108)179/187

Jane - of MA, b1695, m1713 David Webb - desc/o John Snelling
    NE(108)179/187

Jane - of MA, bp 1731, m1751 Philip Lewis - desc/o John Snelling
    NE(108)179/187

Jemima - of MA, b1695, m1722 Obadiah Wheten or Wheatin - desc/o
    John Snelling NE(108)179/187

John - of MA, b abt 1625/1628 d1672, bp as an adult 1667, son of
    John & Frances (Hele) Snelling, m Sarah____ - the immigrant
    GBR268 some aspect of royal descent merits further study;
    NE(52)342/346, (108)179/187; CFA(3)523

John - of MA, b1664 d1699/1700, m abt 1687 Jane Adams b1669
    d1738 dau/o Abraham & Sarah (Mackworth) Adams - desc/o John
    Snelling NE(108)179/187

John - of MA, b abt 1723, m1739 Mary Turner - desc/o John Snelling
    NE(108)179/187

John - of MA, b1739/1740, m(1)1764 Lois Walker, m(2)1769 Mary
    Mann - desc/o John Snelling NE(108)179/187

John - of MA, bp 1753, m (intentions) (1)1777 Elizabeth Neat, m
    (intentions) (2)1783 Katherine Haskins dau/o Capt Christopher &
    Katherine (Miller) Haskins - desc/o John Snelling NE(108)179/187

Capt Jonathan - of MA, b1696 d1755, one of the finest shipmasters
    sailing out of Boston, m(1)1723 Mary Halsey b1696 dau/o
    Nathaniel & Mary (Gross) Halsey, there may possibly be a (2), m
    Mary____ wid/o Alexander Sears - desc/o John Snelling
    NE(108)179/187; CFA(3)523

Col Jonathan - of MA, b1734 d1782, lieut of cavalry of the province
    with the rank of Major, later Col in command of the Governor's Life
    Guards. He was a Tory merchant & went to Halifax with the British
    in 1776., m1758 Elizabeth Barrett b1723 d1811 dau/o Thornton &
    Hepsibah (Williams) Barrett - desc/o John Snelling

SNELLING (cont.)
>NE(108)179/187; CFA(3)524

>Jonathan - of MA, bp 1758 d1809, m Hannah Hutchinson b abt 1729 dau/o Judge Foster & Margaret (Mascarene) Hutchinson - desc/o John Snelling NE(108)179/187

>Jonathan - of MA, bp 1768 d1847, instructor in writing, m1795 Lydia Symmes b1768 d1844 dau/o Col Andrew & Lydia (Gale) Symmes - desc/o John Snelling NE(108)179/187

>Capt Joseph - of MA, b1669 d1726 a shipwright of Boston & sea captain, m(1)1693 Sarah Sedgwick b1677 d1693 dau/o Robert & Sarah Sedgwick, m(2)1694 Rebeckah Adams b1673/1674 d1730 dau/o Jonathan Adams & Rebecca (Andrews) Adams - desc/o John Snelling NE(108)179/187; CFA(3)523

>Joseph - of MA, b1695 d1748, mastmaker, m(1)1718 Mary Payson dau/o Samuel & Mary (Phillips) Payson, m(2)1726 Elizabeth Verein b1704 d1737 dau/o Thomas & Hannah Verein, m(3)1738 Priscilla Clark bp 1712 d1791 dau/o Josiah & Priscilla (Greenwood) Clark - desc/o John Snelling NE(108)179/187

>Joseph - of MA, b1719/1720, m1740 Hannah Fulker - desc/o John Snelling NE(108)179/187

>Joseph - of MA, b1734 d1806, m Elizabeth____ - desc/o John Snelling NE(108)179/187

>Capt Joseph - of MA, bp 1741 d1816, commissary of Issue at cambridge in the Revolution & took a long wagon-train under fire to the Battle of Bunker Hill, m1763 Rachel Mayer b1743 d1837 dau/o William & Rachel (Vaughan) Mayer - desc/o John Snelling NE(108)179/187

>Joseph - of MA, bp 1745, m1771 Abigail Chapman - desc/o John Snelling NE(108)179/187

>Joseph - of MA, bp 1766, m1794 Elizabeth Warner - desc/o John Snelling NE(108)179/187

>Joseph - of MA, bp 1773, m Martha Moss - desc/o John Snelling NE(108)179/187

>Josiah - of MA, bp 1706, barber, m1727 Philippe Pearks or Peakes - desc/o John Snelling NE(108)179/187

>Josiah - of MA, b abt 1735, m1755 Hannah Chamberlain - desc/o John Snelling NE(108)179/187

>Josiah - of MA, b abt 1741 d1821, baker, m Mary____ d1836 aged 94 years - desc/o John Snelling NE(108)179/187

>Josiah - of MA, bp 1757 married & had issue - desc/o John Snelling NE(108)179/187

>Lydia - of MA, b1729 d1789, m (intentions)1749 Col Adino Paddock b1727, a captain of artillery 1774 later colonel in Revolutionary War & best coach-maker in Boston, son of John & Rebecca (Thatcher) Paddock - desc/o John Snelling NE(108)179/187

>Margaret - of MA, bp 1715, m1732 John Jenkins b1710 son of Richard & Mary (Pilkinton) Jenkins - desc/o John Snelling NE(108)179/187

>Mary - of MA, b1718, m1737 Joseph Crouch - desc/o John Snelling NE(108)179/187

>Mary - of MA, b1725, m1745 Henry Atkins, probably son of Henry &

SNELLING (cont.)

Deliverance (Sears) Atkins - desc/o John Snelling NE(108)179/187

Mary - of MA, bp 1743 d1774, m1764 Samuel Greenwood b1741 d1826 son of Capt Nathaniel & Elizabeth (Ventiman) Greenwood - desc/o John Snelling NE(108)179/187

Mary - of MA, bp 1765 probably, m1788 Richard Croome - desc/o John Snelling NE(108)179/187

Mary - of MA, bp 1765 d1837, m1795 Thomas Fletcher - desc/o John Snelling NE(108)179/187

Philippe - of MA, b1732, m1753 Jonathan Low - desc/o John Snelling NE(108)179/187

Priscilla - of MA, bp 1738 d1817, m (intentions) 1766 Nathaniel Greenwood bp 1736 d1823 son of Capt Nathaniel & Elizabeth (Ventiman) Greenwood - desc/o John Snelling NE(108)179/187

Rachel - of MA, bp 1766, m Charles Smith - desc/o John Snelling NE(108)179/187

Rebecca - of MA, b1699, m1719 Richard (Samuel) Phillips - desc/o John Snelling NE(108)179/187

Rebecca - of MA, bp 1737, m (intentions) 1761 Abner Ramsdel - desc/o John Snelling NE(108)179/187

Rebecca - of MA, bp 1744, m1766 Michael Malcolm - desc/o John Snelling NE(108)179/187

Robert - of MA, b1703/1704 d1741 shipwright in 1730, m1726 Lydia Dexter dau/o Richard & Sarah (Bucknam) Dexter - desc/o John Snelling NE(108)179/187

Samuel - of MA, bp 1766 d1836, m Elizabeth Grant b abt 1770 d1859 dau/o Moses & Elizabeth (Brown) Grant - desc/o John Snelling NE(108)179/187; CFA(3)524

Sarah - of MA, b1697/1698, m1719 William Cooper b1693 son of John & Sarah Cooper - desc/o John Snelling NE(108)179/187

Sarah - of MA, bp 1731, m (intentions) 1758 Thomas Masters - desc/o John Snelling NE(108)179/187

William - of MA, b1671, m1692 Mary Tucker - desc/o John Snelling NE(108)179/187

Dr William - of MA 1648, d1674, classical scholar & physician, son of Thomas & Joan Snelling, his nephew was John Snelling who probably accompanied him to New England, m1648 Margaret Stagge d1667 age 46, dau/o Gyles & Anne Stagge - the immigrant EDV132; NE(52)342/346 sufficient proof of alleged royal ancestry is lacking

Dr William - of MA, b1649 d1677/1678, physician, m Margaret d1677/1678, wid/o William Rogers, they had 1 daughter who died with her father & mother in the terrible visitation of small pox the winter of 1677/1678 - desc/o Dr William Snelling NE(52)342/346

William - of MA, bp 1776, m1811 Rachel Lazell b1770 d1866 dau/o Major Isaac & Jane (Byram) Lazell - desc/o John Snelling NE(108)179/187

SOMERSET Mary Joanna - of MD, d1697, m(1)____ Lowther, m(2)1695 Lieut Richard Smith - the immigrant CHB381, 382; sufficient proof of alleged royal ancestry is lacking

SOULE Barnabas - of ME, b1758 d1823, m1781 Jane Dennison - desc/o
Philippe Delano CHB505

John - of NY, b1772 d1812, m1794 Sylvia Marvin - desc/o Philippe
Delano CHB488

Moses - of MA b1676 d1751, m Mercy Southworth - desc/o Capt
Thomas Bradbury J&K174; CHB505

William - of MA, b1738 d1811, m Anna Sewall - desc/o Philippe
Delano CHB487

SOUTHWORTH Alice - b1688 - desc/o Edward Southworth RAA131

Lieut Andrew - of RI, b1709 d1772, m1731 Temperance Kirtland -
desc/o Edward Southworth ECD(2)253; FFF2, 7

Chester - b1764 - desc/o Edward Southworth RAA131

Ensign Constant - of MA 1628, b1614 Leyden d1678/1679 Duxbury
son of Edward Southworth & Alice Carpenter, m1637 Elizabeth
Collier - the immigrant FLW14; ECD(2)253, 257; MCB292; MCS73;
LDS56; DBR(2)399; DBR(3)245, 460, 461, 593; DBR(5)149, 828;
GBR245 some aspect of royal descent merits further study;
EO2(3)281 - desc/o Edward Southworth RAA131; FFF2, 7

Edward - of MA, b1590 d abt 1621 son of Thomas Southworth &
Rosamond Lister, m1613 in Leyden, Holland, Alice Carpenter b abt
1590 d1670 Plymouth, MA age 80 years dau/o Alexander
Carpenter of Wrington, Somersetshire - the immigrant FLW15;
ECD(2)253, 257; MCS73; LDS56; DBR(2)399; DBR(3)161, 593;
DBR(5)149; RAA1, 131; FFF2, 7; GBR245 lists the son Thomas
Southworth & Constant Southworth as - the immigrants

Elizabeth - of MA, d1717, m1664 Joseph Howland - desc/o Thomas
Southworth DBR(3)161; DBR(5)834; GBR245

Elizabeth - of MA, b1686 d1743, m1703 David Little - desc/o Edward
Southworth DBR(5)828

Esther - of CT, b1771, m Howland Marcy - desc/o Edward Southworth
ECD(2)253; FFF2, 7

Gideon - of MA, b1707 d1772, m1728 Mary Wilbur - desc/o Edward
Southworth DBR(3)594; FFF2

Josiah - b1719 - desc/o Edward Southworth RAA131

Mary - of MA, b1676 d1757, m1706/1707 Joseph Rider - desc/o
Edward Southworth ECD(2)257; DBR(5)149

Mercy - of MA, b1638 d1712, m1658 Deacon Samuel Freeman b1639
- desc/o Ensign Constant Southworth MCB293; LDS56;
DBR(2)399; DBR(3)245, 461; RAA131

Nathan - of CT, b1735 d1811, m1758 Hannah Wheeler - desc/o
Edward Southworth ECD(2)253; FFF2, 7

Nathaniel - of MA, b1648 d1710/1711, m1671/1672 Desire Gray -
desc/o Edward Southworth ECD(2)257; DBR(5)149

Nathaniel - b1692/1693 - desc/o Edward Southworth RAA131

Sarah - of RI, b1732 d1775, m1752 Joseph Hawkins - desc/o Edward
Southworth DBR(3)594

Capt Thomas - of MA, b1641 Leyden d1669 son of Edward Southworth
& Alice Carpenter, m1641 Elizabeth Raynor dau/o Reverend John
Raynor - the immigrant FLW14; MCS73; DBR(3)161; DBR(5)834;
GBR245 some aspect of royal descent merits further study

Capt William - of MA & RI, b1659 d1718, m(1)1680 Rebecca Peabody,

SOUTHWORTH (cont.)
   m(2)1705 Martha Kirtland - desc/o Edward Southworth
   ECD(2)253; DBR(5)828; RAA131; FFF2, 7
SPALDING Edward - of MA, b1672 d1739/1740, m abt 1695 Mary
   Adams - desc/o Olive Welby ECD(3)271; RAA93
   Eunice - of CT, b1736/1737 d1801, m1754 Oliver Davidson - desc/o
     Olive Welby ECD(3)271; RAA93
   Jonathan - of MA, b1704 d aft 1761, m abt 1725 Eunice Woodward -
     desc/o Olive Welby ECD(3)271; RAA93
   Mary - b abt 1676 - desc/o Olive Welby RAA93
SPANN Cuthbert - of VA, m Agatha Conway - desc/o Martha Eltonhead
   VG245
   Elizabeth - of VA, m Major Peter Conway - desc/o Martha Eltonhead
     VG245
   Frances Sinah - of VA, m John Conway - desc/o Martha Eltonhead
     VG245
   Richard - of VA, b1738 d1764 son of Captain Cuthbert Spann &
     Agatha Conway, m1760 Priscilla Churchill dau/o Col Armistead
     Churchill & Hannah Harrison & had issue - desc/o Martha
     Eltonhead VG245
SPARKS Simon - of NJ, d1748, m Jane McClane - the immigrant AFA22;
   sufficient proof of alleged royal ancestry is lacking
   Thomas - of NJ, d1791, m Rachel____ - desc/o Simon Sparks AFA22
   Thomas - of NJ, b1760 d1801, m Sarah Biddle - desc/o Simon Sparks
     AFA22
SPAULDING Anna - b abt 1773 - desc/o Alice Freeman RAA132
   Capt Leonard - of MA, b1772 d1854, m Margaretta Warren - desc/o
     Rev Edward Bulkeley ECD(3)74
SPEAKMAN Ann - b abt 1745/1746 - desc/o Hugh Harry RAA102
   Thomas - b1721/1722 - desc/o Hugh Harry RAA102
SPELMAN Capt Henry - of VA 1609, b abt 1588 d1623 - the immigrant
   WAC51; sufficient proof of alleged royal ancestry is lacking
SPENCER Eliphas - b1738 - desc/o Agnes Harris RAA131
   Elizabeth - b abt 1633 - desc/o Agnes Harris RAA131
   Hannah - b1674 - desc/o Agnes Harris RAA131
   Joseph - of CT & WV, d1824, m1777 Deborah Selden - desc/o
     Elizabeth St John CHB222; BCD222
   Mary - of VA, m Capt Joseph Ball - desc/o Col Nicholas Spencer
     CHB529
   Col Nicholas - VA, d1689 son of Nicholas Spencer & Mary Gostwick, m
     Frances Mottram - the immigrant CHB529; WAC25, 26; GBR120
   Samuel - b abt 1638 - desc/o Agnes Harris RAA131
   Samuel - b1668 - desc/o Agnes Harris RAA131
   Sarah - b abt 1636 - desc/o Agnes Harris RAA131
   William - b1708 - desc/o Agnes Harris RAA131
SPICER Nathan - of CT, b1735 d1811, m(2)1765 Abigail Meyhew - desc/o
   Alice Freeman DBR(5)540; RAA132
   Rachel - b1775 - desc/o Alice Freeman RAA132
SPOFFORD Phoebe - m John Grout Jr - desc/o Gov Thomas Dudley
   AAP155; GBR250

SPOONER Mary - d1794, m James Sprague - desc/o Gov Thomas Dudley
DBR(3)520

Samuel - of MA, b1763 d1840, m1798 Hannah Williams - desc/o Dr
Richard Palgrave DBR(4)430

SPOTSWOOD Maj Gen Alexander - of VA 1710, b1676 d1740 lieut
governor of VA, son of Robert Spotswood & Catherine Mercer,
m1724 Anne Butler Brayne dau/o Edward Brayne of London - the
immigrant CHB291; MCB147, 436; MCD296; MCS34; BCD291;
DBR(1)354; DBR(2)205; DBR(3)675; DBR(4)300; EDV100, 101;
WAC47; GBR112; CFA(1)496, 497

Gen Alexander - of VA, major general Revolutionary Army, m Elizabeth
Washington, dau/o Gen Augustine Washington, brother of
President Washington - desc/o Col John West MCB442; MCD296

Anne - of VA, m Lewis Burwell - desc/o Hon Col John West CHB245,
291; BCD245, BCD291; DBR(1)407; DBR(3)163

Ann Catherine - of VA, b1726 d1802, m1745 Col Bernard Moore of
Chelsea, King William Co - desc/o Maj Gen Alexander Spotswood
CHB292; BCD292; CFA(1)497

Dandridge - of VA, m Catherine Brooke - desc/o Col John West
MCB442

Dorothea - of VA, m1747 Col Nathaniel West Dandridge, son of Capt
William Dandridge - desc/o Maj Gen Alexander Spotswood
CHB291; BCD291; GBR112; CFA(1)497

Capt John - of VA, appointed captain Continental Army, m1771 Sallie
Rowsee (Rowzie), dau/o Col John Rowzie, of Farmers Hall, Essex Co
- desc/o Col John West CHB245,291; MCB442; MCD296; BCD245,
291 - desc/o Maj Gen Alexander Spotswood CFA(1)488, 489

John - of VA, d1759, m1745 Mary Dandridge, dau/o Capt William
Dandridge - desc/o Maj Gen Alexander Spotswood CHB291;
MCB441; MCD296; BCD291; CFA(1)497

John - of VA, b1774, m Mary Goode - desc/o Maj Gen Alexander
Spotswood CFA(1)498

Mary - of VA, b1772, m Nicholas Voss - desc/o Maj Gen Alexander
Spotswood CFA(1)498

Robert of VA, m Louisa Bott - desc/o Maj Gen Alexander Spotswood
CHB291; BCD245, 291

Susan - of VA, b1776, m Dr John Bott of Petersburg - desc/o Maj Gen
Alexander Spotswood CFA(1)498

SPRIGG Joseph - of MD, b1760 d1821 in Illinois; credited with service to
the colonists during the American Revolution, m abt 1789 Ann
Taylor dau/o Major Ignatius Taylor - desc/o Henry Corbin
DBR(5)300

SPRING Catherine - b1750, m(1) Joseph Farnham - desc/o Henry Spring
LDS62

Henry - b1628, m(1) Mehitabel Bartlett - the immigrant LDS62;
sufficient proof of alleged royal ancestry is lacking

Henry - b1662, m Lydia Cutting - desc/o Henry Spring LDS62

Henry - b1692, m Kezia Converse - desc/o Henry Spring LDS62

Josiah - b1718, m Catharine Bicknell - desc/o Henry Spring LDS62

SPROAT Mary - b1716 - desc/o John Hawes RAA102

STAFFORD Frances - b abt 1680, m Benjamin Congdon - desc/o Frances Dungan LDS11

Mary - b abt 1678, m Pasco Whitford - desc/o Frances Dungan LDS112

STANARD Mary or Lucy Champe - m Archibald Campbell - desc/o Sarah Ludlow DBR(2)158; DBR(3)236

STANDISH Alexander - b1625/1626 - desc/o Miles Standish RAA131

Elizabeth - b abt 1660/1664 - desc/o Miles Standish RAA131

Miles - of MA, b1584, m(2) Barbara____ - the immigrant RAA1, 131; EDV126; sufficient proof of alleged royal ancestry is lacking

STANLEY Anna or Anne - of CT, bp 1742 Windsor d1803 Windsor, m1761 Thomas Benton b abt 1737 d1815 Windsor - desc/o Col William Leete SMO104

Lois - b abt 1697 - desc/o Agnes Harris RAA131

STANTON Anne - m John Avery - desc/o Bridget Tompson DBR(3)684

Mary - of CT, b1660, m1679 Robert Lay Jr - desc/o Alice Freeman DBR(4)483

STANYAN Anne - of NH, m Thomas Cilley - desc/o Capt Thomas Bradbury J&K165

STANYON Elizabeth - b abt 1700 - desc/o Thomas Bradbury RAA72

James - b1677 - desc/o Thomas Bradbury RAA72

Mehitable - of NH, b1676, m abt 1695 John Robinson - desc/o Capt Thomas Bradbury DBR(3)153; RAA72

STAPILTON Dorothy - b abt 1609 - the immigrant RAA117; sufficient proof of alleged royal ancestry is lacking

STARBUCK David - of MA, b1760 d1843, m1786 Phebe Cartwright - desc/o William Gayer DBR(3)757

Edward - b1719 - desc/o Rose Stoughton RAA119

Hepzibah - b1721 - desc/o Rose Stoughton RAA119

Hepzibah - b1749 - desc/o Rose Stoughton RAA119

Joseph - b1723 - desc/o Rose Stoughton RAA119

Judith - of MA, b1743 d1830, m1753 Joseph Worth II - desc/o William Gayer DBR(1)242, 249, 532; DBR(2)357, 675; DBR(3)51

Lydia - of MA, b1704 d1751, m1722 Benjamin Barney Sr - desc/o William Gayer DBR(3)749, 754

Matthew - b1750 - desc/o Rose Stoughton RAA119

Sarah - of MA, b1697 d1789, m1712 Jabez Macy - desc/o William Gayer DBR(1)270/1, 444; DBR(2)198

Silvanus - of MA, b1727 d1813, m1745 Mary Howes - desc/o William Gayer DBR(3)757

Thomas - of MA, b1706 d1777, m1726 Rachel Allen - desc/o William Gayer DBR(1)56; DBR(2)78; DBR(3)526; DBR(5)857

Thomas - of MA, m Dinah Trott - desc/o William Gayer DBR(1)56; DBR(2)78; DBR(3)526; DBR(5)857

William - of MA, b1699 d1760, m(1)1720 Anna Folger - desc/o William Gayer DBR(1)242, 248, 249, 532; DBR(2)357, 675; DBR(3)51

William - b1748 - desc/o Rose Stoughton RAA119

STARKE Jane - of VA, b1759 d1843, m1782 Capt James Dillard - desc/o Rev Hawte Wyatt DBR(2)21, 25

John Carter - of VA, b1748 d1814, m1769 Sarah English - desc/o Henry Skipwith DBR(1)281

STARKWEATHER Hannah - b1746 - desc/o Alice Freeman RAA132

STEARNS David - of MA, b1729 d1788, m1756 Hannah Burnell - desc/o
Elias Maverick ECD(3)175; DBR(5)737

David Jr - of MA, b1757 d1836, m1782 Susannah Beal(s) - desc/o
Elias Maverick ECD(3)175; DBR(5)737

STEERE Phebe - of RI, b1699 d1767, m John Matthewson - desc/o
Thomas Arnold CHB323; BCD323

STELLE Christiana - m Philip Cox Sr - desc/o Edward FitzRandolph
DBR(2)679; DBR(3)486

John - m Hannah De Bonrepos - desc/o Edward FitzRandolph
DBR(2)679; DBR(3)486

STETSON Jemima - b1694/1695 - desc/o Anthony Collamore RAA82

Robert Cornet - of MA - the immigrant EDV68, 69; sufficient proof of
alleged royal ancestry is lacking

STEUART Christina - of VA, b1741 d1807, m1770 Cyrus Griffin - the
immigrant MCS34; sufficient proof of alleged royal ancestry is
lacking

Gen George H - of MD, m Anne Jane Edmondson - desc/o Dudley
Diggs BCD77

Dr James - of MD, m Rebecca Sprigg - desc/o Dudley Diggs CHB76;
BCD76

Susannah - of MD, m Judge James Tilghman - desc/o Dudley Diggs
J&K255

STEVENS Dolly - b1770/1771 - desc/o John Prescott RAA125

Elizabeth - b1714 - desc/o John Prescott RAA125

Elizabeth - of NJ, b1730, m Rev Charles McKnight - desc/o John
Throckmorton ECD(3)262

Grace - m1657 John Frink - desc/o John Gallup JSW1884

John of NJ, m Rachel Cox - desc/o James Alexander CHB23; BCD23

Joseph - b1710 - desc/o John Prescott RAA125

Mary - b1742 - desc/o John Prescott RAA125

Sarah - of MA, m Rev Joseph Buckminster of Portsmouth, NH, also a
desc/of Bradstreet through his mother Lucy Williams - desc/o Gov
Thomas Dudley NE(8)317

STEVENSON Sarah - m Benjamin Field - desc/o Thomas Lawrence
MCD241

Thomas III- desc/o Thomas Lawrence MCD241

STEWART Lady Charlotte - of NY & VA, dau/o Alexander Steward, 6th
Earl of Galloway & Catherine Cochrane, m1759 John Murray, 4th
Earl of Dunmore, son of William Murray, 3rd Earl of Dunmore &
Catherine Murray, by whom she had eight children - the immigrant
GBR18; NYGBR(40)#4p225/228

Patrick - of NC 1739, d1772, m Elizabeth Menzies - the immigrant
MCD294; sufficient proof of alleged royal ancestry is lacking

William - of NC 1739, m(2) Jane McDougal - the immigrant MCD294;
sufficient proof of alleged royal ancestry is lacking

STICKNEY Nathan - of MA, abt 1760 d1820 a soldier in the Revolutionary
War, m Rachel Phelps dau/o Nathaniel Phelps - desc/o Thomas
Dudley DBR(4)399; DBR(5)360

Elizabeth - of MA, b1733 d1821, m Capt John Evans - desc/o Edward
Carleton DBR(3)493

STIER Henri Joseph, Seigneur of Aertselaer - of MD, son of Albert Jean
Stier & Isabelle Helene de la Bistrate, m Marie Louis Peeters - the
immigrant GBR380; TG(9)45/73

STILEMAN Elias - of NH, d1662 - the immigrant EDV133; sufficient proof
of alleged royal ancestry is lacking

Elias - of NH - desc/o Elias Stileman EDV133

STILLEY William - b1765 - desc/o John Ogle RAA119

STILLMAN Appleton - b1757 - desc/o Samuel Appleton RAA63

John - b1717 - desc/o Samuel Appleton RAA63

STIRLING Margaret - of VA, dau/o George Stirling of Herbertshire, m(1)
David Forbes, m(2)____ Alexander - the immigrant GBR59 some
aspect of royal descent merits further study

STITH Anderson - of VA, d1768 a practicing lawyer in Charles City Co &
major of the county militia, m Joanna Bassett dau/o William
Bassett of Eltham, Kent Co - desc/o Lancelot Bathurst
GVFWM(4)571

Ann - of VA, m1781 William Eaton of North Carolina - desc/o Lancelot
Bathurst GVFWM(4)573

Anne - of VA, m Capt William Parham will dated 1754 - desc/o Col
William Randolph DBR(2)126

Col Bassett - of VA & NC, b1765, m1790 Mary Long dau/o Col
Nicholas Long of Halifax & Mary McKinne - desc/o Lancelot
Bathurst GVFWM(4)575, 594

Capt Buckner - of VA, b abt 1722 of Rock Spring, Brunswick Co
d1791 captain in the county militia, he was the author of an
elaborate essay on tobacco culture, m Susanna____ d1810 - desc/o
Lancelot Bathurst GVFWM(4)573

Buckner - of VA, d1800, m(1)1786 Elizabeth Jones, m(2)1788 Ann
Walker - desc/o Lancelot Bathurst GVFWM(4)573

Lieut-Col Buckner - of VA, lieut-col in Brunswick Co militia & justice of
that county, m Anne Dade of Litchfield, King George Co - desc/o
Lancelot Bathurst GVFWM(4)575

Catherine - of VA, d1795, m1790 Robert Bolling of Petersburg - desc/o
Lancelot Bathurst GVFWM(4)573

Lieut-Col Drury - of VA, b abt 1695 of Prince George & Brunswick Co,
VA, clerk of the county court & county surveyor also interested in
copper mining, m abt 1717 Elizabeth Buckner dau/o Major William
Buckner of Yorktown - desc/o Lancelot Bathurst GVFWM(4)569,
570

Col Drury - of VA, b abt 1718 d1770 surveyor of Brunswick Co, high
sheriff of the county in 1757, justice, major of horse, colonel of foot
& colonel of the county militia, m(1) Martha____, m(2)1762
Elizabeth Jones d1771 wid/o Thomas Eldridge of Prince George Co
- desc/o Lancelot Bathurst GVFWM(4)571/572

Capt Drury - of VA, captain in the Brunswick Co militia & was a
vestryman of St Andrews Parish, m1788 Fanny Love dau/o Allen
Love - desc/o Lancelot Bathurst GVFWM(4)575

Drury - of VA, born in Northampton Co 1755 d1789, clerk of
Brunswick Co court, m Mary Jacobs of Northampton Co - desc/o
Lancelot Bathurst GVFWM(4)575

Elizabeth - of VA, d1792, m Dr William Pasteur of Williamsburg -

STITH (cont.)
    desc/o Col William Randolph GVFWM(4)591

Elizabeth Buckner - of VA, b1745, m John Stringer - desc/o Lancelot Bathurst GVFWM(4)572

Griffin - of VA, b1720 d1784 clerk of Northampton Co, VA, m1743 Mary Blaikley b1726/1727 dau/o William Blaikley of James City Co & Catherine Kaidyee - desc/o Lancelot Bathurst GVFWM(4)572

Griffin - of VA, b1753 d1794 married & left issue - desc/o Lancelot Bathurst GVFWM(4)573

Griffin - of VA, wid/o Samuel Washington & had issue - desc/o Lancelot Bathurst GVFWM(4)573

Lieut-Col John - of VA, d1757 burgess 1718/1726 of Charles City Co, m Elizabeth Anderson dau/o the Reverend Charles Anderson of Charles City Co - desc/o Col William Randolph DBR(2)126; GVFWM(4)590 - desc/o Lancelot Bathurst GVFWM(4)570/571

Col John - of VA, b1755 d1808 distinguished Revolutionary War officer, m Ann Washington d1824 dau/o Lawrence Washington of Choptank, King George Co & had issue - desc/o Lancelot Bathurst GVFWM(4)577

Lucy - of VA, m1797 Mark U Pringle of Baltimore - desc/o Lancelot Bathurst GVFWM(4)573

Mary Randolph - of VA, b1715 d1785, m1733 Rev William Dawson b1704 d1752, second president of William and Mary College, 1743/1752 - desc/o Henry Isham CHB534 - desc/o Col William Randolph DBR(2)672; GVFWM(4)590; PVF132; CFA(5)429

Richard - of VA, of Brunswick Co d1819, m Jane Maclin - desc/o Lancelot Bathurst GVFWM(4)573

Susanna - of VA, b1759 d1838, m Christopher Johnson - desc/o Lancelot Bathurst GVFWM(4)573

Susanna - of VA, m1772 Andrew Meade of Octagon, Brunswick Co - desc/o Lancelot Bathurst GVFWM(4)574

Susanna - of VA, b1759 d1838, m1779 Christopher Johnston b1750 d1819 of Baltimore, MD & had issue - desc/o Lancelot Bathurst GVFWM(4)576

Major Thomas - of VA, b1729 of Brunswick Co d1801 major of the county militia, he was also burgess, justice & county surveyor for Brunswick Co, m1780 Holly Baily - desc/o Lancelot Bathurst GVFWM(4)574

Rev William - of VA, b1707 d1752/1755 William & Mary College, third president of William and Mary College 1752/1755, wrote, *History of VA*, which was printed & bound in the city of Williamsburg 1740, m1738 Judith Randolph (his first cousin) dau/o Thomas Randolph of Tuckahoe - desc/o Henry Isham CHB534 - desc/o Col William Randolph GVFWM(4)568, 590; PVF132; CFA(5)429

William - of VA, d1794 clerk of Northampton Co, VA 1783/1794, m Sarah Smith dau/o Isaac Smith & Elizabeth Custis Teackle - desc/o Lancelot Bathurst GVFWM(4)573

STOCKETT Elizabeth - of MD, b abt 1662, m abt 1678 Thomas Plummer - desc/o Frances White ECD(2)309

STOCKMAN John - of MA, d1686 son of Joseph & Ann (Leigh) Stockman, m Mrs Sarah Pike Bradbury dau/o Major Robert & Sarah (Sanders)

STOCKMAN (cont.)

Pike - the immigrant GBR247; NE(125)263

STOCKTON Richard - of NJ, d1705 - the immigrant EDV99; sufficient proof of alleged royal ancestry is lacking

STODDARD Sampson - of MA, b1740/1741 d1779, m1772 Boston, Jemima White of Boston - desc/o Mary Gye NE(97)56

STODDART Anthony - of MA 1639 - the immigrant EDV58; sufficient proof of alleged royal ancestry is lacking

Daniel - of MA 1723 - desc/o Anthony Stoddard EDV58

Simeon - of MA 1712 - desc/o Anthony Stoddard EDV58

STOKES Lydia - b1710 d1788, m1734 Samuel Haines - desc/o Peter Wright DBR(4)98

STONE Rev Barton Warren - of VA, b1772 d1844, m(1)1801 Elizabeth Campbell - desc/o Col Humphrey Warren CHB318; BCD318

Catherine - of VA - desc/o Capt William Stone WAC48

Elizabeth - of VA - desc/o Capt William Stone WAC48

James - b1727 - desc/o Olive Welby RAA93

John - of VA - desc/o Capt William Stone WAC48

Josiah - b1771 - desc/o Olive Welby RAA93

Mary - of VA - desc/o Capt William Stone WAC48

Matthew - of VA - desc/o Capt William Stone WAC48

Rachel - b1753 - desc/o William Leete RAA107

Richard - of VA - desc/o Capt William Stone WAC48

Thomas - of VA - desc/o Capt William Stone WAC48

Capt William - of VA, b1603 d abt 1695 - the immigrant WAC48; sufficient proof of alleged royal ancestry is lacking

STORRS Samuel - of MA 1663, b1640 - the immigrant EDV70; sufficient proof of alleged royal ancestry is lacking

STOUGHTON Capt Israel - of MA 1632 - the immigrant EDV142; sufficient proof of alleged royal ancestry is lacking

Rose - b1629 - the immigrant RAA119; sufficient proof of alleged royal ancestry is lacking

William - of MA - desc/o Capt Israel Stoughton EDV142

STOUT Deliverance - of NJ, b1701, m Francis Labaw, of New Jersey - desc/o John Throckmorton DBR(5)1012

James - m Catherine Simpson b abt 1691 d1749 - desc/o John Throckmorton DBR(1)178

John - of NJ - desc/o Col St Leger Codd JSW1720

Nancy Deborah - of NJ, b1756 d1844, m1777 Edward Hart - desc/o Col St Leger JSW1721; DBR(4)199, 278

Rebecca - b1725, m Nathan Drake b1726 d1804 - desc/o John Throckmorton DBR(1)178

St Leger Codd - of NJ, b abt 1735 d1767, m abt 1753 Susannah____ - desc/o Col St Leger Codd JSW1720; DBR(4)64, 189, 199, 278; DBR(5)307, 311, 714, 967

St Leger Codd - of NJ, b1755 d1806, m1794 Anna Barcalo - desc/o Col St Leger Codd JSW1720; DBR(4)64, 189; DBR(5)307, 311, 714, 967

STOVER Hannah - b abt 1686 - desc/o Henry Norton RAA118

STOW Sarah - of CT, m Josiah Savage - desc/o Rev Charles Chauncy CHB86; BCD86

STOWELL Elizabeth - b1719, m David Pulsipher - desc/o Robert
   Harrington LDS82
STRACHEY Arabella - of VA, m(1) John Walter, m(2) Henry Cox of
   Rappahannock Co, VA d1675 - desc/o William Strachey APP592;
   GVFWM(4)627/631
   Elizabeth - of VA, b1734 d1789, m Thomas Metcalfe - desc/o John
      Strachey GVFWM(4)629
   Dr John - of VA, b1709 d1756 of King & Queen Co, son of John
      Strachey & Elizabeth Elletson, m Elizabeth Vernon - the immigrant
      GBR410; GVFWM(4)627/631
   William - of VA, b abt 1572 of Wandsworth & Camberwell, Surrey,
      England d bef 1618, 1st secretary of the VA Colony & a member of
      the VA Company, son of William Strachey & Mary Cooke, m 1595
      Frances Forster b1575 dau/o William Forster of Surrey & Elizabeth
      Draper - the immigrant GBR432 some aspect of royal descent
      merits further study; APP590/593
   William - resided at Surrey & London d1634/1635 son of William
      Strachey & Frances Forster, m(1)1620 Eleanor Read dau/o John
      Read of London, m(2)1629 Anne Bourne dau/o William Bourne of
      Greenstead, Essex, m(3) shortly aft 30 Dec 1631 Elizabeth (Cross)
      Jepp b1605 d1672/1673 dau/o William Cross of Norton Fitzwarren
      & Blackmore, Somerset & Grace Perry, & wid/o Samuel Jepp -
      desc/o William Strachey GBR432; APP591; GVFWM(4)627
   William - of VA, b abt 1625 merchant in the Parish of St Augustine,
      London d1686, m(1) Mary Miller dau/o James Miller of York Co,
      VA, m(2) Martha____ - the immigrant GBR432 some aspect of royal
      descent merits further study; APP592
STRAIGHT Aspinwall - of RI, b1774 d1854, m abt 1794 Mary Ann Potter
   - desc/o Jeremy Clarke DBR(5)232
   John - of RI, b1744, m Sarah Austin - desc/o Jeremy Clarke
      DBR(5)232
STRATTON Anne - of MA, m(1) William Lake, m(2) William Stevens -
   desc/o John Stratton GBR425
   Elizabeth - of MA, dau/o John Stratton & Anne Derehaugh, m John
      Thorndike - the immigrant GBR427 some aspect or royal descent
      merits further study; NE(135)287/90
   Elizabeth - of NJ, b1754 d1794, m1774 Esaias Hunt b1752 d1813 son
      of Edward Hunt of Hunterdon Co, New Jersey - desc/o George
      Elkington DBR(2)391
   Hannah - b1678, m John Sanderson - desc/o Mary Knapp LDS27
   John - of MA, son of John Stratton & Anne Derehaugh m____ - the
      immigrant GBR425 some aspect of royal descent merits further
      study; NE(135)287/97; EO2(3)378/381
   Martin - b1730 - desc/o Agnes Harris RAA131
   Owen - of NJ, b1769 d1843, m1808 Mary Hines Shinn - desc/o
      Joshua Owen ECD(2)205
   Stephen - of CT, b1754 d1842, m1777 Sarah Darrow d1841 - desc/o
      Rev Peter Bulkeley DBR(1)809
STREET Nicholas - b1603, m(1) Ann Poole - the immigrant RAA no longer
   accepted as being of royal descent

STRETCHER Edward - of DE - desc/o Thomas Fenwick MCD216
   Fenwick - of DE - desc/o Thomas Fenwick MCD216
STRINGER Grace - of VA, m1754 Northampton Co, John Bowdoin d1775
   - desc/o Col Nathaniel Littleton SMO301
      Hillary III - of VA, d1744 Accomack Co, m1722/1723 Accomack Co,
      Elishe (Alicia) Harmanson d1760 dau/o George Harmanson &
      Elizabeth Yeardly - desc/o Col Nathaniel Littleton APP466; SMO301
      John - of VA, d1751, m(1) Flavia Savage, m(2) Smart___ d1781 -
      desc/o Col Nathaniel Littleton APP466
STRONG Deborah - b1760, m Capt Solomon Tuttle - desc/o Alice
   Freeman DBR(3)430
   Ezra - b1763 - desc/o John Drake RAA87
   Martha - of MA, b1749 d1827, m1773 Rev Ebenezer Moseley - desc/o
   Richard Lyman CHB151; BCD151
   Temperance - b1758 - desc/o John Drake RAA87
STROTHER Agatha - of VA, b1728, m1745 John Madison d1784 - desc/o
   William Strother NFA62; GVFTQ(3)379
   Alice - of VA, b1719, m1738 Henry Tyler - desc/o William Strother
      GVFTQ(3)378
   Alice - of VA, b1732 d1775, m1756 Robert Washington b1729 d1795 -
      desc/o William Strother GVFTQ(3)377; CFA(6)493
   Ann - of NC, m Joel Moody - desc/o William Strother HSF(5)293
   Ann - of NC, b abt 1766, m Garrett Goodlow - desc/o William Strother
      HSF(5)292
   Anne - of VA, b1723, m1744 Francis Tyler - desc/o William Strother
      NFA63; GVFTQ(3)378
   Anne - of VA, m1763 John James - desc/o William Strother
      GVFTQ(3)377
   Anne - of VA, b1750 d1788, m1776 (her cousin) John Strother -
      desc/o William Strother GVFTQ(3)384
   Anthony - of VA, b1710 in Richmond Co d1765 in Stafford Co,
      m(1)1733 Betheland Storke b1716 d1753 dau/o William Storke
      b1690 d1726 & Elizabeth Hart, m(2)1754 Mary James b1736
      dau/o Thomas James & Mary Bruce - desc/o William Strother
      NFA63; GVFTQ(3)377, 389; CFA(6)494
   Anthony - of VA, m Frances Eastham - desc/o William Strother NFA64;
      GVFTQ(3)380
   Anthony - of VA, b1736 d1790 justice & sheriff of King George Co, m
      abt 1760 Frances Elizabeth Kenyon - desc/o William Strother
      GVFTQ(3)389; CFA(6)494
   Anthony - of VA, d1818, m1793 Elizabeth Newton - desc/o William
      Strother GVFTQ(3)389
   Benjamin - of VA, b1712 d1789 major of the Stafford Co Rangers, m
      Mrs Mary (Mason) Fitzhugh dau/o Col George Mason & Sarah
      Fowke & wid/o Col George Fitzhugh - desc/o William Strother
      NFA63; GVFTQ(3)377; CFA(6)493
   Benjamin - of VA, d1752 justice, vestryman & sheriff of King George Co
      also large landed proprietor, m Mary Woffendall - desc/o William
      Strother GVFTQ(3)375; HSF(5)291; CFA(6)493
   Benjamin - of VA, b1750 Stafford Co d1807 Park Forest, Jefferson Co,
      midshipman in the VA Revolutionary Navy & later served in the

STROTHER (cont.)

land forces, m1778 Catherine (Kitty) Price b1753 d1805 dau/o
William Price & Jane Brown of Westmoreland Co, VA - desc/o
William Strother NFA63; GVFTQ(3)392; CFA(6)497

Betheland - of VA m____ Covington - desc/o William Strother NFA65;
GVFTQ(3)380 gives the name of John Wallis as her husband

Charles - of VA & SC, b abt 1730 d1773 Charleston, SC, m Mary Cross
b1730 & had issue William & George who was a lieutenant in
Marion's Brigade in 1781 - desc/o William Strother GVFTQ(3)404;
HSF(13)89

Charles - of SC, b1763 Charleston d1812 Cheraw District, Chesterfield
Co, lieutenant in the Revolution & served in Captain Ellerby's
(Ellerbe) Company, m1782 Jane Ellerbe b1767 d abt 1852 dau/o
Captain Ellerbe & Obedience Galespy (Gillespie) - desc/o William
Strother HSF(13)90, 91

Christopher Judd - of VA & NC, d1795 Franklin Co, NC, moved to NC
1757, served as a soldier in the NC militia, m Anne Kempe - desc/o
William Strother GVFTQ(3)404; HSF(5)292

Delia - of VA, m Joseph Carr - desc/o William Strother GVFTQ(3)416

Dorothy - of VA, m William Walker - desc/o William Strother
GVFTQ(3)376

Dorothy - of NC, m Thomas Floyd (?) - desc/o William Strother
HSF(5)292

Eleanor - of VA, m John Tyler - desc/o William Strother GVFTQ(3)377

Elizabeth - of VA, b1721 d1752, m1738 Major John Frogg - desc/o
William Strother NFA63; GVFTQ(3)378

Elizabeth - of VA, m Capt James Gaines - desc/o William Strother
NFA65; GVFTQ(3)380

Elizabeth - of NC, m Thomas King - desc/o William Strother HSF(5)293

Elizabeth - of VA, b1758 d1823, m1774 Capt John Browning b1749
d1813 enlisted at the beginning of the Revolution & was at Valley
Forge, served through eight years of the War, refusing a discharge
because of ill health. Was at the Yorktown Campaign & when the
flag-staff was shot in two, while he was carrying it, he raised it
again aloft and carried it to the end of the Battle (of Yorktown) -
desc/o William Strother GVFTQ(3)384

Enoch - of VA, b1728 d1772, m1763 Mary Kay - desc/o William
Strother GVFTQ(3)375, 416

Francis - of VA, b1700 d1752, m(1) Elizabeth Forsaker, m(2)1720
Susannah Dabney dau/o John Dabney & Sarah [Jennings ?] -
desc/o William Strother AAP145; NFA62; GBR184; GVFTQ(3)377,
380; HSF(5)292 - desc/o Anthony Savage AAP146; GBR253;
CFA(6)493

Francis - of VA, d1777 lieutenant in the French & Indian War, m Anne
Graves or Fargeson - desc/o William Strother NFA65; GVFTQ(3)381

Francis - of VA, m Elizabeth Fossaker dau/o Richard Fossaker &
Frances Withers of Stafford Co, VA - desc/o William Strother
GVFTQ(3)404

French - of VA, b1733 d1800 prominent in Culpeper Co which he
represented for more than 25 years in the General Assembly,
member of the Conventions of 1776 & 1788 county lieutenant & a

STROTHER (cont.)

Justice, m Lucy Coleman dau/o Robert Coleman & Sarah Anne Saunders of Culpeper Co, VA - desc/o William Strother NFA66; GVFTQ(3)404

George - of VA, d1761, m Mrs Tabitha (Payne) Woffendall d1790 - desc/o William Strother GVFTQ(3)375

George - of VA, b1732 d1767, m Mary Kennerly b1746 d1834 - desc/o William Strother NFA64; GVFTQ(3)381; HSF(13)89

George - of VA, d1811, m1795 (his cousin) Sarah Kenyon - desc/o William Strother GVFTQ(3)389

Rev George - of VA, b1776 d1864, m1796 Mary Duncan b1776 d1851 dau/o James Duncan & Asenith Browning - desc/o William Strother GVFTQ(3)408, 409

James - of VA, d1761 Culpeper Co, sheriff of King George Co 1741, m Margaret French dau/o Daniel French & Margaret Pratt - desc/o William Strother NFA66; GVFTQ(3)404; HSF(5)292

James - of VA, m Elizabeth Purcell - desc/o William Strother GVFTQ(3)416

James - of NC, b1764 d1843, m Patsy Bowers - desc/o William Strother HSF(5)292

James Storke - of VA, b1755 d1819 Revolutionary War soldier with the rank of sergeant in the 2nd VA Regiment & afterwards pensioned by the government, m1788 in Fairfax Co, Elizabeth Battle Morton b1768 d1844 dau/o Parson Morton - desc/o William Strother GVFTQ(3)391; CFA(6)494

Jane - of VA, b1732 d1820, m Thomas Lewis - desc/o William Strother NFA63

Jeremiah - of VA, b1655 d1741 Orange Co, m Eleanor____ who survived him, leaving issue - desc/o William Strother NFA62, 66; GVFTQ(3)375, 403, 404; HSF(5)291, 292; CFA(6)493

Jeremiah - of VA, removed to South Carolina, m Catherine Kennerly or (Kennedy) dau/o Samuel Kennerly or (Kennedy) d1744 & Ellen Kennerly d1756 - desc/o Willian Strother GVFTQ(3)404, 407; HSF(5)292

Jeremiah III - of VA, d1832, m(1) Martha Payne, m(2) Nancy Clayton dau/o Samuel Clayton & Anne Coleman of Culpeper Co - desc/o William Strother GVFTQ(3)408

John - of VA, d1763, m Mary____ - desc/o William Strother GVFTQ(3)376

John - of VA, m Elizabeth Pendleton Hunter - desc/o William Strother NFA63

John - of VA, b1721 d1795 signer of the first protest against the Stamp Act in Culpeper Co on 21 Oct 1765, m1741 Mary Willis Wade b1723 d aft 18 Oct 1802 dau/o Joseph d1757 & Sarah Wade - desc/o William Strother NFA64; GVFTQ(3)380, 382

John - of VA, d1780, m (his cousin) Anne Strother of Wakefield - desc/o William Strother GVFTQ(3)407

John - of VA, b1742 d1805 m____ Price - desc/o William Strother GVFTQ(3)391; CFA(6)494

John - of VA, b1762 d1818 high sheriff, m1782 Helen Piper - desc/o William Strother GVFTQ(3)384

STROTHER (cont.)

John - of VA, m(1)1799 Jane Edwards, m(2) Elizabeth Clopton - desc/o William Strother GVFTQ(3)383

John - of VA, b1771 d1805, m1793 Catherine Fox Price b1772 d1846 dau/o Meredith Price & Elizabeth Fox of Louisa Co, VA - desc/o William Strother GVFTQ(3)390

John - of NC, d1796 Hancock Co, Georgia, served as a soldier from Orange Co, NC during the Revolutionary War, m Jane Fussell d1830 Hancock Co, Georgia - desc/o William Strother HSF(5)292, 293

Joseph - of VA, b1685/1685 d1766 sheriff of King George Co in 1728, m Margaret Berry dau/o James Berry & Grace Powell - desc/o William Strother GVFTQ(3)376; CFA(6)493

Joseph - of VA, b1684 d1762, m Margaret Berry - desc/o William Strother GVFTQ(3)376; HSF(5)291

Joseph - of VA, b1742 captain of Culpeper militia in the Revolution, m1766 Nancy Stewart b1747 - desc/o William Strother GVFTQ(3)382

Joseph - of VA, m(1)1798 Martha Finley, m(2)____ Davenport - desc/o William Strother GVFTQ(3)383

Judd - of VA, d1857, m1801 Rebecca Perry, moved to Illinois - desc/o William Strother HSF(5)292

Katherine - of VA, m Thomas Baker - desc/o William Strother GVFTQ(3)407

Lawrence - of VA, was in Orange Co 1742, m Elizabeth____ - desc/o William Strother HSF(5)292

Lucy - of VA, b1756 d1836, m1774 Capt Francis Covington b1754 d1823 was of the colonial militia - desc/o William Strother GVFTQ(3)384

Lucy - of VA, b1773 d1824, m1792 Francis Wyatt Green b1767 d1826 - desc/o William Strother GVFTQ(3)384

Margaret - of VA, m George Gallagher - desc/o William Strother GVFTQ(3)416

Margaret - of VA, m Thomas Clanahan - desc/o William Strother GVFTQ(3)376

Margaret - of VA, b1725 d1815, m Robert Covington d1766 - desc/o William Strother GVFTQ(3)381

Margaret - of VA, b1726 d1822, m(1)1744 George Morton, m(2)1749 Gabriel Jones b1724 d1806 "The Valley Lawyer" & agent for Lord Fairfax - desc/o William Strother NFA63; GVFTQ(3)378

Margaret - of VA, b1763 d1834, m1781 Col George Hancock b1754 d1820 - desc/o William Strother GVFTQ(3)381

Martha - of NC, m(1) Amos Thompson joined Cornwallis' Army as a British soldier & was killed at the Battle of Guilford Court House 25 Mar 1781, m(2) Mark Stroud fought in the Revolutionary War & marched with the American Army into VA where he met the widow Martha, son of John Stroud - desc/o William Strother HSF(5)293

Mary - of VA, m William Wren d1766 - desc/o William Strother GVFTQ(3)376

Mary - of VA, m____ Detherage - desc/o William Strother NFA65

Mary - of VA, m George Gray - desc/o William Strother NFA66;

STROTHER (cont.)
GVFTQ(3)404

Mary - of VA, m Col William Bronaugh - desc/o William Strother GVFTQ(3)377

Mary Wade - of VA, b1752 d1847, m on or bef 15 Jun 1769 Capt Charles Browning b1746 d1839 later became a captain in the Revolutionary War - desc/o William Strother GVFTQ(3)384, 417

Mary Wade - of VA, b1771, m1790 Col William Menefee b1762 d1841 - desc/o William Strother GVFTQ(3)383

Mildred - of VA, b1760 d1827, m William Covington - desc/o William Strother GVFTQ(3)384

Richard - of NC, b1768, m(1)____, m(2)1832 Mary Black - desc/o William Strother HSF(5)293

Robert - of VA, d1735 King & Queen Co, m Elizabeth Berry - desc/o William Strother GVFTQ(3)375; HSF(5)291, 292; CFA(6)493

Robert - of VA, private in the VA Line during the War of the Revolution, m Martha Radcliffe - desc/o William Strother GVFTQ(3)380

Robert - of VA, d1801, m Elizabeth Dillard - desc/o William Strother GVFTQ(3)381

Sarah - of NC, d1842 aged 93 years, m James Murphy - desc/o William Strother HSF(5)292

Sarah - of VA, b1754 d1820, m William Hughes - desc/o William Strother GVFTQ(3)384

Sarah Dabney - of VA, b1760 d1829, m1779 Col Richard Taylor b1744 d1826 Kentucky, their son was Zachary Taylor b1784 d1850, 12th President of the United States - desc/o William Strother AAP145; NFA65, 65; GBR184; HSF(5)292 - desc/o Anthony Savage AAP146; GBR253

Solomon - of VA, m Nancy Lawler - desc/o William Strother GVFTQ(3)407

Susannah - of VA, m(1)1770 Capt Moses Hawkins killed at the Battle of Germantown 14 Oct 1777, m(2)1781 Thomas Coleman a corporal in the Revolutionary War - desc/o William Strother NFA65; GVFTQ(3)385

Susannah - of VA, m Thomas Gaines - desc/o William Strother GVFTQ(3)380

Susannah Dabney - m(1) John Lawler, m(2) James Hughlett - desc/o William Strother GVFTQ(3)384

William - of VA, b abt 1627/1630 Northumberland, England d1702 Richmond Co, VA son of William Strother & Elizabeth____, m Dorothy [Savage ?] - the immigrant AAP145; NFA62; GBR184 (allegedly - the immigrant to VA) & some aspect of royal descent merits further study; GVFTQ(3)370/443; HSF(5)290/293, (13)88/91; CFA(6)492

William Jr - of VA, b abt 1653 d1726 high sheriff of King George Co, vestryman of Hanover Parish, m abt 1695 Margaret Thornton b1678 dau/o Francis Thornton & Alice Savage - desc/o William Strother APP145; NFA62; GBR184; GVFTQ(3)377; HSF(5)291; CFA(6)493

William - of VA, b1697 d1732/1733 called "Captain" was high sheriff & justice of King George Co in 1727 until the time of his death, m

STROTHER (cont.)

abt 1718 Margaret Watts dau/o Richard & Mary Watts, Margaret, m(2) John Grant of Stafford Co, VA - desc/o William Strother NFA63, GVFTQ(3)378; CFA(6)493

William - of VA, b1709 d1749/1751 Westmorland Co, m1729 Mildred Taliaferro dau/o Charles Taliaferro & Anne Kempe - desc/o William Strother GVFTQ(3)404; HSF(5)292, (13)88, 89

William - of VA, b1726 d1808 in Kentucky, m(1) aft 1750 Sarah (Bayly) Pannill d1774 wid/o William Pannill d1750, m(2)1775 Ann (Cave) Kavanaugh dau/o Benjamin Cave & Hannah Bledsoe & wid/o Philemon Kavanaugh - desc/o William Strother AAP145; NFA64; GBR184; GVFTQ(3)380, 385 - desc/o Anthony Savage AAP146; GBR253

William - of VA, d aft 1779, m(1)1765 Winifred Baker of Westmoreland Co, m(2) (may have) Catherine Dargan dau/o Timothy Dargan, minister & reverend, soldier of Anson Co, NC & Cheraw District, SC - desc/o William Strother GVFTQ(3)404; HSF(13)89, 90

William - served in the Revolution, was a vestryman of St David's Church, 1775/1784, & a representative of the parish 1786. He was Judge in 1784, m(1) Dorothy Singleton, dau/o Thomas Singleton, m(2) Lucy Rogers, dau/o Benjamin Rogers, m(3) Lucy Hicks, dau/o Col George Hicks & had issue by all three wives - desc/o William Strother HSF(13)90

William - of VA, m Margaret Watts - desc/o William Strother GVFTQ(3)377

William - of VA, b1767 d1819, m1790 Milly Medley - desc/o William Strother GVFTQ(3)383

William - of NC, m Sallie Woodward, eldest dau/o John Woodward Sr & Esther McDonald & had issue, one son, Dargan Strother who married & had issue - desc/o William Strother NFA65(?)

William Dabney - of VA, the first person killed in Georgia during the War of the American Revolution - desc/o William Strother NFA65

STUART Catherine - of NC, m1764 William Little Jr - desc/o Patrick Stuart CHB338; BCD337/8

Lady Christian of VA 1773, b1741 d1807 dau/o John, 6th Earl of Traquair & Christian (Anstruther) Stuart, m1769 Judge Cyrus Griffin b1748 d1810 son of Col Leroy Griffin & Marianne Bertrand, last President of the Continental Congress - the immigrant CHB114; MCB140; BCD114; GBR53; NGS(52)25/36

Patrick - of NC 1739, m Elizabeth Menzies - the immigrant CHB337; MCB139; BCD337; sufficient proof of alleged royal ancestry is lacking

STURGES Deborah - b abt 1662, m(1) Benjamin Seeley - desc/o Deborah Barlow LDS59

STURGIS Nathan - b1750 d1827, m1773 Catherine Phillips - desc/o John Evans DBR(1)678; DBR(3)489

Thomas - b1723 d1827, m1747 Katherine Roberts - desc/o John Evans DBR(1)678; DBR(3)489

STURTEVANT Lemuel - b1756 - desc/o Henry Norton RAA118

STUYVESANT Anne - of NY, m Lazarus Bayard - the immigrant EDV26; sufficient proof of alleged royal ancestry is lacking

STUYVESANT (cont.)

Peter - of NY 1647 - the immigrant EDV26; sufficient proof of alleged royal ancestry is lacking

SULLIVAN Daniel - of ME, b1738 d1781, m(1) Anne Paul, m(2) Abigail Bean - desc/o Owen Sullivan BLG2930; AMB265

Ebenezer - of ME, b1753 d1790, m Abigail Cotton - desc/o Owen Sullivan BLG2930

Judge James - of MA, b1744 d1808, m(1)1768 Mehetable Odiorne - desc/o Owen O'Sullivan MCD298; AMB265; AFA240

James - b1769 d1787 - desc/o Owen O'Sullivan AMB265

John - of ME 1623, b1690 d1795, m Lydia Worcester, m Margaret Browne - the immigrant BCD203, royal ancestry not proven - desc/o Owen Sullivan BLG2930

John - of NH, b1740 d1795, m Lydia Worcester - desc/o Owen O'Sullivan AMB265

Mary - of ME & NH, b1752 d1827, m1768 Theophilus Hardy - desc/o Owen O'Sullivan CHB203; BCD203; AMB265

Owen - of ME, b1690 d1795, m1735 Margery Browne - the immigrant BLG2930; AMB265; AFA240; sufficient proof of alleged royal ancestry is lacking

William - b1774 d1839, m1802 Sarah Webb Swan - desc/o Owen O'Sullivan AMB265

SUMNER William - of MA 1635 - the immigrant EDV69; sufficient proof of alleged royal ancestry is lacking

SURRIAGE Agnes - of MA, b1726 d1783, known as Lady Agnes Surriage Frankland, social leader, m Sir Charles Henry Frankland, 4th Baronet, British consular officer - the immigrant GBR43

SWAIN Mary - b1766 - desc/o Peter Bulkeley RAA75

SWAN Dudley Wade - b1729 d1765, m Beulah Gullever b1715 d1790 - desc/o Katherine Deighton DBR(2)571

Mary - of VA, m William Phillips - desc/o John Harris DBR(4)637

Phoebe Wade - b1753 d1808, m Col William Henshaw b1735 d1820 - desc/o Katherine Deighton DBR(2)571

SWANN Capt Alexander - of VA, d1707 - desc/o Dr Richard Edwards DBR(1)224

SWIFT Ruth - b1745 - desc/o Thomas Newberry RAA118

SWINGATE Benedick, later Benedict Calvert - of MD, b abt 1724 d1788, m1748 Elizabeth Calvert - desc/o Charlotte Lee MSC13

SYMMES Anna Tuthill - m William Henry Harrison - desc/o Anthony Collamore AAP145; GBR445

John Cleves - m Anna Tuthill - desc/o Anthony Collamore AAP145; GBR445

Timonty Jr - m Mary Cleves - desc/o Anthony Collamore AAP145; GBR444

SYMONDS Dorothy - of MA, b1670, m1695 Cyprian Whipple - desc/o Dorothy Harlakenden CHB280 ; BCD280; THJ43

Elizabeth - of MA, b1624 d1685, m1644 Daniel Epes - desc/o Dorothy Harlakenden CHB281; BCD281; DBR(1)273; THJ43

Ruth - of MA, b abt 1640 d1702, m Rev John Emerson - desc/o Samuel Symonds AFA18,20, 14

Samuel - of MA, b1595, m Dorothy Harlakenden, m Martha Read - the

SYMONDS (cont.)
   immigrant THJ42, 45; AFA18, 20, 14; EDV144
   William - of MA, m Mary Wade - desc/o Dorothy Harlakenden CHB280;
   BCD280

-- T --

TAINTOR John - of CT, b1760 d1825, m1786 Sarah Hosford (or
   Horseford) b1770 d1856 - desc/o Rev Charles Chauncy CHB88;
   BCD88 - desc/o Rev Peter Bulkeley TAG(36)156

TALBOT Daniel - of MA, b1709 d1788, m1734 Martha Stearns - desc/o
   George (Peter) Talbot CFA(4)
   Dorothy - of MA, b1680/1681, m James Cutting of Watertown - desc/o
   George (Peter) Talbot CFA(4)
   Ebenezer - of MA, b1723 d1764, m1746/1747 Elizabeth Withington -
   desc/o George (Peter) Talbot CFA(4)
   Elizabeth - of MA, b1686/1687, m(1)1713 Eleazer Tupper, m(2)1748
   Samuel Ranes - desc/o George (Peter) Talbot CFA(4)
   Experience - of MA, b1726/1727, m1747 Joseph Smith - desc/o
   George (Peter) Talbot CFA(4)
   Frances - of MD, b abt 1634 d1718, m abt 1650 (her cousin) Richard
   Talbot d1703 - desc/o Anne Arundel CFA(5)288
   Frances - of MD, d1749, m James Butler - desc/o Anne Arundel
   CFA(5)289
   George Jr, known as Peter Talbot - of MA, b abt 1655 near Blackburn,
   Lancashire, England, m(1)1677/1678 Mrs Mary Gold Wodell b1651
   d1687 dau/o Francis Gold (Gould) & Rose____ & wid/o John
   Waddell, m(2)1687 Mrs Hannah Clarke Frizzell b1646 of Woburn,
   MA dau/o William Clark & Margery____ & wid/o William Frizzell of
   Concord - the immigrant GBR441; CFA(4)
   George - of MA, b1688 of Chelmsford d1760 captain on Dorchester
   records of the military co & justice of the peace, m(1)1706/1707
   Mary Turel of Milton, MA b1683 d1736 dau/o Daniel Turel & Anna
   Barrell of Boston, m(2)1737 Elizabeth Withington b1696 d1774
   dau/o Philip Withington & Thankful____ - desc/o George (Peter)
   Talbot CFA(4)
   George - of MA, b1714 d1772, m(1)1742 Hannah Wentworth,
   m(2)1763 Mrs Abigail Dean Bacon - desc/o George (Peter) Talbot
   CFA(4)
   Hannah - of MA, b1712, m1735 David Gay of Stoughton - desc/o
   George (Peter) Talbot CFA(4)
   Jerusha - of MA, b1721, m1746 Jona Capen - desc/o George (Peter)
   Talbot CFA(4)
   John - of MD, m Frances Wogan - desc/o Anne Arundel CFA(5)288
   John - of NJ, b abt 1645 d1727, Anglican missionary clergyman, m(1)
   Isabel Jenney, m(2) Mrs Anne Herbert - desc/o Capt Henry Isham
   GBR339
   Mary - of MA, b1707/1708, m abt 1729 George Allin of Stoughton -
   desc/o George (Peter) Talbot CFA(4)
   Mary - of MD, m1706 Robert Dillon - desc/o Anne Arundel CFA(5)289

TALBOT (cont.)

Capt Peter - of MA, b1716/1717 d1793 Stoughton, served as captain in Revolutionary War, Lexington Alarm, member of the Committee of Correspondence of Stoughton, m(1)1744 Abigail Wheeler b1719 Concord d1750, m(2)1752 Mary Bailey, m(3)1784 Rebecca Decker - desc/o George (Peter) Talbot CFA(4)

Peter IV (called Peter, Jr) - of MA & ME, b1745 Stoughton, MA d1838, representative to MA General Court 1812, surveyor; had lumber & shipping interests; moved from MA to ME at time of marriage, m1771 Brookline, MA, Lucy Hammond b1752 d1831 - desc/o George (Peter) Talbot CFA(4)

Sarah - of MA, b1719, m1739 Benjamin White - desc/o George (Peter) Talbot CFA(4)

Susan - of MD, m Nicholas Morris - desc/o Anne Arundel CFA(5)289

Valentine - of MD, d1749, m Mary Tobin - desc/o Anne Arundel CFA(5)288

TALIAFERRO Col Charles - of VA, b1735 d1798, m1758 Isabel McCulloch dau/o the Reverend Roderick McCulloch - desc/o Col George Reade DBR(2)830

Lieut Colonel John - of VA, commander of VA forces against the Indians 1692, sheriff & justice of Essex Co VA 1699, m Sarah Smith dau/o Major Lawrence Smith - desc/o Col George Reade DBR(2)830

Capt Richard - of VA, b1706 d1748, m1726 Rose Anne Berryman of Goochland Co VA - desc/o Col George Reade DBR(2)830

TALMAN Mary - of CT, b abt 1724 d1778, m1741/1742 Deacon David Dudley - desc/o Anna Lloyd J&K321; ECD(2)193

TANEY Michael III - of MD, d1743, m(1)____, m(2) Sarah____ - desc/o Rev Robert Brooke CHB404

Michael 4th - of MD - desc/o Rev Robert Brooke J&K203; CHB404

Sarah - of MD, m1761/1762 Capt Ignatius Fenwick III - desc/o Rev Robert Brooke CHB404

TANNER Joshua - b1757, m Thankful Tefft - desc/o Joan Vincent LDS98

TASKER Anne - of MD, b1723 d1813, m1741 Samuel Ogle b abt 1702 d1752 governor of MD for three terms - desc/o William Bladen J&K282; CHB46; BCD46; DBR(2)764; GBR152; MG(2)426

Col Benjamin - of MD, b1720 d1760 unmarried, member of Council 1744/1760 & secretary of MD - desc/o William Bladen MG(2)426

Elizabeth - of MD, b1726 d1789, m1747 Christopher Lowndes - desc/o William Bladen CHB45; BCD45; MG(2)426

Frances - of MD, m1754 Robert Carter of Nominy, Westmoreland, VA - desc/o William Bladen MG(2)426

Rebecca - of MD, b1724, m1749 Daniel Dulany b1721 d1797 mayor of Annapolis 1764, member of the council from 1757 & secretary of the state of MD - desc/o William Bladen CHB44; BCD45; GBR151; MG(2)426

TAYLOE Anne Ogle - of VA, m Henry Howell Lewis - desc/o William Bladen CHB46; BCD46

TAYLOR Alice Thornton - of VA, b1773, m abt 27 Sep 1791 Washington Berry - desc/o Anne Lovelace GVFHB(3)340

Ann - of VA, m____ Eastman - desc/o James Taylor NFA27

TAYLOR (cont.)

Ann - of VA, m(1) Robert Taliaferro, m(2) John Todd - desc/o Anne Lovelace GVFHB(3)340

Betsy - b1760, m Elijah Putnam - desc/o Henry Rice LDS39

Rev Daniel - b abt 1690 d1747/1748, an early graduate of Yale & pioneer minister of Orange, New Jersey, m Elizabeth___ & had issue - desc/o Humphrey Davie TAG(23)212

David - b1720, m Betty Houghton - desc/o Henry Rice LDS39

Edmund - of VA, m Anne Lewis - desc/o James Taylor AWW110

Maj Edward - of MA, m Sarah Ingersoll - desc/o Mabel Harklakenden CHB268; BCD268 - desc/o Gov George Wyllys DBR(2)427

Eldred - of MA, b1708 d1777, m(2) Thankful Day - desc/o Mabel Harlakenden CHB268; MCB355; MCD231; BCD268 - desc/o Gov George Wyllys DBR(2)427

Elizabeth - m Nathaniel Greene Jr - desc/o Anne Marbury GBR234 - desc/o Catherine Hamby GBR394

Elizabeth - of VA & KY, m Thomas Bell - desc/o James Taylor NFA4, 30, 59

Elizabeth - b1767 d1856, m1786 Rev Josiah Rucks - desc/o Col George Reade DBR(1)687

Elizabeth - of MA, m Andrew Perkins - desc/o Mabel Harlakenden CHB268; BCD268

Elizabeth - of VA, m1776 Andrew Glassell - desc/o James Taylor NFA29

Elizabeth - of VA, b1763, m Capt Thomas Minor & had issue - desc/o Anne Lovelace GVFHB(3)340

Erasmus - of VA, b1715 d1794, m1749 Jane Moore - desc/o James Taylor NFA29

Frances - of VA, b1700 d1761, m1741 Ambrose Madison - desc/o James Taylor AWW111; NFA2, 27

Frances - of VA, m Garland Burnby - desc/o James Taylor NFA29

Frances - of VA, b1753 d1815, m1789 Rev Nathaniel Moore - desc/o Col George Reade CHB255; ECD214; BCD255

George - of VA, b1711 d1792, m(1)1738 Rachel Gibson, m(2) Sarah Taliaferro - desc/o James Taylor NFA3, 28, 29

Hancock - of VA, m Annah Hornsby Lewis - desc/o Col Richard Lee NFA59

Hannah - of VA, b1718, m Nicholas Battaille - desc/o James Taylor NFA29

Hope - of NJ, b1674 Barnstable d1705 Yarmouth, MA, m abt 1693 Joseph Sturgis b1664 Yarmouth d1747 Yarmouth, son of Edward Sturgis & Temperance Gorham - desc/o Edward FitzRandolph NE(97)276

Howell - b1754 d1845, m Susan Young - desc/o Mildred Reade DBR(1)209

Col Hubbard - of VA, b1760 d1845, m1782 Clarissa Minor b1782 d1842 of Spotsylvania Co, they had issue nine children. Moved to Fayette, later Clark Co, Kentucky in 1790 - desc/o Anne Lovelace GVFHB(3)340

James - of VA abt 1635, b1615 d1698, m(1) Frances___, m(2)1682 Mary Gregory - the immigrant AWW110; NFA1, 26; sufficient proof

TAYLOR (cont.)

of alleged royal ancestry is lacking

James - of VA, b1668 d1729, m Martha Thompson - desc/o James Taylor AWW111; NFA2, 26

James - of VA, b1703 d1784, m(1) Alice Thornton Catlett, m(2) Elizabeth McGrath - desc/o James Taylor AWW111; NFA27

James - of VA, b1732 d1814, m(1) Ann Hubbard, m(2) Elizabeth Fitzhugh - desc/o James Taylor AWW111; NFA28

Gen James - of KY, b1769 d1848, m1795 Keturah Moss moved to Newport, Kentucky & left issue - desc/o Anne Lovelace CHB501; GVFHB(3)340 - desc/o James Taylor AWW111; NFA28

Jane - of VA, m Charles Pitt Howard - desc/o James Taylor NFA29

John - of VA, b1696, m Catharine Pendleton - desc/o James Taylor AWW110; NFA27

Rev John - of NY, b1762 d1840, m1789 Elizabeth Terry - desc/o Mabel Harlakenden MCB355; MCD231

Jonathan - b abt 1692, m Rebecca Powers - desc/o Henry Rice LDS39

Joseph - b1763 d1832, m1777 Mercy Knowles - desc/o Joseph Kirkbride DBR(3)213

Lucy - of VA, m Rev Alexander Balmaine - desc/o James Taylor NFA29

Lucy - of VA, b1759, m James Eubank & had issue - desc/o Anne Lovelace GVFHB(3)340

Martha - of VA, b1702, m Thomas Chew - desc/o James Taylor AWW111; NFA27

Martha - m1710 Rev Azariah Mather of Saybrook, CT b1685 d1736 - desc/o Humphrey Davie TAG(23)212

Martha - b abt 1735 - desc/o Margaret Wyatt RAA61 - desc/o Thomas Newberry RAA118

Mary - of VA, b1688, m(1) Henry Pendleton, m(2) Edmund Watkins - desc/o James Taylor NFA27

Mary - m1704, m Isaac Pratt b1677 son of John Pratt - desc/o Humphrey Davie TAG(23)212

Mary - of CT, b1731 d1807, m1754 Samuel Comstock Betts - desc/o Margaret Wyatt CHB541

Mary Louise - of VA - desc/o Col Richard Lee NFA59

Mildred - of VA, m William Morton - desc/o James Taylor NFA29

Mildred - of VA, b1724 m____ Thomas - desc/o James Taylor NFA29

Naomi - b1695 - desc/o Richard Harlakenden RAA102

Reuben - of CT, b1703 d1754 - desc/o Margaret Wyatt CHB541; RAA61 - desc/o Thomas Newberry RAA118

Lieut Col Richard - of VA & KY, b1741, m1779 Sarah Dabney Strother - desc/o James Taylor NFA6, 30, 49, 59

Robert - of VA, m Frances Pendleton - desc/o James Taylor NFA29

Sarah - of VA, b1676 m____ Powell - desc/o James Taylor NFA26

Seth - of NJ, b1677 Barnstable, m1701 Susanna Sturgis d1751 dau/o Thomas Sturgis & Abigail Lothrop - desc/o Edward FitzRandolph NE(97)276

Sophia - of CT, b1774 d1847, m1798 John Mather - desc/o Gov George Wyllys DBR(2)427

Tabitha - of VA, b1713, m T Wild - desc/o James Taylor NFA29

Wait - of CT, b1693, m Jochin Gregory - desc/o Margaret Wyatt

TAYLOR (cont.)
DBR(3)126
Zachary - of VA, b1707 d1768, m(1) Elizabeth Lee, m(2) Esther
Blackburn - desc/o James Taylor AWW111; NFA2, 28
Lieut Zachary - of VA, m Alice Chew - desc/o James Taylor NFA4, 30,
59
TAZEWELL Littleton Waller - of VA, b1774 d1860 distinguished
statesman; lawyer, United States senator & governor of VA son of
Honorable Henry Tazewell b1753 d1799 & Elizabeth Waller b1754
d1777 - desc/o Col Nathaniel Littleton NE(41)364/368 - desc/o Col
John Waller GVFHB(5)722
TEACKLE Catherine - of VA, b1768, m1786 Charles Smith of Moratico
Hall, Richmond Co & had issue - desc/o Margaret Nelson
HSF(10)199
Elizabeth Custis - of VA, b1742 d1822, m1759 Isaac Smith b1734
d1813 of Selma, near Eastville, Northampton Co - desc/o Margaret
Nelson CRL(2)114; HSF(10)199
Elizabeth Upshur - of VA, b1776 d1837, m(1) Dr George Yerby of
Lancaster Co & had issue, m(2)1808 John Upshur of Brownsville
b1761 d1842 & had issue - desc/o Margaret Nelson HSF(10)199
George - of VA, b1770, m Frances Bowdoin, dau/o John Bowdoin &
Grace Stringer & left no issue - desc/o Margaret Nelson HSF(10)199
Major John - of VA, b1693 of Craddock, Accomack Co d1721
Yorktown, m1710 Susanna Upshur b abt 1693 dau/o Arthur
Upshur II & Sarah Browne - desc/o Margaret Nelson
CRL(2)114,118; HSF(10)188
John - of VA, b1753 of Kegotank, Accomack Co d1817, m Elizabeth
Dennis b1760 d1811 - desc/o Margaret Nelson HSF(10)204
Col John II - of VA, b1762 of Craddock, Accomack Co d1811, m1783
Anne Stockley Upshur b abt 1765 dau/o Thomas Upshur II of
Brownsville & Anne (Stockley) Upshur & had issue - desc/o
Margaret Nelson HSF(10)198
Levin - of VA, b1718/1719 d1794, m(1)1752 Joice Gore Justice
b1735/1736 d1760 - desc/o Margaret Nelson HSF(10)188
Levin - of VA, m(2)1765 Anne Arbuckle b1738 d1794 - desc/o
Margaret Nelson HSF(10)188
Margaret - of VA, b1720/1721 d1794, m1738 Col Edward Robins
b1717 d1779 - desc/o Margaret Nelson HSF(10)188
Sarah - of VA, b1759 d1785, m Dr John Boisnard & had issue -
desc/o Margaret Nelson HSF(10)198
Susanna - of VA, b1766, m (her cousin) John Robins of Salt Grove,
Northampton Co, b1740 & had issue - desc/o Margaret Nelson
HSF(10)198
Thomas II - of VA, b1711 d1769, m1732 Elizabeth (Betty) Custis
b1718 dau/o Thomas Custis of Deep Creek, Accomack Co b abt
1685 d1721 & Anne Kendall - desc/o Margaret Nelson CRL(2)114
Col Thomas III - of VA, b abt 1734 of Craddock, Accomack Co d1784,
m abt 1757 Elizabeth Upshur b abt 1740 d1782 dau/o Abel
Upshur I & Rachel Revell - desc/o Margaret Nelson HSF(10)198
Thomas IV - of VA, b1763, m Catherine Stockley & had issue - desc/o
Margaret Nelson HSF(10)198

TEACKLE (cont.)

Upshur - of VA, b1719/1720 d1774, m Margaret (Custis) Scarburgh - desc/o Margaret Nelson HSF(10)189

TEMPLE Maj Joseph of VA, m Anne Arnold - desc/o William Temple CHB457; WAC84

Joseph - of VA, m Mary Hill - desc/o Maj Joseph Temple WAC84

Sarah or Sally - of VA, m John Tunstall - desc/o William Temple CHB457

Sarah - of MA, bp 1769 d1839, m1786 John Jacob Seibles - desc/o John Nelson DBR(1)611; DBR(2)796

William - of VA, m____ - the immigrant CHB457; sufficient proof of alleged royal ancestry is lacking

William - of MA, bp 1735 d1785, m(1) Sarah Mehitable Whipple - desc/o John Nelson DBR(1)611; DBR(2)796

TERRELL David - of VA, m Mary Ann Mounger - desc/o Thomas Wingfield GVFHB(5)834

Joel - of VA, m Lucy Ragland - desc/o Thomas Wingfield GVFHB(5)834

Peter Burford - of VA, b1764, m1795 Penelope Jones b1776 - desc/o Thomas Wingfield DBR(1)33/34; GVFHB(5)834

Richmond - of VA, m Kitty Garland Butler - desc/o Thomas Wingfield GVFHB(5)834

Thomas - of VA, m Sarah Skelton - desc/o Thomas Wingfield GVFHB(5)834

TERRY Eliphalet - of CT, b1776 d1849, m1817 Lydia Coit - desc/o Richard Lyman CHB149; BCD149

Esther - m William Kibbe - desc/o Richard Lyman MCD249

Mahitable - b1774 - desc/o Amy Wyllys RAA126

Michal - b1736 - desc/o Amy Wyllys RAA126

THACHER Bathsheba - of MA, m1769 Jeremiah Dummer - desc/o Rev John Oxenbridge CHB166; BCD166

Elizabeth - b1682 d1718, m Deacon Samuel Niles - desc/o Rev John Oxenbridge DBR(1)369; DBR(2)511, 609

Lucy - of MA, b1769 d1844, m1788 Abraham Anderson b1758 d1844 son of Abraham Anderson & Ann Collins-Cloutman - desc/o Gov Thomas Dudley NEFGM(1)78

Moses - of MA, b1766 d1845, m(1)1795 Mrs Sarah (Robinson) Read - desc/o Rev John Oxenbridge DBR(1)623, 674; DBR(3)23, 27

Nathaniel - of MA, b1767 d1824, m1787 Lydia Place - desc/o Rev John Oxenbridge DBR(1)276

Rev Oxenbridge - of MA, m Sarah Kent - desc/o Rev John Oxenbridge CHB166; BCD166

Rev Peter II - of MA, b1688 d1744, m1710/1711 Mary Prince - desc/o Rev John Oxenbridge DBR(1)276, 623, 674; DBR(3)23, 27

Rev Peter III - of MA, b1716 d1785, m1749/1750 Bethiah Carpenter - desc/o Rev John Oxenbridge DBR(1)623, 674; DBR(3)23, 27

Capt Samuel - of MA, b1717 d1795, m1758 Mrs Sarah Kent - desc/o Rev John Oxenbridge DBR(1)276

Rev Thomas - of MA, d1640/1641, m Margery____ - the immigrant EDV117; EO2 (3)464, 465 sufficient proof of alleged royal ancestry is lacking

THACKER Alice - of VA, b1671, m1688 William Gough - desc/o Martha
    Eltonhead VG236; CFA(5)136

Anne - of VA, b1728, m Henry Washington son of John Washington &
    Catherine Whiting - desc/o Martha Eltonhead VG236

Edwin - of VA, b1665 d1719, vestryman for Middlesex Parish 1692,
    church warden 1695 & clerk of Middlesex 1694/1704, m
    Frances____ - desc/o Martha Eltonhead VG236; CFA(5)136

Col Edwin - of VA, b1695 d1745 sheriff of Middlesex 1721, burgess
    1723 & vestryman Christ Church Parish 1726/1740, m
    Elizabeth____ d1752 - desc/o Martha Eltonhead VG236

Elizabeth - of VA, b1694, m1712 John Vivian - desc/o Martha
    Eltonhead VG236

Frances - of VA, b1722, m1746 Lewis Burwell b1716 d1779 of
    Kingsmill, James City Co - desc/o Martha Eltonhead VG236

Henry - of VA, b1663 d bef 1714, high sheriff of Middlesex Co 1703 &
    justice 1706, m(1)____, m(2) Elizabeth____ d1714 - desc/o Martha
    Eltonhead VG236; CFA(5)136

Capt Henry - of VA, b1698, m 1727 Mary Elizabeth Clowder dau/o
    Jeremiah Clowder - desc/o Martha Eltonhead VG236

Lettice - of VA, b1704, m1728 Thomas Todd - desc/o Martha
    Eltonhead VG236

Martha - of VA, b1667, m1683 Thomas Hickman - desc/o Martha
    Eltonhead VG236; CFA(5)136

Martha - of VA, b1701, m1723 Rice Curtis - desc/o Martha Eltonhead
    VG236

THOMAS Ann - of PA, b1729 d1809, m1762 Samuel Williams - desc/o Dr
    Thomas Wynne ECD(2)331; DBR(3)762

Daniel - b abt 1754 - desc/o Tristram Thomas RAA131

Daniel - b1776 - desc/o Tristram Thomas RAA131

Elijah - b1775 - desc/o Tristram Thomas RAA131

Sir George - of PA & DE, b abt 1695 d1774 governor of PA & DE, m
    Elizabeth King - desc/o Margaret Tyndale GBR428

Judge Joshua - of MA, b1751 d1821, m1786 Isabella Stevenson -
    desc/o Mary Launce DBR(1)545

Maverick - of MA, b1694, m Joanna English, dau/o James English &
    Love ____ - desc/o Mary Gye NE(96)241

Nathan - b1762 - desc/o Tristram Thomas RAA131

Peter - of MA, b1638, m Elizabeth Burrough - desc/o Mary Gye
    NE(96)241

Philip - of MD 1651/1652 - the immigrant EDV112; sufficient proof of
    alleged royal ancestry is lacking

Rees - of PA, m1758 Elizabeth Harry - desc/o Martha Awbrey CHB299;
    BCD299

Robert - b1733 - desc/o Tristram Thomas RAA131

Samuel - of MD, - desc/o Philip Thomas EDV112

Simon - b1712 - desc/o Tristram Thomas RAA131

Stephen - b1705 - desc/o Tristram Thomas RAA131

Tristram - of MD, chr 1629, m Ann Coursey - the immigrant RAA1,
    131; sufficient proof of alleged royal ancestry is lacking

Tristram - b1666 - desc/o Tristram Thomas RAA131

William - of PA, m1724 Elizabeth Harry - desc/o Martha Awbrey

THOMAS (cont.)
> CHB299; BCD299
> William - of PA, m1786 Naomi Walker - desc/o Martha Awbrey
> CHB299; BCD299

THOMPSON Alice Corbin - of VA, b1763 d1802, m1781 Capt John
> Hawkins - desc/o Col Richard Lee DBR(4)107; DBR(5)877
> Bridget - b1662, m1640/1641 Capt George Denison - desc/o Alice
> Freeman RAA132; TAG(13)1/8
> Charles Raphael - of MD, b1770 d1825, m1798 Ann Fauntleroy -
> desc/o Rev Robert Brooke DBR(2)375
> Dorothy - of CT, bp 1624 d1709, m1644 Thomas Parke - the
> immigrant ECD(2)150; DBR(1)339, 594 - desc/o Alice Freeman
> RAA132; GBR436
> Eunice - b1722 - desc/o Alice Freeman RAA132
> John - of NY 1634 - the immigrant EDV50; sufficient proof of alleged
> royal ancestry is lacking
> John - b1699 - desc/o Alice Freeman RAA132
> Judge John - of VA, m Elizabeth Howison - desc/o Col George Reade
> CHB419
> Littlebury - of NC, b abt 1769 m____ & moved to Mississippi, where he
> grew wealthy & died just before the outbreak of the Civil War -
> desc/o William Strother HSF(5)293
> Martha - of VA, m James Taylor - desc/o Sir Robert Thompson NFA51
> Mary - of MA, m Joseph Wise - desc/o Alice Freeman GBR436
> Mary - bp 1653, m1673 Samuel Hawley - desc/o Alice Tomes THC310
> Mary - of VA, b1679, m James Day - desc/o William Thompson
> AWW110 - desc/o Peter Montague FFF80
> Mildred - of VA, m Capt George Gray - desc/o Col George Reade
> CHB419
> Philip Rootes of VA, m(2) Sally Slaughter - desc/o Col George Reade
> J&K230; CHB249; BCD249 - desc/o Col William Bernard BCD38
> Raphael - of MD, b1736 d1790, m1760 Susannah Cavenaugh - desc/o
> Rev Robert Brooke DBR(2)375
> Robert Lewis - m1761 d1791, m1783 Lucy Hunter - desc/o Col George
> Reade DBR92)836
> Rodes - of VA, b1754 d aft 1780, m abt 1776 - desc/o Charles Rhodes
> ECD(3)243
> Sir Roger - of VA, m____ - the immigrant NFA51; sufficient proof of
> alleged royal ancestry is lacking
> William - of VA - the immigrant AWW110; sufficient proof of alleged
> royal ancestry is lacking
> William - of VA - desc/o Sir Roger Thompson NFA51

THORNDYKE William - the immigrant EDV20; sufficient proof of alleged
> royal ancestry is lacking

THORNTON Elizabeth - of VA, m Thomas Meriwether - desc/o Col George
> Reade DBR(5)159, 210
> Elizabeth - m Edwin Conway Jr - desc/o Anthony Savage GBR253
> Francis - of VA, m Alice Savage - desc/o Anthony Savage AAP143
> Maj George - of VA, m Mary Alexander - desc/o Col George Reade
> DBR(4)847; DBR(5)547, 555, 567, 571
> Lieut Col John - m Jane Washington - desc/o Col George Reade

THORNTON (cont.)
DBR(2)633
Margaret - m William Strother Jr - desc/o Anthony Savage AAP147;
GBR253
Mary - m1762 Gen William Woodford - desc/o Col George Reade
DBR(3)570
Nancy - m1781 Hugh Rogers - desc/o Col George Reade DBR(2)633
THOROUGHGOOD Capt Adam - of VA 1621, b1602 d1640, m Sarah
Offley - the immigrant WAC60; CRL(2)116; CRL(3)121, 122;
sufficient proof of alleged royal ancestry is lacking
Lieut Col Adam - of VA, m ____ Yeardley - desc/o Capt Adam
Thoroughgood WAC60
Elizabeth - of VA, m Capt John Michael - desc/o Capt Adam
Thoroughgood CRL(2)116
THROCKMORTON Albion - of VA, b1740 served in the Revolution as a
cornet in Lee's Legion & received bounty land for his services, m
Mary Webb & had issue - desc/o Robert Throckmorton
GVFWM(5)90
Ann - b1772 d1807, m1807 Joseph (or James) Russell - desc/o Robert
Throckmorton GVFWM(5)91; CFA(1)525
Deliverance - of RI, b abt 1645, m1669 Rev James Ashton, deputy to
the New Jersey General Assembly - desc/o John Throckmorton
ECD(3)262; DBR(1)178; DBR(5)1012
Elizabeth - of VA, dau/o Sir Thomas Throckmorton & Elizabeth
Berkeley, m Sir Thomas Dale d1619 governor of VA - the immigrant
GBR206
Elizabeth - of VA, m John Perry - desc/o Robert Throckmorton
AMB367; GVFWM(5)87; CFA(1)524
Elizabeth - of VA, m Barton Davis of Northumberand Co, VA - desc/o
Robert Throckmorton GVFWM(5)87
Elizabeth - of VA, b1769, m Ebenezer Potter - desc/o Robert
Throckmorton GVFWM(5)90
Frances - of VA, m Francis Whiting - desc/o Robert Throckmorton
GVFWM(5)87
Frances - of VA, b1733 d1794, m(1) William Debnam of Ware Parish,
m(2)1762 James Barbour III - desc/o Col George Reade ECD(2)231
- desc/o Col William Bernard MCD162 - desc/o Robert
Throckmorton GVFWM(5)87
Frances - of VA, b1765, m1783 Gen William Madison - desc/o Col
William Bernard CHB39; BCD38 - desc/o Col George Reade
CHB250; MCD272; BCD250 - desc/o Robert Throckmorton
CHB277, 359; BCD297; GVFWM(5)90
Gabriel - of VA bef 1684, b1665 d1737, justice & sheriff of Gloucester
Co, m1690 Frances Cooke dau/o Mordecai Cooke of Ware Parish,
Gloucester Co, VA - desc/o Robert Throckmorton DBR(1)711;
DBR(5)125; AMB367; GVFWM(5)87; CFA(1)524; CHB297; MCB187,
188, 200; MCD299, BCD297; DBR(5)1011; WAC35
Gabriel - of VA, b1735, m in or bef 1761 Judith Edmundson dau/o
Thomas Edmundson of Essex - desc/o Robert Throckmorton
GVFWM(5)87
Job - of RI, b1650 d1709, m1684/1685 Sarah Leonard b1600

THROCKMORTON (cont.)

> d1743/1744 - desc/o John Throckmorton DBR(3)142; AFA200; NE(98)67/72

Job - of RI, b1720 d1765, m1743 Mary Morford - desc/o John Throckmorton DBR(3)142

Job - of RI, b1761 d1839, m1784 Mary Robinson - desc/o John Throckmorton DBR(3)142, 143

John - of RI, bp 1601 d1687 son of Bassingbourne Throckmorton, citizen & alderman of Norwich & Mary Hill, m bef 1 Jul 1639 Rebecca____ (possibly a kinswoman of Edward Colvile) - the immigrant FLW173; ECD(3)262; DBR(1)178; DBR(3)141, 142; RAA1; AFA200; GBR236; NE(98)67/72, (111)271/279, (117)234

John - of VA, of Ellington & Ware parish b abt 1633 d1678, m Frances Mason dau/o Edward Mason & Elizabeth Locke - desc/o Robert Throckmorton DBR(1)711; DBR(5)125; AMB366; CFA(1)523

John Jr - of RI, b abt 1642 d1690, m1670 Alice Stout - desc/o John Throckmorton GBR236; NE(98)67/72

John - of NJ, b1688 d1741, m Mary____ - desc/o John Throckmorton AFA200

John - of VA, b1731 of Ware Parish, Gloucester Co, m(1) Rebecca Richardson dau/o William Richardson of Ware Parish, m(2) Elizabeth Cooke dau/o John Cooke of Gloucester Co - desc/o Robert Throckmorton GVFWM(5)88

Joseph - of RI, b1693 d1759, m abt 1716 Alice Cox - desc/o John Throckmorton DBR(3)142

Joseph - of NY, b1720 d1800, m1747 Mary Forman - desc/o John Throckmorton AFA200

Joseph Forman - of NJ, b1757 d1800, m Margaret____ - desc/o John Throckmorton AFA200

Lucy of VA, m175_ Robert Throckmorton - desc/o Col William Bernard CHB38; MCD161; BCD38 - desc/o Col George Reade CHB250; MCD272; BCD250 - desc/o Robert Throckmorton AMB367; GVFWM(5)88

Mary - of VA, m Dr William Taliaferro - desc/o Col George Reade AWW83

Mary - of VA, m(1) Richard Powell of Bugden, Hunts - desc/o Robert Throckmorton AMB366; CFA(1)523

Mary - of VA, m John Autrobus of London, m(2) Henry Keene of Bugden - desc/o Robert Throckmorton CFA(1)523

Mary - of VA, m Thomas Throckmorton - desc/o Robert Throckmorton GVFWM(5)87

Capt Mordecai - of VA, b abt 1696 d1767, capt Gloucester Co militia & sheriff of King & Queen Co, VA, m Mary Reade dau/o Thomas Reade of Ware Parish & Lucy Gwyn - desc/o Robert Throckmorton DBR(1)711; DBR(5)125; AMB367; GVFWM(5)88; CFA(1)524; CHB359; MCB186, 187, 200; MCD272, 299

Major Mordecai - of VA, d abt 1788 of Gloucester Co, served in the Revolution as captain of a company of minutemen from Gloucester, m1773 Mary Peyton b1758 dau/o Sir John Peyton, Baronet, of Isleham, Gloucester Co - desc/o Robert Throckmorton GVFWM(5)90/91

THROCKMORTON (cont.)

Patience - of RI, b abt 1640 d1676, m1655 John Coggeshall, deputy governor of Rhode Island - desc/o John Throckmorton NE(98)67/72

Patience - m Hugh Coward - desc/o John Throckmorton GBR236

Robert - of VA, bp 1609 d1664 son of Gabriel Throckmorton & Alice Bedell, m(1) Anne Chace or Chare dau/o Robert Chare or Chace, a citizen of London & Elizabeth Starkle, m(2) Judith Hetley, dau/o Thomas Hetley, alias Hedley of Brampton Hunts & Elizabeth Gore - the immigrant DBR(1)711; DBR(3)443; DBR(5)124, 125; AMB366; RAA1; GBR341; NGS(60)22/24; GVFWM(5)83/109; CFA(1)523

Robert - b1662 VA d1698 England, m Mary Bromsall - desc/o Robert Throckmorton CFA(1)524

Maj Robert - of VA, of Ware Parish, Gloucester Co, m(1)1730 Mary Lewis, m(2) Sarah Smith - desc/o Robert Throckmorton CHB297, 359; BCD297; AMB367; GVFWM(5)87; CFA(1)524

Robert - of VA, of Culpeper Co b1736, m175_ Lucy Throckmorton dau/o Capt Mordecai Throckmorton b1696 d1767, high sheriff of King & Queen Co, VA 1740 - desc/o Robert Throckmorton CHB297, 359; BCD297; GVFWM(5)90

Robert - of VA, d1796 of Roxton, Jefferson Co, justice of Berkeley Co in 1786 & sheriff of Frederick Co 1792, m1776 Catherine Robinson & had issue - desc/o Robert Throckmorton GVFWM(5)91, 92

Sarah - of VA, m1771 Peter Presley Thornton of Northumberland House, Northumberland Co, VA. lieutenant colonel of minutemen at the beginning of the Revolution and a member of the Convention of 1775 - desc/o Robert Throckmorton GVFWM(5)88

Thomas - of KY, b1739 d1826, of Frederick Co, member of the Kentucky House of Representatives & of the state senate from Nicholas Co, 1811/1816, m(1) Mary Throckmorton dau/o Robert Throckmorton, m(2) Mary Hooe dau/o John Hooe & Ann Fowke - desc/o Robert Throckmorton AMB367; GVFWM(5)91; CHB359; MCB186, 187, 200; MCD272, 299; DBR(1)711; DBR(5)126; CFA(1)524

Thomas - of KY, b1775 of Nicholas Co, Kentucky d1835, m Susan Morton b1776 & had issue - desc/o Robert Throckmorton AMB367; GVFWM(5)92; CFA(1)525

Warner - of VA, m Julia Langborne of King William Co - desc/o Col George Reade AWW83 - desc/o Robert Throckmorton GVFWM(5)91

THROOP Daniel - b1669/1670, m Deborah Macey - desc/o William Throop LDS25

Mary - b1708, m Thomas Chapman - desc/o William Throop LDS28

Submit - b1706, m Samuel Murdock - desc/o William Throop LDS25

William (alias Adrian Scrope) - b abt 1637, m Mary Chapman - the immigrant LDS25, 28; EDV48, 49; TAG(63)53/54, (57)110/112; RAA no longer accepted as being of royal descent

William - b1678/9, m Martha Collyer or Colyn - desc/o William Throop LDS28

THURSTON Hannah - of RI, b1701 d1753, m1723 William Cornell - desc/o Jeremy Clarke DBR(3)672

TIBBETTS Abigail - b1700 - desc/o Rose Stoughton RAA119
  Ann - b1697 - desc/o Rose Stoughton RAA119
TICHENOR Daniel - of NJ, b1704 d1776, m(2) bef 1759 Susanna____ -
  desc/o Obadiah Bruen DBR(1)388; DBR(2)498; DBR(5)170
  Susanna - of NJ, b abt 1760 d1822, m abt 1778 Juniah Beach -
  desc/o Obadiah Bruen DBR(1)388; DBR(2)498; DBR(5)170
TILDEN Elder Nathaniel - of MA bef 1628, d1641 - the immigrant
  EDV134; sufficient proof of alleged royal ancestry is lacking
  Phoebe - b1751 d1795, m1774 Joseph Hatch - desc/o Rev John
  Oxenbridge DBR(2)511, 609
TILGHMAN (TILLMAN) Anna Maria - of MD, b1709 d1763, m(1) William
  Hemsley, m(2) Col Robert Lloyd - desc/o Richard Tilghman
  MG(2)449; CFA(5)440
  Anna Maria - of MD, b1737 d1768, m1764 Charles Goldsborough
  b1740 d1769, their son, Charles Goldsborough was governor of MD
  1818, m(2) Right Reverend Robert Smith, Bishop of South Carolina
  d1801 - desc/o Richard Tilghman CRL(1)110; MG(2)450;
  CFA(5)441
  Anna Maria - of MD, b1755 d1843, m1783 Col Tench Tilghman (her
  cousin) who carried the news of Cornwallis' surrender, from
  Yorktown to the Congress in Philadelphia - desc/o Richard
  Tilghman MG(2)454; CFA(5)441
  Anna Maria - of MD, b1759 d1834, m Henry Ward Pearcy of Cecil Co,
  MD - desc/o Richard Tilghman MG(2)449
  Anna Maria - of MD, b1774 d1858, m1797 Judge Nicholas Brice
  b1771 d1851 - desc/o Richard Tilghman MG(2)458
  Christopher - of VA 1638, bp 1612, was a landed proprietor living in
  Accomack Co in 1638, son of Christopher Tilghman, m Ruth
  Devonshire - the immigrant DBR(5)848; RAA1; GBR159
  Edward - of MD, b1713 d1786, high sheriff of Queen Anne Co, MD &
  was a justice of the county, Speaker of the House. He was styled
  captain in 1746 & colonel in 1756 indicating that he held these
  ranks in the militia of the county, m(1) Anna Maria Turbutt, dau/o
  Major William Turbutt of Queen Anne Co, m(2)1749 Elizabeth Chew
  b1720 dau/o Samuel Chew of Dover & Mary Galloway, m(3)1759
  Juliana Carroll b1729 dau/o Dominick Carroll of Cecil Co & Mary
  Sewall - desc/o Richard Tilghman MG(2)450, 451; CFA(5)441
  Edward - of MD, b1750/1751 d1815, m1774 Elizabeth Chew b1751
  dau/o Chief Justice Benjamin Chew of Pennsylvania - desc/o
  Richard Tilghman MG(2)456; CFA(5)441
  Edward - of VA, b abt 1760 d1815, m(2) Sarah (Davis) Smarr - desc/o
  Christopher Tilghman DBR(5)848
  Elizabeth - of MD, b1749 d1836, m1771 William Cooke of Annapolis
  d1817 son of John Cooke of Prince George's Co & Sophia Sewall -
  desc/o Richard Tilghman MG(2)449, 455; CFA(5)441
  Elizabeth - of MD, m Richard Tilghman (her cousin) of the Hermitage,
  son of Richard Tilghman - desc/o Richard Tilghman MG(2)451;
  CFA(5)441
  Col Frisby - of MD, b1773 d1847, m(1)1795 Anna Maria Ringgold
  d1817, m(2)1819 Louisa Lamar - desc/o Richard Tilghman
  MG(2)455 - desc/o Sir Dudley Diggs J&K255

TILGHMAN (TILLMAN) (cont.)

Henrietta Maria - of MD, b1707 d1771, m(1)1731 George Robins, m(2)1747 William Goldsborough - desc/o Richard Tilghman MG(2)449; CFA(5)440

Henrietta Maria - of MD, b1763 d1796, m Lloyd Tilghman (her cousin) son of Matthew - desc/o Richard Tilghman MG(2)452

James - of MD, b1716 d1793, lawyer & represented Talbot Co in the MD assembly, m Anna Francis dau/o Tench Francis of Fansley, Talbot Co, MD - desc/o Richard Tilghman MG(2)452;

James - of VA, b1743 d1809, member of the legislature, attorney general of MD & judge of the court of appeals, m(1)1769 Susanna Steuart d1774 dau/o Dr George Steuart of Annapolis, m(2)1778 Elizabeth Johns dau/o Kinsey Johns of West River - desc/o Richard Tilghman MG(2)454, 455

James - of MD, b1748 d1796, represented Talbot Co in the legislature & was associate judge, m Elizabeth Buely - desc/o Richard Tilghman MG(2)457

John - of VA, b1682 d1738, m Margaret Harrison - desc/o Christopher Tilghman DBR(5)848

John - of VA, b1734 d1785, m1758 Mary Simmons - desc/o Christopher Tilghman DBR(5)848

Lloyd - of MD, b1749 d1811, m1785 Henrietta Maria Tilghman b1763 d1796 dau/o his uncle James Tilghman - desc/o Richard Tilghman MG(2)459; CFA(5)440

Margaret - of MD, b1742 d1817, m1763 Charles Carroll Barrister b1723 d1783, they had two children, twins, who d in infancy - desc/o Richard Tilghman MG(2)454; CFA(5)440

Margaret - of MD, b1744, m Richard Tilghman (her cousin) son of Matthew Tilghman - desc/o Richard Tilghman MG(2)450

Mary - of MD, b1655, m Matthew Ward d1677 of Talbot Co, MD, her only son Major Gen Matthew Tilghman Ward b1677 d1741 was Speaker of the MD Assembly, chief justice of the provincial court & major-general of the Eastern Shore militia, m twice but left no issue - desc/o Richard Tilghman MG(2)448; CFA(5)439

Mary - of MD, b1702 d1736, m1721 James Earle - desc/o Richard Tilghman MG(2)449; CFA(5)439

Mary - of MD, b1753, m Edward Roberts of Talbot Co, MD - desc/o Richard Tilghman MG(2)450

Mary - of MD, m Richard Tilghman (her cousin) son of Matthew Tilghman - desc/o Richard Tilghman MG(2)451; CFA(5)441

Matthew - of MD, b1718 d1790, was adopted at the age of 15 by his childless cousin Maj Gen Matthew Tilghman, was one of the justices of Talbot Co & represented Talbot Co in the MD Assembly. Throughout the Revolution he played a leading part in the affairs of MD. He was a statesman & exerted a profound influence on the policy of MD during the Revolution & upon the formation of the constitution of the state, m1741 Anna Lloyd b1723 d1794 dau/o James Lloyd - desc/o Richard Tilghman MG(2)453, 454; CFA(5)440

Matthew - of MD, b1760, member of the legislature for Kent Co, & Speaker of the House, m1788 Sarah Smyth dau/o Thomas Smyth of Chestertown - desc/o Richard Tilghman MG(2)456; CFA(5)441

TILGHMAN (TILLMAN) (cont.)

Col Peregrine - of MD, b1741 d1807, member of the MD Convention for Talbot Co, state senate & colonel of the 4th Battalion of Talbot Co, m Deborah Lloyd dau/o Col Robert Lloyd of Hope & Anna Maria Tilghman - desc/o Richard Tilghman MG(2)454

Philemon - of MD, b1760 d1797, officer in the British Navy, returned to MD and became a farmer, m Harriet Milbanke, dau/o Admiral Mark Milbanke, R.N. third son of Sir Ralph Milbanke, Baronet - desc/o Richard Tilghman MG(2)458

Rebecca - of MD, d1725, m abt 1681 Simon Wilmer d1699 of Kent Co, MD - desc/o Richard Tilghman MG(2)448; CFA(5)439

Richard - of MD 1661, b1626 d1675/1676, eminent surgeon in London & one of the petitioners for the life of Charles I, doctor in MD from 1669/1671 was commissioned high sheriff of Talbot Co, son of Oswald Tilghman & Elizabeth Packham, m in England, Maria Foxley d1699/1702 - the immigrant CRL(1)110; GBR159; MG(2)443/459; CFA(5)439

Col Richard - of MD, b1672 of the Hermitage, Talbot Co d1738, member MD Assembly & chancellor of the province, m1700 Anna Maria Lloyd b1676 d1748 dau/o Col Philemon Lloyd of Talbot Co, MD & Henrietta Maria Neale - desc/o Richard Tilghman CRL(1)110; MG(2)448, 449; CFA(5)439

Col Richard - of MD, b1705 of the Hermitage, Queen Anne Co d1766, justice of the provincial court of MD 1746/1766, m Susanna Frisby b1718 dau/o Peregrine Frisby of Cecil Co, MD & Elizabeth Sewall - desc/o Richard Tilghman MG(2)449; CFA(5)439

Lieut Col Richard - of MD, b1739 d1810, lieut col of the lower battalion of Queen Anne Co, m Elizabeth Tilghman (his cousin) b1748 d1767 dau/o Col Edward Tilghman - des/o Richard Tilghman MG(2)454

Richard - of MD, b1740 d1809, m1784 Mary Gibson b1766 d1790 dau/o John Gibson of Talbot Co - des/o Richard Tilghman MG(2)456

Maj Richard - of MD, b1746 d1805, First major of the 5th battalion of Queen Anne Co MD, m(1) (his cousin) Margaret Tilghman b1744 d1779 dau/o William Tilghman of Grasse, m(2) Mary Tilghman b1762 d1793 dau/o Col Edward Tilghman of Wye - desc/o Richard Tilghman MG(2)458; CFA(5)440

Roger - of VA, d1716, m(2)1680 Susannah Parham - desc/o Christopher Tilghman DBR(5)848

Susanna - of MD, m Richard Ireland Jones - desc/o Richard Tilghman MG(2)451; CFA(5)441

Col Tench - of MD, b1744 d1786, captain of a Pennsylvania battalion of the Flying Camp; was on duty at Washington's headquarters as military secretary, 1776 & was commissioned lieutenant colonel, aide-de-camp, & military secretary to General Washington 1777. A brave & efficient officer, he was selected to bear to Congress the news of the surrender of Cornwallis at Yorktown. By act of Congress, 29 Oct 1781, it was resolved that the Board of War be directed to present to lieut colonel Tilghman, in the name of the United States in Congress assembled, a horse properly caparisoned & an elegant sword in testimony of their high opinion of his merit &

TILGHMAN (TILLMAN) (cont.)

ability; m1783 Anna Maria Tilghman dau/o Matthew Tilghman - desc/o Richard Tilghman MG(2)457

William - of MD, b1711 of Groves d1782, justice of Queen Anne's Co, MD, m1736 Margaret Lloyd (his cousin) b1714 dau/o James Lloyd & Ann Grundy - desc/o Richard Tilghman CRL(1)110; MG(2)449; CFA(5)440

William - of MD, b1745 d1800, m(1) Ann Kent, m(2) Anna Maria Lloyd dau/o Col Robert Lloyd of Hope, m(3) Eleanor Hall dau/o Francis Hall & wid/o Thomas Whetenhall Rozer - desc/o Richard Tilghman MG(2)455

William - of MD & PA, b1756 d1827, member of MD Convention, legislature & state senator, presiding judge of the third circuit of Pennsylvania, New Jersey & Delaware, president of the court of common pleas & chief justice of Pennsylvania, m Margaret Elizabeth Allen of Philadelphia - desc/o Richard Tilghman MG(2)458

TILLINGHAST John - of MA, b1766 d1839, m1803 Hannah (Sherman) Russell - desc/o Lawrence Wilkinson CHB277; BCD277

Joseph - b1677 d1763, m Freelove Stafford - desc/o Rev Pardon Tillinghast DBR(1)296

Judith - of RI, m John Freebody - desc/o Gov John Cranston GRFHG(1)283

Lydia - b1700, m1717 Job Almy - desc/o Rev Pardon Tillinghast DBR(1)296

Rev Pardon - of RI, b1622 Seven Cliffs, Sussex, England d1718 son of Pardon Tillinghast of Ifield, m Sarah Browne dau/o Rev Benjamin Browne of Ifield, Sussex, England - the immigrant FLW9; MCS25; DBR(1)295; TAG(37)34/38; sufficient proof of alleged royal ancestry is lacking

TILSON Thomas - of VA, b1767 d1829, m1792 Eunice Hubbell - desc/o Mary Wentworth ECD(2)304; FFF90

William - of MA, b1741 d1825, m1762 Mary Ransom - desc/o Mary Wentworth ECD(2)304; FFF90

TILTON Ann - b1763 - desc/o James Prescott RAA124

Josiah - of MA, b Deerfield d Deerfield 1860, m(1)1800 Sarah Dearborn - desc/o Capt Thomas Bradbury DBR(1)357

Sarah - of NH, b1743 d1814, m1764 Lieut Col Nathaniel Emerson - desc/o Henry Sherburne ECD(3)249

Sherburne - of NH, b1699 d1784, m1726 Ann Hilliard - desc/o Henry Sherburne ECD(3)249

TITUS Jacob - b1703 d1792, m1727 Margaret Jermain - desc/o Henry Willis DBR(2)429

John - of NY & NJ, d1761, m Rebecca____ - desc/o Edward Howell AFA50

Mary - of NJ, m Josiah Hard - desc/o Edward Howell AFA50

Philadelphia - m 1750 Adam Carman - desc/o Henry Willis DBR(2)429

TODD ____(Miss) Todd - of VA, m abt 1715 Jonathan Hide b abt 1682 d1718/1719 merchant of Gloucester Co, VA & had issue - desc/o Col William Bernard APP123 - desc/o Anne Lovelace GVFHB(3)288, 350

TODD (cont.)

Ann - of MD, b abt 1697 d abt 1745, m1713 Joseph Johnson of
Baltimore Co, son of Capt Henry Johnson & Elizabeth Goldsmith &
had issue - desc/o Anne Lovelace GVFHB(3)293, 360

Anne - of VA, b abt 1658, m1677 Miles Gibson b1648 d1692 justice of
Baltimore Co, a member of the General Assembly & high sheriff of
Baltimore Co, & had issue - desc/o Anne Lovelace APP406;
GVFHB(3)282, 293, 295, 363, 364

Anne - of VA, b1682 d1720 the first dau/o Capt Thomas & Elizabeth
(Bernard) Todd, m abt 1700 John Cooke of Wareham, Gloucester
Co, VA, son of Mordecai Cooke & had issue - desc/o Col William
Bernard APP119 - desc/o Anne Lovelace GVFHB(2)288, 320

Benjamin - b1693 - desc/o Peter Bulkeley RAA75

Bernard - of VA, b1750 d1814 member of the House of Delegates from
Charlotte 1789/1791, m Elizabeth Pollard dau/o William Pollard of
Hanover Co - desc/o Anne Lovelace DBR(2)725; GVFHB(3)312

Betty Waring - m Temple Walker of King & Queen Co, VA - desc/o
Anne Lovelace GVFHB(3)312

Catherine - of VA, b1750, m1764 Dr James Ware of Gloucester Co -
desc/o Anne Lovelace GVFHB(3)318

Chloe - b1763 - desc/o Peter Bulkeley RAA75

Capt Christopher - of VA, b1690 d1743, justice of Gloucester Co 1727,
m1718/1721 Elizabeth Mason b1701 d1764 dau/o Col Lemuel
Mason, a prominent man in lower Norfolk Co & had issue - desc/o
Col William Bernard APP122 - desc/o Anne Lovelace GVFHB(3)288,
317, 318

Christopher - of VA & TN, married and had a large family, removed to
Tennessee & lived to be over ninety - desc/o Anne Lovelace
GVFHB(3)312

Dorothy - of VA, m(1)____ Gordon, m(2) Thomas Edmundson of Essex
Co d1759 - desc/o Col William Bernard APP121 - desc/o Anne
Lovelace GVFHG(3)315, 316, 332

Elinor - of MD, m1753 John Ensor Jr of Baltimore Co, MD & left issue
- desc/o Anne Lovelace GVFHB(3)303

Elizabeth - of CT, b1690 d1752, m1708 Isaac Dayton - desc/o Rev
Peter Bulkeley DBR(5)971; RAA75

Elizabeth - of VA, b1710, m1728 Benjamin Hubbard - desc/o Anne
Lovelace CHB501; GVFHB(3)332

Elizabeth - b1736 - desc/o Peter Bulkeley RAA75

Elizabeth - of VA, m prior to 1736 James Barbour of Culpeper Co,
justice of Orange Co 1734, vestryman of St Mark's Parish
1730/1740 d1775 - desc/o Col William Bernard APP121 - desc/o
Anne Lovelace GVFHG(3)316, 332

Elizabeth - of VA, m(1) abt 1710 (a Scotsman) Henry Seaton son of
John Seaton of Gair-Miltoun, East Lothian, m(2) abt 1714
Augustine Moore b1685 d1743 of Chelsea, King William Co, VA &
had issue by both husbands - desc/o Col William Bernard APP121
- desc/o Anne Lovelace GVFHB(3)288, 341

Elizabeth - of VA, m Benjamin Hubbard, merchant & member of the
Committee of Safety of Caroline Co d1782 - desc/o Col William
Bernard APP122

TODD (cont.)

Elizabeth - of VA, b1723/1724 d1788, m(1) Nathaniel Wythe, m(2) Mordecai Booth, merchant of Gloucester Co - desc/o Col William Bernard APP122

Elizabeth - of MD, b1732, m John Cromwell of Anne Arundel Co, MD & left issue - desc/o Anne Lovelace GVFHB(3)303

Elizabeth - of VA, m John Wyatt - desc/o Anne Lovelace GVFHB(3)318

Elizabeth - of VA, b1760, m John Patterson of Poplar Grove, Matthews Co & left descendants - desc/o Anne Lovelace GVFHB(3)320

Enos - b1730 - desc/o Peter Bulkeley RAA75

Frances - of VA, b bef 5 Apr 1669, m (may have) Richard Cromwell a wealthy planter & the founder of the Baltimore Co family of Cromwell - desc/o Anne Lovelace APP406; GVFHB(3)283

Frances - of VA, b abt 1709 d1745, m1729 Robert North bp 1698 d1748/1749, captain of militia, justice & commissioner to lay out Jones Town (now part of Baltimore) 1732 & had issue - desc/o Col William Bernard APP123 - desc/o Anne Lovelace GVFHB(3)288, 351, 352

Frances - of MD, m1759 George Risteau of Baltimore Co, MD & left issue - desc/o Anne Lovelace GVFHB(3)303

Gershom - of CT, m Hannah Mansfield - desc/o Rev Peter Bulkeley DBR(3)86; RAA75

Harry - of VA, was a member of the Committee of Safety of King & Queen Co 1774 & was a member of the House of Delegates from the same county in 1784, m Aphia____ - desc/o Anne Lovelace GVFHB(3)311, 312

Isabella - of VA, b1670, m John Madison II - desc/o Anne Lovelace ECD(2)178; DBR(1)121; DBR(2)192, 621; DBR(3)458

James - of VA & MD, b abt 1670 d (drowned) 9 May 1709, m(1) bef Jun 1696 Elizabeth____, m(2)1698 Penelope Scudamore dau/o Thomas Scudamore of Baltimore Co, MD & Abigail Dixon, & had issue - desc/o Anne Lovelace APP406/407; GVFHB(3)282, 288/293

Capt Lancelot - of MD, b1675 d1735, m Elizabeth Rockhold d1741 - desc/o Anne Lovelace JSW1861; DBR(1)652

Lucy - of VA, b abt 1681/1683, m(1) bef 1698____ O'Brien, m(2)1698 John Baylor II born at Tiverton, Devonshire d1721 at Norfolk, merchant & member of the House of Burgesses from Gloucester & King & Queen Co & had issue - desc/o Col William Bernard DBR(3)450; DBR(4)143; APP120 - desc/o Anne Lovelace GVFHB(3)288, 321, 322

Lucy - of VA, b1721 d1791, m1749 Edward Tabb b1719/1720 d1782, of Gloucester Co, son of John Tabb & Martha Hand - desc/o Col William Bernard APP122 - desc/o Anne Lovelace GVFHB(3)318, 319

Lucy - of VA, b1753, m Mr____ Cary who went to Georgia & left numerous descendants - desc/o Anne Lovelace GVFHB(3)319

Mabel - of CT, m Titus Mansfield - desc/o Rev Peter Bulkeley DBR(3)86

Martha - of VA, b1757 d1821, m Reverend Armistead Smith & left issue six children - desc/o Anne Lovelace GVFHB(3)319

Mary - of VA, b abt 1710 d bef 1774, m abt 1728 John Bickerton b abt 1700 d1770 of Hanover Co, captain & major of militia & a justice -

TODD (cont.)

desc/o Col William Bernard APP122; DBR(1)215; DBR(3)132, 334, 692; DBR(4)769; GVFHB(3)332

Mary - of VA, m John Wyatt b1732 d1805 of Gloucester & Prince William Co & left issue - desc/o Col William Bernard APP122 - desc/o Anne Lovelace GVFHB(3)320

Mary - of MD, m John Worthington son of William & Hannah (Cromwell) Worthington & left issue - desc/o Anne Lovelace GVFHB(3)303

Mary - of VA, m____ Buster - desc/o Anne Lovelace GVFHB(3)312

Millicent (Milly) - of VA, m Col Tunstall - desc/o Anne Lovelace GVFHB(3)331

Patience - b1768 - desc/o Peter Bulkeley RAA75

Capt Phillip - of VA, b abt 1688 d bef 1740, lived in Stephen's Parish, King & Queen Co, sheriff of Gloucester Co 1730, m abt 1705/1710 Anne Day dau/o Edward Day of Somerset Co, MD - desc/o Col William Bernard APP122; DBR(1)215; DBR(3)131, 334, 692; DBR(4)769 - desc/o Anne Lovelace GVFHB(3)288, 332

Philip - of VA, b1750 lived at Toddsbury & became the ancestor of the Tabbs of Toddsury d1822, m1780 Mary Mason Booth dau/o Nathaniel Wythe Booth & left issue five children - desc/o Anne Lovelace GVFHB(3)319

Richard - of VA, b1681/1688 d prior to 1723 m____ & had issue sons Bernard & William Todd died without issue - desc/o Col William Bernard APP120 - desc/o Anne Lovelace GVFHG(3)288, 304, 305

Richard - of VA, d abt 1766 father of Justice Thomas Todd of the United States Supreme Court, m prior to 1750 Elizabeth Richards d1777 - desc/o Col William Bernard APP121 - desc/o Anne Lovelace GVFHG(3)312, 313

Richard - of VA, m Mary Lankford - desc/o Anne Lovelace GVFHB(3)314

Ruth - of MD, d1777, m1735 Michael Dorsey - desc/o Anne Lovelace JSW1861

Sarah - m Edward Dorsey b abt 1701 d1767 - desc/o Anne Lovelace DBR(1)652

Sarah - of VA, d1788, m James Barbour - desc/o Col William Bernard APP121

Maj Thomas - of VA, b1660 of Toddsbury on the North River, Mobjack Bay, Gloucester Co, VA d1725, eldest son & executor in his father's will, m Elizabeth Bernard dau/o Col William Bernard & Lucy (Higginson) Burwell & had issue - desc/o Anne Lovelace CHB501; DBR(2)725; APP406; GVFHB(3)282, 284/288

Thomas - of VA & MD, b abt 1681 d1714/1715 vestryman of St Paul's parish Baltimore Co in 1714, m abt 1705 Elizabeth____ d1717 in her 27th year - desc/o Col William Bernard APP119 - desc/o Anne Lovelace GVFHB(3)288, 296/304

Thomas - of MD, b1706 d1739 captain of foot & justice of Baltimore Co, MD, m(1)1728 Lettice Thacker b1704/1705 d1730 dau/o Henry & Elizabeth Thacker of Middlesex Co, VA, m(2) Eleanor Dorsey d1760 dau/o Caleb Dorsey of Baltimore Co, MD - desc/o Col William Bernard APP119 - desc/o Anne Lovelace GVFHB(3)301,

TODD (cont.)
302

  Thomas - of VA, b1710/1711 lived in St Stephen's Parish, King &
   Queen Co d prior to 1761 eldest son of William Todd & Martha
   Vicaries, m(1)____, m(2) abt 1744 Elizabeth Waring b1720 dau/o
   Thomas Waring of Essex Co - desc/o Anne Lovelace DBR(2)725;
   GVFHB(3)309, 311, 331 - desc/o Col William Bernard APP120, 121

  Thomas - of MD, b1738 d1798, m Sarah Wilkinson dau/o Robert
   Wilkinson of Baltimore Co, MD, lived at North Point & left several
   children - desc/o Anne Lovelace GVFHB(3)303

  Thomas - of VA, m Eliza Pendleton dau/o Col Henry Pendleton -
   desc/o Anne Lovelace GVFHB(3)312

  Thomas - of VA, b1765 in King & Queen Co, served in the army in the
   closing days of the Revolution, went to Kentucky with his family abt
   1784/1786. He held various political & judicial positions. He was
   appointed by Jefferson, a Justice of the United States Supreme
   Court, holding this position until his death in 1826, m(1) Elizabeth
   Harris, m(2) Lucy Payne the wid/o Steptoe Washington & had issue
   by both wives - desc/o Anne Lovelace GVGHB(3)314, 315

  Titus - b1730 - desc/o Peter Bulkeley RAA75

  William of VA, b1686 d1736 justice of King & Queen Co, VA, m shortly
   aft 16 Mar 1709/1710 Martha Vicaries dau/o Rev Thomas Vicaries
   of Gloucester Co, VA & had issue - desc/o Anne Lovelace CHB501;
   DBR(2)725; APP120, 121; GVFHB(2)288

  William - of VA, eldest son of Thomas Todd, lived in King & Queen Co,
   VA 1772 member of the Committee of Safety of King & Queen Co
   m____ & had issue - desc/o Anne Lovelace GVFHG(3)311

  William - of VA, married & had one son & two daughters, he was a
   clergyman - desc/o Anne Lovelace GVFHG(3)312

  William - of VA, sheriff of Pittsylvania Co, VA 1786 married & had
   issue - desc/o Anne Lovelace GVFHB(3)314

TOMES Alice - of CT, d abt 1646, m1615 Gov Thomas Welles - the
  immigrant FLW95; FFF115; THC310; NE(80)229/305, 446,
  (89)289; TAG(28)164/167 sufficient proof of alleged royal ancestry
  is lacking

TOMPKINS Col Christopher III - of VA, b1740 d1823, m1774 Ann Fleet -
  desc/o Col George Reade DBR(4)534

  Robert - of VA, b1730 d1795, m1765 Anne Dickinson - desc/o Col
  George Reade DBR(3)383

TOMPSON Bridget - of MA, bp 1622 d1643, m1640/1641 Capt George
  Denison - the immigrant MCS109, 110 - desc/o Alice Freeman
  DBR(3)424, 682; DBR(4)480, 799

  Dorothy - of MA, bp 1624 d aft 1709, m by 1644 Thomas Parke - the
  immigrant MCS110; DBR(2)442, 537; DBR(3)239, 429, 430, 682;
  DBR(5)187, 540, 797 sufficient proof of alleged royal ancestry is
  lacking

  Mary - of MA, bp 1619 d1693, m1641 Joseph Wise - desc/o Alice
  Freeman MCS109

TOOKE James - of VA, d bef 1667 - the immigrant DBR(1)689; RAA1;
  sufficient proof of alleged royal ancestry is lacking

  Mary - of VA, m(2) Edmond Bellson - desc/o James Tooke DBR(1)689

TOOKE (cont.)

Thomas - of VA - desc/o James Tooke DBR(1)689

TORREY Abigail - of MA, b1727 d1778, m1748 Timothy Scranton - desc/o Jane Haviland DBR(4)45

Ann - b1735 - desc/o Jane Haviland RAA135

Deacon Haviland Torrey - of MA, b1684 & left issue - desc/o William Torrey FLW167 - desc/o Jane Haviland FLW167

Lieut John - of MA, m Mary Syme - desc/o Jane Haviland DBR(4)45; RAA135

Joseph - m Deborah Holbrook - desc/o Jane Lawrence J&K216; AAP151; GBR456

Samuel - of MA, b1706 d1745, m Abigail Snowden - desc/o Jane Haviland DBR(4)45; RAA135

Samuel D - ancestor of Hon William Howard Taft - desc/o Jane Lawrence J&K216

Sarah - b1673 - desc/o Alice Baynton RAA66

William - father of Samuel D Torrey - desc/o Jane Lawrence J&K216

William - of MA, b1638 England d1717/1718 Weymouth, m abt 1669 Deborah Greene b1649l Warwick, RI d1728/1729 Weymouth dau/o Deputy-Gov John Greene & Ann Almy - the immigrant FLW167; MCS37 - desc/o Jane Haviland DBR(4)45; RAA135; FLW167

William - m Anna Davenport - desc/o Jane Lawrence GBR456

TOWNELEY Alice - of VA, m Maj John Grymes b1660 d1709 justice 1706, receiver general of VA, son of Lieutenant General Thomas Grymes - desc/o Col George Reade DBR(2)830; PFA Apx D #1

Lawrence - of VA, son of Lawrence Towneley & Alice Calvert, m Sarah Warner, his first cousin, dau/o Augustine Warner & Mary Towneley - the immigrant GBR330; GVFHB(5)559

Margaret Frances - of MD, dau/o Jeremiah Towneley & Frances Andrews, m Richard Chase - the immigrant GBR386 some aspect of royal descent merits further study - alternate descent noted

Mary - of VA, dau/o Lawrence Towneley & Jennet Halstead, m Augustine Warner - the immigrant GBR330

Richard - of NJ, son of Nicholas Towneley & Joanna White, m Mrs Elizabeth Smith Lawrence de Carteret, wid/o William Lawrence & Philip de Carteret - the immigrant GBR386 some aspect of royal descent merits further study - alternate descent noted; GVFHB(5)538/577

TOWNSEND Daniel - of NY, b1676 d1724/1725, m abt 1700 Freelove Dickinson - desc/o Peter Wright ECD(2)318

Gilbert - of NY, b1764 d1843, m abt 1780 Abigail Mead - desc/o Peter Wright ECD(2)318

Isaac - of MA, m Anne Ranger - desc/o Thomas Townsend BLG2943

Isaac - of MA, b1737 d1818, m Elizabeth Hitchcock - desc/o Thomas Townsend BLG2943

Isaac - of MA, b1765 d1841, m Roda Atwater - desc/o Thomas Townsend BLG2943

Jeremiah - of MA, b1711 d1803, m Hannah Cleland - desc/o Thomas Townsend BLG2943

John - of NY, b1712 d1787, m1739 Anne Gedney - desc/o Peter

TOWNSEND (cont.)
>> Wright ECD(2)318
> John III - of NY, b1743 d1821, m1760 Jemina Travis - desc/o Peter
>> Wright ECD(2)318
> John - of CT, b1758, m1785 Mary Kingsbury - desc/o Anne Marbury
>> DBR(3)171
> Lucy - of MA, b abt 1740 d1763/1764, m1758 Ezekiel Jewett - desc/o
>> Grace Chetwode DBR(1)100
> Penn - of MA abt 1727 - desc/o William Townsend EDV44
> Samuel - of MA, b1637/1638 d1704, m Abigail Davis - desc/o Thomas
>> Townsend BLG2943
> Thomas - of MA 1637, d1677, m Mary Newgate - the immigrant
>> EDV44; BLG2943 sufficient proof of alleged royal ancestry is
>> lacking
> William - of MA 1634 - the immigrant EDV44; sufficient proof of alleged
>> royal ancestry is lacking

TRACY Hannah - of MA, b1754 d1797, m1772 Jonathan Jackson -
> desc/o Capt Thomas Lake CHB410
> Lydia - of CT, b1677, m1698 Thomas Leffingwell - desc/o Lieut
>> Thomas Tracy FFF143, 156
> Dr Solomon - of CT, b1651, m1676 Sarah Huntington - desc/o Lieut
>> Thomas Tracy FFF143, 156
> Lieut Thomas - of MA 1636, b1610 d1685, m(1)1641 Mary____,
>> m(2)1679 Martha Bourne - the immigrant FFF143, 156; sufficient
>> proof of alleged royal ancestry is lacking

TRAILL Robert - of NH, son of William of Kirkwall & Isabell (Fea) Traill, m
> Mary Whipple, sister of William Whipple, Jr, signer of the
> Declaration of Independence - the immigrant GBR29

TRAYLOR Joseph - of VA, b1696/1700 d aft 1777, m abt 1720 Elizabeth
> Parkinson - desc/o Henry Randolph DBR(4)171
> Sarah - of VA, b abt 1720/1725 d1798, m Robert Burton - desc/o
>> Henry Randolph DBR(4)171
> William - of VA, b abt 1673/1674 d1753, m1695 Judith Archer -
>> desc/o Henry Randolph DBR(4)171

TREADWELL Mary - of MA, d1825, m1796 Henry Clement - desc/o
> Samuel Appleton DBR(2)647

TREAT Ashbel - of MA, d abt 1780, m Dorcas Waterman - desc/o Rev
> Peter Bulkeley ECD(3)81
> Eunice - of MA, b1704 d1747, m1721 Rev Thomas Paine - desc/o
>> Mary Launce J&K184
> Isaac - of CT, b1701 d1763, m1730 Rebecca Bulkeley - desc/o Rev
>> Peter Bulkeley ECD(3)83
> Lucy - of CT, b abt 1743 d1831, m1766 Joseph Terry - desc/o Rev
>> Peter Bulkeley ECD(3)83
> Moses - of MA, b1771 d1843, m1791 Mahala Manrow - desc/o Rev
>> Peter Bulkeley ECD(3)82
> Rev Richard - of CT, b1694 d abt 1759, m1728 Susanna Woodbridge -
>> desc/o Rev Peter Bulkeley ECD(3)81

TRENT Alexander - of VA, d1751 of Cumberland Co, m Frances____ &
> had sons Peterfield & Alexander, also one daughter Elizabeth Trent
> - desc/o Christopher Branch GVFWM(1)425

TROTH Samuel - b1755 d1815, m Ann Berry Dixon, a widow - desc/o
Robert Lloyd CRFP(1)501

TROTT Mary - b1736 - desc/o Griffith Bowen RAA72

TROWBRIDGE Abigail - of CT, b1670 d1697/1698, m John Marshall -
desc/o Thomas Trowbridge DLJ1855

Abigail - of CT, b1695 d1780, m(1) abt 1715 Daniel Mallory, m(2) abt
1761 Nathaniel Beecher - desc/o Thomas Trowbridge DLJ1858

Abigail - b1712 m____ Green - desc/o Thomas Trowbridge DLJ1860

Ann - of CT, b1688 d1721, m1708 Rev Samuel Cooke - desc/o
Thomas Trowbridge DLJ1856

Caleb - of CT, b1670 d1704, m1704 Mary Lilly - desc/o Thomas
Trowbridge DLJ1854

Caleb - b1706 d1759 New Faifield, m Jemima Keeler dau/o Ralph
Keeler & Jemima____ , & had issue 9 children - desc/o Thomas
Trowbridge DLJ1860

Capt Caleb - of CT, b1747/1748 d1799, m1769 Anna Sherman b abt
1748 d1827 dau/o James Sherman & Sarah Cooke - desc/o
Thomas Trowbridge DLJ1857

Caleb - b1776 d1852 Mansfield, m1799 Abigail Southworth - desc/o
Thomas Trowbridge DLJ1862

Daniel - b1701, m Sarah Seymour dau/o John Seymour & Sarah
Gregory, & had issue, 10 children - desc/o Thomas Trowbridge
DLJ1860

Capt Daniel - of CT, b1703 d1752, m1731 Mehitabel Brown b1711
d1797 dau/o Francis Brown & Hannah Alling - desc/o Thomas
Trowbridge DLJ1857

Daniel - b1750 d1818, m1778 Sybil Atwater b1755 d1831 dau/o Isaac
Atwater & Dorothy Mix - desc/o Thomas Trowbridge DLJ1858

David - b1760 d1812, m abt 1781 Lucy Catlin b abt 1754 d1815
dau/o John Catlin & Margaret Painter - desc/o Thomas Trowbridge
DLJ1865

Ebenezer - b1702 d1777, m1725/1726 Hannah Brown b1796/1797
d1787 - desc/o Thomas Trowbridge DLJ1859

Ebenezer - b1728/1729 d1767, m(1) Esther Catlin b1733 Deerfield,
MA, dau/o John Catlin & Jemima Allen, m(2) Obedience Beecher
b1723/1724 d1807 dau/o Stephen Beecher & Susanna Hale -
desc/o Thomas Trowbridge DLJ1859

Elizabeth - of CT, b1676 d1711, m1691 John Hodshon - desc/o
Thomas Trowbridge DLJ1854

Elizabeth - of CT, b1661, m1678 Peter Mallory - desc/o Thomas
Trowbridge DLJ1855

Elizabeth - of CT, b1693 d1783, m(1)1717/1718 Joseph Miles,
m(2)1758 Stephen Howell - desc/o Thomas Trowbridge DLJ1856

Elizabeth - b1703 m____ St John - desc/o Thomas Trowbridge
DLJ1860

Elizabeth - b1705 d bef 1738, m1725/1726 Isaac Beecher - desc/o
Thomas Trowbridge DLJ1859

Elizabeth - b1710, m1730 Benjamin Nichols - desc/o Thomas
Trowbridge DLJ1860

Elizabeth - b1731 d1806, m(1)1756 Ezra Candee, m(2) Joseph Prindle
- desc/o Thomas Trowbridge DLJ1859

TROWBRIDGE (cont.)

Elizabeth - b1769, m1790 Samuel Sherman - desc/o Thomas
Trowbridge DLJ1862

Elizabeth - b1770, m1794 Elias Parmelee - desc/o Thomas Trowbridge
DLJ1801

Esther - b abt 1694, m James Leavenworth - desc/o Thomas
Trowbridge DLJ1860

Esther - b abt 1726 d1813, m1761 Naboth Candee - desc/o Thomas
Trowbridge DLJ1860

Grace - b1776, m1798 Jabez Dwight - desc/o Thomas Trowbridge
DLJ1864

Hannah - of CT, b1690, m1709/1710 Joseph Whiting - desc/o
Thomas Trowbridge DLJ1854

Hannah - of CT, b1668, m Moses Jackson - desc/o Thomas
Trowbridge DLJ1855

Hannah - b1712, m Jacob Treadwell - desc/o Thomas Trowbridge
DLJ1861

Hannah - b1726/1727, m(1)___ & had issue, m(2) Nathan Smith -
desc/o Thomas Trowbridge DLJ1859

Hannah - b1765 d1831, m1786 Timothy Chittenden - desc/o Thomas
Trowbridge DLJ1862

Isaac - b abt 1693 d abt 1770, m(1) abt 1717 Ruth Perry b1690 d1767
dau/o Arthur Perry & Anna Judson, m(2) Hannah Jones b1709
d1769 dau/o Benjamin & Anna Jones & wid/o Ebenezer Benham -
desc/o Thomas Trowbridge DLJ1859

Isaac - b1721, m(1)1747/1748 Judith Hale dau/o Samuel Hale &
Judith Hodge, m(2) Hannah Scovill b1736 dau/o James Scovill &
Rebecca ___ & wid/o Joseph Way - desc/o Thomas Trowbridge
DLJ1860

Israel - bp 1722 d1795 Fair Haven, VT, m(1) Mary Johnson b1724
dau/o Peter Johnson & Mary___, m(2) Lydia Kilbourn dau/o
Elisha Kilbourn & wid/o Benjamin Palmer - desc/o Thomas
Trowbridge DLJ1860

James - of CT, b abt 1636 d1717 Newton, MA, Deacon, m(1)1659
Dorchester, Margaret Atherton b1638 d1672 dau/o Humphrey
Atherton & Mary Wales, m(2)1674 Margaret Jackson b1649 d1727
dau/o John Jackson & Margaret___ , & had issue 15 children -
desc/o Thomas Trowbridge DLJ1855

James - of CT, b1664 d1732, m(1)1688 Lydia Alsop b1665 d1690
dau/o Joseph Alsop & Elizabeth Preston, m(2)1692 Esther How
b1671 d abt 1697 dau/o Ephraim How & Ann Hough, m(3)1698
Mary Belden b1677 Hatfield, MA d aft 1737 dau/o Daniel Belden &
Elizabeth Foote - desc/o Thomas Trowbridge DLJ1855

James - b1689 d abt 1730, m Susanna___ & had issue, 3 sons -
desc/o Thomas Trowbridge DLJ1859

John - of CT, b1661 d1689, m1683 Ann Leete b1661 d1747 dau/o
William Leete & Ann Paine - desc/o Thomas Trowbridge DLJ1854

John - of CT, b1684 d1739, m1710 Rebecca Eliot dau/o Rev Joseph
Eliot & Mary Wyllys - desc/o Thomas Trowbridge DLJ1856

John - b1709 d1777 Danbury, m Mary Comstock dau/o Samuel
Comstock & Sarah Hanford, & had issue 8 children - desc/o

TROWBRIDGE (cont.)

Thomas Trowbridge DLJ1860

Capt John - b1748 d1791, m1777 Thankful Doolittle b1754 d1827 dau/o Isaac Doolittle & Sarah Todd - desc/o Thomas Trowbridge DLJ1858

Joseph - of CT, b abt 1676 d abt 1715, m abt 1708 Anne Sherwood dau/o Matthew Sherwood & Mary Fitch - desc/o Thomas Trowbridge DLJ1855

Capt Joseph - of CT, b1699 d1763, m(1) abt 1730 Sarah Denison b1708 d1736 dau/o John Denison & Grace Brown, m(2)1739 Mary Woodward b abt 1710 d1771 dau/o John Woodward & Sarah Rosewell - desc/o Thomas Trowbridge DLJ1856

Joseph - b1718 d1801 Danbury, m1741 Trial Morehouse - desc/o Thomas Trowbridge DLJ1859

Joseph - of CT, b1742/1743 d1793, m1766 Sarah Sabin b1745 d1804 Colchester, dau/o Hezekiah Sabin & Mary Power - desc/o Thomas Trowbridge DLJ1587

Joseph - of CT, b1736 d1790 near Savannah, GA, m1762 Elizabeth Bishop b1741 d1794 dau/o Samuel Bishop & Abigail Atwater - desc/o Thomas Trowbridge DLJ1857

Joseph - b1768 d1804, m1796 Lois Mix b1776 d1842 dau/o Nathaniel Mix & Thankful Alling - desc/o Thomas Trowbridge DLJ1863

Joseph - b1772 d1836, m1796 Lois Mix b1774 d1863 dau/o Joseph Mix & Patience Sperry - desc/o Thomas Trowbridge DLJ1862

Joseph - b1776 d1853 Hingham, MA, m1804 Hingham, MA, Susanna Burr - desc/o Thomas Trowbridge DLJ1861

Joseph Easton - b1752 d1801, m1780 Sally Dodd b abt 1752 d1799 dau/o Thomas Dodd & Esther Bishop - desc/o Thomas Trowbridge DLJ1861

Joseph Ebenezer - b1772 d1812 Skaneateles, New York, m1794 Abigail Russell - desc/o Thomas Trowbridge DLJ1865

Justus - b1774 d1810, m1795 Sarah Bontecou b1775 d1861 dau/o Peter Bontecou & Susannah Thomas - desc/o Thomas Trowbridge DLJ1865

Lucretia - b1774, m1804 Ashbel Stillman - desc/o Thomas Trowbridge DLJ1864

Lydia - of CT, b1666 d1731, m1681 Richard Rosewell - desc/o Thomas Trowbridge DLJ1854

Lydia - of CT, b1695, m Charles Moorcock of Boston - desc/o Thomas Trowbridge DLJ1858

Lydia - of CT, b1697, m1721/1722 James Parker - desc/o Thomas Trowbridge DLJ1858

Lydia - b1715, m1735 Eliakim Elmer - desc/o Thomas Trowbridge DLJ1860

Margaret - of CT, b1666, m Joseph Goodwin - desc/o Thomas Trowbridge DLJ1854

Mary - b abt 1697 m____ Brown - desc/o Thomas Trowbridge DLJ1860

Mary - of CT, b1714/1715 d1786, m1743/1744 Rev Benjamin Woodbridge - desc/o Thomas Trowbridge DLJ1856

TROWBRIDGE (cont.)

Mary - of CT, b1691, m1715 Stephen Alling - desc/o Thomas Trowbridge DLJ1856

Mary - b abt 1733, m John Benham - desc/o Thomas Trowbridge DLJ1859

Mary - of CT, b1744 d1789, m1765 Timothy Jones - desc/o Thomas Trowbridge DLJ1857

Mary - b abt 1745 d1827, m abt 1766 John Beecher - desc/o Thomas Trowbridge DLJ1859

Mehitabel - of CT, b1726/1727 d1808, m1744 Titus Smith - desc/o Thomas Trowbridge DLJ1859

Melissa - b1774, m1797 Joseph Dalby of Jamaica, West Indies - desc/o Thomas Trowbridge DLJ1863

Newman - of CT, b1738 d1816, m(1)1764 Elizabeth Bills b abt 1743 d1777, m(2)1778 Rebecca Dodd b1751 d1808 dau/o Thomas Dodd & Esther Bishop & wid/o Richard Cable - desc/o Thomas Trowbridge DLJ1857

Polly - bp 1775, m John Dayton of Hudson, New York - desc/o Thomas Trowbridge DLJ1863

Rachel - b1719, m Moses Bristol - desc/o Thomas Trowbridge DLJ1860

Rutherford - b1744 d1825, m(1)1767 Dorcas Hitchcock b1746 d1788 dau/o Amos Hitchcock & Dorcas Foote, m(2)1793 Thankful Alling bp 1755 d1831 dau/o John Alling & Abiah Hitchcock & wid/o Nathaniel Mix - desc/o Thomas Trowbridge DLJ1858

Samuel - of CT, b1670 d abt 1742, m1697 Sarah Lacy - desc/o Thomas Trowbridge DLJ1855

Samuel - b1700 d1782 New Fairfield, Deacon, m(1)1722 Sarah Seeley b1703 d1752 dau/o James Seeley, m(2)1753 Comfort____ wid/o Joshua Hurlburt, m(3)1774 Ann____ Moger - desc/o Thomas Trowbridge DLJ1860

Samuel - b1761 d1827, m1786 Lydia Johnson b1765 d1843 dau/o Jabez Johnson & Abigail Darrow - desc/o Thomas Trowbridge DLJ1865

Sarah - of CT, b1686, m1707 John Russell - desc/o Thomas Trowbridge AAP149; GBR448; DLJ1856

Sarah - b1715, m Daniel Bennett - desc/o Thomas Trowbridge DLJ1861

Sarah - b1717, m1737 Nathaniel Westcott - desc/o Thomas Trowbridge DLJ1860

Sarah - of CT, b1722 d1795, m1770 John Whiting - desc/o Thomas Trowbridge DLJ1856

Sarah - b abt 1730, m1755 David Johnson - desc/o Thomas Trowbridge DLJ1860

Sarah - b1731, m Levi Clinton - desc/o Thomas Trowbridge DLJ1859

Sarah - of CT, b1753, m1774 Elihu Hall - desc/o Thomas Trowbridge DLJ1857

Lieut Stephen - of CT, b1688 d1734, m1712 Thankful Easton b1687 Hartford d1756 dau/o Joseph Easton & Hannah Ensign - desc/o Thomas Trowbridge DLJ1856

Stephen - of CT, b1726 d1796, m1747/1748 Lydia Burroughs

TROWBRIDGE (cont.)

b1729/1730 d1802 dau/o Joseph Burroughs & Lydia Munson - desc/o Thomas Trowbridge DLJ1856

Capt Stephen - b1746 d1835, m(1)1770 Mary Bassett b1751 d1776 dau/o Ebenezer Bassett & Susanna White, m(2)1778 Margaret Hall b abt 1755 d1799 dau/o John Hall & Abiah Macumber, m(3)1800 Hannah Hall b abt 1751 d1832 dau/o John Hall & Abiah Macumber - desc/o Thomas Trowbridge DLJ1858

Thankful - of CT, b1687, m William Gleason of Brookline, MA - desc/o Thomas Trowbridge DLJ1858

Thankful - of CT, m1745/1746 Benjamin Bristol - desc/o Thomas Trowbridge DLJ1859

Thomas - of CT, b1598 d1672/1673 son of John Trowbridge & Agnes Prowse, m1627 Elizabeth Marshall bp 1602/1603 dau/o John & Alice (Bevys) Marshall - the immigrant AAP149; GBR448, 449; TAG(18)129/137, (57)31/33; EO2(3)515; DLJ1854

Thomas Jr - of CT, bp 1631 Exeter d1702, m(1) Sarah Rutherford b1641 d1687 dau/o Henry Rutherford & Sarah____, m(2)1689 Hannah Nash b1655 d1707/1708 dau/o John Nash & Elizabeth Tapp & wid/o Eliphalet Ball - desc/o Thomas Trowbridge AAP149; GBR448; TAG(57)31/33; DLJ1854

Thomas - of CT, b1659 d abt 1750 Deacon, m1684 Abigail Beardsley dau/o Thomas Beardsley - desc/o Thomas Trowbridge DLJ1855

Thomas III - of CT, b1663 d1711, m1685 Mary Winston b1667 d1742 dau/o John Winston & Elizabeth____ - desc/o Thomas Trowbridge AAP149; GBR448; DLJ1854

Thomas - of CT, b1742 d1782 New York, m1769 Mary Macomber bp 1748 d1811 dau/o Jeremiah Macomber & Sarah Cooper - desc/o Thomas Trowbridge DLJ1857

Thomas - b1764 d1837, m1785 Sally Peck b1766 d1841 dau/o Stephen Peck & Lucy Miles - desc/o Thomas Trowbridge DLJ1865

Thomas - bp 1773 d1797, m1794 Ruhamah Hall b1776 d1842 dau/o Elias Hall & Ruhamah Barker - desc/o Thomas Trowbridge DLJ1863

Wealthy - b1770 d1816, m(1)1791 Samuel Barnes, m(2)1800 Ezekiel Hayes - desc/o Thomas Trowbridge DLJ1863

William - of CT, bp 1633 Exeter d1690, m1656/1657 Elizabeth Lamberton b abt 1632 d1716 dau/o George Lamberton & Margaret Lewen & wid/o Daniel Sellivant - desc/o Thomas Trowbridge DLJ1855

Capt William - of CT, b1657 d1704, m abt 1687 Thankful Stow b1664 d aft 1719 dau/o Samuel Stow & Hope Fletcher - desc/o Thomas Trowbridge DLJ1855

William - of CT, b1700 d1793, m1724 Mehitable Blakeslee b1702 dau/o Samuel Blakeslee & Sarah Kimberly - desc/o Thomas Trowbridge DLJ1858, 1859

William - b abt 1736 d1797, m Rebecca Painter b1734 d1807 dau/o Shubael Painter & Elizabeth Dunbar - desc/o Thomas Trowbridge DLJ1859

William - b1767 d1824, m1788 Lucy Peck b1768 d1819 dau/o Stephen Peck & Lucy Miles - desc/o Thomas Trowbridge DLJ1865

TROWBRIDGE (cont.)

William - b1772 d1818, m(1)1794 Eunice Merriman b1773 dau/o Lent Merriman & Katharine Wright; she div him 1805;, m(2) Sally___ d1813 aged 39 years, m(3) Sally___ - desc/o Thomas Trowbridge DLJ1862

TRUAX John Isaac - of NY, b1749 d1825 drowned in St Lawrence River, m Annatje (Nancy) Van Der Heyden b1754 d1835 - desc/o Joseph Bolles DBR(1)332; DBR(2)424; DBR(4)460

TRUE Deacon Abraham - of MA, b1721 Salisbury d1812 Deerfield, m1744/1745 Sally French b1725 d1814 - desc/o Capt Thomas Bradbury ECD64; DBR(1)356

Anne - b1745 d1800, m Col William Smith - desc/o Capt Thomas Bradbury J&K176

Benjamin - of MA, b Salisbury 1693/1694 d1779 Salisbury, m1717 Judith Morrill b1696 d1782 - desc/o Capt Thomas Bradbury ECD(2)64; DBR(1)356

Benjamin - b1741/1742 - desc/o Thomas Bradbury RAA72

Benjamin - of NH, b1760 d1806, m1782 Molly Batchelder - desc/o Capt Thomas Bradbury ECD(2)64

Lieut Ephraim - b1756 d Washington Co, Ohio 1835, m(1) Mary Martha Mercy Eaton - desc/o Capt Thomas Bradbury DBR(1)110, 111, 440, 491; DBR(2)140, 141; DBR(3)318, 431, 521; DBR(5)122

Capt Henry - b1644/1645 d1735, m1668 Jane Bradbury - desc/o Ephraim True DBR(1)440

Deacon Jabez - of MA, b1686 d1749, m1707/1708 Sarah Tappen - desc/o Capt Thomas Bradbury ECD(2)84; RAA72; FFF90, 102, 107

Jabez - b1714 - desc/o Thomas Bradbury RAA72

Jacob - b1749 - desc/o Thomas Bradbury RAA72

Deacon John - of MA, b1678 d1754, son of Capt Henry & Jane (Bradbury) True, m1702 Martha Merrill b1683 Newberry, MA d1754 Salisbury - desc/o Capt Thomas Bradbury DBR(1)110, 491; DBR(2)140, 141; DBR(3)318, 431, 521; DBR(5)121

John II- of MA, b1703/1704 Salisbury, m1730 Mary Brown d1714 - desc/o Capt Thomas Bradbury DBR(1)110, 491; DBR(2)140, 141; DBR(3)318, 431, 521; DBR(5)121

Jonathan - of MA, m Anne Stevens ancestor of William Mitchell Sargent - desc/o Capt Thomas Bradbury J&K175

Lieut Josiah - of NH, b1776 Seabrook, New Hampshire d1855, m1804 Almira Tuttle b1788 VT d1853 Athens, Ohio - desc/o Capt Thomas Bradbury DBR(1)110, 405, 491; DBR(2)140, 141; DBR(3)318, 431, 521; DBR(5)122

Martha - b1774 - desc/o Thomas Bradbury RAA72

Mary - of MA, b1708 d1767, m1728/1729 Nehemiah Page - desc/o Capt Thomas Bradbury ECD(2)84; FFF90, 102, 108

Sarah - of MA - b1748 Salisbury d bef 1789, m1768 Josiah Tilton b1743 Kingston, New Hampshire d1828 Kingston, New Hampshire 1828 - desc/o Capt Thomas Bradbury DBR(1)356, 357

Deacon William - m Eleanor Stevens - desc/o Capt Thomas Bradbury J&K176

Lieut William - of MA, b1670 d1733, m Eleanor Stevens b1675 d1768 - desc/o Capt Thomas Bradbury ECD(2)64; DBR(1)356; RAA72

TRUE (cont.)

    Capt Winthrop - b1710, m Dorothy Currier - desc/o Capt Thomas Bradbury J&K176; RAA72

TRUMBULL Jonathan - of CT, b1710 d1785, governor of Connecticut - desc/o John Drake J&K311

    Jonathan Jr - of CT, b1740 d1809, governor of Connecticut - desc/o John Drake J&K311

TUCKER Content - b1758 - desc/o Catherine Marbury RAA114

    Frances - of NY, dau/o Thomas Tucker & Mary Nichols, m John Montresor b1736 d1799 British military engineer who served in the American colonies from 1754 to 1778 - the immigrant GBR209

    St George - of VA, b1752 Port Royal, Bermuda d1827 Edgewood, near Warminster, Nelson Co, VA, Revolutionary soldier, jurist & professor of law at William and Mary College, son of Henry Tucker Jr & Anne Butterfield, m(1)1778 at Mataox, Chesterfield Co, Frances Bland, dau/o Col Theodoric Bland & Frances Bolling of Cawsons, Prince George Co & wid/o John Randolph of Mataox, m(2)1791 Lelia Skipwith, dau/o Sir Peyton Skipwith, of Prestwoud, Seventh Baronet & wid/o George Carter of Carotoman, Lancaster Co - the immigrant GBR208; CFA(6)510

TUFTS Sarah - b1725 - desc/o Thomas Dudley RAA89

TULLY Abigail - of MA, b1707 d1773, m(1)1741 Capt John Lee of Lyme, CT, m(2) Deacon Caleb Chapman of Saybrook - desc/o Mary Gye NE(96)364

    John - of MA, b1702 d1776, m(1) Parnell Kirtland d1748 aged 43 years, m(2) Mary Baker wid/o____ Russell - desc/o Mary Gye NE(96)364

    Lydia - of MA, b1711 d1792, m Humphrey Pratt of Saybrook - desc/o Mary Gye NE(96)364

    Sarah - of MA, b1715 d1764, m Capt Joseph Buckingham of Saybrook - desc/o Mary Gye NE(96)364

TUNSTALL Catherine - of VA, m Samuel Matthews - desc/o Edmund Tunstall CHB455

    Edmund - of VA 1636, m1636 Martha____ - the immigrant CHB455; sufficient proof of alleged royal ancestry is lacking

    Edmund - of VA, m Catherine____ - desc/o Edmund Tunstall CHB455

    John - of VA, m Sally Temple - desc/o Edmund Tunstall CHB456

    Capt Joseph - of VA & KY, b1755 d1817, m Jane Pearce - desc/o Edmund Tunstall CHB456

    Richard - of VA, m____ - desc/o Edmund Tunstall CHB456

    Col Richard Jr - of VA, d1872, m Anne Hill - desc/o Edmund Tunstall CHB456

    Richard 3rd - of VA, m Catherine Brooke - desc/o Edmund Tunstall CHB456

    Robert - of VA, a soldier - desc/o Edmund Tunstall CHB456

    Capt Thomas - of VA - desc/o Edmund Tunstall CHB456

    Col William - of VA, m Betsey Barker - desc/o Edmund Tunstall CHB456

TURNER Abigail - of CT, bp 1703 d1756, m1721/1722 Clement Miner Jr - desc/o Mary Wentworth ECD(2)301

    Ezekiel - of MA, b1650 d1703/1704, m1678 Susanna Keeney - desc/o

TURNER (cont.)

Mary Wentworth ECD(2)301

TURPIN Horatio - of VA, m1803 Mary Bancroft - desc/o Christopher
Branch GVFWM(1)426

Mary - of VA, m1761 Richard James - desc/o Christopher Branch
GVFWM(1)426

Mary - of VA, m Robert Goode son of Robert Goode & Elizabeth Branch
- desc/o Christopher Branch GVFWM(1)426

Obedience - of VA, m1754 John Harris - desc/o Christopher Branch
GVFWM(1)426

Philip - of VA, m Caroline Rose - desc/o Christopher Branch
GVFWM(1)426

Thomas - of VA, b1708 d1790 magistrate & sheriff of Goochland Co,
magistrate & lieutenant colonel of militia of Cumberland Co, m
Mary Jefferson dau/o Thomas Jefferson & Mary Field - desc/o
Christopher Branch GVFWM(1)425

Thomas - of VA, m Martha Ward Gaines - desc/o Christopher Branch
GVFWM(1)426

William - of VA, m1773 Sarah Harris - desc/o Christopher Branch
GVFWM(1)426

TUTHILL Mehitable - b1753 - desc/o Roger Ludlow RAA111

TUTT Lieut Gabriel - of VA, b1758 d1833, m1787 Elizabeth Tutt - desc/o
Mary Butler ECD(2)74

Capt James - of VA, b1732/1733 d1789, m1749 Ann Brown - desc/o
Mary Butler ECD(2)74

Col Richard - of VA, d1767, m1731 Elizabeth Johnson - desc/o Mary
Butler ECD(2)74

TUTTLE Mary - of MA, d1707 - desc/o William Tuttle EDV70

William - of MA 1635, m Elizabeth___ - the immigrant EDV70;
sufficient proof of alleged royal ancestry is lacking

TYLER Asa - of MA, b1716 d1776, m1734 Hannah Peabody dau/o
Nathan Peabody - desc/o Gov Thomas Dudley DBR(4)399;
DBR(5)360

Job - b1705 - desc/o Gov Thomas Dudley RAA89

Hannah - m John Spofford IV - desc/o Gov Thomas Dudley RAA89;
AAP155; GBR250

Margaret - of MA, b1735 d1786, m1757 Jedediah Stickney b1735
d1809 - desc/o Gov Thomas Dudley DBR(4)399; DBR(5)360

Sarah - b1738 - desc/o Richard Billings RAA70

TYNDAL Margaret - of MA, b abt 1591 d1647 Boston, MA, dau/o Sir John
Tyndal & Margaret (Anna) Egerton, m1618 Gov John Winthrop
b1587/1588 of Groton, Suffolk d1649 Boston, MA, founder &
governor of the MA Bay Colony - the immigrant FLW193; MCB166;
MCD303; MCS5; DBR(2)676; DBR(3)133; DBR(5)1074; GBR427;
NE(18)182, 183; EO2(3)865

TYNG Anna - of MA, b1639/1640 d1709, m1656 Thomas Shepard Jr
b1635 d1677 son of Mr Thomas Shepard - desc/o Elizabeth
Coytmore AAP144; PFA Apx C #5; GBR165; TAG(32)9/23

Bethia - of MA, b1641 d by 1670, m abt 1659 Richard Wharton d1689,
a merchant adventurer largely concerned with purchase of lands in
ME - desc/o Elizabeth Coytmore TAG(32)9/23

TYNG (cont.)

    Elizabeth - of MA, b1637/1638 d1682, m abt 1656 Thomas Brattle d1683 - desc/o Elizabeth Coytemore ECD(2)101; DBR(5)118; TAG(32)9/23

    Mercy - of MA, b1642/1643 d1670, m1663 Samuel Bradstreet b abt 1629 d1682 came with Winthrop to New England in 1630 later became a physician - desc/o Elizabeth Coytmore TAG(32)9/23

    Rebecca - of MA, m Thomas Dudley in 1722 - the immigrant EDV19; CRL(1)379; sufficient proof of alleged royal ancestry is lacking

    William - of MA, b abt 1605 d1652/1653, m(1) bef Jun 1634 Anne Dersley, m(2) Elizabeth Coytemore - the immigrant RAA1; sufficient proof of alleged royal ancestry is lacking

TYRON William - of NC & NY, b1729 d1788 governor of North Carolina & New York, son of Charles & Mary (Shirley) Tyron, m Margaret Wake - the immigrant GBR45

– U –

UNDERHILL John - of NY, b abt 1597 d1672, military leader & magistrate, son of John Underhill & Honor Pawley, m(1) Helena de Hooch, m(2) Elizabeth Feake, great-niece of John Winthrop, governor of MA Bay Colony - the immigrant GBR398 some aspect of royal descent merits further study; NYGBR(3)#4185/186, (11)#1p20, (64)#1p89/90, #2p207/208; (64)#2p207/208, (80)#2p113, (86)#4p220, (94)#1p50, #4p229

    Mary - of NY, m1780 Mordecai Frost b1758 d1825 son of Isaac Frost - desc/o Rev John Davenport DBR(3)711

    Thomas - of NY, b1738 d1822, m1761 Sarah Weeks b1739 d1825 dau/o Abel Weeks - desc/o Rev John Davenport DBR(3)711

UNDERWOOD Mary - of VA, m Richard Tutt - desc/o Mary Butler ECD(2)73

UPTON John - b1625(?), m Eleanor Stuart - the immigrant RAA no longer accepted as being of royal descent

USHER Hezekiah - of MA 1651 - the immigrant EDV101, 102; sufficient proof of alleged royal ancestry is lacking

    Lieutenant Governor John - of MA, d1726 - desc/o Hezekiah Usher EDV101, 102

– V –

VAIL Amy - b1749 - desc/o Agnes Harris RAA131

    Anne - b1753 - desc/o Edward FitzRandolph RAA96

    Thomas - b1720 - desc/o Edward FitzRandolph RAA96

VALENTINE Elizabeth - of MA, b1739 d1807, m Zaccheus Ballord - desc/o Judge Simon Lynde CHB310; MCB208; BCD310; DBR(3)746; DBR(4)835

    Col Joseph - of MA, b1776 d1845, m(1) Fanny Haven - desc/o Judge Simon Lynde CHB310; BCD311

    Samuel - of MA, b1745 d1834, m1771 Elizabeth Jones desc/o Judge Simon Lynde CHB310; MCD253; BCD310; AWW192

VALENTINE (cont.)

Samuel Jr - of MA, b1773 d1823, m(2)1809 Mary Fiske - desc/o Judge Simon Lynde CHB310; BCD310; AWW192

Col Thomas - of MA, b1713 d1783, m1735 Elizabeth Gooche - desc/o Judge Simon Lynde CHB310; MCB208; MCD263; BCD310; DBR(3)746; DBR(4)835; AWW192

VANDEWALL Martha - of VA, m Col Turner Southall - desc/o Lieut Col Walter Aston FFF271

VAN CORTLANDT Stephanus - of NY - the immigrant EDV14; sufficient proof of alleged royal ancestry is lacking

VAN LODENSTEYN Sophia - of NY, dau/o Jan & Geertruy (Gertrude) Jansdr. van Ilpendam, m Carel de Beauvois or Debevoise - the immigrant GBR365

VAN RENSSELAER Killaen - of NY 1637 - the immigrant EDV15; sufficient proof of alleged royal ancestry is lacking

VAN VOORHEES Steven Coerte - of NY 1660 - the immigrant EDV40; sufficient proof of alleged royal ancestry is lacking

VAN WYCK Cornelius Berents - of NY 1660 - the immigrant EDV39; sufficient proof of alleged royal ancestry is lacking

VANE Sir Henry - of MA, b1613 d1662 Puritan & governor of MA, son of Sir Henry Vane & Frances Darcy, m1639 Frances Wray dau/o Sir Christopher Wray, leaving issue 4 sons & 6 daughters - the immigrant GBR123; NE(2)121/143; EO2(3)573

VARNEY Daniel - b1726/1727 - desc/o Rose Stoughton RAA119

Mercy - b abt 1776 - desc/o Rose Stoughton RAA119

Stephen - b1697 - desc/o Rose Stoughton RAA119

VARNUM Dorothy Prescott - of MA, b1715 d1756, m1736 David Shattuck - desc/o John Prescott DBR(1)525

Elizabeth - b1741 - desc/o John Prescott RAA125

Jonas - b1710 - desc/o John Prescott RAA125

VAUGHAN Col George - of NH, b1676 d1724, m1700 Elizabeth Eliot - desc/o Maj William Vaughan DBR(2)27, 627

Jane, of PA - b abt 1624/1632 dau/o Robert Vaughan & Catherine Nannau, m Robert Owen - the immigrant RAA120; GBR167

Mary - of NH, b1713 d1793, m1741 Cutts Shannon - desc/o Maj William Vaughan DBR(2)27, 627

Maj William - of NH, b1640 d1719, m1668 Margaret Cutts - the immigrant DBR(2)27, 627; RAA1; sufficient proof of alleged royal ancestry is lacking

VEATCH James - of MD, b1628 d1681 sheriff of Patuxent, St Marie's & Potomack, son of Malcolm Veatch of Muirdeen, m1657 Mary Gakerlin - the immigrant DBR(2)521; RAA1; BLG2951; GBR111; TAG(53)152, 153

James - of MD, b1695 d1762, m1719 Rachel Hepburn - desc/o James Veatch BLG2951

James - of MD & SC, b1725, m1751 Eleanor Raymer - desc/o James Veatch BLG2951

John - of MD, b1704 d1767, m1728 Grace Masters - desc/o James Veatch DBR(2)521

Nathan - of MD, b1667 d1705 grand juror & owner of large plantations in Calvert Co, m1689 Anne Clagett - desc/o James Veatch

VEATCH (cont.)
DBR(2)521; BLG2951
Nathan - of MD, b1752 d1829, m1778 Elizabeth Cragg - desc/o James Veatch BLG2951
Silas - of MD, b1729 d1805, m abt 1755 Jean____ - desc/o James Veatch DBR(2)521
Susanna - of MD, b1762 d1825, m1782 Aaron Crain - desc/o James Veatch DBR(2)521

VERNON Samuel - b1683 d1737, m(1)1707 Elizabeth Fleet b abt 1685 d1722, m(2)1725 Elizabeth (Paine) Prince b abt 1680 1754/1759 dau/o Nathaniel & Dorothy (Raynsford) Paine - desc/o Catherine Hamby NE(145)263

VER PLANCK Daniel Crommelin - of NY, b1762 member of Congress 1802/1809 & judge of the court of common pleas of Dutchess Co until 1828, m(1) Elizabeth Johnson dau/o William Samuel Johnson, first president of Columbia College, m(2) Ann Walton only dau/o William Walton & Ann De Lancey - desc/o Robert Sinclair NYGBR(50)#1p48
Samuel - of NY, d1820 prominent both socially & politically, m1761 (his cousin) Judith Crommelin eldest dau/o Daniel Crommelin & Anna Sinclair - desc/o Robert Sinclair NYGBR(50)#1p47/49

de VIMEUR Jean Baptiste Donatien, Count de Rochambeau - b1725 d1807, commander of the French expeditionary army in America during the last three years of the American Revolution, son of Joseph Charles II de Vimeur, Marquis de Rochambeau & Marie Claire Therese Begon, m Jeanne Therese Tellez d'Acosta - the immigrant GBR201

VINCENT Joseph - of RI, b1737 d1823, m1770 Anna Dunbar - desc/o William Arnold MCB396
Joan - b abt 1640, m John Sheldon - the immigrant LDS33 & 98 sufficient proof of alleged royal ancestry is lacking
Nicholas - of RI, d1749, m bef 1724 Elizabeth____ - desc/o William Arnold MCB396

von FERSEN Hans Axel - b1755 d1810, Swedish soldier, aide-de-camp to Rochambeau during the American Revolution, favorite and benefactor of Marie Antoinette, Queen of France, son of Frederick Axel, Count von Fersen & Hedwig Catharina, Countess de la Gardie. died unmarried - the immigrant GBR91

von STEUBEN Friedrich Wilhelm Ludolf Gerhard Augustin, Baron von Steuben - b1730 d1794, Prussian soldier, American Revolutionary commander, son of Wilhelm Augustin & Maria Justina Dorothea (von Jagow) von Steuben, died unmarried - the immigrant GBR63

von WATTEVILLE Anna Dorothea Elizabeth, Baroness Vol Watteville - of PA, dau/o Johann Michael, Baron von Watteville & Henrietta Benigna Justina von Zinzendorf, Countess of Zinzendorf & Pottendorf, m Hans Christian Alexander von Schweinitz - the immigrant GBR195

von ZINZENDORF Nicholas Ludwig, Count of Zinzendorf & Pottendorf - b1700 d1760, religious reformer, son of George Louis von Zinzendorf, Count of Zinzendorf & Pottendorf & Carlotta Justina von Gersdorff, m Errdmuthe Dorothea, Countess Reuss-Ebersdorf -

von ZINZENDORF (cont.)
the immigrant GBR197, 198
VOSE Jerusha - b1702 - desc/o Richard Billings RAA70

– W –

WADDRUP Elizabeth - of VA - desc/o Frances Mason CHB441
Margaret of VA, m William Harwood - desc/o Frances Mason CHB441
WADE Prudence - of MA, b1669, m Thomas Swan b1669 - desc/o
Katherine Deighton DBR(2)571
WAINWRIGHT Francis - of MA - the immigrant EDV111; sufficient proof
of alleged royal ancestry is lacking
Mary - of MA, b1716 d1766, m Judge Chambers Russell - desc/o Gov
Thomas Dudley CRL(1)406
WAITE Jeremiah - b1684, m Mary Graves - desc/o John Leonard LDS70
Joseph - b1702, m Susanna Bancroft - desc/o Rev William Sargent
LDS32; RAA129
Mary - b1708, m Richard Morton - desc/o John Leonard LDS70
Phineas - b1749, m(1) Mehitable Foster - desc/o Rev William Sargent
LDS32; RAA129
WAKEMAN Francis - b1565, m Anne Goode - the immigrant RAA no
longer accepted as being of royal descent
WALCOTT Benjamin - of MA, b1729, m Mary Foster - desc/o John
Putnam CHB428
Benjamin Stuart - of MA, b1755 d1824, m1778 Mary Dexter - desc/o
John Putnam CHB428
William - of MA, b1691, m1711 Mary Felt - desc/o John Putnam
CHB428
WALDEGRAVE Jemima - of MA, dau/o Thomas Waldegrave & Margaret
Holmstead, m Herbert Pelham, 1st treasurer of Harvard College -
the immigrant GBR317; TAG(14)197/202; (18)139/144
WALDO Ann - of CT, b1737 d1779, m1753 Elisha Payne - desc/o John
Drake J&K316
Calvin - of NH, b1759 d1815 soldier in the Revolutionary War & a
lawyer, m(1) Judith Graves - desc/o Rev Thomas Dimmock J&K225
Ebenezer - of CT, m Cynthia Parish - desc/o John Drake J&K313
Edward Jr - of CT, b1709 d1807, m Abigail Elderkin - desc/o Rev
Thomas Dimmock J&K221, 313
Eunice - b1769 - desc/o Edward Carleton RAA78
Jemima - m Henry Lake and had Rev Phipps Waldo Lake - desc/o Rev
Thomas Dimmock J&K223
Jesse - of CT, b1736 d1823 lieut in the Revolutionary War, m(1)1760
Bridget Thompson - desc/o Rev Thomas Dimmock J&K224
John - m Jemima Abbot - desc/o Rev Thomas Dimmock J&K222
John Elderkin - of CT, m Beulah Foster - desc/o Rev Thomas
Dimmock J&K221
Olive - of CT, b1768, m David Taylor mother of General Jonathan
Taylor - desc/o Rev Thomas Dimmock J&K224
Shubael - of CT, b1707 d1776, m(1)1730 Abigail Allen (2) Mary Alden -
desc/o Rev Thomas Dimmock J&K224

WALDO (cont.)

Zechariah - of CT, b1734/1735 d1811, m(1)1758 Elizabeth Wight - desc/o Rev Thomas Dimmock J&K221, 313

Zerviah - m Job Goff of WV - desc/o Rev Thomas Dimmock J&K222

WALES Joshua - b1752 d1859, m1779 Elizabeth Porter - desc/o Rev John Oxenbridge DBR(1)371

Phoebe - b1731 d1799, m1750 Joshua Tilden - desc/o Rev John Oxenbridge DBR(2)511, 609

WALKE Rev Anthony - of VA, son of Anthony Walke of Princess Anne Co, VA & Jane Randolph - desc/o Col William Randolph PVF161

WALKER Anne Hutchinson - m Capt James Sands d1695 - desc/o Anne Marbury DBR(4)311; DBR(5)290

Edward - b abt 1692 d1752, m abt 1712 Mercy Richmond b abt 1693 d1760 dau/o Edward & Mercy (___) Richmond, no children - desc/o Anne Marbury NE(145)265

Hannah - b aft 1693 d aft 1764, m(1)___ Place, m(2) John Atwood, her cousin, b1683 d abt 1764 son of Joseph & Hester/Esther (Walker) Atwood - desc/o Anne Marbury NE(145)265

Helen - m Major William Call, mother of Gen Richard Keith Call - desc/o Sir Richard Everard J&K249; CHB180

James - b abt 1699 d1726, m1725 Mary Walker (his cousin) b1704 d1782, they were the parents of one son, Elisha - desc/o Anne Marbury NE(145)265

Johanna - of MA, b1704 d1786, m1724 David Carpenter II b1701 d1787 son of David Carpenter - desc/o Robert Abell DBR(2)846; RAA59

Katherine - b bef 1694 d bef 1753, m1712 John Blaney 3rd - desc/o Anne Marbury NE(145)265

Mary - b1716, m1737 Daniel Perry - desc/o Lieut Griffith Bowen DBR(1)466

Peter - b abt 1689 d1770, m abt 1710 Sarah Godfrey b1689 d1760 dau/o Richard & Mary (Richmond) Godfrey, parents of six children - desc/o Anne Marbury NE(145)265

WALLACE John - of NJ, b1718 d1783, m Mary Maddox - the immigrant MCB163; sufficient proof of alleged royal ancestry is lacking

WALLER Rev Absolem - of VA, b1741 d1802 exercised an able ministry in the Baptist Church in VA m____ Shelton & had issue 6 children - desc/o Col John Waller GVFHB(5)728; VG383

Agnes - of VA, m____ Johnson - desc/o Col John Waller GVFHB(5)717

Agnes - of VA, m Sharp Smith - desc/o Col John Waller VG383

Ann - of VA, m James Bullock - desc/o Col John Waller GVFHB(5)717

Ann - of VA, m John Beverely Roy - desc/o Col John Waller GVFHB(5)717

Ann - of VA, b1756 d1785, m1773 John Boush of Norfolk - desc/o Col John Waller GVFHB(5)718; VG383

Ann - of VA, m Joel Harris - desc/o Col John Waller VG383

Benjamin - of VA, b1716 d1786 burgess 1745, judge general court 1779/1786, m1746 Martha Hall b1728 d1780 & had issue - desc/o Col John Waller GVFHB(5)718; VG383

Benjamin - of VA, b1749 d1835, m(1) Jean Curtis, m(2) Rachel____ - desc/o Col John Waller GVFHB(5)718; VG383

WALLER (cont.)

Benjamin Carter - of VA, b1757 justice, delegate & clerk of James City Co, m Catherine Page - desc/o Col John Waller GVFHB(5)718; VG383

Clara - of VA, b1757, m(1)1779 Edward Travis, m(2) Mordecai Booth - desc/o Col John Waller GVFHB(5)718; VG383

Dabney - of VA, b1772 d1849, m Elizabeth Minor dau/o Thomas & Mary Minor - desc/o Col John Waller GVFHB(5)764; VG383

Dorothy - of VA, m Thomas Goodloe - desc/o Col John Waller GVFHB(5)717

Dorothy - of VA, b abt 1732 d1792, m1750 Solomon Quarles b1725 d1774 - desc/o Col John Waller GVFHB(5)717; VG383

Dorothy - of VA, m Richard Johnston - desc/o Col John Waller GVFHB(5)717

Dorothy Elizabeth - of VA, b1754 d1777, m1774 Henry Tazewell - desc/o Col John Waller GVFHB(5)718; VG383

Dorothy Jemima - of VA, b1758 d1838, m Benjamin Stephens b1754 d1839 - desc/o Col John Waller GVFHB(5)718

Edmund - of VA, b abt 1718 d1771 qualified to his commission as captain of a company of foot in the Spotsylvania militia, m1740 Mary Pendleton b1720 d1808 dau/o Philip Pendleton & Elizabeth Pollard & had issue - desc/o Col John Waller GVFHB(5)718; VG382

Elizabeth - of VA, m Edmund Eggleston - desc/o Col John Waller GVFHB(5)717

Col John - of VA, b1673 d1754 of Endfield plantation, King & Queen Co, a notable man of his time as an official in both the civil & military establishments of the colony, son of John Waller & Mary Pomfrett, m abt 1696/1697 Dorothy King b abt 1675 d1759 (parentage undetermined) - the immigrant GBR331; GVFWM(5)345/349; GVFHB(5)703/767; VG382

John - of VA, b abt 1701 d1776 of Spotsylvania Co, was a vestryman for St George Parish 1733 & sheriff 1746 for that county, m1730 Agnes Carr b1712 d1779 dau/o Thomas Carr & Mary Dabney - desc/o Col John Waller GVFHB(5)716, 717; VG383

John - of VA, b1735 styled "John Waller, King Wm", m Mary Ann___ - desc/o Col John Waller GVFHB(5)717

John - of VA, b abt 1741 d abt 1775 county clerk of Spotsylvania Co, the fourth of his family to hold that office, m Ann Bowker - desc/o Col John Waller GVFHB(5)717

Rev John - of VA, b1741 Spotsylvania Co d1802 ordained 20 Jun 1770 pastor of a Baptist congregation that had been instituted in his neighborhood, extended his preaching ministry to several VA counties several times coming in conflict with colonial authorities because he refused to seek the legal license required of dissenting ministers, m(1) Elizabeth Curtis, m(2) Rachel___ - desc/o Col John Waller GVFHB(5)718, 728

John - of VA, b1753 clerk Spots Co 1774/1786, m1774 Judith Page - desc/o Col John Waller GVFHB(5)718; VG383

Leonard James Mourning - of VSA, m(1) Agnes Chiles, m(2) Frances Robinson - desc/o Col John Waller GVFHB(5)718

Martha - of VA, m Capt Gabriel Jones - desc/o Col John Waller

WALLER (cont.)
> GVFHB(5)717

> Martha - of VA, b1747, m1767 William Taylor b1739 d1820 of Lunenburg Co, VA - desc/o Col John Waller GVFHB(5)718; VG383

> Mary - of VA, b1699 d1781, m1725 Zachary Lewis b1702 d1765 of Spotsylvania Co, VA, a distinguished lawyer & wealthy planter of his time. He became a member of the vestry of St George Parish Spotsylvania Co in 1728, was King's Attorney & a repesentative in the House of Burgesses 1757/1761 & had issue - desc/o Col John Waller GVFHB(5)716; VG381

> Mary - m Daniel Sackett - desc/o Margaret Wyatt GBR397

> Mary - prob of VA, dau/o John Waller & Mary Pomfrett, m Edward Herndon son of William & Catherine Herndon - the immigrant GBR332 some aspect of royal descent merits further study; GVFWM(5)345/349

> Mary - of VA, m James Overton - desc/o Col John Waller GVFHB(5)717

> Mary - of VA, b1752, m John Tayloe Corbin - desc/o Col John Waller GVFHB(5)718; VG383

> Mary - of VA, m William Wigglesworth - desc/o Col John Waller GVFHB(5)718

> Nancy - of VA, m George Mason - desc/o Col John Waller GVFHB(5)718

> Pomfrett - of VA, b1747 d1799, m Martha Martin - desc/o Col John Waller GVFHB(5)717

> Robert Hall - of VA, b1764, m(1) Nancy Camm, m(2) Martha (nee Langhorne) Crafford - desc/o Col John Waller GVFHB(5)718; VG383

> Sarah - of VA, m Clifton Rhodes b1740 d1819 of Albemarle Co, VA - desc/o Col John Waller GVFHB(5)717

> Sarah - of VA, m Jospeh Spicer - desc/o Col John Waller VG383

> Sarah - of VA, b1766, m John Smith - desc/o Col John Waller GVFHB(5)718; VG383

> Thomas - of VA, b1705 d abt 1765, m abt 1725 Elizabeth Dabney b abt 1705 d1794 & had issue - desc/o Col John Waller GVFHB(5)717

> Thomas - of VA, b abt 1730 d1798, m abt 1750 Susanna [Edwards?] - desc/o Col John Waller GVFHB(5)717

> Thomas - of VA, b1732 d1787, m Sarah Dabney b1740 d1822 dau/o John Dabney & Sarah A J Harris - desc/o Col John Waller GVFHB(5)717; 763; VG383

> William - of VA, b1714 d1760 a man of considerable distinction in the life of his county. He was captain of a troop of horse in 1737 & in 1749 qualified to his commission as colonel of horse in Spotsylvania Co. In 1745 he became a member of the vestry of St George Parish & was a representative from Spotsylvania Co in the House of Burgesses for many years. He was a surveyor of the county & third clerk of Spotsylvania Co in 1751, holding this office until his death; m1738 Mrs Ann (Stanard) Beverley b abt 1716 d1756 dau/o William Stanard & Ann Hazlewood & wid/o Robert Beverley d1733 Esq & had issue - desc/o Col John Waller GVFHB(5)717; VG382

WALLER (cont.)

William - of VA, b1762 d1820, m1786 Elizabeth Macon - desc/o Col John Waller GVFHB(5)718; VG383

Rev William Edmund - of VA, b1747 Spotsylvania Co d1830 removed to Garrard Co, Kentucky 1784 returning to VA in 1803 where he died, m Mildred Smith b1746 d1830 - desc/o Col John Waller GVFHB(5)718, 728

WALTER Harriet Lynde - of MA, m John Odin - desc/o William Browne CHB139 - desc/o Judge Simon Lynde CHB314

WALTHALL Henry - of VA, b1770 d1818/1819, m(2)1801 Elizabeth Chamberlayne Batte - desc/o Lieut Col Thomas Lygon DBR(5)639

Thomas - of VA, b1724 d1787, m(1) Anne Wythe - desc/o Lieut Col Thomas Lygon DBR(5)639

Thomas - of VA, b abt 1740 d1776, m Elizabeth Featherstone - desc/o Lieut Col Thomas Lygon DBR(5)639

WALTON Abraham - m Grace Williams - desc/o Thomas Lawrence GBR456

Daniel - of PA, d1719, m1688 Mary Lamb - the immigrant AFA24; sufficient proof of alleged royal ancestry is lacking

Daniel - of PA, m1714 Elizabeth Clifton - desc/o Daniel Walton AFA24

Daniel - of PA, d1776, m Ann Knight - desc/o Daniel Walton AFA24

Daniel - of PA, b1763 d1836, m Mary Woolens - desc/o Daniel Walton AFA24

Fisher - of MD, d1738, m Elizabeth ____ - desc/o John Fisher APP281

Jacob - m Maria Beekman - desc/o Thomas Lawrence GBR457

John - of MD, d1716/1717, son of William Walton & Rebecca Fisher, m____ - desc/o John Fisher APP281

Reuben - b abt 1734, m Mary Thompson - desc/o Elias Maverick LDS106; RAA115

Reuben - b 1766, m Ruth Peabody - desc/o Elias Maverick LDS106; RAA115

Samuel - b1686, m Hannah Leach - desc/o Elias Maverick LDS106; RAA115

Samuel - b1705, m Rebecca Davis - desc/o Elias Maverick LDS106; RAA115

Sarah - of MA, b1664 d1731, m1688 Thomas Burnap Jr - desc/o Elias Maverick ECD(3)175; DBR(5)736

Stephen - of MD, m Mary____ - desc/o John Fisher APP281

William - m Mary Santvoort - desc/o Thomas Lawrence GBR457

WALWORTH (WAL(S)WORTH) Lucy b1732 d1795, m1753 Capt Veach Williams - desc/o Susan Clinton CHB417 - desc/o Susannah Palmes ECD(3)188; MCD234

Mary - of CT, b1721 d aft 1796, m1742 Deacon Solomon Morgan - desc/o Susan Clinton CHB417 - desc/o Susannah Palmes ECD(3)185

William - of CT 1689 - the immigrant EDV90; sufficient proof of alleged royal ancestry is lacking

WANTON Elizabeth - of RI, b1742 d1814, m1762 Thomas Wickham - desc/o Katherine Deighton ECD(2)111; DBR(5)85 - desc/o Gov Thomas Dudley DBR(5)81

WARD Abigail - b abt 1665 ? - desc/o Mary Gye RAA115

Col Benjamin - of VA, b1747 d1783, m Catherine Crawley - desc/o Thomas Batte DBR(4)394

Catherine Crawley - of VA, m1794 Lieut Francis FitzGerald - desc/o Thomas Batte DBR(4)394

Elizabeth - m John Kittell - desc/o Mary Gye NE(96)359

Ira - b1704 - desc/o Agnes Harris RAA131

John - of VA, m1731 Hannah____ - desc/o Christopher Branch APP137

Martha - of MA, m John Tuttle - desc/o Mary Gye NE(96)359

Mary - of MA, bp 1669 Salem, m____ Doliver - desc/o Mary Gye NE(96)359

Mary - b1750/1754, m John Woodbury - desc/o Edmund Rice LDS114

Merab - b1733 - desc/o Agnes Harris RAA131

Mercy - of MA, m____ Cane - desc/o Mary Gye NE(96)359

Remember - of MA, bp 1669 Salem, m William Wilson - desc/o Mary Gye NE(96)359

Richard - of NC, of Carteret Co - desc/o Christopher Branch APP137

Samuel - of MA, d aft 5 Dec 1698, m Sarah Tittle - desc/o Mary Gye NE(96)359

Thomasine - of MA, dau/o George Ward & Dionis Burrow, m(1) John Thompson, m(2) Robert Buffum - the immigrant GBR355 some aspect of royal descent merits further study

WARING Ann - of MD, m Josiah Hawkins - desc/o Sampson Waring DBR(1)202; DBR(2)299

Basil - of MD, b1654, m Sarah Marsham - desc/o Sampson Waring DBR(1)167, 202; DBR(2)299; DBR(3)768; CRL(2)196

Basil - of MD, b1683 d1733, m1709 Martha Greenfield - desc/o Giles Brent ECD(3)30 - desc/o Sampson Waring DBR(1)168; 202; DBR(2)299; DBR(3)768; CRL(2)196; DBR(2)299; DBR(3)768; CRL(2)196

Basil - of MD, b1717 d1776, m1746 Elizabeth Belt - desc/o Sampson Waring DBR(1)168; DBR(3)768; CRL(2)196

Maj Francis - of MD, b1715 d1769, m1740 Mary Hollyday - desc/o Giles Brent ECD(3)30 - desc/o Sampson Waring DBR(1)202; DBR(2)299

James - of MD, b1755 d1813, m1785 Elizabeth Hilleary - desc/o Sampson Waring DBR(1)168; DBR(3)768; CRL(2)196

Capt Sampson - of VA & MD, b1617/1618 d1670, m Sarah Leigh - the immigrant DBR(1)167, 201; DBR(2)299; DBR(3)766, 768; RAA1; sufficient proof of alleged royal ancestry is lacking

Judge Thomas - of MD, b1752 d1818, m1774 Lydia Walton - desc/o Giles Brent ECD(3)30

WARNER Col Augustine - of VA, b1610 d1674, m Mary Towneley - the immigrant AWW81, 82; NFA69; GVFHB(5)538/577 royal descent is from his wife Mary Towneley

Augustine Jr - of VA, b1643 d1681, m Mildred Reade - desc/o Col Augustine Warner AWW82, 83; NFA70; CRL(3)110 - desc/o Mary Towneley GBR330

Elizabeth - of VA, b1672 d1720, m1690/1691 Col John Lewis b1669

WARNER (cont.)

> d1725 - desc/o Col George Reade CHB420; ECD212; MCD272; BCD255; DBR(1)10, 209, 474, 535, 606, 626, 657, 687; DBR(2)6, 383, 384, 825, 835; DBR(3)186, 187, 331, 352, 448, 587, 615, 623, 701; DBR(4)485, 588, 592, 720; DBR(5)191, 525, 562, 564, 646; AWW83; FFF267; CRL(3)110; APP427; HSF(2)187, 197

Isabella - m1666 Col John Lewis - desc/o Col George Reade NFA71, 77

Mary - of VA, d1700, m1680/1681 Col John Smith d1698 of Gloucester Co, captain of militia, vestryman & land owner - desc/o Col George Reade CHB251; MCD273; BCD251, DBR(1)255, 354, 469, 550, 724, 732; DBR(2)61, 212; DBR(4)496, 773; DBR(5)102, 240, 342; PFA Apx D #1; AWW83; NFA71; CRLL(3)110; APP426; HSF(1)197

Mildred - of VA, d1701, m(1)1690 Lawrence Washington b1659 d1698 captain of militia, justice & sheriff of Westmoreland Co, m(2)1700 Capt George Gale d1712 of Somerset Co MD, justice, major & lieutenant colonel of militia - desc/o Col George Reade J&K146, 227, 228; CHB253; JSW1638; MCS60; BCD253; DBR(1)723, 764; DBR(2)73, 539, 632, 715; DBR(3)446, 570, 614, 615; DBR(4)847; DBR(5)210, 555, 571, 651; AAP139, PFA Apx C #1, Apx D #1; AWW83; FFF124, 268; NFA70, 77; CRL(3)110, 111; GBR183 - desc/o Mary Towneley 330; TAG(51)167/171; APP426; HSF(2)186, 187, 197

Mildred - of VA, b1682, m Robert Porteus - desc/o Col George Reade PFA Apx D #1

Phebe Berrien - of NY, b1772 d1849, m abt 1793 Moses Sayre - desc/o Richard Woodhull ECD238

Ruth - b1705 - desc/o George Morton RAA116

Sarah - of VA, m Lawrence Townley - desc/o Col George Reade DBR(2)830; PFA Apx D #1; AWW82; NFA69, 70

WARREN Alice - of VA, b abt 1645 d abt 1707, m abt 1670 Matthias Marriott d1708 - desc/o Capt Thomas Warren ECD(3)311; DBR(1)189; DBR(2)270; VHG246

Allen I - of VA, b1663 d1738, m Elizabeth Clements - desc/o Capt Thomas Warren ECD(3)313; DBR(1)439; DBR(3)555; VHG249, 250

Allen II (or Jr) - of VA, b abt 1690 d1733, m abt 1715 Anne Hart - desc/o Capt Thomas Warren ECD(3)313; DBR(1)439; DBR93)555; VHG250

Allen III - of VA, d1780, m abt 1740 Mary Phillips - desc/o Capt Charles Barham ECD(2)29; DBR(1)436 - desc/o Capt Thomas Warren ECD(3)313; DBR(1)439; DBR(3)555; DBR(5)793; VHG250

Ann - of MD, m William Dent - desc/o Humphrey Warren CHB317; BCD317

Barton - of MD, d1757, m Elizabeth ____ - desc/o Humphrey Warren CHB317; MCD301; BCD317

Charity - of VA, m____ Smith - desc/o Capt Thomas Warren HSF(18)207

Daniel - of MA, bp 1626/1627 d1715, m1650 Mary Barron - desc/o John Warren CRL(2)143

Capt Daniel - of MA, b1689, m(1)1711 Rebecca Garfield, m(2)1727 Mary Weatherly - desc/o John Warren CRL(2)144

WARREN (cont.)

Elizabeth - of VA, m 1670/1671 John Hunnicutt d1699 - desc/o Capt Thomas Warren VHG249

Elizabeth - of VA, m Thomas Davis d1720 - desc/o Capt Thomas Warren VHG250

Eunice - of MA, b1757 d1796, m1780 Stephen Belknap - desc/o John Warren CRL(2)144

Humphrey - of MD, b1632 d1673, m(1) abt 1652____, m(2) Eleanor____ - the immigrant CHB316; MCD301; BCD316; sufficient proof of alleged royal ancestry is lacking

Col Humphrey - of MD, b Abt 1652 d1689, m(2)abt 1681 Margery____ - desc/o Humphrey Warren CHB316; BCD316, 317

James - of MA, b1726, m 1754 Mercy Otis - desc/o Herbert Pelham NE(4)302

Lieut Jesse - of VA, b abt 1745 d1794 lieutenant in Capt Wilson's Company of Surrey Co, VA, m abt 1770 Martha Thompson - desc/o Capt Charles Barnham ECD(2)29; DBR(1)436; DBR(5)793 - desc/o Capt Thomas Warren ECD(3)313; DBR(3)555; VHG252; HSF(18)213, 214 - desc/o John Harris DBR(4)637

Jesse - of VA & TN, d1840 Robertson Co, TN, m1790 Franklin Co, VA, Rhoda Richards, dau/o Edward Richards & Elizabeth____ - desc/o Capt Thomas Warren HSF(18)209

Jesse Phillips - of VA, b abt 1770 d1829, m1814 Sarah Caroline Bell - desc/o Capt Charles Barnham ECD(2)29; DBR(5)793 - desc/o Capt Thomas Warren ECD(3)313; DBR(1)439; DBR(3)555 - desc/o John Harris DBR(4)637

John - of MA 1630, b1585 d1667, m Margaret____ - the immigrant J&K127; EDV27; PFA Apx C #10; CRL(2)142; sufficient proof of alleged royal ancestry is lacking

Ensign John - of MA, b1665/1666 d1703, m Mary Browne - desc/o John Warren CRL(2)143

John - of VA, b1676 d abt 1700 Old Rappahannock Co, m Rachel Sergent, dau/o William Sergent d1707 Essex Co - desc/o Capt Thomas Warren HSF(18)207

John - of MD b1687 d1713, m Judith____ - desc/o Humphrey Warren CHB316, 17; BCD316, 317

Mary - m John Bigelow - desc/o John Warren J&K127; PFA Apx C #10

Mary - of VA, m(1) Harrison Musgrave, m(2)John Stone - desc/o Humphrey Warren CHB318; BCD318

Mary - of VA, m____ Batts - desc/o Capt Thomas Warren HSF(18)207

Mercy - b1653 - desc/o George Morton RAA116

Patience - b1666 - desc/o George Morton RAA116

Sir Peter - of NY, b1703 d1752 Rear Admiral Royal Navy of New York & the American colonies 1730/1752 son of Michael Warren & Catherine Aylmer, m Susannah De Lancey & left issue - the immigrant GBR217; NYGBR(18)#4p150/152

Rebecca - of VA, m____ Davis - desc/o Capt Thomas Warren HSF(18)207

Robert - of VA, b1667 d1721, m Anne____ & had issue a son Robert Warren - desc/o Capt Thomas Warren VHG249

Sarah - of MA, b1730 d1797, m1755 William Sever - desc/o Herbert

WARREN (cont.)

Pelham CHB196; BCD196; ECD(3)238; NE(4)302

Capt Thomas - of VA, bp 1624/1625 d1669/1670 son of William
Warren & Catherine Gookin, m(1)____, m(2)1654 (marriage
settlement) Elizabeth Shepard dau/o ancient planter William
Spencer & wid/o Major Robert Shepard, m(3) Jane____ wid/o John
King - the immigrant MCB148; RAA1; ECD(3)311, 313; DBR(1)189,
439; DBR(2)267, 270, 568; DBR(3)555; GBR376; VHG244/253;
HSF(18)204/217

Thomas Jr - of VA, b1659 d1721, m Elizabeth____ d1730, leaving
issue, four sons & one daughter - desc/o Capt Thomas Warren
VHG249, 250; HSF(18)206

Thomas - of MD 1663, d1710, m(1)bef 1688 Mary Barton - desc/o
Humphrey Warren CHB317; MCD301; BCD317

Thomas - of VA, b1700 of Surry Co d1759, m Lucy____ d1785 - desc/o
Capt Thomas Warren HSF(18)207

Thomas - of VA, b bef 1740 Old Lunenburg Co d1801 Franklin Co,
served as captain of infantry, VA Line in the Revolutionary War, m
Jane Browne - desc/o Capt Thomas Warrren HSF(18)207, 208

Timothy - of MA, b1715, m(1) 1739 Rebecca Tainter, m(2) abt 1796
Phoebe____ - desc/o John Warren CRL(2)144

William - of VA, b1669/1670 d1702, m____ & had a son James Warren
- desc/o Capt Thomas Warren VHG249

William Barton - of MD, b1738 d1809, m Mary Jane Yates - desc/o
Humphrey Warren CHB317; MCD301; BCD317

William Monroe - of KY, b1775 d1824, m Maria F Fauntleroy - desc/o
Humphrey Warren CHB318; BCD318

WASHBOURNE (WASHBURN) Hepzibah - of MA, d1750, m1702 Benjamin
Leach - desc/o John Washbourne DBR(3)470 - desc/o John
Winslow THC341

John - of MA, bp 1597 d1618 son of John Washburn & Joan Mitton,
m1618 Margery More - the immigrant FLW89 there is no proof that
John Washburn was the son of John Washburn & Joan Mitton;
TAG(36)63; DBR(2)529, 853; DBR(3)230, 469; RAA1

John - of MA, b1621 d1685, m1645 Elizabeth Mitchell - desc/o John
Washbourne DBR(2)529, 853; DBR(3)469

Joseph - of MA, bp 1649, m Hannah Latham - desc/o John
Washbourne DBR(3)470

Mary - of MA, b1661, m Samuel Kingsley - desc/o John Washbourne
DBR(2)529

Sarah - of MA, d1746, m1696 John Ames II - desc/o John
Washbourne DBR(2)853

WASHINGTON Amelia - of VA, m James Clayton - desc/o John
Washington HSF(4)156

Andrew - of VA, m Margaret Bridger - desc/o John Washington
HSF(4)156

Anne - of VA, b abt 1662 d1697/1698, m abt 1680 Maj Francis Wright
- desc/o Col John Washington JSW1750; DBR(1)257, 666;
DBR(2)40, 374; DBR(3)18; DBR(4)406; DBR(5)135, 204; CRL(3)108;
HSF(4)161; CFSSA519

Anne - of VA, m John Stevens - desc/o John Washington HSF(4)158

WASHINGTON (cont.)

Anne - of VA, m William Thompson - desc/o Lawrence Washington CFA563

Anne - of VA, b1752 d1774, m1768 Col Burdett Ashton of Chestnut Hill, King George Co, son of Charles Ashton & Sarah____ - desc/o Col George Reade DBR(5)651; CFSSA521 - desc/o Col John Washington PFA48; CFA(2)744

Arthur - of VA, b abt 1681 d1758/1761, m Sarah Tynes d1764 - desc/o John Washington HSF(4)157, 158

Capt Augustine - of VA, b abt 1694 d1743, m(1)1715 Jane Butler d1728 dau/o Major Caleb Butler of Westmoreland, m(2)1730/1731 Mary Ball b1707/1708 d1789 dau/o Col Joseph Ball of Epping Forest, Lancaster Co & Mary Johnson - desc/o Col George Reade J&K146; CHB253; ECD217; MCS60; BCD253; DBR(1)723, 736, 764; DBR(5)651; AAP1, 139; PFA Apx D #1; AWW81, 83; NFA70; GBR183; TAG(51)167/171; CFSSA520 - desc/o Col John Washington DBR(2)486, 539, 717; PFA39, Apx C #1, Apx C #2; AAP1, 139; FFF124; CRL(3)108, 109; HSF(4)161; CFA(2)742 - desc/o Mary Towneley AAP140; GBR330

Augustine - of VA, b abt 1720 of Westmoreland Co d1762, m abt 1744 Anne Aylett dau/o Col William Aylett & Ann Ashton - desc/o Col John Washington DBR(2)486; DBR(5)651; PFA48; CFA(2)743 - desc/o Col George Reade CFSSA520

Bailey - of VA, b1730/1731, m1749 Catherine Storke - desc/o Col John Washington ECD(2)282; DBR(2)161, 341; DBR(3)389, 392; DBR(5)273

Benjamin - m Penelope____ & had issue, two sons - desc/o John Washington HSF(4)158

Bushrod - of VA, b1762 d1829 Justice of the Supreme Court of the United States, m1785 Ann Blackburn - desc/o Col John Washington PFA55; CFA(2)743

Butler - of VA, b1716 d abt 1729 - desc/o Col John Washington PFA48

Catherine - of VA, m (her cousin) John Washington - desc/o Lawrence Washington CFA(1)563

Catherine - of VA, b1724 d1750, m1746 Col Fielding Lewis of Kenmore, Spotsylvania Co, son of Col John Lewis & Frances Fielding of Warner Hall - desc/o John Washington HSF(4)161 - desc/o Col George Reade CFSSA519

Col Charles - of VA, b1738 of Charlestown, W VA, m Mildred Thornton, dau/o Col Francis Thornton & Mildred Gregory of Fall Hill, Spotsylvania Co - desc/o Col George Reade CHB253; BCD253; CFSSA520 - desc/o Col John Washington CRL(3)109

Corbin - of VA, b1765 d1800, m1786 Hannah Lee - desc/o Col George Reade DBR(1)736 - desc/o Col John Washington PFA55

Elizabeth - of VA, m John Abraham - desc/o John Washington HSF(4)158

Elizabeth - of VA, d1738, m Sampson Lanier - desc/o Col John Washington DBR(1)206, (5)242, 698; HSF(4)158

Elizabeth - of VA, m Reuban Thornton - desc/o Col George Reade AWW83

Elizabeth (Betty) - of VA, b1733 d1797, m1750 Col Fielding Lewis, of

WASHINGTON (cont.)

Kenmore, Spotsylvania Co, son of John Lewis & Frances Fielding of Warner Hall - desc/o Col George Reade CHB254; ECD217; MCS60; BCD254; CFSSA520 - desc/o Col John Washington PFA51; CRL(3)109; HSF(4)162; CFA(2)743

Elizabeth - of VA, b1749 d1814, m1769 Brig-Gen Alexander Spotswood, served with distinction in the Revolutionary War, son of John Spotswood & Mary Dandridge - desc/o Col John Washington PFA48; CFA(2)745 - desc/o Col George Reade CFSSA521

Elizabeth - of VA, b1765, m Charles Carter - desc/o John Washington HSF(4)162

Elizabeth - of VA, b1771 d1795, m Dr George Booth of Gloucester Co & d a few months after marriage - desc/o William Fairfax CFA(2)278

Faith - of VA, m Josiah Barker d1761 son of John & Grace Barker - desc/o John Washington HSF(4)158

Ferdinand - of VA, b1767 d1788 - desc/o Col John Washington PFA53

Fielding - of VA, b1751, m1769 Ann Alexander - desc/o John Washington HSF(4)162

Frances - of VA, m1736 Col Francis Thornton - desc/o Col George Reade AWW83

George - of VA, b abt 1682 d1762, m Mary Wright - desc/o John Washington HSF(4)156

George - of VA, d1783, m Sarah____ - desc/o John Washington HSF(4)156

George - of VA, d1800, m Easter____ - desc/o John Washington HSF(4)158

President George - of VA, b1732 Wakefield, Westmoreland Co d1799 Mount Vernon, Fairfax Co, Commander-in-Chief of the Continental Army, first President of the United States 1789/1797, m1756 Mrs Martha (Dandridge) Custis d1802, dau/o Col John Dandridge & Frances____ of Chestnut Grove, New Kent Co, & wid/o Col Daniel Park Custis of New Kent Co - desc/o Col George Reade J&K228; MCS60; DBR(2)539, 715; AAP1, 139, 140; PFA Apx C #1, Apx D #1, Apx D #2; AWW83, FFF124; NFA70, 71; GBR183; TAG(23)1/11, (51)167/171; CFSSA522 - desc/o Col John Washington PFA39; WAC109; CRL(3)109; GBR243; TAG(53)15; HSF(4)156, 162; CFA(2)743 - desc/o Mary Towneley GBR330

George - of VA, b1757, m Catherine Dangerfield - desc/o John Washington HSF(4)162

Col George Augustine - of VA, m Frances Bassett - desc/o Col George Reade CHB253; BCD253

George Steptoe - of W VA, b1773 Berkeley Co d1809, m1796 Lucy Payne d1846, dau/o John Payne & Mary Coles - desc/o Col George Reade DBR(1)723, 765; CFSSA523 - desc/o Col John Washington PFA53

Gray - of VA, captain in the militia 1780, m1791 Nancy Harrison dau/o James Harrison - desc/o John Washington HSF(4)157

Hannah - of VA, b1765 d1827, m Peter Beverley Whiting d1810/1811 of Elmington, Gloucester Co - desc/o William Fairfax CFA(2)278

Henry - of VA, b1695 d1747, m Mary Bailey - desc/o Col John Washington ECD(2)281; DBR(2)161, 226, 341; DBR(3)389, 392;

WASHINGTON (cont.)

DBR(5)273 - desc/o Lawrence Washington CFA(1)563

Henry - of VA, b1728, m(1)1749 Anne Thacker dau/o Col William Thacker & Elizabeth____ of Middlesex Co, m(2)1760 Charlotte____ - desc/o John Washington HSF(4)161 - desc/o Col George Reade CFSSA519

Henry - of VA, b1760 d1788, m Ann Quarles - desc/o Col John Washington DBR(2)227

Henry Augustine - of VA, b1749, m1772 Mildred Pratt - desc/o Lawrence Washington DBR(2)161, 341; DBR(3)389, 392; DBR(5)273

Howell - of VA, b1771, m Ellen Hackby Pollard - desc/o John Washington HSF(4)163

James - of VA & NC, b abt 1693 Surry Co d1766, moved to Northampton Co, NC where he was a representative, served in the Colonial Assembly & justice of the peace, m abt 1729 Joyce Nicholson dau/o Robert Nicholson & Joanna Joyce of Surry Co - desc/o John Washington ECD233; HSF(4)158

Jane - of VA, b1756 d1833, m1784 Col John Thornton, of Thornton Hill, Madison Co, son of Col Francis Thornton & Frances Gregory of Fall Hill, Spotsylvania Co - desc/o John Washington PFA48; CFA(2)744 - desc/o Col George Reade CFSSA521

Jane - of VA, b1759 d1791, m1777 Col William Augustine Washington - desc/o Col John Washington PFA55; CFA(2)743

Jessie - of VA, m Rebecca Wrenn dau/o Thomas Wrenn - desc/o John Washington HSF(4)157

Joanna - m Charles Thompson d1790 & had issue, six children - desc/o John Washington HSF(4)158

Col John - of VA abt 1657, b1632/1633 of Westmoreland Co d1675 commanded VA forces in the Indian War of 1675 & a member of the House of Burgesses, son of Lawrence Washington & Amphyllis Twigden, m(1)1658 Ann Pope dau/o Lieut Col Nathaniel Pope of MD, m(2) Mrs Anne Gerard Broadhurst Brett dau/o Thomas Gerard of MD as was wife #3, m(3) Mrs Frances Gerard Speake Peyton Appleton - the immigrant ECD(2)281; JSW149, 150; DBR(1)257, 666; DBR(2)40, 132, 225, 226, 241, 281, 301, 341, 485, 486, 715; DBR(3)18, 185, 443, 624; DBR(4)370, 405, 406, 870; DBR(5)135, 204, 242, 547, 564, 711, 1075; AAP139; BLG2961; PFA39, Apx C #2, Apx D #2; WAC109; AWW83; CRL(3)108; GBR243 some aspect of royal descent merits further study; TAG(51)167/171, (53)15; HSF(4)151, 160, 161; CFSSA518; CFA(1)562, (2)742

John - of VA, b abt 1624 d abt 1659/1660 son of Richard Washington (brother of Lawrence) & Frances Browne, m1658 Mary____ wid/o (1) Richard Blunt d1655/1656 & (2) Charles Ford - the immigrant ECD233; MCS21; DBR(1)205, 206; DBR(5)697, 698; GBR243; HSF(4)155

Capt John - of VA, b1661/1663 d1697/1698, m Anne Wickliffe - desc/o Col John Washington ECD(2)281; DBR(2)226, 341, 373, 374; HSF(4)161

John - of VA, b1671, m Mary Townsend dau/o Col Robert Townsend & Mary Langhorne - desc/o Lawrence Washington DBR(2)161;

WASHINGTON (cont.)

DBR(3)389, 392; DBR(5)273; BLG2961; CFA(1)563

Maj John - of VA, b1692 of Highgate, Gloucester Co d1746, m
Catherine Whiting b1694 d1743 dau/o Henry Whiting of Gloucester
Co - desc/o Col George Reade CHB253; BCD253; DBR(3)446, 614;
DBR(4)870; NFA70; CFSSA519 - desc/o John Washington
CRL(3)108; HSF(4)161; CFA(2)742

John - of VA, d1754, m Elizabeth____ - desc/o John Washington
HSF(4)156, 157

John - of VA, m Tamar Rickman dau/o William Rickman - desc/o
John Washington HSF(4)157

John - of NC, b abt 174_ d1768, m1768 Sarah Inman dau/o John (?)
Inman & Sarah Dawson (?) - desc/o John Washington ECD233;
HSF(4)158

Capt John - of VA - desc/o Lawrence Washington CFA(1)563

John - of NC, b abt 1768 d1837, m1799 Elizabeth Heritage Cobb
b1780 d1858 dau/o Jesse Cobb & Elizabeth Heritage - desc/o
John Washington ECD233; HSF(4)159

Capt John - of VA, m1759 Catherine Washington - desc/o Col John
Washington DBR(2)226, 227

John - of VA - desc/o Lawrence Washington MCD306

John Augustine - of VA, b1736 d1787, m1756 Hannah Bushrod -
desc/o Col George Reade DBR(1)736 - desc/o Col John Washington
PFA55; CRL(3)109; CFA(2)743

John Whiting - of VA & KY, b1773, m Frances Guyn Baylor - desc/o
Col George Reade DBR(3)446, 447, 614 - desc/o Col John
Washington DBR(4)870

Joseph - of VA, d1803, m Zilla Branch - desc/o John Washington
HSF(4)156

Joseph - of VA, moved to Robertson Co, TN, m Mary Cheatham dau/o
Frank Cheatham - desc/o John Washington HSF(4)156

Joyce - b abt 1752 d1818, m abt 1770 John Long d1782 & had issue,
six children - desc/o John Washington HSF(4)158

Katherine - of VA, b1767, m Dr John Nelson, son of Roger Nelson of
Frederick City, MD - desc/o William Fairfax CFA(2)278

Lawrence - of VA 1667, bp 1635 d1675 son of Lawrence Washington &
Amphyllis Twigden, m(1)1660 Mary Jones, m(2) abt 1667 Jane or
Joyce Fleming - the immigrant MCD306; DBR(2)161, 486;
DBR(3)388, 389, 392; DBR(4)870; DBR(5)273; RAA1; BLG2961;
CFA(1)562; GBR243; TAG(23)1/10; HSF(4)151; CFSSA518

Capt Lawrence - of VA, b1659 d1697 high sheriff & burgess from
Westmoreland Co, m abt 1689 Mildred Warner dau/o Col
Augustine Warner of Gloucester Co & Mildred Reade - desc/o Col
John Washington DBR(2)132, 241, 539; DBR(4)870; DBR(5)547;
AAP1, 139; PFA39, Apx C #2, Apx D #2; WAC109, 110; CRL(3)108;
GBR243, 330; TAG(51)167/171; HSF(4)161; CFSSA519; CFA(2)742

Lawrence - of VA, d1799, m Catherine____ - desc/o Lawrence
Washington CFA563

Maj Lawrence - of VA, b1718 of Mount Vernon, Fairfax Co d1752,
m1743 Anne Fairfax dau/o Gov William Fairfax & Sarah Walker of
the Bahamas & later of VA - desc/o Col John Washington PFA48;

WASHINGTON (cont.)

CFA92)743 - desc/o Col George Reade CFSSA520

Lawrence - of VA, b1767, m Nelly Custis, granddaughter of Col Daniel Park Custis & Martha Dandridge - desc/o John Washington HSF(4)162

Lawrence Augustine - of VA, b1774 d1824, m1797 Mary Dorcas - desc/o Col John Washington PFA54, Apx C #1

Louisa - of VA, b1775 d1798, m1798 Thomas, ninth Lord Fairfax & d three months after marriage - desc/o William Fairfax CFA(2)278

Lucy - of VA, m E C Williams - desc/o John Washington HSF(4)156

Lucy - of VA, m George Clements - desc/o John Washington HSF(4)157

Lund - of VA, m Elizabeth Foote - desc/o Lawrence Washington CFA563

Lund - of VA, b1767 d1853, m1793 Susan Monroe Grayson b1768 d1823 - desc/o Lawrence Washington MCD306; CFA564 - desc/o William Strother GVFTQ(3)377

Martha - of VA, m John Darden - desc/o John Washington HSF(4)156

Mary - bp 1663, m____ Gibson - desc/o Lawrence Washington CFA(1)562

Mary - of VA, m Robert Hart d1770 & had issue - desc/o John Washington HSF(4)158

Mary - m James Sunday (?) & had issue, one daughter - desc/o John Washington HSF(4)158

Mary Butler - of VA, b1760 d1822, m1780 Dr Valentine Peyton - desc/o Col John Washington ECD(2)282

Mildred - of VA, b1696 d1747, m(1) Roger Gregory, m(2)1733 Col Henry Willis, founder of Fredericksburg - desc/o George Reade JSW1638; BCD255; DBR(2)632; DBR(5)571; AAP1 - desc/o Col John Washington DBR(2)132; DBR(3)570; DBR(4)847; DBR(5)159, 210, 547, 555, 567; CFSSA519; AWW83; NFA71; CRL(3)108; HSF(4)161 - desc/o William Fairfax CFA(2)278

Mildred - of VA, m1740 Col John Thornton - desc/o Col George Reade AWW83

Nathaniel - of VA, m Mary Dade - desc/o Lawrence Washington BLG2961

Nicholson - d1790, m1774 Sarah Holdsworth & had issue, seven children - desc/o John Washington HSF(4)158

Priscilla - of VA, m Robert Lanier b abt 1678 d1756 son of John Lanier - desc/o John Washington HSF(4)158

Richard - of VA, b 1659/1660 d abt 1724, m Elizabeth Jordan dau/o Arthur Jordan & Elizabeth Bevin - desc/o John Washington ECD233; DBR(1)206; DBR(5)242, 698; HSF(4)155, 156

Richard - of VA, m____, moved to Northampton Co, NC & had issue a son Richard Washington - desc/o John Washington HSF(4)156

Robert - of VA, b1729 of Choptank, King George Co, m1756 Alice Strother, dau/o Benjamin Strother & Mary Mason - desc/o Lawrence Washington MCD306; CFA(1)563

Robert - of VA, b1769, m Judith Carter Browne - desc/o John Washington HSF(4)163

Col Samuel - of VA, b1734 Wakefield, of Harewood, Jefferson Co d1781

WASHINGTON (cont.)

(brother of President George Washington) colonel in the Continental Army, m(1) abt 1754 Jane Champe d1758 dau/o Col John Champe of Lambs Creek, King George Co, m(2) abt 1756 Mildred Thornton d1763 dau/o John Thornton of Caroline Co, m(3) abt 1762 Louisa Chapman, m(4)1764 Anne Steptoe - desc/o Col George Reade DBR(1)723; 764; CFSSA522 - desc/o Col John Washington PFA51, 53; CRL(3)109; HSF(4)162; CFA(2)743

Thomas - of VA, d1749 Surrey Co, m Agnes____ - desc/o John Washington HSF(4)157

Thomas - of VA, d1774 Brunswick Co, m Sarah Gray dau/o Gilbert Gray - desc/o John Washington HSF(4)157

Thomas - of VA, furnished supplies to the American army during the Revolution, moved to Tennessee & lived at Leland near Nashville, m1784 Janet Love dau/o Allen Love - desc/o John Washington HSF(4)157

Thornton - of VA, b1760 d1787, m(1)1779 Mildred Berry, m(2)1786 Francis Townshend Washington b1732 dau/o Townshend Washington & Elizabeth Lund - desc/o Col John Washington PFA51; HSF(4)162

Townsend - of VA, b1705 of Green Hill d1778, m1727 Elizabeth Lund - desc/o Lawrence Washington MCD306; CFA(1)563

Col Warner - of VA, b1722 of Gloucester Co d1791, m(1) Elizabeth Macon dau/o Col William Macon, m(2)1764 Hannah Fairfax, youngest dau/o William Fairfax - desc/o Col George Reade CHB253; BCD253; DBR(3)446, 614; CFSSA519 - desc/o Col John Washington DBR(4)870; HSF(4)161

Warner II - of VA, b1751 d1829, m(1) Mary Whiting, m(2)1795 Sarah Warner Rootes - desc/o Col George Reade CHB253; BCD253; DBR(3)446, 614 - desc/o Col John Washington DBR(4)870

William - of VA, m Margaret Tyler dau/o Francis Tyler - desc/o John Washington HSF(4)156

William Augustine - of VA, b1757 of Westmoreland Co d1810, m(1)1777 (his cousin) Jane Washington, dau/o John Augustine & Hannah Bushrod, m(2)1792 Mary Lee, dau/o Richard Henry Lee & Anne Aylett, m(3) Sarah Tayloe, dau/o John Tayloe & Rebecca____ of Mount Airy - desc/o Col John Washington DBR(2)486; PFA48, 50; CFA(2)744 - desc/o Col George Reade CFSSA521

WATERS Lydia - b1721 - desc/o James Neale RAA117

Thomas - b abt 1690 - desc/o James Neale RAA117

William - of VA & MD, d1732/1733 Somerset Co, MD, m Abigail Upshur d1764 Somerset Co, MD - desc/o Nathaniel Littleton HSF(10)190

WATKINS Alice Goode - of VA, b1775 d1866, m1792 Reuben Vaughan Jr - desc/o Lieut Col Walter Aston CHB537

Samuel - of VA, m Elizabeth Goode - desc/o Lieut Col Walter Aston CHB537

WATKINSON Elizabeth - of CT, b1775 d1828, m1801 Alexander Collins - desc/o Sarah Blair TAG(47)69

John Revel - of CT, b1772 d1836, m1805 Hannah Hubbard - desc/o Sarah Blair TAG(47)69

WATKINSON (cont.)

Mary - of CT, b1769 d1840, m1803 Maj Joseph Perkins - desc/o Sarah Blair TAG(47)69

Sarah - of CT, b1771 d1830, m1792 Jacob Pledger - desc/o Sarah Blair TAG(47)69

WATLINGTON Col Armistead - of VA, m Susanna Coleman - desc/o Col George Reade DBR(2)525

Elizabeth - m Peter Barksdale - desc/o Col George Reade DBR(2)525

Paul II - of VA, m Elizabeth Armistead - desc/o Col George Reade DBR(2)525

WATNER David C - b1758 - desc/o Thomas Newberry RAA118

WATTLES Abigail - b1702 - desc/o Richard Billings RAA70

WAUGH Sarah Spotswood - of VA, m James Lyons - desc/o Col John West CHB245; MCD321; BCD245 - desc/o Capt William Claiborne BCD64

WAYLES Martha - m(1) Bathurst Skelton, m(2) Thomas Jefferson b1743 d1826, 3rd President of the United States, her third cousin - desc/o Capt Henry Isham GBR339

WEAVER Clement - b abt 1590, m Rebecca Holbrook - the immigrant RAA no longer accepted as being of royal descent

WEBB Elizabeth - of CT, b abt 1751 d abt 1816, m1769 Samuel Foster - desc/o Grace Chetwood ECD(3)91

WEBSTER Josiah - of CT, b1774 d1852, m1794 Abigail Babcock - desc/o John Drake DBR(2)167; DBR(3)80, 82; DBR(5)50

WELBOURNE Arcadia - of VA, m George Cutler - desc/o Robert Drake DBR(5)381

WELBY Mariann - of MD, dau/o Richard & Anne (King) Welby, m Samuel De Butts - the immigrant GBR37

Olive - of MA abt 1635, bp 1604 Moulton, Lincoln d1691/1692 Chelmsford, MA, m1629 Deacon Henry Farwell of Concord & Chelmsford d abt 1670 - desc/o Frances Bulkeley FLW185; ECD250; ECD(3)271, 275, 278; JSW1710; MCS6; DBR(2)107; DBR(3)620; DBR(4)664; RAA93; GBR107; GPM(1)155, 156

WELD Elizabeth - b1654/1655 - desc/o Griffith Bowen RAA72

Joanna - b1685 - desc/o Griffith Bowen RAA72

John - b1663 - desc/o Griffith Bowen RAA72

WELLER Rhoda - of MA, b1773 d1831, m1792 Sperry Douglas II - desc/o Thomas Newberry ECD(3)224

WELLINGTON Benjamin - of MA, b1646 d1709, m1671 Elizabeth Sweetman - desc/o Dr Richard Palgrave DBR(1)784; DBR(4)430; GBR266

Elizabeth - b1673 d1729, m1690 John Fay Jr - desc/o Dr Richard Palgrave DBR(1)784; DBR(4)430; GBR266

Enoch - b1756 - desc/o Richard Palgrave RAA121

Joseph - b1643 d1714, m(1) Sarah____, m(2)1684 Elizabeth Straight dau/o Capt Thomas Straight & Elizabeth (Kimball) Straight - desc/o Dr Richard Palgrave DBR(1)176; RAA121

Joseph - b1711 d1777 a Revolutionary soldier, m1733 Dorcas Stone b1715 d1801 dau/o Jonathon & Cherry (Adams) Stone - desc/o Dr Richard Palgrave DBR(1)176; RAA121

Mary - b1641, m(1)____ Maddock, m(2) John Coolidge - desc/o Dr

WELLINGTON (cont.)

Richard Palagrave DBR(5)762

Rebecca - b1737 d1770, m1757 Zachariah Hill b1737 d1812 a Revolutionary soldier, son of Zachariah & Rebecca (Cutter) Hill - desc/o Dr Richard Palgrave DBR(1)176, 177

Thomas - b1686 d1758, m(1) abt 1708 Rebecca Whittemore b1690/1691 d1734 dau/o Samuel & Rebecca (Gardner) Whittemore, m(2) Cherry Adams Stone - desc/o Dr Richard Palgrave DBR(1)176; RAA121

WELLMAN Mary - b1650 - desc/o Agnes Harris RAA131

WELLES Ann - b bef 19 Oct 1680, m1646 Thomas Thompson - desc/o Alice Tomes THC310

John - of MA, b1638 d1677, m abt 1664/1665 Sarah Littlefield - desc/o Thomas Welles FFF119

Nathaniel - of MA 1629 - the immigrant FFF119; sufficient proof of alleged royal ancestry is lacking

Richard - of MA 1635 d1672 - the immigrant FFF119; sufficient proof of alleged royal ancestry is lacking

Sarah - of MA, d1735, m(1) Samuel Sibley, m(2)1711 John Sawyer - desc/o Thomas Welles FFF119

Gov Thomas - of CT 1635/1636, b1598, m1615 Alice Tomes - the immigrant FFF117; THC310; RAA no longer accepted as being of royal descent

Thomas - of MA, b1605 d1666 Abigail Warner - the immigrant FFF119; THC322; sufficient proof of alleged royal ancestry is lacking

WELLS David - b abt 1754 d1777, m Mary Hand - desc/o Roger Ludlow CRL(2)365

Gideon Hill - of PA, b1765 of Wellsborough, m Hannah Waln - desc/o Thomas Lloyd CRFP(1)44

Joshua - bp 1716, m(2) Mary Reeves - desc/o Roger Ludlow LDS29; RAA111; CRL(2)365

Mary - of MD, d1698/1699, m(1) Thomas Stockett, m(2)1672 George Yate (Yates) - desc/o Frances White ECD(2)309; JSW1698

Mary - of PA, b1761 or 1764 Burlington d1819, m1785 Benjamin Wistar Morris son of Capt Samuel Morris & Rebecca Wistar of Philadelphia - desc/o Thomas Lloyd CHB123; BCD123; CRFP(1)44

Penelope - b1741, m Oliver Greene - desc/o Frances Dungan LDS76

Sarah - b1732 - desc/o Roger Ludlow RAA111

Sarah Wolcott - of CT, b1708/1709 d1776, m1728 Capt Jonathan Robbins DBR(3)73

Selah - abt 1750, m Mehitable Tuthill - desc/o Roger Ludlow LDS29; RAA111

Silas Hand - b1773, m1809 Sarah Parker - desc/o Roger Ludlow CRL(2)365

William Hill - of PA, d1829, m Elizabeth Dagworthy, US Senator from Delaware 1804 & 1813/1817 - desc/o Thomas Lloyd CRFP(1)44

WENDELL Abraham - of NY, m1698 Maycke Van Ess - desc/o Evert Jansen Wendell CFA565

Abraham - of NY, bp 1716, m1740 Elizabeth Wendell - desc/o Evert Jansen Wendell CFA566

WENDELL (cont.)

Abraham - of MA, b1735, m____, & left issue - desc/o Gov Thomas Dudley NEFGM(1)78

Ann - of MA, b1730, m John Penhallow of Portsmouth - desc/o Gov Thomas Dudley NE(8)315; NEFGM(1)78

Anna - of NY, bp 1709, m1737 Jacob Henry Ten Eyck - desc/o Evert Jansen Wendell CFA566

Anna - of NY, bp 1742, m1765 Col Philip P Schuyler - desc/o Evert Jansen Wendell CFA566

Catherine - of NY, bp 1705, m1727 John A Cuyler - desc/o Evert Jansen Wendell CFA566

Catherine - of NY, bp 1756, m Harmanus A Wendell - desc/o Evert Jansen Wendell CFA567

Cornelius - of NY, b1745, m1768 Anna Lansing - desc/o Evert Jansen Wendell CFA566

Diewertje - of NY, b1653 d1724, m(1) Myndert Wemp, m(2) Johannes Glen - desc/o Evert Jansen Wendell CFA565

Elizabeth - of MA, b1718, m Richard Wibird of Portsmouth, MA - desc/o Gov Thomas Dudley NE(8)315

Elizabeth - of MA, b abt 1742 d1799, m1765 Boston, Rev Peter Thacher b1731 d1826, graduated from Harvard in 1753. After teaching school several years he became pastor of the church of New Marblehead, now Windham, ME 1762 until 1790 but continued to be prominent both in the church & in the town, married a second time but had no issue of that marriage, son of Rev Thomas Smith & Sarah Tyng - desc/o Gov Thomas Dudley NEFGM(1)78

Elsje - of NY, b1647, m1696 Abraham Staats - desc/o Evert Jansen Wendell CFA565

Elsje - of NY, b1689, m1714 Nicholas Schuyler - desc/o Evert Jansen Wendell CFA566

Evert - of NY, b1660, m1681 Elizabeth Sanders Glen - desc/o Evert Jansen Wendell CFA565

Evert - of NY, b1680, m1710 Engeltje Lansing - desc/o Evert Jansen Wendell CFA566

Evert - of NY, bp 1707, m1761 Maria Truax - desc/o Evert Jansen Wendell CFA566

Evert Jansen - of NY bef 1642, b1615 d1709, m(1)1644 Susanna Du Trieux, m(2)1663 Maritje Abrahm De Vosburgh - the immigrant EDV52, 53; CFA565; sufficient proof of alleged royal ancestry is lacking

Gertrud - of NY, bp 1747, m1783 Harper Whitbeck - desc/o Evert Jansen Wendell CFA566

Harmanus - of NY, b1678 d1731, m1699 Anna Sanders Glen - desc/o Evert Jansen Wendell CFA566

Harmanus - of NY, bp 1714 d1771, m1741 Catherine Van Vechten - desc/o Evert Jansen Wendell CFA566

Harmanus - of NY, bp 1742, m Catherine Van Rensselaer - desc/o Evert Jansen Wendell CFA566

Hester - of NY, bp 1686, m1714 Johannes Beeckman - desc/o Evert Jansen Wendell CFA566

WENDELL (cont.)

Jacob - of MA, b1715, m1736 Boston (probably) Elizabeth Hunt - desc/o Gov Thomas Dudley NE(8)315; NEFGM(1)78

Jacob - of NY, bp 1702, m1728 Helena Van Rensselaer - desc/o Evert Jansen Wendell CFA566

Jacob H - of NY, b1754 d1826, m1785 Gertrug Lansing - desc/o Evert Jansen Wendell CFA567

Jeronimus - of NY, b1655, m1676 Ariaantje Visscher - desc/o Evert Jansen Wendell CFA565

Johannes - of NY, b1649, m(1) Maritie Jellise Meyer, m(2) Elizabeth Staats - desc/o Evert Jansen Wendell CFA565

Johannes - of NY, bp 1684, m1708 Susanna Viele - desc/o Evert Jansen Wendell CFA566

Johannes H - of NY, bp 1752, m1785 Cathalina Van Benthugsen - desc/o Evert Jansen Wendell CFA567

John Mico - of MA, b1728, m Catharine Brattle - desc/o Gov Thomas Dudley NE(8)315; NEFGM(1)78

Katharine - of MA, b1726, m William Cooper, Esq, Town clerk of Boston in Revolutionary times - desc/o Gov Thomas Dudley NE(8)315; NEFGM(1)78

Margaret - of MA, m William Phillips of Boston, merchant & had issue Wendell Phillips & one other daughter - desc/o Gov Thomas Dudley NE(8)315; NEFGM(1)78

Maria - of NY, b1677, m1704 Barent Sanders - desc/o Evert Jansen Wendell CFA565

Mary - of MA, b1723, m Samuel Sewall - desc/o Gov Thomas Dudley NE(8)315; NEFGM(1)78

Mercy - of MA, m Nathaniel Oliver - desc/o Gov Thomas Dudley NE(8)315

Judge Oliver - of MA, b1733 d1818 at Cambridge, was in the mercantile business with his father at Boston, judge of probate for Suffolk Co, m1762 Mary Jackson dau/o Edward Jackson & Dorothy Quincy - desc/o Gov Thomas Dudley J&K195; CRL(1)381; NE(8)315; NEFGM(1)78

Philip - of NY, b1658, m1688 Maria Visscher - desc/o Evert Jansen Wendell CFA565

Sarah - of MA, b1721, m(1)1739 John Hunt Jr, m(2) Mr Hewes - desc/o Gov Thomas Dudley DBR(3)597; NE(8)315

Sarah - of MA, b1720, m Rev Dr Abiel Holmes, of Cambridge, b1763 at Woodstock, CT, d1837, Sarah was the mother of Oliver Wendell Holmes - desc/o Gov Thomas Dudley NE(8)315; NEFGM(1)78

Susanna of NY, m1686 Johannes L Teller - desc/o Evert Jansen Wendell CFA565

Susanna - of NY, b1676, m1718 Johannes Symonson Groot - desc/o Evert Jansen Wendell CFA566.

Thomas - of NY, bp 1645 - desc/o Evert Jansen Wendall CFA565

WENTWORTH Abigail - of NH, m1715 Dorchester, Benjamin Jordan - desc/o Elder William Wentworth GDMNH737

Abigail - of NH, b1757 d1812, m Ichabod Butler of South Berwick, ME d1812, was in the Revolutionary War, son of Samuel Butler - desc/o Elder William Wentworth NE(4)332

WENTWORTH (cont.)

Andrew - of NH, b1764 major & brigade inspector of 2d NH Regiment & representative from Somersworth, m Mary Rollins dau/o John Rollins & Mary Carr - desc/o Elder William Wentworth NE(4)333

Ann - of NH, m Woodbury Langdon - desc/o Elder William Wentworth NE(4)338

Ann - of NH, m William Sheafe of Portsmouth - desc/o Elder William Wentworth NE(19)68

Anna - m Ephraim Ham - desc/o Elder William Wentworth GDMNH736

Anna - of NH, b1746 d1813 Bath, England, m Portsmouth 1763 John Fisher d1805 Clifton, England, collector of customs at Salem, MA, who after the Revolution held many important offices in England & left issue - desc/o Elder William Wentworth NE(19)68

Anna Bella - m Francis Gore, Governor of Upper Canada - desc/o Elder William Wentworth NE(19)68

Capt Benjamin - of NH, d1724/1725, representative 1724, m1717 Elizabeth Leighton d1779 - desc/o Elder William Wentworth J&K261; GDMNH736/737

Benning - of NH, b1696 d1770 graduated Cambridge 1715, governor from 1741 to 1766, m(1)1719 Abigail Ruck d1755 dau/o John Ruck of Boston, m(2)1760 Martha Hilton d1805 of New Market, New Hampshire - desc/o Elder William Wentworth J&K262; NE(4)334, (19)65, 65; GDMNH737

Benning - of NH, b1757 at Boston d1808 Halifax, England, m1787 Hereford, England, Anne Bird & had issue - desc/o Elder William Wentworth NE(19)67

Daniel - of NH, b1715/1756 d1747 merchant, m Elizabeth Frost b1714 d1794 of New Castle, New Hampshire - desc/o Elder William Wentworth NE(4)337, 338, (19)68; GDMNH737

Dorothy - of NH, b1680 d1754, m Henry Sherburne b1674 d1757 Counsellor & Chief Justice - desc/o Elder William Wentworth NE(4)338, (19)65; GDMNH738

Ebenezer - of NH, b1677 d1747 captain commanding in 1707 the store-ship of 14 guns & 28 men, sent to reduce the fort at Port Royal, now Annapolis NH m1711 Rebecca Jeffries d1721 Portsmouth, New Hampshire dau/o David Jeffries & Elizabeth Usher & left issue - desc/o Elder William Wentworth NE(4)338, (19)65; GDMNH738

Ebenezer - of NH, b1714 d1757 physician, shopkeeper, m1746 Mary Mendum b1723 d1755 dau/o Nathaniel Mendum & Frances Lloyd - desc/o Elder William Wentworth NE(4)337, (19)68; GDMNH737

Edward - of NH, d1767 aged 74 years, Stoughton, m(1) Keziah Blackman of Stoughton - desc/o Elder William Wentworth GDMNH737

Edward - of NH, b1693, m1728 Stoughton, Martha Kenney & had issue a son John - desc/o Elder William Wentworth GDMNH737

Elizabeth - of NH, m(1) James Sharpe, m(2) Richard Tozier, Jr - desc/o Elder William Wentworth GDMNH739

Elizabeth - of NH, m Capt Samuel Warner - desc/o Elder William Wentworth NE(19)66

Elizabeth - of NH, m 1707 Rowley, Nathaniel Dresser - desc/o Elder

WENTWORTH (cont.)

William Wentworth GDMNH738

Elizabeth - of NH, m1713 Nathaniel Brown of Salisbury - desc/o Elder William Wentworth GDMNH737

Elizabeth - of NH, b1710/1711, m(1) John Lowd, m(2) Capt Benjamin Underwood - desc/o Elder William Wentworth GDMNH737

Elizabeth - of NH, b1737, m(1) John Gould, m(2) Nathaniel Rogers, m(3) William Lee Perkins of Boston - desc/o Elder William Wentworth NE(19)67

Elizabeth - m Edward Minchin of Limerick, Ireland - desc/o Elder William Wentworth NE(19)68

Elizabeth - of NH, b1774 d1836, m1800 Daniel M Durell, graduate of Dartmouth College 1794 - desc/o Elder William Wentworth NE(4)331

Ephraim - of NH, d1748, m(1)1696 Mary Miller, m(2) bef 10 May 1726 Elizabeth Waldron Beard d abt 1737/1738 - desc/o Elder William Wentworth DBR(1)663; DBR(3)714; GDMNH736

Ephraim - of NH, m Martha Grant - desc/o Elder William Wentworth GDMNH736

Ezekiel - of NH, b abt 1651 d1712, m bef 27 Jun 1676 Elizabeth___ d bef 1726 - desc/o Elder William Wentworth J&K261; DBR(1)44, 806; DBR(3)231, 714; GDNNH736

Ezekiel - of NH, m(1) Dorothy Wentworth, m(2) Sarah Nock - desc/o Elder William Wentworth GDNMH736

Ezekiel - of NH, b1702 Somersworth d bef 29 Jun 1757, m Elizabeth (Day) d1768 - desc/o Elder William Wentworth GDMNH737

Frances - of NH, b1745 d1813 at Lurring Hill, Berkshire, England, known as Lady Wentworth, m(1)1762 (her cousin) Theodore Atkinson Jr d1769, m(2)1769 (another cousin) Gov John Wentworth son of Mark Hunking Wentworth - desc/o Elder William Wentworth NE(4)336, 337, (19)67

George - of NH, b1740 d1820 collector of the port of Portsmouth, m (his cousin) Rebecca Wentworth dau/o Ebenezer Wentworth - desc/o Elder William Wentworth NH(19)68

Deacon Greshom - of NH, d1731, m1695/1696 Salisbury, Hannah French (perhaps not his first) - desc/o Elder William Wentworth GDMNH737

Deacon Gershom - of NH, d1758/1759, m Sarah (by tradition Twombly) - desc/o Elder William Wentworth GDMNH737

Hannah - of NH, b1700 d at Portsmouth, NH 1769, m(1) Samuel Plaisted d1731/1732 of Berwick, ME, m(2) Theodore Atkinson b1697 d1791 graduate of Cambridge 1718, clerk of court of common pleas, colonel, collector of the port of Portsmouth, sheriff, councillor, secretary of the colony & judge of Superior Court - desc/o Elder William Wentworth NE(4)338, (19)66; GDMNH737

Hannah - of NH, b1744 d1783 Portsmouth, m1760 Monsieur Bunbury & left issue - desc/o Elder William Wentworth NE(19)69

Hunking - of NH, b1697 d1784 chairman of the Committee of Safety at Portsmouth, m(1) Elizabeth Wibird d1731 in her 23rd year dau/o Richard Wibird, m(2) Elizabeth Keese d1742 in her 32nd year, m(3) Margaret Vaughan b1709 d1788 dau/o Lieut Gov George Vaughan

WENTWORTH (cont.)

& Elizabeth Elliot - desc/o Elder William Wentworth NE(19)66; GDMNH737

Joanna - of NH, b1770, m1790 Capt Hiram Rollins b1767 son of John Rollins - desc/o Elder William Wentworth NE(4)330

Joanna Gilman - of NH, b1755 d1806, m1780 Capt Moses Wingate, a farmer in Dover, son of John Wingate & had issue - desc/o Elder William Wentworth NE(4)332

John - of NH, m abt 1675 Martha____ - desc/o Elder William Wentworth GDMNH737

John - of NH, b1671 d1730 lieut gov of New Hampshire 1717/1730, m Sarah Hunking d1741 in her 68th year, dau/o Mark Hunking of Devonshire & left issue 16 children - desc/o Elder William Wentworth J&K262; NE(4)334, (19)65;; GDMNH737

John - of NH, b1676 of Stoughton d1772 aged 95 years, m Elizabeth Bailey - desc/o Elder William Wentworth GDMNH737

John - of NH, d bet 1717/1718, m1703 Martha Miller d aft 3 Jan 1755 - desc/o Elder William Wentworth NE(4)327; GDMNH736

John of NH, b1703 d1773 judge from 1754 until his death, m Sarah Hall d1790 aged 79 of Bridgewater, Island of Barbados - desc/o Elder William Wentworth NE(19)66; GDMNH737

John - of NH, killed by Indians 1746, m Jane Richards - desc/o Elder William Wentworth GDMNH737

Col John - of NH, b abt 1721 d1781, elected to the colonial legislature at Portsmouth in 1768, called the first revolutionary convention ever held in the state & was made president of it & first judge of the court of common pleas, m(1)1742 Joanna Gilman of Exeter b1720 d1750 dau/o Judge Nicholas Gilman, m(2)1750 Abigail Millet d1767 aged 45 years, dau/o Thomas Millet of Dover, m(3)1768 Elizabeth Wallingford d1776 wid/o Capt Amos Cole of Dover - desc/o Elder William Wentworth J&K261; NE(4)329, 331, 332, 333

John - of NH, b1736/1736 d1820 governor of New Hampshire 1766, lieut governor of Nova Scotia 1792, created a Baronet 1795, m1769 (his cousin) Frances Wentworth dau/o Samuel Wentworth & wid/o Theodore Atkinson Jr - desc/o Elder William Wentworth NE(4)337, (19)67, 68

John - of NH, b1745 d1787 graduated Cambridge 1768, Lawyer appointed register of probate & held the office until his death, four times appointed delegate to Congress where in 1778 he signed the original Articles of Confederation; legislature & senator, m1771 Margaret Frost dau/o Joseph Frost of New Castle - desc/o Elder William Wentworth J&K261; NE(4)330, 331

Jonathan - b1752, m1772 Esther Whitehouse - desc/o Elder William Wentworth DBR(3)714

Jonathan - m1746 Abigail Heard - desc/o Elder William Wentworth DBR(1)663; GDMNH736

Joshua - of NH, b1741/1742 d1809 Portsmouth, colonel of first New Hampshire regiment 1776, representative, councillor in 1786, senator four years, one of the most valuable men in Portsmouth during the American Revolution, m1774 Sarah (Sally) Pierce d1807 aged 50 years & left issue - desc/o Elder William Wentworth

WENTWORTH (cont.)

NE(4)337, 338, (19)69

Katherine - of NH, b1694, m1713 Daniel Chapman of Colchester, CT - desc/o Elder William Wentworth GDMNH738

Lydia - of NH, bp 1752 d1806, m Moses Rand - desc/o Elder William Wentworth DBR(1)663

Mark Hunking - of NH, b1709/1710 d1785 Portsmouth, NH, m Elizabeth Rindge d1794 aged 78 dau/o John Rindge & Ann Odione & had issue - desc/o Elder William Wentworth NE(4)337, (19)67; GDMNH737

Martha - m Joseph Twombly - desc/o Elder William Wentworth GDMNH736

Martha - of NH, b1684, m Samuel Lord - desc/o Elder William Wentworth GDMNH738

Mary - of MA, b abt 1569 d1627, m abt 1591 William Brewster - the immigrant ECD(2)287, 290, 295, 301; FFF90; sufficient proof of alleged royal ancestry is lacking

Mary - of NH, b1673 d abt 1743, m(1) abt 1690 Samuel Rymes d abt 1712 of Portsmouth, New Hampshire, m(2) abt 1717 Dr John Clifton d1731 & left issue - desc/o Elder William Wentworth NE(19)65; GDMNH738

Mary - of NH, b1697, m Capt William Wentworth - desc/o Elder William Wentworth GDMNH737

Mary - of NH, m James Gerrish - desc/o Elder William Wentworth GDMNH738

Mary - of NH, m1712 Boston, James Wright - desc/o Elder William Wentworth GDMNH737

Mary - of NH, b1707 d1743/1744, m(1) Temple Nelson of Boston d1740, m(2)1743 John Steele of Boston - desc/o Elder William Wentworth NE(4)338, (19)67; GDMNH737

Mary - m Nehemiah Kimball - desc/o Elder William Wentworth GDMNH736

Mary - of NH, b1743, m1765 Gen George Brinley d1810, he left the country at the Revolution & was commissary general for British North America & left issue including Catherine Frances Gore, the authoress - desc/o Elder William Wentworth NE(19)67

Mary - of ME, b1763 d1853, m1781 Samuel Brackett - desc/o Elder William Wentworth DBR(4)368

Mercy - of NH, b1686, m1707 Rowley, Joseph Chapman - desc/o Elder William Wentworth GDMNH738

Paul - of NH, m bef 21 Apr 1681 K(C)atharine____ & left issue 13 children - desc/o Elder William Wentworth NE(4)41; GDMNH737

Paul - of NH, d1748 aged 70 years, wealthy merchant, lumber dealer, justice of the peace & public official, m1704 Salisbury, Abra Brown - desc/o Elder William Wentworth GDMNH736

Paul - of NH, b1682 d aft 1746, m(1) Jane Rice & had 4 children, m(2)1724 Rebecca Pickering - desc/o Elder William Wentworth GDMNH738

Paul - of NH, b1743 d1781 major Second NH Reg 1775, representative from Somersworth to Exeter 1776 to 1778, m1769 Molly Higgins d1777 aged 26 years & 10 months dau/o John Higgins - desc/o

WENTWORTH (cont.)

Elder William Wentworth NE(4)330

Rebecca - of NH, b1712 d1738, m Thomas Packer sheriff 1741 to his death 22 Jun 1771 & left issue - desc/o Elder William Wentworth NE(4)338, (19)68; GDMNH737

Rebecca - of NH, b1748 d1818 Portsmouth, m (her cousin) George Wentworth son of Daniel Wentworth - desc/o Elder William Wentworth NE(4)337, (19)68

Deacon Samuel - of NH, d1780, m1725 Joanna Roberts d1780 - desc/o Elder William Wentworth DBR(4)368; GDMNH738

Samuel - of NH, b1640 d1690 of smallpox, hotelkeeper, m1666 Mary Benning & left issue - desc/o Elder William Wentworth NE(4)334, (19)65; GDMNH738/739

Samuel - of NH, b1666 d1736, m(1) Hannah Wiggin dau/o Andrew Wiggin & Hannah Bradstreet, m(2)1691 Elizabeth Hopson, m(3)1699 Abigail Phillips the wid/o Capt Christopher Goff, had issue but none lived to be married - desc/o Elder William Wentworth NE(19)65; GDMNH738

Samuel - of NH, b1699 Salisbury d1758, m1731 Elizabeth French of Salisbury d bef 3 Nov 1737 with all 3 of her children, m(2) Sarah Williams - desc/o Elder William Wentworth GDMNH737

Samuel - of NH, m Patience Downs, the 1st of 3 wives and mother of his children - desc/o Elder William Wentworth GDMNH736

Samuel - of NH, b1708 d1766 graduate of Cambrige 1728, merchant in Boston, m1732 Elizabeth Deering b1715 d1785 London, England, dau/o Henry Deering & Elizabeth Packer - desc/o Elder William Wentworth NE(4)336, 337, (19)67; GDMNH737

Samuel - of NH, b1728 d1776 - desc/o Elder William Wentworth DBR(4)368

Samuel - of NH - desc/o Elder William Wentworth J&K262

Samuel - of NH, m Rebecca Oliver dau/o James Oliver & Rebecca Lloyd of Boston - desc/o Elder William Wentworth NE(19)65

Sarah - of NH, m(1) Benjamin Bernard, m(2) Samuel Winch - desc/o Elder William Wentworth GDMNH739

Sarah - of NH, b1697, m1718 Norwich, Colen Ffesior - desc/o Elder William Wentworth GDMNH738

Sarah - of NH, b1702 d1776, m(1) Archibald McPhedris d1728, m(2)1738/1739 George Jaffrey Jr d1749 aged 66 years, graduate of Cambridge 1736, clerk of the Superior Court, councillor & provincial treasurer - desc/o Elder William Wentworth NE(4)338, (19)66; GDMNH737

Sarah - of NH, m(1) Benjamin Hossum, m(2) John White - desc/o Elder William Wentworth GDMNH738

Sarah - of NH, m Ephraim Ricker - desc/o Elder William Wentworth GDMNH737

Sarah - of NH, m John Penhallow - desc/o Elder William Wentworth NE(19)66

Sarah - of NH, b1735, m1755 James Apthorpe of Braintree, MA & was the mother of Mrs Perez Morton, the distinguished poetess - desc/o Elder William Wentworth NE(19)67

Sarah - of NH, b1736, m John Wendell - desc/o Elder William

WENTWORTH (cont.)

Wentworth NE(19)68

Susanna - of NH, b1760 d1833, m1785 Col James Carr of
Somersworth b1748 d1829 entered the Revolutionary War at its
commencement as a first lieutenant & came out a major, sheriff of
Strafford Co, son of Dr Moses & Mary Carr - desc/o Elder William
Wentworth NE(4)333

Sylvanus - of NH, b1681 d aft 1762, m(1) Mary Key, m(2)1723 Rowley,
Eleanor Davis - desc/o Elder William Wentworth GDMNH738

Sylvanus - of NH, killed by Indians, m Rowley, Elizabeth Stewart -
desc/o Elder William Wentworth GDMNH738

Tamsen - of NH, b1687 d1759, m(1) James Chesley, m(2) Deacon John
Hayes - desc/o Elder William Wentworth DBR(1)44, 806;
DBR(3)231; GDMNH737

Thomas - of NH, d1719 mariner, m Love____ & had one daughter
Elizabeth Wentworth - desc/o Elder William Wentworth GDMNH736

Thomas - of NH, b1739/1740 d1768 Portsmouth, graduate of
Cambridge 1758, m Anne Tasker d abt 1682 dau/o Judge John
Tasker of Marblehead, MA - desc/o Elder William Wentworth
NE(4)337, (19)68

Thomas Millet - of NH, b1753 d1841 lived & died in Lebanon, ME,
m1789 Rebecca Hasey of Lebanon b1767 dau/o Rev Isaac Hasey -
desc/o Elder William Wentworth NE(4)332

Timothy - of NH, d1719, m Sarah Cromwell - desc/o Elder William
Wentworth DBR(4)368; GDMNH738

Timothy - of NH, d1735, m(1) Elizabeth Hodsdon d1735 - desc/o Elder
William Wentworth GDMNH738

Elder William - of NH 1628, b1615/1616 Alford, Lincoln, England
d1696/1697 son of William Wentworth & Susanna Carter,
m(1)____, m(2) Elizabeth Knight - the immigrant J&K261; MCS55;
DBR(1)44, 663, 806; DBR(3)230, 231, 714; DBR(4)368; RAA1;
GBR351 some aspect of royal descent merits further study;
NE(4)321/338, (19)65/69; EO2(3)654/664; GDMNH738, 739

William - of NH, b1680 Dover d aft 1764, m Grace Tucker - desc/o
Elder William Wentworth GDMNH738

Capt William - of NH, b1705 d1767 lived at Kittery, ME, m(1)1729
Margery Pepperrell d1748, m(2)1750 Mary Hall d1790 aged 77,
wid/o Adam Winthrop & had issue 9 children - desc/o Elder
William Wentworth NE(4)335, 336, (19)67; GDMNH737

WESCOTT James - of RI, b1740 d1814, m1767 Martha Tillinghast -
desc/o William Arnold CHB19; BCD19

James Jr - of RI, b1773 d1853, m1795 Mary Dewer - desc/o William
Arnold CHB19; BCD19

WEST Agnes or Ann - of VA, m Richard Gregory - desc/o Col/Gov John
West DBR(3)165, 166, 329, 600

Alexander - of VA, m(1)____, m(2) aft 8 Feb 1726/1727 Mary Robinson,
dau/o Joseph Robinson of Yorkshire, England - desc/o Anthony
West APP665

Ann - of VA, m____ Scarburgh - desc/o Anthony West CFA23

Ann - of VA, b1707, m1730 Thomas Owsley II - desc/o Col/Gov John
West DBR(2)630; DBR(3)128

WEST (cont.)

Anne - of VA, m Henry Fox b1650 d1714 son of Captain John Fox - desc/o Col/Gov John West CHB242; ECD(2)265; LDS100; BCD242; DBR(1)135, 412, 641; DBR(2)31, 206, 370, 371, 560, 807; DBR(3)116, 178, 363; DBR(4)157, 260, 287, 377, 567, 777, 810; DBR(5)558, 840, 858, 871, 896; APP661; SVF(2)399

Anne - of VA, b1685/1686 d1749, m(1) Thomas Sparrow of Anne Arundel Co, MD d1719, m(2)1718 William Sellman b1689/1690 d1742/1743 - desc/o Anthony West APP668

Anne - of VA, m Richard Gregory b abt 1695 d1742 of King William Co justice & sheriff - desc/o Col/Gov John West SVF(2)400

Anthony - of VA 1622, d1652, m Ann____ - the immigrant CFA23; WAC48; CRL(1)118, 119; CRL(2)119; APP661 there is no indication that this family was related to that of Thomas West, Lord De La Warr - royal ancestry has never been proven

Anthony - of VA, d1717, m Elizabeth Rowles d1753 - desc/o Anthony West APP664

Anthony - of VA, d1778, m Comfort Rogers - desc/o Anthony West APP664

Catherine - of VA, m1711/1712 Capt Charles Snead - desc/o Anthony West APP667

Frances - of VA, m Richard Kellam son of Richard & Susan (Ansley) Kellam - desc/o Anthony West APP666

Gov Francis - of VA 1608, b1586 d1633/1634 governor of VA, son of Sir Thomas West & Anne Knollys, m(1)Mrs Margaret Blayney wid/o Edward Blayney, m(2) Temperance Flowerdieu d1628 wid/o Governor George Yeardley, m(3) Jane Davye dau/o Sir Henry Davye - the immigrant MCS3; DBR(2)205; TAG(18)217; GBR115; APP656; FLW23

Col Francis - of VA, b abt 1702 d1796, justice of King William Co, sheriff & burgess, m(1) Susannah Littlepage b1717/1718, m(2) abt 1766 Jane (Cole) Claiborne Bingham dau/o Col William Cole of Boldrup, Warwick Co & wid/o Nathaniel Claiborne & Stephan Bingham - desc/o Col/Gov John West APP660; SVF(2)399, 400

Jean - of VA, m Nathaniel Rogers - desc/o Anthony West APP665

Col/Gov John - of VA by 1618, b1590 d1659, B.A. Magdalen College, Oxford; member of the Governor's Council, VA 1631/1659, governor of VA 1635/1637, Master Muster-General of VA for life, (His commission was in the handwriting of King Charles I, of England 1637/1659) son of Thomas West, 2nd Baron Delaware (de la Warr) & Anne Knollys, m Anne (Shirley?) - the immigrant CHB242; ECD(2)265; MCB159; MCD321; MCS3; LDS100; BCD242; DBR(1)135, 354, 406, 412, 641; DBR(2)29, 30, 206, 367, 368, 371, 524, 560, 629, 807, 842; DBR(3)116, 128, 162, 163, 164, 165, 166, 176, 325, 327, 329, 363, 463, 466, 600, 675; DBR(4)58, 157, 221, 260, 287, 301, 376, 377, 567, 765, 775, 777, 810; DBR(5)558, 840, 858, 870, 871, 896, 1084; WAC51; TAG(18)217; GBR115; APP657; FLW23; SVF(2)398/401

Col John Jr - of VA, b1632 d1689 colonel of militia, 1673, senior justice 1680, burgess for New Kent 1685/1686, granted tax exemption for life, 1660, m by 4 Nov 1664 Unity Croshaw, dau/o

WEST (cont.)

Major Joseph Croshaw - desc/o Col/Gov John West CHB242;
ECD(2)265; MCD321; LDS100; BCD242; DBR(1)135, 406, 412,
641; DBR(2)30, 31, 206, 368, 371, 560, 630, 807, 842; DBR(3)116,
128, 163, 164, 166, 178, 325, 329, 363, 466, 600, 676;
DBR(4)157, 260, 287, 301, 377, 765, 777, 810; DBR(5)558, 840,
858, 871, 896; TAG(18)217; GBR115; APP659

John - of VA, lived at "West Point," served as justice & sheriff of King &
Queen Co, colonel & commander in chief of the militia, m1698
Judith Armistead, dau/o Anthony Armistead of Elizabeth City Co -
desc/o Col/Gov John West APP659; SVF(2)398

John - of VA, b1638/1639 d1703 carpenter & shipbuilder, lieutenant
colonel of militia, m abt 1660 Matilda Scarburgh b abt 1644 d aft 2
Aug 1720, prominent member of the Society of Friends (Quakers) -
desc/o Anthony West CFA23; CRL(1)119; CRL(2)119; APP663

John - of NY, b1693 d1766, m(1)1721 Charlotte MacCarthy - desc/o
Col/Gov John West ECD161

John - of VA, d1718, m(1) Frances Yeardley, m(2) Josepha Maria
Godwin - desc/o Anthony West CFA24; CRL(1)119; CRL(2)119;
APP666

John - of VA, d1751, m Ann Harris - desc/o Col/Gov John West
DBR(2)630; DBR(3)128

John - of VA, b1696 d1773, m____ - desc/o Anthony West APP664

John - of VA, d1755, m Agnes Burton d1760 - desc/o Anthony West
APP665

John - of VA, burgess for King William Co 1756/1758, m Elizabeth
Seaton dau/o George Seaton of King & Queen Co - desc/o Col/Gov
John West SVF(2)399

Jonathan - of VA, d1787, m Ann Smith - desc/o Anthony West CFA24

Katherine - of VA, b1634/1635, m(1) Ralph Barlowe d1652/1653 son
of Edward & Joan (Rushton) Barlow, m(2)1654 (agreement) Charles
Scarburgh, m(3) Major Edmund Bowman d1691/1692 - desc/o
Anthony West APP664

Mary - of VA, m Robert Snead - desc/o Anthony West APP665

Mary Scarburgh - of VA, m Nathaniel Bell d1745/1746 - desc/o
Anthony West APP665

Matilda - of VA, d1742, m(1) Peter Hack d1717, m(2) Jacob Rogers -
desc/o Anthony West APP665

Matilda - of VA, m John Wise - desc/o Anthony West APP666

Capt Nathaniel - of VA, b1592 d1623/1624, m1621 Frances Greville
d1633 - the immigrant CHB243; MCD321; MCS3; TAG(18)217,
218; FLW23; sufficient proof of alleged royal ancestry is lacking

Capt Nathaniel - of VA, b1655 d1723/1734 justice of King William Co,
tobacco agent, captain of militia, m Martha (Woodward) Macon
dau/o William Woodward - desc/o Col/Gov John West DBR(1)406;
DBR(2)842; DBR(3)163, 325, 466, 676; DBR(4)301, 765; GBR115;
APP660; SVF(2)399

Capt Nathaniel - of VA, m Agnes____ - desc/o Col/Gov John West
BCD243; DBR(3)329

Sarah - of VA, m Isaac Smith - desc/o Anthony West CRL(1)119;
CRL(2)119

WEST (cont.)

Sarah - of VA, m Tully Robinson b1658 d1723 - desc/o Anthony West APP665

Scarburgh - of VA, d1760, m____ - desc/o Anthony West APP665

Thomas, 3rd Baron Delaware (de la Warr) - of VA 1610, b1577 d1618 first governor of VA under Capt John Smith's settlement. Delaware Bay & the state of Delaware were named after him, son of Sir Thomas West b1555 d1601/1602, second Baron De La Warr, of Wherwell, Southampton & Lady Anne Knollys, dau/o Sir Francis Knollys & his wife Mary Cary, m1596 Cecily Shirley d1662, his descendants remained in England - the immigrant J&K286; ECD161; MCS3; DBR(2)630; FLW22, 23; TAG(16)40, 129/132, 201/205, (18)42, 137/146, 210/218, (19)197/202; GBR115; APP655/660

Thomas - of VA, m Sarah____ - desc/o Col/Gov John West DBR(3)128, 165, 166, 600

Thomas - of VA, b abt 1670, captain of militia of King William Co & member of the House of Burgesses, m Agnis____ - desc/o Col/Gov John West APP660

Thomas - of VA, d1743, burgess for King William Co, m Mary Cole dau/o Col William Cole of Boldrup, Warwick - desc/o Col/Gov John West APP660; SVF(2)399

Thorowgood - of VA, b1758 d1810, m Susanna Isham - desc/o Anthony West CFA24, 25

Unity - of VA, d1753, m1719 Capt William Dandridge d1747 - desc/o Col/Gov John West CHB243; BCD243; DBR(1)406; DBR(2)842; DBR(3)163, 326, 466, 676; DBR(4)301, 765; GBR115; APP660; SVF(2)399

WESTON Elizabeth - m Roger Conant son of Roger Conant & Elizabeth____ , & had issue a son John Conant - desc/o Thomas Weston EO2(3)687, 688

Thomas - of MA 1644, b abt 1576, bp 1584 d1657 ironmonger son of Ralph Weston & Anna Smyth, m Elizabeth Weaver dau/o Christopher Weaver & Alice (Green) Weaver - the immigrant GBR378; NGS(62) 163/172; TG(7)226/227; NE(141)99/100, 108/109; EO2(3)683/688

WESTOVER Amos - b abt 1753, m Ruth Loomis - desc/o Edward Griswold LDS109 - desc/o Agnes Harris RAA131

Jane - b1672, m(1) John Byington or Boynton - desc/o Edward Griswold LDS45, 89, 109

John - b1711, m Rachel Morton - desc/o Edward Griswold LDS109 - desc/o Agnes Harris RAA131

Jonah or Jonas - chr 1664, m Abigail Case - desc/o Edward Griswold LDS109

WETHERILL Ann - of NJ, m(1) Peter Bishop, m(2) James Moore - desc/o Christopher Wetherill AMB165

Christopher - of NJ 1683, b abt 1648 d1711, m1672 Mary Hornby - the immigrant CHB524; MCD315; MCS58; DBR(2)705; DBR(3)10, 492; AMB165; RAA no longer accepted as being of royal descent

Christopher - of NJ, b1710/1701 d1786, m1735 Mary Stockton - desc/o Christopher Wetherill DBR(3)10; AMB165

WETHERILL (cont.)

Isaac - b1753 d1821, m1776 Rebecca Deacon - desc/o Christopher
Wetherill AMB165

John - of NJ, b1677 d1728, m(1)1700 Sarah Borradell - desc/o
Christopher Wetherill DBR(2)705; AMB165

John - of PA, b1772 d1851, m Susan Garrison - desc/o Christopher
Wetherill AMB166

Joseph - of NJ, b1740 d1820, m1762 Anne Canby - desc/o
Christopher Wetherill AMB165

Mary - of NJ, m Silas Crispin - desc/o Christopher Wetherill AMB165

Mary Noble - of NJ, m1778 Isaac Jones - desc/o Christopher Wetherill
MCD315

Mordecai - b1766 d1826, m Martha Yorke - desc/o Christopher
Wetherill AMB165

Phoebe - of NJ, m Thomas Scattergood - desc/o Christopher Wetherill
AMB165

Samuel - of NJ, m1743 Mary Noble - desc/o Christopher Wetherill
MCD315; AMB165

Samuel - of NJ, b1736 d1816, m1762 Sarah Yarnall - desc/o
Christopher Wetherill DBR(3)10; AMB165

Samuel II - of NJ, b1764 d1829, m1788 Rachel Price - desc/o
Christopher Wetherill DBR(3)10; AMB166

Sarah - b1776 d1840, m1799 Joshua Lippincott - desc/o Christopher
Wetherill AMB166

Thomas - of NJ, b1674 d1759, m1703 Anne Fearon - desc/o
Christopher Wetherill MCD315; DBR(3)10; AMB165

William - of NJ, b1716, m1748 Rebecca Haines - desc/o Christopher
Wetherill DBR(2)705

Rev William - b1762 d1843, m(1)1784 Rebecca Sackett - desc/o
Christopher Wetherill DBR(2)706

WHALLEY Edward - of MA & CT, d1674/1675, English army officer, son
of Richard Whalley & Frances Cromwell, m(1) Judith Duffell, m(2)
Mary Middleton - the immigrant GBR353 some aspect of royal
descent merits further study

WHARTON Rachel - of PA, b1762 d1836, m1781 William Lewis - desc/o
Rebecca Humphrey CHB157; BCD157

William Moore - of PA, b1768 d1816, m(2) Deborah Shoemaker -
desc/o Thomas Lloyd CHB125; BCD125

WHEELER Calvin - b1742 d1838, m Mary Thorpe - desc/o Rev Edward
Bulkeley JSW1883

Eunice - of CT, b1727 d1804, m1746 Capt Joseph Williams - desc/o
Dorothy Thompson ECD(2)150; RAA132

Experience - b1685 - desc/o Alice Freeman RAA132

Experience - of MA, bp 1708 d1785, m1726 William Pollard - desc/o
John Prescott DBR(1)31, 521

Hannah - of CT, b1712, m1731 Simeon Miner - desc/o Dorothy
Thompson ECD(2)153; DBR(1)340, 594; DBR(2)442; DBR(3)239;
DBR(5)187, 797

Martha - b1670 - desc/o Alice Freeman RAA132

Oliver - b1748 - desc/o Olive Welby RAA93

William - of CT, b1681 d1747, m1710 Hannah Gallup - desc/o

WHEELER (cont.)
> Dorothy Thompson ECD(2)150, 153; DBR(1)340; DBR(2)442;
> DBR(3)239; DBR(5)187, 797; RAA132

WHIPPLE Amos - of CT, b1739, m1769 Ann Hewitt - desc/o Dorothy
> Harlakenden CHB280; BCD280

> John - b1765 - desc/o Alice Freeman RAA132

> Malachi - of NY, b1770 d1836, m Priscilla Brown - desc/o Dorothy
> Harlakenden CHB280; BCD280

> Samuel - of CT, b1702, m1726 Bethiah Patch - desc/o Dorothy
> Harlakenden CHB280; BCD280

WHITAKER Alexander - VA, b abt 1585 d1616/1617, Anglican
> clergyman, son of William Whitaker, master of St John's College,
> Cambridge & ____ Culverwell, died unmarried - the immigrant
> GBR331

> Charles - of MD, m Mary Ramsdell - desc/o Mary Bourchier
> DBR(2)459

> Eli B - m Martha Branch - descs/o Mary Bourchier DBR(4)674

> Elijah - b1768 d1826, m1790 Sarah Brashier - desc/o Mary Bourchier
> DBR(2)459

> George - of MD 1650, m Mary____ - desc/o Mary Bourchier DBR(2)458

> Jabez - of VA, son of William Whitaker, master of St John's College,
> Cambridge &____ Culverwell, m Mary Bourchier - the immigrant
> GBR331

> John - of VA, b abt 1694 d abt 1748, m Martha Gough - desc/o Mary
> Bourchier JSW1796; DBR(1)750; DBR(3)69; DBR(4)645, 674

> Rev John - of MD, b1720 d1798, m1741 Mary____ - desc/o Mary
> Bourchier DBR(2)459

> John - b1745 d1823, m(2)1786 Ferebee Pearson - desc/o Mary
> Bourchier DBR(1)751

> John - of NC, m Christienne Benton - desc/o Mary Bourchier
> DBR(4)674

> Lemuel - of VA, d1803, m1800 Elizabeth Brown - desc/o Mary
> Bourchier DBR(4)645

> Capt Richard - of VA, b abt 1643 d abt 1700, m(1)____ Ryland, m(2) aft
> 1672 Elizabeth____ - desc/o Mary Bourchier JSW1796; DBR(2)273;
> DBR(3)69; DBR(4)645, 674

> Richard - of VA & NC, b1720, m Elizabeth Cary - desc/o Mary
> Bourchier DBR(4)674

> Robert - of VA, d1765, m Sarah____ - desc/o Mary Bourchier
> DBR(1)751

> Thomas - of SC, d1818, m Mary Williams - desc/o Mary Bourchier
> DBR(2)273

> Lieut Col William - of VA, b1618 d1662, m____ - desc/o Mary
> Bourchier JSW1796; DBR(1)750; DBR(2)273, 456; DBR(3)69;
> DBR(4)645, 674

> William - of SC, d1788, m(2) Elizabeth Wiggins - desc/o Mary
> Bourchier JSW1796; DBR(2)273; DBR(3)69; DBR(4)645

WHITBY Elizabeth - of VA, (probably), m Joseph Summers - desc/o Anne
> Lovelace APP405

WHITCOMB Abigail - b1688, m Josiah White - desc/o John Whitcomb
> LDS16

WHITCOMB (cont.)

Dorcas - b1729/1730, m Solomon Aikens or Aiken - desc/o John Whitcomb LDS93; RAA84

Elizabeth - b1732 - desc/o James Cudworth RAA84

James - of MA, b1668 d1728, m1694 Mary Parker - desc/o John Whitcomb BLG2913; LDS93 - desc/o James Cudworth RAA84

James - of MA, b1697 d1763, m(4) Sarah Winslow - desc/o John Whitcomb BLG2913

Joanna - of MA, b1745, m1764 Maj Elisha Whitcomb - desc/o John Prescott DBR(1)292

John - of MA, b1588 d1662, m Frances Cogan - the immigrant LDS16, 46 & 93; BLG2913; RAA no longer accepted as being of royal descent

Jonathan - b1628, m Hannah Abigail___ - the immigrant LDS53; sufficient proof of alleged royal ancestry is lacking

Jonathan - b1669, m(1) Mary Blood - desc/o Jonathan Whitcomb LDS53

Jonathan - b abt 1692, m Deliverance Nutting - desc/o Jonathan Whitcomb LDS53

Josiah - b1638, m Rebekah Waters - desc/o John Whitcomb LDS16

Nathaniel - b1697, m(1) Rosilla or Rosanna Combs - desc/o John Whitcomb LDS93; RAA84

Oliver - b1749, m Dorcas Dickinson - desc/o Jonathan Whitcomb LDS53

Oliver - b1772, m(2) Olive Bidlack - desc/o Jonathan Whitcomb LDS53 - desc/o Dorothy Stapilton RAA117

Pliny - of MA, b1775 d1858, m(1) Prudence Fuller, m(2) Margaret Knapp - desc/o John Whitcomb BLG2913

Robert - of MA, b1634 d1683, m1662 Mary Cudworth - desc/o John Whitcomb BLG2913; LDS93

Robert - b abt 1703 - desc/o James Cudworth RAA84

Ruth - b1672, m William Divoll - desc/o John Whitcomb LDS46

Ensign Scottoway - of MA, d1812, m Mary___ - desc/o John Whitcomb BLG2913

William - b1719, m Hannah Darby - desc/o Jonathan Whitcomb LDS53

WHITE (WHYTE) Damaris - of MA, b1723, m Deacon James Briggs - desc/o Frances Deighton DBR(2)163

David - desc/o John Prescott AWW329

Dorothy - of MA, b abt 1717, m bef 1735 Benjamin Whitcomb - desc/o John Prescott DBR(1)292

Eleanor - of VA, m Ananias Dare - the immigrant JSW1540; sufficient proof of alleged royal ancestry is lacking

Elizabeth - of PA, b1705 d1732/1733, m1726 Benjamin Linton son of John Linton, a priest - desc/o Margaret Davis ECD(3)111; DBR(4)230 - desc/o Thomas Bye DBR(5)481

Eunice - b1766, m Luke White - desc/o John Prescott AWW329

Frances - of VA 1637, b1622, m Capt Richard Wells - the immigrant ECD(2)309; JSW1698; sufficient proof of alleged royal ancestry is lacking

Ruth - b1716, m Elisha Sawyer - desc/o John Whitcomb LDS16

WHITFORD John - b1704, m Martha Tefft - desc/o Frances Dungan
    LDS112

   Mercy - b1739, m Daniel Gill - desc/o Frances Dungan LDS112
WHITING Abigail - of CT, b1736, m1757 Daringon Andrews - desc/o
    Elizabeth St John CHB225; MCD310; BCD225

   Benjamin - of CT, b1694 d1773, m1723 Rebecca Parmlee - desc/o
    Elizabeth St John CHB225; MCD310; BCD225

   Charles - of CT, b1692 d1738, m1716/1717 Elizabeth Bradford b1696
    d1777 - desc/o Margaret Wyatt CHB27; BCD27

   Daniel b1768 d1855, m1804 Elizabeth Gilbert Powers b1782 d1859 -
    desc/o Margaret Wyatt CHB27; BCD27

   Dorcas - b1703 - desc/o Edward Bulkeley RAA75

   Dorcas - of MA, d1763, m1720 Joshua Abbott b1685 d1769 - desc/o
    Elizabeth St John CHB218; BCD218; RAA75

   Elisha - b1762 - desc/o Margaret Wyatt RAA61

   Elizabeth - of CT, b1645 d1733, m Rev Jonathan Hobart b1630 d1715
    - desc/o Elizabeth St John J&K299; CHB221; BCD221; DBR(1)683

   Elizabeth - m Rev Stephen Webster of Salisbury - desc/o Gov Thomas
    Dudley NE(8)321

   Elizabeth - of MA, m Samuel Ruggles - desc/o Elizabeth St John
    CHB220; BCD220

   Rev John - of MA, b1681 d1752, m1712 Mary Cotton - desc/o
    Elizabeth St John CHB223; BCD223

   John - b1693 - desc/o Margaret Wyatt RAA61

   John Lake - of MA, b1755, m1782 Olive Wyman - desc/o Elizabeth St
    John CHB224; BCD224

   Rev Joseph - of NY, b1641 d1723 minister at Lynn MA 1680/1682,
    minister at Southampton, Long Island, New York 1682/1723,
    m(1)1646 Sarah Danford - desc/o Elizabeth St John CHB223;
    FLW34, 85; MCD310; MCS74; BCD223

   Katherine - m John Lane Jr - desc/o Elizabeth St John AAP152;
    GBR210

   Margaret - of CT, b1690 d1747, m1710 Rev Jonathon Marsh - desc/o
    Margaret Wyatt DBR(2)613

   Mary - b1672, m(1) Joseph Sheldon, m(2) John Ashley - desc/o Amy
    Wyllys RAA126; TAG(39)89

   Mary - m Rev Daniel Rogers of Littleton - desc/o Gov Thomas Dudley
    NE(8)321

   Mary - of MA, b1743, m(1)1766 Capt William Barron - desc/o
    Elizabeth St John CHB224; BCD224

   Oliver - of MA, b1665 d1736, m1690 Anne Danforth b1668 d1737 -
    desc/o Elizabeth St John CHB218; BCD218

   Rev Samuel - of MA, b1633 d1713 minister at Billerica, MA
    1658/1713, m1656 Dorcas Chester b1637 dau/o Leonard Chester
    - desc/o Elizabeth St John CHB218; FLW34, 85; MCB134; MCS74;
    BCD218; THJ59, 60; RAA75; AAP152; GBR210

   Rev Samuel - of MA 1636, b1597 d1679 - the immigrant EDV71, 72;
    sufficient proof of alleged royal ancestry is lacking

   Samuel III - of MA, m Elizabeth Read - desc/o Elizabeth St John
    CHB220; BCD220; RAA75; AAP152; GBR210

   Judge Thomas - of MA, b1717 d1776, m1742 Lydia Parker - desc/o

WHITING (cont.)

Elizabeth St John CHB223; BCD223

Thomas - resided at Concord, m Mary Lake - desc/o Gov Thomas Dudley NE(8)321

William - b1736 - desc/o Margaret Wyatt RAA61

William Bradford b1731 d1796, m1757 Amy Lathrop b1735 d1815 - desc/o Margaret Wyatt CHB27; BCD27

WHITMAN Jane - b1748 - desc/o Richard Palgrave RAA121

John - b1687 - desc/o Richard Palgrave RAA121

Mercy - of CT, b1690 d1774, m1713 Nathaniel Jacobs b1683 d1772 - desc/o Dr Richard Palgrave DBR(4)693

Zachariah - b1722 - desc/o Richard Palgrave RAA121

WHITMARSH Sarah - b1766 - desc/o Alice Baynton RAA66

Thomas - b1736 - desc/o Alice Baynton RAA66

WHITNEY Abigail - of MA, b1724 m John Rand - desc/o John Whitney AMB331

Abraham - of MA, b1692 d1778, m1714 Mary Stone - desc/o John Whitney AFA226

Deacon Abraham - of MA, b1724 d1818, m1745 Mercy Perry - desc/o John Whitney AFA226

Capt Abraham - of MA, b1752 d1812, m1803 Sarah Jewell - desc/o John Whitney AFA226

Anna - b1660, m Cornelius Fisher - desc/o John Whitney LDS60

Barrett - of MA, b1715, m1737 Elizabeth Adams - desc/o John Whitney AMB331

Benjamin - of MA, b1643 d1723, m(1) Jane ____, m(2) Mary Poor - desc/o John Whitney CHB230; BCD230; AMB330

Benjamin - of MA, b1660 d1736, m(1)1687 Abigail Hagar - desc/o John Whitney CHB228; BCD228

Benjamin - of MA, b1687 d1737, m(1)1710 Sarah Barrett, m(2) Abigail Bridge - desc/o John Whitney AMB331

Cyrus - b1774, m1795 Mary Brewer - desc/o John Whitney AMB332

Ensign Daniel - of MA, b1700 d1775, m Dorothy Taintor - desc/o John Whitney BCD228

Daniel - of MA, m1744 Dorothy Goss - desc/o John Whitney CHB229; BCD228, 229

David - of MA, b1717, m Mercy____ - desc/o John Whitney AMB331

David - of MA, b1761, m(1)1786 Betsy Derby - desc/o John Whitney AMB331

Deborah - of MA, b1711, m Joseph Wheeler - desc/o John Whitney AMB331

Dinah - of MA, b1727, m1756 Elijah Livermore - desc/o John Whitney AMB331

Eleazer - of MA, b1662, m1687 Dorothy Ross - desc/o John Whitney AMB330

Eli - of MA, m(1) 1765 Elizabeth Fay - desc/o John Whitney J&K319

Eli - of MA, b1765 d1825, inventor of the cotton gin - desc/o John Whitney J&K319

George - b1765 d1805 - desc/o John Whitney AMB331

Hannah - of MA, b abt 1708, m Samuel Farr - desc/o John Whitney JSW1808

WHITNEY (cont.)

Henry - of CT, d1672 - the immigrant MCB251; EDV51; sufficient proof of alleged royal ancestry is lacking

Henry - of CT, b1735 d1811, m1761 Eunice Clark - desc/o Henry Whitney MCB252

Isaiah - of CT, b1671, m Sarah Woodward - desc/o John Whitney AMB330

Israel - of CT, b1710 d1746, m Hannah____ - desc/o John Whitney BCD229

John - of MA 1635, b1589 d1673, m(1)1618 Elinor____, m(2)1659 Judah Clement - the immigrant J&K318; CHB228; JSW1808; LDS91; BCD228; AMB330; AFA226; TAG(10)84/88 royal descent refuted; RAA no longer accepted as being of royal descent

John - of MA, b1620 d1692, m1642 Ruth Reynolds - desc/o John Whitney J&K318, 319; CHB228; LDS26, 43, 91; BCD228; AMB330

John - of CT, b bef 1644 d aft 1741, m1674/1675 Elizabeth Smith - desc/o Henry Whitney MCB251

John - of MA, b1684, m1710 Elizabeth Barnard - desc/o John Whitney AMB331

Jonathan - b1634, m1656 Lydia Jones - desc/o John Whitney LDS60; AMB330

Jonathan - of MA, b1680 d1754, m abt 1700 Susanna____ - desc/o John Whitney CHB230; BCD230

Joseph - b1771 d1812, m(1)1793 Sally Collins - desc/o John Whitney AMB330

Joshua - b1635 d1719, m(1) Lydia____, m(2) Mary____, m(3) Abigail Tarball - desc/o John Whitney AMB330

Josiah - of CT, d1750, m1729 Eunice Hanford - desc/o Henry Whitney MCB252

Lucy - b1744, m Asaph Sherman - desc/o John Whitney LDS91

Mary - of MA, b1710 d1788, m Joseph Jones - desc/o John Whitney CHB230; BCD230

Mary - of MA, b1731 d1805, m1762 Maj John Woodbridge - desc/o John Whitney CHB228; BCD228

Moses - of MA, b1655, m1686 Sarah Knight - desc/o John Whitney AFA226

Moses - of MA, b1775 d1816, m1797 Patty Baker - desc/o John Prescott DBR(1)31

Nathan - of MA, m1719 Mary Holman - desc/o John Whitney AMB331

Nathaniel - of MA, b1646 d1731/1732, m1673 Sarah Hagar - desc/o John Whitney J&K319; CHB229; LDS91; BCD229

Nathaniel - of MA, b1675 d1730, m1695 Mary Robinson - desc/o John Whitney J&K319; CHB229; LDS91; BCD229

Nathaniel - of MA, m Mary Child - desc/o John Whitney J&K319

Persis - of MA, b1719, m Nathan Goodale - desc/o John Whitney AMB331

Richard - of MA, bp 1624, m1651 Martha Coldham - desc/o John Whitney J&K318; CHB229; JSW1808; BCD229; AMB330; AFA226

Richard - of MA, b1660 d1723, m Elizabeth Sawtell - desc/o John Whitney CHB229; JSW1808; BCD229

Richard - of MA, m Hannah Whitcomb - desc/o John Whitney

WHITNEY (cont.)
CHB229; BCD229

Ruth - b1645, m(1) John Shattuck - desc/o John Whitney LDS26, 43

Samuel - chr 1711, m Elizabeth Hastings - desc/o John Whitney LDS91

Samuel - of MA, b1734 d1808, m1757 Abigail Cutler - desc/o John Whitney AMB331

Samuel Austin - b1769, m1801 Ruth Perkins - desc/o John Whitney AMB331

Sarah - of MA, b1667, m Charles Chadwick - desc/o John Whitney AMB331

Sarah - of MA, b1723, m Abraham Joslin - desc/o John Whitney AMB331

Silas - of MA, m 1780 Patience Goodnow - desc/o John Whitney CHB229

Stephen - of NY, b1776 d1860, m1803 Hariet Suydam - desc/o Henry Whitney MCB252

Sybil - of MA, b1733 d1812, m Capt Oliver Cummings - desc/o John Whitney CHB229; BCD229

Thomas - of MA, b1629 d1719, m1655 Mary Kedall - desc/o John Whitney AMB330

Thomas - of MA, b1656 d1742, m1679 Elizabeth Lawrence - desc/o John Whitney AMB331

Thomas - of MA, b1681, m1704 Mary Baker - desc/o John Whitney AMB331

WHITON Azariah - b1711, m(1) Elizabeth Barrows - desc/o John Dunham LDS21

Phebe - b1736/1737, m Simon Bradford - desc/o John Dunham LDS21 - desc/o George Morton RAA116

WHITTELSEY Rev Charles - of CT, b1717 d1787, m1745 Elizabeth Whiting - desc/o Rev Charles Chauncy CHB70; BCD70

Chauncey - of CT, b1746 d1812, m1770 Lucy Wetmore - desc/o Rev Charles Chauncy CHB70; BCD70

Lucy - of CT, b1773 d1856, m1797 Joseph Wright Alsop - desc/o Rev Charles Chauncy CHB70; BCD70

Roger Newton - of CT, b1754 d1835, m1775 Ann Woodruff - desc/o Catherine Eyre DBR(1)477

Rev Samuel - b1713 d1768, m1743 Susannah Newton - desc/o Catherine Eyre DBR(1)477

WHITTINGHAM Capt John - of MA, bp 1616 Boston, Lincoln d1639 Ipswich, MA, m Martha Hubbard - desc/o Elizabeth Bulkeley FLW34; MCS74; NE(5)

WICKHAM Elizabeth - of RI, b1773 d1803, m Walter Clarke Gardiner - desc/o Katherine Deighton ECD(2)111; DBR(5)85 - desc/o Frances Dungan EDC(3)138 - desc/o Gov Thomas Dudley DBR(5)81

Frances Amelia - of NY, m Jonathan Burrall - desc/o Gabriel Ludlow NYGBR(50)#1p38

Thomas - of RI, b1700 d1777, m1726 Hannah Brewer - desc/o Frances Dungan ECD(3)138

Thomas - of RI, b1736 d1816, m1762 Elizabeth Wanton - desc/o Frances Dungan ECD(3)138

WIGGIN Abigail - m Mr____ Doe of New Market - desc/o Gov Thomas Dudley NE(8)324

Andrew - m(1)____ & had issue 6 children - desc/o Gov Thomas Dudley NE(8)324

Bradstreet - b1676, m Ann Chase dau/o Joseph Chase of Hampton & left posterity - desc/o Gov Thomas Dudley NE(8)324

Bradstreet - m Phebe Sherburne - desc/o Gov Thomas Dudley NE(8)324

Hannah - m Mr____ Burleigh - desc/o Gov Thomas Dudley NE(8)324

Hannah - d1690 ? in her 24th year, m Samuel Wentworth Jr, leaving one son Samuel - desc/o Gov Thomas Dudley NE(8)324

Martha - m Mr____ Rust - desc/o Gov Thomas Dudley NE(8)324

Mary - of MA, m Captain Jeremiah Gilman b1660 - desc/o Gov Thomas Dudley DBR(5)223; NE(8)324

Mary - m Theophilus Smith - desc/o Gov Thomas Dudley NE(8)324

Mercy - m Mr____ Sherburne - desc/o Gov Thomas Dudley NE(8)324

Sarah - m William Moore - desc/o Gov Thomas Dudley NE(8)324

Capt Simon - b1664, m(1)____ - desc/o Gov Thomas Dudley NE(8)324

Lieut Simon - b1701 d1757, m Susannah Sherburne - desc/o Gov Thomas Dudley NE(8)324

Thomas - b1661, m Martha Denison dau/o John Denison of Ipswich - desc/o Gov Thomas Dudley NE(8)324

WILDER Dorothy - b1686 - desc/o John Prescott RAA125

Eunice - of MA, b1690, m Capt John White - desc/o John Prescott DBR(1)291

Mary - b1679 - desc/o John Prescott RAA125

Reuben - of MA, b1762 d1832, m1784 Mary Pierce - desc/o John Prescott AWW353

WILKINSON Angelica - of VA, m1770 Peterfield Trent - desc/o Christopher Branch GVFWM(1)427

Edward - of VA, m____ Epes a dau/o Lewellin Epes of Charles City Co - desc/o Christopher Branch GVFWM(1)426, 427

Isaac - of RI, b1768 d1843, m Lois Marsh - desc/o Lawrence Wilkinson CHB276; BCD276

John - of RI, b1654 d1708, m1689 Deborah Whipple - desc/o Lawrence Wilkinson CHB276; BCD276

John - of RI, b1690 d1756, m1718 Rebecca Scott - desc/o Lawrence Wilkinson CHB276; BCD276

John - of RI, b1724 d1804, m Ruth Angell - desc/o Lawrence Wilkinson CHB276; BCD276

Joseph - of VA, d1733, m Mary____ - desc/o Christopher Branch GVFWM(1)426

Joseph - of RI, b1682/1683 d1740, m Martha Pray - desc/o Lawrence Wilkinson CHB277; MCB391; MCD330; BCD277

Joseph - of RI, b1721 d1755, m1741 Alice Jenckes - desc/o Lawrence Wilkinson MCB391; MCD330

Joseph 3d - of RI, b1750 d1814, m Elizabeth Brownell - desc/o Lawrence Wilkinson MCB391; MCD330

Lawrence - of RI 1646, d1692 lieut in the army of King Charles I - the immigrant J&K183; MCB390, 391; MCD329; BCD276; DBR(2)201; THJ85, 86; royal ancestry has not been sufficiently proven

WILKINSON (cont.)

Martha - of VA, m____ Howlett - desc/o Christopher Branch GVFWM(1)427

Oziel - of RI, b1744 d1815, m1766 Lydia Smith - desc/o Lawrence Wilkinson CHB276; BCD276

Plain - of RI, b1717 d1791, m1738 John Rogers - desc/o Lawrence Wilkinson MCD330

Priscilla - of VA, m(1) Henry Embry Jr of Lunenburg & Brunswick Co, VA, m(2) William Hill - desc/o Christopher Branch GVFWM(1)426

Prudence - of RI, m Isaiah Angell - desc/o Lawrence Wilkinson CHB277; MCD330; BCD277

Ruth - of RI, b1685/1686 d1738, m William Hopkins - desc/o Lawrence Wilkinson J&K183; CHB277; BCD277; THJ86

Capt Samuel - of RI, d1727, m1672 Plain Wilkenden - desc/o Lawrence Wilkinson J&K183; CHB277; MCB391; MCD330; BCD276, 277

Samuel - of RI, b1674 d1727/1728 - desc/o Lawrence Wilkinson MCD330

WILLARD Abigail - of MA, b1665 d1746, m1694 Rev Benjamin Estabrook, m(2)1700 Rev Samuel Treat - desc/o Mary Launce J&K184; CHB447; DBR(1)545

Eunice - of CT, m Rev Benjamin Chadwick - desc/o Mary Launce CHB448

James - b1762 - desc/o John Prescott RAA125

Maj John - of MA, b1673 d1723, m1703 Frances Sherburn - desc/o Mary Launce CHB448

Rev Dr John - of CT - desc/o Mary Launce CHB448

Rev Dr Joseph - of CT, b1738 d1804, m1774 Mary Sheafe - desc/o Mary Launce CHB449

Mary - of MA, b1669 d1723, m David Melville - desc/o Mary Launce CHB448

Nancy - of MA, m1727 Capt John Parris - desc/o Mary Launce CHB448

Rev Samuel - of MA, b1705 d1741, m1730 Abigail Wright - desc/o Mary Launce CHB448

Rev Samuel - of MA, b1776 d1859, m1808 Susan Barker - desc/o Mary Launce CHB449

Simon - of MA, b1676 d1713, m1702 Elizabeth Alden - desc/o Mary Launce CHB448; DBR(1)545

William - of CT, b1735, m1763 Katherine Wilder - desc/o Mary Launce CHB448

WILLIAMS Abigail - m (a cousin) Thomas Williams - desc/o Margaret Wyatt GBR396

Anna - m Oliver Partridge of Hatfield, son of Edward Partridge, before named who, m Martha Williams - desc/o Gov Thomas Dudley NE(8)323

Anna - of MA, b1752, m1772 Joseph Houghton - desc/o Alice Freeman NE(34)70

Benjamin - of MA, m1689/1690 Rebecca Macy dau/o Capt George Macy - desc/o Frances Deighton DBR(1)419; DBR(4)627; RAA86; NE(5)414

WILLIAMS (cont.)

Benjamin - of MA, b1681 d1757, m Elizabeth Deane - desc/o Frances Deighton NE(5)414

Capt Benjamin - of MA, b1695 d1775 a captain in the French & Indian Wars, m1726/1727 Abigail (Parsons) Johnson - desc/o Frances Deighton DBR(1)419; DBR(4)627

Bethiah - of MA, b1676, m _____ Rice - desc/o Alice Freeman NE(34)70

Bethiah - of MA, b1692, m Major Joseph Hodges of Norton - desc/o Frances Deighton NE(5)414

Damaris - of MA, b1698, m1724 Daniel Howard of Bridgewater - desc/o Frances Deighton NE(5)414

Daniel - of MA, b abt 1682 d1735, m Mercy Deane - desc/o Frances Deighton NE(5)414

Deborah - of MA, b1737 d1774, m1764 Gregory Belcher son of the Rev Joseph Belcher - desc/o Frances Deighton DBR(1)419; DBR(4)627

Desire - b1731 d1821, m Capt Elisha Strong - desc/o Alice Freeman DBR(3)430

Dorothy - of MA, b1721, m1739 Ralph Holbrook of Brookline, MA - desc/o Alice Freeman NE(34)70

Elijah - m Lydia Dwight - desc/o Margaret Wyatt GBR396

Rev Elisha - b1694 d1755 ordained at Weathersfield, CT 1722; chosen rector of Yale College 1726, appointed judge of the Superior Court, m(1) Eunice Chester, m(2) Elizabeth Scott dau/o Rev Thomas Scott of Norwich, England - desc/o Gov Thomas Dudley NE(8)323

Elizabeth - of MA, b abt 1647 d1724, m abt 1670 John Bird of Dorchester b1641 d1732 - desc/o Frances Deighton ECD158; LDS22; DBR(3)61; DBR(5)759; AWW339; NE(5)414

Elizabeth - of MA, b1672, m_____ Tucker - desc/o Alice Freeman NE(34)70

Elizabeth - of RI, b1679 d1723, m(1)1700 Timothy McCarthy, mariner of Newport, m(2)1718 Thomas Paine b abt 1680 d1766 - desc/o Dr Richard Palgrave DBR(2)592; DBR(3)572

Elizabeth - of MA, b1686 d1731, m1707 John Macomber of Taunton - desc/o Frances Deighton DBR(1)762; DBR(2)365; NE(5)414

Elizabeth - m Rev Joseph Crocker of Ipswich - desc/o Gov Thomas Dudley NE(8)323

Elizabeth b1759 d1839, m Ozias McCall - desc/o Susan Clinton CHB417; MCD234

Elizabeth - of NC, m General William Williams (her first cousin) - desc/o William Boddie HSF(1)341

Esther - b1726, m Dr Thomas Williams of Deerfield - desc/o Gov Thomas Dudley NE(8)323

Eunice - of CT, b1775 d1844, m1793 Arunah Metcalf - desc/o Susannah Palmes ECD(3)188

Ezekiel - of MA, b1755, m(1)1777 Susannah Dana, m(2) widow Codner - desc/o Alice Freeman NE(34)70

Freelove - of RI, b1713 d1791, m1732 Daniel Fiske - desc/o William Arnold CHB14; BCD14

Grace - of MA, b1688, m1718 John Metcalf - desc/o Alice Freeman NE(34)70

Hannah - of MA, m John Parmenter of Boston - desc/o Frances

WILLIAMS (cont.)

    Deighton CHB377; NE(5)414

Hannah - of MA, b abt 1670 d1708, m Samuel Bunn of Taunton - desc/o Frances Deighton NE(5)414

Hannah - of MA b1689 d1755, m1712 Joseph Snell of Bridgewater - desc/o Frances Deighton ECD(2)106; DBR(1)563; DBR(2)690; DBR(3)367; DBR(4)861; DBR(5)96; NE(5)414

Hannah - m Rev Joseph Seccomb of Harvard, MA & Chester, Nova Scotia - desc/o Gov Thomas Dudley NE(8)323

Henry Guston - of NC, b1765 Gunston Hall, Warren Co, m1793 Lucy Barker Tunstall b1775 Pittsylvania or Henry Co, VA d1857 Buxton Place, Warren Co, dau/o William Tunstall & Elizabeth (Betsy) Barker - desc/o Col John Alston DBR(1)770; DBR(2)817 - desc/o William Boddie HSF(1)341

John - of PA, son of William ap William &___, m(1) Mary Evans, m(2) Mrs Catherine___ Edwards - the immigrant GBR324 further research should be undertaken to confirm royal descent

John - of MA, b1683, m Dorothy Brewer - desc/o Alice Freeman NE(34)70

John - b1692 - desc/o Alice Freeman RAA132

John - of MA, b1719 d1794 a tanner at Roxbury & always an ardent Revolutionary Whig, m(1)1749 Ann Bird b1724 d1769 dau/o Thomas Bird of Dorchester, m(2)1770 Rebecca Winslow - desc/o Alice Freeman NE(34)70

John - of MA, b1750, m(1) Polly Champney, m(2)1778 Sarah Wheeler - desc/o Alice Freeman NE(34)70

Jonathan - of MA, b1683 d1761, m Elizabeth Leonard - desc/o Frances Deighton NE(5)414

Joseph - of MA, d1692, m Elizabeth___ - desc/o Frances Deighton NE(5)414

Josiah - of MA, b1692, m Martha Howard - desc/o Frances Deighton NE(5)414

Laetitia - of PA, b1771 d1858, m1799 James Poultney - desc/o Dr Thomas Wynne ECD(2)331; DBR(3)762

Lucy - m Rev Joseph Buckminster of Rutland - desc/o Gov Thomas Dudley NE(8)323

Lucy - of MA, b1772, m George Standart - desc/o Alice Freeman NE(34)70

Margaret - of MA, b1723, m1743 Thomas Greggs - desc/o Alice Freeman NE(34)70

Martha - m Edward Partridge - desc/o Gov Thomas Dudley NE(8)323

Martha - b1790 - desc/o Gov Thomas Dudley RAA89

Mary - of MA, b1669, m___ Choate - desc/o Alice Freeman NE(34)70

Mary - of MA, b1670 d1708, m1690/1693 Edward Sands - desc/o Dr Richard Palgrave ECD(3)232

Mary - of MA, b1680, m Ebenezer Robinson of Raynham - desc/o Frances Deighton NE(5)414

Mary - of MA, m Henry Andrews of Taunton - desc/o Frances Deighton NE(5)414

Mary - of RI, d aft 1740, m Epenetus Olney - desc/o William Arnold CHB15; BCD15

WILLIAMS (cont.)

Mary - of MA, b1759, m1779 John Smith - desc/o Alice Freeman
NE(34)70

Mary - of NC, b1776 d1834, m1794 John Anderson - desc/o Edward
Dudley ECD(3)134; DBR(4)669

Mehitabel - of MA, b1676, m Increase Robinson of Taunton - desc/o
Frances Deighton NE(5)414

Mehitable - of MA, b1695, m Rev Benjamin Webb of Eastham - desc/o
Frances Deighton NE(5)414

Miriam - of MA, m Capt James D Colt - desc/o Gov Thomas Dudley
AFA114

Nathaniel - of MA, b1641, m1668 Elizabeth Rogers of Duxbury -
desc/o Frances Deighton CHB376; DBR(1)762, 763; DBR(2)365;
NE(5)414

Peleg - of RI, m Elizabeth Carpenter - desc/o William Arnold J&K294;
CHB14

Phebe - of MA, b1687, m Christopher Richmond of Middleboro -
desc/o Frances Deighton NE(5)414

Rebecca - b1715 - desc/o John Deighton RAA86

Rebeckah - of MA, b1690, m(1) Samuel Pitts of Taunton, m(2) James
Williams of Taunton - desc/o Frances Deighton NE(5)414

Richard - of MA, bp 1606, m1632 Frances Deighton dau/o John
Deighton, of Somersetshire, England & Jane Bassett - the
immigrant CHB375, 376; sufficient proof of alleged royal ancestry is
lacking; royal ancestry is through his wife Frances Deighton;
NE(5)414

Sally - of MA, b1775, m(1) Elisha Esty m(2) Noah Olmstead - desc/o
Alice Freeman NE(34)70

Samuel - of MA, b abt 1680 d1765, m Abigail____ d1779 aged 94 -
desc/o Frances Deighton NE(5)414

Samuel - of MA, b1697, m Mary or Jane Gilbert - desc/o Frances
Deighton CHB378; MCD308; DBR(2)163; NE(5)414

Samuel Jr - of NC, b1751 d aft 1842, m Mary Dudley - desc/o Maj
John Alston Jr JSW1674; DBR(1)619

Samuel - of NC, m(1) Mary Parsons, m(2) Mary Eaton - desc/o William
Boddie HSF(1)341

Sarah - of MA, b1662, m1679 Joseph Bond - desc/o Anthony Colby
ECD(2)96; DBR(4)758; DBR(5)693

Sarah - of MA, m1680 Benjamin Deane of Taunton - desc/o Frances
Deighton CHB377; MCD308; DBR(2)163; NE(5)414

Sarah - of MA, b1668, m ____ Hastings - desc/o Alice Freeman
NE(34)70

Sarah - of MA, b1685, m James Hall - desc/o Frances Deighton
NE(5)414

Sarah - of MA, d1756, m Jonathan Clapp - desc/o Frances Deighton
CHB378

Seth - of MA, b abt 1676 d1761, m Mary Deane - desc/o Frances
Deighton CHB378; NE(5)414

Silas - of RI, father of Thankful Williams - desc/o Frances Deighton
J&K294

Capt Solomon - d1794, m1764 Temple Boddie - desc/o Col John

WILLIAMS (cont.)

Alston DBR(1)766, 770; DBR(2)817; DBR(3)270

Stephen - of MA, b1678, m Sarah Payson - desc/o Alice Freeman NE(34)70

Stephen - of MA, b1757, m1779 Abigail Smith - desc/o Alice Freeman NE(34)70

Temperance Boddie - of NC, m George Tunstall - desc/o William Boddie HSF(1)341

Thankful - b1718 - desc/o Alice Freeman RAA132

Thomas - of MA, d1707, m abt 1679 Mary____ - desc/o Frances Deighton ECD(2)106; DBR(1)563; DBR(2)690; DBR(3)367; DBR(4)860; DBR(5)96; NE(5)414

Thomas - of MA, b1754 Roxbury d1817 Utica, NY, was of the Roxbury Minute Men in Revolutionary times & together with his brother-in-law, Thomas Dana, Jr took part in the famous Boston Tea-Party, m1777 Susannah Dana dau/o Thomas Dana & Martha Williams - desc/o Alice Freeman NE(34)70

Rev William - of MA, b1688 d1760, m Hannah Stoddard dau/o Rev Solomon Stoddard of Northampton - desc/o Gov Thomas Dudley AFA114; NE(8)323

Col William - of MA, b1713 d1788, m Sarah Welles - desc/o Gov Thomas Dudley AFA114

Maj William - of NC, m(1) Ruina Webb, m(2)1789 Elizabeth Kearney - desc/o Col John Alston DBR(1)766 - desc/o William Boddie HSF(1)341

Capt William Ligon - b1771 d1849, m Mary Gannaway - desc/o Thomas Lygon DBR(5)748

William Wheeler - b1760 - desc/o Alice Freeman RAA132

Zipporah - of VT, b1756 d1823, m1775/1776 Timothy Phelps - desc/o Dorothy Thompson ECD(2)150

WILLIS Ann - of VA, b1749, m Thomas Maclin - desc/o Col George Reade HSF(2)198

Anne - of VA, b1731 d1820, m Duff Green of Fauquier Co - desc/o Col George Reade JSW1638; GVFTQ(4)505

Augustine - of VA, b1747 d1799, m1771 Mrs Ann Heath - desc/o Col George Reade HSF(2)198

Augustine - of NC, b1770 d1842 Monroe Co, MS, m1802 Randolph Co, NC, Sally Wood dau/o Reuben Wood & Charity Hayne of SC - desc/o Col George Reade HSF(2)198, 199

Elizabeth - of VA, m Capt John Sale - desc/o Col John Washington DBR(2)132

Elizabeth - of NY, m Robert Zane Sr - desc/o Henry Willis CHB508; MCD334

Elizabeth - of VA, m Mr____ McKain & had issue - desc/o Anne Rich PVF274

Elizabeth - of VA, m1775 Thomas Cocke - desc/o Col George Reade HSF(2)198

Elizabeth Carter - of VA, b1751, m abt 1772 John McKeand - desc/o Sarah Ludlow DBR(1)30

Elizabeth Carter - of VA, b1771 d1802, m Henry Hiot or Hiort, attorney at law - desc/o Anne Rich PVF275; GVFTQ(4)498

WILLIS (cont.)

Esther - of NY, b1677, m1695 William Albertson II d1719/1720 - desc/o Henry Willis DBR(3)315

Francis - of VA, m1742 Elizabeth Carter granddaughter of Robert (known as King) Carter - desc/o Anne Rich PVF274; GVFTQ(4)494

Francis - of VA, b1743/1745 congressman from Georgia, m1769 Elizabeth Edwards - desc/o Anne Rich GVFTQ(4)501 - desc/o Col George Reade HSF(2)198

Francis - of VA, b1744 of White Hall, Gloucester Co d1791, m Elizabeth Perrin b1751 d1791 dau/o John Perrin - desc/o Anne Rich PVF274, 275; GVFTQ(4)494, 498

Henry - of NY, b1628 d1714, who was of royal descent from King Henry I, of France & the Emperor Henry I, of Germany. A Quaker & founder of Westbury, L.I., m Mary Peace b1632 d1714 - the immigrant CHB508; MCD334; DBR(2)429; DBR(3)315; RAA1; sufficient proof of alleged royal ancestry is lacking

Col Henry - of VA, d abt 1740 burgess from Gloucester Co 1718 & 1723, m(1) Anne Alexander dau/o David Alexander & Anne Morgan, m(2) Mildred (Howell) or (Washington) b1723 d1783, m(3) Mildred Washington (aunt of General (Washington) - desc/o Anne Rich GVFTQ(4)502

Henry - of VA, m1742 Elizabeth Gregory dau/o Roger Gregory - desc/o Anne Rich GVFTQ(4)504

John - of VA, b1724, m Elizabeth Madison only sister of Col James Madison, father of the president - desc/o Anne Rich GVFTQ(4)504

John - of VA, d1769, m1743 Mildred Smith d1769 dau/o Augustine Smith of Shooters Hill, Middlesex Co - desc/o Anne Rich GVFTQ(4)500

John - of VA, b1744 Beddingfield Hall, Brunswick Co d Orange Co, NC, farmer & Episcopalian, m abt 1769 Mary Hayes Plummer b Gloucester Co d1824 Warrenton, Warren Co, NC dau/o William Plummer & Mary Hayes - desc/o Col George Reade HSF(2)198

John - of VA, m Nancy____ - desc/o Anne Rich GVFTQ(4)505

John - of NC, d1806, m1792 Eliza Parks - desc/o Col George Reade HSF(2)198

John W - of VA, lieutenant in the Revolutionary army, m____ & had issue who married, respectively, a Hoomes, a Sears & an Epperson - desc/o Anne Rich GVFTQ(4)506

Lewis - of VA, b1734 lieutenant-colonel of 10th VA Regiment, continental troops 1776 to 1778, m(1) Mary Champe dau/o John Champe of King & Queen Co - desc/o Anne Rich GVFTQ(4)506

Lewis - of VA, d1828, m(1)1788 Elizabeth Cocke, m(2) Mary Goodwin - desc/o Col George Reade HSF(2)198

Mary - of VA, b1716, m Lewis Burwell, president of the VA Council 1736 - desc/o Anne Rich PVF271; GVFTQ(4)494, 504

Mary - of VA, m1733 Hancock Lee - desc/o Anne Rich GVFTQ(4)504

Mildred - of VA, m Landon Carter of Cleves & had issue, three daughters - desc/o Anne Rich GVFTQ(4)506

Plummer - of NC, d1818, m Drucilla Ransom Thorn - desc/o Col Goerge Reade HSF(2)198

Priscilla - of VA, m(1) Col William Kennon, m(2) David Flower of

WILLIS (cont.)

Wilmington, NC - desc/o Anne Rich PVF274; GVFTQ(4)494, 495

Rich - of VA, d1812, m Elizabeth Craighill Gray - desc/o Col George Reade HSF(2)198

Robert Carter - of VA, d1783, m Martha____ & had issue - desc/o Anne Rich PVF274; GVFTQ(4)494

Sarah - of NY, b abt 1671 d1729/1730, m John Titus - desc/o Henry Willis DBR(2)429

WILLOUGHBY Elizabeth - of MA, b1641 d1711, m1669 Samuel Camfield - desc/o Francis Willoughby DBR(3)735; DBR(4)348, 651

Elizabeth - of VA, m Isaac Allerton - desc/o Thomas Willoughby AWW118; NFA46

Francis - of MA 1638, d1671, m(1) Mary____, m(2) Sarah Taylor, m(3)1659 Margaret MacGehee dau/o Thomas MacGehee CHB288 - the immigrant ECD(3)281; MCD317; MCS59; BCD288; DBR(1)493; DBR(2)614, 615, 856; DBR(3)341, 342, 734, 735; DBR(4)348, 651; BLG2978; EO2(3)809/820; RAA no longer accepted as being of royal descent; NE(141)108 disproved royal descent

Francis - b1672 deputy & representative 1713, m & had issue - desc/o Francis Willoughby EO2(3)819

Jonathan - of MA, b abt 1635, m Grizzel____ & had issue a dau Mary b1664 & probably other children - desc/o Francis Willoughby EO2(3)819

John - of MA, b1688 - desc/o Francis Willoughby BLG2978

John - of MA, b1707 d1793, m Anna Chamberlain - desc/o Francis Willoughby BLG2978

Jonas - of NH, b1737, m Hannah Bates - desc/o Francis Willoughby BLG2978

Nehemiah - of MA, b1644 d1702 merchant of Salem, m1672 Abigail Bartholomew bp 1650 d1702 dau/o Henry Bartholomew - desc/o Francis Willoughby BLG2978; EO2(3)819

Oliver - of NH, b1764 d1834, m Sarah Baily - desc/o Francis Willoughby BLG2978

Sarah - of MA, bp 1641, m Samuel Canfield bp 1645 eldest son of Matthew Canfield of New Haven - desc/o Francis Willoughby DBR(2)615; DBR(3)342; EO2(3)819

Sarah - of VA - desc/o Thomas Willoughby AWW118

Susannah - of MA & CN, b1664 d1710, m1683 Judge Nathaniel Lynde b1659 d1729 son of Judge Simon Lynde & Hannah Newdigate - desc/o Thomas MacGehee CHB288 - desc/o Francis Willoughby ECD(3)282; MCS59; BCD288; DBR(1)493; DBR(2)856; EO2(3)819

Thomas - of VA bef 1627, b1601 d1658, m Alice____ - the immigrant AWW118; NFA45 sufficient proof of alleged royal ancestry is lacking

Thomas III - of VA, b1632, m Margaret Herbert - desc/o Thomas Willoughby AWW118; NFA45

Thomas IV - of VA, m Sarah Thompson - desc/o Thomas Willoughby AWW118; NFA45

WILSON Deliverance - b1768, m Lovina Fairchild - desc/o Daniel Smith LDS113

WINCHELL Abigail - b1722 - desc/o Thomas Dudley RAA89 - desc/o William Leete RAA107

WINCHESTER Benjamin - b1744 - desc/o John Prescott RAA125

WINDER Elizabeth - of MD, b abt 1691 d1744, m(1) bef 1711 Richard Kenner b1673/1674 d1719, m(2) John Footman d1739 - desc/o Elizabeth Boteler APP190

WINES Barnabas III - of NY, m Anna___ - desc/o Thomas Mapes DBR(2)280

Sarah - of NY, d1733, m abt 1698 Eleazer Luce - desc/o Thomas Mapes ECD(2)194; DBR(2)280

WING Phebe - of MA, b1726/1727 d1787, m1746 Nathaniel Foster - desc/o Mary Wentworth ECD(2)297

WINGFIELD Ann - of VA, m James Garland son of James Garland & Mary Rice of Hanover Co & left issue - desc/o Thomas Wingfield TVG(36)258, 259

Ann - of VA, b1759, m Rev Hope Hull b1763 d1818 & had issue - desc/o Thomas Wingfield GVFHB(5)830

Ann - of VA, b1766, m(1) John Hamner, m(2) John Harrison - desc/o Thomas Wingfield TVG(36)246

Barbara ("Bebby") - b abt 1767, m Dr Frederick Sims & had issue - desc/o Thomas Wingfield GVFHB(5)834

Lieut Charles - of VA, b1728 New Kent Co d1803 Albermarle Co, VA a justice in Albemarle Co in 1771 & a lieutenant in the Revolution, m1750 Rachel Joyner - desc/o Thomas Wingfield DBR(1)775; DBR(5)747; VGS(20)53, 54; GVFHB(5)837; TVG(36)245, 246

Charles Jr - of VA, b1752 d1819, m Mary Lewis - desc/o Thomas Wingfield TVG(36)246

Charles - of VA, d prior to 1819, m(1) Elizabeth Day, m(2) Nancy Giles - desc/o Thomas Wingfield TGV(36)247

Christopher - of VA, b1760 d1821 lieutenant 2nd militia Company, 1794, m Elizabeth Cocke - desc/o Thomas Wingfield GVFHB(5)837; TVG(36)246

Edward Maria - of VA, b abt 1570 d bef 1613, adventurer & 1st president of the VA Colony died unmarried, son of Thomas Maria Wingfield &___ Kerry - the immigrant MCS15; GBR281; NE(103)287/295; HSF(4)165

Eliza - of VA, m Josiah Wingfield son of Robert Wingfield of Louisa Co - desc/o Thomas Wingfield TVG(36)246, 247

Elizabeth - of VA, b abt 1735 d abt 1759, m abt 1756 Charles Cosby b1736 in Hanover Co, VA d1802 Elbert Co, Georgia son of David Cosby & Mary Garland Overton - desc/o Thomas Wingfield GVFHB(5)834

Elizabeth - of VA, b1756 d abt 1792, m in Hanover Co, VA abt 1776 John Grimes, a Revolutionary soldier, son of Capt William Grimes & Mary Sterling - desc/o Thomas Wingfield DBR(1)428, 441; GVFHB(5)832, 833

Elizabeth - of VA, b1752, m1770 Edward Butler b1748 d1809 in Wilkes Co, Georgia son of Edwin Butler & Susanna Wade & had issue - desc/o Thomas Wingfield GVFHB(5)830

Elizabeth - of VA, b1768 Hanover Co d1823 Claiborne Co, MS, m1786 Walter Leake of Albemarle Co, son of Mask Leake & Patience Morris. They moved to Mississippi aft 1799 where Walter was judge, US Senate & finally governor when he died - desc/o Thomas

WINGFIELD (cont.)

Wingfield TVG(36)254

Elizabeth - of VA, b1775, m Hendley Hamner - desc/o Thomas Wingfield TGV(36)246

Frances - of VA, b1736 d1802, m1756 William Terrell b1732 d1812 served in the VA forces during the Revolution, first as an ensign & later as a second lieutenant, son of Joel Terrell & Sarah Elizabeth Oxford & had issue six sons - desc/o Thomas Wingfield DBR(1)33; GVFHB(5)834

Frances -b1763, m David Meriwether & had issue - desc/o Thomas Wingfield GVFHB(5)830

Francis - of VA, b1770 d1866, m Elizabeth Wingfield his cousin, dau/o Thomas Wingfield TGV(36)246

Jemima - of VA, b1773, m Samuel Barkesdale - desc/o Thomas Wingfield TGV(36)246

John - of VA, b abt 1695, m1720 Mary (Polly) Hudson dau/o Charles Hudson & (probably) Sarah Anne Royal - desc/o Thomas Wingfield MCS16; DBR(1)775; DBR(2)505; DBR(5)747; VGS(20)53/58; TVG(36)243/259; GVFHB(5)826;

John - of VA, b1723 Hanover Co, VA d1793 Wilkes Co, Georgia, m1744 Hanover Co, VA, Frances Oliver Buck b1725 d1795 Wilkes Co, Georgia - desc/o Thomas Wingfield DBR(1)328, 581; DBR(2)691; DBR(3)369; GVFHB(5)828, 829

John Jr - of VA, son of John & Mary Wingfield, m(1)____, m(2) Elizabeth____ - desc/o Thomas Wingfield TVG(36)252

John - of VA, b1742 d1814 signed the Declaration of Independence of the Citizens of Albemarle Co 1779, m Robina Langford & had issue - desc/o Thomas Wingfield DBR(5)747; GVFHB(5)837

John - of VA, b1751 d1828, m Susannah Lewis - desc/o Thomas Wingfield TVG(36)246

John - of VA, b1757 d1828, m in VA 1781 Rebecca Nelson & had issue - desc/o Thomas Wingfield GVFHB(5)833

John Jr - 1761 d1802 Wilkes Co, Georgia, m Mary Darracourt & had issue - desc/o Thomas Wingfield GVFHB(5)830

Joseph - of VA, b abt 1734 d1794, m abt 1783 Mary Cocke - desc/o Thomas Wingfield DBR(1)395; DBR(2)505; TVG(36)256

Ensign Joseph - of VA, b1764 d1830 a Revolutionary War soldier, m(1) Mollie Tool & had issue, m(2) Sarah Wingfield dau/o Reuben Wingfield - desc/o Thomas Wingfield DBR(1)775; VGS(20)54; TVG(36)246

Joseph - of VA, m(1) Mary Simms - desc/o Thomas Wingfield TVG(36)

Joseph Benjamin - of VA, m Susannah Wingfield dau/o John Wingfield & Robina Lankford, living in Nelson Co & alive in 1851, they left numerous children - desc/o Thomas Wingfield TVG(36)247

Joseph Cocke - of VA, b abt 1758, m____ Ragland - desc/o Thomas Wingfield DBR(1)395; DBR(2)505 - desc/o Capt Henry Isham DBR(2)508

Maria - b1767, m John Hardin Foster - desc/o Thomas Wingfield GVFHB(5)830

Mary - of VA, b abt 1721, m abt 1736 John Cosby son of John Cosby & Martha Garland - desc/o Thomas Wingfield GVFHB(5)828

WINGFIELD (cont.)

Mary - of VA, b1747, m Peter Terrell d1795 & had issue - desc/o Thomas Wingfield GVFHB(5)830

Mary - of VA, d bef 1795, m Holcraft Norvell killed along with their son George while serving with the VA Line in the Continental Service - desc/o Thomas Wingfield TVG(36)247

Mary - of VA, b bet 1760/1765 d aft 1840, m William Wingfield son of Charles Wingfield & Rachel Joyner of Albemarle Co - desc/o Thomas Wingfield TVG(36)253

Mary - of VA, b1762, m Richard Hamner - desc/o Thomas Wingfield TVG(36)246

Mary - of VA, b abt 1764 d1818, m Richard Warsham b1756 d1826 commissioned ensign in the 14th VA Regiment 1776, second lieut 1777, served in the 10th VA Regiment of the Continental Line in 1778, promoted to first lieutenant 1779, taken prisoner at Charlottesville 1780 & transferred 1781 to the 1st VA Regiment, for his Revolutionary War service he received a pension in 1818, son of Capt John Worsham of Hanover Co, VA & Sophia Watkins of Charlotte Co, VA & had issue - desc/o Thomas Wingfield GVFHB(5)833

Owen - of VA, b1719 - desc/o Thomas Wingfield MCS16

Rebecca - of VA, b bef 1731, m Thomas Pemberton of Albemarle Co - desc/o Thomas Wingfield TVG(36)246

Rebecca - b1765, m John Darracourt - desc/o Thomas Wingfield GVFHB(5)830

Robert - of VA, b abt 1697 d1769, m Ann____ - desc/o Thomas Wingfield MCS16; DBR(5)40; GVFHB(5)826

Robert - of VA, b abt 1736 d1791, m1765 Frances Jordan - desc/o John Wingfield DBR(5)40

Robert - of VA, m Nancy Wingfield, dau/o Nathan Wingfield & lived in Amherst Co - desc/o Thomas Wingfield TVG(36)247

Sarah - of VA & MO, b1790 d1868, m1792 Rev Leonard Ballou - desc/o John Wingfield DBR(5)40, 41

Sarah - of VA, b1754, m(1) Stephen Pettus d1789, m(2) in Wilkes Co, Georgia 1807 William Daniel d1816 in Greene Co, Georgia - desc/o Thomas Wingfield GVFHB(5)830

Sarah - of VA, b1768, m John Martin - desc/o Thomas Wingfield TVG(36)246

Sarah Garland - m(1) Dr Antoine Poullain & had a son Dr Thomas Noel Poullain, m(2) (her cousin) Garland Wingfield - desc/o Thomas Wingfield GVFHB(5)833

Susannah - of VA, m John Cosby b1741 Hanover Co, VA d1827 Frederickstown, Washington Co, Kentucky, son of David Cosby & Mary Garland Overton & had issue - desc/o Thomas Wingfield GVFHB(5)835

Thomas - of VA, b1670 d1720 son of John Wingfield & Mary Owen, m(1) Mary____, m(2) Mary____ - the immigrant MCS16; DBR(1)328, 395, 428, 580, 774, 775; DBR(2)505, 691; DBR(3)369; DBR(5)40, 746, 747; RAA1; GBR121; VGS(20)53/58; TVG(36)243/259; GVFHB(5)822/841

Thomas - of VA, b abt 1693, m Sarah Garland - desc/o Thomas

WINGFIELD (cont.)

Wingfield MCS16; DBR(1)33, 328, 428, 580; DBR(2)691; DBR(3)369; GVFHB(5)826/828

Thomas - of VA, b1733 d1806 Wilkes Co, Georgia, m Hanover Co, VA abt 1754 Elizabeth Terrell dau/o Joel Terrell & Sarah Elizabeth Oxford - desc/o Thomas Wingfield DBR(1)428, 441; GVFHB(5)831

Thomas - of VA, b bet 1740 & 1750 d aft 1830, m Ann Davis dau/o William Davis & Elizabeth Shelton - desc/o Thomas Wingfield TVG(36)248

Thomas - of VA, b1745 d1797 Revolutionary soldier who received bounty land in Georgia for his war service, m1768 in Hanover Co, VA, Elizabeth Nelson b1749 d1802 & had issue - desc/o Thomas Wingfield DBR(1)328, 581; DBR(2)691; DBR(3)369; GVFHB(5)830

Thomas - of VA, b1763 d1857 lived in Appomattox Co, his wife believed to have been a Miss Scott who predeceased him. He left descendants of whom Nancy, Martha, William & Jane were living with him in the 1850 census - desc/o Thomas Wingfield TVG(36)247

William - of VA, b1758 d1836, m Mary Wingfield, first cousin & dau/o John Wingfield Jr - desc/o Thomas Wingfield TVG(37)246

William - of VA, b1761 d1844, m Mary Elizabeth Davis - desc/o Thomas Wingfield TVG(36)252, 253

WINN Minor - of VA & GA, b1759 d1820/1821, m abt 1787 Mary Evans - desc/o Col John Washington DBR(1)666; DBR(2)41; DBR(5)135

WINSHIP Joseph - b1701, m Anna Whitmore - desc/o Robert Harrington LDS17

Joseph - b1727, m Elizabeth Lathrop - desc/o Robert Harrington LDS17

Niber Abigail - b1758, m Luther Barney - desc/o Robert Harrington LDS17

WINSLOW Anne - m John Taylor - desc/o Anne Marbury GBR234 - desc/o Catherine Hamby GBR394

Benjamin - of NC, d1794, m Rachel White - desc/o John Winslow FFF15

Edward - of MA, b1595 - the immigrant EDV45; THC339, 340, 341; EO2(3)847/849; sufficient proof of alleged royal descent is lacking

Edward - of MA, b1714 graduated at Harvard College 1736 & was clerk of the court, register of probate & collector of port, a loyalist, m Hannah Howland dau/o Thomas Howland & wid/o Charles Dyer, & had issue - desc/o Herbert Pelham NE(4)302, 303

Elizabeth - of MA, b1664, m1684 Stephen Burton - desc/o Herbert Pelham NE(4)300

Elizabeth - of MA, b1707, m1729 Benjamin Marston - desc/o Herbert Pelham NE(4)302

Judge Isaac - of MA, b1670 d1738, m1700 Sarah Wensley d1753 aged 80 dau/o John Wensley of Boston - desc/o Herbert Pelham CHB195; BCD195; ECD(3)238; NE(4)300/302

Isaac - of MA, b1739, m(1) E Stockbridge, m(2) T Gay - desc/o Herbert Pelham NE(4)302

John - of MA 1621, b1597 d1673/1674, m1624 Mary Chilton - the immigrant THC341; FFF15; sufficient proof of alleged royal ancestry

WINSLOW (cont.)

is lacking

John - of MA, b1702 Marshfield d1774 Hingham, a distinguished and successful military officer, m(1)1726 Mary Little dau/o Isaac Little, m(2) Mrs Johnson of Hingham - desc/o Herbert Pelham NE(4)302

John - of NC, d1753, m Esther Snelling - desc/o John Winslow FFF15

Joseph - of NC, d1679, m Sarah Lawrence - desc/o John Winslow FFF15

Josiah - of MA - b1629 d1680 in 1675 he was general-in-chief of the whole military force of the United Colonies, raised in King Philip's Indian War, m1657 Penelope Pelham d1703 aged 73, dau/o Herbert Pelham - desc/o Edward Winslow EDV45; Penelope Pelham was of royal descent by her father Herbert Pelham; NE(4)300

Margaret - of MA, m John Miller - desc/o Herbert Pelham MCD321

Pelham - of MA, b1737, m Joanna White - desc/o Herbert Pelham NE(4)302

Penelope - of MA, b1704 d1737, m1724 James Warren d1757 aged 57 he was high sheriff of the county, an office held by his father James Warren - desc/o Herbert Pelham CHB196; BCD195; ECD(3)238; NE(4)302

Susannah - m1649 Robert Latham - desc/o John Winslow THC341

Thomas - of NC, m Elizabeth Clare - desc/o John Winslow FFF15

WINSTON Alice Ann - of MD, b1769 d1813, m 1785 Capt Henry Pendleton of Louisa Co, VA - desc/o Col William Bernard DBR(3)132 - desc/o Anne Lovelace GVFHB(3)338

Barbara - of MD, b1750, m Dr Barrett - desc/o Anne Lovelace GVFHB(3)338

Bickerton - of MD, b1768, m(1) Mary Lyle Smelt, m(2) Mary Smith - desc/o Anne Lovelace GVFHB(3)338

Elizabeth Martha - of MD, b1765, m Col William Overton Callis - desc/o Anne Lovelace GVFHB(3)338

James - of MD, b1753, m Rebecca Johnson - desc/o Anne Lovelace GVFHB(3)338

John Henry - m Mary Johnson - desc/o Col William Bernard DBR(4)769

William Overton - of MD, b1747, m(1) Joanna Robinson, m(2) Anne Kidley (Chamberlayne) Posey - desc/o Anne Lovelace GVFHB(3)338

WINTHROP Adam - of MA, b1620 d1652, m Elizabeth Glover - desc/o Margaret Tyndal FLW194; MCS5; NE(18)183

Deane - of MA, b1633 d1704, m Sarah Glover - desc/o Margaret Tyndal FLW194; MCS5; NE(18)183

John - of MA, b1587/1588 d1649 governor of Massachusetts Bay Colony, m(1)1605 Mary Forth b1583 d1615 daughter & sole heir of John Forth of Great Stambridge Co, Essex, m(2)1615 Thomasine Clopton d1616 her still-born child was buried with her, dau/o William Clopton of Castleins, near Groton, m(3)1618 Margaret Tyndale d1647 dau/o Sir John Tyndale of Great Maplested, Essex, m(4)1647 Martha Nowell, wid/o Thomas Coytmore - the immigrant EDV20; NE(18)182, 183 sufficient proof of alleged royal ancestry is lacking, royal ancestry is through his 2nd wife Thomasine Clopton & his 3rd wife Margaret Tyndale

WINTHROP (cont.)

Joseph - of MA, m Catherine Slicer - desc/o Margaret Tyndale GBR427

Mary - of MA, b1708 d1767, m1729 Gov Joseph Wanton - desc/o Katherine Deighton ECD(2)111; DBR(5)85 - desc/o Gov Thomas Dudley DBR(5)81

Capt Samuel - of MA, bp 1627 d1674, deputy-governor of Antigua, West Indies 1667/1669, m1648 Elizabeth____ - desc/o Margaret Tyndal FLW194; MCS5; DBR(3)133; GBR427; NE(18)183

Sarah - m George Thomas - desc/o Margaret Tyndale GBR428

Col Stephen - of MA, b1619 d1658, m Judith Rainsborough - desc/o Margaret Tyndale FLW194; MCS5; NE(18)183

WISE Edmund - of VA, m(1)1760 Fosque Savage - desc/o Robert Drake DBR(5)1007

George Ayres - of VA, m1795 Elizabeth Oldham - desc/o Robert Drake DBR(5)1007

Sarah - of MA, m Stephen Williams - desc/o Alice Freeman GBR436

WISEMAN John - of MD, d1704, m Catherine Mills - the immigrant DBR(2)834; DBR(3)650; RAA1; sufficient proof - of alleged royal ancestry is lacking

Mary - of MD, m Joseph Leigh - desc/o John Wiseman DBR(2)834

Robert - of MD, d abt 1738, m Elizabeth Heard - desc/o John Wiseman DBR(2)834; DBR(3)650

WISTER John - of PA, b1776 d1862, m1798 Elizabeth Harvey - desc/o Rebecca Humphrey CHB160 - desc/o Thomas Evans CHB192; BCD192

WITHERSPOON Rev John - of NJ, b1722 - the immigrant MCB138; MCD335; sufficient proof of alleged royal ancestry is lacking

WITTER Eunice - b1747 - desc/o Griffith Bowen RAA72 - desc/o Alice Freeman RAA132

Hannah - b1705 - desc/o Alice Freeman RAA132

Joseph - b1698 - desc/o Alice Freeman RAA132

Thomas - of NY, d1786 son of Matthew Witter & Frances Tucker, m(1) Mary Lewis, m(2) 1748 Catherine Van Zandt b1722 d1775 - the immigrant GBR208; NYGBR(61)#4p332

WOLCOTT Alexander MD - of MA, b1712, m(1) Lydia Atwater, m(2) Mrs Mary Allyn, m(3)1745 Mary Richards - desc/o John Drake CHB106; BCD106; DBR(1)729 - desc/o Henry Wolcott BLG2981; CRL(1)153

Alexander - of MA, b1758 d1828, m1785 Frances Burbank - desc/o John Drake CHB106; BCD106 - desc/o Henry Wolcott BLG2981

Amelia - of CT, b1750, m Marvin Lord - desc/o Henry Wolcott CRL(1)150

Anne - of CT, m Matthew Griswold - desc/o Henry Wolcott CRL(1)150

Elizabeth - of CT, b1662 d1708, m Daniel Cooley - desc/o Henry Wolcott CRL(1)151

Elizabeth - of CT, b1706, m1727 Capt Roger Newberry - desc/o Henry Wolcott CRL(1)152

Epaphras - of CT, b1740 d1825, m1762 Mabel Burnham - desc/o Henry Wolcott CRL(1)153

Erastus - of CT, b1722 d1793, m Jerusha Wolcott - desc/o Henry Wolcott CRL(1)153

WOLCOTT (cont.)

George - of CT, b1662, m Elizabeth Treat - desc/o Henry Wolcott
  CRL(1)151

Henry - of CT 1635, b1578 d1655, m1606 Elizabeth Saunders - the
  immigrant EDV47; BLG2981; CRL(1)150, 151; RAA no longer
  accepted as being of royal descent

Henry Jr - of CT, b1610/1611 d1680, m Sarah Newberry - desc/o
  Henry Wolcott CRL(1)150

Hepzibah - of CT, b1717 d1780, m John Strong - desc/o Henry
  Wolcott CRL(1)153

James - of CT, b1766 d1849, m1786 Miriam Munsell - desc/o Henry
  Wolcott CRL(1)154

Dr Jeremiah - of CT, b1733 d1792, m1758 Sarah Goodsell - desc/o
  John Drake DBR(1)729

Lieut Luke - b1755, a soldier in the Revolution, m Mary Wheeler of
  Parma, New York - desc/o Margaret Wyatt DBR(1)148

Mabel - of CT, b1770, m John Richardson - desc/o Henry Wolcott
  CRL(1)154

Mariam - of CT, b1729, m Thomas Williams - desc/o Henry Wolcott
  CRL(1)151

Martha - of CT, b1664, m Thomas Allyn Jr - desc/o Henry Wolcott
  CRL(1)151

Mary - of CT, d1689, m Job Drake - desc/o Henry Wolcott CRL(1)151

Mary - b1694 - desc/o Samuel Appleton RAA63

Mary - of CT, b1742, m Jesse Goodell - desc/o Henry Wolcott
  CRL(1)153

Mary - of CT, b1773, m___ Davis - desc/o Henry Wolcott CRL(1)154

Mehitabal - b1715 - desc/o Samuel Appleton RAA63

Maj Gen Oliver - of CT, b1726 d1797, m Lorraine or Laura Collins -
  desc/o John Drake J&K308; CRL(1)153

Oliver - of CT, b1760 d1833, gov of CT - desc/o John Drake J&K308

Parmenio - of CT, b1746 d1812, m Mary Ballard - desc/o John Drake
  CRL(1)153

Roger - of CT, b1679 d1747, m1702 Sarah Drake - desc/o Henry
  Wolcott BLG2981; CRL(1)151

Maj Roger - of CT, b1704 d1759, m(1)1727 Marah Newberry, m(2)1759
  Eunice Colton - desc/o Henry Wolcott CRL(1)153

Roger - of CT, b1737 d1799, m Dorcas Burnham - desc/o Henry
  Wolcott CRL(1)153

Samuel - b1679 - desc/o Samuel Appleton RAA63

Sarah - of CT, b1686, m1706 Capt Robert Wells - desc/o Samuel
  Appleton DBR(3)73

Sarah - of CT, b1735 d1812, m Elisha Steele - desc/o Henry Wolcott
  CRL(1)153

Sarah - of CT, b1764, m Ebenezer Pomeroy - desc/o Henry Wolcott
  CRL(1)154

Sarah - b1767, m1784 Philemon Harrison - desc/o John Drake
  DBR(1)729 - desc/o Rev John Davenport DBR(2)779

Simon - of CT, b1624 d1687, m(1)1657 Joanna Cook, m(2)1661
  Martha Pitkin - desc/o Henry Wolcott BLG2981; CRL(1)151

Thomas - b1702, son of Lieut Henry & Jane (Allyn) Wolcott, m1725

WOLCOTT (cont.)

> Catherine Loomis b1702 d1738 dau/o Moses Loomis of CT - desc/o
> Margaret Wyatt DBR(1)147, 148

> Thomas - b1726, m Catherine Sackett of Dover, New York - desc/o
> Margeret Wyatt DBR(1)148

> Ursula - of CT, b1724 d1788, m Judge Matthew Griswold - desc/o
> John Drake J&K309; CHB106; BCD106, 354; CRL(1)153

> William - of CT, b1676 d1749, m Abiah Hawley - desc/o Henry Wolcott
> CRL(1)151

WOLSELEY - d1685, m the Reverend Doctor Thomas Knipe b1638,
> graduate of Oxford, Prebendary of Westminster Abbey &
> headmaster of Westminster school - desc/o Sir John Zouch APP731

> Anne - of MD, dau/o Sir Thomas Wolseley & Ellen Broughton, m Philip
> Calvert, governor of MD - the immigrant GBR258

> Helen - b1647 Ravenstone, Staffordshire, m1676 Reverend Thomas
> Sprat, graduate of Oxford, Fellow of the Royal Society, Bishop of
> Rochester & Dean of Westminster Abbey b abt 1636 d1713 -
> desc/o Sir John Zouch APP730, 31

> Mary - of MD, m bef 1687 Roger Brooke b1637 d1700 son of Governor
> Robert Brooke & Mary (Mainwaring) Brooke - the immigrant
> FLW80; DBR(2)333; DBR(3)435; DBR(4)355; GBR258

WOOD Abraham - of PA, b1701/1702 Darby d1733, m Ursula Taylor
> b1701/1703 d1788/1794 Lancaster, Pennsylvania, dau/o Philip
> Taylor & Julian____ of Oxford township, Chester Co, PA - desc/o
> John Bevan Sr CHB80; MCD164; BCD80; DBR(1)376; AFA40, 168;
> CRFP(1)141

> Anne - of PA, b1734 Burlington Co, New Jersey d1799, m1756
> Lancaster Co, William Henry b1701 d1786 Lancaster Co, engaged
> in the manufacture of firearms & did an extensive business with
> Indian traders, took an active part in the public affairs of his
> country & the state, throughout the Revolution ardently espoused
> the cause of the colonists & filled many offices of honor & trust -
> desc/o John Bevan Sr CHB80; MCD164: BCD80, 81; DBR(1)376;
> AFA40; CRFP(1)141, 142

> Charles - b1763 - desc/o Griffith Bowen RAA72

> George - of PA, b1690/1691, m1715/1716 Hannah Hood - desc/o
> John Bevan Sr CRFP(1)141

> Martha - of VA, m Maj Stephen Southall - desc/o Lieut Col Walter
> Aston CHB439

> Mary - of VA, m Judge Peter Johnson - desc/o Lieut Col Walter Aston
> CHB439

> Patty - of VA, m Capt William Merriwether - desc/o Lieut Col Walter
> Aston CHB438

> Richard - of NJ, b1755, m(2)1793 Elizabeth Bacon - desc/o Dorothea
> Scott CHB90; BCD90

> Sally - of VA, m Col William Pryor - desc/o Lieut Col Walter Aston
> CHB438

> Col Valentine - of VA, bp 1724, m1764 Lucy Henry - desc/o Lieut Col
> Walter Aston CHB439

> William - of PA, b1691/1692, m1718 Mary Hood - desc/o John Bevan
> Sr CRFP(1)141

WOODBRIDGE Abigail - b1700, m John Mixer of West Springfield - desc/o Gov Thomas Dudley NE(32)295

Rev Ashbel - d1758 ordained minister at Glastonbury, CT 1728, m1737 Jerusha Pitkin d1799 dau/o William Pitkin of East Hartford & wid/o Samuel Edwards of Hartford - desc/o Gov Thomas Dudley NE(32)296

Benjamin - of MA, b1645 d1736, m1706 Sarah Gerrish - desc/o Gov Thomas Dudley CRL(4)540

Reverend Benjamin - of MA, m(1)1672 Mary Ward d1685 dau/o Reverend John Ward of Haverhill, m(2)1686 Hingham, Deborah Cushing b1651 dau/o Daniel Cushing & wid/o Henry Tarlton - desc/o Gov Thomas Dudley NE(32)293

Benjamin - of MA, b1711 d1797, m Susanna Tappan - desc/o Gov Thomas Dudley CRL(4)540

Deodatus - of CT, b1757 d1836, m(1) Esther Willis - desc/o Mabel Harlakenden CHB271; BCD271

Dorothy - of MA, bp 1650 d1723, m1679 Nathaniel Fryer - desc/o Gov Thomas Dudley CRL(4)539; NE(32)292

Dorothy Lamb - of CT, b1745 d1791, m1766 Lieut Thomas Phelps - desc/o Gov Thomas Dudley DBR(5)613

Dudley - b1677 d1710 of Barbados, m____ & had issue - desc/o Gov Thomas Dudley NE(32)294

Dudley - of MA, d1710 commenced preaching in Simsbury, CT 1695 & ordained there 1697, m Dorothy Lamb dau/o Joshua Lamb of Roxbury - desc/o Gov Thomas Dudley NE(32)293

Dr Dudley - of MA, b1705 d1790 physician in Stonington, m1739 Sarah Sheldon dau/o Isaac Sheldon of Hartford - desc/o Gov Thomas Dudley DBR(1)14; DBR(4)341; NE(32)295   Hon Dudley - of MA, b1747 d1823, m1774 Lucy Griswold - desc/o Gov Thomas Dudley DBR(1)14; DBR(4)341

Elizabeth - of CT, b1673 Windsor d1729 Exeter, New Hampshire, m(1)1694 Rev John Clark of Exeter, m(2)1709 John Odlin of Exeter & had issue of both marriages - desc/o Gov Thomas Dudley NE(32)294

Elizabeth - of CT, b1714 d1754, m1737 Rev Ephraim Little - desc/o Mabel Harlakenden CHB271; BCD271

Rev Ephraim - of CT, b1680 d1725 became minister of the first church in Groton, CT 1704, m1704 Hannah Morgan dau/o James Morgan - desc/o Gov Thomas Dudley DBR(1)14; DBR(4)341; NE(32)295

Haynes - of CT, b1717 d1754, m1742 Elizabeth Griswold dau/o Samuel Griswold of Windsor, CT & had six children - desc/o Dr Richard Palgrave DBR(5)372 - desc/o Thomas Dudley DBR(5)613; NE(32)296

Howell - b1746 d1796 colonel in the Revolutionary army & representative in the CT legislature, m1778 Mary Plummer dau/o Ebenezer Plummer of Glastonbury - desc/o Gov Thomas Dudley NE(32)296

Hon Jahleel - b1728 d1796, m Lucy Edwards - desc/o Gov Thomas Dudley DBR(1)320; DBR(2)415

Jemima - b1706, m Mr Nicholson of New Jersey - desc/o Gov Thomas Dudley NE(32)295

WOODBRIDGE (cont.)

Rev John - of MA, b1644 d1691 began preaching at Killingworth, CT in 1666 & ordained minister 1669, m1671 Abigail Leete dau/o Governor William Leete - desc/o Gov Thomas Dudley DBR(1)14, 319; DBR(2)415; DBR(4)341; DBR(5)1042; RAA89; CRL(4)539; NE(32)293

Rev John - of MA, b1678 d1718 minister at West Springfield, MA 1698, m1699 Jemima Eliot dau/o Rev Joseph Eliot of Guilford - desc/o Gov Thomas Dudley DBR(1)319/29; DBR(2)415; NE(32)295

John - b1702 minister at Poquonnoe, CT 1731, m(1)1729 Tryphenia Ruggles d1749 dau/o Rev Benjamin Ruggles & Mercy Woodbridge, m(2)1750 Mrs Elizabeth Bernard d1783 - desc/o Gov Thomas Dudley NE(32)295

Jonathan - b1767 d1808, m Sarah Meech - desc/o Gov Thomas Dudley DBR(1)320; DBR(2)415

Joseph - b1707 judge of probate Stockbridge, m1730 Mrs Elizabeth (Merrick) Barnard dau/o John Merrick - desc/o Gov Thomas Dudley DBR(1)320; DBR(2)415; NE(32)295

Joseph - of MA, b abt 1657 d1726, m1686 Martha Rogers dau/o Ezekiel Rogers of Ipswich, MA - desc/o Gov Thomas Dudley CRL(4)539; NE(32)295

Lucia (or Lucy) - of MA, b1642 d1710, m(1)1667 Rev Simon Bradstreet of New London, CT, m(2) Capt Epps - desc/o Gov Thomas Dudley J&K196; CRL(4)539; NE(32)292

Mabel - b1718, m Dr Nathaniel Little - desc/o Gov Thomas Dudley NE(32)296

Martha - of MA, b1658 d1738, m1680 Capt Samuel Ruggles Jr of Roxbury - desc/o Gov Thomas Dudley LDS101; DBR(3)520; DBR(4)71; RAA89; CRL(4)539; NE(32)293

Martha - of MA, b1771 d1830, m1794 John Dunlap - desc/o John Whitney CHB228; BCD228

Mary - of MA, d1712, m Samuel Appleton of Ipswich d1693 - desc/o Gov Thomas Dudley NE(32)292

Mary - of CT, bp 1692 d1766, m1724 Judge William Pitkin, governor of CT 1766/1769 & judge of the superior court 13 years - desc/o Mabel Harlakenden CHB271; BCD271 - desc/o Gov Thomas Dudley NE(32)294

Mary - of MA, b1742 d1805, m1773 James Ayer - desc/o Gov Thomas Dudley CRL(4)540

Mary - of CT, b1749 d1833, m1768 Benjamin Bodwell - desc/o John Drake DBR(4)147 - desc/o Dr Richard Palgrave DBR(5)372

Mary - m George Wyllys, secretary of state of CT 1739 - desc/o Gov Thomas Dudley NE(32)296

Mercy - of CT, b1672 d1707, m1696 Rev Benjamin Ruggles of Suffolk, CT - desc/o William Leete CHB366; MCD246; RAA89, 107 - desc/o Gov Thomas Dudley NE(32)293

Russell - of CT, b1719 d1782, m1741 Anna Olmsted (the Cheney brothers, of Manchester, CT, the noted silk manufacturers are descended from him) - desc/o Mabel Harlakenden CHB271; BCD271 - desc/o Gov Thomas Dudley NE(32)296

Ruth - of CT, bp 1695 d1734, m Rev John Pierson of Woodbridge, New

WOODBRIDGE (cont.)

Jersey - desc/o Gov Thomas Dudley ECD256; DBR(2)110; NE(32)294 - desc/o George Wyllys DBR(4)115 - desc/o Mabel Harlakenden DBR(4)118

Rev Samuel - d1746 ordained first minister of the church in East Hartford, CT 1705, m(1)1707 Mabel Russell d abt 1722 dau/o Daniel Russell of Charlestown & wid/o Rev John Hubbard of Jamaica, L.I., m(2) Mrs Content____ Bull d1758 wid/o Benjamin Bull of Newport, Rhode Island - desc/o Gov Thomas Dudley NE(32)295

Samuel - b1740 d1797 minister at Eastbury, CT 1766 & chaplain in the army during part of the Revolutionary war, m1779 Elizabeth Goodman of West Hartford - desc/o Gov Thomas Dudley NE(32)296

Sarah - of MA, b1640 d1691, m____ & leaving issue 5 children - desc/o Gov Thomas Dudley NE(32)292

Susanna - bp 1703, m1728 Richard Treat b1694 son of Thomas Treat of Glastonbury - desc/o Gov Thomas Dudley NE(32)294

Theodore - b1748 major in the Revolutionary army, removed to Pennsylvania, m1783 Esther Plummer dau/o Ebenezer Plummer - desc/o Gov Thomas Dudley NE(32)296

Captain Thomas - of MA, b1649 d1681, m1671/1672 Mary Jones dau/o Paul White of Newbury, MA & Ann____ - desc/o Gov Thomas Dudley CRL(4)539; NE(32)294

Rev Timothy - of MA, b1656 d1732 Hartford, m(1) Mehitable Wyllys dau/o Samuel Wyllys of Hartford, m(2) abt 1703 Mrs Howell, m(3)1716 Abigail Warren dau/o John Warren of Boston & wid/o Richard Lord of Boston - desc/o Gov Thomas Dudley ECD256; DBR(2)110; CRL(4)539; NE(32)294

Rev Timothy Jr - of CT, b1686 d1742 minister at Simsbury, CT 1712, m1712 Dorothy Lamb dau/o Joshua Lamb & wid/o Rev Dudley Woodbridge - desc/o Gov Thomas Dudley DBR(5)613; NE(32)296

Timothy - b1709 d1775, m Abigail Day dau/o Samuel Day of West Springfield & superintendent of Indian Affairs & judge of the court of Hampshire Co - desc/o Gov Thomas Dudley NE(32)295

William - b1755 d1836 Franklin, CT, first preceptor of Phillips Exeter Academy, m Elizabeth Brooks dau/o Deacon Samuel Brooks - desc/o Gov Thomas Dudley NE(32)296

WOODFORD William Catesby - of VA, b1766, m Elizabeth Battaile - desc/o Col George Reade DBR(3)570

WOODHOUSE (WODEHOUSE) Dinah - of VA, m by 24 Apr 1704 Richard Jarvis of Currituck Co, North Carolina - desc/o Capt Henry Woodhouse APP704

Elizabeth - m1638 Thomas Webb - desc/o Capt Henry Woodhouse APP701

Elizabeth - of VA, m abt 1656 Nicholas Meriwether - desc/o Capt Henry Woodhouse JSW1893; DBR(2)709; DBR(5)284

Elizabeth - m by 1655 Giles Collins d1674 - desc/o Capt Henry Woodhouse APP701

Elizabeth - of VA, b bef 1679, m William Oakham d bef 18 May 1687 - desc/o Capt Henry Woodhouse APP703

Elizabeth - of VA, m by 8 Dec 1698 Joel Cornick d1727 justice &

WOODHOUSE (WODEHOUSE) (cont.)

> sheriff of Princess Anne Co - desc/o Capt Henry Woodhouse
> APP703

Grace - of VA, m by 2 May 1704 Capt Richard Sanderson Jr, of
Currituck Co, North Carolina d1733, member of the North Carolina
council - desc/o Capt Henry Woodhouse APP704

Capt Henry - of VA, b1607 d1655 governor of the Bermudas
1623/1626, second son of Sir Henry Woodhouse of Waxham, Co
Norfolk & Ann Bacon dau/o Sir Nicholas Bacon & sister of Francis
Bacon, m in Holland, Judith Manky (Manby) (Haeme) d1666 - the
immigrant JSW1655, 893; DBR(1)93, 347, 570; DBR(2)444, 617,
631, 709; DBR(3)193; DBR(4)484; DBR(5)283, 1090; RAA1;
WAC81; GBR450; APP699/704, GVFWM(5)520/525; RCFA(7)74

Henry III - of VA, b1607 in Holland, d1655 settled in Lower Norfolk,
VA, attorney at law, planter, justice, member of the vestry &
member of the House of Burgesses, m(1) Mary (perhaps Dothron)
d1650, m(2) Mary (Maria)____ she married (2) by 20 Apr 1656
Nathaniel Batts (Batte) of North Carolina - desc/o Capt Henry
Woodhouse JSW1656; DBR(1)93, 347, 570; DBR(2)444;
DBR(5)284; WAC81; APP700

Henry IV - of VA, b abt 1640 d1686/1687, m by 20 Nov 1666 Sarah
Keeling dau/o Thomas & Anne Keeling - desc/o Capt Henry
Woodhouse JSW1656; DBR(1)93, 570; APP702

Henry - of Lynhaven Parish VA, b abt 1665 d bef 1702, coroner, justice
of Princess Anne Co, captain of militia, m(1) abt 1685 Amy Spratt
dau/o Henry & Isabella Spratt, Amy, m(2) by 7 Jul 1709 James
Haynes - desc/o Capt Henry Woodhouse DBR(1)570; APP702

Capt Henry - of VA, b abt 1688 d bef 1743 in Colonial Army, m bef
1722 Mary Lovett - desc/o Capt Henry Woodhouse DBR(1)570;
RCFA(7)75

Henry - of NC 1711/1712, d1750/1751, m(1)____, m(2) Keziah (____)
Jarvis - desc/o Capt Henry Woodhouse APP705

Henry - of VA, d1719, m Elizabeth Dawley - desc/o Capt Henry
Woodhouse APP704

Capt Horatio - of VA, d1719, justice, captain of militia & member of the
House of Burgesses, m Lucy Keeling, his first cousin, living 1719,
dau/o Thorowgood Keeling &, m(2) by 4 May 1720 Reodolphus
Malborne - desc/o Capt Henry Woodhouse JSW1656; DBR(1)93;
APP703/703

John - of VA, d1715, m____ - desc/o Capt Henry Woodhouse APP703

John - of VA, d1693, m by 11 May 1670 Ruth Cason dau/o James &
Jane Cason - desc/o Capt Henry Woodhouse APP703

Maj Jonathan - of VA, of Princess Anne Co, d1775, officer in the
Colonial Army, m Mary____ - desc/o Capt Henry Woodhouse
RCFA(7)75

Judith - of VA, m Hercules Low - desc/o Capt Henry Woodhouse
APP701

Mary - of VA, m by 15 Dec 1671 William Attwood d1712/1713 held
400 acres in Princess Anne Co, 1704 - desc/o Capt Henry
Woodhouse DBR(1)347; DBR(2)444; APP701

Mary - of VA, m bef 1687 William Moore d1705 - desc/o Capt Henry

WOODHOUSE (WODEHOUSE) (cont.)

Woodhouse APP702

Rachel - of VA, m John Totney - desc/o Capt Henry Woodhouse APP701

Ruth - of VA, m John Fulcher - desc/o Capt Henry Woodhouse APP703

Sarah - of VA, d1719, m(1) Cason Moore d1686/1687, m(2) John Sandford d1692/1693, m(3) William Clowes (Clouse) d1699 - desc/o Capt Henry Woodhouse APP702

Sarah - of VA, d1732/1733, m Maximillian Bousch Jr, son of Maximillian Bousch - desc/o Capt Henry Woodhouse JSW1656; DBR(1)93

Capt William - of VA, d1700/1701 captain in the VA Colonial Forces, 1700, Princess Anne Co, m Jane Capps - desc/o Capt Henry Woodhouse APP704; RCFA(7)74

Capt William - of VA, b abt 1739 d bef 1774 church warden of Lynn Haven Parish, military officer, m bef 1756 Betty Dale - desc/o Capt Henry Woodhouse DBR(1)570; RCFA(7)75 this source states he m Pembroke Thoroughgood, dau/o John Thoroughgood

William Dale - of VA, b1762 d bef 1824, m1791 Frances Keeling - desc/o Capt Henry Woodhouse DBR(1)570

WOODHULL Ann - of NY, b1659, m1683 Daniel Tourneur - desc/o Richard Woodhull AMB110

Deborah - of NY, b1654 d1742, m John Lawrence - desc/o Richard Woodhull AMB110

Dorothy - of NY, m William Helme - desc/o Richard Woodhull AMB110

Capt Ebenezer - of NY, d1803, m Abigail Howell - desc/o Richard Woodhull CHB214; BCD214

Elizabeth - of NY, b1762 d1839, m(1) Henry Nicoll, m(2) Gen John Smith - desc/o Richard Woodhull CHB215, 392; MCD324; BCD215

Elizabeth - of NY, b1754 d1795, m1780 Samuel Hopkins - desc/o Richard Woodhull AMB111

Henry - of NY, d1770, m____ Biggs - desc/o Richard Woodhull AMB110

James - of NY, b1752, m(1)1782 Kiturah Strong, m(2) Hannah Helme - desc/o Richard Woodhull AMB111

Jeffrey Amherst - of NY, b1759 d1839, m1784 Elizabeth Davis - desc/o Richard Woodhull AMB111

John - of NY, b1719 d1794, m1740 Elizabeth Smith - desc/o Richard Woodhull ECD239; AMB111

John DD, b1744 d1824, m1772 Sarah Spofford - desc/o Richard Woodhull ECD239

John - of NY - desc/o Richard Woodhull AMB110

John - of NY, b1744 d1824, m1772 Sarah Spofford - desc/o Richard Woodhull AMB111

Josiah - of NY, b1695 d1761, m Clementine Homan - desc/o Richard Woodhull AMB110

Mary - of NY, b1711, m1734 Jonathan Thompson - desc/o Richard Woodhull AMB111

Merritt Smith - of NY, b1748 d1815, m1778 Mary David - desc/o Richard Woodhull AMB111

Capt Nathan - of NY, b1720 d1804, m(1)1751 Joanna Mills, m(2)1786

WOODHULL (cont.)

Elizabeth Smith - desc/o Richard Woodhull AMB110

Nathaniel - of NY, b1693 d1760, m1716 Sarah Smith - desc/o Richard Woodhull J&K257; CHB392; AMB110

Gen Nathaniel - of NY, b1722 d1776, m1761 Ruth Floyd - desc/o Richard Woodhull J&K258; CHB214, 215, 392; MCD324; BCD214

Nathaniel - of NY, d1760, m1716 Sarah Smith - desc/o Richard Woodhull CHB214; MCD324; BCD214

Richard - of NY 1647, b1620 d1690, m Deborah____ - the immigrant J&K257; CHB214, 392; ECD237; MCB167; MCD324; BCD214; AMB110; RAA1; EDV15, 16; TAG(21)69/77, Parentage cannot be determined

Richard II - of NY, b1649 d1699, m1680 Temperance Fordham - desc/o Richard Woodhull J&K257; CHB214, 392; MCD324; BCD214; AMB110

Richard III - of NY, b1691 d1767, m Mary Homan - desc/o Richard Woodhull ECD239; AMB110

Judge Richard - of NY, b1712 d1788, m1738 Margaret Smith - desc/o Richard Woodhull AMB110

Ruth - of NY, d bef 1689, m abt 1678 Samuel Idsall - desc/o Richard Woodhull ECD237; BCD214; AMB110

Ruth - of NY, b1770 d1810, m Selah Strong - desc/o Richard Woodhull CHB214

Stephen - of NY, b1722, m1745 Hannah Cooper - desc/o Richard Woodhull AMB110

Rev William - of NY, b1741 d1824, m1767 Elizabeth Hedges - desc/o Richard Woodhull AMB111

WOODMAN John Sr, b1740 d1808, m abt 1762 Sarah Page - desc/o Thomas Welles FFF119

John Jr - of MA, b1767 d1849, m(1)1790 Abigail Merrill, m(2)1800 Hannah Bates - desc/o Thomas Bradbury FFF90, 102, 108, 120

Remember - of MA, b abt 1673, m1693/1698 Thomas Perkins - desc/o Mary Gye NE(69)360

WOODS Abigail - b1726 - desc/o Olive Welby RAA93

Anna - b1753 - desc/o John Prescott RAA125

Margaret - m John Ashworth - desc/o Michael Woods JSW1889

Michael - of VA, b1684 d1762, m Margaret (Mary) Campbell - the immigrant JSW1889; sufficient proof of alleged royal ancestry is lacking

Richard - of VA, b1721, m Janet____ - desc/o Michael Woods JSW1889

Samuel - m Margaret Holmes - desc/o Michael Woods JSW1889

Samuel - b abt 1690 - desc/o Olive Welby RAA93

WOODSON Agnes - of VA, b1711 d1802, m abt 1730 Joseph Morton - desc/o Col Walter Aston DBR(2)324, 849; DBR(3)508 - desc/o Col Richard Cocke DBR(2)432

Agnes - b1748 d1860, m1765 Francis Watkins - desc/o Col Walter Aston DBR(1)670

Ann - of VA, m1773 Moore Lumpkin - desc/o Col Walter Aston DBR(5)1003

Elizabeth - m Edmund Goode - desc/o Col Walter Aston DBR(2)146

WOODSON (cont.)

John - of VA, d1798, m Elizabeth Anderson - desc/o Col Walter Aston DBR(5)1003

Richard II - of VA, b1690 d1776, m abt 1739 Anne Madelin - desc/o Col Walter Aston DBR(1)670; DBR(2)755

WOODWARD Dorothy - b1734 - desc/o Alice Freeman RAA132

Hezekiah - bp 1731 d1800, m Susannah Meech - desc/o Alice Freeman DBR(2)537

Hezekiah - b1755 d1839, m Eleanor Vail - desc/o Alice Freeman DBR(2)537

WOOLLEY John - b1740 - desc/o Jane Vaughn RAA120

WOOLSEY Rev Theodore Dwight - of NJ, president Yale University - desc/o Rev James Pierrepont J&K241

WOOLSON Elizabeth - b1668, m John Howe - desc/o Saml Hyde LDS92

WORMELEY Col Christopher - of VA, d1685 member VA Council & vestry Christ Church, Middlesex 1666, m(1) Mrs Aylmer, m(2) Francis____ - desc/o Agetha Eltonhead VG230

Elizabeth - of VA, m William Digges - desc/o Agetha Eltonhead VG231

Elizabeth - of VA, d1740, m1703 John Lomax b1674 d1729 son of Rev John Lomax of England, m(2)____ - desc/o Agetha Eltonhead VG230

James - of VA, m(1) Ariana Randolph, m(2) Elizabeth Bullock - desc/o Agetha Eltonhead VG231

John - of VA, Burgess Middlesex Co, m Elizabeth Tayloe dau/o William Tayloe of Lancaster Co - desc/o Agetha Eltonhead VG231

John - of VA, b1689 d1726, m Elizabeth____ d1743 - desc/o Agetha Eltonhead VG230

Judith - of VA, b1695, m1712 Mann Page - desc/o Agetha Eltonhead VG230

Ralph - of VA, d1649 - the immigrant WAC83, 84; sufficient proof of alleged royal ancestry is lacking

Ralph - of VA, b1620 d1665, m Agetha Eltonhead - desc/o Ralph Wormeley WAC84

Ralph III - of VA, b1650 d1703, m(1) Mrs ____ (Peter) Jennings, m(2) Katherine Lunsford d1685 only child of Col Sir Thomas Lunsford, Knight & Baronet, m(3)1687 Madame Elizabeth Armistead of Gloucester, dau/o Col Armistead - desc/o Ralph Wormeley WAC84 - desc/o Agetha Eltonhead VG230

Col Ralph - of VA, d1786 member VA Council 1764, m(1)1736 Sally Berkeley d1741 dau/o Col Edmund Berkeley of Barn Elms, Middlesex, m(2) Jane Bolles dau/o Geoffrey Bolles - desc/o Agetha Eltonhead VG230, 231

Ralph - of VA, b1744 d1806, m Eleanor Tayloe dau/o John Tayloe of Mt Airy - desc/o Agetha Eltonhead VG231

WORTH Eunice - of MA, b1756 d1833, m1776 William Wilson - desc/o William Gayer DBR(3)51

Joseph II - b1729 d abt 1816 - desc/o William Gayer DBR(1)249

Matilda - of MA, b1758 d1843, m1777 Latham Folger - desc/o William Gayer DBR(1)242, 249, 533; DBR(2)357, 675

WORTHINGTON Nicholas - of MA 1650, d1683, m(1) abt 1668 Sarah Bunce, m(2) Susanna____ - the immigrant EDV102; BLG2985;

WORTHINGTON (cont.)
  sufficient proof of alleged royal ancestry is lacking
WRAY Frances - dau/o Sir Christopher & Albinia (Cecil) Wray, m Sir
  Henry Vane b1613 d1662 governor of MA - the immigrant GBR38
WRIGHT Anne - of VA, b abt 1600 d1704/1705, m Lieut Col George
  Nicholas Hack - desc/o Richard Wright ECD(3)285
  Dorothea - of VA & SC - b abt 1740 d1780, m1758 Col John Winn -
    desc/o John Washington DBR(1)666; DBR(2)41; DBR(5)135
  Edmund - of MA, b1670 d1733, m1695 Sarah Townsend - desc/o
    Peter Wright DBR(2)565
  Elizabeth - b abt 1655 - desc/o Oliver Mellowes RAA75
  Elizabeth - of NY, b1653/1654 d1697/1698, m1671 Capt James
    Townsend - desc/o Peter Wright ECD(2)317
  Elizabeth - of VA, b1754 d aft 1839, m1771 Samuel Arnold - desc/o
    Col John Washington JSW1750
  Elizabeth Townsend - b1692 d1756, m Charles Ludlum - desc/o Peter
    Wright DBR(3)302
  Francis - of VA, b1658/1661 d1713, m1680/1682 Anne Washington -
    desc/o Richard Wright BLG2985
  Francis - of VA, b1709 d1742, m abt 1737 Anne Berryman - desc/o
    Col John Washington DBR(1)666; DBR(2)40; DBR(5)135
  James - of VA, b1760/1765 d1823, m1786____ - desc/o Richard
    Wright BLG2985
  James - of GA, d1786 - desc/o Robert Wright MCS26
  Job - m Rachel Townsend - desc/o Peter Wright DBR(3)302
  John - of VA, b abt 1682 d abt 1730, m abt 1706 Dorothy Awbrey -
    desc/o Col John Washington JSW1750; DBR(1)257, 666;
    DBR(2)40, 374; DBR(3)18; DBR(4)406; DBR(5)135, 204 - desc/o
    Richard Wright BLG2985
  John - of VA, b abt 1710 d1792, m abt 1729 Elizabeth Darnall -
    desc/o Col John Washington JSW1750; DBR(1)257; DBR(2)374;
    DBR(3)18; DBR(5)204 - desc/o Richard Wright BLG2985
  Capt John - of VA, b abt 1731 d1789, m1753 Anne Williams - desc/o
    Col John Washington JSW1750; DBR(1)257; DBR(2)374;
    DBR(5)204
  John - of VA & KY, b abt 1765 d bef 1810, m1790 Ann Mason - desc/o
    Col John Washington DBR(3)18
  Joseph - of MA, b1696 d1755, m abt 1719 Elizabeth Jones - desc/o
    Elizabeth Mellowes ECD(3)76
  Jotham - of MA, b1708 d1777, m1745 Tabaiatha Sammis - desc/o
    Peter Wright DBR(2)565
  Jotham - of NY, b abt 1750, m1778 Elizabeth Dusenberry - desc/o
    Peter Wright DBR(2)565
  Lucretia - of NC, d1824, m William Eli Petty - desc/o Col John
    Washington DBR(5)204
  Lydia - of MD, b1655, m1684 Isaac Horner - desc/o Peter Wright
    DBR(4)98
  Martha - of MA, b1659 d1746, m Israel Heald - desc/o Rev Edward
    Bulkeley ECD(3)73
  Mary - of NY, b1642 d1700, m1663 Samuel Andrews - desc/o Peter
    Wright DBR(2)502; DBR(3)636; DBR(4)241, 577

WRIGHT (cont.)

Peter - of NY 1635, b abt 1595 d1675, m1635 Alice____ - the
immigrant ECD(2)317; DBR(2)500, 502, 565; DBR(3)301, 302, 314,
636, 647; DBR(4)97, 98, 241, 575 sufficient proof of alleged royal
ancestry is lacking

Peter - of MA, b1731 d1768, m1755 Ellen Chase - desc/o Elizabeth
Mellowes ECD(3)76

Richard - of VA, b abt 1633 d1663 son of Francis Wright & Anne
Merriton, m1656 Anne Mottrom - the immigrant ECD(3)285;
BLG2985; GBR374; GVFWM(5)562/569

Robert - of SC, d1757, chief justice of South Carolina, son of Sir Robert
Wright & Susan Wren, m Isabella Wright Pitts (widow) - the
immigrant MCS26; RAA1; GBR120

Samuel - of MA, b1661 d1741, m Mary Homer - desc/o Elizabeth
Mellowes ECD(3)76

Sarah - of MA, b1648, m Edmund Wright - desc/o Peter Wright
DBR(2)565

Stephen - of MA, b1764 d1857, m1787 Sarah Prescott - desc/o
Elizabeth Mellowes ECD(3)76

William - of VA, b1732/1733 d1808, m1753____ - desc/o Richard
Wright BLG2985

William - of VA, d1806, m(1) Mary____ - desc/o Col John Washington
DBR(3)18; DBR(4)406

WYATT (WIATT) Ann - of VA, b1631 - desc/o Francis Wyatt CHB423

Ann - of VA, d1818, m Humphrey Haley - desc/o Rev Hawte Wyatt
DBR(1)511

Anne - of VA, m1735 Maj John Starke - desc/o Rev Hawte Wyatt
DBR(2)21, 25; GVFWM(5)575

Anne - of VA, m John Thurston of VA - desc/o Rev Hawte Wyatt
CFSSA543

Conquest - of VA, b1645 d1720, m1668 Sally Pate - desc/o Rev Hawte
Wyatt ECD(2)327; CHB523, DBR(1)212, 615, 706, 930, 932;
WAC60

Conquest - of VA, b1655 d1706/1707 vestryman of Petsworth Parish
in 1690 & Sheriff in 1705, m abt 1675 Sallie____ - desc/o Rev
Hawte Wyatt DBR(1)300, 647; DBR(2)403; DBR(3)407; APP722
states the name of his wife is unknown; CFSSA542

Conquest - of VA, b abt 1672 of Petsworth Parish, Gloucester Co,
m____ & had issue - desc/o Rev Hawte Wyatt CFSSA543

Daniel - of TN - b1750 Gloucester Co d1815 New Orleans, LA, served
with distinction in the Revolutionary War & War of 1812, emigrated
to Tennessee about 1795, m____ & left issue - desc/o Rev Hawte
Wyatt CFSSA544

Edward - of VA, b abt 1621 d1690, m Jane (Conquest - surname has
not been determined with proof) - the immigrant ECD(2)325, 327 -
desc/o Rev Hawte JSW1636; DBR(1)212, 300, 614, 647;
DBR(2)403; DBR(3)407; DBR(5)929, 932; WAC60; APP217/22;
GVFWM(5)571; CFSSA542

Capt Edward - of VA, b1671 d1750, m1705 Frances Newton - desc/o
Rev Hawte Wyatt ECD(2)327; DBR(5)930, 932

Edward - of VA, d by 1731, vestryman, m(1) Ann____ she, m(2) bef 15

WYATT (WIATT) (cont.)

Aug 1734 Martin Conner - desc/o Rev Hawte Wyatt CHB423;
APP722/23

Elizabeth (Betty) - of VA, b abt 1715/1716, m abt 1730/1731 Samuel
Coleman - desc/o Rev Hawte Wyatt DBR(1)615; DBR(3)407

Elizabeth - of VA, b1730 d1803, m1753 Cornelius Collier b1720 King
& Queen Co d1810, son of John Collier & Nancy Eppes - desc/o
Rev Hawte Wyatt ECD(2)325; DBR(1)212, 300, 647; DBR(2)403;
CFSSA544

Elizabeth - of VA, b abt 1705 Gloucester Co, m Capt William Johnston,
of Spotsylvania Co, son of Richard Johnson - desc/o Rev Hawte
Wyatt CFSSA543

Sir Francis - of VA 1621, (Sir Knight) b1575 Allington Castle d1644
twice governor of the VA Colony 1621/1626 & 1639/1641, son of
Sir George Wyatt of Allington Castle & Boxley Manor & Jane Finch,
m Margaret Sandys, dau/o Sir Samuel Sandys - the immigrant
J&K256; CHB422; MCS51; WAC60; CRL(1)270; GBR123;
CFSSA539/549

Francis - of VA, b abt 1670 d1745, m Elizabeth Kennon, dau/o
Richard Kennon - desc/o Rev Hawte Wyatt DBR(1)615; DBR(3)407;
CFSSA543

Francis - of VA, of Gloucester Co, m1742 Lucy Rowe, dau/o James
Rowe & Mary____ of Abingdon Parish, Gloucester Co - desc/o Rev
Hawte Wyatt CFSSA543

Frances Newton - of VA, b1767 d1846, m1787 James Mattison -
desc/o Rev Hawte Wyatt DBR(5)930, 932

George - of VA, bp 1619 St Helen's, Worcester d1671/1672, planter,
probably came to VA with his uncle Sir Francis Wyatt, m
Susanna____ - desc/o Rev Hawte Wyatt CHB423; ECD(2)321;
JSW1636; MCD312; DBR(5)943; WAC60; APP720; CFSSA548

Rev Hawte (Haute) - of VA 1621, b1594 d1638 minister at Jamestown,
VA 1621/1625, second son of Sir George Wyatt of Allington Castle
& Boxley Manor & Jane Finch, m(1)1618 Barbara Elizabeth Mitford,
m(2) Elizabeth____ buried 31 Oct 1626, m(3)1628 Anne Cox
d1631/1632 dau/o John Cox & Ann Lee of Kent, England - the
immigrant CHB423; JSW1636; MCD312; MCS51; DBR(1)211, 299,
511, 614, 647, 706; DBR(2)21, 24, 285, 286, 401, 402; DBR(3)407,
762; DBR(5)929, 931, 932, 943, 1092; WAC60; CRL(1)270;
GBR123; APP718; GVFWM(5)571; CFSSA542

Henry - of VA, b1647 of New Kent Co d abt 1705 vestryman of St
Peter's 1686 & large land holder, m Alice____ d1721/1722 she,
m(2) Major Peter Field d1707 - desc/o Rev Hawte Wyatt CHB423;
ECD(2)321 JSW1636; MCD312; DBR(5)943; APP721;
GVFWM(5)573; CFSSA548

Henry - of VA - desc/o Francis Wyatt CHB423; ECD(2)321

Henry - of VA, b1690, m & had issue - desc/o Rev Hawte Wyatt
CFSSA549

Jane - of VA, m Charles Scott - the immigrant CRL(1)270; sufficient
proof of alleged royal ancestry is lacking

Capt John - of VA, b1630 d1666, m1662/1665 Jane Osborne - desc/o
Rev Hawte Wyatt DBR(1)511; DBR(2)21, 24

WYATT (WIATT) (cont.)

Capt John II - of VA, b1663 d1684, m Anne Jones dau/o Rice Jones of Middlesex Co - desc/o Rev Hawte Wyatt DBR(1)511; DBR(2)21, 24; GVFWM(5)574

John - of VA, b1684 d1750, m1711 Jane Pamplin - desc/o Rev Hawte Wyatt DBR(1)511; DBR(2)21, 24

John - of VA, b1720, mariner, m1745 Martha____ - desc/o Rev Hawte Wyatt CFSSA544

John - of VA, b1631 - desc/o Francis Wyatt CHB423 Capt John W - of VA, b abt 1683/1685 of Petesworth Parish, Gloucester Co d1765/1768, served as captain of the militia, m abt 1718 Elizabeth Buckner - desc/o Rev Hawte Wyatt ECD(2)325; DBR(1)212, 300, 647; DBR(2)403; CFSSA544

John - of VA, b1732 d1805, m Mary Todd dau/o Capt Christopher Todd, of Toddsbury, Gloucester Co, VA - desc/o Rev Hawte Wyatt GVFW(5)572

John - of KY, b1748 London d1833 Millroy, Indiana, served with distinction in the Revolutionary War, emigrated to Kentucky in Mercer Co, m Susan Summit of Spotsylvania Co b1754 d1823 & had issue - desc/o Rev Hawte Wyatt CFSSA546

Joseph - of VA, b1728, served for more than 20 years as a member of the VA Assembly, m1759 Dorothy Peyton - desc/o Rev Hawte Wyatt ECD(2)321; DBR(5)943; GVFWM(5)573; CFSSA549

Margaret - of MA & CT, bp 1594/1595 Braunton, Devonshire d1670/1671, m1626/1627 Matthew Allyn b1605 d1670/1671 son of Richard Allyn, he was a representative to the General Court of Massachusetts, 1636, was deputy & assistant in the CT Colony 1648/1667; a commissioner to the United Colonies, 1660 & 1664. They were the ancestors of Grover Cleveland, President of the United States - the immigrant J&K123; CHB26; FLW57; ECD106, 241; MCD157; BCD26, 353; DBR(1)147, 198; 36, 417; DBR(2)426, 557, 611, 612, 718, 721; DBR(3)126, 687; DBR(5)117; RAA61; CRL(1)184, 185; GBR396; NEFGM(1)153

Nicholas - of VA & MD 1649 d1673, m Damaris____ - desc/o Rev Hawte Wyatt DBR(2)286

Richard - of VA, b1650 of Gloucester Co, m____ & had issue - desc/o Rev Hawte Wyatt CFSSA549

Richard - of VA - desc/o Rev Hawte Wyatt CHB423; ECD(2)321; JSW1636; MCD312; DBR(5)943

Richard - of VA, patented land in New Kent Co, m Catherine____ wid/o Edmund Tunstall of King & Queen Co - desc/o Rev Hawte GVFWM(5)574

Capt Richard b abt 1762 d1845 served in the Revolutionary War, m Nancy Ware & had issue - desc/o Rev Hawte Wyatt GVFWM(5)574; CFSSA548, 549

Sally S - of VA, b1759 New Kent Co d1840 Elbert Co, GA, m(1)1779 Capt William Bibb of Prince Edward Co, son of John Bibb & Susanna Bigger - desc/o Rev Hawte Wyatt ECD(2)321; DBR(5)943; CFSSA549

Sarah - of MD, b bef 1671 d1690, m1688 Col Edward Dorsey - desc/o Rev Hawte Wyatt DBR(2)286

WYATT (WIATT) (cont.)

Sarah - of VA, m Richard Cate - desc/o Rev Hawte Wyatt DBR(1)706

Susanna - of VA, m(1)____ Day, m(2) Thomas Davis - desc/o Rev Hawte
Wyatt CHB435; JSW1636; MCD312

Thomas - of VA, of Spotsylvania Co, justice 1762, m Sukey
Edmondson, dau/o John Edmondson - desc/o Rev Hawte Wyatt
CFSSA543

William - of VA, m____ & had issue, of Gloucester Co - desc/o Rev
Hawte Wyatt GVFWM(5)

William - of VA, patented land in New Kent Co, m Rachel Smith dau/o
Alexander Smith of Middlesex Co - desc/o Rev Hawte Wyatt
GVFWM(5)574

William - of VA, b1707 d1775, m(2)1730 Lettice Nicholls - desc/o Rev
Hawte Wyatt ECD(2)327; DBR(5)930, 932

William - of VA, b1713, m Elizabeth Eggleston - desc/o Rev Hawte
Wyatt DBR(1)511

William Jr - of VA, b1742 d1815, m(1)1766 Frances Newton - desc/o
Edward Wyatt ECD(2)327; DBR(5)930, 932

Dr William E - of VA, b1762 d1802 physician, son of John Wyatt &
Mary Todd, m Mary Graham dau/o John & Elizabeth____ Graham
of Prince William Co, VA - desc/o Rev Hawte Wyatt GVFWM(5)572 -
desc/o Anne Lovelace GVFHB(3)320

WYCHE Abigail - of VA, m George Brewer - desc/o Henry Wyche II
GVFWM(5)601

Amy - of VA, m Ambrose Jackson - desc/o Henry Wyche II
GVFWM(5)601

Ann - of VA, m Armistead Goodwin & they had issue Fanny & Mary
Ann Chapman Goodwin - desc/o Henry Wyche II GVFWM(5)602

Benjamin - of VA, d1769, m Elizabeth Peete dau/o Dr Samuel Peete of
Sussex Co - desc/o Henry Wyche II GVFWM(5)602

Benjamin - of VA, d1817, m Elizabeth Mason & had issue - desc/o
Henry Wyche II GVFWM(5)603

Drury - of VA & SC, moved to South Carolina, m ____ Taylor - desc/o
Henry Wyche II GVFWM(5)603

Elizabeth - of VA, m____ Johnson - desc/o Henry Wyche II
GVFWM(5)601

Elizabeth - of VA, m____ Woodroof - desc/o Henry Wyche II
GVFWM(5)602

George I - of VA, d1757 - desc/o Henry Wyche II ECD(3)294; BLG2987

George II - of VA, d1781, m Sarah Peters - desc/o Henry Wyche II
ECD(3)294; BLG2987

George - of VA, d1757, m____ & had issue - desc/o Henry Wyche II
GVFWM(5)602

Hannah - of VA, m1758 William Howell - desc/o Henry Wyche II
GVFWM(5)602

Henry II - of VA, b1648 d1714 son of Henry Wyche & Ellen Bennett,
m____ - the immigrant ECD(3)294; RAA1; BLG2987; GBR421;
GVFWM(5)596/605

Henry - of VA, d1747 of Brunswick Co, m Frances____ d1747 - desc/o
Henry Wyche II GVFWM(5)600, 601

Henry - of VA, moved to Georgia d1806, m____ - desc/o Henry Wyche

WYCHE (cont.)

    II GVFWM(5)603

James - of VA, d1749, m Elizabeth____ - desc/o Henry Wyche II
    ECD(3)298; GVFWM(5)601

James - of VA, d abt 1760 was one of the first to subscribe the oath of
    gentleman justice of Sussex Co, was a captain in the French &
    Indian War, m1755 Leah Maclin dau/o Capt James Maclin of
    Brunswick Co - desc/o Henry Wyche II GVFWM(5)601

Martha - of VA, m William Stokes - desc/o Henry Wyche II
    GVFWM(5)602

Martha - of VA, m____ Bridges - desc/o Henry Wyche II GVFWM(5)601

Mary C - of VA, m David Putney & had issue - desc/o Henry Wyche II
    GVFWM(5)602

Nathaniel - of VA, d1777 subscribed the oath of gentleman justice of
    Surrey 1763, m Mary____ - desc/o Henry Wyche II ECD(3)298

Nathaniel - of VA, d1816, m1790 Middleton ____Fletcher - desc/o
    Henry Wyche II ECD(3)298

Nathaniel - of VA, d abt 1789, m Mary (Chapman ?) - desc/o Henry
    Wyche II GVFWM(5)602

Peter - of VA, d1756 lived in Brunswick Co, m Alice Scott dau/o
    Thomas Scott of Prince George Co - desc/o Henry Wyche II
    GVFWM(5)602

Peter - of VA, b1748 d1803, m1775 Elizabeth Jenkins - desc/o Henry
    Wyche II ECD(3)294; BLG2987

Rebecca - of VA, m Samuel Lucas - desc/o Henry Wyche II
    GVFWM(5)601

Rebecca - of VA, m John Fletcher - desc/o Henry Wyche II
    GVFWM(5)602

Sarah - of VA, m William Lucas - desc/o Henry Wyche II
    GVFWM(5)601

Tabitha - of VA, m____ Lucas - desc/o Henry Wyche II GVFWM(5)601

William - of VA, d1720 of Surrey Co, m Judith____ - desc/o Henry
    Wyche II GVFWM(5)600

WYLLYS Amy - of CT, b abt 1625 d1698/1699 Springfield, MA, dau/o
    George Wyllys & Bridget Young, m 1645 Maj John Pynchon -
    desc/o George Wyllys FLW64 - the immigrant RAA125; GBR254;
    FLW64; TAG(39)86/89, (44)1/7

Gov George - of MA & CT 1642, b1589/1590 d1644/1645 governor of
    CT, m(1)1609 Bridget Young, m(2) Mary Smith - the immigrant
    DBR(1)335 DBR(4)114; DBR(5)372, 610; EDV103; FLW64;
    GBR254; TAG(39)89, (44)1/7; royal ancestry is through his wife
    Bridget Young

Col George - of CT, b1710 d1796 secretary of the CT colony for sixty-
    six years, m Mary Woodbridge - desc/o Mabel Harlakenden
    J&K253; CHB268; MCB412; MCD230; BCD268, 269; DBR(2)427

Hezekiah - of CT, b1672 d1741 secretary of the CT colony 1712/1734,
    m1704 Elizabeth Hobart - desc/o Mabel Harlakenden J&K253;
    CHB268; MCB412; MCD230; BCD268

Mary - of CT, b1656 d1729, m1684 Rev Joseph Eliot - desc/o Mabel
    Harlakenden CHB272; MCD230; BCD272 - desc/o John Haynes
    MCB236

WYLLYS (cont.)

Mary - of CT, b1742, m1764 Eleazer Pomeroy - desc/o Mabel
Harlakenden CHB269; MCB412; MCD230; BCD269

Mehitable - of MA, b1658 d1697, m(1)1676 Rev Daniel Russell,
m(2)1676 Rev Timothy Woodbridge - desc/o Mabel Harlakenden
CHB269, 271; MCB301, 302; MCD230; BCD269, 271; DBR(4)118 -
desc/o George Wyllys DBR(4)114; DBR(5)610, 613

Ruth - of CT, b1656/1657 d1729, m1692 Rev Edward Taylor - desc/o
Mabel Harlakenden CHB268; MCB355; MCD231; BCD268;
RAA102 - desc/o Gov George Wyllys DBR(2)427

Samuel - of CT, bp 1631/1632 d1709, m abt 1654 Ruth Haynes -
desc/o Gov George Wyllys DBR(2)427; DBR(4)114; DBR(5)610

WYNNE (WYNN) Anne - of PA, m Phineas Roberts - desc/o Dr Thomas
Wynne CRFP(2)1194

Elizabeth - of PA, m Ralph Lewis - desc/o Dr Thomas Wynne
CRFP(2)1194

Hannah - of PA, m1695 Daniel Humphrey, of the Welsh Track in
Radnor & left numerous descendants - desc/o Dr Thomas Wynne
CFP(2)1193

John - of VA, b abt 1726 d1793, m(2) Ann Stone - desc/o Col Robert
Wynne DBR(5)154

Jonathan - of PA & DE, b1669 d1721, m Sarah Greaves & had issue -
desc/o Dr Thomas Wynne GPFPM(3)400/402; CRFP(2)1193

Joshua - of VA, b1663 d1715, m Mary Jones - desc/o Col Robert
Wynne DBR(5)153

Lydia - of PA, m Jonathan Edwards - desc/o Dr Thomas Wynne
CRFP(2)1194

Martha - of PA, m James Kite - desc/o Dr Thomas Wynne
CRFP(2)1194

Mary - of PA, b1659, m1677 Dr Edward Jones & left numerous
descendants - desc/o Dr Thomas Wynne ECD(2)331; CRFP(2)1193

Mary - of PA, m Samuel Pearson - desc/o Dr Thomas Wynne
CRFP(2)1194

Phoebe - of PA, m John Adams, a snuff maker - desc/o Dr Thomas
Wynne CRFP(2)1195

Peter - of VA, b1754 d1808, m Letty (Lettice) Stone - desc/o Col Robert
Wynne DBR(5)154

Rebecca - of PA, m(1) Solomon Thomas of Talbot Co, MD, m(2)1692
John Dickinson of Talbot Co, MD - desc/o Dr Thomas Wynne
CRFP(2)1193

Col Robert - of VA, bp 1622 d1675, m Mary Poythress - the immigrant
DBR(5)153, 564; RAA1; sufficient proof of alleged royal ancestry is
lacking

Sarah - of PA, m Michael Stattleman - desc/o Dr Thomas Wynne
CRFP(2)1194

Sidney - of PA, b1666, m1690 William Chew of MD - desc/o Dr
Thomas Wynne CRFP(2)1193

Sidney - of PA, m Samuel Greaves - desc/o Dr Thomas Wynne
CFP(2)1194

Dr Thomas - of PA, bp 1627 Yskeiviog, Flintshire, Wales, physician &
1st speaker of the Pennsylvania Provincial Assembly, son of

WYNNE (WYNN) (cont.)

Thomas ap John Wynne, m(1)1655/1657 Martha Buttall d1670 of Wrexham, Surey, England, m(2)Mrs Elizabeth Buttall (sister of his first wife) Rawden, widow, m(3)1676 Elizabeth Parr dau/o Rev Thomas Parr & wid/o Joshua Maude - the immigrant ECD(2)33; RAA1; GBR357 some aspect of royal descent merits further study; GPFPM(3)396; CRFP(2)1189/1197

Thomas - of PA, b Wynnestay, Blockley, Philadelphia Co, Pennsylvania d1757, m1722 Mary Warner b1703 dau/o Isaac Warner & Ann Craven of Blockley, & had issue ten children - desc/o Dr Thomas Wynne CRFP(2)1194

Thomas - of PA, b1733/1734 Blockley, Philadelphia d1782, lieutenant in the Flying Camp, 1776, took part in the battles of Long Island & Fort Washington, & taken prisoner at the fall of Fort Washington, 16 Nov 1776, suffered imprisonment in the loathsome warehouses in New York City & the prison ships in the harbor for over four years, not being exchanged until 2 Jan 1781. The hardships endured during his imprisonment contributed to his early death eighteen months after his exchange at the age of forty-eight years; m 1757 Margaret Coulton & left issue two children - desc/o Dr Thomas Wynne CRFP(2)1194

Thomas - of PA, b1762 Wynnestay, Blockley, Philadelphia d1810, m abt 1786 Elizabeth Rees b1762 d1840 & had issue, nine children - desc/o Dr Thomas Wynne CRFP(2)1195

William - of VA, b1699 d1777, m Frances____ - desc/o Col Robert Wynne DBR(5)153, 155

- Y -

YALE Aaron - b1732 of Hartford, Salisbury & Charlotte, VT & Marietta, Ohio d abt 1821, m(1) Ann Hosmer d1773 dau/o Stephen Hosmer, m(2)____ - desc/o Thomas Yale DLJ2036

Abel - b1707 d1784, m(1)1730 Esther Cook b1707 d1740 dau/o Samuel Cook & Hannah Ives, m(2)1742 Sarah Atkins d1800 aged 89 - desc/o Thomas Yale DLJ2037

Abel - b1733 d1797, m1759 Sarah Jerome bp 1739 d1816 dau/o William Jerome & Elizabeth Hart - desc/o Thomas Yale DLJ2037

Abigail - b1660 d1708/1709, m Moses Mansfield - desc/o Thomas Yale DLJ2032

Abigail - b1711 d1730, m1729 Moses Yale - desc/o Thomas Yale DLJ2034

Abigail - b1733, m1754 Samuel Scofield - desc/o Thomas Yale DLJ2036

Amasa - b1747 d abt 1806, m1768 Ann Richards d abt 1800 Sharon - desc/o Thomas Yale DLJ2033

Amasa - b1756 d1797 Salem, Washington Co, New York, m1783 Sally Baxter b1762 Boston d1842 - desc/o Thomas Yale DLJ2038

Ann - b1705, m1733 William Carter - desc/o David Yale DLJ2033

Ann - d1734, m James Cavendish - desc/o David Yale DLJ2031

Anna - b1737, m1758 Elnathan Ives - desc/o Thomas Yale DLJ2036

YALE (cont.)

Anna - b1752, m1770 Aaron Royce of Brighton, New York - desc/o Thomas Yale DLJ2035

Anna - m1776 Amos Mix - desc/o Thomas Yale DLJ2034

Anne - of CT, b abt 1615 d1698 dau/o Thomas Yale & Anne Lloyd, m Edward Hopkins b abt 1600 d1657, governor of CT - the immigrant GBR311; TAG(32)71/80, (56)101/105; EO2(3)889; DLJ2030

Asa - b1709, m1736 Esther Manross dau/o Nehemiah Manross - desc/o Thomas Yale DLJ2037

Asahel - b1764 of Otisco, Onondaga Co, New York d1836, m1786 Sarah Merriman b1764 d1848 dau/o Titus Merriman & Dinah Andrews - desc/o Thomas Yale DLJ2036

Barnabas - b1772 d1794, m1791 Lois Merriam b1771 dau/o Nathaniel Merriam & Martha Berry - desc/o Thomas Yale DLJ2039

Benjamin - b1714 d1781, m1737 Ruth Ives b1714 d1777 dau/o Samuel Ives & Ruth Atwater - desc/o Thomas Yale DLJ2034

Benjamin - b1751 d1852 Guilford, Chenango Co, New York, m(1)1777 Abigail Parker b1755 d1779 dau/o Edward Parker & Sarah Burroughs, m(2)1781 Phebe Rice - desc/o Thomas Yale DLJ2035

Col Braddam - b1772 of Waterford, New York, m(1) Lucy Marsh, m(2) Maranda Bishop - desc/o Thomas Yale DLJ2039

Chloe - b1745 d1771, m1769 Ensign Hough - desc/o Thomas Yale DLJ2037

Daniel - b1750 d1834, m1781 Phebe Merriam b1756 d1835 dau/o William Merriam & Mary Austin - desc/o Thomas Yale DLJ2037

David - of CT, b abt 1613 resident of Boston, MA & London England d1690 aged 76 in England, son of Thomas Yale & Anne Lloyd, m Ursula Knight d1698 aged 74 years in England - the immigrant GBR311; TAG(32)71/80, (56)101/105; EO2(3)889; DLJ2030

David - b1693 d1757, m1718/1719 Martha Bassett b1695 d1759 dau/o Samuel Bassett & Mary Dickerman - desc/o Thomas Yale DLJ2032

Elihu - b1648 Boston d1721, Gov of Madras, m1680 Katharine Elford, wid/o Joseph Hynmers - desc/o David Yale DLJ2030

Elihu - b1696 d1748, m1726 Mehitabel Todd b1704 d1753 dau/o Samuel Todd & Susanna Tuttle - desc/o Thomas Yale DLJ2031

Elihu - b1703 d1745 Cape Breton, m(1)1726 Mary Ives b1702 d1731 dau/o John Ives & Mary Gillette, m(2)1732 Judith How b1706 dau/o Jeremiah How & Judith Cook - desc/o Thomas Yale DLJ2032, 2033

Elihu - b1729 d1797, m(1) Elizabeth___ d1782 age 29, m(2)1783 Sarah Merriman b1742 dau/o Samuel Merriman & Sarah Wiltshire - desc/o Thomas Yale DLJ2033

Capt Elihu - b abt 1747 d1806, m1774 Lucretia Stanley b1748 d1813 - desc/o Thomas Yale DLJ2034

Elijah - b1768 of Amherst, MA d1817, m1798 Lucy Merrick b1757 d1824 - desc/o Thomas Yale DLJ2038

Elisha - b1742 d1825, m1771 Rebecca North - desc/o Thomas Yale DLJ2033

Elizabeth - b1667 d1702, m1788/1789 Joseph Pardee - desc/o Thomas Yale DLJ2032

YALE (cont.)

Elizabeth - b1673, m William Chittenden - desc/o Thomas Yale
DLJ2031

Elizabeth - b1713 d1793, m1739 Stephen Atwater - desc/o Thomas
Yale DLJ2038

Elizabeth - m1784 Levi Robinson - desc/o Thomas Yale DLJ2039

Elsie - b1761 d1813, m John Wright - desc/o Thomas Yale DLJ2039

Emerton - b1756 d1807, m(1) Sarah Merriman d1788, m(2)1790
Mercy Scovill b1767 dau/o James Scovill & Hannah Hough -
desc/o Thomas Yale DLJ2038

Esther - b1737, m Daniel Bunnell - desc/o Thomas Yale DLJ2037

Esther - b1743 d1830, m1762 Jahleel Clark - desc/o Thomas Yale
DLJ2037

Hannah - b1662 d1743/1744, m(1)1682 Enos Talmadge, m(2)1695
Samuel Bishop - desc/o Thomas Yale DLJ2032

Hannah - b1712, m1753 Daniel McKay - desc/o Thomas Yale
DLJ2038

Hannah - b1758 d1813, m Judas Agard - desc/o Thomas Yale
DLJ2039

Hannah - b1773 d1848, m1791 Thomas Foster - desc/o Thomas Yale
DLJ2039

James - b abt 1764, m Charlotte Wilson - desc/o Thomas Yale
DLJ2040

Capt Job - b1738 d1799 Coventry, New York, m1761 Elizabeth
Hendrick b1742 d1806 dau/o William Hendrick & Elizabeth McKay
- desc/o Thomas Yale DLJ2034

Joel - b1759 d1805, m1784 Esther Clark d1848 aged 82 years -
desc/o Thomas Yale DLJ2036

John - b abt 1646 d1711, m Rebecca Mix b1657 d1734 dau/o
Nathaniel Mix & Rebecca Turner - desc/o Thomas Yale DLJ2031

John - b1687 d1782, m1711 Sarah Payne b abt 1691 d1774 dau/o
Philip Payne & Mary____ - desc/o Thomas Yale DLJ2032

John - b1730 d1795, m1750 Eunice Andrews b1729 d1800 dau/o
William Andrews & Mary Foster - desc/o Thomas Yale DLJ2039

John - b1757 d1833, m1804 Betsey Ives - desc/o Thomas Yale
DLJ2039

John - b1775, m1808 Mary Ann Betts - desc/o Thomas Yale DLJ2041

Jonathan - b1747 d1823, m Esther Hall b1751 d1825 dau/o Daniel
Hall & Patience Baldwin - desc/o Thomas Yale DLJ2037

Joseph - b1736 d1776 Harwinton, m1765 Martha Livingston b1745
d1781 dau/o John Livingston & Martha____ - desc/o Thomas Yale
DLJ2040

Joseph - b1756 of Norwich d1813, m1780 Lydia Sanger d1849 aged
89 years, dau/o John Sanger - desc/o Thomas Yale DLJ2034

Capt Josiah - b1752 d1822, m1776 Ruth Tracy - desc/o Thomas Yale
DLJ2039

Justus - b1754 d1826, m(1) Margaret Tracy, m(2) Eunice Sikes -
desc/o Thomas Yale DLJ2039

Katharine - m Dudley North - desc/o David Yale DLJ2030

Katherine - b1720 d1767, m1745 Joseph Hough - desc/o Thomas Yale
DLJ2034

YALE (cont.)

Levi - b1745 d1772, m1768 Agnes Collins b1746 d1833 dau/o
    Jonathan Collins & Agnes Lynn - desc/o Thomas Yale DLJ2035

Lois - b1739, m1759 Asa Barnes - desc/o Thomas Yale DLJ2037

Lois - b abt 1773, m1796 Samuel Butler - desc/o Thomas Yale
    DLJ2040

Lydia - b1735, m1758 Divan Berry - desc/o Thomas Yale DLJ2036

Martha - b1729 d1813, m1748 James Todd - desc/o Thomas Yale
    DLJ2032

Mary - of CT, b1650, m1672 Joseph Ives - desc/o Thomas Yale
    ECD(3)306; DLJ2032

Mary - b1708, m1732 Enos Curtis - desc/o Thomas Yale DLJ2034

Mary - b1729 d1783, m1751 Jonathan Dayton - desc/o Thomas Yale
    DLJ2040

Mary - b1736, m1754 Jotham Curtis - desc/o Thomas Yale DLJ2033

Mary - b abt 1741, m(1)1763 Ozias Gilbert, m(2)1765 William Barker -
    desc/o Thomas Yale DLJ2036

Mary - m Dr John Graham - desc/o Thomas Yale DLJ2034

Mary - b1763 d1799, m Samuel Simpson - desc/o Thomas Yale
    DLJ2039

Mary - b abt 1768, m1786 John Anthony - desc/o Thomas Yale
    DLJ2040

Matthew - b1771 of New Hartford, New York, m1790 Lucy Ives -
    desc/o Thomas Yale DLJ2035

Miles - b1741 d1829, m1772 Rachel Cook b1753 d1819 dau/o David
    Cook & Lois Moss - desc/o Thomas Yale DLJ2034

Moses - b1705 d1748, m(1)1729 Abigail Yale b1711 d1730 dau/o
    Thomas Yale & Mary Benham, m(2)1731 Mary Clark b1713 d1797
    dau/o Josiah Clark & Mary Burr - desc/o Thomas Yale DLJ2036

Moses - b1743 d1813, m Lois Lyman - desc/o Thomas Yale DLJ2036

Nash - b1715 d1802, m1737 Sarah Emerton b abt 1715 d1798 -
    desc/o Thomas Yale DLJ2038

Nash - b1744 d1789, m1768 Ann Coats d1821 - desc/o Thomas Yale
    DLJ2038

Nathaniel - b1681 d1711, m1703 Anna Peck b1686 d1716 dau/o
    John Peck & Mary Moss - desc/o Thomas Yale DLJ2032

Nathaniel - b1652 d1730, m1692 Ruth Bishop b1664 d1739 dau/o
    James Bishop & Mary Lewen - desc/o Thomas Yale DLJ2032

Nathaniel - b1702 d1746, m1728/1729 Thankful Bassett b1702
    d1787 dau/o Samuel Bassett & Mary Dickerman - desc/o Thomas
    Yale DLJ2032

Nathaniel - b1720 d bef 1800, m(1)1746 Hannah Weeks, m(2) Abigail
    G Pratt d1807 - desc/o Thomas Yale DLJ2038

Nathaniel - b1741, m1763 Huldah Foster b1744 d1833 dau/o Thomas
    Foster & Mary Clark - desc/o Thomas Yale DLJ2040

Nathaniel - b abt 1743 d1817, m Esther Franklin b1752 d1841
    Middlebury, VT - desc/o Thomas Yale DLJ2034

Nathaniel - b1753 d1814, m1778 Hannah Scovill b1760 d1847 dau/o
    James Scovill & Hannah Hough - desc/o Thomas Yale DLJ2037

Nathaniel - b abt 1772 d1815, m1791 Abigail Bradley b1779 dau/o
    William Bradley & Rebecca Ives - desc/o Thomas Yale DLJ2040

YALE (cont.)

Noah - b1723 d1803, m1744 Anna Ives b1725 d1809 dau/o John Ives
& Hannah Royce - desc/o Thomas Yale DLJ2035

Ozias - b1766 d1853 Coventry, New York, m1788 Hannah Hotchkiss
b1755 d1810, m(2) Agnes McGeorge b1790 - desc/o Thomas Yale
DLJ2041

Philo - b1775 d1865 Coventry, New York, m(1)1798 Hannah Parker,
m(2)1824 Betsey Bulkeley - desc/o Thomas Yale DLJ2041

Rebecca - b1717 d1806, m(1)1743/1744 Thomas Berry, m(2)____
Hough, m(3)1788 Aaron Lyman - desc/o Thomas Yale DLJ2035

Rebecca - b1737, m1762 Moses Potter - desc/o Thomas Yale DLJ2040

Rebecca - b1773 d1837, m1799 Joseph Hawkins - desc/o Thomas
Yale DLJ2041

Ruth - b1738 d1761, m1756 Samuel Lewis - desc/o Thomas Yale
DLJ2037

Ruth - b1756, m Matthew Rice - desc/o Thomas Yale DLJ2035

Samuel - b1711 d1754, m1736 Susanna Abernathy b1712 d1770
dau/o William Abernathy & Mary Peck - desc/o Thomas Yale
DLJ2033

Samuel - b1737 d1758, m1757 Leah Adams - desc/o Thomas Yale
DLJ2033

Sarah - b1716 d1784, m1740 Joshua Atwater - desc/o Thomas Yale
DLJ2034

Sarah - b1738, m1754 Jesse Curtis - desc/o Thomas Yale DLJ2033

Sarah - b1741, m1761 Daniel McKay - desc/o Thomas Yale DLJ2038

Sarah - b1744/1745 d1775, m Ensign Hough - desc/o Thomas Yale
DLJ2037

Sarah - b abt 1754 d1804, m Nathaniel Hitchcock - desc/o Thomas
Yale DLJ2034

Sarah - b1763, m Isaiah Tuttle - desc/o Thomas Yale DLJ2040

Solomon - b1733 d1790 Harwinton, m1757 Sarah Braddam - desc/o
Thomas Yale DLJ2039

Solomon - b1765 d1794 Galway, Saratoga Co, New York, m1788
Sarah Andrews b1764 dau/o Elon Andrews & Sarah Beach -
desc/o Thomas Yale DLJ2039

Capt Stephen - b1732 d1799, m(1)1757 Sarah Beadles b abt 1740
d1778 dau/o Nathaniel Beadles & Elizabeth Hitchcock, m(2)1780
Phebe Hart b1746 dau/o Nathaniel Hart & Martha Lee & wid/o
Eliasaph Preston - desc/o Thomas Yale DLJ2033

Stephen - b1749 d1818, m1774 Olive Clark b1750 d1811 dau/o
Hezekiah Clark & Abi Curtis - desc/o Thomas Yale DLJ2035

Street - m Mary____ & had issue - desc/o Thomas Yale DLJ2033

Susanna - b1750, m1771 Isaiah Parker - desc/o Thomas Yale
DLJ2033

Sybil - b1743 d1822, m Titus Bunnell - desc/o Thomas Yale DLJ2038

Capt Theophilus - b1675 d1760, m1701 Sarah Street b1681 d1785
dau/o Samuel Street & Anna Miles - desc/o Thomas Yale DLJ2031

Theophilus - b1714 d1759, m1738 Azuba DeWolf, m(2)1764 Ephraim
Allen of Kensington - desc/o Thomas Yale DLJ2033

Theophilus - b abt 1759 of St Andrews, New Brunswick d abt 1805, m
Sarah Andrews - desc/o Thomas Yale DLJ2034

YALE (cont.)

Thomas - of CT, of Plas Grono, Wales d1619, m Anne Lloyd - the immigrant ECD(3)306; RAA1; TAG(32)71/80, (56)101/105; GBR311 lists Thomas as the father of the immigrants & not the immigrant; DLJ2030

Thomas - of CT, b abt 1616 d1683 son of Thomas Yale & Anne Lloyd, m1645 Mary Turner 1704 dau/o Capt Nathaniel Turner - the immigrant GBR311; TAG(32)71/80, (56)101/105; EO2(3)889; DLJ2030

Capt Thomas - b abt 1648 d1736, m(1)1667 Rebecca Gibbard b1650 d abt 1687/1688 dau/o William Gibbard & Anna Tapp, m(2)1688/1689 Sarah Nash bp 1649 d1716, m(3)1716 Mary Wheeler Fairchild Beach wid/o Benjamin Beach - desc/o Thomas Yale DLJ2031

Thomas - b1678/1679 d1750, m1705 Mary Benham b1683 d1747 dau/o Joseph Benham & Hannah Merriman - desc/o Thomas Yale DLJ2031

Rev Thomas - b1739 d1811, m1768 Elizabeth Riggs d1824 aged 84 years, dau/o Samuel Riggs & Abigail Gunn & wid/o Philo Mills - desc/o Thomas Yale DLJ2034

Thomas - b1756 of Lenox, MA d1833, m(1)1778 Mary Couch b1759 d1802 dau/o John Couch & Azuba Andrews, m(2)1803 Phebe____ Butler d1846 - desc/o Thomas Yale DLJ2036

Thomas Garred - b1770 d1793 Dominico, West Indies, m Hannah Hull - desc/o Thomas Yale DLJ2041

Uriah - b1761 d1833 Guilford, New York, m1780 Eunice Merwin - desc/o Thomas Yale DLJ2035

Waitstill - b1744, m(1) Jemima Curtis b1739 d1772 dau/o John Curtis & Jemima Abernathy, m(2) Olive Boardman d1824 aged 77 - desc/o Thomas Yale DLJ2033

YATE George - of MD, b abt 1640 d1691 Anne Arundel Co, MD deputy surveyor, son of John Yate & Mary Tattershall, m Mrs Mary Wells Sockett - the immigrant GBR342; NGS(64)176/180

YATES (YEATES) Catherine - of VA, b1760 d1831, m(2) Dr Robert Wellford, a surgeon in the English Army & settled in Fredericksburg, VA - desc/o Col William Randolph DBR(3)473; DBR(5)861; CFA(5)429

George - of MD, b1674 d1717, m1700 Rachel Warfield - desc/o Frances White JSW1698

John - of VA, son of John Orfeur Yates & Mary Aglionby, m Julia Lovell - the immigrant GBR174

Joshua - of MD, b1741 d1831, m1761 Nancy Boilston - desc/o Frances White JSW1698, 1698

Joshua Jr - of VA, b1772 d1849, m1800 Nancy Higgins - desc/o Frances White JSW1699

Samuel - of MD, b1703 d1778, m Johanna____ - desc/o Frances White JSW1698

YEARDLEY Col Argall - of VA, b1605 d1670, m abt 1650 Sarah Custis - desc/o Sir George Yeardley WAC47; CRL(1)120; CRL(2)120

Argall - of VA, m Sarah Michael - desc/o Sir George Yeardley CRL(2)120

YEARDLEY (cont.)

> Col Francis - of VA, m Sarah Gookin - desc/o Sir George Yeardley WAC47

> Sir George - of VA 1609, m Temperance Flowerdue (knight, governor-general & captain-general of VA) - the immigrant WAC47; CRL(1)119; CRL(2)119; sufficient proof of alleged royal ancestry is lacking

YELLES Deborah - m1747 William Senior of Westmoreland, Jamaica & was ancestress of several officers in Army & Navy - desc/o Sir William Keith GPFHB478

> Elizabeth - m John Merrick Williams of Jamaica & left issue - desc/o Sir William Keith GPFHB478

> Mary - m ____ Brooke - desc/o Sir William Keith GPFHB478

YONGE Francis - of SC, b abt 1682 d1748, m Elizabeth____ - the immigrant AFA10; sufficient proof of alleged royal ancestry is lacking

> Henry - of GA, b abt 1713 d1778, m Elizabeth Bellinger - desc/o Francis Yonge AFA10

> Henry - of GA, b abt 1745 d1789, m1768 Mary Powell - desc/o Francis Yonge AFA10

YOUNG Elizabeth Smith - of VA, b1767 d1822, m1787 Richard Banks - desc/o Capt Henry Woodhouse DBR(5)284

> John - b1763 - desc/o William Goddard RAA99

> Mary - of NH, b1725, m1742 Benoni Rowell - desc/o Thomas Dudley DBR(1)557; DBR(2)687; DBR(4)839

– Z –

ZANE Robert Jr - of NY, b1681 d1774, m Jane Satterthwaite - desc/o Henry Willis CHB509; MCD334

> Robert III - of NY, b1716 d1763, m Mary Chattin - desc/o Henry Willis CHB509; MCD334

> Simon - of NY, b1758 d1832, m Margaret Macomson - desc/o Henry Willis CHB509; MCD334

ZOUCH Elizabeth - of VA, m abt 1646 Col Devereux Wolseley, bp 1617 Colwich, Staffordshire, third son of Sir Thomas Wolseley of Wolseley Bridge, Staffordshire, he was a colonel in the Royalist army - desc/o Sir John Zouch APP730

> Isabella - of VA, to whom her father bequeathed a large part of his estate, explaining that he gave her more because she hath adventured her life in so dangerous a voyage, m Robert Milward, son of Sir Thomas Milward of Eaton, Dovedale, Derbyshire - desc/o Sir John Zouch APP730

> Sir John - of VA 1634, b abt 1585 d1639, knighted aft 1622 & appointed by the king as one of a commission to devise a new plan of government in VA, son of Sir John Zouch b1564 d1611 of Condor Castle, Derbyshire & Lady Mary Berkeley, eldest dau/o Henry, Lord Berkeley by his (1) wife, Lady Katherine Howard, m1605/1606 Isabel Lowe bp 1590 dau/o Patrick Lowe of Denby, Derbyshire & Jane Harpur - the immigrant APP730 royal ancestry

ZOUCH (cont.)

    not sufficiently proven

John - of VA 1634, served as administrator on the estate of his father, land holder in Henrico Co, member of the House of Burgesses, died without issue - desc/o Sir John Zouch APP729/30

Mary - of VA, b aft 1624, m (probably) John Walker - desc/o Sir John Zouch APP730

THE SOURCES

I. Most of the books listed below contain lineages that identify immigrants with reputed royal descent. These lineages include each generation continuously from the royal ancestor to the immigrant and their descendants. This list includes the author's name and the year published, if possible. Several of the books have been revised over the years. This author has tried to include the most recent and updated, and many times, corrected editions. This will aid the genealogical researcher, leading him to many more, original sources, helping him to find more surnames, and ultimately to complete his pedigree to the royal ancestor he is searching for.

code		author(s), *Title*, year published
AAP	=	Gary Boyd Roberts, *Ancestors of American Presidents*, 1989
AFA	=	Ernest Spofford, *Armorial Families of America*, 1929
AMB	=	Arthur Meredyth Burke, *The Prominent Families of the United States of America*, 1975
APP	=	Revised and Edited by Virginia M. Meyer & John Frederick Dorman, *Adventurers of Purse and Person*, 1987 Third Edition, published by the Order of First Families of Virginia, 1607-1624/1625
AWW	=	Annah W. Watson, *Of Sceptred Race*, Memphis: Early Printing & Publishing Co., 1910
BCD	=	Charles Henry Browning, *Some Colonial Dames of Royal Descent*, 1900
BLG	=	Sir Bernard Burke, *Burke's Landed Gentry*, 1939
CFA	=	George Norbury MacKenzie, *Colonial Families of the United States of America*, 1907 (6 vols)
RCFA	=	Nelson Osgood Rhoades, *Colonial Families of the United States of America*, (1 vol)
CFSSA	=	Stella Pickett Hardy, *Colonial Families of the Southern States of America*, 1968
CGA	=	William Armstrong Crozier, *Crozier's General Armory*, 1904
CHB	=	Charles Henry Browning, *Americans of Royal Descent*, 1883.
CRFP	=	John W. Jordan, *Colonial and Revolutionary Families of Pennsylvania*, 1978
CRL(1)	=	The American Historical Company, Inc., *Colonial and Revolutionary Lineages of America*, 1939
CRL(2)	=	The American Historical Company, Inc., *Colonial and Revolutionary Lineages of America*, 1939
CRL(3)	=	The American Historical Company, Inc., *Colonial and Revolutionary Lineages of America*, 1939
CRL(4)	=	The American Historical Company, Inc., *Colonial and Revolutionary Lineages of America*, 1941

DAB	=	Edited by Allen Johnson, *Dictionary of American Biography*
DBR(1)	=	Arthur Adams, *Living Descendants of Blood Royal*, 1959, Vol. I
DBR(2)	=	Arthur Adams, *Living Descendants of Blood Royal*, Vol. II
DBR(3)	=	Arthur Adams, *Living Descendants of Blood Royal*, 1964, Vol. III
DBR(4)	=	Arthur Adams, *Living Descendants of Blood Royal*, Vol. IV
DBR(5)	=	Arthur Adams, *Living Descendants of Blood Royal*, Vol. V
DLJ	=	Donald Lines Jacobus, *Families of Ancient New Haven*, 1923 & 1926
ECD	=	Marcellus Donald Alexander R. von Redlich, *Emperor Charlemagne's Descendants*, Vol. I, 1941
ECD(2)	=	Aileen Lewers Langston, *Emperor Charlemagne's Descendants*, Vol. II. c1941-1974
ECD(3)	=	J. Orton Buck & Timothy Field Beard, *Emperor Charlemagne's Descendants*, Vol. III, 1978
EDV	=	E. De V. Vermont, *America Heraldica*, 1965
FFF	=	Alexander DuBin, *Five Hundred First Families of America*, 1970/1971, Third Edition
FLW	=	Frederick Lewis Weis, *Ancestral Roots of Certain American Colonists*, Seventh Edition, with additions & corrections by Walter Lee Sheppard, Jr., assisted by David Faris, 1992 (Formerly *Ancestral Roots of Sixty Colonists Who Came to New England between 1623 and 1650*.)
GBR	=	Gary Boyd Roberts, *The Royal Descents of 500 Immigrants to the American Colonies or the United States*, 1993
GPM	=	William Richard Cutter, A. M., *Genealogical & Personal Memoirs, Relating to the Families of the State of Massachusetts*, 1910
HSF	=	John Bennett Boddie, *Historical Southern Families*, 1957-1967
J&K	=	Jordan, David Starr & Kimball, Sarah Louise, *Your Family Tree*, 1929
JEB	=	James E Bellarts, C.B., F.A.C.B., *Descent of Some of Our Quaker Ancestors from Adam, the Hebrews, the Egyptians, the Romans, The Irish, Scots, Saxon & British Kings, Charlemagne, the Normans, the Vikings & Others*, 1988
JSW	=	John S. Wurts, *Magna Charta*, 1950
LDS	=	Michel L. Call, *Royal Ancestors of some LDS Families*, 1972
MCB	=	Charles H. Browning, *Magna Charta Barons*, 1898
MCD	=	Charles H. Browning, *Magna Charta Barons & their Descendants*, 1915
MCS	=	Frederick Lewis Weis, *The Magna Charta Sureties, 1215* 1955
NEFGM	=	William Richard Cutter, A.M., *New England Families, Genealogical & Memorial*, 1913 (4 vols)
NFA	=	Annah Robinson Watson, *Some Notable Families of America*, 1898

PFA	=	Burke, *Presidential Families of the United States of America*, 1975
PVF	=	Louise Pecquet Du Bellet, *Some Prominent Virginia Families*
RAA	=	Michel L. Call, *Royal Ancestors of Some American Families*, 1972
SMO	=	Sue Morten O'Brien, *The Register of Americans of Prominent Descent*, 1982
SVF	=	John Bennett Boddie, *Southside Virginia Families*, (2 vols, 1966)
THC	=	Mrs. (Oscar Herbert) Elizabeth M. Leach Rixford, *Three Hundred Colonial Ancestors and War Service: Their Part in Making American History From 495 to 1934*, 1934
THJ	=	W. H. Whitmore & W. S. Appleton, *The Heraldic Journal*, 1865-1868
VG	=	Rev. Horace Edwin Hayden, *Virginia Genealogies*, 1959
VGE	=	Lothrop Withington, *Virginia Gleanings in England*, 1980 Indexed by Thomas L. Hollowak
VHG	=	John Bennett Boddie, *Virginia Historical Genealogies*, 1965
WAC	=	William Armstrong Crozier, *Virginia Heraldica*, 1908

II. Listed below are genealogical dictionaries, helpers, periodicals, quarterlies, and registers. These also contain pedigrees of the royal descent, usually listing any errors that may have been found in the pedigree. Many times there are explanations and corrections to the pedigree from new information that has been found. All references to new and additional information and descendants are given, as are the printed sources in which it can be found. Many times the above sources give several generations of descendants from the original immigrant, and these have for the most part been included in this work.

Each volume is listed with its respective number starting with (1), (2) etc. with the page number or numbers directly after.

EO(1) (2)	=	*English Origins of New England Families From The New England Historical and Genealogical Register*, 1st series (3 vols, 1984), 2nd series (3 vols, 1985), selected and introduced by Gary Boyd Roberts
GDMNH	=	*Genealogical Dictionary of Maine & New Hampshire*, by Sybil Noyes, Charles Thornton Libby & Walter Goodwin Davis, 1979
GPFHB	=	*Genealogies of Pennsylvania Families from The Pennsylvania Magazine of History and Biography*, (1981), introduction by Milton Rubincam
GPFPM	=	*Genealogies of Pennsylvania Families from The Pennsylvania Genealogical Magazine*, (3 vols, 1982)
		(1) - Introduction by Don Yoder
		(2) - Indexed by Thomas Hollowak & Eleanor Antoniak
		(3) - Indexed by Robert & Catherine Barnes

GRFHG	=	*Genealogies of Rhode Island Families from The New England Historical and Genealogical Register*, (2 vols, 1989)

(1) & (2) - Selected and Introduced by Gary Boyd Roberts

GRFRP	=	*Genealogies of Rhode Island Families from Rhode Island Periodicals*, (2 vols, 1983)

(1) - With a Foreword by Paul Campbell, Librarian of the Rhode Island Historical Society & Indexed by Carol Lee Ford

(2) - Indexed by Robert & Catherine Barnes

GVFHB	=	*Genealogies of Virginia Families from The Virginia Magazine of History and Biography*, (4 vols, 1981)

(1) - Introduction by John Frederick Dorman & Indexed by Thomas L. Hollowak

(2) - Indexed by Robert Barnes

(3) - Indexed by John Winterbottom

(4) - Indexed by Toby Drews

GVFTQ	=	*Genealogies of Virginia Families from Tyler's Quarterly Historical and Genealogical Magazine*, (4 vols, 1981)

(1) - Introduction by John Frederick Dorman & Indexed by Judith McGhan

(2) - Indexed by Robert & Catherine Barnes

(3) - Indexed by Raymond B. Clark, Jr.

(4) - Indexed by Gary Parks

GVFWM	=	*Genealogies of Virginia Families from the William & Mary College Quarterly Historical Magazine*, (5 vols, 1982), with an (1) - Introduction by John Frederick Dorman & Indexed by Carol Lee Dorman

(2) - Indexed by Gary Parks

(3) - Indexed by Elizabeth Petty Bentley

(4) - Indexed by Judith McGhan

(5) - Indexed by Robert & Catherine Barnes

MG	=	*Maryland Genealogies, A Consolidation of Articles from the Maryland Historical Magazine*, (2 vols, 1980), Introduction by Robert Barnes & Indexed by Thomas L. Hollowak
NE	=	*New England Historical and Genealogical Register*
NYGBR	=	*New York Genealogical and Biographical Record*
NGS	=	*National Genealogical Society Quarterly*
SCG	=	*South Carolina Genealogies, Articles from the South Carolina Historical (and Genealogical) Magazine*, (5 vols, 1983) Published in Association with the South Carolina Historical Society
TAG	=	*The American Genealogist*
TG	=	*The Genealogist*
TVG	=	*The Virginia Genealogist*, Edited by John Frederick Dorman
VGS	=	*Virginia Genealogical Society Quarterly*

INDEX OF BURIED SURNAMES